LAW AND SOCIETY

2nd Edition

For NBB

Sara Miller McCune founded SAGE Publishing in 1965 to support the dissemination of usable knowledge and educate a global community. SAGE publishes more than 1000 journals and over 800 new books each year, spanning a wide range of subject areas. Our growing selection of library products includes archives, data, case studies and video. SAGE remains majority owned by our founder and after her lifetime will become owned by a charitable trust that secures the company's continued independence.

Los Angeles | London | New Delhi | Singapore | Washington DC | Melbourne

LAW AND SOCIETY

2nd Edition

Matthew Lippman

University of Illinois at Chicago

Los Angeles | London | New Delhi
Singapore | Washington DC | Melbourne

FOR INFORMATION:

SAGE Publications, Inc.
2455 Teller Road
Thousand Oaks, California 91320
E-mail: order@sagepub.com

SAGE Publications Ltd.
1 Oliver's Yard
55 City Road
London EC1Y 1SP
United Kingdom

SAGE Publications India Pvt. Ltd.
B 1/I 1 Mohan Cooperative Industrial Area
Mathura Road, New Delhi 110 044
India

SAGE Publications Asia-Pacific Pte. Ltd.
3 Church Street
#10-04 Samsung Hub
Singapore 049483

Printed in the United States of America

Library of Congress Cataloging-in-Publication Data

Names: Lippman, Matthew Ross, author.

Title: Law and society / Matthew Lippman, University of Illinois at Chicago.

Description: Second edition. | Thousand Oaks, California : SAGE Publications, [2017] | Includes bibliographical references and index.

Identifiers: LCCN 2017018253 | ISBN 9781506362274 (pbk. : alk. paper)

Subjects: LCSH: Sociological jurisprudence. | Law—United States. | Law—Philosophy.

Classification: LCC K370 .L56 2017 | DDC 340/.115—dc23
LC record available at https://lccn.loc.gov/2017018253

Acquisitions Editor: Jessica Miller
Editorial Assistant: Jennifer Rubio
Content Development Editor: Laura Kirkhuff
Production Editor: Tracy Buyan
Copy Editor: Melinda Masson
Typesetter: C&M Digitals (P) Ltd.
Proofreader: Barbara Coster
Indexer: Michael Ferreira
Cover Designer: Michael Dubowe
Marketing Manager: Jillian Oelsen

This book is printed on acid-free paper.

SUSTAINABLE FORESTRY INITIATIVE
Certified Chain of Custody
Promoting Sustainable Forestry
www.sfiprogram.org
SFI-01268

SFI label applies to text stock

17 18 19 20 21 10 9 8 7 6 5 4 3 2 1

■■BRIEF CONTENTS

Available Online: study.sagepub.com/lippmanls2e

Chapter 13. International Human Rights and International Crime

Available Online: study.sagepub.com/lippmanls2e

Appendix A. The Law School Experience

Law and Society on the Web

■■DETAILED CONTENTS

Available Online: study.sagepub.com/lippmanls2e

Chapter 13. International Human Rights and International Crime

Available Online: study.sagepub.com/lippmanls2e

Appendix A. The Law School Experience

Law and Society on the Web

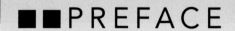

■■PREFACE

■ INTRODUCTION

The academic study of law traditionally focuses on judicial decisions, statutes, and legal commentaries. The law is presented as a logical system of rules. Judges, in the words of Chief Justice John Roberts, are like "umpires who call balls and strikes" and exercise little discretion in deciding cases.

In the 1960s, scholars engaged in the interdisciplinary study of law identified themselves as part of the newly emerging field of "law and society" or "law in society." From the perspective of this multidisciplinary approach, the law is the product of social, economic, political, and psychological forces and is not purely a product of analytical reasoning and logic. Law and society scholars have shifted their focus away from "black letter law" and instead explore questions such as the origin, development, and function of the law; dispute resolution; the psychological and political influences on judicial decision-making; the impact of law; the relationship between law and social change; law and social control; race, class, and gender and the law; and the pluralistic character of law and legal systems. Law and society scholars have called attention to the fact that "law on the books" often is very different from "law in action."

This text reflects the insights of over twenty-five years of teaching and aims to provide an accessible introduction to the field of law and society, with an emphasis on the literature of crime, justice, international human rights, and law. The text is decidedly interdisciplinary and employs concrete examples and social science to illustrate central concepts. The text is organized around the central question of "the influence of law on society and the influence of society on the law."

■ CHAPTER ORGANIZATION

Chapters begin with questions to "**Test Your Knowledge**" and an introduction. The text includes a "**You Decide**" feature, which asks students to apply the concepts in the chapter to contemporary issues. Most chapters also include an **International Perspective** section, which provides a comparative and international focus. The chapters conclude with a **Chapter Summary**, **Chapter Review Questions**, and a list of **Terminology**. **Chapter Outlines** and **Law and Society on the Web** exercises are available on the companion website (**study.sagepub.com/lippmanls2e**).

■ ORGANIZATION OF THE TEXT

The book, in addition to covering the topics traditionally discussed in a law and society text, is unique in the attention devoted to discussion of international human rights and international crimes, privacy and surveillance, and other related contemporary issues. The text includes extensive coverage of the legal profession, juries, criminal courts, and racial and ethnic inequality. The important area of gender is covered throughout the text, and particular attention is devoted to abortion, human trafficking, the global exploitation and sexual abuse of women, and the role of women in the justice system.

Law and society is challenging to teach because students often find it difficult to relate the material to their own experiences and to contemporary concerns. This text makes a conscious effort to make the topics interesting and accessible by including numerous contemporary examples. The organization of the text is outlined below:

An Introduction to Law and Society. The definition of law, the relationship between law and society, the function and dysfunction of law, families of law, and approaches to the study of law.

Theories of Law and Justice. A discussion of the major theoretical approaches to law and society, including natural law, legal positivism, classical sociological theory, sociological jurisprudence, legal realism, and various contemporary approaches.

The Structure and Function of Courts, Legislatures, and Administrative Agencies. An overview of the judicial system, the legislative process, and federal administrative agencies.

The Legal Profession. The historical development of the American legal profession, as well as a discussion of the American Bar Association, various types of legal practitioners, and women and African American lawyers.

Access to Justice and Legal Ethics. Access to justice and legal ethics and the disciplinary process.

Dispute Resolution. The process of dispute resolution, legal consciousness and legal socialization, and alternative forms of dispute resolution.

Criminal Courts. The adversarial trial, defense attorneys, indigent defense, prosecutors, and plea bargaining.

Juries. The development of juries, jury selection and decision-making, and jurors and the death penalty.

Law and Social Control. The capacity of law to deter and to regulate behavior, capital punishment, victimless crimes, and white-collar crime.

The Impact of Law on Society. Law and social change, the impact of law, race relations, abortion, same-sex marriage, the impact of law on criminal justice, and law and social movements.

Law and Racial and Ethnic Inequality. Critical race theory, racial profiling, stand your ground laws, race and drug crimes, hate crimes, and the cultural defense.

Privacy and Surveillance. A history of the law of privacy, the constitutional right to privacy, government surveillance, private sector online data collection, and drug testing.

International Human Rights and International Crime. United Nations and human rights, domestic human rights enforcement, the humanitarian law of war, and torture.

■ DIGITAL RESOURCES

study.sagepub.com/lippmanls2e

Instructor Teaching Site

It's easy to log on to SAGE's password-protected Instructor Teaching Site for complete and protected access to all text-specific Instructor Resources. Simply provide your institutional information for verification, and within seventy-two hours, you'll be able to use your login information for any SAGE title! Password-protected Instructor Resources include the following:

- A Microsoft® Word® test bank is available containing multiple choice, true/false, short answer, and essay questions for each chapter. The test bank provides you with a diverse range of prewritten options as well as the opportunity for editing any question and/or inserting your own personalized questions to effectively assess students' progress and understanding.
- Editable, chapter-specific Microsoft® PowerPoint® slides offer you complete flexibility in easily creating a multimedia presentation for your course. Highlight essential content, features, and artwork from the book.
- Lecture notes summarize key concepts on a chapter-by-chapter basis to help with preparation for lectures and class discussions.
- Sample course syllabi for semester and quarter courses provide suggested models for use when creating the syllabi for your courses.
- Complete answers are provided to all "You Decide" boxes within the text.
- Each chapter includes author podcast links that cover the important topics within the text.
- Carefully selected video links feature relevant interviews, lectures, personal stories, inquiries, and other content for use in independent or classroom-based explorations of key topics.
- EXCLUSIVE! Access is available to certain full-text SAGE journal articles that have been carefully selected for each chapter. Each article supports and expands on the concepts presented in the chapter.

Student Study Site

Use the Student Study Site to get the most out of your course! Our Student Study Site is completely open-access and offers a wide range of additional features. The open-access Student Study Site includes the following:

- Mobile-friendly eFlashcards reinforce understanding of key terms and concepts that have been outlined in the chapters.
- Mobile-friendly Web quizzes allow for independent assessment of progress made in learning course material.

- Carefully selected video links feature relevant interviews, lectures, personal stories, inquiries, and other content for use in independent or classroom-based explorations of key topics.
- EXCLUSIVE! Access is available to certain full-text SAGE journal articles that have been carefully selected for each chapter. Each article supports and expands on the concepts presented in the chapter.

■ SECOND EDITION

I have made a number of changes to the text to incorporate new research and to keep the book as contemporary as possible.

Updated material. The text has been updated throughout to reflect new policy developments in a number of areas, including corporate crime, same-sex marriage, immigration, stop and frisk, police use of deadly force, stand your ground laws, and child soldiers.

New technology. As technology outpaces current legislation, the need for society to explore the legal issues facing our digital age increases. The second edition thoroughly examines issues related to cybercrime, surveillance, identity theft, and new challenges presented by technology, such as Google and the "right to be forgotten," in vitro fertilization and parental rights, and social media and free speech.

New topics. A number of new topics are covered, including the Black Lives Matter movement, homelessness, and the nature of justice.

You Decides. Each chapter includes at least one new You Decide feature, which introduces contemporary topics such as transgender rights. Additional You Decide scenarios are on the study site.

Learning tools. The Test Your Knowledge and Law and Society on the Web features along with other learning tools on the study site have been updated. Chapter 13 on international human rights, along with material on law school and the bar examination that previously appeared in Chapter 5, have been moved to the study site. The Glossary is offered both in the book and on the study site.

■ ACKNOWLEDGMENTS

I profited from the comments of an impressive array of reviewers, who made invaluable contributions to the manuscript. Their comments displayed a significant insight and an inspiring commitment to the educational process.

Reviewers for this edition:

Eric Bellone, Suffolk University

Aaron Lorenz, Ramapo College

Melanie Janelle Murchison, University of Wisconsin–Madison

Boniface Noyongoyo, University of Central Florida

Lydia Brashear Tiede, University of Houston

Anthony Vander Horst, Kent State University

Colin Wark, Texas A&M University–Kingsville

Reviewers for the first edition:

Gordon Abra, University of Oklahoma

Tim Berard, Kent State University

Michelle Brown, The Ohio State University

Sandra Browning, University of Cincinnati

Jake Bucher, Baker University

Candy Cates, Towson University

Laura Woods Fidelie, Midwestern State University

Frank Galbrecht Sr., Johnson County Community College

Karen Hayden, Merrimack College

Kimberly L. Hutson, Norfolk State University

Jeremy Janow, University of Maryland

Amanda Johnson, University of Texas of the Permian Basin

Lynn Jones, Northern Arizona University

Erin Kerrison, University of Delaware

Dae-Hoon Kwak, Texas A&M International University

Murray Leaf, University of Texas at Dallas

Mikaila Mariel Lemonik Arthur, Rhode Island College

Nick Maroules, Illinois State University

Ken Mentor, University of North Carolina at Pembroke

Jesse Norris, Beloit College

Luis Ramirez, Texas Tech University

Sue Siggelakis, University of New Hampshire

Shannon Smithey, Westminster College

Carol Thompson, Texas Christian University

Jerry Van Hoy, University of Toledo

Eric Williams, Sonoma State University

The people at SAGE are among the most skilled professionals an author is likely to encounter. An author is fortunate to publish with SAGE, a company that is committed to quality books. Acquisitions Editor Jessica Miller was extraordinarily supportive and encouraging and provided important guidance in revising the text. Senior Project Editor Tracy Buyan expertly organized a myriad of details associated with the publication of the manuscript and once again proved to be amazingly skilled and competent. The text was immensely improved by the meticulous and intelligent copyediting of Melinda Masson. And thanks to Content Development Editor Laura Kirkhuff for her work on the study site.

At the University of Illinois at Chicago, I must mention colleagues Greg Matoesian, John Hagedorn, Lisa Frohmann, Beth Richie, the late Gordon Misner, Laurie Schaffner, Peter Ibarra, Dagmar Lorenz, Dennis Judd, Evan McKenzie, Dennis Rosenbaum, the late Gene Scaramella, Bette Bottoms, Nancy Cirillo, Natasha Barnes, and Astrida Tantillo. A great debt of gratitude, of course, is owed to my students, who constantly provide new and creative insights.

I am fortunate to have loyal friends who provided inspiration and encouragement. These include my dear friends Wayne Kerstetter, Deborah Allen-Baber, Agata Fijalkowski, Sharon Savinski, Mindie Lazarus-Black, Kris Clark, Donna Dorney, the late Leanne Lobravico, Sean McConville, Sheldon Rosing, Bryan Burke, Maeve Burke, Bill Lane, Ken Janda, Annamarie Pastore, Kerry Petersen, Jess Maghan, Oneida Meranto, Robin Wagner, Jennifer Woodard, Tom Morante, Marianne Splitter, Oliver Mendelsohn, and Marika Vicziany. I also must thank the late Ralph Semsker and Isadora Semsker and their entire family. I will always owe a debt of gratitude to Jerry Westby, who first enlisted me to write for SAGE. Dr. Mary Hallberg has continued to be an important source of support throughout the writing of the text, and the late Lidia Janus remains my true north and inspiration.

I have two members of my family living in Chicago. My sister, Dr. Jessica Lippman, and my niece, Professor Amelia Barrett, remain a source of encouragement and generous assistance. I wrote this book following being victimized by a violent criminal attack, and my sister supported me during my recovery. Finally, the book is dedicated to my parents, Mr. and Mrs. S. G. Lippman, who provided me with a love of learning. My late father, S. G. Lippman, practiced law for seventy years in the service of the most vulnerable members of society. He believed that law was the highest calling and never turned away a person in need. Law, for him, was a passionate calling to pursue justice and an endless source of discussion, debate, and fascination.

AN INTRODUCTION TO LAW AND SOCIETY

TEST YOUR KNOWLEDGE: TRUE OR FALSE?

1. Most definitions of law require that a law is an official government act that is fair and just.

2. A primary difference between the common law and civil law systems is that the common law is based on the opinions of judges and the civil law is based on the enactments of legislatures.

3. Three of the important functions of law in society are social control, dispute resolution, and social change.

4. Law can play a dysfunctional (negative) role in society and can work to the benefit of a small number of individuals; it does not always work to the benefit of the majority of citizens.

5. There is no difference between an approach to the study of law that focuses on "black letter" legal doctrine and an approach that focuses on law and society.

6. A lengthy labor strike over wages, working conditions, and a plant's move outside the United States is an example of the consensus view of law in society.

Check your answers on page 42.

■ INTRODUCTION

We regularly encounter the law in our daily lives in driving cars, in renting apartments, and on the job. Anyone opening the newspaper or reading the news online in recent years would see articles discussing the legal debate over same-sex marriage, abortion, and legalization of marijuana. Other articles would discuss the legality of American drone policy, the latest prosecutions for "insider trading" by Wall Street investors, the prosecution of detainees at Guantánamo, and various high-profile trials.

This chapter provides the first step in the study of the interaction between law and society. Why are we interested in the influence of law on society and the influence of society on law? Why bother to study the relationship between law and society? Why not limit our study to the "black letter" rules of criminal law or personal injury? Consider the Twitter attack on Leslie Jones based on her performance in *Ghostbusters*. In July 2016, Jones, the comedian, actress, and co-star of the remake of the 1984 film, which featured a cast of all-female leading actors, received an avalanche of attacks from trolls on Twitter. She initially spent an entire day retweeting what she described as "hateful and racist" tweets and initially announced that she would "leave Twitter tonight with tears and a very sad heart."

Two days later, after meeting with Twitter CEO Jack Dorsey, Jones announced that she was not leaving Twitter and reactivated her account. Jones stated that the insults "didn't hurt me" although "[w]hat scared me was the injustice of a gang of people jumping against you for such a sick cause. . . . It's so gross and mean and unnecessary." She explained that had she not retweeted the messages, "nobody would have ever known" about the attacks.

Dorsey subsequently deactivated many of the accounts that had sent hateful messages to Jones, including the account of conservative commentator Milo Yiannopoulos, then tech editor of the website Breitbart, who reportedly had roughly three hundred thousand followers. Twitter issued a statement: "People should be able to express diverse opinions and beliefs on Twitter. But no one deserves to be subjected to targeted abuse online, and our rules prohibit inciting or engaging in the targeted abuse or harassment of others."

Yiannopoulos responded that "Twitter doesn't stand for free speech. What they do stand for is a carefully crafted facade of leftist approved ideas, and conservatives that don't stray too far from safe (globalist) ideas. Like so many platforms before them, their efforts to enforce groupthink will be their undoing." Twitter later stated that the company was taking steps to improve the ability to act against abusive behavior (discussed in Chapter 12).

A law student reading these facts likely would conclude that although the First Amendment prohibits government abridgement of expression, Twitter as a private company was free to withdraw Yiannopoulos's account. A law and society analysis would place the attacks against Jones in the context of historic slander against African Americans, investigate the cultural significance of the film *Ghostbusters*, and ask why the casting of Jones and an all-female cast had sparked attacks. Other areas of law and society inquiry would include the role of social media in encouraging group attacks and reflect on the unprecedented role of tech companies in regulating speech. Law and society also might examine whether various racial and gender groups believe hate speech should be protected by the First Amendment. A comparative perspective would ask why the United States is one of the few countries that does not impose civil and criminal liability on individuals for discriminatory comments and compare America's general lack of regulation over online speech with the restrictive approach followed in Europe.

This first chapter introduces various building blocks in the study of law and society (see Table 1.1).

Table 1.1 ■ The Building Blocks in the Study of Law and Society	
Definitions of law	Informal and formal methods of establishing and maintaining social control and approaches to defining law.
Legal families	The major global legal traditions.
Functions of law	The functions of law in a society.
Dysfunctions of law	The negative aspects that law may play in society.
Studying law	The three primary approaches to studying law.
Perspectives on law and society	The principal division in thinking about the relationship between law and society.

Keep the material in this chapter in mind as you read the text.

■ DEFINITIONS OF LAW

Following World War II, the Federal Republic of Germany confronted the problem of individuals who had cooperated with the defeated Nazi regime headed by totalitarian dictator Adolf Hitler. During the war, a woman reported that her husband violated Nazi law by making remarks critical of Hitler. The so-called vindictive spouse's motive in informing on her husband was to enable her to pursue an extramarital affair. Her husband was convicted, imprisoned, and sent to the Russian front, which constituted a virtual death sentence. He survived the war and filed a criminal action against his wife for the unlawful deprivation of his liberty under the 1871 German penal code. A West German court convicted the "vindictive spouse" and reasoned that the Nazi law was contrary to the basic principles of justice.

Prominent Oxford University law professor H. L. A. Hart argued the "vindictive spouse" had followed Nazi law and was improperly convicted (Hart 1958). He reluctantly stated the best course for the new German government would be to pass a law declaring that the Nazi law was "null and void." In response, American law professor Lon L. Fuller contended an immoral law could not be considered a law and that the German court acted properly in convicting the wife (L. Fuller 1958).

The case of the "vindictive spouse" raises questions concerning the definition of law. Is a statute passed by the non-democratic violent and repressive Nazi government a law? How can Nazi law not be considered binding on the democratic German government when the law had been adopted by the governing Nazi regime, enforced by a sitting judge in convicting the husband, and followed by tens of millions of Germans? On the other hand, is an immoral law binding law, or do law and morality exist in separate spheres? Consider that the Nazi regime had passed legislation that authorized the euthanasia of one hundred thousand individuals who were

© iStockphoto.com/Christian Müller

PHOTO 1.1 Lady Justice balancing the scales of justice.

mentally and physically challenged and adopted legislation that authorized the sterilization of as many as three hundred thousand individuals. How can individuals determine whether a law is moral or immoral? Can we expect individuals to determine for themselves whether a law is immoral and whether to obey the law? How can we ask individuals to suffer the consequences of disobeying the law?

There are more definitions of law than we possibly can discuss. Each of the definitions discussed below offers an important insight into the definition of law. Influential legal anthropologist E. Adamson Hoebel remarked that to seek a definition of law is akin to "searching for the Holy Grail" (Hoebel 1979: 18). In reviewing these various definitions, think about what a definition of law should include.

Before turning our attention to law, we need to define the related terms *norms*, *mores*, and *folkways*.

■ NORMS, MORES, AND FOLKWAYS

Values are the core beliefs about what is moral and immoral, good and bad, and acceptable and unacceptable. In the United States, the central values include justice, equality, individual freedom, and the sanctity of human life. There also is a strong ethic of individual responsibility, a respect for the religious beliefs of others, and a high priority placed on family and patriotism.

Norms are the "action aspect" of values and tell us how to act in a situation. We learn norms of behavior at an early age. One type of informal norm is called a folkway. **Folkways** are the customs that guide our daily interactions and behavior. This includes the habits that guide our interactions with teachers and family, our style of dress, our use of language, and even the tip that we leave for a server.

The other type of informal norm is a more. **Mores** are deeply and intensely held norms about what is right and wrong. The violation of a more is met with strong condemnation. An example is the sexual exploitation of children. There also is a strong more that protects private property. Mores can evolve and change. At one point in U.S. history, African Americans were viewed as property and lacked rights, and there was a strong more against recognizing slaves as citizens. In recent years, there has been a developing more against capital punishment for all but the "worst of the worst" killers. Mores also can be uncertain and conflict with one another. The more that life is sacred leads some individuals to oppose abortion and euthanasia while other individuals view the opposition to abortion and euthanasia as conflicting with the mores that protect personal privacy and recognize the right of individuals to control their own bodies. Although patriotism is a strong more in America, some individuals believe that the burning of the American flag must be tolerated in the interests of freedom of speech.

4 ■ Law and Society

Norms provide the foundation for many of our laws. The more against taking the life of innocent individuals is reflected in the law of murder. The equality of individuals is enforced by laws against discrimination. Folkways also may be the basis of laws. Consider laws that require people to shovel the snow from their sidewalk, keep their dog on a leash or pick up after their dog, or recycle trash.

As you recall, mores and folkways are informal norms. In contrast, laws are formal norms enforced by the external controls. The government has sole authority to impose **sanctions** such as fines, imprisonment, suspension of a license to practice medicine or law, or deportation of an individual who is living unlawfully in the United States. Formal norms also may be enforced by private organizations or private groups along with or instead of the government. Professional athletic leagues suspend players for drug use, and the use of these drugs may be against the law. A university may adopt a rule against plagiarism and suspend students who violate the norm that individuals should submit their own work. The student in this instance would not be subject to criminal prosecution by the government.

We now can turn our attention to surveying various approaches to defining law. Folkways and mores, as noted, are informal modes of establishing and ensuring order. As a society becomes more complex, reliance may be placed on the formal mechanism of social control of the law (Pound 1943: 20).

There are various approaches to defining the law, and these tend to be closely related to the research interests of the scholar proposing the definition. There is no correct or incorrect definition of law, and each definition contributes to our understanding of law. Each of the theories tends to have a particular emphasis. Robert Kidder observes that the definitions of law are like designing a car. One designer may sacrifice speed for appearance while another designer may sacrifice both appearance and speed for comfort (Kidder 1983: 20). Keep in mind there are far more definitions of law than we possibly can discuss in this chapter, and the definitions below represent some of the principal approaches to defining law. We will cover the following approaches to defining law:

- Law and Official Authority
- Law in Action
- Law and Physical Force
- Law, Coercion, and Specialization
- Law and Justice
- Law and Social Integration
- Law and Custom

■ APPROACHES TO DEFINING LAW

Law and Official Authority

Most people, if asked for a definition of law, likely would respond that they consider law to be the statutes, rules, and regulations issued and enforced by the government. We may complain about paying taxes, but we nonetheless accept that "the law is the law." Donald Black, a leading law and society scholar, offers a definition of law that reflects the popular conception of law:

Law is governmental social control . . . the normative life of a state and its citizens. (D. Black 1972: 1086)

Black views law as social control by the government. Social control is defined as the regulation over the actions of individuals and groups. The government regulates the actions of individuals and organizations (social control) through official public institutions like courts and police and agencies like the Internal Revenue Service and Department of Motor Vehicles. Consider the web of laws and regulations involved in purchasing, driving, and maintaining an automobile. Black's definition has the benefit of drawing a firm boundary between law and non-law by excluding from law the rules enforced by private entities like fraternities and sororities or the rules that a business adopts to regulate the conduct of employees in the workplace. Black's definition also does not recognize customs and traditions as law. For example, it is a tradition to remove a hat during the national anthem. This tradition is enforced by social pressure and will not result in a governmental fine or punishment and, according to Black, should not be considered a law. The logic of Black's argument is that the government is supreme and its official, authoritative rules and regulations take precedence over the practices of individuals and private organizations. The members of a fraternity are free to regulate their own affairs, although in those instances in which the traditional practice of hazing pledges violates the law, the members of the fraternity may find themselves facing criminal prosecution by the government.

The second portion of Black's definition calls attention to the role of the law in shaping the "normative life of a state and its citizens." The law establishes and reinforces the central values and beliefs in society. The criminal law, for example, supports the core religious values and beliefs in the Ten Commandments. This includes the instructions that "thou shalt not kill" and "thou shalt not steal." Black notes that the law relies on various forms of social control, including penal punishment, compensation to an injured party, reconciliation between conflicting parties, therapeutic or involuntary institutionalization, and the issuance and suspension of licenses.

Black's definition of law builds on the famous command theory of the law developed by nineteenth-century British philosopher John Austin that law is the "command of the sovereign." Austin is credited as one of the originators of *legal positivism*, the notion that the law as written is law regardless of the moral content of the rule (discussed in Chapter 2).

Law in Action

Influential Supreme Court justice Oliver Wendell Holmes offered a definition that focuses on law "in action" rather than law "on the statute books." Holmes offers the practical definition that law constitutes:

The prophecies of what the courts will do in fact and nothing more pretentious, are what I mean by law. (Holmes 1897: 457)

Holmes, like Black, centers his definition of law on an official government institution although he limits his focus to the courts. He differs from Black in that he views law as the actual interpretation of law by the courts rather than law as written in the statute books. Holmes wrote that a "bad man" calculating how to act would want to know how a court will rule and would have little interest in the law as written in the statute books.

The practical approach of Holmes is the foundation of a legal movement called *legal realism* that we will discuss later in the text (see Chapter 2). His puzzling definition actually makes some sense. The First Amendment to the U.S. Constitution provides that Congress shall make no law "abridging freedom of expression." The meaning of the phrase "freedom of expression" requires an examination of Supreme Court cases. The Court has held that freedom of expression does not protect obscenity, child pornography, threats, and incitement to riot. On the other hand, the burning of the American flag is protected symbolic speech. In other words, reading the First Amendment does not give you an understanding of how the courts have interpreted the meaning of freedom of expression. The meaning of freedom of expression is revealed only after examining court decisions, which in Holmes's view involves policy choices and is not merely a mechanical process. The law always is evolving and developing and to some extent remains uncertain. The text of the First Amendment will not tell you whether members of the Westboro Baptist Church have the right to protest at the funerals of members of the military killed in Iraq and in Afghanistan to communicate their view that God hates America and hates the American military because of the country's tolerance of homosexuality (*Snyder v. Phelps*, 561 U.S. 443 [2011]).

Holmes is important for pointing out that the meaning of law as written often is clear only after a court decision interpreting the law. Holmes narrowly focused on courts because he reasoned that courts interpret the meaning of laws adopted by the legislature. As the important legal philosopher Karl Llewellyn noted, Holmes draws our attention to the question "how far the paper rule is real, how far merely paper" (Llewellyn 1962: 24).

Law and Physical Force

Several theorists define law in terms of the application of coercion, particularly physical force. Anthropologist E. Adamson Hoebel writes that a social norm is "legal if its neglect or infraction is regularly met, in threat or in fact by the application of physical force by an individual or group possessing the socially recognized privilege of so acting" (Hoebel 1979: 28).

Hoebel's definition distinguishes social norms from law based on the fact that a violation of the law regularly is met by physical force. A law that rarely is enforced is not considered law under Hoebel's definition because a law is required to be "regularly enforced." He also limits law to the enactments of individuals or official institutions that are authorized to apply physical force. The law of the Old West in which vigilante justice was the order of the day may not be law under Hoebel's definition. Hoebel's definition presents the problem that some legal violations are not enforced by physical force and instead are enforced by non-physical means such as a fine or forfeiture of property.

Law, Coercion, and Specialization

Max Weber is one of the most influential sociological theorists and articulated his theories on law in his monumental work *Economy and Society*. His definition highlights that physical or psychological coercion is a fundamental aspect of the law. Although Weber's definition of law may appear to be the same as Hoebel's, there is a slight difference. "An order will be called law if it is externally guaranteed by the probability that physical or psychological coercion will be applied by a staff of people in order to bring about compliance or avenge violation" (Weber 1954: 34).

Weber's definition focuses on the application of physical or psychological coercion to achieve conformity with the law. Coercion is applied by a "staff of people" or individuals in official positions charged with enforcing the law, such as judges and police. Government authorities are able to employ physical and psychological coercion, whereas individuals in private organizations typically are limited to psychological coercion. Weber recognizes people obey the law not only because of the threat of physical coercion. Conformity to the law also may be motivated by the desire to avoid embarrassment and humiliation.

Weber differs from Hoebel in providing that law may be enforced by either physical or psychological coercion. Both Weber and Hoebel fail to account for individuals' adherence to rules based on a sense of duty, tradition, and obligation even in the absence of external threat.

Law and Justice

Philip Selznick and other adherents of what has been labeled the University of California at Berkeley school of the sociology of law argue that a definition of law must incorporate a justice or moral component (Kidder 1983: 25).

A definition of law that excludes a moral component likely recognizes Hitler's decrees as law. This would mean that the individuals who in 1941 met at the Wannsee Castle in Berlin and drew up the plans for the extermination of the Jews of Europe could plead they were "only following lawful orders." The response of the victorious Allied powers at the Nuremberg trials following the war was to proclaim that mass murder is wrong whatever the requirements of domestic German law and that Nazi officials must have known that their involvement in exterminating Jews, Poles, Russians, and other groups constituted murder. Introducing a moral component into the definition of law provides a basis for distinguishing between the "lawful" and "unlawful" orders and laws (Nonet 1976; Nonet and Selznick 1978; Selznick 1961).

The question in defining law from a moral perspective is not whether the law is issued by a public official and carries a threat of punishment. The question rather is whether the law serves and promotes the dignity and welfare of individuals. A law that lacks a moral content cannot be considered law (Sutton 2001: 150).

An obvious difficulty with Selznick's formula is that individuals inevitably will disagree over whether a law promotes human dignity and the public welfare. There is disagreement, for example, over whether affirmative action promotes equality or is a form of discrimination. Some people believe individuals have the right to die while other individuals view this as a form of murder. Despite the difficulty with determining which laws promote human dignity and the public welfare, Selznick raises the important question whether law can be separated from morality.

Lon Fuller agrees with Selznick that a law must satisfy certain moral standards. Fuller focused on the characteristics of a "good law." Fuller sets forth the standard to be met by a "good law" in his famous parable of King Rex. Rex, on his ascendancy to the throne, wanted to solve the problems of his subjects. He quickly became frustrated by the complexities of drafting a legal code and decided to assume the role of the judge of all disputes. King Rex once again experienced extraordinary difficulties, his subjects talked of open revolt, and Rex died without achieving his aims.

Fuller explains that Rex failed in eight ways to make a "good law." These eight standards comprise what Fuller calls the "inner-morality" of the law. A legal system that fails to satisfy these standards cannot be considered to be just. An example of a violation of "inner-morality" is retroactive legislation. King Rex declared acts unlawful after the fact. Individuals who believed that they were acting lawfully later found that they had broken the law. Another violation of the "inner-morality" of the law is requiring contradictory obligations. An example is a law that requires the installation of new license plates on New Year's Day and a separate statute that punishes individuals who work on New Year's Day (L. Fuller 1964: 33–92).

Law and Social Integration

A very different notion of law is proposed by Bronislaw Malinowski, one of the pioneers of legal anthropology. Malinowski offers the following definition:

> Law is a body of binding obligations . . . kept in force by the specific mechanisms of reciprocity and publicity inherent in the structure of society. (Malinowski 1982: 2, 46–47)

Malinowski studied the islands of the South Pacific. These societies did not possess a formal government, courts or police, or a written set of legal rules. In his study of the South Pacific, Malinowski in a famous example describes how social relationships were maintained through a complex system of the exchange of necklaces, armlets, fish, and yams. These gifts created social ties between individuals that connected individuals with one another and integrated the society into a cohesive social order. The rules of gift giving were based on the social expectation that individuals share with one another. Individuals learned the rules of gift giving at a young age, and individuals who did not follow the rules regulating gift giving were subject to public embarrassment, ridicule, and rejection.

Malinowski viewed the customary law of gift giving as performing the function of integrating society by creating social relationships and is credited with helping to establish the structural functionalist approach to law. In your own experience, you and your friends may take turns paying for dinner checks or bar bills. This exchange helps to create ties that bind you and your friends together. Malinowski's approach has been criticized for blurring the distinction between tradition and customary modes of behavior and the law. On the other hand, Malinowski highlights that the nature of law may differ in small-scale societies from the nature of law in western industrial societies.

Law and Custom

Legal anthropologist Paul Bohannan views law as based on custom. Customs are patterns of behavior that develop in a society.

> Law is custom recreated by agents of society in institutions specifically meant to deal with legal questions. (quoted in Kidder 1983: 30)

People learn customary practices through observation and education, and through participation as children in customary practices. Bohannan argues that at some point a conflict arises in a community over whether to continue following a customary practice and the custom is weakened. The custom then is affirmed and strengthened by being incorporated into law. Bohannan terms this process *reinstitutionalization*, or the embodiment of custom into law. Once the custom is incorporated into law, the enforcement of the custom is vested in official institutions such as the police or the courts. Custom, according to Bohannan, is the first step toward law.

Hoebel illustrates the process of reinstitutionalization by telling the story of Cheyenne brave Wolf Lies Down. Contrary to the customary practice among the Cheyenne, Wolf Lies Down's horse was borrowed by another warrior without his consent. He complained to the Chiefs Society that without his horse he could not hunt or fish. The Chiefs compelled the borrower to apologize, and the borrower offered to return the horse. The Chiefs in response to this incident translated custom into the formal rule that horses should not be borrowed without consent. The individual whose horse is borrowed without consent under this rule is authorized to ask for return of the horse. A borrower who refuses to return the horse is subject to a whipping. The horse is central to the Cheyenne, and the Chiefs recognized that the taking of horses, unless halted, could disrupt tribal society. Custom was translated into a law enforced by the tribal elders (Hoebel 1979: 18–28).

The relationship between law and custom may be somewhat more complicated than Bohannan suggests. In some instances, the law is a reaction to custom, and law attempts to change customary practice. A frequently cited example is the requirement that Utah, in order to be admitted to the Union in 1896, prohibit the practice of polygamy in its constitution. Various small and isolated Mormon sects defied the Mormon religion's rejection of polygamy and continue to recognize multiple wives.

Consider a more contemporary example. In 2006, in *Georgia v. Randolph*, the Supreme Court held that the police had improperly relied on the consent of the defendant's spouse to enter the couple's home to seize narcotics. The majority held that the "customary expectation of courtesy" is a foundation of the Fourth Amendment and a social guest standing at the "door of shared premises would have no confidence that one occupant's invitation was a sufficiently good reason to enter when a fellow tenant stood there saying 'keep out'" (*Georgia v. Randolph*, 547 U.S. 103 [2006]).

■ SUMMARY OF DEFINITIONS OF LAW

In summary, the definitions of law discussed above differ from one another. Several of the central differences are summarized in Table 1.2.

Table 1.2 ■ Summary of Definitions of Law	
Public law and private rules	Some definitions of law are limited to the acts of public officials. Other definitions are sufficiently broad to include private individuals and organizations.
Written law and law in action	Several definitions focus on written laws in the statute books while other definitions focus on law "in action" as interpreted by courts.
Written law and coercion	Some definitions require that law should be written while other definitions consider any rule that is enforced by physical or psychological coercion or force as law.
Morality and law	Most definitions of law do not require law to possess a moral dimension. Other scholars believe that law cannot be separated from morality.
Law and custom	Some definitions are sufficiently broad to include written law as well as customary law.

■ DEFINITIONS OF JUSTICE

We commonly equate the law with justice and talk about bringing a criminal to the "bar of justice." Observers may greet a verdict that they support by proclaiming that "justice is served" or that the outcome of the case is a "just" result. On the other hand, the losing party in a case may describe the result as "unjust" or complain about the "injustice" of the judge's rulings at trial.

There are more definitions of **justice** than we can possibly discuss ranging from the promotion of virtue to maximizing the welfare of society. Perhaps the most influential definition of justice is articulated in the *Corpus Juris Civilis*, a legal code drafted under the Emperor Justinian (ca. 482–565 CE). The so-called Justinian Code defined justice as "the constant and perpetual wish to give everyone that which they deserve." This definition is interpreted by Raymond Wacks as containing three central elements: the importance of valuing individuals, the consistent and impartial treatment of individuals, and the equal treatment of individuals (Wacks 2006: 59).

Wacks notes that the Roman notion of justice is embodied in the figure of Themis, the goddess of justice and law whose statue typically is found at the entrance of courthouses (see Photo 1.1). She customarily is portrayed with a sword in one hand and a pair of scales in the other hand. The sword signifies the power of the judiciary, the scales symbolize the neutrality and impartiality with which justice is administered, and the blindfold highlights that justice is blind and is immune from pressure or influence.

The Greek philosopher Aristotle (384–322 BCE) defines justice as the distribution of equal amounts to those who are equal. Aristotle poses the question of what standard should be used in determining equality and asks how we should determine which of several flute players should be provided with the largest supply of flutes. Should each flute player receive the same supply of flutes? Should the most promising players who have the greatest potential receive the largest number of flutes? In the alternative, should the best player receive the largest number of flutes? Aristotle points out that using the standard of justice as equality is likely to result in different outcomes in different societies depending on how equality is defined. His personal answer is that the best player should receive the largest number of flutes because he or she will create the highest quality of music and benefit society. The purpose of a flute is to be played, and the best player will realize the true purpose of the flute (Sandel 2009: 186–190).

In 2001, the U.S. Supreme Court was asked to decide whether 25-year-old golfer Casey Martin, who suffers from a congenital circulatory condition, was entitled to use a golf cart rather than walk when competing on the Professional Golfers' Association (PGA) Tour. Martin stated that he was able to hit the ball as well as any other professional golfer but required the golf cart to position himself nearby the ball. The PGA argued that walking tested a competitor's stamina and strength during a round of golf and that walking was an essential part of the PGA competition. Martin contended that under the Americans with Disabilities Act (ADA) he had the right to ride a cart because he otherwise would be unable to compete in professional golf tournaments. He argued that a cart would not provide him with an advantage over the other golfers, and that allowing him to ride in a cart would not fundamentally modify the nature of the competition. The Supreme Court ruled in favor of Martin. Justice Antonin Scalia along with Justice Clarence Thomas dissented and noted that athletic competition is based on physical attributes that are not evenly distributed and that the Court should not be involved in redesigning the rules. What is the just result in the case of Casey Martin? (*PGA Tour v. Casey Martin*, 532 U.S. 661 [2001]).

The primary categories of justice that we will encounter in reading the text are shown in Table 1.3.

Table 1.3 ■ Categories of Justice

Category of Justice	Definition
Comparative justice	Individuals in similar situations should be treated in a similar fashion.
Discriminatory justice	The law is selectively enforced against an individual based on characteristics such as race, class, ethnicity, or gender.
Distributive justice	The government directs resources (e.g., tax deductions, financial assistance) to individuals.
Procedural justice	Government decisions are reached through fair procedures. (See Chapter 6.)
Restorative justice	Individuals who are harmed are compensated for their injuries and for the damage to their property.
Retributive justice	The government punishes individuals who harm others and/or society.
Substantive justice	The fundamental civil and political and property rights of individuals such as freedom of speech and the right to be represented by a lawyer at trial are protected against government interference.

■ FAMILIES OF LAW

This section discusses **families of law**. There are four major legal traditions in the world: the common law, the civil law, socialist law, and Islamic law. The emerging system of international law also is briefly discussed.

John Henry Merryman, a prominent scholar of comparative law, notes that these different legal families reflect the fact that the globe is divided into countries with their own histories and traditions. Merryman, when he speaks of traditions, means attitudes about how law is made and should be applied and the process of legal change (Merryman and Pérez-Perdomo 2007: 1–5).

The legal systems of England and the United States differ in many respects. Despite their differences, these two legal systems are considered part of the same legal family because they share a common heritage and a commitment to the evolution of the law through the decisions of judges. This is very different from the Islamic law tradition. The Islamic tradition spans the globe and encompasses a wide diversity of legal systems. These diverse legal systems share the views that *Shari'a* law as set forth in the Koran is the word of God as transmitted to the Holy Prophet Muhammad.

Keep in mind that most legal systems are the product of a "mix of traditions." The majority of the countries in the world have been influenced by trade, travel, colonialism, and immigration. Turkey is one of the most influential Muslim countries and a major world power. Turkish law has been influenced by Swiss, German, French, and Roman law along with Islamic law and local customs and more recently by U.S. law and various developments in Europe. The larger lesson is that legal systems continue to grow and change and integrate foreign developments and are not frozen in time (Orucu 2007).

The Common Law

The origin of the English **common law** is traced to the Norman victory in 1066 at the Battle of Hastings by William the Conqueror. At the time of the Norman invasion, English law varied across the country and combined customary practice with the laws of the former Roman and Germanic tribal occupiers along with the lingering influence of the church law introduced during the effort to convert the British population to Christianity. Disputes were settled by the local lords who controlled large tracts of land or by shire (county) courts.

Matters of concern to the king such as the collection of taxes were the responsibility of royal courts. The issues of daily justice were taken care of by decentralized local courts. The royal courts gradually became perceived as fairer than the local courts. As a result, the royal judges of the king's court as they traveled throughout the country began to be asked to decide local disputes. There was no written law, and these royal judges in deciding cases followed the local customs.

The Norman kings, in an effort to unify the justice system, recorded the customary practice and decisions of royal judicial officials. The process of compiling decisions largely was complete by the reign of Henry II (1154–1189), who was known as the "father of the common law." These judgments provided precedents that local judges began to rely on in deciding the cases that came before them. The effect was to unify the law of England. This body of recorded law is known as the common law because it is the law common to all of England. One of the first comprehensive compilations of English law and procedure was authored in 1188 by Ranulf de Glanville, an advisor to King Henry II, who wrote a *Treatise on the Laws and Customs of the Realm of England*. The second important recording of the decisions of local judges was Henry de Bracton's *On the Laws and Customs of England* written between 1220 and 1260.

Suzanne Samuels illustrates the benefits of a uniform approach to legal decisions. She notes that local English judges adopted various approaches in matters of inheritance. Estates might be equally divided between the sons of the deceased or transferred to the youngest son, or a portion might be reserved for daughters. Common law judges followed the practice of the Norman conquerors and adopted primogeniture, which reserved the inheritance to the oldest son. The policy, however unfair to the other children, provided certainty and clarity, and uniformity and limited disputes over inheritance. Younger male children realized at an early age that they needed to prepare to make their own way in the world (Samuels 2006: 59).

The distinctive aspect of the common law is that it is "judge-made" law. The common law is the product of the decisions of judges providing solutions to practical problems. This contrasts with the civil law tradition (discussed below), which is based on statutes drafted by legal specialists. The common law traces its origins to the experiences and decisions of local judges and is not the product of elites imposing their views on local judges.

A common law judge deciding a case looks to **precedent** (*stare decisis*) and follows the decision of other judges. Precedent ensures a judge bases his or her decisions on the law rather than his or her own personal view. In other words, "like cases are treated alike." The practice of following precedent provides uniformity and predictability in legal decisions and respect for the judicial decisions of other judges and allows a judge to rely on the insights and wisdom of other judges confronting similar problems.

Of course, judging is not an entirely automatic and mechanical process. Deciding a case is not like putting the facts of a case into a slot machine, pulling a lever, and receiving a decision. The facts of each case are different, and a judge may distinguish the case before him or her from the previous case. The mill owner in the precedent case may be liable for failing to grind the farmer's grain as promised. The rule that a mill owner who fails to deliver the grain on time is liable for monetary damages may be modified in a second case where a flood washes out the roads and prevents the delivery of grain. In a third case, a court may find that the mill owner was unable to deliver grain because of a storm that the mill owner should have anticipated. As you can see, the common law has an ever-developing and dynamic character.

Another important aspect of the common law that is discussed later in the text is the adversarial nature of trials. In contrast to other legal traditions, the facts are revealed by the lawyers zealously representing each side of the case through the examination and cross-examination of witnesses. The common law also allows for the participation of members of the community at trial, a practice that developed into the jury system.

The common law tradition embodies a strong concern with individual rights and liberties. The Magna Carta of 1215, known as the "Great Charter," was a significant step in the development of the common law. This document was drafted by English barons to limit the power of King John. The charter established the foundation for certain rights that we take for granted today, including the right to trial by jury, the right against self-incrimination, and limitations on criminal punishment.

A second important event in the development of civil rights and liberties was the Glorious Revolution of 1689, which resulted in the installation of King William II and Mary II and led to the adoption of the Bill of Rights. William and Mary agreed to accept the Bill of Rights and announced that the monarchy would be subject to the laws of Parliament and would not impose taxes without parliamentary approval. The Bill of Rights established a number of rights to protect individuals against the Crown, including the election of Parliament, the prohibition on cruel and unusual punishment, and the right to petition the government for the redress of grievances. These principles proved important when the common law spread to the British colonies in North America.

William Blackstone's *Commentaries on the Laws of England*, written between 1765 and 1769, stands as one of the most significant documents in the spread of the common law to America and Canada. Blackstone's four-volume work compiled the common law on individual rights, torts, legal procedure, property, and criminal law. It is said that only the Bible had a greater impact on the thinking of the Founding Fathers. The vocabulary of "inalienable rights" and the claim of "no taxation without representation" are derived from Blackstone's commentaries and profoundly influenced the drafting of the Declaration of Independence and the U.S. Constitution.

The common law is the predominant legal system in Great Britain, Ireland, Northern Ireland, Canada (except Quebec), New Zealand, Australia, and most of England's former colonies. In reality, there is no pure common law system. In the United States from the early days of the founding of the Republic, there was a distrust of lawyers and a resistance to relying on judge-made law, which was viewed as undemocratic. State legislatures and the U.S. Congress reacted by embodying common law rules in written legislative statutes. American judges continue to use common law precedents and principles in interpreting the statutes passed by the legislative branch. In other countries, the common law tradition has been combined with other influences. South Africa, for instance, combines English common law with Roman-Dutch law, and India combines the common law with Hindu law.

The Civil Law Tradition

Civil law for most Americans means the law that addresses private disputes (e.g., contracts) and wrongs (personal injuries) as distinguished from criminal law, which addresses penal offenses that are prosecuted by the state. The **family of civil law** has a very different meaning.

The family of civil law embodies a legal tradition in which statutes passed by the legislature are the only recognized source of law. The civil law is the oldest and most widely used system of law and is the dominant legal tradition in Europe, Latin America, Africa, and most of Asia (Merryman and Pérez-Perdomo 2007: 6, 23).

The origins of civil law are traced to Rome. The Roman emperor authorized various jurists to issue written opinions that were binding on parties to a dispute. These jurists also were free to write opinions on hypothetical (imaginary) cases. A large body of written opinions was produced, some of which contradicted one another. The emperor Justinian in 527 CE appointed sixteen experts to organize these opinions, resolve conflicts, eliminate wrong decisions, and produce a written legal code. The result was the great *Corpus Juris Civilis,* published in 533 CE. Justinian proclaimed that the code henceforth would be considered the definitive version of legal rules and prohibited any written interpretation or commentary on the document (Merryman and Pérez-Perdomo 2007: 6–14).

Roman law existed alongside religious law. Roman law addressed the secular world although ecclesiastical courts applied canon law and addressed issues of faith. The primary source of religious law was the decrees issued by the Pope. Cannon law shared Roman law's written character and was consulted for guidance on secular issues of concern to the Church, such as divorce and child custody (Reichel 2008: 114–115).

Roman law and ecclesiastical law were replaced by Germanic law following the sack of Rome by Teutonic tribes in the fifth century. An interest in these codes was revived during the eleventh-century medieval Renaissance. Thousands of students flocked to Bologna to study Roman and ecclesiastical law and returned to their countries with an appreciation of the value of a written and organized legal code. The secular Roman and religious church law eventually combined with the customary law that developed to regulate commercial relations between merchants in Europe to form the three pillars of a new European-wide legal tradition (Glendon, Carozza, and Picker 2016: 24–27).

The rise of European nationalism in the seventeenth and eighteenth centuries led to the development of European national legal codes. The French Civil Code of 1804, drafted by a commission of four eminent jurists, is considered the first modern civil code. Napoleon viewed the code as his legacy to the French people and claimed the title of the "Great lawgiver." The more than two thousand provisions in the code did not merely summarize existing law. Instead, the Napoleonic Code introduced a profound reform in the French legal system and reflected the values of the French Revolution. Written in a clear and understandable fashion, it was intended to be understood by the average citizen. The code repealed all previous legal enactments and was meant to be a complete and comprehensive statement of the law. The drafting commission stressed that there was no need to look beyond the four corners of the document. In theory, the average person could easily understand the text and could handle his or her own case in the courtroom (Glendon et al. 2016: 24–36).

The Napoleonic Code's code's concern with individual rights is reflected in the provisions protecting private property and contractual rights. Napoleon viewed the code as a universally applicable set of legal principles that would live forever and imposed the code on conquered territories in Belgium, the Netherlands, Italy, parts of Poland, and the western regions of Germany. French legal influence continued to grow in the nineteenth and twentieth centuries as a result of French colonialism and the spread of French culture to North America, Latin America, Africa, and Asia (Glendon et al. 2016: 39–40, 49–50).

The German Civil Code also proved to be an influential document. The long and complicated code took almost thirty years to draft and went into effect at the dawn of the twentieth century. The drafters of the German code surveyed the entire course of German history and selected the rules that should form the basis of the new code. The code has proven influential in the drafting of legal codes in a number of countries, including Austria, former Czechoslovakia, Greece, Hungary, Italy, Switzerland, former Yugoslavia, Brazil, Portugal, and Japan (Glendon et al. 2016: 39–48, 53–55).

You might already have concluded that there is a philosophical divide between the common law and civil law traditions. The common law is a system that stresses the role of the judge in the development of the law. English law developed as a result of judges addressing practical problems. The civil law system, in contrast, is embodied in a clear written code that addresses every problem and is the product of scholars and legislators. The judge is limited to the code and is not authorized to "make law."

The common law developed through judges applying precedents and gradually developing the law. In the civil law tradition, the "code is king." The judge looks to the code rather than to the decisions of other courts and applies the law as stated in the statute. The Italian Civil Code of 1942 specifies that "no other meaning" can be attributed to a statute "than that made clear by the actual significance of the words . . . and by the intention of the legislature." In practice, the civil code is not always crystal clear, and judges often look to the decisions of other judges (Merryman and Pérez-Perdomo 2007: 44).

In the United States, judges are authorized to review the constitutionality of a statute. The practice of judicial review allows the Supreme Court to find that a state or federal law is contrary to a provision of the Constitution. In most civil law countries, the belief is that courts should not overturn the decision of elected representatives and are not authorized to review the constitutionality of statutes. Higher courts in the civil system may overturn a verdict of a lower court on the grounds that the lower court improperly interpreted the requirements of the statute.

The legal procedures of the courts in the civil law system are discussed in greater detail later in the text. In the civil law inquisitorial system, the judge and lawyers work together and cooperate in gathering information in an effort to compile a full and accurate account of the facts. In contrast, in the common law system, the belief is that the truth emerges in the adversarial competition between opposing lawyers. The civil law provides the accused with a limited number of rights during the investigation of a crime because the stress is placed on developing a truthful account. In practice, common law systems and civil law systems each have adopted aspects of the other approach.

The Socialist Legal Tradition

The socialist legal tradition is identified with the political ideology of communism. In this discussion, communism and socialism are used interchangeably although the two are not identical. There are socialist political parties and governments in Europe that endorse many of the economic aims of communism although they are committed to a democratic form of government.

The central ideas of communism were articulated by the nineteenth-century political theorist Karl Marx and his collaborator Friedrich Engels and in the twentieth century by V. I. Lenin. Any effort to summarize communist ideology inevitably oversimplifies what is a complex doctrine characterized by various schools of thought. Law for Marx and Engels is a mechanism to support the political and economic domination of the powerful ruling class and to exploit the working class. The law, according to Marx and Engels, is a tool to legitimize long and dangerous working conditions, low wages, and exploitation of the working class. Workers accept these conditions because they are taught to believe the law is an objective and fair set of rules. The notion of legal equality and opportunity diverts workers' attention from the inequality of rich and poor. An analysis of law cannot be separated from economics. For example, socialist legal scholars note individuals who own media organizations have a much greater capacity to be heard than does the average citizen. In the famous sarcastic observation of Anatole France, the law in its majestic equality forbids both the rich and the poor from sleeping under bridges, begging on the street, or stealing bread (H. Berman 1963: 20–21).

Marx and Engels believed that workers eventually would begin to recognize they were exploited. They predicted the tension between rich and poor inevitably would lead to a revolt of the working class and to the creation of a classless society. In this communist state, the workers collectively would own the factories and farms and other means of production and would no longer be exploited. There would be no need for law in this utopian society because the only purpose of law is to legitimize the exploitation of workers. Society in the Marxian utopia would be regulated through social pressure and through each individual's commitment to a classless society (H. Berman 1963: 20–21).

Following the Russian Revolution and the overthrow of the czar in 1917, the Soviet Union looked to spread communism across the globe. In the aftermath of World War II, Eastern Europe fell within the Soviet sphere of influence, and Russia used an iron fist to impose communist rule on Czechoslovakia, East Germany, Hungary, Poland, and Romania, and to some extent on Yugoslavia, Albania, and Bulgaria. Today communism is limited in varying degrees to China, Cuba, North Korea, and the Soviet Union. Several other former communist countries are moving rapidly toward introducing western-style market economic reforms (Fijalkowski 2010).

The former Soviet legal code is the oldest and most important of the codes in the socialist legal tradition and is the focus of the discussion in this section. Following the Bolshevik Revolution, the new Russian communist regime continued the traditional system of a written civil code. The code combines the systematic and comprehensive approach of the Germanic code with the revolutionary approach of the Napoleonic code (Glendon, Gordon, and Osakwe 1982: 268).

The philosophy underlining socialist law is that human beings are imperfect and flawed. This imperfection results from the fact that human beings are the product of societies that are characterized by slavery, feudalism, serfdom, and capitalist exploitation. The purpose of socialist law is to cleanse the past and to prepare individuals for the transition to a classless society in which the people collectively own property. In the pure socialist state, the individual has duties and obligations to ensure the success of the socialist state. There is no right to dissent or to protest and to interfere with the transition to a pure communist state.

Socialist law is not neutral and objective; the law advances the political goals of the government and imparts socialist values. For example, the law of self-defense in socialist systems generally does not follow the common law rule that an individual should exhaust every alternative before employing deadly force. In the socialist systems, individuals are expected to "stand their ground" because this rule promotes courage and integrity and wrongdoers forfeit the right to life. There are several fundamental principles that constitute the foundation of socialist law (Samuels 2006: 98).

- *Property.* The development of an economy based on public ownership of land and industry.
- *Security.* The limitation on individual rights and liberties in an effort to safeguard the government against internal and external threats.
- *Education.* Promotion of the benefits of socialism and criticism of the negative aspects of free enterprise. The law promotes a spirit of service and self-sacrifice for the welfare of society and patriotism.

Socialist judges are selected by the legislative branch and are subject to removal and punishment if they fail to follow the law. One unique aspect of the socialist legal tradition is "comrade courts," which hear minor disputes. These courts are established in factories, farms, villages, apartment buildings, and unions and hear cases involving vandalism, the use of obscene words in public, neglect of traffic laws, failure to demonstrate respect toward government officials, and misconduct in the workplace. Defendants who are convicted may be asked to apologize or may receive a warning or a fine (Glendon et al. 1982: 300, 309–312).

The socialist legal tradition places a premium on the welfare of society and subordinates individual rights to the "greater good" of society. Individuals have no right to engage in racist or sexist speech or speech critical of the government, which could lead to societal conflict.

The Islamic Legal Tradition

Islam means "submission" or "surrender." In relation to the Islamic religion, individuals should "submit" to God. **Shari'a** is the term for Islamic law and is translated as the "path to follow" for salvation. In contrast to other legal traditions, Islamic law is contained in a religious text, the Koran. The law is not merely intended to regulate society. The Koran establishes the obligations of individuals who seek to follow the divine path to human salvation. The text of the Holy Koran regulates all aspects of human existence ranging from religious ritual to diet and sexual relationships (Lippman, McConville, and Yerushalmi 1988: 24–33).

The Koran is the word of God as revealed to the prophet Muhammad in a series of divine revelations beginning in 626 BCE (which extended over twenty-two years). The Koran encompasses 6,342 verses, most of which address religious values and obligations. *Shari'a* law is set forth in roughly 148 verses: family and civil law in 70 verses; constitutional law in 10 verses; criminal law in 30 verses; legal jurisdiction and procedure in 13 verses; economic and finance in 10 verses; and international relations in 25 verses. The religious basis of *Shari'a* law contrasts with other major legal systems, which are based on the decisions of secular courts and legislatures and leaders (Lippman et al. 1988: 29).

Keep in mind that Koranic law in most Islamic societies exists along with modern legal codes that are based on common or continental law. These European legal codes were first introduced through treaties that were designed to be applied to foreigners living in Islamic societies. European law also was introduced into the Muslim world as a result of the colonial rule of England, France, Italy, and the Netherlands. Muslim countries in recent years also have introduced western commercial law to encourage foreign trade and investment (Lippman 1989: 34–35).

Despite modern legal developments in the Muslim world, *Shari'a* remains highly significant. Islam has a strong emphasis on social justice, and a ruler who deviates from the requirements of Islam forfeits his legitimacy and may be overthrown by the population. Fundamentalist critics attack regimes as illegitimate that fail to follow *Shari'a*. These regimes are viewed as having ushered in a new age of *jahiliyya,* the misguided rule of human "evildoers," rather than the rule of God. *Shari'a* is the symbol of a return to a true Islamic state and is portrayed by dissidents as the central step in the cleansing of western influences from society. Muslim governments typically anticipate criticism and adopt *Shari'a* law to establish their legitimate claim to the loyalty of the population (Ruthven 1984: 361).

Shari'a law at the time of the Prophet was reformist and aspired to limit the system of "blood revenge," which led to endless cycles of retribution and tribal violence. A number of current commentators view various aspects of *Shari'a* as ill suited for a modern society and as contrary to contemporary human rights norms. Islamic religious thinkers, in contrast, insist that *Shari'a* is compatible with human rights norms. They argue *Shari'a* cannot be understood absent an appreciation of the structure of Islamic society. Theft, for example, is harshly punished under Islamic law. However, in theory, stealing should be unnecessary because Muslims have an obligation to make charitable contributions (*zakat*) and an Islamic government has the obligation to care for the disadvantaged. An individual who steals to survive is subject to a more moderate punishment. Muslim legal scholars contend an individual who steals for personal gain under these circumstances demonstrates a dangerous anti-social attitude and deserves to be severely punished. There also is the claim that Muslim societies, because of the harsh punishment for *Shari'a* offenses, have little or no crime (Lippman 1989: 36–37).

The most controversial aspect of *Shari'a* is the criminal law. The four central sources of *Shari'a* law are the Koran, *Sunna*, consensus (*ijima*), and rule by analogy (*qiyas*).

The Koran is the word of God as revealed by the angel Gabriel to the holy prophet Muhammad as recorded by scribes. The second most authoritative source of the law is *Sunna*, or the recorded statements, judgments, and acts of the prophet Muhammad, which explain, elaborate, or reinforce the Koran. The verses of the *Sunna* are called *Hadith* and are ranked according to their degree of authenticity (Lippman et al. 1988: 23–33).

In those instances in which the meaning of the Koran or of a *Hadith* is unclear, there is a resort to consensus. Consensus is the accumulated wisdom of Koranic scholars. It is the basis for setting compensation for injury to a woman at half that of a Muslim male. Analogical reasoning is used to extend the law to similar situations. It was used to expand the Koranic prohibition on alcohol to narcotics based on the fact that both substances produce similar reactions. There are several other supplementary sources of the law, the most important of which is custom. Custom is employed to adapt *Shari'a* to the practice in a community. It is the basis for determining whether women are required to be veiled or to cover various portions of their body. Keep in mind that there are various schools of Islamic law. Two central disagreements are whether there may be a resort to sources beyond the Koran and *Hadiths* and whether Islamic law should be viewed as continuing to evolve or whether the evolution of *Shari'a* law was halted in 900 BCE (Lippman 1989: 37–38).

Criminal acts are divided into three categories: *Hudud, Quesas,* and *Ta'zir.*

Koranic crimes. *Hudud* offenses are crimes against God whose punishment is set forth in the Koran and in the *Sunna.* The state as God's agent initiates prosecution of the accused. *Quesas* are crimes of physical assault and murder that are punished by retaliation, the taking of a life for a life in the case of murder. These offenses are prosecuted by the victim or the victim's family. The victim or his or her family may waive punishment and ask for compensation or pardon the offenders.

Non-Koranic crimes. *Ta'zir* are offenses that are not set forth in the Koran. These offenses, like *Quesas,* are private wrongs, and the victim or the victim's heirs initiate the prosecution and may waive punishment. Punishment for *Ta'zir* is at the discretion of the judge (*qadi*).

Hudud Offenses

The most controversial area of Islamic law are the seven *Hudud* offenses (Lippman et al. 1988: 38–42).

Theft. The taking of designated types of property. The first and second acts are punishable by amputation of the hands, and the third and fourth offenses are punishable by amputation of the feet.

Adultery (zina). Adultery (sexual relations between two individuals, at least one of whom is married) and fornication (sexual relations between unmarried individuals) undermine marriage and may lead to family conflict, jealousy, divorce, illegitimate births, and the spread of disease. Married persons are punished by stoning to death, and unmarried persons by one hundred lashes.

Defamation (qazaf). A false allegation of adultery or illegitimacy of a child is punished by eighty lashes.

Highway robbery (haraba). Highway robbery is punishable by amputation and in some instances by execution. This offense interferes with commerce and creates fear among travelers.

Alcohol (khamr). The drinking of intoxicating beverages is punishable by eighty lashes. Alcohol encourages laziness and inattentiveness to religious duties.

Apostasy (ridda). The voluntary renunciation of Islam by a member of the faith is punishable by death. An individual commits apostasy by converting to a non-Islamic religion, engaging in idol worship, or rejecting the principles of Islam. Apostates are considered legally dead, and if they leave the country, their property is distributed to their heirs. Apostasy is considered high treason and creates conflict and discord.

Rebellion (baghi). The forceful overthrow of a legitimate leader of an Islamic state is a war against Allah and his messenger. The leader is obligated to consider the rebels' demands, and once having concluded that they lack merit, the leader is justified in ordering the army to attack rebels who refuse to lay down their arms. Rebels who are not killed in combat are subject to beheading. If the rebels' allegations possess merit, the leader is to be removed from office and punished.

Quesas Offenses

Quesas crimes are divided into offenses against the person (murder) and offenses against the body (bodily injury).

Murder. Islam considers murder to be the most serious crime against the person. Muhammad reportedly stated that Allah's first act on the Day of Judgment would be to punish murderers. The killer is executed unless compensation is demanded by the victim's family or they pardon the offenders.

Bodily injury. The offender is subject to the same harm that was inflicted on the victim. The victim may waive punishment and ask for compensation or may pardon the offenders.

Ta'zir Offenses

Ta'zir means "chastisement," and these offenses are contained neither in the Koran nor in the *Sunna*. The power to punish these crimes is based on the sovereign's duty to protect the public welfare.

The judge (*qadi*) has discretion to impose a punishment that reflects the seriousness of the offense, the offender's background, and the public interest in deterring the conduct. Punishments entail flogging, banishment, fines, and the death penalty. These offenses include the consumption of pork, demanding excessive interest, false testimony, bribery, and misleading the public through sorcery, fortune telling, astrology, or palmistry (Lippman et al. 1988: 52–53).

Prosecuting Criminal Offenses

The procedures for prosecuting criminal offenses are not set forth in detail in the Koran and are at the discretion of the ruler. The customary procedure is simple and straightforward. The accused is entitled to the essential guarantees of the right to be informed of the charges, the presumption of innocence, the right to counsel, and the right to be free from abuse and torture during pre-trial interrogation. The *qadi*, or judge, is appointed by the ruler and is required to be a virtuous and honest male of religious faith who is well versed in *Shari'a*. The *qadi* is accountable to Allah for his decisions and is subject to punishment for convicting an innocent individual.

The *qadi* convenes the trial in a mosque. The evidence that is introduced at trial is required to possess a high degree of reliability, and a conviction requires a certainty of guilt. If the defendant denies his or her guilt, the prosecution presents its evidence. The number of eyewitnesses are established in the Koran. Adultery and fornication require four eyewitnesses. Other offenses require two eyewitnesses. Eyewitnesses are required to be Muslim males of good character and integrity. Two female witnesses are required for each required male eyewitness. Testimony is limited to direct observation and all witnesses must agree on the details of the crime. An individual also may be convicted by a confession in open court that is repeated as many times as the number of witnesses required to convict the defendant of the crime with which he or she is charged (Lippman et al. 1988: 68–71).

In those instances in which the plaintiff is unable to produce the required number of qualified witnesses, the defendant is asked to take a religious oath attesting to his or her innocence. If the defendant takes the oath, the case is dismissed; if he or she declines after three requests, a judgment is entered for the plaintiff. Practicing Muslims believe in an all-powerful God who will punish individuals making a false oath. A distinctive aspect of Islamic criminal procedure is the absence of appeal. The remedy for an individual who is convicted lies in a petition to the ruler.

The intensity of feelings surrounding Islamic law is illustrated by the controversy over the blasphemy law in Pakistan. The law was first introduced by colonial English authorities and punished "deliberate and malicious acts intended to outrage the religious feelings of any class by insulting its religious beliefs." In 1977, the Pakistan government amended the law to punish the defiling and desecration of the Koran. In 1986, the law was modified to provide death for defiling Islam. Between 1986 and 2010, roughly 1,274 prosecutions for blasphemy were filed in Pakistan although the death penalty has yet to be imposed.

The United Nations (UN) Committee on the Elimination of Racial Discrimination noted the number of prosecutions of innocent individuals brought by angry or jealous neighbors called for the repeal of Pakistan's blasphemy law.

In 2010, Oklahoma voters supported a referendum to prohibit state courts from referencing *Shari'a* law in their legal decisions. The referendum vote was dismissed by some observers as an irrational overreaction because American courts simply do not decide cases based on *Shari'a* law. Supporters of the referendum pointed to the prospect that judges might consult *Shari'a* law in questions of marriage, child custody, the division of marital property, and in considering the legality of polygamous relationships. A federal court held that the Oklahoma law was unconstitutional because it discriminated against the Islamic religion and that Oklahoma failed to present a single instance in which Islamic law had been applied by an Oklahoma court.

In the United Kingdom, devout Muslims may agree to bring non-criminal disputes that do not involve children before a Muslim Arbitration Tribunal. Decisions may be appealed to a secular court in those instances in which a decision is alleged to violate human rights or is contrary to the "public interest." There are roughly thirty *Sharia* courts that individuals may agree to consult to decide issues of divorce, child custody, and family law in accordance with Islamic law.

International Law

International law is the law that regulates the relationships between countries in the world. International law is not considered part of the family of laws although it is increasingly important. The shrinking of the world and the increased interaction between countries in trade, culture, and the movement of people has brought the world closer together. This process is termed *globalization*. In music and in food, for example, there is an interesting fusion of cultures.

In Europe, there is a formal economic integration of countries into the European community. Members of the community are required to open their borders to the movement of goods and people from member countries. The European Court of Human Rights reviews the policies of European states to ensure that their national law respects rights such as freedom of speech and freedom from torture and abuse (Shaw 1986).

Public international law regulates the relationships between nation-states and encompasses areas such as the law of the sea, trade, and outer space; the treatment of diplomats; the law of war; and the extradition of offenders. Following World War II, a movement developed toward the protection of international human rights. The law of human rights regulates a state's treatment of individuals and contains many of the protections already available to individuals in the United States. *Private international law* regulates businesses across international borders. This law would be relevant to an American corporation doing business in Africa, Asia, or Europe.

The focus in the text is on public international law. The field of international law can be confusing because the international community is not organized like a state political system with a president and legislature that possess the authority and power to tell states and individuals how to act.

The UN is an organization of countries across the globe, and there are regional organizations such as the Organization of American States that are affiliated with the UN. The UN does not have an army to persuade member states to follow the organization's decisions. The UN may be able to pressure a state to comply with its decisions and in extreme situations is able to punish a state economically. In rare instances such as Korea, Kuwait, and Libya, the UN has been able to organize a coalition of member states to act militarily.

The primary sources of international law are treaties or agreements that states agree to accept. The treaty provisions then must be incorporated into a nation-state's domestic law before it is enforceable. An example is the International Convention on the Prevention and Punishment of the Crime of Genocide, which has been incorporated into U.S. federal law.

There also are treaties establishing various international legal institutions that nation-states may voluntarily join. For example, the International Court of Justice is a court that is part of the

UN that hears complaints by one state against another state. This may involve a state alleging that another state has unfairly diverted a river and has deprived a state of its fair share of a water supply. The recently established International Criminal Court has jurisdiction over various international crimes committed in the territory of a member state or crimes committed against the nationals of a signatory state.

American laws increasingly are extending their reach beyond the territorial boundaries of the country. Various criminal statutes allow for jurisdiction over crimes committed abroad. An example is the prosecution of individuals residing in the United States for acts of torture or genocide committed outside the country.

One difficulty with formulating and enforcing international law is that the world is composed of a diverse group of states. A claim that the *Shari'a* punishments violate human rights will be resisted by those states that view these punishments as the word of God.

■ THE FUNCTIONS OF LAW

Law serves various "jobs" or functions in society (Hoebel 1979; Schur 1968). The **functions of law** include social control, dispute resolution, and social change.

Social Control

Social control is the process of ensuring individuals engage in "right conduct." In small-scale societies in which the population shares a similar background, ethnic identity, and values, social control may be achieved through social pressure from friends and neighbors. Individuals who challenge the values of the group tend to be expelled from the community (banishment), and less serious violations of the group's values may result in shaming the individual as a method of deterring others from violating the law. A small-scale society simply cannot tolerate dissent that challenges the core beliefs and may create divisions within the group (L. Friedman 1977: 11).

In a larger and more diverse society, social pressure remains important. People respond to the critical remark of a friend or relative and are inspired by the praise of a teacher or parent. Individuals in a large-scale society live a portion of their lives in various institutions, each of which may have its own methods of social control. An employee who constantly is late may be fired or suspended or may suffer a loss of pay, returning books late to the library may result in a fine, a bar may refuse to serve a troublesome or inebriated patron, a hotel may cancel the reservation of an individual who arrives late in the evening, and a restaurant that fails to meet health standards may have its license suspended. A parent may "ground" a son or daughter who does not return home on time from a date.

The law is the primary institution that is relied on to ensure social control in large and diverse societies. People have different values, various income levels, and attitudes, and informal social pressures often may not be sufficient to ensure social control. An individual may identify with a subculture that encourages and supports the use of drugs or dog fighting. Lawrence M. Friedman lists the functions of the law in maintaining social control. First, the law defines, usually in written form, the deviant behavior that is subject to legal punishment. Second, the law defines the institutions and procedures that will punish individuals who engage in deviant behavior.

PHOTO 1.2 The law as pictured here affects our daily lives in various major and minor ways ranging from picking up after dogs and traffic tickets to access to marijuana. Despite frustrations with the legal system, Americans express respect for the rule of law.

This typically is a court and may involve lawyers and a jury. Third, the law defines the procedures that are used to investigate and detect crime. For example, the law defines the ability of the police to conduct searches and seizures and to interrogate suspects (L. Friedman 1977: 11).

Of course, merely because a law is passed does not mean that the law will succeed in the social control of deviant behavior. Controversy was stirred in various cities when local ordinances required dog owners to pick up the defecation of their canines. A vocal group of dog owners resented being forced to pick up the waste of their dogs, and sanitation workers did not want to handle the waste in the garbage. New York City responded to these complaints by imposing fines as high as $250 for a failure to pick up after your pet. Most dog owners undoubtedly comply with the "poop scoop" law. The law nonetheless is difficult to enforce, and compliance in many cases depends on social pressure from neighborhood residents and other dog owners.

Friedman notes that the law performs the additional function of secondary social control. A thief sentenced to prison is both punished and taught a lesson. The lesson is communicated to the thief as well as everyone who attends or reads or hears about the conviction. The conviction encourages law-abiding behavior and deters violations of the law (L. Friedman 1977: 14).

The law also controls behavior through rewards. Individuals may obtain tax deductions for contributing money to a charitable cause or for installing solar panels on their house.

Dispute Resolution

A second function of the law is dispute resolution. Friedman defines a dispute as the "assertion of inconsistent claims over something of value." He notes that disputes can be "dangerous" because they can easily get out of hand and lead to retaliation and to violence. An example is dueling, which was an accepted method of vindicating an individual's honor and settling disputes in the United States until well into the nineteenth century, when every state passed laws prohibiting the practice (L. Friedman 1977: 12).

Friedman distinguishes between minor disputes involving small-scale disagreements over contracts, divorce, and land ownership and major disputes involving fundamental disagreements between workers and employers or between consumers and the manufacturers of a defective product.

Disputes and conflicts may be resolved through negotiation between the parties. A dispute or conflict that is translated into a legal disagreement may lead to a complaint before a court. The parties to the case may settle the suit rather than pursue a time-consuming or expensive legal action and may want to avoid the uncertainty of a court decision.

The legislature also may intervene to resolve a dispute by passing a law that resolves a conflict. The U.S. Congress responded to pressure from the African American community and declared Martin Luther King's birthday a federal holiday in 1983. The effort to persuade Congress to recognize King's birthday as a federal holiday was first proposed in 1968, and it required six million signatures on a petition and fifteen years of lobbying to pass the law. Arizona did not recognize the Martin Luther King holiday until 1993, and South Carolina finally acknowledged it in 2000 (L. Friedman 1977: 12).

Social Change

A third function of law is social change. The U.S. Supreme Court ordered the desegregation of American schools in *Brown v. Board of Education* while Congress in a series of laws ensured equal access to restaurants, hotels, and other facilities across the country and protected the right of individuals to vote. Law also can be used to bring about less far-reaching change such as requiring drivers to wear seat-belts or to require hands-free use of cell phones while driving. There is a question whether law is effective in bringing about social change absent support from a political movement that supports the change (L. Friedman 1977: 12–13).

Brown v. Board of Education and civil rights legislation told the states and private businesses that "thou shalt not" discriminate. Friedman observes that the law also "creates rights." Congress may pass a law that enables a wounded veteran to receive medical care for post-traumatic stress disorder (PTSD) or to receive pension payments for the disabilities associated with PTSD. Section 1983 of the U.S. Code allows individuals to sue state and local governments for the violation of their civil rights and liberties (L. Friedman 1977: 13).

An additional function of the law identified by Friedman is record keeping. The state keeps track of births, deaths, marriages, house sales and purchases, and professional licenses (L. Friedman 1977: 13–14).

■ THE DYSFUNCTIONS OF LAW

Law does not always protect individuals and result in beneficial social progress. Law can be used to repress individuals and limit their rights. The respect that is accorded to the legal system can mask the **dysfunctional role of the law**. Dysfunctional means that the law is promoting inequality or serving the interests of a small number of individuals rather than promoting the welfare of society or is impeding the enjoyment of human rights.

The early legal history of Native Americans in the United States reflects nineteenth-century biases and prejudices. In 1823, in *Johnson v. M'Intosh* (21 U.S. 543 [1823]), the U.S. Supreme Court held that North America had been discovered by Christian Europeans and that the indigenous Native American inhabitants of the United States did not possess title to the land they occupied. Justice John Marshall wrote that Native Americans were "an inferior race of people . . . under the perpetual protection and pupilage of the government" who "could have acquired no proprietary interest" in the land that they "wandered over." Native Americans were tenants who occupied the land at the pleasure of their government landlords.

In 1830, President Andrew Jackson obtained congressional endorsement for the Indian Removal Act, which authorized him to transfer Native Americans living east of the Mississippi River to unoccupied lands west of the Mississippi in Oklahoma. Between 1838 and 1839, four thousand of the fourteen thousand Cherokees who were forcibly removed perished during what is known as the Trail of Tears. The General Allotment Act of 1887 allowed the U.S. government to allot land on reservations to individual Native Americans and to sell the remainder of the land to outsiders. The act permitted the federal government to seize nearly ninety million acres of reservation land, most of which was sold to white farmers and developers. In 1903, in *Lone Wolf v. Hitchcock*, the U.S. Supreme Court held that Congress was authorized to seize and to sell the land on which Native Americans resided. The Court held that the "power of the general government over these remnants of a race once powerful, now weak and diminished in numbers, is necessary to their protection, as well as to the safety of those among whom they dwell" (*Lone Wolf v. Hitchcock*, 187 U.S. 553 [1903]).

The judicial decisions that allowed the dispossession of Native American land were based on the principle that Native Americans lacked written deeds and documents to establish their ownership over the land on which they resided. North America under the common law was considered to have been unoccupied territory that had been "discovered" by Europeans. As a result, Native Americans had no rights to the land and, as tenants, could be removed by the federal government (Harring 1994; Wilkinson 1987).

In 1927, revered Supreme Court justice Oliver Wendell Holmes writing for an 8–1 majority held that Virginia was constitutionally justified in carrying out the sterilization of Carrie Buck, a "feeble minded white woman." Holmes wrote that this operation was required because heredity plays an important role in the "transmission of insanity" and "imbecility." The sexual sterilization and discharge of Buck and others like her would permit them to be self-supporting and prevent them from continuing to present a "menace." Holmes noted that given the self-sacrifice required of the "best citizens" to fight for their country, "it would be strange if it could not call upon those who already sap the strength of the State" for "lesser sacrifices . . . to prevent our being swamped with incompetence." He ended his opinion with a famous epigram: "It is better . . . [if] instead of waiting to execute degenerate offspring for crime or to let them starve . . . society can prevent those who are manifestly unfit from continuing their kind. . . . Three generations of imbeciles are enough" (*Bell v. Buck*, 274 U.S. 200 [1927]).

Virginia by 1979 had sterilized 7,450 individuals, and nationally a total of between sixty and seventy thousand individuals had been sterilized, twenty thousand in California alone. In 2002, Governor Mark Warner of Virginia "sincerely apologized" for the Commonwealth's practice of eugenics. Two state legislators presented a commendation from the General Assembly to Raymond W. Hudlow who was sterilized against his will as a runaway at age 16 and went on to become a decorated soldier in World War II. Virginia subsequently agreed to provide $25,000 to each surviving victim, and North Carolina earlier had apologized and agreed to provide $50,000 to each surviving victim (Cohen 2016).

Courts in other instances are employed as conscious instruments of repression. In Nazi Germany during the twelve years of the Third Reich, at least thirty-two thousand individuals were sentenced to death because of protest against the regime or because they were Jews or political dissidents. Individuals who committed anti-Semitic acts of violence were acquitted and praised. In other instances, individuals were criminally convicted because of "who they were" rather than "what they did." In 1942, Oswald Rothaug, head of the Special Court in Berlin, convicted Leo Katzenberger, the leader of the Berlin Jewish community, of the racial defilement of Irene Seiler, age 32. The evidence indicated that Seiler was a family friend of Katzenberger and that he had kissed her on the cheek and as a youngster she had sat on his lap. Although racial defilement was defined in the law as sexual relations between a Jew and an Aryan, and although evidence indicated that Katzenberger was medically incapable of committing such an act, Rothaug nonetheless ruled that the "Jews are our misfortune" and that any physical contact between a Jew and a German was sufficient to constitute racial defilement. Katzenberger was executed by use of the guillotine (Lippman 1997).

Courts also can be used to stifle freedom of expression. Roughly twenty-six U.S. states have laws against so-called strategic lawsuits against public participation (SLAPP). These legal actions are used to intimidate critics of businesses and organizations. Legal actions typically are dropped if the critic will enter into an agreement to halt his or her criticism. Justin Kurtz, a 21-year-old college student, was sued by a towing company for $750,000 after he created a Facebook page that criticized the company for allegedly unlawfully towing his automobile. The company dropped its legal action after Kurtz agreed to take down his Facebook page and to stop criticizing the towing company.

One of the most prominent SLAPPs involved a legal action brought by Texas ranchers against Oprah Winfrey for $12 million in damages after she commented that she would not eat a hamburger following a program on "mad cow disease." A jury found in favor of Winfrey. Individuals posting critical reviews on Yelp have been the target of recent legal actions. There is a trend for doctors and other professionals to have patients sign an agreement that they will not post negative reviews online.

At least twenty-eight states have anti-SLAPP laws that provide individuals with varying types of protection. California has the most far-reaching law that allows courts to dismiss legal actions found to be motivated by intent to punish and to deter individual comment on matters of "public interest."

Several of the dysfunctions of law are listed in Table 1.4 (L. Friedman 1977: 15–16).

Table 1.4 ■ Dysfunctions of Law	
Harassment	Legal actions may be brought to harass individuals or to gain revenge rather than redress a legal wrong.
Bias	The law may reflect biases and prejudices or reflect the interest of powerful economic interests.
Repression	The law may be used by totalitarian regimes as an instrument of repression.
Rigidity	The law is based on a clear set of rules. Self-defense requires an imminent and immediate threat of violence. Battered women who have been subjected to a lengthy period of abuse and who, as a result, kill their abuser while he is asleep typically are denied the justification of self-defense. The denial of self-defense to "battered women," according to some legal commentators, is unfair because the women reasonably can anticipate that the abuser will continue the pattern of violence in the near future.

(Continued)

Table 1.4	(Continued)
Precedent	The law, because of the reliance on precedent, may be slow to change. Judges also are concerned about maintaining respect for the law and hesitate to introduce change that society is not ready to accept. In 1896, in *Plessy v. Ferguson*, the U.S. Supreme Court held that the Constitution's prohibition on racial discrimination under the Fourteenth Amendment is satisfied by separate but equal facilities (*Plessy v. Ferguson*, 163 U.S. 537 [1896]). The Supreme Court slowly limited this precedent, and in 1954, *Brown v. Board of Education* finally broke with precedent and ruled that separate educational facilities were not equal educational facilities (*Brown v. Board of Education*, 347 U.S. 483 [1954]).
Unequal access to justice	An individual who is able to afford a powerful law firm and talented private attorneys and who can afford to retain experts and investigators has a better chance of being acquitted of a criminal charge or winning a civil suit than an individual who lacks resources. In the criminal arena, a defendant who can afford bail has a better chance of being acquitted than a defendant who is forced to remain in jail while awaiting trial.
Conservatism	Courts are reluctant to second-guess the decisions of political decision-makers in times of war and crisis. The U.S. Supreme Court during World War II upheld the internment of 112,000 Japanese immigrants and Japanese Americans (*Korematsu v. United States*, 323 U.S. 214 [1944]).
Decrease political activism	A reliance on law and courts can discourage democratic political activism. Individuals and groups, when they look to courts to decide issues, divert energy from lobbying the legislature and from building political coalitions for elections. The reliance on unelected judges to make public policy decisions is criticized as undemocratic.
Impede social change	The law may limit the ability of individuals to use the law to vindicate their rights and liberties. For example, in 1996, Congress passed the Prison Litigation Reform Act, which was intended to limit the ability of state prisoners to sue in federal courts for the violation of their civil rights. The number of federal lawsuits filed dropped from forty-two thousand in 1995 to twenty-six thousand in 2000 (Calavita 2010: 40).

This introductory chapter thus far has provided a foundation for the study of law and society. You might want to review the definitions, families, and functions and dysfunctions of law. In the next section, we discuss the three principal approaches to studying law.

■ THE STUDY OF LAW

There are various approaches to the study of law. This section distinguishes between the study of legal doctrine, jurisprudence, and law and society. This distinction is somewhat overstated because any study of law likely will combine elements of all three types of analysis.

The Study of Legal Doctrine

The typical law student is interested in the **"black letter" law**, the rules that are followed in writing a will, drafting a contract, or determining the liability of a driver involved in an automobile accident. Law school education focuses on rules and applying the rules to various situations that may arise. The rules are found in cases and legislative statutes and, in some cases, in regulations issued by government agencies.

The study of legal doctrine is an applied and practical discipline intended to train practicing attorneys. Law students typically have little tolerance for the history of the law or philosophical questions on the definition of law. They want to walk out of class knowing the difference between the elements of larceny, robbery, and burglary.

The common law that was transported to the colonies from England provided a comprehensive set of legal rules. In the United States, there was a distrust of judges and a desire for the law to be accessible to the average person. The common law was incorporated into laws or statutes adopted by state legislatures and the U.S. Congress. These materials were supplemented by administrative regulations issued by government agencies regulating areas such as trucking, standards for radio broadcasting, food safety, and grazing and oil exploration on public lands.

The study of law is based on various areas of study or foundation building blocks that will be discussed later in the text. The two primary divisions in the law are public law, which addresses the relationship between the citizen and the state, and private law, which addresses the relationship between individuals and groups in society.

Public law. Public law is composed of three areas. Criminal law and criminal procedure focus on the definition of criminal conduct and the punishment of crimes and on the procedures for the investigation and detection of crime. Constitutional law focuses on (a) the structure and functioning of the branches of government, (b) the interrelationship between the branches of government, and (c) the limits of governmental power and the rights of individuals. Administrative law governs the authority of government to regulate various activities. Agencies regulate virtually every aspect of society, from consumer protection and broadcasting to the conduct of elections and the environment and taxation.

Private law. Private law includes the areas of contract, torts, and property. Contract involves the formation and enforcement of agreements between individuals and between organizations. Torts address rights and remedies for injuries to the person, property, privacy, reputation, and mental harm to individuals. The law of property defines what is property (e.g., whether an idea is property), who owns property, and what the rules are for resolving ownership disputes. There are other areas that might be included in private law, for example, corporate law, which deals with the organization and functioning of businesses and partnerships. Family law regulates marriage, divorce, children, and the claims to marital property, and copyright and patent law protects the creators of creative works.

In law school, students study the written appellate opinions of judges in legal cases interpreting statutes and regulations and provisions of the Constitution. In interpreting these materials, judges rely heavily on the precedent created by the decisions of other judges in deciding similar cases. The appellate opinions of judges generally assume the facts are clearly established and focus on the law. The opinions in most instances employ technical legal terms and phrases and are not easily comprehended by the average reader. Limited attention is paid in legal education to the trial process.

In the minds of students and law professors and most of the public, the law is viewed as a logical system in which legal precedents and other materials will provide an answer, much like putting money in a slot machine. A law student learns various methods of logical reasoning that are used to reach a result. Legal decisions for the "black letter" lawyer are determined by the law, and a judge's personality or political point of view has little role in determining the outcome of a case. In 2005, Supreme Court chief justice John Roberts, in his confirmation hearing, stated like an umpire who calls balls and strikes that he would fairly and objectively apply the law.

We will return to the notion that law is a science later in the book. Most law professors today would recognize that precedent is a starting point that may not always provide the answer to a problem. A judge inevitably will bring a measure of independent judgment to the task of deciding a case. Alan Hutchinson observes that law is a "living tradition" that is never complete. He compares the law to a work-in-progress in which judges are constantly adapting the law to changed conditions and new challenges (Hutchinson 2011: 1–8).

In the famous 1805 case of *Pierson v. Post*, Lodowick Post was foxhunting with his friends on Long Island, near New York City. The hunting party had scented a fox and was in hot pursuit along a beach. Jesse Pierson, a local resident who harbored resentment toward new residents like Post, suddenly appeared and shot the fox, grabbed the carcass, and ran away. Who was the rightful owner of the fox: Post, who had detected the fox and was closing in for the kill, or Pierson, who killed the fox?

Judge Tompkins in a 2–1 decision in favor of Pierson drew on Roman and common law texts and held the fox is a natural and free animal and that the property right over the fox is determined by "occupancy only." "Pursuit alone" does not constitute ownership. Dissenting judge Henry Brockholst Livingston based his decision on custom. He argued the fox was the enemy of the world and that Post should be rewarded for making the effort to rid the community of this pest. *Pierson* remains the rule on ownership of wild animals—the legal right is vested in the individual who deprives the animal of its natural liberty and subjects the animal to control. Ownership is lost if an animal escapes. Cases have awarded possession of a school of mackerel to the fisher who netted the fish rather than to the fisher who tracked and enclosed the fish. In cases of whales, courts have followed Judge Livingston and have recognized the custom among whale hunters is that ownership resides in the individual who harpoons the whale rather than in the individual who secures the carcass on the beach.

Pierson v. Post reappeared on the legal landscape in 2001 when Barry Bonds of the San Francisco Giants hit a record-breaking seventy-third home run into the stands of Pac Bell Park. Fans struggled for the ball, which was valued in the six figures. Alex Popov caught the ball in his mitt, and in the pushing and shoving, the ball was grabbed by Patrick Hayashi. Popov sued Hayashi and claimed he was the rightful owner. Major League Baseball (MLB) also filed an ownership claim to the ball. Who is the owner of the ball? Judge Kevin McCarthy held that the ball had been abandoned by MLB when it left the park, that Popov had only momentarily caught the ball, and that Hayashi had taken legal possession. The judge, however, split the difference and divided the $450,000 auction price between Popov and Hayashi (Hutchinson 2011: 67–88).

The Study of Jurisprudence

The term **jurisprudence** is derived from the Latin word *jurisprudentia*, or "the study, knowledge, or science of law." Jurisprudence typically involves a consideration of the philosophical questions that underlie the law. One branch of jurisprudence involves normative questions or the ethical aspects of the law. In Plato's dialogue *Crito*, Socrates is in jail awaiting the punishment of death by poison. He has been convicted of the crime of corrupting the youth of Athens. Socrates's student Crito visits him and tells him that he has arranged for Socrates to escape from prison. Socrates asks whether it is right for someone who has been convicted of a crime, however unjustly, to avoid punishment? Socrates also poses the question whether there is an obligation to obey the law and what are the consequences for society of disobeying the law. Other questions arise during their dialogue, such as how to determine whether a court's decision is unjust and whether justice is a necessary aspect of law. What are the permissible goals of punishment? Under what conditions is the death penalty justified? These are normative questions, or questions that relate to the ethical aspects of the law. Jurisprudence also includes what are termed *analytic questions*. These are questions that involve a study of the definition of law, the origins of law, and how judges reason and make decisions (Golding 1975).

One of the most famous cases in legal history is the English case of *The Queen v. Dudley and Stephens* (14 Q.B.D. 273 [1884]). Australian maritime lawyer John Henry Want purchased the fifty-two-foot, twenty-ton boat the *Mignonette* while in England and hired Captain Tom Dudley to find a crew and to sail the vessel back to his homeland. Dudley hired a three-man crew consisting of Edwin Stephens, Edmund Brooks, and a 17-year-old orphaned cabin boy named Dick Parker. The light and small ship was considered somewhat flimsy to navigate some of the globe's most treacherous waters (Hutchinson 2011: 13–39).

The ship set sail on May 19, 1885, and on July 5, the vessel was hit by a gigantic wave and a large hole was punched in the lee bulwarks. Dudley ordered the crew to abandon ship. The *Mignonette* sank within five minutes, and the crew was left in the middle of the South Atlantic 680 miles from the nearest landmass with two cans of turnips and no water, no shelter, and no fishing equipment. After several days at sea, they managed to capture and kill a turtle, which along with the remaining turnips was the only food they had to sustain themselves.

The crew became desperate after not having eaten for eight days or drunk any water for five days. Parker became seriously ill and delirious from drinking seawater. Dudley raised for the second time the question whether they should follow the customary practice among sailors and draw lots to determine which member of the crew should be killed and eaten. Stephens was receptive to the proposal although Brooks continued to express his opposition. On the twentieth day, Dudley argued that if no vessel appeared to rescue them, he would take responsibility for killing Parker and explained that he would only be accelerating Parker's anticipated death by a few days. Stephens hesitated and agreed; Brooks remained silent and did not respond.

Dudley proceeded to slit Parker's throat, and Dudley, Stephens, and Brooks drank Parker's blood and consumed Parker's remains over the next three days. On the fourth day after Parker was killed, the three men were losing hope when they were rescued by the German freighter the *Montezuma*, and by September 1885, the surviving crew members arrived back in England.

Despite the ordeal that the three sailors had endured, they were brought to trial and charged with killing Parker. The case made its way to a five-judge appellate court, which in a unanimous decision convicted the three defendants. The court, although recognizing the suffering the defendants endured, held they had no right to kill a "weak and unoffending boy" to ensure their own survival. The judges rejected the argument that the defense of necessity permitted taking one life to save a greater number of individuals. The judges asked, "By what measure is the comparative value of lives to be measured? Is it strength, or intellect or what?" The court could find no justification for singling Parker out to be eaten and sentenced the three defendants to death. The court asked the Crown to exercise mercy and to spare the three defendants, and as a result, their sentences were commuted to six months in prison.

The defense of necessity recognizes a crime at times may be required to avoid a greater and imminent crime. *Dudley and Stevens* established the principle that continues to be followed by American, Canadian, and English judges that necessity does not justify the taking of human life. The fear is that recognizing that necessity may justify the taking of human life is a slippery slope that may lead to the killing of a grandparent or physically challenged child because of the economic burden on a family. On the other hand, the challenge confronting the crew of the *Mignonette* is difficult to compare with any other situation. The crew may have found themselves in a state of nature in which they exercised their natural right of self-preservation.

In 2000, an English court deviated from the precedent in *Dudley and Stephens* and held conjoined twins might be separated although one would die. A failure to separate the twin would have resulted in the death of the healthy twin as well as the weaker twin, who suffered from an undeveloped brain and lacked a functioning heart and lungs.

In another interesting case, Israeli agents in 1961 unlawfully abducted Adolf Eichmann, one of the central figures in the Nazi extermination of six million Jews. Eichmann had been openly living in Argentina where he had fled following World War II. He was brought to Israel and tried for war crimes and crimes against humanity committed between 1939 and 1944 against the Jewish people and other groups. Eichmann was prosecuted under an ex post facto law adopted in 1950 for crimes committed in Europe before Israel was recognized as a nation-state against individuals who at the time were citizens of European countries rather than citizens of the state of Israel. His claims that he had merely followed orders and that as a government official he was immune from legal liability were rejected by the court. Eichmann was unanimously convicted by three Jewish judges and remains the only individual executed in the history of the state of Israel. The Eichmann case raises a host of interesting jurisprudential issues, including whether Israel was justified in abducting, prosecuting, and executing Eichmann. The reality is that if Israel had not acted, Eichmann likely would not have been brought to the bar of justice. The question remains whether the ends justified the means in the Eichmann case (Lippman 2002).

The Study of Law and Society

Both "black letter" law and jurisprudence consider law to be a self-contained system that is isolated from economics, politics, psychology, and history. Law and society takes the opposite approach and studies the influence of external events on the law. In the words of Kitty Calavita, law and society examines the "influence on law of forces outside the box." In pursuing this project, law and society takes a multidisciplinary approach and draws on anthropology, history, political science, psychology, sociology, and philosophy, as well as law and jurisprudence (Calavita 2010: 4–5).

Calavita illustrates her point by pointing to the First Amendment protection of freedom of speech, a constitutional provision that is considered a defining aspect of American democracy. She notes that freedom of speech has been reduced or expanded by the courts depending on the political climate (Calavita 2010: 4–5).

Courts, for example, are particularly concerned with protecting national security during wartime. Geoffrey R. Stone of the University of Chicago, a leading constitutional lawyer, describes how the Supreme Court during World War I retreated from protecting freedom of expression in the interests of protecting national security (G. Stone 2004: 135–234). The late Harry Kalven observes the decisions are "dismal evidence of the degree to which the mood of society" can "penetrate judicial chambers" (Kalven 1988: 147). In *Schenck v. United States*, Schenck distributed a pamphlet that strongly denounced the draft and called on individuals to write their members of Congress to repeal what he termed a monstrous wrong. The Court noted that "when a nation is at war many things that might be said in time of peace . . . will not be endured so long as men fight and no Court could regard them as protected by any constitutional right" (*Schenck v. United States*, 249 U.S. 47 [1919]).

Another example of outside wartime influences on legal decisions is the internment of Japanese Americans during World War II. President Roosevelt, following the Japanese attack on Pearl Harbor in Hawaii, signed Executive Order 9066, which led to the removal of 120,000 individuals of Japanese descent—primarily from California, Washington, Oregon, and Arizona—and their assignment to detention camps. Two-thirds of the individuals removed and detained were American citizens.

The wholesale internment was intended to counter a threat to national security although the FBI already had detained two thousand individuals of Japanese ancestry who the agency determined posed a threat to the United States and opposed mass internment. The U.S. Supreme Court in *Hirabayashi v. United States* (320 U.S. 81 [1943]) and in *Korematsu v. United States* (323 U.S. 214 [1944]) held that the internment was based on national security rather than on racial prejudice. The dissenting justices asked how individuals could be detained without proof that they constituted a threat to national security. Justice Frank Murphy denounced the decisions as the "legalization of racism" and pointed out that only those German and Italian residents who were considered to pose a threat to the United States had been interned.

In 1944, after the Roosevelt administration announced it was releasing the internees, the U.S. Supreme Court ordered the release of Mitsuye Endo, who the court determined was a loyal American and posed no threat to national security (*Ex parte Endo,* 323 U.S. 283 [1944]). The Court noted that loyalty is "a matter of the heart and mind, not of race, creed, or color." A number of liberal Supreme Court judges later would write that they regretted their decisions approving the internment of Japanese Americans.

In 1988, President Ronald Reagan in signing the Civil Liberties Act of 1988 declared that the Japanese internment had been a "grave injustice" that was based on "racial prejudice, wartime hysteria, and a failure of political leadership" rather than on the grounds of national security. The act provided a presidential apology and reparations to Japanese Americans. Federal courts later set aside the convictions of Fred Korematsu and Gordon Hirabayashi, both of whom had refused to comply with internment orders, based on the government's suppression of evidence that indicated that Japanese Americans did not pose an internal threat (G. Stone 2004: 283–307).

The examination of the impact of wartime on judicial decisions challenges the notion that legal decisions are as mechanical as an umpire's calling balls and strikes. The law instead is influenced by a range of factors, including the pressures of wartime; the desire of judges to maintain public support; the pressure to support the decisions of the president, Congress, and the military; and racial stereotypes.

Lawrence Friedman and his co-authors provide another way to think about law and society. They distinguish between *internal* and *external* approaches to law. Internal scholarship focuses on court cases, statutes, and constitutional provisions and aims to provide an answer to a legal problem. Law and society relies on the tools of the social sciences and looks at law from the "outside" and explores the *external* social factors that influence the law and how law influences social attitudes and practices (L. Friedman, Pérez-Perdomo, and Gómez 2011: 2–3).

In the next section, two perspectives on law and society are sketched that you might find helpful as you read the remainder of the text.

■ TWO PERSPECTIVES ON LAW AND SOCIETY

Law and society scholars tend to view the relationship between law and society through the lens of two opposing theoretical perspectives. The **consensus perspective** views society as sharing common values and as relatively stable. Law is a mechanism for resolving the occasional disputes that may arise and serves to keep society stable and balanced. A central function of law is to help ensure that people will cooperate with one another and that society will operate in a smooth and integrated fashion.

At the other end of continuum is the **conflict perspective**. Conflict is viewed as a central aspect of society. This is the mirror opposite of the consensus model. Society is viewed as composed of competing groups, and the law is an instrument of coercion that is employed by dominant and powerful groups to maintain their power and control.

The debate between these two perspectives has been a persistent theme in law and society and is unlikely to be resolved. The consensus and conflict approaches provide two useful perspectives through which to view the relationship between law and society.

A Consensus Perspective

The consensus perspective views society as based on shared values. Americans, despite their diversity of race, religion, and attitudes, share common beliefs including principles embodied in the First Amendment such as freedom of religion and expression and a belief in individual responsibility.

Roscoe Pound is the theorist most closely identified with the consensus perspective: the view that the role of law is to reconcile interests and to ensure that society remains in balance. This at times requires that individuals' rights and desires be compromised to ensure society remains strong and stable. Law is like a respected friend who smooths over the occasional misunderstandings that may arise between his or her friends and ensures disputes are settled without resort to bitterness or force. The role of the judge or legislator is to engage in "social engineering" and to find a balance between the claims of the individual and society to achieve social harmony. Pound measured law by how effectively it served society (Pound 1942, 1943, 1954).

Pound identified six "social interests" that are promoted by law and are essential to the maintenance of a secure and stable society. A social interest is a "claim, a want, a demand, an expectation" and encompasses a broad range of areas. Interests include the quality of life, preservation of morals, and conservation of resources. The interest in security includes providing individual health and safety and enforcing contractual obligations. At times, these interests may conflict, and a balance must be struck. Individuals boarding a plane are subjected to searches of their person and property in the interest of countering the social threat of terrorism. In this instance, the law limits individuals' privacy and freedom from intrusion in the interest of the safety and welfare of society.

The notion that society is based on consensus should not be mistaken for a stagnant society stuck in the past or present. Pound used the term *socialization of law* to describe the continuing growth and expansion of the law to respond to various interests and to provide for individual fulfillment. In the past decades, American society has been relatively stable although we have seen an expansion of the rights of women, minorities, individuals who are physically and mentally challenged, consumers, and even animals.

Pound viewed law as the most important of various mechanisms of "social control" that ensure that the societal machine functions smoothly and efficiently. He perhaps underestimates the role of other mechanisms of social control. For example, education imparts a historical understanding and provides the skills that are needed for individuals to become productive members of society. Along with religion, education helps to shape our values and beliefs.

Talcott Parsons elaborates on Pound's vision and describes law as integrating society to ensure a cooperative community of individuals. Law is the tissue that keeps the parts of the body functioning and cooperating together. Individuals on a daily basis obey the rules of the road, businesses follow the terms of contracts, and landlords and tenants respect the terms of a lease. In other words, law establishes the understandings and expectations that keep society functioning in a smooth and integrated fashion (Parsons 1962).

John Sutton views the expansion of voting rights to African Americans living in the South as an example of how the law responds to integrate individuals into society and to protect the interest in maintaining the integrity of the political process. In 1947, only 12 percent of the voting-age African American population was registered to vote in the eleven states of the old Confederacy, and only 1 percent of the voting-age population in Mississippi was registered to vote. A variety of mechanisms were used to disenfranchise African Americans; these mechanisms included a poll tax on African Americans, a literacy test, and the use of so-called white primary elections that excluded African American voters. Congressional efforts to protect voting rights in 1957 and 1960 proved ineffective because the laws depended on individuals to bring legal actions in each county where election officials discriminated against African Americans. The atmosphere changed with the reelection of President Lyndon Baines Johnson in 1964, whose own impoverished background had given him a deep and abiding commitment to equal rights. Public opinion galvanized behind voting rights for African Americans after witnessing the beating of civil rights activists marching from Selma to Montgomery, Alabama. Congress responded by overwhelmingly supporting a strong voting rights measure that authorized the federal government to take control of the voting process in jurisdictions with a history of discrimination. The Voting Rights Act of 1965 transformed politics in the South by increasing African American voting registration and breaking the back of white domination of the political process. The voting rights bill was an important step toward the end of second-class citizenship for African Americans and reflects a strong belief in the right of each individual to participate as an equal in the political process. American democracy could not retain legitimacy in the eyes of the world so long as African Americans, comprising a significant percentage of the population of southern states, were excluded from the political process (Sutton 2001: 163–174).

In 2013, the Supreme Court held a central provision of the Voting Rights Act was unconstitutional. Justice John Roberts explained that this so-called pre-clearance provision that required the "covered" states to obtain the authorization of the Department of Justice before changing voting laws no longer was required. African American registration, voting, and the election of African American political officials had improved dramatically in these states and "approach[ed] parity" with whites. Justice Ruth Bader Ginsburg in dissent noted that Congress in reauthorizing these provisions found that African Americans continued to confront barriers to voting. The decision left intact the provisions of the act that authorized legal actions to challenge practices that abridge or deny any individual to vote on account of race (*Shelby County v. Holder*, 570 U.S. ___ [2013]).

In another example, Lennard Davis traces the history of the Americans with Disabilities Act and ADA Amendments Act of 2008. Davis notes that people with disabilities are the nation's largest disadvantaged minority. They historically were among the poorest citizens, had limited access to public transportation, found buildings inaccessible, and confronted barriers to education. The ADA recognized that disability was a civil rights issue and established the equal rights of individuals with disabilities. The act prohibits private and public discrimination in employment, requires accessibility of public accommodations and private facilities, and requires access to telecommunications. Davis notes that the ADA has provided a uniform set of standards, and although falling short in ensuring employment for people with disabilities, the ADA has been responsible for ramps, electronic doors, curb cuts, accessible bathrooms, and American Sign Language interpreters at public events (L. Davis 2015).

In 2004, in *Tennessee v. Lane*, the U.S. Supreme Court upheld the constitutionality of the ADA. Lane suffered a crushed hip and pelvis during a car accident. Both of Lane's legs were in a cast, and because he was confined to a wheelchair, he was unable to climb the stairs to the second floor of the courthouse. The judge and courthouse personnel reportedly laughed at him as he dragged himself up the stairs for his arraignment. On the trial date, Lane refused to scale the stairs and was arrested for a failure to attend his trial and later pled guilty to driving with a revoked license. His lawyer during the trial shuttled up and down the stairs to communicate with Lane. The U.S. Supreme Court held in a 5–4 decision that Congress had acted in a constitutionally appropriate fashion to protect the fundamental right of an individual with a disability to gain access to court proceedings and that Tennessee was required to provide reasonable means of access in public buildings to individuals with disabilities. Justice John Paul Stevens wrote that the legislative record demonstrates that "discrimination against individuals with disabilities persists in such critical areas as . . . education, transportation, communication, recreation, institutionalization, health services, voting, and access to public services. This finding, together with the extensive record of disability discrimination . . . makes clear . . . that inadequate provision of public services and access to public facilities was an appropriate subject for prophylactic legislation" (*Tennessee v. Lane*, 541 U.S. 509 [2004]).

Lawrence Friedman and Jack Ladinsky's article on the law of industrial accidents is a classic example of law balancing the interests of business and workers (L. Friedman and Ladinsky 1967). Workers who were injured in industrial accidents could sue their employer for damages. However, the fellow-servant rule provided that a worker could not sue an employer for injuries caused by fellow workers. During the Industrial Revolution in nineteenth-century America, workers suffered an increasing number of accidents. Industrialists avoided liability by blaming the injury on workers in the plants. As a result, workers with disabilities were left without compensation for debilitating injuries. This type of situation, however unfortunate, was viewed as the price of economic growth and progress (L. Friedman and Ladinsky 1967).

Courts began to create exceptions to the fellow-servant rule under pressure from the rising number of victims of industrial accidents. It is estimated that beginning in 1900, thirty-five thousand deaths and two million injuries resulted from workplace accidents. The injury rate for railroad workers doubled between 1889 and 1900. Industrialists confronted growing unrest among workers along with the prospect of escalating legal fees and jury awards and the rising costs of insuring their businesses against litigation costs. The solution was for states to adopt workers compensation schemes that strictly limited the amount an employee could receive while recovering from an accident. In Wisconsin, if an accident caused partial disability, the worker received 65 percent of his or her weekly loss in wages during the period of disability. Fixed death benefits were payable to the worker's dependents.

Friedman and Ladinsky note that neither industry nor workers viewed workers compensation as an ideal solution. However, the scheme offered a compromise that was acceptable to both sides, and reaching an agreement was preferable to continued struggle and conflict over the issue of worker health and safety. The legal system responded to a problem by offering a solution that averted labor unrest and continued litigation over industrial responsibility for injuries to workers. Friedman and Ladinsky note that "solutions" very often are compromises that both sides find acceptable.

Despite Pound's optimism, he recognized that law could not solve every problem or provide redress for every grievance. Filing a legal complaint or lobbying for legal reform is expensive and time-consuming and is beyond the financial capacity of most individuals. In other instances, individuals recognize that "you can't fight city hall" and accept injustice. Government agencies suffer from limited budgets and are unable to enforce laws protecting the environment and the health and safety of workers in factories and miners in coal country.

The conflict approach challenges the view that law is a mechanism that provides for social stability and integration. The conflict perspective views disagreement and tension as a central characteristic of society. Recent conflicts over gun rights, abortion, the right to die, and the federal deficit raise the question whether any consensus that may have existed in the past has broken down.

A Conflict Perspective

The conflict perspective is based on the view that society is characterized by competition over money, power, and values. Society is shaped like a pyramid, with the wealthy and the powerful at the top and the mass of people near or at the bottom. The law is one tool used by the powerful to maintain their dominance and to attain their goals.

The noted late radical historian Howard Zinn writes that in the past it was obvious to serfs that they were being exploited by their royal masters who expropriated much of the produce from the land on which the serfs worked. In the modern era, most people tend to view the law with awe and with respect and do not fully grasp that the law is one of the primary instruments used to exploit them. The ability of individuals to understand the law is limited by confusing complexities and by the endless "library of statutes." Most people likely only are vaguely aware of the provisions of the tax code that benefit large corporations. The corporate share of the tax receipts in the United States declined from 30 percent of all revenues in the mid-1950s to 6.6 percent in 2009. General Electric, the largest corporation in the United States, in 2010 paid no taxes on its $14.2 billion in profits and claimed a tax benefit of $3.2 billion. Zinn captures this critical perspective by offering an anecdote involving a powerful mine owner who, when asked why the coal mine operators pay so little in taxes while the local people starve, replied, "I pay exactly what the law asks me to pay." The question Zinn asks is who makes the law and who benefits from the law (Zinn 1971: 18).

One of the foremost proponents of a conflict approach is the criminologist Richard Quinney, who writes that criminal law and presumably law in general is an "instrument" of the ruling class and of the state to support the "existing" political and economic arrangements. The law for Quinney lulls people into the false belief that the system is fair and that all individuals possess equal rights and are able to influence the law. Consider the familiar observation that freedom of speech only is meaningful if you possess a printing press (Quinney 1974: 16, 24).

A number of propositions underlie the conflict theory (Quinney 1974: 16; F. Williams 1980: 214–215).

1. Society is characterized by conflict and conflicting groups.

2. Society is dominated by groups with the greatest economic and political power, and these groups draft and enforce the law and use the law to promote their own self-interest and point of view.

3. Dominant groups use the police and other social control agencies to enforce the laws that promote their self-interest and values.

4. The less powerful groups in society possess limited political power and exert little influence on the formulation of law and on the enforcement of the law.

5. Dominant groups define criminal and unlawful behavior, and the behavior of groups that lack power is more likely to be considered criminal and the members of these groups are more likely to be punished more harshly. An example of a dual standard of justice is the failure to pursue criminal charges against the individuals on Wall Street responsible for the mortgage schemes that led to the global economic downturn.

6. People tend to view the prevailing legal structure as the natural and inevitable order of society and do not stop to ask whether the existing legal structure is fair or just and cannot even imagine how things could be different.

William Chambliss's essay on the English law of vagrancy is a classic study of the role of the law in serving the interests of dominant economic groups. In 1348, the Black Death (the bubonic plague) ravaged Europe and killed roughly 50 percent of the population of England and drastically reduced the number of available workers. Chambliss argues that vagrancy laws were passed to ensure a continuing supply of cheap labor. In 1349, a vagrancy law was adopted in England, which required individuals to work at the pre-epidemic wage level and forbade individuals from moving to a better-paying job or accepting a higher wage. The law also attempted to force individuals to work by declaring it a crime to give alms to the unemployed. In 1360, the punishment for violation of the work provisions by an individual under 60 years of age was fifteen days. In 1499, the law was modified to provide that violators were to be secured in the stocks without bread or water for three days and released (Chambliss 1964).

As the years passed, the vagrancy laws rarely were enforced. Feudalism was being rapidly replaced by an industrial factory economy. The new industrialists and merchants had little interest in tying workers to the land because they required a free and mobile workforce that was available to work in factories and shops. Serfdom gradually declined and was abolished in the sixteenth century.

The Chambliss essay is a case study of how the law of vagrancy initially served the powerful economic interests of feudal landlords and later shifted to protect the interests of the new merchant class. The other message from Chambliss's work is that the law of vagrancy discriminated against and disadvantaged the poor while favoring the "wealthy and the powerful" (Deflem 2008: 123).

In the United States, vagrancy laws historically adopted the language of English statutes and were used against the homeless, beggars, prostitutes, gamblers, the unemployed, gang members, and individuals regarded as a "nuisance." Vagrancy laws in the United States were employed as in England to control crime, to force individuals into the labor force, and to segregate undesirables from the rest of society by consigning them to "skid rows" and "red light districts" (Foote 1956). The laws' broad and elastic language eventually led to their being declared unlawful because they provided the police with an unconstitutional degree of discretion (*Papachristou v. Jacksonville*, 405 U.S. 156 [1971]).

Keep in mind that the conflict model views competition between groups as political as well as moral. Joseph Gusfield, in his classic study of the temperance movement, argues that the "dry forces" primarily were composed of rural, middle-class evangelical Protestants who were threatened by the arrival of urban immigrant Catholics and German Lutherans. Although they lacked political and economic power, these immigrant groups posed a long-term threat to the dominance of rural Protestants. The Protestant groups responded by attempting to reform these "hard-drinking" and "immoral" immigrants and to encourage them to embrace middle-class American values.

In the 1840s and 1850s, rural, evangelical Protestant groups promoted abstinence from alcohol as a status symbol and as a central characteristic of middle-class America. At the beginning of the twentieth century, the United States was rapidly becoming increasingly urban and Catholic. Protestant groups feared their influence was slipping away and confronted the reality that they would soon lose political control. They responded by successfully pushing for passage of the Eighteenth Amendment to the Constitution, which prohibited the manufacture, sale, and transportation of alcohol. Gusfield argues the debate over prohibition, although formally about the dangers of "demon alcohol," really symbolized a struggle between the middle-class Protestant culture of abstinence and the immigrant, working-class drinking culture. The prohibition of alcohol assured Protestants their way of life would be preserved despite the influx of Southern and Eastern Europeans (Gusfield 1986). A central target of the prohibition forces was the local saloons, which were the center of immigrant culture and political organizing. Immigrants were portrayed as threatening the American way of life as a result of their alleged immorality, criminal activity, Catholicism, and lack of work ethic. The anti-alcohol campaigns in the southern states targeted African Americans and working-class whites and in California targeted Hispanics (McGirr 2016).

The repeal of the Eighteenth Amendment fourteen years after its ratification marked a decline in the supremacy of Protestant middle-class abstinence as a sign of social acceptability and the simultaneous increase in the influence of urban immigrant groups and drinking culture. Can you find a contemporary struggle that is reminiscent of the conflict between Protestants and immigrant Catholics described by Gusfield?

The conflict approach asks us to consider who wins and who loses when considering the law and legal system. Critics of the conflict approach are understandably critical of the notion that law and enforcement of the law can be understood as nothing more than servants of the rich and powerful. You nonetheless should keep the critical perspective along with the consensus perspective in mind as you continue to read this textbook.

1.1 YOU DECIDE

Lon Fuller, in one of his well-known jurisprudential problems, recounts the dilemma of the "grudge informers." He asks the reader to assume the role of the Minister of Justice in a country of twenty million people (L. Fuller 1964: 245–253). The country was characterized by a peaceful and democratic government. A deepening economic depression led to the formation of various small activist groups divided by race, religion, and politics and to a breakdown of stability. The Headman and his Purple Shirt party emerged out of the disorder and promised to restore peace, order, and stability.

The Purple Shirts swept into power based on various falsehoods, misrepresentations, and the physical intimidation of the opposition, which kept many people away from the polls. After assuming power, the Purple Shirts did not change the constitution or civil and criminal codes and did not remove any government officials or remove judges from the bench. Elections were held as scheduled, and votes were accurately counted.

The Purple Shirts, however, subjected the country to a reign of terror. Judges whose decisions were in disagreement with the policy of the Purple Shirts were

(Continued)

beaten and murdered. The laws were interpreted to enable the jailing of political opponents, and secret statutes were adopted, the content of which was known only to the Purple Shirt government elite. Retroactive statutes were adopted that declared as crimes acts that were legally innocent when committed. Opposition political parties were outlawed, and thousands of political opponents were executed following their criminal conviction or were assassinated. A general amnesty was declared for individuals who were Purple Shirt loyalists who had been convicted of crimes in defense of the "fatherland against subversion."

At one point, members of the former Socialist-Republican Party, which had been the most formidable opposition force to the Purple Shirts, were physically intimidated into transferring their property to Purple Shirt activists. These strong-arm tactics later were legalized by a secret statute ratifying the transfer of the property to members of the Purple Shirts.

The Purple Shirts subsequently were overthrown, and a democratic and constitutional government was installed. During the Purple Shirt regime, a number of individuals retaliated against individuals against whom they had grudges by reporting them to authorities. These individuals were accused of such acts as criticizing the government, listening to foreign radio broadcasts, associating with known opponents of the regime, hoarding more than the authorized amount of eggs and other food, and failing to report lost identification papers within five days. These acts were subject to capital punishment. In some instances, the penalties were imposed pursuant to "emergency" statutes adopted by the Purple Shirt regime, and in other instances, the penalties were imposed by legally installed judges without any written law.

As Minister of Justice under the new democratic government, you must decide whether the "grudge informers" who reported violations of the law should be prosecuted although they were following the law under the Purple Shirt regime.

1.2 YOU DECIDE

A number of small cities and towns throughout the country have passed ordinances prohibiting individuals from wearing "saggy pants" in school and even in public. In 2004, the Louisiana state legislature voted down a bill that would have made it "unlawful for any person to wear clothing in any public place or place open to public view which either: (1) Intentionally exposes undergarments; or (2) Intentionally exposes any portion of the pubic hair, cleft of the buttocks, or genitals," with certain exceptions such as "clothing worn in a private residence" or "swimming attire worn at a swimming pool or beach." Violators would have been subject to three days of community service

and a maximum fine of $175. The following year, the Virginia House of Representatives passed a bill that died in the Senate that would have fined any person who "intentionally wears and displays his below-waist undergarments, intended to cover a person's intimate parts, in a lewd or indecent manner."

These laws inspired small towns across the country to adopt anti-saggy-pants ordinances. Some of these ordinances provide for a fine of several hundred dollars and/or several months in jail although towns differ on the energy with which the police enforce these ordinances. President Barack Obama reportedly weighed in on saggy pants and lectured that "brothers should pull up their pants. You are walking by your mother, your grandmother, [and] your underwear is showing. What's wrong with that? Come on. Some people might not want to see your underwear. I'm one of them."

The saggy-pants style reportedly originated in prison where inmates were issued pants that often were too large and in which belts were prohibited.

Civil liberties groups argue that saggy-pants ordinances target young African American and Hispanic males, and that these broad and imprecise laws provide the police with an unreasonable degree of discretion in determining what pants fall within a saggy-pants ordinance and invite racial profiling and restrict young people's freedom of expression. Saggy pants, it is argued, are no more objectionable than skimpy clothing or males walking around shirtless.

Social commentators note that saggy-pants ordinances are reminiscent of the type of condemnation that historically has been directed at the hair and clothing styles of young people and that saggy pants are part of a long tradition of young people using their appearance to create a sense of identity and to express rebellion. Local officials respond that these laws are directed at public indecency rather than youth culture or freedom of expression.

In 2008, Riviera Beach, Florida, became the first town to adopt a saggy-pants law by popular referendum with the support of 72 percent of the electorate. Mayor Thomas Masters, who had sponsored the law, proclaimed, "I am thankful to the people who came out and voted with their conscience and defined what is indecent in our city." A violation of Riviera Beach's saggy-pants law was punishable with a $150 fine or community service for a first offense; a second offense resulted in a $300 fine or additional community service, and habitual violators could be sentenced to up to sixty days in jail.

In April 2009, Riviera Beach's saggy-pants ordinance was held to be unconstitutional under any and all circumstances by County Judge Laura Johnson. Judge Johnson found that there was no legitimate government interest and declared that no matter how "tacky or distasteful" the saggy-pants style is perceived to be by citizens of Riviera Beach, the Fourteenth Amendment's freedom of choice and liberties requirements must prevail.

In 2010, Judge Ruben Franco dismissed the arrest of Julio Martinez in New York City for disorderly conduct for wearing low-hanging and underwear-exposing pants. Disorderly conduct requires causing "inconvenience, annoyance, or alarm to a substantial segment of the public." Judge Franco noted that Martinez had the "right to look ridiculous."

Are saggy-pants ordinances an example of the dysfunction of law? Are they an example of the consensus or conflict approach to law? Should high schools and localities regulate student dress? As a judge, would you hold that saggy-pants laws violate the civil rights and liberties of individuals?

CHAPTER SUMMARY

The establishment and maintenance of order in society is based on a combination of informal and formal modes of social control. As society becomes more complex, greater reliance is placed on the formal mechanism of social control of the law.

There are various approaches to defining the law, each of which tends to reflect the perspective of the individual proposing the definition. One focus is on formal rules enforced by authoritative governmental institutions; other definitions focus on rules enforced by coercion or force.

The law, however defined, performs various functions in society: social control, dispute resolution, and social change. The law, despite its importance, also can be dysfunctional or have a negative impact on society. A clear example is the use of law as a mechanism of repression.

The legal systems of countries across the globe may be categorized as failing within various legal traditions.

A tradition is an attitude about how law is made and should be applied and the process of legal change. The four primary traditions or families of law are the common law, civil law, Socialist law, and Islamic law. International law plays a role in regulating the relationship between nation-states. There are various perspectives on analyzing a legal system. The focus may be on the study of legal principles, jurisprudence, or law and society.

The various approaches to studying the relationship between law and society generally can be categorized as reflecting a consensus perspective or a conflict perspective. Keep these approaches in mind as you read about theories of the relationship between law and society. In the next chapter, we review the primary theoretical approaches to law and society.

CHAPTER REVIEW QUESTIONS

1. Discuss the various approaches to defining law.

2. Distinguish between norms, mores, and folkways.

3. Compare and contrast the common law, civil law, and social law legal traditions. Which legal tradition best protects rights and liberties?

4. Does international law have the central characteristics of law?

5. Distinguish between the study of legal doctrine, the study of jurisprudence, and the study of law and society.

6. Compare and contrast a consensus perspective with a conflict perspective on law. Which approach most accurately describes law in contemporary America?

TERMINOLOGY

"black letter" law   28
common law   13
comparative justice   12
conflict perspective   34
consensus perspective   33
distributive justice   12
dysfunctional role of the law   25
families of law   12

family of civil law   14
folkways   4
functions of law   23
international law   22
jurisprudence   30
justice   11
mores   4
norms   4

precedent   13
restorative justice   12
retributive justice   12
sanctions   5
Shari'a   18
socialist law   17
substantive justice   12
values   4

ANSWERS TO TEST YOUR KNOWLEDGE

1. False

2. True

3. True

4. True

5. False

6. False

WANT A BETTER GRADE?

Get the tools you need to sharpen your study skills. Access practice quizzes, eFlashcards, author podcasts, SAGE journal articles, hyperlinks for Law and Society on the Web, and more at **study.sagepub.com/lippmanls2e**.

THEORIES OF LAW AND JUSTICE

TEST YOUR KNOWLEDGE: TRUE OR FALSE?

1. Both natural law and legal positivism consider an unjust law to be a valid law.

2. A legal system based on utilitarianism would provide economic benefits to economic elites that do not benefit most people in society.

3. A society based on Immanuel Kant's categorical imperative likely would provide medical care for everyone in society.

4. Henry Maine's theory that law progresses from "status" to "contract" is illustrated by the transition from slavery to wage labor.

5. Karl Marx viewed law as independent of the economic structure of society.

6. Max Weber made an important contribution to types of authority and to types of legal thinking.

7. Legal realism and sociological jurisprudence focus on factors outside the law to explain how judges decide cases.

8. Functionalism questions whether law is essential to the operation of society.

9. Statistical analysis on how judges decide cases in various areas of the law is an example of legal behavioralism.

10. Libertarianism favors increased government regulation.

11. Critical legal studies, critical race theory, and feminist jurisprudence all endorse the existing legal system.

Check your answers on page 68.

■ INTRODUCTION

In this chapter, we review some leading theories of the origins and basis of law. These thinkers and schools of thought address a number of broad questions about the law. As you read this chapter, ask yourself what problem the theorist is attempting to explain and how the various approaches differ from one another. The problems addressed by these various theorists include the following:

What factors account for the development of law?

How have laws evolved historically?

What are the philosophical principles on which law is based?

Is there a relationship between law and society?

Can law be used to impact and to reform society?

What factors account for the decisions of judges and juries?

What methods should be used to study law and society?

Is law neutral, or does law serve certain interests in society?

■ LEGAL SYSTEMS

Before we turn to examine various theories on the origins, development, and purpose of law, it might be helpful to consider that the law is part of a *legal system* with various component parts. Martin Golding proposes that a legal system requires the "jural activities" shown in Table 2.1 (Golding 1975: 17).

Table 2.1 ■ Components of a Legal System	
Laws	The laws define the formal rules regulating society.
Legislation	There is an agency for changing and making laws.
Enforcement	There is an agency for enforcing the laws.
Dispute resolution	There is an agency for settling disputes between individuals.

Golding notes that not all legal systems satisfy these requirements.

In thinking about legal systems, we tend to focus on legal systems in the United States and in Europe. These legal systems have detailed, written civil and criminal codes drafted by legislatures, interpreted by a network of trial and appellate courts, and enforced by the police and other law enforcement agencies. Administrative agencies regulate areas such as banking, food and drug safety, education, and transportation.

There are other, less detailed systems of law that do not include all the elements thought to be required for a legal system. E. Adamson Hoebel describes the Comanche Native American tribe, whose native land in the nineteenth century was in the headwaters of the Yellowstone and Missouri Rivers. The chieftains in charge of the tribes lacked formal legal authority and exercised little control over members of the tribe. There was no judicial or legislative authority or formal mechanisms for resolving disputes or for establishing the law. The law was enforced by each individual member of the tribe based on customary practice (Hoebel 1979: 127–141). Wife-stealing and adultery were prevalent and at times were used by warriors to assert their masculinity and strength. The warrior in most instances willingly paid reasonable restitution for the "adulterous wife." If payment was not forthcoming, the husband was entitled to call on friends and neighbors or a "mighty warrior" to exact physical retribution. The husband, in turn, was subject to retaliation from the dead warrior's friends and family.

Various Eskimo societies lack government, courts, police, or written law. Disputes tend to result from homicide, adultery, and marriage. Conflicts at times are settled as an alternative to blood revenge through wrestling, head butting, and straight-armed blows to the side of the head. Other Eskimos settle dispute through "song duels." The winner is decided by the response of the crowd. In West Greenland, the singer is accompanied by a chorus comprising the entire household (Hoebel 1979: 67–99).

As you can see, legal systems are diverse and different. Legal systems do not evolve by accident. There is fairly widespread acceptance of the notion that legal systems develop in response to the nature of society—some would say in response to the economic requirements of society. Developmental models of law are premised on the view that legal systems move from "simple" to "complex" forms as society evolves. Law, in turn, also can influence society by prohibiting destructive practices and providing conditions for economic development (Schwartz and Miller 1975).

As shown in Table 2.2, we can sketch three phases of evolution for legal systems.

Table 2.2 ■ Phases of Evolution for Legal Systems

Phase	Description
Premodern legal systems	These legal systems primarily are found in hunter and gatherer societies in which individuals share a common ethnicity and in which history and individuals are unified by face-to-face cooperation and by a communal lifestyle. Customary law regulates marriage, child-rearing, incest, homicide, and sexual offenses. Individuals resort to self-help to settle disputes.
Transitional legal systems	In the transition to an agricultural society, landowners accumulate wealth and institutions develop to settle disputes over land, crops, employment, and the sale of goods. Agriculture leads to the development of transportation, banking, consumer goods, and educational institutions.
Modern legal systems	An extensive body of civil and criminal laws develops, and specialized agencies are required to regulate increasingly specialized areas such as banking, food and drugs, and the economy. A system of local, national, and specialized police forces is instituted. Procedural rules for bringing legal cases and the law of evidence are developed, and the court system provides for a system of appeals to ensure fair results. Legal precedents are relied on by courts to ensure predictability and continuity of results.

Legal philosophers have developed various theories to explain the origin, nature, development, and purpose of law in these diverse systems of justice. Most theories fall far short of providing a comprehensive explanation that applies to all types of legal systems.

These theories are best thought of as ways of thinking about law. You will encounter references to various theories throughout the remainder of the text. We begin with natural law.

■ NATURAL LAW

The **natural law** school views law as a set of universal principles applicable to all societies in all historical epochs. These principles are discoverable through reason. The ideal society should be ordered in accordance with natural law principles, which reflect the divine will for the ordered plan of the universe. Positive law that is inconsistent with natural law is considered to be unjust and to lack legitimacy and is not to be obeyed.

The notion of natural law is nicely captured by Aristotle, who in describing natural law notes that it "everywhere has the same force and does not exist by people's thinking this or that." The Roman philosopher Cicero writes that "there is in fact a true law, namely right reason, which is in accordance with nature, applies to all men and is unchangeable and eternal." Cicero lists various principles drawn from the law of nature including the obligation to avoid harming others, the right of self-defense and to protect others from harm, and the prohibition on cheating (J. Kelly 1992).

Saint Thomas Aquinas by Carlo Crivelli, 1476. The Yorck Project via Wikimedia Commons

PHOTO 2.1 Saint Thomas Aquinas (1225–1274) was an Italian Dominican friar and priest who in *Summa Theologiae*, written between 1265 and 1274, articulated a comprehensive religious statement of natural law.

Thomas Aquinas (1225–1274) in *Summa Theologiae*, written between 1265 and 1274, articulated a comprehensive religious statement of natural law. Aquinas contends there are four categories of law: the eternal law (known to God); natural law (eternal law, which may be known to human beings); divine law (revealed in scripture); and human law (law enacted by government authorities). A human law that conforms to eternal or natural law is just because it serves the good of humanity; a law that fails to conform to eternal or natural law is "no law at all."

Aquinas does not accept that any law that is enacted has the status of law. An unjust law is "violence" rather than "law." The categories of unjust law include laws intended to benefit lawmakers rather than the common good, laws intended to benefit society but that unfairly burden certain members of society, and laws that go beyond the legal authority of the lawmaker.

Natural law often is identified with the Roman Catholic Church or with other religious traditions although there is not necessarily a relationship between religion and natural law. Secular humanists, for example, argue there are universal values all societies should aspire to achieve, including freedom from hunger, protection against violence and abuse, and access to education and health care. The difficulty, of course, is reaching an agreement on the content of natural law. Natural law has experienced a renaissance in the twentieth century, providing an intellectual foundation for the trials of Nazi war criminals at Nuremberg following World War II and for the UN adoption of various documents on international human rights. Oxford University legal theorist John Finnis revived natural law theory in his book *Natural Law and Natural Rights*. Finnis argues there are "self-evident" principles that are "really good for human persons" (Finnis 2011). We can see echoes of natural law in the contemporary debate over the "right to die" (discussed in You Decide 2.3 on the study site).

Legal positivism, in contrast to natural law, finds law in the "four corners" of government, laws, orders, and enactments.

■ LEGAL POSITIVISM

John Austin (1790–1859) was a British philosopher known for his advocacy of **legal positivism**. Positivism is based on the Latin *positum*, which means law as set forth or posited. Austin articulated his views in a set of lectures at the University of London published in 1832 under the title *The Province of Jurisprudence Determined*.

Austin pioneered a branch of legal positivism that is variously termed *formalistic, conceptualistic,* or *analytical jurisprudence* (Schur 1968: 26).

Austin was unconcerned with the "goodness" or "badness" of legal rules, and considered such questions "extra-legal" (Schur 1968: 26). He took the position that law is the command of the sovereign. A command is an order accompanied by a threat to impose a disability or punishment for disobedience. He believed that even an immoral law enacted in accordance with established procedures should be obeyed. Austin argued to proclaim that laws that are bad or contrary to the will of God are "void and not to be tolerated, [and to obey such laws] is to preach anarchy" (John Austin 1995: 157, 186). There is some confusion because of Austin's use of the term *sovereign*, which he considers to include any individual or specified group of individuals to whom most of society "has the habit of obedience." Contemporary legal scholar Donald J. Black broadens Austin's definition of law by stating that law is "governmental social control." Black's definition has the advantage of clearly indicating that the sovereign includes the executive and legislative branches of government as well as the courts (D. Black 1976).

Austin's theory of legal positivism was anticipated by the famous English political philosopher Thomas Hobbes (1588–1679), who in *Leviathan* viewed people as originally living in a state of nature in which life was "nasty, brutish, and short." Individuals in order to escape this deadly environment formed a social contract in which they traded their freedom for the security of rule by a strong sovereign. The law for Hobbes simply is the commands of the sovereign with which individuals are contracted to obey. He wrote that "[a] law . . . is the speech of him who by right commands . . . to others [what is] to be done or omitted" (J. Kelly 1992: 237).

The benefit of positivism is that it clearly states what constitutes the law and where to find the law. Positivists do not necessarily embrace the existing law; they merely state that it should be obeyed until it is changed or modified.

Hans Kelsen (1881–1973) was an Austrian scholar who taught in Europe and later at Harvard Law School. Kelsen advocated what he called the "pure theory of law." He called his theory a pure theory because he argued that morality should play no role in evaluating the legitimacy of a law. A law is valid so long as it is obeyed (Kelsen 1967).

H. L. A. Hart (1907–1992) endorsed legal positivism although he argued that the law should be viewed as comprising both primary rules (e.g., obligations to act or not act) and what he terms "secondary rules." Secondary rules include rules of recognition that establish standards for identifying what is recognized as a law (e.g., constitutional requirements for a law such as non-discrimination), a rule of adjudication for determining whether a rule has been violated (e.g., courts), and a rule of change (e.g., how rules are modified) (Hart 1961).

Hart's contribution is to argue that the law is more complicated than whatever the sovereign commands.

You can see that there is a tension between natural law, which holds that only laws that are consistent with the natural order are legitimate, and positivism, which stipulates that laws enacted in accordance with established procedures are legitimate and are to be obeyed. This tension often arises when discussing civil disobedience (see Chapter 10).

■ UTILITARIANISM

Jeremy Bentham (1748–1832) is best known for his utilitarian philosophy and the notion that law should maximize the "greatest good for the greatest number." This greatest happiness principle is the foundation of **utilitarianism** and is based on the belief that individuals in their personal lives act to maximize their pleasure and to minimize their pain. Bentham argued this same principle should guide social policy.

Bentham was a proponent of *legal instrumentalism*, the view that law should be designed to achieve specific goals and purposes. He rejected the notion of natural law and natural rights as "nonsense on stilts" because he argued that rights only exist when embodied in concrete law. He asked how rights can be said to exist when one person's right to food and a loaf of bread may result in the denial of another's right to food and a loaf of bread. Bentham noted that rights inspire people to passionately pursue what they believe they are entitled to possess when the role of law should be to discourage passion and competition.

PHOTO 2.2 Jeremy Bentham (1748–1832) was an English social theorist and social reformer known for his utilitarian moral philosophy.

Martin Golding illustrates Bentham's philosophy by noting that if the fine for "overtime parking" is one dollar and the cost to park in a parking garage is two dollars, then the incentive to violate the law will not be counterbalanced by the incentive to obey the law. On the other hand, Golding notes that a ten-dollar fine may be more than is required to persuade individuals to park in the garage (Golding 1975: 77).

Bentham, along with Italian criminologist Cesare Beccaria (1738–1794), was critical of what he viewed as the lack of fairness in the criminal justice system. Defendants were incarcerated without charge, judges and prosecutors were corrupt and extracted bribes, confessions were obtained through torture, and individuals were incarcerated in atrocious conditions. The death penalty in England was imposed for more than two hundred crimes, including for pickpocketing and stealing food, and sometimes individuals were disemboweled or dismembered before being executed.

Beccaria, in *On Crimes and Punishments* (first published in 1764), argued that criminal sanctions should be proportional to the offense and designed to deter the individual offender and other individuals from committing a crime. The purpose of punishment was not revenge or suffering. Beccaria argued an effective punishment was required to be severe, swift, and certain. The severity of the punishment should slightly outweigh the pleasure of the crime. Punishment beyond this point is unnecessary, excessive, and inhumane. A swift and certain punishment reinforces the connection between the crime and the punishment (Beccaria 1988).

Beccaria's ideas spread across Europe to the United States and inspired Bentham to criticize American criminal justice policies. Utilitarianism continues to have an influence in the debate over deterrence and punishment (see Chapter 9).

■ THE CATEGORICAL IMPERATIVE

In 1785, German moral philosopher **Immanuel Kant** (1724–1804) wrote *Groundwork of the Metaphysics of Morals*, which was intended as an alternative approach to utilitarianism.

Kant believed human beings are capable of ordering their life based on reason and are not controlled by emotion and impulse. He argued human beings should rely on their capacity for reason and self-consciously act with respect and regard for all individuals at all times and to act as if this was a universal law of nature. Kant writes that human beings are worthy of absolute respect because they are rational and reasoning: "I say that man, and in general every rational being, exists as an end in himself, not merely as a means for arbitrary use by this or that will" (Kant 1993: 30). This "formula of humanity" leads Kant to formulate what he terms the **categorical imperative**: "Act in such a way that you always treat humanity, whether in your own person or in the person of any other, never simply as a means, but always at the same time as an end." Kant's categorical imperative dictates that we treat all human beings, whoever they are and wherever they live, with respect because of their rational capacity (Sandel 2009: 122).

Kant treats human beings as "ends in themselves" and criticizes utilitarianism for a willingness to treat human beings as a "means to an end" (Sandel 2009: 110). For example, Kant would condemn the utilitarian notion that health care should be devoted to the young rather than to the old because the young have a longer life expectancy than the old and likely will make a greater contribution to the future of the country. Law that lacks a moral foundation should not be obeyed because it is the command of the sovereign.

The European historical school, discussed next, was yet another reaction to natural law. This school explained law based on historical forces.

■ HISTORICAL SCHOOL

The nineteenth-century **historical school** directly linked law to society and located the source of law in the historical development of society. As society develops industrial factories, banking, transportation, and large-scale food production, the historical school argued the legal system responds by developing laws and regulations that are not required in a simpler agricultural society. For example, once individuals had begun to work in factories and to purchase food at stores or at restaurants rather than gather their own food, a system of food safety inspection and rules was put into place.

Friedrich Carl von Savigny (1779–1861) was an important early advocate of studying law from a historical perspective. Savigny was a German academic at the University of Berlin who researched the history of Roman law and the influence of Roman law on contemporary law in Europe. He rejected the notion there was a uniform and timeless natural law and also dismissed the notion that law was the product of the command of a sovereign ruler. Savigny, instead, contended that law was linked to society and reflected what he termed the "spirit" of the people, which reflected the values, customs, and beliefs of a society. The ruler would have a difficult time imposing a law that conflicts with the "spirit" of a society (Savigny 1975).

Sir Henry Maine (1822–1888) was an academic at Cambridge University in England who published his lectures in the book *Ancient Law.* Maine argued legal scholars should study the historical evolution of the law, and in his lectures, he traced the development of law from ancient societies to the nineteenth century. He argued societies, although differing in certain respects, evolve in accordance with similar patterns.

Maine's most famous observation is that society develops from family and status to contract. In a family-based society, individual privilege and opportunity are based on family prestige, power, and reputation. The father of the family exercises absolute authority over his wife and children, and all property is in his name.

Maine argues that as society evolves, powerful families lose their grip on power. Social relations come to be based on contracts or signed agreements between individuals. Maine illustrates his argument by noting that the "status" of the slave is replaced by a contractual relationship between servant and master. Feudal serfs are superseded by unionized workers whose union negotiates their conditions of employment. Maine's most famous observation is that "the movement of progressive societies has hitherto been a movement from status to contract" (Maine 1970: 165).

Herbert Spencer (1820–1903) wrote at the same time as Henry Maine and provided a detailed description of the historical relationship between law and society. He sketched five stages of legal evolution and, like Maine, believed the process of industrialization leads to a legal system based on inherited status and privilege being replaced by a legal system based on individual equality, rights, and opportunity. A system of laws emanating from the command of the sovereign and on religious principle inevitably would be replaced by a legal system based on the "consensus of society." Spencer believed that as society develops, there increasingly is less need for government other than to provide public safety (Spencer 1884).

Spencer was an adherent of Charles Darwin and viewed the biological theory "survival of the fittest" as a model for society. He greatly influenced a number of scholars, including William Graham Sumner (1840–1910) of Yale University who is strongly identified with "social Darwinism" and advocated self-reliance and rugged individualism (Sumner 1911).

Photos.com/Thinkstock

PHOTO 2.3 Karl Marx (1864–1883), in writing about the exploitation of the working class under capitalism, established the theoretical foundation for communism.

Sumner articulated a harsh philosophy based on economic competition, the free market, and a limited government that did not intervene to protect the poor and disadvantaged. He opposed government-supported education, health care, and support for the poor and disadvantaged because these activities interfered with the law of natural selection.

■ CLASSICAL SOCIOLOGICAL THEORISTS

The three leading early sociologists—Émile Durkheim, Max Weber, and Karl Marx—wrote on the relationship between law and society. **Classical sociological theory** accepts the notion that law and society interact with one another. Marx and Durkheim, in particular, theorize that law is influenced by society and that law changes in accordance with the influences of society.

There are few thinkers whose work has been as influential as that of **Karl Marx** (1818–1883). You undoubtedly are familiar with the basic tenets of Marxism. Marx described society as developing through various socioeconomic stages although he concentrated on the transition from capitalism to communism.

Marx's primary focus was the industrial capitalism that existed in England. Under capitalism, the bourgeoisie own the *means of production*, such as tools, machinery, and factories. The proletariat or workers own almost no property whatsoever and work under exploitative conditions in the factories. The bourgeoisie perpetuate this inequity because of their interest in exploiting the workers and maximizing their profits.

Marx argued that under industrial capitalism the elites own the means of production and the working class works long hours for subsistence wages in unsafe conditions. Marx viewed the law as part of the *superstructure*, which is determined by the economic relations (the economic base) between individuals in society. Marx wrote in *The Poverty of Philosophy* (1900: 197) that "legislation . . . never does more than . . . express in words, the will of economic relations." The law, on the surface appearing to be fair, serves the interests of capitalism. Legal rules are interpreted and used by the economic elites to maintain their control of property and to induce a false consciousness among the proletariat by convincing them that society is fair and just. Marx addressed the bourgeoisie in his famous *Communist Manifesto* and wrote that "jurisprudence is but the will of your class made into a law for all, a will whose essential character and direction are determined by the economic conditions of existence of your class" (Marx and Engels 1955: 47).

Marx wrote a series of newspaper articles criticizing the Forestal Theft Act of 1837 adopted in the Rhineland and similar laws adopted in other German states. The law prohibited the peasantry from engaging in their traditional practice of gathering wood and other materials to help support themselves and to warm themselves in the winter months. The rapid growth of the German economy meant that this material was needed by business for the construction of ships, machinery, and roads. Marx pointed to the law as an example of how law is used by the economic elites to promote their own self-interest. He wrote that criminalizing the gathering of loose wood on the ground resulted in the "sacrifice of the poor to a lie." Marx also condemned a series of laws censoring the press, arguing that the laws were intended to punish opinions critical of the government (Trevino 2008: 102).

Marx, in *A Contribution to the Critique of Political Economy* (1972: 263), predicted that capitalism would collapse and be replaced by communism, the "dictatorship of the proletariat" based on the principle of "from each according to his ability, to each according to his needs." In this stage, private property is abolished, and in this utopian and blissful society, there is no need for law. Marx's theory of "dialectical materialism" is a dialectic that views the revolutionary clash between capitalism and labor as inevitable.

Max Weber (1864–1920) was a prominent German professor of political economy and is regarded as one of the most influential and significant sociological thinkers of the modern age. Weber's most important contribution to law and society is his discussion of political domination, which he defines as the probability that specific commands will be obeyed by a group of persons. Compliance may be obtained through the physical or psychological coercion of reluctant members of the group. A second, less costly way to obtain compliance is through authority or because the commands of a leader are viewed as "rightful" or "deserved." Weber identifies three types of authority, which help us understand different types of legal reasoning and why people obey the law. In reality, any ruler combines aspects of all three of these types of authority (Weber 1954).

Charismatic authority. A charismatic authority is an individual whose pronouncements are obeyed because of what are viewed as his or her extraordinary qualities whether based on magic or supernatural or heroic powers of connection with God. The charismatic authority may make decisions based on his or her insights, intuition, or revelations and is not limited by precedent, logic, or consistency. Weber's primary examples of charismatic authority are the Hebrew prophets Amos, Isaiah, Jeremiah, Ezekiel, and Hosea.

Traditional authority. The legitimacy of traditional authority is based on the status of an individual's office or position, typically an inherited status. Examples are the pharaoh and the feudal lord. The ruler has discretion to decide cases and to make policy based on his or her discretion.

Rational-legal authority. Individuals exercising rational-legal authority come to power in accordance with established procedures and make decisions based on objective and impersonal rules embodied in written documents. Such an individual is obeyed because of the legitimacy of the rules on which his or her decision is reached rather than based on personal loyalty to the ruler.

Weber provides a definition of law emphasizing that law, unlike custom or ethical guidelines, is backed by the power of coercion. "An order will be called law if it is externally guaranteed by the probability that physical or psychological coercion will be applied by a staff of people in order to bring about compliance or avenge violation" (Weber 1978: 34).

Weber proceeds to develop four ideal types of legal thinking (described below). In Weber's typology, legal procedures are either formal or substantive. Formal law proceeds in accordance with established and uniform rules, regardless of the outcome of the analysis. Substantive law involves a case-by-case analysis. Legal procedures also may involve rational or irrational law. Rational procedures involve logical analysis or an established method of analysis. Irrational procedures involve magic, divine revelation, or the supernatural.

Formal irrational thought. Established and strictly required procedures are employed by charismatic or traditional authorities although decisions are irrationally derived without explanation and are based on magic, divine revelation or guidance, or personal insight. A commonly cited example is the Azande tribe in Sudan in which an individual's innocence or guilt is determined by the reaction of chickens who are fed poison.

Substantive irrational thought. Decisions are made by a charismatic and traditional authority on a case-by-case basis and are guided by ethical, religious, and political considerations rather than on the basis of general rules. There is no concern with consistency between various judgments or with offering an explanation. The legitimacy of the decision is based on the wisdom of the law giver. Weber notes this mode of decision-making resembles the *khadi*-justice, or *qadi*, the Muslim judge who arbitrates disputes between buyers and sellers in the market.

Substantive rational thought. Substantive decisions are made by charismatic and traditional authorities and are based on principles drawn from non-legal, political, and religious sources. There is a concern with consistency with religious, ethical, or political ideals rather than with the "factual truth" of the matter. Weber had in mind the Buddhist emperor Ashoka (ca. 264–226 BCE), whose decisions followed the religious and spiritual principles of the Buddha.

Formal rational thought. Decisions are based on logical analysis of legal rules found in legal sources with little concern for moral or religious considerations. Universal rules are set forth in written documents and applied in a uniform fashion. Outcomes have a high degree of predictability. A crucial aspect of formal rational thought is the development of a secular legal system that is separate from religious courts.

Weber connects law to society when he argues that formal rational thought made an important contribution to the development of modern European industrial capitalism. He does not contend that there is a causal relationship between the economy and law. The law is shaped by social, cultural, and political factors. He instead argues that economic development is encouraged by an insistence on clear, certain, definite, and predictable legal rules that regulate relationships between people. Formal legal rationality nonetheless is crucial to the development of industrial capitalism. Individuals can enter into contracts to sell goods when there are universally established and accepted rules regulating the delivery of goods and the payment of monies, and sellers are confident that courts will award damages for a breach of the contract. The number of laws increases as society grows more complex, and the challenge is to ensure that these rules are communicated and explained.

Émile Durkheim (1858–1917) is a third leading legal sociologist. Durkheim is considered to be the first French sociologist and was named a professor at the Sorbonne in Paris, where he devoted himself to the scientific study of society. Durkheim in *The Division of Labor* explored social solidarity, the "glue" that keeps a society together.

A society is united by a sense of solidarity, and societies have different types of solidarity as they evolve. Durkheim viewed law as reflecting the type of solidarity in a society. *Mechanical solidarity* exists in small, homogeneous preindustrial societies in which individuals share attitudes, beliefs, values, lifestyles, and habits. People generally engage in identical types of labor, hunting, crop raising, handicraft making, and child-rearing. Individuals adhere to the same values, religion, and lifestyle, and there is little tolerance of dissent or individuality. Durkheim terms the beliefs and sentiments common to the average members of a society "collective consciousness." Durkheim writes that "we should not say that an act offends the common consciousness because it is criminal, but that it is criminal because it offends that consciousness" (Durkheim 1964: 40).

Organic solidarity, in contrast, is found in large-scale, diverse societies with an economic division of labor. Social cohesion is based on the interdependency of individuals rather than on a shared sense of community and common values. Organic solidarity is characteristic of large, industrial societies. Individuals, although they have different points of view and values, are tied together by the fact that each person is able to perform a task required by other individuals.

Durkheim theorized that societies evolve from mechanical to organic solidarity. Each of these forms of social organization is characterized by a different approach to legal regulation. Mechanical solidarity is associated with repressive sanctions. Repressive penalties are severe punishments that reflect moral outrage and anger over acts that offend social values. Infractions of the rules are an attack on the values that unite society, and for that reason, they are harshly punished.

Organic solidarity is characterized by restitution. The stress is on financially compensating individuals for the injuries they suffered. The goal is to achieve reconciliation and restorative justice and to maintain positive social relations between individuals. The primary legal form in societies based on organic solidarity is the contract, which people use to order their interdependent relationships with one another. Criminal punishments involve imprisonment and fines rather than physical punishment because the law recognizes the humanity of offenders. A society based on organic solidarity is more complex than a society based on mechanical solidarity and as a result will have more laws and agencies regulating activities ranging from banking and taxation to transportation.

Durkheim notes we cannot observe a society's form of solidarity. The type of law, however, provides insight into the type of social organization in a society.

■ LEGAL REALISM

American **legal realism** was a movement that argued that the focus should be actual functioning of the law. Realism united a diverse group of scholars, all of whom believed legal decisions were explained by extra-legal factors, such as a judge's experiences, prejudices, and psychology and powerful social interests and forces, rather than by legal logic or precedent. Scholars accordingly should focus on the "real" reasons that explain the decisions of judges and juries.

Oliver Wendell Holmes Jr. (1841–1935) was son of a justice of the Massachusetts Supreme Judicial Court. He followed in his father's footsteps as a judge on the Massachusetts high court. In 1902, President Theodore Roosevelt appointed Holmes to the U.S. Supreme Court, where he distinguished himself as one of the greatest justices in the twentieth century. Holmes's legal philosophy later became known as "legal realism."

Holmes challenged legal formalism, the notion that legal rules are the product of logical analysis and that the outcome of cases is dictated by the mechanical application of legal rules. He argued the "life of the law has not been logic, it has been experience."

According to Holmes, judges first find a result that reflects their own personal prejudices, political philosophy, or public policy preferences and then find a legal rule that supports and justifies their personal viewpoint. As Edwin M. Schur notes, Holmes argued judges "make" rather than "find" the law (Schur 1968: 43). His philosophy became known as legal realism because he advocated looking at how law actually functioned rather than focusing on the outcome that would result by applying the legal rule.

Law, according to Holmes, is not a mathematical enterprise in which there is a mechanical and predetermined result. In most instances, there is conflict over the legal rules, and the outcome of a case is dictated by powerful political and economic interests. He wrote that "ultimate victory" invariably belonged to the "strongest."

Holmes looked at how courts actually decided cases rather than focusing on legal rules. He wrote that predictions of what courts "will do in fact and nothing more . . . are what I mean by the law." He stated that the lawyer, in predicting judicial decisions, should look at the law from the view of the "bad man" who does not care about moral considerations or ethical rules and only cares about the outcome of the case. In other words, the focus should be on the actual functioning of courts rather than an analysis of legal rules (Holmes 1938: 461).

Holmes argued that juries also decide cases based on their sense of what is right and what is wrong and do not automatically follow the law in reaching a result.

Holmes's focus on how the law actually functioned rather than on legal rules on the books inspired scholars like Karl Llewellyn (1893–1962), E. Adamson Hoebel (1906–1993), and Jerome Frank (1889–1957). Llewellyn and Hoebel are known for *The Cheyenne Way* (1941), their empirical study of the law of the Cheyenne Indians. In *Law and the Modern Mind* (1930) and *Courts on Trial* (1949), Frank focused on judges and juries in trial courts rather than on the decisions of appellate courts and argued lawyers were so intent on winning, the testimony of witnesses was so inaccurate and biased, and the evidentiary record was often so incomplete that the trial process did not necessarily result in a fair and balanced verdict. He compared the unpredictability and reliability of a trial to throwing pepper in the eyes of a surgeon during an operation, and he advocated a radical reform of the trial process. Frank suggested that Freudian psychological analysis might be a fruitful approach to explaining the behavior of judges. Thurman Arnold in a book that continues to be important argued that law plays a symbolic function by focusing attention on the ideals that unite society and by diverting attention from society's shortcomings (Arnold 1962: 23–70).

Holmes and the legal realists were early advocates of the view that is widespread among legal academics today that there is a difference between law on the books and law in action and that judicial decisions are based on factors other than legal logic. He advocated demystifying the law and viewing legal rules as reflecting choices about public policy rather than viewing legal rules as the product of rationality and logic.

Legal realism made an important contribution in calling for legal scholars to go beyond legal rules and to undertake an empirical study of the decisions of judges and jurors. The realists also believed society continuously evolved and that the law must be adjusted to these new developments. Their concern with public policy and legal reform inspired a number of the individuals who worked for President Franklin Delano Roosevelt during the New Deal.

■ SOCIOLOGICAL JURISPRUDENCE

Roscoe Pound (1870–1964), professor of general jurisprudence at Harvard Law School, first articulated the ideas that formed the foundation of **sociological jurisprudence** in a 1906 address to the American Bar Association. He argued law should be evaluated based on the "results it achieves" rather than based on the logical consistency of legal rules. The true purpose of the law is to make people's lives easier and happier. He rejected the notion of law as a "slot-machine" in which the judge pulls the lever and a logically consistent decision emerges from the machine. Pound wanted the law to be engaged in "social engineering," directed at solving societal problems rather than focusing on the logical consistency between legal rules.

Pound wrote during a period of urbanization, immigration, concentration of economic power and growing poverty, and exploitation of labor. His purpose in writing was to get lawyers and judges to examine the impact of law and to use the law to address social problems.

Pound urged lawyers and judges to consult the new and growing literature in political science, sociology, and economics and to analyze the relationship between law and society, a project that he labeled sociological jurisprudence. Pound advocated an action-oriented and practical jurisprudence in which laws and judicial rulings were designed and evaluated based on their impact on society rather than based on legal analysis (Pound 1908: 605).

Pound drew on psychology to identify various social interests—such as physical safety, economic progress, and environmental conservation—that were central to society and theorized that the function of law was to secure these interests to individuals and to adjust the competing claims, such as demand for economic development against the claims of environmentalists to conserve resources.

A lasting impact of sociological jurisprudence is to link the study of law and the social sciences and to pioneer the use of social science data in legal briefs and decisions. Sociological jurisprudence also is important for drawing attention to the gap between law on the books and law in the books.

Oxford professor A. V. Dicey (1835–1922) in a series of lectures at Harvard Law School argued that the development of English law was dependent on public opinion. He contended that at any given time there is a dominant set of beliefs, sentiments, and accepted principles, which together "make up the principle of public opinion of a particular era." These ideas shape the law and originate in the ideas of a single thinker or group of thinkers. Dicey had in mind the influential thinkers who have changed the way we look at the world, for example, Charles Darwin with his theory of evolution. These ideas are repeated and spread by disciples. The success of these new ideas in persuading public opinion depends on the strength of the ideas, the enthusiasm of adherents, and, most important, the changed circumstances that cause people to question their beliefs. Shifts in public opinion and the resulting change in the law move at a slow pace except when society is confronted with an emergency or crisis.

Legal innovation, according to Dicey, typically is the product of the ideas that lawmakers acquire in their youth and only are implemented decades later when they assume positions of influence and power. The ability of the older generation fully to implement their ideas is limited by the influence exerted by the younger generation who, because of their different social circumstances, typically hold a different point of view. A successful change in the law, however, encourages a change in public opinion, which, in turn, becomes receptive to even more far-reaching reforms (Dicey 1905: 1–42).

■ FUNCTIONALISM

Functionalism was the predominant approach to law and society in the 1940s and 1950s. The origin of this approach can be traced to the work of French scholar Auguste Comte (1798–1857). Comte made an analogy between the biology of the body and the social organism of society. Each of the various parts of the body performs a function that is essential to the maintenance of the body just as various social practices and institutions perform roles that maintain society. Education, for example, is important for transmitting skills, attitudes, values, and history.

Functionalism views law as performing an important function that assists in keeping the social system in equilibrium and performing in an effective fashion. Émile Durkheim, discussed earlier in the chapter, provided a unique perspective on crime, arguing that deviance plays an important role in ensuring a healthy and fully functioning society. Durkheim asserted that the condemnation and punishment of deviance helps to reinforce social values, unites people against a common threat, creates jobs for criminal justice professionals, and may lead activists to protest the law and to bring about social change.

Functional analysis was applied by prominent social anthropologist Arthur R. Radcliffe-Brown (1881–1955) and by Bronislaw Malinowski (1884–1942) in his study of the Trobriand islanders (Malinowski 1982: 46–47).

An interesting modification was introduced by sociologist Robert K. Merton. Merton called attention to the fact there are "manifest functions" and "latent functions." Manifest functions are those "consequences which make for the adaptation or adjustment of the system." Latent functions are those outcomes that are "neither intended nor recognized." Merton also notes that a social practice or institution may have a dysfunction, which "lessens the adaptation or adjustment of the system" (Merton 1968).

Talcott Parsons (1902–1979) was perhaps the most influential advocate of functionalism. Parsons, in his 1951 book *The Social System,* viewed society or any part of society as a social system. Law may be viewed as a subsystem of society or, in the alternative, studied as a separate social system. Parsons wrote at a high level of abstraction, and in this discussion, we address only the broad generalities of Parsons's complicated functional theory in which law was only one of a number of important components.

Parsons theorized that to survive and prosper, social systems and subsystems must satisfy four functional imperatives (AGIL, shown in Figure 2.1):

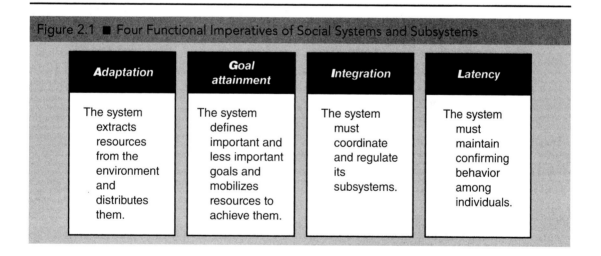

Figure 2.1 ■ Four Functional Imperatives of Social Systems and Subsystems

Adaptation	Goal attainment	Integration	Latency
The system extracts resources from the environment and distributes them.	The system defines important and less important goals and mobilizes resources to achieve them.	The system must coordinate and regulate its subsystems.	The system must maintain confirming behavior among individuals.

The law performs an integrative function by settling disputes and by maintaining harmony and order between the various subsystems, and it performs an adoptive function by continually adjusting subsystems to ensure that they address current challenges. The legal system helps to achieve normative consistency, promoting values such as liberty and freedom and respect for individuals that are cherished by most Americans (goal attainment). The law also functions as a form of social control, meaning that the law regulates what is considered deviant behavior and channels individuals to act in a lawful fashion (latency).

The law, in functional analysis, is part of the glue that binds society together and keeps society from breaking apart. Consider how the law settles disputes between consumers and businesses and between labor and business and has responded to changed circumstances by prohibiting unscrupulous business practices and by outlawing the exploitation and abuse of workers.

Karl Llewellyn, whom we discussed earlier, developed the notion of "law-jobs" to describe the various functions performed by law. Llewellyn's approach was followed by important scholars E. Adamson Hoebel and J. Vilhelm Aubert (1922–1988). Lawrence Friedman lists a number of functions performed by the law (L. Friedman 1977: 17–20). This includes settling disputes, social control, creation of norms and values, recording the thousands of transactions that take place, announcing the rules and standards that help people decide how to act, and providing people and groups with the fair adjudication of disputes.

Functionalism's view that law maintains social balance and equilibrium is at odds with theories that view society in constant stress, conflict, and disagreement.

We next turn our attention to more recent approaches to understanding law. English jurisprudential scholar Roger Cotterrell notes that these approaches owe much to the work of the legal realists (Cotterrell 1989: 207).

■ LEGAL BEHAVIORALISM

Political scientists engaged in the study of judicial politics have pioneered the quantitative analysis of judicial decisions. Statistical techniques are relied on in *judicial behavioralism* to test whether there is a correlation between the personal characteristics of judges and the content of their judicial opinions. Categorizing judicial opinions as "liberal" or "conservative" provides insight into whether party identification, gender, race, or religion are correlated with judges' decisions. This quantitative approach assumes that judges' social and political beliefs, rather than legal analysis, determine how a judge decides a case (Epstein, Landes, and Posner 2013).

Judicial behavioralism is one aspect of **legal behavioralism**, a larger empirical approach to the study of law and society. Legal sociologist Donald Black in a 1972 article argued the sociology of law should be objective and value-free and rely on quantitative measures of law. Issues of public policy, morality, and justice cannot be reduced to quantitative measurement and should not be the concern of sociologists. This approach was roundly rejected by Philippe Nonet, who argued for a normative approach in which sociology of law addresses the moral and public policy issues confronting society (Nonet 1976).

Black, in several important books, measures law by the frequency with which laws are passed, regulations are issued, complaints are filed, calls for police service are made, prosecutions are initiated, individuals are convicted, and civil actions are filed and a verdict is returned. He theorizes that different societies have different quantities of law.

Black presents a complex framework for measuring the quantity, direction, and style of law. *Quantity of law* refers to whether a type of conduct is regulated by law and whether or not a sanction is imposed. *Direction* relates to whether there is a social distance between the parties to a conflict. The *style of law* can be penal, compensatory, therapeutic, or conciliatory. Black uses a complex framework to develop various propositions about the law. These propositions are based on the variation in stratification (inequality), morphology (division of labor), richness of the culture (diversity of backgrounds in society), formal organization (centralization in political and economic spheres), and non-legal social control (peer pressure).

An example of Black's "geometry of the law" is a crime by a homeless person against a wealthy individual. Black argues that, in measuring the "amount of law," the social distance between a victim and an offender is more important than the seriousness of the crime. A crime with an "upward direction" committed by the homeless person against the wealthier individual will involve more law than a crime with a "downward" direction. The wealthier individual who is a crime victim is more likely to call the police, insist that the prosecutor file charges, file a suit for civil damages, and appear at court for sentencing. In contrast, a crime by the wealthier individual against the homeless person likely will result in a fine (compensatory), mediation (conciliatory), or psychological counseling (therapeutic). Black's framework predicts that the same crime will result in different types of legal actions and different punishments depending on the class position of the offender and of the victim (D. Black 1976: 28). A significant number of studies cited in the text that involve quantitative or statistical analysis are part of the behavioral approach to legal analysis.

■ LIBERTARIANISM

The core principle of **libertarianism** is the maximization of individual freedom. According to libertarianism, individuals possess the right to do whatever they want and to use their personal property however they choose so long as they do not interfere with the freedom of other individuals or harm other individuals. Libertarians believe government should be limited to combating crime, protecting private property, enforcing contracts, and safeguarding the national defense. They object to various types of government policies (Sandel 2009: 60):

Paternalism. Laws intended to prevent individuals from harming themselves are unjust. This includes laws requiring seat-belts, motorcycle helmets, and the purchase of insurance. Individuals who risk personal injury or harm are required to assume responsibility for their own medical expenses and may not impose this cost on society.

Morals legislation. Libertarians view laws that use the power of the state to promote virtue or morality as unjust. They accordingly oppose laws that prohibit prostitution, narcotics, and same-sex marriage.

Redistribution of income. Libertarians oppose laws that require people to assist others, most notably the use of taxation to redistribute wealth. Individuals' tax dollars should not be used to support low-cost housing, public education, or health care for others.

Freedom. Individuals also should not be prohibited from discriminating based on race, ethnicity, or gender in employment and should decide for themselves whom they serve in their business. Libertarians also oppose licensing. The government should not prevent individuals from working as a hairstylist, plumber, or real estate agent.

Robert Nozick in *Anarchy, State, and Utopia* (1977) articulates what Michael Sandel observes is the "moral crux of the libertarian claim," the notion of self-ownership. Nozick reasons that when taxing money produced by an individual's labor for purposes of redistribution, the government in essence is requiring an individual to engage in work without compensation: "If people force you to do . . . unrewarded work . . . this . . . makes them a part-owner of you; it gives them a property right in you" (quoted in Sandel 2009: 65).

Each of us may be willing to pay a dollar to see the Rolling Rocks rock group perform. In time, the Rolling Rocks will be wealthier than other individuals. Nozick argues a system of redistribution of the money earned by the Rolling Rocks to a less successful band will distort the free decisions of the individuals who paid a dollar to see the Rolling Rocks. Karen Lebacqz notes that for Nozick, "justice is determined by how the distribution came about, not by what the distribution is." The fact that some people are more prosperous than others may be "unfortunate," but it is not "unfair" (Lebacqz 1987: 56–58).

Free market philosophy advocates agree with libertarians that the free exchange of goods maximizes individual freedom. They also argue the primary benefit of markets is that they promote the general social welfare and result in the delivery of better services.

An example is "school choice" in which parents are issued vouchers that may be used at any public school or partially to offset the cost of a private education. In theory, parents will use their vouchers to send their children to the "best" schools, which will provide an incentive for schools to improve their performance. Poor-performing schools will not attract students and will be unable to continue.

Libertarianism was challenged by John Rawls (1921–2002) in his controversial volume, *A Theory of Justice* (1999). Rawls wipes the slate clean and returns all of us to the state of nature. He asks what principles we collectively would agree on as the foundation of a new society if we were unaware of our individual age, nationality, race, gender, income, and other characteristics. Rawls finds two principles that he believes would be chosen. The first is that each person is to have an equal right to the most "extensive basic liberty compatible with a similar liberty for others." The second principle is that, although equality of wealth and income is not required, any inequalities must work to the benefit of the least affluent members of society.

Rawls's "difference principles" dictate that as an accident of birth some people may have certain inherited financial and intellectual advantages over other people. As a result, people begin the race of life at different points. He argues these advantages are undeserved and in a free market system these individuals enjoy advantages in areas such as college admissions. Rawls believes these advantages should be viewed as a community resource and everyone should share in these individuals' achievements. The privileged individuals accordingly should be expected to pay higher taxes to compensate, to provide special programs like childhood education, and to create economic growth for the less advantaged.

Rawls notes that the talents rewarded in society are somewhat accidental. In another country, a skilled baseball player or popular television personality would not be worth the millions of dollars that she or he earns in the United States. The tax system and system of compensation that favor the wealthy reflect a decision to organize society in a certain fashion. Rawls contends this organizational scheme is not written in stone and that we should share the benefits of our natural advantages with the entire society.

In thinking about Rawls, consider how professional sports leagues regularly change the rules to attract fans to the game. We grumble at the modification of the rules but accept that the rules regularly are changed to make the game more attractive or to shorten its length.

■ LAW AND ECONOMICS

Law and economics applies economic principles and econometric quantitative analysis to legal rules. One branch of law and economics attempts to demonstrate that existing legal rules are based on economic principles, and the other branch proposes reforms of legal principles to make them more efficient. This theoretical approach has the advantage of using quantitative techniques and evidence to evaluate the merits of legal rules (Posner 1973).

Law and economics is heavily based on the thinking of Italian economist Vilfredo Pareto (1848–1923) and is premised on several principles:

Efficiency. The law should attempt to achieve the most efficient results rather than focus on individual rights.

Private resolution. Disputes are best settled through private negotiation and the free market rather than through governmental regulation.

Data. Legal analysis should rely on quantitative analysis rather than rely solely on logical analysis.

A major focus of law and economics has been the law of torts or personal injury although in recent years scholars have applied economic principles to a range of legal areas (Calabresi 1970).

The influence of law and economics can be illustrated by a familiar approach to the deterrence of crime. Gary Becker in his 1968 article "Crime and Punishment: An Economics Approach" argues that criminals are "utility maximizers" and base their decision of whether to commit a crime on opportunity and the costs and benefits of criminal activity. Becker contends that criminal activity like any other economic activity may be increased or decreased by adjusting the "price" or likelihood and amount of criminal punishment. Under this approach, the price of criminal activity will be increased until most criminal activity is deterred. Critics of Becker's approach argue that the question of limitations on police tactics and on the fairness of the length of criminal punishments is subordinated to efficiency in preventing crime (G. Becker 1968).

Law and economics often is criticized as unduly harsh although its principles have been extremely influential in debating the need for government regulations in areas such as the environment. Should we think about "cost maximization" and weigh the expense of worker safety rules against the financial burden involved for industry?

■ CRITICAL LEGAL STUDIES

The **critical legal studies** (CLS) movement was initiated at a 1977 meeting in Madison, Wisconsin. Alan Hunt writing in 1989 found roughly seven hundred articles in print whose authors identified themselves as "Crits." Hunt notes there are various strands to CLS, which loosely are united by an "uncompromising offensive on law and legal theory" (Hunt 1989: 3).

CLS has been called a direct descendant of American legal realism and shares the view that politics and law are one and the same. CLS differs from realism in that it focuses more intently on legal reasoning and on the substance of legal rules. There are several themes that characterize the CLS movement (Trevino 2008: 391–398):

Indeterminacy. There is no single correct answer. Judges may reach various decisions while appearing to rely on the law. This is referred to as the "flippability" of the law.

Antiformalism. Law is not a logical and rational system of reasoning. Judges employ the law to reach decisions that reflect their own ideology.

Contradiction. There are no consistent values underlying the approach to legal issues. In some instances, legal rules regarding search and seizure seem to be concerned about individuals' rights, and in other instances, the rules seem to tilt in favor of the police.

Marginality. Most people do not consult the law in their interpersonal relationships, and the importance of the law is exaggerated. A significant part of our interpersonal relationships are conducted through a "handshake" and trusting one another.

Ideology. Law provides an ideology—a set of values, beliefs, and categories that are used to benefit the powerful and wealthy. America celebrates freedom of expression. The category of freedom of expression, however, has been interpreted by the U.S. Supreme Court to permit individuals to contribute unlimited amounts of money to politicians based on the view that money is a form of speech. Equal protection of the law, which prohibits discrimination, is not interpreted as preventing more money from being spent on wealthy suburban schools than on urban schools.

Trashing. CLS scholarship reveals the gap between the assumptions underlying the law and social reality. The notion that all individuals are equally positioned to compete for entry to college and that affirmative action is unnecessary is an example of the difference between the law and the barriers to upward mobility confronting economically disadvantaged minorities.

Utopian reform. Roberto Unger, a central figure in CLS, proposed "deviationist doctrine," the application of principles from one area to another area. He argued, for example, that democratic principles should be extended from the public sphere to the workplace (Unger 1986).

Feminists and critical race theorists took issue with the fact that CLS did not pay sufficient attention to discrimination and its issues.

■ CRITICAL RACE THEORY

Critical race theory (CRT) focuses on race and the law. CRT grew out of CLS and shares the view that the law is neither neutral nor objective but rather is a mechanism for supporting the dominance of powerful economic and political interests. CRT differs from CLS in that race is viewed at the center of American law and law is viewed as a primary mechanism to perpetuate racism, which it views as a permanent and deeply embedded aspect of American society rather than the product of isolated, discriminatory decisions. CRT views the law as a mechanism for supporting and perpetuating racism in virtually every area of American life, questions whether law has the capacity to modify patterns of discrimination and segregation that is deeply embedded, and is more concerned than CLS with public policy reform.

CRT has pioneered reliance on telling the story of victims to convey the impact of racism. This methodology is a technique for articulating the voice of individuals who in the past were excluded from the academic literature. Storytelling brings home the reality of racism without the weightiness of a technical legal discussion.

Richard Delgado and Jean Stefancic list several characteristics of CRT, including skepticism toward the legal system's endorsement of color blindness and merit-based achievement as an effective antidote to racial disenfranchisement and disadvantage; documentation of how the history of racism continues to impact the law and to perpetuate "white privilege"; recognition of the knowledge and insights of ordinary people who have been the victims of racism; and social activism directed at the elimination of "racial oppression" (Delgado and Stefancic 2001: 6–12).

CRT also developed the notion of intersectionality, which looks at how race, gender, class, sexual orientation, and national origin can work in combination to compound discrimination (Crenshaw 1995).

■ FEMINIST JURISPRUDENCE

Feminist jurisprudence was developed by scholars who concluded CLS was not adequately addressing the "gendered" nature of the law and legal system. Feminist legal scholars are dedicated to documenting how the law has been used to subordinate women.

There are various approaches to feminist legal theory, all of which are committed to reformulating the approach of the law to gender. It is not possible in this brief overview to adequately represent the thinking of this diverse group of scholars. These different perspectives all share a concern with the role of the law in subordinating women to men (Levit and Verchick 2016).

Liberal feminists and *equal treatment feminism* are committed to reforming the legal system to ensure equality between men and women. Liberal feminist lawyers successfully challenged laws excluding women from juries and from various occupations. They also worked to reform laws that victimized women. An example is the repeal of state statutes that provided "marital immunity" for men charged with the rape of their spouse. Another set of laws were challenged that were intended to protect but disadvantaged women such as by limiting the number of hours that they could work. The struggle for equality is far from finished: women still lack equal pay for equal work, continue to encounter a "glass ceiling," and are not provided with adequate maternity and parental leave and access to day care.

Cultural feminism or difference feminism challenges the notion that men and women are the same and advocates a wholesale transformation and "feminization" of legal doctrine. Cultural feminism argues that formal legal equality does not ensure that women are treated fairly. For example, judges typically calculate monetary damages for injuries resulting from torts based on anticipated future earnings. This approach disadvantages injured women whose damages typically are discounted based on projected work absences during child-rearing. Individuals who voluntarily leave a job are disqualified from unemployment compensation, a requirement that disadvantages women who leave work because of the demands of family life.

The solution for cultural feminism is to treat women differently than men based on their different circumstances.

The notion that men and women are not the same is heavily influenced by the "different voice" theory of educational psychologist Carol Gilligan. Gilligan argues that girls and boys differ in their moral development. Girls are taught compassion, empathy, and community. In contrast, boys are inculcated with individualism and independence. Women as a result of their early influence are characterized by an "ethic of care" and with a sense of connection and concern for the welfare of other individuals. Men, in contrast, possess an "ethic of justice" and are concerned with concepts like rights, rules, and obligations. In other words, women are about people, and men are about abstract rules (Gilligan 1982).

Dominance feminism views legal doctrine as a matter of power. Men dominate society and the legal system and as a result have developed legal rules and procedures that reflect male values. Dominance feminists point to the law on pornography and administration of the law in the areas of domestic violence, sexual harassment, prostitution, and rape. The existing adversarial legal system and male-designed legal rules cannot provide for female equality with men, and the entire justice system requires a feminist reformation.

"Anti-essentialist" and "intersectionalist" feminist scholars argue that there is no uniform feminist position and that any analysis should include an exploration of how race and class interact with gender to impact women. Critical race feminists, for example, argue that the study of housing discrimination should consider how gender, race, and income all combine to affect the ability of single mothers of color to rent an apartment. In other words, any analysis must consider how various factors interact together. It also is important to appreciate that each and every woman does not confront the same situation.

The notion of "multiple consciousness" was developed by Professor Mari Matsuda to advocate the analysis of laws from the perspective of groups whose point of view often is not appreciated or taken into consideration by scholars. The concern that raising the minimum wage for female fast-food workers will result in higher prices for consumers should be balanced by an appreciation of the difficulty confronting single mothers to support themselves and their children on current minimum wage salaries. The process of adopting multiple perspectives is part of the process of "consciousness raising" or developing a sense of the solidarity of women and the various challenges that women confront (Matsuda 1989).

Feminist methods are used to reveal aspects of legal issues that typically are not revealed by traditional (male) modes of analysis. This involves "asking the women's question," which involves analyzing an issue from the perspective of a female rather than from the perspective of a male, which is the predominant mode of analysis. This involves reviewing the data on the impact of a law or policy on women. The first question is whether the law is being enforced in a differential fashion. Is child custody in most instances awarded to a man rather than to a woman? Are more men than women promoted or more girls than boys expelled from school? The next question is whether the difference in the application of a law or policy is justified by the evidence or whether it is based on a discriminatory application of the law. Pregnant women, for example, earlier in the twentieth century were denied the opportunity to use disability leaves from work based on what proved to be the false assumption that pregnancy leaves were longer and more expensive than other health-based disabilities.

An important part of feminist methods is telling women's personal stories to document the impact of a law or policy and to identify discriminatory laws or policies that may not be apparent until women share their stories. These conversations can result in an awareness that women share a common experience such as sexual harassment in the workplace and lead to women joining together to address the discriminatory actions. Keep these perspectives in mind as you read about topics such as abortion in the text (see Chapter 10).

■ LAW AND HUMANITIES

Law and humanities is a movement that draws on the insight of art, media, English, and philosophy to understand the law (Sarat, Anderson, and Frank 2014).

Judith Resnick and Dennis Curtis illustrate how art and architecture provide insight into the view of the law in various cultures. An example is an exploration of why justice historically has been portrayed as a lady with a sword (law's violence) and scales (law's fairness) and why "Lady Justice" has been portrayed with and without a blindfold at various points in time. The blindfolded Lady Justice, which initially was a symbol of the ability to trick and fool judges, gradually took on the symbolism of a law that meted out justice in a fair and neutral fashion. In recent years, there has been a return to the view that the blindfold needs to be removed so that Lady Justice is no longer prevented from confronting the truth of the inequities in the legal system (Resnick and Curtis 2013: 62–105).

2.1 YOU DECIDE

The four defendants are members of the Speluncean Society, a group of amateurs interested in the exploration of caves. The four defendants, along with Roger Whetmore, another member of the society, entered into a limestone cavern. A landslide trapped them in the cave. Heavy boulders blocked the entrance to the cave. The secretary of the Speluncean Society became alarmed when the five failed to return as scheduled. A rescue party was organized, and workers and machines were transported to the cave. The rescue effort was obstructed several times by fresh landslides. One landslide killed ten of the workers. The treasury of the Speluncean Society quickly was exhausted, and additional money was raised from the public and from the government. On the thirty-second day, the explorers were rescued. The total cost of the rescue was $800,000.

Following the rescue, the defendants recounted their experience inside the cave. The explorers reported that they quickly exhausted their provisions. On the twentieth day, it was learned that they had a portable machine with them capable of receiving and sending information. The rescuers made contact with the five men inside the cave. The men asked how long it would be before they were rescued, and the engineers in charge of the rescue effort replied that it would take ten more days even with no additional avalanches. The men asked to speak to a doctor and asked whether they could live for ten additional days without food. The physician replied that it was doubtful. The machine went silent for eight hours. The cave explorers asked a doctor whether they could live for ten days if they ate one of the individuals who were trapped. The doctor reluctantly answered yes.

(Continued)

(Continued)

Whetmore asked the doctor whether it was advisable to draw lots to determine who would die. None of the doctors involved in the rescue effort was willing to answer the question. The trapped men asked to speak to a judge, minister, or priest, but none was willing to advise the men inside the cave.

There was no further communication from the cave. It was discovered on the twenty-third day after their entrance into the cave that Whetmore had been killed and eaten by his colleagues. It was Whetmore who had proposed that one of the explorers should be eaten to allow the others to survive. He had a pair of dice, and the five eventually agreed on a procedure to determine who would be eaten. Whetmore withdrew from the plan before the dice were rolled and explained that he favored waiting another week. The other explorers accused him

of acting in bad faith because he had proposed the plan and now wanted to withdraw. They rolled the dice for Whetmore after he was asked whether he objected to someone throwing the dice for him, and he expressed no objections. The throw went against Whetmore, and he was killed and eaten.

The four defendants were charged and convicted of murder. The statute reads that "[w]hoever shall willfully take the life of another shall be punished by death."

As a judge, would you recommend to the chief executive of the country that the four defendants be given clemency, which has the effect of releasing an individual following the service of less than his or her complete criminal sentence? In answering the problem, explain which legal theories will prove helpful.

CHAPTER SUMMARY

There is significant diversity among legal systems. There are various theories that explain the origin, evolution, function, and nature of law. A number of these approaches to law may best be considered perspectives on law rather than comprehensive explanations.

The natural law school views law as a set of universal principles that are discoverable through human reason and applicable to all societies in all historical epochs. This contrasts with legal positivism, which views law as officially declared rules and regulations.

Utilitarianism focused on public policy and asked, "What is the greatest good for the greatest number?" Immanuel Kant directly criticized utilitarianism's willingness to disadvantage some individuals to benefit a greater number of individuals and argued that all human beings are deserving of respect and should be treated as "ends" rather than "means."

The nineteenth-century historical school linked law to society and found the source of law in the historical development of society. The legal rules in an agricultural society are different from those required in an industrial society. Classic sociological theorists took the next step in directly connecting law and society. Marx and Durkheim in particular viewed law as a product of the economic arrangement of society. Weber explored the nature of authority and the sources of obedience to law.

Legal realism liberated legal analysis from an analysis of legal rules and argued that the decisions of judges and juries could be explained by extra-legal factors. Oliver Wendell Holmes Jr. argued that the law is not a mathematical enterprise in which there is a mechanical and predetermined result. He asserted that the outcome of cases in most instances is dictated by powerful political and economic interests. Sociological jurisprudence analyzed law as embedded in society and focused on the social influences on the law and, most important, on how law could be used to improve society. Functionalism views law as performing important roles that assist in keeping the social system in equilibrium.

Libertarianism is based on maximization of individual freedom. According to libertarianism, individuals possess the right to do whatever they want and to use their personal property however they choose so long as they do not interfere with the freedom of other individuals or harm other individuals. Law and economics focuses on using the law to achieve the most efficient use of resources and agrees with libertarianism that this is achieved through the private market rather than through government regulation.

The libertarian platform of liberating individuals from as much legal regulation as possible contrasts with critical legal studies, critical race theory, and feminist jurisprudence, which, though viewing law as protecting class, race, and political privilege, fundamentally believe law can be used as an instrument of social change and improvement. Law and humanities highlights the contribution of the arts and humanities to our understanding of law.

CHAPTER REVIEW QUESTIONS

1. Compare and contrast natural law and legal positivism. How would these two theories differ in their approach to a state statute authorizing the death penalty for atrocious and cruel acts of murder?

2. How would a utilitarian analyze the desirability of a law providing for the euthanasia of older individuals who have a limited life expectancy and whose medical treatment is paid for by federal funds? How would an approach based on the categorical imperative differ?

3. Explain the thinking of Henry Maine.

4. Briefly summarize the contributions to law and society of Karl Marx, Émile Durkheim, and Max Weber.

5. Summarize the contribution of legal realism and sociological jurisprudence to law and society. How do these approaches differ from legal positivism?

6. How do functionalists view the role of law?

7. What is legal behavioralism? How does this relate to legal realism and sociological jurisprudence?

8. Summarize the underlying philosophy of libertarianism.

9. List the distinguishing characteristics of critical legal studies and critical race theory.

10. What is the unifying theme of feminist jurisprudence?

11. Which of the theoretical approaches discussed in the text most closely describes your view of the nature of law?

TERMINOLOGY

categorical imperative   49

classical sociological theory   51

critical legal studies   61

Durkheim, Émile   53

feminist jurisprudence   63

functionalism   56

historical school   49

Kant, Immanuel   49

legal behavioralism   58

legal positivism   47

legal realism   54

libertarianism   59

Marx, Karl   51

natural law   46

sociological jurisprudence   55

utilitarianism   48

Weber, Max   52

ANSWERS TO TEST YOUR KNOWLEDGE

1. False
2. False
3. True
4. True

5. False
6. True
7. True
8. False

9. True
10. False
11. False

WANT A BETTER GRADE?

Get the tools you need to sharpen your study skills. Access practice quizzes, eFlashcards, author podcasts, SAGE journal articles, hyperlinks for Law and Society on the Web, and more at **study.sagepub.com/lippmanls2e**.

CHAPTER

3

THE STRUCTURE AND FUNCTION OF COURTS, LEGISLATURES, AND ADMINISTRATIVE AGENCIES

TEST YOUR KNOWLEDGE: TRUE OR FALSE?

1. The Federalists and anti-Federalists disagreed over the role of the federal government in the newly established United States of America.

2. The United States has a unified court system rather than a dual court system.

3. Courts want to hear as many cases as possible and reject the use of technical procedural mechanisms to limit their caseload.

(Continued)

■ INTRODUCTION

American lawmaking is the product of courts, legislatures, and administrative agencies. Legislators spend their time and energy passing laws to address matters of pressing social policy and delegate various responsibilities to administrative agencies with expertise in technical areas such as nuclear power, transportation safety, consumer affairs, and environmental protection.

The executive branch of government is charged with carrying out the laws passed by the legislature. The actions of the administrative agencies and legislature, and the executive in turn, are subject to judicial review by the courts.

This chapter discusses the structure and function of courts, legislatures, and administrative agencies and their involvement in lawmaking.

■ COURTS AND CONFLICT RESOLUTION

The primary function of courts is **conflict resolution**. Disputes may arise between two parties who are unable to resolve a disagreement. One of the parties asserts a claim, demand, or right, and the other disagrees (see Table 3.1).

Table 3.1 ■ Elements of a Dispute	
Element	**Example**
Claim	"You took the watch that my mother specifically stated in her will was meant to be given to me."
Demand	"Return the watch immediately that my mother conveyed to me in her will."
Right	"You violated my property rights when you took the watch. You have no legal right to the watch."

Disputes may involve individuals, organizations, and the government. A dispute may be settled in a court proceeding or informally settled out of court, or an individual may drop the complaint. There are several types of disputes (Goldman and Sarat 1989: 4–6).

Private disputes. Private disputes involve two individuals, neither of whom is part of the government. A complainant may sue in court for damages if he or she is unable to reach a satisfactory settlement. You may sue another person seeking compensation for injuries suffered in an auto accident.

Public-initiated disputes. The government may rely on the courts to protect the public health, safety, and welfare. An example is a legal action against a corporation to enforce laws against air or water pollution or a legal action against a locality or state that is depriving citizens of their right to vote. A public-initiated dispute may be based on the civil law or the criminal law. The government may sue for damages or to enjoin (stop) a polluter or may pursue criminal penalties.

Defendant-initiated public disputes. An individual or organization claims the government is violating the requirements of a law or the Constitution. An example is a challenge to the state's imposition of the death penalty against juvenile offenders or individuals who are mentally challenged.

The final decision issued by a court in a dispute is termed **adjudication**. Court decisions may resolve one set of issues and, in the process, create new issues that must be resolved in future disputes. In *Roper v. Simmons*, the Supreme Court struck down the death penalty for juveniles (*Roper v. Simmons*, 543 U.S. 551 [2005]). This decision led to the question whether juveniles may be sentenced to life in prison for homicide offenses and for non-homicide offenses (*Graham v. Florida*, 560 U.S. ___ [2010]; *Miller v. Alabama*, 567 U.S. ___ [2012]). In 2015, in *Montgomery v. Louisiana*, the Supreme Court held that *Miller* applied retroactively to juveniles sentenced to life without parole before the decision in *Miller* and that states were required to provide the incarcerated juveniles with an opportunity to demonstrate that they should be resentenced or granted parole. The decision in *Montgomery* applied to roughly 2,300 juveniles serving a sentence of life without parole for murder (*Montgomery v. Louisiana*, 577 U.S. ___ [2015]).

Judges do not control the issues they are asked to decide. A judge presented with a case has no choice other than to address the issues raised by the litigants, whether this involves affirmative action, the treatment of the homeless, abortion, or gun control. In other words, courts cannot address problems that have yet to appear on their docket.

The U.S. Supreme Court each year receives thousands of applications from individuals seeking a review of their case and only reviews a small percentage of these cases. The Court may indicate in a decision that there is an unresolved issue that it is looking to address in the future.

State and federal judicial courts in the United States are supported by public funds and are open to any individual who makes a legal demand, makes a legal claim, or asserts a legal right. This is different from specialized tribunals whose jurisdiction extends to a limited number of individuals and performs a specialized function. A university judicial board adjudicates whether students have violated university regulations, and the National Collegiate Athletic Association conducts hearings to determine whether a university's sports programs have violated NCAA rules and should be placed on probation.

A judge in the U.S. system is expected to be an objective and neutral decision-maker and should not favor one side or the other in a dispute. The notion that judges are "above the fray" is essential for public acceptance of court decisions as fair and objective. Individuals who view the judicial process as a neutral and legitimate mechanism for dispute resolution are likely to accept the outcome, even if they are unhappy with the result. As a result, they are less likely to settle their disputes through the use of force, intimidation, or self-help. In this sense, the judicial function contributes to social stability. Another important function of courts that we will discuss later in the chapter is lawmaking (Jacob 1996: 1–15; Shapiro 1981).

■ THE DEVELOPMENT OF FEDERAL COURTS

A major issue with the Articles of Confederation was that there was no national court to resolve conflicts between the courts of the different states. In 1787 at the Constitutional Convention in Philadelphia, a resolution was adopted calling for the creation of a national judiciary (Corsi 1984: 162–166; Richardson and Vines 1970: 16–35).

The structure of the judicial system continued to be the subject of significant debate. The anti-Federalists opposed a national judicial system, arguing this would impinge on states' rights, interfere with the power of Congress, and threaten civil liberties. State courts, according to the anti-Federalists, should be left alone to decide cases without the federal courts looking over their shoulder. The Federalists, on the other hand, supported a strong national government that could unite the country and promote economic development. State courts could not be relied on to give outsiders from other states a fair hearing in a suit involving residents of the state.

The anti-Federalists and Federalists reached a compromise. Article III of the Constitution created a single Supreme Court and left it to Congress to fill in the details of a national judicial system. Article III provides that "the judicial power of the United States, shall be vested in one Supreme Court, and in such inferior courts as the Congress may from time to time ordain and establish." Courts created under the authority of Article III of the Constitution are termed **Article III courts**.

The Federalists succeeded in the first Congress in passing the Judiciary Act of 1789, which created a separate system of thirteen federal district courts. The act constituted a compromise. The jurisdiction of federal district courts was to be drawn along state lines. The understanding was that federal district court judges were to be selected from the state where the court was located. The district courts were grouped within three circuits. Each circuit court was composed of one district court judge and two federal Supreme Court justices. Circuit courts had original jurisdiction over serious crimes, civil cases of $500 or more involving citizens of different states, and cases in which the United States was the plaintiff. Circuit courts also were given appellate jurisdiction over district court cases. The circuit court system took a heavy toll on Supreme Court justices who were required to "ride the circuit" and travel across the country to serve as appellate court judges. As a result, the circuit court convened only on rare occasions. The justices were not relieved of this responsibility until 1875.

The debate between proponents of a strong central government and proponents of decentralized government continued throughout the nineteenth century. Politicians opposing an expansion of federal power continued to argue that the problem of the mounting federal caseload could be addressed by expanding the jurisdiction of state courts to hear federal cases. Individuals favoring a strong federal government countered that the number of federal judges and federal courts should be enlarged to ease the burden on Supreme Court justices.

Individuals favoring a strong national government after almost one hundred years of debate finally carried the day and passed the Judiciary Act of 1891, which created circuit courts of appeals.

These new courts would hear appeals from federal trial courts and relieve the Supreme Court from reviewing minor cases. The Judiciary Act of 1925 made most of the Supreme Court's jurisdiction discretionary with the Court. These two laws in combination freed the Court to only address questions of national importance. This was a significant step because the Supreme Court now was free to focus on a limited number of important cases that held the promise of shaping the course of the country (G. White 2016: 371).

■ THE STRUCTURE OF THE JUDICIAL SYSTEM

Most countries in the world have a single, unified court system. The United States, in contrast, has a **dual court system** comprising a federal court system and a state court system. The federal system is based on the U.S. Constitution and on statutes passed by Congress; the state court systems are created by state constitutions and by state statutes.

The fifty state court systems significantly differ from one another, and the reality is that there are fifty separate systems of state courts. Each state has its own laws, court procedures, legal precedents, and system of appeals of state court decisions.

In some instances, federal and state courts both have jurisdiction over a dispute or what is called *concurrent jurisdiction.* A state, for example, would have jurisdiction to prosecute an individual for drug possession within the geographical boundaries of the state, and the federal government would have jurisdiction over the same crime as part of its authority to regulate the national market in drugs and narcotics. Appeals may be taken from state courts to federal courts if a federal issue is involved, such as whether a state law violates the First Amendment freedom of expression.

One interesting twist is that the Fifth Amendment to the U.S. Constitution protects individuals from **double jeopardy**, or being prosecuted twice for the same offense. The **dual sovereignty doctrine** permits an individual to be prosecuted for the same act in both federal and state court. Terry Nichols was convicted in federal court for involvement in the 1995 Oklahoma City bombing of the Murrah Federal Building resulting in the death of 168 persons and in countless injuries. The jury deadlocked on whether to impose the death penalty, and Nichols was sentenced to life imprisonment. Oklahoma felt strongly that Nichols deserved the death penalty and prosecuted him in an Oklahoma state court. The jury deadlocked, and Nichols once again avoided the death penalty. Oklahoma did derive some satisfaction from the fact that Timothy McVeigh, who was responsible for organizing the bombing and igniting the bomb, was convicted in federal court and executed in 2001.

An individual also may be prosecuted in a state or federal criminal court and be sued for damages. O. J. Simpson was acquitted in criminal court of the murder of Nicole Brown Simpson and Ron Goldman and later was found guilty of wrongful death in civil court and ordered to compensate the victims' families in the amount of $33.5 million.

■ JUDICIAL GATEKEEPING

The first requirement for a court to hear a case is that the tribunal has jurisdiction over the dispute. **Jurisdiction** is authority of a court to hear a case and is established by a legislative statute or by the Constitution.

Judges have developed rules limiting the ability of courts to decide cases before the issues have been thoroughly developed. These requirements ensure that individuals bringing a case have a personal stake in the outcome of the litigation and will function as zealous advocates. The restrictions also preserve the time and energy of judges by restricting the number of cases that they are asked to decide. *Justiciability* is a term that describes a number of preconditions that must be met before a court will consider a case.

Mootness. Courts will not hear a moot case, a case in which the plaintiff will not be affected by the outcome. In *DeFunis v. Odegaard*, DeFunis claimed that he had been discriminated against in the law school admissions process. DeFunis had been provisionally admitted pending the outcome of the case. As a consequence, the Supreme Court refused to hear his case because he would have graduated by the time the Court issued a decision (*DeFunis v. Odegaard,* 416 U.S. 312 [1974]).

Standing. An individual must be affected by the law that he or she is challenging. In *City of Los Angeles v. Lyons*, the defendant had been subjected to a potentially lethal chokehold by the police. The Supreme Court held the defendant lacked standing because he was unlikely to be a victim of a chokehold by the police in the future (*City of Los Angeles v. Lyons*, 461 U.S. 95 [1983]). The standing doctrine also has been relied on in criminal cases to deny individuals the ability to rely on a defense. Members of the military who have refused to serve in foreign engagements lack standing to rely on the "Nuremberg defense" on the grounds they have not received direct orders to commit a war crime (*Levy v. Parker*, 396 U.S. 1204 [1969]).

Ripeness. Courts limit their jurisdiction to "cases and controversies." Courts will not issue "advisory opinions." A student cannot ask the court to rule on whether a proposed policy subjecting all students to drug testing is constitutional until he or she is asked to submit to a drug test.

Collusion. The Supreme Court will not hear cases in which individuals have agreed to "stage a conflict" in order to get the issue before the Court.

Exhaustion. An individual bringing a case is required to have exhausted all administrative remedies. A student challenging school policies would first have to make an effort to persuade school authorities and the school board to change the policies before filing a legal challenge.

Political question. Courts will not decide issues that are within the constitutional authority of other branches of government. During the Vietnam War, individuals facing the draft filed cases asking courts to block their induction into the military on the grounds the war was unlawful. Federal courts refused to decide whether U.S. military intervention was legal based on the fact that the decision whether to employ armed force is assigned by the Constitution to the president and to Congress.

State secrets. Evidence is excluded from trial based on the fact that information will be disclosed that might endanger national security. The doctrine was first used to block a legal action for damages against the Air Force based on the claim that disclosure of the details of a plane crash would result in the release of information regarding the crew's top-secret mission (*United States v. Reynolds,* 345 U.S. 1 [1953]). Most recently, the Supreme Court held that a group of journalists, lawyers, and human rights activists lacked standing to challenge the government surveillance policy of

American citizens on the grounds the surveillance program was classified and the plaintiffs were unable to demonstrate they had been subject to the government surveillance (*Clapper v. Amnesty International*, 568 U.S. ___ [2013]).

The ability of an individual to bring a legal action also may be limited by his or her lack of access to legal assistance and/or inability to afford the costs of a legal action.

■ THE JURISDICTION OF FEDERAL COURTS

Jurisdiction for the purposes of this discussion means the legal authority of a court to hear and decide a case. The term is derived from the Latin *juris* ("law") and *deciere* ("to speak").

Federal courts under Article III of the Constitution have so-called **federal question doctrine** over cases in which the United States is a party, cases involving a law passed by the U.S. Congress, cases raising constitutional issues, and cases requiring the interpretation of international treaties. Congress also has given federal courts jurisdiction over diversity cases involving citizens of different states in which an individual is suing for damages of at least $75,000. A number of legal issues do not fall within federal jurisdiction and, instead, fall within the "subject matter" jurisdiction of state courts, including personal injury suits, divorces, breaches of contracts, and landlord–tenant disputes. State courts generally possess "territorial jurisdiction" over these matters when they occur in whole or in part within the territorial authority of the court.

The primary courts comprising the federal judicial system are district courts, courts of appeal, and the Supreme Court. The federal judicial system also includes various courts of specialized jurisdiction, including bankruptcy courts, the U.S. Court of International Trade, and the U.S. Court of Federal Claims. There also are courts that are not part of the federal judicial branch, such as military courts, the U.S. Court of Appeals for Veterans Claims, and the U.S. Tax Court.

■ FEDERAL DISTRICT COURTS

The ninety-four federal district courts are the workhorses of the federal system and are the first stop for almost every case that enters the federal judicial system. The district courts have diversity jurisdiction or jurisdiction over civil cases involving citizens from different states in which an individual is suing for at least $75,000. The theory behind diversity jurisdiction is that a state court judge would favor the individual from his or her state while a federal court judge would not favor either party.

There is at least one district court in each state, and California and Texas have four or more district courts. There are roughly 678 federal district court judges. District court trials are conducted before a single judge. Between two and twenty-nine judges are assigned to conduct trials in a district, depending on the district's geographical size. An important though rarely mentioned group of judicial officers is the 429 magistrate judges assigned to handle minor matters in the districts. These judges perform minor, day-to-day legal matters that otherwise would consume the time of district court judges. Magistrates, for example, hear police requests for arrest or search warrants and conduct bail hearings.

Roughly 361,689 civil and criminal cases were filed in 2015 in district courts, over 280,000 of which were civil and over 80,000 of which were criminal cases. The greatest number of criminal cases involved immigration, and almost one-third involved narcotics. Other criminal cases related to white-collar crime, bank robbery, mail fraud, and civil rights abuses. District courts in 2016 considered over 48,000 petitions for *habeas corpus* from prisoners challenging the constitutionality of their confinement. *Habeas* petitions are claims from individuals who are incarcerated, have exhausted their state remedies, and claim to have been unjustly convicted and imprisoned.

A federal district trial court would be familiar to anyone who has watched a Hollywood movie depicting a trial. The lawyers present witnesses who are subject to cross-examination. The judge issues rulings on the admissibility of various forms of evidence and instructs the jury on the law they are to apply in evaluating the facts of the case. A losing party in a civil case who believes that the judge has made an error or a defendant in a criminal case who is convicted may file an appeal based on the claim the judge has made a mistake. This might entail admitting evidence that is alleged to be inflammatory and prejudicial, issuing inaccurate instructions to the jury, or admitting evidence in a criminal case that is alleged to have been unlawfully seized by the police.

■ FEDERAL COURTS OF APPEAL

Appeals from district courts may be taken to federal courts of appeal or what also are referred to as circuit courts. There are thirteen courts of appeal, eleven of which have jurisdiction over the district courts in their circuit. The Ninth Circuit is the largest circuit and includes Alaska, Hawaii, California, Nevada, Arizona, Idaho, Oregon, Washington, Montana, Guam, and the Northern Mariana Islands. Congress over the years has expanded the number of courts of appeal in response to the pleas of federal circuit court judges that they lacked the resources to cope with their caseloads.

The Twelfth Circuit Court of Appeals focuses exclusively on the District of Columbia because of the large number of appeals from the decisions of federal agencies. The Thirteenth Circuit Court of Appeals was created by Congress in 1982 and has nationwide jurisdiction to hear appeals in specialized areas including patent claims, government contracts, trademarks, and veterans' benefits.

There are 179 judicial positions on courts of appeal although several remain vacant. The Ninth Circuit is staffed by twenty-nine judges while the Second Circuit—which has jurisdiction over Maine, Massachusetts, New Hampshire, and Puerto Rico—is staffed by six judges.

Three court of appeal judges together hear appeals from district courts. The judges read a written argument submitted by the lawyers called a **brief** and then listen to oral arguments and question the lawyers. The judges vote whether to uphold or overturn the district court decision. In particularly important cases, all the court of appeal judges may hear a case *en banc* (together). The decision of a court of appeals is binding precedent within the appellate court's circuit unless the judgment is overturned by the U.S. Supreme Court.

The court of appeal may affirm the lower court judgment or reverse the lower court judgment on the grounds that the judge's error affected the judgment at trial. A reversal opens the door for a new trial.

There were roughly fifty-four thousand appeals filed in federal courts of appeal; nearly 20 percent were criminal cases involving narcotics, immigration, firearms and explosives, and property offenses. The courts of appeal also consider a large number of petitions for *habeas corpus* on appeal from district courts, most of which involve petitions filed by inmates. The Supreme Court, as discussed below, considers only a limited number of the appeals that are filed from the decisions of the courts of appeal. As a result, the courts of appeal are the courts whose precedents control the decisions of district courts within the circuit. The holdings of courts of appeal may differ from one another, and the Supreme Court typically will resolve these conflicts by issuing a judgment clarifying the law.

The Supreme Court sits at the top of the hierarchy of federal courts.

■ THE U.S. SUPREME COURT

Article III, Section 2 of the Constitution defines the Supreme Court's jurisdiction and provides the Court with appellate jurisdiction over cases in the federal system, cases in state courts that raise a federal constitutional issue (e.g., whether police interrogation violated a suspect's Fifth Amendment right against self-incrimination), and cases involving the interpretation of an international treaty. An example of treaty interpretation is whether international diplomatic agreements require states to arrange for Mexican citizens who are arrested for offenses punishable by death to meet with a representative of the Mexican embassy.

The Supreme Court has original jurisdiction over several types of cases. This includes disputes between states, disputes between the U.S. government and a state, and disputes between a state and a foreign citizen. The Court is not required to hear a case that falls within its original jurisdiction, and there have been fewer than two hundred such cases in the Court's history. In this narrow category of cases, the Supreme Court acts as a trial court and hears the testimony of witnesses and the arguments of the lawyers.

The Court exercises discretionary jurisdiction over appeals from the federal courts of appeal and state supreme courts. In other words, the justices on the Court choose specific cases they will decide and those they will not decide.

The Court typically receives over seven thousand petitions for review, and despite the familiar threat by individuals that they will "take their case all the way to the Supreme Court," the reality is that the Court votes to hear fewer than ninety cases each term. In other words, the Court does not play the role of a "court of last resort" for every criminal defendant.

An individual who wants the Supreme Court to consider hearing his or her case files a *writ of certiorari*, or an order issued to a lower court to send the record of the case to the Supreme Court. The *rule of four* requires that four of the nine Supreme Court judges must vote to hear a case. A petition that fails to attract four judges is denied, and the decision of the lower court stands.

PHOTO 3.1 The Supreme Court building, home of the U.S. Supreme Court in Washington, D.C., built in 1935.

The decision of the Court not to hear a case does not mean that the Court approves the decision of the appellate court or disapproves the decision of the court of appeal.

Most of the appeals heard by the Supreme Court are appeals from the federal courts of appeal or state supreme courts. A small number of cases originate from federal district courts. In the 2015–2016 term, the Court issued eighty-one decisions. Lawrence Baum records that in 2013–2014, 90 percent of Supreme Court decisions were on appeal from lower federal courts and only ten were from state courts. Seventy-four percent were civil cases, and 26 percent were criminal cases (Baum 2016: 154).

Contrary to conventional wisdom, the Supreme Court does not intervene to correct every miscarriage of justice in the federal and state court systems. A Court decision is a precedent that controls the future decisions of all lower federal courts and all state courts and plays a supervisory role over the judicial system to ensure uniformity. The Court will hear an appeal from a court of appeal when several courts of appeal disagree with one another on an issue or with a state supreme court or when state supreme courts disagree with one another. For example, the Supreme Court stepped in when courts of appeal disagreed whether lethal injection constitutes cruel and unusual punishment and when courts of appeal differed on whether it is constitutional for a judge to permit victim impact statements during the sentencing phase of a criminal trial.

The second type of appeal the Supreme Court generally is willing to hear involves cases presenting significant constitutional issues that must be addressed in the interests of the country. Examples include a series of cases addressing the treatment of detainees at Guantánamo and the *Bush v. Gore* case in which the Court upheld the results of the presidential vote in Florida, resulting in the election of George W. Bush (*Bush v. Gore*, 531 U.S. 98 [2000]).

The Supreme Court and other multiple-judge panels may issue a unanimous or a non-unanimous written decision. Five Supreme Court judges are required for a **majority opinion**. A judge may agree with the majority, although for a different reason, and write a **concurring opinion**. In a case in which a majority of judges favor a particular result but cannot agree on the reason for the decision, the majority will comprise a **plurality opinion** and one or more concurring opinions. In those instances in which the chief justice is in the majority, he or she selects the judge to write the majority opinion. In those instances in which the chief justice dissents, the senior justice in the majority either writes the decision or selects the justice to write the decision. A decision that is written by the chief justice or by a prominent justice often carries more weight than a decision written by other justices.

Justices who disagree with the majority decision may write their own **dissenting opinion** or join other justices in issuing a joint

Xinhua/Yin Bogu via Getty Images

PHOTO 3.2 U.S. associate justice Anthony Kennedy administers the oath of office to Judge Neil Gorsuch as his wife Marie Louise Gorsuch holds a bible and President Donald J. Trump looks on during a ceremony in the White House Rose Garden on April 10, 2017.

dissenting opinion. Dissenting opinions are important because they may attract enough justices in the future to constitute a majority (Urofsky 2015). For example, in *Payne v. Tennessee,* the Supreme Court reversed two earlier decisions and upheld the constitutionality of victim impact statements during the sentencing phase of death penalty cases (*Payne v. Tennessee,* 501 U.S. 808 [1991]).

The influential website SCOTUSblog analyzed U.S. Supreme Court decisions between the 2009 and 2013 terms and determined that roughly 51 percent of the cases were decided by a unanimous vote, 8 percent were decided by an 8–1 vote, 11 percent were decided by a 7–2 vote, 10 percent by a 6–3 vote and 20 percent were decided by a 5–4 vote.

A Supreme Court opinion may result in various outcomes. The U.S. Supreme Court may agree with the appellate court and *affirm* the lower court decision or disagree with the appellate court and *reverse* the decision. It also is possible to affirm part of a decision and to reverse part of a decision. In other instances, the Supreme Court may find that the lower court used the wrong legal standard; in these cases, the Supreme Court may lay out guidelines for the lower court and *reverse and remand* the case to the lower court to carry out the instructions of the Supreme Court.

The Background of Supreme Court Judges

Federal court judges are nominated by the president of the United States, and their nomination must be confirmed by a majority vote of the U.S. Senate. There is no requirement for federal judges to be lawyers, although all appointees to the federal bench have had law degrees.

Federal district court and court of appeal judges are drawn from a relatively small slice of the legal profession. Lawrence Baum writes that most federal judges are from high-status families, 63 percent of court of appeal judges attended private universities, and 23 percent of court of appeal judges attended Ivy League schools. The typical career path for a federal judge involves experience as a prosecutor or working for a politician and then moving on to a profitable law practice in a private firm before being appointed to a judgeship. Over two-thirds of federal district and court of appeal judges have a net worth of at least $500,000, and nearly 50 percent of district court judges and over 50 percent of court of appeal judges are millionaires (Baum 2013: 124).

A significant number of federal judges were active in politics prior to their appointment. Presidents often use judicial appointments to reward their political supporters, and many of these political activists also have relationships with the members of their party in the U.S. Senate, the body constitutionally charged with confirming the president's judicial appointees.

The president, of course, is looking to appoint justices who agree with his legal philosophy, and appointees' records are thoroughly reviewed by the president's staff.

Federal judges who distinguish themselves on the bench can climb the judicial career ladder. Eight of the last nine appointments to the U.S. Supreme Court formerly were judges on circuit courts of appeal. Presidents and members of the Senate do not want to be embarrassed by supporting a nominee who does an "about face" on the bench and for this reason favor nominees who have an established judicial record.

The most profound change in the judiciary is the diversity of sitting judges. Thirty years ago, the federal bench was a "white boys' club." Today, women comprise over 30 percent of judges on courts of appeal, and racial minorities constitute roughly 25 percent of the judges on courts of appeal (Baum 2013: 124).

The Supreme Court has been criticized as an elitist governmental body that is unrepresentative of the United States. The Court is composed of nine judges: a chief justice and eight associate judges. As of the spring of 2017, there have been 113 Supreme Court justices, 17 chief judges, and 95 associate judges. The first Catholic justice, Roger Taney, was not appointed until 1835. There have been only nine other Catholics on the Court, five of whom presently are serving on the Court. The first Jewish justice, Louis Brandeis, was appointed in 1916, and there have been five other Jewish justices, three of whom currently are serving on the Court.

Thurgood Marshall, appointed to the Court in 1965 by President Lyndon Johnson, was the first African American named to the Court. Clarence Thomas, who currently serves on the Court, was the second African American appointed to the Court.

Justice Sonia Sotomayor, named to the Court by President Barack Obama, is the first Hispanic justice. There has yet to be an Asian American justice. Sandra Day O'Connor, appointed by President Ronald Reagan in 1981, was the first female justice, and three other women subsequently have served on the Court. Historically, most justices have been from the upper middle class or upper class, although two current justices—Thomas and Sotomayor—are from lower-middle-class backgrounds and the other members of the current Court are from middle-class backgrounds. Five of the eight judges on the Roberts Court in the 2015–2016 term had a net worth of at least $1 million.

Supreme Court justices tend to be drawn from elite private undergraduate colleges and law schools. Five members of the current court graduated from Harvard Law School, three from Yale Law School, and one from Columbia (who transferred from Harvard). Most of the judges are from the East Coast corridor between Boston and Washington, D.C., or have spent considerable time living on the East Coast.

In recent years, there has been a significant change in the professional background of individuals serving on the Supreme Court. In the past, individuals named to the high court held elected office or served in presidential administrations. For example, Chief Justice Earl Warren was governor of California and was appointed by Republican president Dwight D. Eisenhower. Warren is credited with persuading his fellow justices to join him in holding segregated schools unconstitutional in *Brown v. Board of Education.* Thurgood Marshall was a famous civil rights attorney who served on the Warren Court and had extensive experience litigating in trial and in appellate courts across the country. These two justices typified the type of practical background that characterized appointees to the Supreme Court.

Recent decades have witnessed a strong shift toward appointing individuals with extensive experience as sitting judges and, to a lesser extent, as law professors or practicing corporate attorneys. Critics assert that although sitting judges who are elevated to the Supreme Court possess obvious legal competence, the Supreme Court also should include individuals who can bring practical experience as a politician, trial attorney, or businessperson to the Court.

Appointment to the Supreme Court also involves a measure of good fortune and luck. Between 1969 and 1992, every Supreme Court appointment was made by a Republican president, meaning that an entire generation of qualified Democratic lawyers and judges had very little likelihood of being nominated to the Court.

In February 2017, newly elected president Donald Trump named Judge Neil M. Gorsuch, a federal appeals court judge in Denver, Colorado, to fill the court vacancy created by the death of Justice Antonin Scalia. Justice Gorsuch's judicial philosophy of constitutional interpretation follows that of Justice Scalia, and his appointment restored a 5–4 conservative majority on the Court. Gorsuch at age 49 is the youngest Supreme Court nominee in the past twenty-five years. Although he brings a measure of regional diversity because he is a Colorado native and served on the Tenth Circuit Court of Appeals in Denver, Justice Gorsuch conforms to the pattern of recent appointments. His mother was head of the Environmental Protection Agency under Ronald Reagan; he was educated on the East Coast and attended Harvard Law School, as well as Oxford University in England; and he served as a Supreme Court clerk to Justice

Anthony Kennedy. He was appointed to the federal bench in 2006 by President George W. Bush, and his judicial opinions suggest that he will join Justice Thomas as the most conservative justice on the Court.

Should we be concerned about the elitist character of the Supreme Court? The perception that the Court is representative of the population is important because the Supreme Court is an unelected body with judges serving life terms on "good behavior." The Court's rulings have a profound impact on the lives of Americans on issues ranging from abortion to gun control to the regulation of business, and the perception that justices are representative of America helps to maintain popular support for the Court's decisions. A justice also brings his or her background and experience to the Court. A justice from the West is likely to have sensitivity toward, if not an understanding of, land conservation, the environment, and immigration.

The other side of the argument is that the Supreme Court is an elite institution and the judges should be drawn from the "best and the brightest." A judge's privileged background is less important than his or her ability to draft a fair and reasoned legal opinion. People respect the rulings of the Supreme Court because of the intelligence and impartiality of the justices. In any event, the composition of the Court also has been changing as the demographic profile of the United States has changed. As noted, there currently are three female justices (one of whom is Hispanic) and three Jewish justices. In the past, the Court was dominated by Protestants, and today there are five practicing Catholic justices and one who attends an Episcopalian church.

It is worth mentioning that there is a continuing controversy over when a justice should voluntarily retire from the Court. The justices are eligible for generous pensions if they retire, and finances for that reason are unlikely to be a significant consideration in a justice's decision whether to leave the bench. It is speculated that since World War II, seven justices remained on the Court for a period of time despite a noticeable decline in their physical or mental capacities. On the other hand, Sandra Day O'Connor retired in 2008, David Souter retired in 2009, and both were in good health. A consideration on the part of justices as to whether to retire is whether there is a president in office who is likely to appoint a justice to their seat who shares their legal outlook. There also are well-documented cases of presidents pressuring justices to resign. President Lyndon Johnson famously persuaded Arthur Goldberg in 1965 to take the position of ambassador to the United Nations so as to create a vacancy on the Supreme Court (Baum 2016: 61–63).

The Supreme Court's assertion and use of the power of judicial review is the most hotly debated aspect of the Supreme Court.

PHOTO 3.3 In August 2009, Sonia Sotomayor was confirmed as the 111th justice of the U.S. Supreme Court. Justice Sotomayor was raised in a Bronx, New York, housing project, attended Princeton and Yale Law School, and is the first Hispanic justice on the Court.

© iStockphoto.com/EdStock

Judicial Review

Alexander Hamilton argued in the *Federalist Papers* that Americans had no reason to fear the development of a powerful judicial branch. The judiciary was the "least dangerous branch." He pointed out that courts depend on the legislature for funding and rely on the executive branch to enforce their rulings.

The Supreme Court decided very few significant cases between 1790 and 1799. The Court was held in such low esteem that individuals refused appointment to the Court and Chief Justice John Jay left the Court to take what he considered a more important position in New Jersey. The Court achieved unanticipated national dominance with the appointment of John Marshall as chief justice by President John Adams in 1801.

In 1803 in *Marbury v. Madison*, Justice Marshall changed the course of American history when he held that the Supreme Court was constitutionally authorized to exercise the right of **judicial review**. The Court, based on this authority, claimed the right to determine the meaning of the Constitution and to evaluate whether acts of Congress and the president were authorized by the Constitution.

In *Marbury*, President Adams appointed a number of loyal Federalist judges as he left office. One of these "midnight judges" was William Marbury, who, although confirmed by the Senate, had not received his commission as justice of the peace for Washington, D.C., by the time Adams left office. Adams's successor, Republican president Thomas Jefferson, instructed his secretary of state, James Madison, not to convey the commission to Marbury. Marbury asked the Supreme Court to order Madison to deliver his commission. Chief Justice Marshall found that although Marbury was entitled to his commission, the section of the Judiciary Act of 1789 that established the Supreme Court's original jurisdiction to act in this situation was unconstitutional. Justice Marshall explained that the Constitution is the supreme law of the land and when a statute is inconsistent with the text of the Constitution, the Court is required to declare the law unconstitutional and to refuse to enforce the law (*Marbury v. Madison*, 5 U.S. 137 [1803]). Thirteen years later, in *Martin v. Hunter's Lessee*, the Court claimed the right to strike down state laws that conflicted with the requirements of the federal Constitution and later asserted the authority to review the decisions of state courts (*Martin v. Hunter's Lessee*, 1 U.S. 304 [1816]).

There is continuing debate whether the framers of the Constitution intended for federal judges to exercise the power of judicial review. The power of judicial review, whatever the intent of the drafters of the Constitution, has involved the Court in major issues in American life ranging from abortion to gun control to the death penalty to the treatment of detainees at Guantánamo. Journalist Anthony Lewis writes that at times the Court does not resemble a court so much as an "extraordinarily powerful" god sitting on a "remote throne" (Lewis 1964: 11).

Judges that favor the Court's employing the power of judicial review to overturn state and federal laws are considered to support **judicial activism**. Judges who favor issuing a ruling that avoids directly overturning a law adopted by elected representatives are said to favor **judicial restraint**. Activists broadly interpret the Constitution and laws and believe the law should adapt to changing conditions. Judges adhering to judicial restraint are reluctant to go beyond the letter of the text. The conventional view is that activist judges tend to be liberal Democrats and judges favoring judicial restraint are conservative Republicans. There are examples of both liberal and conservative judges engaging in judicial activism as well as judicial restraint. The criticism of unelected judges engaging in judicial activism may come down to a question of "whose ox is being gored."

The primary criticism of judicial activism is that unelected judges are "legislating from the bench" and are engaging in the type of lawmaking that should be reserved for elected legislators. In *Miranda v. Arizona*, the Court held that the Self-Incrimination Clause of the Fifth Amendment of the U.S. Constitution extended beyond the courtroom and protected individuals subjected to police interrogation. The Supreme Court held that police across the country were required to recite the *Miranda* warning and in the past forty years has considered close to fifty cases on police interrogation and added layer upon layer of rules regulating the practice (*Miranda v. Arizona*, 384 U.S. 436 [1966]).

The Supreme Court, when it exercises judicial review, can find itself in the middle of political controversy. In a series of hotly contested cases in the 1960s, the Court erected a "wall of separation" between church and state. In 1962 in *Engel v. Vitale*, the Court defied public opinion and held that a non-denominational prayer violated the First Amendment prohibition of "establishment of a religion." The Court held it is "no part of the business of government to compose official prayers for any group of the American people to recite as part of a religious program carried on by government" (*Engel v. Vitale*, 370 U.S. 421 [1962]).

In 2000, in *Santa Fe School District v. Doe*, the Court held that allowing student-led prayer at the football games was an unconstitutional violation of the First Amendment Establishment Clause that separated church and state. Justice Stevens in his majority decision held that school sponsorship of a religious message is impermissible because it sends the "message to members of the audience who are nonadherents that they are outsiders, not full members of the political community, and an accompanying message to adherents that they are insiders, favored members of the political community" (*Santa Fe School District v. Doe*, 530 U.S. 290 [2000]).

In 2015, in *Obergefell v. Hodges*, the U.S. Supreme Court held that same-sex couples had a fundamental right under the Equal Protection Clause of the Fourteenth Amendment to marry. The late Justice Antonin Scalia dissented on the grounds that the decision had no basis in law and argued that the Court had short-circuited the ongoing democratic debate in the country over same-sex marriage. He wrote that to "allow the policy question of same-sex marriage to be considered and resolved by a select, patrician, highly unrepresentative panel of nine is to violate the principle even more fundamental than no taxation without representation: no social transformation without representation" (*Obergefell v. Hodges*, 576 U.S. ___ [2015]).

In 2010, in *Citizens United v. Federal Election Commission*, a five-judge majority of the Supreme Court struck down a congressional statute restricting corporations and labor unions from using their funds to pay for "electioneering communications" in presidential primaries and elections. The Court majority held that the federal campaign law was an unconstitutional limitation on the freedom of expression of corporations and when the government uses the law to determine "where a person may get his or her information or what distrusted source he or she may not hear, it uses censorship to control thought. . . . This is unlawful. The First Amendment confirms the freedom to think for ourselves," and that speech is not less important because the "speech comes from a corporation rather than an individual" (*Citizens United v. Federal Election Commission*, 558 U.S. 310 [2010]).

President Barack Obama used the occasion of his State of the Union address to Congress in 2010 to criticize the decision as a victory for powerful corporations that use their power to "drown out the voices of everyday Americans" and threaten the integrity of the electoral process.

In 2012, the Court found itself once again involved in political controversy when Chief Justice John Roberts joined four liberal justices in voting in *National Federation of Independent Business v. Sebelius* to uphold the constitutionality of the Affordable Care Act ("Obamacare"). Justice Roberts surprised Court observers who predicted he would join the other conservative justices in holding the statute unconstitutional. The chief justice noted that decisions are "entrusted to our nation's elected leaders, who can be thrown out of office if the people disagree with them" (*National Federation of Independent Business v. Sebelius*, 567 U.S. ___ [2012]).

The Supreme Court also has not hesitated to hold that the president has exceeded his constitutional authority. One of the most famous examples was the "Steel Seizure Case" in which the Court held that President Harry Truman had acted unconstitutionally during the Korean War in ordering a federal takeover of the nation's steel mills to prevent a labor strike (*Youngstown Sheet & Tube Co. v. Sawyer*, 343 U.S. 579 [1952]).

President Obama also had his policies rejected by the Court. In 2016, the U.S. Supreme Court failed to uphold President Obama's executive order that protected roughly five million undocumented immigrants from deportation and would have allowed them to legally work in the United States (*United States v. Texas*, 579 U.S. ___ [2016]).

President Trump, frustrated over district and appellate court injunctions on his proposed travel ban, leveled personal attacks on the federal judges, characterizing the decision of a "so-called" judge as "ridiculous," a "disgrace," and "political" (J. Davis 2017).

There is a question whether an unelected group of judges with life tenure should overturn laws that are passed by elected representatives or to compel states to accept polices that they oppose. The thinking is that judicial intervention in the "political thicket" discourages a vigorous democracy. Questions such as the role of prayer in school or whether corporations and unions should be free to expend an unlimited amount of funds to influence political elections or same-sex marriage should be debated and decided by elected representatives rather than by unelected judges.

Alexander Bickel in his famous book *The Least Dangerous Branch* over fifty years ago called the exercise of judicial review by unelected justices the "counter-majority difficulty" and characterized judicial review as a "deviant institution" in American democracy (Bickel 1962). This argument subsequently has been echoed by a long list of prominent commentators (Ely 1980).

On the other hand, the Supreme Court's exercise of judicial review ensures that Congress and the president do not assume powers that are not authorized by the Constitution and safeguards the rights and liberties of citizens against governmental abuse. In the famous 1943 case of *West Virginia v. Barnette*, the Supreme Court struck down a law that required students to salute the flag. Justice Robert Jackson noted that the purpose of the Bill of Rights is to "withdraw certain subjects from . . . political controversy" and to "place them beyond the reach of majorities and officials." Jackson famously wrote that "if there is any fixed star in our constitutional constellation, it is that no official, high or petty, can prescribe what shall be orthodox in politics, nationalism, religion, or other matters of opinion" (*West Virginia v. Barnette*, 319 U.S. 624 [1943]).

Judicial review in recent years has been used by conservative judges to strike down federal laws that are thought to intrude on the states' rights. In *United States v. Lopez*, the Supreme Court struck down the federal Gun-Free School Zones Act. Justice William Rehnquist noted Lopez was "a local student at a local school; there is no indication that he had recently moved in interstate commerce, and there is no requirement that his possession of the firearm have any concrete tie to interstate commerce" (*United States v. Lopez*, 514 U.S. 549 [1995]).

In *United States v. Morrison*, the Court invalidated a portion of the Violence Against Women Act, which authorized women to sue the perpetrators of domestic violence in federal court. Studies indicated the fear of violence deterred women from moving across state lines and domestic violence interfered with interstate commerce. The Court held the law obliterated the distinction between state and national jurisdiction: "Were the Federal Government to take over the regulation of entire areas of traditional State concern, areas having nothing to do with the regulation of commercial activities, the boundaries between the spheres of federal and State authority would blur. . . . It is difficult to perceive any limitation on federal power, even in areas such as criminal law enforcement or education where States historically have been sovereign" (*United States v. Morrison*, 529 U.S. 598 [2000]).

There is evidence that although Supreme Court justices and federal district and appellate court judges are unelected, they pay close attention to public opinion in writing their decisions. Popular respect for the Supreme Court depends on the justices' remaining in touch with public sentiments. In those instances in which a judgment is out of step with prevailing opinion, the justices respond in many instances by issuing a decision in a second case moderating their initial ruling (B. Friedman 2009).

The Supreme Court receives a large number of **amicus curiae** ("friend of the court") briefs from interest groups in an effort to bolster the argument of the litigants before the court whose point of view they share. The arguments in these briefs in some instances have been adopted by judges who shared the point of view in the amicus brief. In 2013, the Court received eleven amicus briefs for each case heard by the Court. These groups include associations of businesses and unions, groups that represent specific groups in the population such as the National Association for the Advancement of Colored People Legal Defense and Educational Fund, and groups specifically concerned with civil rights and liberties such as the American Civil Liberties Union. In cases affecting criminal justice, the Court is likely to hear from prosecutors and the police as well as associations of defense attorneys. The Court received 147 amicus briefs in considering same-sex marriage and in 2012 received 136 amicus briefs in considering Obamacare.

Keep in mind that the Court may uphold the constitutionality of a law. The Court's stamp of approval assures the public that a controversial law is a proper exercise of constitutional power. Prominent scholar James MacGregor Burns argues the problem with judicial review is that the Court has been too quick to place its stamp of approval on legislation that limits the civil liberties and rights of individuals and that federal courts have not been sufficiently aggressive in guaranteeing individuals access to education or a job (J. Burns 2009; Hirschl 2004).

There is a body of opinion that absent judicial review a "popular constitutionalism" would develop in which elected officials would act in a responsible fashion in enacting laws to ensure that they did not violate the Constitution (Tushnet 2000: 161–164). There is no reason, according to this argument, why the views of Supreme Court justices should be considered superior to the views of the state legislatures and of Congress. These elected officials after passing a law have the flexibility to easily amend a law or to pass a new measure (L. Kramer 2005). On the other hand, Erwin Chemerinsky notes that elected officials have demonstrated little interest in protecting prisoners and other groups who lack political power and are unlikely to voluntarily spend money on issues such as the reduction of prison overcrowding and medical care for inmates. Chemerinsky asserts that there is a risk that without judicial review there will be a patchwork of laws on abortion, gun rights, and other rights across the country (Chemerinsky 2014: 216–218).

The Supreme Court and Congress

The U.S. Constitution insulates federal judges from political pressure and retribution by providing judges with lifetime appointments "during good behavior." Their salaries may not be reduced as long as they are in office. This protects them against political retaliation by lawmakers who may disagree with their decisions.

The U.S. Supreme Court depends on other branches of government to enforce its decisions. Congress has supported Supreme Court decisions by exercising the "power of the purse." In 2000, the Supreme Court in *Boy Scouts of America v. Dale* held the Boy Scouts were constitutionally entitled to exclude gay men and boys. Various school districts announced that they would no longer cooperate with the Boy Scouts. Congress responded by passing a law stating these school districts would be ineligible for federal funds unless they provided the Boy Scouts with "equal access" (*Boy Scouts of America v. Dale*, 530 U.S. 640 [2000]).

President Dwight D. Eisenhower, in 1957, sent troops to Little Rock, Arkansas, to enforce a federal court desegregation order directed at Central High School. President Eisenhower, in a nationwide address, stressed that mob rule cannot be allowed to override the dictates of a federal court.

The Supreme Court, Congress, and the president may interact with one another to shape legislation. In 2007, the U.S. Supreme Court limited the ability of an individual to file a suit for pay discrimination (*Ledbetter v. Goodyear Tire and Rubber Co.*, 550 U.S. 618 [2007]). President Obama promised to overturn the decision, and Congress subsequently passed a law protecting the ability of individuals to file a legal action for pay discrimination.

In *Boumediene v. Bush*, the U.S. Supreme Court held that various aspects of the military commissions established by Congress were unconstitutional. Congress responded by reforming the process to meet the Court's objections in the Military Commission Act of 2009 (*Boumediene v. Bush*, 553 U.S. 723 [2008]).

In 2013, Congress responded to a court decision by amending a statute that criminalized making false claims of military honor by requiring that claims be made with the intent to obtain money, property, or other tangible benefit (*United States v. Alvarez*, 567 U.S. ___ [2012]).

In 2006, Congress extended the Voting Rights Act for twenty-five years after extensive hearings detailing racial discrimination at the polls by "covered jurisdictions." In 2013, in a 5–4 decision, the Supreme Court in *Shelby County v. Holder* held Section 4 of the Voting Rights Act of 1965 unconstitutional. The law is considered the crown jewel of the civil rights movement of the 1960s. The statute required nine southern states and various counties and municipalities in other states with a history of electoral discrimination to receive authorization ("pre-clearance") from the Department of Justice or a federal court in Washington, D.C., before modifying their voting laws.

The Supreme Court in the past had upheld the Voting Rights Act, noting that the law is an important mechanism to combat racial discrimination in voting rights. Chief Justice Roberts reversed course in *Holder* and held that the focus on the nine southern states and other jurisdictions was unconstitutional because it is "based on 40-year-old facts having no logical relationship to the present day." He explained if "Congress . . . must identify those jurisdictions to be singled out on a basis that makes sense in light of current conditions . . . it cannot simply rely on the past." Chief Justice Roberts argued that the law's "strong medicine" no longer was needed, pointing to the fact the act had increased African American voter turnout in most of the "covered jurisdictions" to a higher level than white turnout and that many southern towns now had elected African American mayors. Justice Roberts invited Congress to draft another formula "based on current conditions."

Justice Ruth Bader Ginsburg in her dissent noted that "thanks to the Voting Rights Act, progress once the subject of a dream has been achieved and continues to be made." She noted that the court "errs egregiously" by "overriding Congress's decision."

Congress failed to amend the Voting Rights Act, which led to a series of state laws that federal courts have held unconstitutionally impeded access by African Americans and other minorities to the ballot box (A. Berman 2015).

On occasion, the Supreme Court has held that a law is beyond the constitutional authority of Congress. The only course open to Congress is to begin the process of amending the Constitution, which is a complicated, difficult, and lengthy task. In 1989 and 1990, the Supreme Court held state and federal laws prohibiting the burning of the U.S. flag were unconstitutional. Efforts to amend the Constitution to prohibit desecration of the flag proved unsuccessful (*Texas v. Johnson*, 491 U.S. 397 [1989]).

Another recent example is the 2013 Supreme Court decision in *United States v. Windsor* striking down the federal Defense of Marriage Act. The act denied federal benefits to same-sex couples married in states recognizing same-sex marriage. The result was to deny over one thousand types of federal benefits to one or both members of these marriages, ranging from social security to tax benefits. Justice Anthony Kennedy, in a 5–4 decision, wrote that the "federal statute is invalid, for no legitimate purpose overcomes the purpose and effect to disparage and to injure those whom the State, by its marriage laws, sought to protect in personhood and dignity." The law, according to the Court majority, was motivated by an intent to denigrate the "moral and sexual choices" of same-sex couples and "ten thousands of children now being raised by same-sex couples." Justice Antonin Scalia in dissent criticized the majority decision for ignoring the views of "our respected co-ordinate" branch of government, the Congress, and stripping "the power of the people to govern themselves" (*United States v. Windsor*, 570 U.S. ___ [2013]).

Lawrence Baum reports that as of 2014, the Supreme Court had overturned 177 federal laws in whole or in part. The Court was most active between 1963 and 2014, a period in which 106 statutes were overturned as unconstitutional. Baum notes that this constitutes a small percentage of congressional statutes passed by Congress and that five of every six times that the Court reviews a Congressional statute it upholds the constitutionality of the law (Baum 2016: 159). However, the laws rejected by the Court include important measures like the Missouri Compromise of 1820 restricting slavery in some territories on the grounds that the law deprived individuals of property without due process of law (*Dred Scott v. Sandford*, 60 U.S. 393 [1857]) and *in Schechter Poultry Corp. v. United States,* the Court overturned President Franklin Delano Roosevelt's signature legislation to bring the country out of the Great Depression (*Schechter Poultry Corp. v. United States*, 295 U.S. 495 [1935]). Another series of cases invalidated the congressional effort to reform campaign finance. In *Buckley v. Valeo*, for example, the Court overturned certain limits on campaign expenditures and contributions on the grounds that financial donations constituted speech protected under the First Amendment (*Buckley v. Valeo*, 424 U.S. 1 [1976]).

Keep in mind that between 1790 and 2014 the Court overturned 1,080 state and local laws as unconstitutional. An additional 241 laws were rejected because they infringed on areas reserved for federal laws (Baum 2016: 163).

A controversial and unsettled question is whether Congress can tamper with the Supreme Court's jurisdiction and limit the types of cases that the Supreme Court can hear on appeal. Between 1974 and 2002, more than 130 congressional bills were introduced in an unsuccessful effort to limit the Court's ability to hear abortion, affirmative action, and school segregation cases, as well as cases involving the reference to God in the Pledge of Allegiance and challenges to the Defense of Marriage Act. In 1996, Congress passed the Prison Litigation Reform Act, which limited the ability of prisoners to file federal court suits challenging their conditions of confinement (Baum 2016: 202–215).

In some instances, Congress has taken the radical step of attempting to modify Supreme Court decisions by changing the composition of the Court. Presidents James Madison, James Monroe, and John Quincy Adams all argued that the Supreme Court should be expanded in size. Congress reduced the number of justices to eight to prevent President Andrew Johnson from filling vacancies. The size of the Court was reestablished at nine members when President Ulysses S. Grant assumed office. The most famous attempt to influence the Court by increasing its size was President Franklin Roosevelt's "court-packing plan" in 1937. Roosevelt proposed expanding the court from nine to fifteen justices in an effort to ensure support for his New Deal legislation. His proposal lost momentum when the Supreme Court in a series of decisions upheld the constitutionality of several of Roosevelt's New Deal programs (J. Burns 2009: 139–178).

Judicial Nominations and Congress

The greatest shifts in Supreme Court decisions have resulted from presidential appointments to the Court. The president fills vacancies on district courts and courts of appeal as well as the Supreme Court and typically appoints individuals from his own party who share his philosophical outlook. Senate approval for district court judges is virtually automatic. Appointments to the circuit courts of appeals are contested when the Senate is controlled by the opposition party and the party wants to leave appellate slots vacant in hopes that it may wrest control of the White House in the future and fill the vacancy with one of its members.

Twelve of the 159 Supreme Court nominations that presidents have submitted to the Senate as of 2015 have failed to receive Senate confirmation. The first nominee rejected was John Rutledge, nominated by George Washington as chief justice in 1795, and another failed nominee was Robert Bork, nominated in 1987 by President Ronald Reagan. Twenty-four nominees withdrew—for example, Harriet Miers withdrew from consideration in 2005. Most recently, the Senate failed to act on President Obama's nomination of Merrick Garland, the thirteenth nominee who failed to receive Senate confirmation. Neil Gorsuch, nominated by President Trump, was the 161st Court nominee (see You Decide 3.4 on the study site).

Presidents whose party held a Senate majority had 90 percent of their nominees confirmed. In contrast, presidents whose party held a minority of the Senate had only 60 percent of their nominees confirmed. One-third of unsuccessful nominations were made by presidents who had not been elected to office.

President Obama successfully appointed two accomplished female nominees to the Supreme Court: Sonia Sotomayor and Elena Kagan. He experienced somewhat less success in gaining confirmation for lower court judges.

Six years into Obama's presidency, 86.9 percent of his judicial nominees to circuit courts of appeals were successful as compared to 75 percent of President George W. Bush's nominees and 50 percent of President Clinton's nominees after six years in office. Ronald Reagan, in contrast, was successful in 97 percent of his nominations (McMillion 2015).

As for district courts, President Obama after six years in office was successful in the confirmation of 92 percent of his nominations. President Reagan once again experienced the greatest success with the confirmation of 97 percent of his nominees after six years in office. President Clinton was successful in 90 percent of his nominations, and President Bush was successful in 86.8 percent of his nominations.

Each of these presidents has left his stamp on the federal judiciary. President Obama, although appointing fewer federal judges than Presidents Reagan, Clinton, and Bush, nonetheless appointed 55 judges to federal courts of appeal and 268 judges to federal district courts, a total of 323 federal judges. President Reagan, in contrast, appointed 384 judges, and President Clinton 379 judges.

After President George W. Bush left office, Republican-appointed judges controlled nine of the twelve federal circuit courts, and judges appointed by Democrats controlled one circuit court of appeal. As President Obama left office, Democratic appointees constituted a majority on eight circuit courts of appeal, and Republican nominees constituted a majority on four federal circuit courts of appeal (Savage 2016).

In the next several years, the federal judiciary likely will be significantly more conservative in orientation because President Trump has inherited 112 vacancies, 33 of which have been unfilled for over two years. In contrast, when President Obama came into office, there were 58 vacant federal judgeships. Considering the age of current federal court judges, President Trump may have the opportunity to appoint 38 percent of judges. In 2013, the Senate agreed that a simple majority would be required to appoint district court and appellate court judges although sixty votes would continue to be required for Supreme Court appointments. The thinking was that Supreme Court appointments are so important that Senate confirmation should require a "super-majority" of sixty votes. A limitation on the appointment of district court judges is the so-called "blue slip" policy, which gives senators a veto over district court judges appointed in their state (J. Katz 2017). Note that the Senate Republicans voted to modify the rules to allow Justice Gorsuch to be confirmed by a majority vote (54–45) and threaten to revoke the "blue slip" rule.

The public interest group Alliance for Justice in a January 2016 statement documented that President Obama had "dramatically improved demographic diversity of the federal judiciary." After seven years in office, President Obama nominated more than twice as many women (164) than did President George W. Bush during his eight-year term in office. Forty-three percent of Obama's judicial nominees were female. Bill Clinton, 29 percent of whose appointees were women, has the second-best record of appointing women to the judiciary. President Obama nominated more than twice as many non-Caucasian judges (19 percent African American; 11 percent Hispanic; 7 percent Asian American and Pacific Islander) as President George W. Bush and somewhat more non-Caucasian judges than President Clinton. Obama named fourteen lesbian, gay, bisexual, and transgender (LGBT) nominees, far more than any other president. President Clinton was the only other president to nominate an LGBT candidate to a federal judgeship. President Obama also was the first president to nominate a Muslim to a federal district court.

President Obama, according to the Alliance for Justice, was equally attentive in promoting a diversity in the personal backgrounds of his nominees although most have fairly traditional professional backgrounds. Roughly 50 percent of his district and appellate court nominees at the time of their appointment were state or federal judges. Three times as many nominees who worked in private practice worked on behalf of corporate clients than represented non-corporate clients or a mix of corporate and non-corporate clients. Somewhat more nominees served as prosecutors than served as public defenders or as private defense attorneys. A relatively small percentage worked as public interest attorneys on behalf of consumers or as civil rights attorneys, and only a small percentage had been law school professors (Alliance for Justice 2016).

Before we leave the topic of Supreme Court and judicial nominations, note that the process has become highly controversial and contested in recent years. In 1987, President Reagan nominated Robert Bork to succeed the retiring Supreme Court justice Lewis Powell. Bork ultimately would prove to be the twelfth Supreme Court nominee rejected by the Senate and forced to withdraw.

Bork was critical of the notion of a living and evolving Constitution. He stated that he would have no difficulty overturning existing precedents. It was anticipated that Bork's vote would tilt the balance of the Court in a more conservative direction on issues such as abortion, school prayer, affirmative action, and criminal procedure. Liberals viewed Bork as a threat to the Constitution. Democratic senator Edward Kennedy of Massachusetts described Bork's America as a country in which "women would be forced into back alley abortions, blacks would sit at segregated lunch counters, [and] rogue police could break down citizens' doors in midnight raids."

Bork's testimony lasted for five days and more than thirty hours, and 101 witnesses testified for and against the nomination. Conservative and liberal lobby groups raised millions of dollars to support or oppose the Bork nomination. At the end of the Bork hearings, the public firmly opposed his nomination. The Judiciary Committee voted 9–5 against Bork, and the full Senate rejected his nomination by a vote of 58–42. The process of attacking and exaggerating a nominee's record has come to be known as "being Borked." Bork's extensive "paper record" of writings and open and honest responses undermined his candidacy. Subsequent nominees have learned they should offer bland and evasive answers and that their ambitions to be appointed to the federal judiciary can be undermined by an extensive written "paper trail."

The Constitution specifies that judges "shall hold their offices during good behaviour." The House of Representatives may bring impeachment charges against a judge for "treason, bribery, or other high crimes and misdemeanors," and the judge then is to be prosecuted before the Senate. A two-thirds vote of the senators present is required to convict and to remove a judge from office. Thirteen federal judges have been impeached by the House, and seven of these judges have been convicted by the Senate. Three impeachments have occurred since 1986. As for the Supreme Court, in 1804 the Jeffersonian Republicans unsuccessfully attempted to impeach Supreme Court Justice Samuel Chase. Supreme Court Justice Abe Fortas resigned in 1969 after his financial improprieties threatened to lead to his impeachment and removal from the Court.

The federal court system is dwarfed in size and in the number of decisions by the state court systems, which are discussed as follows.

The Supreme Court and Public Opinion

The U.S. Supreme Court holds an important and unique place in America. Despite the fact that the Court has a profound impact on public policy, the judges hold lifetime appointments and are not subject to elections or even to formal evaluation. Very little is known about the inner workings of the Court, and the Court's deliberations are not televised. The average American does not receive the opportunity to visit Washington, D.C., and to visit the Court and witness a Supreme Court case. Most people do not read the Court's opinions and instead depend on the news media to interpret the Court's decisions (Drake 2016).

Popular opinion of the Court was at a thirty-year low in 2015 because of its upholding of Obamacare and legalization of same-sex marriage. These decisions resulted in a high level of unpopularity among Republicans. The death of Justice Scalia left the Court with only eight members, and as a consequence, the Court heard fewer high-profile cases. As a result, the Court gradually regained its popularity. In August 2016, 60 percent of Americans had a favorable view of the Court, and only 32 percent viewed the Court unfavorably. Fifty-seven percent of Republicans and 73 percent of Democrats viewed the Court favorably.

Republicans and Democrats starkly differ on their view of how the Court should interpret the U.S. Constitution. Sixty-nine percent of Republicans believe that the Constitution should be interpreted as originally written although 70 percent of Democrats favor interpreting the Constitution as an evolving document in accordance with current times. Ninety percent of political conservatives support a so-called originalist point of view as compared to 83 percent of liberals who favor interpreting the Constitution in light of contemporary events.

Sixty-five percent of registered voters reported that selections to the Supreme Court were important in their voting decision, ranking it ninth on a list of fourteen issues. Seventy-seven percent of conservative Republican and Republican-leaning voters stated that Court nominees were very important as opposed to 69 percent of liberal Democrats and Democratic-leaning voters. Selections to the Court were viewed as less important by moderate and liberal Republicans and by moderate and conservative Democrats.

Americans believed by 56 to 38 percent that the Senate should have held hearings on the nomination of Merrick Garland to the Supreme Court. Forty-six percent of individuals believed that Garland should be confirmed, 30 percent opposed his confirmation, and 24 percent had no opinion (see the You Decide feature on the study site).

There are various proposals to make the Supreme Court more democratic, including televising hearings and increasing the number of seats available to the public to attend oral arguments. The justices generally oppose televising the Court proceedings because they believe it would invite "grandstanding" by lawyers and justices and encourage the participants to simplify their arguments. Chief Justice John Roberts has responded to demands for public access by making the tapes of oral arguments available. Other reforms include term limits for justices and some form of merit selection (Chemerinsky 2014: 293–330).

■ THE ORGANIZATION OF STATE COURTS

State courts are the centers of legal activity. Over 95 percent of all legal cases are filed in state courts. An estimated one billion cases were filed in state courts over the past decade. State cases are brought under state laws and state constitutions. In some instances, cities and counties are authorized to adopt municipal codes, which are another source of state law. For example, roughly thirteen cities prohibit the ownership of certain breeds of dogs that are considered a public danger. The National Center for State Courts reports that 94.1 million cases were filed in state courts in 2013. This includes the type of cases that affect the lives of most Americans, traffic cases, civil and criminal cases, domestic relations, and juvenile cases. In 2013, 21 percent of cases filed in state courts were criminal, 18 percent were civil cases, 6 percent involved domestic relations, 1 percent related to juveniles, and 54 percent were traffic cases (George and Yoon 2016: 4). There are more cases filed in California, Illinois, and Florida than in all the federal courts combined (LaFountain et al. 2015). Ninety-six percent of the judges in the United States sit on state courts. California, Georgia, New York, and Texas have judicial systems that are larger than the federal judiciary (M. Hall 2008: 236; National Center for State Courts 2006: 15).

State constitutions give the legislature the power to create state courts. Article VI, Section 1 of the California Constitution provides that the judicial power is vested in the Supreme Court, courts of appeal, and superior courts. The legislature under this provision is responsible for dividing the state into judicial districts and creating one or more superior courts in each district.

State court systems are independent of one another. A decision by a court in New York does not constitute a precedent for courts of other states. At times, a state court may look to the decisions of courts in other states to see how they have dealt with an issue. Keep in mind that state laws may differ from one another. In thirty-two states, a defendant may receive the death penalty for first-degree murder although eighteen states have abolished capital punishment. In non-death-penalty states, individuals convicted of first-degree murder may receive a sentence of life imprisonment.

Various efforts have been made to provide for uniform state laws. The American Law Institute (ALI)—a group of distinguished lawyers, judges, and academics—drafted the Model Penal Code, which incorporates what the drafters of the code consider to be the best definition of various crimes. States are encouraged by ALI to adopt these model laws.

There is significant variation in state court structures. The typical state court system is composed of courts of limited jurisdiction, courts of general jurisdiction, intermediate appellate courts, and a supreme court of last resort. State judiciaries may differ in the mix of cases on their docket, the content of their laws, and whether cases are settled or adjudicated at trial. These differences are due to a range of factors, including whether the state is heavily rural or urban. A higher percentage of personal injury cases are settled in small, homogeneous, and rural states in which people generally are familiar with one another than in large, diverse, and urbanized states (M. Hall 2008: 240).

■ STATE COURTS OF LIMITED JURISDICTION

Courts of limited jurisdiction hear minor criminal offenses and civil cases. Most people who come into contact with the state court system find themselves before courts of limited jurisdiction. Sixty-six percent of all state cases are tried before these courts. Various names are used for these courts including county courts, justice of the peace courts, magistrate's courts, and municipal courts.

Think of courts of limited jurisdiction as courts that adjudicate minor matters. These tribunals have jurisdiction over a limited category of cases, which typically include traffic cases, minor criminal cases, and violations of municipal ordinances such as a failure to leash a dog. Courts of limited jurisdiction also may hear small claims, domestic relations or family matters, and juvenile delinquency cases. These trials are conducted in an informal fashion before a single judge. Appeals may be taken to a state court of general jurisdiction, and an appeal typically requires that the parties undertake a trial de novo (new trial), which involves a complete retrial of the case.

Nationally there are 13,500 trial courts of limited jurisdiction presided over by 18,500 judicial officials. The caseload of these courts is roughly sixty-eight million cases per year, 40 percent of which are traffic cases, 15 percent criminal cases, and 10 percent civil cases. The rest of the docket comprises domestic and juvenile matters. In the past few years, states and cities have introduced a number of specialized courts dealing with drugs, domestic violence, and veterans (Neubauer and Fradella 2011: 96).

■ STATE COURTS OF GENERAL JURISDICTION

Courts of general jurisdiction are the primary trial courts for criminal and civil cases that do not originate in courts of limited jurisdiction. Think of these courts as trial courts that handle more serious matters. A case can be brought in a court of general jurisdiction if it involves a designated monetary amount, is a felony charge, involves a state constitutional issue, or is brought under a state law that provides for jurisdiction in a court of general jurisdiction.

The losing party in a trial before a court of limited jurisdiction has the right to appeal to a court of general jurisdiction. An unusual aspect of the appeal is that the court will conduct a trial de novo, meaning that the case is tried all over again.

Courts of general jurisdiction commonly are called circuit courts, district courts, or superior courts. A single judge hears cases in courts of limited jurisdiction and in courts of general jurisdiction. There are 2,040 courts of jurisdiction with eleven thousand sitting judges in the fifty states, which hear roughly 34 percent of cases filed in state court.

The dockets of most trial courts are dominated by criminal cases although trial courts in sixteen states process more civil cases than criminal cases and focus their efforts on divorce and child custody, inheritance, personal injury, and contract (M. Hall 2008: 238).

■ STATE APPELLATE COURTS

Forty-two states have **state appellate courts** below the state supreme court. Individuals have the right to appeal a case from courts of general jurisdiction to appellate courts. These courts variously are called appellate courts, appellate divisions, and appeals courts. State appellate courts are three-judge courts that read briefs submitted by the lawyers and hear oral arguments. Alabama and Tennessee have separate courts of appeal for civil and criminal cases. Eleven small states do not have appellate courts, and appeals are taken directly to the state supreme court. State appellate courts recorded 262,230 cases in 2013 (LaFountain et al. 2015).

■ STATE SUPREME COURTS

The state supreme court is at the top of the judicial hierarchy and has discretion over which cases to review. In some smaller states, there are no appellate courts, and the state supreme court reviews all appeals. Oklahoma and Texas have separate civil and criminal supreme courts. States variously call these courts supreme courts, supreme judicial courts, supreme courts of appeal, courts of appeal, and courts of criminal or civil appeal. A party that loses a case in the state supreme court that raises a federal question may appeal to a federal district court.

The state supreme court is the final arbiter in matters of state law and establishes binding precedents on courts within the state. A movement called the **new judicial federalism** encourages state supreme courts to broadly interpret state constitutional provisions to provide more rights than the U.S. Supreme Court holds is required under the Constitution. For example, the Illinois Supreme Court has held that the state constitution's protection of due process of law provides defendants undergoing police interrogation with greater access to a lawyer than according to the U.S. Supreme Court is required by the federal Constitution.

Studies indicate that supreme court judges in two-thirds of the states are hesitant to issue rulings that will place them at odds with governors and state legislatures and rarely overturn state laws on the grounds the statutes conflict with their state constitution. Supreme court judges in the remaining states overturn a significant percentage of the laws that are challenged on constitutional grounds. In 2004, for example, the Kansas and New York high courts threw out their state's death penalty laws (M. Hall 2008: 250–252). In 2013, the Connecticut Supreme Court overturned the state's death penalty.

■ STATE JUDICIAL SELECTION

State court judges clearly have an impact on our lives. They preside over trials that determine whether people will be criminally convicted, pay fines, receive or pay monetary damages, and be awarded child custody. Despite the importance of judges, most people are unaware of how their state court judges are selected.

In selecting judges at the state level, there is disagreement over whether judges should be completely independent of the voters or whether judges should be responsive to the public and stand for election. Another obvious tension is disagreement over the personal qualities that make a "good judge." A selection system based on "merit" may result in the selection of judges who possess excellent legal training, experience, and skills although a system that allows the voters to select judges may result in "less qualified" judges who are more attentive to the problems confronting the average person.

In European countries, students entering law school prepare for a judicial career by undergoing specialized training. In contrast, in the United States, there isn't even a handbook on how to prepare for a career on the bench.

The system for selecting judges has undergone significant changes over the past two hundred years. A central grievance of the American colonists was the king of England's appointment of judges, who were dependent on the king and unresponsive to popular opinion. Following the American Revolution, seven states provided for selection by the legislature, five called for selection by the colonial governor and his council, and in one state, judges were jointly selected by the governor and by the legislature. States newly admitted to the union followed one of these three models.

In the 1840s, a movement developed for democratic control of the judiciary, which led to the election of judges. The judges were elected in partisan elections for limited terms.

Political parties by the 1880s began to be perceived as corrupt, and judicial elections were viewed as vehicles for political parties to reward unqualified loyalists. States responded by adopting nonpartisan elections. Absent party labels, voters had no easy way to determine which candidates to support. The nonpartisan election of judges also was criticized for elevating ambitious and wealthy candidates to the bench rather than resulting in the selection of the best-qualified candidates.

In 1937, the American Bar Association endorsed a "hybrid plan," which three years later was adopted by Missouri. The so-called **Missouri Plan**, or merit selection, involves a non-political nominating commission that sends the names of candidates who the commission believes are "best qualified" to the governor. The governor appoints a candidate from the list to the judicial vacancy. The judge serves a term of service, and the electorate then votes whether to retain or to reject the judge. A vote to reject a judge results in a vacancy and the appointment of a new individual to the bench. The Missouri Plan combines selection based on legal qualification with a popular veto and insulates the process of judicial selection from party politics. In the past, roughly 1 percent of judges appointed by governors were rejected by voters (Corsi 1984: 104–114).

Several systems are used to select state court judges; most states use a combination of these methods, which accounts for the fact that more than fifty states are included below (Baum 2013: 104).

1. *Partisan elections.* Candidates run for judicial office under the label of a political party (ten states).

2. *Nonpartisan elections.* Candidates run for election without party identification (twenty-one states).

3. *Merit selection.* The governor appoints candidates considered qualified by a nonpartisan commission. The individuals appointed to the judiciary following a period in office either are retained or are rejected by popular vote (twenty states).

4. *Appointment.* Judges are appointed by the governor with the confirmation of the legislature or are appointed by the legislature (seven states).

5. *Legislative selection.* The legislature elects judges (two states).

The striking aspect of these selection systems is that in forty-one states, *at least some of the judges* must go before the voters during their judicial career. The most common length of a judicial term is six years, although New York judges serve fourteen years in office. Rhode Island judges serve life terms, and judges in New Hampshire hold office until age 70. Salaries for state supreme court judges are in the six figures.

Despite the differences in the methods used to select state court judges, these systems result in judges who are similar in background, qualifications, gender, diversity, and quality. Over half of all state court judges are white males. Women constitute less than one-third of state court judges, and no state has as many female as male judges. People of color account for fewer than 20 percent of state court judges, and in four states, there are no members of the judiciary who are people of color. Women of color account for roughly 8 percent of state court judges. Commentators advocating greater diversity on state courts point out that these courts decide cases that directly affect the lives of Americans and should be representative of society (George and Yoon 2016: 3, 7).

It is difficult to determine whether any of the selection systems result in judges who are "better" than the judges selected in other selection systems. Do judges who are elected differ from judges who are selected? Chief Justice John Roberts wrote, "Judges are not politicians, even when they come to the bench by way of the ballot. . . . A judge . . . must 'observe the utmost fairness,' striving to be 'perfectly and completely independent.'" There nonetheless is evidence that judges who are required to go before the voters pay more attention to public opinion in their decisions and that monetary awards for in-state plaintiffs who sue out-of-state defendants are larger in jurisdictions with elected judges (Helland and Tabarrok 2002). Appointed judges who are free from popular control reverse criminal convictions at a higher rate than do elected judges although elected judges are more likely to impose harsher sentences, including the death penalty, than appointed judges (Pinello 1995). Even the harshest judges become more punitive as an election approaches (Liptak 2016).

Studies indicate that elected judges are less likely to support gay rights than appointed judges. State supreme court judges elected in partisan elections supported gay rights 53 percent of the time as compared to judges in nonpartisan elections who supported gay rights 70 percent of the time. Judges who confronted retention elections supported gay rights 76 percent of the time, and judges in appointed systems supported gay rights 82 percent of the time (Liptak 2016).

One troubling development is the increased amount of money spent on judicial elections by interest groups seeking to influence judicial decisions. The role of "big money," or what is termed the problem of "cash in the courtroom," risks giving the impression that justice is "for sale." Survey data indicate seven of ten Americans believe the decisions of state court judges are influenced by cash contributions, and nearly half of all state court judges agree.

One well-known example of interest group involvement in judicial elections is the 2004 defeat of the chief justice of the West Virginia Supreme Court, Warren McGraw. A coal company executive spent $3 million to defeat McGraw and succeeded in electing a candidate whose views were more sympathetic toward the coal industry. The successful candidate subsequently cast the decisive vote in a 3–2 verdict overturning a $50 million judgment against the coal company. The U.S. Supreme Court subsequently held that Judge Benjamin should have recused himself or withdrawn from the case (*Caperton v. A. T. Massey Coal Company*, 556 U.S. 868 [2009]). Other judges have been defeated in elections because of their votes on same-sex marriage, the death penalty, or abortion or because they are viewed as "soft on crime."

The Brennan Center for Justice at New York University School of Law and the National Institute on Money in State Politics found that political parties and special interest groups accounted for 40 percent of total spending in state judicial races in 2013–2014. Another way of looking at financial contributions is that the contributions of lawyers and lobbyists accounted for 63 percent of all donations. The report finds that multimillion-dollar races are common and that judicial elections increasingly are being bankrolled by groups intent on affecting the outcome of judicial decisions. Supreme Court candidates in nineteen states spent a total of over $34 million in 2013–2014. The result is that judicial candidates and judges hoping to be elected or retained are increasingly dependent on contributions from groups that expect them to decide a case in a specific fashion. In the twenty-three states that held elections during 2013–2014, the candidate who spent the most money won the election 90 percent of the time. The study raises the issue whether states should reconsider electing judges (Brennan Center for Justice and National Institute on Money in State Politics 2015).

Judicial elections are important for holding judges accountable to the public. On the other hand, elections may result in judges "looking over their shoulder" and issuing decisions that appeal to public opinion. Because of the low turnout in state judicial elections, a motivated group of "one issue" voters can have a significant impact on the result. The question of which selection system results in a better brand of justice remains unanswered (Bright and Keenan 1995).

The U.S. Supreme Court, in an effort to maintain the appearance and reality of judicial integrity in selection systems in which judges confront popular election, held that states may prohibit judicial candidates and judges from personally soliciting financial contributions. The court recognized that the impartiality of judicial decisions may be compromised if judges were allowed to ask for money from lawyers and powerful interests who may appear in the judge's court (*Williams-Yulee v. Florida Bar*, 575 U.S. ___ [2015]).

■ HOW JUDGES DECIDE DISPUTES

Talking about how judges decide cases can be like mixing apples and oranges. A trial court judge in cases that do not involve a jury will be asked to weigh and balance the facts and to reach a verdict based on the law. Trial court judges also are charged with determining the appropriate criminal sentence. This is a very different task from appellate court and Supreme Court judges. These judges typically sit in multi-judge panels and receive a factual record from the trial court, read written briefs and hear oral arguments from lawyers, and issue judgments based on the law.

A U.S. Supreme Court justice who is in a position to establish a precedent that is binding on lower court judges and considers the public policy aspects of a decision is in a very different position from a lower court trial judge or appellate judge who is bound by the established law in making a decision. Studies of judicial decision-making typically are based on studies of the U.S. Supreme Court and on studies of federal circuit courts of appeal. In the 2014–2015 term, there were thirty-nine unanimous opinions, and there was at least one dissent in sixty-nine cases. In contrast, in the 2015–2016 Supreme Court term, the Court issued thirty-nine unanimous decisions, and there was at least one dissent in forty-nine cases. The Court reversed appellate courts in 72 percent of the cases in the 2014–2015 term and reversed appellate courts in 54 percent of the cases in the 2015–2016 term. Eight circuits had at least 50 percent of the cases reviewed by the Court overturned (M. Bell 2016).

Judges typically explain that their decisions are based on the law (Epstein and Knight 1998). According to this "robes on" theory, once judges slip into their black judicial robes, they disregard all considerations other than the law. The primary decision-making tool of the judge is *stare decisis*. Reliance on precedent involves locating a case that is factually similar to the case before the judge. The judge then applies the rule established in the previous case to reach a decision. *Stare decisis* ensures that the law is predictable and stable and that decisions reflect the judgment of the legal community and are not solely the product of the judge who is making the decision (Carter 1979: 236–152; Epstein and Kobylka 1992: 11–12).

The extreme version of "mechanical jurisprudence," or **legalism**, was articulated by Supreme Court Justice Owen Roberts who stated the "judicial branch . . . has only one duty; to lay the article of Constitution which is invoked beside the statute which is challenged and decide whether the latter squares with the former" (*United States v. Butler*, 297 U.S. 1 [1936]).

This "robes on" theory does not easily account for how judges decide cases when the precedent is outdated or even objectionable. The Supreme Court slowly eroded the "separate but equal" doctrine established in *Plessy v. Ferguson* (163 U.S. 537 [1896]) and held in *Brown v. Board of Education* (347 U.S. 483 [1954]) that separate schools did not constitute equal schools and ordered desegregation with "all deliberate speed." The justices reasoned that "separate" could not be "equal" because of the stigma attached to segregated facilities.

There are various legal tools in addition to precedent to help judges navigate through the legal thicket. A judge may employ **originalism** and ask what the creators of the law or the framers of the Constitution intended at the time that the law or constitutional provision was drafted. In interpreting a constitutional provision, a judge might examine the records of the Constitutional Convention, ratification debates in the states, and the statements of the drafters of the Constitution and American legal history. According to originalists, this approach makes sense because a judge should interpret the constitutional text rather than impose his or her point of view (Brest 1980).

Antonin Scalia is the judge most closely identified with the originalist perspective. Scalia, for example, criticized his fellow judges for holding that a child who is frightened to testify in the presence of her alleged abuser should be permitted to testify on closed-circuit television. Scalia noted the Sixth Amendment provides that in "all criminal prosecutions the accused shall enjoy the right . . . to be confronted with the witnesses against him." He pointed out that at the time the Sixth Amendment was drafted, children were expected to confront their alleged abusers and the only change that had occurred over the past two hundred years was that society developed an awareness of the trauma experienced by a child witness. Justice Scalia conceded that society may be perfectly happy with the protection accorded to child witnesses although there was no avoiding the fact that the Supreme Court had restricted defendants' Sixth Amendment rights to confront their accusers (Scalia 1997). Judge Richard Posner in noting the limited perspective of originalism expresses doubts whether the Fourteenth Amendment Equal Protection Clause from an originalist perspective can be interpreted to prohibit school segregation (Posner 2008: 340–346).

The intent of the framers of the Constitution may not always be crystal clear. In *Lawrence v. Texas*, the Supreme Court held that the right to privacy protected the right of same-sex couples to engage in sexual relations within the home (*Lawrence v. Texas*, 539 U.S. 558 [2003]). The Court in deciding *Lawrence* rejected the earlier historical analysis in *Bowers v. Hardwick* that concluded that there was no historical acceptance of same-sex relationships (*Bowers v. Hardwick*, 478 U.S. 186 [1986]).

Originalism encounters the obvious difficulty that the framers of the Constitution did not always speak with a single voice and in any event did not anticipate many of the technological advantages such as DNA that challenge the law today. The question asked by critics is why the intent of "long dead people" should dictate a judge's decision in the twenty-first century. A constitution frozen in place would mean, if Justice Scalia is correct, that children must confront their alleged abusers in the courtroom and that racial segregation and gender discrimination are lawful. Originalists respond to this criticism by asserting that judges are required to follow the law and that they betray this obligation by "legislating from the bench." The solution is to amend the U.S. Constitution or for state court judges to provide greater rights than are required by the federal constitution (Levinson 1982).

Other judges in approaching an issue for the first time employ strict constructionalism or **textualism**, which most frequently is used in interpreting a statute. The literalists look at the words of a statute or constitutional provision and do not analyze the intent of the drafters of the law or constitutional provision. In other words, they do not examine what is termed "legislative history." Efforts to unearth the intent of the drafter is a dead end because there rarely is a single, clear statement of intent. The best indication of what the drafters of a measure intend is the words in the text. This approach encounters the problem that words may not reveal the full meaning of the law.

There is a danger, according to literalists, that if a decision is not based on the words on the page, judges will make policy rather than follow the law (Scalia and Garner 2012). In *Texas v. Johnson*, the Supreme Court seemingly stretched the notion of freedom of expression beyond the commonsense meaning of the words and held that the First Amendment protected symbolic speech, such as the burning of the American flag, when undertaken to communicate ideas (*Texas v. Johnson*, 491 U.S. 397 [1989]).

A third perspective is to view the U.S. Constitution as a "living document" that should be interpreted to meet contemporary needs of society. At the time the Constitution was drafted, the death penalty for juveniles was accepted as a permissible mode of punishment. Should the phrase "cruel and unusual" be interpreted in light of contemporary values, or should judges adhere to the view that the death penalty for juveniles was not viewed as cruel at the time the Constitution was drafted and therefore does not constitute cruel punishment today?

An example of this evolutionary approach is the Supreme Court's decision in 1965 in *Griswold v. Connecticut*. In *Griswold*, the Court overturned a Connecticut statute that prohibited the use of contraceptives by married as well as by unmarried couples and punished anyone who assisted another person in the use of contraceptives. The Court held that a "zone of privacy" is created in the Constitution by "penumbras" of various amendments. In other words, a right to privacy was created by the collective meaning of various provisions of the Bill of Rights. The First Amendment right to freedom of expression, for example, involves a right to be free to think and reflect, and the Fourth Amendment right to be free from unreasonable searches and seizures involves a right to be left alone. The problem with this analysis is that the word *privacy* does not appear in the Constitution. As Justice Hugo Black noted in his dissenting opinion, "I like my privacy as well as the next one, but I am nevertheless compelled to admit that government has a right to invade it unless prohibited by some specific constitutional provision. . . . But there is not." Justice Potter Stewart questioned what acts fell within the right to privacy. Does it protect the right to take drugs or to engage in prostitution in the home? (*Griswold v. Connecticut,* 381 U.S. 479 [1965]).

Judges who view the law as a "living" body of rules often employ a **balancing of interests** approach in reaching a decision. The judge identifies the contending policy interests at stake in a case and decides which interest should take precedence. In *Tennessee v. Garner,* the Supreme Court established the standard for police use of deadly force against a "fleeing felon." The common law in England authorized the police to use deadly force to apprehend a "fleeing felon," and this historically had been the rule in the United States. In *Garner,* the Court asked whether it is reasonable under the Fourth Amendment to the Constitution for the police to use deadly force to seize a suspect. A strict adherence to precedent would result in holding that deadly force is justified against a felon who disregards a police order to "halt." The Supreme Court majority balanced the life and liberty of a felon against the interest in apprehending felons and held deadly force was justified only against a felon who posed a threat of violence against the police or the public. Deadly force would not be justified to apprehend a felon in other circumstances.

The difficulty with the balancing of interests approach is that judges may place different weights on different interests and reach different results. In *Garner,* Justice Sandra Day O'Connor dissented and argued that the police officer was justified in killing the fleeing felon because of the danger posed by burglars to the residents of homes. A rule that allows fleeing felons to avoid apprehension undermines police authority and the rule of law (*Tennessee v. Garner,* 471 U.S. 1 [1985]).

Various legal commentators (as discussed in Chapter 2) questioned the notion that the solution to legal issues is as "certain and exact as an answer to a problem in mathematics" (Frank 1930: 10). Jerome Frank, writing in 1930, argued judges first reach a conclusion about a case and then write an opinion supporting their viewpoint. A judge's decision in a case, according to this view, reflects his or her personal biases, experiences, and background. A judge whose parent died as a result of medical negligence likely will be hostile toward a doctor being sued for medical malpractice. Frank concludes that the personality of the judge is more important than legal rules in the judicial process (Frank 1930: 33, 34, 136).

Frank and legal realists laid the foundation for the **attitudinal approach**. Herman Pritchett, writing in 1941, argued Supreme Court decisions could be explained by the "conscious and unconscious preferences and prejudices" of the justices. Social scientists analyzed the voting behavior of federal judges and found that judges tend to vote consistently in a liberal or conservative direction on civil liberties and economic issues. Liberal attitudes tend to be associated with Democratic judges, and conservative attitudes tend to be associated with Republican judges (Schubert 1965: 131–157).

Jeffrey Segal and Harold Spaeth, two of the leading proponents of the attitudinal approach, conclude that judges decide cases based primarily on their ideological preferences rather than based on precedent and other methods of legal reasoning (Segal and Spaeth 2002). Segal and Spaeth analyzed Supreme Court decisions between 1962 and 1998 in Fourth Amendment search and seizure cases and found that the justices' political ideology explained roughly 71 percent of the decisions.

A series of more recent studies concluded that federal courts of appeal judges, in adjudicating asylum claims, are significantly impacted by their views toward immigration (Epstein, Landes, and Posner 2013: 81). The impact of a judge's ideology on his or her judgments tends to be weakest in criminal cases (Segal, Spaeth, and Benesh 2005: 237–238) and strongest in cases involving freedom of expression and privacy (Pinello 1999: 219).

The attitudinal approach assumes that lifetime tenure of justices and the Supreme Court's position at the top of the judicial hierarchy liberate justices to vote in accordance with their personal and political points of view. Cass Sunstein argues that ideology is less important than a judge's view of his or her judicial role. The "heroic" judge is comfortable with bold decisions although the minimalist is more comfortable with small, modest steps. Other personality types include the "soldier" and the "mute" (Sunstein 2015).

What role does a judge's background play in his or her decisions? Justice Sonia Sotomayor later apologized for a remark at her confirmation hearing that a "wise Latina" could decide a case better than a white male. Religion, socioeconomic background, and education have been found to have little influence on the voting behavior of federal district court and court of appeal judges. There also are no stark differences between female and male judges in their decisions other than in cases involving gender discrimination (Cross 2007: 48–53, 92–93). Studies also indicate that the difference between the sentencing decisions of male and female judges and between African American, Hispanic, and white judges is modest at best. Judges appear to be more influenced by the seriousness of the crime and the offender's background than by their personal background (Spohn and Hemmens 2012: 224–225).

A judge's race and gender is not without significance. A number of studies find that "panel composition" exerts an influence on voting. Cass Sunstein and his colleagues find that federal courts of appeal judges are more favorable toward affirmative action when all the judges on the three-judge panel are appointed by Democratic presidents and are opposed to affirmative action two-thirds of the time when all three judges are the appointees of Republican presidents. Male judges are more likely to vote in favor of a female bringing an employment discrimination case when at least one of the members of the judicial panel is a woman. The likelihood of a white judge voting in favor of the plaintiff bringing a voting rights case rises when at least one member of the panel is an African American (Boyd, Epstein, and Martin 2010; Peresie 2005). Judge Richard Posner attributes the "panel composition" effect to the fact that most judges want to avoid conflict with a colleague who expresses strong beliefs about a case that he or she views as involving deeply held personal beliefs about race or gender (Posner 2008: 33–34).

Kevin T. McGuire makes the interesting argument that a Supreme Court justice's "birth order" impacts his or her judicial decisions. The oldest in the family identifies as a child with the parents and is concerned with maintaining family discipline and order. The younger siblings are more adventurous and rebellious. As a result, justices who were older members of the family tend to be conservative and are reluctant to vary from precedent and to hold legislative enactments unconstitutional. In contrast, judges who were younger members of the family tend to be "less rule bound" and because they were at the bottom of the family barrel are more likely to identify with the disenfranchised members of society. As a result, these justices are more likely to adopt an activist stance and to challenge legal rules and reject legislative enactments as unconstitutional. Does this make sense to you? (McGuire 2016).

The **strategic approach** views judges as motivated by certain goals, such as the abolition of capital punishment. To attract their judicial brethren to their point of view, judges rely on persuasion, bargaining, and social interaction. A judge, for example, may decide not to write a dissent and to support the majority decision so as to maintain good relationships with his or her judicial colleagues in hopes of attracting the support of the other judges in cases in which he or she is highly motivated to achieve a policy goal (Murphy 1964; Spiller and Gely 2008). Epstein and Knight write that "justices are strategic actors who realize that their ability to achieve their goals depends on a consideration of the preferences of other actors, of the choices they expect others to make, and of the institutional context in which they act" (Epstein and Knight 1998: 10).

An extreme version of the contention that judges decide cases based on factors other than the law to achieve policy goals is the argument that the five conservative Supreme Court judges appointed by Republican presidents cast votes in *Bush v. Gore* to ensure the election of George W. Bush knowing he would appoint conservative judges to the bench. The four liberal judges, all of whom were appointed by Democratic presidents, dissented. They undoubtedly wanted to see Al Gore elected because he would appoint judges who agreed with their ideological point of view (Posner 2008: 30).

Judges are aware that respect for the law and compliance with their decisions depends on popular support for judicial judgments and support from elected officials.

Under the leadership of Chief Justice Earl Warren, the Supreme Court delayed a judgment in *Brown v. Board of Education* until the Court was able to reach a unanimous decision. The chief justice believed that respect for a decision ordering the integration of schools required a unanimous and united court. Following *Brown*, the Supreme Court waited to hear a challenge to a Virginia law prohibiting intermarriage between whites and African Americans, fearing that too much change would provoke a backlash. The Court subsequently ruled these anti-miscegenation laws unconstitutional in *Loving v. Virginia* (388 U.S. 1) in 1967 (Murphy 1964).

The attitudinal and strategic approaches are premised on the belief that judges focus on advancing their own policy preferences. The **historical-institutional approach** is based on the view that judicial decisions are shaped by judges' awareness that they are part of an important political institution. They take seriously their role as responsible and professional members of the judicial branch of government, and their decisions are shaped by an awareness of the need to maintain respect for the judiciary. A radical turn in a conservative or liberal direction or a disregard of public opinion will diminish the prestige of, and respect for, the judiciary (R. M. Smith 2008). There is evidence that U.S. Supreme Court justices will write clearer and more accessible opinions in high-profile judgments that they believe are contrary to public opinion in an effort to persuade the public and to maintain public support (R. Black et al. 2016).

Observers of the Supreme Court have argued that Chief Justice John Roberts in 2012 voted with the liberal justices to uphold the main provisions of the Affordable Care Act (Obamacare) because he did not want to risk the Supreme Court being viewed as a partisan and political institution (*National Federation of Independent Business v. Sebelius*, 567 U.S. ___ [2012]).

Lower court judges are particularly sensitive to the fact that they are part of a judicial organization. These judges in a phenomenon known as "reversal aversion" have been found to adjust their decisions to be consistent with Supreme Court precedents when they anticipate being reversed (Westerland et al. 2010).

Judges when interviewed note the overwhelming number of cases are routine. The precedents are clearly established, and the outcomes of the cases are uncontroversial and clear. The judges' political beliefs are irrelevant. They claim in such situations that they will follow precedents even when they disagree with the legal rule. A judge who did not adhere to precedent would quickly lose the respect of his or her colleagues.

There is no guiding precedent in 5 percent to 15 percent of the cases in which judges' opinions are guided in part by their own philosophy. Assuming judges are to be believed, it is equally as inaccurate to claim that law plays no role in judges' decisions as to claim that ideology plays no role in judges' decisions. No single theory of judicial decision-making adequately explains why a judge reaches a particular decision (Tamanaha 2010: 121–124, 143–144, 147–148).

3.1 YOU DECIDE

The U.S. Constitution of 1787 accommodated the states of the American South and provided that African American slaves were to be counted as "three-fifths" of a person in the apportionment of Congress and taxes, and Congress was barred from prohibiting the importation of slaves until 1820. Another provision provided that enslaved or indentured individuals who escaped to a non-slave state or territory did not shed the shackles of involuntary servitude. In 1793, Congress authorized slave owners to "seize or arrest" fugitives. The Fugitive Slave Act of 1793 later was amended to require federal marshals to assist in the apprehension of fugitives.

The Supreme Court in *Prigg v. Pennsylvania* held that the act was a valid exercise of the "positive and unqualified" federal constitutional authority to safeguard the property interest in fugitive slaves. The federal law was held to take precedence over all state legislation on the topic (*Prigg v. Pennsylvania*, 41 U.S. 539 [1842]).

Between 1810 and 1850, estimates are that the Underground Railroad spirited as many as one hundred thousand fugitive slaves, valued at $30 million, to safety. In Philadelphia alone, more than nine thousand fugitives were sheltered between 1830 and 1860.

The most direct legal confrontation between the ideologies of abolitionism and slavery occurred during the federal jury trials of individuals charged with harboring and safeguarding fugitive slaves. The trials typically took place in non-slave states adjacent to slave states. Federal judges justified the conviction of abolitionists on the grounds of states' rights, property rights, and law and order.

The defendants were portrayed as common criminals, and juries were instructed that they were required to uphold the rule of law. Questions of human rights and the natural right to freedom were dismissed as irrelevant to the question of the defendant's guilt.

What course was open to a conscientious anti-slavery judge? Should a federal judge have resigned rather than enforce the law or removed himself from the case? What about instructing the jury to acquit the defendants on the grounds that the law was immoral? A local judge in Ohio imprisoned nine deputy marshals who apprehended a fugitive slave and ordered the individual's release. What is the responsibility of a judge who finds an abortion or death penalty law morally objectionable? (See Cover 1975.)

■ LEGISLATURES

A legislature is a group of individuals elected or selected as members of a government assembly of individuals established by a state or national constitution. The legislature is concerned primarily with lawmaking. Legislatures also play conflict management and legitimizing functions.

In America, the U.S. Congress is concerned with federal matters, and fifty state legislatures are responsible for state concerns. The federal and state legislatures, although different in many respects, are organized in a similar fashion and perform similar roles.

The primary role of legislatures is lawmaking. Unlike courts that must wait for a dispute to be placed on their docket, legislatures are free to reach out and to address issues. The legislature controls the issues that it addresses while the courts respond to the issues that are raised by litigants.

The Constitutional Role of the Legislature

The American colonies were ruled by legislatures that shared power with governors appointed by the English Crown. The elected legislatures followed procedures established in England and played a major role in lawmaking. These legislatures provided the model for the first Continental Congress of 1774, which met throughout the Revolutionary War and was incorporated into the Articles of Confederation as part of the governing structure of the United States.

The early Continental Congress was a weak institution that lacked the power to regulate commerce between the states or to raise taxes. There was no national executive or judicial branch to enforce the laws adopted by Congress, and as a result, the Constitution depended on the cooperation of state governments.

The U.S. Constitution of 1787 envisioned a strengthened legislative branch. At the same time, the document guarded against the type of tyrannical rule practiced by King George III and his colonial governors. The genius of the American Constitution is the creation of a governmental structure characterized by separation of powers, checks and balances, and federalism. In this system of divided government, no single branch of government is able to monopolize power or to enforce its will. The branches of the federal government must cooperate with each other and with the state governments to govern effectively.

Separation of powers. Power is distributed among the branches of government to prevent any one branch from becoming too powerful. The various branches of government must cooperate to effectively govern.

Checks and balances. Each branch of government is able to place a brake on the power of other branches of government.

Limited powers. Each governmental branch is prohibited from certain types of actions.

Federalism. Power is divided between the national and state governments. National laws and treaties are supreme within the national scope of authority. However, powers not granted to the federal government are reserved to the states.

This constitutional structure has stood the test of time and has helped the United States grow and develop from an isolated, agrarian power to an industrialized, urban world power.

The Constitution assigns Congress "all legislative power" and establishes a bicameral legislative branch divided between the House of Representatives elected from local districts and the Senate whose members represent the entire state. The number of congresspersons from a state is based on the size of the state population although each state is apportioned two senators. A congressperson represents the interests of a particular district within a state, whereas a senator must run statewide and represents a broad and diverse slice of the electorate.

Every ten years, the number of congressional districts in a state is adjusted in accordance with the population. The population shifts in the United States have resulted in an increase in congressional delegations from western states, Florida, and several other southern states and a corresponding decrease in congressional delegations from the "rust belt" states in the Midwest. This "redistricting" of congressional boundaries in most states is the responsibility of state governors and state legislatures, which makes these state-level elections crucially important for the composition of the federal Congress. A common complaint is that the parties in control of redistricting create "safe districts" to ensure that the party continues to control local and national legislative elections. California and several other states have taken steps to insulate redistricting from politics.

The House, Senate, and president all must cooperate to pass a law. If the president vetoes or objects to a law, the measure still may become a law if the veto is overridden by two-thirds of the members of the House and of the Senate. The Supreme Court is able to exercise the power of judicial review to determine whether the law is consistent with the requirements of the Constitution.

The Constitution places a high value on stability and makes rapid change difficult to achieve. The entire House of Representatives is elected every two years along with one-third of the Senate. The president is elected every four years and is limited to two terms. One-third of the Senate turns over every two years. This ensures that the entire government does not change in a single election in response to particular events and issues and that there is a measure of stability among elected officials. A senator who is elected every six years does not have to be as concerned about responding to public opinion as does a member of the House of Representatives who must run for reelection every two years.

The federal and state constitutions establish the criteria for membership in the legislature. Members of the House of Representatives must be 25 years old, must have been a U.S. citizen for seven years, and must be a resident of the state they represent. Senators must be at least 30 years old, must have been a citizen for seven years, and must be a resident of the state in which they run for office.

The framers of the Constitution viewed the legislative branch as the primary source of law and national policy. Congress is given specific enumerated powers to tax, to regulate interstate and foreign commerce, to create courts subordinate to the Supreme Court, to create and regulate military force, and to declare war. Congress also must approve all government spending. Article I, Section 9 provides that "[n]o money shall be drawn from the treasury, but in consequence of appropriations made by law." The Senate, among other powers, is authorized to ratify treaties and to confirm the president's nomination of cabinet officials and judges.

The broad scope of congressional power is indicated by the "elastic clause" (Section 8 of Article I), which empowers Congress to make "all Law which shall be necessary and proper for carrying into Execution" its specific powers. In addition, Congress is empowered to conduct investigations into areas that fall within its constitutional powers.

The Constitution and the Bill of Rights restrict the exercise of congressional powers. For example, the First Amendment protects freedom of speech, assembly, and religion. The Supreme Court exercises the power of judicial review to ensure Congress does not enact laws that are beyond its constitutional authority.

The Constitution is largely silent on the organization and functioning of the Congress and leaves each chamber of the Congress free to decide how to organize itself. Members of Congress are elected in virtually every instance as members of either the Democratic or Republican party. An elected representative's congressional career is almost entirely dependent on his or her party affiliation. Legislation is introduced by a member of the Congress and, with isolated exceptions, goes through one or more relevant legislative committees with jurisdiction over the topic of the proposed legislation. The chair and members of the committee are named by the Democratic and Republican parties in proportion to each party's representation in the House of Representatives or in the Senate. The two parties take the lead in setting the priorities for bills that the committees should consider.

The committees have responsibilities over specific areas, and longtime members of each committee develop an expertise over the policy issues that fall within the committee's jurisdiction. The committees hold hearings on legislation, and witnesses are heard who both support and oppose the law. In most instances, the committee members divide along party lines and hold opposing views toward proposed law.

Those bills approved by the committee are sent to the floor of each chamber, and the committee members' recommendation typically is followed by members of their party. Most congresspersons and senators do not possess the knowledge or expertise to make a judgment on the wisdom of legislation addressing issues from endangered species to alternative energy and job creation. As a result, legislators tend to rely on the knowledge and expertise of members of the committee whom they respect and trust. Representatives also rely on members of their legislative staffs who monitor and research legislation and in many instances help to write the laws.

Once a bill is passed in one legislative chamber, it is sent to the other chamber. The House and the Senate versions of bills invariably are different from one another. A conference committee comprising members of each legislative chamber meets and irons out any differences, and the legislation then is sent back to each chamber for reconsideration. There is a particular urgency to agree on bills, such as the budget, that are essential for the government to function.

The process of a bill becoming a law is even more complicated than described above. Typically, only a small percentage of bills that are introduced by members ever make it to the floor of the chamber. It is said that there are at least one hundred points in the process in which a bill may fail to gain approval. As a bill is shepherded through the legislative process, the party leadership often must offer incentives to attract the required votes. In the case of important legislation, the leadership may offer benefits to reluctant members, including campaign funds, office space, visits from well-known personalities to the member's district, and other perks. During the consideration of President Obama's health care law, two Democratic senators were offered a $300 million subsidy to help with health care costs in their states in return for their votes.

The House of Representatives has 435 members and the Senate 100 members. The large size of the House requires stricter and less flexible procedures than the Senate. Unlike the House, the Senate has unlimited debate, and amendments to legislation or a single senator can prevent a bill from reaching the floor.

The Function of the Legislature

The legislative branch, in addition to lawmaking, performs other functions.

Conflict management. The legislative process is organized to give legislative minorities influence in the lawmaking process. The system dampens conflicts between the political party in the legislative majority and the political party in the minority. Committee hearings, floor debates, and conference committees all provide an opportunity for various points of view to be heard. The president is constitutionally authorized to veto legislation with which he or she disagrees although the veto can be overridden by the vote of two-thirds of both houses of Congress.

The legislative process facilitates conflict resolution by forcing individuals to modify legislation to attract a legislative majority. In those instances in which the House and the Senate pass bills that conflict with one another, the conference committee forces the representatives of the two houses of Congress to seek a compromise that will appeal to their fellow legislators. In other instances, Congress and the president may reach a compromise to avoid a veto.

In recent years, the two parties have been less willing to compromise; this has led to "legislative gridlock" and an inability to pass legislation through both the House of Representatives and the Senate.

Adjudication. The power of impeachment allows Congress to indict and prosecute government officials and remove them from office. President Richard Nixon resigned before he could be prosecuted for "high crimes and misdemeanors." Each chamber also has ethics committees, which investigate whether members violated congressional ethics standards and which are authorized to impose various disciplinary punishments. In 2010, 80-year-old Charles Rangel, the powerful chair of the House Ways and Means Committee in charge of taxes, was censured by the House because of his failure to pay taxes and his filing of misleading financial statements and other improprieties. Congress also conducts investigation into issues of public importance, such as the BP (formerly known as British Petroleum) oil spill.

Governmental responsiveness. Legislative representatives perform constituent service and intervene to help citizens who encounter problems with the government, such as late social security checks, poor mail service, or problems with the Internal Revenue Service (IRS). This helps to ensure the government is responsive to the needs of individuals and provides people with a sense that the government works effectively.

Appointments. The Congress, as the elected representatives, approves the appointment of judges and cabinet officials and the heads of agencies such as the FBI.

Legitimation. Congressional approval of domestic programs, military interventions, and foreign treaties is a symbol of public acceptance of a policy decision. A decision undertaken by the president without congressional support may be perceived as arbitrary and undemocratic.

Participants in the Legislative Process

There are a number of players in the legislative process, including the media and the public, lobbyists and interest groups, legislators, and the executive branch.

Media and public opinion. The media and public opinion also play a role in the legislative process. The media can highlight various issues and influence public opinion. Sophisticated public opinion polling allows legislators and political parties to determine the issues that are important to the public and how to articulate their arguments to attract voter support. New technologies also have given the public a direct and instantaneous method of communicating with lawmakers.

Lobbyists and interest groups. Lobbyists and interest groups attempt to influence lawmakers to support laws that they favor and to vote against laws that they oppose. They engage in a range of activities, including educating lawmakers, organizing individuals to write letters and call legislators to oppose or support particular legislation, and making campaign contributions.

Legislators. There are two theories of the role of legislators. One theory is that legislators are *trustees* who should use their own judgment in voting on issues. As trustees, their role is to lead public opinion. A second approach is that legislators should be *delegates* whose votes reflect the individuals whom they represent.

A conflict between constituency (delegate) and conscience (trustee) rarely arises because legislators generally share the views of their constituents and are reluctant to cast votes that may jeopardize their reelection. Studies suggest that legislators overestimate the conservatism of the electorate and are willing to defy the opinion of their voters only on moral issues such as abortion, capital punishment, and same-sex marriage (Rosenthal 2009: 97–100; Squire and Moncrief 2010: 199–200). Most representatives describe themselves as trustees, although a significant percentage describe themselves as *politicos* who try to balance both the delegate and trustee orientations (Rosenthal 2009: 97–100; Squire and Moncrief 2010: 199–200).

Another way to think about representation is to ask whether legislators fit the demographic profile of the areas they represent. Congress and state legislatures continue to be dominated by white, male, educated, upper-income Protestants who have lived in the same community for a number of years (Rosenthal 2009: 34).

This pattern is changing. Women and minorities, although underrepresented in Congress relative to their percentage of the population, have been steadily increasing their numbers in Congress. In recent years, the number of women and minorities has stabilized, and in 2017, there were 104 women in the House of Representatives (19 percent) and 21 in the Senate. There were 49 African Americans in the House and 3 in the Senate, 34 Hispanics in the House and 4 in the Senate, and 12 Asian Americans and Pacific Islanders in the House and 3 in the Senate. Seven members of Congress are self-identified as LGBT, as is one in the Senate. These numbers do not tell the full story. The Congressional Black Caucus, the Congressional Hispanic Caucus, and the Congressional Caucus for Women's Issues are important parts of the Democratic Party, and women head a number of important Democratic Party congressional posts. Congress also includes Jews, Hindus, Buddhists, and Muslims. In financial terms, Congress is unrepresentative: more than half of the members are millionaires (Marcos 2016; S. Smith, Roberts, and Vander Wielen 2009: 15–16).

There are roughly two hundred lawyers and an equal number of businesspeople in Congress, and the changing face of America is indicated by the fact that there are fewer than ten farmers and ranchers. There are no veterans of World War II currently serving in Congress although seventy-nine members of the House of Representatives and twenty-one members of the Senate have military experience (S. Smith et al. 2009: 17).

State legislatures have a higher percentage of women than does the U.S. Congress (24 percent), which is explained, in part, by the fact that women are taking the first steps on the road to political careers. The percentage of African Americans, Hispanics, and Asian Americans is similar to representation at the national level although it varies by state and region (Squire and Moncrief 2010: 55–56).

In terms of geography, in the House of Representatives, representation from the South and West is increasing while the number of representatives from the East and Midwest is decreasing. The most dramatic change is that the South, which once was a Democratic Party bastion, has become solidly Republican. There also is a trend for both the Republicans and Democrats to become more ideological and partisan. Moderate candidates increasingly find it difficult to win the party primaries or state conventions that select the candidate to be nominated to run in the general election. The result is that the Republicans are more conservative and the Democrats more liberal than in the past (S. Smith et al. 2009: 14).

The conventional wisdom is that legislators are concerned only with reelection. This should not be surprising because most people want to keep their jobs. It often is overlooked that legislators also want to make good public policy, particularly on issues that they feel strongly about. They understandably want to move up the political ladder and increase their political clout, in part because they want to shape public policy. Legislators also feel a sense of satisfaction when they are able to help constituents with problems that they may encounter with government agencies like the IRS or Social Security Administration.

Polls indicate that although the public views Congress and state legislatures as ineffective, people believe their own members are doing a good job. This helps to account for the fact that most members of Congress and state legislators are reelected with a high percentage of the vote.

Executives. Presidents and governors are the chief executive officers of the government. The executive and legislative branches are mutually dependent. The president depends on Congress to pass laws, fund programs, and approve his appointments to the judiciary and to the heads of cabinet departments. Under even the best of circumstances, the president and Congress likely will disagree over the details of legislation and need to find ways of reaching agreements.

The president and state governors have a significant impact on the legislative process. The executive helps establish the legislative priorities for the coming session. The president, for example, may run for election and promote certain ideas that he wants the Congress to adopt. Health care was at the center of Barack Obama's campaign. The president has a "bully pulpit" and commands media attention. He is in a position to attract public support for his proposals and to place pressure on members of his party to support his legislative agenda.

The Congressional Budget and Impoundment Control Act of 1974 requires the president to submit a budget to Congress for the coming year on or before the first Monday in February. The presidential budget provides a foundation for congressional deliberations over public expenditures.

The president's agenda is important when his party is in control of one or both houses of Congress and the president is popular. Members of his party will want to support the president and push through his agenda to improve their own chances for reelection.

The president and governors also can offer incentives to members of the legislature to support their policy proposals. The president can offer to campaign for a legislator's reelection, raise money during the campaign, or appoint a legislator to a high-profile study commission or invite the member on a presidential trip abroad.

The president and state governors can veto legislation that can be overcome only at the national level by a vote of two-thirds of the members of the House of Representatives and Senate. The president and congressional leaders may negotiate a bill that is acceptable because both sides want to avoid a confrontation. Historically, Congress rarely has been able to overturn a presidential veto. State governors have the added weapon of a line-item veto, which enables them to veto a particular provision in a law. At the national level, the president must veto an entire law. In the past few years, presidents who have not vetoed a law with which they disagree have signed the law and added a signing statement that is the president's interpretation of the law. The legal status of a signing statement is unclear.

The executive branch also must enforce the law. A president, although he cannot disregard a law, can drag his feet in implementing the legislation. The president can try to get around Congress by relying on his power as head of the executive branch to issue executive orders. These are directives issued by the president or by a governor to administrative agencies under his authority or control. President Truman desegregated the military by executive order. In what is commonly referred to as the Steel Seizure Case, the Supreme Court held that President Truman's executive order seizing the steel mills during World War II was beyond the president's powers and was unconstitutional (*Youngstown Sheet & Tube Co. v. Sawyer*, 343 U.S. 579 [1952]).

President Obama found himself frustrated by Congress and relied on executive orders to achieve certain goals, such as raising the minimum wage for federal workers. President Trump on assuming office issued executive orders implementing his campaign promises and reversing a significant number of President Obama's orders. These executive orders included a controversial travel ban, calling for funds to build a wall on the Mexican border, loosening financial and environmental regulations, and taking initial steps toward the repeal of the Affordable Care Act (White House 2017).

Congress is not powerless; for example, members used the power of the purse to prevent President Obama from expending funds to close the Guantánamo prison camp and to intern and prosecute Guantanamo detainees in the continental United States.

3.2 YOU DECIDE

In ancient Rome and Greece, an offender guilty of a serious offense against society was subject to the forfeiture of property and civil death—the loss of all rights and privileges. In the early common law, certain categories of offenders were subject to banishment and the loss of all property and civil rights. The practice of the "civil death" of offenders in England inspired laws in American states disenfranchising felons from the right to vote. These laws became widespread following the American Civil War when southern governmental officials relied on felony disenfranchisement laws to restrict African Americans' access to the ballot box. Scholars have found that the larger the African American population, the more likely a state is to adopt a felony disenfranchisement law (Lai and Lee 2016; Sentencing Project 2016).

In the 2016 election, roughly 6.1 million individuals were prohibited from voting in various states as a result of states' felony disenfranchisement laws, which declare convicted felons ineligible to vote. The number of individuals disenfranchised has grown at a rapid rate as a result of drug laws and the enhancement of crimes that formerly were misdemeanors to felonies. In 1976, 1.17 million individuals were disenfranchised, which grew to 3.34 million in 1996, to 5.85 million in 2010, and to 6.1 million in 2016.

In every state with the exception of Maine and Vermont, incarcerated felons are prohibited from voting. Four states extend this prison disenfranchisement to felony parolees until the completion of their parole, and eighteen states disenfranchise prisoners and felony parolees and probationers until the completion of their supervision. There are twelve states that disenfranchise some or all felons following the felons' release from prison, as well as felony parolees and probationers following the termination of their judicial supervision.

States with felon disenfranchisement provide for an array of requirements for reinstating the voting rights of convicted felons although certain categories of offenders are permanently disenfranchised in various states. The Virginia Constitution prohibits felons from voting although Governor Terry McAuliffe used his clemency powers to restore voting rights on an individual basis. Florida has a five-year waiting period before an individual can apply for reinstatement.

The twelve states that disenfranchise felons account for roughly 50 percent of the felons who are disenfranchised nationally. Twenty-six percent of individuals who are disenfranchised are parolees and probationers, and roughly 22 percent of individuals who are

(Continued)

disenfranchised are felons presently incarcerated. In six of the states that disenfranchise former felons following their release, more than 7 percent of the adult population is disenfranchised.

One in thirteen African Americans of voting age is prohibited from voting under felony disenfranchisement laws. In aggregate, 2.2 million African American citizens are banned from voting, although as a result of reform efforts between 1999 and 2016, roughly 840,000 African Americans and citizens of other races have had their voting rights restored.

Felony disenfranchisement is based on the argument that individuals who break the law should not participate by voting for individuals who make the law. In the case of homicide, victim advocates claim that felons should

not exercise a right that no longer is available to their victims. Individuals who oppose the disenfranchisement of felons argue that these laws prevent former offenders from being integrated into society and rehabilitated. The constitutionality of felony disenfranchisement remains a point of contention (*Richardson v. Ramirez*, 418 U.S. 24 [1974]).

According to the Sentencing Project, disenfranchisement policies in states probably affected the results of seven Senate races and the 2000 presidential election. Public opinion polls indicate that eight out of ten Americans support voting rights for individuals who have completed their prison sentences and two-thirds support voting rights for individuals on probation and parole.

What is your view of felony disenfranchisement?

Interest Groups and Lobbyists

An interest group is a coalition of individuals or organizations that attempts to influence government decisions. There are three categories of interest groups. *Traditional membership groups* comprise individuals promoting economic, social, or political concerns. Examples include senior citizen groups, environmentalists, teachers, farmers, civil liberties advocates, students, and individuals committed to reforming the economy. Second, there are *associations comprising affiliated organizations* such as an association composed of unions, an organization that represents small businesses or manufacturing firms, or an organization that represents urban areas. A third category is *institutional interest groups*, such as a university that wants government support or authorization to build a hospital or a foreign country that wants foreign assistance. In other instances, a bank or corporation may lobby on its own to obtain favorable legislation. Another category is groups of citizens who informally come together to influence foreign or domestic policy or the fate of a prisoner on death row.

Many of these groups have their own full-time lobbyists. In other instances, an interest group may contact a lobbying firm to represent its interests on particular issues. Ordinary citizens on occasion join together and serve as citizen lobbyists to work on specific issues such as intervention abroad or the protection of an endangered forest or park.

The First Amendment to the Constitution protects the rights of these organized groups of individuals to assemble for the purposes of influencing governmental policy (Nownes, Thomas, and Hrebenar 2008: 99–100). Roughly five thousand organizations and eighteen thousand individuals are involved in working to influence government policy in Washington, D.C. (S. Smith et al. 2009: 338). The Center for Responsive Politics estimates that in 2016, $3.12 billion was spent on lobbying and 11,143 individuals were employed as registered lobbyists. The top five lobbying firms earned between $9 million and $19 million for their efforts. The largest expenditures are from health care and pharmaceuticals, insurance, oil and gas, utilities, electronics, securities, and hospitals and nursing homes.

The increase in lobbying activity is due to a number of factors, including the expanding role of the federal government. Industries want to be exempt from environmental regulation, oil companies want tax incentives to help them explore and drill for oil, the auto industry wants protection from foreign competition, and the National Rifle Association has an interest in resisting the regulation of firearms. The growth of defense spending has led to the growth of groups lobbying for the development of new weapons systems and foreign countries seeking foreign military assistance. Lobby groups also have proliferated as a result of new social movements concerned with women's rights, gay rights, and the rights of various religious, ethnic, and racial minorities.

Lobbying groups find themselves competing against groups advocating the opposite point of view. Groups favoring merit pay for teachers and an end to tenure and school vouchers are opposed by educational groups and teachers unions that want to preserve the existing system. This pluralistic system means that all points of view are represented and that legislators attempt to strike a balance between competing viewpoints. This *pluralistic theory* of democracy is challenged by the *elitist theory* of democracy. The elitist theory views the political system as favoring the rich and powerful and contends that groups acting on behalf of consumers, the environment, economic justice, and the poor are overwhelmed by groups representing the privileged and powerful. The result is that the legal system protects the interest of the most privileged and advantaged individuals and corporations.

Lobbyists employ inside strategies and outside strategies. Inside strategies involve directly approaching lawmakers to educate them and persuade them to introduce laws or support particular laws, testifying during committee hearings on legislation, and writing speeches that lawmakers can deliver during floor debates. Lobbying firms hire retired lawmakers and former legislative staff members to ensure access to lawmakers.

Lobbyists play an important role in the political system. They provide lawmakers with the information to make an informed decision. Legislators confronted with the issue whether to support offshore drilling will look to lobbyists to educate them on the impact of drilling on the natural environment, the safety risks of this drilling, the impact of an accident, and whether offshore drilling will advance energy independence for the United States, and to inform them whether there are available alternative sources of energy. A crucial determination in a legislator's vote is the impact of a vote on a lawmaker's reelection. Legislators, in addition to looking at the arguments for and against offshore drilling, will consider the electoral influence of oil companies and environmental groups within their electoral district.

Lobbyists also rely on outside strategies. This involves "astro turfing," or generating outside letters and e-mails. Other outside strategies involve outreach to the media, using social media, and organizing public demonstrations.

The twenty companies that spent the most on lobbying in 2007 hired an average of eighteen full-time lobbyists and employed twenty-eight different Washington lobbying firms. On average, their lobbyists were involved in seventeen different issues before twenty agencies and on sixty-three different laws (Drutman 2015: 85–88).

The most controversial technique that lobbyists use to influence politicians is campaign contributions. There are limits on individual contributions, and lobbyists "bundle" contributions from a number of individuals that they direct to candidates. It is not unusual for a lobbyist to donate money to both candidates in an electoral race in an attempt to ensure influence with both candidates. Another tactic is to form a political action committee (PAC) that receives contributions from individuals and corporations or unions and then contributes the money to various candidates. In 2010, unions and businesses spent a reported $800 million to support sympathetic congressional candidates, the bulk of which was spent by business interests. Despite the criticism of lobbyists' use of money to influence elections, there is continuing debate over whether lobbyists are able to buy the support of politicians (Drutman 2015; A. Katz 2015: 158).

A major public concern is the so-called revolving door in which individuals leave Congress, a congressional staff position, or the executive branch and are hired as lobbyists to influence their former colleagues. Retired members of Congress are required to wait a least two years during this so-called cooling-off period after they retire before lobbying their former colleagues. High-level staff members are required to wait at least a year. Nonetheless, between 2001 and 2011, roughly 5,400 former congressional staffers had registered as lobbyists and may earn as much as $300,000 per year (Drutman 2015: 161).

In recent years, financial donors to presidential and congressional candidates have taken advantage of various aspects of the Internal Revenue Code to create "social welfare organizations," which engage in independent political activity without being required to disclose the names of donors. The stress on money in politics has led to incidents of congressional corruption. In 2004, former congressman Randall "Duke" Cunningham of California was convicted of accepting $2.4 million in bribes from defense contractors, and two years later former congressman Bob Ney from Ohio pled guilty to accepting bribes from lobbyist Jack Abramoff. Abramoff earlier had been criminally convicted for showering lawmakers with money and gifts in return for sponsoring legislation favored by his clients. In 2000, Abramoff sponsored a trip for House Majority Whip Tom DeLay to play at the historic St. Andrews golf club in Scotland, and DeLay subsequently "killed" a bill opposed by Abramoff's clients in the gambling industry. DeLay also blocked legislation that would have required manufacturers in the Northern Mariana Islands to comply with U.S. labor laws after Abramoff received a $1.36 million payment from the government of the Northern Marianas. DeLay, considered the most powerful figure in Congress at that time, subsequently found himself caught up in the Abramoff lobbying scandal and was convicted of money laundering by a Texas court. A Texas appeals court subsequently overturned DeLay's conviction.

Former Illinois congressman Aaron Schock was indicted in 2016 for various financial offenses committed between 2008 and 2015 while a member of Congress. Shock famously decorated his congressional office in the style of the television program *Downton Abbey*. The indictment alleged that Schock among other crimes reimbursed himself with government funds for 150,000 miles he falsely claimed that he drove, used campaign funds to buy himself a new car and camera equipment, and used government and campaign funds to redecorate his Capitol Hill apartment and to take a private plane to Chicago for a football game. Philadelphia congressman Chaka Fattah was convicted of financial fraud in 2016 for using government and charitable funds to repay campaign debts and to pay student loan debts among other crimes and was sentenced to ten years in prison.

In response to continuing scandals, the federal government and most states now regulate lobbyists. Lobbyists are required to register and to file reports revealing their clients, the issues they were hired to influence, and their fees. Legislators are prohibited from accepting travel and various gifts.

President Obama addressed the "revolving door" by blocking individuals registered as lobbyists in the preceding year from working in his administration and by restricting members of his administration from contacting the agencies in which they worked for two years after leaving office. President Trump issued an executive order placing somewhat looser restrictions on lobbyists working in his administration and prohibiting most individuals in his administration from contacting the agency in which they worked for one year after leaving his administration but allowing them to lobby other portions of the government. He also imposed a lifetime ban on lobbying on behalf of foreign governments. Former administration officials, however, have developed strategies to evade these restrictions.

We now turn our attention to administrative agencies.

■ ADMINISTRATIVE AGENCIES

The United States has a dual system of administrative agencies. There are roughly 50 federal administrative agencies, and the average state may have as many as 170 agencies. Federal and state agencies often share the same field of regulation such as the environment or worker safety. State agencies in these instances enforce federal standards as well as state laws that are stronger than the federal requirements. Both the federal and state departments of labor monitor worker health and safety and enforce minimum wages and maximum hours of work.

Many of these agencies issue and enforce administrative regulations and hold enforcement hearings and in essence combine legislative, executive, and judicial functions.

The federal and state bureaucracies employ roughly twenty million people, fifteen million of whom are employed by the states. This does not include independent contractors, which are private companies hired to perform government functions.

Administrative law is the law regulating government administrative agencies. The law specifies the process that agencies must follow in developing and enforcing rules and regulations. The study of administrative law also involves an examination of how individuals and groups within the agency's jurisdiction implement the guidelines established by the agency. The U.S. Department of Education, for example, requires universities to develop and gain approval of policies and procedures to combat sexual harassment on campus.

The Interstate Commerce Commission (ICC) was created in 1887 to regulate the costs of shipping on the nation's railroads and to prevent the railroads from charging exorbitant fees to farmers and merchants. This was followed by the Federal Trade Commission (FTC) in 1914, established by Congress to promote free and fair competition in interstate commerce by preventing unfair competition. In the early 1900s, Upton Sinclair in the book *The Jungle* focused attention on the unhealthy conditions in meatpacking plants. Congress responded by creating the Food and Drug Administration (FDA) to monitor the nation's food supply as well as drugs. The Federal Communications Commission (FCC) was created in 1934 in response to developing communications technologies to set standards for privately owned radio stations; the FCC later was authorized to regulate television. In 1938, the Civil Aeronautics Board (CAB) was created to regulate the newly developing air traffic system, and the agency's powers were transferred to the Federal Aviation Administration (FAA) in 1958.

The number and power of administrative agencies greatly expanded in the 1930s and 1940s during President Franklin Delano Roosevelt's New Deal. The agencies established during the New Deal were designed to stabilize, and restore confidence in, the economic system. The Securities and Exchange Commission (SEC), for example, was created in 1934 to regulate the stock market and protect the investments of Americans. The National Labor Relations Board (NLRB) was established in 1934 to regulate the relationship between businesses and workers and to protect the right of workers to organize unions and strike against management.

As society has become more complex, new administrative agencies have been created to address newly emerging problems and priorities. The Environmental Protection Agency (EPA) was created in 1970 to set standards for the protection of the environment, and in the same year, the National Highway Traffic Safety Administration (NHTSA) was established to set safety standards for automobiles and highways. The next year, the Occupational Safety and Health Administration (OSHA) was created to protect worker safety. The Consumer Product Safety Commission (CPSC) was created in 1972 to ensure safe products for consumers. Two years later, the Nuclear Regulatory Commission (NRC) was established to set safety standards and inspect nuclear power plants. The newest agency is the Consumer Financial Protection Bureau (CFPB), which in 2012 was charged with protecting consumers' relationship with credit card companies, banks, and loan and mortgage businesses.

The rules issued by federal and state agencies have a pervasive impact on our lives. These agencies have been called the "fourth branch of government" and a "shadow government" and likely have more influence on our daily lives than either the legislative or judicial branch of government.

The food you eat for breakfast may have been inspected by the FDA, which also is responsible for ensuring that the label on the cereal box you opened accurately informs you of the content of what you are eating. The rate for the electricity you use to make your coffee and scramble your eggs is established by a state regulatory commission, and the coffeemaker has been manufactured to meet safety standards established by the CPSC. As you leave for school, the car you drive complies with safety standards established by the NHTSA, which also is responsible for requiring the seat-belts and safety bags in your car. The emission standards in your auto have been established by the EPA. You turn on the radio in the car and find stations, licensed by the FCC, which are required to meet the decency standards the FCC established. You park your car with a credit card that was issued in accordance with standards established by the CFPB.

Another example of the wide-ranging impact of administrative agencies is the U.S. Fish and Wildlife Service, which in 2015 ruled that lions in Africa would be considered protected under the Endangered Species Act. This rule makes it increasingly difficult to import live lions and lion heads, paws, and skins into the United States. This new regulation was adopted in reaction to the killing of Cecil the lion by a now deceased Minnesota dentist.

Keep in mind that there is debate and disagreement about various administrative rules. The FCC in 2015 adopted net neutrality, a rule that considers the Internet a public utility, guarantees fair access and equal treatment on the Internet for all users, and prohibits broadband companies from creating a fast lane for wealthy and powerful content providers with fast download speeds and a slow lane for businesses and consumers (so-called tiered service). Advocates of net neutrality like Al Franken from Minnesota claim that net neutrality will encourage free speech and democratic participation. Senator Franken characterizes net neutrality as the "First Amendment issue of our time" by guaranteeing that individuals and websites have access to the Internet whatever their financial resources and will not have to pay to express their point of view. The newly constituted FCC under President Trump has taken steps to reverse net neutrality and to allow broadband and cable companies to function with less regulation based on free-market principles. The argument is that this will allow broadband and Internet companies to offer certain content at a reduced price or entirely free to consumers although critics note that some content may be blocked entirely (C. Kang 2017).

The Legal Basis of Administrative Agencies

Administrative agencies go by various names, including commissions, bureaus, boards, officers, departments, and offices. These agencies are delegated powers by the legislature to carry out the legislature's constitutional powers. The ICC was created by Congress as part of the chamber's authority to regulate interstate commerce. The authorization to create the agencies is based on Article 1 of the U.S. Constitution, which states that Congress shall have the power "to make all Laws which shall be necessary and proper" for carrying out its powers. As Congress passes new laws, the number and authority of agencies expands to enforce the congressional measures. The National Environmental Policy Act of 1969 created the EPA. In the past decades, the EPA has been given authority to regulate air quality, clean water, noise control, pesticides, and the handling and disposal of toxic wastes. As the agency's responsibilities have increased, the number of employees has expanded. The EPA employs roughly seventeen thousand individuals who work in Washington, D.C., and at ten regional headquarters and twenty-two laboratories. Half of the employees are scientists, engineers, and environmental protection specialists.

Legislatures do not possess the time and expertise to draft rules and regulations and to inspect the safety of mines, the workplace, or nuclear power plants. Administrative agencies are staffed by experts who understand the issues that arise in the areas of their expertise. The EPA, for example, has responsibility for toxic dump sites. These sites can seep into the groundwater and cause cancer and leave an area uninhabitable. There is considerable expertise involved in identifying dangerous chemicals, regulating the handling of these chemicals by industry, designing methods of cleaning toxic sites, and burying these chemicals to prevent them from endangering the public. Mine Safety and Health Administration (MSHA) inspectors are responsible for monitoring air quality in the nation's mines and ensuring that the mining is being conducted in a safe fashion.

Regulation is expensive, and costs are balanced against benefits. The annual budget for OSHA is well over $500 million, and the agency employs roughly 1,100 inspectors. OSHA claims to identify roughly ninety thousand workplace violations a year, to have levied fines totaling more than $90 million against industry, and to have significantly decreased workplace injuries, illnesses, and deaths. Walsh and Hemmens state that regulation costs each American household over $15,000 (Walsh and Hemmens 2016).

Congress in creating agencies found it could not anticipate all the issues that may arise and in 1914 provided the FTC with virtually unlimited power to protect consumers against unfair labeling and trade practices. This type of broad delegation of powers was designed to provide knowledgeable experts with the flexibility required to develop regulatory policies. Critics warned against government by unaccountable bureaucrats who, absent meaningful legislative oversight, would "run wild" and impose unrealistic and burdensome standards on industry (M. Horwitz 1992: 213–246).

Congress responded to these fears in 1946 by adopting the Administrative Procedure Act. This act established the procedures to be followed by federal agencies in issuing regulations and adjudicating violations of regulations; it also established procedures for judicial review of agency rules and procedures. Under the act, agencies are required to follow due process procedures in hearings.

Administrative agencies, in carrying out their delegated responsibilities, perform three primary functions: rule-making, investigation, and adjudication.

Rule-making. Agencies develop rules and regulations to be followed by individuals and institutions that fall within their jurisdiction. Agency rules have the binding force of law. The NHTSA is charged with ensuring automobile safety and reducing automobile accidents and deaths. The agency has broadly interpreted this mandate and issued rules on airbags, seat-belts, tires, brakes, and child safety.

Proposed rules are published in the *Federal Register*, a government publication. There is a notice period in which anyone can read the rule and submit a comment. Following the comment period, agency officials review the comments and determine whether to implement, modify, or abandon the rule.

Investigation. Agencies often are given the authority to investigate and to prosecute violations of the rules established by the agency. Information is gathered through requiring reports or through on-site visits by inspectors. Agencies that experience difficulty in obtaining information may subpoena witnesses and documents and conduct searches of facilities. They also rely on complaints from employees who report misconduct. In some instances, agencies investigate violations although prosecutions are carried out by the federal or state attorney general. The Equal Employment Opportunity Commission (EEOC), for example, investigates allegations of workplace discrimination.

Adjudication. A number of agencies are authorized by law to adjudicate disputes. These agencies are concerned with employment discrimination, occupational health and safety, consumer products, and immigration. Agencies process a significant number of complaints and have a large docket of cases to decide. Government agencies typically attempt to settle cases to conserve time and resources. Most corporations settle disputes in order to maintain good relations with the agency and to avoid the expense and embarrassment. A party who enters into a consent order agrees to abide by the terms of the agreement although the party may not be required to admit to having violated the law.

In those instances in which a settlement is not reached, the agency has the discretion to overlook the violation or to bring the violation before an administrative law judge, a judge who is an expert in administrative procedures and in the agency's sphere of regulation. Administrative judges are civil servants who are appointed based on competitive exams. The administrative law judge is responsible for determining the facts and for applying the proper legal standard. These proceedings, although less formal than a trial, are conducted in accordance with the due process standards established by the Administrative Procedure Act.

The agency and the defendant have the right to be represented by a lawyer.

The losing party may appeal the decision of the administrative law judge to a court. Judges, because they lack expertise in the technical details of the administrative law judge's decision, will not question the reasonable factual findings of an administrative judge and only will overturn an administrative tribunal's decision based on a legal error. This may involve a failure to follow required procedures, a finding that the rule was beyond the agency's authorized powers, or the application of an incorrect legal standard.

Controlling Administrative Decision-Making

There is a continuing tension between the view that agencies are staffed by professional experts who should be free to adopt rules to regulate industry and the notion that these agencies have become too powerful and are largely unaccountable to the public. Agencies are identified with "big government," "red tape," and "pointy-headed bureaucrats" and with impeding business competitiveness.

Administrative agencies are politically accountable to the legislative branch. Congress lacks the time and expertise to monitor the decisions of administrative agencies and in most cases has written agencies a "blank check."

There are situations, however, in which Congress has intervened in response to a public outcry over agency policies. Congress, for example, responded to consumer protest and prohibited the NHTSA from requiring seat-belt systems that prevented an automobile from starting or sounded a continuous alarm when the belt was unfastened. Another congressional initiative was the National Environmental Policy Act of 1969, which required federal agencies to evaluate the environmental impact of agency decisions.

In 1996, in an effort to control administrative agencies, Congress passed the Congressional Review Act. The act required agencies to submit all recently enacted rules to Congress, which then had sixty days to disapprove of the rule. This law was used to reject OSHA's rule on ergonomic (repetitive motion) injuries.

In 2012, agricultural interests were able to block a regulation that imposed limits on children under 18 from working for hire in "hazardous" areas such as operating motorized farm machinery (Steinzor 2015: 34–35). One of the first acts of the newly elected Republican majority in 2017 was to repeal a rule enacted by the SEC requiring oil companies to publicly disclose payments made to governments in developing energy resources across the globe and to repeal a consumer protection rule on overdraft fees on prepaid debit cards. This was followed by repeal of a regulation that would incorporate certain individuals who are mentally challenged into the national background check system for the purchase of firearms (Shear 2017). As of July 2017, Congress had revoked fourteen rules adopted by the Obama administration.

A number of presidents have placed their stamp on agencies by appointing administrators who share the president's priorities. The EPA under President George W. Bush turned down a request from California to impose tighter air quality emission standards on automobiles. This policy was reversed by the EPA under President Obama. The Obama administration also changed a Bush administration policy and imposed tighter controls on coal-burning power plants in thirty-one states. Critics were quick to point out that this change in policy would cost private industry close to $3 billion and that these costs would be passed on to consumers.

President Donald Trump has taken steps to fulfill his campaign promise to promote economic growth by repealing administrative regulations that he believes discourage growth in the American economy. In his view, businesses are weighed down by unnecessary and burdensome regulations that raise costs for businesses and consumers and limit profits and job creation. President Trump characterized 75 percent of regulations as "horrible." He accordingly directed each agency to establish a task force to remove "job killing regulations and increasing economic opportunity" and issued an additional executive order requiring agencies that issue a new rule to repeal two orders. One priority item is for the EPA to eliminate President Obama's environmental rules on global warming and the regulations on the prevention of pollution in lakes, streams, and rivers and to replace these regulations with more industry-friendly rules (Davenport 2017a, 2017b). Another example of deregulation is reducing the allegedly lengthy period required for the FDA to approve the marketing of newly developed medical drugs (Thomas 2017). In education, there is the prospect of repealing a number of regulations, including regulations that adversely affect online, for-profit educational institutions (Hutteman and Alcindor 2017). A larger goal expressed by influential advisors in the White House may be to go beyond the modification of specific regulations and to effectively dismantle various agencies altogether (Davenport 2017a, 2017b). This almost certainly will be weakening the enforcement power of the CFPB, which since its inception in 2011 has provided $12 billion in financial savings to twenty-seven million consumers (Rappeport 2017).

There are internal checks on administrative agencies. Most agencies provide for ethical accountability through inspector generals who monitor the financial management and conflict of interest and ethical conduct of agency personnel.

The judiciary as noted above has adopted a policy of "limited review" of administrative decisions and is reluctant to substitute the judgment of the court for the judgment of the agency (*Chevron U.S.A. Inc. v. NRDC*, 467 U.S. 83 [1984]). The Endangered Species Act prohibits the taking of an endangered species by a private individual unless the individual has a permit. Logging companies challenged a regulation issued by the secretary of the interior, which interpreted the word *take* to include modification of the habitat of the spotted owl.

Logging companies contended that *take* was intended to be limited to the direct use of force against an endangered or threatened species such as shoot, kill, or capture. The Supreme Court noted that Congress expressed the purpose of providing "comprehensive protection" to the listed species and the Court "owe[d] some degree of deference" to the secretary based on his "expertise" (*Babbitt v. Sweet Home Chapter of Communities for a Greater Oregon*, 515 U.S. 687 [1995]).

The Public Health Service Act of 1970 prohibits family planning funds from going to any program where abortion is used as a method of family planning. In *Rust v. Sullivan*, the Supreme Court upheld a "gag rule" regulation issued by the secretary of health and human services prohibiting doctors in organizations that receive federal funds from advising pregnant women that abortion is one possible response. The regulation indicated that one permissible response to an inquiry from a patient is that the organization "does not consider abortion an appropriate method of family planning and therefore does not counsel or refer for abortion" (*Rust v. Sullivan*, 500 U.S. 173 [1991]). Critics assert that this judicial policy of limited review concentrates too much power in administrative agencies.

Administrative Agencies and Regulated Industries

Administrative agencies are charged with regulating industries but risk becoming too close and too sympathetic to industry's point of view while disregarding the public interest. **Agency capture** occurs when an agency works on behalf of the individuals or industry regulated by the agency rather than on behalf of the public interest. Agency regulations have significant economic consequences for regulated industries and, as a consequence, businesses devote significant resources to influencing decisions. The public is unorganized and generally unaware of the significance of agency rules and decisions and may find its interests are not taken into consideration by administrative decision-makers.

Industry regulators are aware that in the future they may have the opportunity to move into a well-paying job in the businesses they are regulating. In many cases, the individuals who represent industry are former co-workers of regulators. Regulation also is frustrated by the fact agencies lack enough inspectors to keep informed of what is going on in private industry.

In April 2010, the Deepwater Horizon drilling rig exploded in the Gulf of Mexico, spilling roughly 172 gallons of oil into the Gulf. The Minerals Management Service (MMS) was responsible for ensuring drilling was carried out in a safe and responsible fashion. The MMS also was charged with the task of promoting offshore drilling and collecting lease payments. The agency placed a priority on promoting offshore drilling and collecting lease payments and, as a result, safety took a back seat. MMS allowed BP and other firms to engage in offshore drilling in the Gulf of Mexico without complying with the requirements that companies evaluate the impact of their activities on the environment and on endangered species.

MMS was understaffed, with only sixty inspectors for the more than four thousand drilling rigs in the Gulf of Mexico and, as a result, was heavily dependent on industry to monitor compliance with regulations. Inspectors were underpaid compared to industry technicians and regularly accepted gifts from industry executives. A presidential commission investigating the explosion concluded MMS was an agency "systematically lacking the resources, technical training or experience in petroleum engineering that is absolutely critical to ensuring that offshore drilling is being conducted in a safe and responsible manner. . . . For a regulatory agency to fall so short of its essential safety mission is inexcusable."

There is evidence MMS was aware of the risk of a blowout of the Deepwater Horizon drilling rig and disregarded the threat. For example, in 2009, the National Oceanic and Atmospheric Administration (NOAA) warned MMS that drilling posed the risk of a major oil spill and criticized the agency for minimizing the risk of an oil spill.

In 2010, an explosion at the Upper Big Branch coal mine in West Virginia resulted in the death of twenty-nine miners, the worst mine disaster in the United States since 1970. The MSHA released a report in December 2011 concluding that safety violations including a faulty ventilation system contributed to the disaster and issued 369 citations for safety violations and assessed $10.8 million in fines. The new owners of the mine agreed to pay a $209 million settlement to the families of the miners who died in the explosion at the mine. A supervisor pled guilty to conspiring to impede MSHA's enforcement efforts, and Don Blankenship, the CEO of Massey Energy, was convicted in 2013 of conspiring to willfully violate safety standards.

An independent investigation in 2011 condemned Massey for a reckless failure to meet basic safety standards in order to increase profit margins. The investigation also criticized the U.S. Department of Labor and its MSHA for failing to act to ensure safety at Big Branch mine even after having issued 515 citations for safety violations and three methane explosions in the mine in 2009. The MSHA, according to the report, should have issued a "flagrant violation citation" and notified miners and their families that they were working in a mine that did not meet minimal safety standards. The report also noted that the MSHA inspectors failed to enforce safety standards at Massey Energy's Aracoma Alma Mine No. 1. This resulted in "deplorable conditions" and a "preventable" fire that led to the death of two miners.

The report noted that West Virginia politicians were afraid to challenge Massey because of the company's ability to bankroll electoral campaigns against state officials. In May 2015, U.S. District Judge Karen Caldwell sentenced former state representative W. Keith Hall to seven years in prison and fined him $25,000 for bribing state mine inspector Kelly Shortridge, whom he arranged to be assigned to inspect his Pike County coal mines. Hall occupied important legislative positions on the regulation of mines, which enabled him to provide inspectors with a confidence that they would not be held criminally liable for accepting bribes. In return for the bribes, the inspector overlooked or delayed reporting violations of Kentucky law on surface mines.

Congress, by failing to adequately fund administrative agencies to keep up with the growth in the workforce, limits the investigative capacity of agencies. In 2011, 4,609 workers were killed on the job, roughly 50,000 died from occupational illnesses, and a large number of workers were injured. Many of these injuries resulted from a failure of industry to adhere to OSHA regulations on areas such as machine safety features. In 1997, there were 2,405 OSHA inspectors for every 28,000 workers, and by 2012, this ratio had grown to one inspector for every 58,687 workers (Steinzor 2015: 22, 56).

In Japan, the Nuclear and Industrial Safety Agency (NISA) approved a ten-year extension for old nuclear reactors at Fukushima Daiichi one month before an earthquake and tsunami damaged the reactors and caused a meltdown. The approval was granted despite the fact the plant had reached the forty-year limit for plant stability and evidence that the operators of the plant had been concealing defects in the plant's operation. Nuclear opponents pointed out that NISA was affiliated with the Ministry of Economy, Trade and Industry, which was charged with encouraging the development of Japan's nuclear industry. As a result, NISA served a rubber stamp for the nuclear industry and regularly overlooked safety violations. Administrators regularly were rewarded with well-paying positions in the nuclear industry (Onishi and Belson 2011).

3.3 YOU DECIDE

In May 2014, the European Court of Justice heard a case against Google brought by Spanish lawyer Mario Costeja González, who requested the removal of a link to a digitized 1998 article in *La Vanguardia* newspaper about an auction for his foreclosed home. Costeja complained that although the auction took place twelve years ago, the link continued to appear when his name was Googled. The European court, which hears cases on human rights involving European states, ruled in *Costeja* that search engines as well as websites ("data controllers") are required to respect European-wide data protection regulations, that Google was required to remove information that is "inaccurate, inadequate, irrelevant or excessive," and that individuals have a human right to have this information removed. The court held that the article about Costeja's foreclosure was permitted to remain on the original site although Google was required to delink the article from its search engine. On its first day that the court order was to be enforced on May 30, 2014, Google received twelve thousand requests to have personal details removed from its search engine.

The "right to be forgotten" is based on the claim that individuals have the right to have certain types of information about themselves contained in articles, videos, and photographs deleted from the Internet

to prevent the information from being accessed by others. The right to be forgotten differs from the right to privacy, which protects information that is not publicly known from being disclosed. In contrast, the right to be forgotten entails removing information that at one point was widely available to the public on the Internet. An individual who wants to exercise the right to be forgotten applies to the administrators of a search engine to have an item removed. The search engine in making the decision must weigh the individual's request against the public interest. An individual whose request is refused may appeal to a national government regulatory agency.

Most of the information removed from sites like Google, Yahoo, and Bing reportedly is private and personal information rather than information of public concern such as criminal activity or information regarding public corruption. Individuals favoring the free flow of information express concern that rather than risk a fine for improperly maintaining information, a company will be tempted to remove an item from its site. The removal of links to information according to critics is a form of censorship and threatens the integrity of Internet searches. Critics ask whether this differs from forcing the removal of an objectionable book from the library. There is a concern that the right to be forgotten will be extended to sites such as Wikipedia and other compilations of information.

Proponents of the right to be forgotten note that roughly 41 percent of the estimated one million links that have been requested to be removed as of 2016 (more than thirty-eight thousand requests to Google alone as of February 2016, 40 percent of which have been removed) have been deleted, which is a relatively small percentage of all entries on the Internet. Keep in mind that information removed may be obtained from non-European sites. In one instance, Google was subjected to criticism for removing information regarding a surgeon's "botched operation." Critics asserted that the removal of this information placed the public at risk. Examples of other items removed include excerpts from a mass shooter's manifesto and a slide show that characterized a reality TV star as "an annoying, unbearable hag." A European musician sought to have a link to the *Washington Post* review of his performance removed on the grounds it was "defamatory, mean-spirited, opinionated, offensive and simply irrelevant for the arts."

Do you believe that the "right to be forgotten" is contrary to the free flow of information that is essential to a vigorous exchange of ideas?

Administrative Regulation of Sexual Harassment on Campus

In October 2010, the members of Delta Kappa Epsilon fraternity at Yale University marched on campus chanting, "No means yes! Yes means anal! No means yes! Yes means anal!" A video of the demonstration went viral, sparking nationwide outrage. Fraternity pledges also were photographed holding signs that said, "We love sluts."

Yale issued a letter condemning the use of the fraternity's language. Sixteen current and former Yale students responded by filing a twenty-six-page complaint with the Education Department's Office for Civil Rights alleging that the university's inadequate response creates a climate on campus that prevents women from enjoying the same access to an education at Yale as men.

The complaint was based on Title IX of the Education Amendments of 1972, which prohibits any educational institution that accepts federal funds from discriminating against women. This includes sexual harassment, sexual assault, and rape. Federal law requires colleges and universities to disclose campus security policies and crime statistics, including sexual assaults and rapes.

Yale was only one of several schools under investigation by the Office for Civil Rights under President Obama. The statistics on sexual assault on campus are jaw-dropping. One in five college women (and 6 percent of college men) are the victims of sexual assault over the course of their college career, and less than 5 percent of these assaults are reported to the university administration or to the police. Women know the assailant in 80 percent of the sexual attacks. Researchers conclude that women often do not immediately recognize they have been the victim of a crime because they have a difficult time accepting that an individual whom they know could sexually attack them. In other instances, women do not want to be subjected to humiliation or social ostracism, or they blame themselves for trusting the man or for drinking alcohol.

In 2015, the Association of American Universities administered the *Campus Survey on Sexual Assault and Sexual Misconduct* to nearly eight hundred thousand students at twenty-seven universities. The survey found that 11.7 percent of students had experienced non-consensual sexual contact by physical force, threats of physical force, or incapacitation since enrolling in college.

The number of undergraduate students experiencing this type of assault was 18.1 percent, and female undergraduates at Yale reported an even higher rate—28.1 percent, or 5 percent higher than undergraduate women at other institutions in the survey.

Federal guidelines issued by the Department of Education under President Obama are the first comprehensive statement of institutions' obligations under Title IX. The guidelines stress that a school or university that "knows or reasonably should know of possible sexual violence" is obligated to "act to end the violence, protect those who have reported it and investigate to find out what happened." The guidelines require educational institutions to conduct Title IX investigations even if a criminal investigation is being conducted. The Department of Education recognizes that disregarding an incident can result in women leaving school, impeding their access to education. Institutions in some instances should move the alleged perpetrator to a different dorm, change the victim's classes, or remove the accused from school.

The guidelines instruct institutions to establish systems for grievances employing a preponderance of the evidence standard, the burden of proof used in civil cases. All individuals involved in the incident should be permitted to testify before the panel, and the panel should determine whether "it is more likely than not" that sexual violence occurred. In the past, most schools employed a much higher standard of proof. Institutions also should keep women informed of the progress of the investigation and of the outcome of the case. Should the Department of Education, which is part of the executive branch of government, be involved in dictating how colleges and universities should handle allegations of sexual assault?

Stanford University, in light of the serious consequences involved in finding a student guilty, requires a unanimous verdict by a panel composed of three faculty members. Critics ask why a woman must persuade three individuals to sustain a complaint and a man can avoid liability with a single vote. Stanford also has a provision for a "non-hearing resolution" in which a Title IX coordinator can propose a non-judicial resolution of the matter. Critics point to the fact that women may feel pressured to accept a compromise that allows a man to avoid full responsibility (Drape and Tracy 2016).

Keep in mind that a university also may be found reckless and legally liable for its handling of complaints about sexual molestation and harassment. Studies find that somewhere between 25 and 63 percent of rapists are repeat offenders, and several universities are being sued by victims who claim that universities were slow to remove an accused rapist from the campus (Saul 2017).

The Trump administration is reviewing the question of sexual assault on campus and whether the federal government should dictate the required procedures that are to be followed under Title IX in response to allegations of sexual molestation. Expectations are for a reduced federal role.

■ LAW ENFORCEMENT

The police are part of the executive branch of government. They enforce the criminal laws enacted by the legislature. The police also indirectly have an impact on the content of laws. For example, searches and seizures under the Fourth Amendment to the U.S. Constitution are to be based on a warrant issued by a judge that provides probable cause to search a home and to seize evidence. The police found this restriction unrealistic and entered homes without a warrant to prevent the destruction of evidence. The courts recognized the police indeed were justified in entering a home in emergency situations and accordingly recognized an "exigent circumstances" exception to the Fourth Amendment prohibition on unreasonable searches and seizures. Each time the police stop a pedestrian or motorist, they are interpreting a legal rule and applying it to a factual situation. For example, the police are interpreting the meaning of "reckless driving" or "drunk and disorderly" in public.

The origins of American law enforcement may be traced to England. In the nineteenth century, England adopted a "mutual pledge" system of public safety in which individuals were responsible for maintaining order. Each community was divided into groups of ten families (a tithing), and each citizen had the duty to raise the "hue and cry" in the event of a crime. Tithings were subject to a royal fine if they failed to apprehend a wrongdoer. The next step was to vest responsibility for criminal control in the "hundred," which was composed of ten tithings. The local lord appointed custodians to arm and supervise the "hundred." There was a need to coordinate local groups, and the next step was the appointment of a "shire reeve" or sheriff. The sheriff administered "shires" or units that encompassed geographical areas roughly the size of a county. Justices of the peace were appointed by the Crown to assist the sheriff and in time assumed a judicial role (President's Commission on Law Enforcement and Administration of Justice 1967b: 3–5; J. Rubinstein 1973: 3–11).

This system of self-policing was unable to effectively regulate the large number of individuals who poured into large industrial towns during the Industrial Revolution of the 1700s. Various civic associations were formed to patrol streets and highways, and the government appointed "police offices" to maintain public safety and order. By the nineteenth century, nine police offices had been established in London. These offices lacked coordination and largely proved ineffective in protecting citizens. In the early 1800s, gaslights were introduced on the streets as a crime prevention tool.

In the 1820s, Home Secretary Sir Robert Peel persuaded the English Parliament to adopt an "Act for Improving the Police In and Near the Metropolis." The one thousand members of the police force wore uniforms and were commanded by a commissioner. The home secretary (the cabinet secretary concerned with domestic affairs) was responsible for providing a budget for the police, who became known as "bobbies." The home secretary, in turn, was under the authority of the democratically elected Parliament, guaranteeing popular control over the police. The system soon spread throughout the country.

The seventeenth- and eighteenth-century American colonists brought the early English rural law enforcement system to America. Constables were appointed to enforce the law in towns, and sheriffs were in charge of policing the counties. Colonial governors appointed wealthy landowners who were loyal to the English Crown to these law enforcement positions. Following the American Revolution, the system of appointed law enforcement officials was replaced by popular election, a system that continues today in many jurisdictions within the United States.

Colonial cities in the seventeenth century relied on a system of volunteer night watchmen. New York City was the first city to pay the night watchmen. These men were known as the "rattle-watch" because they carried rattles on their rounds to assure the residents they were present and to create apprehension among offenders.

As cities expanded, many American urban areas developed organized metropolitan police forces. New York City was the first jurisdiction to abolish the night watch and to create a unified police force to patrol the city during the day as well as in the evening. By the early 1900s, virtually every major city had adopted the New York model. Most urban police forces were headed by a chief or commissioner, typically appointed by a mayor with the approval of the city council.

Politicians appointed their supporters to police forces who, in turn, were expected to contribute to the politicians' campaign. Reformers instituted a number of policies designed to create a professional police force insulated from political interference. These reforms included the integration of the police into the civil service system, merit hiring based on test scores, educational requirements, and the development of police training academies.

The sheriff–constable system proved unable to counter the growing crime problem. Local police agencies lacked coordination with one another, and lawbreakers were able to flee safely across city and county lines. States responded after World War I by creating statewide police forces to help enforce "crime across borders" and to address the problem of automobile traffic and theft. State police jurisdiction in some instances was limited to statewide highways, and other state police exercised authority throughout the state.

There are a wide variety of police law enforcement agencies in the United States. These include the state police and criminal investigation agencies at the state level, the sheriff's police at the county level in over three thousand counties, and local police departments in one thousand cities, twenty thousand townships, and fifteen thousand villages, boroughs, and towns. There also are special-purpose police, such as state park or hospital district police.

Finally, a number of federal departments possess enforcement personnel, with arrest and firearm authority. The Revenue Cutter Service, established in 1789 to prevent smuggling, was the first federal law enforcement agency. The development of federal law enforcement culminated in 1924 with the establishment of the FBI.

A number of federal law enforcement agencies address specific areas of concern. The Secret Service, for example, protects the president and investigates counterfeiting and forgery, and the Drug Enforcement Administration (DEA) is charged with countering the drug trade. The Postal Inspection Service investigates the use of the mail for unlawful purposes, and the IRS possesses criminal investigative authority over taxes. The U.S. Marshals Service is a law enforcement agency within the Department of Justice with responsibility for maintaining order in the courtroom, delivering legal papers, apprehending fugitives from justice, and transporting prisoners and other courtroom-related duties.

As the twentieth century drew to a close, policing was transformed into a technologically sophisticated enterprise. The use of fingerprints in the early twentieth century was followed by radio and telephone communication, the introduction of the squad car, DNA, and surveillance cameras. Policing in urban areas no longer is "guesswork." The police increasingly have college and advanced degrees and rely on large-scale data analysis to map "crime hot spots" and to identify "networks" of offenders thought to be responsible for a disproportionate share of criminal behavior.

Critics in the 1960s complained the police were isolated in squad cars and removed from the community. The police responded by hiring an increasing number of minorities and women. This was followed in the late 1990s by departments embracing **community policing**, which was intended to enlist the community as partners with the police in combating crime. The goal was to make the community the "eyes and ears" of the police and to help the police focus on individuals and activities that threatened the stability of the community. Policing was viewed as a coordinated activity requiring, for example, the demolition or renovation of abandoned housing, the creation of recreational opportunities for young people, the maintenance of the physical appearance of neighborhoods, and the implementation of educational and employment programs. The "broken windows" approach to policing was a related development. The thinking was that tolerating small acts of criminality, such as graffiti, weakened the stability of neighborhoods and led to a downward spiral of criminality.

As you read the remainder of the text, we will discuss various aspects of policing, including stop and frisk and interrogation.

■ A STATISTICAL PROFILE OF THE POLICE

State and Local Police

Local departments have differing organizational structures although some basic features are shared by departments. The chief of police and his or her deputies are at the top of a three-legged organizational stool. The operational leg is divided into patrol, traffic, juvenile, vice and narcotics, gangs, and detectives. These units may be divided into local precincts or districts. The administrative leg includes hiring and training and internal investigation, public information, and legal advisor. The services leg includes forensic laboratories, data processing, purchasing, and upkeep of equipment. Departments increasingly provide for a community relations branch that is concerned with ensuring community support, communication, and understanding. Local laws also provide for various outside mechanisms for ensuring police accountability in cases of alleged police misconduct (Vago 2012: 137–139).

As of January 1, 2013, an estimated 605,000 employees worked at more than twelve thousand local police departments. An estimated 47,700 individuals were sworn officers with general arrest powers, which is a 35 percent increase from 1987. One-third of local police departments used unpaid reserve or auxiliary officers, numbering twenty-nine thousand unpaid officers. The 128,000 non-sworn personnel are involved in accounting, dispatch, information technology, and forensics (Bureau of Justice Statistics 2015).

In 2013, 27 percent of police officers were members of racial or ethnic minority groups compared to 15 percent in 1987. Between 2007 and 2013, the percentage of minority police officers increased from 25.3 percent to 27.3 percent.

In 2013, about 12 percent of local police officers were African American, an increase from 9 percent in 1987. Roughly 11 percent of officers were Hispanic or Latino in 2013, which was more than double the percentage of Hispanic officers in 1987. Three percent of officers were Asian, native Hawaiian, Pacific Islander, Native American, or Alaska Native in 2013, four times higher than 1987. Larger police departments were more diverse than smaller departments. More than two in five officers in departments serving five hundred thousand or more were minorities as compared to one in five officers in departments serving a population of fewer than fifty thousand.

The number and percentage of full-time sworn female officers also has increased. In 2013, an estimated one in eight police officers was female. In 2013, fifty-eight thousand female officers were employed as compared to roughly twenty-seven thousand officers in 1987. This is an increase from 8 percent to 12 percent of all sworn officers. The percentage of supervisory personnel who were women increased during this same period from 5 to 10 percent.

In 2013, 17 percent of officers in departments serving jurisdictions with 250,000 or more residents were women as opposed to 7 percent in departments serving fewer than 25,000 residents. Fifteen percent of supervisors were female in departments serving 25,000 or more residents as opposed to 6 percent in departments in jurisdictions with 5,000 or fewer residents. Overall, 3 percent of police chiefs were female although 7 percent of chiefs were women in jurisdictions of 250,000 or more residents.

The popular conception is that the police departments are large bureaucratic institutions. An estimated 48 percent of departments employ fewer than ten officers although these departments employ roughly 4 percent of all full-time local police officers. A total of 645 (5 percent) departments employed one hundred or more officers and accounted for 63 percent of all officers.

In 2013, 71 percent of departments policed fewer than ten thousand residents and employed 13 percent of all full-time local police officers. An estimated 3 percent of departments policed a population of a hundred thousand or more and employed 54 percent of all officers. (See Table 3.2.)

The average base starting salary for an officer in 2013 was $44,000 for all jurisdictions but higher in departments policing larger jurisdictions. An estimated 10 percent require a two-year college degree, and 1 percent require a college degree. Most departments consider military service as an alternative to education. Smaller departments tend to require a high school degree.

In 2013, about seven in ten local police departments, including nine in ten serving a population of twenty-five thousand or more, had a mission statement that included community policing. Departments with a community policing component employed 88 percent of officers. A majority of departments serving ten thousand or more residents trained new recruits for eight hours or more in community policing skills. About half of the departments serving a population of fewer than ten thousand provided this type of training.

Most departments organize beat assignments based on geography, and nine out of ten local police departments employing one thousand or more officers had personnel designated to address specialized areas such as drugs, juvenile crime, domestic violence, child abuse, and special weapons and tactics (SWAT).

Table 3.2 ■ Ten Largest Local Police Departments in the United States by Number of Full-Time Sworn Personnel		
	Number	Per 10,000 Residents
New York, NY	34,454	41
Chicago, IL	12,042	44
Los Angeles, CA	9,920	26
Philadelphia, PA	6,515	42
Houston, TX	5,295	25
Washington, D.C.	3,865	61
Dallas, TX	3,478	28
Phoenix, AZ	2,952	20
Baltimore, MD	2,949	47
Miami-Dade, FL	2,745	22

Source: Figures based on Bureau of Justice Statistics, Local Enforcement Management and Administrative Statistics (LEMAS) Survey 2013.

Federal Law Enforcement

Twenty-four federal agencies employ 250 or more officers with arrest and firearms authority and employ 96 percent of federal officers. Four of five federal officers are employed by the Department of Homeland Security (DHS) and the Department of Justice (DOJ). DHS employs roughly 55,000 or approximately 46 percent of all federal officers, and DOJ employs one-third of federal officers. U.S. Customs and Border Protection (CBP) employs 36,863 officers with arrest and firearm authority, most of whom are stationed either at ports of entry or on the U.S.–Mexico and U.S.–Canada borders. The second-largest law enforcement agency within the DHS is Immigration and Customs Enforcement (ICE), employing roughly 12,446 officers. The Federal Bureau of Prisons (BOP) employs 17,000 officers, and the FBI employs almost 13,000 individuals with arrest and firearm authority.

Private Security

Any review of police cannot overlook the rapidly expanding area of private policing. A private security company is a for-profit company that provides armed and unarmed security services to the private and public sectors. These various functions fall into three broad categories.

1. *Physical security* of people and facilities, including bodyguards, dog guards, alarm installation and maintenance and surveillance, protection of buildings, and crowd control

2. *Information security*, including the storage of information and protection against cybercrime

3. *Employment-related security*, background checks of employees, protection against employee theft, and drug testing

Private security personnel may work for a private firm that provides services or may be directly hired by a corporation or entertainment venue. The industries that tend to hire their own security personnel are restaurants, casinos, entertainment venues, and medical centers (Strom et al. 2010).

In 2009, there were roughly fourteen thousand private security firms in the United States. Seventy percent of employees worked for firms of one hundred or more employees. The industry employs more than one million full-time and part-time employees. Forty-six percent of private industry employees are minorities, the median salary is $23,460, and salaries range to slightly less than $40,000.

Estimates place the total revenue of the security industry at roughly $25 billion. The ten largest firms account for 67 percent of total revenues. Most firms are global, and total international revenues are close to $100 billion. The British firm G4S generated revenues of $12 billion in 2012. Other leading revenue-generating firms are Securitas AB, ADT, AlliedBarton, DynCorp, GardaWorld, Control Risks, Booz Allen Hamilton, CACI International, Brink's, and Pinkerton. The sectors of the economy spending the highest percentage of their revenues on security are education, hospitals, insurance and banking, and government.

Private military companies also function abroad and supplement the U.S. military. They contract with the Department of State, the Pentagon, and other agencies and provide bodyguards, embassy security, protection for critical infrastructure, and security for military transport. They operate in more than fifty countries and have the ratio of one private contractor for every ten members of the U.S. military. They also provide security services for foreign countries by, among other functions, training military personnel. The industry generates over $100 billion in revenues (Singer 2007).

INTERNATIONAL PERSPECTIVE: THE UN SYSTEM

In 1919, the League of Nations was founded as an international organization dedicated to maintaining international peace and security. The League attracted fifty-eight member states and was dissolved in 1954 after failing to control the wars of aggression waged by Germany and Japan.

The name *United Nations* was first proposed in 1942 by British prime minister Winston Churchill and by U.S. president Franklin Delano Roosevelt to describe the World War II alliance between the United States, Great Britain, and the Soviet Union. The proposal for a United Nations organization that included countries across the globe was discussed at a series of international meetings during World War II. In August 1945, the details of the proposed United Nations organization were agreed on by France, the Republic of China, the United Kingdom, the United States, and the Soviet Union at Dumbarton Oaks in Washington, D.C.

The United Nations (UN) was founded in 1945 with the drafting and approval of the UN Charter by fifty nation-states at the United Nations Conference on International Organization in San Francisco. The UN formally came into existence on October 24, 1945, with the signatures of fifty state representatives. The first meeting of the UN occurred in London in January 1946. In 1951, the UN headquarters in New York City officially opened with associated agencies operating in Geneva, The Hague, Nairobi, Vienna, and Rome.

The UN, according to the Charter, is devoted to the enforcement of international law, the prevention of war, the protection of human rights, the promotion of equal rights and economic development, and the social progress of people across the globe. There are five primary branches of the United Nations:

General Assembly. The General Assembly is composed of representatives of each of the member states and is headed by an elected president. The assembly meets each year, and nation-states have one vote regardless of their population and global importance. Significant decisions require a two-thirds vote. The General Assembly passes non-binding resolutions and declarations that reflect the sentiments of member states toward international issues and also approves formal treaties that member states may adopt and ratify and incorporate into their domestic legal systems.

Security Council. The Security Council has the responsibility for maintaining international peace and security and may commit the UN to intervene to prevent a breach of the peace. The Security Council is authorized to pass resolutions that are binding on member states and has ordered UN troops to intervene to expel Iraq from Kuwait and to protect South Korea against aggression from North Korea. In recent years, the Security Council has sent peacekeeping forces into Bosnia, Democratic Republic of Congo, Darfur, Somalia, and other countries and has negotiated the destruction of chemical weapons in Syria. The Security Council, as part of its responsibility to maintain peace and security, has authorized international criminal tribunals in Rwanda and in the former Yugoslavia, Sierra Leone, Cambodia, East Timor, and other countries. There are five permanent members (China, France, Great Britain, Russia, and the United States), each of whom has a veto, and ten rotating non-permanent members. A veto prevents the Security Council from adopting a resolution.

International Court of Justice. The International Court of Justice (ICJ) hears allegations by countries that another country is violating international law and determines whether a state is liable for breaching international law. States must accept the jurisdiction of the ICJ before the court will adjudicate a dispute. The new International Criminal Court (ICC) hears criminal allegations against leaders and citizens of states that have accepted the tribunal's jurisdiction. The ICC is independent and is not part of the UN system. The Security Council, however, may refer cases to the ICC or may prevent the ICC from prosecuting a case for six months.

Economic and Social Council. The Economic and Social Council (ECOSOC) is concerned with issues of economic development, the environment, population, human rights, crime, and the rights of women and minorities. The ECOSOC supervises a number of specialized agencies that address these issues. States are elected by the General Assembly to serve three-year terms.

Secretariat. This branch is headed by the secretary-general, the head of the UN. The secretary-general's staff of international civil servants administers the UN and undertakes studies and provides information to other branches of the UN. The secretary-general is an important world figure and is called on to resolve disputes between countries, direct peacekeeping operations, and speak out on global issues. The secretary-general is nominated by the Security Council, and his or her appointment is confirmed by the General Assembly. The post of secretary-general is rotated between various regions of the world and may not be held by a citizen of one of the permanent members of the Security Council.

There are a number of agencies in the UN system that work on specialized issues and are the main centers of activity in the UN. These agencies include the World Health Organization (WHO), the Food and Agriculture Organization (FAO), the United Nations Children's Fund (UNICEF), the International Atomic Energy Agency (IAEA), the United Nations Educational, Scientific and Cultural Organization (UNESCO), the World Bank, the United Nations High Commissioner for Refugees (UNHCR), and the International Labour Organization (ILO).

Virtually every independent country in the world, with the exception of Taiwan, Kosovo, and Vatican City, is a member of the UN. There currently are 193 member states. A state is eligible for membership if it agrees to accept the principles of the UN Charter and meet the obligations of a member state. The General Assembly votes on whether to admit a nation to the UN. The UN is supported by contributions from the member states and operates in six official languages.

The UN performs a number of functions in the global community:

Peace and security. The UN secretary-general and the Security Council intervene to negotiate conflicts between states. The Security Council is authorized to peaceably resolve disputes and also may require member states to provide troops to intervene to control situations that threaten international peace and security. In recent years, UN troops known as the "Blue Helmets" have intervened in situations of conflict within states, such as the conflict between Serbs, Croats, and Muslims in Bosnia and conflicts in Haiti, Burundi, and Ivory Coast. The UN acted in Korea (1950–1953) and in Kuwait (1990) to halt wars of aggression. The Security Council has been criticized for failing to intervene in 1994 to halt the Rwandan genocide. In 1995, Dutch peacekeepers established a safe haven in Srebrenica for Muslims fleeing Serbian military forces and were overrun by Serb forces, resulting in the killing of seven thousand Muslim men. The UN also has been involved in encouraging disarmament and in agreeing to restrictions on the development and deployment of nuclear weapons.

Human rights and humanitarian assistance. The UN provides assistance to nation-states in areas such as conducting elections, implementing political reform, improving the functioning of the judiciary, and drafting constitutional protections. The organization also provides food, shelter, and water to individuals displaced by natural disasters and war and works to eradicate poverty and illiteracy and to protect refugees. In 1948, the General Assembly adopted the non-binding Universal Declaration of Human Rights, which lists the rights possessed by all people in the world that governments are morally obligated to protect and preserve. This was followed in 1977 by two legally binding treaties, the International Covenant on Civil and Political Rights and the International Covenant on Economic, Social and Cultural Rights. These three instruments comprise the "International Bill of Rights."

Self-determination. The UN has helped eighty former European colonies attain independence.

Social and economic development. UN agencies provide financial assistance and experts in areas such as AIDS, tuberculosis, and malaria and family planning, child mortality, and health.

The UN is a source of law in the international legal system through both adjudication and legislation.

Adjudication. ICJ decisions, although they have no binding authority on domestic courts, establish principles of international law. The international criminal tribunals for Rwanda and the former Yugoslavia, along with tribunals in Sierra Leone, Cambodia, and East Timor, established by the UN have made important contributions to the international law of war and to human rights.

Legislation. The UN makes law in several ways. The UN formulates treaties that countries are given the opportunity to sign and integrate into their domestic law. An example is the 1948 Convention on the Prevention and Punishment of the Crime of Genocide. Security Council decisions create precedents that establish international legal rules. The decision to authorize intervention to protect Libyans against the forces of dictator Momar Quadafi, for example, is a precedent that may be used to justify intervention in future threats to a civilian population. General Assembly resolutions, although not legally binding, help define the unwritten principles of customary international law.

The United States is the largest provider of financial contributions to the United Nations, providing an annual appropriation of $13 billion, which was 22 percent of the UN budget and 28 percent of the peacekeeping budget in 2015. There is a question whether the United States should continue to contribute $13 billion to the United Nations or even continue to remain a member of the organization.

CHAPTER SUMMARY

Most countries in the world have a single, unified court system. The United States, in contrast, has a dual court system comprising a federal court system and a state court system. The federal system is based on the U.S. Constitution and statutes passed by Congress; state court systems are created by state constitutions and state statutes.

The U.S. Constitution provides a divided government structure, and power is divided between the presidency, Congress, and the courts. The federal government structure is based on separation of powers and on checks and balances between the three branches of government.

Article III of the U.S. Constitution created a single Supreme Court and left it to Congress to fill in the details of a national judicial system. Article III provides that "the judicial power of the United States, shall be vested in one Supreme Court, and in such inferior courts as the Congress may from time to time ordain and establish." This provision was a compromise between the Federalists, who favored a strong federal judicial system, and the anti-Federalists, who viewed federal courts as a threat to liberty and who as a consequence favored concentrating the judicial power in state courts. This debate continued throughout the first hundred years of the country and was not resolved until the end of the eighteenth century with the creation of a three-tiered federal court structure.

Federal district courts are the trial courts in the federal system, and appeals may be taken to courts of appeals. The Supreme Court sits at the top of the federal hierarchy, and its decisions are binding precedent on all federal and state courts. The Supreme Court, for the most part, has discretion over the cases that it reviews on appeal, and its decisions are intended both to resolve conflicts between lower courts and to address significant legal questions. The Court exercises the power of judicial review to determine the constitutionality of the acts of Congress and of the presidency.

There is continuing debate whether the framers of the Constitution intended for federal judges to exercise the power of judicial review. The power of judicial review, whatever the intent of the drafters of the Constitution, has involved the Supreme Court in major issues in American life ranging from abortion to gun control to the death penalty to the treatment of detainees at Guantánamo.

State courts are the centers of legal activity. Ninety-eight percent of all legal cases are filed in state courts. State cases are brought under state laws and state constitutions. There is significant variation in state court structures. The typical state court system is composed of courts of limited jurisdiction, courts of general jurisdiction, intermediate appellate courts, and a supreme court of last resort. State judiciaries differ in the mix of cases on their docket and in how they rule.

U.S. states rely on various mechanisms to select judges, and most provide for at least some democratic procedures. There is no single philosophy of judging that is accepted by all state and federal judges. State and federal judges are influenced by various methods of analysis in deciding cases, including legalism, originalism, literalism, balancing of interests, the attitudinal approach, and the strategic approach.

The United States has a dual system of administrative agencies, and federal and state agencies at times share common concerns. Agencies engage in rule-making, investigation, and adjudication. Congress has exercised limited oversight over agency decision-making. The courts have adopted a policy of "limited review" of administrative decisions and are reluctant to substitute the judgment of the court for the judgment of the agency. There is a tendency for agencies to become "captured" by their constituents rather than to provide meaningful regulation.

The United States has a dual system of state and federal law enforcement agencies, which are supplemented by private security.

CHAPTER REVIEW QUESTIONS

1. Trace the development of the federal court system.

2. Discuss the dual court system in the United States and the relationship between the federal and state court systems.

3. What is the significance of the concept of justiciability? Define mootness, exhaustion, standing, the political question doctrine, ripeness, and collusion.

4. Describe the organization and function of federal district courts, courts of appeals, and the Supreme Court.

5. Are Supreme Court judges selected from a cross section of the population? Does the United States need a more diverse Supreme Court?

6. What are the arguments for and against judicial review?

7. Describe the structure and function of state courts and the selection process of state court judges.

8. How do judges decide cases?

9. Discuss the function of the legislative branch of government and the structure of the U.S. Congress. What is the role of interest groups and lobbyists in the legislative process?

10. Outline the function of administrative agencies.

11. Discuss the development of the modern police.

TERMINOLOGY

ANSWERS TO TEST YOUR KNOWLEDGE

1. True

2. False

3. False

4. False

5. False

6. False

7. False

8. False

9. False

10. True

WANT A BETTER GRADE?

Get the tools you need to sharpen your study skills. Access practice quizzes, eFlashcards, author podcasts, SAGE journal articles, hyperlinks for Law and Society on the Web, and more at **study.sagepub.com/lippmanls2e**.

CHAPTER 4

THE LEGAL PROFESSION

Additional information on law school can be found in Appendix A: The Law School Experience, available online at **study.sagepub.com/lippmanls2e**

TEST YOUR KNOWLEDGE: TRUE OR FALSE?

1. Commentators point to ancient Rome as the beginning of the legal profession.

2. In England, only a special class of lawyers called barristers argue cases in court.

3. Following the American Revolution, lawyers were respected and embraced by the American people.

4. The American Bar Association is an organization of lawyers in small as well as large firms.

5. Practicing law as a solo practitioner or in a medium-sized firm is similar to practicing law in a large corporate firm.

6. The term *Washington lawyer* commonly is used to refer to lawyers who work for the federal government.

7. An in-house corporate counsel works in a law firm and advises corporations.

8. The American legal profession reflects the demographic breakdown of American society.

9. The American legal profession is described as "stratified" because of the differing prestige, income, and work of lawyers.

Check your answers on page 177.

■ INTRODUCTION

This chapter describes the structure and composition of the American legal profession.

Public opinion polls indicate that Americans hold "mixed" views when it comes to lawyers. On the one hand, lawyers are celebrated for standing up for the little person against powerful institutions. On the other hand, lawyers are viewed as materialistic and manipulative and are blamed by individuals who remain angry over, for example, their divorce settlements, loss of child custody, or criminal convictions.

In recent years, we have witnessed an increased skepticism toward the legal profession. Only stockbrokers and politicians evoke less confidence from the American public, and respect for the justice system has experienced significant decline. Michael Asimow, in his study of close to three hundred movies featuring lawyers, finds that in the past few decades the image of lawyers in films has undergone dramatic change. Lawyers have gone from the type of ethical, virtuous, competent, and courageous individual portrayed by Gregory Peck in *To Kill a Mockingbird* (1962) to literally being portrayed as the devil by Al Pacino in *The Devil's Advocate* (1997). The general trend in fictional films has been toward viewing lawyers as embodying an uneasy balance between "virtue" and "corruption." In the 1962 film *Cape Fear*, Sam Bowden (Gregory Peck) is a skilled lawyer and loving family member who is tormented by Max Cady (Robert Mitchum), whom he helped send to jail by testifying against him in a rape trial. In the 1991 remake, Bowden (Nick Nolte) is transformed into a morally ambiguous figure who is unfaithful to his wife and is a flawed father. As a public defender, Bowden represents Cady (Robert De Niro) and unethically suppresses evidence of the "promiscuity" of the victim in order to ensure Cady's conviction (Asimow 2000; Sherwin 2000: 172–186).

In the initial portion of this chapter, we trace the historical development of the American legal profession.

■ PERSPECTIVES ON THE LEGAL PROFESSION

Lawyers, doctors, and the clergy historically were characterized as the three "learned professions." What does it mean to be a profession? A **profession** is an occupational group that has high status and prestige. This high respect does not result from waving a magic wand. Power and prestige in the past primarily were monopolized by aristocratic and prominent families and were passed on to their sons and daughters. The rise of the market economy resulted in power and prestige being based on economic accomplishment rather than family privilege.

Lawyers responded to this changed economic reality by relying on various strategies to create a demand for their services and to ensure that non-lawyers did not pose a threat to their dominance. In technical language, lawyers pursued a strategy intended to maintain their high social status by asserting "monopolistic control over the economic market."

As you read the chapter, pay attention to the policies that lawyers have relied on to protect their prestige and power as professionals (summarized in Table 4.1). Some of these strategies are listed below (Larson 1977).

- *Specialized educational training*
- *Restricted access to the profession*
- *Special knowledge and expertise*
- *Self-regulation*

In brief, lawyers undergo a lengthy and demanding education (specialized educational training) and are qualified to practice law only after they have passed the bar examination (restricted access to the profession). This training provides lawyers with knowledge in areas that are not understood by most people and justifies their high legal fees (special knowledge and expertise). Lawyers, as skilled professionals, claim that they are in the best position to regulate themselves and to evaluate when a fellow lawyer's conduct has breached professional ethics (self-regulation).

Table 4.1 ■ Characteristics of the Legal Profession	
Specialized education	Legal education affiliated with universities that only is available to qualified applicants
Restricted access	Bar examination; continuing legal education limitations on practicing law across state boundaries
Monopoly over expertise and skills	Restriction on practicing law without a license; difficulty of non-lawyer representing himself or herself in court
Self-regulation	Self-enforcement of code of ethics drafted by bar associations
Professional ideology	Protection of the client and respect for the law

From the perspective of the sociology of professions, lawyers are similar to plumbers, teachers, or other occupations in their campaign to capture control of essential services, achieve social status, and assert independence from government control. Commentators point out that many of the simple tasks that we depend on lawyers to perform could be adequately performed by non-lawyers (Sutton 2001: 228–229).

Other scholars argue that the legal profession is as concerned with making a public contribution as with its own economic advancement. In this view, lawyers make a valuable contribution by representing both the poor and the privileged and are guardians of our rights and liberties. Professional legal associations provide a valuable source of solidarity, support, and identity for lawyers and do not merely constitute organized efforts to pursue lawyers' own self-interest.

Another critical perspective on the legal profession is that lawyers have fallen on hard times and are fast becoming paid employees without a great deal of professional freedom or economic security. In other words, lawyers no longer are able to control their work, income, and careers and are slowly becoming reduced to the status of workers. Yet another competing perspective views lawyers as a powerful part of the economic establishment and as part of the problem rather than part of the solution (Abel 1989: 14–39, 249–318).

As you read the chapter, pay attention to how developments in society have influenced the legal profession and the practice of law. Consider how the legal profession and society interact with one another to help shape the world of lawyers.

■ THE HISTORICAL DEVELOPMENT OF THE ENGLISH LEGAL PROFESSION

Disputes historically were settled according to unwritten customary laws without the assistance of lawyers. As society and modes of dispute resolution became more complicated, there was an increasing demand for individuals who were able to guide the average person through the legal thicket. The earliest lawyers likely were the orators of ancient Athens (146–100 BCE). The orators were skilled in oral argument rather than the law. Athenian law required that individuals present their own case. Litigants, however, were entitled to ask a friend for assistance and asked for help from orators who they claimed were close acquaintances. In the mid-fourth century, the limitation on representation in court was repealed, and the law recognized the right of individuals to be represented by an orator in court. The Athenians feared that orators might be tempted to "bend the truth" to ensure their clients were successful and insisted that orators could not be paid for representing individuals.

The orators, as you recall, were advocates and generally were not trained in the law. As a result, most commentators point to ancient Rome rather than Athens as the starting point for the legal profession (L. Friedman 1977: 21).

The Romans shared the Athenians' fear that advocates who were paid would have an incentive to twist the facts at trial. A Roman law enacted in 204 BCE prohibited advocates from accepting a fee. Emperor Claudius (41–54 CE) later legalized advocacy although he limited the fees that advocates could charge. The advocates were talented orators, but they were not trained in law. Individuals seeking a legal opinion consulted a class of part-time legal specialists, or jurisconsults (*iuris consulti*), who offered legal opinions to the public. Jurisconsults also were consulted by judges who were uncertain how to decide a case.

The legal profession in Rome by the rule of Emperor Hadrian (117–138 CE) had become regulated with restrictions on who could function as an advocate and on the fees that could be charged. The advocates were required to undergo a four-year course of study and to submit letters of reference from their instructors before being admitted to practice before a specific court.

Despite the decline of the Roman Empire, the body of legal rules developed by the jurisconsults and the digests or books that recorded Roman law spread throughout Europe and formed the basis of the modern continental European system of civil law. The tribes of Great Britain, despite being occupied by Rome for almost four centuries, maintained their own customary forms of law and dispute resolution and resisted adopting Roman law. The British gradually developed a unique legal system that formed the basis of the British common law that later was transported to America by English colonists.

The crucial event in English legal history is the Norman Conquest of 1066 over the Saxons. William the Conqueror created a system of royal courts. The Court of Common Pleas was a traveling court that resolved disputes between ordinary individuals revolving around land, trespass, debt, and personal property. The judges would follow local customs in deciding cases. These decisions gradually were compiled into a system of law common to the English people and formed the basis of the common law, or law that was shared by the English people. The judges' decisions formed the precedent (*stare decisis*) that was to be followed by other judges.

An individual wishing to file a legal action had to obtain a writ or a license to bring a case to court. The writ (or "form of action") had to meet highly technical and involved language. An individual who failed to follow the required form could not proceed ("where there is no writ, there is no right"). The defendant then was required to follow an exact formula in response. The system proceeded with each individual trading highly technical complaints and responses (Glendon, Gordon, and Osakwe 1982: 142–152).

A judge and individual filing a complaint had to be well versed in the law to participate in this system of common law pleading, and there clearly was a need for some formal system of legal training (Tigar and Levy 1977: 157). The solution was the Inns of Court. These started out as residence halls and working rooms in London for judges, lawyers, and students and were located near the king's courts (Hogue 1966: 246). In 1292, King Edward I assigned judges responsibility for legal education, and the judges responded by creating an apprentice program at the Inns of Court. This was an eight-year program involving lectures, moots (or mock trials), and reading writs. Students undergoing training (pupilage) were assigned to a master who supervised the pupil's education. The term *barrister* likely originated to describe the lawyers who argued in these moot courts. The Inns of Court were full of rituals and ceremonies and were based on a rigid hierarchy that reinforced a sense that the lawyers were part of a professional elite (Lemmings 2003).

Serjeants of the king were a special rank of senior barristers who accompanied the common law judges as they traveled around the country and provided legal assistance to individuals. The serjeants also represented the king in the royal courts in London in tax disputes (the Court of Exchequer), in disputes with local officials (King's Bench), and in courts created to achieve justice where there was no available writ (Court of Chancery). The institution of serjeant was abolished in the eighteenth century, and barristers were given the exclusive right to appear in court (Hazell 1978).

A separate group of lawyers, or *solicitors*, developed who directly advised clients, prepared documents (conveying property and drafting wills), and negotiated settlements. Solicitors originally were a class of lawyers within the Inns of Court but were excluded from the Inns in 1794. The solicitors proceeded to develop their own system of professional preparation. Although the barristers and solicitors today are technically co-equal branches of the law, barristers—because of their appearance in court and monopolization of judgeships—remain the more prestigious branch of the British legal profession (Hazell 1978).

In 1758, Cambridge University took the first steps toward making the study of law a university subject when the famous barrister Sir William Blackstone was appointed to the Vinerian Chair of Jurisprudence. Two decades later, law faculties were established at both Cambridge and Oxford. The thinking was that prospective lawyers required a broad curriculum of study that could serve as a foundation for the technical education in the Inns of Court. The new law program included the basic common law subjects (e.g., contracts, property, and criminal law) as well as legal history, legal philosophy, and Roman and ecclesiastical law. Blackstone's four-volume *Commentaries on the Laws of England* was the central text relied on by lawyers in England, and later in the United States, for understanding the common law (Fidler 2003).

Today, a law degree from one of the roughly one hundred English institutions offering a law degree is required to enter legal practice in the United Kingdom. Individuals who major in other subjects are required to pass an examination before they can undertake the required training to become a solicitor or barrister. An individual seeking a career as a barrister registers with one of the four Inns of Court and attends classes for a year covering legal procedure, the law of evidence, and various substantive areas of law. Following this course of study, individuals are required to pass the Part II examinations, and the fortunate few who pass are accepted for a one-year pupilage with a junior barrister. Individuals who complete the pupilage are eligible to take their own cases. Solicitors go through their own course of study and then spend a year as an article clerk with a solicitor. There are roughly thirty thousand solicitors, and they outnumber barristers seven to one. Roughly 10 percent of the barristers who comprise "the bar" are considered worthy of the title of Queen's Counsel (QC), which authorizes them to "take silk" and to wear silk robes. Judges in England generally are selected from the ranks of the QC (Glendon et al. 1982: 192–210).

As we turn our attention to the development of the legal profession in the United States, you perhaps can appreciate why the early American colonists were suspicious of lawyers, virtually all of whom had been educated in the Inns of Court in England and were viewed as supportive of the British Crown. As you read about the history of the American legal profession, keep in mind the tension between lawyers who wanted to restrict access to the legal profession to preserve the "quality of lawyers" and lawyers who advocated opening the legal profession to a broader and more diverse portion of the population.

■ THE GROWTH OF THE AMERICAN LEGAL PROFESSION

The Early Years

The early American colonists distrusted lawyers. Thomas Morton, the first attorney to arrive in Plymouth Bay, Massachusetts, was expelled by the Puritans in 1629 for atheism, drinking, dancing, and instructing the Native Americans on how to use firearms. In 1645, Virginia prohibited trained lawyers from appearing in court. Connecticut and the Carolinas followed the same policy (L. Friedman 2005: 53).

Why this animosity toward attorneys? The early colonists had confidence in the average person and viewed lawyers as members of the social elite who made money by taking advantage of the problems of small farmers and workers. They believed individuals should represent themselves in the courtroom and that a lawyer should not stand between the individual and the judge. Angry riots were carried out against lawyers who were viewed as helping bankers imprison debtors and seize their property. Lawyers in North Carolina were accused of perverting justice. They were described as "cursed hungry Caterpillars" whose fees "eat out the very Bowels of our Commonwealth" (quoted in L. Friedman 2005: 53).

The lawyers in colonial America had been educated in England, a country many of the early settlers had fled and distrusted and wanted to leave behind. The disdain for lawyers was particularly intense in the colonies such as Massachusetts that had been established by religious sects that looked to the clergy and to other pious officials to interpret and apply the law of God (Erikson 1966). The Quakers in Pennsylvania believed disputes should be resolved in a peaceful and cooperative fashion rather than through the argument of opposing lawyers (L. Friedman 2005: 54). Judges wanted to control their courtroom without being challenged by lawyers and had little interest in defending lawyers (K. Hall 1989: 22).

© iStockphoto.com/GeorgiosArt

PHOTO 4.1 Early American colonial lawyers were trained in England and brought the common law tradition to the United States. Their close connection to England led to a distrust of lawyers.

The famous American author James Fenimore Cooper in his novel *The Pioneers* (1823) captured the common perception that law was divorced from the values of the ordinary person in his description of the plight of the frontier guide and man of the people Natty Bumppo. Natty always hunted freely for food on untamed land in upstate New York. The land had been granted by the government to Judge Marmaduke Temple, who announced that hunting was to be prohibited. On the same day Natty rescues the daughter of Judge Temple from an attack, he kills a deer on the land granted to Judge Temple. Judge Temple issues a search warrant for Natty's home to find evidence of the dead deer and orders Natty's arrest when Natty resists arrest by pointing a rifle at a constable. Judge Temple acknowledges Natty's heroism although he proclaims that resistance to lawful authority cannot be tolerated. Natty pleads there is no guilt in doing what is right but nonetheless is convicted and sentenced to a fine and a month in prison. This story reflects the popular reaction against lawyers' involvement in debt collection, land foreclosure, and sympathy for the landed elites (P. Miller 1965: 101–102).

Civil and criminal trials generally were conducted without lawyers. The gradual acceptance of the legal profession led to a relaxing of the exclusion of lawyers from trials. In New York, lawyers could appear in felony trials to advise individuals on "points of law," and in South Carolina, a law adopted in 1731 allowed an individual to be represented by up to two lawyers. Virginia in 1734 recognized the right to legal representation in cases in which defendants confronted the death penalty (L. Friedman 1993: 57).

Their relatively limited courtroom role does not mean that lawyers did not make an important contribution to American life. Historian Kermit Hall argues that those trained lawyers who favored separation from Great Britain were crucial in serving as spokesmen for independence and explaining why the policies of the British Crown violated the rights of the individual. Lawyers like James Otis achieved notoriety for representing colonists charged with defying the British. Hall points out that "twenty-five of the fifty-six signers of the Declaration of Independence and thirty-one of the fifty-five delegates to the Constitutional Convention in 1787 were lawyers" (K. Hall 1989: 53; Hoffer 2010: 69).

In the early colonial era, lawyers either had emigrated to the colonies or were the sons of wealthy farmers and merchants who had trained in the Inns of Court in London. By 1750, the situation had changed, and most lawyers qualified for practice by "reading law" with an attorney in the American colonies. An individual who aspired to be a lawyer was mentored, tutored, and supervised by the lawyer with whom he apprenticed. In return for this opportunity, the aspiring lawyer would copy documents, run errands, and file papers with the court. After a year or two of working for the practitioner before hanging out his own shingle, the apprentice was required to pass a relatively undemanding state bar exam administered by a local court. This was the path followed by the future president Thomas Jefferson and by Alexander Hamilton of New York, who was appointed as secretary of the treasury by President George Washington.

The first formal program of legal instruction for individuals aspiring to take the state bar exam was established by Judge Tapping Reeve in 1784 at the Litchfield Law School in Connecticut. Between 1784 and 1833, more than eight hundred students graduated from Litchfield. Another famous law scholar, George Wythe, began tutoring students at William and Mary in 1779, and other professorships of law were established at Harvard in 1817 and Yale in 1843. These courses were composed of brief informal lectures; at the end of the lectures, students were required to pass a single oral examination. In the early colonial era, most lawyers and judges relied on the small number of English law books that were available. Legal scholars such as Joseph Story and James

Kent for the first time started to compile textbooks of American law that replaced the texts written by English commentators (Hurst 1950: 259).

The growing influence and importance of the legal profession in the early years of the nineteenth century was remarkable given the early hostility toward the legal profession (P. Miller 1965: 109). French essayist Alexis de Tocqueville, in writing of his visit to the United States in 1835, observed that the legal profession was the "most powerful" group in America, which, through lawyers' dedication to the rule of law, helped ensure that the passions of the people did not overwhelm democracy in periods of crisis. The American legal profession, in Tocqueville's view, provided the same stability in the United States that the aristocracy provided in Europe (Tocqueville 1973).

The number of individuals entering the legal profession increased in response to the growing demand for lawyers to assist in the sale and purchase of land and agricultural crops and to collect debts, draft wills and contracts, defend petty crimes, and address the range of issues involved in maritime commerce. Consider a farmer in Virginia shipping cotton to a factory in New England. A lawyer was required to draw up a contract that addressed issues such as whether the seller would still be paid if the ship transporting the cotton sank in transit, if the shipment were delayed, or if the cotton did not meet the expected quality. A lawyer would be needed to go to court in the event that the buyer neglected to pay. Another area of legal specialization developed after insurance companies offered to insure goods shipped at sea against loss or damage. Lawyers also began running for local office and became increasingly prominent in politics (Hurst 1950: 295–300).

Practicing lawyers wanted to limit access to the profession. In 1731, New York City granted seven lawyers a monopoly over the practice of law, and in 1756, the seven lawyers agreed that they would accept only their own sons as apprentices for the next fourteen years. In Rhode Island, eight lawyers signed a compact in which they agreed not to compete with one another over the fees that they charged. An attempt also was made in some states to distinguish barristers from solicitors and to create an elite category of practitioner (L. Friedman 2005: 58–59).

These attempts to limit the number of lawyers and to distinguish barristers from solicitors proved unsuccessful. States responded by passing legislation to ensure the legal profession remained open to both rich and poor. In 1851, the Indiana Constitution was amended to declare that "every person of good moral character . . . shall be entitled to admission of practice of law in all courts of justice." Law in the United States, in contrast to England, was thought of as a democratic profession open to the sons of wealthy farmers and merchants as well as to individuals from modest backgrounds. Between 1740 and 1840, the number of lawyers in Massachusetts increased ten times in proportion to the population. By 1860, only eleven of thirty-nine jurisdictions required a minimum period of preparation before taking the bar exam. Abraham Lincoln advised young people seeking to enter the law that the "cheapest, quickest and best way" into the legal profession was to apprentice, get a license, and keep reading and learning the law (L. Friedman 2005: 58, 463).

In the 1840s, law firms (groups of lawyers who practice law together) began to be established in most major cities. The firms concentrated their practice on the drafting of documents, debt collection, and maritime law and rarely appeared in court. The vision of the lawyer in the popular imagination during this era nonetheless remained the romantic "country lawyer" who, like Abraham Lincoln, "rode the circuit" from one county seat to another county seat. Lincoln and other lawyers followed a judge as he traveled from one town to another and acquired clients as they traveled the territory within the judge's jurisdiction. There was little time for research, and these trial lawyers were skilled orators who possessed the ability to think on their feet in the courtroom (L. Friedman 2005: 231–233).

It is important to note that lawyers throughout the nineteenth century were engaged in the struggle over slavery. Southern courts regularly litigated questions relating to the sale of slaves, including whether a "buyer" had a right to return a slave who later was found to suffer from a physical disability or whether the "buyer" or "seller" was to absorb the economic loss of a slave who committed suicide while in transit. A case also might involve a suit for damages by the owner of a slave who claimed that the slave had been mistreated and injured by an individual who had rented the slave for work on his farm. Families often litigated for years over the ownership of slaves who had not been accounted for in the will of a deceased parent. Creditors brought suit to claim ownership of slaves in payment of debts owed by their owner. Criminal codes demanded strict obedience from slaves and punished whites who challenged the institution of slavery (Stamp 1956: 192–236). A number of idealistic lawyers challenged the institution of slavery in various states and represented fugitive slaves who managed to escape to other states and slaves who mutinied and seized control of slave ships (Cover 1975).

In summary, the early American settlers distrusted and disliked lawyers. This negative view of lawyers was based primarily on the view that lawyers were part of the English elite and were antagonistic to the interests of working people. The role of lawyers in forming the new American Republic and the involvement of lawyers in the expanding American economy led to the realization that lawyers were necessary to the success of the United States. The legal profession in America, in contrast to that in England, was open to both rich and poor.

The Middle Years

In 1850, there were almost 22,000 lawyers in the United States. By 1880, the number of lawyers almost had tripled, and twenty years later, the number of lawyers in the country had reached 114,000. The profession continued to be broadly based and attracted the sons and occasional daughters of the small businessperson, farmer, government employee, and office worker (L. Friedman 2005: 484; K. Hall 1989: 216).

In the twentieth century, a number of public universities established law schools. A formal legal education was viewed as offering a broader introduction to the law than an apprenticeship and appealed to young people who did not want to spend several years under the thumb of an established attorney. There also were more individuals seeking apprenticeships than there were available opportunities. The introduction of the law school further democratized the legal profession by breaking the hold of the practicing bar on who could obtain an apprenticeship and obtain the necessary experience to practice law (L. Friedman 2005: 463–465).

The development of the typewriter and other technological devices meant large numbers of apprentices were no longer needed to copy documents in longhand. Apprentices were replaced by a pool of young women who were employed as typists and stenographers (L. Friedman 2005: 464).

The number of law schools increased from 15 in 1850 to 102 in 1900. In 1850, twelve states had at least one law school; in 1900, thirty-three states had law schools. The largest law program was at the University of Michigan, which expanded from 1,611 students in 1870 to 7,600 students in 1894. Michigan took the unprecedented step of recruiting students from across the country. In 1869, Howard University was founded and grew to be the most prominent of the twelve African American law schools (L. Friedman 2005: 464).

Enrollment in a law program generally did not require any previous education. In the twentieth century, schools desiring to set themselves apart began to require one or two years of undergraduate education. The number of years required to receive a law degree increased from one year in 1850 to two years at the turn of the century. Harvard instituted a three-year program that gradually became the standard period of study. Most law instructors were practicing lawyers and judges. Harvard was the first school to introduce a full-time law faculty. Examinations tended to be based on rote memorization of the material (L. Friedman 2005: 464–465).

The teaching of law was revolutionized with the appointment of Christopher Columbus Langdell as dean and professor at Harvard Law School. Students admitted to Harvard were required to possess an undergraduate degree or to pass a demanding entrance exam and were expected to demonstrate a knowledge of either French or Latin. The course of study was extended in 1876 to three years. Langdell divided the curriculum into a series of discrete courses carrying different credit hours, which were to be taken in a defined order. Students were required to pass a final exam at the end of the year to matriculate to the next year of study (L. Friedman 2005: 468).

Langdell's long-lasting contribution was his replacement of the textbook with the **casebook**. The instructor no longer stood in front of the class and lectured out of a textbook written by one of the leading legal commentators. The casebook contained a collection of carefully selected cases that reflected what Langdell viewed as the "correct" legal rule. The casebook did not contain essays, comments, or text. The teacher was the leader who, through the **Socratic method** of question and answer, helped students uncover the legal rules in each case. Langdell viewed law as a "science." The cases were the laboratory that enabled the teacher and the students to discover through the exercise of "human wisdom the legal principles which had evolved over the course of years."

PHOTO 4.2 Christopher Columbus Langdell (1826–1906) was appointed dean of Harvard Law School in 1870. Langdell's development of the casebook and Socratic method of instruction revolutionized legal education in the United States.

Langdell famously observed that law is a science and that all the materials of that science are contained in the casebook. The Harvard system also was distinguished by the fact that law was viewed as a single set of rules and principles that were applied in a uniform fashion regardless of the city or state in which the judge presided. Critics complained Langdell's approach overlooked that law was the product of social forces and politics and was not a predictable series of equations. Other observers claimed the "baby had been thrown out with the bath water." Lawyers required an introduction to document drafting, contract negotiation, and court practice, and the case method disregarded the "nuts and bolts" of legal practice and overlooked the interpersonal skills that are so vital to lawyer–client relationships (L. Friedman 2005: 468; Hurst 1950: 165–170).

Langdell also replaced part-time instructors with full-time faculty members who were academic researchers rather than practitioners. In 1873, Langdell shocked the legal world when he hired James Barr Ames to the faculty despite the fact that Ames had no experience in the practice of law. Other law schools followed the lead of Harvard. The

Socratic method became the standard approach to the teaching of law, and Harvard law graduates were hired by law schools across the country. Law now took its place alongside other academic disciplines as a specialized and demanding course of study that could be mastered only through several years of intense study. The notion that law was an academic discipline rather than a practical trade was encouraged by the establishment of the *Harvard Law Review* in 1887 and the *Yale Law Journal* in 1891 and by the development of casebooks in various fields of study (L. Friedman 2005: 473–475).

The other important development was the proliferation of night schools. Jerome Corsi writes that after Harvard began requiring a college degree for admission to its law school and other elite schools began requiring two years of prior education, attendance at law schools was placed out of reach for the working class and immigrants (Corsi 1984: 56). By 1900, there were twenty evening programs and seventy-seven day programs, and the University of Minnesota and four other schools offered both day and night legal education. The night schools were proudly practical and opened the door of the legal profession to the working class, to Catholics and Jews, and to new immigrant groups from Poland, Italy, Ireland, and eastern Europe. Conventional day programs often placed quotas on the admission of these groups (L. Friedman 2005: 474).

In 1905, one-third of law students attended a night program. In Boston, between 1900 and 1910, the number of lawyers increased by 35 percent, and the number of foreign-born lawyers increased by 77 percent. This rapid rate of growth in the number of foreign-born lawyers continued into the next decade in Chicago, Philadelphia, St. Louis, and other cities (Auerbach 1976: 95–97).

The established bar felt threatened by the expansion of law graduates, and many established lawyers feared the quality of the legal profession would be undermined by these newly minted ethnic lawyers. There undoubtedly was a measure of anti-immigrant bias motivating those lawyers who urged that standards for admission to law school should be raised to impede the movement of individuals from the "grocery-counters" to "gentlemen of the bar." Several states repealed their "diploma privilege," a policy that granted admission to the bar to any graduate of a local law school. States began to require applicants to pass a bar exam as a condition for being admitted to practice law. In an effort to control the quality of legal education, the law schools formed the Association of American Law Schools (AALS), which, in 1921, agreed to cooperate with the American Bar Association in accrediting law schools. The graduates of unaccredited schools now would be required to overcome various barriers before taking the bar exam (L. Friedman 2005: 474).

Jerold Auerbach argues that the accreditation process was an attempt to preserve "elite privilege" and to limit the continuing entry of immigrants into the legal profession (Auerbach 1976: 100, 107–114). Only eighteen of the ninety-four law programs accredited in 1936 offered both a day and a night program, and only one night school was accredited (Hurst 1950: 274).

An equally controversial question was whether access to a legal license and the ability to practice law should be strictly regulated and restricted. As we previously noted, prior to the Civil War, entry to the practice of law was relatively unregulated. Following the war, there was a movement toward regulating both the legal and the medical professions, and by 1914, admission to the legal profession had been centralized in a state board of examiners in virtually every state and more stringent standards had been introduced (Hurst 1950: 280).

The case method of instruction highlighted the importance of legal decisions, and the California Constitution proclaimed that in a democracy, the state supreme court should provide written decisions that could be examined by the public. As the country expanded, the number of published volumes of state and national reports grew from eighteen volumes in 1810 to eight thousand volumes one hundred years later. The first system of organizing reports by topic was introduced in 1879. There was a corresponding expansion of supplementary texts analyzing and discussing these legal decisions (L. Friedman 2005: 475–482).

The heart of the law remained the solo practitioner and small firm lawyer whose practice addressed the "bread and butter" practical problems confronting the average individual. This work included divorces, real estate, foreclosure of mortgages, and collecting debts owed to an individual or to a small business. The most admired lawyers in the nineteenth century were the "lawyer statesmen" who argued important cases before the courts, moved in and out of the political arena, and exhibited a commitment to public service.

The model was Daniel Webster, who argued before the Supreme Court and served as a member of the House of Representatives, a senator from Massachusetts, and secretary of state before his death in 1852 (Kronman 1993). The lawyer-statesman continued to make a mark in the twentieth century. A number of presidents after 1850 were lawyers, including James Buchanan, Abraham Lincoln, Chester A. Arthur, James Garfield, and Grover Cleveland. Two-thirds of senators and roughly one-half of the House of Representatives were trained as lawyers. At any given time, between half and two-thirds of state governors were lawyers (L. Friedman 2005: 494; Hurst 1950: 352).

The great power and prestige in the legal profession was slowly shifting to the Wall Street lawyer as the country witnessed the continued expansion of the railroad and industry and commerce. Kermit Hall quotes an 1893 article from *American Lawyer* that the primary work of the lawyer was "transferred from the court house to the office. Litigation has declined and counsel work has become the leading feature of practice." Hall records that although large firms were a relatively "insignificant" percentage of the profession, they were growing at a wild and rapid rate, and attorneys who were familiar with the world of business and commerce had become the model to be emulated by other lawyers (K. Hall 1989: 212–213). These lawyers worked behind the scenes and drafted documents and negotiated contracts rather than appearing in court. They were viewed by their clients as "wise men" who were consulted on business decisions and were invited to serve on corporate boards of directors. Law firms rapidly expanded to meet the need for shipping contracts between the railroads and farmers and factories, the purchase of land and rights of way across land, the issuance of corporate stock to raise money, loans to purchase equipment, personal injury suits against corporate clients, and the drafting of insurance agreements.

Major cities across the country witnessed the development of two or three large firms that serviced the needs of corporate America. A second significant development was the hiring of in-house corporate lawyers. The railroads and insurance companies employed lawyers to advise them and to monitor the work of the firms. Another new trend was the hiring of lawyers by state and local governments to draft and enforce administrative regulations in areas such as housing and fire codes and to defend against lawsuits. In 1895, the Law Department of New York City had become the largest law office in the United States (L. Friedman 2005: 486–487, 495).

The literature on lawyers often portrays the profession as a unified group that pursues the self-interest of lawyers. As previously discussed, lawyers joined together to restrict access to the legal profession by requiring individuals to attend law schools, accrediting law schools, and introducing strict licensing standards.

The twentieth century witnessed the beginning of a "stratified" legal profession in which the lawyers in elite corporate law firms had a different background and inhabited a different world than the small-town solo practitioner. In 1927, John Foster Dulles rose to become head of the famous

Cravath law firm and later served as secretary of state under President Dwight David Eisenhower. He recounted that, despite his undergraduate degree from Princeton and year at the Sorbonne in Paris, his law degree from a non–Ivy League law school was a hindrance and he was hired by the Cravath law firm only because of his grandfather's personal connections with one of the founding figures of the firm (Corsi 1984: 56–57).

The remainder of the chapter provides a detailed description of American lawyers. The next section provides a sketch of the contemporary American legal profession.

■ THE CONTEMPORARY LEGAL PROFESSION

There are roughly 1.45 million lawyers in the United States, or 1 lawyer for every 265 persons. The number of lawyers has increased over seven times in the past sixty years. You can appreciate the increase in the legal profession by considering that in 1991 there were roughly 800,000 lawyers in the United States. The number of lawyers per capita has increased from 1 in every 627 individuals in 1960 to 1 in every 265 persons, according to the latest statistics (Barkan 2009: 246). The growth in the number of lawyers is due primarily to the number of women entering the legal profession. Nationally, there are roughly 40 lawyers per 10,000 population (M. Kelly 2007: 351). Some additional statistical data drawn from the latest survey conducted by the American Bar Association are listed in Table 4.2. Keep this snapshot of the legal profession in mind as you continue to read the chapter.

Table 4.2 ■ The Legal Profession

Licensed lawyers	1,300,705 (eligible to practice law)
Gender	The legal profession is predominantly male. Roughly 65 percent of lawyers are men.
Race and ethnicity	The legal profession is *predominantly Caucasian*. Approximately 89 percent of lawyers are white (not Hispanic), 5 percent are African American, 4 percent are Hispanic, 3 percent are Asian American, less than 1 percent are Native Hawaiian or Pacific Islander, and less than 1 percent are Native American.
Age	Roughly a quarter of lawyers are between the ages of 35 and 44, and roughly 60 percent are over the age of 45.
Practice area	Roughly three-quarters of lawyers are in private practice, and the remainder are divided between government and private industry, the judiciary, and education or are retired.
Solo practitioners	Well over half of the legal profession in private practice are solo practitioners or work in firms of between two and five lawyers. An estimated 16 percent of lawyers practice in firms of over one hundred lawyers.
Location	Lawyers live where there is legal business. Washington, D.C., has almost 277 lawyers per 10,000 residents, and New York has 20.4 lawyers for every 10,000 residents. Other states with the most lawyers per capita include Massachusetts (14.5), Illinois (14.0), Colorado (13.0), Connecticut (12.3), Georgia (12.0), Pennsylvania (11.9), and Florida (11.7). On the opposite side of the scale, Iowa (6.2), Idaho (6.1), Kansas (5.8), South Dakota (5.8), Arkansas (5.3), and North Dakota (4.4) have the lowest number of lawyers per capita.

Source: American Bar Association. Lawyer Demographics 2015.

We next discuss the American Bar Association, which is the national legal organization of lawyers in the United States. The trend has been for the association to broaden its membership by encompassing a larger and more diverse portion of the legal profession and to serve as an organization that unapologetically protects the interests of the legal profession.

The American Bar Association

The late nineteenth century witnessed the development of associations of engineers, doctors, and educators as well as lawyers. The licensing of lawyers was controlled by state legislatures. Lawyers began to band together to demand a voice in the rules regulating their livelihood. Their central concern was to tighten entry into the practice of law and to limit competition. We already have seen that between 1870 and 1890, the requirements for practicing law were tightened with a written exam replacing the oral examination (K. Hall 1989: 211–215).

Historians trace the beginning of the bar association to 1870 in New York City. The association proclaimed that the integrity of the legal system was one of its major goals.

New York lawyers were concerned the rampant corruption among politicians would lead to the bribery of judges and lawyers and to a loss of respect for the legal profession and for the system of justice. The culture of corruption ultimately might lead businesses to leave the city, which would affect the livelihood of lawyers.

In 1878, the **American Bar Association** (ABA) held its first meeting. Simeon E. Baldwin, a judge on the Connecticut Supreme Court, and Francis Rawle, a member of a prominent Philadelphia family, invited one hundred attorneys to the upscale New York resort of Saratoga Springs. This was a decidedly elite group of lawyers who had little interest in reaching out to the vast number of sixty thousand lawyers in the country. The ABA Charter proclaimed that the organization's purpose was to improve the administration of justice, provide for a uniform approach to the law in the various states, uphold the honor of the legal profession, and encourage friendly relations between lawyers (K. Hall 1989: 215).

The ABA in the early years was an exclusionary organization intent on limiting access to the profession by immigrants and religious and racial minorities. In 1909, the ABA called for the exclusion of "aliens" from the practice of law. The organization's advocacy of tighter standards for entry into the state bar exams, a mandatory minimum of study prior to taking the bar, higher standards for being a licensed attorney, and the drafting of a code of ethics (in 1908) was intended to pressure states into raising the standards regulating the profession. These "reforms" made it more difficult for immigrants and minorities to be admitted to the practice of law (K. Hall 1989: 257–258).

The ABA remained an all-white-male organization until 1918 when the first woman was admitted (in 1995, Roberta Cooper Ramo became the ABA's first female president, and in 2016, the ABA elected the organization's seventh woman president, Linda A. Klein). The exclusion of African Americans led African American attorneys to establish the National Bar Association in 1925.

The ABA inspired the growth of local and state bar associations, and by 1925, there was an organization of lawyers in every state and territory. By 1930, more than 1,100 local and state bar associations had been established. These local bar associations were stronger and more vibrant than the ABA because they opened membership to all lawyers. The ABA started to experience a decline in influence and prestige and as a result began to reverse course and to open its membership to lawyers across the country. In 1880, the ABA had 552 members or 0.9 percent of the lawyers in the United States. In 1912, the ABA took steps to broaden its base of support, and by 1940, its membership had reached 31,000 or 17 percent of all lawyers (Hurst 1950: 288–289).

In truth, most lawyers had been suspicious of the ABA. In the early twentieth century, small-town lawyers and solo practitioners viewed their legal business as threatened by collection agencies and banks and other organizations that were taking work from attorneys. A collection agency, for example, could pursue debtors more efficiently than could lawyers. The ABA's call for raising standards for access to the practice of law and for codes of ethics was viewed as yet another attack on the small-town practitioner by corporate elites. Magali Sarfatti Larson writes that small-town lawyers changed their viewpoint and flocked to the ABA because of the organization's aggressive support for America's war effort in World War I and the growing fear that immigrants and ethnic and religious minorities would invade the legal profession (Larson 1977: 174–175).

Membership in state bar associations also expanded because of *bar integration.* Bar integration requires that all lawyers in a state join the local bar association. The drive for integration was based on the consideration that an integrated bar could collect dues from all lawyers within the state and speak with a unified and powerful voice on behalf of the legal profession. An integrated bar association also would make it easier for the state bar to supervise and to monitor the ethical conduct of all lawyers within the state. North Dakota, Alabama, Idaho, and New Mexico adopted integrated bars in the early 1920s, and by 1960, roughly thirty states and the District of Columbia had integrated bars (K. Hall 1989: 259). According to Jerold Auerbach, the move toward integration was resisted in those states in which corporate lawyers feared the domination of lawyers from immigrant backgrounds (Auerbach 1976: 118–120).

It is fair to say that in the early twentieth century, the ABA reflected the views of conservative lawyers. In 1936, lawyers unhappy with the ABA's opposition to President Franklin Delano Roosevelt's New Deal reforms formed the left-wing National Lawyers Guild (NLG). Allegations that the NLG was dominated by communists and disloyal Americans led to members fleeing the NLG, and the organization exists today as a small and active group of politically progressive lawyers (K. Hall 1989: 260).

The contemporary ABA, although it continues to be dominated by conservative lawyers, has endorsed both conservative and liberal policies and has taken controversial positions such as calling for a moratorium on capital punishment. The membership includes more than four hundred thousand lawyers, which constitutes over one-third of lawyers in the United States, and is one of the largest professional membership organizations in the country. The internal structure of the ABA today has a great degree of internal democracy and no longer is administered by a small elite. The president of the ABA remains the public face of the organization, although the authority to take positions on public policy issues is vested in the House of Delegates, which includes representatives from local and state bar associations. The Board of Governors administers the organization. More than two thousand separate sections, divisions, and committees encompass every conceivable area of legal practice and demographic group within the legal profession.

The ABA today is concerned with helping improve the practice of law rather than with restricting access to the legal profession. The organization has four primary purposes: assisting members in law office management (e.g., technology), improving professionalism (e.g., continuing education and ethical enforcement), increasing diversity within the profession, and advancing the rule of law (e.g., public education and law reform).

The ABA has not entirely succeeded in shaking its elitist orientation. A survey of Chicago lawyers finds that Protestant graduates of elite schools who practice law in large firms are more likely to be members of the ABA than are solo practitioners and lawyers who practice in smaller firms. On the other hand, solo practitioners and lawyers in smaller firms are more likely than lawyers in large firms to be active and energetic members of specialized legal organizations in areas such as criminal law or immigration law and in organizations of lawyers of various religious, ethnic, or racial backgrounds (Heinz, Nelson, Sandefur, and Laumann 2005: 54–56).

An important function of the ABA since the 1950s has been to appoint a committee of prominent lawyers to evaluate the U.S. president's federal judicial nominees as either "unqualified," "qualified," or "highly qualified." The ABA traditionally has reported its findings to the Senate Judiciary Committee. President George W. Bush announced that because of the ABA's liberal orientation and hostility toward conservative nominees, he no longer would include the ABA in the selection process. This decision was reversed by President Barack Obama (Baum 2013: 99). President Trump announced that he would not consult the ABA on judicial appointments (Liptak 2017b).

The ABA and other associations of lawyers actively lobby the government to shape legal policy. Trial lawyers have opposed limits on damages a court can award for "pain and suffering" resulting from medical negligence and personal injuries. Trial lawyers contributed more money than any other group to political candidates in the 2008 campaign. A number of large law firms contributed close to $2 million. The trend for lawyers and law firms to heavily donate to political campaigns continued in the 2012 presidential election. President Barack Obama received over $27.5 million, and Mitt Romney received over $14.2 million. In 2016, lawyers and law firms continued to be active in the presidential campaign, contributing $36.4 million to Hillary Clinton and $942,000 to Donald Trump. This amounted to 5.2 percent of Clinton's total financial contributions and 3.4 percent of Donald Trump's financial contributions. Five unsuccessful Republican and Democratic candidates received more money from the legal profession than Donald Trump (Center for Responsive Politics n.d.).

In 2016, the legal profession hired 319 lobbyists and spent nearly $15 million in an effort to advance the interests of the legal profession. These issues ranged from criminal justice reform to supporting legal assistance to the indigent to immigration and tort reform to intellectual property rights over material posted on the Internet. It must be kept in mind that on some issues, lawyers are divided. Trial lawyers, for example, are opposed to the limits on pain and suffering for damages that have been adopted in several states, a policy that is favored by large firms that represent corporate clients (Center for Responsive Politics n.d.).

Another continuing focus of associations of lawyers has been lobbying for laws that prohibit the unauthorized practice of law (UPL). Lawyers have argued that people require protection against online legal forms and computer software for divorces or wills, which may lead to people improperly executing legal documents. Opposition to UPL is motivated primarily by a desire to protect lawyers from competition from non-lawyers in areas such as drafting wills and preparing documents for house sales (Hurst 1950: 318–322).

Although she is a law professor, Deborah Rhode argues that the prohibition on UPL is costing the public money and that there is no reason that paralegals or specialized professionals should not be permitted to complete routine forms in divorce, landlord–tenant disputes, bankruptcy, and immigration (Rhode 2000: 136).

The next sections discuss the "stratified legal profession" in which the experience and interests of solo practitioners and lawyers in small firms differ significantly from the experience and interests of lawyers in large firms.

Solo Practitioners and Small Firm Lawyers

There is a large body of research on **solo practitioners** and small firm lawyers (e.g., five or fewer lawyers). These lawyers embody the American spirit of independent professionals. The scholarly research has yielded several important insights:

Hierarchy. The American legal profession is a pyramid in which there is a large gap in income and lifestyle between the corporate attorneys in law firms and the solo practitioners and small firm lawyers at the bottom of the hierarchy.

Integration. There is little contact or connection between corporate lawyers and the lawyers at the bottom of the hierarchy.

Quality of legal representation. There is some indication that clients represented by solo practitioners may receive less skilled representation than the corporate interests represented by large firms.

Ethics. Research indicates that solo practitioners and lawyers in small firms may be more likely than corporate lawyers to disregard ethical codes of professional conduct.

Chicago with a rich history of sociological research has been the site of a number of studies of the legal profession. In 1959, Dan C. Lortie, in articles based on his doctoral dissertation at the University of Chicago, identified that the career paths of lawyers were strongly determined by the law school they attended. Students who attended the elite private law schools of the University of Chicago and Northwestern University tended to be hired at law firms (58 percent of graduates) while graduates of two private proprietary institutions (owned by a single individual or group of individuals) that offered a part-time legal curriculum taught by practitioners tended to pursue careers as solo practitioners (46 percent of graduates). Graduates of Chicago's two Catholic law schools were less likely to be hired into firms than were graduates of Chicago and Northwestern (32 percent) and less likely than graduates of the two part-time programs to pursue careers as solo practitioners (36 percent).

The graduates of Chicago and Northwestern were more likely to be Protestants from a higher socioeconomic background than the graduates of the other four schools and were more likely to have an undergraduate bachelor's degree. They were hired into firms that were larger and more prestigious than the firms that hired graduates of the four competing law programs. Chicago and Northwestern graduates in law firms worked in the downtown Chicago loop under the supervision of senior lawyers in cases involving large and powerful corporate interests. This contrasted with solo practitioners, who worked in neighborhood offices on small cases involving individual problems such as divorce, personal injury, the purchase of homes, and minor criminal matters. The significance of Lortie's early study is that the graduates of the two elite programs were hired into firms with the prospect of progressing to the rank of a well-paid partner. In contrast, the graduates of the two part-time programs relied on their neighborhood and religious and ethnic connections to make ends meet.

The stratified nature of the Chicago legal profession was confirmed by Jerome E. Carlin in another important early work (Lortie 1959). Carlin's *Lawyers on Their Own* reports on his study of more than ninety solo practitioners in Chicago. In the late 1950s and early 1960s, solo practitioners accounted for roughly 50 percent of the close to twelve thousand lawyers in Chicago. Carlin observed that, although the independent and virtuous solo practitioner who tells truth to power was the popular image of a lawyer, these practitioners, in fact, lived professional lives of "quiet desperation."

First, the lawyers in Carlin's study generally were the sons of uneducated eastern European immigrants who passionately pursued the American Dream. Most of the lawyers in Carlin's study decided to study law after having unsuccessfully pursued a career in engineering, medicine, pharmacy, or dentistry. These individuals, like their parents, were animated by the American Dream. Two-thirds studied law in the evening at one of Chicago's Catholic law schools or at one of the local law schools that at the time accepted almost every applicant. Most of the solo practitioners passed the bar following several attempts. These young lawyers started out working for another lawyer or small firm while building their own practice (Carlin 1962: 1–23).

Carlin found that the working life of solo practitioners is radically different from the working life of lawyers in large firms. Solo practitioners operate in what Carlin terms an "invisible market" in which they are continually scrambling to attract clients. Their practice is like a jigsaw puzzle in which they generate an income by piecing together small cases from a broad range of the law. The low-level practitioners interviewed by Carlin were engaged in a legal rat race in which they employed a limited range of legal skills and knowledge. They might slightly modify a standard form for a landlord leasing out a storefront or apartment, draft a simple will, file the necessary papers for an individual opening a local restaurant, or draft a letter for a business demanding payment of a bill. Financial pressures forced them to rapidly settle personal injury cases, persuade defendants to plead guilty, and encourage divorcing couples to settle their disputes as quickly as possible (Carlin 1962: 41–103).

The solo practitioners in Carlin's study had very few regular clients and were in constant competition with other lawyers for clients. A solo practitioner might one day handle a divorce and the next day find him- or herself handling a drunk driving charge and two days later file a personal injury claim. The most successful solo practitioners maintained contacts with a broad range of individuals who referred clients to them, including police officers, accountants, doctors, bail bondsmen, and other lawyers. They were able to expedite a hearing on reducing a homeowner's property tax or a hearing on a claim for workers compensation through their contacts with court clerks and secretaries. Ethical concerns were raised when referral sources and clerks and secretaries expected compensation in return for their help (Carlin 1962: 157–205).

Carlin finds that most of the lawyers in his study were stuck at the bottom of the profession and rarely were able to obtain employment with a large firm. They lived in a world in which they were isolated from "higher level lawyers." Solo practitioners and lawyers in small firms rarely found themselves in a case in which the opposing attorney was a member of a large firm, and they generally did not participate in local bar associations or lawyers' organizations, which were dominated by higher-status lawyers. Most of the solo practitioners that Carlin interviewed hoped to attract clients through their involvement in ethnic organizations or neighborhood associations (Carlin 1962: 169).

Solo practitioners and small firm lawyers, according to Carlin, were the "bottom feeders" of the legal profession and frequently were "dissatisfied, disappointed, resentful," and "angry" (Carlin 1962: 169). They compensated for their low status by claiming that they valued their independence and that, in contrast to lawyers in large firms, they "practiced real law" and directly interacted with clients, tried cases, and negotiated settlements (184–200). The lawyers in Carlin's study in moments of honesty admitted that they viewed themselves as occupying a "pariah position in a highly stratified professional community" and believed that they were considered by other lawyers to be shouldering the "dirty work" of the profession (177, 181). Law for these attorneys was viewed as a business rather than a profession in which connections rather than talent were the key to success (192–193).

A particular cause of complaint by the solo practitioners in Carlin's Chicago study was that the actions required to maintain their practice frequently were at odds with the code of professional conduct. They believed that they were unfairly criticized by corporate lawyers for the occasional monetary "tip" or "present" they gave a clerk who moved their case up on the courtroom calendar (Carlin 1962: 155–164). Solo practitioners and small firm lawyers in one study defended "ambulance chasing," the practice of approaching accident victims in person or through a paid "runner" and offering to represent them in court. Lawyers went so far as to monitor police radio communications and rush to the scene of accidents. The attorney typically offered to take the personal injury case without payment in return for one-third of the damages awarded in the case. Solo lawyers and small firm lawyers defended *contingent fees* as a way of providing legal representation to individuals who otherwise could not afford to hire a lawyer. Corporate lawyers condemned "ambulance chasing" as beneath the dignity of the legal profession and pointed out that "stirring up litigation" was contrary to the code of legal ethics. Lawyers working on a contingent fee had an incentive to reach a quick settlement rather than take a case for trial. There was little left for the client after paying expenses and the contingent fee to the lawyer (Reichstein 1965).

The question is whether Carlin's relatively small sample accurately described solo practitioners in Chicago and whether his findings may be generalized to other cities (A. Sutherland 1963). In 1963, Jack Ladinsky published a study of 100 solo practitioners and 107 lawyers from firms of more than ten persons; his results confirmed Carlin's finding in virtually every aspect. He described a vicious cycle in which working-class kids from ethnic backgrounds lacked the money for tuition and were forced to work to attend law school at night. These part-time law graduates found that they lacked the training, social connections, and credentials to land a job with a large law firm. Their only option was to work as solo practitioners and to take care of what they described as the "dirty work" of the legal profession. They barely made enough to live on and generated business through family, friends, neighbors, and membership in organizations (Ladinsky 1963).

Carlin returned to the world of small practitioners in his 1966 study of solo practitioners in New York City (Carlin 1966: xxii). Carlin responded to the criticism that he had failed to support his earlier work with objective evidence (Frey 1963) by exhaustively compiling statistical evidence on legal practitioners in New York City. Carlin found that New York had the same "stratified legal profession" he earlier had found in Chicago and in Detroit. The "old school" Protestant law firms were at the top of the legal pyramid, and the small firms and solo practitioners were at the bottom (Carlin 1966: 41–65).

Carlin surveyed 801 lawyers in his New York study and concluded that solo and small firm lawyers were significantly more likely than lawyers in corporate firms to engage in unethical conduct despite the fact they recognized that the rules they violated were important for maintaining public respect for the legal profession. These violations included kickbacks for client referrals, tolerating a client's bribe of a government official in return for dropping a tax violation, and agreeing with a married couple to fabricate grounds for divorce. Carlin was sympathetic to solo practitioners and recognized that they functioned on an economic shoestring and faced pressure from clients who wanted their problems solved and from government officials who expected a bribe in return for bending the rules (Carlin 1966: 165–182).

A follow-up study of New York solo practitioners forty years later found that new lawyers entering into solo practice or small firm practice had learned from their mentors that, when there was a clash between ethical norms and making money, making money came first. One young lawyer reported that his mentors had told him to walk out of the room and overlook the fact that his client had paid cash under the table in return for the seller signing a contract to sell the lawyer's client a desirable piece of real estate (Levin 2004).

Carlin and Ladinsky challenge the notion of a unified legal profession and instead find that solo practitioners and most lawyers in small firms work in a separate world from that of lawyers in large firms. Their studies stand as an indictment of a legal profession in which the best trained, most technically skilled, and ethically most responsible lawyers represent the upper reaches of business and society while the "least competent, least well-trained, and least ethical lawyers" represent small businesses and the working class. The result is that the "most helpless clients who most need protection are least likely to get it" (Carlin 1966: 177).

Does Carlin and Ladinsky's claim of a stratified bar stand the test of time? A comprehensive survey in 1975 of the Chicago legal profession found the profession was divided into two "hemispheres" and that the occupants of these two spheres rarely "cross the equator" (Heinz and Laumann 1994). The lawyers in these two "hemispheres" differ in social origin, prestige of the law schools they attended, professional history, membership in legal organizations, and political views and values. Solo practitioners and small firm lawyers represented individuals, whereas large firms represented corporate interests (129–130). A similar study conducted in 1995 indicated that Chicago lawyers continued to occupy two hemispheres divided by social origin, education, the class of clients, type of work, and income (Heinz et al. 2005: 29–73). The most recent Chicago survey finds a "greater presence of women and minorities in lower-status practice settings who to some extent have taken [the] place of Catholics and Jews at the economic bottom of the legal profession" (72).

We should be cautious in generalizing Carlin's fairly critical view of solo practitioners to all solo practitioners and small firm lawyers. An important study of divorce lawyers in Maine and New Hampshire found that these lawyers are divided between lawyers who specialize in divorce and "generalist" lawyers who only occasionally are involved in divorce work. The "specialists" consider themselves part of what the authors of the study term a "community of practice" with other divorce lawyers. The lawyers in this "community of practice" take pride in their professional approach to divorce law. These "specialist" lawyers adopt a legal approach to issues such as child custody and the division of marital property and place the welfare of the client before the temptation to quickly settle a case. It is worth noting that a significant percentage of the "specialist lawyers" in the study were women who placed a priority on providing emotional support to their clients, most of whom were middle-class females (Mather, McEwen, and Maiman 2001).

A study of solo practitioners and small firm lawyers who specialize in immigration also found these lawyers maintained a strong sense of belonging to a "community of practice" (Levin 2009).

On the other hand, the authors of the study of divorce lawyers found that attorneys who were part of the "old boys network" of solo practitioners who handled the occasional divorce had a very different idea of what constituted a "reasonable" approach to divorce. The "old boys" could not afford to spend more than a few hours on a divorce case and sought quick settlements and asked their predominantly working-class clients to negotiate their own agreements on issues such as child custody and child visitation. These solo practitioners were critical of the specialists who made "a mountain out of a mole hill" and turned a divorce into a "federal case" (Mather et al. 2001).

Carroll Seron, in her important 1996 study, found that solo practitioners and small firm lawyers confront the continuing challenges of attracting business, satisfying client demands, and administering their offices. They echoed the lawyers in Carlin's study in complaining their professional lives often were lonely and full of stress from "trying to be in two places at once" and felt disrespected by their peers. The lawyers in Seron's study, however, did not share the dark and depressed view of the lawyers in Carlin's study. They believed the advantages of solo and small firm practice outweighed the disadvantages and viewed themselves as making a positive contribution to their clients. These lawyers, like the divorce lawyers we previously discussed, prided themselves on their independence and on their professional approach to the practice of law. Seron concludes none of the lawyers she interviewed would sacrifice the interests of their clients in order to rapidly dispose of a case and collect a fee (Seron 1996).

Jerry Van Hoy, in his interviews with solo practitioners in Chicago, also found that these lawyers believed that they were providing clients a valuable service and that the solo practitioners were critical of the "high turnover," "mass production," and lack of attention to the individual problems of clients in newly established "corporate franchise law firms" (Van Hoy 1997: 77–85).

Seron also discovered that a number of women found that solo practice enabled them to balance the demands of work and the demands of family (Seron 1996). We should note that lawyers in small towns tend to be solo practitioners or members of small firms and that these lawyers enjoy considerable prestige and respect. Small-town lawyers, of necessity, practice in a number of areas of the law and tend to represent their friends and neighbors, and their ability to attract clients depends on their integrity, professionalism, and reputation (Landon 1990).

What can we conclude about solo practitioners and lawyers in small firms? We have seen that these lawyers in the words of John Conley are under constant pressure to attract clients and to turn over their caseload. Despite enjoying a measure of independence and flexibility in their schedule, these lawyers express a desire to confer with other lawyers and complain their professional lives are isolated and lonely. Solo practitioners and lawyers in small firms continue to view themselves as at the "bottom of the barrel" of legal practice and believe that they are unfairly labeled as unethical and unprofessional (Conley 2004: 1995).

Carlin's views of solo practitioners and small firm lawyers have been somewhat modified by recent studies. A number of solo practitioners and small firm lawyers now specialize in particular areas of the law rather than offer a full range of legal services. These "specialist" lawyers pride themselves on maintaining a significant degree of independence, expertise, and professionalism and view themselves as making an important contribution to their clients (Heinz et al. 2005: 35–38).

Keep in mind that the ranks of solo practitioner, although a declining part of the legal profession in the city of Chicago, have been growing in the suburbs and rural areas and constitute roughly 48 percent of the legal profession. These suburban and rural solo practitioners likely experience many of the same challenges that confronted the lawyers in Carlin's pathbreaking studies (M. Kelly 2007: 357).

In the next section, we survey the lawyers at the top of the legal profession who practice in large law firms.

Large Corporate Law Firms

The lawyers who practice law in large law firms are the royalty of the legal profession. These lawyers represent powerful corporate clients, make the most money, and are engaged in what are considered the most prestigious and intellectually challenging areas of the law (Heinz et al. 2005).

At the very pinnacle of the legal pyramid are a number of "mega-firms" that have offices across the United States and in many cases across the globe. Roughly twenty-seven U.S. firms have more than one thousand lawyers. In the past, all of the large and prominent firms were headquartered in New York City and served the financial community and for that reason were referred to as Wall Street firms. Today, you can find leading firms that possess "global reach" throughout the country.

The Chicago-based firm of Baker McKenzie is one of the largest in the world. Baker McKenzie advertises that it has well over 4,200 lawyers and generates over $2.6 billion in revenue a year. The firm has seventy-seven offices across forty-seven countries. Four of the ten largest global firms are headquartered in London. The English firm Clifford Chance has over 3,200 lawyers and thirty-five offices in twenty-six countries and generates over $2 billion in revenue. The one hundred largest law firms, according to the Web-based legal publication *Above the Law*, made $96.6 billion in 2015 (Zaretsky 2016b). The lawyers affiliated with these mega-firms are generously compensated. A young lawyer hired by a top-tier New York law firm right out of law school can expect a salary in the range of $180,000 with a bonus at the end of the year of at least $15,000. In their eighth year, young associates in New York may earn as much as $315,000, with a significant year-end bonus. Partners at Cravath, Swaine & Moore each reportedly earned $3.15 million in 2015 (E. Olson 2016c).

The 1995 survey of Chicago lawyers confirms that money, resources, and prestige are concentrated in large corporate law firms (see Table 4.3).

Table 4.3 ■ Corporate Law Firms and the Legal Profession

Status	Prestigious legal work for corporations is the preserve of the large firm. Low-status work for individuals and families is concentrated in solo practice and small firms (Heinz et al. 2005: 100–101).
Resources	Lawyers in firms of over one hundred lawyers have the advantage of more support staff than other attorneys and have access to expensive and sophisticated technology (Heinz et al. 2005: 105–106).
Law practice	More than one-third of profits from the practice of law are concentrated in large firms while the income of smaller firms and solo practitioners is decreasing (Heinz et al. 2005: 99–100). The trend is for the income of lawyers whose practice is devoted to business to be increasing while the income of lawyers who devote themselves to representing individuals is steeply declining (Heinz et al. 2005: 162).
Clients	The time devoted by lawyers to large organizations (e.g., business, unions, foundations, government) is roughly two times the time devoted by all lawyers to individual and family practice (Heinz et al. 2005: 43).
Number of law firms	The U.S. legal profession in 2000 included 47,563 law partnerships; 10 percent included more than ten lawyers (4,926). Roughly 10 percent of these partnerships (Heinz et al. 2005: 356) employed a hundred or more lawyers. Michael Kelly points out that these statistics do not fully communicate the importance of these "mega-firms" for the practice of law.
Size	In the 1950s, the largest U.S. law firm numbered 125 attorneys. The average number of lawyers in the 250 largest firms in 1983 was 150, and these firms included 37,400 attorneys. The firms expanded in 1993 to include 66,855 lawyers, and by 2003 to include 110,061 lawyers or 16 percent of all lawyers in private practice in the United States. In 2003, the average number of lawyers in the 250 largest firms had reached 440. Twenty-one firms had at least 900 lawyers. Two years later, an additional 6,600 lawyers had joined these large firms (M. Kelly 2007: 357, 359–360).
Geography	Ninety-five percent of the 250 largest firms have multiple offices. Ten thousand lawyers in these firms are living abroad (M. Kelly 2007: 360). Carol Silver notes that before 1970, only two U.S. law firms had offices in London. Fifteen New York firms and eight firms headquartered in other cities opened London branches during the early 1990s. In 1999, 57 of the 72 firms in her study had branches in London (Silver 2000).

Revenue	In 2002, the one hundred largest income-generating U.S. law firms reported gross revenues of $46 billion. The income of these one hundred largest firms represents roughly 40 percent of the gross (and net) revenues generated by all law partnerships (M. Kelly 2007: 361–363).
Profits	In 2005, the average profit per partner of the one hundred largest-grossing firms was over $1 million. In nine firms, the average profit per partner was over $2 million. The average revenue for a lawyer in the one hundred most profitable firms in 2005 was $960,000 (M. Kelly 2007: 362). In 2015, the websites Law360.com and AbovetheLaw.com report that the ten largest law firms generated revenues of between $1.7 billion and $2.1 billion. Profits per partner were well over $2.5 million.

An important development is that the number of lawyers in firms of fewer than one hundred lawyers is slowly decreasing because these moderate-sized firms are being absorbed into larger law firms. Those lawyers who are not absorbed into large firms have swelled the increasing number of solo practitioners and lawyers in firms of fewer than five lawyers (M. Kelly 2007: 357).

The organization of large, powerful firms follows the model pioneered by Paul D. Cravath, who is credited with introducing the so-called *Cravath system* in the beginning of the twentieth century at the venerated Wall Street firm of Cravath, Swaine & Moore. Cravath recruited talented, male law graduates from elite law schools who were part of the northeastern upper class. Erwin Smigel, in his 1969 study of Wall Street lawyers, found that 83 percent of the partners in large firms graduated from an elite undergraduate program or law school, and this figure rises to 88 percent if the universities of Virginia, Michigan, and Chicago are included (Smigel 1969: 74).

The young law graduates at Cravath, Swaine & Moore were mentored by senior lawyers in the firm and gradually were assigned increasingly important responsibilities as they developed an area of specialization. The policy at Cravath, Swaine & Moore was to promote from within the firm, and the "best and brightest" of these young lawyers, after proving their ability over the course of eight to ten years, were elevated to "partner." Associates who achieved partner were given equity (ownership) in the firm. At the end of the year, equity partners were entitled to a percentage of the firm's profits in addition to their salary. Associates were paid far less than partners and were provided with a bonus at the end of the year based on the firm's profits (Smigel 1969).

There was a harsh policy of "up or out" for associates. This policy was "softened" by the practice of finding positions for young lawyers who did not attain the rank of partner or who concluded that they were not suited for the time demands of life in a corporate firm. The firm's policy of discriminating in hiring against Jews, Catholics, women, and minorities was justified on the grounds that clients preferred individuals who shared their background. There was a strict quota on Jews, and no women or minorities and very few Catholics were hired into the firms. These groups responded by forming their own firms (Smigel 1969: 74–118).

Firms generally have abandoned their discriminatory hiring practices, and today Jews, Catholics, women, and a small number of minorities can be found in prestigious practice areas that formerly were the preserve of Protestant males. Firms also have broadened their pursuit of legal talent and have hired an increasing number of associates from local second-tier law schools (Heinz et al. 2005: 67–68, 73, 155, 317).

The Wall Street firms studied by Smigel typically were headed by a founding patriarch or patriarchs. These were "name partners," whose names appeared on the front door of the firm. These senior partners were well-known personalities who established personal relationships with the "captains of industry," sat on the boards of directors of corporate clients, and supervised the young associates who attended to the full range of legal needs of the partners' clients (Smigel 1969).

The informal "gentlemen's agreement" that formed the basis of the firms in the earlier era has been replaced by formal "partnership agreements" that establish the organization of the firm and the rights and responsibilities of members of the firm (Silver 2000). The firms are organized around specialty areas, and a number of associates work under the direction of one or two partners who head a particular "practice area." The firms offer a "full-service stop-and-shop" for clients. These specialty areas typically include corporate governance (e.g., legal issues arising in running the corporation), securities (selling stock to the public), anti-trust, mergers and acquisitions (buying businesses), taxation, labor law (relations with unions), and litigation (lawsuits). The firms also often have senior partners specializing in wills and trusts to help corporate executives convey their assets to their family. The firms typically refer their wealthy clients' personal concerns to a solo practitioner or small firm that specializes in divorce, personal injury, or minor criminal matters.

The firms have added practice areas in response to developments in society. Today, a firm may have partners who specialize in the environment, cyberspace, the media, and intellectual property (e.g., ownership of music and content in cyberspace). Firms also have regional specialties. A firm in Texas likely will possess expertise in oil and gas law while firms in Los Angeles may offer a specialty in entertainment law. Highly specialized areas often are the preserve of smaller *boutique firms* that focus on areas such as maritime or airline law or patents (the ownership of technological design) or nonprofit foundations (e.g., the American Cancer Society).

Members of the firm have been categorized as managers, entrepreneurs, or grinders. A managing partner is in charge of administering the firm, and a "hiring partner" is in charge of interviewing and hiring young lawyers. The managing partner typically consults with an executive committee comprising various powerful partners, and another committee is charged with establishing the compensation or salaries.

The planning committee is in charge of attracting new business. This typically is composed of "rain makers" (entrepreneurs) or partners who are adept at attracting business based on their relationships with the business community. Various partners often are active in electoral politics or are appointed to jobs in the state or federal governments, and their visibility and political connections attract clients to the firm. For example, James Baker, who formerly was chief of staff for President Ronald Reagan and secretary of the treasury under President George H. W. Bush, is senior partner in the Houston firm of Baker Botts. The "grinders" are the associates who work under the supervision of partners and devote themselves to the "grunt work" of legal research, writing memorandums, and drafting documents (Nelson 1988: 70–80).

Scholars in the 1980s and 1990s devoted a significant amount of attention to explaining why corporate firms continued to expand their size and profits (Sander and Williams 1989). This expansion has been variously explained by the pressure to promote associates to partner ("the tournament of lawyers") (Galanter and Palay 1991), the firms' desire to expand their areas of specialization to cushion themselves against a decline in particular areas of practice (the "portfolio theory") (Gilson and Mnookin 1985), and the need for firms to provide expertise in new specialty areas of legal practice (e.g., environmental law) required by their corporate clients (Nelson 1988).

The world of the corporate law firms has been shaken in recent years by the temporary weakening of the U.S. economy and the bankruptcy of thirty-seven large firms since 1988. A number of venerable firms have collapsed, including Thacher Proffitt, a 160-year-old New York City law firm that at its height employed 350 lawyers and leased five floors in a downtown office building. In 2007, the firm had revenues of over $194 million, and each partner enjoyed revenues of more than $1 million. The closing of Thacher Proffitt left 195 lawyers unemployed, although 40 immediately were hired by a Chicago law firm looking to strengthen its presence in New York City. Thacher was the third New York City firm to collapse in 2008, and thereafter a long list of leading law firms announced that they were terminating lawyers and staff (Fortado 2008). It is estimated that large corporate law firms released roughly 4,600 lawyers in 2009 and that between 2007 and 2010 roughly 14,000 lawyers and legal staff were terminated (A. Williams 2010).

In 2012, the prominent firm of Dewey & LeBoeuf went out of business in the largest law firm collapse in history. At its height, the firm had employed 1,400 lawyers in twenty-six offices, and in 2011, it generated $935 million in revenues. Four members of the firm confronted criminal charges for falsification of business records, but only one of them was convicted (Goldstein and Moyer 2017).

Corporate firms are becoming increasingly cost conscious and have modified their business practices in response to the changing economic climate (Heinz et al. 2005: 288–315). Administrative partners now are assisted by professional administrators, and the pursuit of business is aided by public relations firms and publicists (293).

Large firms are introducing two tracks of partners. Equity partners are owners of the firm and share in the profits. A second, ever-increasing group of associates who are promoted to partnerships remain on a fixed salary. Firms also have sought to merge with competing firms in order to develop business in other cities or to add to their legal expertise (Heinz et al. 2005: 290, 294).

Firms no longer reserve partnerships for lawyers who have worked their way up through the associate track and instead are hiring partners from other firms in an effort to strengthen their legal expertise. These "lateral hires" typically bring clients to the firm and command salaries far beyond those paid to other partners in the firm.

The firms cannot afford for associates to ease into their positions and thus increasingly assign associates to specialty areas early in their careers. Roughly a quarter of associates entering the firm will make partner, and most associates anticipate that they will move on to other firms after four or five years to avoid being terminated. They may spend their professional life bouncing from one firm to another in hopes of eventually achieving a partnership. Other associates may find themselves working in a satellite firm or as an in-house counsel for a corporate client of the firm.

There is growing resentment among the ranks of associates over their ever-increasing workload and their ever-diminishing quality of life. Instead of hiring additional associates, firms are saving money by hiring lawyers on a temporary basis to work on specific projects or are relying on **paralegals**. Paralegals are non-lawyers who have basic legal training and who work as secretaries while performing uncomplicated legal work that previously may have been undertaken by lawyers. This might include completing the forms a corporation is required to submit in applying for a work visa for a foreign computer software engineer or engaging in basic legal research. Paralegals earn roughly one-third the salary of a new associate, and the firms make a substantial profit by billing clients several hundred dollars per hour for their services (Heinz et al. 2005: 293–294).

Younger lawyers in a number of firms have been frustrated by the fact that older partners who may no longer attract clients continue to reap profits based on their longevity with the firm. In some instances, younger partners and associates have left firms and have taken clients along with them to their own firms.

Older partners increasingly are being pressured to retire and to work as consultants to the firm on specialized assignments. These senior attorneys typically are given the title of "senior attorney" or "of counsel" (Heinz et al. 2005: 292, 307). The Chicago firm of Sidley Austin demoted thirty-two senior partners to create opportunity for younger lawyers. In another example, seventeen senior partners at the old-line New York firm of Cadwalader, Wickersham & Taft were pressured to retire by partners who believed that these older lawyers were not "pulling their weight." At Shearman & Sterling, the decision to "de-equitize" several partners occurred when its average profit per equity partner fell 4 percent to under $1.85 million and gross revenues grew less than 2 percent to $860.5 million. The trend toward shedding equity partners promises to continue.

In 2014, non-equity partners comprised somewhat more than 40 percent of all partners at "premier" firms while comprising 17 percent of these firms a decade ago (E. Olson 2016b).

The major law firms no longer can count on being retained to provide all of a corporate client's legal work. Corporations have developed in-house corporate legal counsel offices to handle much of their less complicated work. These in-house lawyers divide the outside work between several firms and at times place the law firms in the position of competing against one another for work (Heinz et al. 2005: 297–298). Various firms, in order to increase their profitability, have resorted to diversifying into non-legal fields such as private investigation, money management, governmental lobbying, and real estate (310).

Law firms are considering modifying their billing practices in order to attract business. Partners in elite firms may bill as much as $800 an hour, and young associates, although billing at a lower rate, are expected to bill well over two thousand hours a year. This translates into twelve-hour days six or seven days a week. Associates are required to keep time sheets recording the billable hours they spend on each task. The understanding is that a lawyer will not bill for the hours required to develop the background required to work on a client's case.

The ABA has been critical of this system of hourly billing for creating competition between young associates over billable hours and penalizing lawyers who reach settlements rather than take cases to trial. Billing by the hour also provides an incentive for firms to "pad" bills by assigning several lawyers to the same task, and it creates tension between lawyers and clients over the fairness of the amount charged by the firm (American Bar Association 2001–2002).

The early critics of corporate law firms attacked the firms as "sweat shops" that exploited young lawyers and served the interests of corporations at the expense of the public interest. The founding patriarchs of these firms responded that they provided a brake on the excesses of corporate clients by ensuring that these financial titans adhered to the law (Galanter and Henderson 2008; Galanter and Palay 1991: 11, 16–18).

In recent years, this criticism has been echoed by prominent members of the legal profession, who complain that lawyers in large firms have been reduced to narrow specialists driven by money and personal advancement. Corporate lawyers, according to critics, need to maintain the business of corporate clients and as a result are reluctant to tell corporate officials they risk violating the law (Kronman 1993; Linowitz 1994).

Eighty percent of corporate lawyers report they have never refused a client or a work assignment "because of personal values" (Heinz et al. 2005: 119). Robert Nelson, in his study of corporate lawyers in Chicago, concluded the evidence does not support Smigel's view that lawyers "mediate social conflict" by modifying the unreasonable demands of clients. "The notion that lawyers struggle with clients over fundamental questions about the common good is simply wrong." In other words, a lawyer who represents a corporate client is likely to tell a client how to get around environmental regulations rather than to discourage the client from drilling in an environmentally sensitive area (Nelson 1988: 258).

The late Sol Linowitz, in his discussion of the transformation of law from a profession into a business, discusses a number of the most prominent law firms in the country that in the early 1990s collectively paid more than $19 million to settle claims of alleged malpractice stemming from their assisting clients to commit financial fraud. Some of these malpractice suits involved the most well-respected and prominent lawyers in the country who knowingly involved themselves in unscrupulous financial schemes that defrauded the poor and elderly out of millions of dollars (Linowitz 1994: 40–42). There also are a number of recent cases of individual criminality by lawyers in which associates have been indicted and convicted of "insider trading." This involves purchasing stock in a corporate client based on confidential information that a company was about to announce a medical breakthrough or to announce a potentially profitable business venture that would result in the value of the stock increasing (K. Kirkland 2005). Several former leaders of the now defunct Dewey & LeBoeuf law firm were prosecuted for larceny and securities fraud for hiding the firm's desperate financial situation from creditors, investors, auditors, and other partners although the government failed to convict them at trial (Goldstein 2014: A1).

The corporate firm now also is under siege by a developing trend toward outsourcing legal work abroad. American, British, and Indian lawyers are being hired by outsourcing firms to undertake the basic work previously undertaken by junior associates in U.S. firms. In 2009, there were 140 outsourcing law firms in India, and revenues were predicted to reach $1 billion by 2013. These outsourcing firms charge between one-tenth and one-third of the fee of a U.S. law firm (Timmons 2010).

The last two sections have provided a snapshot of the **stratified private legal profession**. The next two sections sketch government lawyers and in-house counsel.

4.1 YOU DECIDE

In 2013, the world's largest law firm, DLA Piper, settled a suit over legal fees with a client. The firm sued the client for $675,000 in unpaid legal bills, and the client, in turn, filed a counterclaim alleging the firm overcharged for handling the bankruptcy of one of his businesses. Internal e-mails indicated the associates working on the case were in the typical "churn that bill, baby!" mode. One e-mail commented, "We are already 200k over our estimate—that's Team DLA Piper!" and another indicated the bill "shall know no limits." DLA later explained that the e-mails were "an inexcusable effort at humor."

Steven J. Harper, a former partner at the firm of Kirkland & Ellis and an adjunct professor at Northwestern University Law School, explained in the *New York Times* this type of overbilling is not unusual. Associates are expected to bill two thousand hours a year, which at $400 an hour results in a profit of $800,000 for the firm. An associate who meets the minimum number of billable hours receives a bonus and salary.

The partners supervising the associates push the lawyers who work for them to compile billable hours. Hourly fees escalate to as high as $600 to $800 an hour when a partner spends his or her own time on a case. The higher a partner's billable hours are, the greater the partner's annual share of the firm's profits will be.

Despite the dissatisfaction of clients with the practice of billable hours, alternative fee arrangements in 2010 accounted for only 16 percent of fees at the largest law firms. Billable hours remain the standard approach and are used by courts to evaluate the reasonableness of attorney fees.

The situation at DLA Piper is only part of a larger problem. Webster Hubbell, a former Arkansas Supreme Court justice and associate attorney general for President Bill Clinton, went to prison for billing for work that he never performed.

As a young associate in a law firm, how would you be tempted to exaggerate your billable hours?

Government Lawyers

Roughly 11 percent of lawyers are employed by the federal, state, county, or municipal governments. One-third, or roughly thirty thousand, of these **government lawyers** work for the federal government. This does not include the judicial branch, which we discussed earlier in the text (Baum 2013: 66). The great influx of lawyers into government occurred during President Franklin Delano Roosevelt's New Deal. Roosevelt inspired some of the "best and brightest" law students to abandon careers on Wall Street and join his administration in Washington, D.C. (Shamir 1995). Many of these young people would later make their mark as influential federal judges, leading lawyers, and high-profile academics. Two-thirds of the editors of the *Harvard Law Review* from the classes of 1930 through 1932 were employed at some point during the 1930s by the Roosevelt administration. This was not merely a matter of idealism. Many of these law graduates, despite their intellectual accomplishments, found themselves discriminated against when applying for employment with "white shoe" Wall Street law firms (Auerbach 1976: 181, 186).

Today, government jobs provide an avenue for law graduates to obtain valuable skills and knowledge and, after several years, to move into private practice. For example, a young attorney may work for an environmental agency and translate this into employment with a firm that specializes in assisting corporations to comply with environmental regulations (Spector 1972). Lawyers also may be attracted to governmental work because they believe in public service or are strongly committed to an agency's mandate to protect the environment or the financial sector. Other lawyers find that government jobs offer an attractive lifestyle that does not involve the stress of private practice (Spangler 1986: 132). Government positions attract a disproportionate number of women and minorities who perceive these jobs as providing greater opportunity than is available in private firms. The trade-off is that starting salaries for government workers lag far behind those of the private sector (Heinz et al. 2005: 163, 167).

The U.S. attorney general in Washington, D.C., is the chief law enforcement officer of the United States. Appointed by the president with the approval of the Senate, the attorney general leads the U.S. Department of Justice, which has eight specialized divisions; these divisions are antitrust (mergers between businesses), civil law, criminal enforcement, civil rights, the environment and natural resources, tax, national security, and justice management. The attorney general establishes priorities for the enforcement of federal law. For example, in recent years white-collar crime, which for many years had a low priority in federal prosecutions, has taken on increased importance. The attorney general also advises the president of the United States on the legality of various programs (this usually is undertaken by the Office of Legal Counsel within the Justice Department) and brings civil and criminal prosecutions (N. Baker 1995). He or she also supervises the FBI, the DEA, and the federal prisons. The Office of the Solicitor General and the lawyers on staff there are in charge of determining whether to bring appeals on behalf of the United States to the Supreme Court (Salokar 1995).

The president of the United States appoints a personal lawyer, the counsel to the president, who is headquartered in the White House Office of General Counsel. The counsel to the president and his staff provide legal advice on issues regarding the administration of the executive branch. This involves questions of ethics, the preservation of records, and the assertion of executive privilege (e.g., when the government may refuse to share information with Congress) and provides the president with background information on potential judicial and Supreme Court nominees (Lund 1995; Rabkin 1995).

The Watergate scandal during the Nixon administration led the U.S. Congress to adopt the Ethics in Government Act of 1978, which authorizes the president to appoint a special counsel to investigate and to prosecute corruption by high-ranking officials within the executive branch. Between 1978 and 1992, thirteen independent counsel investigations were authorized by Congress (Harriger 1995).

Other lawyers work in various federal "alphabet" agencies. These include the Federal Communications Commission (FCC), Securities and Exchange Commission (SEC), Federal Trade Commission (FTC), Environmental Protection Agency (EPA), and the National Labor Relations Board (NLRB); each of these agencies has a general counsel in charge of the agency's legal work. The general counsel and his or her staff draft regulations, bring enforcement actions on behalf of the agency, and defend agency decisions before the courts (Devins 1995; Herz 1995). For example, the FCC has successfully enforced regulations that impose fines on television stations that broadcast isolated profane language. The constitutionality of these regulations was upheld by the U.S. Supreme Court (*FCC v. Fox,* 556 U.S. 502 [2009]). A number of lawyers also work in congressional offices and with congressional committees on Capitol Hill.

In the states, lawyers can be found in each state's office of the attorney general. State attorneys general are elected statewide office holders who are charged with the criminal and civil enforcement of state laws. In the criminal area, prosecutors who work for the attorney general enforce the state criminal code. Lawyers assigned to the civil division enforce state laws in civil prosecutions ranging from taxation to consumer protection and the environment. The state attorney general also defends state laws against challenges to their constitutionality.

Other government lawyers work for cities or suburban jurisdictions in enforcing zoning regulations, housing codes, and health codes and defending legal actions brought against the city by individuals, who, for example, claim that they have been victims of police abuse. Lawyers also serve as public defenders for indigent defendants and work as legal aid lawyers representing indigents in civil cases such as actions against landlords who neglect to maintain rental units.

The growth of the government bureaucracy has proved a bonanza for legal work and has resulted in the development of what is termed **Washington lawyers**. These are lawyers and firms specializing in representing business interests before federal agencies and in influencing congressional legislation affecting their clients. Firms like Covington & Burling are located in the heart of the nation's capital, and Covington's partners regularly move from the firm to posts within Democratic presidential administrations and then back to the firm. Other firms are closely tied to the Republican Party. A Washington office now has become a requirement for firms representing corporate interests. The firms represent their clients before administrative agencies and are involved in areas such as the rate structure for trucking established by the Interstate Commerce Commission, licenses for ownership of radio and television stations, and licenses for building nuclear power plants and obtaining authorization for a merger between airlines. Washington firms go beyond legal representation and are involved in lobbying government agencies. For example, the firms advocate on behalf of foreign governments seeking to influence congressional legislation on favorable trade policy or foreign aid (Goulden 1971).

Eve Spangler notes that government lawyers' work is dependent on the political priorities of elected officials. A number of career attorneys left the voting rights section of the Department of Justice in protest over what they viewed as the George W. Bush administration's lack of commitment to protect the voting rights of minorities. Working for the government can be frustrating. Merit often is not rewarded, salaries remain far below the private sector, and a lawyer's decisions must be approved by his or her supervisors. Promotions in some instances may be more dependent on a lawyer's political affiliations than the lawyer's performance on the job. As individuals grow older, Spangler observes, they may find it difficult to leave the government and may find it increasingly challenging to achieve a satisfying professional life (Spangler 1986: 142–143).

Government lawyers confront the dilemma of whether their loyalty rests with the politicians who have been elected to office or whether their loyalty is to the even-handed enforcement of the law. A number of allegations were made regarding the alleged politicalization of the Department of Justice during the George W. Bush administration. The allegation was made that lawyers were being hired based on their political point of view rather than based on their professional accomplishments (Bruff 2009; Goldsmith 2007).

In-House Corporate Counsel

There is a trend for large corporations to hire their own **in-house corporate counsel**. These lawyers spend their time on work that formerly was performed by corporate law firms. These tasks might include negotiating and drafting contracts to supply goods to a national department store chain, entering into franchise agreements with local businesspeople who are contracting to operate a branch of a fast-food restaurant, purchasing land or negotiating a lease for a store in a mall, and ensuring that the firm submits all required environmental and tax forms. Complex areas like issuing stock or engaging in litigation continue to be the work of law firms.

Corporations are looking to cut costs and now are spending almost as much on their own internal law firms as on outside law firms. Some corporations have internal law firms with branches across the country that number well over five hundred lawyers. One of the primary responsibilities of corporate lawyers is to negotiate fees with law firms and to monitor the firms' work (Abel 1989: 168–172).

In an important study, Robert L. Nelson and Laura Beth Nielsen found that in-house lawyers adopt one of three roles. The "cop" views his or her role as telling businesspeople when they cross legal lines. The "counsel" acts as a general advisor and combines objective legal analysis with an ethical and business perspective. The role that is increasingly prevalent is the "entrepreneur," who works as part of a team with business executives in an effort to maximize profits (Nelson and Nielsen 2000).

Consider the case of Ford Motor Company, which marketed the Pinto knowing that the gas tank was in danger of exploding when rear-ended by a car going as slow as 21 mph. The company reasoned in 1971 that the cost of being sued by the victims of a crash would be less than the cost ($11 per car) of installing a safety device on 12.5 million cars and trucks. Ford feared that new safety standards being considered by Congress would force the company to install safety devices on its gas tanks and cost the company roughly $21 million. Ford responded by hiring powerful lobbyists who persuaded Congress to postpone the new fuel tank standards until 1977. Internal Ford memos leaked to the press in 1979 documented that corporate executives knew about and intentionally decided against fixing the defective gas tanks. The company subsequently recalled 1.5 million Pintos and Bobcats manufactured between 1971 and 1976.

A "cop" reading the engineering report in 1971 might tell Ford the company was liable in the event of a serious injury and that the Pinto should be recalled for refitting regardless of the fact the new standard would not go into effect until 1977. The "counsel" also would raise ethical considerations and point out that a serious accident would harm Ford's standing with the public. He or she also might advise against lobbying to delay the safety standards. An "entrepreneur" might prove sensitive to economic considerations and, because Ford was in compliance with current safety standards, may have been less insistent that the company recall the automobile for modification (Luban 1988: 207–210).

In-house corporate counsel positions attract some of the best and brightest law graduates and individuals who formerly worked as associates for large law firms. A significant number of female attorneys also work as in-house corporate counsels. The pay scale has been steadily increasing for corporate counsel positions, and these jobs offer more employment security than jobs in a law firm. These positions have proven to be stepping-stones for corporate careers. A number of CEOs of large corporations began their career as in-house corporate counsel (Heinz et al. 2005: 298).

We have outlined the primary career paths pursued by lawyers: private practice, government, and in-house corporate counsel. In the next two sections, we discuss the challenges confronting female lawyers and African American lawyers in the practice of law. Some commentators have argued that, in addition to stratification in the legal profession based on the type of legal practice, there is stratification based on gender and race. Consider whether the barriers women and African Americans have confronted in society are similar to the barriers that these groups confront in the legal profession.

Female Lawyers

Joanne Belknap documents the historical sexual segregation of the legal profession. She writes that in 1890 there were 135 female lawyers in the United States. Women comprised 1.0 percent of all lawyers in 1910 and 2.1 percent of all lawyers in 1930. As recently as 1970, women constituted only 2.8 percent of all lawyers. In recent decades, the number of female lawyers has increased dramatically. In 1980, Belknap records that 13 percent of all lawyers, or 59,000 lawyers, were women. The number of African American female lawyers increased from 446 to 4,272 in the decade between 1973 and 1983. By 2003, women constituted roughly half of all graduates from law school. Women now comprise 34 percent of all practicing attorneys (Belknap 2007: 447–448).

You likely are well aware of the reasons for excluding women from the practice of law. Females were viewed as inferior in mind and body and were thought to be naturally destined to be wives and mothers and domestic homemakers. Unscrupulous women also would employ their feminine charms to sway judges and juries. These stereotypes were so firmly embedded that in 1971 women taking the bar exam in New York were required to sit

PHOTO 4.3   The number of female lawyers has risen dramatically and women comprise roughly 34 percent of the legal profession and slightly fewer than 50 percent of all law students.

© iStockphoto.com/Deborah Cheramie

separately from men because of the presumption that women would excite the men and divert their attention from the test (Belknap 2007: 441).

The first female lawyer is thought to have been Arabella Mansfield, who was admitted to practice in Iowa in 1869. Only a handful of women were able to follow in her footsteps. In 1872, the Supreme Court upheld the refusal of Illinois to issue a license to practice law to Myra Bradwell. Justice Joseph P. Bradley famously reasoned that as a married woman Bradwell could not enter into contracts with clients and therefore was unsuited to the practice of law. He wrote:

> Man is, or should be, woman's protector and defender. The natural and proper timidity and delicacy which belongs to the female sex evidently unfits it for many of the occupations of civil life. The Constitution of the family organization, which is founded in the divine ordinance as well as in the nature of things, indicates the domestic sphere as that which properly belongs to the domain and functions of womanhood. The harmony, not to say identity, of interest and views which belong, or should belong, to the family institution is repugnant to the idea of a woman adopting a distinct and independent career from that of her husband. . . . A married woman is incapable, without her husband's consent, of making contracts which shall be binding on her or him. This very incapacity was one circumstance which the Supreme Court of Illinois deemed important in rendering a married woman incompetent fully to perform the duties and trusts that belong to the office of an attorney and counselor. (*Bradwell v. Illinois*, 83 U.S. 130 [1872])

In *Ex Parte Lockwood*, the Supreme Court upheld a challenge to a Virginia law that excluded women from the definition of a "person" eligible to practice law in the state (*Ex Parte Lockwood*, 154 U.S. 116 [1894]).

Women in those states in which they were eligible to practice had to depend on reading law with relatives or with their husbands in order to qualify for legal practice. A study of forty-five states at the turn of the twentieth century found ten states had not yet admitted women to practice. Most of the states that admitted women to practice had admitted fewer than ten women, although forty-seven women were practicing in Massachusetts in 1900. Virginia did not license the first woman to practice law until 1920. The ABA only admitted women to membership in 1918, and the prestigious Association of the Bar of the City of New York admitted its first female member in 1939 (Abel 1989: 90).

There were limited opportunities for women to attend law schools. Michigan in 1870 was the first school to admit women. This was followed by Yale in 1886 and Cornell in 1887 (K. Hall 1989: 218). These schools were the exception. Women generally were not admitted to leading law schools until well into the twentieth century and in most instances were admitted to the limited number of schools that offered part-time legal education to women (Abel 1989: 90–91). The dean of Columbia Law School resisted pressure during the early twentieth century to admit women and proclaimed that if women were admitted, the school would be overwhelmed with "freaks or cranks." Columbia relented and admitted women in 1928. Harvard remained firm in its refusal to admit women until 1950. Notre Dame did not welcome its first female students until 1968, and Washington and Lee opened its doors to women in 1972 (Auerbach 1976: 295).

As noted, women now comprise roughly one-third of all practicing lawyers. Women who entered the practice of law before 1975 tended to possess elite credentials and had some access to elite law firms. As women and minorities have gained greater access to the legal profession, they have tended to replace Catholics and Jews on the "lower rung of the ladder." Heinz and his co-authors, in their 1995 study of the Chicago Bar, concluded that the legal profession remains "clearly stratified" and that this stratification now is based on "presence of woman minorities in lower-status practice settings and in lower-status roles." The Chicago study found that as more women have entered the profession, female lawyers have become diverse in terms of social background and increasingly have earned degrees from less prestigious law schools. Does this explain why women are concentrated at the bottom of the legal profession? A quantitative analysis of the survey data indicates that the fact that women and minorities are at the lower rung of the profession cannot be fully explained by factors other than discrimination (Heinz et al. 2005: 72–73). This finding is echoed by Belknap, who concludes women continue to be overrepresented in government work and underrepresented in the more prestigious areas of private practice (Belknap 2007: 450–451). In other words, women face a "sticky floor" as well as a "glass ceiling" (J. Baker 2003).

Even when women enter the ranks of the elite firms, they have difficulty breaking through the "glass ceiling" and being elevated to an equity partner. The ninth annual report of the National Association of Women Lawyers (NAWL) on the two hundred largest law firms concludes that women have made "no appreciable progress in reaching the top rung" (NAWL 2016). In 2016, the ABA Commission on Women in the Profession reported that women comprised 44.7 percent of all associates in law firms, 21 percent were partners, 18 percent were equity partners, and 18 percent of the managing partners of the two hundred largest law firms were women (ABA Commission on Women in the Profession 2016). Among non-equity partners who graduated from law school in 2004, a year in which roughly 50 percent of law graduates were women, 62 percent of non-equity partners were men, and 38 percent of non-equity partners were women (NAWL 2016). Men are two to five times more likely than equally qualified women to make equity partnership (Rhode 2015: 61).

The NAWL finds that women are not fully represented on the committees that make key decisions on hiring and compensation in law firms. There typically are eight men and no women on the compensation committee that decides salaries and bonuses. Female equity partners customarily make 80 percent of the salary of male equity partners. This figure rises to 87 percent of the salary of male equity partners when there are three or more women on the firm compensation committee. Women represent only 8 percent of partners making a million dollars or more. There are various explanations for the difference in compensation for men and women, one of which is that although female equity partners work the same number of hours as their male peers, the clients of female partners are billed less for their work than for the work of male partners. Women also are asked much more often than men to undertake uncompensated work such as mentoring younger lawyers.

Heinz and his co-authors concluded that women working in firms are more likely than men to believe that they have been denied the opportunity to work on significant cases and to work with important clients. Women when interviewed offer the alarming conclusion that while "high performing women do at least as well as comparable men . . . 'mediocre' men appear to be more likely to get the benefit of the doubt than are mediocre women" (Heinz et al. 2005: 153–154). It is perhaps understandable that one of the studies cited by Heinz and his co-authors concluded that while both men and women are increasingly likely to leave law firms, this trend is much more prevalent among women because of their lack of career opportunities (Kay and Hagan 1998, 2003).

Another interesting finding is that women partners tend to be somewhat more prevalent in firms that are outside of the leading one hundred firms. The firms with the highest percentage of female partners tend to be located outside of New York City and to have been established by forward-thinking lawyers and specialize in areas like entertainment law or real estate rather than mainstream corporate practice in banking and corporate law. The firms with women partners are supportive of women who decide to have children and base promotion on an individual's total contribution to the firm rather than solely on billable hours. The firms with a significant percentage of female partners also have gone out of their way to recruit women from other firms, to study how to retain and advance women, and to have generous pregnancy and family leave policies (Tribe 2017). An earlier study found that the highest percentage of women partners were located in firms in Miami, New Orleans, Denver, and San Francisco, whereas the smallest percentage of female partners could be found in the suburban rings that surrounded Los Angeles and Washington, D.C., and in Charlotte (North Carolina) and Salt Lake City (Utah) (O'Brien 2006). Note that the preeminent firm of Cravath, Swaine & Moore in 2016 named Faiza J. Saeed, a prominent female attorney, as the sixteenth presiding partner in the firm's history (de la Merced 2016).

Women also are underrepresented at the top ranks of in-house corporate counsel. Roughly 24 percent of the general counsel of Fortune 500 firms are women, and 19 percent of general counsel of Fortune 501–1000 are women. As for law schools, 31 percent of the deans of law schools are women, although roughly 54 percent of associate deans and 68 of assistant deans are women (ABA Commission on Women in the Profession 2016).

An interesting study by Professor Katherine Shaw of the Cardozo School of Law analyzed the lawyers appointed by the U.S. Supreme Court to argue as a "friend of the court" issues that are not presented in the briefs of the parties before the Court. Ten percent of the fifty-four "friend of the court" lawyers in the study were women, and 5 percent were African American or Hispanic. Most lawyers appointed as a "friend of the court" were arguing their first case before the Court, and these appointments can give a significant boost to a young lawyer's career. In 2015–2016, 23 percent of the lawyers arguing before the Court were women (Liptak 2016).

Women, according to surveys, are frustrated by their experiences in the legal profession, and there is a concern about women leaving the practice of law, particularly leaving large firms. Commentators point to the continuing gap between the number of female law graduates and the number of women practicing law. In 2008, women comprised roughly 31.6 percent of the practicing bar despite the fact that they comprised roughly 47 percent of law graduates in the same year, a trend that has continued (ABA Commission on Women in the Profession 2009).

Fiona Kay and her co-authors as part of a study asked why women leave the practice of law. They conclude that women who felt marginalized in a largely male environment left firms because they lacked mentors and colleagues and experienced a lack of social life in the firm. Women were unhappy with a system in which billable hours rather than the quality of work was rewarded. They also expressed apprehension that their careers would suffer when they started a family (Kay, Alarie, and Adjei 2016).

The Defense Research Institute (DRI), an organization of lawyers who defend defendants in civil cases, sponsored a study of the gender discrimination experiences of 765 female members (see Table 4.4). It must be remembered in considering the results of the study that litigation perhaps is the most competitive and combative area of the legal practice (Defense Research Institute 2005).

The ABA Commission on Women in the Profession (2016) found that women in other areas of legal practice had similar experiences. A 2010 report by the Women Lawyers of Utah found that 37 percent of women in firms reportedly experienced verbal or physical interactions with male colleagues that created an unpleasant or offensive work environment. Twenty-seven percent of these women felt that this rose to the level of harassment, and 86 percent of these women believed that the objectionable conduct amounted to sexual harassment. In contrast, 22 percent of males said they had experienced an unpleasant work environment, and 4 percent of these individuals believed that the conduct constituted harassment. The report notes that women in other types of legal practice also experienced harassment (Women Lawyers of Utah 2010).

Table 4.4 ■ Findings of Defense Research Institute	
Bias	More than 70.4 percent of women report experiencing gender bias in the courtroom. This included judges and court personnel referring to women as "baby" and "honey" and using their first name.
Leaving the profession	Of the women surveyed, 61.6 percent considered leaving the practice of law due to gender-related issues.
Glass ceiling	Roughly 65 percent of women surveyed believe that there is a glass ceiling for women defense attorneys.
Personal life	More than 52 percent of women surveyed said that the practice of law influenced their personal decision on the timing of motherhood. A number of women said that they postponed having children so that they could satisfy the requirements for partnership. Women feared that having a child or taking maternity leave would result in their being perceived as lacking commitment to a legal career and would prevent them from receiving important assignments and from being promoted.
Mentors	Roughly 62 percent of women reported having a mentor; only 25 percent of these mentors were female.
Clients	Female lawyers reported that male clients often did not respect them and requested representation by a male lawyer during consultations. Roughly 70 percent reported pressure to be a "rain maker" and to generate business.
Perception of professionalism	The report found that women continued to struggle with balancing the requirement of being assertive as a litigator with the fear that they would alienate their colleagues, judges, and jurors by appearing overly aggressive. This is the classic "no-win situation" in which women risk being perceived as either lacking aggression or being overly aggressive and appearing either too emotional or too cold and calculating.

The Utah survey also found that 21 percent of women felt that they had been treated unfairly in the firm and 42 percent of these respondents believed that their mistreatment constituted discrimination (10 percent of women in firms). The unfair treatment was based on a lack of fair compensation (44 percent), a lack of respect (13 percent), and "lesser" assignments (13 percent).

There are several legal actions filed by women partners in large firms who claim that despite their strong performance, they are paid less than men who have a lower level of performance. Women as noted are paid 80 percent of what men receive. This translates into roughly $125,000 per year and $1 million over a decade (E. Olson 2016a). One survey reports that women partners on average make one-third or roughly $300,000 less annually than male law partners (E. Olson 2017).

A number of commentators have cautioned against concluding that the underrepresentation of women in positions of authority is explained solely by discrimination. These arguments are nicely summarized by Richard L. Abel in his study of American lawyers. The contention is that women gravitate toward government and solo and small firm work because lawyers in these practice areas find it somewhat easier to balance the demands of work with their family responsibilities and are able to work part-time in the early years of raising a family. The assertion also is made that women generally are more liberal and are drawn to areas of the law representing the disenfranchised that do not pay as well and are considered less prestigious than business-related practice areas. Other writers have argued that women may anticipate that they will face discrimination and simply do not apply for jobs in large firms. Yet another argument is that women are making steady progress and, although change is inevitable, it is unrealistic to expect that change will occur overnight (Abel 1989: 90–99).

Commentators are divided on whether the professional disadvantage experienced by women results from the fact that they are discriminated against or that they generally have primary responsibility for raising children. A study of law graduates of the prestigious University of Michigan Law School indicates that fifteen years following graduation, women who make a commitment to children and family "work significantly fewer hours . . . and are much less likely to be found in the highest paid types of practices or as partners in private practice." In other words, there is a "substantial price to pay" in terms of the probability of achieving a partnership and in terms of income for devoting time to raising children. Women who work part-time or take a leave of absence report "dropping off the planet" of the firm and being assigned to tedious and relatively unimportant work (Chambers 1989; Dau-Schmidt, Galanter, Mukhopadhaya, and Hull 2009).

On the other hand, there are studies that conclude that women's lack of professional mobility appears to be explained more by discrimination than by choices that women make regarding "work–life balance" (Heinz et al. 2005). An ABA survey found that 60 percent of women and women of color and only 4 percent of men felt isolated in their work environment and more women than men wanted better mentoring. Forty-four percent of women of color and 39 percent of white women, as well as 25 percent of minority men and only 4 percent of white men, believed they were passed over for attractive assignments (Rhode 2015: 69-70). Which view do you find more persuasive? Will women continue to be placed in the position of choosing between their career and family?

The question is whether the increased entrance of women into the practice of law will make a difference in the way that lawyers approach their jobs. There were predictions that women would bring a more conciliatory style to the practice of law, bringing the parties to disputes together to reach solutions that recognized the interests of all the parties (Menkel-Meadow 1986).

Jennifer Pierce conducted a qualitative study of female lawyers and paralegals in a litigation firm and in the office of an in-house corporate counsel. Pierce found that women are more likely than men to question the adversarial model of litigation. Women tend to compensate for the adversarial demands of the courtroom by bringing a humane orientation into their relationships outside the courtroom. For example, one of the lawyers in the study brought the parties in a contract dispute together to explore the underlying emotions that seemed to be responsible for the dispute. It soon emerged that one of the parties was angry with the other individual for marrying his ex-wife. The other party expressed surprise that this remained an issue, and once the air was cleared, the two individuals entered into a settlement. An adversarial stance would have resulted in this case going to court with only one of the two parties in the lawyer's office emerging as the "winner." A small number of women in Pierce's limited sample patterned themselves after male litigators, although these women were troubled by their conformity to the "male model." Pierce's study raises the issue whether it is realistic to expect that women can change the nature of the practice of law without changing how we structure the world of employment and the adversarial legal system (J. Pierce 1995: 124, 133–134).

A related characteristic of legal practitioners is a tendency to focus clients on legal questions rather than emotional issues. Austin Sarat and William Felstiner, in their study of divorce lawyers, recount the story of a female client who voluntarily left the home she shared with her husband following their separation and felt angry over her treatment and wanted some gesture by her husband that recognized that she had lost her home. They observed a male lawyer lecture the client not to let her emotions get in the way of a financial settlement on the property (Sarat and Felstiner 1986). Mather and colleagues found that female divorce lawyers tend to be "sensitive listeners" who recognize clients "not only as an assemblage of facts and figures about marital finances but also as a fragile human being in need of help through the divorce" (Mather et al. 2001: 82). Other studies have questioned whether women and men differ in their understanding of the importance of bringing a sensitive and supportive approach to the practice of law. These studies find that the difference between lawyers in terms of their interactions with clients is explained by a different approach to the practice of law rather than to gender (Seron 1996: 109–114). In the next section, we discuss the challenges that confront African American lawyers and other minority lawyers.

4.2 YOU DECIDE

In 2017, a panel of federal judges suspended Chicago attorney Jason R. Craddock Sr. for twelve months from practicing law in federal court. As a pre-condition to the lifting of the suspension, Craddock was ordered to address what the judges viewed as his anger management issues. Craddock's suspension could be limited to six months based on a demonstration that he was ready to return to the practice of law.

Craddock admitted that he twice used "gender-based, vulgar terms" to address Courtney Lindbert, a lawyer who represented the defendant restaurant in a sex discrimination case brought by Craddock on behalf of a waitress. Craddock addressed Lindbert in a hallway

outside the courtroom as "C---ney," substituting an objectionable term for the female anatomy for Courtney's first name. He later wrote an e-mail addressed to "C---ney Lindbitch." Lindbert alleged that Craddock in addition to insulting her made her fearful for her physical safety. The judicial panel found that Craddock's insults were intended to "intimidate" Lindbert in her representation of her client and that there was no evidence that supported Craddock's contention that Lindbert had belittled and insulted him and provoked him to lash out at her.

Was Craddock's suspension from the practice of law in federal court justified?

African American Lawyers

There is a history of excluding minority lawyers from the legal profession. Richard Abel writes that minority groups were "virtually excluded from the profession until the 1960s." The first African American male lawyers were admitted to practice in the mid-1840s in Massachusetts; the first female African American lawyer was admitted to practice in the District of Columbia in 1872 after graduating from Howard University.

These lawyers were the exception; very few African Americans managed to be admitted to the practice of law. In 1900, there were 730 African American lawyers in the United States (or 0.5 percent of the profession); a decade later, there were only 795 African American attorneys. At the turn of the century, roughly 50 percent of the states had fewer than 10 African American lawyers.

The barriers to African Americans' admission to law school and discrimination within the legal profession were most severe in the South but also existed in other parts of the country. Only twenty African Americans were admitted to practice in Philadelphia between 1909 and 1945; none was admitted between 1933 and 1943 (Abel 1989: 99–100). As late as 1932, there were only 1,200 African American lawyers in the entire country (K. Hall 1989: 218).

The small number of African American lawyers was due to a combination of discrimination and lack of educational opportunity. As late as 1960, African Americans constituted 10.6 percent of the American population and only 0.8 percent of the legal profession; in 1970, African Americans constituted 11.2 percent of the population and 1.3 percent of the legal profession (Abel 1989: 100).

The ABA mistakenly admitted three African Americans in 1912 and quickly passed a resolution rescinding their admission because the prevailing practice was to admit only "white men" as members. A compromise was reached that permitted the three lawyers to maintain their membership in the ABA on the condition they immediately resign. The ABA did not officially welcome African American lawyers as members until 1943 (Auerbach 1976: 65).

Since that time, the ABA has established the expansion of the number of minority lawyers and the employment of minority lawyers as primary goals (American Bar Association 2016). Progress for all minority lawyers has been slow.

African Americans constitute 4.2 percent of all lawyers (1.9 percent are female); Hispanics constitute roughly 3.4 percent of all lawyers (1.2 percent are female); and Asian Americans constitute approximately 2.2 percent of all lawyers (1.0 percent are female). Native Americans constitute an estimated 0.2 percent of all lawyers (0.1 percent are females). In the past few years, despite the decline in law school enrollment, minority enrollment has remained at around thirty-five thousand or roughly 28 percent of all law students. African American enrollment has held steady at around ten thousand (American Bar Association 2016).

The Chicago Bar study concludes that African American and Hispanic lawyers are "disadvantaged in every way—in socioeconomic status of origin, in law school prestige, in attainment of partnership status, and in income." These groups had "significantly lower probabilities" of an income in the top range or partnership in a firm of any size. Thirty-six percent of all white lawyers reported incomes below $70,000, whereas 72 percent of minorities and 85 percent of African Americans reported incomes below $70,000. The segregation of the legal profession by race and gender has led to a dual justice system in which minority and female lawyers by and large serve the less affluent and educated (Heinz et al. 2005: 73, 269).

A particular concern has been the modest percentage of African American, Hispanic, Asian American, and Native American lawyers in large corporate law firms. Minority lawyers in 2016 comprised 15 percent of lawyers at corporate firms as compared to 13.8 percent in 2007 (Chung 2016) and are 8 percent of equity partners (National Association of Women Lawyers 2016; Rhode 2015: 62). Deborah Rhode states that African American lawyers constitute 3 percent of lawyers at major law firms and less than 2 percent of partners. Minority lawyers constitute 9 percent of the general counsel of Fortune 500 firms (Rhode 2015: 62).

Stephen J. Harper lists the demographic breakdown of the firm Cadwalader, Wickersham & Taft in 2012. The firm lists 452 lawyers, 104 of whom were partners. Ninety-one of the partners were men, and thirteen were women. Five of the men were Asian American, one was Latino, one was Hawaiian/Pacific Islander, one was American Indian/Native, and no partners were African American. One of the female partners was Asian, and the rest were white (Harper 2013: 95).

The figures for minority women equity and non-equity partners rose from 1.88 percent in 2009 to 2.55 percent in 2015. African American women were 0.64 percent of all equity and non-equity law firm partners, and Hispanic women were 0.63 percent of equity and non-equity law firm partners. Asian or Asian American women comprised 1.07 percent of partners in 2016. Minority women in aggregate constituted 2 percent of equity partners at the two hundred largest firms, according to NAWL (McQueen 2016).

Forty-two percent of male associates of color leave their law firms within twenty-eight months of being hired, and 78 percent leave their firm within fifty-five months of being hired. The figures for female minority attorneys are that 41 percent leave their firms within twenty-eight months of being hired, and the ABA reports that 85 percent of minority female women leave large firms within seven years (Chung 2016).

The figures for African Americans certainly are an improvement over Smigel's earlier finding of only three African American lawyers who had been hired at Wall Street firms (Smigel 1969: 45). The fact nonetheless remains that fewer African American lawyers are being hired and more African American lawyers are leaving large firms than eight years ago (Chung 2016). Scholars have spilled a great deal of ink debating why there are not more minority attorneys in corporate law firms. David Wilkins and Mitu Gulati, in their studies of African American lawyers, adopt a structural perspective. They argue that partners want to generate billable hours and to work efficiently and effectively for their clients. They compete with one another for bright associates. Most associates are fairly indistinguishable from one another in terms of grades and credentials, and partners naturally are attracted to white associates with whom they identify and feel comfortable. Another explanation is that the pattern is for African American associates to leave firms early and partners may not want to invest time and effort in mentoring minority lawyers.

African American lawyers report that they do not receive mentoring or important assignments and are not given the opportunity to attend meetings with clients. As noted above, a high percentage of African American lawyers leave the firms before five years, and the overwhelming majority pursue careers in government or in in-house corporate legal departments. Only 17 percent of African American lawyers leaving law firms move to other large firms (Wilkins and Gulati 1996).

A study by the private research firm Nextions illustrates the bias confronting African American lawyers. A research memo was drafted by researchers that was full of minor spelling and grammatical oversights and errors in analysis. The memo was represented as having been written by a junior associate. The memo was evaluated by sixty partners in twenty-two law firms who agreed to participate in a "writing analysis study." The lawyers were told that the memo was written by Thomas Meyers, a third-year associate who graduated from New York University. Half of the partners were told that Meyers was a Caucasian, and half of the partners were told that Meyers was an African American. The partners found more errors in the memo written by the "African American Thomas Meyers" than in the memo written by the "Caucasian Thomas Meyers." The comments on the memo written by the "Caucasian Thomas Meyers" generally were positive and his work was ranked as 4.1 out of 5, while the comments on the memo written by the "African American Thomas Meyers" generally were negative and his work was ranked as 3.2 out of 5 (Reeves 2015).

A survey of African American graduates of Harvard Law School find that most are highly successful and pursue careers comparable to Caucasian graduates of Harvard Law School. However, even among this group of highly talented lawyers, over half report experiencing racism from colleagues, clients, or public officials; 86 percent report that African American lawyers continue to confront discrimination; and 27 percent note that they are the only African Americans in their workplace. These responses of course may not reflect the experience of more recent Harvard graduates (Wilkins et al. 2002).

In 2017, Imelme Ubana, the daughter of Nigerian immigrants, was elected president of the prestigious *Harvard Law Review*, the first African American female to ascend to this position. Forty-one percent of members of the law review are minority students as compared to roughly 32 percent of the school. Most of these students are either Asian or Hispanic. Only 5.7 percent of male and 9.6 percent of female students at Harvard are African Americans. The law review was founded in 1887, and in 1990, Barack Obama became the first African American student to be elected president of the law review (Seelye 2017).

Richard Sander disputes this institutional explanation and, while not dismissing that racism plays a role, argues that the large law firms are based on merit and that the lack of success of African American lawyers in corporate law firms is explained by grades and qualifications (Sander 2006). Sander's "human capital" argument is effectively refuted by a comprehensive study that found that African American lawyers' decision to leave large corporate firms is based on "institutional discrimination." In other words, the decision of African Americans to leave the firms is based on a lack of contact with partners and mentorship, which leads to a feeling of isolation and alienation rather than being based on an inability to satisfy expectations (Payne-Pikus, Hagan, and Nelson 2010).

Each of these reasons may explain why a New York firm, which in the 1990s hired a "critical mass" of African American, Hispanic, and Asian American associates, found that virtually all of those lawyers left the firm (Baynes 2012).

African American lawyers have found government and in-house corporate counsel to be more receptive environments. David Wilkins has documented the difficulties confronting African American firms. Many of these firms relied on business from governments that traditionally hired law firms to represent cities in legal actions or to draft legal documents required to sell bonds to the public. The government budgetary crisis, the retreat from "set-asides" for minority businesses, and the competition for talented African American lawyers all have created a climate in which these firms have found it difficult to survive (Wilkins 2008).

You might ask yourself, given the pressures on lawyers and the challenges confronting female and African American lawyers, whether minority lawyers would pursue a legal career if they started all over again. We explore the question of lawyers' job satisfaction in the next section.

Professional Satisfaction

Patrick Schlitz, in a roundly criticized essay, cites evidence that lawyers disproportionately suffer from depression, anxiety, alcoholism, drug abuse, and suicide and that much of this behavior stems from unhappiness with the practice of law. Schlitz concludes that the legal profession is one of the most "unhappy and unhealthy [professions] on the face of the earth" and that "lawyers seem to be among the most depressed people in America" (Schlitz 1999: 872–874).

Heinz and colleagues, in their study of Chicago lawyers, provide little support for Schlitz's conclusions in their study (Heinz et al. 2005: 256–274). The Chicago study indicates that 84 percent of the respondents stated they were either satisfied or very satisfied with their legal career; roughly 10 percent were neutral, 5 percent were dissatisfied, and 1.6 were very dissatisfied (257). Although women expressed unhappiness over the lack of understanding of the challenges of motherhood, there was no significant difference between the satisfaction expressed by men and women (258), a finding that is supported by a study of lawyers in Toronto, Canada. The Toronto study also found that a significant percentage of lawyers (77.7 percent of men and 78.7 percent of women) stated that if they were starting their career all over again, they would choose to become a lawyer (Hagan and Kay 2007: 68–71).

There is some speculation that women are reluctant to articulate their frustrations and may have greater job dissatisfaction than is indicated by the data. One study finds that women have a sense of "despondency" over their lack of opportunity and responsibility and recognition and over the difficulties of combining a career with motherhood (Hagan and Kay 2007; Rhode 2015: 62, 72). African American lawyers are satisfied with the choice of a legal career but very dissatisfied with the conditions of their workplace and with their limited opportunity for advancement (Rhode 2015: 16).

Lawyers uniformly express concern that the profession focuses on the financial bottom line and that lawyers are less civil and are more likely to mislead one another than in the past (Rhode 2000: 9). The findings of lawyer career satisfaction also must be tempered by the fact that the surveys typically do not include individuals who have left the practice of law.

We have painted with a broad brush in discussing lawyer satisfaction. One study found that recent graduates of elite law schools are less satisfied than graduates of less selective schools who work in less prestigious settings. It would appear that the graduates of elite universities find life as an associate in a large law firm disappointing while graduates of less prestigious schools see a legal career as an opportunity for upward mobility (Dinovitzer and Garth 2007).

The surveys generally find that the happiest lawyers are the lawyers who believe their work is "meaningful" despite the fact they may not earn as much money as highly compensated lawyers. Lawyers who are dissatisfied also point to public hostility toward the legal profession and to the fact that they are required to adopt a negative mindset of doom and gloom in which they are required to protect their clients from the worst possible set of circumstances (Quenqua 2015). A study of sixty-five thousand individuals on workplace satisfaction ranked associate in a law firm as the least satisfying position and law clerk as the seventh least satisfying position (Patrice 2013).

The latest figures from the Centers for Disease Control and Prevention find lawyers rank fourth in the proportion of suicides as compared with other occupation groups. The leading categories are dentists, pharmacists, and physicians. Lawyers are 3.6 times more likely to suffer from depression than non-lawyers and two times as likely to suffer from substance abuse (Rhode 2015: 15).

You should now have a basic understanding of the structure and organization of the legal profession. We turn our attention in the next chapter to legal education and the process of becoming a lawyer. Our first topic is law school, and we then look at the bar examination. As you recall, restricting access to a job and controlling training are two of the central characteristics of a "profession."

 ## INTERNATIONAL PERSPECTIVE: THE LEGAL PROFESSION IN CHINA

The People's Republic of China is experiencing the first stages of the evolution of its legal profession. The ascendancy of Communist rule in 1949 resulted in the elimination of the Chinese legal profession. Lawyers were persecuted, imprisoned, and banished to rural areas as part of the "cultural revolution." In 1978, following the death of Mao Zedong, the Chinese leadership proclaimed that the development of a legal profession was essential for the development of a modern economy. The government moved cautiously and in 1982 adopted provisional regulations on lawyering that proclaimed that although lawyers are responsible for protecting the "legitimate" rights and interests of citizens, their primary loyalty should be to the Communist state. Lawyers initially were classified as "state workers" and in some instances were admitted to the bar based on political connections rather than on legal qualifications or ability. The 1997 Lawyers Law labeled attorneys as

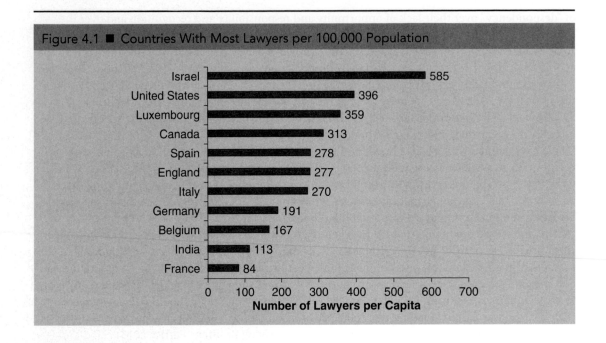

Figure 4.1 ■ Countries With Most Lawyers per 100,000 Population

Country	Number
Israel	585
United States	396
Luxembourg	359
Canada	313
Spain	278
England	277
Italy	270
Germany	191
Belgium	167
India	113
France	84

Number of Lawyers per Capita

professionals free from state control charged with providing legal services to society. Soon thereafter, a legal degree was instituted as a prerequisite to taking the bar examination (Terrill 2016).

For the number of lawyers in various countries, see Figure 4.1.

In 1979, there only were two law schools in China; by 2008, there were roughly 560 law programs enrolling three hundred thousand students. Entrance to Chinese universities is based on a highly competitive examination, and roughly 50 percent of the one million students who sit for the exam in a given year gain admission to a university. Students follow a standard fourteen-course legal curriculum for three years of study. Teaching is by the lecture system, and there is little focus on practical skills or case analysis (G. Clark 2008: 841).

In 2002, a unified national examination for lawyers and judges was established. Applicants must possess a college degree to take the exam. The two-day examination includes an essay and a multiple choice section. The pass rate is under 10 percent, although the Ministry of Justice is authorized to waive the exam for qualified persons. A year of apprenticeship is required after passing the examination and before being authorized to practice. Lawyers are automatically enrolled as members of the All China Lawyers Association (ACLA), which is under the control of the Ministry of Justice. The ACLA has promulgated a code of professional conduct and regulates lawyers (G. Clark 2008: 840).

The growth of the legal profession in China has been remarkable. There were 21,546 lawyers in 1986, and the latest figures indicate that there now are over two hundred thousand lawyers and well over ten thousand law firms. A significant percentage of lawyers work for the government or for corporations. As a result, there is a shortage of lawyers available to represent individuals. In 2003, a system of legal aid was established in which every lawyer is obligated to participate (G. Clark 2008: 440).

The average per capita income for an individual in China is below $2,000, and representing individual clients is not lucrative for most lawyers. Lawyers in firms are required to return a minimum of 50 percent of their fees to the firm with which they are affiliated. Competition for business among the nineteen thousand Chinese law firms is intense, and lawyers tend to refuse to represent clients in cases that promise to be time-consuming or in cases in which clients have questionable claims. The state also ensures that the damage awards are limited in cases involving automobile accidents, defective products, and workplace injuries, among other areas, which discourages lawyers from filing these types of cases (Michelson 2006).

The development of the Chinese legal system continues to be hampered by state control of the more than two hundred thousand judges that staff courts. Less than 20 percent have a college degree, and most are party loyalists and military veterans. Judges owe their appointment and loyalty to local party activists and government officials and rarely will rule against powerful interests (Hung 2008).

President Xi Jinping took office in March 2013 and in January 2015 proclaimed that the legal profession would henceforth be considered a "knife held firmly in the [hands of] the Party." The government initiated a series of criminal prosecutions of outspoken lawyers and legal activists. This culminated in a July 2015 crackdown that led to the temporary detention of nearly three hundred lawyers and to the arrest for terrorism of lawyers viewed as "hardcore" opponents of the regime (Human Rights Watch 2016).

The new directive on Management Methods on Law Firms and Management Methods on Lawyers require lawyers and law firms to "support the leadership of the Chinese Communist Party," and to establish party branches in law firms. Lawyers are prohibited from expressing views that "reject the fundamental political system" of China or "endanger national security." The directive sets forth a number of vague prohibitions such as a prohibition on lawyers publishing or signing joint letters (of protest), using the Internet and media to "provoke discontent," and instigating individuals to file law suits. Lawyers also may not organize or sign joint letters (critical of the legal system).

The Ministry of Justice each year determines whether to renew a lawyer's license to practice, and may order fifteen days of detention for disturbing the order of the court. More than 250 lawyers associated with the *weiquan* movement (human rights) since 2015 have been arrested on charges of falsifying evidence. In most instances, the lawyers were incarcerated and then released without charge although four remain in jail and roughly thirteen are in detention and likely will face trial (Buckley 2017a; Ran 2009).

In a prominent trial in December 2015, well-known human rights activist Phu Zhiqiang was convicted and received a three-year suspended sentence and lost his law license for "provoking trouble" and "inciting ethnic hatred on the internet." In a televised trial, another lawyer, Zhou Shifeng, confessed to subversion and was sentenced to seven years in prison. Xie Yang alleged along with other lawyers that during his interrogation he was deprived of water and sleep and was beaten, kicked, head-butted, and forced to sit in a stress position; clouds of smoke were blown in his face; and his wife was threatened. Although Xie Yang signed a confession, he refused to implicate other lawyers and after a year was charged with inciting subversion of state power (Buckley 2016, 2017a; Perlez 2015).

In May 2016, Xie Yang withdrew his claims of torture and pled guilty and stated that he had been "brainwashed" while abroad by human rights activists. A number of other lawyers in the last two years have made televised confessions and have pled guilty. The defense lawyer who revealed Xie Yang's allegations of torture was himself detained prior to Yang's recantation (Buckley 2017b).

There is a growing presence of American, Austrian, and English law firms in China, and law firms from at least nine other countries also have established offices in China. In 2016, there were 179 foreign law firms practicing in ten Chinese cities. These firms hire Chinese lawyers to handle the work of multinational corporations doing business in China and also represent Chinese companies exporting goods to the United States and to Europe (Liu 2006).

CHAPTER SUMMARY

Early American lawyers were educated in the English Inns of Court and were viewed with suspicion. The elitist character of the legal profession was out of step with the democratic ethos of the newly established Republic, and state legislatures resisted efforts to restrict access to the legal profession and proclaimed that a legal career should be open to any qualified applicant. The law was rapidly embraced as an avenue for upward mobility by the sons of middle-class merchants and farmers. The important role played by lawyers in the drafting of the U.S. Constitution and Bill of Rights led to a renewed respect and regard for lawyers.

The American law school fully developed in the late nineteenth and early twentieth centuries when Christopher Columbus Langdell introduced the casebook and Socratic method and a coherent curriculum at Harvard Law School. Law schools are organized into a hierarchy with a small group of highly selective schools at the top. The graduates of these top-ranked programs tend to monopolize the best-paying and most highly coveted jobs.

The end of the nineteenth century witnessed rapid economic expansion and the growth of the railroad. The corporate law firm that serviced these corporations began to emerge as the most powerful and prestigious branch of the law. This trend accelerated in the twentieth century, and the United States today is characterized by a "stratified legal profession" with a large income gap between lawyers in corporate firms at the top of the legal pyramid and solo practitioners and small firm practitioners at the bottom of the legal pyramid. The lower rungs of the legal profession once dominated by Catholics, Jews, and immigrants increasingly are populated by women and minorities who remain underrepresented among partners at large law firms. The twentieth century also saw growth in the number of lawyers in government and in-house legal counsel positions.

In the past several years, the ability of elite lawyers to maintain professional independence has been threatened by the economic downturn. Large firms must compete with one another for a portion of a corporate client's business and are cutting costs by terminating staff and lawyers and by forcing older lawyers into retirement. The remaining associates face the prospect of being denied partnerships and remaining as salaried employees. The studies on lawyer satisfaction indicate that lawyers are happy to have entered the practice of law even though they are unhappy about their conditions at work.

CHAPTER REVIEW QUESTIONS

1. Trace the development of the legal profession from Athens through Rome and in England.

2. Outline the development of the American legal profession in the early and middle years.

3. What are the characteristics of solo practitioners and small firm lawyers?

4. Discuss the characteristics, organization, and function of large corporate law firms.

legal representation to an inmate confronting a hearing for loss of parental rights (*Lassiter v. Department of Social Services*, 452 U.S. 18 [1981]). In 2011, the Supreme Court rejected the claim that the state was required to provide legal representation to an individual who was held in civil contempt and jailed for one year as a result of a failure to pay child support (*Turner v. Rogers*, 564 U.S. 431 [2011]). State courts also have resisted creating a state constitutional right to representation in civil cases or what is called a "civil *Gideon*."

In the next sections, we briefly review three efforts to increase access to legal services: advertising, contingent fees, and group legal services plans. In our discussion of criminal courts in Chapter 7, we will look at representation in criminal cases.

Advertising

You are arrested for driving while intoxicated or for a minor fight at a party, or you are sued by your landlord. How will you find a lawyer you can trust? Most of you undoubtedly will ask a friend or a relative for a recommendation. You also might be watching television and notice a lawyer advertising his or her services or see an advertisement in a school newspaper. Does it strike you as strange to see lawyers advertising their services?

Advertising by lawyers was a common practice during the early twentieth century. Elite lawyers decided to put a stop to this and, in the 1930s, supported a prohibition on advertising. Lawyers in firms were able to rely on a steady stream of business from their corporate clients and wealthy individuals and considered such advertisements demeaning to the profession and inconsistent with the professional stature of lawyers (Abel 1989: 125).

It took almost forty years for solo practitioners and lawyers in small firms to reverse the prohibition on advertising. The key developments that ushered in this change were a series of U.S. Supreme Court cases that struck down bar association rules that limited the ability of lawyers to compete for clients. In 1975, the Court ruled that a local Virginia bar association was restraining competition by requiring that lawyers charge a minimum fee for handling home sales. The result of the bar association's policy was that no lawyer in Fairfax County, Virginia, would handle a sale for less than 1 percent of the value of the home (*Goldfarb v. Virginia State Bar*, 421 U.S. 773 [1975]). Two years later, the U.S. Supreme Court struck down ethical rules established by the State Bar of Arizona that prohibited lawyers from advertising. The two attorneys who brought the case had opened a legal clinic that handled routine matters such as uncontested divorces, name changes, and simple wills for a standard fee. The thinking was that the lawyers could turn a profit by handling a large number of cases for a modest fee. The lawyers decided to place an advertisement in a Phoenix newspaper offering "legal services at very reasonable fees" (*Bates v. State Bar of Arizona*, 433 U.S. 350 [1977]). The U.S. Supreme Court held that advertising would introduce competition into the legal marketplace that inevitably would result in lawyers competing to offer low-cost legal services to consumers. The Court stressed that false, deceptive, or misleading advertising should not be permitted. A claim, for example, that "we are successful in virtually all of our cases" is unclear and imprecise.

The Court later clarified that while lawyers are permitted to advertise their services, a bar association may prohibit lawyers from engaging in "in-person solicitation" of potential clients. The Court reasoned that there was a risk that the public would be misled and pressured into retaining an attorney and that lawyers would "stir up litigation." There is no limitation on lawyers informing individuals of their legal rights and prospects for obtaining a recovery so long as the lawyer does not seek to represent the individual (*Ohralik v. Ohio State Bar Association*, 436 U.S. 447 [1978]). The Court has approved mail solicitation of clients because a "truthful and nondeceptive" letter does not pose the same risk of pressure as does face-to-face solicitation (*Shapero v. Kentucky Bar Association*, 486 U.S. 466 [1988]).

State and local bar associations differ significantly on their standards for advertising, and some localities remain resistant to video images of accidents, testimonials from clients, and lawyers purchasing advertisements in newspaper lists of "super lawyers" or the "best lawyers." The U.S. Supreme Court upheld a controversial Florida prohibition against written solicitation to accident victims within thirty days of the accident (*Florida Bar v. Went For It Inc.*, 515 U.S. 18 [1995]).

The question is how to balance lawyers' freedom of speech and the social interest in informing consumers of the availability of legal representation against the interest in protecting the public from advertising that is misleading or inaccurate or omits essential information. An upstate New York law firm's television spot that portrayed lawyers racing at superhuman speeds to consult with a group of space aliens regarding a dented flying saucer initially was found in violation of a statewide prohibition against portrayals that were clearly unrelated to legal competence and that misled clients and demeaned the legal profession. New York courts later ruled that the advertisement was constitutionally protected freedom of speech. Personal injury and divorce lawyers tend to be more aggressive than other lawyers in their advertising. A lawyer in Chicago bought space on a billboard on a major highway that proclaimed, "Life's short. Get a divorce." The billboard portrayed a woman in lingerie and a shirtless and muscular man separated by the scales of justice. The Florida Supreme Court reprimanded two lawyers because of a television advertisement that featured the logo of a pit bull with a spiked collar and used the words "pit bull" in the firm's telephone number. The court reasoned that the "logo does not assist the public in ensuring that an informed decision is made prior to the selection of the attorney" (*Florida Bar v. Pape*, 918 So.2d 240 [Fla. 2005]). Other law firms find creative ways to advertise, such as sponsoring race car drivers or Little League teams (Baum 2013: 75).

Peter Dench/Reportage Archive/Getty Images

PHOTO 5.1   A billboard advertisement for the Rad Law Firm in downtown Dallas, Texas.

Some of the most controversial advertising involves lawyers contacting the victims of a disaster. In October 2003, ten people died and dozens were injured in an accident involving the Staten Island Ferry in New York City. Lawyers immediately began contacting the one thousand survivors in an effort to attract clients. This resulted in claims being filed for $1.3 billion in damages on behalf of the victims. A thirty-second television advertisement by one firm showed the grim picture of a ferry washed over by waves of green dollar signs and a voiceover proclaiming that people on board the ferry were entitled to damages and that it soon may be too late to file a legal action (Saulny 2003).

In September 2009, the Institute for Legal Reform, an arm of the U.S. Chamber, published a study in support of its advocacy of a restraint on legal suits against business. Television advertising for medical malpractice lawsuits by lawyers increased from roughly 10,150 advertisements in 2004 to more than 156,000 ads in 2008. In this same period, spending on advertisements by lawyers increased from $3.8 million to nearly $62 million, a roughly 1,300 percent increase in 2008-adjusted dollars. In 2015, lawyers advertising on television reached $892 million, a 68 percent increase over 2008. Large law firms tend to devote 3–5 percent of their revenues to advertising despite the uncertain impact of such advertising. In 2001, the firm of Brobeck, Phleger & Harrison spent $3.1 million on television advertising targeting high-tech firms. Despite this broad advertising campaign, Brobeck was forced into bankruptcy in 2003 (Heinz et al. 2005: 309–310). Another study determined that in 2003 lawyers spent more than any other business or profession on yellow-page ads, roughly $1 billion (Baum 2013: 75).

A study of lawyer advertising in the yellow pages in San Diego, California, found widespread disregard of the standards for advertising established by the State Bar of California. For example, of the 835 advertisements examined, 76 made the claim of "no recovery, no fee" while failing to disclose whether an individual would be held liable for the expenses and costs of the litigation. Lawyers referenced their past success and claimed they had collected "millions of dollars for clients" without indicating the basis for such claims or noting that past success did not provide a basis for predictions of future success.

The same study found that between 1988 and 2001, state bar associations disciplined several lawyers for unethical advertising. Ten actions were brought against lawyers in Florida, and seven complaints were filed in Texas and in three other states. In the other forty-five states in the study, a total of sixty-five complaints were filed (Rossi 2002).

In 2015, a number of law firms spent $10 million or more in advertising, and a Houston firm spent $25 million, according to the U.S. Chamber Institute for Legal Reform. Spending for legal-related television advertisements was $892 million in 2015, an increase of 68 percent since 2008. Legal advertising on television is focused on three topics: prescription drug claims, medical device claims, and asbestos and mesothelioma. The leading market for broadcast ads aired by personal injury lawyers is Tampa, followed by Orlando, Atlanta, and Las Vegas. There were over 165,000 legal advertisements in Tampa alone in 2015. Law firms are paying top dollar to buy keywords on Internet searches. Twenty-three of the twenty-five and seventy-eight of the one hundred most expensive search terms are legally related. The most expensive Google keyword search terms were "San Antonio car wreck attorney," costing $670 per click, and "accident attorney Riverside CA" ($626 per click) (Weiss 2015b).

The impact of advertising is not at all clear. An early study in Iowa and in Wisconsin found that lawyers who advertised are perceived as less competent, honest, helpful, effective, and reliable than lawyers who do not advertise. There also appears to be a risk that heavy-handed advertising will decrease confidence in the legal profession. On the other hand, there is evidence that advertising results in competition between lawyers for clients and leads to a lowering of legal fees for basic services such as the drafting of wills (Rossi and Weighner 1991).

Lawyers in large firms generally are not compelled to resort to direct advertising to the public and continue to regard blatant advertising as demeaning to the profession. Firms instead rely on websites, newsletters, and high-profile partners whose star power can attract clients, and encourage their partners to sit on the boards of directors of corporations where they mix and mingle with individuals from the world of high finance and business. Corporate firms increasingly rely on publicists, who issue press releases, contact journalists to write stories on the firm, and arrange for lawyers to appear on talk shows. Law firms also circulate "league tables" that rank firms on items such as the amount of money firms have recovered for clients. Another method of promoting a firm is to send out letters or take out notices in legal publications announcing new partners or associates (Heinz et al. 2005: 313).

There remains resistance among "old guard" lawyers to advertising. Carroll Seron, in her study of the business of legal practice, found that although advertising is accepted, traditionalists continue to view advertising as demeaning to the profession and as giving the false impression that lawyers can produce results with little effort. Traditionalists continue to rely on referrals, community ties, and membership in community organizations to attract clients (Seron 1996: 50–53). In contrast, younger and more business-oriented lawyers are comfortable with aggressively marketing themselves (50–53, 95–97). Seron notes that these youthful lawyers could just as easily be marketing pizzas or hamburgers and that they are more excited by the business aspects of law than with the actual practice of law. In this fast-paced world of the entrepreneurial lawyer, efficiency and generating a profit are more important than quality and personal relationships between lawyers and their clients (95–97, 104, 107).

Contingent Fees

Most lawyers charge by the hour, and their hourly rate is based on their expertise, their experience, and the difficulty of the task. Solo practitioners and small firms in a local area charge roughly the same fee for routine tasks such as the purchase of a home. The ABA Model Rules of Professional Conduct (1.5[a]) state, "A lawyer shall not make an agreement for, charge, or collect an unreasonable fee or an unreasonable amount of expenses."

Deborah Rhode reports that less than 5 percent of Americans believe lawyers' fees are fair. She accuses lawyers of "padding charges" by intentionally or unintentionally exaggerating the time devoted to a case, a practice that apparently is common in large corporate firms. There is clear fraud in 5–10 percent of cases and questionable practices in another 25–35 percent of cases. In one survey, 40 percent of lawyers conceded they inflate their charges, and roughly half of in-house corporate lawyers believe they are being overcharged by law firms. Lawyers report they bill for social conversations although corporate clients state that they do not expect to be billed for these conversations (Rhode 2000: 169–171). Former federal judge Jed Rakoff reported that the fee for hiring a lawyer has increased a greater rate than the average increase in income or wages and increased at more than three times the rate of inflation. Between 1985 and 2012, the average billing rate for law firm partners increased from $112 per hour to $536 per hour, and for associates from $79 to $370 per hour. These fees have contributed to most civil cases being settled; in 2015, only 1 percent of civil cases in state and federal court were decided on the merits at trial (Rakoff 2016: 4).

The following is a list of some classic abuses in corporate firms (Rhode 2000: 171–174).

- A lawyer may charge for the time an associate engages in non-legal work such as unpacking a box of documents.
- A senior partner may charge a large fee for completing a routine task that does not require legal expertise.

- Lawyers violate their ethical obligations by charging a client for learning the law required to represent a client on a legal matter.

- Large firms use "unit billing" in which charges are broken down into fifteen- or twenty-minute time segments. A brief phone call may cost a client one-fifth of a lawyer's hourly fee.

- Lawyers engage in double billing. They charge one client for travel time on a plane while charging another client for the time spent working on their case while on the plane.

- Firms inflate the costs of routine services such as photocopying and even charge for heating and air conditioning.

- Lawyers may require retainers (advance payments) and will keep the entire fee despite the fact that they quickly resolve the problem.

An alternative method of charging for legal services is a **contingent fee** arrangement. In a contingent fee arrangement, the client does not pay the lawyer. The lawyer is paid an agreed-on percentage of any legal settlement or of any court judgment that a plaintiff may receive. The contingent fee agreement covers only the legal fees in a case, and the plaintiff remains liable for expenses such as photocopying. It is estimated that 90 percent of personal injury cases are filed by lawyers working on a contingent fee basis (Baum 2013: 77–78). Keep in mind that contingent fee arrangements are between lawyers and plaintiffs bringing a legal action and do not cover the representation of defendants who are being sued (Rakoff 2016: 4).

A central criticism of contingent fees is that a lawyer will try to settle the case rather than go to court so as to spend as little time as possible on the case (Corsi 1984: 215–216). Defenders of contingent fees argue lawyers working on contingent fee will not settle a case and disregard the interest of the client because the lawyer will want to make a client happy to ensure the client retains the lawyer in the future. Lawyers also will want to ensure a client receives a fair settlement to maintain a reputation as a zealous advocate among other potential clients (Kritzer 2002a, 2002b).

The primary argument for contingent fees is that absent a contingent fee, lawyers may be unwilling to represent a client in a complicated case. This is particularly important for poor clients who may not be able to afford to hire a lawyer on an hourly basis. Critics of contingent fees respond that lawyers carefully screen cases before undertaking contingent fee representation and refuse to take cases where there is a risk of "losing." This explains why lawyers report they are successful in 90 percent of the cases. It also is pointed out that lawyers generally will not take cases on a contingent fee that may not result in a large settlement, and an individual whose recovery is likely to amount to less than $100,000 may not be able to find a lawyer willing to represent him or her on a contingent fee basis (Brickman 2003).

One of the chief criticisms of contingent fees is that lawyers at times obtain large fees for a moderate amount of work. The typical contingent fee is one-third the amount of the settlement or legal judgment. For example, a lawyer represented a widow whose husband was killed in the 2001 attack on the World Trade Center and obtained a $6.6 million settlement. The lawyer earned a $2 million fee for his work. A contingent fee, if broken down into the amount of money the lawyer is earning per hour, in some cases may translate into thousands or tens of thousands of dollars (Lansing, Fricke, and Davis 2009). In 1989, a soft-drink delivery truck struck a school bus, killing twenty-one children and injuring dozens of others. The bottling company's insurance company immediately settled for $122 million. The attorneys earned one-third of the settlement and generated a fee of roughly $25,000 per hour (P. Bell and O'Connell 1997: 216).

There also is the criticism that **class action** settlements at times have resulted in a significant percentage of the settlement going to the lawyers rather than to the plaintiffs. A class action is a legal action in which a lawsuit is brought on behalf of a small number of plaintiffs who are certified by the court as representatives of all "similarly situated individuals." The "members of the class" are contacted by the lawyers and are invited to join or opt out of the lawsuit. A class action makes sense when there are thousands of individuals, each of whom may have a small claim for damages. It would not be financially worthwhile for lawyers to file lawsuits on behalf of each individual client on a contingent fee basis because the recovery in each case would not be sufficiently large to meet the expenses of the litigation. Combining the claims provides an incentive for a law firm to take the consolidated case on a contingent fee basis. Class actions in the past have been filed against companies that manufactured defective medical devices, investors who have been defrauded by firms that misrepresented their financial condition, and consumers who purchased defective products or harmful medication, and on behalf of the victims of employment discrimination. In 2002, federal court of appeals judge Richard Posner refused to accept a settlement between the tax preparer H&R Block and a group of plaintiffs that would have resulted in the roughly seventeen million members of the class each receiving between $15 and $30 although the lawyers would have received $4 million in attorney fees in addition to expenses. Other judges in refusing to accept settlements have explained that allowing lawyers to receive large fees might make the public skeptical about the motives of lawyers and result in individuals being reluctant to join class action suits in the future. Keep in mind that arbitration clauses in most contracts (discussed in Chapter 6) preclude class actions (Rakoff 2016: 4).

Defenders of contingent fees argue that the hourly income of a lawyer working on a contingent fee case works out to be roughly similar to that of a lawyer working on an hourly basis. The lawyer also cannot predict how many hours a case will take and cannot predict whether he or she will be successful. The Minneapolis law firm of Faegre & Benson earned a contingent fee of over $100 million in successfully representing the Alaska fishermen whose livelihood was damaged by the *Exxon Valdez* oil spill. The firm had worked on the case for more than seventeen years and sacrificed other sources of income (Kritzer 2002a, 2002b).

Some commentators recognize the need for contingent fees and recommend keeping attorney fees at a reasonable level by capping the amount a lawyer may earn on a case, by allowing lawyers to earn a fee based on the number of hours they spend on a case, or by allowing lawyers working on a contingent fee to increase their hourly fee by 30 percent or 35 percent if they win the case (Lansing et al. 2009).

Elite members of the legal profession view the contingent fee as resulting in lawyers profiting from the suffering of their clients and as beneath the dignity of lawyers. On the other hand, lawyers who charge on the basis of contingent fees question whether the elite lawyers who oppose contingent fees are motivated by a desire to make it difficult for their corporate clients to be sued (Auerbach 1976: 44–48).

Various states have introduced reforms that limit the amount a lawyer may recover in a contingent fee, which critics allege discourages lawyers from taking all but the most lucrative cases. Stephen Daniels and Joanne Martin studied the impact of a 2003 Texas law that imposed a "hard cap" of $250,000 on noneconomic injuries (e.g., pain and suffering) in medical malpractice cases. The thinking of the Texas legislature was that large non-economic recoveries were driving up insurance rates and health care costs. Daniels and Martin find that "caps" on recovery for noneconomic harm resulted in a significant number of tort lawyers deciding against taking all but the most obvious medical malpractice cases because the risk and amount of work was not worth the amount of money that might be recovered on a contingent fee. Tort lawyers particularly avoided taking cases in those instances in which individuals did not suffer a significant loss of wages (e.g., children, unemployed, or elderly) (Daniels and Martin 2015: 205–230).

Benjamin Barton argues that tort reform of contingent fees has contributed to the rise of "settlement mills" that provide legal representation in cases that are unattractive to personal injury lawyers. These are high-volume personal injury practices that engage in nationwide advertising and negotiate quick and bargain basement settlements with insurance companies. These settlement mills have close working relationships with insurance companies and settle hundreds of cases at a time without even bothering to file a legal claim. Individuals with significant injury claims represented by a settlement mill typically receive a lower settlement than they would have received in the absence of a "cap" on recovery (Barton 2015: 107, 110-114).

A new development is investments by large banks and financial firms in lawsuits. The average person finds it difficult to afford to bring a case to court, and lawyers working on contingent fee lack the money to support the litigation. The typical run-of-the-mill civil action in federal court costs an average of $15,000; a medical malpractice case requiring expert witnesses may run well over $100,000. Lawyers have begun to borrow money in order to finance cases. The lawyers representing "ground zero" workers borrowed $35 million and settled the case for $712.4 million. The lenders earned roughly $11 million. Borrowing money is defended as allowing the average person to afford to sue a large corporation. Lawyers in most states are not required to inform their clients that they have borrowed money. The interest rate on a loan is as high as 15 percent, and the cost may be more than the financial award in the case. Lenders may be eager for a return on their investment and may place pressure on the lawyer to settle the case. Delays in settlement may result in interest fee payments taking an increasingly greater amount of the ultimate settlement (Appelbaum 2010).

In the next section, we outline two other approaches to providing individuals access to justice. Group legal services plans provide access to legal assistance as part of an individual's employment or union membership. Legal aid provides assistance to individuals who fall below the poverty line.

5.1 YOU DECIDE

In 2016, the news site Gawker was found guilty of harming former professional wrestling superstar Hulk Hogan (aka Terry Bollea) by subjecting him to embarrassment and to humiliation in posting a video recorded by a security camera of Hogan in a behind-closed-doors sexual interaction. The video was posted on Gawker for six months and reportedly was watched by millions of individuals. The 62-year-old

Hogan was pictured interacting in 2007 with the wife of his former best friend, "shock jock" Todd A. Clem, known on the radio as Love Sponge Clem. Clem's now former wife testified that Clem had encouraged her to have sex with Hogan. Clem could be heard at the end of the tape telling his wife that they could become rich from the sale of the tape. Gawker refused to take the video off the site despite several requests from Hogan.

(Continued)

(Continued)

A six-person Florida jury composed of four women and two men returned a guilty verdict against Gawker, Gawker owner Nick Denton, and Gawker editor Albert J. Daulerio and awarded Hogan $115 million in compensatory damages ($55 million for economic harm and $60 million for emotional distress) and $25 million in punitive damages.

It later was revealed that Hogan's suit against Gawker, which dragged on for nearly three years, was secretly funded by Peter Thiel, a co-founder of PayPal, who reportedly spent $10 million in support of the legal action. Thiel later would become a subject of controversy himself when it was revealed that he was one of the few tech entrepreneurs who supported and donated a significant amount of money to the presidential campaign of Donald Trump.

Thiel, unlike the typical investors who fund legal actions, apparently was looking for retribution against Gawker rather than looking for a profit. He allegedly was angry at Gawker for "outing" him and several of his friends as gay. Hogan's lawyers following the guilty verdict characterized Gawker as engaging in "morbid and sensational prying" rather than journalism and expressed the hope that the verdict would deter others from victimizing "innocent people."

Gawker argued throughout the trial that journalists are charged with revealing the activities of public personalities like Hogan who promote an image of sexual prowess. Gawker also pointed out that there was no question that the video was accurate and had not been modified. As a result of the damage award, Gawker media was forced into bankruptcy and sold to Univision although the Gawker.com site was dissolved.

Is press freedom in the United States at risk when a wealthy Silicon Valley billionaire can bankroll a legal action against an Internet site for publishing truthful material about a celebrity?

Legal Services Plans

An alternative avenue for people to obtain legal services involves **group legal services plans**. These may be organized either as "access plans" or as "prepaid legal services plans." Access plans provide individuals with access to lawyers as a benefit of their union membership or employment or membership in an organization. In contrast, individuals enrolled in a prepaid legal services plan pay a fee and in return are provided legal assistance for certain types of legal needs (Baum 2013: 77). It is estimated that between 30 percent and 40 percent of the public have access to some type of prepaid legal services plan (Rhode 2004: 97).

Legal services plans have existed in Europe for well over one hundred years. The first plans in the United States were introduced in 1973 when Congress amended the labor relations law to permit unions to bargain with management over the provision of legal services for union members. In 1971, the Laborers' International Union became the first union to provide legal assistance for its members. Various corporations and professional organizations followed this example and began to provide free legal assistance to their employees.

How do group legal services plans work? In an access plan, individuals who are covered by the plan are given a list of lawyers near their home with whom they may consult without having to pay a fee. The lawyer will make a phone call, write a letter, or review a contract or other document. An individual who wants the lawyer to pursue a more complicated matter such as providing representation on a reckless driving charge will be charged a reduced fee. AARP (formerly the

American Association of Retired Persons) is an example of an organization that offers an access plan to its members (Corsi 1984: 246–249). Former federal judge Jed Rakoff, although praising legal services plans, notes that the decline of labor unions in the United States has meant that over 90 percent of the private workforce does not have access to these plans as part of employment (Rakoff 2016: 5).

In a prepaid legal services plan, you pay a monthly fee of roughly $25 and, in return, are provided with free consultation with a lawyer and a number of basic services, including preparation of the documents required to purchase or sell a home, drafting a will, and reviewing an employment contract. Individuals can pay an additional fee to receive assistance with other matters such as a divorce, bankruptcy, representation in a minor criminal or civil case, or adoption. The lawyers who provide legal consultation generally are local attorneys who supplement their private practice by working for the prepaid plan or lawyers who work for the plan full-time. Under a "closed" plan, an individual is restricted to lawyers who contract with the plan. An "open" plan permits an individual to consult with any attorney who agrees to set a ceiling on fees (Rhode 2004: 98).

Benjamin Barton notes that a promising development in access to prepaid legal services is online sites like *LegalZoom.com*, *RocketLawyer.com*, and *LegalShield.com* that offer subscription plans that include online legal forms, attorney review of legal documents, and access to a lawyer for consultations (Barton 2015: 204). *LegalServicesLink.com* is an online service on which individuals post legal problems and lawyers enrolled on the site respond by listing their professional background and proposed fee.

Legal services plans ensure individuals will have the opportunity to consult with a lawyer on basic legal matters. Critics maintain that the plans enter into agreements with newly minted lawyers to save money, there is little quality control (Rhode 2004: 98), and the lawyers tend to spend as little time as possible with a client and often rely on paralegals (Van Hoy 1997).

Bar associations help provide legal representation to the middle class through referral services. These are "clearinghouses" that refer individuals to qualified lawyers in the community. The first organized efforts by local bar associations to address the needs of the middle class were experiments with referral services in the 1930s in Philadelphia and Chicago. In 1946, the ABA House of Delegates encouraged local bar associations to establish referral services to direct individuals to qualified lawyers willing to provide legal services at a reasonable rate (Hurst 1950: 326–329).

In the next section, we discuss programs to meet the legal needs of the poor.

Meeting the Legal Needs of the Poor

The German community in New York City created the country's first legal aid society in 1876 to protect newly arriving immigrants from dishonest landlords and exploitative employers and shopkeepers. Legal assistance to the poor gradually came to be viewed as a mechanism to assure the poor and working class that the legal system served the interests of all citizens and did not merely cater to the wealthy and privileged. In 1890, the German legal society was expanded to provide for the needs of individuals from every background and was renamed the New York Legal Aid Society. Four years earlier, the Protective Agency for Women and Children was established to protect women and children from being exploited by unscrupulous employers (Batlan 2015: 47–86). Shortly thereafter, the Bureau of Justice was created in Chicago to provide legal services to the poor. Lawyers in other cities thereafter formed legal aid societies modeled after the organizations in New York and in Chicago, and by 1917, legal aid societies had been formed in forty-one cities. These organizations provided assistance to the indigent in issues ranging from landlord–tenant disputes to divorce and employment (Shepard 2007: 2–4).

In 1919, Reginald Heber Smith, the 24-year-old director of the Boston Legal Aid Society, published the influential book *Justice and the Poor* based on his study of legal aid societies. Smith argued the poor were denied access to justice because they could not afford to hire lawyers and pay the costs of litigation. As a result, the indigent could not rely on the legal system to protect their rights. This led the poor to believe the American legal system was stacked against them. Smith predicted that this unequal access to the legal system would lead to social unrest and disorder. The solution was for the legal profession to expand its commitment to legal aid. Smith was a Harvard-trained lawyer and was a great believer in the American system of justice, and he did not doubt the poor and working class would be treated fairly by the judiciary if they were provided with legal representation (R. H. Smith 1919).

Smith painted a portrait of the fairness and justness of the American legal system that appealed to the legal establishment, and in 1917, the ABA passed a resolution encouraging state and local bar associations to assist the "worthy poor" (Rhode 2004: 59). Between 1921 and 1937, Smith chaired the ABA Standing Committee on Legal Aid and encouraged local bar associations to form legal aid societies.

Emery Brownell, in 1961, updated a study of legal aid that he had taken ten years earlier and found that although there had been growth in legal aid, roughly 20 percent of the nation's largest cities did not have legal aid offices (Brownell 1951, 1961). A study by Jerome Carlin and two other eminent researchers determined there was one legal aid lawyer for every 120,000 eligible clients. As a result, the average legal aid lawyer only had time to meet with 25 percent of the individuals seeking assistance and only possessed the resources to address straightforward and uncomplicated matters (Carlin, Howard, and Messinger 1966: 58). In 1963, it was estimated that legal aid was reaching only 1 percent of those in need, and two-thirds of low-income Americans had yet to consult with a lawyer. The bulk of the funding for legal aid was contributed by private charities rather than by the legal profession. The ABA warned of the danger of government involvement in the delivery of legal services (Rhode 2004: 60) as a step toward public control of the legal profession (Auerbach 1976: 136–137).

In 1964, U.S. attorney general Robert F. Kennedy, in a Law Day address at the University of Chicago School of Law, observed that the "the tenants of slums, and public housing projects, the purchasers from disreputable finance companies, the minority group member who is discriminated against" are all unable to assert their legal rights because of their lack of legal representation. In contrast, the wealthy are able to afford lawyers to guide them through the legal thicket. Attorney General Kennedy criticized lawyers for permitting the development of "two systems of law . . . one for the rich, one for the poor" (quoted in Shepard 2007: 1–2). Kennedy's address had been inspired by two Yale law graduates working on behalf of poor people, Edgar Cahn and Jean Cahn, who argued that the government should hire lawyers to work in local neighborhoods to represent poor people in legal matters and to bring legal actions challenging the conditions and practices that disadvantage the poor (Cahn and Cahn 1964).

President Lyndon Johnson fulfilled the vision of the assassinated president John F. Kennedy and worked with the Democratic Congress to pass the Equal Opportunity Act of 1964 to combat poverty in the United States. Johnson boldly declared a "war on poverty" designed to eliminate and prevent poverty in America. The statute created the Office of Economic Opportunity, which contributed funds to existing legal aid offices across the country, established more than one hundred new neighborhood legal offices, and funded the hiring of almost two thousand anti-poverty lawyers. The centers were to provide legal assistance to individuals whose income was less than 125 percent of the poverty level (in 2014, this was $27,563 for a family of four and amounted to fifty-four million people).

Jean Cahn was named as director of these new programs. Neighborhood lawyers, while representing poor people in their day-to-day legal problems, also employed law as an instrument to challenge public policies that disadvantaged the poor and marginal members of society. Examples of this type of social reform litigation included legal actions establishing that landlords had an obligation to provide habitable and safe residences for tenants, asking courts to take over the operation of public housing projects that were unsafe and unhealthy and infested by drugs and gangs, and arguing that people should not be deprived of public assistance without a hearing. Legal aid lawyers also brought actions to desegregate schools and argued that a California requirement that voters should have a knowledge of English was unconstitutional (E. Johnson 1974: 71). In other words, the mission was "to change the structure of the world in which poor people live" (Auerbach 1976: 270).

A number of lawsuits were filed challenging the working conditions of migrant workers in California and the policies of the state's chief executive, Governor Ronald Reagan. Governor Reagan was a vocal critic of federally funded legal aid and raised the question whether the government should be supporting lawyers in California Rural Legal Assistance to pursue what he considered to be a liberal social agenda. Governor Reagan's criticism was reiterated by Vice President Spiro Agnew, who described legal aid lawyers as "ideological vigilantes" who employed public funds to pursue their own "theories of how society should be structured and how the resources, rights and benefits of that society should be distributed." Legal aid in the view of Agnew should be limited to problems confronting individuals in housing and employment and as consumers rather than focusing on social reform. The bread and butter of legal services should be to prevent evictions and homelessness, protect battered women from abusers by obtaining orders of protection, and ensure that fathers pay child support to feed their children. Legal aid lawyers responded by arguing that the larger issues of discrimination in education, housing, and social services must be addressed if poor people are to have a chance to lift themselves out of poverty (Corsi 1984: 148–149).

The ABA originally viewed legal services for the poor as a threat to the economic independence of the legal profession and criticized legal aid as a step toward "Communist control." The ABA eventually endorsed federally funded legal services although various local bar associations continued to oppose federally funded lawyers whom they viewed as depriving local lawyers of clients and as promoting radical social reform (Auerbach 1976: 236, 272–273).

As President Nixon was about to leave office under the cloud of a threatened impeachment for his role in the Watergate scandal, he placed legal services under the control of the newly created **Legal Services Corporation** (LSC). The corporation was to be run by an eleven-person board of directors appointed by the U.S. president with the approval of Congress. The delivery of legal services was to be under the control of regional directors. On the one hand, the creation of the corporation ensured that legal services would be removed from direct control by the president and could not be eliminated with the stroke of a pen. On the other hand, the directors were appointed by the president and could exercise their authority to limit the activities of legal aid lawyers funded by the corporation (Shepard 2007: 102).

PHOTO 5.2   The Legal Services Corporation funds local nonprofit groups providing access to civil justice for low-income Americans. It is estimated in 2015 that 1.8 million individuals benefited from legal assistance. Agencies lack adequate resources and turn away close to 50 percent of individuals seeking assistance.

The delivery of legal services was strongly supported by President Jimmy Carter, who noted that although the United States had the "highest concentration" of lawyers in the world, it did not have "more justice." President Carter noted that no professional service was "more wastefully or unfairly distributed than legal skills. Ninety percent of our lawyers serve ten percent of our people. . . . We are over-lawyered and under-represented" (quoted in Shepard 2007: 123).

President Reagan, on taking office in 1980, unsuccessfully attempted to eliminate the LSC although he succeeded in severely reducing funding for the agency and in restricting the activities of legal aid lawyers. These restrictions were intended to return lawyers to their traditional role of representing individual clients in remedying specific problems such as divorce, child support, landlord–tenant issues, and claims for veterans' benefits rather than devoting themselves to "politically controversial activities." Legal aid lawyers under Reagan were prohibited from engaging in litigation involving abortion, school desegregation, immigration, prisoners, and public housing residents facing eviction because of drug use. They also were barred from lobbying, voter registration, political organizing, class action suits against the government, and seeking attorney fees. The prohibition on class actions suits was a direct effort to limit law to achieve social reform such as asking a court to take over a jail that fails to provide safety and security and basic human needs or a challenge to the electoral system in a city that is alleged to underrepresent African Americans. The prohibition on attorney fees meant that lawyers were prohibited from accepting fees that were provided as a matter of law to lawyers who brought cases resulting in the protection of consumers or tenants or employment discrimination. The reduction in funding for legal services, along with the prohibition on the receipt of attorney fees, severely restricted the budget of the LSC. This resulted in staff cutbacks, and various offices decided that with staff reductions, they no longer had the resources to represent clients in areas such as divorce, child custody, and bankruptcy (Luban 1988: 242, 298–300).

Legal services were not a priority for the administration of President George W. Bush (Shepard 2007: 240). At the time President Obama assumed office, federal funding was roughly one-half of the 1980 level (Rhode 2004: 106). Local legal service programs typically supplemented federal funds with monies contributed by state and local bar associations and other sources. The majority of the funding in roughly one-third of the states at present is based on state and local sources, which constituted 58 percent of all funding in 2007. The so-called federal poison pill rule prevents a legal aid office receiving federal funds from using any outside funds to engage in activities prohibited by federal law. At the same time as local legal aid programs have experienced a cutback in federal funding, the availability of local funding has been shrinking as a result of the downturn in the economy. These funds typically are based on interest in accounts held by lawyers for their clients (IOLTA, or Interest on Lawyer Trust Accounts), which, with a decline in interest rates, no longer generate the several hundred million dollars that they yielded in the past (Baum 2013: 74). Total funding in the United States for civil legal assistance is roughly $2.25 for every eligible individual as compared to $32 in England and $12 in New Zealand (Rhode 2004: 106, 112). A 2007 study by the LSC (outlined below) documented the continuing gap between the legal needs of the poor and the provision of legal services. The report concludes that "in large portions of the country the justice gap is wider than it was twenty-five years ago" (Legal Services Corporation 2007).

For every client served by an LSC-funded program, at least one person was turned away because of insufficient resources. The largest number of people who are turned away have issues regarding housing and family and consumer affairs. This means that these people may experience evictions, a lack of child support, or domestic abuse.

Only a "very small percentage" of legal problems of low-income people (one in five or less) are addressed by a private attorney or a legal aid lawyer. Individuals explained they were unable to afford a lawyer despite the fact that most households surveyed were financially eligible for free assistance from legal aid. Other respondents who did not obtain legal representation believed that a lawyer could not help them.

President Obama increased spending on legal assistance by $30 million and distributed close to $400 million to 137 legal aid centers across the United States. He also lifted restrictions on the ability of legal aid lawyers to obtain court-awarded attorney fees for certain types of cases. Forty-five states provide attorney fees to lawyers who successfully bring an action for violation of consumer protection laws while federal law provides attorney fees for enforcement of housing discrimination laws (Dillard and Savner 2009).

The LSC 2015 report documents that legal aid lawyers closed 755,774 cases. Nearly 129,000 clients of the LSC were 60 years of age or older, and roughly 528,000 clients were women. Somewhat over 116,000 cases involved domestic violence. The households benefiting from LSC assistance included roughly 1.8 million individuals (Legal Services Corporation 2015).

LSC grantees nonetheless are progressively limited in their ability to provide legal services. The 2015 LSC report states that 50 percent of individuals seeking assistance from grantees were turned away because of a lack of adequate resources. A recent study by the Boston Bar Association found that in Massachusetts civil legal aid programs turn away 64 percent of eligible cases. Nearly thirty-three thousand low-income residents in Massachusetts were denied the aid of a lawyer in life-essential matters involving eviction, foreclosure, and family law cases involving child abuse and domestic violence. People seeking assistance with family law cases were turned away 80 percent of the time. In New York City, roughly 90 percent of individuals in child custody proceedings do not have lawyers in child support matters in family court, and 99 percent of tenants are unrepresented in eviction proceedings.

Polls indicated that roughly 80 percent of the public support the provision of basic legal services for the poor. Legal aid programs nonetheless have suffered a cutback in funding and may once again find that they may be barred from challenging the broad social conditions that affect the poor (Rhode 2004: 104). President Donald Trump's initial 2017 budget rejected the $500 million appropriation requested by LSC and instead cuts the budget to zero. A congressional budget agreement restored the LSC budget to the existing $385 million appropriation, which is roughly a 17 percent reduction from the LSC 2010 budget appropriation (in inflation-adjusted dollars) (Snell and O'Keefe 2017).

Pro bono is yet another method of delivering legal services to the public.

Pro Bono

We should not overlook that lawyers donate their professional expertise to individuals who ordinarily cannot afford a lawyer's services. **Pro bono publico** ("done without compensation for the public good") is viewed as part of a lawyer's obligation to ensure equal justice and reminds lawyers that their primary responsibility is to uphold the rule of law. There also is the practical consideration that providing legal representation promotes respect for lawyers and enhances confidence in the fairness of the legal system. Large firms also find that pro bono work can assist in recruiting idealistic young attorneys (Rhode 2004: 146–147).

In 1908, the non-binding ABA Canons of Professional Ethics advised in Canon 12 that "a client's poverty" might dictate that a lawyer offer his or her services for a reduced fee or "even none at all." The ABA's current Model Rules of Professional Conduct provide that a lawyer should have as a goal the provision of fifty hours a year of free legal services. This provision has been adopted in some form by virtually every state bar association's code of professional conduct.

The thinking is that lawyers are provided a monopoly on legal representation and, in return for this privilege, should assist the public in gaining full and fair access to the legal system. Pro bono work also ensures that lawyers will appreciate the problems that confront the average person and appreciate those areas of the legal system that require reform (Rhode 2015: 54).

In the 1980s, a survey indicated that lawyers donated an average of between five and fifteen hours per year and that the overwhelming majority of this work was devoted to friends, family, and employees of lawyers or their clients or to local organizations in which lawyers might make valuable contacts with potential clients (Rhode 2004: 65–66).

Should lawyers be required to donate services to the poor? This type of requirement has been rejected as an interference with lawyers' ability to earn an income and as a form of "involuntary servitude." Most lawyers do not necessarily possess the required expertise to assist people with ordinary problems. There also is the consideration that lawyers who represent bankers or retailers or other businesses are reluctant to bring a case against a firm that is part of the industry that they depend on for their livelihood (see You Decide 5.3 on the study site).

Although the ABA has rejected mandatory pro bono, it suggests lawyers should aspire to provide fifty hours per year without charge primarily to "persons of limited means" or to organizations assisting them. This responsibility also could be fulfilled by providing legal services to charitable, religious, community, or educational organizations or by making financial contributions to these groups. Most states follow some version of this ABA standard. Florida, Maryland, and New Jersey impose the most stringent requirements for pro bono work by lawyers. Nationally, between 15 percent and 18 percent of lawyers engage in pro bono activity, and American lawyers on average donate less than half an hour of pro bono work per week. The approximately fifty thousand lawyers at large firms average ten minutes per day on pro bono activities, and pro bono activity in the most profitable firms has been rapidly declining. Eighteen of the one hundred most profitable firms have agreed to meet the challenge of donating 3–5 percent of their revenues to support legal assistance (Rhode 2004: 151–155). Lawyers generally are ranked as one of the top paid professions, and yet the average lawyer donates $85 a year to pro bono organizations (Rhode 2000: 5).

Deborah Rhode conducted a comprehensive survey of pro bono work. She found that lawyers in most large firms quickly learn that pro bono work is not rewarded as highly as work for paying clients and is at odds with the firm's stress on profits. Many young lawyers are burdened with debts from their student years and want to spend time accumulating billable hours and pursuing bonuses. Lawyers also do not have the time to undertake additional work. Lawyers note they help paying clients on a daily basis in their traditional practice (Rhode 2004: 160–172).

Rhode reports that most lawyers would welcome more pro bono work. The lack of pro bono opportunities is a source of dissatisfaction among newly minted lawyers and that fully half of lawyers would like to devote more time to pro bono work. Yet, only a quarter of lawyers work in organizations or firms that fully credit pro bono work as billable hours, and nearly two-thirds believe that pro bono work is a negative or unimportant in determining promotion and compensation (Rhode 2015: 19).

Rebecca L. Sandefur's statistical analysis of lawyers' self-reported pro bono activity provides a somewhat more sophisticated analysis of pro bono activity. She finds pro bono activity is highest in state bar associations that directly recruit lawyers to undertake legal assistance, in states with the highest per capita income for lawyers, and in states in which lawyers are concerned that individuals may seek assistance from non-lawyers (e.g., accountants) who constitute a threat to the continuing income of the state's legal profession (Sandefur 2007).

In another recent study, Robert Granfield finds that attitudes of young lawyers toward pro bono work are determined by the lawyers' "workplace setting" rather than by the value placed on pro bono activity during the lawyers' legal education. For example, in contrast to Rhode, he finds the greatest support for mandatory pro bono work is by lawyers in large firms because the lawyers are able to count pro bono work toward their "billable hours" and obtain valuable legal experience. Lawyers in large firms embrace pro bono as a means of countering the perception that they are "money hungry servants of corporate interests." African American lawyers tend to have a strong sense of community responsibility and, as a consequence, have a greater involvement in pro bono work than white lawyers (Granfield 2007).

Benjamin Barton notes that the problem of the lack of legal representation cannot be fully addressed through pro bono work and that much of lawyers' pro bono work is devoted to cultural and arts organizations rather than to the indigent. There also is the persistent objection that a mandatory pro bono obligation would constitute an unlawful taking of a lawyer's expertise without payment (Barton 2015: 195–196).

We next focus on lawyers whose legal practice is based on representing clients who share their ideological commitment rather than on making money.

Cause Lawyering

We usually think of lawyers as "hired guns" who represent any client who walks in the door and is willing to pay the attorney's fee. Lawyers employ their skills on behalf of the client despite their personal view of the client or the client's claim. We know that although lawyers tend to gravitate toward those areas of practice that reflect their personal views, lawyers' personal opinions or political ideology on issues such as the environment generally do not determine whether they are willing to represent an oil company or the Sierra Club.

Some lawyers devote their energies to representing "causes" rather than individuals or large corporate entities and organizations. Lawyers engage in **cause lawyering** when they use the law to advance a social movement or social policy they believe is in the "public interest." Lawyers engaged in cause lawyering typically share the goals of the social or political movement they represent. Cause lawyering may involve working full-time for a social justice organization or may involve lawyers who supplement their legal practice with cases on behalf of a political or social movement. Scholars who study cause lawyering observe that it involves an intent to advance a political cause as well as behavior that advances the cause (Scheingold and Bloom 1998).

Lawyers involved in cause lawyering may work on behalf of organizations such as the American Civil Liberties Union (which is committed to the protection of freedom of expression and civil liberties), the Natural Resources Defense Council (which works on behalf of the environment), or the National Organization for Women (which works to defend the rights of women). One of the most storied examples of cause lawyering was the legal strategy designed and implemented by attorneys for the National Association for the Advancement of Colored People (NAACP) that resulted in the integration of the public schools. During the 1960s, Ralph Nader, a young Harvard Law School graduate, inspired young lawyers to work in "public interest law" on behalf of consumers. "Nader's Raiders" made important reforms in areas ranging from automobile safety to occupational safety for workers (Sarat and Scheingold 2006; Scheingold and Sarat 2004). Although "cause lawyering" traditionally has been identified with liberal causes, the past decades have witnessed a growth in cause lawyering on behalf of conservative groups and foundations. An example is the American Center for Law and Justice, founded by Reverend Pat Robertson, which defends and advances freedom of religion, the "right to life," and the sanctity of marriage (Southworth 2008).

Lawyers make various contributions to social movements. Even an unsuccessful case can prove important to a movement (Scheingold 1974). Several wealthy individuals have established legal organizations that recruit plaintiffs to challenge issues like affirmative action and connect them with sympathetic lawyers that the organization pays to take the case (Mencimer 2016).

Legitimacy. Lawyers file cases that contend that a group possesses a legal right and entitlement to what it is seeking to achieve. The NAACP achieved court rulings recognizing that the denial of integrated educational opportunities for African American young people violated their constitutional right to equal protection under the law. This sometimes is referred to as "framing" an issue.

Political platform. A legal case allows a group to articulate and highlight its views and to persuade the public of the merits of its claims. Focusing on the harm suffered by a particular individual in litigation can "humanize" an issue by drawing attention to the suffering of a specific member of the group. Individuals who defended segregation were placed on the defensive when confronted with young children who were denied equal educational opportunity.

Inspiration. Legal actions may inspire protests, encourage social activism, bring attention to a cause, and place pressure on elected officials to pay attention to a movement. A legal strategy was important in the movement against the Vietnam War in the 1960s and has proven significant in the movement against nuclear weapons and by both sides in the abortion debate.

On the other side of the scale is the risk that an unsuccessful legal challenge may damage a movement's legitimacy. An intense debate took place over whether the movement for same-sex marriage would be hurt in the event that a legal case claiming that the prohibition on same-sex marriage violated equal protection of the laws proved unsuccessful. The alternative was to continue to focus on swaying public opinion and persuading state legislatures to amend their laws to recognize same-sex marriage.

Movement activists at times are critical of cause lawyers who do not put themselves at risk by engaging in political protests and political organizing. There also can be tension between lawyers who may want to make conventional legal arguments and activists who may want to use the courtroom to make political points.

Lawyers who engage in cause lawyering generally have a different perspective than other lawyers in their view of the role of a lawyer. Studies indicate that most students who enter law school because they want to use the law to achieve social change quickly abandon their altruistic aspirations (McGill 2006). They shift their priorities and place a premium on working in a setting in which they can develop their legal skills, earn a competitive salary, and achieve professional prestige. Most students also come to accept that the role of a lawyer is to represent anyone in need of representation rather than to pursue a personal political agenda (Stover and Erlanger 1989).

Cause lawyers generally have aspirations for reform that go beyond a single issue or single case. Lawyers committed to human rights are committed to litigating issues ranging from immigration to Native American and workers' rights and torture (Kawar 2015; Lee 2014). These lawyers appreciate that social change requires in addition to litigation that they educate the public and the media on the issues, help organize rallies and protests, and form coalitions with lawyers and groups that share their commitments (D. Cole 2016: 149–220). A fairly recent development involves state attorneys general who share a common political point of view combining to bring multistate litigation on issues ranging from abortion, gun control, and same-sex marriage to global warming. State attorneys general have worked across party lines in suing pharmaceutical and tobacco companies (Nolette 2015). Most recently, state attorneys general collaborated in challenging President Donald Trump's February 2017 immigration order, and their efforts have been augmented by a renewed commitment by liberal legal activist groups (Savage 2017).

What accounts for the fact that some lawyers commit some portion of their career to cause lawyering? Ann Southworth in her study of conservative cause lawyers found that lawyers working on behalf of conservative religious groups generally share the views of their clients and question whether lawyers should be morally neutral about the causes they represent.

A number of lawyers in Southworth's study attended law school with the goal of using the law to achieve social change. Other lawyers shifted to cause lawyering after finding they derived little satisfaction from conventional legal practice. There is another group of lawyers who, while committed to advancing a political cause, also viewed their involvement in cause lawyering as a good strategy for attracting clients (Southworth 2008: 71–88).

Amanda Hollis-Brusky (2015) documents the impact of the conservative Federalist Society, which is what she terms an "epistemic (knowledge) community"—a group of lawyers, academics, and students devoted to the advancement of conservative constitutional principles. Hollis-Brusky illustrates how the Federalist Society has propagated its views through conferences, law review articles, networking, appointment of conservative judges on state and federal courts, organizing amicus curiae briefs, legal advocacy, and drawing attention to judicial decisions that support its philosophy. In *District of Columbia v. Heller*, recognizing the Second Amendment right of individuals to possess arms, four of the five Supreme Court justices in the majority along with the judge who wrote the appellate court decision had deep ties to the Federalist Society. Three Federalist Society members orchestrated the legal strategy and twenty-one members of the society signed on to eight different amicus curiae briefs. The Supreme Court opinion relied on articles written by prominent academic members of the society (*District of Columbia v. Heller*, 554 U.S. 570 [2008]). The American Constitution Society performs a similar though less influential role in promoting liberal interpretations of the U.S. Constitution.

Self-Representation

Courts are gradually recognizing the right to **pro se** representation (or self-representation). The organized legal profession during the 1930s sought to preserve a monopoly over the law and successfully lobbied state legislatures to enact statutes prohibiting the "unauthorized practice of law." These statutes were directed against non-lawyers representing clients in court. Judges also created procedural barriers against individuals representing themselves in court (Rhode 2004: 75–76).

The movement for pro se representation has been fueled in recent years by the availability of "do-it-yourself" legal materials and efforts to make legal remedies less complicated, such as "no-fault divorce." Another new development is laws passed in forty-one states that have "unbundled legal services" and permit individuals to represent themselves in court while hiring lawyers to address technical matters such as writing legal documents. This modifies the traditional rule that a lawyer is required to represent an individual throughout the entire legal process.

This has been accompanied by the first stages of a movement to establish special courts for pro se cases, to employ attorneys to assist pro se litigants, and to provide advisory hotlines, self-help centers, and online manuals on pro se representation (Rhode 2015: 49).

Deborah Rhode reports that pro se filings constitute a quarter of all new civil cases. One party appears without the assistance of a lawyer in between 65 percent and 90 percent of uncontested divorces. Rhode also notes self-representation is increasingly the norm in landlord–tenant disputes, bankruptcies, and minor criminal charges. She cites a study that indicates that roughly half of the individuals representing themselves believed that the matter was sufficiently straightforward that they could represent themselves or explained they could not afford a lawyer (Rhode 2004: 82–83).

Jona Goldschmidt attributes the increase in pro se filings to increased literacy, rugged individualism, the expense of litigation and attorney fees, and negative views of attorneys. He argues that preserving the ability of individuals to proceed pro se is crucial to maintaining confidence in the fairness of the judicial system. Goldschmidt attributes the opposition to pro se to the economic self-interest of lawyers in maintaining control over courtroom practice (Goldschmidt 2002).

Rhode notes that most judges claim they have an obligation to remain impartial between the parties in a case and refuse to assist individuals desiring to represent themselves and prohibit court personnel from assisting individuals to act pro se. She writes that complicated legal forms and procedures and the long, drawn-out legal procedures make it difficult for individuals to represent themselves. Judges find themselves with heavy caseloads and typically do not want to encourage pro se representation, which likely will slow down the adjudication of cases. Court systems are strapped for cash and will find it difficult to provide the resources required to assist pro se litigants (Rhode 2004: 82–85).

A related approach to limit the costs of representation was adopted in Colorado, which now allows non-lawyers to represent claimants in unemployment hearings. Washington state allows licensed real estate brokers to perform some of the tasks formerly reserved for lawyers in real estate transactions (Rhode 2015: 50).

We end our sketch of lawyer–client relationships with a discussion of the system of regulating the ethical practices of lawyers. As you recall, self-regulation is one of the characteristics of a profession.

■ LEGAL ETHICS

Lawyers historically have been viewed as having little regard for ethics. The philosopher Plato criticized their "small and unrighteous souls" while the great Roman Seneca noted that lawyers act as instruments of injustice who are "'smothered by their prosperity" (Rhode 1998: 284).

Deborah Rhode notes the catalogue of public criticisms of lawyers would fill a lengthy book. The primary complaint is greed. Rhode observes it is commonly remarked that a lawyer is an educated individual who "rescues your estate from your enemies and keeps it for himself." In an ABA survey, three-fifths of Americans describe lawyers as greedy, and as many as three-quarters believe legal fees are excessive. A second complaint is that lawyers are impolite, arrogant, and insensitive and neglect their clients. Only one-fifth of respondents describe lawyers as caring and compassionate. It should come as no surprise that over 90 percent of parents do not want their children to grow up to be lawyers. Rhode humorously asks why New Jersey has so many toxic waste dumps and California so many lawyers? The answer is because New Jersey got first choice (Rhode 2000: 5).

Discipline of the legal profession in the nineteenth century was the responsibility of judges, and there was no formal system of regulation. Richard Abel notes that state and local bar associations professed to be interested in ethics but made little effort to regulate themselves. There was a move to formalize ethical rules in the early twentieth century, which resulted in the 1908 Canons of Professional Ethics. Jerold Auerbach writes that the canons were directed at solo practitioners and focused on prohibiting advertising, banning referral fees, promoting litigation by individuals, and barring lawyers from listing legal specialties (Auerbach 1976: 42–43). Abel observes that self-regulation is an essential component of an occupation's claim to the status of a profession and that self-regulation provides protection against state regulation (Abel 1989: 142).

The most obvious explanation for ethical codes of conduct is that these documents reflect lawyers' view that they perform an important social function in defending the rights and liberties of the individual and hold themselves to the highest standards. Ethical codes are intended to assure individuals that they are in safe and secure hands when they consult a lawyer: in other words, you can trust your lawyer. The now-deceased prominent lawyer and diplomat Sol Linowitz writes that the primary feature of the legal profession is *credit emptor* ("let the buyer trust") rather than *caveat emptor* ("let the buyer beware") (Linowitz 1994: 5).

The legal profession clearly is concerned with ethics, judging by the constant concern with revising ethical codes, the requirement that law schools offer classes in professional ethics, and the provision of a separate section of the bar exam on legal ethics. Most state bars require that a portion of a lawyer's **continuing legal education** include a component on ethics. The ethical system is based on the premise that if lawyers are taught their ethical responsibilities, they will adhere to these standards regardless of pressures from clients and colleagues, the temptations of financial fraud, or other financial misconduct.

Another aspect of the ethical system is that individuals who apply for admission to a state bar must submit to a "character" review in which they submit references and disclose all information that may call their "good character" into question. Individuals convicted of a felony (a crime punishable by a year or more) generally will have a difficult time gaining admission.

Despite this focus on ethics, surveys indicate a significant number of lawyers are uninformed about their ethical responsibilities or simply disregard them. Lawyers generally are prohibited from paying a lawyer who refers a client to them. The reason is that the referral fee will be passed on to the client, resulting in an increase in the cost of legal services. The practice of law is a profession rather than a business, and attorneys should not be paid for a simple referral. Yet 62 percent of lawyers in one poll approved of payments for referrals, and 67 percent thought the practice was permissible or did not know whether it was permissible (Abel 1989: 143). Lawyers in firms often are taught that ethical guidelines do not apply by their mentors who tell them that kickbacks and referral fees are a customary part of the practice of law (Abel 2008: 498).

The legal profession was rudely awakened to the reality of the disciplinary system in 1970 when former U.S. Supreme Court justice Thomas Clark reported that a three-year study revealed a "scandalous situation" in which lawyers viewed the disciplinary system with reactions ranging from "apathy to outright hostility." The Clark Commission found that disciplinary action was "nonexistent in many jurisdictions" and that procedures were outdated and ineffective (M. Devlin 1994: 369–379).

As part of the reform effort, the **Model Rules of Professional Conduct** were adopted by the ABA in 1983. This document is intended as a model to be followed by state bar associations. The Model Rules of Professional Conduct replaced the 1969 Model Code of Professional Responsibility, which, in turn, replaced the 1908 Canons of Professional Ethics. The model rules have been adopted by virtually every state bar association although there are significant differences in certain areas such as the standards for advertising.

The Model Rules of Professional Conduct address a number of areas, the most important of which are listed below.

Lawyer–client relationships. Fees for legal representation, information that should be kept confidential, safekeeping of money and property, declining and terminating legal representation, and the obligation to provide competent and diligent representation.

The lawyer as counselor. The obligation to offer objective and disinterested advice and the duty, when dealing with two individuals, to fairly resolve a dispute.

The lawyer as advocate. The obligation to avoid litigating claims that lack merit and to avoid unnecessary delay, trial publicity, lawyers as witnesses, and responsibility of prosecutors.

Relations with persons other than the client. The duty to communicate with an opposing party through his or her lawyer and guidelines for communicating with unrepresented parties.

Law firms and associations. Responsibilities toward partners, associates, and paralegals, and procedures for practicing in jurisdictions where a lawyer is not admitted to practice.

Public services. Pro bono activities and obligation to accept court appointment to represent indigents.

Information regarding legal services. Limitations on advertising and on soliciting clients.

The integrity of the profession. Disciplinary proceedings and misconduct, duty to report misconduct, prohibition on political contributions intended to assist in obtaining legal business or judicial appointments.

In August 2016, the American Bar Association amended its ethics rules to provide that it is professional misconduct for a lawyer to engage in "conduct that the lawyer knows or reasonably should know is harassment or discrimination on the basis of race, sex, religion, national origin, ethnicity, disability, age, sexual orientation, gender identity, marital status or socioeconomic status related to the practice of law." This includes statements of bias or prejudice toward others as well as derogatory verbal or physical conduct. The rule extends to legal settings as well as the workplace and professional social activities.

The rule change, in part, was in response to a number of complaints by female lawyers that they are subjected to sexist and demeaning comments by opposing lawyers. Opponents objected that the rule stifles lawyers' freedom to express themselves and that the amendment to the rules was driven by "political correctness" rather than by norms of professional conduct. The rule excludes statements made in the course of legitimate legal representation such as courtroom advocacy or comments made when consulting with a client.

Each rule in the model code is followed by comments elaborating on the particular obligation. The violation of several of these ethical rules constitutes a crime and may result in criminal liability. As a result, a lawyer's ethical violations may result in criminal prosecution and, as discussed below, a civil suit brought by a client for malpractice. The basic definition of professional misconduct is reprinted in Table 5.2.

Table 5.2 ■ Rule 8.4 Misconduct	
It is professional misconduct for a lawyer to	(a) violate or attempt to violate the Rules of Professional Conduct, knowingly assist or induce another to do so, or do so through the acts of another;
	(b) commit a criminal act that reflects adversely on the lawyer's honesty, trustworthiness or fitness as a lawyer in other respects;
	(c) engage in conduct involving dishonesty, fraud, deceit or misrepresentation;
	(d) engage in conduct that is prejudicial to the administration of justice;
	(e) state or imply an ability to influence improperly a government agency or official or to achieve results by means that violate the Rules of Professional Conduct or other law; or
	(f) knowingly assist a judge or judicial officer in conduct that is a violation of applicable rules of judicial conduct or other law.

A violation of ethical standards is subject to professional discipline. The ABA in 1993 adopted the Model Rules for Lawyer Disciplinary Enforcement, which have been amended on several occasions and have been adopted by most state bar associations. The model rules establish state boards to hear ethics complaints; these boards are composed of lawyers and of members of the public appointed by the state supreme court. The board is assisted by a full-time legal staff of lawyers who investigate and prosecute complaints. An "intake office" is charged with assisting members of the public to file a complaint. The hearings initially are conducted by local hearing boards composed of lawyers and members of the public who hear from the staff lawyer as well as from the lawyer charged with an ethics violation. Appeals may be taken to the state board and to the state supreme court. Punishment that results in a limitation on a lawyer's ability to practice law is required to be approved by the state supreme court. The state supreme court in most states has responsibility for licensing lawyers to practice and is the appropriate body to determine whether a lawyer has violated the terms of the license and whether he or she should be disciplined. State bars generally try to avoid these types of hearings for matters such as claims of excessive legal fees and provide for mediation or efforts to assist the parties to resolve their differences.

The available sanctions or penalties include the following:

Disbarment. A permanent prohibition on the ability of a lawyer to practice law, which is imposed for the most serious violations.

Suspension. The lawyer is prohibited from the practice of law for a limited period of time.

Probation. A lawyer is allowed to practice while undergoing rehabilitation for a problem such as alcoholism or drug abuse that contributed to the ethics violation. A failure to satisfactorily complete the rehabilitation program results in a more serious penalty.

Reprimand. A letter is sent to the lawyer noting minor misconduct. These matters can be disposed of without a formal hearing if the lawyer agrees to accept responsibility.

Restitution. Disciplinary sanctions generally require the lawyer to provide financial reimbursement to the client, and the lawyer also is directed to reimburse the state disciplinary board for all expenses.

The model rules list various aggravating as well as mitigating factors. A penalty likely will be more severe when there is a pattern of misconduct, a failure to cooperate with the investigation, a refusal to admit misconduct, a fraud on the court, or a vulnerable victim, and when a lawyer should be aware of ethical rules based on long experience in the practice of law. Mitigating factors include a history of ethical conduct, documented personal or emotional problems, a cooperative attitude, professional help for any problems, and making restitution or taking steps to restore the damage caused by the misconduct.

The results of the adjudication of the complaint are communicated to the individual bringing the complaint and to the lawyer charged with an ethical violation. Reprimands for serious ethical violations and suspensions and disbarments typically are made public ("public penalties"). Penalties for minor misconduct typically are not publicized ("private penalties"). State bars generally issue statistical reports that summarize activities over the course of a year. Oregon is the only jurisdiction that makes the results of all complaints public (Abel 2008: 504).

In 2008, disciplinary agencies received 114,283 complaints, and 32,302 were pending from prior years. Most cases were dismissed because the complainant failed to submit a complaint that constituted a violation of the ethical code or because evidence of a violation was lacking. Ultimately, 3,360 lawyers were charged with an ethical violation. Roughly 6,670 individuals were sanctioned (including complaints from prior years). This included over 900 disbarments, almost 2,000 suspensions, and more than 850 reprimands (ABA Standing Committee on Lawyers' Professional Liability 2008). Bar associations understandably want to be certain that a public sanction is merited, and thus they closely examine complaints. The result is that a complainant may grow frustrated with the fact that the time from the filing of a complaint to the imposition of a public sanction can take on average 505 days in California, 400 days in Georgia, fifteen months in Maryland and in Minnesota, and 951 days in Alaska (ABA Standing Committee on Lawyer Disciplinary Systems 2015; State Bar of California 2014). One improvement is the creation of a nationwide online database by the ABA in 1994 that allows disciplinary agencies to determine whether a lawyer has been subjected to discipline in another state.

Benjamin Barton analyzed disciplinary complaints in 2009 and finds that 125,596 complaints were filed, which amounted to one complaint for every 10 lawyers. Following investigation, 6,900 (5 percent) of the complaints led to formal charges. Public sanctions were imposed on 5,009 lawyers, and 798 were disbarred (0.6 percent of complaints). Barton notes that because only public sanctions are made available to the public, the disposition of the vast majority of complaints remain confidential (Barton 2015: 213). An analysis of disciplinary data from 2014 indicates that state disciplinary boards in all but a handful of states continue to receive very few complaints and to impose public sanctions on a handful of lawyers (American Bar Association Standing Committee on Lawyer Disciplinary Systems 2015).

It should be recognized that the decisions of state disciplinary boards may differ significantly from one another. South Carolina suspended a lawyer who stole $1,800 from her daughter's Girl Scout cookie sales although other states imposed a suspension or additional ethics education on lawyers who stole a client's funds. The process has been criticized for not fully protecting the public because clients cannot obtain a record of past complaints filed against a lawyer that did not result in sanction, and in most states a lawyer who has been disbarred is able to reapply for admission (Rhode 2000: 160–161).

As you undoubtedly recall, Jerome Carlin found that solo practitioners and individuals from small firms who attended lower-status law schools and who experienced difficulty in attracting clients were most likely to engage in ethical violations (Carlin 1966). A study of a small midwestern city (Handler 1967) and an Australian study (Gandossy 1985) supported Carlin's findings. A review of disciplinary proceedings in California, Illinois, and the District of Columbia in 1981–1982 found 80 percent of disciplinary complaints were brought against solo practitioners and no complaints were brought against lawyers who practiced in a firm with more than seven lawyers. Nationally, solo practitioners accounted for less than half of all lawyers (48.6 percent), and firms with more than seven lawyers accounted for roughly the same proportion of the legal profession (Abel 1989: 145). The question is whether solo practitioners are more unethical than other lawyers or whether their ethical lapses result from being overworked and living on the economic edge. There also is the possibility that disciplinary boards are willing to overlook violations by corporate lawyers or that corporate firms are able to reach private settlements with clients who complain about ethical violations (Abel 2008: 506).

The statistics on disciplinary violations likely do not provide a full picture of the extent of disciplinary violations among the legal profession. A significant percentage of clients lack knowledge of the availability of disciplinary procedures or choose not to file a complaint. A survey found only 13 percent of clients knew where to file a complaint. Clients also are not fully informed about the ethical responsibility of lawyers and may not understand that their lawyer has acted in an unethical fashion (Abel 2008: 500). In many instances, lawyers' ethical violations are undertaken to promote the interests of clients, and the clients clearly are not about to complain. Lawyers also are reluctant to complain about their colleagues. Only a tenth of all grievances are filed by lawyers against their fellow practitioners (Abel 1989: 145). Why? Lawyers do not want to take the time and effort to file a complaint, create "bad blood" with a fellow attorney, and draw attention to the ethical abuses of their profession (Rhode 2000: 159).

Another aspect of the disciplinary process is that not all behavior that lowers respect for the legal profession constitutes a violation of the code of professional conduct. Deborah Rhode catalogues a list of perfectly ethical trial tactics that transform trials into a "war" between the parties rather than a search for the truth. These tactics include creating delays, humiliating witnesses, and coaching witnesses to offer evasive replies (Rhode 2000: 83, 97–102). In some instances, disciplinary bodies have determined that this type of conduct constitutes "excessive zeal" (Abel 2008: 377–378).

Legal disciplinary procedures have been criticized as slow and secret and insulated from public accountability. Only one-third of Americans believe that disciplinary procedures are effective in controlling abuse. One survey showed that only 20 percent of lawyers in California believed the disciplinary system was effective and 90 percent wanted to keep control over discipline within the legal profession.

Disciplinary procedures are not the only mechanism to monitor lawyers. Judges may hold lawyers in contempt of court (a fine) for misconduct during a trial. This might involve destroying or concealing evidence or criticizing the judge throughout a trial as biased or unfair. A Seattle law firm was fined over $300,000 by the Washington Supreme Court for withholding documents in a case in which a young child suffered a brain injury as a result of taking an asthma drug. The document only was discovered after four years of litigation as a result of a leak from a "whistle blower" (Rhode 2000: 87). Rule 11 of the Federal Rules of Civil Procedure authorizes judges to fine lawyers who intentionally bring unfounded or frivolous (silly) legal proceedings or drag out trials in an effort to harass the defendant (Abel 2008: 503).

Another option available to defendants is to file a malpractice action. Oregon is the only state that requires lawyers to possess malpractice insurance. Between 20 percent and 50 percent of lawyers in other states lack malpractice insurance. Malpractice insurance is an important safeguard for the public because an individual who sues the lawyer knows the insurance company will pay the costs of any legal judgment against the lawyer or can be confident the insurance company will settle the claim against the lawyer (Abel 1989: 154). Roughly half of all claims arise out of a lawyer's failure to file an action on time, a neglect to respond to a complaint resulting in the client being held liable, a failure to conduct adequate investigation, or a lack of knowledge of the law or fraud or theft (Abel 1989: 154–155). Malpractice is difficult to prove because you must establish that your lawyer's obvious negligence caused you to lose the case. You then must prove a financial loss as a result of the negligence. In 2007, thirty-five thousand individuals filed malpractice claims, and close to one-half of individuals filing claims were successful. Roughly one-quarter of malpractice claims stem from personal injury cases, 20 percent involve real estate, and 10 percent concern wills, pensions, and small business (ABA Standing Committee on Lawyers' Professional Liability 2008). Rhode reports that between 10 percent and 20 percent of lawyers engage in behavior that may expose them to a malpractice suit in any given year and that insurance payouts are estimated at $6 billion per year. Two-thirds of successful malpractice claims result in a recovery of over $100,000. It must be remembered the costs of a legal action and legal fees significantly limit the amount that a plaintiff actually receives from a malpractice claim (Rhode 2000: 165).

Lawyers are not above the law and may be criminally prosecuted. In 2017, Kathleen Kane, the former state attorney general of Pennsylvania, was convicted of perjury, false swearing, and obstruction of justice and other crimes and was sentenced to serve ten to twenty-three months in county jail and eight years' probation for during her term in office leaking confidential grand jury testimony, then denying the leak to law enforcement investigators (Hurdle and Pérez-Peña 2017).

What is the motivation of lawyers who engage in misconduct? Richard Abel studied lawyers found to have engaged in ethical misconduct and found the attorneys were experienced lawyers who engaged in a pattern of misconduct over a number of years. Each of the lawyers was in need of money to keep his or her office functioning or to meet household expenses. They found themselves overwhelmed and resorted to desperate solutions. One lawyer failed to keep track of his client's cases and neglected to appear in court and covered up his errors by drafting false judicial judgments indicating the judge had ruled against the client. The motivation of pure greed led real estate lawyers in New York City to use their expertise to assist individuals who they mistakenly believed were wealthy foreign leaders to sneak money into the United States which then was used to purchase luxury homes (Story 2016).

Another lawyer viewed himself as "above the law" and justified paying kickbacks to insurance agents who were willing to settle his clients' cases on the grounds that "everyone did it." This lawyer's ego was so fragile that he could not accept losing a case and he explained that the kickback guaranteed the insurance company would compensate his client for his or her injury.

The lawyers who committed ethical violations considered themselves "special" and that their personal problems entitled them to disregard the rules. One lawyer stated that he could not be expected to meet deadlines when his mother was sick. It also was important that most of the clients who were the victims of unethical conduct were injured, jobless, immigrants, or elderly and were easily exploited by the lawyers (Abel 2008: 491–497, 513).

5.2 YOU DECIDE

In 1982, public defender Marc Miller was assigned to represent Edgar Hope, who along with Alton Logan was charged with killing a security guard and wounding a second security guard during a robbery at a McDonald's restaurant. Hope shared with Miller that he did not know Logan, that Logan was innocent, and that his co-perpetrator was Andrew Wilson, standing trial at the time for killing two police officers. Miller told Logan's lawyer that his client was innocent. Miller also stated to the public defenders representing Andrew Wilson, Dale Coventry, and W. Jamie Kunz that their client had been involved in the McDonald's killings.

Coventry and Kunz questioned Wilson, who admitted to being the shooter at the McDonald's robbery. The two lawyers knew that Wilson was truthful because ballistics tests connected a shotgun shell discovered at McDonald's with a weapon found at Wilson's residence. The deceased police officers' firearms also were seized at the same location.

Coventry, Kunz, and Miller, after consulting other lawyers and experts, concluded they were barred by the attorney–client privilege from revealing that Logan was innocent. The three swore an affidavit that did not name Wilson but indicated that they had knowledge through privileged sources that Logan was innocent, which was placed in a sealed envelope and deposited in a locked box in Coventry's bedroom.

Logan avoided the death penalty and was sentenced to life imprisonment. Wilson, who was confronting capital punishment, agreed that the lawyers could reveal Logan's innocence after his death. Wilson's death sentence, however, was reversed when it was discovered that his confession had been obtained as a result of police torture.

Wilson and Hope never came forward with the truth, and when confronted by Logan in prison, Wilson reportedly smiled and walked away.

Wilson ultimately passed away after twenty-six years in prison, and Coventry and Kunz finally produced an affidavit that resulted in the release of the 54-year-old Logan.

Kunz, when asked about remaining silent for all these years, responded, "If I had ratted him out . . . then I could feel guilty, then I could not live with myself. . . . I'm

(Continued)

(Continued)

anguished and always have been over the sad injustice of Alton Logan's conviction. Should I do the right thing by Alton Logan and put my client's neck in the noose or not? It's clear where my responsibility lies and my responsibility lies with my client."

A Cook County, Illinois, judge issued a certificate of innocence to Logan, and the City of Chicago reached a $10.25 million settlement with Logan based on evidence that now-imprisoned Chicago police officer John Burge had concealed implicating Wilson in the homicide.

The ethical rules vary from state to state although several states provide that a lawyer may break a confidence to halt an execution but not to free an innocent inmate. Massachusetts seems to be unique in allowing lawyers to violate a privilege to prevent a "wrongful execution or incarceration of another." Most states consider that the attorney–client privilege is not waived by the death of a client. This is because the family still may be concerned about the deceased's reputation, civil liability, or retribution. There is the complicating factor of whether a lawyer has proof of a wrongful conviction other than the statement of his or her client.

Should a lawyer violate the attorney–client privilege when he or she knows an innocent individual is imprisoned or sentenced to death?

 ## INTERNATIONAL PERSPECTIVE: LEGAL EDUCATION IN GERMANY AND FRANCE

The U.S. system of legal education is fairly unique. Consider that legal education in European civil law systems is an undergraduate degree. Classes typically are taught as a lecture and focus on how to read statutes rather than on cases. There is even less focus on preparing students to practice law than in the American system, and most European countries require an apprenticeship following the completion of law school.

In Germany, a law graduate must pass the "first state examination" as the initial step toward entering an apprenticeship. The *Referendar* system involves spending two years as an apprentice in a variety of legal settings. For example, a young lawyer may spend time working in a private firm, government agency, or court. The apprentice lawyer, after passing a second state exam, is ready to embark on the career of his or her choice. A young lawyer once having decided to pursue a particular legal career will find it difficult to change careers (Glendon, Carozza, and Picker 2016: 94–103).

France possesses a much more complicated system. A French student must first study for three years and obtain a university degree (*licence en droit*) followed by an additional year for a master's degree. This last year involves classes in legal ethics and the drafting of documents and two internships. He or she then must pass the bar exam to become eligible to enter a period of practical training (*Referendarzeit*). This entails a two-year internship spent rotating between various branches of the legal profession. Following the completion of the internship, the individual is eligible to take a second state bar examination. The successful applicant then becomes an *avocat*. The historical evolution of the French legal profession led to the requirement that an *avocat* retain the services of an *avoué* to handle the paperwork on appeals. These two branches of the French legal profession were partially merged in 1971. There are some remaining distinctions. For example, only a select group of senior *avocats* may practice before the highest court in France (the Court of Cassation), and an *avoué* continues to prepare paperwork for appeals. There is yet a third group of *conseils juridiques* who are licensed to provide legal advice to individuals, businesses, and corporations. In 1992, *avocats* were merged with *conseils juridiques*, creating a single profession of *avocats* authorized to appear in court, prepare documents, and provide advice to individuals and corporations.

The *notary* is an important legal institution in European civil law and very different from the American notary public. The *notary* is authorized to prepare documents such as wills, property transfers, mortgages, and marriage and divorce contracts and has various other responsibilities relating to legal documents. Notaries also authenticate documents (indicate that they are "real") that are introduced at trial and are obligated to retain archives of all the documents they prepare. There are a limited number of *notaries*, and a law graduate must pass a special exam to become a *notary* and then must wait for a vacancy. A *notary* is expected to be neutral and objective and is to provide professional advice to clients on how best to draft a will or to structure a prenuptial agreement (Merryman and Pérez-Perdomo 2007: 106).

What about a law graduate aspiring to be a judge? In Germany following the second bar examination, the young lawyer serves a three- to four-year probationary period as a lower court judge and then is eligible for a permanent appointment. In France, students desiring to be a judge during their last year in law school prepare to pass a competitive exam. Successful applicants then are enrolled in a special thirty-one-month course of study at the National School for the Judiciary. This period of academic study is followed by a series of internships with agencies ranging from the police to prisons and a judicial apprenticeship. The third part of the program includes placement with various judges and working in the office of an *avocat*. Candidates then are eligible for permanent appointment as a judge (Glendon et al. 2016: 102–109).

The civil law system has the advantages of ensuring well-prepared judges and provides for full access for women and minorities to the judiciary. On the other hand, judges are civil servants who are concerned about promotion and are hesitant to make controversial decisions.

Another aspect of the civil law system that we would find unusual is the procurator (the equivalent of the district attorney). The procurator, in addition to prosecuting criminal cases, is authorized to intervene in civil cases to represent the public interest (e.g., on the issue of affirmative action). The procurator technically is a member of the judiciary and undergoes the same training as a judge and may move between the prosecutor's office and the judiciary. In France, the judges are referred to as *magistrature assise* (sitting judiciary) and the procurators as *magistrature debout* (standing judiciary) (Terrill 2016: 169–170).

Professors in both the common law and civil law systems must demonstrate academic excellence. Professors in the civil law system must undergo a lengthy training period and in Germany are required to produce a major piece of research (*Habilitationsschrift*) after completing a doctoral degree in order to obtain the rank of "private docent." Judges and lawyers in the civil law system tend to look to a small number of respected legal academics to guide their interpretation of the legal statutes (Merryman and Pérez-Perdomo 2007: 108–110).

CHAPTER SUMMARY

The ABA has helped increase the access of the poor and middle class to the justice system by supporting legal aid and pro bono representation. The involvement of ideologically inclined lawyers in cause lawyering has led to significant legal victories for minorities and the poor and for conservative causes. Law schools also have demonstrated a strong commitment to affirmative action admissions to law schools although minorities remain underrepresented among law students.

Solo practitioners and small firm lawyers have managed to expand access of the working class to the justice system through advertising, contingent fees, group legal services plans, and challenges to minimum fee schedules. There also is a growing movement among ordinary citizens for pro se representation.

The legal profession has avoided government regulation of legal services by providing dissatisfied clients with the opportunity to file ethics complaints against their lawyer. This system of professional regulation is criticized as slow and ineffective and for focusing almost exclusively on solo practitioners and lawyers in small firms.

CHAPTER REVIEW QUESTIONS

1. List the areas in which the legal needs of the middle and working classes are unmet. What are the barriers to middle- and working-class access to a lawyer?

2. Why is advertising by lawyers a controversial practice?

3. What are the arguments for and against contingent fee arrangements?

4. Describe how legal services plans operate.

5. What is cause lawyering? Are lawyers acting unprofessionally who engage in cause lawyering rather than representing a wide variety of clients?

6. Describe the core principles of legal ethics. What is the process of adjudicating legal ethics complaints? Why do lawyers commit ethical violations?

7. After reading the chapters on lawyers in the text, are you more or less inclined to become a lawyer?

TERMINOLOGY

cause lawyering   195

class action   186

contingent fee   185

continuing legal education   199

group legal services plans   188

Legal Services Corporation   191

Model Rules of Professional Conduct   200

pro bono publico   194

pro se   198

ANSWERS TO TEST YOUR KNOWLEDGE

1. False

2. False

3. False

4. True

5. False

6. False

7. True

8. False

9. False

WANT A BETTER GRADE?

Get the tools you need to sharpen your study skills. Access practice quizzes, eFlashcards, author podcasts, SAGE journal articles, hyperlinks for Law and Society on the Web, and more at **study.sagepub.com/lippmanls2e**.

CHAPTER 6

DISPUTE RESOLUTION

TEST YOUR KNOWLEDGE: TRUE OR FALSE?

1. The primary difference between mediation and arbitration is whether there is a binding decision.

2. The method of dispute resolution used in a society depends on a number of factors. The diversity and population size of a society are two of several determinants of whether individuals will overlook, settle, or litigate a dispute.

3. Most Americans view the legal process as helpful and fair.

4. Americans are quick to pursue their grievances in court, and the critics who claim that the United States is a litigious society have a valid point in this regard.

5. Alternative dispute resolution is discouraged by judges.

Check your answers on page 242.

■ INTRODUCTION

A **dispute** is a disagreement between two or more individuals or groups. Richard Lempert and Joseph Sanders write that legal disputes involve "conflicting interests. Usually one person has something the other wants and both parties make claims of entitlement." If both claims cannot be satisfied, there is a "true conflict" (Lempert and Sanders 1986: 137). Richard E. Miller and Austin Sarat note that a dispute begins as a **grievance**. A grievance is an "individual's belief that he or she (or a group or organization) is entitled to a resource which someone else may grant or deny" (R. Miller and Sarat 1980–1981: 527).

You may have a grievance with a professor over a grade. A dispute arises because you believe that you deserve an A rather than a B in class. Brian C. Marquis, a 51-year-old paralegal, returned to study law and sociology at the University of Massachusetts. Marquis sued the university, claiming that the teaching assistant in his political philosophy class failed to follow the grading scale on the syllabus and instead "curved" the final grades in class. Marquis argued that he deserved an A–, that the C would impede his ability to get into law school, and that the grade had transformed his transcript into a "dismal record on non-achievement" and proclaimed that he would not take "no" for an answer and appealed to federal district court.

The teaching assistant wrote Marquis that "the students' numerical scores seemed too high to him so he graded everyone on a curve before assigning a letter grade" and that he "thought a 'C' was a good reflection of Marquis' work in the class." The head of the Department of Philosophy explained that the instructor made clear that the "number" on the tests had "[no] absolute meaning." Catharine Porter, the University of Massachusetts–Amherst ombudsman who was a defendant in the case, pointed out that "if every student that didn't like his or her grade started to do this, we'd have to hire . . . 25,000 attorneys." Peter Michelson, a lawyer for the university, told the judge that Marquis's suit was "more or less, baloney." He posed the question, "Does the court really want to put itself in the business of reviewing, under some constitutional or federal statutory doctrine, the propriety of the grades which a student has received?" Federal district court judge Michael Ponsor dismissed the legal suit on the grounds that the university had rejected Marquis's appeal of his grade and that his legal rights had not been violated.

The stages in the disputing process are described in the following section of the chapter.

■ STAGES OF DISPUTING

Anthropologists Laura Nader and Harry F. Todd Jr. have developed a three-stage typology of the disputing process (Nader and Todd 1978: 14–15).

1. *Grievance or preconflict stage.* An individual believes he or she has been "wronged or injured." The slight may be real or imagined. The individual now must choose whether to escalate the grievance into a confrontation or walk away.

2. *Conflict stage.* The individual who feels wronged (aggrieved party) confronts the offending party and communicates his or her feeling of injustice. At this point, both individuals are aware of the disagreement. The offending party may attempt to diminish the conflict by pressuring the aggrieved party to accept the situation, by offering to negotiate, or by settling the dispute.

3. *Dispute stage.* The conflict is made public, and a third (outside) party becomes involved in the dispute. The outside party may intervene at the request of one or both of the parties or their supporters or based on his or her own initiative.

A dispute may not progress through each stage. An individual may take his or her grievance directly to the dispute stage and file a complaint in court. The individual may take a grievance to the conflict stage and then deescalate the conflict or may enter into a negotiation with the offending party.

A second description of the disputing process was developed by law and society scholars William Felstiner, Richard Abel, and Austin Sarat (Felstiner, Abel, and Sarat 1980–1981). The crucial step is the transformation from an "unperceived injurious experience (UNPIE)" to a "perceived injurious experience (PIE)." People who live downwind from a nuclear test site may experience physical problems and at some point realize they have contracted cancer. The individual at this point progresses to the first stage, which is learning of his or her illness and **naming** the grievance as cancer. Some cancer victims will attribute the cancer to the test site. This second stage is termed **blaming**. Other victims may harbor a generalized feeling of injustice without linking their illness to the test site. This general sense of injustice is a *complaint*. In the final stage, the aggrieved individual confronts the individual thought to be responsible for the harm and asks for a remedy. This stage of confronting the government about the operation of the nuclear test site is termed **claiming**. A claim that is rejected or greeted with inaction may lead to a dispute.

Each of these descriptions of disputing requires an individual to recognize that he or she has been harmed, identify the cause of the harm, and confront the individual or group thought to be responsible for the harm. The disputing process is driven by an individual's perception that he or she has been treated unfairly. Lawrence M. Friedman notes that a behavior that is condemned by some people may be considered completely acceptable by other individuals (L. Friedman, Pérez-Perdomo, and Gómez 2011). In some societies, there is an emphasis on peaceful coexistence, and individuals may be reluctant to "make waves" and enter into disputes. In other societies, individuals may be encouraged to assert their rights and file complaints. Individuals and societies, as discussed below, differ in the mechanisms used to settle disputes (S. Roberts 1979: 45–55).

Research on torts (personal injuries) shows that the number of cases are reduced as grievances progress to disputes and ultimately to trial. Richard Miller and Austin Sarat found that for every 1,000 grievances, 200 became disputes, 116 were referred to a lawyer, and only 38 (approximately 4 percent of grievances and 19 percent of disputes) were filed in court. The success rate for individuals bringing tort complaints is somewhat better than 52 percent at trial although this differs based on the type of claim. They found that legal actions for damage resulting from motor vehicles that were brought to trial proved much more successful than claims based on allegations of medical malpractice (R. Miller and Sarat 1980–1981).

Why do so many grievances for personal injury not find their way into court? Individuals who do not pursue claims may not view themselves as seriously injured, may not blame others for their injury, may find the remedy too expensive in terms of time or money, may find conflict emotionally difficult, or may lack understanding of the legal process (Robbennolt and Hans 2016).

■ METHODS OF DISPUTE RESOLUTION

There are various methods commonly used to resolve disputes. Most societies use several types of disputing procedures (S. Roberts 1979: 57–79).

Keep in mind there always is the alternative of *lumping*, deciding against pursuing a grievance and living with the situation. The individual swallows his or her pride and continues the relationship. Marc Galanter observes the decision to "do nothing" may be based on an individual's lack of awareness that he or she has suffered a wrong that may be remedied by the law. An individual also may calculate that the costs of pursuing the matter outweigh the possible benefits. Individuals may not pursue a claim the first time they are victimized by a harmful act although the next time they may reach the "breaking point" and pursue the claim. A power or status difference between individuals also can discourage the weaker party from pursuing a claim because the weaker party may believe that "you cannot fight city hall." Consider the circumstances in which you are likely to "lump" a poor grade on an exam or on a paper (Galanter 1974: 124–125).

Galanter distinguishes between types of litigants based on the frequency with which they go to court. One shotters (OSs) are contrasted with repeat players (RPs) who tend to be business firms and corporations that make frequent use of the courts over a significant period of time in similar types of cases. An example of an OS is an individual suing another individual for injuries suffered during an automobile accident or an individual suing a hospital for medical malpractice. RPs tend to be large and powerful organizations that constantly are in court: landlords, insurance companies, and large automobile manufacturers. An OS seeking return of a security deposit is at a decided disadvantage against an RP who knows how housing court operates, possesses the resources to hire expert and experienced lawyers, and is willing to devote significant resources as part of his or her property management business to winning in court. The landlord also has learned, based on past experience, to insert various clauses in the lease to the apartment signed by the renter, which makes it difficult for the renter to succeed in court. Under the circumstances, an OS may find "lumping" the best option and accept the loss of his or her security deposit.

"Lumping it" differs from *avoidance*. In avoidance, the individual who believes he or she is harmed decides to walk away from a situation and end the relationship rather than pursue the grievance. You may be tempted to drop a class and "exit" the course if the teacher is unresponsive or if you receive a second poor grade. Of course, this may be a required class, or the add/drop period may have passed and you may have no available alternatives (Hirschman 1970). A society may make the decision for an individual and "avoid" a conflict by banishing or expelling troublemakers. Consider a school that expels a troublemaker or a coach who kicks a player off the team (S. Roberts 1979: 65–66).

One of the individuals in a conflict may resort to *coercion* or to self-help. Coercion includes violence, public ridicule, revealing embarrassing information, and blackmail. The greater the stakes are, the more tempting it is to resort to coercion. An extreme and tragic example is the lynching of African Americans falsely accused of theft, rape, and murder by white mobs in the nineteenth and early twentieth centuries (L. Friedman 1993: 189–191). Sally Engle Merry, in an early study of disputing in a multiethnic housing project, found a surprising reliance on violence to settle disputes. The disputes rarely were permanently settled, and individuals' continuing sense of grievance led to the eruption of periodic acts of retribution (Merry 1979).

In some societies, blood revenge is an accepted part of dispute resolution. The tribe of an individual who is killed may obtain revenge by taking the life of a member of the offending tribe or group (S. Roberts 1979: 55–56). Another form of violent dispute resolution is trial by combat, which was part of the English common law between the eleventh and mid-fifteenth centuries and even has been unsuccessfully invoked by some litigants in American courts who claim that trial by combat continues to be part of American law.

Dueling or arranged combat between two individuals with matched weapons in accordance with agreed-upon rules was practiced in Europe and in colonial America to settle disputes. Duels followed strict rules articulated in the so-called twenty-six commandments first developed in Ireland. Dueling was condemned by figures such as George Washington and Benjamin Franklin and by religious figures. The most famous duel involved Vice President Aaron Burr and Federalist and former secretary of the Treasury Alexander Hamilton in 1804, which led to Hamilton's death. President Andrew Jackson participated in several duels before assuming the presidency and in one duel killed a Nashville attorney. On September 22, 1842, future president Abraham Lincoln arranged to duel Illinois state official James Shields before supporters intervened to persuade the two principals to walk away from the confrontation. Between 1795 and the Civil War, the U.S. Navy lost two-thirds as many soldiers to dueling as the Navy lost to combat. Following the Civil War, dueling came to be viewed as institutionalized murder rather than as a means of defending honor but continued to be practiced in the southern states as late as the early twentieth century. Today, most states and the federal government have laws prohibiting dueling.

John Hagedorn has documented the use of violence by Chicago street gangs to settle disputes with other gangs over the control over turf and to retaliate for violent attacks. The resort to violence was so deeply ingrained that it undermined an effort to unify Latin gangs so as to maximize the gangs' profit from the drug trade (Hagedorn 2015).

Various forms of disputing direct an individual's frustration and anger into rituals. An example is the Eskimo *nith*-song. The parties to the dispute express their viewpoints through singing and dancing before the entire community. The community then decides which individual won the song contest (S. Roberts 1979: 59–61).

Talking is a central method of settling disputes. Talking allows individuals to express their points of view, release their frustrations, and reach an acceptable settlement. *Negotiation* involves a discussion between the two parties in which each individual attempts to persuade the other to change his or her mind. In some instances, individuals entering into a dialogue are able to reach a compromise solution. A successful negotiation requires individuals who are willing to recognize the other person's point of view has merit and who are willing to accept "half a loaf." Negotiation is particularly attractive when the time and costs of continuing to pursue the grievance outweigh the benefits of "winning." An instructor may be willing to negotiate a higher grade or an extra-credit assignment rather than take the time and energy to defend the grade before an administrative grade appeal board. There also is consideration that university administrators may support the student and the instructor will have wasted his or her time and appear irresponsible (Nader and Todd 1978: 10).

In *mediation*, the parties agree to the presence of an outside party who assists the parties to reach an agreement they likely could not reach on their own. In some instances, a mediator may be imposed on the parties. A family court may require the parties to enter into mediation before filing for a divorce. It is important the parties view the mediator as impartial and trustworthy. The goal of a mediator is to find a compromise solution through a process of "give and take." Each party is encouraged to give something to the other party in exchange for something that he or she wants. A department head may meet with both a student and a professor and encourage them to reach a compromise over a disputed grade (Nader and Todd 1978: 10).

In *arbitration*, the principals consent to the intervention of an outside party whose decision they agree to accept as binding. Arbitration, like mediation, involves an outside and impartial party that helps the parties to settle their dispute. The arbitrator considers the competing claims of the disputing parties and reaches a binding decision regarding the dispute. In arbitration, one of the parties likely will win, and the other party may lose (win-lose), whereas in mediation, the stress is on helping the parties voluntarily reach a compromise solution (win-win) (Nader and Todd 1978: 11).

Adjudication involves an impartial third party who, in response to a request, has the authority to intervene and issue a decision. In an arbitration, the two parties agree to accept the decision of an arbitrator. In contrast, in an adjudication, one of the parties files a claim, and the other party is required to appear and accept the decision of the decision-maker, in most cases a judge. A party who fails to appear risks a judgment for the other party.

An individual may decide to engage in litigation, which involves the referral of the dispute to the official, formal court system.

Dispute resolution may not end a dispute and instead may lead to a continuing cycle of dispute or to a proliferation of disputes. A dispute between neighbors over property boundaries may lead to litigation over the placement of a fence. This in turn may result in a physical fight and lead to criminal complaints for assault and battery and to a cycle of complaints over zoning violations, overhanging trees, a failure to keep dogs on a leash, and complaints to the police over unnecessary noise.

■ PRECONDITIONS FOR ADJUDICATION

Various procedural preconditions or hurdles must be satisfied before a judge will adjudicate a dispute. A dispute that satisfies these conditions is called **justiciable**, meaning that it is ready to be decided. These procedural requirements include the following (Nader and Todd 1978: 11):

Timeliness. A claim must be filed within a fixed number of years from the time of the original incident. This is known as the statute of limitations.

Jurisdiction. A tribunal or court may be authorized by law to hear a particular type of case (subject matter jurisdiction) that occurs in a particular geographical area (jurisdiction over the person).

Controversy. Courts limit themselves to deciding active and actual cases and controversies and do not issue advisory opinions or decisions on hypothetical questions. An individual bringing a case must actually be harmed by the law. You may not challenge a policy that the police are considering because the policy has not yet been implemented and you are not yet affected by the policy.

The results of an adjudication typically may be appealed to superior court in the judicial hierarchy. The decisions that result from adjudication have the advantage of being the product of established and respected judicial institutions. Adjudication has the disadvantage of being costly and time-consuming, and losing parties may find new and creative ways to return to court and to pursue their grievance. "Hot button" issues rarely are settled. Consider the steady stream of cases presenting innovative challenges to issues like abortion procedures, gun control, affirmative action, health care, capital punishment, same-sex marriage, and campaign finance.

Laura Nader, in her important study of disputing in a Mexican Zapotec court of law, makes the point that there are various styles of adjudication. Adjudication can aim at a "win-win" rather than a "win-lose" result. The Rincon is an isolated region populated by two thousand Zapotec Spanish-speaking individuals who earn their livelihood through agriculture. In the United States, adjudication involves a confrontation between two individuals. The judicial decision typically results in a victory for one side and a defeat for the other side. In contrast, the *presidente*, the Zapotec judicial official, seeks to achieve a "balance" or "equilibrium." This means locating a middle ground in which neither side leaves the court with a feeling of anger or resentment. The *presidente* allows the parties to articulate their side of the story without interruption. He then issues a brief decision. The *presidente*'s goal is to provide a compromise solution that allows the parties to live with one another rather than to punish the wrongdoer and risk a continuing conflict. In one example, the *presidente* heard a case involving an angry husband who alleged his wife acted without consulting him, and an angry wife who accused the husband of not fulfilling his responsibilities to the family and a sick child. The *presidente*, rather than becoming embroiled in the heated dispute between the husband and the wife, directed the parties to focus on their child rather than on themselves (Nader 1969).

The important point is that a society typically has various mechanisms to settle disputes. An individual may seek to negotiate and mediate before turning to arbitration or adjudication. Each procedure may be appropriate for a different type of dispute and for a particular time and place. Mechanisms to settle disputes are part of all varieties of societies, including pirates, shipwrecked sailors, leper colonies, and miners during the California gold rush of the 1800s (Robinson and Robinson 2015). Mitchell Duneier documents how the largely homeless sidewalk magazine vendors in New York City developed their own system to settle disputes over the location of their tables and how other unhoused individuals supported themselves by charging the vendors to guard the tables overnight (Duneier 1999). Rebecca Solnit in her study of societies experiencing disasters demonstrates that when formal legal institutions collapse, people come together to regulate themselves (Solnit 2009).

■ SOCIAL INFLUENCES ON DISPUTING

Both the social structure of a society and a society's legal culture influence the form of disputing.

Anthropologist Max Gluckman observes that the nature of the relationships between individuals determines the type of dispute-processing procedure that will be used (Gluckman 1955: 18–20).

In a small-scale society in which people know one another and join together to fish, hunt, and raise crops, people are conscious of the fact that they depend on one another, and they go out of their way to avoid conflict. Another reason people in small-scale societies avoid conflict is that most people are connected to a large number of individuals through intermarriage and friendship. Pursuing a dispute runs the risk of dividing families and undermining relationships. As a result, individuals will tend to "lump it" or negotiate or mediate disputes. Anthropologists describe these societies in which people are tied together by a web of connections as being characterized by **multiplex relationships** (Gluckman 1955: 18–20).

Laura Nader and Harry F. Todd Jr. note that multiplex relationships require settlements that will "allow . . . relations to continue" (Nader and Todd 1978: 13).

Other observers caution that disputes in small-scale societies will not necessarily be settled in a cooperative fashion. In a dispute, an individual may place a greater value on land or crops than on a relationship, particularly when the property is scarce and in short supply (J. Starr and Yngvesson 1975).

Larger and more diverse societies are characterized by **simplex relationships**. In contrast to the multiple connections that tie people together in closely knit societies, simplex relationships in larger societies are limited to a specific type of connection. You likely will never see the nurse who assists you in the emergency room again, and your relationship with the postal worker is limited to the delivery of the mail. In simplex relationships, people are not greatly concerned about maintaining relationships and likely will not place a high priority on compromise and negotiation. Grievances generally will result in adjudication or arbitration, and individuals will pursue "win-or-lose decisions" (Nader and Todd 1978: 13).

The nature of relationships in a society influences the nature of dispute processes. Dispute processing is also affected by the distribution of political power in a society. In a small-scale multiplex society, there are relatively few people with greater wealth or greater power than other individuals. Individuals are dependent on one another and have a large number of family connections and ties. The dispute process reflects individual equality and is based on avoidance, negotiation, and mediation. In multiplex societies, power tends to be concentrated in the wealthy and politically influential. The powerful are not dependent on maintaining good relations with the rest of society, and they will attempt to control and manipulate legal institutions to reflect their own self-interests and will pursue adjudication. In contrast, an individual who lacks power will make every effort to mediate a dispute with an upper-class individual who has the power to control the outcome of the dispute (Nader and Todd 1978: 19–22).

A third factor in determining the nature of dispute resolution in a society is culture. Legal culture refers to a society's view of the law and of legal institutions. One aspect of legal culture is views toward dispute resolution. Does the society have an approach to disputes that encourages non-confrontational modes of resolving disagreements ("win-win"), or does the society promote an adversarial approach and encourage formal adjudication ("win-lose") (Rosen 2006)?

In a study of the decline of the use of tort law in Chiang Mai in northern Thailand, David Engel and Jaruvan Engel found that in the past individuals looked to customary law administered by village elders to adjudicate disputes and only turned to the formal justice system when a litigant refused to provide a monetary remedy that was consistent with traditional Buddhist principles. The development of a more mobile, western-style economy resulted in the dismantling of village societies, and individuals resisted using the courts to seek remedies that they did not view as linked to the Buddhist religious principles of goodness, justice, and virtue (Engel and Engel 2010: 21–32).

Japan is a clear contrast to the American pattern of adjudication. Japan has relatively low rates of litigation and one of the smallest numbers of lawyers and judges per capita in the world. Litigation rates in Japan per one hundred thousand members of society are rising, but remain ten times lower than rates in the state of California.

The Japanese place a high value on compromise, harmony, and mutual understanding rather than enforcing the letter of the law. Sometimes a dispute can be resolved by offering an apology. This type of cultural commitment to compromise is incompatible with a system of "winners and losers." Takeyoshi Kawashima, in a much cited article, argues the Japanese prefer extra-judicial informal means of settling disputes. He notes that during a housing and land shortage in Japan in the early twentieth century, the government anticipated an avalanche of lawsuits that would overwhelm the judicial system and organized a mediation process between tenants and landlords. The number of cases submitted to mediation was much greater than the number of cases filed in court. Kawashima explains that in Japan, the tenant is expected to defer to the landlord-owner who, in turn, is obligated, based on his or her greater power, to act in a kind and considerate fashion. This social expectation rules out reliance on "winner takes all" adjudication (Kawashima 1969).

The predominant mode of settling disputes in Japan is for the parties to reach a mutually desirable solution through personal discussion. Kawashima found that of the roughly 2,500 traffic accidents involving four Japanese taxi companies that resulted in either personal injury or property damage, only a single case resulted in litigation and was settled out of court. Kawashima notes the

Japanese are uncomfortable with the notion that there is a conflict in which one party is adjudged to be morally at fault. They prefer to negotiate a compromise solution.

The cultural explanation for a society's method of dispute resolution is criticized as being difficult to measure. It is difficult to accept that everyone in a society shares the same approach to resolving conflicts. Consider the variation in the personalities of Americans toward disputes.

Takao Tanase takes issue with Kawashima's explanation that Japan has a culture of conciliation and harmony. He argues that the Japanese in the world of business are as cutthroat as any people in the world. The reason the Japanese settle, according to Tanase, is that the government has created a structure that encourages out-of-court settlements and discourages adjudication. Court-affiliated mediation services resolve cases in 50 percent less time than court adjudication, and the total cost is one-seventh as expensive as a formal trial. There are limitations on the amount an individual can collect in court, and it makes sense to settle a case rather than wait years for a judicial decision that may not result in a significantly more lucrative financial award than can be obtained in a settlement. In Japan, alternatives to judicial adjudication are available in medical malpractice, construction disputes, environmental claims, and consumer complaints (Tanase 1990).

Eric Feldman, in his study of the Tuna Court at the Tokyo Central Wholesale Market's tuna auction, found that Japanese merchants are not necessarily opposed to litigation. He found that merchants do not hesitate to bring disputes to the court despite the tribunal's reliance on formal rules and procedures. Feldman notes the court offers quick, efficient, inexpensive, and reliable decisions that treat disputes as normal events in the buying and selling of fish rather than issues of right and wrong. He concludes that the Tuna Court, by avoiding declaring "winners" and "losers," dampens conflict and contributes to a harmonious and ordered marketplace (Feldman 2006).

Robert Kidder explains Japanese failure to sue as an expression of self-interest that is not terribly different from the motivation of Americans. He cites the example of the Japanese fishing village of Minamata in which babies were born deformed and brain damaged and adults were paralyzed. The disease was traced to the dumping of mercury into the village's fishing waters by a nearby chemical factory. Most villagers refused to sue and were content to rely on the good faith of the company to compensate them. Kawashima undoubtedly would point to the villagers of Minamata as an example of the desire for compromise and harmony.

Kidder dismisses the notion that this failure to sue was based on a cultural rejection of conflict and notes that the factory was the main employer in the town and the inhabitants were fearful of "rocking the boat." The company warned that if they were dragged into court, they would be forced to close medical clinics and schools. A similar mercury-induced epidemic broke out in Niigata, a fishing village farther downstream. Because the residents were not dependent on the factory and did not fear economic retaliation, they immediately filed legal actions (Kidder 1983: 46, 50–51, 77–78, 103).

The response of the villagers in Minamata is not terribly different from the response of workers in West Virginia who were victims of the Buffalo Creek disaster. The Buffalo Creek disaster resulted from a breach in a Pittston Coal Company's coal-waste refuse pile, which was used to artificially dam a stream. The breach allowed a twenty- to thirty-foot tidal wave of water and sludge traveling as fast as thirty miles per hour to sweep through sixteen small communities. More than one hundred people died, one thousand homes were devastated, and four thousand were left homeless. In the end, only two hundred adults chose to sue Pittston Coal, which was virtually the only source of employment in the area (Stern 2008). Kidder concludes by asking whether the Japanese really are more reluctant to sue than Americans and whether Americans are as "trigger-happy" as commonly described (Kidder 1983: 46–47).

A fourth factor influencing dispute resolution involves the economic and legal costs and time required to pursue adjudication. The United States, as we shall see later in the chapter, is viewed by many commentators as a **litigious** society in which people regularly resort to adjudication to remedy harms. Stewart Macauley, in his classic study of contractual relations in the American business community, found business executives prefer to bargain informally with one another rather than to bring a legal action to enforce the terms of the contract. A legal action is expensive and time-consuming, and it strains relationships between businesses and harms a firm's reputation (Macaulay 1963).

Oliver Mendelsohn documents that the Indian business community developed the practice of informally settling disputes rather than resorting to the courts. The Palanpuris in northern Gujarat are a tight-knit community who dominate the Indian and global diamond market. Disputes are settled among diamond merchants by enlisting a distinguished member of the community. In one instance, a Palanpuri diamond broker lost a valuable packet of diamonds. The broker would lose his livelihood if required to compensate the manufacturer for the full value of the lost diamonds. A respected diamond manufacturer intervened and after five hours of negotiation persuaded the trader to accept a reduced amount of money in compensation. Indian cotton traders in various cities enlist merchant associations to resolve disputes between traders and between traders and customers (Mendelsohn 2014).

An additional factor that may influence dispute resolution is the identity of the parties. Individuals may adopt different forms of dispute resolution depending on the identity of the other party. David Engel describes Sander County (a pseudonym), Illinois, as a traditional farming community that in the 1970s was experiencing social change as a result of increased diversity. Farm accidents in the past had been viewed as an accepted part of working life. This reflected a strong ethic of personal responsibility and accountability. An effort to blame others and seek monetary compensation for an injury was considered unethical and immoral. This attitude was reinforced by the close-knit nature of the community in which virtually everyone was connected through family or friendship. Even in the strongest of cases, juries awarded a modest financial recovery; as a result, most personal injury cases were settled before trial. Insurance companies, once having compensated an injured motorist, rarely sued the motorist who caused the accident to recover the payment. The pressure against litigation resulted in a woman accepting $12,000 in settlement for the death of her son in an automobile accident without even filing a legal claim (Engel 1987).

The roughly one in fifteen personal injury cases that did proceed to trial shared a common characteristic: the individuals were separated by a social distance that made any form of dispute resolution short of adjudication difficult. For example, a Mexican immigrant sued the owner of a bar for injuries suffered during a brawl. The plaintiff claimed that the workers behind the bar had passed a weapon to the assailant. The Latino family, although anticipating that people would view them as outsiders and as troublemakers, believed they had been wronged. The tavern owner was an established member of the community who owned a small business that was an important social center in the community. The parties viewed one another with a suspicion that prevented negotiation, and the parties only confronted one another at trial and ultimately reached a settlement.

In another case, a mother brought a case against an automobile dealership for injuries suffered by her 5-year-old daughter when a large trash container on which she had been climbing fell on her. The mother sued for $250,000, and the case ultimately was settled before trial for $3,000. The woman was new to the community and considered herself an outsider. Long-time residents indicated they would have accepted personal responsibility for the injury to the child and would have privately communicated any disappointment to the dealership. New residents believed they were viewed as outsiders and felt discriminated against and typically used the law to communicate their resentment over being dismissed as second-class citizens. Because the newly arrived residents had no relationship with long-time residents, there were no social or economic costs to bringing a legal action.

An interesting twist is that it was considered socially acceptable to sue an individual for a breach of a contractual obligation. A farmer might be sued for failing to meet the payments for a tractor or for failing to pay for animal feed. Long-time residents accepted that although some flexibility might be provided, people were responsible for failing to meet their commitments.

Sander County illustrates the impact of a culture of long-time residents that rejects adjudication as a method of dispute resolution for personal injury claims. In the case of personal injury claims by newly arrived individuals against traditional residents, adjudication provided the only method to bring outsiders and insiders to the negotiation table. These two groups of residents existed in separate worlds, and new residents did not want to risk retribution or retaliation for pursuing adjudication.

As Sander County changes, there likely will be increased adjudication on personal injury claims, and filing these claims will no longer be viewed as an attack on a way of life based on a shared commitment to common values.

Engel's description of Sander County is similar to descriptions by Carol Greenhouse of Hopewell, located near a major southern metropolis, and Barbara Yngvesson of Riverside, Massachusetts. In each instance, long-term "insider" residents viewed themselves as part of a culturally homogeneous community in which disputes were overlooked or settled in a non-confrontational fashion. This "insider" ethic of law avoidance contrasted with the view of the "outsider" newcomers whose resort to the law was denounced as litigiousness and illustrated their refusal to integrate into the community and to settle disputes in "civilized" fashion (C. Greenhouse, Yngvesson, and Engel 1994).

After reviewing the factors influencing the type of dispute resolution that individuals will pursue, we consider the attitudes of Americans toward the law and the legal system.

■ AMERICAN ATTITUDES TOWARD THE LAW

A number of studies have explored the **legal consciousness** of Americans. Legal consciousness is the attitudes and views of individuals toward the law and how these attitudes and views influence individuals' willingness and ability to pursue legal remedies. Legal consciousness is a dynamic process that is the product of a variety of influences. Your early education and experience with government agencies may be positive, and you may learn in school that America is unique in protecting the civil and political rights and liberties of all of its citizens. These positive attitudes and beliefs may change as a result of a bad experience with the police, difficulties and frustrations with the Internal Revenue Service, or learning that, despite the fact that your landlord is mistreating you, you cannot easily get out of the lease you signed (Nielsen 2004: 6–10). A number of studies of legal consciousness are summarized below.

Styles of legal consciousness. A leading study of legal consciousness is Patricia Ewick and Susan S. Silbey's 1998 book, *The Common Place of Law: Stories From Everyday Life*. The authors conducted far-ranging interviews with 430 New Jersey residents in order to explore how people think about and use the law in their daily lives.

Ewick and Silbey identify three types of legal consciousness. The *before the law* consciousness is held by individuals who view the law with awe and respect and as an objective and respected set of institutions and rules. They turn to the law when they experience severe problems and often experience frustration at trying to accomplish something in the legal system. Individuals who possess the *with the law* legal consciousness view the law as a "game" with a set of rules that can be used and manipulated by skillful players to achieve concrete goals. The last type of legal consciousness is *against the law*. Individuals with this consciousness view themselves as caught in the complexity and power of the law and engage in what the authors call "acts of individual resistance" to avoid being controlled by the law. Examples include claiming to be disabled to avoid jury service, using a high-pitched voice "like a woman" to ensure the police respond to a call for assistance, or a juvenile's lying about her age at a hospital emergency room to receive treatment without her parents' permission (Ewick and Silbey 1998).

The authors tell the story of Millie Simpson, a housekeeper earning $18,000 per year, who drove a series of old gas-guzzlers. She parked her 1984 Mercury automobile in front of her house and left it there because she could not afford the insurance payments required to operate the car. Millie was surprised to receive a summons to appear in court for leaving the scene of an accident and driving without insurance. She appeared in court and truthfully explained to the judge her son's friend had taken the car without her permission. The judge accepted Millie's explanation and her plea of not guilty. At her second appearance, Millie assumed the second judge was aware of her earlier explanation and that there would be no problem obtaining an acquittal. She was surprised when she was found guilty (*before the law*). Millie's wealthy employer intervened and hired a powerful law firm that managed to reopen the case and succeeded in having the verdict overturned and Millie's fine returned to her (*with the law*). Millie subsequently was convicted of three charges relating to the condition of her automobile and, unknown to the court, performed her community service at the church where she had been active for many years (*against the law*).

Monica Bell documents that African American mothers view the police with distrust as a result of police violence, lack of responsiveness, racial bias, and a failure by the police to pursue offenders (*against the law*). As a result, they generally rely on self-help to resolve conflicts (M. Bell 2016).

The mothers in Bell's study, however, employ the police in a strategic fashion (*with the law*). One strategy is "domain specificity" in which the police are trusted for problems related to the home such as escorting violent partners out of the house, locating runaway children, or calming noisy neighbors. On the other hand, the police are unlikely to be called to address drug dealing or violent crime where there is a strong norm against "snitching," a risk of retribution, and the prospect of lengthy imprisonment for the offender. Another strategy is "therapeutic consequence" in which calling the police is viewed as a mechanism to get a family member into a social service program, to prevent a young person from slipping into criminality, or to protect a friend who is a victim of domestic violence.

Legal consciousness and working-class Americans. Sally Engle Merry studied white working-class individuals in two New England towns and the legal consciousness that motivated them to pursue legal remedies in court (Merry 1990).

Merry found that before bringing a complaint to the legal system, people typically first resort to gossip, zoning boards, complaints to the police and social welfare agencies, and self-help. Individuals threaten to pursue legal remedies more often than they actually file court actions. They recognize that filing a complaint in court intensifies and escalates the conflict and as a result pursue a legal remedy only as a last resort after exhausting other alternatives.

Merry found that working-class individuals turn to the legal system to solve their problems because they believe as Americans they are entitled to the assistance of the legal system and that the courts have a responsibility to protect the rights, safety, and security of Americans. They appreciate that settling disputes through "legal rules and authorities is more civilized and reasonable than violence." Complainants are disappointed when they find the disputes they brought to court are dismissed by prosecutors and judges and by the other criminal justice personnel as insignificant "garbage cases" in which the courts are being asked to solve a problem with a noisy neighbor, an unfaithful lover, a violent husband, or an undisciplined child. These types of small-scale disputes fall within the jurisdiction of lower criminal courts, juvenile courts, and small claims courts (Merry 1990: 2).

Working-class individuals' experience with the courts typically is discouraging. They find the "system complex, the judge hard to find, and the penalties surprisingly light" (Merry 1990: 3). The reaction of litigants is that courts are indifferent to the problems of the average person. Plaintiffs, rather than receiving legal protection, are met with lectures and advice about how to organize their lives and are told to return for mediation. Mediation is viewed as a dead end. The discussion is not a calm and cool meeting of the minds. It instead is a war of words, an emotionally intense exchange in which the participants shout and accuse one another of being a "bad person" and unwilling to compromise.

Individuals who pursue a legal remedy in a family or neighborhood dispute experience the satisfaction of embarrassing and inconveniencing a resistant neighbor or family member who is forced to appear in court. The downside of seeking a legal remedy is that the judge now is able to dictate the outcome of the dispute.

Merry found that women are more likely than men to resort to the courts because they feel that they lack personal power and are in need of a strong ally to protect themselves against domestic violence, to retain child custody, or to gain leverage in conflicts with neighbors or local merchants. They are disappointed because they find that domestic violence complaints, rather than being treated as serious claims, are dismissed as emotional outbursts. Women say their domestic violence complaints antagonize the men against whom the complaint is filed and place the women at risk of violent retribution (Merry 1990: 70, 180).

An important aspect of Merry's study is that people are combative and resist the efforts of judges and lawyers to minimize the importance of their complaints and dismiss their cases. They refuse mediation, insist on going to court, and challenge the judge in the courtroom. Individuals are not deterred when a judge dismisses their criminal case. They respond by filing new charges in small claims courts or suing for civil damages.

Merry discovered that despite the disappointment with the legal process, working-class Americans have a strong sense of their legal rights and view themselves as entitled to seek legal remedies. The legal system, by stressing that each individual has a right to his or her "day in court" and that the "courthouse door is open to every American," and by highlighting the power of law to protect individuals, reinforces the belief that individuals have the right to ask the courts to protect them. The more people make use of legal institutions, the more comfortable they are in turning to the courts.

Merry's study showed that working-class Americans feel the same sense of entitlement to use the courts as wealthier Americans. The difference is whereas working-class Americans employ the courts for family matters and for neighborhood disputes, middle-class Americans tend to use the courts for disputes over real estate, construction contracts, and consumer problems.

The last point is that although Americans are encouraged to use the courts, they are disappointed with their treatment and with the outcome of their cases. It appears this negative experience affects their belief in the American system of justice. Merry writes that litigants "come to see the particular court . . . as corrupt and flawed . . . [and] come to see that their entitlements are not taken as seriously as those of other people." Working-class people have learned that although they have access to the courts, it takes skill and determination to be taken seriously. Despite their experiences, they continue to believe strongly that it is their right to ask courts to protect their rights and liberties (Merry 1990: 145, 161, 171).

Offensive speech. Laura Beth Nielsen's study of offensive public speech explored the attitudes of Americans toward freedom of speech. She found that individuals' experiences shape their view of the law. Nielsen studied the reactions in three Northern California cities to offensive public speech (including racist and sexually suggestive speech aimed at women and at gays) and the reactions to individuals soliciting funds on the street (begging) (Nielsen 2004). In the United States, unlike in most other countries in the world, the First Amendment protects racist and sexist speech as part of the marketplace of ideas. One woman interviewed by Nielsen reported a man walked up to her and said, "I hate women, they're all sluts." Another commented, "Suck my d---." Yet another man commented, "I would have liked to have been there this morning when your man put that smile on your face. . . . I'll bet he f---ed you so long you'll be smiling all day" (Nielsen 2004: 1).

Nielsen explores whether people believe that offensive speech should be protected under the First Amendment despite the fact that protecting this type of speech creates a "license to harass" (which is also the title of Nielsen's book). Nielsen asked a sample of white men, white women, and people of color whether they believed that such speech should be prohibited. The three groups that were interviewed agree that racist and sexist speech is offensive although they believe the speech should be protected under the First Amendment. The interesting finding is that the groups differed on the reason why the speech should be protected under the First Amendment.

It is not surprising that people of color were much more likely than whites to view racist speech as the "most serious [personal] problem" and women were much more likely than men to view sexually suggestive speech as the "most serious [personal] problem." There nonetheless was recognition among all groups that racist and sexist speech constituted a "social problem" (Nielsen 2004: 75, 81, 97).

Whatever their personal reaction to offensive speech, the individuals interviewed by Nielsen generally did not support legal regulation of offensive speech. The interesting point is that various groups offer different reasons for protecting offensive speech. A majority of white men believe racist and sexist speech should be protected under the First Amendment (before the law). White women and people of color tend to oppose regulation of offensive speech because they believe it would be difficult to draw the line between offensive and inoffensive speech and the restriction on offensive speech could be used to restrict their own speech (against the law). A significant percentage of women also believe the police lack the resources to enforce laws against offensive speech and that offensive speech is best addressed by the individual who is confronted with the comments (with the law).

Nielsen speculates individuals' views toward racist and sexist speech reflect their personal experiences. She speculates white men adopt a First Amendment approach because they are not the target of verbal insults and attacks and do not fully appreciate the impact of verbal assaults. Women have learned that they cannot rely on the law to combat gender bias and, as a consequence, they doubt the capacity of the law to protect them from offensive speech. Views toward regulation of sexist and racist speech have little relationship to individuals' occupation or income (Nielsen 2004: 92, 93, 106, 112–127, 129–130).

There is no significant difference between groups in terms of their views toward begging. Eighty percent of individuals in Nielsen's study reported encountering "beggars" on the street, and 35 percent of respondents favor restricting begging. The individuals who oppose restrictions on begging believe individuals have no alternative to begging and should have the ability to do what is required to survive. Nielsen notes that while racist and sexist speech is tolerated, begging that directly impacts white men and businesses is prohibited in various cities, suggesting legal regulation reflects the public policy preferences of influential business owners who are fearful beggars will interfere with shoppers (Nielsen 2004: 163–164, 176).

Calvin Morrill and colleagues studied "rights consciousness" among young people. They found that although minority youth experience a violation of their rights in school to a greater extent than do Asian and white young people, they are no more likely to pursue a legal remedy. Regardless of race, students are more likely to take extra-legal rather than legal action in response to discrimination. Examples of extra-legal remedies are the rallies and lobbying efforts relied on by undocumented young people intent on securing legal protection. The authors theorize the experience of minority youth with the legal system has convinced them that pursuing legal remedies is not likely to result in the vindication of their rights (Morrill et al. 2010).

This study, along with Nielsen's findings, confirms that Americans view legal remedies as a last resort and are reluctant to make legal complaints.

Sexual harassment. Sexual harassment is an issue of concern to both private industry and the government. Most large corporations and government agencies have training programs and detailed regulations addressing sexual harassment, and there are examples of companies like ESPN that have terminated employees for inappropriate remarks and conduct. A number of studies have found that sexual harassment is most likely to occur in male-dominated workplaces that tolerate and even encourage discriminatory attitudes toward women. This, of course, is not the only explanation. Most universities have strong policies against sexual harassment, and yet roughly 60 percent of college students state that they have been harassed, in most instances by fellow students. The number of complaints of sexual harassment filed with the federal Equal Employment Opportunity Commission continues to rise at a rate of roughly 12 percent a year (Boland 2005; L. Howard 2007).

The data indicate only about one-sixth of sexually harassed women pursue legal action. Phoebe A. Morgan studied thirty-one women who considered filing a complaint and found that only four of them ultimately pursued legal action. Most of the women feared a legal action would strain relations with their husbands or significant others and would cause their children to experience stress and strain (Morgan 1999).

Sexual harassment claims are very different from the local family and neighborhood disputes discussed by Merry and by Ewick and Silbey. Women must hire expert lawyers, engage in years of litigation against powerful governmental or business organizations, and subject themselves to intense examination of their personal lives. The women interviewed by Morgan believe they were victimized and are entitled to legal remedies although they have reluctantly concluded that practical considerations prevent them from pursuing their claims (Morgan 1999).

Abigail C. Saguy found very different attitudes in France toward sexual harassment. She found that sexual harassment statutes in France are not entirely respected and that lawyers and plaintiffs who bring these suits are "discredited" and "stigmatized." In France, sexual remarks and flirting tend to be accepted as part of the natural relationship between the sexes, and the American laws are viewed as intrusive and as an interference with personal freedom.

French female employees hesitate to condemn sexual harassment at work because of a fear of being identified with American feminism. Judges also want to avoid being criticized for adopting the ideology of American feminism and are reluctant to award significant monetary compensation (Saguy 2003).

Employment discrimination. Kristin Bumiller studied the response of African American women to job discrimination. Bumiller notes that the individuals she interviewed did not decide against pursuing claims of discrimination based on a lack of knowledge of their rights or a lack of access to a lawyer or as a result of being frustrated by technicalities (Bumiller 1987).

The individuals in Bumiller's study for the most part were angry over their treatment by employers whom they viewed as "tyrants." They prided themselves as possessing a strong "ethic of survival," strength, integrity, and a sense of self-sacrifice that allowed them to continue to work despite discrimination.

The women resisted filing a legal claim for discrimination based on their "group identity." They rationalized that "everyone confronts mistreatment" or that the individual who discriminated against them was a "bad apple" who was not representative of the people in their workplace. The women, though recognizing that they had a strong legal claim of discrimination, did not want to disrupt their work environment and were skeptical about the prospects for success, believing that their supervisor would deny what was said, their colleagues would resent them, and they would be subject to retaliation.

In sum, although they were aware of their legal rights, the individuals interviewed by Bumiller did not view legal protections against discrimination as effective protection because they perceived the costs and consequences of litigation as outweighing the rewards.

Rights consciousness and the Americans with Disabilities Act. David M. Engel and Frank W. Munger interviewed sixty individuals with learning disabilities or physical disabilities regarding the impact on their lives of the Americans with Disabilities Act (ADA) of 1990. The ADA was intended to combat the day-to-day areas of discrimination confronting people with disabilities. Despite confronting discrimination, none of the individuals interviewed by the authors had filed a claim under the ADA. They possess an understandable fear that requesting an accommodation will result in a perception that they are unable to achieve their career potential without special treatment (Engel and Munger 2003).

Engel and Munger asked whether the law has made

PHOTO 6.1 The Americans with Disabilities Act (1990) is intended to combat the day-to-day areas of discrimination confronting individuals with disabilities.

a difference in individuals' lives. They found that a large number of individuals with mental and physical challenges have come to view themselves as fully able to reach the heights of their profession. The ADA has helped individuals reinterpret their past and understand that their life situation is the product of discrimination and a lack of support rather than a result of a lack of ability or intelligence. The law also has educated the larger community about the need to take affirmative steps to assist individuals who are intellectually and physically challenged.

The authors found that individuals differ in their ability to take advantage of the opportunities afforded by the ADA. Individuals possess differences in drive, ambition, and resilience and in their capacity to avoid viewing themselves as limited by their disability. Individuals with strong family support and with economic advantage have opportunities that are not available to individuals who find their lives limited by a lack of money or by race or gender. Individuals' opportunities also may be limited by the nature of their disability and how late in life they became disabled. Individuals who lack resources and whose mental disability is undetected may go through life without realizing the extent of their disability.

Engel and Munger conclude that despite the positive impact of the ADA on the lives of individuals, the general pattern is for Americans with disabilities to "lump" a denial of their rights rather than to pursue a legal remedy. They characterize Americans as a nation of "law avoiders." As a result, the violation of rights remains unchallenged, wrongdoers remain undeterred and continue to engage in unlawful behavior, and victims continue to suffer because of their failure to pursue legal remedies. The very individuals the ADA is designed to protect are the least likely to bring claims that their rights are being violated.

Rights consciousness. Anna Kirkland interviewed activists in the "fat acceptance advocates." Federal law does not prohibit discrimination based on obesity, and only a handful of state and local jurisdictions prohibit discrimination based on obesity. These activists experienced discrimination and yet resisted the notion that they merited legal protection. Although "fat acceptance advocates" adopted various defense techniques to counter discrimination and negative remarks in their daily lives and argued that they deserved accommodation based on their weight, they conceded that their condition was based on voluntary behavior and was different from disabilities protected from discrimination under the law. They stressed that individuals deserved to be judged based on their performance and should be free from discrimination and yet resisted the notion that they merited legal protection (A. Kirkland 2016).

Kirkland's findings confirm other studies that found although Americans may not view themselves as possessing legal rights, they are committed and concerned with expanding the protections provided by the law. George Lovell analyzed letters written by American citizens to the newly established Civil Rights Division of the Department of Justice between 1939 and 1941, long before the scope of civil rights and liberties protected under the Constitution was expanded by the U.S. Supreme Court. Lovell found that individuals expansively interpreted the Constitution as extending to areas that had not yet been recognized by the Supreme Court such as the rights of criminal defendants in state courts. The Department of Justice explained in almost every instance that the citizen's complaint had no legal basis. Roughly 12 percent of individuals responded by writing back and insisting that their complaint was grounded in the Constitution. Lovell notes that a significant number of individuals did not passively accept the prevailing view of their rights and wrote letters that viewed rights in idealistic terms and as a dynamic and evolving legal concept (Lovell 2006).

American "legal consciousness." Americans have a strong commitment to the Constitution and to the core principles of the American Republic. Regardless of their social class and income, they strongly believe that they are entitled to their "day in court." Contrary to common belief, Americans are not "quick to pull the trigger" and view the filing of a legal challenge as a last resort. It is surprising that despite the fact that the system of justice does not always meet expectations, there is a strong commitment to resolving conflicts through the legal system rather than through intimidation or coercion (D. Engel 2016).

Most individuals find that pursuing a legal remedy exacts considerable emotional and financial costs for themselves and for their families. The prospect of taking on a large organization in a long drawn-out sexual harassment or discrimination claim is particularly intimidating and requires significant resources and self-confidence.

Average Americans' interactions with the legal system leave them with a sense of being disrespected and disappointed. Individuals resent their claims being channeled into mediation, which they consider to be an unsatisfactory substitute for adjudication in court. They are confused by legal procedures and quickly come to understand that they must fight to be heard and to enjoy their "day in court." Women and minorities are particularly skeptical about the ability of the law to protect them. There is a perception that the legal system seems to be more interested in addressing the problems that confront the wealthy and well-off members of society and that judges and lawyers have little interest in expending the time and resources to address the family and neighborhood "garbage" problems that concern working-class Americans. The end result is that the average American "lumps it" rather than pursue legal remedies. It is the better-off members of society who are less likely to "take no for an answer."

Numerous studies conclude that the extent to which injured Americans "lump" their injuries is startling. Nine out of ten injured Americans do not pursue a claim. Only 3 percent of individuals suffering a minor injury, for example falling on an icy sidewalk, hire a lawyer. Among those who suffer modest injury, 78 percent of individuals "lump" their injury. Even in the case of severe, life-threatening injuries, two out of three individuals do not take an action (Hensler et al. 1991). Only 3–4 percent of individuals pursued cases involving medical errors (T. Baker 2005).

David Engel in a recent book challenges the view that individuals make a conscious and rational decision whether to proceed from one level on the "pyramid" of dispute resolution to the next level on the pyramid. He argues that the decisions of "real human beings" whether to pursue tort claims are determined by a range of factors, including the debilitating impact of physical pain, the stigma attached to people who complain, the societal ethic of accepting personal responsibility for injuries, and the influence of family and friends on decisions. The complex factors that combine to cause Americans to "lump" their injuries, according to Engel, are not accounted for by the notion that individuals make a rational decision whether to lump or to pursue a legal claim (Engel 2016: 31–36).

The failure to pursue claims and lumping unlawful conduct means that tortfeasors will be undeterred in continuing their harmful conduct such as distributing harmful products. The costs of injury will be absorbed by individuals who are harmed rather than by those responsible for the injury. The trajectory of an individual's entire life can be changed by an injury. Consider the costs and consequences of failing to bring a legal action against a construction company for the use of cancer-inducing building materials. A successful case can inspire other individuals to pursue legal remedies and force the company to change the type of building materials that are employed (Engel 2016: 180–181).

A crucial dimension of legal consciousness is **procedural justice**. The perception whether a case was "justly" decided is dependent on whether the procedures are viewed as fair. Americans are concerned about whether they are given the opportunity to articulate their views and to be heard and whether decision-makers are fair, neutral, and unbiased and treat them with respect and regard. In those cases in which procedures are viewed as fair, a significant percentage of individuals will accept the result, even when they lose the case. Tom Tyler notes that individuals who are allowed to participate in reaching a decision are likely to accept the result (Tyler 2006: 163–165).

Individuals at times resort to extra-legal and legal methods of resistance to an unresponsive legal system or employ these tactics to call attention to an issue.

Resistance, according to James Scott, is the "weapon of the weak" and involves creative methods to attack an institution ranging from a waiter spitting in a customer's soup to a worker sabotaging an assembly line (Scott 1985). Mindie Lazarus-Black and Susan Hirsch in *Contested States* (1994) discuss how oppressed groups use law as a tool to combat powerful institutions and to achieve a measure of personal independence. Susan Coutin documents how church groups defied what they viewed as the American government's unlawful refusal to recognize the asylum claims of Central American refugees fleeing civil war and offered the individuals sanctuary in churches and community centers (Coutin 1993). Kitty Calavita, in her book on law and society, discusses how prison inmates flood the courts with complaints to harass guards and swamp the prison administration with paperwork, thereby expressing their anger while maintaining a sense of dignity (Calavita 2010: 41).

Despite the reluctance of Americans to rely on the legal system, commentators warn that the American court system confronts a crisis and is at risk of being overwhelmed by an avalanche of litigation. The claim is made that we have too many laws that have opened the door for too many "nonsense cases" that do not belong in court. These cases limit the ability of the judicial system to devote attention to important legal issues. Businesses respond to these "nonsense suits" by raising their prices to pay the costs of defending themselves in court against these groundless cases. The next section asks whether the litigation crisis in America is a reality or a myth.

■ THE DEBATE OVER LITIGATION IN AMERICA

The conventional wisdom is that the United States is characterized by rampant litigiousness. *Litigiousness* is derived from Latin and characterized by a quarrelsome, contentious individual. For purposes of this discussion, it connotes an eagerness to litigate. Our response to any insult or slight is "I will see you in court," and we urge our friends and relatives "to sue the bastards" (Lieberman 1981; W. Olson 1991).

The issue of litigiousness has been of concern for a number of years. In 1970, Chief Justice of the United States Warren Burger in a talk to the American Bar Association urged a solution to what he viewed as the crisis created by increased litigation. Chief Justice Burger noted that federal judges had a backlog of cases and called for an increased number of judges and appointment of professional court administrators to manage court dockets, and endorsed a study by the late Harvard law professor Paul A. Freund calling for a new National Court of Appeals to alleviate the workload of the U.S. Supreme Court. In 2005, President George W. Bush condemned the rush to the courthouse when he observed that "we're a litigious society; everybody's suing . . . there are too many lawsuits in America" (Haltom and McCann 2004: 291).

Why is litigiousness considered a problem? After all, everyone has a right to have "his or her day in court." According to critics, the courts are jammed and overwhelmed with cases that have little legal merit. The entire system is in danger of collapse. The tyranny of law has replaced logic and reason, and Americans suffer from the tyranny of too much law and too many lawyers. Philip K. Howard complains that more than sixty steps are required in New York City to suspend a student for more than five days. A school principal recounts being required to suspend a first grader for carrying a weapon to school, who, after being asked by the teacher to bring her favorite possession to class, brought a pen knife given to her by her grandfather (P. Howard 2009: 104, 106). In the criminal area, defendants raise what Alan Dershowitz terms "abuse excuse," blaming their diet, parents, genes, or childhood trauma for their criminal activity (Dershowitz 1994: 3).

As a result of what Lawrence M. Friedman calls "hyperlexis," courts are unable to focus their full attention on important issues. There are considerable costs to this avalanche of litigation. Taxes are raised to support the judicial branch; businesses are dragged into court, driving up the prices they charge consumers; and insurance rates for doctors skyrocket, forcing them to abandon medical practice. In a society where students sue teachers, patients sue doctors, consumers sue businesses, and neighbors sue one another, trust is undermined. Doctors practice defensive medicine, teachers hesitate to discipline students, and people walk on eggshells. According to this narrative of "hyperlexis," the United States has become a nation in which individuals sue at the drop of a hat and blame others for their problems rather than assume individual responsibility for their actions (L. Friedman 1994: 16).

Caesar Barber is exhibit A of the litigation explosion. At the time of his legal suit, Barber was a 56-year-old maintenance worker who was 5 feet, 10 inches tall and weighed 270 pounds. He filed a legal action claiming that fast-food chains failed to disclose the fat and salt content in their food and that their cuisine had endangered his health (Haltom and McCann 2004: 179–181).

Nutritionists, doctors, and dieticians appreciated the important dietary issues raised by Barber's lawsuit. The popular reaction in the media, however, was to ask whether it was fair for Barber to argue fast-food restaurants were legally liable for the fact that he ate too much inexpensive, fattening food. Critics humorously asked whether Barber wanted "fries with his lawsuit."

 ## 6.1 YOU DECIDE

In 2002, a suit was filed on behalf of two Bronx, New York, teenagers who alleged that McDonald's had made them "fat and sick." One plaintiff was a 51-year-old woman who was 5 feet, 6 inches tall and weighed 270 pounds, and the other plaintiff was 14 years old and 4 feet, 1 inch tall and weighed 170 pounds. The case was thrown out by the judge on the grounds that the plaintiffs had failed to demonstrate that McDonald's food was more dangerous to health than was entirely obvious and that McDonald's food was responsible for their condition. In reaction to this case and other cases, twenty-six states enacted "commonsense consumption" laws prohibiting consumers from suing food sellers for making them fat, giving them diabetes, or creating high blood pressure. Proponents of these "cheeseburger" laws argued that individuals' physical challenges result from a combination of genetics and poor choices in nutrition and in personal lifestyle. Prohibiting individuals from suing and blaming fast-food companies for their physical challenges has the beneficial effect of encouraging individuals to take responsibility for their own health and to lose weight. On the other hand, individuals who advocated imposing responsibility on fast-food companies argued that the companies conceal the high salt and fat content of their food; the companies spend billions of dollars on advertising, particularly targeting children; and the food that fast-food outlets sell is psychologically and physically addictive.

Should individuals be prohibited from suing fast-food companies for the health risks created by fast-food?

In 1976, Judith Richardson Haimes sued Temple University Hospital. She claimed that an iodine-based dye used in conjunction with a CAT scan had caused an extreme and serious allergic reaction, including headaches, and sued, based in part on the claim the headaches had ended her practice as a professional psychic. In the past, she claimed to have assisted the police in solving crimes. The jury deliberated forty-five minutes before returning a verdict in her favor for $600,000 and interest for a total of close to $1 million. The judge overturned the monetary award as "grossly excessive" and ordered a new trial. A second judge dismissed Haimes's case, and she was left with nothing to show for her efforts. Despite the fact that it ultimately was dismissed, the Haimes case became a frequently cited example of the litigation explosion in the United States (Haltom and McCann 2004: 1–2).

Other instances of so-called nonsense cases include suits against a woman for standing up a man for a date, legal actions brought by a child against his parents for failing to properly raise him (L. Friedman 1994: 21), a self-described "milk-a-holic" suing the dairy industry for clogged arteries, an individual suing the phone company for the loss of a leg that occurred when a car hit the phone booth he was using, and a man who sued an industrial manufacturer because the stress caused by pushing the lawnmower the company manufactured caused a heart attack. In another example, California teenager Rick Bodine climbed onto the roof of a high school to steal a floodlight. He fell through a covered skylight, and the resulting injuries left him a quadriplegic. He sued the school on the grounds school officials were aware of the danger on the roof because of an injury that had occurred to a worker several months earlier (Haltom and McCann 2004: 64–66).

William Haltom and Michael McCann studied newspaper coverage of litigation. They conclude that the media coverage overrepresents "crank cases." It is the old story that "human bites dog" is covered while "dog bites human" is not considered newsworthy. They find that the outrageous "tort stories" reported in the newspapers are an insignificant percentage of the cases litigated in court. The media is under pressure to sell papers, so they focus on controversial cases and rarely cover cases in which plaintiffs are unsuccessful or reports that a verdict was overturned on appeal (Haltom and McCann 2004: 174–177).

Lawrence M. Friedman cautions against accepting claims of a litigation explosion. He echoes Haltom and McCann in arguing that most of the cases featured in the media are unrepresentative of the typical tort case and there is no evidence of a litigation explosion. Despite the fact the American population has increased, the number of cases filed per hundred thousand people has remained relatively stable. Thus, although the number of cases filed has increased, the rate has remained relatively stable. The figures that typically are relied on to support the claim there is a litigation explosion are based on filings in federal courts, yet 95 percent of cases in the United States are brought in state courts. A determination of the number of cases filed in state courts is complicated by the fact that state court statistics are notoriously inaccurate. Laurence Baum, after examining the number of case filings in state courts in recent years, concludes that filings have been "flat or [have] decreased" and that the "arrow is either flat or facing down" (Baum 2013: 224–225).

Friedman also notes there are problems in measuring the concept of "litigation." Do we include cases that are filed? Cases that are filed and settled before trial? Cases that are dropped during the trial? An increase in the number of cases filed in court does not necessarily mean judges are overwhelmed. In California, the largest category of cases that are filed is divorce. These cases typically are not time-consuming. Divorce orders are drafted by lawyers prior to divorce hearings and rubber-stamped by the judge. Most automobile accident claims in California are settled prior to trial: less than 1 percent of automobile accident claims result in a trial (L. Friedman 1994: 17–19).

The United States undoubtedly has experienced an increase in the number of laws as society has become more complex, although this does not necessarily translate into increased litigiousness. The automobile, for example, has led to volumes of new traffic laws, the licensing of drivers, registration of vehicles, environmental regulations, laws on taxis and ride services, trade agreements regulating the import of foreign automobiles, consumer protection laws, franchise agreements between manufacturers and dealers, and laws regulating the content of fuel as well as countless other rules and regulations. Some lawyers make a living by concentrating on arrests for drunk driving and moving violations.

The increase in the number of laws has not necessarily translated into an increase in the amount of litigation. One explanation is that the law is fairly predictable and certain in certain areas. For example, state courts follow established formulas for the amount of child support required following a divorce, and there is very little room for argument and the parties have no reason not to reach a settlement.

Businesses try to anticipate problems when they enter into contracts in order to avoid litigation. Most apartment leases and car sales contracts cover every conceivable issue that may arise and leave little room for litigation. Next time you check a bag with an airline, take a look at the baggage claim tag to see how the airline has limited its liability for lost or damaged baggage. Businesses, landlords, and employers also have developed mediation or arbitration mechanisms for resolving and settling disputes. The end result is that there is an increase in legal activity by lawyers in writing contracts, in drafting leases, and in representing clients in arbitration and mediation although this does not translate into an increase in litigation.

Lawrence M. Friedman concludes that although the number of cases filed has not greatly increased, there are new types of cases being brought to trial in areas that formerly were not viewed as subject to legal regulation. He characterizes the development of these new areas of litigation as an expression of Americans' desire for "total justice." Many of these cases are complicated, and this accounts for the fact that judges feel overwhelmed. Friedman cites several areas in which we have seen an increase in litigation; see Table 6.1 (L. Friedman 1994).

Friedman's argument is supported by a study by J. Mark Ramseyer and Eric B. Rasmusen, who found that the amount and type of litigation in the United States generally was the same as in Canada, France, Germany, and the United Kingdom. The court dockets in all these countries focused on bankruptcies, divorces, and automobile accidents. However, Americans radically differed in what the authors term "second order litigation," cases that would never be litigated in other countries. These "second order" cases included legal actions seeking significant amounts of damages against tobacco companies and asbestos and automobile manufacturers and litigation against

Table 6.1 ■ New Areas of Litigation	
Civil rights	Federal civil rights laws in the late 1960s and the Americans with Disabilities Act and other laws have resulted in the filing of employment discrimination cases, voting rights cases, and cases on university admissions and disability access that largely were unknown in the past. In some cases, individuals sue on behalf of themselves as well as on behalf of similarly situated individuals (a class action).
Judicial intervention	Courts have responded to legal actions by intervening to monitor the treatment of prisoners and residents of mental institutions and the clean-up of environmental hazards. In a significant number of cases, judges have found violations of civil liberties and have appointed "special masters" to implement court-ordered reforms.
Megacases	Megacases are "monster" lawsuits. In 1969, the federal government filed suit against IBM, claiming that the company's size had provided a monopoly over the market for business technology. The complicated case did not go to trial for six years; during this period, hundreds of witnesses testified, nine thousand documents were received into evidence, and ten thousand pages of pretrial testimony were recorded.

Pokémon Go for the invasion of privacy by causing individuals to trespass on private property (Kritzer 2002a; Ramseyer and Rasmusen 2010).

Litigation that some people regard as interfering with the sound judgment and flexibility of public administrators is regarded by other individuals as protective of rights and liberties. In past decades, law students have been able to enroll in a class on education law, an area of the law that did not even exist fifty years ago. In the 1960s and 1970s, there were seventy-five federal cases addressing students' hair length, sideburns, and mustaches. There also are countless cases on desegregation, the rights of students with mental and physical challenges, and bilingual education. These developments, on the one hand, may be viewed as expanding the rights and liberties of public school pupils. On the other hand, other individuals regard this expansion of the law to be part of an overbearing and intrusive activist judiciary (L. Friedman 1994: 22–34).

An important perspective discussed in the next section is that "clogged" courts are not the major challenge confronting the justice system. The primary problem with the legal process is that it is too complicated and expensive and is not serving the needs of the average person.

6.2 YOU DECIDE

On February 27, 1992, Stella Liebeck, age 79, bought a cup of coffee from the drive-through window at a McDonald's in Albuquerque, New Mexico. Her grandson, Chris Tiano, drove the car out of the drive-through and stopped in the parking lot.

Liebeck placed the coffee between her legs and used both hands to open the lid. As she removed the lid, the cup spilled into her lap. Liebeck screamed in pain and went into shock, and Tiano rushed her to the hospital. The doctors concluded that Liebeck suffered

(Continued)

(Continued)

third-degree burns that resulted in permanent scarring over 16 percent of her body, including her thighs, buttocks, genitals, and groin area. Liebeck was diagnosed with one of the worst burn cases from hot liquids the doctors had ever seen and remained in the hospital for over a week, where she was subjected to a series of painful skin grafts. She was partially disabled for roughly two years following the accident.

Liebeck initially wrote McDonald's, asserting that coffee "that hot" should "never have been given to a customer." She requested McDonald's to evaluate the temperature at which coffee should be served to customers and asked for compensation for her medical expenses and related costs. Liebeck's request for McDonald's to change its policy was rejected, and the company offered to pay $800 in compensation (her expenses were roughly $20,000).

McDonald's sells a billion cups of coffee per year, which results in daily revenues of $1.35 million.

Liebeck retained an attorney who filed suit and unsuccessfully offered to settle for $300,000. A mediator recommended a settlement of $225,000, which McDonald's rejected.

At trial, Liebeck's attorney contended that the coffee was an "unreasonably dangerous product" and that McDonald's had placed consumers at risk. McDonald's company manual stated that coffee should be served at temperatures of between 180 and 190 degrees, a temperature that can cause severe skin burns if not removed within seven seconds. McDonald's coffee was served at a temperature above that of other fast-food restaurants, and McDonald's had received over seven hundred complaints regarding hot coffee over the previous decade. The company had paid nearly three-quarters of a million dollars to settle these claims. The warning on the cup ("Caution:

contents hot") was difficult to read because of its color, size, and position.

McDonald's responded that Liebeck had spilled and failed to remove the coffee from her skin and that McDonald's should not be held responsible for her negligent conduct. According to McDonald's, Liebeck's legal suit exemplified the over-litigiousness of American society.

The jury held McDonald's liable for $160,000 in compensatory damages and roughly $2.7 million in punitive damages. The jury concluded that Stella Liebeck was responsible for 20 percent of the accident, which led to a reduction in the award for compensatory damages. The $2.7 million in punitive damages was intended to discourage fast-food restaurants from continuing to serve hot coffee. The $2.7 million comprised roughly two days' revenue for McDonald's from coffee sales. Trial judge Robert H. Scott later reduced the punitive award from $2.7 million to $480,000 using the formula of three times the compensatory damages. Liebeck later reached a settlement with McDonald's on the compensatory damage award presumably to avoid the expense and risk of defending the verdict on appeal.

McDonald's reported that it had reduced the temperature of the coffee at the Albuquerque outlet to 158 degrees. Coffee lids carried the warning "HOT, HOT, HOT," and signs at local McDonald's warned, "Coffee, tea, and, hot chocolate are VERY HOT!"

William Haltom and Michael McCann find that the media coverage focused on four elements of the Liebeck case: the severity of her injuries, the large jury award, the claim that McDonald's coffee was too hot, and a description of the coffee spill (Haltom and McCann 2004).

Why did this case receive extensive coverage in the media? As a juror, would you have ruled in favor of Liebeck?

■ ALTERNATIVE DISPUTE RESOLUTION

A growing movement toward **alternative dispute resolution** (ADR) developed in the last several decades of the twentieth century. ADR involves the use of negotiation, mediation, arbitration, and other methods as an alternative to the formal judicial adjudication of disputes.

We previously learned there are various forms of dispute resolution. Negotiation involves the parties to a dispute sitting down and talking in an effort to reach an agreement that both sides can accept. An example may be plea bargaining between prosecutors and defense attorneys before trial. Mediation involves a neutral individual who attempts to encourage discussion between the parties. The mediator helps the parties focus on the main points of agreement and disagreement

PHOTO 6.2   Alternative dispute resolution provides a method of resolving disputes without resorting to the courtroom.

and assists them in crafting a solution. The disputants in a negotiation or mediation must voluntarily accept the results of the process. The most formal form of ADR is arbitration, in which a neutral third party hears the claims of the two parties and reaches a binding decision. Most union contracts (collective bargaining agreements) provide for the mandatory settlement of disputes.

One goal of ADR is to expand the availability of the legal process to the poor, elderly, and working class. The expense and intimidating nature of the traditional legal process may discourage people from taking a landlord to court for failing to provide adequate heat, challenging the legality of an exploitative consumer contract, or seeking protection from domestic or family violence. The streamlined and simple procedures of ADR and the absence of lawyers and judges provide a more equal and less intimidating playing field than the courtroom (Kidder 1983: 171–174).

A History of Alternative Dispute Resolution

Jerold Auerbach traces the American origins of ADR to the early colonial settlements. These tight-knit religious communities of believers were based on harmony and devotion to religious doctrine. Individuals were expected to embrace their fellow believers with love and tolerance and to put aside their disagreements to preserve unity and stability. The reliance on courts and lawyers to settle disputes was discouraged because it was feared that legal actions would promote even greater divisions and disagreements. Attorneys were caricatured as weeds that extinguish every plant and every vegetable that inhabits the same soil. Whenever possible, conflicts and disputes were to be decided outside of the legal system through the use of mediation (Auerbach 1983: 3–5, 10).

The Puritans settled individual disputes before the entire congregation; this encouraged members to forgive and forget and to embrace one another in the spirit of Jesus. The congregation was empowered to expel individuals who did not follow the "church way" (Auerbach 1983: 23–25).

The distrust of law and reliance on alternatives to adjudication characterized settlements throughout New England. In the big and busy city of Boston, a town meeting in 1635 directed that inhabitants should not sue one another until an arbitration panel had heard the dispute. In Connecticut, local towns were advised to consider arbitration as an alternative to jury trials. Outside of New England, New Jersey, Pennsylvania, and South Carolina experimented with dispute resolution. The Quakers in Pennsylvania preached that disputes should be resolved with love and gentleness among friends of the parties, and if this failed, individuals were to submit their disagreement to arbitration by disinterested Quakers. A refusal to accept the judgment of arbitration resulted in expulsion from the Society of Friends (Auerbach 1983: 25–31).

The Dutch colony of New Netherlands, during the tenure of Governor Peter Stuyvesant between 1647 and 1664, established a rotating arbitration board to mediate disputes involving wages, debts, and contracts. Individuals who filed legal suits were referred by the court to arbitration, and courts resisted efforts to adjudicate disagreements (Auerbach 1983: 31–32).

Despite the gradual development of fully functioning state judicial systems, alternative forms of dispute resolution existed in religious and political communities, including the Shakers, Seventh Day Baptists, and Mormons (Auerbach 1983: 47–68). The Scandinavian immigrant groups arriving in the early twentieth century in Minnesota and in North Dakota had strong traditions of conciliating disputes, and the Chinese continued the practice of looking to family elders to settle disputes. Newly arriving Jews relied on rabbinical courts to settle disagreements. These groups all stressed the importance of preventing disputes from disrupting their communities and did not want to display their dirty linen to outsiders.

In the twentieth century, the growing embrace of alternatives to the formal judicial system was motivated by a disillusionment with the fairness of the judicial system and by a desire to provide the working class and poor with greater access to the legal system. Roscoe Pound, professor of law at Harvard, in a 1912 address to the American Bar Association condemned the "horse-and-buggy" character of the urban legal system. Courts were crowded, the costs prohibitive, and legal representation out of the financial reach of the working class. There was a drive to develop faster, more affordable, and less divisive alternatives to the adjudication of disputes in courts. There was the added recognition that not all disputes belonged in court or could be easily settled by a judge without a formal trial. Issues ranging from child custody to disputes between neighbors were best settled by the parties themselves.

The famed legal reformer Reginald Heber Smith observed that whereas litigation inflamed the parties and fueled anger, reconciliation offered "moderation" and "honorable compromise" (R. H. Smith 1919).

The city of Cleveland, in 1912, pioneered conciliation of disputes. Parties in a dispute involving $35 or less were encouraged to appear without lawyers before a judge who would work with the parties to reach a mutually satisfactory result based on reason rather than on anger or recrimination. The "Cleveland plan" spread to major cities, including Chicago, Philadelphia, and New York.

Store owners historically have agreed to rely on commercial arbitration. Eighteenth-century New York merchants complained that the legal process was slow and expensive and created bad blood and that few judges understood technical business questions. In 1768, the merchants established a private tribunal staffed by an impartial referee to settle commercial disputes.

The acceptance of commercial arbitration is indicated by the founding of the American Arbitration Association in 1926. Arbitration is used today to determine whether an employee has been justifiably penalized, suspended, or terminated by his or her employer or to iron out disputes in business and industry. Various professional sports leagues such as Major League Baseball and the National Hockey League provide for arbitration of salary disputes between players and management. There also is an arbitration court that presides over disputes within the Olympic movement.

In recent years, even the most diehard opponents of ADR have accepted that court procedures are too complicated and slow and too expensive. There also is a realization that a "winner-take-all" approach does not resolve a dispute. The losing party carries resentments that may result in an increase in tension and conflict. In some instances, a specialized panel may possess more expertise than a court to resolve questions like medical malpractice.

In 1980, the U.S. Congress adopted the Dispute Resolution Act and declared that for most citizens, legal mechanisms for the resolution of "minor" disputes were "largely unavailable, inaccessible, ineffective, expensive, or unfair." Congress provided financial assistance for states and industry to offer inexpensive ADR procedures. Ten years later, Congress adopted the Administrative Dispute Resolution Act, which required federal agencies to offer to settle disputes through mediation and arbitration. The solution was to provide access to community-based dispute resolution mechanisms that are "effective, inexpensive, and judicious." In 1998, the Congress passed the Alternative Dispute Resolution Act, which requires federal district court judges to offer parties in civil disputes access to ADR before the case proceeds to trial.

On taking office, President Barack Obama appointed Harvard law professor Laurence Tribe as senior consular for access to justice with a mandate that included, among other goals, the improvement in access of the poor and middle classes to alternative forms of justice. ADR takes various forms. Several innovative methods are listed in Table 6.2.

Table 6.2 ■ Innovative Litigation Methods	
Court-annexed arbitration	Judges refer civil suits to an arbitrator, who issues a quick, non-binding decision. Either party can return the case to court if the arbitration award is viewed as inadequate.
Med-Arb	The disputing parties agree to a third party acting as a mediator and consent to the mediator arbitrating any unresolved issues.
Rent-a-judge	The parties agree to accept the decision of a privately retained judge, often a retired judicial official.
Multi-door courthouse	A center offers the parties a range of ADR services.
Screening panels	Various states have created medical arbitration. A patient bringing a medical malpractice case must first go before a panel of doctors who decide whether the case has sufficient merit to proceed to court.
Ombudsmen	A corporation or government institution employs an individual to handle the grievances of customers or citizens.

One example of the type of initiatives pioneered by local governments is neighborhood justice centers. These centers hear all types of disagreements and are not limited to legal conflicts. The centers provide an inexpensive form of dispute resolution for minor housing, family, and criminal disputes. They tend to rely on mediators from the local community, who tend to be available at all hours of the day.

Supporters of ADR point out that disputants who rely on ADR and disputants who pursue their claims in courts are equally as pleased with the results. Studies indicate that the small, intimate setting of ADR in which the mediator or arbitrator provides both parties with a fair opportunity to talk tends to result in less heated discussion than disputes settled in a courtroom (Travers 2010: 130–131).

ADR is not free from criticism. Critics claim individuals deserve their day in court regardless of income and education, and there is reason to believe individuals often are pressured into outcomes that are not in their best interest. According to critics, ADR is not about ensuring justice to the disenfranchised; it is about efficiently riding the judicial system of what powerful interests regard as "garbage" cases. The focus should not be on providing people remedies for yapping dogs or screeching cats or rowdy teenagers who keep people up at night; rather, the focus should be on providing individuals with access to health, healthy food, and the tools to control the environmental hazards that litter their communities (Auerbach 1983: 144). A focus on solving a particular problem, like teenagers who gather on the corners and intimidate residents, fails to address the underlying justice issues that cause the problem. Defenders of ADR respond that these larger concerns are questions of public policy that are better suited for the legislature than for the courts (Auerbach 1983: 144) (see You Decide 6.5 on the study site for the use of dispute resolution to settle injury claims of the victims of the 9/11 terrorist attacks).

6.3 YOU DECIDE

American corporations as a matter of routine include clauses in their contracts that are written in fine print that require individuals to agree in advance to arbitrate any disputes that arise rather than pursue a remedy in court. In 2009, the public interest group Public Citizen found that 80 percent of credit card companies, 70 percent of banks, and 90 percent of cell phone companies currently have arbitration clauses in their consumer contracts (Staszak 2015: 19, 38). The proliferation of these clauses is troubling because individuals in many instances are unknowingly forfeiting their constitutional right to file a legal action against the company. American consumers, as a result of these arbitration clauses, in many cases have lost the right to pursue legal actions against automobile dealers, banks, construction firms, and a large number of other types of businesses.

Arbitration clauses, in addition to restricting individuals from bringing legal claims in court, also typically prohibit individuals from organizing class action suits in which individuals combine their individual small claims so as to make the claims economically worthwhile for a lawyer to bring to court. Absent a class action, it simply is not financially feasible to pursue a legal action for even several thousand dollars.

Corporations under arbitration clauses typically have the right to name the arbitrator and to establish rules of evidence and at times shift the cost of unsuccessful claims to individuals. The arbitration proceedings, other than the names of the complaining party and the corporation, typically are sealed from public examination. Some contracts contain opt-out clauses that allow an individual to avoid the arbitration clause if invoked within thirty to forty-five days of signing the contract although most people are unaware of this provision. The data indicate that companies select the same arbitrators to conduct arbitrations, which gives arbitrators seeking continued employment an incentive to rule for the company. The *New York Times* found that forty-one arbitrators each handled ten or more cases for a single company between 2010 and 2014. In one instance, an arbitration firm had handled over four hundred cases for a corporation.

The evidence suggests that individuals are reluctant to pursue arbitration. The *New York Times* found that between 2010 and 2014 only 505 consumers went to arbitration over a claim of $2,500 or less. Verizon, with more than 125 million subscribers, only confronted sixty-five consumer arbitrations between 2010 and 2014; Sprint, with more than 57 million subscribers, only entered into six arbitrations; and Time Warner Cable, with 15 million subscribers, only confronted seven arbitrations.

Consumers perhaps realize that they are not likely to be successful in company-required arbitration. One study in 2007 found that arbitrators in California ruled against consumers 94 percent of the time (Staszak 2015: 19, 38).

The use of forced-arbitration clauses was upheld by the U.S. Supreme Court in decisions in 2011 and in 2013, and in response to these decisions, the use of arbitration clauses has rapidly increased. It is difficult to obtain a credit card, cable service, or cell phone or to shop online without agreeing to an arbitration clause, buried in the contract. The use of arbitration clauses is not confined to disputes about money. Doctors, nursing homes, and private schools are increasingly relying on forced-arbitration clauses to limit claims for discrimination, elder abuse, fraud, medical malpractice, and wrongful death. The family of a 94-year-old woman in a nursing home in Murrysville, Pennsylvania, who died from a head wound, was required to settle the dispute through arbitration, as was a woman in Jefferson, Alabama, who sustained injuries when the brakes failed on her Honda automobile. The parents of an infant born with serious deformities in Tampa, Florida, had their lawsuit filed in state court dismissed because there was an arbitration clause that precluded a legal action against the hospital. A cruise ship employee who claimed that two crew members had drugged and raped her and left her unconscious also had her case for an unsafe workplace filed in court dismissed because of an arbitration clause.

Another example of a class action that was barred from being litigated was a claim by African American employees at Taco Bell who claimed they were denied promotions, required to work the least desirable shifts, and subjected to degrading comments by supervisors.

The baby of Leydiana Santiago of Tampa, Florida, was born with hearing loss and thumbs that required amputation. She claimed that her doctor had mistakenly determined that she had a miscarriage and, as a result, she resumed taking medication for lupus, which caused birth defects. In April 2014, a Florida appeals court held that Ms. Santiago was required to enter into arbitration. Judge Chris Altenbernd held that "I obey what appears to be the rule of law without any enthusiasm. . . . I have disappointed Thomas Jefferson and John Adams."

The *New York Times* found 1,179 class action suits filed between 2010 and 2014 that companies objected should be filed in arbitration. Judges ruled in their favor in four out of five cases. In 2014 alone, judges ruled for corporation class action bans in 134 of 162 cases.

The arbitration clause reportedly was developed in a series of meetings between credit card companies, businesses, and lawyers at large firms. The lawyers who developed the arbitration clause explained in their defense that arbitration clauses advantage consumers because they do not have to undergo the expense of litigation. However, the *New York Times* found that approximately two-thirds of consumers with claims of credit card fraud, fees, or other issues received no monetary awards in arbitration.

In 2013, Supreme Court Justice Elena Kagan in dissenting from the Court's upholding of an arbitration clause in an American Express contract noted that "the monopolist gets to use its monopoly power to insist on a contract effectively depriving its victims of all legal recourse" and wrote that the Court was telling the victims, "Too darn bad" (*American Express Co. v. Italian Colors Restaurant*, 570 U.S.___ [2013]). The Consumer Financial Protection Bureau plans to issue a rule prohibiting financial institutions from using arbitration clause. Congress has threatened to revoke the rule.

Do you agree with Justice Kagan's characterization of arbitration clauses?

INTERNATIONAL PERSPECTIVE: GACACA COURTS IN RWANDA

In the past decades, countries across the globe have confronted the challenge of putting the country back together following years if not decades of massive human rights violations in which people were arrested, imprisoned, and executed without trial. Once a new government comes to power, the regime confronts the challenge of creating a society in which people no longer live in fear and instead feel safe and secure.

Transitional justice is the process by which a newly installed regime seeks to redress the human rights violations and wrongs committed by members of the previous repressive government. One of the challenges of transitional justice is creating a sense of respect for the law. This requires confidence in the fairness of legal procedures. Another important goal is to educate the next generation about what occurred in the country to ensure that people will appreciate the importance of maintaining a democratic government that respects the rights of individuals.

Countries across the globe confront the challenge of transitional justice, including states in Africa, Eastern Europe, and South Asia. There are various mechanisms used in transitional justice. One is a truth commission. South Africa for decades languished under an apartheid (racial separation) regime in which the majority African population lived under harsh and unequal conditions. Following the fall of the apartheid regime, South Africa adopted a truth commission in which individuals who come forward and testify about their crimes are relieved of criminal and civil liability for their acts. The theory is that individuals, by admitting their crimes and by acknowledging the harm their acts caused, help bring people together.

Another approach, adopted in Argentina, Chile, and Guatemala, is truth and reconciliation commissions, composed of a panel of distinguished individuals who investigate and compile a historical record of events. South Africa and a number of other countries combined these two mechanisms of transitional justice with monetary reparations for victims.

The international community in Sierra Leone, East Timor, and Cambodia established mixed tribunals comprising domestic judges along with judges representing the international community.

Most of these approaches to transitional justice stress reconciliation rather than vengeance or retribution (Van Der Merwe, Baxter, and Chapman 2009).

You might ask yourself, why not merely criminally prosecute the perpetrators? It often is difficult to determine the identity of individuals who engaged in torture or carried out assassinations. A regime would have to conduct thousands of trials, anger the supporters of the previous government, and risk igniting social conflict and animosity. It also is problematic to hold individuals criminally liable for following what at the time were the lawful orders of government officials.

Between April and mid-July 1994, as many as one million individuals were slaughtered in the Rwandan genocide. Rwanda had experienced almost fifty years of ethnic violence that pitted the majority Hutu population against the minority Tutsi population. In April 1994, the plane carrying the presidents of Rwanda and Burundi was shot down, triggering the slaughter of Tutsi civilians. Lists of Tutsi and moderate Hutu were circulated to killing squads. The radio urged Hutu to kill the "cockroaches" and vowed that in the future young children would have to consult books to see a Tutsi because they all were to be slaughtered. The Rwandan Patriotic Front (RPF), a Tutsi guerrilla organization, responded by launching attacks against Hutu in Rwanda. The RPF ultimately proved successful in defeating the Hutu forces and installing a Tutsi-led government (Des Forges 1999).

In the aftermath of the 1994 Rwandan genocide, the United Nations formed the International Criminal Tribunal for Rwanda (ICTR) to prosecute "serious violations" of international law. The theory behind the tribunal is that the global community has an interest in bringing to justice high-ranking Rwandan government leaders and officials responsible for the major international crimes of genocide, torture, and systematic rape. The ICTR focused its prosecutions on top-ranking Hutu government, military, and political party leaders and declared an end to the "culture of impunity" for government leaders (N. Jones 2010: 104–131).

Rwanda announced it would bring every individual accused of crime and anyone who was not prosecuted by the ICTR before domestic courts. The Rwandan justice system had been destroyed during the genocide, and although several thousand individuals were brought to trial, the prisons overflowed with an estimated 130,000 individuals awaiting trial (Burnet 2010: 98).

The international community pressured Rwanda to prosecute lower-level criminals detained in prison. The solution developed by Rwanda in 2005 was to return to a traditional form of village dispute resolution, the **gacaca** court. The gacaca is a patch of grass in the inner courtyard of a village home, which is the location for private discussions. Roughly twelve thousand gacaca courts were established, which were staffed by twenty thousand lay judges. In June 2012, the jurisdiction of the gacaca courts expired, and the courts were closed.

The official goals of gacaca were to reveal the truth about the Rwandan genocide, expedite the prosecution of serious crimes, and hold individuals (regardless of their official status) responsible for their crimes, thereby demonstrating that Rwandans were able to settle their own differences (Meyerstein 2011).

The fundamental idea behind gacaca was for the local community to listen to the testimony of surviving victims, perpetrators, and witnesses and to ask questions and discuss the case. Following the hearing, the judges were to meet in private and arrive at a verdict and an appropriate sentence. A defendant who confessed to his or her crimes received a lesser sentence, half of which might be served in community service. Defendants were encouraged to combine their confessions with pleas for forgiveness. A defendant also could be ordered to pay reparations to victims or to pay damages into a fund established for the victims of genocide. Appeals were permitted from gacaca to a special appeals panel.

The vast majority of the roughly one million cases before the gacaca resulted in defendants confessing their guilt. The confession was the first step toward individuals publicly accepting responsibility for their crimes and seeking forgiveness from the victims and from the local community. This allowed family members and friends to learn the fate of their loved ones and, in some instances, to unearth their remains. The confession also eased the perpetrators' return to the village. Victims who had kept their suffering to themselves were provided the public opportunity to describe their pain and suffering.

The gacaca is credited for bringing Hutu and Tutsi together after years of separation and animosity.

The local community was educated on the events surrounding the genocide and learned to work with one another to solve problems. Critics of gacaca point out that the idealistic picture painted by the Rwandan government of perpetrators and victims reconciling with one another overlooks that the Tutsi victims often continue to live in fear and cannot forgive or forget the death of their family members and friends at the hands of the Hutu (P. Clark 2010: 195, 224). The perpetrators have not always let go of their resentment toward the Tutsi who at the time of the genocide were viewed as a privileged group that monopolized the best education and the best jobs and enjoyed the highest incomes (Hazfeld 2005, 2007). The process also has been criticized for focusing exclusively on crimes committed by Hutu and for disregarding killings committed by Tutsi militia groups invading the country from Uganda.

Gacaca courts, despite their shortcomings, were a unique village-based experiment in transitional justice, which combined punishment of defendants with restorative justice. Some individuals have argued the United States should create a truth commission to document American abuses of detainees during the war on terror. Do you agree?

6.4 YOU DECIDE

In the 1975 case *Goss v. Lopez*, the U.S. Supreme Court held that high school students were entitled to a hearing before being suspended (*Goss v. Lopez*, 419 U.S. 565 [1975]). A number of students were suspended from high schools in Columbus, Ohio, based on disobedient and disruptive conduct committed in the presence of a school administrator.

In 1971, high school students in Ohio organized a series of protests against school policies. Tyrone Washington disrupted a class in the school auditorium at Marion-Franklin High School and was ordered to leave by the school principal. He refused and was suspended. Ralph Sutton attacked a police officer who was attempting to remove Washington from the auditorium and also was suspended. Four other students were suspended for joining Washington in protesting school policy. None of the students was provided with a hearing although they were invited to attend a conference along with their parents to discuss their suspensions.

Dwight Lopez and Betty Crome were students involved in the protest at Central High School and McGuffey High School, respectively. Lopez was suspended during a disturbance in the lunchroom, which resulted in the destruction of property. Lopez alleged that he was not a party to the destruction of property and was an innocent bystander. Crome also was present at the incident at Central High School and was suspended for a ten-day period. Roughly seventy-five students along with Lopez and Crome were suspended.

The Fourteenth Amendment to the U.S. Constitution applies to the states and provides that an individual may not be deprived of liberty or property without due process of law. Ohio, according to the U.S. Supreme Court, had chosen to provide a free education to all young people between the ages of 5 and 21 years of age and to require these individuals to attend school for at least thirty-two weeks per year. The state, once having created this entitlement, may not deprive students of this entitlement by suspending them without a due process hearing. A hearing also is required because a suspension interferes with a student's liberty by damaging a student's reputation in the school and opportunity to pursue higher education and employment. The Supreme Court explained that "having chosen to extend the right to an education Ohio may not withdraw that right on the grounds of misconduct, absent fundamentally fair procedures to determine whether the misconduct has occurred."

At a minimum, students confronting a suspension have the right to oral or written notice of the charges against them, an explanation of the facts on which the charges are based, and the opportunity to be heard. This due process requirement is intended to ensure that decision-makers base suspensions on accurate facts. The Supreme Court noted that fairness "can rarely be obtained by secret, one-sided determination of facts."

The Court stopped short of requiring that students be provided with a lawyer or with the opportunity to confront the witnesses against them or to call their own witnesses. These types of requirements would make suspensions so time-consuming and burdensome that they rarely would be employed. The Court cautioned that suspensions beyond ten days may require more extensive procedures.

Justice Lewis Powell, writing in a dissenting opinion joined by three other judges, criticized judicial interference with the decision-making of school authorities. He argued that suspensions are one of the traditional mechanisms that administrators rely on to maintain school discipline. The requirement that students should be provided with a hearing interferes with the ability of administrators and teachers to rely on suspensions to ensure the security and stability of the school. Requiring an adversarial hearing before a suspension is made is incompatible with the teacher–student relationship in which the teacher guides the development of the student. The next step toward the erosion of the authority of teachers and administrators undoubtedly will be to require that judges review the decision to give a student a B rather than an A or a decision to deny a student promotion to the next grade.

Powell also argued that education is a state and local responsibility, and the federal courts do not have a role in local educational policy. The country has relied for generations on the judgment and good sense of teachers and administrators, and judicial intervention only can undermine their authority.

Do you agree that students should be provided with an informal hearing prior to their suspension?

CHAPTER SUMMARY

A dispute is a disagreement between two or more individuals or groups. A legal dispute involves conflicting interests. Usually one person has something the other wants, and both parties make claims of entitlement. A dispute goes through various stages in which an individual recognizes that he or she has been harmed, identifies the cause of the harm, and confronts the individual or group thought to be responsible for the harm.

There are various styles of dispute resolution, including acceptance, avoidance, self-help, and talking. Talking may involve negotiation, mediation, arbitration, and/or adjudication. Various procedural hurdles typically must be satisfied before pursuing a "talking remedy." Both the social structure of a society and a society's legal culture influence the form of disputing that is practiced in a society.

A number of studies have explored the legal consciousness of Americans. Legal consciousness is the attitudes and views of individuals toward the law and how these attitudes and views influence individuals' willingness and ability to pursue legal remedies.

Americans have a strong commitment to the Constitution and to the core principles of the American Republic. Regardless of their social class and income, Americans strongly believe that they are entitled to their "day in court." Contrary to common belief, Americans are not "quick to pull the trigger" and view the filing of a legal challenge as a last resort. Americans' interaction with the legal system leaves them with a sense of being disrespected and disappointed. They are confused by legal procedures and quickly come to understand that they must fight to be heard and to enjoy their "day in court." The end result is that the average American "lumps it" rather than pursues legal remedies. It is the better-off members of society who are less likely to "take no for an answer."

An individual's perception as to whether a case is "justly" decided is dependent on whether the procedures are viewed as fair. Americans are concerned about whether they are given the opportunity to articulate their views and to be heard and whether the decision-maker is neutral and unbiased and treats them with respect and regard.

The conventional wisdom is that America is a litigious society. This is challenged by commentators who contend that unrepresentative "nonsense" cases are overly represented in the media and question the accuracy of the data. The alternative dispute resolution movement is premised on the view that disputes can be resolved efficiently through mediation, arbitration, and other methods as an alternative to the formal judicial adjudication of disputes.

CHAPTER REVIEW QUESTIONS

1. Distinguish between a grievance and a dispute.

2. Discuss the stages of a dispute.

3. What are various ways in which individuals may respond to a dispute?

4. List various methods of dispute resolution.

5. How does the social structure of a society and a society's legal culture influence the form of disputing?

6. What are the main characteristics of the legal consciousness of Americans?

7. Is America a "rampantly litigious society"?

8. Discuss the development of the alternative dispute resolution movement and the types of ADR. What are the arguments for and against ADR?

TERMINOLOGY

alternative dispute resolution   233
blaming   211
claiming   211
dispute   209
gacaca   239

grievance   209
justiciable   214
legal consciousness   219
litigious   218
multiplex relationships   215

naming   211
procedural justice   227
resistance   227
simplex relationships   215
transitional justice   238

ANSWERS TO TEST YOUR KNOWLEDGE

1. True

2. True

3. False

4. False

5. False

CHAPTER 7

CRIMINAL COURTS

TEST YOUR KNOWLEDGE: TRUE OR FALSE?

1. The crime control model is distinguished from the due process model of criminal procedure, in part, based on the fact that the crime control model is somewhat more concerned with speed and efficiency than with the protection of individual rights.

2. Defense attorneys feel respected by the public, which appreciates that they represent individuals who are charged with criminal conduct.

3. Public defenders by every measure are less effective in representing defendants than private defense attorneys.

4. Prosecutors exercise complete discretion in deciding whether to prosecute a defendant.

5. Grand juries are an effective check on prosecutorial discretion.

6. Judges, prosecutors, and defense attorneys have a mutual interest in encouraging plea bargaining.

7. An argument in favor of plea bargaining is that it ensures that the punishment fits the crime.

Check your answers on page 273.

■ INTRODUCTION

The classic vision of a trial involves two lawyers zealously representing their clients in a courtroom in front of a judge and jury. This adversarial process is described as the "fight theory of justice" or the "sporting theory of justice." The courtroom in the **adversarial model** is described as a "battlefield" in which the combatants struggle for supremacy. The "fight theory of justice" is based on the belief that the "truth" will emerge from the confrontation between two committed advocates. Critics of "adversarial legalism" assert that the trial process does not always produce accurate results because trials are tainted by lawyers who stretch the facts, witnesses who shade and withhold the truth, and attorneys whose arguments are calculated to appeal to the jury's emotions rather than to the jury's rationality (Frankel 1978; Kagan 2001).

The reality is that the criminal trial is an endangered species. A criminal trial requires enormous preparation, time, expense, and resources and has been criticized as an "unworkable" method of adjudicating "ordinary cases." In the United States, most criminal cases are plea bargained, and full-blown trials tend to be reserved for serious felonies in which the defendants possess the wealth and resources to insist on a trial or in which defendants believe the outcome is a close call and they may succeed in persuading a jury of their innocence. There also are a small number of "high-profile" cases, which prosecutors believe are sufficiently important to merit a full airing of the facts in a public trial (Geis and Bienen 1998).

In the plea bargaining or **consensus model** of the criminal justice process, most cases are disposed of by striking a plea agreement before trial. The goal of this consensus model is to efficiently and speedily move cases through the system. The reliance on plea bargaining is based on the recognition that the judicial system would grind to a halt if most cases were brought to trial rather than disposed of by a plea bargain (Langbein 1979).

In this chapter, we examine criminal trial courts, the role of prosecutors and defense attorneys, and plea bargaining. As you read the chapter, consider the gap between how criminal courts work in theory and how criminal courts work in reality. Ask yourself whether criminal courts function in a fair fashion.

■ CRIME CONTROL AND DUE PROCESS

Herbert Packer developed two conflicting models of criminal procedure, a crime control model and a due process model, which are based on the differences between the consensus model and the adversarial model of criminal justice (Packer 1968; Weigend 1980: 421).

The **crime control model** is based on the premise that the repression of crime is one of the most important functions of government. The emphasis is on the rapid arrest, screening, charging, and acquittal or conviction and sentencing of the guilty and on limiting the appeals process in order to remove anti-social individuals from society. The criminal justice system is an assembly line in which the goal is for suspects to have their cases dismissed or to plead guilty and for the police and prosecutors to move on to the next case rather than spend time establishing guilt or innocence at trial or responding to appeals.

The crime control model may be contrasted with the **due process model**. The due process model, while recognizing the importance of preventing and punishing crime, stresses the need for protecting suspects against the power of police, prosecutors, and judges. Detailed procedures are viewed as the best protection against human error, mistreatment, corruption, and false convictions. Speed and efficiency are sacrificed in the interest of protecting individuals' rights, providing equal treatment, and, most important, ensuring reliable results. The due process model is an obstacle course; the crime control model is an assembly line.

The American criminal justice system attempts to balance the processing of crime with due process protections. We first look at prosecutors and defense attorneys and then turn our attention to the plea bargaining process. In the next chapter, we will look at criminal trials, jury decision-making, and judicial sentencing. As you read these chapters, pay attention to the process by which cases are disposed of at various points in the criminal justice process.

■ DEFENSE ATTORNEYS

Defense lawyers are required to provide competent and effective representation. In 1984, in *Strickland v. Washington*, the U.S. Supreme Court held that even when a lawyer commits a serious error at trial, the verdict will not be reversed unless "there is a reasonable probability that but for counsel's unprofessional errors, the result of the proceeding would have been different" (*Strickland v. Washington*, 466 U.S. 668 [1984]).

In 1967, Arthur Wood conducted a valuable early survey of criminal lawyers, but it does not fully describe the diversity of the current criminal bar (A. Wood 1967). Wood's work was updated by Paul Wice in his 1978 study of criminal lawyers in nine cities. Although conducted before the entry of large numbers of women and minorities into the legal profession, Wice's study provides some sense of the characteristics of criminal lawyers in private practice; the survey does not include **public defenders** (Wice 1978).

Wice found that 70 percent of criminal lawyers were between 30 and 50 years old. The absence of younger lawyers is explained by the fact that 75 percent of the lawyers in the sample had experimented with various areas of legal practice before settling on criminal law. The small percentage of older lawyers is due to the fact that more senior attorneys found they lacked the energy and passion required for criminal law. A surprising number of private defense lawyers had been prosecutors and, after having gained experience, moved into defense work. Only 12 percent had been public defenders. Wice speculates that public defenders either remained as public defenders or became disillusioned with criminal law and decided to pursue other areas of practice (Wice 1978: 63–65, 82–86).

Wice observes that most African American and minority lawyers worked for the public defender and as a

PHOTO 7.1   James Holmes (born December 13, 1987) pled not guilty by reason of insanity to the killing of 12 individuals and to the injuring of 70 individuals in an armed attack on a movie theater in Aurora, Colorado, on July 20, 2012. Holmes's insanity defense was rejected by the jury and he was sentenced to 12 consecutive life sentences without the possibility of parole.

result were not in his sample of private lawyers. Nonetheless, 11 percent of the lawyers he surveyed were African American, which at the time was a larger percentage than the number of African American lawyers in the legal profession as a whole. Wice estimates that over 60 percent of the clients of the lawyers in the survey were African American. Almost 50 percent of the lawyers in Wice's sample were Jews, 31 percent Catholics, and the remainder Protestants. Wice attributes the large percentage of ethnic lawyers to the fact that these attorneys had been excluded from corporate law firms and carved out a niche for themselves in the practice of criminal law. Criminal law was a natural specialization for ethnic lawyers because criminal law generally is concentrated in urban areas and is not sufficiently profitable to be of interest to corporate lawyers. Wice does note that an increasing number of corporate lawyers have turned their attention to white-collar crime (Wice 1978: 71–75).

Despite the ethnic character of the defense bar, Wice identifies 63 percent of criminal lawyers as coming from middle-class backgrounds and 23 percent from professional backgrounds. Criminal lawyers in general were "in-bred," with almost 60 percent having been raised in the cities in which they practiced law. A surprising number of these criminal lawyers attended elite law schools or schools with a national reputation (25 percent), and only 16 percent attended lower-quality schools. The lawyers in Wice's study tended to minimize the importance of education for the practice of criminal law and instead stressed the importance of experience (Wice 1978: 63–75).

Criminal lawyers are well aware they command little respect. The public identifies defense lawyers with the "criminals" they represent and does not understand how defense lawyers can defend the "guilty" (Wice 1978: 122). Female defense attorneys who represent defendants who are charged with crimes against women experience a moral tension, which they resolve by accepting the importance of providing individuals accused of crimes with legal representation and by viewing themselves as protecting individuals' rights (Siemsen 2004).

Most defense lawyers are unhappy because they believe they are not respected by other lawyers and find themselves working long hours in crowded urban courtrooms earning much less money than other lawyers in private practice. Defense lawyers also confront the constant challenge of attracting business, and they depend on referrals from clients and from other lawyers. They generally have little money and expend considerable time collecting fees from clients, many of whom are incarcerated. The result is that most criminal lawyers cannot support themselves by only focusing on

PHOTO 7.2 Actor Bill Cosby and criminal defense attorney Brian McMonagle (right) return to court for a preliminary hearing on criminal charges against Cosby for sexual assault on April 3, 2017, in Norristown, Pennsylvania. Cosby's trial ended in a mistrial and he will be retried on the same charges.

Table 7.1 ■ Justifications of Public Attorneys' Defense of Criminal Defendants	
Perceived Role	**Rationale**
The Garbage Collector	It is dirty work, but someone has to ensure that the police and prosecutors adhere to the law and check the abuse of power.
The Constitutionalist	Criminal defendants possess a Sixth Amendment right to counsel.
The Civil Libertarian	The protection of a defendant's constitutional right upholds the rights of all American citizens.
The Legal Positivist	The question of guilt or innocence is a question for the fact finder (judge or jury) rather than for the defense attorney.
The Philosopher	There is a difference between factual or moral responsibility and legal guilt. A defendant only is legally guilty if the prosecution establishes his or her legal guilt beyond a reasonable doubt in a court of law.
The Oddsmaker	It is better that ten guilty people go free than one innocent person is convicted.
The Political Activist	A lawyer acts in a moral fashion when defending the impoverished and disadvantaged and attempting to assist them to avoid imprisonment, which will make it difficult to find employment and make a life for him- or herself.
The Social Worker	A defendant's relationship with a caring and concerned lawyer can give the defendant a sense that there is someone who cares about the defendant and will assist in his or her rehabilitation.
The Humanitarian	The lawyer should come to the assistance of individuals in need of help.
The Egoist	Criminal defense work is interesting.

criminal cases and must devote at least 40 percent of their time to noncriminal cases (Wice 1978: 90–114).

There are several justifications offered for public attorneys' defense of criminal defendants (Babcock 2013). Several of these are listed in Table 7.1. Which do you find most persuasive?

In a number of local courts, criminal defendants are represented by "courthouse regulars" who have long-standing relationships with prosecutors and judges. Abraham Blumberg notes that the "lawyer-regular" rarely is able to exercise his or her full legal skills because most cases are plea bargained. He also finds that defense lawyers believe that they contribute to the welfare of society by protecting the rights of defendants and resent the fact that they are dismissed by better paid corporate lawyers as "second-rate lawyers" (Blumberg 1979: 242).

In 1967, Blumberg drew on his experience as a defense attorney to reveal the reality of the defense attorney as a "double agent" engaged in "the practice of law as a confidence game." Blumberg argues that defense attorneys are central performers in a theatrical performance in which the lawyer assures the client that the lawyer has the skills required to rescue the defendant from a harsh punishment. The defense lawyer, after persuading the client to plead guilty, "cools out" the client to keep the client from turning against the defense lawyer for failing to keep the client out of jail. The judge may even assist the defense lawyer by praising his or her skillful representation. Blumberg offers the important insight that the defense lawyer is a double agent who, rather than representing his or her client, is engaged in serving the organizational goals of the judge and prosecutor by persuading the defendant to plead guilty. The defense attorney benefits because he or she collects a fee without having to spend time defending the case at trial. Blumberg writes that the imperative of the court bureaucracy to "clear" cases from the docket takes precedence over the interests of defendants and the requirements of due process of law. The result is that courtrooms have been reduced to "betting parlors and commodity exchanges" (Blumberg 1979: 161, 227–246).

Rodney J. Uphoff, in his study of criminal courts in Dane and Milwaukee Counties (Wisconsin) and Cleveland County (Oklahoma), challenges Blumberg's view that defense attorneys are motivated by a desire to clear cases as quickly as possible to make money. He finds that even the most well-intentioned defense attorney finds him- or herself in a weak bargaining position (Uphoff 1992). Lawyers often have no option other than to enter into unattractive bargains because clients cannot afford the cost of trial or prosecutors may have a strong case and possess little incentive to offer concessions.

The defendants in Uphoff's study believe judges and prosecutors encourage plea agreements and fear they will be punished if they insist on going to trial. Many of these defendants had prior criminal convictions that undoubtedly would be introduced by the prosecutor at a trial and would make it difficult to gain an acquittal. Defendants who could not arrange for bail also faced the prospect of a lengthy pretrial detention.

Uphoff concludes that criminal trials are not a "fair fight." Defense attorneys are unable to match the resources, investigators, and forensic experts available to prosecutors. Uphoff also stresses that the prosecutor possesses a range of "bargaining chips" (e.g., additional charges carrying lengthy prison sentences) that deter defendants from going to trial. In other words, Blumberg's criticism of defense lawyers as "double agents" fails to appreciate that even the most well-intentioned defense attorney has no alternative other than to strike a plea bargain with prosecutors. Defense lawyers are not the confident "double agents" that Blumberg describes and might better be viewed as powerless pawns (Uphoff 1992).

The question is whether a skilled defense lawyer makes a difference. Harry Kalven Jr. and Hans Zeisel in a survey of judges found that in three-quarters of criminal trials, judges believe there is no significant imbalance between the skills of the prosecutor and the skills of the defense attorney. Judges viewed the prosecutor as the superior lawyer in 13 percent of the cases and viewed the defense attorney as the superior lawyer in 11 percent of the cases. Lawyers representing poor defendants were somewhat less likely to be viewed as superior and somewhat more likely to be viewed as inferior than defense lawyers representing non-indigent defendants. Kalven and Zeisel estimate that the defense counsel made a difference in 1 percent of the trials studied; the impact of defense lawyers was greater in cases tried before a jury. The important point is that the defense counsel provided competent representation and maintained a balance between the prosecution and defense in three-quarters of all cases (Kalven and Zeisel 1966: 355–357, 372).

Roger Hanson and Brian Ostrom studied indigent defense in nine cities using public defenders, assigned counsel, and contract attorneys and found that they are as "successful" as privately retained lawyers in terms of length of time to dispose of a case, obtaining dismissals or acquittals for their clients, and reduction of charges. Private attorneys perform modestly better in keeping a defendant out of prison although six out of ten of these defendants are incarcerated. Hanson and Ostrom suggest that defendants' dissatisfaction with the time and attention they receive from a public defender should not obscure the results achieved by these lawyers (Hanson and Ostrom 2012).

The bulk of cases in criminal courts are handled by public defenders. A perennial question is whether public defenders provide the same quality of representation as private defense lawyers.

■ INDIGENT DEFENSE

The U.S. Supreme Court in *Gideon v. Wainwright* held that the Sixth Amendment to the Constitution guarantees individuals charged with a felony access to a lawyer in criminal prosecutions. The Court explained that it was an "obvious truth" that the right to an attorney is central to the guarantee of a fair trial. Absent a lawyer, a defendant could not adequately present evidence in his or her defense, cross-examine prosecution witnesses, or navigate through the technicalities of the law of evidence and court procedures (*Gideon v. Wainwright*, 372 U.S. 335 [1963]). The Court later clarified that the right to an attorney at trial applied to any case in which a defendant might be incarcerated. A court could not sentence to prison a defendant who did not have legal representation (*Argersinger v. Hamlin*, 407 U.S. 25 [1972]). On the same day that the Court decided *Gideon*, the justices held that the guarantee of a right to a lawyer extended to an individual's initial appeal following conviction (*Douglas v. California*, 372 U.S. 353 [1963]). The right to an attorney subsequently was extended to all "critical stages" of the criminal justice process, such as an appearance in a lineup

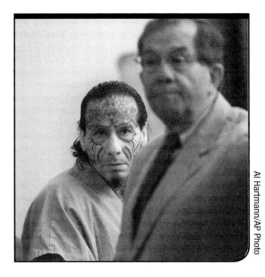

PHOTO 7.3   The landmark Supreme Court case of *Gideon v. Wainwright* established the right of criminal defendants to be guaranteed legal representation in criminal cases. States either provide public defender services or pay private attorneys to represent indigent defendants. Public defender offices suffer from heavy caseloads, poor pay, and limited resources.

following a formal criminal charge. A critical stage is any stage in which the absence of a lawyer strongly prejudices a defendant's case and makes it highly likely that he or she will be convicted at trial (*United States v. Wade*, 388 U.S. 218 [1967]) (Lewis 1964).

   Gideon meant that every state would be required to provide defense attorneys for indigents (L. Silverstein 1965). States rely on three major systems for defending indigent defendants: assigned counsel, contract attorneys, and/or public defenders.

Assigned counsel. Judges appoint to cases private lawyers who are willing to represent indigent defendants. The lawyers typically are paid on an hourly basis although some states provide for a flat fee. Lawyers must ask for funds for investigators, expert witnesses, and other purposes. This model tends to be used in small cities and counties of fewer than fifty thousand residents where there are not enough criminal cases to justify a permanent public defender system. In jurisdictions in which lawyers are required to be "prescreened" to participate in the program, the court is able to ensure that competent lawyers are involved in indigent defense. At $40 or $50 an hour, these programs are not appealing to experienced attorneys.

Contract attorneys. Private lawyers, bar associations, law firms, or a group of attorneys contract with the state or local government to represent indigents. This contract model also is used in cities and counties with small populations. Budget-conscious government officials under this system are able to determine in advance how much money they will spend on indigent defense. On the other hand, attorneys have an incentive to maximize their profits by spending as little time as possible on each case, and firms may assign their least experienced attorneys to represent indigents to hold down their expenses. Some attorneys are required to pay expert witnesses out of the flat fee they receive to represent indigents (Houppert 2013: 18).

Public defenders (PDs). Salaried lawyers paid by the government work full-time to provide indigent defender services.

Many larger cities and counties have a "mixed" system, which combines PDs with assigned counsel or contract attorneys. Authority over these various models of defender services may be centralized in a state or county agency or may be administered by a statewide indigent defense commission that funds local indigent defense.

PDs are the primary mechanism for representing indigent defendants in urban criminal justice systems. Ninety of the nation's 100 largest counties have public defender systems although assigned counsel programs operate in 2,800 of the nation's 3,100 counties (Wice 2005: 10). PDs represent about 79 percent of indigent defendants.

The first public defender office was established in Los Angeles County in 1914, and the idea spread across the United States. The public defender office in Los Angeles was established because indigent defendants could not afford lawyers or were represented by lawyers who failed to provide them with a vigorous defense. Public defender services were created to counter the power of prosecutors by providing indigent defendants with adequate representation at trial and at sentencing (McIntyre 1987: 38). Other cities and localities responded to the Supreme Court decision in *Gideon v. Wainwright* by following the Los Angeles example and establishing a public defender service. In 1951, there were only 7 public defender organizations in the United States, and by 1973, 573 defender organizations had been established (McIntyre 1987: 29).

A number of studies report that clients have little faith in PDs. Clients know that PDs are paid by the state and believe PDs have little incentive to do a good job because they will continue to put bread on their table whatever the outcome of the case. PDs are viewed by indigent defendants as part of the court bureaucracy who, instead of zealously representing defendants, cooperate with prosecutors in rapidly plea bargaining defendants' cases (Sudnow 1965: 273). The primary basis for distrust of PDs is that defendants perceive that when you receive something for free, it cannot be very good. The suspicion toward PDs is expressed in such shorthand as the PD's office is the "only working railroad in the state . . . you are railroaded straight to prison" or PD stands for "place in detention." Critics often repeat the statement of a defendant who reportedly stated that he "did not have a lawyer when he went to court, [he] had a public defender" (Casper 1971, 1972). In Cook County (Illinois), PD is said to stand for "penitentiary dispenser," and defendants question whether they would have been convicted if afforded a "real lawyer" (Bogira 2005: 126).

Studies of PD offices in Cook County (Illinois) and in Essex County (New Jersey) provide a more balanced perspective on PDs. Most defenders in these jurisdictions attended local law schools and are from solidly middle-class backgrounds. The studies find that a significant percentage of public defenders are experienced and skilled lawyers who are motivated by a passion for litigation and who derive satisfaction from protecting clients from being "screwed" by prosecutors. PDs are more diverse than the legal profession as a whole: roughly 30 percent are women, and 30 percent are minorities. Female lawyers are attracted by the opportunity to work with clients and to help them improve and transform their lives. Minority lawyers feel an obligation to defend individuals who share their background and believe that they face less discrimination in the PD's office than in the private sector.

PDs perceive they lack respect from judges and other lawyers. They constantly confront the "cocktail party question" from the public, which wants to know "How can you defend those people?" The PDs typically respond with some pride that they are upholding their clients' constitutional right to a free and fair trial (K. Davis 2007; McIntyre 1987; Wice 2005).

The Bureau of Justice Statistics compared the effectiveness of publicly funded lawyers who represent indigent defendants to that of private lawyers who represent somewhat more economically advantaged defendants. Virtually no difference was found in the conviction rates of defendants represented by public attorneys versus private attorneys. A lower percentage of individuals represented by private attorneys were sentenced to prison (53.9 percent as opposed to 71.3 percent), and these defendants received shorter prison sentences (31.2 months as opposed to 38.3 months). The lengths of defendants' sentences, with the exception of drug offenses, were generally the same whether defendants were represented by a publicly funded lawyer or by a private attorney. These differences do not necessarily indicate that private attorneys are more competent because public attorneys tend to be involved in "less winnable cases." Defendants who believe they have a chance of acquittal also may manage to find the money to hire a private attorney (Harlow 2000).

A study of nine courts confirmed that the differences between public and private attorneys are not as stark as the conventional wisdom suggests. Assigned lawyers, contract attorneys, and public defenders process cases in less time than do privately retained lawyers. This means that defendants represented by these lawyers spend less time in jail awaiting the final disposition of their case. Does this mean public defenders plead their clients guilty to clear their caseload? Contrary to conventional wisdom, roughly the same percentage of defendants represented by PDs and those represented by private attorneys plead guilty (Hanson, Ostrom, and Lomvardias 1992). Consider the following:

Convictions. The conviction rates of defendants represented by assigned counsel, contract attorneys, public defenders, and private attorneys are virtually identical.

Acquittals. The four categories of lawyers all have similar acquittal rates for cases that go to trial.

Charge reductions. Another measure of effectiveness is charge reduction, whether or not the charges to which a defendant pled guilty were less serious than the original charges. Public attorneys once again generally do as well as privately retained lawyers.

Prison. A smaller percentage of clients represented by private attorneys end up in prison. The difference is misleading when considering that private lawyers have the luxury of selecting the clients that they represent and that their clients are more likely to have close ties to the community and to have less lengthy prior criminal records.

Plea bargaining. Jerome Skolnick found that there was no difference between private defense attorneys and public defenders in their ability to negotiate pleas for their clients (Skolnick 1967).

What accounts for the view that private attorneys are far superior to public defenders, who are considered second-rate lawyers unconcerned about their clients? Skolnick notes that commentators usually compare public defenders with the most skilled private attorneys rather than with the average private practitioner. He nonetheless finds that, compared to PDs, private attorneys are more fully engaged in their cases, file more motions, and consult more frequently with the client and family members (Skolnick 1967: 67–68). This is explained, in part, by the fact that a public defender handles between 200 and 2,225 felonies and misdemeanors a year as compared to the average private attorney who would consider 100 cases a "crushing burden" (Houppert 2013: 13).

The economic downturn over the past years led to the slashing of state budgets for public defenders. In 2004, the American Bar Association Standing Committee on Legal Aid and Indigent Defendants held hearings in twenty-two states and concluded that forty years after *Gideon v. Wainwright*, indigent defense "remains in a state of crisis resulting in a system that lacks fundamental fairness and places poor persons at constant risk of wrongful conviction." The funding is "shamefully inadequate" and has resulted in escalating caseloads for lawyers engaged in the defense of indigents. More than 70 percent of county-based public defender offices exceeded the caseloads recommended by the ABA. Defendants can spend months or as long as a year in jail waiting to meet with a PD. The ABA report finds that in rural southern states, over 40 percent of defendants plead guilty immediately after meeting their lawyer for the first time. These "meet 'em and plead 'em" lawyers typically arrange plea bargains even before meeting with their clients.

States spend far more money on prosecutor offices than on defense services, which means that PD offices do not have the same number of lawyers, investigators, experts, and support staff as prosecutor offices do. Fordham law professor John Pfaff reports that in 2008, state and local governments spent 30 percent less on defense services than on prosecution (Pfaff 2017: 137). Tennessee is typical: in 2007, the state spent twice as much on prosecution as on defense for criminal cases. In Cumberland County (New Jersey), PDs handle 90 percent of all cases. The prosecution has twice as many lawyers and seven times as many investigators as the PD office. The question is, how many individuals might have been acquitted or would have received convictions on less serious offenses if public defender services had had the same access to experts and investigators as the prosecutors had (American Bar Association 2004: 12, 16, 21; Houppert 2013)?

In 2010, Justice Tom Chambers of the Washington Supreme Court noted that defense services in the state failed to fulfill the promise of *Gideon* (*State v. A. N.J.*, 225 P.3d 956 [2010]).

> Although the vast majority of public defenders do sterling and impressive work, in some times and places, inadequate funding and troublesome limits on indigent counsel have made the promise of effective assistance of counsel more myth than fact, more illusion than substance. It is clear, even if not calculated, that the prosecution benefits from a system that discourages vigorous defense and creates an economic incentive for indigent defense lawyers to plea bargain.

Professor Andrew Manuel Crespo of Harvard makes the interesting point that criminal defendants who are convicted and are in a position to take their case all the way to the U.S. Supreme Court are at a distinct disadvantage as compared to the government. Experienced lawyers represent defendants in less than one-quarter of Supreme Court criminal appeals. Highly qualified lawyers from the Office of the Solicitor General participated in 72 percent of the criminal cases and sided with the state attorney general against criminal defendants in 96 percent of these cases. Government lawyers on average had argued twenty-five cases before the Court, five times the experience of the criminal defense lawyers in the cases before the Court. Six members of the current Court have experience as prosecutors although there is no justice with experience in criminal defense (Liptak 2016).

Now that we have discussed defense attorneys, we turn our attention to prosecutors.

7.1 YOU DECIDE

Public defenders across the United States represent more than 85 percent of criminal defendants, many of whom are poor and indigent minorities. Between 1995 and 2015, spending on indigent defense fell by 2 percent even as the number of felony cases rose by approximately 40 percent. Roughly 70 percent of county-based public defenders nationwide carry caseloads that exceed the standard of 150 felonies and 400 misdemeanors.

State and county spending on indigent defense is roughly $2.3 billion, approximately 1 percent of the more than $200 billion spent on criminal justice. In forty-three states, indigent defendants are made to pay a portion of the expense of their defense although many of them are economically destitute. South Dakota charges $92 an hour for public defense, and a failure to pay is a criminal offense. The result is that a defendant represented by a public defender who is acquitted may find him- or herself both in debt and subject to imprisonment as a result of an inability to reimburse South Dakota for the expense of representation. In New Orleans, indigents must pay $40 to apply for representation and an additional $4 if they plead guilty or are found guilty. Fresno, California, public defenders have caseloads that are four times the ABA-recommended maximum of 150 cases.

In August 2016, Michael Barrett, director of the Missouri State Public Defender, wrote then Missouri governor Jay Nixon complaining that the governor had repeatedly cut funding for the state's indigent defense system that continues to rank forty-ninth in the United States in terms of funding. After cutting $3.47 million from public defense in 2015, Governor Nixon announced a reduction of an additional 8.5 percent in the public defender's budget. At the same time that the Missouri State Public Defender was unable to hire additional lawyers, the caseload increased by

12.5 percent. Barrett, in order to express his dissatisfaction, invoked a Missouri law that gives the director of the Missouri public defender system the authority to require any member of the state bar to serve as a public defender and directed Governor Nixon to represent an indigent defendant.

Governor Nixon responded that the Missouri State Public Defender lacked authority to appoint private lawyers to represent indigents absent a finding by a circuit court judge that the appointment would not cause "undue hardship" and dismissed Barrett's request as a "publicity stunt." A court later agreed with Governor Nixon and blocked his appointment.

The budget cuts in Missouri followed a report by the Civil Rights Division of the Department of Justice that determined that the Missouri public defender system was stretched beyond all reasonable limits and that poor African American children were being systematically deprived of their rights in Missouri due in large measure to a lack of public defenders.

A 2014 American Bar Association study estimated that Missouri's public defenders, because of their heavy caseloads, were budgeted less than a quarter of the money required to be "reasonably effective" in felony cases and that the system required an increase of 75 percent of the number of public defenders to be "reasonably effective." Barrett pointed out that the system's caseload had increased to roughly 82,000 cases, which meant that each of the state public defenders spends less than one-fifth the recommended time preparing a felony case and spends an average of two hours preparing a misdemeanor case when twelve hours are required.

A Missouri Bar report concluded that Missouri's public defender system had reached a point where what it provides is often nothing more than the "illusion of a

(Continued)

(Continued)

lawyer." The great fear expressed by public defenders in Missouri is that innocent individuals will be sent to prison because the state cannot provide adequate defense. The Constitution Project in 2009 issued a report, *Justice Denied: America's Continuing Neglect of Our Constitutional Right to Counsel*, that found that to clear their caseloads, public defenders across the country would have to dispose of a case every 6.6 hours each and every day (Constitution Project and National Legal Aid & Defender Association 2009).

The Louisiana public defender system also has experienced severe shortages. Public defenders assigned to the public defender office in Orleans Parish in 2014 handled 18,000 cases or 431 cases per lawyer, providing a public defender an average of seven minutes for every client. Felony attorneys managed caseloads of 350, more than two times the recommended 150-case limit, and the misdemeanor caseload was nearly five times the recommended limit of 400 cases.

New Orleans judge Arthur Hunter subsequently ordered the release of the seven indigent felony defendants who had spent months in jail without legal representation. Judge Hunter concluded that the defendants' right to legal representation should not be dependent on the failure of the legislature to adequately fund indigent defense. He announced, "We are now faced with a fundamental question, not only in New Orleans, but across Louisiana. What kind of criminal justice system do we want? One based on fairness or injustice, equality or prejudice, efficiency or chaos, right or wrong?" Derwyn Bunton, chief district defender for Orleans Parish (New Orleans), observed, "There's no such thing as Cadillac justice and Toyota justice. There's justice, and there is injustice. . . . And we are not going to be complicit in any injustice."

The American Civil Liberties Union has brought successful legal actions against a number of states including Michigan, New York, and Washington for failing to provide "meaningful and effective counsel" for indigents. Then attorney general Eric Holder on the fifth anniversary of *Gideon v. Wainwright* stated that our public defender system is in a state of crisis.

Professor John Pfaff has written that a federal government appropriation of $4 billion or 0.3 percent of the federal discretionary spending budget would triple the amount spent on indigent defense.

Should states continue to fund indigent defense? Would you favor federal financial assistance? Should public defenders resign rather than continue to work under conditions in which defendants are not provided with adequate defense?

■ PROSECUTORS

The American colonies followed the English model and relied on victims to prosecute crimes. This system of private prosecution presented several problems. Victims found it burdensome to make their way to urban centers to initiate criminal complaints. The system also was abused by individuals who used the threat of prosecution to blackmail individuals into paying them for not filing a criminal complaint. In the early 1700s, the colonial authorities began to assume control of criminal prosecutions. It soon became apparent that the workload could not be shouldered by a single prosecutor, and a system of decentralized deputy prosecutors was established. The decentralized system of prosecution reflected the traditional American distrust of centralized governmental authority. The shift to public prosecution signified a recognition that crime threatened social stability and that there was a public interest in creating a publicly funded, professional prosecutor's office.

The democratic revolution ushered in by the election of Andrew Jackson in 1820 led to the movement for elected prosecutors. In 1832, Mississippi amended its constitution to require that prosecutors be popularly elected. In the next twenty-five years, virtually every state provided for the election of prosecutors who were vested with "absolute discretion" whether to prosecute a criminal offender (Jacoby 1980).

The system of decentralized prosecutors continues today. Local prosecutors variously are referred to as the prosecuting attorney, state's attorney, commonwealth's attorney, or county attorney and are elected in forty-six of the fifty states and typically serve four-year terms. There are roughly 2,341 local prosecution offices across the United States. Eighty-five percent of prosecutors are full-time officials, and in the remaining 15 percent of jurisdictions, public prosecutors also have private law practices. Prosecutors typically have jurisdiction over offenses committed in their district.

Almost 60 percent of prosecution offices are in communities with fewer than 100,000. Eleven percent of offices are in jurisdictions of more than 250,000, which process nearly 60 percent of all felony cases. The 2 percent of offices that serve areas of over 1 million people handle over 20 percent of all felony cases (Pfaff 2017: 129).

In smaller jurisdictions, there may be a single prosecutor whereas in urban areas the elected prosecutor may supervise hundreds of attorneys. The prosecutor's offices in both Cook County (Illinois) and Los Angeles County (California) have more than 850 lawyers. These large offices are bureaucratic organizations. The elected prosecutor is assisted by a number of deputy prosecutors who, in turn, supervise various divisions within the office (e.g., juvenile, narcotics, criminal prosecution). Young attorneys who usually are several years out of law school are employed as assistant prosecuting attorneys and handle most of the day-to-day work of the office. The number of prosecutors has continued to increase. Pfaff found that between 1990 and 2007, the number of prosecutors increased by 30,000 (Pfaff 129: 2017).

Assistant prosecutors are paid far less than lawyers in private practice. A survey of 2,119 prosecutors by the American Prosecutors Research Institute found that 90 percent of the prosecutors were still paying off student loans and a number of them worked second jobs to pay off their debts. Despite the modest pay, young lawyers are attracted to the prosecutor's office because of the opportunity to develop their legal skills and eventually move on to a job in a private firm. Elected prosecutors often have political ambitions and at times use their office to position themselves to run for higher office (Siegel, Schmalleger, and Worrall 2011: 225).

Pfaff notes that roughly 95 percent of incumbent prosecutors are reelected and that nearly 70 percent are reelected when challenged in an election. Most prosecutors run in low-turnout elections in which voters have little information about the candidates. The result of this insulation from public accountability is a relatively small turnover in prosecutors. One survey found that 72 percent of prosecutors had served at least five years (a term typically is four years) and 40 percent of prosecutors had served at least twelve years in office. After establishing themselves in office, prosecutors often look to run for higher office. A prosecutor with plans to remain in office or to run for higher office has little reason to bring attention to him- or herself by taking a soft view on crime that may come back to haunt him or her in a future election. Pfaff attributes much of the growth in the prison population to prosecutors' decisions to charge defendants with felony offenses carrying prison terms rather than with misdemeanors (Lantigua-Williams 2016; Pfaff 2017).

Roy Flemming, Peter Nardulli, and James Eisenstein, in their study of nine counties, found that elected prosecutors adopt one of three styles. Courthouse insurgents want to "shake things up" and will openly criticize judges whom they consider "soft on crime." Insurgents instruct assistant prosecutors to insist on lengthy sentences in plea bargains with defense attorneys. Courthouse reformers share the goals of the insurgents although they assume a more conciliatory and low-key approach and avoid open conflict with judges. Courthouse conservatives accept the traditional way of doing things and do not criticize judges or modify existing practices. They hire lawyers based on the individual's political connections and support (Flemming, Nardulli, and Eisenstein 1992).

The important point to keep in mind in thinking about prosecutors is that chief prosecutors face election every four years and need to avoid angering the electorate. The challenge for a prosecutor is that with limited time and resources, some cases must be dismissed or plea bargained (A. Davis 2007). This means that a number of guilty individuals may not be brought to the bar of justice or receive a sentence that fits their crime. In the next section, we will explore how prosecutors decide which cases to pursue.

Prosecutors and the Dismissal of Cases

The prosecutor has been called the most powerful figure in the criminal justice system. Prosecutors exercise the **discretion** to charge defendants with a crime, drop charges, or bring a case to trial (M. Kadish and Kadish 1973). Pfaff describes prosecutors' offices as "invisible empires" that function in a "black box" with little public accountability (Lantigua-Williams 2016).

Defendants' legal challenges to the exercise of prosecutorial discretion typically are rejected by courts on the grounds that prosecutors are in the best position to determine what crimes to prosecute and what charges to bring against a defendant.

Prosecutors are the "traffic cops" of the criminal justice system. Prosecutors have broad discretion whether to prosecute a case and determine the charges that are brought against a defendant. The U.S. Supreme Court, in rejecting a claim that the death penalty in Georgia was administered in a racially discriminatory fashion, noted that discretion performs a "fundamental role" in the criminal justice system and that the "capacity of prosecutorial discretion to provide individualized justice" is "firmly entrenched in American law" (*McCleskey v. Kemp*, 481 U.S. 279 [1987]).

The Supreme Court has held that "so long as the prosecution has probable cause to believe that the accused has committed an offense defined by statutes, the decision whether or not to prosecute, and what [to] charge . . . generally rests entirely in his [the prosecutor's] discretion" (*Wayte v. United States*, 470 U.S. 598 [1985]). This discretion is limited only by the fact that the prosecutors must not base their decisions on the grounds of individuals' race, religion, ethnicity, or gender or exercise of their civil rights or liberties.

Prosecutors generally are concerned with maintaining a "high batting average." As an elected official, the chief prosecutor knows that public support for his or her reelection depends on high conviction rates. Young prosecutors are aware that too many acquittals can be a "career killer." As a result, prosecutors avoid spending their limited time and resources on weak or minor cases and typically plea bargain these cases or drop the charges (Frohmann 1991: 213, 215).

Pfaff illustrates the power of prosecutors by noting that New York State has twenty-three separate and distinct assault offenses. A second-degree assault on a judge is a Class D felony. A prosecutor by charging an assault on a judge as a Class C felony can double the potential sentence from seven to fifteen years in prison (Pfaff 2017: 31).

Studies of sexual assault cases provide insight into the exercise of prosecutorial discretion in determining which cases to prosecute. There are three primary explanations for whether a prosecutor will pursue a case. First is the strength of the case. This includes the number of eyewitnesses to the crime and whether there are fingerprints or DNA. Second is the seriousness of the offense. Prosecutors are more likely to pursue a case in which the perpetrator used a weapon, the victim was injured, or the victim was young. The third factor (discussed below) is the credibility of the victim (Albonetti 1987).

Lisa Frohmann studied the non-prosecution (*nolle prosequi*) of rape cases and found that prosecutors make decisions based on their "downstream" prediction of how juries will decide a case. This downstream prediction is based on the prosecutor's view of what jurors consider a typical rape. Prosecutors compare the "typical rape" to the victim's account. The question is whether the victim's account will ring true with the average juror or whether the average juror will conclude that the victim consented to the sexual encounter. Prosecutors also are concerned that jurors may conclude the victim irresponsibly placed him- or herself in a situation in which a sexual encounter was inevitable and therefore the defendant should be acquitted.

Frohmann finds that prosecutors' version of the "typical rape" is based on several "typifications of rape-relevant behavior." A difference between this ideal version of a rape and the victim's account will lead the prosecutor to dismiss the case as "unwinnable." Consider the following "typifications" (Frohmann 1991: 213).

Typifications of rape scenarios. The victim claims to have been kidnapped and was subjected to involuntary intercourse. The prosecutor's experience is that the typical kidnapping involves a variety of sexual acts and doubts the victim's account.

Other "typifications" include whether the victim's behavior following the reported rape is consistent with rape (e.g., timely post-incident reporting), whether the victim's relationship with the perpetrator following the rape is typical of rape victims (e.g., an absence of post-incident interaction), and whether the victim's facial expressions, body language, and mannerisms (demeanor) and lifestyle are typical of rape victims (e.g., the victim was a prostitute and likely entered into a consensual relationship) (Frohmann 1991: 217–221).

In a second study, Frohmann argues that prosecutors viewing rape allegations through the lens of the "typical rape scenario" results in the dismissal of cases in which the victims' behavior varies from "middle-class expectations." The important point made by Frohmann is that most typifications have very little relationship to the question whether a complainant was sexually assaulted (Frohmann 1997).

Frohmann finds that a prosecutor's decisions whether to pursue a case at times is based on what the prosecutor perceives is jurors' stereotypical image of a geographic area, the residents, and their lifestyle, attitudes, and values. Frohmann cites the example of prosecutors deciding against pursuing a prosecution because they anticipate that jurors will view a rape victim in a low-income neighborhood as a prostitute who was trading drugs for sex rather as a poor and admirable individual who was victimized. Frohmann expresses concern that prosecutors' reliance on "discordant locales" in their analysis results in a failure to protect victims of sexual assault.

Casia Spohn, Dawn Beichner, and Erika Davis Frenzel replicated Frohmann's study in Dade County (Florida). They found that roughly 53 percent of sexual assault cases are "screened out" by prosecutors. The authors explain that prosecutors want to "avoid uncertainty" and pursue charges when there is a good chance of conviction and screen out cases when a conviction is unlikely.

Prosecutors' downstream evaluation involves an assessment of the strength of the evidence and of the rape victim's credibility and behavior. Spohn and her co-authors also found that a significant number of cases are screened out because the victim fails to appear, wishes to avoid the humiliation and trauma of pursuing the case, or concludes a conviction is unlikely (Spohn, Beichner, and Davis Frenzel 2001).

Jamie L. Small adds to our understanding of prosecutorial decision-making in her study of the disposition of sex offenders in Michigan. Small finds that prosecutors have internalized a sensitivity toward the impact of sex offenses on victims. Perpetrators are viewed with disgust and as lower-class males who are easily identified by their unkempt physical appearance and poor grooming (the "hillbilly look"), non-traditional family situation, and unstable employment. Small observes that the danger is that privileged individuals, including celebrities, who do not fit the image of the stereotypical defendant may not be viewed as perpetrators by prosecutors or jurors. She recounts that the prosecutors she studied believe that they are able to differentiate sex offenders in photographs from other offenders based on their appearance alone (Small 2015: 130–133).

Prosecutors in different jurisdictions have different priorities and, for example, may decide to devote resources to serious drug cases and drop charges for the possession of marijuana. Another prosecutor may view marijuana as a "gateway" drug and prosecute marijuana cases (Baum 2013: 163).

The next decision for the prosecutor is whether to plea bargain a case or bring the case to trial.

7.2 YOU DECIDE

In the 2015 case of *People (of California) v. Efrain Velasco-Palacios*, a California court of appeal found that Kern County prosecutor Robert Murray committed "outrageous government misconduct" when he added two lines to the transcript of the defendant's confession to make it appear that the defendant who was charged with child molestation had admitted to the rape of the victim. When Velasco-Palacios refused a plea bargain to eight years in prison, Murray threatened to file a rape charge carrying life imprisonment. Murray only admitted changing the transcript after the defense attorney requested to hear a taped recording of the interrogation. Murray explained that the alteration was a "joke." California judge H. A. Staley held that Mr. Murray's falsifying of the transcript of a confession was "egregious, outrageous, and . . . shocked the conscience" and dismissed the charges against Velasco-Palacios.

Murray was placed on probation for thirty days from the practice of law; if he failed to satisfactorily establish his fitness to continue to practice law, he faced a suspension of his law license for a year.

Federal judge Alex Kozinski, appointed by President Ronald Reagan, has written that a "non-trivial number of prosecutors—and sometimes entire prosecutorial offices—engage in misconduct that . . . undermines the fairness of criminal trial" (Volokh 2015).

Prosecutorial misconduct entails a prosecutor breaking a law or violating professional ethics in the course of a criminal prosecution. In *Berger v. United States*, Justice Joseph Sutherland explained prosecutorial misconduct means "overstepp[ing] the bounds of that propriety and fairness which should characterize the conduct of such an officer in the prosecution of a criminal offense" (*Berger v. United States*, 295 U.S. 78 [1935]). This may involve concealing evidence, making improper arguments at trial, or offering false testimony.

The most frequent area of prosecutorial abuse involves *Brady* material. In *Brady v. Maryland*, the U.S. Supreme Court held that the Due Process Clause requires prosecutors to disclose exculpatory (exonerating) evidence within their possession that is relevant to the innocence, guilt, or sentence of the accused. The purpose of the *Brady* rule is to prevent miscarriages of justice by requiring the disclosure of evidence that may prevent the conviction of an innocent individual. A prosecutor's violation of *Brady* will result in the reversal of a conviction unless the prosecutor is able to establish that there is no reasonable probability that the material would have influenced the outcome of the case (*Brady v. Maryland*, 397 U.S. 742 [1970]).

The Supreme Court has held that prosecutors who are sued for a violation of a defendant's civil rights under Section 1983 (42 U.S.C. § 1983) are entitled to absolute immunity. This means that prosecutors enjoy complete immunity from being sued. This is intended to ensure that the legal process works efficiently and smoothly because prosecutors will not be concerned that they will be held civilly liable for their decisions. In *Burns v. Reed*, the U.S. Supreme Court held that a prosecutor was immune from liability for failing to disclose that the defendant had consistently denied shooting her son and that her murder confession had been obtained through hypnosis (*Burns v. Reed*, 500 U.S. 478 [1991]). In another case, prosecutors were held to have absolute immunity for failing to disclose that a jailhouse informant who was a key witness at trial had testified for the government on numerous occasions in return for a sentence reduction (*Van de Kamp et al. v. Goldstein*, 555 U.S. 335 [2009]).

Courts are reluctant to find prosecutorial misconduct. According to the California Innocence Project, judges are "casting a blind eye to prosecutors who cast their thumbs on the scales of justice." The report *Preventable Error: A Report on Prosecutorial Misconduct in California 1997–2009* examined 4,000 California and federal appellate court rulings addressing prosecutorial misconduct. The courts found prosecutorial misconduct in 707 of these cases. In only six instances were prosecutors disciplined by the State Bar of California. A Texas study found that between 2004 and 2012 state courts found prosecutorial misconduct in 91 cases and in no instance were prosecutors disciplined.

Criminal charges against prosecutors are rarely filed. An important exception is the 2006 Duke Lacrosse case in which Durham County (North Carolina) district attorney Mike Nifong was charged with criminal contempt, sentenced to one day in jail, and disbarred for concealing DNA evidence that exonerated the defendants. Former Williamson County (Texas) district judge Ken Anderson entered into a plea bargain, pled guilty to contempt of court, and was sentenced to ten days in jail, a fine, and community service and agreed to give up his law license for having concealed evidence in the 1987 trial of Michael Morton, who served almost twenty-five years in prison for the murder of his wife, a crime he did not commit.

Georgetown law professor Paul Butler notes that although defense attorneys at times are asked "How can you defend those people?" it should be much more difficult for a prosecutor to explain "How can you prosecute those people?" He asks whether a prosecutor can be a "good person." Butler notes that prosecutors carry heavy caseloads and do not have the time or inclination to consider whether a defendant may be innocent. They nonetheless seemingly care very little about victims beyond the victims' capacity to assist in convicting defendants. Prosecutors in pursuing low-level drug crimes and in asking for lengthy prison terms are primary participants in a system that produces vast racial disparities and mass incarceration and results in a number of false convictions. Other critics of prosecutors point out that prosecutors aggressively fight for restrictions on the constitutional rights of defendants, turn a blind eye to the police shading of the truth at trial, and are main cogs in the plea bargaining process (Butler 2013).

How would you answer Paul Butler's question whether a prosecutor can be a "good person"? Does he overlook the positive contribution of prosecutors in combating violent crime?

■ THE GRAND JURY

In the federal system and in twenty-two states (for serious crimes), prosecutors are required to obtain an indictment from a **grand jury** before bringing a case to trial. Grand juries are panels of citizens who determine whether there is sufficient evidence (probable cause) to proceed to trial. In the federal system, the grand jury is composed of twenty-three individuals; in the state system, as few as twelve (Missouri). The grand jury can be traced to 1166 in England and is intended to protect citizens against prosecutors' abuse of power. In theory, the grand jury is independent of the prosecutor and may call witnesses and require individuals to submit documents and other physical evidence.

A number of features of the grand jury enable the prosecutor to obtain indictments (Frankel and Naftalis 1977). The standard for indictment is probable cause. The Supreme Court has explained that probable cause is not a high bar: it requires only a "fair probability." In practice, the grand jury is dominated by the prosecutor, and as former New York judge Sol Wachtler famously remarked, a prosecutor could persuade a grand jury to "indict a ham sandwich."

According to a study of 162,000 federal cases by the Bureau of Justice Statistics, grand juries failed to return an indictment in only 11 instances.

Listed below are the some of the features of the grand jury that help prosecutors obtain criminal indictments.

Legal representation. Individuals may not be represented by a lawyer before the grand jury. The individual must leave the room to consult with his or her attorney.

Testimony. Individuals may refuse to testify on the grounds of their Fifth Amendment right against self-incrimination. The prosecutor may offer witnesses immunity from prosecution to pressure them to testify.

Prosecutor. The prosecutor, in practice, determines the witnesses who will testify before the grand jury and questions the witnesses. The suspect is not represented during the proceedings. The prosecutor is not required to disclose evidence favorable to the accused.

Proceedings. The proceedings are conducted in secret, and an individual who discloses grand jury proceedings may be held in contempt of court. An individual is not informed that he or she is being investigated by a grand jury, although prosecutors may inform an individual that he or she is a "target" of a grand jury investigation.

Evidence. Unlawfully seized evidence and illegally obtained confessions may be considered by the grand jury.

Double jeopardy. A prosecutor who fails to persuade a grand jury to return an indictment may convene a second grand jury in hopes of obtaining an indictment.

Testimony before a grand jury is to be kept secret, and an individual who leaks grand jury testimony may be held in contempt of court, fined, and even imprisoned. The reform of grand juries was proposed following the failure of grand juries to indict police officers in the deaths of African American Michael Brown in Ferguson, Missouri; the shooting of 12-year-old Tamir Rice; and the chokehold death of Eric Garner in Staten Island, New York. These high-profile cases are part of a pattern of a failure to indict police officers by grand juries. In Houston, Texas, grand juries have failed to indict police on 288 consecutive occasions. Reform proposals include making grand jury proceedings publicly available following a non-indictment, appointing a special prosecutor in police excessive and deadly force cases, and allowing judges to actively question witnesses during proceedings. These changes are intended to restore public confidence in grand juries and to counter the conflict of interest that confronts prosecutors required to investigate police officers they work with and depend upon on a daily basis. California will no longer use grand juries in police excessive and deadly force cases.

Once an indictment is brought against an individual, the next step is to bring that individual before a preliminary hearing and formally charge him or her with a crime. In practice, only about 10 percent of cases proceed to trial. The vast bulk of criminal cases are plea bargained.

■ PLEA BARGAINING

Most definitions of **plea bargaining** describe it as a process in which a defendant pleads guilty in return for a promise to receive some benefit from the state. The state typically offers three types of incentives to defendants; see Table 7.2.

Table 7.2 ■ Types of Plea Bargains	
Charge bargaining	The defendant pleads guilty to a less serious charge. This results in the defendant's serving a shorter prison sentence than he or she originally faced.
Count bargaining	The defendant pleads guilty to some of the charges that originally were filed against him or her, and in return, the remaining charges are dropped.
Sentence bargaining	The defendant pleads guilty in return for a lenient sentence or probation.

The prosecutor may promise to recommend that the defendant serve his or her sentence in a nearby or minimum-security institution.

There also is what we might term *extraordinary bargaining*. This typically involves the defendant's agreeing to plead guilty and undertaking extraordinary actions such as making a large charitable contribution or performing community service in return for the prosecutor's offering a suspended sentence or other consideration.

The Development of Plea Bargaining

Isolated instances of plea bargaining can be found in the early years of the republic. Judges were suspicious of the practice and went to great lengths to ensure that guilty pleas were free and voluntary. In 1804, in the Massachusetts case of *Commonwealth v. Battis*, before accepting a guilty plea, the court conducted an examination of the sheriff, the jailer, and the judge who accepted the preliminary plea "as to the sanity of the prisoners; and whether there had been tampering with him, either by promises, persuasion, hopes of pardon if he would plead guilty" (*Commonwealth v. Battis*, 1 Mass. 95 [1804]). A Michigan court in 1878 expressed concern over the "serious abuses" by

Figure 7.1 ■ The Pretrial Criminal Process

Arrest
- The suspect is seized based on probable cause.

Charging Decision
- The prosecutor charges the suspect with a crime.

Initial Appearance
- The suspect is arrested, booked, and confined; must be brought "without unnecessary delay" before a judicial official; and is informed of the charges, the right to a lawyer, and the right to a trial.

Bail
- Bail is set at initial appearance or at a bail hearing.

Information
- The prosecutor signs a document informing the defendant of facts supporting the criminal charge.

Grand Jury
- A grand jury may indict or refuse to indict the suspect.

Indictment
- Indictment is required for various crimes by twenty-two states and may not rely on information.

Arraignment
- The defendant enters a formal plea.

Discovery
- Exculpatory evidence and various other types of evidence must be turned over to the defense. Some states require the defense to turn over evidence to the prosecution and to inform the prosecution of defenses and witnesses.

Pretrial Motions
- Various motions are made to dismiss charges, change location of trial, and suppress evidence.

prosecutors who were tricking defendants into pleading guilty by making "false assurances . . . when a fair trial might show they were not guilty, or might show other facts important to be known" (*Edwards v. People*, 39 Mich. 760 [1878]).

Lawrence Friedman writes that the frequency of plea bargaining continued to increase, and by the late nineteenth century, a significant number of cases were disposed of by plea bargaining. This trend continued, and by 1926 in Chicago, almost 80 percent of defendants were "copping a plea." In the same period in the Northern District of California and in Connecticut, over 90 percent of all cases were disposed of by guilty pleas. Defendants were offered significant incentives to plead guilty. In the 1920s, a defendant in New York who pled guilty was twice as likely to receive a suspended sentence as a defendant who was convicted at trial. Friedman concludes that "bargain justice" was evolving into the standard approach to disposing of criminal cases. He notes plea bargaining was attractive to the judges and lawyers because it was "quick and it was cheap . . . [and it] did not depend on the wild unpredictable notions" of a jury (L. Friedman 1993: 252–253).

Concern continued to be expressed about the fairness of "negotiating pleas" rather than providing defendants with their "day in court," and a number of states formed commissions to review plea bargaining. A review of these commission reports indicates that even in a largely rural state like Georgia, over 70 percent of criminal cases were plea bargained. State reports recommended that an increased number of cases should be brought to trial. Critics attacked plea bargaining as an "incompetent, inefficient, and lazy method of administering justice" that undermined respect for the legal process (Alschuler 1979: 211).

There also has been a decline in jury trials in federal court. In 1997, 3,200 of 63,000 defendants were convicted in jury trials as compared to 2015 in which 1,650 defendants out of 81,000 defendants were convicted in jury trials. Former judge John Gleeson in a 2013 court opinion noted that 81 percent of federal convictions in 1980 were the product of guilty pleas, and in one recent year, the figure was 97 percent. Judge Jesse M. Furman noted that in the four-plus years he has spent as a judge in the federal district court in Manhattan, he has presided over only a single criminal trial. Judge J. Paul Oetken in half a decade on that bench noted that he has had four criminal trials including one retrial for following a deadlocked jury (Weiser 2016b).

In 1971, in *Santobello v. New York*, the U.S. Supreme Court proclaimed that plea bargaining was fully consistent with the U.S. Constitution. Chief Justice Warren Burger called plea bargaining "an essential component of the administration of justice" that is to be "encouraged." The chief justice noted that absent plea bargaining, the judiciary would be overwhelmed and that we would "need to multiply by many times the number of judges and court facilities." Chief Justice Burger stressed that plea bargaining had the advantage of leading to the "prompt and largely final disposition of most criminal cases" (*Santobello v. New York*, 404 U.S. 257 [1971]). A year earlier in *North Carolina v. Alford*, the U.S. Supreme Court held that a judge may accept a plea of guilty from a defendant who denies his guilt and who nevertheless enters a guilty plea to second-degree murder in order to avoid conviction of first-degree murder and the imposition of the death penalty. The Court held that a defendant "may voluntarily . . . consent to the imposition of a prison sentence even if he is unwilling . . . to admit his participation in the . . . crime." In this instance, the Court noted that there was overwhelming evidence implicating Alford in the killing, and the state court was justified in accepting his plea (*North Carolina v. Alford*, 400 U.S. 25 [1970]).

In 2012, the U.S. Supreme Court issued two decisions that commentators view as the first steps toward greater judicial regulation of plea bargaining (*Lafler v. Cooper*, 556 U.S. ___ [2012]; *Missouri v. Frye*, 566 U.S. ___ [2012]). The Court in these cases observed that plea bargaining is a critical phase of the criminal justice process and is as central to the criminal justice system as are trials. Negotiated pleas are not an "adjunct" to the criminal justice system. They "are the criminal justice system." According to the Court, 97 percent of federal trials and 94 percent of state trials result in guilty pleas.

In *Frye*, the Court held that defense attorneys have an obligation to communicate offers to defendants from prosecutors. Frye had been prejudiced by his attorney's failure to communicate the prosecutor's plea offers because there was a reasonable probability that he would have accepted the prosecutor's original offer had it been communicated to him and he would have avoided a four-year prison sentence. The Court indicated that jurisdictions might ensure that pleas are communicated to defendants by requiring that offers be made in writing or in open court before a judge. In *Lafler*, the Court noted that the defense attorney had been deficient in advising Cooper to reject a plea bargain because the prosecution would be unable to establish criminal intent at trial. The defendant was convicted at trial and received a harsher sentence than he would have received had he accepted the plea bargain.

In 2013, in *United States v. Davila*, the Supreme Court held that a federal magistrate had improperly encouraged Davila to enter into a plea bargain by stating that being "open and honest" may ensure a two- or three-level reduction in his sentence. The Court held that the federal rules of criminal procedure prohibit a judge from such active involvement with a defendant in plea discussions because a judge may easily influence a defendant's decision to plead guilty" (*United States v. Davila*, 569 U.S. ___ [2013]).

In the next sections, we look at the plea bargaining process.

Working Groups

Dean Nathan Roscoe Pound of Harvard Law School in 1922 conducted a study of the criminal trial courts in Cleveland, Ohio. Pound's study punctured the myth of fair and equal justice in the criminal courts. He later would observe in a series of lectures that our institutions had been developed in a rural and frontier society and were ill suited to the demands of an industrialized urban society. He observed that the "bad physical surroundings, . . . the want of decorum, the undignified . . . disposition of cases at high speed . . . create . . . a general suspicion . . . which . . . gravely prejudices the law" (Pound 1930: 190–191).

In 1954, Caleb Foote described the Philadelphia Magistrate Court in which forty defendants were discharged and fifteen were convicted of vagrancy and sentenced to three months in jail within fifteen minutes. Four defendants were sentenced to jail within seventeen seconds (Foote 1956).

A number of scholars have pointed out that courts remain the least studied institution in the criminal justice system. Pound's and Foote's analyses would prove influential in directing the attention of journalists and socio-legal scholars in the 1960s to the functioning of criminal courts. *Washington Post* reporter Leonard Downie Jr. observed a number of urban courts and reported that over 90 percent of defendants pled guilty in exchange for a reduced charge. Downie observed the chaos of big-city courts and concluded, in the words of one judge, that the criminal courts resembled "factories" in which "defendants are quickly processed like so many sausages." Downie noted in the rush to judgment that the penalty rarely fits the crime. There was a risk that the guilty were being punished too lightly and the innocent were being falsely convicted. Individuals who refused a plea and insisted on a trial could expect to be punished with a harsher sentence (Downie 1972: 18–51).

Sociologist David Sudnow provided insight into the negotiation of pleas in his discussion of "normal crimes." Sudnow studied public defenders and explained that defense lawyers, when examining a "charge sheet," have learned that various crimes tend to be committed under similar circumstances. Burglary typically is viewed as involving repeat, unarmed offenders who operate alone; limited property damage; and the theft of items of modest economic value. The defense lawyer and prosecuting attorney each have come to understand that a "normal burglary" will be reduced to petty theft to induce a guilty plea. The defense attorney assumes that the defendant is guilty and focuses on the appropriate charge and punishment rather than on mounting a vigorous defense. An effort is made to reduce the sentence sufficiently to induce a guilty plea while ensuring that the penalty roughly "fits the crime" (Sudnow 1965). Jerome Skolnick found that there was no difference between private defense attorneys and public defenders in their negotiation of pleas for their clients (Skolnick 1967). Peter Nardulli explains that courtroom regulars establish a consensus view on the terms of plea negotiations for various offenses and that there is no difference in the treatment of courtroom regulars and lawyers who, on occasion, represent defendants in criminal court (Nardulli 1986: 415).

James Eisenstein and Herbert Jacob, in their study of Baltimore, Chicago, and Detroit, found that prosecutors, judges, and defense attorneys comprise a **working group** and that this informal and interdependent organization of lawyers and judges works to evaluate and dispose of cases. The group is united by a common interest in clearing the case docket, and each of the participants recognizes that this requires cooperation in disposing of cases. Eisenstein and Jacob find that although a similar percentage of cases result in convictions in all three cities, there is variation between the cities in the number of cases dismissed before trial, the length of sentences, and the number of cases brought to trial before a judge (Eisenstein and Jacob 1977: 291–292, 300). Eisenstein, Flemming, and Nardulli explain that the variation between courts is due to the fact that each court is subject to different "cultural environments." Prosecutors in one jurisdiction may not place a priority on prosecuting possession of small amounts of marijuana, whereas prosecutors in other jurisdictions may view this offense as a more serious crime (Eisenstein et al. 1988: 22–73).

Although we know very little about the factors that determine whether a prosecutor will offer a plea agreement, most of the research finds a greater uniformity among prosecutors in various cities than Eisenstein and Jacob suggest. Prosecutors are least likely to offer a concession to defendants charged with a serious offense who possess a lengthy criminal record where there is strong evidence of guilt. On the other hand, prosecutors are more likely to offer a bargain to defendants who have committed minor offenses and in cases in which the evidence of guilt is weak (Mather 1979).

Not enough data are available to draw any firm conclusions on the impact of race on plea bargaining (Spohn, Gruhl, and Welch 1987: 189). Several studies have found that African Americans and Hispanics are "more likely than white suspects to be charged with a crime and fully prosecuted." Federal prosecutors are authorized to ask courts to depart from the specified sentence for individuals who assist in prosecutions. The U.S. Sentencing Commission found that federal prosecutors were "more likely" to ask courts to reduce the sentence of white defendants and that these offenders received a "larger sentence reduction" than either African American or Hispanic defendants (Walker, Spohn, and Delone 2007: 192–193).

Nicole Gonzalez Van Cleve, in her long-term observational study of Cook County (Illinois) courts, finds that race permeates the plea bargaining process. Nearly twenty-three thousand individuals pass though the courthouse at 24th and California Streets in Chicago each year. Nearly 70 percent of the defendants are African American, 17 percent are white, and 11 percent are Hispanic although 84 percent of state's attorneys, 69 percent of public defenders, and 74 percent of judges are white. Three-quarters of the judges are former prosecutors, and one-quarter are former public defenders, most of whom have spent their careers as part of the courthouse culture (Van Cleve 2016).

Lawyers and judges divide defendants of color into "mopes" and "monsters." Mopes are viewed as incompetent, indecent, lazy, uneducated, and unable to delay gratification. Hispanics are viewed as mopes because they are identified as "illegally" residing in the United States and a drain on the resources of taxpayers. In the plea process, the mopes are not valued but viewed as undeserving of due process protections, and there is little concern about their future (i.e., they're "de-futured"). In contrast, a white defendant who is viewed as middle class is presumed to have committed a misstep that can be corrected through drug rehabilitation or being "scared straight."

Monsters are predominantly people of color who are believed to pose a serious social threat. Prosecutors believe that the most important aspect of their job is the prosecution and punishment of monsters. If not for the mopes, the courts could devote their time and attention to the disposition of these monsters.

Public defenders, according to Van Cleve, to be successful must accept these stereotypes, share demeaning inside jokes, participate in mocking of defendants by the prosecutors and judges, and participate in disposing of cases as quickly as possible. Defense attorneys who fight too hard for their clients and resist the "racialist" culture are dismissed as "clueless," "difficult," "incompetent," and as "mope lovers" or even mopes themselves. They suffer petty indignities like being left in a locked cell with a client or having a client denied participation in a drug program.

The obvious reason for the prevalence of plea bargaining is the "mutuality of advantage" for lawyers and judges.

The Mutuality of Advantage in Plea Bargaining

Why did plea bargaining replace the trial as the primary mechanism for determining guilt in criminal courts?

The most obvious reason is the mutuality of advantage for prosecutors, defense attorneys, and judges. Prosecutors are elected officials, and plea bargaining allows them to maintain a "high batting average" of convictions and enables prosecutors to avoid the uncertainty of a formal trial. Young assistant prosecutors often are evaluated based on their "clearance rate" of cases, and their career advancement may depend on their ability to "clear the docket." Another important consideration is that prosecutors will not have to concern themselves with legal challenges to police procedures because defendants pleading guilty waive their capacity to challenge searches and seizures, interrogations and lineups, and other constitutionally mandated procedures. Plea bargaining has the added advantage of freeing prosecutors to focus their resources on the trial of serious crimes.

Defense attorneys are able to rapidly dispose of cases and secure considerations from the prosecutor for their clients and do not have to devote time and energy to preparing for trial. By pleading guilty, the defendant avoids the uncertainty of the sentencing process. Experienced defendants also are aware that individuals convicted at trial generally receive longer sentences than individuals who strike a bargain with the prosecutor. Defendants who strike a bargain also do not have to spend time in a jail waiting for their case to come to trial.

Defendants who negotiate a plea may be able to bargain for concessions such as being incarcerated in an institution near their family. A trial can be enormously expensive for individuals who are represented by a private attorney; a plea bargain can save an individual significant amounts of money. In some cases, victims may welcome a plea bargain that permits them to avoid testifying in court and reliving the traumatic events of the crime.

Plea bargaining allows judges to clear their case docket and to avoid the various decisions that surround a trial that typically are the subject of appeal. A defendant's willingness to plead guilty also is looked at as the first step toward a defendant's rehabilitation.

Plea bargaining serves the "mutuality of interest" of lawyers and judges in pushing cases through the system and avoiding trials and is not only a response to a heavy caseload. Caseload, however, cannot be entirely dismissed as a factor, because the more cases there are on the court calendar, the greater the pressure there is to process cases through the system and to avoid the time and energy required to bring a case to trial (Heumann 1978). Another explanation for plea bargaining is that plea bargaining was developed by elected district attorneys who wanted to avoid the prosecution and severe punishment of members of newly enfranchised immigrant groups (McConville and Mirsky 2005).

One of the more interesting arguments traces the origins and continuation of plea bargaining to the development of the legal profession. Historically, criminal trials for felonies were conducted before a judge without lawyers. It was believed that the truth would best be discovered by the judge's directly confronting the defendant. The trial tended to be informal. As lawyers became involved in criminal trials, the proceedings became highly technical and complex and weighed down by rules. A felony trial that might last an hour during the eighteenth century averaged 7.2 days by the end of the 1960s. The result is that a trial is simply too burdensome for lawyers and judges and too expensive to be provided to the majority of defendants, and the plea bargain naturally developed as a mechanism to avoid bringing cases to trial (Bach 2009: 93).

Critics point to the Supreme Court case of *Bordenkircher v. Hayes* as an illustration of the use of plea bargaining to punish defendants who insist on taking their chances at trial (*Bordenkircher v. Hayes*, 434 U.S. 357 [1978]). In *Bordenkircher*, Hayes was indicted by a grand jury for forging a check for $88.30, a crime punishable by two to ten years in prison. The prosecutor offered a sentence of five years and threatened Hayes with indictment under the Kentucky habitual offender law if he refused to accept the plea bargain. Hayes had two prior felonies for robbery and "detaining a female," and his conviction as a habitual offender resulted in his being sentenced to life in prison. The Court upheld Hayes's sentence of life imprisonment and explained that Hayes had been given a choice whether to plead guilty or to go to trial.

Defendants know that they risk a longer sentence by insisting on a trial. Law professor John Langbein has made the controversial comparison between plea bargaining and the medieval practice of torturing suspects to obtain an admission of guilt. He argues that plea bargaining, like torture, is intended to coerce defendants to plead guilty. There is no other explanation for prosecutors "piling on charges" against a defendant that they are willing to eliminate in return for a guilty plea. The obvious risk is that an innocent individual will enter a guilty plea to avoid a harsh punishment (Langbein 1978).

Langbein also argues that plea bargaining weakens the "moral force" and respect for the criminal justice process. Offenders plead guilty to offenses that do not fit the facts of their crime and are convicted without being provided their "day in court." As a result, the defendant's guilt is not established in open court beyond a reasonable doubt and the defendant is not afforded the opportunity to cross-examine witnesses or to present his or her own evidence in court. A bargain may result in a punishment that is too lenient or too harsh, although in either case the penalty does not fit the crime. A bargain also avoids public exposure of constitutional violations by the police, and the deterrent effect of penalizing the police for disregarding the law is undermined. An additional criticism is that plea bargaining vests too much power in prosecutors who have the authority to offer bargains to defendants (Alschuler 1968, 1975; Langbein 1978).

The claim is made that a guilty plea and an individual's accepting responsibility for his or her actions is the first step toward an offender's rehabilitation. Robert A. Kagan, however, notes that plea bargaining "transforms the act of confession from a ritual of moral and social healing into a cynical game, reinforcing the criminal's alienated view of society" (Kagan 2001: 85). He also argues that plea bargaining encourages manifestly guilty defendants to insist on a trial and on their innocence in order to extract a favorable bargain (85).

The interests of the lawyers, judges, and defendants may make plea bargaining inevitable. Alaska successfully banned plea bargaining. Studies found that defendants continued to plead guilty and that the number of trials did not significantly increase. Defendants apparently believed that they would be more harshly treated by going to trial and thus informally negotiated with prosecutors for lighter sentences. The ban on plea bargaining later was withdrawn to bring "policy in line with the prevailing practice." In 1982, California voters approved a ballot measure that prohibited plea bargaining. The ballot proposition provided for substantial exceptions, and the percentage of felony defendants pleading guilty rose from 78 percent in 1982 to 90 percent in 1991. The effort to abolish plea bargaining in Alaska was abandoned in 1994 after having little impact on the incidence of guilty pleas (Baum 2013: 174; M. Rubinstein and White 1979).

Defendants will continue to plead guilty so long as they are offered a lower sentence and other incentives in return for a guilty plea. A study by Human Rights Watch in New York found that 97 percent of drug offenders pled guilty. Defendants who tried their luck at trial and were convicted were sentenced to an average of sixteen years in prison as compared to a sentence of five years and four months for defendants who plea bargained.

What of the risk that innocent individuals will plead guilty? Ten percent of all individuals imprisoned and later exonerated based on DNA in state courts over the past two decades pled guilty. In 2015, 68 of the 157 exonerations involved defendants who pled guilty, more than in any other year on record. According to the University of Michigan Law School National Registry of Exonerations, more than 300 of the 1,900 individuals in the database who have been exonerated pled guilty (Richer and Anderson 2016).

Are there reforms that might curb the worst abuses of plea bargaining?

7.3 YOU DECIDE

The English Bill of Rights of 1689 prohibited "excessive bail" but did not define those offenders eligible and ineligible for bail. Defendants in the newly established United States awaiting trial could gain release from jail by depositing money or title to property with the court. A failure to appear resulted in forfeiture of the deposit. The thinking was that an individual should not be detained absent a finding of guilt (Harvard Law School Program on Criminal Justice Policy 2016).

The Eighth Amendment to the U.S. Constitution states that "excessive bail" shall not be "required." This constitutional provision is not applicable to the fifty states although all state constitutions have similar provisions and provide for bail in the case of all non-capital offenses. The U.S. Supreme Court has held that the purpose of bail is to ensure that an individual appears for trial and should not be set at an amount to ensure that the accused remains imprisoned.

The United States historically has relied on the monetary bail system. An individual who cannot fund the bail amount typically contacts a bail bondsperson who posts the amount for the bail with the court. The defendant is required to deposit 10 percent of the bond with the bondsperson to compensate the bondsperson for posting bail.

The amount of bail is established by the judge in a pretrial hearing and is based on the amount of money that is required to ensure that the defendant appears for trial. A greater amount is considered "excessive bail." A defendant will be denied bail if it is determined that the defendant poses a risk of flight or poses a risk to others. In some jurisdictions, judges follow a bail schedule in which the amount of bail is fixed based on the offense rather than on a defendant's risk of flight.

Defendants who do not have the financial resources to make bail may find themselves incarcerated for lengthy periods prior to trial, experience difficulty in preparing for trial, lose their job, and risk a loss of custody of their children. In some instances, individuals who are incarcerated stand trial in prison clothes, which may prejudice the jury against them. Studies find that individuals who stand trial while incarcerated are more likely to be convicted and are more likely to receive longer prison sentences. The difficulties of confinement in a local jail may motivate a defendant to plead guilty to begin serving his or her sentence in a less crowded state in prison.

At any given time, there are more than 450,000 individuals in local jails because they lack the money for bail, which costs the taxpayers an estimated $14 billion a year. Studies find that individuals who cannot meet bail are in the lowest third economically. The United States, according to the National Institute of Corrections of the U.S. Department of Justice, has more pretrial detainees than any other country in the world.

Individuals arrested for minor offenses may spend more time awaiting trial than the sentence accompanying the crime with which they are charged. Defendants who are acquitted will have served time in prison but be found innocent. Studies show that racial minorities are assigned higher amounts of bail and are twice as likely as whites to be incarcerated pending trial. The result is that individuals are incarcerated because of a lack of financial resources. Critics assert that this is the modern-day equivalent of "debtors' prison."

Six states and various localities have abolished money bail in favor of a system in which individuals are released on their own recognizance. Statistics indicate that this has had no impact on the percentage of individuals appearing for trial.

The District of Columbia has demonstrated that cash bail can be replaced by the use of a pretrial risk assessment program that evaluates defendants' fitness to be released on their own recognizance under minimal

(Continued)

(Continued)

supervision. Fifteen percent of defendants in the District of Columbia are held pending trial, and the appearance rate for trial is 89 percent, which is equivalent to the appearance rate for defendants in a cash bail system.

In a number of cities, individuals are forming bail funds to provide bail for indigent defendants. Do you agree with this effort? Would you abolish the cash bail system?

7.4 YOU DECIDE

In 1961, in *Mapp v. Ohio*, the U.S. Supreme Court held that evidence seized by the police in violation of the Fourth Amendment's prohibition on unreasonable searches and seizures should be excluded from evidence at a criminal trial. The Court majority reasoned the exclusionary rule is an "essential ingredient" in protecting individuals' Fourth Amendment right to privacy, deterring the police from disregarding the requirements of the Constitution, and excluding tainted evidence from the courtroom (*Mapp v. Ohio*, 367 U.S. 643 [1961]). Critics of the exclusionary rule assert it harms society, frustrates prosecutors, and has little impact on the police. A better remedy would be disciplining the police officer and allowing the defendant to sue for damages. The Supreme

Court has limited the scope of the exclusionary rule, holding in several cases, for example, that there is a "good faith" exception to the exclusionary rule (*Herring v. United States,* 555 U.S. 135 [2009]). Social science studies are unable to draw a firm conclusion regarding the deterrent impact of the rule on the police. We know lawyers file motions to suppress physical evidence in a relatively small number of cases, and relatively few individuals escape punishment as a result of these motions to suppress evidence.

Do you favor the exclusionary rule?

(For You Decide 7.5 on the admissibility of rap music at trial, visit the study site at study.sagepub.com/lippmanls2e.)

INTERNATIONAL PERSPECTIVE: INQUISITORIAL LEGAL SYSTEMS

Critics of the American adversarial approach to justice contrast the "fighting theory" of the U.S. system with the **inquisitorial system** followed in continental Europe. European countries have moved much closer to the adversarial model, and the U.S. system has adopted a number of features of the inquisitorial system. Nonetheless, it is worthwhile to examine the general features of the continental European system to help us evaluate the strengths and weaknesses of the adversarial model of criminal justice. France, Germany, Italy, and the Netherlands all differ from one another in important respects, and we will talk about the general features of continental trials, some of which may not be applicable to each of these countries (Merryman and Pérez-Perdomo 2007).

The inquisitorial system comprises three stages: the investigative phase, the examining phase, and the trial. In the investigative phase, the police investigate the crime. This is different from the United States in that the prosecutor is kept distant from the police investigation of the crime. In the investigation stage, the police compile the evidence that supports guilt as well as the evidence that supports a suspect's (or suspects') innocence.

In the examining phase, which has been abolished in several countries, the examining judge reviews the dossier prepared by the police, interrogates various witnesses, and makes a determination whether the case should proceed to trial. The defense attorney and the defendant are present during the examining phase and can bring facts to the attention of the judge and suggest witnesses that should be heard. A finding of "reasonable cause" results in the case being forwarded to the court for prosecution. The final report is available to the defense attorney, the prosecutor, and the court itself (Kagan 2003: 88).

It is at the trial phase that we see the clear differences between the inquisitorial and adversarial systems. In Germany, "serious cases" historically were required to be brought to trial (mandatory prosecution). The German Code of Criminal Procedure provides that prosecutors must "take action against all prosecutable offenses" with some exceptions for minor offenses (Langbein and Weinreb 1978: 1563–1567).

The Europeans prefer multi-judge tribunals. The judges control the trial and ask questions of the witnesses, decide the witnesses to call and in what order, and determine the expert witnesses who will testify at trial. Following the judges' examination, the prosecutor and the defense may ask questions of the witnesses. They typically limit their questions to clarifying points made by witnesses in response to the judges' interrogation. Judges generally want to hear all the evidence and are much more flexible than American judges in terms of allowing witnesses to testify to matters like hearsay (e.g., what another person said). The lawyers may submit written summaries of their cases at the end of trial and may make closing arguments (Pizzi 1999: 16).

In Germany, the judicial panel includes both professional judges and citizens (called lay judges, who serve four-year terms), who jointly decide the verdict in the case. France and Spain provide for juries in the case of criminal prosecutions, and the jury panel is compiled without the examination of potential jurors that we have in the United States. There is some provision for jurors to ask questions during the trial, although the jurors are much less powerful than their American counterparts (Terrill 2016: 247–248, 267–268, 270).

As you can see, the inquisitorial system is controlled by judges rather than lawyers and has very few of the theatrics of the adversarial system because the judge controls the courtroom. The goal at every stage is to compile the factual evidence and ultimately to attempt to arrive at the truth of the matter. Technical procedures are subordinated to the interest in unearthing the facts of the case. The continental system is less concerned than the American system with procedures and with protecting the rights of defendants. William T. Pizzi describes the continental inquisitorial system as analogous to the fluid game of soccer while the American system is analogous to the heavily regulated game of football. In the U.S. adversarial model, a defendant who takes the stand is subject to cross-examination and may decide to avoid telling his or her side of the story. In the inquisitorial system, the accused may choose to make an unsworn statement during the examination phase and at trial and thereby avoid cross-examination (Pizzi 1999: 15–45).

European prosecutors are civil servants, and their careers do not depend on whether they win every case. The official code of legal ethics makes clear that defense attorneys are to serve as independent organs of the administration of justice and are to be independent from both the defendant and the interests of the government. In the United States, prosecutors and defense attorneys consult with witnesses. In Germany, the ethical rule strongly discourages lawyers from having contact with witnesses to preserve the witnesses' independence and the truthfulness. This rule prevents lawyers from coaching and influencing the testimony of witnesses (Luban 1988: 96–97).

Several additional points are worth making. In the United States, legal education often is approached from the point of view of the two competing lawyers formulating their respective arguments. In Germany, legal education is approached from the perspective of a judge attempting to reach a just result. In addition, legal fees in Germany are strictly regulated, and lawyers have no incentive to drag out trials to generate increased fees (Luban 1988: 97). In some countries, the victim may join the criminal prosecution with a civil suit and the judges may award damages at the end of the trial. In other countries, the victim is allowed to intervene on the side of the prosecution and bring a separate civil action following the trial (Glendon, Gordon, and Osakwe 1982: 95–96).

We have somewhat exaggerated the differences between the inquisitorial and adversarial approaches to a criminal trial. In recent decades, European legal systems have experienced a growth in caseloads as a result of prosecutions of white-collar crime, narcotics offenses, and human trafficking and have introduced various mechanisms similar to the American practice of plea bargaining to avoid full-blown trials. European prosecutors generally do not possess the ability to pressure defendants to enter a guilty plea, and any agreements typically must be approved by a judge. Defendants who pursue a case to trial do not receive a more severe penalty. In Italy, the defense and prosecution may agree for the defendant to receive a punishment of two years or less, and this agreement must be approved by a judge. A defendant also may request the judge to engage in a streamlined trial procedure in return for a reduction in his or her sentence. Section 152 (II) of the German Penal Code states that prosecutors are required to "take action against all prosecutable offenses, to the extent that there is sufficient factual." There are provisions for prosecutors in the case of minor offenses to offer a charge to the accused that may result in a suspended prison sentence of up to one year and a forfeiture of profits from a crime. Agreements between the prosecution and the defense generally must be approved by a judge, defendants have the ability to examine a prosecutor's files to determine the strength of the evidence against them, victims have the right to challenge a bargain, and prosecutors may not bring multiple offenses to pressure a defendant to plead guilty (Ma 2002).

John Henry Merryman and Rogelio Pérez-Perdomo quote one anonymous law professor's remark that if he were innocent, he would prefer to be prosecuted in a European court, and if guilty, he would prefer to be prosecuted in a common law (U.S.) court (Merryman and Pérez-Perdomo 2007: 133).

CHAPTER SUMMARY

The U.S. system of criminal justice strikes a balance between the due process and crime control models. On the one hand, the United States has an adversarial system of justice in which the defense attorney zealously represents his or her client at trial against the prosecutorial resources of the state. On the other hand, jury trials have proven so burdensome and time-consuming that only 10 percent of cases are brought to trial.

Most cases are plea bargained. Trial court working groups cooperate to dispose of cases through plea agreements. This informal system is based on an established set of expectations regarding the sentence that is appropriate for a "normal" crime. Plea bargaining works to the advantage of prosecutors in clearing cases and ensuring convictions. Defense attorneys are able to dispose of their clients' cases, secure considerations from the prosecutor in return for a guilty plea, and collect a fee without having to devote a significant amount of time and energy to preparing for trial. Defendants, by pleading guilty, avoid the uncertainty of leaving it to the judge to impose a criminal sentence if they are convicted. This may prove particularly important because defendants who are convicted in a trial typically receive longer sentences than individuals who strike a bargain with the prosecutor.

The prevailing perspective is that defense attorneys are "double agents" who work against the interests of their clients. This harsh view of defense attorneys overlooks that they themselves are at a great disadvantage in negotiating with prosecutors. Public defenders are viewed with particular suspicion because they are paid by the state. There in fact is little difference between the competence of private defense attorneys and public defenders.

Prosecutors possess discretion to dismiss a case, bargain a case, or bring the case to trial. Cases that proceed to trial are those in which a plea bargain cannot be reached or which are in the prosecutor's political interest to bring to trial.

CHAPTER REVIEW QUESTIONS

1. Distinguish between the crime control and due process models.

2. Discuss the differing views of defense attorneys.

3. Why are public defenders generally viewed as less skilled than private defense attorneys? Is there justification for the negative view of public defenders?

4. How do prosecutors differ in their prosecutorial styles?

5. Why do prosecutors drop charges of rape in some cases and bring charges of rape against defendants in other cases?

6. What accounts for the high number of cases that are plea bargained rather than brought to trial?

7. How does the American adversarial approach to criminal trials differ from the inquisitorial system?

TERMINOLOGY

adversarial model   244

consensus model   244

crime control model   244

discretion   256

due process model   244

grand jury   260

inquisitorial system   270

plea bargaining   261

public defenders   245

working group   265

ANSWERS TO TEST YOUR KNOWLEDGE

1. True

2. False

3. False

4. False

5. False

6. True

7. False

WANT A BETTER GRADE?

Get the tools you need to sharpen your study skills. Access practice quizzes, eFlashcards, author podcasts, SAGE journal articles, hyperlinks for Law and Society on the Web, and more at **study.sagepub.com/lippmanls2e**.

8

JURIES

TEST YOUR KNOWLEDGE: TRUE OR FALSE?

1. There is a decline in the number of federal and state jury trials.

2. A jury in every state is required to have twelve jurors.

3. Individuals who believe a defendant is guilty are eligible to serve on a jury so long as they can be fair and objective toward the defendant.

4. Lawyers can strike or dismiss a limited number of individuals from the jury based on no reason whatsoever.

5. A jury may disregard the law in determining whether a defendant is innocent or guilty.

6. Judges and juries in most instances reach the same result in determining a defendant's guilt or innocence.

7. A minority of jurors are able to persuade a majority of jurors to change their point of view in a large number of instances in determining a defendant's guilt or innocence.

Check your answers on page 312.

■ INTRODUCTION

Trials at times attract our attention, in part, because large moral questions are presented and debated. Is the murder of an abusive spouse justified? May a doctor comply with a dying patient's request to inject the patient with a toxic drug and ease the pain of death? Trials bring to the surface human impulses that we keep under control. Trials force us to ask ourselves whether we would ever be tempted to commit murder for money or fame or revenge. We become fascinated with stories of violence and corruption and wonder how people with money and fame could have risked everything by engaging in criminal conduct. As observers, we participate in the process from a distance and ask ourselves whether the defendant is guilty and whether we have the capacity to commit similar acts of criminality (Geis and Bienen 1998).

In this chapter, we examine the role of the trial and ask how ordinary citizens serving on a jury respond when asked to decide a defendant's guilt or innocence and whether the person should receive the death penalty. The last part of the chapter discusses sentencing and the alarming problem of "false convictions."

■ THE TRIAL

Criminal trials serve important functions in the criminal justice system (R. Burns 2011; Ferguson 2007).

Values. Trials highlight important values that underlie our system of justice. These values include the right to a public trial, in which individuals confront their accusers in open court and are given the opportunity to explain their version of the facts and to have their guilt or innocence determined by a jury of their peers. Individuals are presumed innocent, and the prosecution must establish an individual's guilt or innocence beyond a reasonable doubt.

Legitimacy. The fact that guilt is determined in accordance with regular and fair procedures encourages respect for the rule of law and the legal system.

Security. The trial assures us that the government will intervene to protect citizens by prosecuting wrongdoers. The trial also reminds us that we will not be picked up off the street and incarcerated without trial.

Symbolism. Trials tell us that crime does not pay and will result in fair and certain punishment.

Democracy. A trial provides popular knowledge about a case, and a jury trial allows popular participation in the administration of justice.

Law. Trials often result in appeals to appellate courts. These appellate decisions at times allow judges the opportunity to establish important legal principles that ensure that the Constitution continues to develop to meet contemporary challenges. An example is the right to counsel at trial and the right of a defendant to be informed of his or her rights before being subjected to police interrogation.

We have already seen that a number of cases are "screened out" and that the vast majority of cases are then plea bargained out of the system. A number of observers have commented on the "twilight" of the trial (L. Friedman 1993: 388). Albert Alschuler offers the provocative observation that "the American jury trial . . . has become one of the most cumbersome and expensive fact-finding mechanisms that humankind has devised" (Alschuler 1986: 1825).

Why have we witnessed the decline of the trial? The desire for certain outcomes, along with heavy caseloads and the culture of working groups, has motivated prosecutors and defense attorneys to bargain cases rather than to risk the "crap shoot" of a trial (Pizzi 1999: 74, 184). Trials involve considerable time and expense. Consider that a study of county courts in 1980 indicated that one-third of trials in Oakland, California, involved homicides and that the average case lasted nearly two weeks. In 1991, the average capital punishment prosecution cost North Carolina $80,000, and some capital punishment trials cost the state as much as $150,000 (Kagan 2001: 82).

The average defendant simply cannot afford the costs of defending him- or herself in a criminal case, and in the words of Malcolm Feeley, a trial simply is not a "viable alternative" to a plea bargain. A high-profile criminal prosecution such as the O. J. Simpson murder case undoubtedly costs millions of dollars while a criminal defense for a felony can cost $10,000 to $15,000 (Feeley 1979: 187; Kagan 2001: 82).

Some commentators have argued that the desire to protect the rights of defendants has led to such complicated and involved procedures that the criminal justice system has been forced to rely on plea bargaining and to limit trials to roughly 10 percent of the cases. The result is that the vast number of defendants do not have "their day in court" (Weigend 1980: 411).

Criminal trials generally are limited to those cases in which a defendant refuses to accept a plea bargain or to important "high-profile cases" in which there is a public demand for the punishment of an individual to the "full extent of the law" (Baum 2013: 171).

The American trial, of course, is premised on the belief that by pitting the zealous advocacy of a defense attorney against the dedicated prosecutor, the truth will emerge. There is a lengthy list of critics who contend that there is a vast gap between the "fight theory" or "sporting theory" of justice and the "truth theory." The argument is that lawyers distort the facts in order to win and that this process does not serve the cause of justice (Frank 1949: 80–81). Andrew E. Taslitz writes that the competition between lawyers does not improve the discovery of truth. Instead, the "fight theory" encourages lawyers to do whatever is required within the limits of ethics and the law to win at all costs. The only measure of lawyers' skill at trial is whether they win (Taslitz 1999: 103). Consider some of the tips offered by the late Irving Younger on cross-examination of witnesses. Younger advises that you should "never permit the witness to explain his or her answer," and if the opposing lawyer is "holding the jury spellbound," you should "leap" to your feet and make loud and irrelevant objections to divert the jurors' attention (Luban 1988: 70).

There is no better illustration of what critics assert is the problem with criminal trials than the work of Greg Matoesian on the cross-examination of rape victims. Matoesian relies on the analysis of courtroom language to demonstrate how lawyers skillfully cross-examine rape victims to discredit their testimony. He writes that the result is to "revictimize" women. An example is the "sexual double bind." This entails asking questions in which a rape victim "cannot win." Her answer is used by the defense attorney to portray her either as overly emotional and perhaps vengeful or as calm, cool, and calculating and as a woman who is unlikely to have been dominated by a male (Matoesian 1993, 1995, 2001). As Taslitz writes in supporting Matoesian's "double-bind" analysis, rape trials "reinforce oppressive social norms. . . . [A] woman should not go out at night . . . should dress modestly . . . and should not openly express sexual interest in a man. . . . Violating these norms risks rape" (Taslitz 1999: 113).

In his analysis of the William Kennedy Smith rape trial, Matoesian demonstrates how a talented defense lawyer like Roy Black employs his control over the questioning to suggest that the victim's inability to recall when she removed her pantyhose after leaving the bar with Smith calls her character into question. The victim alleged that she drove Smith home, took a tour of the historic Kennedy compound, and took a walk on the beach with Smith, and that he later raped her on the front lawn. Black asks whether the victim was wearing her pantyhose in the car when she drove

Smith home. He then asked whether she had them on when she went into the house, walked through the kitchen, walked through the house, walked across the lawn, and walked on the beach. The victim in each instance responded, "I'm not sure." Matoesian notes that the victim's removal of her pantyhose is a normal act before walking on the beach and irrelevant to whether she consented to the sexual interaction with the defendant. Why did Black pursue this line of questioning? John M. Conley and William M. O'Barr, in discussing the questioning with their male students, report that from the male perspective, people wear outer clothing and underwear. "Decent" women do not "lose track of their underwear" when they are with a man. The question that arises is whether a man should be "held responsible for his actions toward such a woman" (Conley and O'Barr 2005: 32–34). Smith was acquitted by a jury within five minutes of their consideration of the case. Was the jury merely swayed by the fact that the defendant was a member of the revered Kennedy family? In the next sections, we will explore whether the type of questioning relied on by Roy Black is likely to prove successful with juries.

Headline Trials

Lawrence M. Friedman notes that an exception to the "vanishing trials" is the "headline trial" or "big trial." These are criminal trials that "make a splash" and receive significant media and public attention and discussion. Headline trials entertain, appeal to the interest in celebrity culture, and highlight public concerns. These trials appeal to the public, in part, because they tend to focus on the fault lines that divide society such as race and gender. The trials may involve celebrities or previously unknown individuals who are transformed into public figures. Headline trials tend to be long and drawn-out proceedings with time-consuming jury selection, arguments over the evidence, detailed examination of witnesses, and careful consideration of the facts by juries. Because these are the trials that are televised, written about, and discussed in the media, they shape the public perception of the administration of justice (L. Friedman 2015).

Headline trials tend to be dramatic, rarely are an "open and shut" case, and typically involve questions such as whether the individual sitting in the courtroom possessed the capacity and motive to commit a crime. Who else could have been the perpetrator? Was the killing an act of self-defense? What really went on behind closed doors? Did the victim deserve his or her fate? Is the evidence reliable, and was there tampering with the evidence? Friedman lists several categories of headline trials.

Political trials. Friedman defines a political trial as a trial that has "political meaning." This may involve a prosecution for a political act of rebellion or betrayal such as the prosecution of a spy or terrorist. The message to the citizenry is that the government will pursue individuals who pose a threat and keep the public safe. An example is the 1996 trial, conviction, and execution of Timothy McVeigh for the bombing of the Alfred P. Murrah Federal Building in Oklahoma City that killed 160 people including children in a day care center. A political trial also may be directed against opponents of the regime to deter dissent. This may involve a show trial of a political opponent for a non-political crime. The Russian government's prosecution of members of the punk rock group Pussy Riot for hooliganism that offended religious sensibilities, in part, was intended to deter protest against Russia's anti-LGBT policies.

Corruption and fraud. Prosecution of government officials for economically or politically motivated misconduct reflects the modern belief that government officials should serve the interests of the public rather than the interests of themselves or the interests of their friends. A recent example is the prosecution and conviction of former Illinois governor Rod Blagojevich in 2013 for attempting to sell the U.S. Senate seat vacated by President Barack Obama following his election and extorting campaign funds from state contractors.

Justice denied. These cases take on importance because of doubts whether the case will be fairly conducted or decided. The jury decision to acquit George Zimmerman for the alleged killing in self-defense of Trayvon Martin was greeted with disbelief among individuals who pointed to evidence that Zimmerman targeted a young African American wearing a hoodie who Zimmerman likely believed had no reason to be in the neighborhood other than to commit vandalism or a burglary.

Tabloid trial. These are notorious and scandalous trials that are appealing because of their entertainment value. An example is the lurid Milwaukee, Wisconsin, trial in 1992 of Jeffrey Dahmer who killed and mutilated as many as a dozen men before or after sexual relations. Following their death, Dahmer dismembered the victims and in some instances engaged in cannibalism. The soap-opera trial involves killings provoked by love, jealousy, and hate and the complications of a love triangle. In 1991, Betty Broderick was convicted of the double homicide of her former husband, Dr. Dan Broderick, and his second younger wife and former secretary Linda Kulkena. Betty had helped pay for Dan's education, and although she received a lucrative divorce settlement, she could not contain her rage toward Dan for having left her.

Celebrity trial. These trials receive notoriety because of the identity of the defendant and/or the victim rather than because of the type of crime involved. A celebrity is a famous person who is well known to the public. An example is the 1994 double murder trial of O. J. Simpson, a member of the Pro Football Hall of Fame and media personality. The trial proceedings were beamed across America and mesmerized the entire country. Nightly programs were devoted to discussing the events at trial. These proceedings often overlap with tabloid trials.

Mystery and identity. The *whodunit* trial involves doubts about what happened, who did it, and why. A famous example is the acquittal of Claus von Bülow for the attempted murder of his sickly wife Margaret Crawford. Von Bülow, a European aristocrat, had an unhappy marriage to the rich American, and the question was whether she had brought on her own coma by her alcoholism and medication or whether von Bülow had given her a potentially fatal drug injection. The trial was recounted in a best-selling book and Hollywood film.

Worm in the bud. These trials expose the underside of wealthy and privileged individuals. The trial attracts the public because it provides insight into the life of the rich and famous that generally is inaccessible to the average person. An example may be the 1991 trial and acquittal of William Kennedy Smith, a member of the famous Kennedy family, for rape. A subcategory is the *who would have thought* trial. These prosecutions involve the shock of discovery. The McMartin day care trial in the 1980s involved accusations that workers in a child day care center were sexually abusing children. Although it was revealed that the mother who lodged the accusations was a mentally disturbed alcoholic, the accusations brought on a moral panic in which dozens of parents came to believe that their children had been molested and were victims of cult-like abuse.

In the next sections of the chapter, we explore the role and function of the jury in a trial.

■ THE JURY IN CRIMINAL CASES

The origin of the criminal **jury** is uncertain. In 1066, William the Conqueror defeated King Harold's army in the Norman Conquest of England. The Norman kings would summon a "body of neighbors" to offer sworn testimony on who owned various pieces of property, and this information was used to impose taxes. A group of neighbors also was asked to investigate criminal activity. A presenting jury of twelve "lawful men" (a "presenting jury") was charged with informing the king's judges of individuals in a local jurisdiction who had committed a crime and should be brought to trial (T. Green 1985: 7).

In 1215, the church prohibited trial by ordeal (e.g., various physical tests employing fire and water or combat). The king's judges responded by creating an alternative mode of determining a defendant's guilt or innocence. Twelve individuals acquainted with the defendant or with the events surrounding the criminal accusation were ordered to appear and to swear an oath attesting to the defendant's guilt or innocence. The interesting point is that this is very different from the modern notion that jurors are to be impartial and to have formed no opinion regarding a case. Sworn oaths may have continued to be relied on in some areas of England as late as the fifteenth century (Hans and Vidmar 1986: 27–28).

In the fourteenth and fifteenth centuries, the determination of a defendant's guilt or innocence at trial began to be based on the testimony of witnesses. The petit jury (small jury) was created to evaluate the evidence that was presented during a trial, and jurors no longer were expected to rely on their own knowledge of the facts. The jurors' judgments were to reflect the conscience of the community, and jurors were to be selected from the community in which the crime had been committed. In those instances in which jurors were unable to be fair, the trial was to be moved to a different location.

A defendant was authorized to waive a jury trial and, instead, to submit to "strong and continuing pain," typically involving being crushed to death. Individuals at times accepted this harsh alternative because a conviction at trial resulted in the forfeiture of all possessions, an act that deprived offspring of an inheritance. This harsh alternative was not entirely abandoned until 1772, when it was declared that an individual who waived a jury trial was presumed guilty. A hundred years later, this rule was slightly modified, and a refusal of a jury trial was considered to be equivalent to a plea of guilt (Vidmar and Hans 2007: 25).

Trials were not elaborate affairs. The judge would question witnesses, and the jury would meet and return a verdict. Judges exercised stringent controls over the jury and punished jurors who returned the "wrong verdict." In 1554, heavy fines were imposed on eight of the twelve jurors who acquitted Sir Nicholas Throckmorton of high treason for conspiring and plotting the death of Queen Mary (Vidmar and Hans 2007: 27).

The trial of Quakers William Penn and William Mead in 1670 was a historical turning point in the development of the jury. Penn addressed a group of Quaker worshippers outside of the Friends Meeting House on Gracechurch Street in London. Penn was held to be in violation of the Conventicle Act, which prohibited worship that did not conform to the requirements of the Anglican Church. Penn and Mead were charged with what in modern terms may be considered as unlawful assembly and a disturbance of the peace. Penn proclaimed that praising God and assembling to worship God was a lawful act. When asked by the judge whether he pled guilty, Penn responded that the question was not "whether I am guilty of this Indictment but whether the Indictment is legal" (Abramson 2000: 70–71). As he was removed from the courtroom, Penn appealed to the jury to refuse to cooperate with the prosecution, which was "devoid of all law" (T. Green 1985: 224).

The jury adjourned for ninety minutes, and when they returned, they acquitted Mead but could not agree on whether to convict or acquit Penn. The judge ordered the jurors to continue to deliberate. When the jurors returned to the courtroom, they once again acquitted Mead and refused to convict Penn, proclaiming that his only "crime" was speaking on Gracechurch Street. The court ordered the jury to continue its deliberations; the jury once again returned with not guilty verdicts. The judge then ordered the entire jury incarcerated. The next morning, the jury again refused to convict the defendants. The same scenario was repeated for a fourth time; again, the jury stood firm and returned a verdict of not guilty for both Penn and Mead (Abramson 2000: 70–71). Historian Thomas Green writes that the jury, by "assessing the law themselves, had rebuffed the tyranny of the judiciary and vindicated their own true historical and moral purpose" (T. Green 1985: 225–226).

This did not end the matter. A number of jurors were fined for refusing to follow the law. Juror Edward Bushel refused to pay his fine and was imprisoned. Bushel and three other jurors filed a suit in the Court of Common Pleas and claimed that Bushel's imprisonment, as well as the fine imposed on the three jurors, was unlawful. Chief Justice John Vaughan upheld Bushel's claim and held that jurors rather than judges are the finders of fact and that jurors may not be fined or imprisoned because officials disagree with their verdict (T. Green 1985: 137–148).

English juries continued to assert their independence. In 1685, King James II, a convert to Catholicism, rescinded all anti-Catholic laws in England. He directed that this edict was to be read to Anglican congregations. Seven Anglican bishops petitioned the king to exempt them from reading the order to their congregants. James was angered at the bishops' opposition to the repeal of anti-Catholic laws and charged them with seditious libel and ordered them interned in the Tower of London. The prevailing practice was for judges to require juries to answer specific factual questions relating to the defendant's conduct (special verdict). The judge would then apply the law and evaluate whether the defendant was guilty. In this instance, a finding by the jury that the bishops had petitioned the king would have been all that was required to convict the bishops of seditious libel. The jury, however, returned a verdict of not guilty (general verdict) to prevent the judges from convicting the bishops of seditious libel (Vidmar and Hans 2007: 30–31).

As late as 1800, English law provided for the death penalty for 230 offenses, many of which resulted in only minimal social harm. Juries responded by regularly acquitting defendants to avoid the death penalty. Juries, for example, excused thefts by their neighbors known to be of decent character and background who may have acted out of momentary weakness. The death penalty for theft tended to be reserved for highway robbers who killed during the course of the crime (T. Green 1985: 28–54).

The English jury was transported to the American colonies and to other British colonies, and today fifty-two countries employ some form of jury decision-making. In the early colonial period, American juries followed the independent pattern established by the English jury. The trial of John Peter Zenger, which is discussed in the next section, marked a turning point in the development of the American jury.

■ THE DEVELOPMENT OF THE AMERICAN JURY

The jury as noted was transported from England to the American colonies. The jury provided for popular participation in the legal process and ensured that the outcome of legal disputes reflected the views of the local community. The 1606 charter of the Virginia Company provided for juries in civil and criminal cases. In 1628, the Massachusetts Bay Colony introduced jury trials, and in 1647, juries were introduced in New Jersey. Juries were provided for in the Colony of West New Jersey in 1677. Pennsylvania followed suit in 1682 and recognized trials before juries (Vidmar and Hans 2007: 47).

John Peter Zenger was the German-born publisher and editor of the *New York Weekly Journal*. He ran a series of articles and satirical advertisements that were critical of English governor William Cosby's greed and corruption. Cosby ordered Zenger's arrest and detention for seditious libel. The judge, a political ally of Governor Cosby, imposed an exorbitant bail (Vidmar and Hans 2007: 42–43).

At his trial in 1735, Zenger was represented by Alexander Hamilton, perhaps the most famous lawyer of his day. The jury's role was limited to determining whether a statement had been published. The judge applied the law and evaluated whether the statement constituted seditious libel. Truth was not a defense. Hamilton argued that the jury should not be a captive of the court and that the jurors should determine for themselves whether the articles published in Zenger's newspaper constituted seditious libel. The jury, in Hamilton's opinion, also should decide whether truth constituted a defense (Vidmar and Hans 2007: 44–46).

This was a radical revision of prevailing practice. Hamilton was not merely arguing that the jury should determine the facts and apply the law to the facts. He contended that the jurors were the "judges of the law" and possessed the authority to disregard a law that was contrary to the "law of nature." Nature, according to Hamilton, gave every person "the liberty . . . of exposing and opposing arbitrary power, by speaking and writing truth." The jurors were "to make use of their consciences and understanding" in judging Zenger's guilt. The jury adjourned and a short time later returned a verdict of not guilty (Abramson 2000: 74–75).

The Zenger trial symbolized the role of the jury as a bulwark of liberty against overzealous British prosecutors. Colonial juries consistently refused to convict defendants who resisted British authorities. Trial by jury was viewed as central to democracy, and the British abrogation of trial by jury for violation of the Navigation Acts (that required American ships to send goods destined for foreign jurisdictions through English ports) was listed as a central grievance in the Declaration of Independence. Keep in mind that the notion of a democratic jury was limited to a jury of white males who owned property (Abramson 2000: 23–24, 27).

The jury reached the height of its influence during the founding of the American Republic. Throughout the debate over the drafting of the Sixth Amendment to the U.S. Constitution, the Federalists (favoring strong central government), although believing in the importance of the jury, rejected the prevailing practice of forming a jury from the vicinage (county) of the crime. The thinking behind forming juries from the vicinage was that the members of a local jury would be knowledgeable about the personal lives of the defendant and the victim, and their verdict would constitute the "conscience of the community" and reflect local values and beliefs. The Federalists argued that a jury should be impartial and objective and should be composed of individuals distant from the site of the crime. The anti-Federalists responded that in the newly formed American democracy, the government was distant from the local population and the local jury was an important avenue for democratic participation. A compromise was reached in the drafting of the Sixth Amendment, providing that a jury should be formed from the "State and district wherein the crime shall have been committed." The language vindicated the Federalist position because the Congress, in drawing the lines of districts, made these identical to state boundaries. In other words, juries no longer were required to be from the locale of the crime. A second important point is that the Sixth Amendment refers to an "impartial jury," which is a rejection of the anti-Federalist belief that a jury should be formed from friends and neighbors. The jury now was to be impartial rather than acquainted with the events that gave rise to the trial (Abramson 2000: 22–36).

An additional factor in the development of the jury in the United States was the emergence of an educated and well-qualified judiciary. In the early years of the Republic, American judges often lacked legal training and were content to let jurors determine what the law was and apply the law to the facts of the case. The notion was that the common law of England was based on natural justice, and knowledge of the law was inherent in human beings. The jury would decide for itself whether self-defense required an imminent and immediate threat and whether individuals possessed a duty to retreat before using deadly force in self-defense. The jury then would apply this standard to the facts of the case and reach a decision. The professional judiciary insisted that it was the role of the judge to tell the jury the law and that the jury was limited to finding the facts and returning a verdict based on an application of the law as dictated by the judge to the facts. Every state—with the exception of Maryland and Indiana—required the judge to instruct the jury that the jury was to follow the law articulated by the judge and that jurors were prohibited from applying their own views of the law in deciding the case. In the past, jurors had been permitted to question witnesses. The increasing reliance on lawyers at trial meant that jurors were to assume a more passive role at trials. As Jeffrey Abramson notes, the jury entered the nineteenth century with the prerogative to determine the law for itself and even to disregard the law when required by justice. The jury left the nineteenth century with the duty to follow the law articulated by the judge (Abramson 2000: 30–33, 37).

Jury trials in the eighteenth and nineteenth centuries were relatively brief proceedings. Trial procedures were uncomplicated, and there was no scientific evidence or expert witnesses. As many as six trials were held in a courtroom in a single day. The number of jury trials steadily has declined as trial procedures have become more complex. Roughly 149,000 state jury trials and 5,550 federal jury trials are conducted in the United States each year. Roughly 47 percent of the trials are for felonies, 19 percent are for misdemeanors, 31 percent are civil trials, and 4 percent are listed as others. An estimated 32 million individuals are called for jury service each year, and in the neighborhood of 1.5 million individuals are selected to serve on juries (Devine 2012: 6).

Jury trials nonetheless remain important. They typically are conducted for serious felonies, including charges carrying a possible penalty of death. These often are high-profile trials that help shape our perception of the fairness of the legal system. Juries remain a safeguard against overly aggressive prosecutors and politically motivated prosecutions and biased judges. Keep in mind that a jury determines guilt and innocence and in many instances also has the option of convicting a defendant of a lesser included offense. A defendant, for example, may be charged with assault with intent to murder, and the jury may find that the defendant lacked a homicidal intent and should be convicted of assault, which carries a significantly lower sentence.

This chapter in discussing juries draws on the over 1,500 published jury studies that employ various methodologies including interviews, surveys, laboratory experiments, and statistical analysis (Devine 2012: 8).

■ JURY DECISION-MAKING

Historically, unanimous verdicts were required in the criminal justice system. The requirement of unanimity among a group of twelve individuals necessitates that juries consider the views of all jurors to reach a consensus. In 1972, the U.S. Supreme Court held that the Constitution permits state criminal juries to decide noncapital cases by a 10–2 or 9–3 margin (*Apodaca v. Oregon*, 406 U.S. 404 [1972]; *Johnson v. Louisiana*, 406 U.S. 356 [1972]). The Court concluded that reducing the size of the jury would not impact the accuracy of jury verdicts because a majority of jurors are required to agree that a defendant's guilt has been established beyond a reasonable doubt. The fact that a verdict was non-unanimous would not mean that verdicts were decided without a vigorous debate and a close consideration of the evidence.

The Court also held that the twelve-person jury is not constitutionally required (*Williams v. Florida*, 399 U.S. 78 [1970]). The Court subsequently held that the minimum size of the jury in criminal cases is six (*Ballew v. Georgia*, 435 U.S. 223 [1978]). Five-person juries are not considered to be sufficiently large to represent the community, and a state may not evade the requirement that a jury must consist of six persons by permitting convictions based on votes of 5–1 (*Burch v. Louisiana*, 441 U.S. 130 [1979]).

Roughly thirty states employ juries of fewer than twelve members for some criminal offenses. Louisiana and Oregon are the only states that authorize non-unanimous verdicts while some states permit defendants to waive unanimous verdicts (Abramson 2000: 181).

We have limited information about jury decision-making because the deliberations take place behind closed doors. Jurors confront the challenge of listening to testimony and making a judgment about a defendant's guilt or innocence. This information often is not presented in chronological order, and various witnesses may contradict one another. Jurors also must put themselves in the position of the various parties at the time of the events at issue in the trial rather than evaluate the evidence based on "twenty-twenty hindsight." Jurors must resist being influenced by their own preconceptions and concluding that, for example, because a suspect was shot and killed by a police officer, the officer must have acted in either a reasonable or an unreasonable fashion.

Political scientists Lance Bennett and Martha Feldman in an influential analysis argue that jurors draw on their own life experience and knowledge to assist them in developing a story about what happened in a case. They then determine whether a guilty or not guilty verdict best fits the story. Jurors might draw on experiences from their own lives in determining whether a driver who in a fit of "road rage" killed another driver acted in self-defense or was the aggressor. Jurors' judgments at times may not be based solely on the facts. They may in some cases weigh and balance various factors and ask themselves whether the defendant deserves to be criminally convicted. Jurors, for example, may conclude that a defendant who has killed an abusive spouse should be convicted of a lesser degree of homicide rather than being convicted of first-degree murder (Bennett and Feldman 1981).

Studies find that jurors' race has little or no impact on whether they will convict or acquit a defendant.

On the other hand, female jurors are more likely to favor conviction in cases involving sexual offenses (Devine 2012: 113). The most important factor in jury decision-making tends to be the interaction between jurors in the jury room.

The first order of business inside the jury room is to select the foreperson or leader of the group. Jurors tend to elect people who have experience serving on juries or individuals with leadership skills. They tend to elect educated individuals of higher socioeconomic status and favor men over women.

The second step is for the jury to agree on a procedure to be followed in determining the defendant's guilt or innocence. A jury that begins with an informal vote is termed a *verdict-driven deliberation*. As you might expect, the *verdict-driven* approach results in jurors quickly dividing into various camps. People find it difficult to change their mind publicly; as a result, jurors encounter difficulty in reaching a unanimous agreement. A second approach is the *evidence-driven* deliberation in which jurors discuss the evidence in an effort to reach a consensus before voting. These two deliberative styles are equally likely to be employed by jury panels (Devine 2012: 156–157).

Studies indicate that the decision reached by a majority of jurors on the first vote ultimately tends to emerge as the jury's verdict. The jurors who disagree with the majority gradually accept the majority view (Vidmar and Hans 2007: 142–144). Harry Kalven Jr. and Hans Zeisel, in their classic jury study, find that the initial majority view eventually attracts support from all of the jurors in 90 percent of the cases (Kalven and Zeisel 1966: 488). Dan Simon notes that agreement may not reflect a true consensus. A study by the National Center for State Courts of three thousand juries finds that in half of the juries that reached a verdict, one or more jurors bent to the will of the majority despite their personal disagreement. These jurors tend to lack self-confidence and to lack conviction in their viewpoint (D. Simon 2012: 200).

It is typical that only a small number of jurors actively participate in the deliberations. Most jurors look to several outspoken people to represent their views. As you might expect, educated men with high-status occupations tend to dominate the discussion. Jury forepersons speak for between 25 and 30 percent of the time spent deliberating the verdict. As the divisions in the jury are clarified and intensified, fewer people are comfortable with conflict, and fewer are willing to participate in the discussion. This is particularly the case in those instances in which the debate becomes personal and insults are traded and exchanged. Juries deliberate between two and four hours in a straightforward "garden variety" case before reaching a verdict (Devine 2012: 156–157).

The portrayal in the movies of the lonely juror who persuades the entire array to his or her point of view rarely occurs during actual jury deliberations. Kalven and Zeisel find that in 10 percent of the cases, a minority of jurors succeed in persuading a majority of jurors to switch their point of view. In roughly one case out of twenty, the jurors are unable to reach an agreement. This is called a *hung jury* and typically requires that four or five jurors band together to resist the majority of jurors on the first vote. Non-unanimous verdicts, according to Kalven and Zeisel, would reduce the modest number of hung juries by 45 percent (Kalven and Zeisel 1966: 460–461, 489–490).

In those instances in which the jury is able to reach an agreement, the last phase is the reconciliation stage in which the jurors smooth over their disagreements and support a verdict.

Juries that are authorized to return non-unanimous verdicts tend to stop deliberations when a majority of jurors agree on a verdict and do not continue to make an effort to persuade the dissenting jurors. As a result, verdicts are reached more rapidly. There is some indication that jurors are less confident in verdicts that are non-unanimous. On the other hand, jurors in non-unanimous states likely would reach a consensus if the discussion continued. We have seen that in most instances, dissenting jurors ultimately join with the majority. As a result, studies indicate, unanimous and non-unanimous juries tend to reach similar results (Hastie, Penrod, and Pennington 1983). In the next section, we examine the factors that account for jury decisions.

■ JUDGES AND JURIES

We now turn our attention to understanding why juries decide to convict or to acquit a defendant.

Kalven and Zeisel in their 1966 book, *The American Jury*, report the results of their massive Chicago Jury Project, which remains the most important academic study of the jury (Kalven and Zeisel 1966). Contemporary jury studies continue to confirm the general results of Kalven and Zeisel's study (Vidmar and Hans 2007: 151).

The most frequently cited aspect of the Chicago Jury Project is a survey of 555 judges who reported whether they agreed or disagreed with the jury verdict in 3,576 criminal cases in their courts. The results were as follows. The judge and the jury agreed in 78 percent of the cases on the jury verdict (e.g., 64 percent of the defendants were guilty, and 14 percent of the defendants were not guilty). As for the remaining cases, in roughly 19 percent of the cases, the jury acquitted a defendant, and the judge would have convicted the defendant; in nearly 3 percent of the cases, the jury convicted the

PHOTO 8.1 Every individual in the United States charged with a crime punishable by six months or more in prison is entitled to a trial before a jury of his or her peers. There are roughly 150,000 jury trials conducted in the United States each year; 67 percent are criminal cases.

defendant while the judge would have acquitted the defendant (Kalven and Zeisel 1966: 56–57). In other words, the judge and jury agreed in four out of five cases, and in those cases in which the jury and judge disagreed, the jury was roughly six times more likely to be more lenient than the judge. A defendant whose case is heard by a judge without a jury is roughly 12 percent more likely to be convicted (Vidmar and Hans 2007: 148, 150–151).

What accounts for the different decisions of judges and juries? The judges in the survey provided a range of explanations. Juries were more likely to be affected by sympathy for a defendant in roughly 4 percent of the cases. Younger and older defendants, defendants with physical challenges, and defendants with appealing wives or young children in the view of judges elicited a sympathetic response from jurors. In a small number of cases, the judges concluded that the jury disagreed with the law. An example was the popular belief in the 1950s that drunk driving did not merit criminal punishment. In other instances, judges knew information that did not enter into evidence, such as a defendant's prior criminal record or that some charges were dropped by the prosecutor (Kalven and Zeisel 1966: 121–220).

What of the cases in which the jury convicted a defendant and the judge would have convicted the defendant of a lesser offense or acquitted the defendant? In these cases, the defendant's demeanor at trial, his or her prior criminal record, and the jury's negative view of the defendant's lifestyle tipped the balance where the evidence of guilt was weak (Hans and Vidmar 1986: 142–144).

Kalven and Zeisel stress that the weaker the prosecution's case, the more likely that factors other than the evidence will enter into the jury's calculus. In other words, juries generally decide cases based on the strength of the evidence presented at trial along with the believability (credibility) of the defendant and of the victim. Juries also tend to be influenced by the youth and vulnerability of the victim (Kalven and Zeisel 1966: 149–181), and at least some jurors start with a bias in favor of the prosecution (D. Simon 2012: 196). An important point to keep in mind is that judges overwhelmingly support the jury system and, even when disagreeing with the decisions of juries, accept the verdicts as reasonable (Vidmar and Hans 2007: 150–151).

Juries, although praised for their ability to evaluate the evidence at trial, do not receive the same high marks for their ability to understand the jury instructions issued by a judge. Judges issue instructions at the completion of the prosecution and defense cases that instruct jurors on the law that they are to apply in determining whether the prosecution has established the defendant's guilt beyond a reasonable doubt. Studies find that between 13 and 73 percent of jurors comprehend a judge's instructions. One study found that two-thirds of jurors claimed to understand the judge's instructions although when tested only one-third actually understood the instructions. A study of Florida jurors found that after receiving jury instructions on the burden of proof, one-quarter of jurors incorrectly believed that the defendant should be convicted if the evidence was equally likely to support an acquittal as a conviction (D. Simon 2012: 196, 200).

Jurors tend to evaluate the evidence in accordance with their own sense of what makes sense regardless of the judge's instructions (D. Simon 2012: 185). So-called limiting instructions are issued throughout the trial instructing the jury on evidentiary matters. For example, a defendant's prior criminal record for crimes of dishonesty under some circumstances may be introduced into evidence when a defendant takes the stand in his or her own defense. The judge informs the jury that these prior criminal convictions may be considered in evaluating the defendant's credibility and are not to be considered in determining a defendant's guilt or innocence. Studies indicate that juries that hear evidence of a defendant's prior conviction cannot separate this information from their evaluation of the defendant's guilt or innocence. They inevitably consider this evidence in formulating their verdict and are more likely to convict the defendant. Keep in mind that judicial instructions tend to be full of technical jargon and challenge even the most advanced law students (Hans and Vidmar 1986: 125–126).

Studies also indicate that jurors tend to credit eyewitness testimony even when the witness is discredited on cross-examination as not having had a clear view of the defendant. An identification by a witness who displays confidence in his or her identification is particularly likely to be believed by jurors. Scientific research, however, indicates that there is no correlation between individuals' confidence in their identification and the accuracy of their identification (Vidmar and Hans 2007: 194–195). The impact of eyewitness testimony is particularly powerful when consistent with other evidence presented at trial (Devine 2012: 129).

Another problematic area is juror consideration of expert witnesses. For example, in a rape case, a judge may permit a psychological expert to testify that the victim's behavior following the alleged rape is consistent with the "rape trauma syndrome" that is characteristic of rape victims. The defense may cross-examine the expert, and the judge may permit the defense to present its own experts. Studies indicate that better-educated jurors and jurors who have a background related to the expert testimony are more likely to understand and consider expert testimony. Other jurors are likely to disregard the expert testimony. Jurors have particular difficulty understanding the notion of "statistical probability" and tend to accept arguments by the opposing counsel that the scientific evidence lacks reliability (Vidmar and Hans 2007: 182).

The complicated judicial instructions for applying the insanity defense are a good example of how jurors disregard expert witnesses and jury instructions. The insanity defense relieves individuals of criminal responsibility. The reason is that these individuals are incapable of forming a criminal intent and are not "morally culpable." It would advance neither deterrence nor retribution to punish legally insane defendants. Instead, they are institutionalized and treated in a mental health facility. There is significant opposition to the defense among the American public, which vastly overestimates the number of cases in which the defense is relied on and proves successful. Defendants rely on the defense in fewer than 1 percent of cases, and the defense is estimated to be successful between 1 percent and 25 percent of these cases (Vidmar and Hans 2007: 216).

Of the various legal tests for insanity, the test used most often by the federal government and in most states is the *M'Naghten* test ("right-wrong test"). The *Durham* test is much broader than the *M'Naghten* test and at one time was used in several states but now is limited to New Hampshire. Rita Simon conducted a number of jury simulations and found that the nature of the crime with which a defendant is charged is more important than the legal test in determining whether an individual is determined by a jury to be legally insane. None of the jurors applying *M'Naghten* found a defendant charged with the incest of his two daughters was insane; 19 percent of the jurors who applied the *Durham* test found the defendant insane. In a simulation involving a housebreaking charge, an equal number of jurors who applied the *M'Naghten* test and jurors who applied the *Durham* test found the defendant legally insane (R. Simon 1967).

More recent studies support Simon's conclusions. The strength of the evidence of a defendant's insanity and the testimony of medical experts, for example, is less important in determining a juror's determination of insanity than evidence that the defendant planned the crime. The fact that a defendant planned a killing, purchased a weapon, and stalked the victim is viewed by most jurors as inconsistent with legal insanity. It is entirely possible, however, for a legally insane individual to plan a killing that is "commanded" by the "voice of God" or in which the victim is viewed as a "demonic figure" responsible for the world's ills. To counter jurors' reluctance to find defendants legally insane, a number of states have provided juries with the option of finding a defendant guilty but insane rather than not guilty by reason of insanity. The guilty but insane verdict results in a defendant's receiving treatment while incarcerated in prison (Finkel 1995).

The crime of rape is another area in which juries tend to rely on their own commonsense notions. Kalven and Zeisel's study was published almost fifty years ago, and the law of rape and social attitudes have undergone significant change since then. Their basic findings nonetheless continue to have relevance. Kalven and Zeisel found that the jurors divided rape between simple rape and aggravated rape. In "simple rape" cases, females were viewed as "assuming the risk" of the offense by visiting the defendant's apartment, drinking with the accused, or getting into a car with several males. In 60 percent of the simple rape cases in which the jury acquitted a defendant, the judge would have convicted the defendant. In those cases in which the judge and the jury agreed to convict, the jury would have convicted the defendant of a crime that is less serious than rape. The jury viewed a rape as "aggravated rape" in those cases involving violent attacks, assaults by several assailants, and attacks in which the defendant and the victim were strangers. The jury acquitted defendants in only 12 percent of the aggravated rape cases in which the judge would have convicted the defendant (Kalven and Zeisel 1966: 252–253).

Studies continue to find that jurors are guided by strong prejudices in deciding allegations of rape and are reluctant to convict a defendant when they perceive that a woman "assumed the risk" of a rape as a result of her dress and lifestyle. A woman who goes to a man's apartment on the first date continues to be viewed as having invited sex by her behavior (Vidmar and Hans 2007: 198–201). On the other hand, jurors are more likely to convict a defendant of rape when there is evidence that a weapon was involved or when a defendant was unemployed and had no family relationships and had made a bad impression on the jurors. We all, of course, base our views on impressions of other people. The troubling aspect of these findings is that jury verdicts are based on personal prejudices rather than on the relevant evidence presented at trial (LaFree, Reskin, and Vishner 1985).

In summary, the judge and the jury agree on the verdict in most cases. In those instances in which they disagree, jurors are somewhat more lenient. Juries also appear to be overly influenced by eyewitness testimony while giving limited weight to expert witnesses. Jurors find technical jury instructions confusing and apply their own standards in areas such as the insanity defense.

Juries in many instances clearly do not mechanically apply the law, as given to them by the judge, to the facts in reaching a verdict. A controversial question discussed in the next section is whether jurors may simply disregard the law and acquit a seemingly guilty defendant.

■ JURY NULLIFICATION

Jury nullification is the conscious and deliberate decision of a jury to acquit a defendant despite the jury's awareness that the defendant is guilty based on the facts and the law. We have seen that juries historically have been willing to disregard the requirements of the law so as to vindicate the rights of defendants like William Penn and John Peter Zenger. The practice of jury nullification was relied on by juries that acquitted defendants who assisted fugitive African Americans fleeing slavery in the South and by juries that acquitted protesters against the Vietnam War. Kalven and Zeisel, in reviewing the history of jury nullification, observe that the jury has served both as a "bulwark against grave official tyranny" and as a "moderate corrective" against the prosecution of unpopular crimes such as selling alcohol during Prohibition (Kalven and Zeisel 1966: 296–297).

We earlier noted that beginning in the mid-nineteenth century, judges asserted the authority to define the law and limited juries to the determination of the facts. In 1895, the U.S. Supreme Court formally recognized the division of responsibility between the judge and the jury in *Sparf and Hansen v. United States.* In this decision, the Court clearly stated that juries were to evaluate the facts and to follow the law as stated by the judge. The Supreme Court warned that permitting juries to decide the law would allow each jury to become "a law unto themselves" and to overthrow the rule of law (*Sparf and Hansen v. United States*, 156 U.S. 51 [1895]).

A typical jury instruction directs the jury that it is the duty of the judge to instruct jurors on the law to be applied and that the jury is required to follow the law as explained by the judge. Georgia, Indiana, Maryland, and Oregon recognize, in their constitutions, the right of the jury to disregard the law. New Hampshire recently adopted a law allowing lawyers to inform jurors of their right to disregard the law and exercise their independent judgment. The general practice in other states and in the federal courts is for judges to instruct juries that they are obligated to follow the law as recited by the judge. Defense lawyers typically are warned by the judge against urging the jury to nullify the law in their closing arguments.

Courts continue to praise juries as a bulwark against overzealous prosecutors and as the conscience of the community while insisting that jurors follow the law as stated by the judge

(*Duncan v. Louisiana*, 391 U.S. 145 [1968]; *Taylor v. Louisiana*, 419 U.S. 522 [1975]). In *United States v. Dougherty*, a group of antiwar protesters vandalized the offices of Dow Chemical Company to protest the company's manufacture of napalm for use in Vietnam. A federal court of appeals affirmed the trial court's refusal to inform the jury of its right to nullify the law. The appellate court recognized that juries historically had exercised the power of nullification. However, the court held that to inform juries of this right would lead to anarchy and undermine the rule of law. The outcome of a case would depend on the composition and mood of the jury rather than on the requirements of the law. Any change in the law should take place through the legislative process rather than through the judgment of a group of jurors. In any event, the court reasoned that juries were well aware of this right and it was not necessary to inform jurors of this right (*United States v. Dougherty*, 473 F.2d 1113 [D.C. Cir. 1972]).

An illustration of the possible impact of nullification instructions is a 2012 New Hampshire case in which the judge issued a jury nullification instruction and the jury acquitted Doug Darrow of drug offenses stemming from his cultivation of medical marijuana in his backyard.

Jury nullification may not always result in a verdict that protects rights and liberties. In the 1960s, nullification was relied on by jurors in the American South to acquit defendants charged with the abuse of civil rights activists. One of the most infamous cases of southern juries practicing nullification involved the acquittal of the defendants accused of murdering Emmett Till. Fourteen-year-old Till was from Chicago and was visiting his family in Mississippi. The husband of a white woman considered Till's alleged whistling at his wife grossly insulting and insolent and together with a friend shot Till and dumped his body into the river. Despite the overwhelming evidence identifying the defendants as the murderers, an all-white jury took one hour and seven minutes to acquit the defendants. One juror noted that if the jurors had not stopped to drink a soft drink, they would have reached the verdict more quickly. In 1987, a New York jury refused to convict Bernard Goetz of attempted murder. After being attacked by muggers, Goetz purchased a firearm that he used to shoot four young African American men who asked him for $5 on the New York subway.

In 2016, Ammon Bundy and his brother Ryan and five other individuals involved in an armed takeover of the Malheur National Wildlife Refuge in southeastern Oregon were acquitted in a surprise verdict in federal district court. The seven defendants were charged with conspiring to use "force, intimidation, and threats" to keep federal employees from working at the refuge during the takeover and with unauthorized possession of a firearm in a federal facility. Eleven individuals already had pled guilty to the charge. The defendants admitted entering the 188,000-acre wildlife preserve to protest federal land policy and to return the land to local control but denied that there was a conspiracy (Sherwood 2016).

The general argument for nullification is that there are situations in which the jury believes that an individual should not be subject to criminal penalties. Acquitting individuals in such situations enhances respect for the law. As Dean Roscoe Pound of Harvard Law School famously remarked, jury lawlessness is the "great corrective" to the inflexible application of the law. The question remains whether juries should be informed of their ability to exercise jury nullification. Keep in mind that studies suggest that nullification instructions likely will influence the jury only in highly emotional cases in which the jurors view the application of the law as unjust. Studies indicate that there will not be an avalanche of acquittals (Benforado 2015: 71). As a juror, would you nullify the law in the case of a doctor who engages in the mercy killing of a long-suffering and seriously ill cancer patient who has expressed a desire to die (I. A. Horowitz 2008)?

Former U.S. prosecutor and Georgetown University professor Paul Butler recounts a case he prosecuted against a 19-year-old African American male for possession of cocaine. The young man claimed that he did not know the envelope containing cocaine was in his pocket. Butler, an African American and a graduate of Harvard Law School, thought that this was an "open-and-shut case." He was shocked when the jury returned a verdict of not guilty. Butler explains that he came to understand that the older African American jurors viewed themselves as advancing the cause of justice. In the District of Columbia, one-third of young African Americans at any given time are in prison, on parole or probation, or awaiting trial, and two-thirds of African American males can expect to be arrested before reaching the age of 30. On reflection, Butler realized that these jurors understood that African Americans are singled out for arrest and prosecution on drug crimes and that nothing is accomplished by sending another young African American to jail when there are more African American young men in prison than in college.

Butler argues for "strategic jury nullification" to reduce mass incarceration and to communicate the need for fundamental change in the criminal justice system. He calls for jurors to refuse to convict defendants prosecuted for possession of small amounts of drugs for personal use or for selling a small quantity of drugs to a consenting adult (Butler 2009: 74–78).

Butler concludes that, given the bias in the criminal justice system, working as a prosecutor because you hope to reform the criminal justice system is as counterproductive as working for an oil company because you want to help the environment. Butler argues that prosecutors have little discretion because they must follow the policy established by the chief prosecutor, who can remain in office only by getting tough on crime. He views prosecutors as workers on an assembly line devoted to mass incarceration that has made the drug problem worse rather than better. Butler asks us to consider the moral costs of complicity with a system that degrades "our fellow human beings."

Do you agree with Butler?

■ JURY SELECTION

The jury selection process is intended to result in a fair and impartial jury. Jeffrey Abramson argues that in recent years the Supreme Court has been equally concerned with ensuring that individuals are not excluded based on race, ethnicity, or gender.

The initial jury pool is required to be selected from a comprehensive source such as lists of voters or motor vehicle license holders. In 1880, in *Strauder v. West Virginia*, the Supreme Court held that a West Virginia law that limited jury service to white males stamped African Americans with a badge of inferiority, encouraged racial discrimination, and violated equal protection (*Strauder v. West Virginia*, 100 U.S. 303 [1880]). It was not until the 1940s that a majority of states on their own initiative provided that women were eligible to serve as jurors. A few decades later, the Supreme Court held that the constitution required that the jury pool include women as well as men (*Taylor v. Louisiana*, 419 U.S. 522 [1975]). The Court also held that the pool of individuals from which the jury is selected must represent a fair cross section of the community. The Supreme Court has stopped short of requiring that the actual jury represent a cross section of the community, although several justices have strongly indicated that a jury that does not include an array of groups is unable to fully reflect the views of the community (*Taylor v. Louisiana*, 419 U.S. 522 [1975]).

The next step is to select the jury panel from the pool of individuals who have been summoned to serve on the jury. Individuals in the jury pool are subjected to pretrial questioning, or *voir dire* ("to speak the truth"), which in most states and in the federal system is conducted by the prosecutor, the defense attorney, and the judge. The purpose is to determine whether an individual, if selected to serve on the jury, can be fair and objective. An individual may be excluded on two grounds:

Challenge for cause. An unlimited number of jurors may be excused for cause with the consent of the judge. Removal for cause requires that a juror is unable to be fair because the juror has made up his or her mind or the juror has a personal relationship that makes it likely that he or she cannot be objective. An example would be a juror who is married to a police officer in a case involving the killing of a law enforcement officer.

PHOTO 8.2   A white, male jury in Sumner, Mississippi, after deliberating for one hour acquitted Roy Bryant and his half brother John W. Milam on September 23, 1955, for the murder of Emmett Till, a 14-year-old African American. Newly revealed evidence calls into question the accuracy of the not guilty verdict.

Bettmann/Getty Images

Peremptory challenge. The defense and prosecution have a limited number of peremptory challenges. This allows the exclusion of jurors for no reason whatsoever. A lawyer may anticipate that a juror is biased or may be apprehensive that the individual has been irritated by the questioning during *voir dire.* The U.S. Supreme Court has ruled that peremptory challenges may not be used to exclude jurors based solely on their race (*Batson v. Kentucky*, 476 U.S. 79 [1986]) or based solely on their gender (*J.E.B. v. Alabama, ex rel. T.B.*, 511 U.S. 127 [1994]). In January 2014, the Ninth Circuit Court of Appeals held that individuals who are gay may not be excluded from a jury considering a case involving the pharmaceutical industry and human immunodeficiency virus (HIV).

The U.S. Supreme Court recently affirmed the *Batson* doctrine in ruling that the peremptory challenge of two African American jurors had been substantially motivated by a discriminatory intent. Chief Justice John Roberts held that "the State's . . . prosecutors were motivated in substantial part by race when they struck Garrett and Hood [the African American jurors] from the jury. . . . Two peremptory strikes on the basis of race are two more than the Constitution allows" (*Foster v. Chatman*, 578 U.S. ___ [2016]).

Voir dire typically involves the brief questioning of prospective jurors in open court. Studies indicate the procedure is not entirely effective in identifying potential jurors who have made up their mind or who are likely to favor the prosecution or the defense. Researchers have found that individuals fail to reveal that members of their family work in law enforcement, that they have been crime victims, or that they do not believe defendants should be presumed innocent (Seltzer, Venuti, and Lopes 1991). Jurors have a tendency to want to present themselves in a positive light in response to a question. For example, potential jurors may not want to admit that they are unable to be fair and objective or may be embarrassed to admit they have been arrested. It is important to note that lawyers typically are more skilled at *voir dire* than judges, and when the lawyers are allowed to extensively question jurors, a greater number of jurors are struck from the jury for cause (Nietzel and Dillehay 1982).

Studies find that despite the holding in *Batson*, race continues to play a role in peremptory challenges. Prosecutors in some cases want to exclude from the jury pool minority jurors whom they view as more liberal, whereas defense attorneys may want to exclude white jurors and older jurors whom they view as more conservative. Absent a clear pattern of excluding minorities or women from a jury, it is difficult for a judge to determine whether a lawyer is relying on a nonracial reason for excluding a juror. A study conducted by the nonprofit group Equal Justice Initiative found a continuing pattern of discrimination in jury selection in southern states. The study, for example, finds that there are counties in Alabama where more than 75 percent of African American jurors have been struck from serving on a jury in death penalty cases. In North Carolina, at least twenty-six individuals on death row were sentenced by all-white juries (Vidmar and Hans 2007: 98–99).

Adam Benforado notes that between 2005 and 2009 in Harris County, Alabama, four out of five African Americans were struck from jury panels in capital cases. As a result, half of the juries in death penalty cases had no African American jurors, and the other half had a single African American juror. The Louisiana Capital Assistance Center found that between 1999 and 2007 African Americans were struck from juries at more than three times the rate as whites. Benforado concludes that despite all the procedural safeguards, the "core problem" of discrimination in jury selection remains (Benforado 2015: 245).

Research indicates that, contrary to the conventional wisdom, age, gender, employment, and race have very little value in predicting how a juror will decide a case (Hans and Vidmar 1986: 76–78). Studies also find that even the more skilled attorneys are unable to identify a significant percentage of the jurors whose views may be prejudicial to their case. The result is that the attitudes of jurors selected for a jury in most instances do not significantly differ from the attitudes of jurors who were not selected by lawyers to serve on the jury (C. Johnson and Haney 1994).

Do you believe that peremptory challenges should be eliminated in order to prevent racial and sexual discrimination in the jury selection process? Should individuals only be struck from the jury for cause?

Before we turn our attention to lawyers' use of jury consultants to select juries, it is important to note the challenge posed by pretrial publicity. The First Amendment to the U.S. Constitution protects freedom of expression. The media are a particularly important check on governmental abuse and are essential to an informed and active citizenry. The media's right to freedom of expression in some instances may conflict with the protection of the defendant's right to an impartial and objective jury. Particularly gruesome crimes or high-profile crimes may receive extensive media coverage in which the details of the crime are described and the suspected perpetrators are identified. Studies indicate that jurors who have been exposed to media coverage are likely to view the prosecution's case as stronger than the defense case and are more likely to view the defendant in a negative light as compared to jurors who have not been exposed to this publicity. Jurors may state that they are able to be fair, but this claim is unlikely to be true where there is saturation coverage of a crime. Various procedural remedies are available to the judges to limit the impact of media coverage. This includes sequestering the jury, prohibiting the lawyers from talking to the media, and, as a last resort, moving the trial to another jurisdiction (Vidmar and Hans 2007: 107–123).

Defense lawyers have turned to jury consultants in an effort to employ the power of science to improve their ability to select sympathetic jurors.

■ SOCIAL SCIENCE AND JURY SELECTION

Trial lawyers often remark that when the jury selection is over, the outcome of the trial has been decided. In other words, lawyers tend to believe that the composition of the jury will decide the outcome of the case regardless of the strength of the evidence. In the past, lawyers relied on their own intuition or insight into human nature to guide the selection of the jury. This conventional wisdom involves beliefs such as if the defendant is a woman, it is best to favor men on the jury because they will follow their protective instinct and favor the woman. Female jurors should be selected if the defendant is a good-looking young man. Women are viewed as harder on other women, and ethnic groups differ in terms of their receptivity to emotional as opposed to intellectual appeals (Abramson 2000: 146–147).

One of the first cases in which lawyers used "scientific" or "systematic" jury selection was the 1972 conspiracy trial of Catholic priests Philip and Daniel Berrigan and five other individuals charged with conspiracy to engage in unlawful acts of protest against the Vietnam War. A team of social scientists conducted telephone surveys and interviews with residents of Harrisburg, Pennsylvania, the site of the trial. They discovered that, contrary to their expectations, college graduates in the area were conservative and were likely to favor conviction. As a result, the defense attorneys concentrated on eliminating college graduates from the jury pool through challenges for cause or through preemptory challenges. The defendants were acquitted, and the successful reliance on social science research in selecting the jurors led to the employment of the same strategy in the trial of other activists during the 1970s. In 1985, the use of scientific jury selection techniques is credited with the acquittal of businessman John Z. DeLorean, who was charged with selling cocaine to fund his auto company (Abramson 2000: 148–149).

Expert consultants on jury selection typically employ scientific surveys of the local community to determine the demographic profile of individuals who are likely to be sympathetic and unsympathetic to their client (Abramson 2000: 147).

Jury consultants have become a growth industry: the number of jury consultants increased from 25 in 1982 to 250 in 1995. The firm Litigation Sciences, Inc., reported gross revenues of $25 million in 1984, and the industry as a whole generated over $200 million in revenues (Abramson 2000: 147, 149).

Consultants have moved beyond surveys to body language and handwriting analysis and even have investigated the lifestyle and background of potential jurors. Consultants also coach lawyers during the jury selection process and suggest questions. A second area of consulting is the use of mock juries to test the persuasiveness of arguments prior to the actual trial. Consultants also have placed "shadow jurors" in the courtroom. The background of these individuals matches the profile of jurors hearing the case, and consultants rely on these "shadow jurors" to evaluate the effectiveness of the lawyer's arguments during the trial (Abramson 2000: 150–153).

Adam Benforado writes that consultants now are being used to shape the attitudes of potential jurors rather than used exclusively to select favorable jurors. Jurors in an experiment who were asked two questions as to whether they could be fair if they learned that the defendant was a gang member were more likely to convict than jurors who heard the same evidence but were not asked these questions (Benforado 2015: 255).

Studies indicate that scientific jury selection largely has been unsuccessful in predicting the behavior of specific jurors. There are simply too many variables in a trial to predict a juror's reaction to the testimony in the courtroom or to predict jurors' reaction to a victim or to a defendant or how they will be affected by the jury deliberations (Abramson 2000: 147; Kassin and Wrightsman 1988: 60–62). Dennis Devine concludes that scientific jury analysis results in a "modest improvement" in the selection of favorable jurors over the performance of attorneys who did not rely on jury consultants although Devine recognizes that this small difference might be "decisive in some cases" (Devine 2012: 55). Defense attorneys nonetheless understandably want to present the strongest possible case at trial and are attracted to the use of jury consultants. Should courts prohibit prosecution and defense lawyers from gaining a possible advantage at trial by relying on jury consultants? We next sketch the research on jury decision-making in death penalty cases.

■ THE JURY AND THE DEATH PENALTY

In 1972, in *Furman v. Georgia*, the U.S. Supreme Court held that the death penalty violated the prohibition against cruel and unusual punishment. The Court in a 5–4 decision reasoned that although the death penalty is constitutional, the lack of standards to guide the jury results in a situation in which there is "no meaningful basis for distinguishing the few cases in which [the death penalty] is imposed from the many cases in which it is not." The "wanton and freakish" application of the death penalty means that different juries might reach different decisions and that there is a risk of racial bias in the imposition of capital punishment (*Furman v. Georgia*, 408 U.S. 238 [1972]). In response to *Furman*, thirty-five states passed new death penalty statutes between 1972 and 1976.

In 1976, in *Gregg v. Georgia*, the U.S. Supreme Court held that a Georgia statute satisfied the constitutionally mandated requirements for the imposition of the death penalty. The central aspect of the Georgia approach is the separation of the guilt phase of the trial from the sentencing phase of the trial (a bifurcated trial process). Under the Georgia statute, a lawyer could argue in the guilt or innocence phase of the trial that his or her client is innocent and, if the defendant is convicted, argue in the sentencing phase that the defendant does not deserve to die.

In the sentencing stage, the jury determines whether the state has proven beyond a reasonable doubt that the killing involved one or more aggravating circumstances set forth in the statute. In the event the jury finds one or more of these aggravating circumstances, they are to balance these aggravating factors against any mitigating factors presented by the defense attorney. The jury may impose the death penalty if they find that the aggravating factors outweigh the mitigating circumstances. Decisions are to be automatically reviewed by the state supreme court to ensure that the death penalty is applied in a consistent and uniform fashion (proportionality review). This procedural process is intended to ensure that the death penalty is imposed in a uniform fashion on the "worst of the worst" offenders (*Gregg v. Georgia*, 428 U.S. 153 [1976]).

We will discuss the death penalty and deterrence and the death penalty and race later in the text. At this point, the focus is on "death qualified juries." In a 1968 decision (*Witherspoon v. Illinois*, 391 U.S.

510 [1968]) and in a second opinion in 1985 (*Wainwright v. Witt*, 469 U.S. 412 [1985]), the Court held a juror may be removed for cause in a death penalty case if his or her personal views toward the death penalty will "prevent or substantially impair the performance of his [or her] duties as juror in accordance with his [or her] instructions and his [or her] oath." A judge under this standard may exclude a juror who has reservations regarding the death penalty that may interfere with his or her performance as a juror (so-called *Witherspoon* excludables); a judge also may remove those jurors who automatically would vote for the death penalty. The Court subsequently held these jurors may be excluded both from the guilt stage and from the sentencing stage (*Lockhart v. McCree*, 476 U.S. 162 [1986]).

Neil Vidmar and Valerie Hans, in reviewing studies of death penalty cases, conclude that despite *voir dire*, a significant number of individuals who serve on capital juries are predisposed to find the defendant guilty and to recommend the death penalty. They also find jurors who believe in an "eye for an eye" and that death is the only appropriate punishment for murder are likely to vote for death on the first ballot of the penalty phase of the trial (Vidmar and Hans 2007: 250–251).

Psychologist Phoebe Ellsworth in a survey of Californians found that roughly 40 percent of individuals would be excluded from serving on a jury hearing a capital punishment case based on their professed inability to impose the death penalty. The typical juror in a death penalty case tends to be an economically advantaged Protestant or Catholic, Republican white male. These individuals, although honestly believing they are fair and impartial, are more likely to find a defendant guilty in simulated studies than are "*Witherspoon* excludables." In other words, the *Witherspoon* standard results in juries that are drawn from a narrow segment of the population who are predisposed to convict defendants (Ellsworth 1984).

Studies find that asking potential jurors during *voir dire* whether they are capable of following the law and imposing the death penalty tends to create a perception among jurors that the judge expects them to vote in favor of the death penalty. The impression that a judge disapproves of individuals who are unable to impose the death penalty is reinforced when individuals who oppose capital punishment are dismissed from the jury panel. The discussion of the death penalty during *voir dire* also has been shown to desensitize individuals to the consequences of voting for the death penalty (Haney 2005: 93–114).

Research indicates that as many as 55–60 percent of jurors have a difficult time comprehending the jury instructions in death penalty cases (Luginbuhl and Howe 1995), do not understand the basic information (D. Simon 2012: 190), and possess significant skepticism toward expert testimony at the sentencing stage of capital punishment cases (Sudby 1997).

One of the most important research findings involves what Craig Haney refers to as "moral disengagement." This is the process through which jurors deflect or avoid responsibility for the sentence of death. Jurors rationalize that their decision to sentence a defendant to death will be reviewed by an appellate court and reversed if incorrect. They also take comfort in the belief that sentences of death rarely are carried out (Haney 2005: 93–114).

In summary, Hans and Vidmar conclude that a death qualified jury is not like other juries. These juries are less diverse, are more inclined to convict defendants, and do not represent a true cross section of the community. Despite the procedural protections surrounding death penalty prosecutions, the decision whether to impose capital punishment tends to be tilted in favor of death (Hans and Vidmar 1986: 236).

As we shall see in the next section on wrongful convictions, the trial process does not always yield accurate results. A study of Texas juries concluded there was little difference in the backgrounds and post-conviction behavior of defendants who jurors found posed a "continuing threat to society" and merited the death penalty and defendants who were not viewed as posing a "continuing threat to society" and received a sentence of life in prison. The authors conclude that inaccurate decision-making had resulted in a number of individuals being sentenced to death who deserved life imprisonment (Marquart, Ekland-Olson, and Sorensen 1989). In some instances, as we shall see in the next section, what appear to be innocent individuals have been convicted and sentenced to death.

8.2 YOU DECIDE

In a controversial Texas case, Cameron Todd Willingham, age 23, was convicted of the arson murder of his three young daughters in Corsicana, Texas, on December 2, 1991. Arson investigators testified that Willingham spread accelerant on the floor of the house and ignited a fire with the intent of killing his young daughters. John H. Jackson, the assistant prosecutor who was assigned to prosecute the case, told the newspapers that Willingham's motive was to rid himself of his young children because they interfered with his "beer drinking and dart throwing." In the past, Willingham had experienced minor scrapes with the law and had been known to drink and to abuse his wife, Stacie. It later was alleged that Willingham had killed the children to conceal Stacie's abuse of the children (Grann 2009).

The prosecutor, Jackson, wanted to avoid a trial and offered life imprisonment in return for a guilty plea to murder. One of Willingham's two assigned attorneys was a former state trooper and the other a local general practitioner. Willingham refused to listen to his lawyers' advice and insisted on his innocence and turned down the plea bargain. Murder charges were filed in January 1992, and the case proceeded to trial.

At trial in August 1992, the prosecutor primarily relied on the testimony of the two arson investigators. Johnny Webb, a jailhouse informant awaiting trial for robbery, testified Willingham had confessed to him in prison. The informant, who later was diagnosed with bipolar personality disorder, later recanted his testimony and then turned around and affirmed his original testimony. The informant subsequently was sentenced to fifteen years in prison and five years later was released

based on the recommendation of the prosecutor in the Willingham case. Other witnesses modified their earlier statements to the police. One witness initially told the police Willingham was devastated and had to be restrained from risking his life by reentering the burning house to save his daughters. The same witness later testified Willingham's emotional reaction appeared inauthentic and that he had a gut feeling Willingham "had something to do with the setting of the fire." Willingham's lawyers presented a single defense witness, a babysitter who could not believe Willingham would kill his children.

Jackson, in his argument to the jury, read from a Bible that had been in Willingham's home. He concluded his closing argument by reciting a passage spoken by Jesus that whoever harmed one of his children is to be cast in the seas with a millstone around his neck.

Following Willingham's conviction, the prosecutor in the sentencing phase of the trial highlighted Willingham's tattoo of a skull encircled by a serpent, which together with other evidence allegedly fit the profile of a sociopath. The prosecutor presented two psychological expert witnesses. Tim Gregory, a family counselor, analyzed the posters of rock groups such as Iron Maiden and Led Zeppelin that had hung on Willingham's wall and suggested they were indicative of an interest in violence and Satanism and cult activities. The primary psychological expert, Dr. James Grigson, a forensic psychiatrist, had testified so frequently for the prosecution in Texas capital punishment cases that he commonly was referred to as "Dr. Death." Grigson concluded Willingham was an "extremely severe sociopath" who was beyond treatment. He previously had been expelled from the American Psychiatric

Association for unethical conduct in testifying regarding the psychological state of defendants whom he had not personally examined and for having claimed he could predict dangerousness with 100 percent accuracy.

Willingham was sentenced to death. An independent examination of the forensic evidence by Dr. Gerald Hurst, a leading world expert on explosives and fires, concluded the forensic report was flawed on all of the twenty indicators that allegedly supported the conclusion that Willingham was guilty of arson. Four days before Willingham's execution, the Texas Board of Pardons and Paroles rejected a plea for clemency based on Hurst's report, and Texas governor Rick Perry refused to stay the execution. On February 17, 2004, Willingham was executed by lethal injection. He insisted, "I am an innocent man convicted of a crime I did not commit. I have been persecuted for twelve years for something I did not do."

In 2005, a report by outside experts submitted to a Texas commission established to investigate allegations of error and misconduct by forensic scientists concluded the arson investigation in the case of Todd Willingham was flawed. Governor Perry continued to insist that Willingham was a "monster," and allegedly pressured the head of the commission to decide against pursuing the investigation of the Willingham case. Governor Perry subsequently removed the head of the commission and two other members of the commission in a step critics alleged was intended to prevent the continuing investigation of Willingham's conviction. The *Chicago Tribune* reported in August 2009 that nine of the country's top fire analysts concluded the investigation of the Willingham fire had been based on outmoded theories and folklore.

In 2014, the lead prosecutor, John H. Jackson, was accused of misconduct by the State Bar of Texas based on evidence that he struck a deal with his chief witness, inmate Johnny Webb. Jackson in exchange for Webb's false testimony against Willingham intervened to help Webb, reduced his aggravated robbery conviction, requested an early parole hearing, and arranged for him to serve the remainder of his sentence in the county jail rather than in prison. Jackson denied the allegations, and he was acquitted of misconduct in a jury trial in 2017.

Consider how some of the points discussed in this chapter contributed to what may have been the wrongful conviction of Todd Willingham.

■ SENTENCING

A defendant who is convicted confronts the reality of criminal punishment. There are various reasons why we punish offenders. Sentences typically are intended to achieve several of these sentencing goals (see Table 8.1).

Table 8.1 ■ The Goals of Sentencing	
Retribution	An individual is punished in proportion to the harm caused by his or her criminal act. Punishment is the "just deserts" for an individual's criminal conduct.
Deterrence	Punishment is intended to discourage other individuals from committing crime. Specific deterrence is punishment intended to deter the offender from repeating his or her criminal act (recidivism), whereas general deterrence is intended to deter other individuals from engaging in criminal conduct.
Incapacitation	Punishment is intended to remove an individual from society in the interest of safety and security.
Rehabilitation	Punishment is intended to transform individuals spiritually and psychologically to turn them into productive members of society.
Restoration	Restorative justice requires the offender to compensate the victim for the harm that was inflicted.

These goals are achieved through various sentencing schemes. Sentencing primarily is the responsibility of the judge, although six states provide that sentencing is the responsibility of the jury. The U.S. Supreme Court in recent years has expanded the role of juries in sentencing. In 2000, in *Apprendi v. New Jersey*, the Court held that any fact that increases a sentence beyond the statutory maximum, such as for possession of a weapon, must be submitted to the jury and proven beyond a reasonable doubt. A failure to submit a question to the jury that enhances a defendant's sentence, such as whether a defendant acted with "deliberate cruelty," is a violation of the Sixth Amendment right to a trial by jury (*Apprendi v. New Jersey*, 530 U.S. 466 [2000]; *Blakely v. Washington*, 542 U.S. 296 [2004]). States typically employ a combination of sentencing schemes.

The general approach to sentencing has been to vest the decision in the judge who exercised his or her discretion in setting the sentencing. In the past few decades, the trend has been for state legislatures to limit the sentencing discretion of judges and to fix the term of sentences. The goal is to limit the disparity or difference between the sentences handed down to various offenders for the same crime.

We should note that the federal government and most states also provide for assets forfeiture or seizure pursuant to a court order of the "fruits" of illegal narcotics transactions (along with certain other crimes) or of the "instrumentalities" that were used in such activity. The following are the primary sentencing schemes that are used by state criminal justice systems. As a rule, states use various approaches to sentencing.

Indeterminate sentence. The legislature specifies a minimum and maximum sentence for an offense. The judge imposes a minimum and maximum sentence, and the parole board reviews the offender's sentence and determines the actual time that the offender serves in prison. In some jurisdictions, the legislature fixes the minimum sentence, and the judge sets the maximum to be served.

Determinate sentences. The judge establishes the actual time to be served by the offender within the range established by the legislature (minus any good-time credits earned by the offender). The offender may receive a shorter or longer sentence, but this must be justified by the judge. A variant of this sentence is the "three strikes" laws that require individuals to be sentenced to lengthy terms following their third felony conviction.

Mandatory minimum sentences. The legislature requires judges to sentence an offender to a minimum sentence, regardless of mitigating factors. Prison sentences in some jurisdictions may be reduced by good-time credits earned by the individual while incarcerated.

Presumptive sentencing guidelines. A legislatively established commission provides a sentencing formula based on various factors, stressing the nature of the crime and the offender's criminal history. Judges may be strictly limited in terms of discretion or may be provided with flexibility within established limits. The judge must justify departures from the presumptive sentence on the basis of various aggravating and mitigating factors that are listed in the guidelines. A prosecutor may file a motion for a downward departure for a defendant who provides substantial assistance to the prosecutor. Appeals are provided in order to maintain "reasonable sentencing practices" in those instances in which a judge departs from the presumptive sentence in the guidelines.

Types of Sentences

Sentences for misdemeanors typically are announced immediately following the trial. In the case of felonies, probation officers usually prepare a presentence report that provides the judge with background on the defendant and the various options for sentences. Both the prosecutor and the defense attorney are provided the opportunity to present their views of the appropriate sentence during the sentencing hearing. There are factors outside of the legal process that at times can impact a judge's sentencing decision. Public opinion, political pressure, and media attention can influence a judge to impose a stringent sentence on high-profile personalities. There often is the added pressure to harshly penalize a well-known defendant to assure the public that the legal system "does not play favorites." Virtually every state and the federal system provide for some form of "victim impact" statement that provides victims with the opportunity to balance the focus on the offender at sentencing with a focus on the harm and suffering of the victim.

Most states and the federal system provide for appeals from the sentences. Forty states have "truth in sentencing," which provides that offenders are to serve at least 85 percent of their sentence. Various types of sentences are available to judges; see Table 8.2.

Table 8.2 ■ Types of Sentences	
Fines	State statutes usually provide for fines as an alternative to incarceration or in addition to incarceration.
Probation	Probation involves the suspension of a prison sentence so long as an individual continues to report to a probation officer and adhere to certain required standards of personal conduct. This may entail psychiatric treatment or a program of counseling for alcohol or drug abuse. The conditions of probation are required to be reasonably related to the rehabilitation of the offender and the protection of the public.
Intermediate sanctions	This includes house arrest with electronic monitoring, short-term "shock" incarceration, community service, boot camps, and restitution. Intermediate sanctions may be imposed as a criminal sentence or a condition of probation or following imprisonment or in combination with a fine.
Imprisonment	Individuals sentenced to a year or less generally are sentenced to local jails. Sentences for longer periods are typically served in state or federal prisons.
Death	Thirty-two states and the federal government provide for the death penalty for homicide. The other states provide for life without parole.

Factors in Sentencing

Hundreds of studies have analyzed the factors that influence judges' sentencing decisions. A judge must first decide whether to imprison a defendant or whether to use another type of sanction. The next question is the length of the sentence. The most important factors in sentencing are listed below.

Seriousness of offense and defendant's prior record. Studies indicate that the principal basis for sentences is the seriousness of the offense and the defendant's criminal history. Offenders who commit more serious crimes receive longer sentences and are more likely to be incarcerated than individuals who commit less serious offenses. There are a number of approaches to determining the seriousness of an offense. This may entail whether the offense is categorized as a serious felony or minor misdemeanor, the type of injury to the victim, the value of the property that is stolen or damaged, whether the defendant used a weapon, and society's view of the threat posed by the offense. The other primary determinant of the severity of a sentence is the defendant's prior criminal record. The National Academy of Sciences Panel on Sentencing Research in 1983 confirmed the seriousness of the offense and the defendant's prior record are the "key determinants of sentences" (Blumstein et al. 1983: 83).

Offender characteristics. Judges consider a defendant's personal stability in formulating a sentence. A defendant with a strong social support network may be viewed as less likely to continue to engage in criminal activity in the future and to be more likely to rehabilitate him- or herself. The unemployed, uneducated, young, and poor are viewed as more likely to continue to engage in criminal activity, and studies indicate that they receive longer sentences and are more likely to be incarcerated. Judges are reluctant to imprison individuals who have a job and support a family because their incarceration will affect an entire family unit (Spohn 2009: 92–94).

Victims. Several studies of the death penalty and sexual assault suggest defendants who kill Caucasians are more likely to receive a death sentence than defendants who kill African American victims. The killing of white female victims when accompanied by sexual abuse is the offense most likely to result in the death penalty (M. Williams, Demuth, and Holcomb 2007).

Impact. In 1971, in *Payne v. Tennessee*, the U.S. Supreme Court held that immediate family members may give statements describing the effect of the death of the deceased on their lives (*Payne v. Tennessee*, 501 U.S. 808 [1991]).

Procedural factors. There is some evidence defendants who plead guilty receive more lenient sentences than defendants who stand trial. Defendants who are not released on bail prior to trial are disadvantaged in preparing for trial and generally receive longer sentences than defendants who are released on bail (Spohn 2009: 97–104).

What of the gender or race of the judge? In reviewing the literature on judges and sentencing, Cassia Spohn finds the "differences between male and female judges and between black or Hispanic judges and white judges are not large. . . . All judges based their sentencing decisions primarily on the seriousness of the crime and the offender's prior criminal record" (Spohn 2009: 122). In the area of civil law, there is evidence that female judges are more sympathetic than male judges to female plaintiffs in sex discrimination cases and are able to influence the votes of male judges when serving on a multi-judge panel (Boyd, Epstein, and Martin 2010). There is evidence that the number of African American and Hispanic attorneys per capita in a jurisdiction moderates racial disparities in sentencing (R. King, Johnson, and McGeever 2010).

In recent years, various efforts have been made to reform the sentencing process.

Sentencing Reform and "Three Strikes" Laws

In 1980, Minnesota adopted sentencing guidelines in an effort to provide for uniform, proportionate, and predictable sentences. Currently, more than a dozen states employ guidelines.

In 1984, the U.S. Congress passed the Sentencing Reform Act. The law went into effect in 1987 and established the U.S. Sentencing Commission, which drafted binding guidelines to be followed by federal judges in sentencing offenders. Sentences under the federal guidelines are based on a complicated formula that reflects the seriousness and characteristics of the offense and the criminal history of the offender. The judge employs a sentencing grid and is required to fix a sentence within the narrow range where the offender's criminal offense and criminal history intersect on the grid. A series of Supreme Court cases beginning with *United States v. Booker* have established that the guidelines are advisory and do not bind federal judges in sentencing (*United States v. Booker*, 543 U.S. 220 [2005]).

The guidelines were part of a movement to limit the discretion of judges in sentencing. Mandatory minimum sentences are another sentencing reform that requires judges to sentence offenders to fixed sentences. Mandatory minimums were first introduced in Maine in 1976 and then adopted by California, Illinois, and Indiana in 1977.

States also have introduced sentence "enhancers." Sentences are enhanced for individuals who used a weapon or acted on behalf of a gang as well as other factors. The Michigan Felony Firearm Statute of 1977 requires a two-year sentence enhancement for the use of a firearm in the course of committing a felony.

Between 1993 and 1995, twenty-four states and the federal government passed a "three strikes" law in which offenders were required to be sentenced to lengthy prison terms when convicted of a third felony. The thinking was that this uniform sentencing policy would reduce disparities or differences in the sentencing of offenders. There also was a sense that parole boards were releasing individuals back on the street who had not served a significant portion of their sentence. As previously noted, "truth in sentencing" laws in over forty states require offenders to serve at least 85 percent of their sentence.

Sentencing reform and a move toward fixed-term sentences reflected disillusionment with rehabilitation. State officials concluded that this goal had proven unsuccessful and the focus should be on swift and certain retributive punishment and on deterrence. In the past few years, as states have confronted budget deficits, the pendulum has begun to swing toward alternatives to the policy of mass incarceration of offenders.

California is an example of a trend toward reconsideration of harsh sentencing policies. California's "three strikes" law adopted in 1994 signaled a shift in states' sentencing policies toward incapacitating and deterring repeat offenders who threaten the public safety. The law was designed to provide longer prison sentences for individuals who have committed multiple felonies. The measure was sparked by the kidnapping and murder of 12-year-old Polly Klaas. Her killer, Richard Allen Davis, had a lengthy prison record including two prior convictions for kidnapping. He had served half of his most recent sentence before being released. If Davis had served his entire sentence, he would have been incarcerated at the time of the kidnapping and murder of Klaas. The "three strikes" law was passed by the California legislature and signed by Governor Pete Wilson in March 1994. California voters subsequently expressed support for the measure in November 1994 by a margin of 72 percent to 28 percent.

The California law originally required that the first two felonies must be designated as "strikable" felonies while the third strike may be any felony. Defendants received sentences of between twenty-five years and life in cases in which the third strike included stealing a slice of pizza, stealing cookies from a restaurant, and stealing meat from a grocery store. The law also provided for enhanced penalties for two-time offenders (Spohn 2009: 265).

In 2003, the U.S. Supreme Court in *Ewing v. California* affirmed Ewing's sentence of twenty-five years to life under the California "three strikes" law for stealing three golf clubs (each valued at $399) while on parole for convictions of three counts of residential burglary and one count of robbery. Ewing was no stranger to the criminal justice system, having served nine separate prison terms. The U.S. Supreme Court found that Ewing had not been deterred by his past criminal punishment and that his lengthy sentence was justified based on California's "public-safety interest in incapacitating and deterring recidivist felons" and "amply supported by his own long, serious criminal record." The Court clarified that this was not cruel and unusual punishment because it was not "grossly disproportionate" to Ewing's criminal acts (*Ewing v. California*, 538 U.S. 11 [2003]).

Studies indicate that prosecutors and judges avoided the harshest aspect of the law by offering plea bargains and by limiting the third-strike cases to serious criminal conduct (Engen 2008).

The prediction was that the law would result in one hundred thousand inmates being added to the California prison system, although by the end of 2004 fewer than forty-three thousand inmates were serving time for a second or third strike. This nonetheless was a significant increase in the number of long-term inmates to be added to California's overcrowded prison population (Spohn 2009: 265–266).

In 2012, California voters by an overwhelming margin voted to require that the third strike is a violent or serious felony. It is estimated the change in the "three strikes" law will allow 2,800 individuals to petition for release from prison and save the state of California $100 million. California voters by a narrow 6 percent margin also voted to maintain the state's death penalty. In 2014, California voters further limited the scope of the state's "three strikes" law by converting various nonviolent felonies to misdemeanors, which allowed roughly thirteen thousand individuals sentenced under the "three strikes" law to be released from prison (Tonry 2016: 17–18). In the state of Washington, which has limited its "three strikes" laws to violent criminals, the law has resulted in the long-term incarceration of a small number of dangerous offenders (James Austin and Irwin 2001: 191–195).

In the last twenty-five years, there has been an expansion of federal mandatory minimum sentences for crimes ranging from child pornography to identity theft. According to the U.S. Sentencing Commission, there are more than 190 federal offenses carrying a mandatory minimum sentence and an estimated 40 percent of all federal inmates are incarcerated under mandatory minimum sentences, three-quarters for narcotics offenses and roughly 12 percent for firearms offenses. The number of federal prisoners interned under a mandatory minimum sentence increased from 29,603 in 1995 to 75,579 in 2010. Virtually every state has followed the example of the federal government and provided for a significant number of mandatory minimum sentences. Most apply to drug offenses, aggravated rape, committing a crime with a deadly weapon, and drunk driving (U.S. Sentencing Commission 2012).

A study of mandatory minimum sentences for drug offenders under federal law found that one-third of the individuals incarcerated for drug offenses did not have a record of violence or prior criminal convictions and yet were serving an average of 81.5 months in prison. These individuals could be "effectively sentenced to shorter periods of time at an annual savings of several hundred million dollars" (Vincent and Hofer 1994: 1).

Two other sentencing innovations that increased the terms of imprisonment were "truth in sentencing" laws requiring that individuals serve at least 85 percent of their sentence, which states introduced as a condition of receiving federal funds, and the increased use of life without parole (LWOP) sentences for homicide (Tonry 2016: 77–91).

Drug crimes are explored in greater depth in the chapter on race and the law (Chapter 11). (For judicial corruption in the sentencing of juveniles in Pennsylvania, see You Decide 8.4 on the study site.)

■ WRONGFUL CONVICTIONS

Lawyers and judges are haunted by the prospect that an innocent person will be executed. In England in 1660, William Harrison vanished from sight. Harrison's servant was suspected of the crime and swore that his mother and brother had killed Harrison. All three were executed, and two years later, Harrison appeared and alleged that he had been kidnapped by a criminal gang. There are at least two recent executions of inmates that many observers believe may have involved the killing of an innocent man, Ruben Cantu in Texas in 1994 and Larry Griffin in Missouri in 1995.

There is no way of knowing how many innocent individuals are convicted and imprisoned each year as a result of what Brian Forst describes as an "error of justice" (Forst 2004: 3–4).

In 2015, the National Registry of Exonerations, a joint project of the University of Michigan and Northwestern University, reported the number of exonerations of individuals wrongfully convicted increased to a record 149 individuals in twenty-five states, the District of Columbia, and Guam, a record 65 of whom had pled guilty. Nearly 40 percent of exonerees had been convicted of homicide, five of whom were sentenced to death, and roughly 30 percent had been convicted for drug crimes. These individuals served an average of more than fourteen years in prison. A record 27 exonerations were based on false confessions, 65 involved official misconduct by criminal justice officials, and a record 65 exonerations were cases in which no crime actually was committed (e.g., a false claim of arson). The report notes that since 1989, there have been 1,735 exonerations, most following convictions for murder, rape, or other sexual assaults, and since 2011, the number of exonerations has more than doubled. Seventeen percent of the exonerations in the registry were based in whole or in part on DNA evidence.

Between 1973 and the beginning of 2006, 123 inmates in twenty-five states were removed from death row because of sufficient evidence to exonerate them or because of evidence that raised serious doubts about their guilt. In 2003, Illinois governor George Ryan commuted the death sentence of 167 individuals on death row, explaining that a significant number of innocent individuals had been sentenced to death in Illinois and there was a significant risk that an innocent individual would be executed. Thirteen individuals on death row in Illinois subsequently were exonerated (Vidmar and Hans 2007: 226).

There is a general consensus that since 1976, between 0.5 percent and 1.3 percent of individuals sentenced to death are innocent (Scheck, Neufeld, and Dwyer 2000). Samuel R. Gross, Barbara O'Brien, and their colleagues in a study published in the *Proceedings of the National Academy of Sciences* find 4.1 percent of individuals sentenced to death are innocent. A conservative estimate is that between 0.5 percent and 1.0 percent of criminal cases per year involve false convictions. Marvin Zalman and his colleagues note that this would mean that five thousand innocent individuals are convicted and two thousand individuals are wrongfully incarcerated each year (Zalman, Smith, and Kiger 2008).

The Innocence Project at Cardozo School of Law in New York has pioneered the use of DNA to establish the innocence of incarcerated individuals and has been involved in advocacy on behalf of more than 350 individuals who have been exonerated through DNA evidence since 1989. The Cardozo Innocence Project finds that misidentifications by eyewitnesses to a crime are the leading cause of false convictions. Other causes of wrongful convictions include inaccurate forensic evidence, false confessions, erroneous information from informants, and false reports from jailhouse snitches (Scheck et al. 2000). A study of false confessions conducted by Northwestern University Law School concludes that false confessions are "amazingly common" (Warden and Drizin 2009: vii).

Samuel Gross and a team of researchers found that 340 defendants (327 men, 13 women) were falsely convicted between 1989 and 2003 and ultimately were exonerated. **Exoneration** means that there was a formal acknowledgment the defendant is innocent. Ninety-five percent of these individuals served at least ten years in prison, and 80 percent served at least twenty-five years in prison. An exoneration may result from a pardon from the governor of the state (42 cases), a dismissal of the charges by a court when presented with evidence of innocence (263 cases), or an acquittal on retrial (31 cases). Four individuals, following their death, were acknowledged by the prosecutor in their case to be innocent. Most of those exonerated were convicted of murder (205 cases), rape (121 cases), and other crimes of violence (11 cases). Drug and property crimes accounted for a small number of charges (3 cases). Only 20 of these convictions resulted from guilty pleas (Gross et al. 2005: 524, 529).

Examining the convictions for rape, 107 of the 121 exonerations for rape involved eyewitness misidentification. In 105 of these cases, the defendant was cleared by DNA. African Americans comprise 29 percent of individuals convicted of rape and 64 percent of the individuals convicted of rape who were exonerated. In 78 percent of the rape cases in which an African American was exonerated for rape, the victim was white. Gross and his colleagues explain that these false convictions likely are due to the notoriously inaccurate results of cross-racial witness identifications (Gross et al. 2005: 318–320). They conclude a "plausible guess" is that the "total number of miscarriages of justice" in the United States "must be in the thousands, perhaps tens of thousands" (151).

Brandon L. Garrett's study of 250 individuals exonerated between 1974 and 2008 finds that the main causes were false confessions (16 percent), faulty eyewitness identification (76 percent), inaccurate forensic evidence (61 percent of analysts), and false testimony by informants (21 percent). Exonerated individuals spent an average of thirteen years in prison (Garrett 2011: 1–13).

In these cases, the defendants' DNA from the crime scene was preserved, which enabled the defendants to petition a court to order DNA testing. In those cases in which there is no match between the defendant's DNA and the DNA preserved from the crime scene, a judge, before releasing the defendant from custody, must be persuaded there is no scenario that might explain the absence of the defendant's DNA from the crime scene and that the defendant therefore is innocent. Individuals also may be pardoned by the governor of the state.

Garrett reports that only 16 of the 250 individuals in his study pled guilty and did not go to trial. This is very different than most criminal defendants who enter into plea bargains. Garrett speculates the small number of guilty pleas among the exonerated in his study is due to the defendants' desire to establish their innocence and refusal to falsely admit their guilt. Prosecutors also may have refused to offer attractive bargains because of the seriousness of the defendants' crimes (Garrett 2011: 150–151).

What accounts for the fact that most innocent individuals in Garrett's study were convicted at a criminal trial rather than following a guilty plea? Why was an innocent defendant convicted following a trial with all the associated due process protections? There is no single explanation. These trials all had some aspect that tilted the judge or jury toward returning a guilty verdict. The prosecution in each instance presented a strong evidentiary case based on police testimony, confessions, victim testimony, eyewitnesses, and forensic testimony. The defendants typically relied on court-appointed lawyers, public defenders, or "bargain basement lawyers," most of whom did not have the time or resources to investigate the crime, hire experts, or effectively cross-examine the prosecution's experts or other witnesses (Garrett 2011: 145–177).

Defense lawyers representing 68 percent of the exonerees relied on the relatively inexpensive and uncomplicated "alibi defense," which jurors tend to dismiss as a defense offered by most guilty defendants.

The explanations for a false finding of guilt include prosecutorial or police misconduct, inaccurate forensic evidence, inflammatory closing arguments by prosecutors, jury and judicial bias, ineffective defense lawyers, and the exclusion of minorities from juries. Garrett concludes that the primary cause of false convictions is the vast difference in the resources between the prosecutor and the defense, which tilts the playing field in favor of the prosecution. This imbalance of resources is especially important because of the difficulty of persuading the judge or jury that the prosecution failed to establish the defendant's guilt beyond a reasonable doubt.

Garrett points to the case of Dennis Fritz, who relied on a court-appointed bankruptcy and personal injury lawyer to defend him in a murder trial. Fritz took the stand and claimed he was innocent. The prosecution, in contrast, presented more than twenty witnesses, including a jailhouse informant and fourteen forensic experts. Fritz was sentenced to death, later was exonerated, and remarked that he felt like a lamb being led to the slaughter.

An important development is the creation of a **Conviction Integrity Unit** (CIU) in over twenty prosecutors' offices. These units prevent, identify, and correct false convictions and are credited with over one hundred exonerations in 2014 and 2015.

In the next section, we introduce the newly established International Criminal Court, which is an important component of the international legal system. We will be referencing the court throughout the text.

8.3 YOU DECIDE

On June 18, 2006, Jennifer Thompson wrote an article in the *New York Times* recounting her devastating ordeal in 1984 when a male assailant broke into her locked apartment while she was asleep and raped her. Jennifer had the presence of mind to maneuver her attacker into the dimly lighted area of her otherwise dark apartment in order to observe his distinguishing features.

Jennifer later provided the police with a detailed description of her attacker. A few days later, Jennifer,

who is Caucasian, identified her African American attacker from a number of photographs and subsequently identified him in a lineup. She explained that her memory was relatively fresh and that Ronald Cotton looked exactly like the man who raped her and matched her assailant's height and weight. It turned out that Ronald Cotton's alibi was fabricated and that his family's explanation that he was asleep on the couch on the evening of the rape was contradicted by testimony that he was seen riding his bike late at night. The police subsequently seized a flashlight under Cotton's bed that

(Continued)

(Continued)

was similar to a flashlight allegedly used by the assailant, and the rubber on Cotton's shoes was consistent with the rubber found at the crime scene.

In 1986, Jennifer took the stand and identified Cotton as her rapist, and he was convicted and sentenced to life imprisonment. Cotton's conviction was overturned on appeal. At his subsequent retrial, a second woman who had been raped the same evening as Jennifer identified Cotton as her rapist and explained that she had been too scared to have identified him at the time of his original trial. Cotton once again was convicted and sentenced to two life terms in prison.

In 1995, DNA evidence indicated that the man responsible for raping both women was Bobby Poole, an inmate who had bragged for a decade that he was responsible for the attacks. Ronald Cotton subsequently was pardoned by the governor of North Carolina. Jennifer to this day recounts that when she relives her rape her rapist is Cotton.

The primary explanation for false convictions for rape is inaccurate eyewitness identifications. In 2014, the National Research Council of the National Academies, an organization of distinguished scholars, in its study *Identifying the Culprit: Assessing Eyewitness Identification*, concluded that faulty witness identifications are present in almost three-quarters of DNA exonerations. Cross-racial identifications are particularly inaccurate.

Identifications typically are conducted in three ways:

Photo arrays. An eyewitness or victim is asked to identify the suspect from a catalogue of photos.

Lineups. An eyewitness or victim is asked to identify a suspect from a lineup that typically includes five other "fillers" or individuals who are not suspects.

Showup. An eyewitness or victim is presented with a single suspect and asked whether the individual is the perpetrator.

These procedures at times are used in conjunction with one another. The eyewitness or victim at trials typically is asked to identify whether the individual at the defense table is the perpetrator and whether this is the same individual the witness identified. It is conventional wisdom among criminal lawyers that there is little that is more convincing to a jury than a witness who takes the stand and identifies an individual as the perpetrator of the crime.

How common are the type of misidentifications that occurred in the Ronald Cotton case? There have been more than 450 lineup studies and thousands of studies on facial recognition. Dan Simon in summarizing these studies writes that when a guilty individual is in a lineup, one in every three individuals selected is in fact innocent (D. Simon 2012: 51, 54).

There is a strong impulse for witnesses to want to identify someone in the lineup as the perpetrator. Witnesses who select a suspect in a lineup when shown an identical lineup without the perpetrator they originally identified simply select someone else (Benforado 2015: 112–113).

Eighteen states have reformed their identification procedures to improve accuracy in accordance with social science research. These reforms include a lineup administrator, who is unaware of the suspected perpetrator, instructing the eyewitness that the real perpetrator may or may not be in the lineup; placement in the lineup of non-suspects who match the witness's description of the suspect; and asking eyewitnesses about their confidence in their identification. Another reform in improving accuracy is to view suspects one at a time rather than as a group.

Why is there such a high incidence of misidentifications? How could these identifications be made more accurate? Should the jury receive instructions on the inaccuracy of eyewitness identification?

INTERNATIONAL PERSPECTIVE: THE INTERNATIONAL CRIMINAL COURT

In 1998, the **Rome Statute** creating the International Criminal Court (ICC) was opened for signature. The statute came into operation when sixty countries signed the treaty and their legislatures incorporated the statute into their domestic law.

This was the culmination of a 150-year effort to create an international court. The structure of the Rome Statute is a balance between two theoretical perspectives.

1. *Realism.* Realists believe that nations are selfish and protect their self-interest. The world is based on political power and military might rather than the rule of law. Countries will refuse to assist the new court when their self-interest is threatened. The court will become an instrument that serves the need of powerful states rather than an instrument to achieve global justice.

2. *Social constructiveness.* There is a new global vision of a world based on the rule of law, and the ICC fills the need for an institution that will help realize the dream of social justice based on the rule of law.

The notion that there are limitations on the right of countries to wage war in the western world was first articulated by the theologian Saint Augustine in the fifth century BCE. Saint Augustine developed the theory of a "just war" and argued that war is justified if all other avenues of redress have been exhausted and if the war is intended to prevent a greater harm. The idea that there should be a limitation on the resort to armed force by nation-states, limitations on the types of weapons that are utilized, and restrictions on the targeting of civilians and civilian objects was a prominent theme of political philosophers in the seventeenth and eighteenth centuries.

The first modern military code was drafted in 1863 by Columbia University law professor Francis Lieber at the request of President Abraham Lincoln. The "Lieber Code" codified the customs and practices that were recognized by nation-states as limiting the employment of armed force during warfare. A parallel development was the establishment of the International Committee for Relief to the Wounded (1876), later renamed the International Committee of the Red Cross. The committee, as one of its main tasks, worked for international conventions to regulate warfare. The Red Cross called for the creation of an international court to enforce what the organization called the "humanitarian law of war." The first major international effort to regulate the conduct of war was the drafting of the Hague Conventions of 1899 and 1907, which regulated land and naval warfare.

The mass casualties of World War I led the Allied powers to insist that Germany turn over alleged war criminals for prosecution before an international tribunal. A similar tribunal was contemplated to prosecute government officials responsible for alleged Turkish atrocities against the Armenians. In the end, these tribunals were never formed, and a small number of Germans were brought to trial before German domestic courts rather than before international courts. This nonetheless was a significant step. In the past, states accused of violating the customary practices regulating warfare paid compensation to the aggrieved state. There was no notion that government officials and military leaders might be held liable before international courts. States traditionally had been viewed as sovereign entities, and a state should not be judged by the court of another state or by an international court.

The events of World War II led to the formation of the International Military Tribunal (IMT) at Nuremberg (1945–1946). The IMT was created by the Nuremberg Charter signed by the United States, Great Britain, France, and Russia. The tribunal convened in 1946 and convicted nineteen high-level Nazi war criminals of crimes against peace (waging an aggressive war), war crimes (crimes against combatants), and crimes against humanity (crimes against civilians). The Nuremberg judgment stands as one of the most significant legal developments of the twentieth century. The decision established that the dictates of international law take precedence over the demands of domestic law. In other words, the laws of a country are subordinate to the demands of international law. The international community will hold individuals liable for the commission of international crimes regardless of whether they are high-ranking government officials or high-ranking members of the military, and the fact an individual may have acted pursuant to superior orders does not constitute a defense. Following Nuremberg, the IMT at Tokyo convicted a number of high-ranking Japanese leaders for waging aggressive wars and for war crimes.

The four Allied powers, who defeated and occupied the Third Reich, drafted a joint document, Control Council Law No. 10, providing uniform procedures for prosecuting Nazi officials who were in charge of law, medicine, diplomacy, economic development, and the administration of concentration camps and of the occupied territories of Europe. Trials of lower-level Nazi and Japanese officials were conducted in countries that had been occupied by Germany and by Japan during the war.

The trend toward the international criminal liability of individuals was continued with the formation of the United Nations (UN) in 1948. The UN agreed to various international treaties that provided for international criminal liability. The areas covered by these treaties ranged from genocide to torture and war crimes. An important development was the Geneva Conventions of 1949, which required signatory states to prosecute grave breaches of the law of war. The Geneva Conventions subsequently were updated in 1977 and made applicable to non-international (internal) conflicts.

The foundation for an international court was laid when the UN established special criminal courts to prosecute war crimes in Yugoslavia (1993) and Rwanda (1994). Special courts subsequently were created to prosecute crimes committed in Cambodia, Sierra Leone, and East Timor. The movement for an international criminal court gained momentum with the endorsement of this idea by the U.S. Congress and the American Bar Association and by the drafting of a model statute by the UN International Law Commission.

In 1993, the UN convened a Preparatory Committee (PrepCom) to develop a draft statute. This three-year effort culminated in 1998 in the Rome Statute, which in 2002 attracted the required sixty signatures and ratifications to begin to function.

The Rome Statute is directed at the "most serious crimes of concern to the international community." As with any treaty, states are required to sign the treaty and make the treaty obligations part of their domestic law. Once a nation-state ratifies the document, the ICC can assume jurisdiction over the crimes listed in the treaty that are committed on the state's territory or committed by a national of the state. There are four categories of crimes over which the tribunal has jurisdiction. These are the three Nuremberg offenses of crimes against humanity, war crimes, and crimes of aggression, and a fourth category, genocide. The drafters of the Rome Statute could not agree on a definition of a "crime of aggression," and as a result, the court is not yet authorized to exercise jurisdiction over government officials who unlawfully use armed force against other states. Realists might argue that this illustrates how the self-interest of states limits the effectiveness of the ICC.

The Rome Statute holds individuals responsible for their criminal conduct regardless of whether they are governmental leaders or military officials. The Rome Statute is modeled on the civil law system and specifically lists and defines the elements of all the crimes punishable by the ICC. The ICC as noted has jurisdiction over war crimes and crimes against humanity, including the mistreatment of prisoners of war, intentional attacks on civilians, and torture. The ICC statute also prohibits acts that only recently have been recognized as international crimes, such as environmental damage during warfare, crimes against women, the enlistment and use of child soldiers, and the practice of abducting and imprisoning civilians ("disappearances"). These offenses are punishable when they take place during wartime (war crimes), during non-international conflicts (war crimes), and during widespread and serious attacks on civilians (crimes against humanity). The ICC also has jurisdiction over genocide and aggressive war.

A distinctive feature of the ICC is that it is "complementary" to domestic, national courts. This means that the court only may exercise jurisdiction over cases in those instances in which a country that is a signatory to the treaty has failed to make an effort to bring individuals to the bar of justice. In other words, the ICC is a "back-up" tribunal. The ICC may assert jurisdiction over individuals from states that are not signatories of the ICC when the matter is referred to the court by the UN Security Council.

The ICC has eighteen judges who are elected by those states that have ratified the Rome Statute. There are various methods for a case to reach the court. A state party to the treaty may refer a case to the court, the UN Security Council may ask the court to take jurisdiction over a case involving both signatory and non-signatory states, or the prosecutor may independently examine a situation.

The prosecutor may proceed with an investigation only with the approval of the Pre-Trial Chamber. A limitation of the treaty is that the prosecutor must depend on signatory states to assist with investigations and to detain and turn suspects over for trial. The Pre-Trial Chamber also must approve any charges brought against individuals. In deciding whether to indict an individual for a criminal offense, the prosecutor should consider the seriousness of the crime, the interests of the victims, the role of an individual in a crime, and the health of the accused.

The Rome Statute addresses the plight of the victims of international crimes. The statute establishes a trust fund for victims and may order reparations for the damages victims may have suffered. There also is a provision for victims to participate in the proceedings. The criminal punishment of offenders is explicitly intended to deter violations of the law. The court may impose a prison sentence of up to thirty years and may impose life imprisonment for crimes of "extreme gravity." Offenders also may be subject to a fine or to the forfeiture of property obtained as a result of criminal conduct.

In March 2005, the UN Security Council referred the situation of violence in Darfur in Sudan to the ICC. The prosecutor subsequently issued arrest warrants for a number of Sudanese government officials, including President Omar al-Bashir. The decision to issue an arrest warrant for a sitting head of a country is an unprecedented step and was viewed by the Sudanese as an invasion of their sovereign jurisdiction. President al-Bashir defiantly refused to recognize the warrant and expressed confidence that he would never be brought to trial before the ICC.

In 2012, Congolese warlord Thomas Lubanga was the first individual convicted by the ICC and received a prison sentence of fourteen years for the recruitment and use of child soldiers. Former vice president of the Democratic Republic of Congo Jean-Pierre Bemba was convicted in 2016 of command responsibility over a rebel group that had engaged in rape as a war crime and as a crime against humanity committed in 2002–2003. Bemba's conviction marked an important development in the protection of women during wartime. In the same year in another landmark case, Ahmad al-Faqui al-Mahdi pled guilty to his rebel army's destruction of historical and religious monuments in the northern Mali city of Timbuktu in 2012 and was sentenced to between nine and eleven years in prison. In 2016, prosecution was initiated against former Ivorian president Laurent Gbagbo and youth leader Charles Blé Goudé for murder, rape, and other crimes against humanity committed during post-election violence in Côte d'Ivoire in 2010–2011. Lord's Resistance Army commander Dominic Ongwen is scheduled to stand trial for crimes committed in attacks on internally displaced persons camps in northern Uganda. Ongwen's crimes include forced marriage, forced pregnancy, torture, murder, and conscription and use of children under 15 in armed conflict. A major setback was the dropping of charges against Kenyan government officials for post-election violence in 2007–2008 that resulted in over 12,000 injured because of a "troubling pattern" of suspected witness tampering. In a more positive development, an estimated 180,000 individuals have received financial assistance through the ICC Trust Fund for Victims.

The ICC prosecutor has limited resources, and the decision to investigate some countries rather than others is a source of political controversy. African countries led by Kenya, Libya, and Sudan complain that they are being singled out for investigation and prosecution and that the ICC is an instrument of "modern colonialism." Burundi and South Africa announced their withdrawal from the ICC, and there is the threat of a mass exodus of the thirty-four African members of the ICC. South Africa's decision to leave the court, which may be reversed, was undertaken in response to criticism that the country had ignored an ICC order to detain President al-Bashir of Sudan who was visiting the country. It should be noted that since 2011 the ICC chief prosecutor has been from Gambia and that virtually all of the indictments against African warlords and opposition figures have been referred to the ICC by the countries themselves or by the UN Security Council. The suspicion is that the leaders of some African countries who advocate withdrawal from the ICC fear that they will be indicted for international crimes. The ICC concedes that it is easier to conduct investigations in Africa than in war-torn areas of the globe like Afghanistan, Colombia, and Palestine. A promising investigation involves crimes by Russian forces in South Ossetia, Georgia, in 2008 during the Russo-Georgian conflict. Some of the worst atrocities in the global community are outside the reach of the ICC because neither Iraq nor Syria is a member of the ICC and Russia and China have vetoed a Security Council resolution to authorize ICC jurisdiction over Syria (Chan and Simons 2016).

The effectiveness of the ICC is limited by the fact that the United States, China, Israel, Pakistan, India, and Russia have not recognized the jurisdiction of the ICC. President George W. Bush was opposed to U.S. recognition of the court and repudiated President Bill Clinton's decision to sign the Rome Statute. The Bush administration feared that U.S. military personnel involved in peacekeeping operations on the soil of a signatory to the ICC might find themselves subject to the jurisdiction of the ICC. The United States responded to the possible assertion of ICC jurisdiction by asking countries that receive American financial assistance to guarantee they will not refer American military personnel for trial before the ICC. The Congress passed legislation stating that the United States would use military force to free any American soldier detained by the ICC.

The United States historically has distrusted international institutions. The belief is that American officials should not be subject to the jurisdiction of foreign judges sitting on the ICC. There is an abiding fear that a future U.S. president or military officials will be indicted for war crimes before the ICC. On the other hand, the decision not to cooperate with the ICC means that the United States will not play a role in shaping the court. Should the United States sign the Rome Statute and participate as a member of the ICC (Schiff, 2008)?

CHAPTER SUMMARY

Trials, although relatively infrequent, are important for affirming the constitutional commitments to due process procedures and to a trial before a jury of an individual's peers.

The jury was part of the legal culture transported from England to the American colonies. This common law institution ensured popular participation in the administration of the law and provided a check on prosecutorial discretion.

Jury trials, despite the prevalence of plea bargaining, remain important. They typically are conducted for serious felonies, including charges carrying a possible penalty of death. These often are high-profile trials that help shape our perception of the fairness of the legal system. Juries remain a safeguard against overly aggressive prosecutors and politically motivated prosecutions and biased judges.

There is limited solid information on the jury decision-making process. Studies indicate that the decision reached by a majority of jurors on the first vote ultimately tends to emerge as the jury's verdict. As the deliberations progress, the jurors who disagree with the majority gradually come to accept the majority view. A small number of jurors typically participate in the deliberations. Most jurors look to several outspoken people to represent their views. The dissenting jurors are able to persuade the majority to change their minds in roughly only 10 percent of jury deliberations.

The judge and the jury agree as to the outcome in most cases. In those instances in which judges and juries disagree, the juries are somewhat more sympathetic to defendants. Juries generally decide cases based on the evidence presented in court, and the weaker the prosecution's case is, the more likely jurors are to be influenced by their reaction to defendants and to victims.

Juries give a great deal of credit to eyewitness testimony while giving limited weight to expert witnesses. Although jurors are instructed to follow the law given by the judge, jurors possess the ability to nullify or to refuse to follow the law. Jurors find technical jury instructions confusing and apply their own standards of "right and wrong" in areas such as sexual offenses and the insanity defense.

The jury selection process is subject to constitutional safeguards against discrimination on the grounds of race and gender. Social scientists have been shown to possess limited ability to predict the type of individual who is likely to be sympathetic to the prosecution or to the defense.

Death qualified juries are not like other juries. These juries are less diverse, are more inclined to convict defendants, and do not represent a true cross section of the community. Despite the procedural protections surrounding death penalty prosecutions, the decision whether to impose capital punishment tends to be tilted in favor of death.

There is a trend toward limiting the discretion of trial court judges in sentencing, although this may be reversed by the decline in state budgets and the increasing costs of incarceration.

Despite the time and attention devoted to ensuring the fair adjudication of cases, there are cases in which individuals have been wrongfully convicted. These erroneous convictions lend support to critics who argue that the European inquisitorial system results in more accurate outcomes than the American adversarial system of plea bargaining and trials. The new International Criminal Court is the culmination of the growth of international criminal law over the past 150 years and promises to accelerate the evolution of international criminal justice.

CHAPTER REVIEW QUESTIONS

1. What function do trials perform in the criminal justice system?

2. Trace the development of the jury in England.

3. Why did the jury take hold in the United States?

4. What do we know about how juries make decisions?

5. Do judges and juries generally agree? On what types of cases do they differ?

6. What is jury nullification? Are jurors informed of jury nullification?

7. Are lawyers and social scientists able to scientifically predict how jurors will decide a case?

8. What is the difference between juries in regular criminal cases and juries in death penalty cases? Are juries in death penalty cases more or less likely to impose the death penalty?

9. List the factors that a judge considers in sentencing a defendant.

10. Describe the purpose of "three strikes" sentencing laws. Have these laws been proven effective in deterring crime?

11. Do you favor mandatory minimum sentences?

12. What accounts for wrongful convictions?

TERMINOLOGY

Conviction Integrity Unit   305
exoneration   304

jury   279
jury nullification   288

Rome Statute   307

ANSWERS TO TEST YOUR KNOWLEDGE

1. True
2. False
3. True

4. True
5. True

6. True
7. False

CHAPTER  9

LAW AND
SOCIAL CONTROL

 TEST YOUR KNOWLEDGE: TRUE OR FALSE?

1. General deterrence is the threat of a penalty that causes individuals who would have committed a crime to refrain from committing the criminal act. Specific deterrence is the capacity of the law to deter an individual who has committed a crime from once again violating the same law.

2. If a law is passed penalizing a crime and the number of individuals violating the law declines, we can confidently conclude that the law deterred the crime.

3. A comparison between the effectiveness of one type of threatened punishment and the effectiveness of another type of threatened punishment is called marginal deterrent effect.

4. A law is not considered to have a deterrent impact if the threat of a legal penalty results in a change in behavior but the modified behavior remains unlawful.

5. A deterrence curve plots the number of individuals deterred at increasingly severe levels of punishment.

6. The consensus of research studies is that the death penalty deters homicides.

7. American law historically has imposed relatively modest penalties for "victimless crimes" like gambling and prostitution.

8. Both individual corporate officials and the corporation itself can be held criminally liable.

Check your answers on page 380.

■ INTRODUCTION

A central function of law is to discourage individuals from acts that threaten social stability and the safety and security of individuals. This is the deterrent function of law. **Deterrence** is based on the proposition that individuals are "rational actors" and will avoid behavior, however attractive, when the costs outweigh the benefits. The assumption is that, absent the imposition of a punishment or penalty, most individuals will disregard rules and regulations and society will degenerate into disorder.

The law, of course, is only one mechanism for maintaining social stability. In some small and homogeneous groups, like college fraternities and sororities or a college athletic team, individuals learn and willingly follow customs and traditions and respond to social pressure. The law takes on increasing importance in large, diverse, and complex societies in which social conformity cannot be achieved through education, religion, family, and/or social pressure.

Customs and traditions may pose a barrier to adherence to the law. College cheating on exams and papers, once roundly condemned, appears to be on the increase. Students no longer accept that cheating is wrong, and peer pressure against cheating has diminished. Polls indicate that most students believe that cheating is necessary to "get ahead" and that "everyone cheats." These students for the most part believe that the purpose of college is to get a job rather than to learn and intellectually broaden horizons. As many as 70 percent of students admit to cheating on exams, 84 percent state that they have cheated on written assignments, and over 50 percent have copied material from a website without citing the source. Colleges with honor codes in which students pledge to conduct themselves honorably have a greater extent of cheating than other campuses. Students believe that the honor code is a "paper tiger" and that the administration and faculty will not enforce rules against cheating. Students are confident they are sufficiently skillful to avoid being detected.

Colleges like the University of Minnesota and the University of Florida report that cheating has increased by over 50 percent in recent years. Colleges are responding by increasing efforts to curb cheating, and students are being warned that cheating will lead to expulsion and that the evidence of cheating will be transmitted to potential employers. The question is whether this increased concern with deterring cheating will prove effective.

As you read the text, take the time to reflect on the theory and effectiveness of deterrence. Deterrence is explored in the remainder of the chapter by looking at capital punishment, victimless crimes, and white-collar crime.

■ INFORMAL AND FORMAL SOCIAL CONTROL

Émile Durkheim in *The Division of Labor in Society* writes that small, traditional societies are bound together by **mechanical solidarity**. People in these societies engage in the same type of work and cooperate in farming, hunting, producing handicrafts, and raising children. There is a strong sense of solidarity and loyalty to the group. People tend to hold the same beliefs, share common values (a "collective consciousness"), and define themselves as members of a group rather than as individuals. The society is held together by a shared morality, and there is little tolerance for individuality or nonconformity. A deviation from expected behavior is viewed as an attack on universally shared values or what Durkheim refers to as the "collective consciousness." He famously wrote, "We must not say that an action shocks the conscience because it is criminal but rather that it is criminal because it shocks the common conscience" (Durkheim 1964: 40, 81).

Mechanical solidarity typifies what commonly are considered "primitive," "ancient," and "preindustrial" societies. There are elements of mechanical solidarity preserved in the Old Amish communities in Indiana, Pennsylvania, Ohio, and portions of Canada. The Amish dress in black; the men wear wide-brimmed hats, and the women bonnets and long dresses. The Amish largely are an agricultural society: the men farm, and the women assume domestic responsibilities. The traditional Amish reject modern conveniences and adhere to common values and customs and to a shared religion and lifestyle. Individuals who do not conform to the Amish way of life are expelled from the community (Trevino 2008: 236–237).

The U.S. Supreme Court in *Wisconsin v. Yoder* upheld the religious right of the Amish to defy the compulsory schooling law in Wisconsin and to withdraw their children from school after the eighth grade. The Court accepted the Amish argument that secondary schooling would expose their young people to "worldly influences" and substantially interfere with the religious development of Amish children. This would "gravely endanger if not destroy the free exercise" of the Amish religion (*Wisconsin v. Yoder*, 406 U.S. 205 [1972]).

Another example of mechanical solidarity is the Massachusetts Bay Colony in Massachusetts, founded by the Puritans in 1628. The Puritans executed and banished religious dissidents and in 1692 executed a series of women who were determined to be witches possessed by the devil (Erikson 1966).

Durkheim argues that societies based on a division of labor are characterized by **organic solidarity** rather than mechanical solidarity. In societies held together by organic solidarity, individuals with different interests and talents perform interdependent roles. Doctors provide health care to workers who build houses using materials provided by manufacturers, all of whom eat food sold in grocery stores supplied by farmers. Although they may possess different points of view, individuals are linked by this interdependent division of labor and are reliant on one another (Durkheim 1964: 85).

Law plays a role in maintaining both mechanical solidarity and organic solidarity. Durkheim argued that law in societies based on mechanical solidarity is repressive and reflects the community's outrage toward acts that threaten the community's collective consciousness. Repressive law is characterized by "an eye for an eye" (*lex talionis*) and is enforced through harsh punishments such as torture, the death penalty, and blood revenge. In contrast, the law in societies based on organic solidarity is based on contractual relationships between people, and a violation of the law results in restitution to the injured party. Why this difference in approach? A violation of the law in a society based on mechanical solidarity is viewed as an attack on society, and harsh punishment is an act of self-defense. In contrast, a violation of the law in a society based on organic solidarity is viewed as an attack on the individual rather than the entire society and is punished by compensation to the victim (Trevino 2008: 240–241).

Scholars generally have rejected Durkheim's contention that mechanical solidarity is characterized by repressive law and that organic solidarity results in restitution. The important point to keep in mind is that small, closely knit, and homogeneous societies and groups are able to rely on individuals' internalization of shared values and social pressure to maintain social solidarity. Diverse, economically complex, and large-scale societies lack a sense of shared values and rely on a web of formal legal relationships and legal institutions to maintain social control (Spitzer 1975). The President's Commission on Law Enforcement and Administration of Justice noted that an individual who lives in a small town is likely to be under "surveillance" by his or her community and "therefore under its control." In contrast, a resident of a city is "almost invisible, socially isolated from his neighborhood and therefore incapable of being controlled by it. He has more opportunities for crime" (President's Commission on Law Enforcement and Administration of Justice 1967a: 6).

Richard Schwartz studied two Israeli agricultural settlements. The first was a collective, or *kvutza*, with no private property in which the land was owned and worked in common by all the members. The members of the commune lived in community-owned housing, ate in a communal dining hall, showered and did their laundry in communal facilities, and educated their children in communal nurseries and schools (Schwartz 1954).

The other settlement was a *moshav*, which means that it was based on private property in which individuals worked on their own land and lived in their own homes and only joined together to buy fertilizer and sell produce.

Two-thirds of the residents of the *kvutza* stated that they would go along with the community even if they disagreed with communal policy. In contrast, three-fifths of the members of the *moshav* stated that they would insist on following their own view. Residents of both communities were asked what the phrase "amongst us" means. In the *kvutza*, 98 percent stated that it referred to their community, whereas one-half of the *moshav* responded that the phrase referred to their family or close friends.

As Durkheim might have predicted as an example of organic solidarity, the *moshav* established a judicial committee to hear complaints by residents against one another that operated in accordance with written procedures and enforced written rules and was authorized to enforce its rulings by fines or even banishment. In the *kvutza*, which resembles mechanical solidarity, there were no formal judicial proceedings or written rules. Informal pressures from members of the commune and popular pressure were relied on to persuade individuals to fulfill their responsibilities to the collective. In contrast, a group of young persons in the *moshav* stole melons intended to be served at a wedding. The residents of the *moshav* concluded that lecturing the young people would fall on deaf ears and that "nothing could be done."

Sarah L. Boggs studied formal and informal social controls in cities, suburbs, and small towns in Missouri. She found 83 percent of residents of small towns and rural areas believed informal relationships and the willingness of their "decent" and "law-abiding" neighbors to intervene was the primary factor in keeping their neighborhoods safe and secure as compared to 70 percent of individuals in the suburbs and 68 percent of individuals in urban areas. The residents of suburbs and urban areas were more likely to believe their neighbors would not report an ongoing burglary and were more likely to see their safety as dependent on the police. Residents of urban areas were the most likely to purchase watchdogs and weapons (Boggs 1971).

The community policing movement in the United States is based on the notion that the police working in partnership with an active and alert community in urban areas are able to combat crime. A central component of this strategy is for the police to work with community organizations and with local leaders who act as the "eyes and ears" of the police. "Beat meetings" between the police and the community provide an opportunity for residents to inform the police of problems that need to be addressed and about crime "hot spots." Community policing is a recognition that a strong neighborhood working in conjunction with the police can combat crime. In Chicago, community policing succeeded in reducing the crime rate and increasing confidence in the police although the initiative was not entirely successful in developing a trust in the police in minority communities (Skogan 2006).

Societies maintain social control by relying on a combination of informal social pressure and by formal rules enforced by institutions such as the police. This chapter primarily focuses on the effectiveness and ineffectiveness of the criminal law as a method of formal social control.

■ LEGAL CONTROL

Lawrence M. Friedman, in his discussion of law and society, claims that there are four reasons why people obey the law (L. Friedman 1977: 115–116):

1. *Self-interest.* Individuals drive at a reasonable rate of speed because it is in their interest to avoid an accident and to avoid the consequences of an arrest.

2. *Sanctions.* Individuals are afraid of the consequences of violating the law. This may entail monetary fines, loss of a privilege such as a driver's license, community service, imprisonment and probation, and supervision by correctional authorities.

3. *Social influence.* Individuals obey the law to avoid embarrassment, criticism, and condemnation from their friends, family, and community.

4. *Conscience.* Individuals follow the law because it coincides with their own sense of right and wrong.

The criminal law is intended to control the socially harmful activity of individuals and of groups of individuals. A crime also may violate the civil law, which is designed to compensate individuals for injury caused by individuals and by groups of individuals. The standard of proof in civil law is less than is required for a crime. For example, O. J. Simpson was acquitted of murder, but a jury found that he was liable for the wrongful death of the crime victims.

Criminal punishments serve a number of functions (see Table 9.1).

Table 9.1 ■ Functions of Criminal Punishments	
Retribution	Criminal punishment expresses society's desire for *retribution* or revenge for the harm caused by the crime.
Incapacitation	Criminal punishment isolates offenders and safeguards society.
Deterrence	Criminal punishment deters violation of the law.

Perhaps the primary purpose of criminal punishment is to deter potential offenders from breaking the law and to deter former offenders from resuming their criminal careers.

Deterrence is based on the proposition that people will follow rules to avoid a penalty or punishment. While you may be in a hurry to get home, you know it is better to be late than to risk a heavy fine for speeding. In most instances, most of us are willing to take the time to search for a parking place rather than park unlawfully in a handicapped parking space and risk getting a traffic ticket and an expensive fine.

The United States relies heavily on the criminal law to maintain social control as indicated by the fact that the United States has the highest rate of imprisonment in the world.

■ CRIMINAL PENALTIES

The enforcement of the criminal law in large part relies on the ultimate sanction, that is, the confinement of offenders. The United States has the largest prison population in the world with a total prison population of more than 1.5 million prisoners (Allen, Latessa, and Ponder 2012: 36–37, 178–181, 203–205). *PrisonPolicy.org* reports that, combining all penal institutions, the total incarcerated population in the United States is 2.3 million. The United States has a larger prison population than China, a country that has four times the population of the United States. There are roughly 666 prisoners per 100,000 population in the United States. Russia has the second highest rate of imprisonment, 615 prisoners per 100,000 population. England's imprisonment rate is 148 per 100,000, Germany has a rate of 76 per 100,000, and Japan has a rate of 62 per 100,000. The median incarceration rate among all nations is about 125 per 100,000, roughly a sixth of the American rate (Liptak 2008b; Wagner and Rabuy 2016).

In the United States, there is a federal prison system and state prison systems along with local jails (Allen et al. 2012: 36–37, 178–181, 203–205; see also Table 9.2). Thirty-six states and the District of Columbia reportedly have a higher incarceration rate than Cuba, which imprisons 510 people per 100,000 population (Wagner and Rabuy 2016).

Conservative federal judge Alex Kozinski puts the size of the American prison population in stark perspective when he writes that with 5 percent of the global population, the United States has almost a quarter of the world's prison population. China, in contrast, has roughly 20 percent of the world's population and 16 percent of the world's prison population. Judge Kozinski goes on to note that the United States also has some of the longest prison sentences in the world and cites an informal survey of twenty trials in which the jurors believed the defendant merited a much lower sentence than the judge was legally required to issue to the defendant (Volokh 2015).

A central challenge confronting correctional institutions is overcrowding. The federal system operates at 137 percent of capacity while 22 percent of state prison systems operate at or above their capacity. The California prison system is designed to house 80,000 inmates and has experienced a population as high as 165,000 in recent years. In 2011, in *Brown v. Plata*, the U.S. Supreme Court ordered California to decrease its prison population from 143,435 to 109,805 within two years. A federal judge in California found that an average of one inmate per day was dying due to the inability of the institutions' medical system to treat inmates. Justice Anthony Kennedy in a 5–4 decision wrote, "A prison that deprives prisoners of basic sustenance, including adequate medical care, is incompatible with the concept of human dignity and has no place in civilized society" (*Brown v. Plata*, 563 U.S. 493 [2011]).

Overcrowding has led to a number of creative programs in the states to supervise individuals outside of the correctional institution. These include electronic monitoring, supervision with periodic reporting requirements, sentencing reforms, diversion into treatment programs, community service, and short-term "shock incarceration."

Roughly 3.8 million Americans are on probation, meaning that following their criminal conviction, the judge, rather than incarcerating the individuals, placed them under the supervision of the department of probation and imposed requirements that were to be satisfied as a condition of

Table 9.2 ■ U.S. Correctional Facilities and Population

Federal prisons	The Federal Bureau of Prisons operates 102 correctional institutions with a prison population of 211,000. Roughly 15 percent of federal prisoners, as a result of contractual arrangements, are housed in local or state facilities. Approximately 105,000 inmates are incarcerated for drug offenses, 33,000 for firearms offenses, 19,000 for immigration violations, and 13,000 for property offenses. Roughly 45 percent of inmates are serving between five and fifteen years in prison.
State prisons	The 1,719 state prisons house roughly 1.351 million individuals. Ninety-three percent of inmates are males, 37 percent are white, and 41 percent are African American. Hispanics account for 22 percent of the state prison population. The average age of an inmate is 32 years of age. Fifty-three percent of inmates are incarcerated for crimes of violence, 19 percent of inmates are imprisoned for property offenses, and 16 percent of inmates are in prison for drug offenses. Roughly 70 percent of inmates have not received a high school diploma or GED.
Jails	There are 2,283 local jail facilities and 79 Native American Country jails in the United States. These institutions house individuals awaiting formal charge or trial, individuals who have not yet been sentenced, and convicted offenders who are serving a term of imprisonment of less than a year. The average daily population of jails is roughly 646,000 nationwide, and it is estimated that over 11 million individuals are admitted to jail during the course of a year. Roughly 195,000 individuals have been convicted of a crime, and over 450,000 individuals have not yet been convicted. The jail population is 87 percent males, most of whom are in their 20s. The twenty-five largest jails have 31 percent of the jail population, and 36 percent of these institutions exceed capacity. In 2007, jails functioned at 96 percent of their capacity. The U.S. military and U.S. territories also have prison systems.
Juvenile detention	There are 34,000 youth in 942 juvenile detention facilities. Roughly 7,000 are locked up for technical violations of the law such as a violation of probation, 8,100 are incarcerated for property offenses, and 13,600 have been detained for crimes against the person.
Immigration	Roughly 33,000 undocumented immigrants are detained awaiting deportation or a decision on an application for asylum.

Source: Wagner, Peter, and Bernadette Rabuy. 2016. *Mass Incarceration: The Whole Pie.* Northampton, MA: Prison Policy Initiative.

the defendants' continued freedom. A violation of probation results in an individual's imprisonment. An additional 820,000 individuals are on parole, meaning they were released before completing their prison sentence and are required to adhere to certain specified conditions.

There are nearly seven thousand juveniles incarcerated for violating the conditions of their parole, and another six hundred juveniles are incarcerated for status offenses such as truancy or running away.

In 2015, according to the Bureau of Justice Statistics, roughly 6.7 million people were under some form of adult correctional supervision in the United States, either prison or jail or probation or parole. This was the first time since 2002 that the number of individuals under correctional supervision dipped below 6.8 million and constitutes roughly 1 in 37 U.S. adults or approximately 2.7 percent of the adult population, the lowest rate of adults under correctional supervision since 1994. The rate for African Americans is 1,745 per 100,000 adults, for Hispanics 820 per 100,000, and for white adults 312 per 100,000 (Liptak 2008a; T. Williams 2016a).

Roughly nineteen thousand people are in federal prison for criminal convictions based on a violation of federal immigration laws. More than thirty-three thousand other individuals are civilly detained by U.S. Immigration and Customs Enforcement (ICE) and are confined in immigration detention facilities or in local jails under contract with ICE.

A much-overlooked component of criminal penalties is monetary fines. Statutes typically provide judges with discretion to impose a fine up to a designated amount. An individual who fails to pay a fine may be resentenced by a judge, and additional prison time may be imposed (O'Malley 2009).

The number of individuals incarcerated suggests that the criminal law and punishment are only partially successful in deterring criminal conduct.

■ DETERRENCE

The theoretical foundation of deterrence is traced to two classical theorists, Cesare Beccaria and Jeremy Bentham. The Italian Cesare Beccaria in his 1764 essay *On Crimes and Punishments* wrote that the intent of punishment is to "instill fear in other men" (Beccaria 1988: 30). Jeremy Bentham was a nineteenth-century thinker known for his utilitarian philosophy. He advocated a practical approach to public policy premised on the belief that public policy should "advance the greatest good for the greatest number of individuals" in society. In *Principles of Penal Law* (1843), Bentham argued the purpose of punishment is to provide individuals with the incentive to obey the law. He explained that for deterrence to be effective, the "pain of punishment" must outweigh the benefits derived from the crime (Bentham 1962: 396, 399).

Bentham's approach is termed *utilitarianism* and also is referred to as the classical school of criminology. Deterrence theory builds on the foundation of utilitarianism. It assumes that people weigh the costs against the benefits of their actions and will be deterred from criminal behavior when they realize the benefits of crime are outweighed by the costs of crime. Criminal conduct based on this theory can be prevented by continuing to increase the penalty attached to criminal behavior until individuals find that the cost of crime is too high (Barkan 2009: 137).

Several terms employed in deterrence theory are defined in Table 9.3 (Zimring and Hawkins 1973: 71–74).

Table 9.3 ■ The Terminology of Deterrence	
Deterrence	The threat of a penalty causes individuals who would have committed the behavior to refrain from committing the act.
General deterrence and specific deterrence	General deterrence refers to the capacity of a law to deter individuals from engaging in the prohibited conduct. Specific deterrence refers to the capacity of a law to deter an individual who already has been penalized for the prohibited behavior from repeating the prohibited behavior.
Channeling effect	There is a change in behavior resulting from a law. For example, an individual may respond to a tuition increase required by the state legislature by paying the tuition, transferring schools, or dropping out of school.
Absolute deterrent effect	The number of prohibited acts prevented by a law are weighed against the number of prohibited acts that otherwise would have occurred absent the law prohibiting the behavior. Zimring and Hawkins (1973) cite the example of a $100 fine that is imposed for walking on the grass. Absolute deterrence is weighing the number of individuals who now avoid walking on the grass against the number of people who would walk on the grass without the imposition of a fine.

Marginal deterrent effect	A comparison is made between the effectiveness of one type of threat and the effectiveness of another type of threat. The net deterrent effect measures the number of people who will avoid walking on the grass when a $100 fine is imposed versus the number of people who will avoid walking on the grass when a fine of $25 is imposed or who will avoid walking on the grass if individuals violating the ordinance are prohibited from using the park for a month.
Partial deterrence	The threat of a legal penalty results in a change in behavior although the modified behavior remains unlawful. Decreasing the speed limit from 65 miles per hour (mph) to 55 mph causes drivers to reduce their speed from 70 mph to 60 mph. Increased penalties for robbery may persuade muggers to reduce their street crime from three to one mugging per week. In the alternative, the mugger may shift his or her focus to residential burglaries.
Deterrence curve	A graph can be used to plot the number of individuals deterred at increasingly severe levels of punishment. Initially, a modest punishment may result in very few people being deterred. The number of individuals deterred increases as the punishment is enhanced.

Various factors are viewed as important in determining the extent to which a law will deter behavior.

Requirements for Deterrence

The conventional wisdom is that there are a number of fundamental requirements for deterrence to be effective (L. Friedman 1977: 122–124):

Communication. The law, penalty, and enforcement must be communicated to the target audience.

Certainty. There must be a belief that violating a legal rule will result in the imposition of a penalty. One crude measure of certainty is the percentage of violations of a specific type of crime that result in arrest and the percentage of arrests that result in convictions.

Severity. The punishment must be sufficiently severe to deter individuals from engaging in the prohibited behavior. This is determined by the sentences actually imposed on offenders or by the maximum sentence available for the crime under the law.

Speed. The punishment must be inflicted without delay. This is measured by the time between the arrest and sentencing.

Stigma. The greater the shame attached to an act is, the more effective the deterrent effect of the law will be.

Procedural justice. The law to be obeyed must be viewed as moral and must be viewed as enforced in a fair and equal fashion. The individuals or agency enforcing the law must be respected and regarded as acting in the public interest. These requirements generally are measured by surveys of public opinion (Tyler 2006).

Lawrence Friedman cautions that there is a difference between *actual risk* and the *perceptions of risk*. Individuals may lack knowledge of the law and of the enforcement of the law or may believe, regardless of the objective facts, that there is little likelihood they will be apprehended.

General Deterrence

Everyday experience suggests **general deterrence** is effective. As David M. Kennedy observes, only a small number of individuals voluntarily will place their hand on a hot stove, run across a six-lane expressway, or violate road regulations when followed by a police officer. Burglars tend to avoid breaking into a home with a sign reading "Beware of Dog," and individuals avoid smoking marijuana in the presence of a police officer (D. M. Kennedy 2010: 9).

Early studies found that American states with a greater certainty and a greater severity of punishment had lower rates of crime per hundred thousand residents than states with less certainty and severity. These results were challenged on the grounds that crime rates might be explained by factors such as poverty or the age of the population rather than the certainty and severity of criminal punishment.

A number of more recent studies also find that the number of police and the likelihood of arrest have a deterrent impact and reduce crime (Marvell and Moody 1994, 1995). A study in Orlando, Florida, over six months found that an increase in arrests resulted in an immediate decrease in crime because potential offenders presumably learned of the arrests and decided that the risk of apprehension was too great (D'Alessio and Stolzenberg 1998).

A much-cited example of the relationship between the number of police and the probability of arrest and crime is a study of Nazi Germany's occupation of Denmark during World War II. In 1944, Germany occupied Denmark and arrested nearly the entire police force. Individuals no longer feared that crime would be detected, and the crime rate quickly escalated (Hood and Sparks 1972: 174).

There is limited support for the notion that longer prison sentences have a deterrent impact on crime (Chamlin 1991; Doob and Webster 2003; Walker 2006). Tom Tyler notes individual behavior is affected more by the prospect of being apprehended and punished than by the harshness of the punishment (Tyler 2006: 142–143). A study of laws in forty-four states that increased the penalty on individuals who committed a crime while in possession of a firearm failed to find these laws deterred individuals from using a gun to commit a crime (Marvell and Moody 1995: 274). Studies of the imposition of mandatory sentences for crimes involving firearms in Massachusetts and in Detroit (Michigan) also found there was no impact on gun crimes (Loftin and McDowell 1981; G. Pierce and Bowers 1981).

There is a question whether even certain and severe punishment can deter chronic offenders, particularly those individuals with a personality disorder. Individuals motivated to rob, rape, burglarize, or kill in many instances believe there is a low risk of being apprehended. They are not intimidated by the threat of penalty, do not consider the consequences of their behavior, and believe they can manipulate the criminal justice process and escape a harsh punishment.

Evaluating General Deterrence

Frank Zimring and Gordon Hawkins note that decision-makers make certain "common errors" in evaluating the deterrent impact of criminal laws and policies (Zimring and Hawkins 1973: 24–32).

The first is "Aunt Jane's Cold Remedy." Aunt Jane's is a mixture of alcohol, sugar, and hot water that some people believe will be effective in curing a common cold within ten days. Individuals who believe in this folk remedy report their colds disappear and credit their recovery to Aunt Jane's. Most colds in fact will be cured within ten days without any treatment.

Zimring and Hawkins compare "Aunt Jane's Cold Remedy" to measures adopted to combat crime. Adopted when there is an increase in the crime rate, these countermeasures are credited with returning the crime rate to a "normal historical level." Zimring and Hawkins observe that there is a historical fluctuation in the crime rate and that crime would have dropped whether or not new laws and penalties were adopted, police dogs were introduced, police patrols were increased, or a crackdown on gangs was initiated. The difficult challenge is to determine the percentage of the drop in the crime rate attributable to the change in policy and the percentage of the drop in the crime rate attributable to the natural cycle of criminal conduct. Government officials are quick to credit the reduction in crime to the new laws and programs. When crime rates remain the same or continue to increase, officials proclaim their policies prevented crime from rising to an even greater extent (Zimring and Hawkins 1973: 24–26).

The second threat to an accurate evaluation of the impact of a law on crime is the "tiger prevention" fallacy. Zimring and Hawkins use the example of an individual running down the streets of a large American city. The police stop the woman and ask why she is interfering with traffic. The runner responds that she is keeping "tigers away from the city." The officer points out that there is no tiger within five thousand miles, and the runner responds, "I must be doing a really good job." This story illustrates the tendency of public officials to believe the heavy criminal penalties they have instituted are preventing a "crime wave." Both the runner and public officials believe their actions are effective despite the absence of evidence. In fact, the enhanced criminal penalty may have little or nothing to do with the number of burglaries or murders (Zimring and Hawkins 1973: 26–30).

Decision-makers questioning the effectiveness of deterrence may fall victim to the "fallacy of the warden's survey." In this story, a prison warden asks inmates whether they are deterred by high prison penalties. Zimring and Hawkins observe that the warden's study is problematic because the warden's sample is composed of inmates, a group who has not been deterred from breaking the law. The inmates do not represent the public, and any study that relies on their responses to reach conclusions on deterrence is flawed (Zimring and Hawkins 1973: 31–33).

Another issue is the fallacy of underreporting. In 1927, Norway responded to an increase in sex offenses by increasing the punishment for these offenses. The curious result was that comparing the five-year period before the change with the five-year period after the change reveals that the rate of sexual offenses rose by 68 percent. Professor Johannes Andenaes explains that the increased discussion regarding sexual offenses resulted in a new willingness among the public to report sexual offenses (Andenaes 1974). As a result, it is difficult to measure whether the enhanced penalties decreased the incidence of sex crimes (Zimring and Hawkins 1973: 279).

A fifth mistake in evaluating deterrence is the error of diminishing returns. The enhancement of punishment may result in no additional deterrence effect and the crime rate remaining steady. The temptation is to believe that deterrence has failed. The explanation may be that most individuals already are deterred by existing punishments and the increased level of punishment is not sufficiently severe to deter individuals who continue to engage in criminal behavior (D. M. Kennedy 2010: 36).

Last, there is the fallacy of attributing deterrence to conviction of a crime rather than to the "secondary effects" of conviction of a crime. One study found shame was a more powerful deterrent than law for tax offenses and drunk driving (Grasmick and Bursik 1990). Charles R. Tittle determined that disapproval by friends and family is a more powerful deterrent than the imposition of criminal penalties (Tittle 1977; Tyler 2006). Informal disapproval is a particularly powerful deterrent for women (Richards and Tittle 1981).

Individuals also may be less concerned about punishment than by the fact a criminal conviction may make it difficult to obtain or to keep a job. There also is the loss of privileges such as the right to vote in some states or ability to practice various professions (Zimring and Hawkins 1973: 172–194).

The capacity of law to deter criminal behavior also differs based on the offender and the type of crime.

Types of Crime and General Deterrence

William Chambliss makes the point that some types of crime are more easily deterred than others. *Instrumental offenses* are committed for material gain and are carefully planned. Individuals undertaking offenses like robbery, burglary, and motor vehicle theft carefully weigh and balance the possibility of detection and may be deterred by the threat of criminal punishment. The individual who contemplates an instrumental offense has the time to abandon his or her criminal plans and find a lawful or unlawful avenue to achieve his or her goals. *Expressive offenses*, in contrast, are based on an emotional reaction, and individuals typically do not take the time to weigh and balance the consequences. The primary examples in Chambliss's view are murder in the heat of passion or reckless homicide and narcotics addiction (Chambliss 1967).

The notion that individuals act in a calculated and rational fashion in committing a crime fails to account for the fact that a crime may be motivated by greed, revenge, economic desperation, jealousy, psychological disturbance, and a host of other factors (D. M. Kennedy 2010: 17). Another factor is that group pressure may push individuals into criminal behavior and overwhelm the deterrent impact of the law (D. M. Kennedy 2010: 3).

Chambliss further argues that offenders with a high commitment to carrying out crimes or pursuing criminal careers are less likely to be deterred than offenders with a low commitment to crime. Offenders with a low level of commitment may weigh and balance the consequences of committing a crime and conclude that they should abandon their plan. Daniel Nagin and Raymond Paternoster suggest individuals with low self-control are less easily deterred because they have not invested in education or in a career and therefore have less to lose if they are apprehended (Nagin and Paternoster 1993).

The importance of Chambliss's argument for policymakers is that certain types of offenders and certain types of crime are more difficult to deter than other types of offenders and crimes (Zimring and Hawkins 1973: 138–141).

An additional limitation on general deterrence is that offenses that are committed in private are much more difficult to deter because there is a reduced risk of detection and arrest (Barkan 2009: 139). Location is important; for example, a college student may believe that the risk of being detected and punished for selling narcotics on campus will be much less than the risk of selling narcotics to strangers on the street (D. M. Kennedy 2010: 30–31).

People may differ in how they weigh and balance the benefits of following the law against the costs and consequences of violating the law. Convicted drunk drivers in one study were evenly divided over whether a two-week jail term or a six-month suspension of a driver's license constituted a more severe punishment (Grasmick and Bryjack 1980). An economically secure college student may find the consequence of an arrest for selling drugs outweighs the economic benefits. A college student who lacks money for tuition may come to a very different conclusion. The important point is that advantaged and disadvantaged college students are engaging in calculations and reaching very different conclusions. The penalty for drug trafficking may have to be doubled or tripled before the destitute student is deterred from selling drugs (Hood and Sparks 1972: 174).

Another limitation on the effectiveness of deterrence is a lack of knowledge of the law. A drug dealer may not be aware that he or she will be harshly punished for selling narcotics within one thousand feet of a school. Studies indicate that members of the public lack an accurate perception of the penalties attached to various criminal offenses. As a result, in most instances, increasing the punishment attached to a crime will not effectively deter criminal conduct. Individuals already may view certain crimes as harshly punished, and adding ten or fifteen years to a sentence that already is viewed as harsh may result in little increased deterrence (D. M. Kennedy 2010: 31). Sentencing structures in fact are so complex that even the police, prosecutors, defense attorneys, and judges are uncertain about penalty levels (Kleck et al. 2005).

Lawrence Friedman observes that the knowledge of the law is not distributed equally in society. Federal income tax regulations are so complicated that only accountants and tax attorneys are fully informed of the details of the tax code (L. Friedman 1977: 114–115).

Studies indicate the importance of communicating increased enforcement and punishment to the public although in most instances these types of campaigns are not part of government strategy (Cook 1980). In New Zealand, France, and England, widespread publicity warned drivers of enhanced enforcement of laws against drunk driving and increased Breathalyzer testing. As a result, drunk driving decreased in New Zealand even before the initiation of enforcement. In England and France, drunk driving decreased despite the fact that the police never followed the publicity campaign with increased enforcement. Enhanced penalties for drunk driving in England undertaken without publicity had no impact on drunk driving whatsoever (L. Ross 1973, 1977; L. Ross, McCleary, and Epperlein 1982). Publicity also proved effective in a British burglary prevention campaign (S. D. Johnson and Bowers 2003).

In another study, warning letters sent to over sixty persons stealing cable television transmission with descramblers led roughly two-thirds of the individuals to deactivate the devices (G. Green 1985). Zimring and Hawkins cite a study at a university in which illegal parking by faculty significantly decreased after letters were sent warning that faculty who parked illegally would have the fines deducted from their salary (Zimring and Hawkins 1973: 129).

Individuals who modify their behavior in response to a threat unfortunately eventually resume their former patterns. The power of deterrence deteriorates over time. This typically is due to the fact that the level of enforcement fails to meet the level individuals anticipated or the level of enforcement diminishes over time. Consider that despite the "zero tolerance" of drunk driving, 80 percent of drivers convicted of drunk driving continue to drive after their licenses have been suspended (D. M. Kennedy 2010: 11, 30, 55).

The next section focuses on specific deterrence.

9.1 YOU DECIDE

In 2013, New York City mayor Michael Bloomberg announced an ordinance prohibiting restaurants, sports venues, and movie theaters from selling soda and other specified sugar drinks in containers larger than sixteen ounces. The New York Court of Appeals overturned the ordinance on the grounds that it was beyond the authority of the mayor's health commission.

The ordinance recommended that males consume roughly 130 calories of sugar a day and women consume roughly 100 calories of sugar per day. A sixteen-ounce soda contains twice the amount of sugar an individual should consume on a daily basis. Individuals generally consume the proper quantity of sugar in fruits and vegetables. The ordinance was based on scientific evidence that excessive sugar consumption leads to obesity, diabetes, and cancer. Roughly one-third of Americans consume more than 400 calories per day of sugar, and a small number consume 1,000 calories of sugar or one-half the daily total calories.

Childhood obesity rates for children ages 10 through 17 over the past eight years have increased 10 percent for all children and 23 percent for "poor" children. Portion sizes also have significantly expanded.

Mayor Bloomberg in announcing the ordinance stated, "I've got to defend my children, and yours, and do what is right to save lives. . . . Obesity kills." He stated that he was particularly concerned about poor people who he claimed lacked access to a full range of food choices.

Critics objected to the New York City government telling people what to consume and pointed out that fast-food restaurants were not regulated under the ordinance. Milk shakes and other high-calorie drinks and fat-laden food also were unregulated. Individuals were free to order two eight-ounce drinks.

Other jurisdictions adopted a different approach to taxing sugary drinks, imposing a tax on each ounce of soda rather than on the size of the container. The tax in most instances is imposed on the manufacturer and typically is passed on to the consumer. In 2015, the Philadelphia City Council approved a 1.5-cent-per-ounce tax on sodas and other sugary drinks. Drinks that are more than 50 percent fruit juice, vegetable juice, or milk are exempt. It is estimated that the tax will raise $91 million per year to fund the expansion of pre-kindergarten, the creation of community schools, and investments in parks and in recreation centers. Critics who opposed the tax argue that it will disproportionately affect the poor and contend that the tax will gradually increase and be used to fund other budgetary items. The Cook County, Illinois, board subsequently adopted a similar law, which applies to the city of Chicago and to nearby suburbs. In November 2016, a sugary-drink tax was adopted by voters in Boulder, Colorado, and in Oakland, San Francisco, and Albany, California.

In November 2014, Berkeley, California, was the first jurisdiction to adopt a soda ordinance, and the early evidence indicates that there has been a decrease in the consumption of sugar-sweetened beverages and an even greater increase in the consumption of water among lower-income residents.

The World Health Organization has urged countries to tax sugary drinks based on the fact that 39 percent of adults across the globe are overweight and at risk of obesity-linked diseases. Mexico and to a limited extent England also have adopted legislation regarding sugary drinks. Studies find that the tax in Mexico has reduced the consumption of sugary drinks for the past two years.

Will these ordinances succeed in changing individuals' intake of sugary drinks? Should the government play the role of "big brother" and attempt to influence individuals' diets?

Specific Deterrence

Specific deterrence is the capacity of the law to deter an individual who has committed a crime from once again violating the same law. This is extremely difficult to measure. The reality of the American criminal justice system is that most crimes are not reported to the police and most perpetrators are not apprehended, prosecuted, and imprisoned. This "filtering effect" detracts from the deterrent impact of criminal penalties (D. M. Kennedy 2010: 42–53, 57). Steven E. Barkan observes that crime involves minimal risk for offenders and points out the following statistics from 2005 (Barkan 2009: 142):

Arrests. The police make an arrest in eight of every one hundred serious street crimes.

Prosecution. Four in every one hundred serious crimes are prosecuted; the charges are dropped in other cases.

Incarceration. One in every one hundred serious crimes results in incarceration.

Anthony N. Doob and Cheryl Marie Webster interviewed sixty incarcerated burglars and robbers who report that they did not even consider the possibility that they would be caught and prosecuted for their criminal conduct. This, of course, does not mean that there are individuals who in fact have been deterred by the threat of punishment (Doob and Webster 2003). Studies of offenders and non-offenders find offenders believe that they have less of a chance of being apprehended for committing a crime than do non-offenders (Zimring and Hawkins 1973: 102–103).

"Project Exile" was a federal program to combat gun crime that was accompanied by widespread publicity. Individuals possessing unlawful firearms would be prosecuted and sentenced to a minimum prison term of five years. A study of inmates incarcerated in Rochester, New York, found that most inmates were aware of the program and viewed the five-year sentence as harsh. A number of inmates knew of individuals prosecuted under the program, and a significant number also knew of individuals who had been apprehended with a firearm who had not been prosecuted for unlawful possession. The inmates tended to view the federal prosecution for possession of a firearm as unpredictable, uncertain, and "hit or miss" and did not view the threat of an enhanced penalty as a deterrent. Those instances in which inmates were prosecuted and received a mandatory five-year sentence were viewed as the exception rather than the rule and were dismissed as resulting from a prosecutor's ego or racial bias.

Inmates who had been incarcerated for gun violations viewed the federal effort to combat gun possession as yet another example of an empty threat by federal officials and doubted whether they would serve their complete sentence. The important point is that these inmates incarcerated for gun violations believed their conviction and punishment for possession of a firearm was the exception rather than the rule and resulted from factors other than the seriousness of their crimes. This perception suggests the enhanced penalty for possession of a firearm had little deterrent effect (D. M. Kennedy 2010: 57–58).

There is some indication that offenders in prison relatively quickly adjust to their situation and that the deterrence value of their imprisonment diminishes over time. Arrestees when surveyed viewed a five-year prison sentence as twice as severe as a one-year sentence and a twenty-year sentence as 1.6 times as severe as a ten-year term (McClelland and Alpert 1985). The diminished threat posed by punishment is evident from the recidivism rate among offenders who have been imprisoned. A 2002 Bureau of Justice study found that 67.5 percent of individuals released from prison in 1995 were rearrested within three years for a new crime. Inmates with the highest rearrest rates are robbers, burglars, larcenists, motor vehicle thieves, individuals arrested for possessing or selling stolen property, and individuals convicted of weapons charges (D. M. Kennedy 2010: 12). The length of imprisonment does not appear to affect the recidivism rate. Studies find inmates who have been released early to alleviate prison overcrowding do not have higher rates of recidivism than inmates who serve their full sentence (James Austin 1986).

Numerous factors may undermine specific deterrence. Zimring and Hawkins observe that harsh punishment for a crime may lead prosecutors to become reluctant to charge offenders under the statute and may lead jurors to return not guilty verdicts. In jurisdictions in which the police, prosecutors, judges, and jurors are personally acquainted with offenders, are sympathetic to offenders, or distrust the government, there may be resistance to enforcing the law. Zimring and Hawkins cite drunk driving as an example of a behavior that society in the past seemed to tolerate, limiting the deterrent effect of the law (Zimring and Hawkins 1973: 59, 66).

The lack of consistent enforcement of drug crimes and domestic violence and the tolerance of prostitution can lead to the view among offenders that the police tolerate crime in certain communities or are on the payroll of local gangs. David M. Kennedy notes that the failure to enforce the law may result in the law being viewed as serving the interests of the rich and powerful and as undeserving of respect. Crime can become rationalized by offenders as a justified rebellion against illegitimate authority. In an interesting experiment, observers witnessed drivers making illegal right-hand turns and found other drivers did not follow the example of drivers who made the unlawful turns. Researchers then placed a man in an Air Force uniform at the street corner to represent an authority figure. The researchers found that the illegal turns were "contagious" and drivers witnessing the illegal turns themselves made unlawful turns. The explanation is that the figure in uniform provided official approval of the unlawful behavior (D. M. Kennedy 2010: 59–60).

Kennedy observes that an arrest and incarceration can so damage an individual's life prospects that the arrest undermines deterrence. The individual has little to lose and much to gain by continuing a pattern of criminal conduct. Arrests throughout a community can disrupt families, create unemployment, and lead to a neighborhood in which crime is a way of life. Young people may view criminals and "gang bangers" as deserving of respect and status (D. M. Kennedy 2010: 58–65). Sam Walker notes that widespread arrests, prosecutions, and imprisonment in a community can create an expectation that this is a "normal life activity" with "little deterrent effect" (Walker 2006: 111). Crime becomes a vehicle to gain respect, honor, and a lifestyle (Gibbs and Shelly 1982).

Before we leave the topic of deterrence, there are ethical concerns that are worth considering.

The Ethics of Deterrence

The eighteenth-century philosopher Immanuel Kant in his well-known categorical imperative urged that an individual should never be used as a "means to an end."

An objection to general deterrence is that individuals are punished as a means of deterring other individuals from committing crimes. Ernest van den Haag quotes an English judge's remark that "men are not hanged for stealing horses, but that horses may not be stolen" (quoted in van den Haag 1975: 41).

Lawrence Friedman describes a deterrence curve. A $25 fine will deter some people from parking illegally. Raising the fine to $50 will deter another group of individuals. To achieve near perfect deterrence, the fine may have to be raised to $250. You may be one of the people who would have been deterred by a $25 fine, and yet you are fined $200 because this is required to deter those individuals who are not deterred from parking illegally with a fine of $25 or $50 (L. Friedman 1977: 123).

Zimring and Hawkins cite the example of a street robber whose dangerous behavior merits his punishment. The legislature has established a penalty ranging from one to ten years. The judge sentences the offender to five years in prison, and the parole board refuses to release him after he has served three years of his five-year sentence.

Zimring and Hawkins pose the dilemma that a two-year sentence normally would satisfy the social interest in punishing robbery. A two-year sentence also is sufficient to have convinced the robber to abandon his life of crime. The robber complains that he is being punished with two years based on his own behavior and three additional years to deter other people. A related concern is the cost of incarcerating the robber and other robbers for three additional years (Zimring and Hawkins 1973: 37–38, 50–66).

Van den Haag contends that a robber's punishment reflects a balancing of various goals and, once having committed a serious criminal act, an individual voluntarily has subjected him- or herself to punishment and is in no position to complain that he or she is being unfairly sanctioned. Deterrence theory requires that offenders serve sentences that will deter others from committing crimes.

Individuals often are asked to sacrifice in the interests of society. Consider a tax system that asks the rich to pay more than the poor or a military draft that asks some young people to defend the society while others are not subject to military service. The robber may have an argument if a harsh penalty is imposed for an act, such as parking illegally, that does not greatly harm society (Hart 1968).

In some instances, the possible benefits of deterrence must be weighed against the possible social costs. Consider that according to the National Conference of State Legislatures, ten states explicitly authorize the concealed carry of firearms on public college campuses by licensed gun owners. These state legislatures reason that there is no reason that universities should be "no go zones" for the Second Amendment. This policy is welcomed by some students who feel safer knowing that their fellow students are armed. On the other hand, there is the consideration that students are under stress and that conflicts can easily escalate, that individuals intent on campus violence may not be deterred, and that some instructors feel that the presence of firearms in the classroom are not conductive to learning.

In the next section, we examine one of the most controversial issues involving deterrence, whether the death penalty deters criminal behavior.

9.2 YOU DECIDE

In early America, shaming punishments were used such as placing individuals in stocks and subjecting them to public humiliation. The notion was that public embarrassment would deter the individuals and others from crime. These were small, close-knit communities in which individuals' relationships and reputations were important to their self-perception and status.

(Continued)

(Continued)

In the past decades, judges have resorted to shaming punishments rather than fining or incarcerating individuals who have committed minor offenses. Although this seems a more humane and effective form of punishment than a short jail sentence or fine, critics assert that shaming punishments allow judges to treat individuals like "animals in a zoo" and to subject individuals to immense and unnecessary public humiliation. There also is a danger that these shaming punishments will be selectively applied to certain offenders. Judges, rather than focusing on humiliating offenders, should think about positive alternatives like requiring an individual to devote time to community service.

Several state legislators nonetheless have gone so far as to advocate giving offenders a choice between imprisonment and public flogging. Examples of shaming punishments include the following:

In 2012, Shena Hardin was arrested for passing a school bus by driving on a sidewalk and was required to stand at an intersection wearing a sign that read, "Only an idiot would drive on the sidewalk to avoid a school bus." A year later, Richard Dameron, who had threatened police officers, was required to stand outside a police station for three hours a day for one week with a sign stating, "I was being an idiot and it will never happen again." In 2014, Edmond Aviv pled guilty to disorderly conduct and was directed to remain on a street corner for five hours with a sign that read, "I AM A BULLY! I pick on children that are disabled, and I am intolerant of those that are different from myself. My actions do not reflect an appreciation for the diverse South Euclid community that I live in."

Cleveland, Ohio, Housing Court judge Ray Pianka ordered landlord Nicholas Dionisopoulos, who was convicted of violating multiple requirements of the Cleveland housing code, to live in one of the units for six months and fined him $100,000.

In 2003, a Texas man was ordered to sleep for thirty consecutive nights in a two- by three-foot doghouse for whipping his stepson with a car antenna.

Oklahoma District Court judge Mike Norman in December 2012 ordered Tyler Alred, 17, to attend church for ten years as a condition of his sentence for DUI manslaughter. The Oklahoma American Civil Liberties Union condemned the sentence as a "clear violation of the First Amendment" protection of the free exercise of religion and filed a complaint against Norman. Alred also was required to graduate from high school and welding school, submit to regular drug and alcohol tests, and participate in victim impact education seminars.

Cameron County, Texas, Justice of the Peace Gustavo "Gus" Garza allowed parents to spank their daughter in his courtroom in lieu of paying a $500 fine for their daughter's truancy. He was admonished by the State Commission on Judicial Conduct on March 9, 2009, which concluded that "Judge Garza exceeded his authority by providing parents and the school district with a 'safe haven' for the administration of corporal punishment . . . with no legal authority to impose the sanction either by the Texas Education Code or Texas Code of Criminal Procedure."

In August 2014, a Pennsylvania superior court struck down part of a shaming sentence imposed on former state Supreme Court justice Joan Orie Melvin. Melvin had been convicted of misusing public funds and using her government-funded staff to work on her election campaigns. The trial court judge's order that Melvin send pictures of herself wearing handcuffs to other state court judges was overturned because the use of handcuffs as a "prop is emblematic of the intent to humiliate Orie Melvin in the eyes of her former judicial colleagues. . . . It was solely intended to shame her."

Do you support shaming sentences?

■ CAPITAL PUNISHMENT

Executions

In 1608, Captain George Kendall was executed by a firing squad in Jamestown Colony, Virginia, for treason and mutiny. This was the first of an estimated 10,598 executions between 1608 and 1929 in what commonly is referred to as the "early period" of **capital punishment** in the United States.

Roughly 70 percent of these executions took place after 1850, and 51 percent of the individuals executed were African Americans (Paternoster, Brame, and Bacon 2008: 5).

The law in the American colonies and states reflected a combination of English common law, religious doctrine, and the repressive requirements of slavery in the South.

In the New England colonies, the death sentence was imposed for crimes against the person, such as murder, manslaughter, and rape or repeated acts of burglary or robbery. The religious character of the colonies also

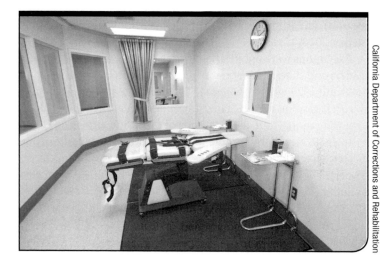

PHOTO 9.1   All states with the death penalty and the federal government use lethal injection as the primary method of executing individuals.

led several settlements to impose the death penalty for crimes against God, such as witchcraft, idolatry, blasphemy, bestiality, adultery, and various sexual offenses. One of the most infamous examples was the execution of twenty accused witches in Salem, Massachusetts, in 1692 (Paternoster et al. 2008: 5–7).

The southern colonies imposed capital punishment for property offenses including stealing hogs and tobacco. Capital punishment also was imposed for undermining the institution of slavery. These offenses included concealing a slave with the intent to free him, inciting slaves to rebel, and circulating seditious literature (Paternoster et al. 2008: 6). In the South, murder or revolt by a slave as well as the murder of a husband by his wife were considered forms of "petit treason" punishable by particularly painful deaths. In 1739, African American slaves involved in the "Stono slave revolt" were beheaded and their heads mounted on stakes as a warning to other slaves who might contemplate rebelling (Steiker and Steiker 2016: 8).

Lawrence Friedman documents that prior to the declaration of American independence, capital punishment was directed primarily against African Americans. Between 1706 and 1784, 555 slaves were sentenced to death in Virginia. In 1741 in New York, 30 slaves were executed for joining in a conspiracy to revolt (L. Friedman 1993: 44).

Between 1688 and 1820, the "Bloody Code" in England imposed the death penalty on more than two hundred offenses. Many of the leaders of the American Revolution reacted by advocating limiting capital crimes. Following the American Revolution, states restricted the number of crimes carrying the death penalty. Capital punishment no longer was imposed for religious offenses or for property crimes. The Pennsylvania statute of 1786 limited capital punishment to eight offenses and abolished the death penalty for sodomy and buggery and for robbery and burglary. Pennsylvania also became the first state to distinguish between degrees or types of murder and limited the death penalty to the most serious form of homicide. Virginia restricted the death penalty to murder and certain offenses committed by slaves (L. Friedman 1993: 73–75; Paternoster et al. 2008: 10). Michigan in the midcentury abolished the death penalty for murder (although retaining it for treason), and Rhode Island and Wisconsin abolished capital punishment altogether (Steiker and Steiker 2016: 11).

Executions were public affairs and were accompanied by speeches from political and religious leaders and statements of remorse by the accused. Roughly 80 percent of the executions between 1608 and 1929 were by hanging. The hangings at times were gruesome affairs, and the condemned were left gasping for air. States responded to calls for the abolition of capital punishment by exploring more "humane" methods of execution.

In 1889, New York became the first state to sentence a prisoner to die through the use of the electric chair and made the decision to conduct executions in private, behind prison walls. By 1929, 68 percent of executions were carried out through the use of electricity, and the trend was toward excluding the public from executions. The last public execution was carried out in Kentucky in 1936 and was attended by between ten thousand and twenty thousand persons with vendors selling popcorn, hot dogs, and drinks (L. Friedman 1993: 75–76; Paternoster et al. 2008: 5–20; Steiker and Steiker 2016).

In the 1840s, states began to modify statutes that required juries to impose the death penalty on defendants who were found guilty. Jurors at times acquitted sympathetic defendants, and states responded by providing jurors with the discretion to impose a sentence of either death or life imprisonment. By 1963, every state had adopted a discretionary sentencing scheme (Paternoster et al. 2008: 27–28).

The electric chair almost completely replaced death by hanging, although by the mid-1960s, execution through the use of the gas chamber was used in roughly 30 percent of all executions. Between 1890 and 1990, roughly four thousand people were killed by electrocution in twenty-six states. In gas chamber executions, individuals were killed through the use of hydrogen cyanide gas, which cuts off oxygen to the brain. Prisoners reportedly turned purple and experienced seizures and spasms; the last execution through gas occurred in Arizona in 1999. At the time the use of the gas chamber was abandoned, 594 individuals had been executed through the use of lethal injection. Utah and Nevada continued to provide individuals the option of death by firing squad. In recent years, states have executed individuals through the use of lethal injection (Paternoster et al. 2008: 27–35; Steiker and Steiker 2016: 14–15).

In 1972, in *Furman v. Georgia*, the U.S. Supreme Court ruled that while the imposition of capital punishment was constitutional, allowing juries complete discretion whether to impose capital punishment led to the imposition of capital punishment in a "freakish" and "unpredictable" fashion. Various judges suggested that the death penalty did not always fit the circumstances of the crime or background of the offender and that capital punishment was being disproportionately imposed on the poor and on minorities rather than on the "worst of the worst" offenders. Justice Potter Stewart captured the mood of the Supreme Court when he wrote that the random application of the death penalty is cruel and unusual punishment under the Eighth Amendment "in the same way that being struck by lightening is cruel and unusual" (*Furman v. Georgia*, 408 U.S. 238, 309–310 [1972]). The *Furman* decision resulted in states halting executions and modifying their capital punishment statutes.

States reacted by passing mandatory death penalty laws that required that defendants convicted of intentional homicide receive the death penalty. The U.S. Supreme Court ruled in *Woodson v. North Carolina* that treating all homicides alike resulted in death being cruelly inflicted on undeserving defendants. The Court held that a jury "fitting the punishment to the crime" must consider the "character and record of the individual offender" as well as the "circumstances of the particular offense." The uniform system adopted in North Carolina treated "all persons convicted of a designated offense not as uniquely individual human beings, but as members of a faceless, undifferentiated mass to be subject to the blind infliction of the penalty of death" (*Woodson v. North Carolina*, 428 U.S. 280 [1976]).

The last step in the evolution of due process procedures in death cases was the 1976 Supreme Court decision in *Gregg v. Georgia*. In *Gregg*, the U.S. Supreme Court approved a Georgia death penalty statute that provided for three procedural reforms. First, in a separate (bifurcated) hearing, the jury is to determine guilt or innocence and then in a separate hearing is to consider whether the death penalty should be imposed. Second, in determining whether to impose the death penalty, the jury is to be provided with a list of statutory aggravating factors and is to weigh these factors against any mitigating factors presented by the defense. Last, there is to be an automatic appeal to the state supreme court, which is to determine whether the death penalty is being imposed in a uniform fashion. These procedures are intended to ensure that capital punishment is imposed in a uniform fashion on offenders who constitute the "worst of the worst" (*Gregg v. Georgia*, 428 U.S. 153 [1976]).

The decision in *Gregg* opened the door to the reintroduction of the death penalty. The decision was quickly followed by the 1977 execution by firing squad of Gary Gilmore in Utah. At present, thirty-two states and the federal government have death penalty statutes. The U.S. Supreme Court following *Gregg* has considerably narrowed the type of offenses for which capital punishment may be imposed and has narrowed the categories of offenses and offenders who may be subject to the death penalty.

Types of crimes and the death penalty. In 1977, the U.S. Supreme Court held it is excessive to impose the death penalty for the kidnapping of an adult (*Eberhart v. Georgia*, 433 U.S. 917 [1977]). In *Coker v. Georgia* in 1977, the Supreme Court ruled it is grossly disproportionate and excessive punishment to execute a defendant convicted of aggravated rape. The Court reasoned that "the murderer kills; the rapist . . . does not" (*Coker v. Georgia*, 433 U.S. 584 [1977]). Twenty-one years later, in *Kennedy v. Louisiana*, the Supreme Court held that imposition of capital punishment for the rape of a child is a disproportionate punishment as measured by evolving standards of contemporary society and constituted cruel and unusual punishment (*Kennedy v. Louisiana*, 554 U.S. 407 [2008]).

In *Enmund v. Florida*, the Court held it is unconstitutional to execute the driver of a getaway car who lacked a criminal intent and who did not participate in a robbery and murder (*Enmund v. Florida*, 458 U.S. 782 [1982]). On the other hand, in *Tison v. Arizona*, the Court noted that "major participation" in a felony "combined with reckless indifference to human life is sufficient to satisfy the . . . culpability requirement" (*Tison v. Arizona*, 481 U.S. 137 [1987]).

Types of offenders and the death penalty. The U.S. Supreme Court in a series of cases restricted the category of individuals subjected to capital punishment. In 1988, in *Thompson v. Oklahoma*, the Supreme Court held that the execution of a defendant who is under the age of 16 at the time of his or her offense constituted cruel and unusual punishment. Justice John Paul Stevens wrote that "inexperience, less education, and less intelligence make the teenager less able to evaluate the consequences of his or her conduct while at the same time he or she is much more apt to be motivated by mere emotion or pressure than is an adult" (*Thompson v. Oklahoma*, 487 U.S. 815 [1988]). In *Roper v. Simmons*, the Court held that the execution of an individual under 18 years old constituted cruel and unusual punishment. Justice Anthony Kennedy explained that juvenile offenders "cannot with reliability be classified among the worst offenders. . . . Their . . . vulnerability and comparative lack of control . . . mean juveniles have a greater claim than adults to be forgiven for failing to escape negative influences in their whole environment" (*Roper v. Simmons*, 543 U.S. 551 [2005]).

In 2002 in *Atkins v. Virginia*, the Supreme Court held that it is unconstitutional to execute individuals who are mentally retarded. The Court explained these individuals lack the capacity to control and to comprehend the consequences of their behavior. Individuals who are mentally challenged as a result cannot be held morally responsible for their actions and do not constitute the "worst of the worst" who are appropriately subject to the death penalty (*Atkins v. Virginia*, 536 U.S. 304 [2002]). The Court earlier had held that it was an affront to human dignity to execute an inmate who has mentally deteriorated during his or her confinement and is mentally ill at the time of the scheduled execution (*Ford v. Wainwright*, 477 U.S. 399 [1986]).

Methods of execution and the death penalty. The Supreme Court has yet to find that any method of execution constitutes cruel and unusual punishment. The Court upheld the constitutionality of the use of firing squads for executions (*Wilkerson v. Utah*, 99 U.S. 130 [1878]) and approved the use of electrocution on the grounds that it results in "instantaneous and therefore painless death" (*In re Kemmler*, 136 U.S. 436 [1890]). In 2008, the U.S. Supreme Court addressed the constitutionality of the execution of individuals through the use of lethal injection. In *Baze v. Rees*, the Court upheld the constitutionality of Kentucky's lethal injection protocol. Every death penalty state provides for lethal injection to be the primary method of execution although a handful of states also provide for electrocution, the gas chamber, hanging, and the firing squad (*Baze v. Rees*, 553 U.S. 35 [2008]). In 2015, in *Glossip v. Gross*, the Supreme Court upheld the use of midazolam as the first chemical in a three-drug cocktail (*Glossip v. Gross*, 576 U.S. ___ [2015]).

Between 1976 and 2016, there were 1,442 executions in the United States, 3 of which were carried out by the federal government. There were 98 executions in 1999, the highest number of executions since 1951. The number of executions since 1999 has been declining. In 2010, there were 46 executions, a 12 percent drop from the 52 executions in 2009. In 2016, there were only 20 executions, a decrease from the previous modern low figure of 20 in 2015. The Death Penalty Information Center reports there were 2,902 individuals on death row in the United States. California, with 741 individuals on death row, has the largest death row population followed by Florida (376) and Texas (254) (Death Penalty Information Center 2016).

Southern states, since the reinstatement of the death penalty in *Gregg v. Georgia* in 1976, have accounted for over 90 percent of executions. Texas has carried out over one-third of all executions since 1976 (538) and, along with Oklahoma (112) and Virginia (111), accounts for over 50 percent of executions.

Jurors demonstrate a continuing disinclination to impose the death penalty. Juries handed out 118 death sentences in 2009, 114 in 2010, 85 in 2011, 82 in 2012, 83 in 2013, 73 in 2014, 49 in 2015, and 29 in 2016. This is a significant decline from the peak year of 1996 when 315 death sentences were handed down.

Only seven states carried out executions in 2014, and five of these states executed more than a single person. Six states carried out executions in 2015, five of which carried out more than one execution; five states carried out executions in 2016, but only Alabama, Georgia, and Texas carried out more than a single execution. California, Maryland, Pennsylvania, and some other states have not had an execution in almost five years (Death Penalty Information Center 2016).

As noted above, a significant factor contributing to the decline in the number of executions is a shortage of sodium thiopental, a component of the mixture that is used for executions; this shortage caused executions to be delayed in Arkansas, California, Kentucky, Oklahoma, and Tennessee. The shortage was caused by the refusal of European manufacturers to provide chemicals to be used in executions. A number of states are introducing new "chemical cocktails" to enable them to continue to execute individuals or are finding alternative suppliers of chemicals.

In January 2014, Dennis McGuire was executed by the state of Ohio. The execution was conducted with a largely untested combination of drugs and required twenty-five minutes from the time the chemicals were started to the declaration of death. A court approved the drug protocol although lawyers for McGuire argued the drugs could cause a struggle to breathe, resulting in "agony and terror."

In April 2014, the Oklahoma execution of Clayton D. Lockett, convicted of shooting a 19-year-old woman and burying her alive, was halted sixteen minutes following the insertion of the intravenous line and injection of a sedative. Despite the administration of lethal drugs, Lockett twitched and mumbled and attempted to lift his head and shoulders off the gurney. Officials discovered Lockett's vein had ruptured, preventing the delivery of the chemicals, and he died of a heart attack twenty-seven minutes after the decision was made to call off the procedure (Eckholm 2014).

This was followed by what appears to have been excruciatingly painful executions of Randolph Wood in July 2014 in Arizona and Ronald Bert Smith in Alabama in December 2016. Supreme Court justice Sonia Sotomayor, in dissenting from the U.S. Supreme Court's refusal to reconsider the constitutionality of the use of an execution cocktail that includes the sedative midazolam, wrote in February 2017 that "prisoners executed by lethal injection are suffering horrible deaths beneath a 'medically sterile aura of peace.' . . . [W]e should not blind ourselves to the . . . evidence that midazolam is simply unable to render prisoners insensate to the pain of execution. The examples abound" (*Arthur v. Dunn*, 80 U.S. ___ [2017]). In April 2017, Arkansas, concerned about the state's expiration of a dwindling supply of midazolam, executed four convicted murderers in one week.

The Application of the Death Penalty

The possibility that a defendant will confront the death penalty depends on whether a defendant is subjected to one of the thirty-two states with capital punishment that executes individuals sentenced to death. In an interesting development in November 2016, Nebraska voters overturned a state legislative ban on capital punishment. Carol and Jordan Steiker divide states into four categories based on their approach to the death penalty (Steiker and Steiker 2016: 118–120):

1. *Abolitionist states.* States by law that prohibit the death penalty; primarily located in the Midwest and in the Northeast (e.g., Michigan and Vermont).

2. *De facto abolitionist states.* States with capital punishment that sentence a small number of individuals to death and infrequently carry out death sentences; located across the country (e.g., Colorado and Wyoming).

3. *Symbolic states.* States that sentence a significant number of individuals to death but carry out a relatively small number of executions; located across the country (e.g., California and Pennsylvania).

4. *Active death penalty states.* States that sentence individuals to death and carry out executions; primarily located in the South and in border states (e.g., Oklahoma and Texas).

Prosecutors within death penalty states differ in their willingness to charge defendants with capital crimes. In Maryland, which recently abolished the death penalty, prosecutors pursued the death penalty in roughly 27 percent of the cases in which a defendant was eligible for capital punishment. The death penalty was sought in 65 percent of the eligible cases in Baltimore County and in only 5 percent of the eligible cases in adjacent Baltimore City (Paternoster et al. 2008: 59–64).

Between 2010 and 2016, Los Angeles County, California, imposed more death sentences than any county in the United States. In 2016, only twenty-seven of the nation's three thousand counties imposed death sentences. In the last four decades, fifteen counties (0.5 percent of U.S. counties) have carried out 30 percent of executions (Death Penalty Information Center 2016).

The death penalty is disproportionately imposed on individuals who kill Caucasians. Seventy-six percent of individuals executed killed a white victim, 15 percent killed an African American, and 7 percent killed a Hispanic victim (Death Penalty Information Center 2016). A majority of individuals executed are Caucasians who killed white victims (54 percent). Roughly 36 percent of individuals executed are non-whites who killed white victims. Roughly 3 percent of individuals executed are Caucasians who killed non-white victims, and 18 percent are non-whites who kill non-whites (Paternoster et al. 2008: 47–49). In Louisiana, individuals who kill a Caucasian are six times as likely to receive the death penalty and fourteen times as likely to be executed when the victim is white (Editorial Board 2016).

African Americans are disproportionately sentenced to death. Forty-two percent of individuals on death row are African American, 42 percent are Caucasian, and 13 percent are Hispanic.

In 2016, there were 55 women on death row or roughly 1.87 percent of the individuals on death row. Fifteen women have been executed since 1976, and 571 women have been executed since the death penalty was instituted in the United States, comprising almost 3 percent of all executions (Death Penalty Information Center 2016).

The Death Penalty Information Center reports that since 1973 more than 156 individuals on death row in twenty-six states have been exonerated and released. In the past decades, there have been an average of five exonerations each year. In 2015, 6 individuals on death row were exonerated. These individuals were convicted and incarcerated in Alabama, Arizona, Florida, Georgia, Mississippi, and Texas and had spent an average of nineteen years in prison. Roughly 50 percent of individuals exonerated were African American, 40 percent were white, and the remainder were Hispanic (Death Penalty Information Center 2016).

In Illinois, 298 individuals were sentenced to death between 1977 and 2000, and 13 of them were exonerated. One individual was exonerated within forty-eight hours of his scheduled execution. Republican governor George Ryan, a supporter of capital punishment, declared the process was fatally flawed and declared a moratorium on executions in Illinois. Three years later, Governor Ryan commuted the death sentences of 167 other men on death row. Eight additional individuals on death row in Illinois have been exonerated (Paternoster et al. 2008: 65–67; Turow 2003). A 1992 study contends that there are more than four hundred instances in which innocent individuals were convicted and sentenced to death in the United States (Radelet, Bedau, and Putnam 1992).

Andrew Gelman and his co-authors found that close to two-thirds of death sentences are reversed on appeal. Eighty-two percent of the defendants who were retried received a sentence less than death, and 7 percent were found not guilty. These lengthy appeals have slowed the pace of executions. Between 1977 and 1983, the average time between conviction and execution was four years. At the end of 2003, the time between conviction and execution had lengthened to ten years (Gelman et al. 2004; Liebman et al. 2000). In Louisiana, 82 percent of the 155 death sentences handed down since 1976 were later reversed (Editorial Board 2016).

As we have seen, explanations for the overturning of death penalty verdicts range from overzealous police and prosecutors to flawed forensic evidence and mistaken eyewitness identification to "junk science" and reliance on "jailhouse snitches." The most troubling aspect of the Gelman study is that 40 percent of the reversals of capital cases by state courts and roughly 30 percent of the reversals by federal courts are based on "ineffective assistance" of counsel (Gelman et al. 2004). In these cases, the appellate courts determined that the performance of the defense attorney fell below "prevailing professional norms" and that there is a "reasonable probability" that the result would have been different absent the lawyer's deficient performance (*Strickland v. Washington*, 466 U.S. 668 [1984]).

Most death row defendants cannot afford to pay attorney fees let alone hire expert witnesses and investigators and must depend on court-appointed attorneys who receive modest payment from state funds. Only a handful of lawyers possess the skill and experience to defend a death penalty case, and these lawyers cannot handle more than two or three cases at any given time. Newspaper investigations consistently have found that defendants confronting the death penalty are represented by defense counsel of questionable quality. A *Chicago Tribune* report on the administration of the death penalty in Texas found that roughly 20 percent of inmates on death row were represented by lawyers who had been disciplined for professional misconduct, and in half of these cases, the misconduct occurred before the lawyer was appointed by the court to handle the death penalty case. The *Tribune* found that in the prosecution of 30 percent of the 131 individuals executed during the term of former governor George W. Bush, the defense counsel failed to offer any mitigating evidence at the sentencing stage or presented only one witness in mitigation (Armstrong and Mills 1999a, 1999b). The absence of lawyers who are competent to bring death penalty appeals has contributed to the fact that the average delay between sentencing and execution is fifteen years (Steiker and Steiker 2016: 206–207).

Public Opinion and the Death Penalty

In September 2016, the Pew Research Center found that for the first time in forty-five years, fewer than half of Americans (49 percent) support the death penalty. Forty-two percent of respondents told Pew they oppose capital punishment, the highest percentage of opposition since a May 1966 Gallup poll found that 47 percent of Americans opposed the death penalty. Six in ten respondents stated that the death penalty does not deter serious crimes. Fifty percent of individuals believed that minorities are more likely than whites to be sentenced to death although 41 percent said that whites are equally as likely as minorities to be sentenced to death. Seventy-one percent said that there is a risk that the innocent will be executed, a view endorsed by 84 percent of individuals opposing the death penalty and 63 percent of individuals supporting the death penalty. In an interesting response, 90 percent of individuals endorsing the death penalty believe it is morally justified, a view shared by only 26 percent of individuals opposing the death penalty (Masci 2016).

Fifty-seven percent of whites support capital punishment as compared to 29 percent of African Americans and 36 percent of Hispanics. More men (55 percent) than women (43 percent) favor the death penalty. Seventy-two percent of Republicans support the death penalty versus 34 percent of Democrats and 44 percent of Independents.

A Gallup poll in 2015 found that 60 percent of individuals supported the death penalty and 37 percent opposed the death penalty. Fifty percent of individuals believe the death penalty is applied fairly, and 44 percent believe it is applied unfairly, the highest perception of a lack of fairness in the administration of the death penalty in seventeen years. Various polls indicate that a majority of Americans favor sentencing individuals to life without parole rather than to death (Steiker and Steiker 2016: 214).

Public support for the death penalty undoubtedly reflects the commonsense notion of retribution that is based on an "eye for an eye" and a "tooth for a tooth." An individual who has taken a life in a premeditated and deliberate fashion has voluntarily taken a life and has decided to place him- or herself outside society. The requirement that the jury find at least one aggravated punishment that is not outweighed by mitigating circumstances ensures that the death penalty is reserved for the "worst of the worst" offenders (van den Haag 1975: 213). On the other hand, support for the death penalty is declining because of doubts about whether the government should be empowered to take a life, the belief that individuals will be fully punished who are imprisoned without the possibility of parole, and fear that an innocent individual will be executed.

David Garland argues that the acceptance of the death penalty is based on five "frames" that legitimize reliance on capital punishment (Garland 2010: 39–69).

1. *Rules.* The death penalty is constitutional.

2. *Crime.* The death penalty deters crime and is central to the war on crime.

3. *Retribution.* The death penalty provides "order and balance" by repaying the offender "in kind."

4. *Healing.* The death penalty heals the victims and removes the offender from the community.

5. *Democracy.* The death penalty reflects the will of the people.

The Debate Over Capital Punishment

Philosopher Walter Berns argues that murder is a crime against society because it undermines the foundations of society by threatening the safety and security of individuals and the sanctity of human life. The failure to take the life of a murderer cheapens human life and places society at risk (Berns 1987).

It is argued that the death penalty deters individuals who commit serious offenses such as kidnapping and rape from taking the next step and killing their victims. The argument also is made that a death sentence is the only deterrent available to prevent inmates who are serving life sentences or extremely lengthy prison sentences from killing other inmates. There is the additional consideration that capital punishment provides the families of victims with a sense of closure and satisfaction that the murderer of their loved one has been fully punished (van den Haag 1975: 214–217).

In response to the moral argument in favor of capital punishment, individuals favoring the abolition of capital punishment argue that retribution or an "eye for an eye" is not required to be precisely equivalent to the harm inflicted by the offender. Life without parole is sufficiently severe to demonstrate respect for the life of the victim (Reiman 2007). Hugo Bedau proposed a "minimal invasion principle." According to Bedau, a democracy is obligated to respect human rights and should only use the degree of force that is necessary to achieve its goals. Bedau concluded life imprisonment without parole is as effective as capital punishment in providing retribution and there is no need to resort to the death penalty (Bedau 2004).

The execution of offenders ensures that these individuals will no longer pose a threat to society. Offenders sentenced to life imprisonment may escape from prison or pose a threat to other inmates. On the other hand, individuals convicted of homicide if they escape or are released on parole are unlikely to commit another serious offense (Paternoster et al. 2008: 135–138).

A study of 6,835 inmates who were serving sentences for homicide offenses and were paroled from state prisons found that 4.5 percent later were convicted of another crime and 0.31 percent committed another murder (Sellin 1980). James Marquart and Jonathan Sorensen compared the post-release criminal conduct of 28 individuals on death row in Texas who were released following the decision in *Furman v. Georgia* with the post-release criminal conduct of 109 inmates serving life terms for murder or rape who were released on parole. One of the death row inmates committed a murder following release although none of the parolees committed a murder. Fourteen percent of the death row inmates committed a crime as compared to 6 percent of the inmates sentenced to life terms. The crimes committed by the individuals released from death row included one rape and two burglaries. This same pattern of criminal conduct was found in a national study of 239 individuals released from death row (Marquart and Sorensen 1988, 1989).

The "brutalization thesis" posits that the death penalty actually increases rather than deters crime by creating a climate tolerant of law breaking, violence, and murder (Bailey 1998).

Capital Punishment and Deterrence

A central justification for capital punishment is the deterrence of homicide. There are a number of studies that conflict with one another on this question. The general consensus is that there is no evidence that executions are any more of a deterrent than sentences of life imprisonment (Paternoster et al. 2008).

Thorsten Sellin is responsible for the initial work on the deterrent impact of the death penalty. He compared the homicide rates between 1920 and 1935 of adjacent states that were similar on various dimensions but differed on whether they used the death penalty. Sellin's thesis was that if capital punishment was more effective than life imprisonment in deterring homicide, states that employed the death penalty should have lower homicide rates than contiguous states that imposed life imprisonment. He found no significant difference in the homicide rate between death penalty states and life imprisonment states within the same geographic regions (Sellin 1959). Sellin's findings were confirmed by a study conducted by Ruth Peterson and William Bailey based on data gathered between 1973 and 1984. They found that the homicide rate in death penalty states (8.5 per 100,000) was somewhat higher than the homicide rate in non–death penalty states (7.6 homicides per 100,000) (R. Peterson and Bailey 1988).

The flaw in Sellin's analysis is that the homicide rate in states may be determined by factors that have nothing to do with whether a state imposes the death penalty or limits punishment for homicide to life imprisonment. David Baldus and James Cole's comprehensive comparison of the capital punishment and non–capital punishment states nonetheless generally confirms Sellin's results (Baldus and Cole 1975).

The economist Isaac Ehrlich emerged as a strong critic of Sellin's work. Ehrlich argued it was not sufficient to look at whether a state imposed the death penalty. He combined data from all states and employed a sophisticated statistical technique (regression analysis) to determine the impact of the imposition of the death penalty on homicides in the United States between 1933 and 1969. Ehrlich's model also allowed him to eliminate factors other than whether a state provided for the death penalty that might explain homicides. He reached the provocative conclusion that an additional execution per year on average may have resulted in seven or eight fewer murders (Ehrlich 1975: 414). In 1985, Stephen Layson, a student of Ehrlich, concluded each additional execution may have prevented eighteen additional homicides (Layson 1985).

Ehrlich's methodology was criticized (Passell and Taylor 1977), and the prestigious National Academy of Sciences appointed a panel on deterrence headed by Nobel Prize–winning economist Lawrence Klein to clarify the relationship between the death penalty and homicide. The panel relied on the same data and techniques as had Erhlich and concluded the results failed to establish that the death penalty affected the homicide rate (Klein, Forst, and Filatov 1978: 359).

John Donohue and Justin Wolfers found that a close examination of the Ehrlich data failed to "clearly indicate" whether the "preponderance of evidence suggests that the death penalty causes more or less murder" (Donohue and Wolfers 2006: 843).

Reviewing the literature on deterrence and the death penalty, Richard Berk concluded that "for the vast majority of states, for the vast majority of years, there is no evidence for deterrence in these analyses" (Berk 2005: 330).

A study of television coverage found that neither the amount nor the type of newspaper coverage of an execution had a deterrent effect on the homicide rate in the United States (Bailey 1990).

In reviewing the evidence on the deterrent impact of the death penalty, Zimring and Hawkins reach the troubling conclusion that the death penalty takes the lives of convicted murderers without evidence to suggest that capital punishment is a more effective deterrent than the threat of a lengthy term of imprisonment (Zimring and Hawkins 1973: 188–190).

Michael Radelet and Traci Lacock asked a prestigious panel of criminologists whether the empirical evidence indicated the death penalty constituted a deterrent to murder. Roughly 78 percent of the individuals surveyed stated that the death penalty does not lower the murder rate in a state. Ninety-four percent agreed that there was little evidence to support the deterrent effect of the death penalty. Furthermore, 91.6 percent said that increasing the frequency of executions would not increase the deterrent effect of the death penalty, and 87.6 percent stated that speeding up executions would not increase the deterrent effect of the death penalty. Ninety-one percent stated that politicians support the death penalty to appear tough on crime. Seventy-five percent stated that the death penalty distracts legislatures from discussing the real solutions to crime (Radelet and Lacock 2009).

In 2012, the National Research Council of the National Academies appointed a committee to consider whether "capital punishment deters homicide." The committee concluded the "research to date is not informative about whether capital punishment decreases, increases, or has no effect on homicide rates." As a result, existing research is flawed and should not be relied on in formulating public policy. The committee found fundamental flaws in the literature of the death penalty and deterrence. For example, in calculating the deterrent impact of capital punishment, the studies fail to consider that death penalty state statutes provide for both capital punishment and life imprisonment. Studies need to consider whether individuals are deterred solely by the threat of death or whether the threat of life imprisonment also has a deterrent impact. Future research needs to involve interviews with actual murderers to determine whether they are deterred by the threat of capital punishment (Nagin and Pepper 2012).

As state budgets shrink, the comparative costs of the death penalty and life imprisonment likely will be of increased relevance. As of 2016, there were 2,902 individuals on death row, a decline from 2,984 in 2015 and from 3,539 in 2000. The prosecution of a capital case is more expensive than a homicide prosecution in which the prosecution does not seek the death penalty. A death penalty prosecution is more complicated and time-consuming and involves a number of appeals. Florida would save an estimated $51 million a year if it sought life without parole rather than the death penalty. It is estimated that between 1976 and 2000, Florida spent $24 million on each death penalty prosecution. The death penalty in California will cost taxpayers $130 million more per year than it would cost to house the prisoners for life terms. The trial costs for capital cases in Los Angeles County are three times the costs of non-capital cases and have strained the funds in death penalty states available for indigent defense (Paternoster et al. 2008: 131–133). Carol and Jordan Steiker estimate that the cost per execution (which includes costs associated with capital trials, legal representation, and enhanced security on death row) in California is nearly $250 million (Steiker and Steiker 2016: 206).

In November 2013, California voted 53 percent to 47 percent to continue capital punishment. California has executed six individuals since reinstating the death penalty in 1978, and the death row population in that state has grown to 741 individuals. The estimates are that the death penalty has cost California $4 billion since 1978. In 2016, in an effort to cut the costs associated with keeping individuals on death row for lengthy periods, California voters adopted a law designed to speed the time required for death penalty appeals.

■ INTERNATIONAL PERSPECTIVES ON CAPITAL PUNISHMENT

The United States is one of a small, but significant, number of countries that use capital punishment. The Death Penalty Information Center reports that ninety-five countries have abolished the death penalty, nine countries have abolished the death penalty for ordinary crimes, and thirty-four nation-states that provide for capital punishment no longer carry out the death penalty. Capital punishment is retained by fifty-eight countries.

Amnesty International reports that 1,634 individuals were executed in twenty-five nation-states in 2015, an increase of 50 percent from 2014 and the highest number of executions since 1989. This total does not include China, which considers the number of individuals executed to be a state secret. The number of executions in China in 2015 likely numbered in the thousands. Iran in 2015 executed at least 977 individuals; Saudi Arabia 158; Pakistan 328; and the United States 28. China, Iran, and Saudi Arabia execute individuals for crimes that are not considered "the most serious" under international law, including drug trafficking, corruption, adultery, and blasphemy.

Eighty-four states have ratified the Second Optional Protocol to the International Covenant on Civil and Political Rights aiming at the abolition of the death penalty, which obligates signatory states to suspend executions and to take all necessary measures to abolish the death penalty. A majority of countries through either law or practice have abolished capital punishment. In November 2010, the United States, China, and India voted against a UN General Assembly non-binding resolution calling for a moratorium on the death penalty. The resolution received support from 107 countries and was opposed by 38 countries; 36 countries abstained.

In the next section, we look at the ability of the law to deter so-called victimless crimes or offenses that individuals voluntarily pursue and generally do not view as harmful. The question is whether the law is capable of deterring this type of consensual criminal conduct (you can find You Decide 9.8 on deterrence on the study site).

■ VICTIMLESS CRIMES

The law in the United States historically has criminalized various consensual acts that are considered harmful as well as immoral. Prostitution, for example, involves two mutually consenting adults although it is criminalized in every jurisdiction in the United States outside of Nevada. Crimes like prostitution, gambling, vagrancy, euthanasia, and the possession of obscenity and various types of narcotics are called **victimless crimes** because there allegedly is no identifiable victim (Schur 1965).

© iStockphoto.com/microgen

PHOTO 9.2 Prostitution is illegal in the United States with the exception of several rural counties in Nevada. Prostitution frequently is associated with the abuse of women and illegal sex trafficking although it remains a profitable enterprise. The Urban Institute reports Atlanta's sex trade was valued at $290 million in 2007, and Miami's unlawful sex economy generated $235 million.

A case nonetheless can be made that these acts do harm the individuals involved as well as society. Some commentators contend it is more accurate to view these so-called victimless crimes as consensual crimes or as crimes against public order (Barkan 2009: 149–156).

Legal philosopher Richard Wasserstrom writes that the fundamental issue is whether the law should punish conduct because society views the act as immoral (Wasserstrom 1971). The most famous statement on law and morality is John Stuart Mill's essay *On Liberty* (1859). Mill believed that the law may not, without justification, interfere with individuals' independence and autonomy. He wrote that the "only purpose for which power can be rightfully exercised over any member of a civilized society against his will is to prevent harm to others." Mill argued that an individual cannot be made to act or to refrain from acting because society believes it will be "better" for the individual or that it will make him or her "happier" or "wise." Society may criticize an individual's behavior or provide rewards or benefits although, according to Mill, absent a demonstrated harm to others, it may not pass a law requiring an individual to act or pass a law punishing an individual for failing to act. Mill argued that society is equally as likely to be correct as incorrect when it comes to issues of right and wrong and virtue and sin (Mill 1979: 141–162).

Lawyer and judge James Fitzjames Stephen in *Liberty, Equality, Fraternity* (1873) challenged Mill and argued that Mill's notion of unlimited individual liberty would lead to social chaos and that the survival of society required the coercion of individuals into moral behavior.

The debate over law and morality was renewed in August 1954 when John Wolfenden was appointed to head a committee to evaluate English laws regarding prostitution and homosexuality. The committee recommended that homosexual relations between consenting adults should no longer be a crime. This recommendation was based on "individual freedom of choice" in matters of "private morality." The commission reasoned that there must remain a realm of "private morality and immorality" that is "not the law's business" (Wolfenden Report 1957: para 61).

In 1962, the American Law Institute, which is composed of a number of prominent American lawyers, judges, and legal scholars, published the Model Penal Code (MPC). The code is a comprehensive set of criminal statutes that reflect the opinion of this respected group of legal thinkers on the best approach to defining crimes and criminal defenses. States are asked to consider adopting some or all of the provisions of the MPC. The MPC followed the philosophy that it is "inappropriate" for the law to attempt to prohibit conduct on the grounds that it constitutes immoral behavior. The encouragement of moral behavior is best left to educational and religious institutions.

In 1958, one hundred years after the publication of *On Liberty*, English lord Patrick Devlin delivered a public lecture criticizing John Stuart Mill and the Wolfenden Report for asserting that law and morality inhabited separate spheres. Lord Devlin published his lecture under the title *The Enforcement of Morals* and argued that a common and uniform moral belief system binds society together and prevents society from degenerating into disarray. Every society has the right to preserve its existence, and the criminal law is the instrument for protecting those moral values that are essential for a community's existence. Lord Devlin lectured that "there is a compelling justification" for criminalizing behavior that elicits "intolerance, indignation and disgust" and "we cannot . . . condemn ourselves to inactivity against evil because of the chance that we may by mistake destroy good." He concluded, "Suppression of vice is as much the law's business as the suppression of subversion" (P. Devlin 1965: 7, 11, 16, 17, 123).

In 1963, H. L. A. Hart of Oxford University responded to Lord Devlin's talk in his volume *Law, Liberty, and Morality* by questioning whether there was agreement on moral values and whether the criminal law was the appropriate vehicle to enforce morality. Morality should be discussed and debated and ultimately left to the judgment of the individual. The fact that a majority condemns a practice does not justify the punishment of the minority who does not support the majority view. This would limit freedom to what conduct the majority finds acceptable and would deny the possibility that morality may evolve and change. There also was little evidence that actions in private, consensual acts damaged society (Hart 1963).

The criminalization of various "consensual crimes" can be traced to their condemnation in colonial America. In the New England colonies, there was no separation between crime and religious sin. A failure to attend church, blasphemy, and working on the Sabbath were crimes. Sexual acts condemned in the Bible resulted in religious reprimand or excommunication as well as a modest criminal penalty. Sodomy with juveniles and buggery were punished by the death penalty. In 1642, 16-year-old Thomas Granger of Plymouth, Massachusetts, was convicted of buggery (bestiality) with a horse, a cow, two goats, five sheep, two calves, and a turkey and was executed along with the animals (L. Friedman 1993: 34–35).

Fornication was the most widely punished seventeenth-century criminal offense. Unmarried individuals who slept together were prosecuted, fined, and whipped or placed in stocks. Women who bore a child out of wedlock might be punished with twenty-one lashes. In Massachusetts, it was unlawful to gamble or to play shuffleboard. A Virginia law punished individuals for drunkenness, swearing and cursing, adultery, and fornication (L. Friedman 1993: 35–36, 54).

A study of prosecutions in six counties in Massachusetts between 1760 and 1774 found that fornication accounted for 38 percent of the prosecutions, and 13 percent of prosecutions were for religious offenses (e.g., profanity, failure to attend church). The fornication prosecutions for the most part were brought against women and were intended to compel a woman to reveal the name of the man who had defied the bonds of holy matrimony and who should be held responsible for supporting any children produced by the illicit fornication (L. Friedman 1993: 54).

In the nineteenth century, the focus on what Lawrence Friedman refers to as "crimes against morality" continued. The approach to these offenses was based on what Friedman refers to as the **Victorian Compromise**. Society accepted that the human impulse toward pleasure meant that full enforcement of crimes against morality was not realistic and that a measure of immoral behavior should be tolerated so long as the activity took place below the public radar. There also was a recognition that it was virtually impossible to fully enforce laws against adultery and fornication in large and diverse urban areas. In Michigan, for example, adultery and fornication were tolerated and were punished only if "open and notorious." Criminal charges for the seduction of a "virtuous unmarried female" by a male who persuaded her to "yield to his lustful embrace" were dropped if the defendant agreed to marry the woman. Alabama limited punishment for abusive, insulting, or obscene language to epithets uttered in the presence of a woman (L. Friedman 1993: 130, 219–220).

Gambling continued to be punished in the nineteenth century. An 1839 Illinois law imposed a fine on anyone who sold or imported for sale "any pack or packs of playing cards, or any dice, billiard table, billiard balls . . . or any obscene book." It also was a criminal offense to "play for money, or other valuable thing, any game with cards . . . checks, or at billiards; or to bet on any game." The Victorian Compromise resulted in a toleration of gambling. Only fifty-nine indictments for gambling were handed down in New York between 1845 and 1851, roughly half of women arrested paid fines, and the charges against the other defendants were dismissed. Periodic efforts were made to limit state-sponsored lotteries because the public endorsement of gambling allegedly promoted unrealistic hopes for a "life of luxury" among the working class, who should be devoting their time and energy to work and industry (L. Friedman 1993: 133–134).

Excessive drinking had always been a crime. In the nineteenth century, drinking was blamed for undermining the work ethic and for creating an inebriated population that could not be trusted with the vote. Drinking was associated with foreign immigrants from Germany and Ireland and was described as bringing about social decay. A temperance movement developed, which in 1851 persuaded Maine to prohibit the manufacture and sale of alcohol (L. Friedman 1993: 134).

The Victorian Compromise began to break down after 1870. Societies for the "suppression of vice" developed as a backlash against what was viewed as the loose morality of the working class and immigrants. A young salesman from Connecticut, Anthony Comstock, succeeded in persuading Congress to pass the 1873 Comstock Law, which declared that it was a crime to mail any "obscene, lewd, or lascivious" publication or any "article or thing designed or intended for the prevention of conception or procuring of abortion." This law was the model for state laws, which also raised the age of consent for statutory rape from 14 to 16. The U.S. Congress made it a crime to sell lottery tickets across state lines, and various states prohibited the manufacture and sale of liquor or heavily regulated the sale of liquor. An 1879 ordinance in Oakland, California, required individuals swimming in the harbor to wear trunks reaching from the waist to the thigh and a shirt or jersey covering all of the upper part of the body except the head or arms (L. Friedman 1993: 139).

States and localities declared it a crime to operate a brothel and passed laws against "nightwalkers" and "vagrants" and "lewd and lascivious" behavior. Prostitution generally was tolerated by the police so long as it was confined to "red light" districts. Religious leaders, however, condemned prostitution as an attack on the family and the domestic role of women. The police responded to pressure from church groups and anti-vice organizations by periodically cracking down against women who solicited on the street, but they demonstrated little interest in enforcing the law against high-priced call girls and male customers. The arrestees were led through the street and jeered at and harassed by onlookers, jailed, and released after paying a modest fine. There was a measure of hypocrisy behind this entire exercise. The consensus among males was that prostitution provided men with a private outlet for their sexual impulses while allowing "good women" to preserve their virginity and chastity until marriage (L. Friedman 1993: 223–228).

In 1880, there were 58,000 prisoners in prisons and in local jails, 4,768 of whom were imprisoned for offenses against "public morals." Most of these individuals were arrested for "drunk and disorderly" conduct, but there were also individuals imprisoned for incest, homosexual activity, bigamy, adultery, seduction, fornication, lewdness, indecent exposure, and possession of obscene materials (L. Friedman 1993: 139).

"Victimless crimes" continued to be a focus of criminal justice in the twentieth century. The fear of foreigners became intertwined with sexual morality in 1910 with the passage of the Mann Act. The American public feared that the country was being infiltrated by foreign networks of pimps and degenerates who threatened to lure innocent farm girls into what was called sexual "white slavery." The Mann Act declared it a crime to "transport . . . any woman or girl" across state lines "for the purpose of prostitution or debauchery, or for any other immoral purpose." The Mann Act was stretched beyond the original purpose and was used to enforce sexual morality. In the famous Supreme Court case of *Caminetti v. United States* in 1917, the Court upheld the conviction of two young men who had traveled with their girlfriends across the California border into Nevada (L. Friedman 1993: 327; see also *Caminetti v. United States*, 242 U.S. 470 [1917]).

An infamous example of the abuse of the Mann Act was the prosecution of Jack Johnson, the heavyweight champion of the world. Johnson, an African American, was convicted of sending a ticket from Chicago, Illinois, to his white girlfriend in Pittsburgh, Pennsylvania. Johnson was convicted and sentenced to a year in prison. Between 1910 and 1915, more than a thousand defendants were convicted of "white slavery." Although the Mann Act primarily was used against men, women also were targeted. A study of 156 women imprisoned between 1927 and 1937 indicated that almost one-quarter of the women were not connected with commercial prostitution and had been arrested for traveling across state lines with a man whom they planned to marry (L. Friedman 1993: 328).

The dawn of the twentieth century also witnessed the "red-light abatement movement" dedicated to the eradication of brothels. Chicago was typical. In October 1909, twelve thousand men and women marched on the red-light district to reclaim the area for Christianity. Two years later, ten thousand residents paraded in support of the eradication of this "kingdom of vice." A Chicago report labeled prostitution as an evil that must be eliminated to safeguard the moral integrity of the city. Thirty-one states passed abatement laws that gave the state attorney general as well as citizens the right to file a legal action to close brothels. Prostitutes, though arrested across the country, evaded these abatement actions by moving into other areas of the city. Despite the public condemnation of prostitution, sexual services continued to be in great demand (L. Friedman 1993: 228–331).

In the early twentieth century, laws against fornication and adultery continued to be enforced. In Boston in the first six months of 1920, seventy-seven men and eighty-one women were charged with fornication, twenty-five men and twenty women were charged with adultery, and forty-six men and forty-nine women were charged with lewd and lascivious cohabitation. A number of states raised the age of consent for sexual relations to 18, and Tennessee law declared that it was a felony to have sexual relations with a woman under 21 (L. Friedman 1993: 332–334).

The prohibition on homosexuality was largely unenforced by the police until the early twentieth century. Only six appellate cases were reported before 1870, twenty-three between 1870 and 1900, and two hundred in the first part of the twentieth century. In the 1940s alone, there were sixty-eight reported cases. By the early 1950s, one thousand individuals were being arrested per year in the District of Columbia for homosexual activity. Sodomy laws were broadly interpreted to include any sexual activity that did not have the potential to lead to procreation (L. Friedman 1993: 343–344).

The war against vice culminated in 1919 with the passage of the Eighteenth Amendment to the U.S. Constitution, which prohibited the manufacturing, shipping, importing, or selling of liquor. In 1929, in Columbus, Ohio, there were 1,958 arrests for violations of liquor laws. This was ten times the arrest rate for auto theft and more than twenty times the rate of arrest for robbery. Prohibition played into the hands of organized crime groups that pioneered the bootlegging of liquor. In 1927, Al Capone, the "boss of bosses" in Chicago, generated over $60 million from the sale of illicit liquor and gambling (L. Friedman 1993: 339–341).

Prohibition was abolished in 1933. Joseph Gusfield, in his well-known book *Symbolic Crusade: Status Politics and the American Temperance Movement*, argues that prohibition was a movement predominantly comprising small-town rural Protestants who identified drinking with Catholic immigrants from Ireland and Italy who had settled in urban areas. Gusfield contends that the temperance movement was a symbolic crusade against immigrants and was an effort to stamp out "demon rum," which was viewed as the first step in the eroding the moral structure of American society (Gusfield 1963).

By the second half of the twentieth century, the war on vice had lost some of its considerable steam. Nevada legalized gambling in 1931, and state lotteries gradually were established. New Jersey, in need of revenues, established casino gambling in Atlantic City, and a number of states authorized casinos. Prosecutions under the Mann Act numbered 157 in 1961 and dropped to 36 by the end of the 1960s. Various states repealed their criminal laws against fornication and adultery (L. Friedman 1993: 341–347).

The Supreme Court put the nail in the coffin of sodomy laws when it overturned the sodomy convictions of two gay men in *Lawrence v. Texas* (*Lawrence v. Texas,* 539 U.S. 558 [2003]).

So-called victimless or consensual crimes continue to be a center of debate. Norval Morris and Gordon Hawkins in their classic work, *The Honest Politician's Guide to Crime Control*, criticize what they call the "overreach" of criminal law (N. Morris and Hawkins 1969: 5–6), or what Stanford Kadish refers to as "overcriminalization" (S. Kadish 1967: 158–176). Morris and Hawkins note that the issue of victimless crimes is of concern because almost half of all arrests are for drunk and disorderly behavior, gambling, and prostitution (N. Morris and Hawkins 1969: 4). They articulate a number of objections to the criminalization of acts of individual morality (5–6).

Crime tariff. The financial cost of gambling, narcotics, and prostitution is driven higher by the unlawful nature of these activities, which limits competition between suppliers.

Organized crime. The extraordinary profit that can be earned attracts organized crime and gangs to the illicit activities. The money that is made funds other unlawful activities or is invested in lawful businesses that generate additional profits.

Secondary crime. The high cost of supporting a narcotics or gambling habit can lead addicts to commit crimes to "feed their habit." Individuals who engage in illegal behavior also can be blackmailed.

Quality control. There is no health and safety control over items sold in the "black market." Legalizing activity would allow for health inspections for prostitutes and government control over the quality of narcotics.

Deterrence. Arresting individuals who are addicted to narcotics or alcohol does not deter this behavior. Individuals arrested for drunk and disorderly behavior or prostitution generally are arrested and quickly released. The revolving door of arrest and release does not provide a deterrent.

Arrests. The difficulty of enforcing laws against prostitution and other victimless crimes often requires law enforcement personnel to engage in troubling tactics such as entrapment to enforce the law. The failure to arrest individuals involved in "victimless crimes" undermines the deterrent value of the law.

Double standard. The legitimacy of the prohibition of "moral crimes" is undermined by the inconsistency in enforcement. Individuals are sent to jail for possession of marijuana at the same time that twenty-nine states and the District of Columbia allow for medical marijuana. The law also may appear arbitrary. We tolerate tobacco, one of the most harmful drugs, but we criminalize marijuana (with the exception of Washington State, Colorado, Alaska, California, Maine, Nevada, Massachusetts, and Oregon).

Corruption. The absence of a complaining witness or victim and the large amounts of money to be earned from illicit activity provide temptations for police and judicial corruption. The police may be bribed or may rob drug dealers and resell the narcotics.

Social harm. The laws on "victimless crimes" are based on moral objections, and these acts do not cause significant social harm.

Forbidden fruit. The declaration of acts as unlawful makes them more attractive to young people.

Budget deficits. A significant amount of money and resources are spent enforcing laws against victimless crimes. Legalization of narcotics or prostitution would generate significant state revenues and provide a needed source of funds to the states.

Consider the arguments for and against victimless crimes when reading the brief discussions of prostitution and gambling.

9.3 YOU DECIDE

California adopted a law prohibiting the sale or rental of "violent video games" to minors unless accompanied by an adult. These games were to carry the label "18." The law covers games "in which the range of options available to a player includes killing, maiming, dismembering, or sexually assaulting an image of a human being, if those acts are depicted" in a manner that "a reasonable person, considering the game as a

(Continued)

whole, would find appeals to a deviant or morbid interest of minors," that is "patently offensive to prevailing standards in the community as to what is suitable for minors," and that "causes the game, as a whole, to lack serious literary, artistic, political, or scientific value for minors." Violation of the law is punishable by a civil fine of up to $1,000. The video game industry has in place a voluntary rating system designed to inform consumers about the content of games.

Video game and software firms challenged the law as a violation of the First Amendment to the U.S. Constitution.

In 2011, in *Brown v. Entertainment Merchants Association*, the Supreme Court overturned the law as unconstitutional. The Court held California was unable to demonstrate a causal relationship between exposure to video games and violence among juveniles, that it impermissibly singled out video games for regulation, and that the law was under-inclusive because children had access to games purchased by adults (*Brown v. Entertainment Merchants Association*, 564 U.S. 786 [2011]).

Would you restrict the sale of violent video games to juveniles?

Prostitution

Prostitution is a criminal offense in forty-nine states in the United States and in thirteen of the fifteen counties in Nevada. In other states and localities, prostitution generally is considered a misdemeanor punished by a jail sentence of up to a year and by a fine. The jail term typically is increased with each subsequent arrest. State laws usually punish an act of sex in return for something of value, soliciting for prostitution, and agreeing to engage in an act of prostitution. An individual may lose his or her driver's license for using an automobile to carry out a prohibited act of prostitution. In 2006, according to FBI estimates, there were 79,700 arrests for prostitution, slightly more than the 77,600 arrests for prostitution in 2007. In recent years, arrests for prostitution and commercialized sex activity have significantly declined. According to the Uniform Crime Reports, there were roughly 42,000 arrests in 2013, 37,000 arrests in 2014, and 31,000 arrests in 2015. The sex trade is a lucrative business for pimps and sex traffickers, generating $290 million in Atlanta, Georgia, and $235 million in Miami, Florida, in 2007 (Lowrey 2014).

The traditional objection to prostitution is that the Bible and other religious texts view it as a sin. In recent years, the focus has shifted to the impact of prostitution on the women involved in the sex trade. This includes the risk of pregnancy and venereal disease, abuse from customers, exploitation by pimps, and loss of self-esteem. There also is a concern that street activity by prostitutes drives businesses and families out of a neighborhood. Individuals visiting prostitutes may become crime victims and be reluctant to report the crime to the police. The arrests for prostitution tend to focus on prostitutes rather than on male customers. The reason that is offered for this discriminatory application of the law is that the prostitute, by soliciting customers on the street, offends public decency (Packer 1968: 328–331).

The argument for legalizing prostitution is that sexual activity between consenting adults should not be a criminal offense and there is no reason why sexual activity should be prohibited because it involves an exchange of money. According to this argument, prostitutes have the right to use their bodies as they see fit. Prostitutes also provide a sexual outlet to individuals whose disabilities and limitations make it difficult to attract sexual partners.

Criminalizing prostitution has had little impact on limiting the prevalence of prostitution. Arresting prostitutes reinforces their dependence on pimps who post bail, hire lawyers, and protect prostitutes against abuse from customers. Criminalizing prostitution makes it unlikely that prostitutes will report abuse by pimps or customers or robberies to the police. Enforcing the laws against prostitution generally requires that the police spend significant resources in surveillance and in sting operations.

The Netherlands has legalized prostitution and has developed a $1 billion sex industry with thirty thousand sex workers who comprise 5 percent of the Dutch economy. Large German cities have created "amusement zones" that include brothels. Sweden has successfully limited public solicitation for prostitution by repealing its law against selling sexual services and passing a law that punishes purchasing a sexual service.

The argument for legalization of prostitution is challenged by the global phenomenon of sex trafficking, which also illustrates the ineffectiveness of the criminal law to curb this practice.

The FBI describes human sex trafficking as the "most common form of modern-day slavery" and estimates that the number of domestic and international victims is in the "millions." As many as fifteen thousand individuals are trafficked for sex and forced labor in the United States each year.

Human sex trafficking is the fastest growing international enterprise and one of the most profitable forms of illegal activity for organized crime. Most of the victims are women and children from impoverished circumstances who are forcibly abducted or persuaded under false pretenses to accompany traffickers. The women are confined, raped, psychologically abused, and often sold into slavery and prostituted. Foreign women typically lack language skills to seek assistance and are fearful that they will be sent back home where they will be stigmatized as prostitutes.

The federal Trafficking Victims Protection Act (TVPA), first adopted in 2000, defines a human trafficking victim as an individual induced to perform labor or a commercial sexual act through "force, fraud, or coercion." An individual under the age of 18 is categorized as a victim even when force, fraud, or coercion is absent. The TVPA does not require that an individual is transported across state or international boundaries to be considered a trafficked person.

The TVPA combats trafficking by prosecution, protection, and prevention ("3 Ps").

1. *Prosecution.* Criminal prosecution and jailing of individuals involved in human trafficking under various federal and state laws prohibiting sex trafficking.

2. *Protection.* Protection of victims and providing them medical care, shelter, and a visa to allow them to remain temporarily in the United States.

3. *Prevention.* Raising awareness of human trafficking and working to decrease demand for trafficked persons.

The Department of State compiles a yearly report on global sex trafficking, and countries failing to act against trafficking risk the termination of U.S. foreign assistance.

Relatively few visas have been issued to victims of sex trafficking, and despite the high priority placed on the prosecution of traffickers, the number of individuals trafficked in the United States continues to grow at a rapid rate. Do you favor legalization of prostitution? (The international dimension of trafficking is discussed in Chapter 13 on the study site.)

In 2015, Amnesty International (AI), a leading, global human rights organization, or what is termed a non-governmental organization (NGO), adopted a policy calling for recognition of the human right of sex workers to enter into contracts to provide sexual services. AI means by *decriminalization* removing criminal penalties on the solicitation and act of prostitution and removing all regulation on prostitution. The removal of criminal penalties would take prostitution out of the shadows, allow sex workers to make use of the justice system to protect themselves from violence and discrimination, and allow them access to social security and to banking services. AI does not advocate what the NGO terms legalization because AI fears that prostitution, like any other commercial enterprise, would be subject to extensive regulation including limiting the location of services, restricting advertising, and controlling the ability of sex workers to solicit for prostitution. AI recognizes that decriminalization of prostitution will necessitate the repeal of various laws such as "brothel keeping," "promotion of prostitution," "solicitation," and "living off the proceeds of prostitution" that AI argues may be used to arrest and to punish sex workers and that critics contend protect sex workers against exploitation by pimps and sex traffickers.

Sex workers, according to AI, are one of the most "marginalized groups in the world." Their categorization as criminals allows them to be subjected to a host of abuses, including rape, beatings, trafficking, extortion, and forced eviction. In some instances, these abuses are carried out by the police along with clients and pimps.

AI's proposed public policy has been criticized by various feminist groups and groups of "survivors" of prostitution who argue that prostitution should be criminalized and eliminated rather than accepted as a legitimate commercial enterprise.

Organizations of survivors of prostitution argue that AI's use of the terms *sex work* and *sex workers* obscures that prostitution is not conventional employment that

individuals freely choose to pursue. Most individuals are forced into prostitution at an early age or are forced by economic circumstance or by threats of violence to work under oppressive and often violent conditions. Individuals emerge from sex work psychologically and often physically scared. Amnesty International's plan for decriminalization, according to critics, will increase human trafficking and aligns AI with the oppressors of human rights rather than with the protection of human rights. In the end, critics assert that AI overlooks that prostitution is created and advantages men.

An intermediate approach to decriminalization and legalization is the so-called Nordic model. In 2016, following two years of debate, the French Parliament approved a new law on prostitution that is based on the approach to prostitution followed in Sweden, Norway, and Iceland. The French law focuses on punishing the customer rather than the sex worker, imposes a fine of roughly $1,700 for a first offense and roughly $4,000 for a second offense, and provides that a conviction will be recorded on the defendant's criminal record. Individuals arrested for paying for prostitution also will be required to attend classes on the harm caused by prostitution and learn how sex workers often are the victims of trafficking and abuse. The French law declares that solicitation for prostitution by a sex worker no longer is considered a crime and repeals legislation that made "passive soliciting a crime" that resulted in arrests of sex workers for standing in public with revealing clothing. An additional provision provides over $5 million to assist sex workers to leave the profession and provides temporary six-month visas to foreign sex workers unlawfully in France who enter the "exit program." Roughly 80 percent of the forty thousand sex workers in France are from outside the country.

What is your view of criminalizing individuals who pay for prostitution rather than sex workers who solicit prostitution? How would AI view the French approach to regulating prostitution? What of AI's critics?

9.5 YOU DECIDE

In 1983, the city of Minneapolis, Minnesota, hired well-known feminist scholars Catharine MacKinnon and Andrea Dworkin to draft an anti-pornography statute. The law was passed by the city council and vetoed on two occasions by the mayor of Minneapolis. The next year, the Indianapolis city council learned of the MacKinnon-Dworkin draft statute and adopted the law as a city ordinance, which subsequently was signed into law by Mayor William Hudnut.

The U.S. Supreme Court has held that obscenity has no redeeming social value and is unprotected speech. The test for obscenity is difficult to apply. In *Miller v. California*, the Court held that in evaluating a publication, the publication must be taken as a whole, appeal to the prurient (sexual) interest, contain patently offensive depictions of ultimate sexual conduct, and on the whole be judged in accordance with the standards of the local community (*Miller v. California*, 413 U.S. 15 [1973]). A less strict standard is used for judging whether material constitutes unlawful child pornography (*New York v. Ferber*, 458 U.S. 747 [1982]).

The Indianapolis ordinance prohibited material that did not fall within the Supreme Court's definition of obscenity. The statute broke new ground and prohibited the "sexually explicit subordination of women, whether in pictures or in words." The "pornographic" portrayal of women under the ordinance includes the portrayal of women in any or all of six types of situations. These portrayals include women as sexual objects who enjoy pain or humiliation, women as sexual objects who experience sexual pleasure in being raped, women being penetrated by objects or animals, and women in scenes of physical abuse. The ordinance also prohibits portraying women as sexual objects for "domination, conquest, violation, exploitation, possession, or use, or

through postures or positions of servility or submission or display."

The ordinance prohibits trafficking in pornography, coercing individuals into performing pornographic works, and forcing pornography onto other individuals. Anyone injured by an individual who has seen or read pornography is recognized as possessing the right to bring a legal action against the maker or seller of the pornography.

Indianapolis contended that pornography shapes thoughts and perceptions. Men who view women in subordinate positions are likely to treat women as inferior. This lack of respect for women translates into low pay, domestic violence, and rape. The ordinance, according to Indianapolis, was required to combat the influence of the multimillion-dollar pornography industry.

The American Booksellers Association challenged the constitutionality of the Indianapolis ordinance on the grounds that the law violates the First Amendment. The federal Seventh Circuit Court of Appeals agreed with the Booksellers Association and struck down the law. The court held that the law discriminates on the grounds of the content of speech. Speech treating women in the approved way is lawful "no matter how sexually explicit." Speech treating women in the "disapproved way . . . is unlawful no matter how significant the literary, artistic, or political qualities of the work taken as a whole" (*American Booksellers Association v. Hudnut*, 771 F.2d 323 [1985]).

The Seventh Circuit Court of Appeals explained that the First Amendment does not permit the government to prohibit speech that it does not agree with and to permit speech that coincides with what the government views as the "truth." The First Amendment is based on a "marketplace of ideas" in which citizens challenge

(Continued)

speech with which they disagree with more speech. The Indianapolis ordinance unconstitutionally had excluded one point of view from the marketplace of ideas.

Obscenity is not constitutionally protected speech because it erodes society's moral standards and has no redeeming social value. The Seventh Circuit accepted the argument that the pornographic depiction of women

subjected to violence may encourage sex discrimination and yet concluded that the Indianapolis ordinance intrudes on protected speech.

Do you agree violent portrayals of women constitute sex discrimination? Should pornographic portrayals of women be protected under the First Amendment? Would you support a local law similar to the Indianapolis law?

Gambling

Gambling generally describes an activity that is prohibited under criminal law.

Gaming refers to games of chance, which are considered legal. A card game among friends, for example, may be exempted from criminal statutes in some states.

States apply a dominant factor or predominance test to determine whether an activity constitutes gambling. An activity involves gambling if the element of luck is the dominant factor or predominates over skill. Social gambling between friends on card games is permitted under most state statutes. This generally is defined as a "social context" in which everyone participates in the activity and no one profits by conducting or sponsoring the game. Some states limit the amount of money that an individual may win in a single hand and require that the game be conducted in a residence or other "private place." All states allow nonprofit charitable organizations to raise money by sponsoring certain types of gambling activities. Another common exception is "drawings" conducted by stores in which the "winner" receives a prize. Virtually every state treats gambling as a misdemeanor, although several states treat subsequent arrests for gambling as felonies.

The early American colonists brought with them games of chance that were popular in England, and there were few restrictions on gambling. Lotteries were used in the eighteenth and nineteenth centuries to raise revenues for universities and to support education. By the early twentieth century, gambling had become viewed as immoral and was driven underground. Unlawful gambling, along with the illegal sale of alcohol, became the cash cow for organized crime.

In 1931, Nevada legalized most forms of gambling, and over the next thirty years, Las Vegas became known as the center of gambling in the United States. In 1977, New Jersey established legalized gambling in Atlantic City. Twenty-four states now allow commercial casinos in some form. According to the American Gaming Association, the more than one thousand river-based, land-based, and racetrack commercial casinos and card rooms in these states produced a gross gaming revenue of $38.54 billion and contributed $8.85 billion in tax revenues in 2015. The total gaming revenue is $68.44 billion including Native American casinos (discussed below) (American Gaming Association 2016).

Each state determines whether to allow gambling, what forms of gambling to permit, and who may gamble. States differ on whether to permit betting on horse races and dog races, allow card or table games, and permit slot machines and video poker, as well as on where these forms of gambling may be located. Some states require a minimum age for gambling, and in other states, a minimum age is established for particular forms of gambling. In New Jersey, you can buy a lottery ticket and bet on horse racing at age 18 although you must be 21 years of age to enter an Atlantic City casino. Every state allows gambling activities such as bingo games that benefit charities.

Native American tribes are legally entitled to establish casinos on tribal land. In 1979, the Florida Seminole tribe began sponsoring bingo games. Native American gaming is regulated by the federal Indian Gaming Regulatory Act of 1988, and jurisdiction over various aspects of Native American gaming is shared by the federal and state governments and the tribes. Profits may be used only for community welfare purposes. There are roughly 473 Native American–owned gaming enterprises in twenty-eight states, and 241 of the 500 tribes in the United States operate gaming establishments. In 2015, Native American casinos earned a total of $29.9 billion.

New Hampshire established a state lottery in 1963, which marked the first time in the twentieth century that a state directly established a lottery. By 1999, thirty-seven states had established lotteries to raise money, and today, forty-three states have lotteries.

In the past decade, Internet gambling has become enormously popular. Delaware, New Jersey, and Nevada are the only states to have legalized Internet gambling, although several other states likely will provide for online gambling in the near future.

Gambling historically has been condemned as immoral for focusing attention on material gain rather than on spiritual matters. The modern justification for criminalizing gambling is that it diverts money from the support of families and can lead to addictive behavior. The American Psychiatric Association labels pathological gambling as an impulse control disorder. Addictive gamblers may engage in crime to support their habit, and their compulsive behavior may lead to borrowing money at high interest rates. Gambling disorders can severely disrupt families and lead to financial chaos, domestic violence, and divorce. Studies indicate between 1 percent and 2 percent of the population are problem gamblers, and in Las Vegas, problem gamblers may constitute as much as 7 percent of the population. In recent years, a large number of older individuals increasingly have turned to gambling to escape boredom and to increase their incomes (Lesieur 1992).

There is obvious inconsistency in allowing gambling in casinos, in state-sponsored lotteries, and at racetracks while prohibiting other forms of gambling. Gambling laws are difficult to enforce because most unlawful gambling is hard to detect. Gambling is a lifestyle, and making gambling illegal has failed to deter individuals from wagering. Organized crime has been able to fill the demand for gambling and controls most large-scale betting on sports outside of Las Vegas. Wagering is one of the largest sources of income for organized crime, and individuals who owe money may be subjected to threats and retaliation. The unlawful nature of gambling means that cheating and threats often are unreported to the police. The large amount of money involved in unlawful gambling operations makes the police susceptible to bribery. Another concern is that with well over $4.2 billion wagered on the Super Bowl and $9.2 billion on March Madness in 2015, there is the danger of athletes being bribed to influence the outcome of athletic events. In recent years, there have been betting scandals in the English and German football leagues, in college and professional basketball, and in Major League Baseball.

Police investigation of gambling is time-consuming and requires the cultivation of informants and the use of electronic surveillance. Relatively few arrests are made for unlawful gambling. According to the FBI Uniform Crime Report, in 2006 there were 12,300 gambling arrests, and in 2007 there were 12,200 arrests for gambling. Since then, there has been a steady decline in gambling arrests: 9,900 arrests for gambling in 2010, 8,600 in 2011, 9,900 in 2012, 5,055 in 2013, 4,363 in 2014, and 3,587 in 2015. Studies of prosecutions for unlawful gambling indicate that most individuals receive modest fines and rarely are imprisoned.

There is particular concern over the growth of gambling among college students. A study sponsored by the National Center for Responsible Gaming in conjunction with Harvard Medical School found that 40 percent of college students reported having gambled in the past year, and between 3 percent and 11 percent of college students are considered to have a "gambling problem." Only about one-fifth of colleges have written policies on gambling.

Gambling in the United States has been transformed by the fantasy sports industry. The two largest companies, FanDuel and DraftKings, which represent 90 percent of the industry, have attracted well over $400 million in investments and are each valued at more than $1 billion and scheduled to merge. Professional sports leagues that traditionally have opposed gambling are some of the largest investors along with major media companies. Investors include the National Basketball Association, Major League Baseball, NBC Comcast and Fox Sports, and various prominent owners of sports teams (J. Kang 2016).

This fantasy industry has been made possible by the fact that in 2006 Congress enacted a provision in the Unlawful Internet Gambling Enforcement Act that declared fantasy sports legal. An estimated fifty-seven million people play fantasy sports (FS), and over four million play daily fantasy (DF) sports, by paying an entry fee and compiling teams of players. Winning and losing in FS is based on the performance of the players over the course of the season. Daily fantasy is based on a player's performance on a single day in a 182-game baseball season or 82-game basketball season.

The legality of FS in various states continues to be uncertain. New York, which is one of the biggest FS markets, in 2016 after opposing FS as unlawful gambling recognized fantasy sports as a game of skill in time for the 2016 National Football League season. A number of states, however, continue to categorize DF sports as unlawful gambling rather than as a game of skill. The primary source of controversy is over DF sports in which players compete against other players for money paid into the pool by each player based on the performance of professional sports athletes in a single day of competition, which critics contend involves more luck than skill.

Individuals insisting that FS involve skill point to the need to keep abreast of player performance and statistical trends and the fact that competitors possess varying levels of preparation and knowledge. Analysts, however, contend that individuals using sophisticated statistical software dominate FS, particularly in those competitions in which players compete head-to-head. The overwhelming percentage of people who play FS, similar to gamblers, lose money. A study by the consulting firm McKinsey of Major League Baseball found that 91 percent of profits were won by 1.3 percent of players. A survey of 1,400 DF sports players by Eilers Research (now Eilers & Krejcik Gaming) found that 70 percent of players lost money. McKinsey found that the top 11 DF sports players risked an average of $2 million in entry fees and profited $135,000 per person over three months, and the remaining individuals in the top 1.3% paid $9,100 and made an average of $2,400 per person (E. Miller and Singer 2015). Despite the fact that most bettors lose money, surveys indicate that an overwhelming number of players love playing DF sports.

FS, however controversial, ultimately may be eclipsed by the legalization of betting on sporting events by Congress. Well over 60 percent of the public favor legalization of betting on sports.

The sports betting market is a "sleeping giant," with an estimated $149 billion wagered illegally in 2015.

An estimated 28 percent of the American adult population have bet on sports in the past year.

The question is whether society has the right to dictate to people that they cannot use their money to gamble. By choosing to keep some forms of gambling in the shadows, society forfeits the ability to tax the proceeds from unlawful gambling activity.

Vagrancy and Homelessness

William Blackstone, the venerated eighteenth-century English legal theorist, observed that "idleness" constitutes "high offense against the public economy." Incorrigibles in some instances were incarcerated in irons and kept on bread and water until they joined the working economy. Vagrancy laws were imported into colonial America and remained a part of state criminal codes well into the twentieth century. In 1837, in *New York v. Miln*, the U.S. Supreme Court proclaimed that "[w]e think it as competent and as necessary for a state to provide precautionary measures against . . . [the] pestilence of paupers, vagabonds, and possibly convicts as it is to guard against the physical pestilence . . . [of] infectious disease" [*New York v. Miln*, 36 U.S. 102 [1837]).

A Jacksonville, Florida, ordinance was typical in criminalizing a long list of "vagrants" including "rogues and vagabonds, or dissolute persons who go about begging, . . . persons who use juggling or unlawful games or plays, common drunkards, . . . common railers and brawlers, persons wandering or strolling around place to place without any lawful purpose or object, habitual loafers, [and] disorderly persons." The police often expanded on this list by broadly interpreting the laws' provisions to hold individuals criminally responsible for such acts as "prowling by auto."

Risa Goluboff, in *Vagrant Nation: Police Power, Constitutional Change, and the Making of the 1960s*, recounts that vagrancy laws until well into the twentieth century were used against unemployed workers who traveled in search of higher wages and better working conditions. The laws also were employed to arrest individuals who begged for food or money. A failure to work a steady job was viewed as a moral failure rather than as a product of the introduction of technology, and a social stigma was attached to individuals who chose to live the "hobo life." These vagrancy and "tramp" laws also were used in some cases against workers striking against labor conditions and wages (Goluboff 2016: 116).

In addition to the unemployed, vagrancy laws were directed at the "lewd and dissolute" and "sex perverts" and were applied against prostitutes and lesbian, gay, bisexual, and transgender (LGBT) individuals gathered in public. The police frequently invoked the "loitering" provision in these laws, which punished appearing in public with no visible means of support, to arrest individuals whom they suspected of contemplating criminal conduct. Vagrancy laws also proved an important tool in arresting members of gambling interests and individuals involved in drugs (Goluboff 2016: 8–66).

Legal commentators and courts viewed vagrancy laws as an exception to the requirement that a crime requires an act and may not be based on a status such as being poor and employed. The Virginia Supreme Court in 1937 unapologetically stated that vagrancy does not involve "particular affirmative acts of a person" and instead punishes a "mode of life, habits, and character."

A 1935 report from the New York State Law Revision Commission echoed the views of the Virginia Supreme Court, and for the next several decades, courts pronounced that the purpose of vagrancy laws was to prevent crime and that if the police must wait for a crime to be committed, the preventive aspects of the law would be undermined. Judges went so far as to observe that individuals' "attitudes" may place them in the class of individuals subject to vagrancy laws (Goluboff 2016: 28, 60).

In the 1960s, African Americans and other people of color were particular targets of vagrancy laws. An Alabama vagrancy law carried a penalty of a $500 fine and imprisonment for up to a year and was used against "outside [civil rights] agitators" in the South. The Reverend Martin Luther King denounced these laws as a "new low in the tactics that some southerners are willing to use to maintain the system of segregation." The Kerner Commission appointed by President Lyndon B. Johnson in the wake of urban protests following the assassination of Martin Luther King singled out loitering and vagrancy laws as a source of community tension with the police (Goluboff 2016: 62, 65, 114–115, 267, 269).

Another group targeted by vagrancy laws in the 1960s were so-called hippies, young, long-haired youth who opposed the Vietnam War and were identified in the public mind with a "counterculture" of drugs and "free love." For example, two Colorado young people were arrested while baking pies in a "hippie hangout" under a law that criminalized any individual "able to work and support himself in some honest and respectable calling, who shall be found loitering or strolling about, frequenting public places, or where liquor is sold, begging or leading an idle, immoral or profligate course of life, or not having any visible means of support." A federal district court overturned the defendants' convictions and noted that this vagrancy law could be used against "every member of the community who is not living . . . the [accepted life] style . . . [at] the whim of the authorities." The court noted that an individual is "free to be a hippie, a Methodist, a Jew, a Black Panther, a Kiwanian or even a communist, so long as his conduct does not imperil others, or infringe upon their rights. In short, it is not a crime to be a hippie" (*Goldman v. Knecht*, 295 F. Supp. 897 [D. Colo. 1969]).

Broadly drafted vagrancy laws were held unconstitutional by the U.S. Supreme Court in *Papachristou v. Jacksonville* over twenty years after the Court first heard a challenge to these laws (*Papachristou v. Jacksonville*, 405 U.S. 156 [1972]). In *Papachristou*, the Court held that vagrancy laws were void for vagueness and reasoned that these laws failed to provide individuals with adequate notice of the acts, which were criminalized at the same time that the police were provided with an unreasonable amount of discretion in enforcing the laws. The lack of clear standards "permits and encourages an arbitrary and discriminatory enforcement of the law" and "results in a regime in which the poor and unpopular are permitted to 'stand on a public sidewalk . . . only at the whim of . . . police officers.'" Justice William O. Douglas, a fiercely independent justice from Oregon, added that Americans "walking . . . wandering [and] loafing," along with the right to be "nonconformists," historically have been part of American freedom, pluralism, and diversity.

The declaration that vagrancy laws were unconstitutional left cities and towns with a depleted arsenal to regulate individuals viewed as a threat to public safety and stability. As homelessness expanded in certain parts of the country, government officials turned to new strategies to control the homeless population.

The National Law Center on Homelessness and Poverty estimates that there are between 2.5 and 3.5 million individuals experiencing homelessness each year in the United States, including at least 1.6 million children. There are roughly 7.5 million people who have lost housing and live with relatives or friends. The homeless are concentrated among African Americans, individuals with disabilities, and individuals under 60. Roughly 15 percent of the homeless are victims of domestic violence, and 1 percent are military veterans. These figures are rough estimates because different agencies employ different definitions of homelessness, employ different methods of collection, and survey at different times of year (National Law Center on Homelessness and Poverty 2016a).

The National Law Center attributes homelessness to the shortage of affordable housing and to a shortage of shelter housing, which forces people to live on the street. The Los Angeles City and County estimate that there are only 11,933 shelter beds to serve a homeless population of roughly 53,706. The National Law Center periodically surveys 187 cities and concludes that municipal codes, in effect, "criminalize" the "necessary human activities" of the homeless. These laws are designed to move the visibly homeless out of commercial and tourist districts and increasingly to exclude them from entire cities (National Law Center on Homelessness and Poverty 2016b).

Reliance on these "quality of life" laws is justified by political officials based on the protection of public health and public safety. The National Law Center argues that the application of these laws has transformed cities into "no-homeless zones." These laws include the prohibition on a range of activity including camping, begging, sitting, lying, or storing personal possessions in public; loitering; sleeping in a vehicle; and food sharing in public. In 2016, the Law Center named Denver, Colorado; Puyallup, Washington; Honolulu, Hawaii; and Dallas, Texas, to the "hall of shame" for the treatment of the homeless (National Law Center on Homelessness and Poverty 2016b).

Although these municipal polices and laws profess to be based on the view that the criminal law is the most effective mechanism to motivate homeless individuals to take advantage of the availability of shelters, critics assert they are based on the view that the homeless are an impediment to economic development. The National Law Center contends that providing housing is much less expensive than a strategy of criminalization of homelessness and does not address the fundamental causes of homelessness.

Forest Stuart, in his study of "skid row" in a major American city, finds that the police conduct constant surveillance of the homeless population. The average individual on skid row is stopped by the police an average of 5.4 times a year. As a result, individuals learn to be "cop wise" and are constantly adjusting their behavior to avoid attracting the attention of the police (Stuart 2016).

The National Law Center cites the example of Lawrence Lee Smith, who was left homeless after a degenerative joint disease left him unable to continue to work in construction and to support himself. He lived in a camper van for a number of years, and when the van was towed, he could not afford to retrieve it, leaving him homeless. The shortage of shelters in Boise, Idaho, forced him to sleep on the street. He subsequently was arrested for unlawful camping and jailed for one hundred days, and in the process, his tent, his stove, and other equipment he depended on to live were stolen.

Jerome Murdough, a 56-year-old homeless veteran, took shelter from the cold in the stairwell of a public housing building. He was arrested for trespassing, and because he did not have $2,500 for bail, he was incarcerated at Rikers Island in New York City. Murdough was left unattended in a hot cell and died there of a heat-related disease.

The National Coalition for the Homeless documented 1,650 acts of violence against the homeless between 1999 and 2013 in which 375 individuals lost their lives. The perpetrators tended to be under age 30, and these acts occurred in forty-seven states. In 2013, there were 109 attacks, 18 of which resulted in death. These assaults appeared to have been motivated by resentment toward the homeless, the ability to target the homeless without fear of retaliation, and the thrill of collective violence (National Coalition for the Homeless 2014).

The National Coalition for the Homeless has proposed a Homeless Bill of Rights to ensure that the homeless are free from discrimination, that their persons and property are safe and secure, that they have access to shelter and city services, and that their children are provided the opportunity for education.

American policies toward the homeless have been criticized by international organizations, in effect, as the criminalization of homelessness. In 2014, the United Nations (UN) Human Rights Committee, in its Concluding Observations on the review of the U.S. government's record of implementation of the International Covenant on Civil and Political Rights, expressed concern about "reports of criminalization of people living on the street for everyday activities such as eating, sleeping, [and] sitting in particular areas" (Kittrie 1971).

Do you agree or disagree that various cities, in effect, are criminalizing homelessness? What is society's responsibility, if any, toward the homeless? The next section shifts the discussion to the deterrence of "crime in the suites."

■ WHITE-COLLAR CRIME

James Bryce's *The American Commonwealth* (1888) and Henry Demarest Lloyd's *Wealth Against Commonwealth* (1894) condemned the corruption of politicians and greed of corporate executives in the United States. Lloyd noted that large corporations had gobbled up the competition and had secured monopolies over vital resources like oil and, as a result, were able to charge exorbitant prices. The Standard Oil Company headed by John D. Rockefeller symbolized this corporate dominance of the American economy. The U.S. Congress bowed to popular pressure and passed the Sherman Antitrust Act in 1890, which prohibited firms from combining to fix prices and from merging to control the market.

Muckraking journalists and writers documented corporate dominance of the economy. Frank Norris's book *The Octopus* (1901) was a fictionalized account of a conspiracy among four companies to control the railroad industry in the western states. Upton Sinclair's novel *The Jungle* (1906) documented the exploitation of immigrant workers and the dangerous working conditions in the meatpacking industry in Chicago. Sinclair's work led to the establishment of the Food and Drug Administration (FDA), which was authorized to regulate the meatpacking industry. Louis Brandeis, later to be named to the U.S. Supreme Court, in *Other People's Money and How the Bankers Use It* (1914) condemned bankers like J. P. Morgan, who Brandeis alleged betrayed the trust of their depositors through risky investments.

Sociologist Edward Alsworth Ross was one of the first academics to study corporate America. He developed the concept of *criminaloid* to describe the well-respected members of the business community whose public esteem masked their corrupt business and political practices (E. Ross 1965).

The term **white-collar crime** first was introduced in 1939 by sociologist Edwin H. Sutherland in his presidential address to the American Sociological Association. Sutherland discussed the need for academics to expand the study of crime to include the misconduct of business and professional elites (E. Sutherland 1940). Ten years later, Sutherland defined white-collar crime as "crimes committed by a person of respectability and high social status in the course of his occupation." This definition focused on offenses committed by highly respected individuals in pursuit of their professional goals. A doctor may submit a bill to the government for health care that he or she did not provide (occupational crime) or a corporate executive may bribe a government official to give the executive's firm a lucrative government contract (corporate crime). Sutherland's definition of white-collar crime excludes crimes unrelated to commercial activity such as murder, adultery, and intoxication. He highlighted the costs of white-collar crime by citing the example of the manager of a chain grocery store who in one year embezzled an amount of money six times greater than the amount of money lost in the five hundred burglaries and robberies of the firm's grocery stores (E. Sutherland 1949: 7, 9).

Sutherland explained that corporate criminality is not always apparent to the public because many laws regulating corporations categorize firms' legal violations as civil violations rather than criminal offenses. As a result, corporate excesses are not labeled as crimes. In a study of seventy large corporations, Sutherland found 980 official violations (criminal convictions, civil judgments, and actions taken by government agencies), only 158 (16 percent) of which were categorized as criminal offenses. Forty-one of the seventy corporations had been convicted of criminal charges, with an average of almost four convictions per firm. He argued that individuals who are recidivists generally are treated more harshly and that corporations that engage in repeated criminality also should be punished more severely (E. Sutherland 1945, 1949: 13–15, 19–23, 227).

An updated version of Sutherland's study by Clinard and Yeager (1980) confirmed his findings on the extensive nature of corporate crime and civil violations. Three-fifths of the 477 manufacturing firms studied had been charged with civil, criminal, or administrative violations between 1975 and 1976. The study found that 38 companies were responsible for 52 percent of the criminal offenses and civil violations and that corporate illegality was concentrated in the largest firms in the oil, pharmaceutical, and auto industries. Clinard and Yeager also found that 60 percent of the 582 largest corporations had been charged with at least one legal violation and the average number of legal violations was 4.4. Reviewing studies of corporate criminal conduct and white-collar crime, three leading scholars conclude that white-collar crime is "relatively commonplace" and that "at some point most major firms or their executives will be accused of committing business crimes" (Rosoff, Pontell, and Tillman 2010: 2).

Brandon L. Garrett in his important study of white-collar crime prosecutions finds that 5 percent of companies listed on the stock market were criminally prosecuted between 2001 and 2012. Forty-six percent were convicted, and 54 percent entered into a deferred prosecution or non-prosecution agreement (discussed below). The firms paid an average fine of $45 million, a miniscule amount compared to their value. Another study estimates that 14.5 percent of large publicly traded companies commit fraud (Garrett 2014: 260–261).

Most Americans view street crimes as a much more serious problem than white-collar crime. Stephen Rosoff, Henry Pontell, and Robert Tillman estimate that the economic cost of common crimes amounts to only 6 percent of the annual losses from white-collar crime. In 1992, Lincoln Savings and Loan, a bank run by Charles Keating, was seized by the federal government, which assumed responsibility for the payment of the $3.4 billion debt accumulated by Keating's irresponsible loan policy. The total cost of all the bank robberies in the United States in 1992 was $35 million. The total cost of all the American bank robberies in the past one hundred years likely is less than the cost of paying off the debts of Lincoln Savings and Loan (Rosoff et al. 2014: 23).

The FBI estimates that the "total amount" stolen in property crimes in 2014 was $14.4 billion, which pales in comparison to the losses associated with white-collar crime, which are estimated to be as low as $456 billion and as high as $1.6 trillion (Reiman and Leighton 2017: 119).

The following are some of the primary areas of white-collar crime (Payne 2013) and examples of fraudulent schemes (FBI 2011).

Falsification of corporate information. At the end of 2011, 728 fraud investigations were being pursued by the FBI. Petters Group Worldwide, a Minneapolis firm, obtained loans from investment groups to finance sales to big-box retailers. In fact, the sales contracts were fabricated, and investors were defrauded of $3.4 billion. Petters was convicted on various counts, including wire fraud. The energy company Enron created a false financial statement that overstated its actual profitability by billions of dollars using fictitious companies to borrow money that was transferred to Enron for largely worthless stock. These monies were reported as profit to inflate Enron's value and stock price.

Enron in 2001 declared the largest corporate bankruptcy in the history of the United States, and over thirty executives were criminally prosecuted.

Stock fraud. At the end of 2011, the FBI was investigating over 1,800 cases of stock fraud. A couple years earlier, Bernard Madoff was convicted of running a $20 million Ponzi scheme in which he used money from new investors to pay individuals who already had invested in the firm. In fact, the financial transactions were fictitious, and the firm was insolvent. Madoff paid himself and his sons multimillion-dollar salaries. Joseph Blimline was convicted of selling fraudulent investment opportunities in oil and gas leases in Michigan and in Texas between 2003 and 2009. Over 7,700 investors were defrauded of $485 million. Money from individuals who invested in the later stages of the scheme was used to pay early investors in the scheme and to pay Blimline a lucrative salary and provide him with millions of dollars in loans. In 2012, Blimline was sentenced to twenty years in prison.

Health fraud. Between 2009 and 2011, the FBI brought 1,676 indictments and obtained 736 convictions for health care fraud. Dr. Hany M. Iskander pled guilty to charging the federal government for medical operations performed on the elderly under the Medicare program. The operations either were not performed or were unnecessary. Dr. Iskander and his wife, Evat Hanna, also were convicted of obstruction of justice for shredding documents. Dr. Iskander was sentenced to fifty-one months in prison and agreed to forfeit his medical license and to return home to Egypt. Hanna was sentenced to home detention for a year. In 2011, the presidents of two South Florida companies pled guilty to collecting over $200 million in bogus Medicare claims. The companies paid kickbacks to assisted living facilities and to halfway houses in return for delivering patients for unnecessary mental health treatment and hospitalization. In addition to restitution, Lawrence Duran was sentenced to fifty years in prison and Marianella Valera to thirty-five years in prison.

Mortgage fraud. As of 2011, the FBI had 2,691 pending mortgage fraud cases. Investigations between 2009 and 2011 resulted in 1,082 convictions. Viktor Kobzar and various co-conspirators purchased luxury homes and filed false documents inflating the value of the homes, which they then sold to unqualified purchasers or to "straw purchasers" who were paid by Kobzar to act as purchasers of the home. These purchasers obtained loans to purchase the property from Kobzar based on false documents that inflated the purchasers' incomes. The purchasers then typically defaulted on the loan and walked away from the home. Kobzar was sentenced to five years in prison for arranging fraudulent mortgage loans totaling $46 million. Luis Belevan pled guilty to conspiring to commit fraud between 2009 and 2010. Belevan defrauded at least 1,800 individuals who paid him a fee of roughly $1,500 each based on the false claim that he could help them save their homes from mortgage foreclosure. Belevan generated nearly $3 million in nine months.

Insurance fraud. In 2009, the FBI investigated 152 cases of insurance fraud, which led to forty-three indictments, two arrests, and forty-two convictions. Alan Teale established Victoria Insurance Company in Atlanta, Georgia. Victoria collected $16 million in insurance premiums, and when the company was shut down, there were $20 million in unpaid claims. A number of famous athletes paid over $100,000 for policies that would protect them in the event of a career-ending injury only to discover later that the company lacked the money to pay any potential claims. Another of Teale's companies offered insurance to high school athletic programs. The company went under because of a lack of funds to pay claims, leaving sixty seriously injured high school athletes without monetary compensation. Teale died in prison serving a seventeen-year sentence.

Mass marketing fraud. At the end of 2011, the FBI was investigating ninety-six cases of mass marketing fraud. A Vancouver, Canada–based marketing firm sent letters to thousands of elderly U.S. residents falsely claiming they were the winners of a lottery. The letter was accompanied by a fraudulent check, which the residents were told would help to pay some of their expenses. The elderly were asked to send money to pay for the processing of their lottery winnings. The Vancouver firm pocketed over $10 million in money transfers. In 2009, two of the central figures in the fraud were arrested. A company based in England defrauded fifty-two elderly Americans out of $2.7 million by claiming that the individuals had won a lottery prize although they owed taxes payable to the English company on the prize money. The individual behind the scheme was convicted of fraud and sentenced to fourteen years in prison.

Money laundering. At the end of 2011, the FBI had investigated 303 cases leading to 37 indictments and 45 convictions for money laundering. The FBI documented that various businesses and banks cooperated with organized crime interests and state sponsors of terrorism. Barclays (New York) and Credit Suisse (New York) both had conducted illegal transactions on behalf of Iran and Sudan and other governments.

Tax avoidance. In 2015, a leak of 11.5 million documents from the Panamanian law firm of Mossack Fonseca revealed a global network of unethical and at times illegal conduct by wealthy and powerful individuals. Mossack Fonseca, with five hundred employees and offices in forty countries, was in the business of creating shell companies (fictitious companies whose ownership is concealed) across the globe that were used by wealthy investors to avoid income, gift, and inheritance taxes and luxury taxes on yachts (which appear in 19,389 of the documents). The documents known as the **Panama Papers** indicate that Mossack Fonseca had at least 14,153 clients worldwide and 2,400 clients in the United States, and established as many as 214,000 shell companies on its clients' behalf in the British Virgin Islands, Panama, the Seychelles, and other countries that hold themselves out as tax havens. Clients of Mossack Fonseca included world leaders such as former British prime minister David Cameron and close associates of Russian president Vladimir V. Putin, who had moved over $2 billion into offshore accounts, and family members of leading officials of the People's Republic of China. It is estimated that 8 percent of global wealth or more than $76 billion is hidden in shell companies in offshore accounts and in tax havens in various American states (Lipton and Creswell 2015).

Environmental crime. In March 1989, the oil tanker *Exxon Valdez* struck Bligh Reef in Prince William Sound, Alaska, resulting in the spill of more than eleven million tons of crude oil. Exxon paid a criminal fine of $100 million and a civil penalty of $900 million. BP pled guilty to fourteen criminal charges and agreed to pay $4 billion in penalties for the explosion of an oil rig, which polluted hundreds of miles of Gulf of Mexico beaches and wetlands and resulted in the death of eleven workers. In 2013, a low-level BP engineer was convicted of obstruction of justice for deleting text messages relating to the BP oil spill. Princess Cruises in 2016 pled guilty to seven felony charges based on the illegal dumping of oil-contaminated waste and covering up its intentional pollution of the seas. In another case in 2016, a number of Michigan officials were charged with criminal contamination of the Flint, Michigan, water supply and cover-up of the lead contamination of the water supply (Davey and Smith 2016).

Sutherland theorized that white-collar crime is explained by *differential association*. People who enter the world of business are surrounded by individuals who engage in unlawful behavior. These illegal practices spread throughout the industry and become common practice. The complicated laws regulating business and the difficulty of understanding the corporate world tends to isolate businesspeople from public criticism and legal investigation (E. Sutherland 1989: 227–257).

A related theory explains white-collar crime as an expression of the American *cultural ethic* that "winning is the only thing." The competitive drive to dominate the competition motivates even the most honest corporate executive to do whatever is necessary to succeed. The manic drive to accumulate money is described as bordering on a sickness and has been labeled as "psychopathic wealth accumulation." The income of the CEO of top companies is five hundred times the income of the average worker (Rosoff et al. 2014: 587–588).

A third explanation for white-collar crime is that the structure of certain industries is *criminogenic*, or produces crime. These businesses generally are industries in which employees are under intense pressure to achieve results and as a result feel compelled to bend the rules in order to keep their jobs. In these industries, the financial rewards for a strong performance on the job are so significant that many individuals will do whatever is necessary to succeed. It also is difficult for law enforcement to detect fraudulent behavior in complex industries.

The auto repair business generally is viewed as characterized by unnecessary and phantom repairs, overcharging, and the installation of defective parts. The used car business is known for odometer rollbacks. This practice involves changing an automobile's title and odometer to conceal the mileage on a late-model car. A rollback can add $4,000 or $5,000 to the price of a late-model used car. In 2008, an estimated 450,000 car buyers were victimized by rollbacks, resulting in $10 billion in unnecessary costs and expenses (Rosoff et al. 2014: 591–592).

© iStockphoto.com/EdStock

PHOTO 9.3 White-collar criminal Bernard Madoff was sentenced to 150 years in federal prison based on his bilking investors out of close to $20 million.

Yet another explanation for white-collar crime considers the cause of corporate crime to be the *corporation's pursuit of profit*. Corporate profits are elevated over all other considerations. Corporate executives are focused on cutting costs and maximizing profits and engage in the dumping of hazardous waste, selling of tainted baby food, and exposing of workers to dangerous working conditions. A well-known example is the decision of Ford Motor Company executives in the 1970s not to correct a defect in the design of the gas tank of the Pinto. Ford executives reasoned that the $11 cost per vehicle to recall the vehicles and repair the design defect would damage the company's financial bottom line. They calculated it was less expensive to pay the damages that may be awarded by a court to individuals who might sue Ford for injuries suffered in an accident. Ford's worst nightmare occurred in 1978 when three Illinois teenagers died after another vehicle struck their 1972 Ford Pinto in the rear and the gas tank of the Pinto automobile exploded. Ford succeeded in having the reckless homicide charges dismissed (Rosoff et al. 2014: 99).

In March 2014, it was revealed that General Motors officials and engineers at least since 2007 were aware of a defect in the ignition switch of hundreds of thousands of cars that disabled the air bags. This problem reportedly led to the death of 124 individuals. General Motors told families of accident victims that the company lacked evidence of a defect. In February 2014, the company recalled 1.6 million vehicles to remedy the defect (Jensen 2014).

Christopher Stone, in evaluating the various incentives and pressures toward corporate wrongdoing, questions whether the law can be effective in controlling the criminal conduct of corporations. He instead advocates a movement toward the development of corporate social responsibility (C. Stone 1975).

A crucial factor in each of these explanations for corporate crime is the ability of perpetrators to justify their criminal conduct or engage in what criminologists refer to as "techniques of neutralization." Neutralization allows an individual to engage in criminal conduct without pangs of conscience. These "distancing" techniques include the notion that "everyone is doing the same thing" and that "no one was harmed" and "jobs are saved." Donald Cressey found that most embezzlers persuade themselves that they are borrowing the money and will return it after they succeed in using the money to make a profit. Another justification used by embezzlers is that they are underpaid and deserve the money (Cressey 1953).

Eugene Soltes interviewed some of the most infamous white-collar criminals of the past decade. He notes that the students he taught at Harvard Business School all were exposed to business ethics and on graduation aspired to "do the right thing" as corporate executives. He asks why some of these very same students engaged in white-collar crime. Soltes argues that corporate executives live in an isolated environment that places a premium on profit and personal success and that they are surrounded by subordinates who support their every decision. These executives cannot appreciate that in their single-minded pursuit of profit, their conduct may be unethical, yet alone criminal, and may have a detrimental impact on consumers and investors. Soltes concludes that the solution to white-collar crime is in the creation of a corporate culture in which decisions are questioned and examined and contends that white-collar crime will not be effectively deterred by exclusive reliance on the criminal law (Soltes 2016).

Studies find that white-collar criminals are treated more leniently than offenders who commit "common crimes," most of whom are from lower socioeconomic classes (Hagan and Nagel 1982). The significant economic profits accumulated by white-collar criminals and the relatively light sentences handed down by judges undermine the deterrent effect of the criminal law. These light sentences are explained by the "status shield" accorded to white-collar criminals. Judges do not view educated corporate criminals as typical criminal types. White-collar criminals also are able to afford skilled and influential lawyers and are able to mount a strong defense (Rosoff et al. 2014: 599).

A study of California Medicaid health providers charged with grand theft found that defendants were half as likely to be incarcerated as a control group of non-corporate defendants charged with grand theft. The Medicaid fraud consisted of submitting bills to the State of California for fictitious and unnecessary medical services. Medicaid providers, a number of whom were doctors, received more lenient treatment despite the fact the financial losses from their offenses were more than ten times the losses caused by the crimes of the control group (Tillman and Pontell 1992).

One of the largest scandals in the past decades involved the savings and loan (S&L) industry. These institutions were created in the 1930s to loan money to the builders and buyers of new homes. The deposits were insured by a federal government agency, the Federal Savings and Loan Insurance Corporation (FSLIC). As restrictions on the S&L industry were lifted, the S&Ls started to issue risky loans, and bank owners started to use the S&Ls' money for their own benefit. The entire industry collapsed, the FSLIC ran out of cash to cover the costs, and the American taxpayer was stuck with a bill for roughly $480 billion. Jeffrey Reiman and Paul Leighton cite a study from the University of California at Irvine that finds the average prison term for a defendant involved in the S&L scandal was thirty-six months as compared to fifty-six months for burglars and thirty-eight months for motor vehicle thieves. S&L offenders did receive longer sentences than first-time property offenders, who were sentenced to an average of twenty-six months in prison. Note that the average financial loss in an S&L prosecution was $500,000; the average financial loss in a first-time property offense in 1995 was $1,251 (Reiman and Leighton 2017: 135).

Reiman and Leighton compare the "crimes of the poor" with the "crimes of the affluent." They note that each of the crimes of the affluent cost the public more than all of the property crimes combined. Ninety-six percent of the individuals convicted of robbery in their study were sentenced to prison and served an average of sixty-seven months; 74 percent of individuals convicted of burglary were sentenced to prison and served an average of twenty-one months; and 80 percent of individuals convicted of auto theft were sentenced to prison and served an average of ten months in prison. In comparison, 63 percent of individuals convicted of fraud were sentenced to prison and served an average of seventeen months; 66 percent of individuals convicted of violation of the tax law were sentenced to prison and served an average of thirteen months; and 47 percent of individuals convicted of embezzlement were sentenced to prison and served an average of eleven months (Reiman and Leighton 2017: 119, 134).

There is evidence that white-collar criminals are receiving longer sentences. In 2009, Bernard Madoff, aged 71, was sentenced to 150 years in prison for bilking investors out of $20 million. This reportedly is the fourth longest white-collar sentence handed down in the past few years. In another example, a federal judge in Colorado sentenced Norman Schmidt, aged 73, to 330 years in prison for a fraudulent investment scheme in which he diverted investors' money to buy racing cars, a racetrack, and other racing-related properties. Financer Allen Stanford was sentenced to 110 years in prison after being convicted of defrauding investors. In 2010, Thomas J. Petters received a 50-year prison sentence for defrauding investors of as much as $3.7 billion. A year later, Lee B. Farkas was sentenced to 30 years for financial fraud. Stewart Parnell, former president of the Peanut Corporation of America, was sentenced to 28 years in prison for knowingly selling peanuts contaminated with salmonella. The peanuts resulted in the death of nine individuals and sickened more than seven hundred in forty-six states. His brother was sentenced to twenty years in prison, and another executive was sentenced to five years in prison. The longest sentence on record is the 835-year sentence against Sholam Weiss for insurance fraud and other related crimes.

These lengthy sentences remain the exception. The Department of Justice reports that roughly 14 percent of individuals convicted of white-collar crimes receive prison sentences of over five years. Reiman and Leighton cite a study of 440 high-profile corporate fraud prosecutions that finds that the bulk of white-collar criminals convicted at trial received sentences of between five and twenty years. Fifty-seven percent of the defendants pled guilty, and the majority of these defendants received sentences of less than five years. Only two defendants were sentenced to more than fifteen years in prison (Reiman and Leighton 2017: 146). There is continuing criticism of the Department of Justice for failing to aggressively pursue prosecutions against the individuals responsible for the 2008 financial crisis.

There is continued disagreement over how severely to punish white-collar criminals. Andrew W. W. Caspersen, age 39, a member of a privileged New York City family, educated at the best private schools and at Princeton University and Harvard Law School, and a successful Wall Street executive, in 2016 pled guilty to two counts of financial fraud. His victims included friends, brothers, his own mother, family of a former girlfriend killed in the 9/11 attack on the World Trade Center, and a charity dedicated to protection of the environment. Caspersen was able to attract nearly $40 million in his investment firm, virtually all of which he used for his personal private stock purchases and to pay interest to investors in fictitious business ventures (Goldstein 2016).

Caspersen at sentencing contended that he suffered from a pathological gambling addiction. A Yale University psychiatrist submitted an analysis that Caspersen had started with gambling and sports betting and that his addiction had driven him into risky stock market investments. An investment analyst testified that many of Caspersen's investments were risky and irrational, and another witness testified that Caspersen compulsively checked the stock market on a continual basis.

Prosecutors asked for a fifteen-year sentence, noting that Caspersen had methodically created false documents to support his schemes and had used his personal pedigree in an attempt to solicit nearly $150 million in investments. Judge Jed Rakoff recognized that Caspersen had engaged in a "substantial fraud" and had betrayed the trust of countless individuals. He nonetheless sentenced Caspersen to four years in prison and nearly $28 million in restitution. Judge Rakoff announced that it was "more likely than not" that Caspersen suffered from a gambling addiction and that cognitive neuroscience held out the promise of assisting judges in understanding and evaluating criminal conduct. He explained that "no purpose would be served" by a lengthy prison sentence, and federal sentencing guidelines that called for the imposition of a harsher sentence were "absurd." Judge Rakoff added that individuals who might question the leniency of the sentence simply do not know all the facts. Although Judge Rakoff may be correct, the question remains whether an ordinary defendant could have mounted the same high-price defense as Caspersen.

The FBI's focus on terrorism and budget cutbacks to other federal agencies reportedly has weakened the government's ability to investigate white-collar crime. It is becoming increasingly difficult for the government to compete with private industry for individuals who possess the expertise in complicated financial matters to oversee the conduct of corporations (Lichtblau, Johnston, and Nixon 2008; Moyer 2009).

■ CORPORATE LIABILITY

A fundamental debate is whether to hold individuals criminally liable for white-collar crime or whether to hold the corporation itself criminally responsible.

The U.S. Supreme Court in *New York Central and Hudson River Railroad v. United States* held that a corporation along with its employees may be held criminally liable. The Court noted, "If . . . the invisible, intangible essence or air which we term a corporation can level mountains, fill up valleys, lay down iron tracks and run railroad cars," it should be held to account when it acts "viciously" rather than "virtuously" (*New York Central and Hudson River Railroad v. United States*, 212 U.S. 481 [1909]). Criminal prosecution was required to control corporate behavior. Absent punishing the corporate entity, corporate crime would not be deterred. In the words of Edward Turlow, first Baron Thurlow, in the late eighteenth century, "[D]id you ever expect a corporation to have a conscience, when it has no soul to be damned, and no body to be kicked?" (Steinzor 2015: 45–46).

In 2003, President George W. Bush, when confronted with fraud scandals at Adelphia, WorldCom, HealthSouth, and other companies, argued that the solution to criminal conduct was a "change in corporate culture" and in the rehabilitation of corporations. The focus was on entering into deferred prosecution agreements (DPAs) with large corporations. A criminal prosecution would be put on hold in return for the firm agreeing to accept responsibility, pay a fine and restitution, and reform the firm's organization and approach to doing business. A failure to fully implement the agreement over a period of two years may result in criminal prosecution of the corporation.

Attorney General Eric Holder under President Barack Obama continued a policy of entering into DPAs rather than prosecuting corporations or corporate officers. The logic of this policy of not prosecuting individual corporate officers is that in many instances it was difficult to blame an individual or small group of individuals for corporate criminal conduct. A number of corporate officials, plant managers, and engineers all were aware of the defects in the General Motors ignition system that resulted in the death of over one hundred individuals. The logic of DPAs, which Attorney General Holder had advocated eighteen years earlier as a young lawyer, in part was based on the fact that large corporations were "too big to fail" and that a criminal prosecution would damage the reputation of the corporation, harm sales, reduce the value of stock held by investors, and lead to unemployment and hardship for workers. The focus on corporate rather than individual liability also reflected a philosophical retreat from mass incarceration. Fundamental fairness dictated that a corporation that benefited from criminal activity should be punished. A portion of the fines paid by corporations were to be paid to private organizations working in the public interest rather than to the federal government, a policy which has been reversed by the Trump administration.

The Justice Department came under intense criticism following the 2008 financial crisis because prosecutions were not brought against Wall Street executives responsible for bundling and selling subprime (questionable) mortgage loans. Mortgage fraud cost the American economy an estimated $15 trillion. Prosecutions of white-collar criminals under Eric Holder are said to have fallen to a twenty-year low. Attorney General Holder countered that the federal government collected over $6 billion in fines from corporations including megabanks like Bank of America, JPMorgan Chase, and Citigroup. In most cases, these large banks paid civil fines and did not confront criminal charges, and bank officials were not prosecuted. Bank of America paid the government a civil penalty of $13 billion to settle a charge of selling billions of dollars of overvalued mortgages to investors although neither the bank nor bank officers were criminally charged (Ramirez and Ramirez 2017: 2–3).

A significant number of corporate criminal cases as noted were resolved by a DPA. HSBC, headquartered in London, operates in eight countries and has $2.5 trillion in assets and nearly ninety million customers. The bank overlooked the deposit of large amounts of cash by Mexican drug cartels and by the terrorist states of Iran and Syria and then laundered the money by sending large amounts of funds to the United States. HSBC paid $1.92 billion in fines and forfeiture and entered into a DPA, which required the bank to create an effective money laundering compliance structure (Garrett 2014: 84–85, 259–261).

Criminal cases, when filed, focused on holding corporations rather than individuals responsible. BNP Paribas, France's biggest bank, in a criminal case paid a record $8.9 billion penalty and pled guilty to the crime of "trading with the enemy" by concealing financial dealings with Sudan, Iran, and Cuba although no BNP employee was subject to prosecution (Buell 2016: 126–127).

In 2012, BP settled the Deepwater Horizon case by pleading guilty to several charges including Clean Water Act violations, obstruction of justice, and negligent homicide of eleven rig workers and paying a fine of $1.26 billion. BP also paid $2.4 billion to the National Fish and Wildlife Foundation and $350 million to the National Academy of Sciences and established on its own accord a fund to compensate victims. Two individuals pled guilty to a misdemeanor Clean Water Act charge, and a third BP employee also pled guilty to a misdemeanor charge for deleting text messages.

Judge Emmet G. Sullivan in a lengthy opinion in the General Motors case criticized DPAs that allowed corporate executives to escape criminal prosecution by paying a corporate civil penalty although this same opportunity was not offered to common criminals. He characterized the $900 million settlement with General Motors over concealment of a defective ignition system that resulted in as many as 124 deaths and more than two hundred injuries a "shocking example of potentially culpable individuals not being criminally charged . . . despite the fact that the reprehensible conduct of its employees resulted in the deaths of many people." He went on to note that he was "disappointed that deferred-prosecution agreements . . . are not being used to provide the same opportunity to individual defendants to demonstrate their rehabilitation without triggering the devastating collateral consequences of a criminal conviction."

Federal district court judge Jed Rakoff in a decision later overturned by an appellate court rejected a DPA between the Department of Justice and Citigroup in which the bank paid a $285 million fine without admitting guilt for selling flawed mortgage-backed investments while betting its own money against the securities making a profit. He claimed that the settlement was "neither fair, nor reasonable, nor adequate, nor in the public interest."

In 2016, the newly named attorney general Loretta E. Lynch announced that she would urge Department of Justice lawyers in prosecuting white-collar criminals to place a priority on prosecuting individual corporate employees rather than focus on holding corporations liable or negotiating DFAs. The attorney general's reasoning was that crimes are committed by individuals rather than by organizations. Deputy Attorney General Sally Yates explained that the "public needs to have confidence that there is one system of justice and it applies equally regardless of whether that crime occurs on a street corner or in a boardroom." She added that prosecuting "flesh-and-blood people" for corporate crimes is crucial for deterring corporate misconduct and increasing confidence among the public. The newly implemented policy also required corporations seeking to avoid criminal prosecution to cooperate in singling out the individuals in the firm primarily responsible for the criminal activity. This new policy resulted in several prosecutions (Ramirez and Ramirez 2017: 57–58).

Following the explosion of Upper Big Branch Mine in West Virginia that killed twenty-nine workers, the company entered into a DFA. After obtaining guilty pleas from three lower-level mine supervisors, in 2013 executive officer David Hughart pled guilty to conspiracy to impede mine safety and was sentenced to forty-two months in prison. In 2016, Don Blankenship, the CEO of Massey Energy, which owned Big Branch, was convicted of conspiracy to violate federal mine safety regulations, sentenced to a year in jail and to a year of supervised release, and fined $250,000 or twelve and a half days for each of twenty-nine miners who died in the mine explosion.

In 2016, Volkswagen engineer James Robert Liang pled guilty for involvement in a ten-year conspiracy to defraud American regulators and customers by installing software designed to evade U.S. emissions tests.

In 2017, the Japanese auto parts maker Takata pled guilty to wire fraud for providing false data on the safety of automobile airbags and agreed to pay a $1 billion fine. Three Takata executives were charged with covering up the defects in the safety bags, which resulted in eleven deaths and 180 injuries (Soble 2017).

Keep in mind that state prosecutors have continued to charge corporations with homicide. In 2005, Far West Water and Sewer, along with the company president and other executives, was convicted of causing the death of two workers who died from toxic chemicals while working on an underground sewer tank. The company was fined $1.7 million and required to pay restitution to the families of the dead workers.

The next section briefly examines the use of civil commitment to control individual behavior.

9.6 YOU DECIDE

In 2012, Rajat K. Gupta was convicted of conspiracy and three counts of securities fraud and was sentenced to twenty-four months in prison to be followed by one year of supervised release. The court imposed a fine of $5 million along with restitution to the victims. Gupta's crime was to breach his duty of confidentiality as a member of the board of directors of Goldman Sachs, a major New York investment firm. He informed Raj Rajaratnam, the head of the investment firm Galleon, that investment guru Warren Buffett was about to invest $5 billion in Goldman Sachs. Rajaratnam promptly bought Goldman stock. Gupta later advised Rajaratnam to sell the stock. These tip-based trades resulted in an illegal gain for Rajaratnam of over $5 million. Prominent individuals wrote letters on Gupta's behalf attesting to his "big heart and helping hand" as evidenced by his involvement in the Global Fund to Fight AIDS, Tuberculosis and Malaria; the Public Health Foundation of India; the Indian School of Business; and the Pratham Education Foundation providing education to underprivileged youth. Gupta already was a multimillionaire based on his prior employment as head of McKinsey, perhaps the best and most powerful consulting firm in the world. There is no evidence that Gupta personally benefited from conveying the information to Rajaratnam although the prosecution argued that he was trying to position himself to enter the world of Wall Street investing.

Judge Jed Rakoff said that he had "never encountered a defendant whose prior history suggests such an extraordinary devotion, not only to humanity . . . but also to individual human beings in their times of need." However, Rakoff characterized Gupta's crimes as "disgusting" and as a "terrible breach of trust" and concluded that it was necessary to punish him to deter other individuals from engaging in insider trading. Gupta's two-year sentence nonetheless was far less than the eight- to ten-year sentence he would have received under the advisory federal sentencing guidelines.

Did it make sense to send Gupta to prison? What of the defense attorney's unsuccessful proposal that Gupta be required to work in Rwanda in a program to combat HIV and malaria?

■ CIVIL COMMITMENT

The government has the authority and obligation to provide for the health and safety of society and has the recognized "police power" to civilly commit individuals who pose a threat to themselves and to others. The additional justification for the commitment of individuals is to provide treatment and rehabilitation, although the law is somewhat unclear whether the government is obligated to treat dangerous individuals who are involuntarily committed.

Every state and the federal government has **civil commitment** laws. There is a constitutional requirement to provide individuals with a hearing before a legal tribunal before they are involuntarily committed. Individuals may be committed because of a mental illness or because they are a dangerous sex offender or because they are a chronic alcoholic or narcotics addict. Roughly one hundred thousand juveniles are detained in juvenile institutions.

Virtually every state and the federal government have a violent offender act. These laws provide that an individual who has been convicted of a sexually violent offense and is scheduled for release may be civilly committed to a mental institution based on a finding before a judge and jury that the individual is a "sexual predator." Individuals who have been charged with a sexually violent offense and acquitted by reason of insanity also are eligible for confinement. The Supreme Court has upheld these laws as part of the government's power to protect society and has ruled that this does not constitute "double jeopardy" (punishing an individual two times for the same offense). A confined sexual predator's psychiatric condition is subject to periodic review by a court to determine whether continued confinement is required. In theory, the individual may be indefinitely committed to a mental institution, and critics contend that the claim that individuals are being interned to provide treatment is used as a pretext to justify individuals' indefinite incarceration (*Kansas v. Hendricks*, 521 U.S. 346 [1997]).

A number of regimes, most particularly Russia, have controlled dissidents by alleging that they are mentally disturbed and institutionalizing them in mental institutions (Bloch and Reddaway 1977).

Another type of social control over sex offenders involves registration laws. These obligate individuals who are convicted of criminal offenses to register with the local government authorities and to keep authorities informed of their employment, residence, and other personal details. The individual's name and other details are posted on a website. The Supreme Court has held that these laws do not constitute double jeopardy because a requirement of registration does not constitute punishment. States and localities prohibit registered sex offenders from living nearby to schools and from entering parks and public facilities that attract young children. Critics assert that these laws paint with too broad of a brush in defining sex offenders and that not all sex offenders pose a continuing threat. The question remains whether society is justified in singling out sex offenders for tight controls. The argument is that sex offenders can never be rehabilitated and are likely to engage in a renewed pattern of sexual abuse years after they seemingly are "cured" (*Smith v. Doe*, 538 U.S. 84 [2003]).

■ INTERNATIONAL PERSPECTIVE: GENOCIDE

Raphael Lemkin was a Polish lawyer who had emigrated to the United States to escape Nazi persecution. In 1944, Lemkin wrote a series of essays in which he proposed an international convention on the prevention and punishment of the crime of genocide. Lemkin developed the term

genocide by combining the Latin word *genos* (race, tribe) with *cide* (murder). Lemkin suffered a loss of more than fifty family members during the Holocaust and explained that the new proposed crime of genocide should punish acts directed against individuals based on their membership in a national, racial, religious, or national group. Certainly if an attack on an individual was a crime, it also was a crime to attack a collection of individuals (Lemkin 1944).

Lemkin is an example of how a single individual can bring about social change. As a result of his efforts, the United Nations (UN) General Assembly in 1948 adopted the international Convention on the Prevention and Punishment of the Crime of Genocide. The Genocide Convention was the first international human rights document adopted by the newly established UN. The Convention was a response to the Nazi extermination of six million Jews and millions of Poles and Russians and other Eastern Europeans and Roma. The Preamble notes that in order to "liberate" humankind from the "odious scourge of genocide," "international cooperation is required."

The Convention is a bold and forward-looking document. Article I declares that genocide—whether committed in time of peace or time of war—is an international crime that the signatories to the treaty undertake to "prevent and to punish." This language indicates that genocide is a matter of concern to all nations and the signatories pledge to halt genocide and punish the perpetrators. It is significant that genocide is punishable, whether it occurs during wartime or peacetime. Consider that under the Convention, a state is unable to commit acts of genocide against individuals who are part of its own population and claim that the international community lacks the authority to intervene to punish the act. Article IV provides that individuals will be held criminally liable regardless of whether they are high-ranking government or military leaders or low-ranking followers. Each state agreeing to adhere to the Convention pledges to adopt laws that give effect to the provisions of the Convention. Jurisdiction over an act of genocide is vested in a tribunal of the country in the territory of the state in which an act of genocide occurs. Article IX gives jurisdiction to the International Court of Justice (ICJ) over disputes between states, including those "relating to the responsibility of a State for Genocide." The ICJ is a UN court that hears complaints by states against other states. As a result, one state may bring an action before the ICJ complaining that another state is committing genocide.

Article II defines genocide, and Article III punishes conspiracy to commit genocide as well as incitement to genocide, an attempt to commit genocide, and complicity in genocide. The definition of genocide is somewhat awkwardly expressed and reads as follows:

> In the present Convention, genocide means any of the following acts committed with intent to destroy, in whole or in part, a national, ethnical, racial or religious group, as such:
>
> (a) Killing members of the group;
>
> (b) Causing serious bodily or mental harm to members of the group;
>
> (c) Deliberately inflicting on the group conditions of life calculated to bring about its physical destruction in whole or in part;
>
> (d) Imposing measures intended to prevent births within the group;
>
> (e) Forcibly transferring children of the group to another group.

Genocide requires a specific intent or purpose to exterminate a group included in the definition. This is different from a hate crime, which requires an attack on an individual because of his or her membership in a group. Genocide requires the intent to exterminate the group and is limited to the acts listed in the Convention. The required intent is to exterminate a numerically substantial part of the group although some courts have accepted that the intent to exterminate a prominent and important part of a group is sufficient (Quigley 2006: 9–14).

A domestic genocide prosecution requires a state signing the Convention to incorporate the Convention into its domestic criminal statutes. Genocide also is one of the crimes that fall within the jurisdiction of the new International Criminal Court, and the court already has indicted President Omar al-Bashir of Sudan for genocide in Darfur (Schabas 2009: 107, 400–490).

The U.S. criminal statute on genocide goes beyond the formal requirements of the Genocide Convention and establishes federal jurisdiction over individuals within the United States responsible for the crime of genocide, even when committed outside the United States. It also is possible for the victims of genocide to bring a civil action in U.S. federal court against a perpetrator for an act in "violation of the law of nations" (*Kadic v. Karadzic*, 70 F.3d 232 [2d Cir. 1995]).

Genocide today is considered an international crime along with torture, war crimes, and widespread and systematic inhumane acts against a civilian population (crimes against humanity). These offenses carry universal jurisdiction, which means that international law recognizes that any country may claim jurisdiction to punish an act of genocide. Genocide is considered to be the most serious international offense and continues to be considered the "king or queen" of international crimes.

Why does genocide have this moral status and stature? Mass exterminations are clearly unacceptable, and all efforts should be taken to prevent and to punish the taking of human life. Genocide has the added component that the extermination must be directed at a specific group and that the intent must be to exterminate the group. Laws against genocide are a recognition that each group makes an important contribution to the human family and that diversity is a central global value. There also is an acknowledgment that people define themselves in part based on their religious, racial, national, and ethnic identity. The destruction of a group deprives individuals of a sense of identity and tradition (May 2010).

As previously noted, individuals' status and stature do not insulate them from criminal liability. In 2016, in one of the most important contemporary genocide trials, former Bosnian Serb leader Radovan Karadzic, age 70, was found guilty of genocide by the International Criminal Tribunal for the former Yugoslavia and was sentenced to forty years in prison. The trial court found that Karadzic failed to intervene to prevent the killing of eight thousand captured non-combatant Muslim men and boys at Srebrenica in Bosnia. The trial chamber found that Karadzic failed to intervene because he intended that every male Muslim was to "be killed."

There is no statute of limitations on the international crime of genocide because of the compelling interest in punishing this crime against "humankind." In 2015, Oskar Groening, age 94, dubbed "accountant of Auschwitz," was convicted in Germany of accessoryship to the murder of three hundred thousand prisoners at the Auschwitz concentration camp between 1942 and 1944. Groening was a small cog in the Nazi killing machine and was responsible for cataloguing the cash and valuables seized from individuals transported to the camp. His involvement in the atrocities at Auschwitz was nonetheless sufficiently serious to justify his indictment and conviction.

Despite the international prohibition against genocide, Daniel Goldhagen estimates that during the twentieth century, more people died at the hands of what he terms governmental eliminationist policies than were killed in all the wars combined. Despite the claim following the Holocaust that "never again" would the world community tolerate genocide, since World War II the world has witnessed genocides in Bangladesh, Burundi, Cambodia, East Timor, Rwanda, Bosnia, and Darfur and against aboriginal peoples in Guatemala, Paraguay, and other Central and Latin American countries (Goldhagen 2009: 55–56).

Before we proceed, it should be noted that some commentators argue that only three events satisfy the strict standard for genocide: the Nazis' holocaust against the Jews, the Turkish extermination of the Armenians, and the mass killing of the Tutsi in Rwanda. These critics argue that broadening the definition to include other mass atrocities risks blurring the significance of the term *genocide* (Destexhe 1994).

The determination of what atrocities are labeled a genocide may be as much a question of politics as a question of objective analysis. Indigenous peoples throughout the world historically have been pushed off their lands and exterminated and have lacked the political power to draw attention to their plight. We often forget that the Sinti-Roma (Gypsies) were exterminated in massive numbers by the Nazis during World War II (Bodley 2002).

Turkey, although acknowledging that Armenians were killed during World War I, views these deaths as part of the war effort by the Ottoman Empire against internal subversion. Armenia and twenty-eight countries and Pope Francis have condemned the death of 1.5 million Armenians as a systematic and planned genocide. This intense disagreement and debate was highlighted in 2016 when celebrity Kim Kardashian in a full-page *New York Times* advertisement attacked the *Wall Street Journal* for running an advertisement by a group called Fact Check Armenia denying that Turkey had committed genocide against the Armenians. In 2015, the European Court of Human Rights in *Perincek v. Switzerland* held that a Swiss law that declared that it was a crime to deny the "Armenian genocide" was a violation of freedom of speech. The Court stressed that it was not reaching a conclusion on whether the events in Armenia constituted genocide (*Perincek v. Switzerland*, ECHR 325 [2015]).

The world community has reached a consensus that Islamic State or ISIS has committed genocide against the Yazidi minority group. The Independent International Commission of Inquiry on the Syrian Arab Republic appointed by the UN High Commissioner for Human Rights in 2016 reported that ISIS has sought to "erase" the Yazidis through "killings; sexual slavery, enslavement, torture and inhuman and degrading treatment and forcible transfer causing serious bodily and mental harm; the infliction of conditions of life that bring about a slow death; the imposition of measures to prevent Yazidi children from being born, including forced conversion of adults, the separation of Yazidi men and women, and mental trauma; and the transfer of Yazidi children from their own families and placing them with ISIS fighters, thereby cutting them off from beliefs and practices of their own religious community." The European Parliament, U.S. House of Representatives and State Department, and U.S. Holocaust Memorial Museum all affirmed that ISIS is committing genocide against the Yazidis as well as against Christians and against adherents of other religions.

A lingering question is whether mass killing constitutes genocide even when the perpetrator lacks a specific intent to exterminate the group. The French philosopher Jean-Paul Sartre made the controversial argument that the U.S. bombing campaign in Vietnam was designed to further America's dominance in the developing world. The Vietnamese people, according to Sartre, confronted the choice between surrender and genocide. The American philosopher Hugo Bedau responded that the United States was waging a war intended to contain Communism, and there was no evidence that, American decision-makers intended to exterminate the Vietnamese people (Bedau 1973).

Keep in mind that atrocities that are committed without the specific intent to destroy a group are punishable under international law as crimes against humanity. A UN commission in 2005 condemned killings and the displacement of various tribes in Darfur and noted that there was no "specific intent to annihilate" the victims although these acts constituted crimes against humanity.

Genocides are motivated by various reasons or goals. Frank Chalk and Kurt Jonassohn, after reviewing various proposed typologies of genocide, developed the following overlapping categories of genocide (Chalk and Jonassohn 1990: 35–40).

Genocide to eliminate the threat of a rival. The genocide in Rwanda in 1993 was carried out by the Hutu majority to eliminate the minority Tutsi, who historically dominated government and business.

Genocide to acquire economic wealth. The genocide of aboriginals in Australia and Latin America and of Native Americans in North America was designed to clear native peoples off the land and to seize the land and minerals.

Genocide to create terror. The Bosnian Serbs and their allies in Serbia in the late 1990s engaged in acts of genocide to intimidate Bosnian Muslims and drive them out of those portions of the country that they viewed as part of "Greater Serbia."

Genocide to implement an ideology. The Nazi regime implemented the "Final Solution" to eliminate the Jews, who were viewed as evil incarnate.

There are a number of explanations for genocide. These causal factors are sufficiently powerful to overcome the moral and legal restraints on individuals' willingness to engage in mass murder (Baum 2013; Newman and Erber 2002). Psychologist Ervin Staub identifies a number of factors that are preconditions for genocidal violence (Staub 1989).

Difficult life conditions. Economic problems and a decline in the power and prestige of a country create frustration.

Group conflict. There is a preexisting conflict or tension between groups.

Cultural devaluation. There is a history of stereotypes that devalue the victims as human beings. This is a process of dehumanization and scapegoating.

Cultural superiority. The perpetrators view themselves as culturally superior.

Respect for authority and obedience. There is a tradition of obeying authority and not questioning orders.

Unhealed wounds. There is a history of grievances by the perpetrators against the victims.

History of aggression. There is a history of using violence to settle disputes between groups, which makes it easier for groups to resort to violence.

Ideology. There is an ideology or belief system that incorporates cultural devaluation and cultural superiority, and draws on unhealed wounds to justify violence. This utopian belief system blames the victims for society's problems.

Leaders. Political leaders and the media articulate an ideology that justifies violence.

Mobilization. The political structure possesses the capacity to mobilize groups to commit violence against the victims.

Isolation of victims. The victims are identified and isolated to facilitate their killing or internment.

Bureaucracy. An administrative organization allows individuals to justify their actions on the claim that they are obeying orders and are responsible for only a small part of the genocide. Bureaucratic organization allows individuals to justify their actions on the grounds that the individuals at the top are responsible and that they are merely part of a complicated organization. In other words, individuals are able to feel that they are not responsible.

Bystanders. The global community, by remaining silent, endorses the genocide and does not force the perpetrators to come to terms with their actions. The failure to speak out against genocide or to intervene to halt genocide encourages other regimes to resort to mass murder (Midlarsky 2005).

There are a host of theories on the factors that trigger or spark a genocide. These theories include a regime targeting a minority to build the regime's power base (I. L. Horowitz 2005), particularly revolutionary regimes seeking to mobilize the population in support of a common cause (Weitz 2003). Other theories explain genocide by the competition between ethnic groups for power (Mann 2005); the targeting of a group viewed as a drain of resources (Rubenstein 1983); the desire of a group to expand its national territory (Kiernan 2007); and the human instinct toward a distrust and suspicion of individuals who are from a different background (Hinton 2002).

Daniel Goldhagen is a persistent critic of the notion that the factors promoting genocide are so powerful that "anyone" could commit genocide. Christopher Browning wrote a well-known book, *Ordinary Men* (1998), which is a study of Reserve Police Battalion 101. The battalion was a "killing squad" of men who were assigned the task of executing Jews and dissidents in occupied Poland. Browning found that the men were not ardent and ideological Nazis but instead succumbed to group pressure. In other words, they were ordinary individuals who acted out of a sense of group solidarity. Goldhagen, in *Hitler's Willing Executioners* (1996), argues that this type of social science analysis reduces individuals to automatons and absolves individuals of moral responsibility. He also argues that anti-Semitism was part and parcel of German culture and that the killings of Jews in Poland was an expression of the hatred of the Jews that was an accepted part of German society (Goldhagen 1996).

George H. Stanton has outlined eight stages in the development of genocide (Stanton 1998).

1. *Classification.* Societies begin to distinguish between groups based on race, religion, and ethnicity. Societies with two major groups are most likely to experience genocide.

2. *Symbolization.* Groups are distinguished based on symbols, such as requiring Jews to wear the yellow star in Nazi Germany.

3. *Dehumanization.* A group is dehumanized and is equated with animals, vermin, insects, or diseases. Propaganda is spread through the newspapers, the radio, and film.

4. *Organization.* The state organizes groups to carry out genocide. This may involve militia groups or gangs that are secretly sponsored by the state.

5. *Polarization.* Groups are polarized and driven apart. Laws may prohibit intermarriage or require segregation of groups. Moderates are arrested, killed, and driven out of the government and out of the country.

6. *Preparation.* The victims are identified and distinguished on the grounds of ethnicity and religion. Lists of victims are developed, and they are confined to ghettoes, deported to concentration camps, or forced to live in harsh and difficult isolated conditions.

7. *Extermination.* A process of killing and mass extermination is initiated.

8. *Denial.* The perpetrators deny responsibility for the killings and blame other governments or the victims for carrying out the extermination.

The genocide in Rwanda in 1994 is a textbook case of an extermination that followed Stanton's "The 8 Steps of Genocide." Rwanda is marked by two distinct ethnic groups, the Hutu and the Tutsi. Roughly 85 percent of the population of two million at the turn of the twentieth century were Hutu. The Tutsi herded cattle; the Hutu cultivated the land and labor. The distinction between the two peoples is mythologized as being based on a difference in origin and appearance. The Hutu are stereotyped as stocky, round-faced with bolder features. The Tutsi are thought of as taller with finer features. In reality, these two groups are best viewed as fluid. Historically, they spoke the same language, followed the same Catholic religion, shared a common culture, and intermarried. A Hutu might improve his or her economic situation and achieve the power and status of an honorary Tutsi, and a Tutsi might lose his or her property and assume the status of an honorary Hutu. A Hutu's bravery and courage in battle also might result in his elevation to the status of a Tutsi. The differences between Hutu and Tutsi widened with the ascendancy of the Tutsi Mwami (Chief) Kigeri Rwabugiri (1860–1895), who promoted the Tutsi at the expense of the Hutu (Gourevitch 1998: 47–50).

Beginning in the 1970s, the Hutu and Tutsi engaged in a series of acts of mass violence and racially provocative rhetorical attacks against one another. In 1990, for example, a leading newspaper published the "Hutu Ten Commandments," which denounced the Tutsi as dishonest and condemned Hutu who had business relationships with the Tutsi as traitors who were to be killed. The eighth commandment proclaimed, "Hutus must stop having mercy on the Tutsi" (Gourevitch 1998: 88).

In August 1993, President Juvénal Habyarimana, the Hutu head of Rwanda, entered into the Arusha Accords with the Rwandan Patriotic Front, which guaranteed free elections. A UN peacekeeping force entered Rwanda to ensure that the agreement was implemented (A. Jones 2006: 237).

Hutu extremists could not accept the peace accords. Preparations were made for a genocide. Hundreds of thousands of machetes were imported, youth gangs (the *interahamwe*) were trained to carry out killings, and lists of Tutsi were prepared (A. Jones 2006: 238).

On April 6, 1994, President Habyarimana was killed when his plane was shot down as it landed at the Kigali airport. The killing of Tutsi and moderate Hutu leaders was rapidly initiated in a thoroughly planned and organized onslaught. The UN troops who were in Rwanda to oversee the implementation of the Arusha Accords were driven out of Rwanda when ten Belgian peacekeepers were detained and killed by Hutu extremists. Individuals were stopped at roadblocks, and individuals with Tutsi identity cards were hacked to death with machetes. Tutsi who had sought safety in churches and hospitals and stadiums were slaughtered. On April 20, in the parish of Karama, between thirty-five and forty-three thousand people were killed in less than six hours (A. Jones 2006: 239).

Political leader Léon Mugesera called on the Hutu to "wipe out this [Tutsi] scum" and urged the Hutu to dispatch the Tutsi interlopers back to Ethiopia. In April 1994 during the height of the genocide, the Nyabarongo River, which flowed into the Egyptian Nile, was full of dead Tutsi symbolically sent back to their mythical homeland of Egypt (Gourevitch 1998: 53).

The radio and the media played an important role in the genocide. The media maintained a drumbeat of anti-Tutsi propaganda and provided the names and addresses of individuals targeted for death. The Hutu were reminded that the graves "are only half full" and that they should unite to pursue and kill the enemy. A unique aspect of the Rwandan genocide was that, unlike the Holocaust in which the Germans carried out much of the killing by herding large numbers of people into "gas ovens," the killings in Rwanda were carried out face-to-face with crude scythes and hatchets and hammers. The politicians and the intellectuals who planned and directed the killings took advantage of the tendency of Rwandans to obey the dictates of authority. Perhaps as many as five hundred thousand Hutu participated in the process of exterminating the Tutsi (Des Forges 1999: 10–11).

The genocide only drew to a halt when the invading forces of the Rwandan Patriotic Front, composed of Tutsi living in exile in neighboring Uganda, took control of the country. Alison Des Forges estimates that beginning on April 4, 1994, half a million Tutsi, or roughly 75 percent of the Tutsi population of Rwanda, were killed in thirteen weeks (Des Forges 1999: 16).

Samantha Power, in her study of the international community's historical failure to protest against genocide, points out that the UN Security Council studiously avoided using the term *genocide* when confronted with the events in Rwanda and that the international community dragged its feet to avoid intervening. The U.S. Department of State, as a matter of policy, avoided referring to events in Rwanda as genocide (Power 2002: 329–389). Following the genocide, a UN Commission of Experts determined that although both the Tutsi and the Hutu had committed acts of violence, the Hutu had carried out planned systematic acts of mass extermination that had constituted genocide (Gourevitch 1998: 203).

Eighty defendants were convicted, and twelve were acquitted before the International Criminal Tribunal for Rwanda. A number of defendants were convicted before domestic courts in Belgium, Finland, Germany, and Sweden and other European countries.

In 2001, the UN appeared to turn over a new leaf in the struggle against genocide when the organization adopted a resolution on "The Responsibility to Protect." In the resolution, member states pledged to act collectively to prevent genocide and, where necessary, to intervene militarily to defend the victims of genocidal violence (Evans 2008). In 2014, the UN Security Council commemorated the twentieth anniversary of the genocide in Rwanda by calling on states to recommit to the prevention of and fight against genocide and other serious crimes under international law. The next year, the U.S. Senate also adopted a resolution affirming the national interest in preventing acts of genocide against innocent individuals across the globe.

A blue-ribbon American panel working under the sponsorship of the U.S. Holocaust Memorial Museum earlier recommended that the president make the prevention of genocide a core component of American foreign policy and recommended a series of steps to detect, prevent, and punish genocide. A central recommendation was a "genocide early warning system" to anticipate areas of the world at risk for genocide. President Obama adopted the recommendations in the report and formed an Atrocities Prevention Board in the government to coordinate efforts to prevent genocide and other atrocities (Albright and Cohen 2008).

A review of the events in Rwanda illustrates the role of historical grievance, ethnic division, ideology, propaganda, societal disruption, and international inaction in genocidal violence and the limited capacity of international and domestic law to contain genocidal violence.

CHAPTER SUMMARY

Small and close-knit societies primarily rely on the internalization of values and social pressure to achieve social solidarity. In contrast, economically complex and diverse societies depend on formal law and formal legal institutions to maintain social control.

In both types of societies, the criminal law is an important mechanism for achieving stability. A primary purpose of punishment is to deter violations of the law. In the United States, one in every thirty-one adults is under some form of correctional supervision; this is roughly 2.9 percent of the population.

Deterrence is based on the calculus that individuals are rational and will not commit a crime when the costs of punishment outweigh the benefits of violating the law. Research differs on the general deterrent effects of increasing police patrols and increasing punishment. The conventional wisdom is that the effectiveness of deterrence depends on certainty, severity, speed, and procedural fairness. An evaluation of deterrent effects is complicated by various methodological issues. William Chambliss points out that the law is more effective in deterring instrumental offenses than in deterring expressive offenses and that the law is more effective in deterring low-commitment offenders than in deterring high-commitment offenders. A number of other factors influence deterrence, including the communication of criminal penalties.

Specific deterrence is limited by the relatively small number of crimes that result in arrest, prosecution, and imprisonment. The deterrent effect of criminal penalties has a limited effect on prison inmates, which helps account for the relatively high recidivism rate in the United States.

The death penalty, victimless crimes, and white-collar crime all illustrate the limitation of the law in deterring criminal conduct. The international prohibition on genocide has proven to have little deterrent impact when confronted by various socioeconomic factors, which in combination push a society toward genocidal violence.

9.7 YOU DECIDE

Suicide attacks have been carried out in a long list of countries and regions, including Afghanistan, Algeria, Chechnya, India, Iraq, Kashmir, Kenya, Kuwait, Lebanon, Pakistan, Syria, Tajikistan, and Yemen. Perpetrators of these attacks are not limited to Islamic terrorist groups. Suicide bombings have been carried out by the Hindu Tamil Tigers in Sri Lanka and Sikhs in India. Suicide bombers are able to conceal weapons on their body and penetrate the most well-protected targets. Between 1980 and 2003 (not including September 11, 2001), suicide attacks comprised 3 percent of all terrorist acts but accounted for 48 percent of all deaths resulting from terrorism. Suicide attacks tend to target civilians. These attacks killed an average of twelve persons while other terrorist attacks killed an average of one person (not counting September 11, 2001) (Pape 2005: 28). In recent years, the number of suicide attacks and the number of victims in the Middle East have increased as terrorist groups have found themselves under direct attack. Suicide attacks in other parts of the world have been employed to assassinate government leaders such as Indian prime minister Rajiv Gandhi (Burleigh 2009: 394). The Chicago Project on Security and Terrorism

in its online database documents that between 1982 and June 2016, 5,292 suicide attacks were launched in forty countries and occurred at a rate of one a day between 2003 and 2016.

Suicide attacks communicate that terrorist acts cannot be deterred or defended and that no location is immune from attack. The terrorists may lack a military arsenal but are able to mobilize an unlimited number of "human missiles" who are willing to die for a cause. The goal is to kill enemy military and civilians and to spread fear and insecurity among the population. A bomb and suicide belt can be constructed with easily obtained materials for roughly $150. The suicide bomber's family members are celebrated, and the parents usually receive money in compensation for the loss of their son or daughter (Pape 2005: 28).

Mia Bloom observes that spectacular acts of suicide bombing enable a terrorist organization to elevate its prestige in the deadly cycle of competition with other groups for money and recruits. Suicide bombings, however horrific, are justified by pointing to the brutality of the state that is the target of the attack. The plight of individuals must be unbearable for them to willingly sacrifice their lives (Bloom 2005: 76–77).

(Continued)

(Continued)

Various radical Muslim clerics have concluded that suicide bombing does not violate the Koran's prohibition on suicide. Suicide bombing is considered one of the few effective methods of resistance available to Muslims who face an imbalance of power in confronting the "aggressor nations" of the United States and Israel. The clerics reason that the suicide bomber is indistinguishable from the soldier who fights with the realization that he or she ultimately will be killed. Suicide bombers are advised that they should welcome their deaths because they will "enjoy beautiful life in paradise and with joy at having dealt the enemy a damaging blow" (M. Kramer 1998: 146–148).

Nasra Hassan, an international relief worker, interviewed nearly 250 individuals involved in suicide operations (N. Hassan 2001). S was one of her interviewees who at the age of 22 had boarded a bus on the outskirts of Jerusalem filled with Israelis with the intent of igniting a bomb. S and two other young Palestinians unsuccessfully attempted to detonate bombs strapped to their bodies, opened fire, and wounded five passengers and killed one passenger. They hijacked a car, and in a shootout with Israeli military forces, two of the young men and their hostage were killed. S was pronounced brain dead and miraculously survived, and all three men were named *shaheed batal*—"martyr heroes." S today is honored as a young person whom Allah brought back to life.

S was told that the first drop of the martyr's blood instantaneously eliminated his sins. The martyr can bring seventy of his or her closest friends and relatives to Heaven, and males will be surrounded by seventy-two virgins in Paradise. Palestinian neighborhoods feature posters with suicide bombers and flocks of green birds based on the statements by the prophet Muhammad that the soul of the martyr is carried to Allah in the bosom of the green birds of Paradise. Calendars are illustrated with the "martyr of the month," and children are taught the names of martyrs.

S was one of eleven children from a middle-class family that fled their home in Israel to a refugee camp during the 1948 war. He joined the fundamentalist Palestinian group Hamas at a young age and, before volunteering as a suicide bomber, had served two terms in prison for attacking Israeli soldiers. One of his brothers was serving a life term in an Israeli prison. S explained that he volunteered to act as a suicide bomber because they can "immediately open the door to Paradise—it is the shortest path to Heaven." S explained that in heaven, he would be rewarded with a place in the garden of Paradise that is the home of martyrs and prophets. A martyrdom that is carried out for Allah "hurt[s] less than a gnat's bite." He had sworn an oath on the Koran to carry out the martyrdom.

The suicide bombers Hassan interviewed ranged from 18 to 38 years of age; most were middle class and educated with full-time jobs. Hassan describes them as normal, polite, serious, deeply religious, and articulate with rage at the humiliation suffered at the hands of Israel. They had no qualms about suicide bombing, explaining that the Israelis kill civilians and that this is "war, and innocent people get hurt." Suicide is forbidden in Islam, and the prospective martyrs insisted on the term *sacred explosion*. They explained they did not have tanks or rockets and instead rely on "our exploding Islamic human bombs. In place of a nuclear arsenal, we are proud of our arsenal of believers."

Hassan reports that young men and women clamor to join the ranks of suicide bombers. Young people under age 18 or who have children are rejected, and only one brother in a family may be enlisted as a suicide bomber. Individuals who are selected are closely monitored and observed as they interact with their family and friends and in the mosque. As the date of attack approaches, two individuals remain with the bomber at all times. The trainers keep the individual's focus on Paradise, on joining the prophet Muhammad, on the seventy-two virgins, and on fighting the Israelis. Individuals may be taken to visit their own gravesite to help them come to terms with death.

The foundation of the preparation for suicide bombing is the "suicide cell." The cell consists of a leader and two or three young men. Following months or even years of study, they are assigned the title of a "living martyr" ("he who is waiting martyrdom"). Cell members undergo a regimen of prayer, Koran reading, religious lectures, and lengthy fasts. As the date of the scheduled attack approaches, the "living martyr" prepares a will and records a video statement encouraging others to join him in a Jihad. The living martyr watches the videos of other martyrs. The living martyr performs a final ritualistic cleansing and attends a communal prayer at the mosque. He recites the Islamic prayer for battle, places a Koran in the pocket above his heart, and straps the explosives around his waist, and the planner bids him farewell with the words, "May Allah be with you, may Allah give you success so that you achieve Paradise." The living martyr responds, "We will meet in Paradise." As the martyr presses the detonator, he states "Allahu akbar" (Allah is great. All praise to Him). The martyr is celebrated in sermons and leaflets and posters, and his video is distributed. The families are congratulated and sponsor celebratory parties.

On December 25, 2009, Umar Farouk Abdulmutallab, a 23-year-old Nigerian, attempted to ignite a bomb as his plane descended into Detroit. Abdulmutallab's father is one of the wealthiest and most powerful figures in Nigeria, and Abdulmutallab had attended one of the best private secondary schools in Africa. His intense religion left him feeling isolated and alone. The preliminary evidence indicates that as a mechanical engineering student at the University College, London, he was persuaded to engage in Jihad by radical Islamists that he met at the London Muslim Center. Abdulmutallab also traded e-mail messages with American-born cleric Anwar al-Awlaki, whom he may have visited in Yemen. Abdulmutallab left London for Yemen and wrote his parents he had found the true Islam and that they should forget about him. It is probable that while in Yemen he was trained by the Yemenese branch of al Qaeda. Abdulmutallab left Yemen and soon thereafter boarded an airliner bound for Detroit.

In the last several years, the Islamic State (ISIS) has undertaken suicide attacks across the Middle East and Europe although the group has focused on Iraq, Syria, and Turkey. ISIS has relied in some instances on children because they are easily indoctrinated and because they do not raise suspicions and are able to infiltrate targets. The young suicide bombers reportedly are prepared for

their assignment by being buried alive or shot with rubber bullets to demonstrate that they are able to defy death.

Political scientist Robert Pape in his study of suicide bombers challenges the notion that contemporary terrorism is inspired by religion, particularly Islam. He argues that the central objective of terrorism is to coerce a foreign democratic state that has military forces in the terrorists' homeland to withdraw its troops. The targeted states tend to be democracies that the terrorists consider to be "vulnerable to coercion."

Pape's analysis indicates that suicide attacks are animated by the goal of forcing the United States to withdraw from Afghanistan, Iraq, and the Middle East. An occupying country, as in the case of the United States, tends to be particularly offensive to the indigenous population when the foreign troops are of a different religion than the country's inhabitants. In brief, Pape concludes that it is "wrongheaded" to view suicide terrorism as an act committed by religious fanatics or by individuals motivated by religious hatred. He finds that suicide bombing is a deliberate tactic undertaken in response to foreign occupation that is intended to force a government to withdraw its troops. The motivation for suicide bombing is political rather than religious. The United States, according to Pape, was targeted by al Qaeda only after American troops were sent to Saudi Arabia in 1990, which led Osama bin Laden to proclaim the goal of driving the United States out of the Middle East. Democracies whose policies are dependent on public support are vulnerable to pressure from suicide bombers and typically are targeted for attacks. Pape argues that suicide bombing provides terrorists with a weapon that they can rely on to counter the military advantage of stronger opposing powers (Pape 2005; 2010).

Australian academic Riaz Hassan studied suicide bombers and generally supports Pape's analysis. She finds that suicide bombing provides an avenue for individuals to seek revenge against an occupying power that has humiliated their country and religion (R. Hassan 2009).

What is the relevance of suicide bombing to the capacity of law to control international violence?

CHAPTER REVIEW QUESTIONS

1. Discuss Durkheim's distinction between mechanical solidarity and organic solidarity. What is the role of law in each type of society?

2. Why do individuals obey the law? What is the purpose of criminal punishment?

3. Distinguish between special and general deterrence. List and discuss the various approaches to measuring deterrence.

4. What are the difficulties in achieving special and general deterrence? Discuss the ethical considerations in deterring crime.

5. Can capital punishment deter homicide?

6. What are the challenges of deterring prostitution? Gambling? White-collar crime?

7. Discuss whether law can deter genocide.

TERMINOLOGY

capital punishment   331

civil commitment   369

deterrence   314

general deterrence   322

genocide   370

mechanical solidarity   314

organic solidarity   315

Panama Papers   361

specific deterrence   327

victimless crimes   342

Victorian Compromise   344

white-collar crime   358

ANSWERS TO TEST YOUR KNOWLEDGE

1. True

2. False

3. True

4. False

5. True

6. False

7. False

8. True

WANT A BETTER GRADE?

Get the tools you need to sharpen your study skills. Access practice quizzes, eFlashcards, author podcasts, SAGE journal articles, hyperlinks for Law and Society on the Web, and more at **study.sagepub.com/lippmanls2e**.

CHAPTER  10

THE IMPACT OF LAW ON SOCIETY

 TEST YOUR KNOWLEDGE: TRUE OR FALSE?

1. There is a persuasive case that change in the law causes social change and that in other instances social change causes legal change.

2. Supreme Court decisions are the law of the land and are implemented without controversy.

3. Same-sex marriage would have been recognized in all fifty states even if the U.S. Supreme Court had not held that the Constitution required recognition of same-sex marriage.

4. The *Miranda* decision succeeded in ensuring that confessions by criminal suspects are free and voluntary and eliminated false confessions.

5. Social movements play almost no role in bringing about legal change.

Check your answers on page 440.

■ INTRODUCTION

In this chapter, we examine the relationship between law and social change. The question is whether law merely reflects social attitudes, customs, and practices or whether law shapes society. Does law follow society, or does law lead society? The reality is that social change is determined by a combination of factors and there is no single perspective that we can rely on to explain social change.

We will look at several case studies of the impact of judicial decisions on school integration, abortion, and same-sex marriage. Is law capable of bringing about a fundamental shift in how people think, live, act, and interact with one another? We also consider the impact of the Supreme Court decision in *Miranda v. Arizona* that regulates police interrogations as well as the topic of prison reform. In looking at these two case studies, ask yourself whether a law can effectively impact the behavior of individuals, organizations, police officers on the street, and guards in a prison.

The first part of this chapter asks whether law reflects social attitudes and practices or whether law changes social attitudes and practices. In other words, is law a reflection or product of society, or does law transform society? The second part of the chapter explores the capacity of courts to bring about social change by considering several case studies. The third section of the chapter discusses a social movement perspective. The law from this point of view can help to achieve social change when it is employed as one of many tactics used by an organized movement that is working for social change. This discussion is followed by a brief consideration of the role of civil disobedience by individuals who attempt to bring about social change by violating the law. The chapter concludes by looking at the movement against female circumcision and legal and social change in the international arena.

■ THE IMPACT OF SOCIETY ON THE LAW

German theorist Friedrich Carl von Savigny (1779–1861) and American social anthropologist William Graham Sumner argued that law was a reflection of what Sumner termed "folkways" and "mores," which Sumner defined as the customs and practices and moral beliefs of society. In a famous remark, Sumner noted that "legislation, to be strong, must be consistent with the mores." Sumner believed that people were uncomfortable with change and that they preferred to live by "tradition and habit." Traditional and familiar patterns and practices could be changed only through patience and persuasion. The best approach to legal change was to get people to change their views and practices and then to introduce new laws.

Von Savigny and Sumner believed the law must be tailored to the culture and history of each society, and the effort to institute universal rights, however admirable, would have little impact (Savigny 1975; Sumner 1906: 55, 113). Some commentators have gone so far as to argue that custom is the glue that binds society together and is far more effective than law in maintaining social order. Anthropologist Stanley Diamond in a provocative essay writes, "Law and order is the historical illusion; law versus order is the historical reality" (Diamond 1971: 140).

Yehezkel Dror in his article on law and social change makes the point that law inevitably lags behind social developments. The first drivers of the automobile confronted laws developed for the horse and buggy. Dror explains that the legislative process is slow and cumbersome, and it takes time to change the law (Dror 1959).

The early years of computer hacking illustrate Dror's argument that law lags behind social developments. In the early years of the Internet, the prosecution of hackers often failed because the law of theft and the law of trespass protected physical objects, and judges held that the statutes did not cover the theft of "intangible" objects like passwords or trespassing into a website. The federal and state governments responded by passing statutes regulating cyberspace.

The Internet has raised a host of other issues that continue to be debated, including whether a social network is legally responsible for all items posted on its site, whether "fake news" and racist posts should be restricted, who owns the content of an e-mail, and what the extent is of an individual's privacy on the Internet (Lessig 2006).

Several important studies typically are relied on to illustrate how social change shapes the law. William J. Chambliss in an important essay illustrates the development of the law of vagrancy. Vagrancy is defined as an individual in public with no visible means of financial support or what today we may term a "homeless person."

In 1348, the bubonic plague ravaged England and caused the death of almost 50 percent of the population. The wealthy, landed elite found themselves in need of workers to care for the land and to cultivate the soil. The elite solved this problem by persuading Parliament to adopt a vagrancy law. The purpose of the law was to force the unemployed into the workforce. The vagrancy law declared it a crime to beg for alms and refuse employment and made it an offense to leave a job. The prohibition on individuals leaving a job was intended to prevent individuals from migrating to jobs offering higher wages. A freeze on wages was instituted to protect employers from being forced to compete with one another for workers by offering higher wages than their competitors.

In the eighteenth century, England evolved from an agricultural to a commercial society. Merchants shipping goods across the country for export to other countries found their shipments threatened by robbers and thieves. The law of vagrancy was slightly modified and was used to detain individuals who were viewed as potential robbers and thieves; the punishment of vagrancy was elevated from incarceration to whippings and to the severing of the ear.

Chambliss concludes that his essay illustrates how the law of vagrancy responded to the needs of agricultural and business elites. He makes the point that these economic interests formed the economic backbone of English society and that society as a whole benefited from the use of the law of vagrancy to ensure a steady supply of workers (Chambliss 1964).

The notion that changes in society help shape the law is illustrated also by Lawrence Friedman and Jack Ladinsky in their study of the evolution of workers compensation (L. Friedman and Ladinsky 1967) and Jerome Hall in his study of the evolution of the law of theft (J. Hall 1952). Richard Schwartz's study of the law in two Israeli communities also illustrates the close relationship between the structure of society and the law (Schwartz 1954).

The evolution of divorce law in the United States provides an additional example of how law responds to cultural and social change. Divorce was prohibited in England until 1857. The solution for the unhappily married couple was for one of the partners to desert the home or for the couple to pursue adulterous affairs (L. Friedman 2005: 142).

In colonial America, most colonies continued the prohibition on divorce. The Pennsylvania legislature in 1682 recognized the right to divorce on the grounds of adultery. New Hampshire and New Jersey adopted similar laws, all of which were overturned by British colonial authorities (L. Friedman 2005: 142).

The states in the newly proclaimed American Republic were divided on whether to recognize divorce. The South maintained an absolute prohibition on divorce. Couples hoping for a divorce depended on a private bill passed by both houses of state legislatures. The legislatures were not a rubber stamp. In Virginia, only one of every three couples was granted a legislative divorce. Between 1798 and 1833, only 291 legislative divorces were granted in Georgia (L. Friedman 2005: 142).

In the northern states, state legislatures authorized judges to grant divorces based on the grounds listed in the state statutes. Pennsylvania, in 1785, was the first state to recognize judicial divorce. The grounds for divorce in New York were limited to adultery while other states recognized various grounds for divorce, including impotence, adultery, cruelty, desertion and presumption of death, or joining a minority religious faith (L. Friedman 2005: 143).

Friedman notes that the pressures on the American family in the late eighteenth and nineteenth centuries led to a growing demand for divorce. Continuing to prohibit divorce meant that both partners would be required to tolerate adultery, domestic violence, and alcoholism. The southern and border states gradually abolished legislative divorces and allowed for divorce in courts of law.

Nineteenth-century divorce laws struck a balance between the popular demand for divorce and the opposition of religious authorities who prophesized the disintegration of American society. The "innocent" party was required to establish that his or her partner was at fault. In other words, there was no acceptance of the notion of a consensual separation (L. Friedman 2005: 144, 377).

The acceptance of judicial divorce led to an increased incidence of divorce. Between 1860 and 1900, the incidence of divorce increased 70 percent. There were 7,380 divorces in 1869, or 1.2 per 1,000 marriages. In 1920, there were 167,105 divorces or 7.7 per 1,000 marriages. Roughly two-thirds of the divorces were granted to women (K. Hall 1989: 166).

In the twentieth century, the growth of government and industrialization and the decline of an agricultural society transformed marriage. A large family no longer was needed to work on farms. Men worked outside the home, public schools replaced home education, and government welfare meant the family no longer was the only institution available to support the sick and the elderly. Marriage slowly evolved into an institution based on love, romance, and friendship and no longer was a purely economic arrangement. Divorce was increasingly accepted as an alternative to an unhappy union (K. Hall 1989: 300–301). A study of divorce in two California counties between 1850 and 1890 indicated that divorce was pursued by individuals of every social stratum (L. Friedman 2005: 379–380).

National divorce laws were a crazy and irrational quilt. The only consistent pattern was that divorce was available only to the "innocent party." An inability to prove fault meant that the parties were unable to sever their marriage. New York limited divorce to adultery. In contrast, Wyoming provided for divorce on the broad ground of "indignities" that made the marriage "intolerable." Virginia recognized divorce if a woman had worked as a prostitute, and Hawaii proclaimed leprosy as grounds for divorce. Some states permitted the innocent party to remarry but prohibited the "guilty party" from remarrying. South Carolina continued to resist divorce and only recognized divorce in 1949 (L. Friedman 2005: 381, 577).

By the mid-twentieth century, the system of divorce was in crisis. Couples increasingly resorted to "manufactured" divorces. Testimony was falsified, and individuals were paid to falsely testify they had an affair with a husband or with a wife. The rigid system of divorce began to weaken when roughly twenty states recognized divorce based on the consensual separation between the parties for periods ranging from two to twenty years (L. Friedman 2005: 579).

The death knell of "fault divorce" occurred in 1970 when California adopted "no-fault" divorce. The judge was authorized to dissolve a marriage when there were "irreconcilable differences" and an "irremediable breakdown." In practice, divorces were automatically granted. No-fault divorce quickly spread across the country, and either party could go to court and ask for an end to the marriage—the agreement of the other party was not required (L. Friedman 2005: 579).

A surprising number of states quickly embraced no-fault divorce, including Arkansas, Oklahoma, Colorado, Florida, Michigan, Oregon, Kentucky, and Nebraska. No-fault divorce was accompanied by changes in the law regulating custody of children, the distribution of property, and the monetary support required to be provided to help an ex-spouse develop a self-sufficient career (Jacob 1988: 2–3, 92).

The late Herb Jacob termed the movement for no-fault divorce the "silent revolution" because of the speed with which the entire country adopted this reform. He identifies a number of factors that he believes led to the transition to no-fault divorce. An important factor, according to Jacob, is the fact people were living longer and, after their children left home, looked to change their lives. Women increasingly were working outside the home and achieved economic independence and no longer found themselves trapped in unhappy marriages. Birth control and the acceptance of "sex outside of marriage" liberated men and women from being forced to remain married in order to find sexual fulfillment. Jacob also argues that the feminist movement helped engender the belief among women that they had equal rights with men and no longer were compelled to tolerate abuse and cruelty or exploitation.

These developments, according to Jacob, helped to promote the view that the purpose of marriage is happiness and companionship and that marriage is not primarily devoted to raising children or to supporting a family farm or small business. The argument that no-fault divorce made divorce too easy persuaded very few people to oppose the reform of divorce laws (Jacob 1988: 1–29).

Jacob, in reviewing the explanation for the spread of no-fault divorce, fails to find a determined social movement that pushed for this innovation or high-profile politicians who argued for this change. He argues that no-fault divorce spread across the country "because the time was ripe for such a measure" (Jacob 1988: 92–93).

What is the impact of no-fault divorce? We have no way of determining whether individuals who divorce would have remained together under a system of divorce based on fault or would have "manufactured" a divorce under the fault system. Individuals may not have been able to financially afford the costs of a divorce based on "fault" and may have decided to separate or to continue to live together.

Divorce rates also decrease with education. As more women earn college degrees, the rate of divorce decreases. Other relevant variables are a woman's age at the time of her marriage, whether she was raised in a two-parent family, whether the couple is religious, what the family income is, whether the husband or wife is unemployed, and whether one or both spouses previously has been divorced. Calculating the extent of divorce is difficult because of the government's failure to keep accurate statistics. We also are unable to account for individuals who decide to live together rather than to marry and who then may separate (Centers for Disease Control and Prevention 2017).

A new version of Jacob's book published today would perhaps focus on marriage rather than on divorce. According to a Pew study, marriage as an institution seems to be in decline; unmarried American adults outnumber married adults. Twenty percent of Americans 25 years of age and older have never been married. In 1960, this figure stood at 10 percent of all Americans 25 years of age and older.

Individuals are delaying marriage. Half of the men who marry for the first time are nearly 29 years of age or older; half of women who marry for the first time are 27 years of age or older. The average age for a first marriage in the 1990s was in the early 20s.

Why this decline and delay in marriage? People perceive that living together as an unmarried couple or living alone is socially acceptable. Another explanation is that Americans increasingly are intent on establishing their careers and gaining financial stability before they consider marriage. Marriage increasingly is an institution that is affordable only for the college educated. Marriage rates have rapidly declined for individuals in lower economic categories. Even among the young and educated middle class, a "good marriage" no longer is perceived as important as it was to previous generations.

Another example of the changing approach to marriage is the crime of adultery. Adultery, sexual relations between two individuals, one of whom is married, was punished in colonial America with fines, banishment, whipping, and even death. There was a "double standard"; the law was enforced most frequently against women rather than men. As social norms in the mid-twentieth century began to encourage individual fulfillment and social tolerance, adultery, although continuing to be viewed as immoral, rarely was criminally prosecuted. In 1953, the influential Model Penal Code recommended that states repeal laws against adultery and fornication, and today sixteen states surprisingly continue to keep adultery statutes on the books, which in most instances punish adultery as a misdemeanor. Adultery rarely, if ever, is prosecuted. Roughly 20 percent of men as well as women report engaging in adulterous affairs, and less rigorous polls report much higher rates of extramarital sex. Although adultery is overwhelmingly viewed as immoral, only one-third of Americans favor continuing to punish adultery as a crime (Rhode 2016).

In summary, there is persuasive argument—supported by illustrations of the evolution of vagrancy and development of no-fault divorce—that law is a reaction to society. Consider another example based on the technological advancement in the birth process.

■ LAW AS THE CAUSE OF SOCIAL CHANGE

In contrast to the view that law reflects society is the view that law is a dynamic force that changes society (Dror 1959). Dror argues that there are two mechanisms through which law causes social change. Law indirectly brings about social change by influencing institutions. Requiring young people to attend school, for example, resulted in a more educated labor force. This, in turn, created competitive and productive workers who staffed the steel plants and auto factories, which in the last half of the twentieth century transformed the United States into the leading industrial and military power in the world. The development of patents protected scientific innovations and discoveries. This gave individuals an incentive to pioneer new products because they knew they would own their inventions and profit from their discoveries. The patent also enabled inventors to sue anyone who infringed on their patent by copying their concept.

Dror also points out that law can directly bring about social change. He gives the example of a law prohibiting polygamy as the condition of Utah being admitted as a state.

Dror cautions that law may fail to achieve social change. An example is Prohibition. The Eighteenth Amendment to the U.S. Constitution took effect in 1920 and declared the production, transportation, and sale of alcohol illegal. The Volstead Act defined "intoxicating liquor" and articulated methods of enforcing the prohibition on the sale of alcoholic beverages. The inability to enforce alcohol prohibition resulted in the Twenty-First Amendment repealing Prohibition.

Dror suggests that we can study law and social change by examining the change a law brings about in individuals' attitudes and opinions and by determining whether we can find measurable change such as the number of schools that desegregated in response to the 1954 Supreme Court decision in *Brown v. Board of Education* (Dror 1959: 76).

Leon H. Mayhew offers another perspective on the capacity of law to bring about social change (Mayhew 1971). He notes that a law can create new procedural rights. An example is *Gideon v.*

Wainwright in which the Supreme Court recognized that states were obligated to provide lawyers to indigent defendants charged with felonies. As a result of *Gideon*, many jurisdictions created public defender services to provide legal representation to indigent defendants (*Gideon v. Wainwright*, 372 U.S. 335 [1963]).

Friedman offers three additional categories that are useful in thinking about law and social change. First is "planning" the creation of a new social arrangement. Two examples are President Barack Obama's health care plan and his creation of a consumer agency to protect individuals against unfair banking and credit card practices. Second, Friedman describes a "veto" as a law that tears down an existing structure and creates a new set of arrangements. An example is the Supreme Court decision in *Brown v. Board of Education*, which declared segregated schools and facilities an unconstitutional denial of equal protection of the law. The repeal of "don't ask, don't tell" in the military and medical marijuana are other examples. Third, Friedman also distinguishes "deep defense" from "slack." A deep defense is an issue in which society strongly supports a certain legal arrangement and pushes back against a legal effort at change. An example is opposition to Prohibition or opposition in some states to gay marriage and to abortion rights. Slack is a law that most people do not feel strongly about, and it allows a motivated minority to push to pass a law. Legislatures regularly fund the building of monuments, construction of highways, and naming of new buildings after famous personalities. The people who support the bill often deeply care about the bill while most people do not feel strongly about the legislation (L. Friedman 1977: 157–188).

Edwin M. Schur argues that law has a significant role in social change and that the law is not solely a reflection of society. He focuses on the indirect change in attitudes that results from legal reform. Schur uses the example of civil rights and argues that the laws and court decisions establishing racial equality slowly led to a change in popular attitudes and an acceptance of racial integration. Federal laws and court decisions supporting the rights of African Americans also mobilized individuals who supported equality to push for the continuing integration of schools and other public facilities. He argues that as people came into contact with one another, they began to question, and eventually abandoned, their prejudices (Schur 1968: 135–140).

We are left to question whether law reflects society or whether law changes society. The most realistic view of the relationship between law and society is to appreciate that in some instances law may reflect society, and in other instances law may be a source of social change.

10.1 YOU DECIDE

In the United States, there is an increased use of surrogacy. In 2014, more than two thousand babies were born by hiring a woman to bring a baby to term. This does not include the use of women in India, Thailand, and other developing countries that allow the hiring of surrogates to bring a baby to term. The practice of employing surrogates is unlawful in most other western democracies.

(Continued)

(Continued)

There is no explicit federal regulation of surrogacy in the United States, and states vary in their approach to the issue. Roughly seventeen states have laws regulating surrogacy. In seven states, there is at least one court opinion upholding the practice although in five states surrogacy contracts are unenforceable. In other states, there is an absence of case law or legislative enactments addressing surrogacy, and in some states, lawmakers have unsuccessfully attempted to criminalize surrogacy.

Surrogates can make as much as $20,000 and often remain in contact with the child through visits, communication, and photos. Surrogacy has drawn opposition from individuals favoring adoption and from anti-abortion groups because of the production of eggs that may not be fertilized or may be destroyed. Opponents of surrogacy also include individuals who object to child-rearing by same-sex couples, feminists who view the practice as exploitative of women, and individuals who view surrogacy as a step toward designer babies or as resulting in unforeseen medical complications for surrogates and for the children.

Television personality Sofia Vergara, age 44, best known for her role in Modern Family, and her former fiancé Nick Loeb, age 41, conceived together through in vitro fertilization (IVF) two female embryos that they preserved during their engagement. After being together for four years, their engagement ended. Loeb brought a legal action against the ART Reproductive Center and Vergara to prevent the destruction of the embryos. The reproductive center's legal forms drafted in accordance with the couple's wishes provided for the destruction of the embryos in the event of death of either Vergara or Loeb and otherwise left the disposition of the embryos to whatever arrangement they agreed upon. Absent an explicit agreement to insert the embryos in a surrogate, the embryos would remain frozen indefinitely.

Vergara, who has an adult son and presently is married to actor Joe Manganiello, stated that as a Catholic she would never destroy a fetus although she also would not consent to Loeb obtaining custody. Sofia explained that a child should be the product of a loving relationship rather than a contentious relationship. Loeb countered that he had strong pro-life views and believed that life started at conception. Vergara countered that Loeb had been with two women who twenty years ago had abortions. Loeb dropped his lawsuit when ordered by a California court to reveal the names of the women.

Loeb in April 2015 in a newspaper editorial in the New York Times contended, "A woman is entitled to bring a pregnancy to term even if the man objects. . . . [S]houldn't a man who is willing to take on all parental responsibilities be similarly entitled to bring his embryos to term even if the woman objects?"

States have yet to address the issue presented by the disagreement between Vergara and Loeb and have left it to the courts to develop a solution. There is a strong policy that the law will not compel an individual like Vergara to be a parent absent his or her consent. In most instances, unlike Vergara and Loeb, the parties enter into a contract that anticipates all the issues that may arise in the future.

In 1989, a Tennessee court during a divorce action between Mary Sue and Junior Davis awarded custody to Junior, who wanted to destroy the fertilized embryos despite the fact that Mary Sue was infertile and wanted to preserve the embryos. There subsequently have been at least eleven cases across the country involving custody of a fetus, and in eight of the cases, the courts have followed the Tennessee approach and have ruled in favor of the party who did not want the fetus gestated.

Courts in Illinois, Maryland, and Pennsylvania have recognized a "last chance" doctrine exception to the "Tennessee rule." In an Illinois case, shortly after Karla Dunston and Jacob Szafranski began dating, Dunston was diagnosed with lymphoma. The treatment presented a high risk of leaving Dunston infertile, and Szafranski agreed to provide his sperm and fertilize Dunston's embryos in the hopes that one day she would be able to conceive a biological child. Dunston subsequently recovered and claimed custody over the embryos. Szafranski objected to Dunston's being awarded custody of the embryos because he did not want to be forced into fatherhood, which he argued would affect his ability to enter into a relationship in the future. Szafranski relied on the fact that the IVF facility contract provided that a party to the agreement could not obtain custody of the embryo without the consent of the other party. Judge Sophia H. Hall held that "Karla's desire to have a biological child in the face of the impossibility of having one without using the embryos outweighs Jacob's privacy concerns and his speculative concern that he might not find love with a woman because he unhesitatingly agreed to help give Karla her last opportunity to fulfill her wish to have a biological child" (*Szafranski v. Dunston*, 2015 Il. App. [1st Dist.] 122975-B).

Nick Loeb, unlike Karla Dunston, had the opportunity to procreate in the future. He nonetheless stated that this does not mean that "I should let the two lives I have already created be destroyed or sit in a freezer until the end of time."

Loeb continued to assert that each fetus was a potential life, and after dropping the California case, filed suit on behalf of the fetuses against Vergara in the strongly pro-life state of Louisiana. Loeb contended that "Emma" and "Isabella" by not being born were being denied their inheritance from a trust he established in their name in Louisiana. Loeb asked the Louisiana court to give him full custody over the embryos and "authority to release them for transfer, continued development, and birth."

Would you award custody to Sofia Vergara or to Nick Loeb? Should the state or federal government develop standards to regulate custody disputes involving IVF or leave this to judicial decisions? What basic principles should guide custody disputes involving IVF?

■ COMPLIANCE, REJECTION, AND EVASION OF THE LAW

William M. Evan states there are two steps in the implementation of a new law. First, the law must be institutionalized and communicated to the public, and the methods of enforcement must be established. The second step is the internalization of the law. Individuals must voluntarily accept and follow the law.

Evan sketches a hypothetical continuum of acceptance and rejection of a law. On the one hand, there may be complete acceptance and **compliance** with the law. On the other hand, a law may be openly *rejected* and *resisted*. A third possibility is for people to engage in **evasion** or attempts to find loopholes in the law.

A regime may resort to massive enforcement to obtain *involuntary compliance* with a law. The challenge is to convert this involuntary compliance into *voluntary compliance*. Individuals may realize that the costs of resistance are too high or come to appreciate the merits of the law. The practical question is how much resistance can be tolerated and for how long before government officials reverse course and abandon the law.

Evan recognizes that in a large and diverse society, resistance to law is inevitable. He articulates various "necessary" though perhaps "not sufficient" conditions that determine whether a legal rule will be internalized and accepted. Keep in mind that individuals inevitably will differ in their reaction to the law and no single factor determines that reaction. Individuals initially may evade or resist a law and eventually may accept and comply with a law. Noncompliance may be too costly, or an individual may come to see that a law does not have the negative consequences that he or she anticipated.

The factors that influence individuals' acceptance of legal change include the following (Evan 1980):

Source of law. The source of the law must command respect. The source of law may be legislative (e.g., Congress, state legislature), executive (e.g., the president, a governor), administrative (e.g., a school board), or judicial (e.g., courts). Evan argues that most people believe laws should be developed and drafted by an elected legislature and are likely to respect and obey legislative enactments more easily than a decision handed down by an unelected government official or agency or by an unelected judge. It is particularly important that fundamental change is initiated by an authoritative source.

Existing values. A law that is viewed as consistent with existing values and beliefs and is not perceived as a radical change is more likely to be accepted than a law calling for fundamental change.

Reference group. The ability to point to communities that have successfully adopted the new law may persuade individuals that the new law is beneficial. Individuals are more likely to accept a law that is supported by their friends and neighbors and people they respect. In other words, you likely will accept or resist a law because you desire to fit in with your friends.

Implementation. Significant change is best implemented before there is time for opposition to develop. The lengthy debate and discussion of President Obama's health care law allowed opposition to the law to gain momentum, and opponents almost succeeded in defeating the law.

Enforcement. Individuals implementing and enforcing the law must believe in the law and should not be perceived as corrupt, discriminatory, or hypocritical. The legitimacy of the law is undermined by the perception that there is one standard for the wealthy and another standard "for the rest of us."

Punishment and rewards. A law is most likely to achieve compliance when there is punishment for individuals who refuse to comply with the law and there are rewards for individuals who comply with the law. Punishment is most effective when individuals may lose something important like their liberty, job, or income. A law may gain acceptance by rewarding people who comply with the law.

Protection. A law is most likely to be effective when there is an adequately funded agency or organization to monitor compliance. There are allegations that mine safety legislation, in some instances, is ineffective because federal officials are understaffed and cannot monitor the safety of mines on a regular basis.

External support. A law also is more likely to be accepted when it is supported by a well-organized and vocal social movement. Mothers Against Drunk Driving (MADD) has been instrumental in persuading politicians to adopt laws increasing the penalties for drunk driving.

Responsibility. A specific agency or entity should be charged with implementing the law and protecting the rights of individuals who would suffer if there was noncompliance with the law.

Two additional features of a law influence whether it will be effectively implemented:

Information. A law must be communicated to people in a clear and understandable fashion. A failure to inform people of a change in the law will result in noncompliance. People also are reluctant to accept or follow or to take advantage of a law they are unable to understand.

Individual resources. Individuals will obey laws that take little time or effort and may resist or evade or disregard laws they view as entailing a significant amount of effort. Many people find recycling of their garbage to be too complicated and time-consuming. Some find their taxes so complicated that they decide against claiming all their possible tax deductions.

Based on these factors, it is not surprising that Supreme Court rulings prohibiting prayers and religious Bible study in schools encountered considerable resistance. In 1962, in *Engel v. Vitale*, the Court held a "denominationally neutral" prayer that the New York State Board of Regents required to be recited at the start of the school day violated the constitutional prohibition against governmentally sponsored religious activity (*Engel v. Vitale*, 370 U.S. 421 [1962]). Justice Hugo Black wrote that the prayer violated the First Amendment prohibition on the establishment of religion. The important point was that the government was promoting religion and placing its stamp of approval on "non-sectarian religion."

The next year, in *School District of Abington Township v. Schempp*, the Supreme Court held that a Pennsylvania statute requiring Bible reading and recitation of the Lord's Prayer violated the Establishment Clause of the Constitution (*School District of Abington Township v. Schempp*, 374 U.S. 203 [1963]). *Engel* and *Schempp* were attacked by members of the U.S. Congress for making "God unconstitutional," and 146 bills were introduced to amend the U.S. Constitution to make clear that prayer in the schools and Bible reading was a constitutionally protected activity.

A survey of studies finds "minimal compliance" with the Supreme Court's prohibition on prayer in schools (Corsi 1984: 311–312). One study found that only five of the twenty-nine states whose schools engaged in Bible reading completely abandoned this practice following the decision in *Schempp* (E. Katz 1965). A second study undertaken by Robert H. Birkby found that of the 121 school districts in Tennessee, only 1 had eliminated all of its religious activities, and 51 made some modifications to their religious practices. Birkby speculates that the members of school boards in the districts that did not follow the Supreme Court decision either questioned the authority of the Supreme Court to intervene in religious affairs or strongly believed in the value of religious activities (Birkby 1966).

Two well-known political scientists studied compliance with the Supreme Court's religious decisions in four school districts in a state they called Midway. The authors found at least half of the schools engaged in "some form of unconstitutional religious activity" (Dolbeare and Hammond 1971: 72–73).

How do you explain the resistance to the Supreme Court decisions limiting state-sponsored religious prayers and Bible reading? Do you believe unconstitutional activity continues in public schools? There is evidence that religious practice in the public schools is more prevalent today than at any time in recent years.

■ COURTS AND SOCIAL CHANGE

The traditional role of a court is to hear a complaint between two individuals or in a criminal case between the state and the defendant. In a civil case, for example, the court issues a judgment that may result in an individual who drove through a red light and hit another automobile paying monetary damages to the individual whose car was damaged.

The late professor Abram Chayes of Harvard Law School in an important article in 1976 described the "role of the judge in public law litigation." These cases involve public policy rather than disputes between private parties. Chayes notes that in this type of case, the judge is less interested in providing a defendant with compensation for past wrongs than with gathering a broad range of facts and providing standards to guide future behavior. In crafting a remedy, the judge attempts to balance various policy considerations (Chayes 1976).

In 1954, the U.S. Supreme Court in *Brown v. Board of Education* assumed a broad social policy role when it combined cases from Kansas, South Carolina, Virginia, and Delaware and held that African American students who were required to attend segregated schools were denied equal protection of the law guaranteed under the Fourteenth Amendment to the U.S. Constitution (*Brown v. Board of Education*, 347 U.S. 483 [1954], 349 U.S. 294 [1955]).

Gordon Silverstein notes that appellate courts' traditional role has been to approve or to block laws passed by the legislative branch. The Supreme Court, for example, rejected as unconstitutional the effort to create a national income tax, and a tax was imposed only after the U.S. Constitution was amended to permit a national personal income tax with the passage of the Sixteenth Amendment in 1913. *Brown*, according to Silverstein, was the first in a series of cases in which the Court assumed a command function. Silverstein explains that this involves the Court telling other branches of government what to do. Despite criticism of judges assuming this degree of power, Silverstein notes that both liberals and conservatives have come to see courts as a mechanism to achieve social change without having to go through the challenges of achieving change through the complicated political process (G. Silverstein 2009: 42–43).

The issuance of a decision like *Brown* (discussed below) is the beginning of the process. A judicial decision must be *communicated* to the sectors of society who are affected by the law. The question is whether there is *compliance* with the decision or whether there is *resistance, evasion,* or *noncompliance* with the judgment.

A related question is to evaluate the impact of a judicial decision. Did the court decision result in social change or fail to bring about social change? Was social change due to a change in public attitudes that occurred prior to the court's decision (T. Becker 1969)?

Gerald Rosenberg writes that courts can play two different roles in social change (G. Rosenberg 2008: 7).

Judicial path. Judges issue a decision that is obeyed based on the prestige and authority of and respect for legal institutions.

Extra-judicial path. The court's decision highlights an important issue, influences public opinion, leads to discussion of the issue by candidates running for elected office, and results in state legislatures and the U.S. Congress adopting laws that reinforce the court's judgment.

Whereas courts on the judicial path are able to bring about social change, courts on the extra-judicial path are able to bring about social change in conjunction with political activism. This brings us full circle, back to the original debate over whether law reflects societal developments and thereby helps to contribute to social change or whether law is an independent force that is able to bring about social change.

The United States has a strong tradition of judges believing their judicial decisions can bring about social change and employing the law as an instrument of public policy. Rosenberg terms this the dynamic court view. This *dynamic court view* is disputed by theorists who believe that change is achieved most effectively by elected officials. Rosenberg terms this the *constrained court view*.

The dynamic view stresses that judges, as unelected officials, are able to make decisions that elected representatives may want to avoid for political reasons. Elected representatives, for example, have nothing to gain and much to lose by becoming involved in prison reform. Judges can make decisions that cannot attract a majority in the legislative process. In the 1950s, individuals and groups dedicated to the elimination of racial discrimination confronted the challenge of either working to repeal discriminatory legislation in roughly sixteen southern and border states or persuading thirty-six of the forty-eight state legislatures to amend the U.S. Constitution to adopt an amendment prohibiting racial discrimination. The best approach to eliminating racial discrimination was thought to be asking the federal courts to hold that racial discrimination was contrary to equal protection under the U.S. Constitution. Judges are able to write opinions that explain their views, thus increasing the likelihood that the decision will be understood and accepted by the public; judges also are able to monitor the implementation of their decisions to ensure there is compliance with the judgment (G. Rosenberg 2008: 32–36).

The reliance on judges and courts to achieve social reform raises the philosophical question whether unelected judges should be involved in implementing social reform (Bickel 1962; Ely 1980).

There are good reasons for believing that courts are limited in their ability to bring about fundamental social change. Courts must wait for an issue to be placed on their dockets before they act. In some instances, a court may be prohibited from issuing a decision by various technical requirements. During the Vietnam War, individuals challenging the legality of the war were turned away by courts because judges reasoned that the president and Congress had sole control over foreign affairs. Individuals in the military who claimed they might be involved in war crimes if sent to Vietnam were told by the courts that only individuals asked to engage in unlawful actions in Vietnam had standing, effectively making it impossible to bring this claim before a court.

There also are significant financial costs involved in legal trials and appeals, and a case may take years to wind through the judicial system. An issue also must be translated into a legal question. The right to employment or to be free from poverty are important public policy issues that courts have ruled are not protected by the U.S. Constitution.

Judicial decisions may be resisted by political officials who may adopt legislation intended to frustrate the decision. This may require courts to issue additional decisions interpreting the decision in the original case. The Supreme Court has held that individuals have a right to bear arms under the Second Amendment to the Constitution. The Court, however, will be asked to decide a number of cases determining whether a city's gun control ordinances are reasonable regulations or whether the ordinance violates the Second Amendment. Consider whether you can carry a firearm to class at a university or in a bar or movie theater. It will take a number of years for the Court to fully articulate the full scope of the Second Amendment right to bear arms.

Elected legislators may be better positioned than judges to achieve fundamental change. A judge depends on the lawyers to present arguments and information. Legislators, in contrast, are able to hold hearings and conduct investigations to consider all the relevant facts before addressing a social problem. As a result, elected representatives likely will have a greater understanding and expertise than unelected judges. Legislation typically results from discussion and compromise. At the conclusion of the legislative process, a law in many cases has attracted the support of a broad cross section of the community. A statute is able to go into greater detail than a legal decision and is easily amended as new situations arise. Elected representatives also are able to use the "power of the purse" to provide the resources required to support the implementation of the law (D. Horowitz 1977).

Courts and legislatures should be viewed as part of an integrated political system. Courts decide cases, and these decisions in many cases provoke a reaction from the legislative branch. The legislature may decide to pass a law or adopt a constitutional amendment modifying or limiting the ruling or may even attempt to strip the court of jurisdiction over a category of cases. A group may organize a popular referendum to reverse a judge's decision, and individuals and other courts may evade or resist the ruling. Highly motivated individuals may engage in civil disobedience to articulate their displeasure and organize rallies and interject the issue into political campaigns. In other words, impact is a dynamic and constantly evolving process, and it may take a number of years to determine the outcome of a decision (Goldman and Jahnige 1968, 1971).

An example is the Supreme Court's 1973 decision in *Roe v. Wade* (discussed below) declaring that women have a fundamental right to an abortion during the first two trimesters of pregnancy (*Roe v. Wade*, 410 U.S. 113 [1973]). State legislatures opposing the decision responded by modifying their laws to restrict access to abortion. The U.S. Congress limited funding for abortions, and various states imposed waiting periods and prohibited the use of publicly funded facilities for abortions (*Planned Parenthood of Southeastern Pa. v. Casey*, 505 U.S. 833 [1992]; *Webster v. Reproductive Health Services*, 492 U.S. 490 [1989]). There also has been a continuing effort by members of the U.S. Congress to adopt a constitutional amendment limiting or prohibiting abortions, and various doctors and hospitals have refused to perform abortions. In 2006, the Supreme Court upheld a federal law prohibiting partial-birth abortions, the first time the Court approved a law that did not make an exception to preserve the life of the mother (*Gonzales v. Carhart*, 550 U.S. 124 [2007]).

President George W. Bush and most recently President Donald Trump limited funding to international institutions that promoted abortion as a form of birth control. Anti-abortion groups like Operation Rescue have engaged in continuing protests at abortion clinics, and anti-abortion groups have organized mass rallies in Washington, D.C., on the anniversary of *Roe v. Wade*. There also have been isolated and tragic attacks on abortion clinics and on doctors who perform abortions. The Republican Party platform historically has opposed abortion, and abortion has been a central issue in elections.

Pro-choice groups have responded by working to preserve *Roe v. Wade* and have lobbied for the appointment of pro-choice judges to the federal bench. Public opinion, although supportive of abortion, is receptive to limitations on abortions and strongly supports sex education for juveniles (G. Rosenberg 2008: 175–246).

The next section discusses case studies of the impact of judicial decisions in the areas of school integration, abortion, same-sex marriage, regulation of police interrogations, and reform of prisons. Each case study presents an important aspect of the impact of judicial decisions and the capacity of judicial decisions to bring about social change.

Predicting the consequences of the outcome of a legal decision is difficult because of numerous factors that must be considered. Arthur S. Miller has urged social scientists to develop sophisticated tools to predict the impact of a law (A. Miller 1965).

School Integration

In 1954, in *Brown v. Board of Education*, the U.S. Supreme Court held that racially segregated public schools denied African American students equal protection of the law. *Brown* reversed the

Court's 1896 decision in *Plessy v. Ferguson* that held that African Americans were not deprived of equal protection of the law when assigned to "separate, but equal, facilities" (*Plessy v. Ferguson*, 163 U.S. 537 [1896]).

Brown overturned more than fifty years of precedent when Chief Justice Earl Warren relied on social science studies in concluding that "separate but equal" stamped African American young people with a "badge of inferiority." Warren observed that to separate African American students "from others of similar age and qualifications solely because of their race generates a feeling of inferiority as to their status in the community that may affect their hearts and minds in a way unlikely ever to be undone." The chief justice accordingly held that "in the field of public education the doctrine of 'separate but equal' has no place because separate educational facilities are inherently unequal" (*Brown v. Board of Education*, 347 U.S. 483 [1954]).

Photo 10.1 The Little Rock Nine was a group of African American students whose attendance at the segregated Little Rock Central High School in 1957 was prevented by Governor Orval Faubus, who called out the Arkansas National Guard. On September 24, 1957, President Dwight D. Eisenhower sent the 101st Airborne Division to protect the students and to escort them to class. The high school continues to function and has been designated as a national historic site.

United States Army

Keep in mind that the Court recognized that there was a vast difference in the funding of white and African American schools. The per pupil spending for white schools in the South typically was more than four times the spending on African American students, the pupil–teacher ratios were significantly lower in white schools, and the facilities and programs offered to white students were far superior to those offered to African American students.

The Court subsequently issued a second opinion implementing *Brown*. The judgment in *Brown* II proclaimed that school systems must desegregate with "all deliberate speed." The holding in *Brown* II recognized that school administrators required additional time to implement the decision. There may be a need to construct new schools, arrange for transportation, and organize the administration and teaching staff (*Brown v. Board of Education*, 349 U.S. 294 [1955]).

The Court was aware of the radical change required by their decision in *Brown*. The judges waited until they had reached unanimity before issuing their decision and recognized their decision could not be immediately implemented (Kluger 1976: 543–747).

The decision in *Brown* meant that all segregated public elementary and secondary school systems were unconstitutional and would be required to integrate. This affected segregated school systems in seventeen southern and border states and in the District of Columbia, along with school systems in four states (Arizona, Kansas, New Mexico, and Wyoming) that allowed local school districts to establish segregated schools. Eleven other states had no law on the books on segregated schools, and sixteen states had laws prohibiting discrimination in public education (G. Rosenberg 2008: 42).

The decision in *Brown* was the culmination of a long-term legal strategy adopted by the National Association for the Advancement of Colored People (NAACP). The litigation strategy had been developed by lawyers who later would be recognized as some of the most gifted attorneys in twentieth-century legal history, the most prominent of whom was Thurgood Marshall, who later would be named a Supreme Court justice. Two of the central cases that established the foundation for *Brown* were *Sweatt v. Painter* (339 U.S. 629 [1950]) and *McLaurin v. Oklahoma State Regents for Higher Education* (339 U.S. 637 [1950]). In *Sweatt*, the Court held that the state-funded Texas law school for African Americans was not "equal" to the all-white University of Texas Law School because it lacked the same facilities, high-quality faculty, and reputation as the University of Texas law program available to white applicants. In *McLaurin*, the Court held on similar grounds that the graduate education offered to the plaintiffs was not equal to that available to white students.

Brown is without question one of the most famous Supreme Court decisions in U.S. history. The question is whether *Brown* caused the desegregation of public schools.

In the so-called border states that were not part of the confederacy, there was significant and almost immediate compliance. Within ten years, 55 percent of African American students attended school with white students (Lempert and Sanders 1986: 362; Sutton 2001: 176). The eleven southern states of the old Confederacy are a different story entirely. Ten years following *Brown*, less than 1 percent of African American students in the South were in integrated schools (Sutton 2001: 176).

John Sutton notes that southern politicians rallied to oppose *Brown*. In 1956, 101 southern senators and members of the House of Representatives signed what has become known as the "Southern Manifesto." The manifesto condemned *Brown* as an abuse of judicial powers, and the signatories pledged to use "all lawful means" to prevent the enforcement of *Brown* (Sutton 2001: 176).

Southern governors and state legislatures followed the lead of their national representatives and developed various tactics to frustrate the implementation of *Brown*. Politicians such as Governor George Wallace of Alabama proclaimed "segregation now, segregation tomorrow, segregation forever" and condemned "black-robed judicial anarchists" (G. Rosenberg 2008: 78). School boards in 2,200 school districts in the southern states refused to integrate, forcing the government to file legal actions against the school board in each district (Sutton 2001: 176).

President Dwight D. Eisenhower reluctantly sent federal troops to Little Rock, Arkansas, to desegregate Central High School when Governor Orval Faubus called in the Arkansas National Guard to prevent African Americans from entering the school. The Kennedy administration, although quietly supportive, also did not actively promote school desegregation. Lyndon Johnson, whose presidency was destroyed by the Vietnam War, proved to be the most effective and persistent champion of civil rights (Sutton 2001: 177).

Civil rights organizations tried to recruit local parents to bring legal actions to desegregate the schools. African Americans, however, remained reluctant to file suit because of the threat of harassment and retribution and possible loss of employment, particularly in small towns (Sutton 2001: 176). White Citizens' Councils were formed to intimidate politically active African Americans. In 1953, in Yazoo City, Mississippi, the White Citizens' Council posted in stores the names of fifty-three African Americans who had signed a petition calling for the desegregation of schools (G. Rosenberg 2008: 82–83).

The U.S. Supreme Court in the years following *Brown* seemingly retreated from deciding cases involving school desegregation, which may have resulted in a perception that the Court had weakened in its resolve to order schools to desegregate with "all deliberate speed."

The Supreme Court between 1954 and 1964, when Congress passed the Civil Rights Act (discussed below), issued only three opinions on school desegregation cases. In each instance, the Court struck down the local school board's scheme as an unconstitutional effort to evade *Brown*.

In *Cooper v. Aaron*, the Supreme Court rejected an effort by Arkansas to prevent the desegregation of Central High School in Little Rock. The Court held that the rights of African American students are not to be "sacrificed or yielded to . . . violence and disorder" (*Cooper v. Aaron*, 358 U.S. 1 [1958]).

In *Goss v. Board of Education of Knoxville*, decided eight years following the decision in *Brown*, the Court rejected a plan that allowed students to transfer from a school in which their "race" was in the minority to a school in which their "race" was in the majority. The Supreme Court reasoned that the plan was intended to ensure that schools remained segregated (*Goss v. Board of Education of Knoxville*, 373 U.S. 683 [1963]).

The next year, the Court addressed "massive resistance" in Virginia and held that Prince Edward County had acted unconstitutionally in shutting down its public school system five years earlier and diverting the money to support private segregated education for white students (*Griffin v. School Board of Prince Edward County*, 377 U.S. 218 [1964]). Prince Edward County's policy, which was endorsed by the State of Virginia, resulted in a denial of an education to a significant number of African American children who lacked the ability to pursue their education in other parts of Virginia or outside the state (K. Green 2015).

In summary, despite the resolve of the U.S. Supreme Court in the ten years following *Brown*, the mandate to desegregate the schools in the South was "flagrantly disobeyed" (G. Rosenberg 2008: 52).

The Civil Rights Act of 1964

A number of events combined to inspire the U.S. Congress to pass the Civil Rights Act of 1964. These events included the massive freedom march on Washington led by the Reverend Martin Luther King Jr., the violence against civil rights workers in the South, and the desire to honor the legacy of the assassinated young president, John F. Kennedy. Scholars agree that *Brown* had little impact on congressional passage of the Civil Rights Act (Lempert and Sanders 1986: 363). The act authorized the U.S. attorney general to file desegregation suits on behalf of students. Title VI of the act provided that

> [n]o person in the United States shall, on the ground of race, color, or national origin, be excluded from participation in, be denied the benefits of, or be subjected to discrimination under any program or activity receiving Federal assistance.

The Department of Health, Education and Welfare (HEW) was authorized to issue regulations cutting off assistance to school districts that discriminated on the basis of race.

In 1965, the Elementary and Secondary Education Act (ESEA) provided over a billion dollars per year in federal assistance to local school districts with a significant percentage of low-income students. A school system that discriminated risked the loss of this federal aid.

The threat of the withdrawal of funds meant that there now was a direct cost to school districts that maintained segregated school systems. Between 1963 and 1970, the number of students attending desegregated schools in the border states and in the District of Columbia increased rapidly, and by 1970, roughly 77 percent of African American students were attending desegregated schools. The desegregation in the South was even more immediate and impressive, and by 1972, roughly 91 percent of African American students were in desegregated schools.

The desegregation of schools in some instances resulted from the filing of vigorous enforcement actions by the Department of Justice and in other instances from pressure exerted by HEW. A court order to desegregate, if not obeyed now, might result in the withdrawal of federal funding (G. Rosenberg 2008: 51–53). The impact of the threat of the withdrawal of funds can be seen from the fact that by the end of 1967, of the 4,588 school districts in seventeen southern and border states, only 350 school districts remained under a court order to desegregate and 1,225 districts had entered into an agreement voluntarily to desegregate. In other words, two-thirds of the school districts in the South and in border states voluntarily were respecting the civil rights of minority students (Lempert and Sanders 1986: 333).

Greater progress toward school desegregation was made in the five years following the adoption of the Civil Rights Act of 1964 than had been made in the previous ten years. Richard Lempert and Joseph Sanders assert that the explanation is that Congress authorized HEW to act to deny funds to segregated school systems and that the Department of Justice was empowered to pursue the desegregation of school systems. Under Johnson's successor, President Richard Nixon, HEW and the Department of Justice had little interest in pursuing desegregation; as a result, urban school districts in the North remained predominantly African American and Hispanic (Lempert and Sanders 1986: 368).

Rosenberg also observes that the broad political landscape had begun to change following 1964, which helped to create an atmosphere that encouraged and supported desegregation. President Johnson was strongly supportive of civil rights, and numerous studies document that a crucial factor in explaining desegregation was the rise of a new generation of mayors, governors, and local educational and business leaders who supported desegregation.

An important factor was the passage of the 1965 Voting Rights Act, which authorized federal intervention to protect the right of African Americans to vote. Between 1964 and 1970, African American voter registration increased almost 27 percent. This meant that politicians in the South no longer could disregard the demands of African Americans. The continuing migration of African Americans to the large electoral states of California, Illinois, Michigan, New Jersey, New York, Ohio, and Pennsylvania also contributed to political support for civil rights by politicians in these states (G. Rosenberg 2008: 96–97).

Rosenberg concludes that *Brown v. Board of Education* remained a dead letter and did not play a central role in accelerating school integration. *Brown* only proved important when combined with support from President Johnson and Congress. He speculates that even without *Brown*, integration was inevitable. In support of his argument, Rosenberg points to the impassioned African American protests, sit-ins, bus boycotts, and marches; expanding African American voting and economic power; the need for the United States to protect its global image following World War II as the defender of human rights; and the rise of mass media communication, which turned public opinion against segregation by vividly portraying southern violence against African American demonstrators.

In summary, Rosenberg contends that *Brown* was a minor footnote and that integration of the schools was inevitable. *Brown* had a significant impact only when combined with the decision of Congress to employ the "power of the purse" to bring about school integration (G. Rosenberg 2008: 107–169). Rosenberg's arguments have been challenged by studies that conclude that *Brown* drew attention to the issue of desegregation and sparked a national debate that had a profound impact on public opinion and public policy (Flemming, Bohte, and Wood 1997).

The issue today is de facto segregation based on housing patterns throughout the United States. Although schools are desegregated as a matter of law (de jure), a significant number of students continue to attend schools in which the students predominantly are of a single race. In 2016, a federal study of K–12 public schools found that between 2001 and 2014, the percentage of public schools that had at least 75 percent poor African American or poor Hispanic students increased from 9 to 16 percent. These schools as compared to other schools offered fewer math, science, and college preparatory classes and had disproportionately higher rates of students who were held back in the ninth grade or suspended or expelled. Schools with concentrations of poverty regardless of their racial composition generally have lower test scores, graduation rates, and rates of college attendance than economically diverse or economically privileged schools (U.S. Government Accountability Office 2016).

The U.S. Supreme Court initially responded by endorsing the mandatory bussing of students across district lines to achieve racial integration (*Swann v. Charlotte-Mecklenburg Board of Education*, 402 U.S. 1 [1971]), although the Court later limited bussing as a remedy to counter segregated schools to those instances in which district lines intentionally had been drawn to maintain segregated schools (*Milliken v. Bradley*, 418 U.S. 717 [1974]). The Court in recent years has been divided and generally skeptical about the use of modest race-conscious assignment of students to schools to achieve school integration within school districts (*Parents Involved in Community Schools v. Seattle School District No. 1*, 551 U.S. 701 [2007]). School districts increasingly are relying on magnet schools and publicly funded charter schools in an effort to achieve school integration and are introducing the evaluation of teachers to raise achievement scores. The Trump administration promises to extend the use of vouchers that students can use to attend private schools. Most studies find that although parents, whatever their race, believe that diversity in education is important and that students benefit from a diverse education, they also believe that diversity is less important than maintaining a local school.

Do you believe that educational diversity in K–12 schools is an important value that local school districts should continue to pursue?

The next section discusses Rosenberg's view that the Supreme Court's controversial abortion decision in *Roe v. Wade* reflected preexisting social values and therefore had a limited impact on social change.

Abortion

Abortion before "quickening" was permitted under English common law. Quickening was determined to occur when the fetus began to move inside the womb in the fourth or fifth month of pregnancy. The belief was that at this time, the soul entered the fetus. The laws in the American colonies and states followed the quickening doctrine and imposed criminal liability on individuals conducting abortions after quickening rather than on the woman seeking an abortion.

State laws in the United States started to diverge from the quickening doctrine in the eighteenth century. Several states recognized that an abortion could be performed following quickening if undertaken on the advice of a physician to preserve the life of a woman. Other states did not regulate abortions whatsoever. As a result, the number of abortions increased during the 1850s and 1860s from one in every twenty-five to thirty births to one in every five or six births. The increase in abortion numbers was concentrated in the white middle class and was condemned by religious leaders as a "fashionable" form of homicide (L. Friedman 1993: 229; K. Hall 1989: 162).

Between 1820 and 1860, abortion was widely available to American women. The American Medical Association (AMA) reacted by launching a campaign against abortion. The AMA professed to be concerned about the dangers posed to women by unscrupulous abortionists, although there also was alarm at the declining birthrate among middle-class white women and a fear America would be overwhelmed by the children of immigrants (L. Friedman 1993: 229–230). In 1857, the AMA appointed a Committee on Criminal Abortion, whose report proclaimed that abortion was the "wanton murder and destruction of a child," which was deserving of "all hatred and detestation" (American Medical Association 1859).

The popular perception of abortion gradually changed as a result of pressure from the AMA. Between 1880 and 1910, virtually every state declared abortion a crime unless undertaken to save the life of the mother. The quickening doctrine was abandoned, and criminal liability was extended to both the doctor and the woman (K. Hall 1989: 162–163).

This was to be the prevailing pattern in the United States. The period between the 1930s and 1960s has been called the period of silence on abortion. Abortions by and large were limited to relatively wealthy women who could afford to hire a doctor willing to perform an illegal abortion or who possessed the financial resources and freedom to travel abroad for an abortion. Women who lacked resources confronted the prospect of risking dangerous "back-alley abortions" or putting their baby up for adoption (Garrow 1998; Graber 1999).

Attention was refocused on abortion as a result of the health threat to infants posed by the pregnancy drug thalidomide and by an epidemic of German measles. These developments coincided with the growth of a new grassroots pro-abortion movement comprising a coalition of feminist groups dedicated to providing women control over their bodies and lives. The coalition also included the AMA, which had grown alarmed over the negative health impact of the illegal abortion industry, and lawyers and judges who saw little reason to criminally prosecute women for seeking abortions. These diverse groups coalesced in the National Association for the Repeal of Abortion Laws (NARAL), which in 1969 called for abortions to be undertaken by women in consultation with their doctors and without legal restrictions. NARAL argued that the decision whether to undertake an abortion was a decision for the woman in consultation with her doctor and that the government should have no role in this decision. The philosophy of the movement was captured in the term *pro-choice* (Epstein and Kobylka 1992: 143–150).

The tactics of the pro-choice movement ranged from picketing and demonstrations and sit-ins in hospitals to educational campaigns and lobbying. The arguments in support of abortion were based on safeguarding the health of women, the need to curb the predicted global population explosion, and the right of women in the workforce to determine when to start a family. By 1970, nineteen states had relaxed their abortion laws. The abortion movement now had reached the political limits of its popular appeal; the remaining states unalterably opposed relaxing restrictions on an abortion (L. Greenhouse and Siegel 2011: 2038–2047).

The first states to extend access to abortions were Colorado, North Carolina, and California, whose 1967 laws permitted abortions to safeguard the health or mental health of the mother, in the case of rape or incest, or where there was a substantial risk the child would be born with a grave physical or mental defect. Seven additional states adopted reform laws the following year: Arkansas, Delaware, Georgia, Kansas, Maryland, New Mexico, and Oregon (G. Rosenberg 2008: 262–263).

Pro-choice advocates argued these "reform" abortion statutes were overly restrictive, a view supported by a presidential commission on the status of women that recommended the repeal of restrictions on abortion. In 1970, Hawaii adopted a law that permitted free choice in abortions of a "nonviable" fetus, provided the abortion was performed in a hospital, and imposed a ninety-day residence requirement on access to an abortion. The Hawaiian approach subsequently was adopted by Alaska, New York, and Washington (G. Rosenberg 2008: 263).

Silverstein notes there was little prospect for additional progress on abortion rights. In 1971, thirty-four states considered and rejected the Hawaii model and refused to lift their restrictions on abortion. As a result, reformers turned to the courts to guarantee broader abortion rights for women (G. Silverstein 2009: 113).

The judicial strategy culminated in the 1973 U.S. Supreme Court abortion decisions (Epstein and Kobylka 1992: 149–167) in *Roe v. Wade* (*Roe v. Wade*, 410 U.S. 113 [1973]) and in the companion case of *Doe v. Bolton* (*Doe v. Bolton*, 410 U.S. 179 [1973]).

In *Roe* and in *Bolton*, the U.S. Supreme Court held that the constitutional right to privacy protects the right of a woman to an abortion. This fundamental right could be overridden by a compelling state interest. A woman retained the right to an abortion without "undue interference" by the state during the first trimester. During the second trimester, regulation was permitted that "reasonably relates to [the] preservation and protection of maternal health." In the third trimester, the fetus obtained "viability" and was capable of living outside the womb; at this time, the state has a compelling interest in the potential life of the fetus. The Constitution now permitted the restriction of abortions except where required to preserve the life or health of a woman (Epstein and Kobylka 1992: 149–167).

In 1983, in *City of Akron v. Akron Center for Reproductive Health*, the Supreme Court stressed that in the twenty years since *Roe*, the Court had continued to affirm that a "woman has a fundamental right to make the highly personal choice whether or not to terminate her pregnancy" (*City of Akron v. Akron Center for Reproductive Health*, 462 U.S. 416, 420, n.16 [1983]).

Did the number of abortions increase as a result of *Roe v. Wade*? Gerald Rosenberg finds the number of abortions had been increasing before the decision in *Roe v. Wade*. His findings indicate the following (G. Rosenberg 2008: 178–181):

Pre–Roe v. Wade. The number of abortions had been increasing prior to the decision in *Roe v. Wade*. The largest increase in the number of abortions occurred between 1970 and 1971, and the second highest increase in the number of abortions was between 1972 and 1973.

Post–Roe v. Wade. The number of abortions following the decision in *Roe v. Wade* in 1973 continued to increase, although the rate of increase stabilized and began to decline by the early 1980s.

In other words, the "largest numerical increases in legal abortions occurred in the years prior to the initial Supreme Court action" (G. Rosenberg 2008: 178).

Rosenberg explains *Roe* reflected a developing social trend and did not affect the prevailing practice in states like New York, which was derided as the "abortion center" of the nation.

A significant minority of states prior to *Roe v. Wade* modified their abortion laws to ease barriers to the termination of a woman's pregnancy, and in 1972, almost six hundred thousand abortions were performed, an increase of over one hundred thousand abortions from the previous year. According to Rosenberg, the fact that abortions continued to increase following *Roe* indicates the decision did result in an easing of restrictions on abortion and led to a modest increase in the number of abortions performed (G. Rosenberg 2008: 179–184).

Popular support for abortion already was substantial before *Roe v. Wade* and did not increase significantly following the decision. Unscientific polls of doctors, nurses, and social workers found overwhelming support for elective abortion. Rosenberg notes this is additional evidence that *Roe* generally reflected existing attitudes and that the decision did not significantly transform public opinion (G. Rosenberg 2008: 238, 260–261).

Rosenberg also argues that *Roe* had little impact on public attitudes in those states and regions generally opposed to abortion. In 1974, 20 percent of women lived in California and in New York, and 37 percent of abortions were performed in these states. In 1973, only 4 percent of abortions were performed in the eight states constituting the East South-Central and West South-Central census divisions in which 16 percent of all women resided (G. Rosenberg 2008: 190). Abortion opponents portrayed abortion as murder rather than as a health measure and relied on support from the Catholic Church, religious fundamentalists, and political conservatives. Abortion was portrayed as part of a liberal political ideology that also endorsed drugs, sexual freedom, and an opposition to American military intervention abroad (L. Greenhouse and Siegel 2011: 247–274). Linda Greenhouse and Riva B. Siegel make the important point that *Roe* intensified a debate over abortion that was taking place before the Supreme Court's decision, and that *Roe* provided a focus for both sides of the debate (L. Greenhouse and Siegel 2011: 277).

Nearly fifty years following *Roe v. Wade*, the impact of the decision is difficult to evaluate. Following *Brown v. Board of Education*, there was a growing acceptance of racial desegregation in the schools and in society. In contrast, the country has not fully embraced abortion and remains divided. One important difference, according to Rosenberg, is that the pro-choice movement continued to rely on the courts to protect abortion rights and did not work politically to broaden the number of individuals and groups supportive of abortion.

The years following *Roe* witnessed an increasing opposition to abortion. The U.S. Congress adopted a number of anti-abortion measures, the most significant of which was the Hyde amendment in 1976. This law decreased the number of federally funded abortions from 250,000 in 1976 to 2,421 in 1978. Many of the women ineligible for federal funding are able to receive state funding for abortions (G. Rosenberg 2008: 187).

Various state legislatures aggressively opposed *Roe v. Wade* and passed laws designed to limit access to abortions. These laws included provisions for spousal and parental consent, written consent forms describing the "pain" that abortion inflicts on the fetus, pre-abortion counseling and mandatory waiting periods for abortions, prohibitions on the most common technique of carrying out abortions, limitations on the facilities in which abortion may be performed, and allowing private insurance plans to refuse coverage for abortions. Other states have passed statutes that only allow abortions to save the life of the mother and have threatened to withdraw the license of any doctor performing an abortion.

In recent years, there has been a renewed effort by various state legislatures to limit abortion. This includes attempts to restrict abortion to the first twenty weeks of pregnancy, the requirement that women undergo an ultrasound prior to an abortion, and laws requiring that the fetus is provided with a formal burial.

Most of these efforts, although declared unconstitutional by courts of appeals, have forced the pro-choice movement to expend considerable time and resources challenging these laws (G. Rosenberg 2008: 188).

In 2013, legislatures in twenty-two states enacted seventy new laws restricting reproductive rights. More laws restricting abortion passed between 2011 and 2013 than in the previous decade.

In 2000, thirteen states had at least four types of abortion restrictions and were considered by the Guttmacher Institute to be "hostile" to abortion rights. Fifteen years later, the number of "hostile" states had more than doubled, and the proportion of women between 15 and 44 years of age living in "hostile" states increased from 31 percent to 56 percent. The number of states "supportive" of abortion between 2000 and 2015 decreased from seventeen to twelve, and the proportion of women of reproductive age living in "supportive" states decreased from 40 percent to 30 percent during this period. The entire southern region of the United States along with much of the Midwest currently is considered to be "hostile" to abortion. Consider that between 2011 and July 2016, states enacted 334 abortion restrictions that accounted for 30 percent of all restrictions adopted since *Roe v. Wade*.

A restrictive provision like the requirement of an ultrasound requires women to make two visits to a clinic is burdensome for women in rural areas without a nearby abortion provider. A woman may have to take time off of work and arrange for child care and transportation. This raises the cost of an abortion and discourages women from obtaining an abortion.

There also has been a growth in the political prominence and impact of the anti-abortion movement. The anti-abortion movement includes groups like Americans United for Life, the National Right to Life Committee, and Operation Rescue. As noted above, the anti-abortion movement has countered the claims of a "woman's right to choose" with the counterclaim that abortion is murder.

Anti-abortion groups engage in rallies, lobbying, and demonstrations and financially support sympathetic political candidates and coordinate legislative initiatives. Operation Rescue also engages in direct action, picketing abortion clinics to dissuade women from seeking abortions. According to the Guttmacher Institute, the leading public policy group on issues of reproduction, 80 percent of abortion clinics reported being picketed. In 2014, the U.S. Supreme Court held that a thirty-five-foot buffer zone around the entrance to an abortion clinic violated the First Amendment rights of anti-abortion demonstrators (*McCullen v. Coakley*, 573 U.S. ___ [2014]).

Fringe elements of the anti-abortion movement have protested against doctors that perform abortions and have engaged in vandalism and even violence against clinics and doctors and workers in abortion clinics. In 2015, an armed attack on an abortion clinic resulted in the killing of three individuals and the wounding of nine others. Since 1993, eleven abortion providers have died in attacks (G. Rosenberg 2008: 188).

In the years following *Roe v. Wade*, the American public has developed a sophisticated view of abortion that reflects a balance between the arguments of pro-abortion and anti-abortion groups. The public generally supports abortion to protect the health and life of the mother, where the pregnancy results from rape or incest, or where there is a high likelihood that the baby will be born with a severe defect. Public opinion is somewhat more divided when abortion is pursued based on an "unwanted pregnancy" (G. Rosenberg 2008: 188). Public opinion has been remarkably stable, with most people taking the position that abortion should be legal only under certain circumstances, 29 percent believing it should be legal under any circumstances, and 19 percent believing abortion should be illegal in all circumstances.

Locating an abortion provider remains a challenge in some parts of the United States. Eighty-seven percent of U.S. counties lack hospitals or clinics that perform abortions. The figure rises to 97 percent in non-metropolitan counties. Thirty-two states today lack abortion providers in more than 80 percent of their counties. Roughly 33 percent of U.S. women of reproductive age live in one of the 87 percent of counties in the United States without an abortion provider. The latest data indicate that women have to travel an average of thirty miles to obtain an abortion.

This can become a financial burden in states that require multiple visits to an abortion provider before a woman can obtain an abortion (Guttmacher Institute n.d.).

Hospitals are increasingly reluctant to carry out abortions, and abortions increasingly only are available from specialized clinics. A mere 4 percent of hospitals at present perform abortions, and a study by the American Congress of Obstetricians and Gynecologists found that most doctors bend to pressure from hospitals and from their colleagues and do not perform abortions (Freedman 2010). As a result, in 1983, 13 percent of providers performed 56 percent of all abortions, and in 1985, 15 percent of providers performed 60 percent of all abortions. Abortions are difficult to obtain past the first trimester. In 1985, only 43 percent of providers performed post–first trimester abortions (G. Rosenberg 2008: 193–195).

The Guttmacher Institute reports that in 2008, 1.21 million abortions were conducted in the United States. In 2011, roughly 1.08 million abortions were performed, a decrease of 13 percent from 2008. The abortion rate in 2011 was 16.9 percent per one thousand women aged 15 to 44 as compared to 19.4 percent per thousand in 2008. This is the lowest rate since abortion was held constitutional in 1973. The Centers for Disease Control and Prevention of the federal government documents that between 2004 and 2013, the total number of abortions decreased 20 percent; the rate of abortions per one thousand women aged 15–44 decreased 21 percent; and the rate of abortions per thousand live births decreased 17 percent. In 2013, all three of these measures reached their lowest levels. Experts attribute this decline to an increase in use of birth control, to the growing number of restrictions on abortion, and to a culture that questions abortion. It should be noted that non-Hispanic white women accounted for nearly 40 percent of abortions. Among all racial groups, white women had the lowest rate of abortions and lowest ratio of abortions per thousand live births although the rate and ratio of abortions decreased among all racial groups between 2007 and 2013. Abortions tend to be concentrated among poor women with incomes below or slightly above the federal poverty level who already have children and who tend to be the sole breadwinner of their family (Guttmacher Institute n.d.).

The Guttmacher Institute reports that two-thirds of abortions occur at eight weeks of pregnancy or earlier and 91 percent occur in the first thirteen weeks of pregnancy. Most women who have an abortion base their decision on various reasons including their inability to afford a child; a belief that a baby will interfere with work, school, or their ability to care for dependents; the fact that they did not want to be a single parent; or the fact that they were experiencing difficulties with a husband or partner.

Silverstein attributes the continuing fragile status of *Roe* to the fact that the pro-choice movement invested all its resources in a legal strategy and allowed the anti-abortion force to emerge as a politically powerful force in local and national politics and elections. He writes that abortion rights hang in the balance based on the composition of the U.S. Supreme Court.

Abortion opponents were encouraged by the Supreme Court decision in *Planned Parenthood of Southeastern Pa. v. Casey*, 505 U.S. 833 (1992). *Casey* replaced the trimester framework of *Roe* with a framework based on the viability of the fetus (ability to live outside the womb). The plurality opinion held that advancements in medical technology established that a fetus could be viewed as viable at 22 or 23 weeks rather than the 28 weeks established in *Roe*. The state's interest in the potential life of the fetus now was established to begin earlier in the pregnancy. Prior to viability, the Court held that states may regulate abortion so long as the regulations do not impose an undue burden on a woman's right to an abortion. At viability and after viability a state may regulate and even prohibit abortions other than when the life of the mother is at stake. *Casey* proceeded to uphold the constitutionality of a Pennsylvania requirement that women wait to consent to abortion twenty-four hours after receiving information about the risks of an abortion and information about the fetus along with a requirement for parental consent before a minor may obtain an abortion.

Roe v. Wade, however, is far from a dead letter in the Supreme Court. In 2016, in *Whole Woman's Health v. Hellerstedt*, 59 U.S. ___ (2016), the U.S. Supreme Court held 5–3 that a Texas law placed an undue burden on women seeking an abortion and was unconstitutional. Justice Stephen Breyer held that the law's requirement that doctors obtain "admitting privileges" at a local hospital and that abortion clinics have expensive difficult-to-obtain facilities equivalent to an ambulatory surgical center "places substantial obstacle in the path of women seeking a pre-viability abortion . . . [and] constitutes an undue burden on abortion access, and . . . violates the federal Constitution." Justice Breyer noted that Texas was unable to present any evidence that these requirements would provide a single woman with a better or safer operation. The law already had resulted in the closing of almost half of the abortion clinics in the state, and approval of the Texas law would have increased the number of Texas women living more than two hundred miles from the nearest abortion clinic from 10,000 to 750,000.

Rosenberg's case studies of school integration and of abortion suggest that the Supreme Court standing alone cannot bring about instant social change. A decision will be effective when supported and reinforced by the actions of the other branches of government or when the judgment follows social changes that already are under way. In a federal system like the United States, state and local governments with the support of active political movements are able to limit the impact of Supreme Court decisions and influence the Court's willingness to aggressively implement these judgments.

How do you explain the rapid acceptance of same-sex marriage discussed in the next section of the chapter?

Same-Sex Marriage

In May 2012, Barack Obama became the first sitting U.S. president to openly declare support for the legalization of same-sex marriage.

The American public was first introduced to the issue of the legality of same-sex marriage in 1993 when the Hawaii Supreme Court held in *Baehr v. Lewin* that the denial of marriage licenses to same-sex couples constituted unconstitutional discrimination on the basis of gender in violation of Hawaii's constitution. According to the court, Hawaii failed to demonstrate that the state possessed a compelling reason for prohibiting same-sex couples to marry (*Baehr v. Lewin*, 852 P.2d 44, clarified in 852 P.2d 74 [Haw. 1993]).

The decision in *Baehr* ignited a firestorm. In 1995, the Hawaii legislature passed a law that restricted marriage to heterosexual couples. Conservative family groups and churches opposed to same-sex marriage placed a constitutional amendment on the ballot stating that the question of same-sex marriage was reserved to the state legislature and that courts had no role in this determination. The amendment was passed in 1998 by a vote of 69.2 percent to 28.6 percent and affirmed the legislature's earlier decision that marriage was limited to relationships between a man and a woman. In November 2013, Hawaii reversed course, and the governor signed a legislative act recognizing same-sex marriages.

In 1996, the U.S. Congress passed the Defense of Marriage Act (DOMA). The law defined marriage as "only a legal union between one man and one woman as husband and wife" and denied federal marriage benefits to same-sex partners (e.g., health insurance, tax deductions, social security benefits; there are a total of 1,138 federal benefits). The legislation advised states they need not recognize same-sex marriages performed in other states. There also was an unsuccessful effort to amend the U.S. Constitution to define marriage as between a man and a woman.

In 1999, Vermont became the next state to take a position on same-sex marriage. In *Baker v. Vermont*, the Vermont Supreme Court held that the state was acting unconstitutionally by failing to recognize same-sex marriage. The court provided the legislature the option of providing gay individuals a "domestic partnership" or "registered partnership," making available "all or most of the same rights . . . provided . . . to married partners" (*Baker v. Vermont*, 744 A.2d 864 [Vt. 1999]). In April 2000, following an intense debate in the Vermont legislature, Governor Howard Dean signed a bill making Vermont the first state to recognize civil unions for same-sex couples. The act provided same-sex couples the same benefits available to married couples.

Over the next eight months, 1,704 civil unions were consecrated in Vermont; in 2000, 6,271 civil unions were performed in Vermont (G. Rosenberg 2008: 345–347). On September 1, 2009, the Vermont legislature adopted same-sex marriage, the first legislature to adopt same-sex marriage without being ordered to take this step by the state's supreme court.

In the aftermath of *Baker*, a number of states passed laws prohibiting same-sex marriage. In 2000, Nebraska and West Virginia adopted constitutional amendments prohibiting same-sex marriage; Nevada in 2002 and Wyoming in 2003 followed Nebraska and West Virginia's example. In 2004, thirteen additional states prohibited same-sex marriage.

Massachusetts was the next state to address the issue of same-sex marriage. In July 2002, the state legislature, despite a petition signed by 130,000 individuals, refused to take a vote on whether to amend the Constitution to prohibit same-sex marriage. In November 2003, the Massachusetts Supreme Judicial Court held that by denying same-sex couples the benefits and protections of marriage, the state had made these individuals into "second-class citizens." The court noted that the prohibition on same-sex unions does not advance the aim of encouraging "adult stable relationships" and instructed the legislature that the Constitution required same-sex couples the right to marry (*Goodridge v. Department of Public Health*, 798 N.E.2d 941 [Mass. 2003]).

On May 17, 2004, the first same-sex marriages in the United States were performed. This was the first of six thousand same-sex marriages conducted in Massachusetts over the course of the next twelve months (G. Rosenberg 2008: 348–349).

President George W. Bush reacted by warning that marriage was in danger of being redefined by activist judges and urged the amendment of the U.S. Constitution "to protect marriage as a union of man and woman as husband and wife" (G. Rosenberg 2008: 49). Groups opposed to same-sex marriage, joined by then governor of Massachusetts Mitt Romney, collected a record 170,000 signatures calling on the state legislature to adopt a constitutional amendment defining marriage as between a man and a woman. These groups failed to attract the necessary votes, and same-sex marriage remained the law in the Commonwealth of Massachusetts, the thirteenth largest and one of the most diverse and liberal states in the country. Although Governor Romney opposed same-sex marriage, a number of mayors and local officials along with prominent local bar associations supported same-sex marriage. Opinion polls also consistently indicated that roughly 50 percent of the Massachusetts public supported same-sex marriage. On the other hand, Massachusetts's adoption of same-sex marriage was surprising given the Commonwealth's large religiously oriented population.

The Massachusetts decision in *Goodridge* inspired both opponents and proponents of same-sex marriage. A range of gay rights organizations became engaged by the issue (G. Rosenberg 2008:

356–357). A number of local officials throughout the country disregarded the requirements of their own state law and began to recognize same-sex marriages. Marriage ceremonies were conducted in San Francisco (California), New Paltz (New York), Portland (Oregon), and Sandoval County (New Mexico). San Francisco issued 4,037 marriage licenses to same-sex couples in February 2004 before being ordered to stop by the California Supreme Court, which later voided all of the marriages (G. Rosenberg 2008: 358–360).

Following the Massachusetts decision in *Goodridge*, civil unions were adopted by legislatures in Connecticut (2005) and in New Hampshire (2007) despite the fact that both state supreme courts had not ruled on the question. The state legislatures in these two New England states clearly were influenced by developments in Massachusetts and Vermont and extended various protections to same-sex couples. New Jersey, in response to a state supreme court ruling, adopted civil unions in 2006. Several states provided domestic partnerships with all or a significant number of the rights accompanying marriage.

PHOTO 10.2 A number of states recognize marriage between same-sex couples. In June 2013, the U.S. Supreme Court in *Windsor v. United States* declared the federal Defense of Marriage Act, which denied federal benefits to same-sex couples, unconstitutional. The decision opened the door to the recognition of same-sex marriage by lower federal courts in various states that previously did not provide for same-sex marriage.

In 2008, Connecticut became the next state to provide for same-sex marriage when the Connecticut Supreme Court held that "interpreting our state constitutional provisions in accordance with firmly established equal protection principles leads inevitably to the conclusion that gay persons are entitled to marry the otherwise qualified same-sex partner of their choice. . . . To decide otherwise would require us to apply one set of constitutional principles to gay persons and another to all others."

Rhode Island announced that it would recognize same-sex marriages performed in adjacent Massachusetts and in other states. In May 2008, New York also announced that it would recognize same-sex marriages performed in other jurisdictions. Maryland adopted a similar law in 2010.

In 2009, Iowa became the first midwestern state to recognize same-sex marriage when the Supreme Court held that "we are firmly convinced the exclusion of gay and lesbian people from the institution of civil marriage does not substantially further any important governmental objective. . . . We have a constitutional duty to ensure equal protection of the law." The same year, the New Hampshire and Vermont legislatures adopted laws providing for same-sex marriage, and the District of Columbia City Council also provided for same-sex marriage.

The debate over same-sex marriage in the next phase was dominated by events in California. The California Supreme Court held the state law prohibiting same-sex marriage unconstitutional. This ruling was overturned by a popular vote ("Prop 8") that defined marriage as being limited to a union between a man and a woman. The California Supreme Court upheld the ban while allowing the eighteen thousand marriages that had been carried out under the earlier Supreme Court ruling to stand.

In August 2010, federal district court judge Vaughn Walker held Proposition 8 unconstitutional and directed that gay marriage ceremonies should begin to be conducted in California after the Ninth Circuit Court of Appeals had the opportunity to either affirm or overturn his ruling. Judge Walker wrote that limiting marriage to a man and a woman was "an artifact of a foregone notion that men and women fulfill different roles in civil life." He concluded that by every measure, "opposite-sex couples are no better than their same-sex counterparts . . . as partners, parents and citizens, opposite-sex couples, and same-sex couples are equal."

The State of California refused to appeal Judge Walker's judgment, and an appeal to the Supreme Court was undertaken by a private party. In 2013, in *Hollingsworth v. Perry*, the Court held by a 5–4 vote that the activists who placed Proposition 8 on the California ballots in 2008 did not possess standing to defend the law in federal courts after the state refused to appeal the trial verdict. Chief Justice John Roberts wrote, "We have never before upheld the standing of a private party to defend the constitutionality of a state statute when state officials have chosen not to. . . . We decline to do so for the first time here" (*Hollingsworth v. Perry*, 570 U.S. ___ [2013]).

In the companion case of *United States v. Windsor*, the Supreme Court held that DOMA was a violation of the Equal Protection Clause of the Fifth Amendment. Justice Anthony Kennedy held that the law impermissibly refused to recognize and discriminated against one category of marriages recognized by the state. Justice Kennedy reasoned that the "purpose and effect" of DOMA was "to disparage and to injure those whom the State, by its marriage laws, sought to protect in personhood and dignity" (*United States v. Windsor*, 570 U.S. ___ [2013]).

A year earlier in November 2012, Maine, Maryland, and Washington were the first states to adopt same-sex marriage by popular vote. Minnesota became the second state to reject by popular vote a constitutional ban against same-sex marriage. In 2013, state court decisions in New Jersey and in New Mexico recognized same-sex marriage, and six additional states enacted laws recognizing same-sex marriage.

Attorney General Eric Holder, in February 2014, announced that the Justice Department would recognize same-sex marriage in the department's policies. For example, the privilege of a spouse not to testify against his or her spouse and the right to prison visitations would be extended to same-sex couples.

Federal district and appellate courts throughout the country subsequently struck down additional state prohibitions on same-sex marriage. The U.S. Supreme Court had no alternative other than to clarify the constitutionality of same-sex marriage when the Sixth Circuit Court of Appeals upheld the same-sex marriage bans in Kentucky, Michigan, Ohio, and Tennessee, which were in direct conflict with other circuit court opinions.

James Obergefell and John Arthur entered into a long-term relationship. When Arthur became seriously ill, the two traveled from Ohio to Maryland to marry one another. They returned to Ohio, which did not recognize same-sex marriage, and as a result, local officials refused to list Obergefell as the spouse on Arthur's death certificate. Obergefell challenged the constitutionality of the Ohio law, which in the words of his lawyers dictated that "they must remain strangers even in death, a state-imposed separation Obergefell deems hurtful for the rest of time." Obergefell's challenge to the Ohio law, along with the cases of several same-sex couples, was consolidated and heard before the U.S. Supreme Court.

In 2015, in *Obergefell v. Hodges*, the Supreme Court struck down state laws prohibiting same-sex marriage as a denial of the plaintiffs' liberty to exercise the fundamental right to marry and as a denial of equal protection of the law. The Court also held that the interest in providing same-sex couples with a sense of certainty and security in their relationships also required states to recognize same-sex marriages performed in other states (*Obergefell v. Hodges*, 576 U.S. ___ [2015]).

Justice Kennedy, writing for a five-justice majority in *Obergefell*, held that the right to marry is a fundamental right, which is an expression of an individual's freedom to chart the course of his or her life and to enter into the most intimate of relationships with another individual free of state interference. Virtually every state already recognized the right of same-sex couples to adopt children. Marriage provides protection, security, and stability for children and gives them a sense that they are no different from other children. Last, "[M]arriage is a keystone of our social order," and "[t]here is no difference between same- and opposite-sex couples with respect to this principle." Denying same-sex couples the opportunity to marry deprives them of the various benefits of marriage, and introduces an unnecessary degree of instability into their relationship. Justice Kennedy concluded that

> [t]he limitation of marriage to opposite-sex couples may long have seemed natural and just, but its inconsistency with the central meaning of the fundamental right to marry is now manifest. With that knowledge must come the recognition that laws excluding same-sex couples from the marriage right impose stigma and injury of the kind prohibited by our basic charter. . . . [The plaintiffs'] plea is that they do respect it [marriage], respect it so deeply that they seek to find its fulfillment for themselves. Their hope is not to be condemned to live in loneliness, excluded from one of civilization's oldest institutions. They ask for equal dignity in the eyes of the law. The Constitution grants them that right.

Chief Justice Roberts in his dissenting opinion argued that the universal definition of marriage involves a man and a woman and that the prohibition on same-sex marriage was rationally related to the state interest in the sanctity of marriage. The logical extension of the majority's reasoning that same-sex couples possessed the right to legal recognition of their relationships as marriage would lead to a constitutional right to polygamy. The Court by intervening to decide the issue of same-sex marriage has short-circuited the democratic process. Several dissenters expressed concern that the Court's decision disregarded the interest of individuals whose religion opposed same-sex marriage and who now would be labeled as prejudiced and as bigots. The dissenting justices also expressed concern that same-sex marriage would break the link between marriage and procreation and lead to fewer individuals believing it was necessary to be married before having children.

The constitutionality of gay marriage has not been entirely accepted. The 2016 Republican Party platform recognized that marriage only is between a man and a woman. In a section titled "Defending Marriage Against an Activist Judiciary," *Obergefell v. Hodges* is described as "lawless" and as having robbed "320 million Americans of their legitimate constitutional authority to define marriage as the union of one man and one woman." The platform supported overruling *Obergefell* and leaving the matter of same-sex marriage to the states.

Chief Justice Roy Moore of the Alabama Supreme Court defied a federal court order and instructed probate judges in Alabama to stop issuing marriage licenses to same-sex couples. He condemned the Supreme Court decision in *Obergefell* as a "wasteland of sexual anarchy" and proclaimed that there was a "duty to disregard illegal orders." Justice Moore called the Supreme Court's decision "immoral," "tyrannical," and "unconstitutional" and urged all other state judges to resist the decision. In response to Moore's defiance of federal court orders, state judicial officials suspended Moore from office until the end of his term in 2019. Judge Moore subsequently resigned from the Alabama Supreme Court.

Kim Davis, the clerk of Rowan County, Kentucky, defied a federal district court order to issue marriage licenses to same-sex couples. Davis continued to articulate religious objections to issuing marriage licenses and was found in contempt of court and jailed in September 2015. She agreed to allow deputy clerks in her office to issue and sign marriage licenses and was released after five days.

Indiana adopted a Religious Freedom Restoration Act (RFRA), which stipulated that a governmental entity may not "substantially burden" a person's exercise of religion . . . [unless it] is in furtherance of a compelling government interest; and is the least restrictive means of furthering that compelling governmental interest." Critics interpreted this law as opening the door to individuals to refuse services to same-sex couples epitomized by a refusal to make and sell a wedding cake to a same-sex couple contemplating marriage. A week after the bill was signed into law, Memories Pizza in Walkerton, Indiana, announced that the restaurant would refuse to cater a same-sex wedding as a result of the law. In reaction to intense pressure from business interests that threatened to move from Indiana and objections from various organizations that threatened to withdraw their conventions from Indiana, the law was amended to make clear that the statute was not a defense of discrimination against individuals based on sexual orientation. Indiana as a result of the boycott lost an estimated $60 million in revenue. Similar laws were amended in several other states or were vetoed by the governor under business pressure to clarify that these laws also did not justify discrimination. A number of laws burdening same-sex marriage nonetheless continue to be introduced across the country. The issue of the right to refuse services based on a religious opposition to same-sex marriage will be decided by the U.S. Supreme Court.

The estimate based on 2014 tax returns is that there are 183,280 same-sex marriages in the United States, approximately a third of 1 percent of marriages. Female same-sex couples comprised 55 percent of same-sex married couples. Male same-sex couples generally are concentrated in dense cities like New York, Los Angeles, and San Francisco although female same-sex couples tend to live in smaller and medium-sized cities like Madison, Wisconsin, and Burlington, Vermont (Bui 2016).

Public opinion is increasingly receptive to gay marriage, and state laws are changing in response to these evolving views. At the time that Congress passed DOMA, only 25 percent of Americans said that gay couples should have the right to marry. Today, this percentage has more than doubled (Gelman, Lax, and Phillips 2010). In May 2016, a Gallup poll found that support for same-sex marriage had risen to 61 percent of Americans. The Pew Research Center finds that 57 percent of Americans support same-sex marriage and 37 percent oppose same-sex marriage. The greatest gap in support is unsurprisingly based on age, with younger people more heavily supporting same-sex marriage. Another differentiation in support is based on political party identification. Seven in ten Democrats, 64 percent of Independents, and 33 percent of Republicans support same-sex marriage. Seventy-eight percent of liberals, 66 percent of moderates, and 29 percent of conservatives favor same-sex marriage. In 2016, 57 percent of whites and 42 percent of African Americans supported same-sex marriage.

Polls indicate an increased willingness by employers to hire gay employees and an increased number of individuals who have a gay friend or relative and who regularly watch a television program that includes gay characters. One indicator in the growth of acceptance of gay romantic relationships is the fact that roughly three thousand private companies, colleges and universities, and state and local governments offer domestic partner health coverage to both same-sex and different-gender couples (G. Rosenberg 2008: 407–414).

In 2001, the Netherlands became the first country to recognize same-sex marriage, and at present there are roughly twenty-three countries that recognize same-sex marriage. In July 2010, Argentina became the first country in Latin America to legalize same-sex marriage. There is no country in Asia that authorizes same-sex marriage; Israel recognizes these marriages when performed abroad.

10.2 YOU DECIDE

Massachusetts passed one of the nation's most comprehensive bullying prevention laws in response to the suicide of two Massachusetts students: Phoebe Prince (age 15) from South Hadley and Carl Joseph Walker-Hoover (age 11) from Springfield. Massachusetts was on the leading edge of an effort to stem what is viewed as an increased prevalence of bullying in schools, much of which is taking place online.

The bill requires that teachers and school staff report bullying to the school principal, mandates training for teachers on bullying, and requires education for students on bullying behavior. Bullying is defined as

> [t]he *severe or repeated* [emphasis added] use of one or more students of a written, verbal or *electronic expression* [emphasis added] or a physical act or gesture, or any combination thereof, directed at another student that has the effect of: (i) causing physical or emotional harm to the other student or damage to the other student's property; (ii) placing the other student in a reasonable fear of harm to himself or of damage to his property; (iii) creating a hostile environment at school for the other student;

(iv) infringing on the rights of the other student at school or (v) materially and substantially disrupting the education process or the orderly operation of a school.

Virtually every state has a bullying statute. Only a handful of state statutes carry a criminal penalty. Most stipulate that students are to be punished by the school and that schools adopt anti-bullying policies. Subsection (v) of the Massachusetts law is somewhat controversial in that it potentially reaches conduct outside of school that affects the educational process.

Most bullying, according to government data, takes place in or around school or online.

About 49 percent of children in Grades 4–12 reported being bullied by other students at school at least once during the past month, whereas 30.8 percent reported bullying others during that time.

A similar number of students report being "frequently bullied," defined as two or more incidents in one month. This likely is an underestimate because only about 20 percent of bullying incidents are reported to adults.

Today, traditional forms of bullying, though still accounting for the majority of incidents, are being replaced by cyberbullying. The Pew Internet & American

(Continued)

Life Project in a 2007 survey found that one-third of teens report that they have been harassed online, defined as "receiving threatening messages; having their private emails or text messages forwarded without consent; having an embarrassing picture posted without permission; or having rumors spread about them online." A 2006 Harris poll reports that 43 percent of teens report having experienced cyberbullying in the past year. Sameer Hinduja and Justin Patchin, who direct the Cyberbullying Research Center, report that 22 percent of kids report engaging in online bullying on at least two occasions in the past month, and 29 percent report that they have been bullied. Hinduja and Patchin note that traditional forms of bullying continue to pose a problem: 34 percent of middle schoolers report having bullied at school, and 44 percent of middle schoolers report having been a victim (Hinduja and Patchin 2010).

The Gay, Lesbian and Straight Education Network conducted a survey that determined that nine of ten gay, lesbian, transgender, or bisexual middle and high school students suffered physical or verbal harassment in 2009, including taunts and beatings. The stopbullying .gov site states that 55.2 percent of lesbian, gay, bisexual, and transgender students experienced cyberbullying. The harassment of young gay men emerged as a major concern in October 2010 when 18-year-old Rutgers freshman Tyler Clementi committed suicide by jumping off the George Washington Bridge. Clementi, a talented musician, apparently was embarrassed and humiliated when his roommate and another student viewed his intimate interaction with another male on a webcam and streamed the encounter on the Internet. Tyler's death coincided with a two-year campus program to teach the importance of "civility" and the use and abuse of the new technology. The previous month, a 13-year-old gay sixth grader, Seth Walsh, hanged himself in his backyard after being subjected to a relentless regimen of abuse by his peers. Seth apparently had been harassed for years with comments such as "You should kill yourself" and "You should go away" and "You're gay, who cares about you." Two other young gay students committed suicide in the same month after being subjected to relentless bullying.

What accounts for the sudden identification of bullying as a serious problem that deserves criminal punishment? Is bullying really on the increase, or is this "crisis" being manufactured by a generation of overly protective parents and school administrators? Can bullying be addressed through law or through training programs? Is this a matter that schools should address, or should bullying be left to parents? (For another question on the relationship between social change and law, see You Decide 10.5 on the study site.)

■ THE IMPACT OF COURT DECISIONS ON CRIMINAL JUSTICE

Courts have a particularly important role in reviewing the practices of the police and other criminal justice organizations to ensure individual rights and liberties are being respected by the guardians of societal safety and security. The preservation of liberties understandably may be viewed as unnecessarily impeding and interfering with the primary mission of criminal justice organizations. The Supreme Court and other appellate courts, in the context of hearing appeals, have established broad constitutionally required procedures that criminal justice agencies and institutions are required to follow.

In establishing these procedural requirements, courts generally have been mindful of the need to balance individual liberties with the societal interest in safety and security. Critics nonetheless assert that judges lack the expertise to establish standards for criminal justice professionals. The question is, what impact do these decisions have on the conduct of the police and other criminal justice professionals (Milner 1971)?

A significant amount of work has been done on the **impact of law** on organizations. Organizations will be more likely to comply with the law when there is outside pressure monitoring their performance (Edelman 1990, 1992). Researchers find organizations that are not strictly monitored will indirectly evade the decisions by attempting to persuade courts to accept the organization's definition of compliance (Edelman 1990, 1992; Edelman, Uggen, and Erlanger 1999). A more optimistic view is that various legal mandates come to be accepted by the organization as "good practices" and take on a life of their own and become part of the organization's routine (Dobbins and Sutton 1998).

In the next two sections, we look at case studies of police implementation of the *Miranda* rule on interrogations and the implementation of reform policies by correctional institutions. In considering the discussion of *Miranda*, note how the police have adjusted to the requirements of *Miranda* so that it does not pose a barrier to obtaining confessions.

The discussion of prison reform illustrates the importance of administrative support for legal decisions that require reform. The judgment in the case of *Ruiz v. Estelle* on the Texas prison system also suggests that courts may lack the expertise to anticipate the consequences of the reforms that they require. Last, the decision illustrates how external events may overwhelm reforms.

Interrogations and Confessions

In 1929, President Herbert Hoover appointed an eleven-member National Commission on Law Observance and Enforcement, which was chaired by Attorney General George Wickersham and included some of the most prominent individuals in the fields of law and criminal justice. The section on police interrogation documented the widespread police use of the "third degree" in the questioning of defendants (National Commission on Law Observance and Enforcement 1931).

The report describes prolonged incommunicado interrogations that lasted as long as ninety-six hours. During these interrogations, suspects were deprived of food, sleep, and hygiene; were isolated from family, friends, and legal assistance; and were shuttled from one jail to another to keep them disoriented and confused. The police had a strong incentive to obtain confessions because a suspect's admission of guilt virtually guaranteed that a jury would return a guilty verdict. As a result, once suspects confessed, they were motivated to enter into a plea bargain.

The Wickersham Commission condemned the third degree as having corrupted the criminal justice system. The use of the third degree led to false confessions, police cover-ups, and perjury in court to conceal the employment of physical force and the tainting of the integrity of the criminal justice process. Jurors increasingly were losing confidence in the criminal justice system, and there was a risk they would begin to disregard confessions and acquit defendants.

Various police officers in their statements to the Wickersham Commission defended the third degree.

They relied on what Richard Leo calls a "working ideology" in which use of physical force to extract confessions is a necessary arsenal in the war against crime (Leo 2008: 66). The officers viewed the third degree as an indispensable tool to extract confessions from obviously guilty defendants who otherwise would rely on their Fifth Amendment right against self-incrimination and refuse to talk to the police. These "sophisticated" defendants, once having maintained their silence, hired slick and sophisticated lawyers and were able to obtain acquittals at trial. The third degree in the view of the police was deployed against dangerous and clearly guilty defendants, and a prohibition on the third degree would lower police morale (National Commission on Law Observance and Enforcement 1931: 137, 146–147, 178–179).

In *Brown v. Mississippi*, the U.S. Supreme Court held that police interrogations that resulted in involuntary confessions violated the Due Process Clause of the Fourteenth Amendment and were inadmissible in evidence. In *Brown*, the police extracted confessions from three African American defendants through "physical torture." The Court observed that it "would be difficult to conceive of methods more revolting to the sense of justice." Chief Justice Charles Evans Hughes observed that the account of the abuse of the defendant in *Brown* read "more like pages torn from some medieval account than a record made within the confines of a modern civilization which aspires to an enlightened and constitutional government" (*Brown v. Mississippi*, 297 U.S. 278 [1936]).

Influential law enforcement officials across the country realized that the police risked losing respect and that a change in the approach to interrogations was required. J. Edgar Hoover, the director of the FBI at the time, was at the forefront of a movement to promote police professionalism and scientific interrogation. The centerpiece of this movement was interrogation manuals, first issued in the late 1940s, that were used to train the tens of thousands of police officers in techniques of scientific interrogation. The leading manual was authored by the late professor Fred Inbau of Northwestern University School of Law, who, along with various co-authors, developed a nine-step process of interrogation. These tried and tested techniques were designed to allow interrogators to psychologically dominate and manipulate suspects to obtain confessions (Inbau et al. 2001). One edition of the Inbau handbook provided 1,600 scenarios for the police to use when interrogating suspects on more than fifty possible offenses (Leo 2008: 153).

The stage now was set for the Supreme Court's decision in *Miranda v. Arizona* (384 U.S. 436 [1966]). The Supreme Court observed that in recent years the third degree had been replaced by use of psychological coercion. Individuals subjected to incommunicado police interrogation found themselves isolated and alone and overwhelmed by the sophisticated psychological practices of the police.

The *Miranda* decision mandated that prior to interrogation the police provide a suspect with a four-part warning. The warning is designed to protect defendants' right against self-incrimination by informing suspects they are not required to talk to the police, that anything they say may be used against them, that they have the right to be assisted by a lawyer, and that if they cannot afford a lawyer, one will be appointed or retained for them. The four-part *Miranda* warning is intended to "even the playing field" between the police and suspects by providing individuals with the information required to protect their right against self-incrimination. The warning serves to alert suspects that they are involved in an adversarial process and that the police are not on their side in this battle of wits. The four-part *Miranda* warning contains the elements shown in Table 10.1.

A suspect may invoke his or her right to silence or right to an attorney or waive these rights. In the event a suspect invokes the *Miranda* rights, the police may not undertake an interrogation. A suspect ordinarily is asked to sign a *Miranda* form indicating he or she has received the *Miranda* rights and that he or she wants to waive the rights. The prosecution has a "heavy burden" to establish that a suspect knowingly, voluntarily, and intelligently waived his or her rights. In a series of cases, the Supreme Court has held that there are a number of situations in which the police are not required to provide the *Miranda* warnings. For example, without reading the *Miranda* rights, the

Table 10.1 ■ Four Elements of the Miranda Warning	
1. **Silence**	You have the right to remain silent.
2. **Consequences of talking**	Anything you say may be used against you in court.
3. **Lawyer**	You have the right to consult with a lawyer and to have the lawyer present during interrogation.
4. **Appointed lawyer**	In the event you cannot afford a lawyer, an attorney will be appointed to represent you.

police generally may interrogate a suspect who is not under arrest or "deprived of his or her freedom in a significant way."

The Supreme Court in *Miranda* created a set of legal protections intended to safeguard the rights of suspects during police interrogation. The Court in effect was telling the police they no longer would be able to rely so heavily on interrogations to investigate crimes and would be required to rely on other investigative techniques.

Miranda drew an immediate reaction from the U.S. Congress and state politicians who viewed the decision as yet another example of the Supreme Court's "coddling of criminals." The Congress responded by passing a bill requiring the admission into evidence of any voluntary confession. The Court later rendered the congressional statute an unconstitutional "dead letter" by holding that the Fifth Amendment required that the police administer the *Miranda* warnings (*Dickerson v. United States*, 530 U.S. 428 [2000]).

Richard Leo, a leading expert on police interrogation, concludes that the *Miranda* warnings have made "no practical difference" in limiting the ability of the police to obtain confessions from suspects. Leo observes that studies indicate that between 78 percent and 96 percent of suspects waive their rights and talk to the police. He cites the comments of one scholar that next to the warning labels on cigarette packages, *Miranda* is the most widely ignored official warning. Leo observes the police have over forty years of experience with *Miranda* and are skilled at obtaining waivers or at creating situations in which the Supreme Court has held that the Constitution does not require the reading of *Miranda* rights to suspects. Leo lists various strategies used by the police to conduct interrogations without *Miranda* posing a barrier to obtaining a confession and concludes that sophisticated police tactics ensure that "virtually all suspects waive their *Miranda* rights." These tactics include the following (Leo 2008: 124–127, 280):

Free to leave. The police officer asks a suspect to come to the police station and tells the suspect that he or she is not under arrest. The Supreme Court has ruled that a suspect in this situation is not in custodial interrogation for purposes of *Miranda* and may be interrogated by the police without being read the *Miranda* warnings.

Implied waiver. The police officer reads the *Miranda* rights and immediately moves into questioning. A suspect who responds is considered to have "implicitly waived" his or her Miranda rights.

De-emphasizing the significance. The police officer engages in "small talk" and casually blends the *Miranda* warning into the conversation without indicating it is significant. A suspect may waive his or her rights without realizing the consequences of the waiver.

Incentive. The police officer may tell a suspect that by waiving the *Miranda* rights, the suspect can tell his or her side of the story. The officer may indicate that if the suspect talks, the officer will contact the prosecutor about filing a lesser charge or seeking a lesser sentence. The officer also might mention that he or she cannot discuss the case or inform the defendant of the charges unless the suspect talks.

Avoid warnings. The police may avoid giving the *Miranda* warnings. The Supreme Court has ruled that although the confession is inadmissible in evidence, it may be used to cross-examine the suspect in the event that he or she takes the stand at trial. In certain circumstances, the police, after interrogating the suspect without the *Miranda* warnings, may administer the warnings and obtain a second, admissible confession.

Public safety. The U.S. Supreme Court developed a "public safety" exception to reading the *Miranda* rights. This exception is relied on in interrogating suspected terrorists.

Stephen Wasby reviewed the early empirical work on the impact of the *Miranda* decision and found that Yale University graduate students did not understand the *Miranda* warnings and even those students whose rights had been thoroughly explained to them by a law professor prior to the interrogation felt compelled to talk to the police. Wasby concludes that absent the presence of a lawyer, individuals find it difficult to assert their *Miranda* rights (Wasby 1970: 161–162).

Following a suspect's waiver, *Miranda* no longer poses a barrier to the police, and the police typically will adopt an aggressive approach to interrogation. The interrogation manuals assume every suspect is guilty and that the goal is to obtain a confession. One effective technique is the "accusation." The officer refuses to believe the suspect's denials of guilt and proclaims that no one will believe the suspect is innocent.

Another tactic involves "false-evidence ploys." Evidence ploys involve a false claim by the police that they have hair or blood evidence or DNA implicating the suspect in the crime. The police may rely on the "promise threat dynamic" in which the police suggest that a confession will result in lenient treatment whereas silence may result in harsher punishment (Leo 2008: 147, 154, 158–159).

Some suspects react by feeling intimidated and overwhelmed by the police whom they perceived as determined to convict them. They come to believe a confession is in their self-interest because it may result in a reduced charge or a more lenient sentence. The next step is for the police to help the suspect develop an account of the crime that will ensure the suspect is found guilty. This story typically includes the suspect's motives, lack of remorse, knowledge of facts of the crime that only would be known to the perpetrator, and a statement that the confession was voluntary. The police even may write a confession and hand it to the suspect to sign. The police typically will include an error in spelling or grammar and ask the suspect to correct the text so that it appears that the defendant read, understood, and corrected the confession. They also often will insert facts that only the defendant would know, such as where he or she went to high school, to make the confession appear to be composed by the defendant (Leo 2008: 163–164, 171–177).

As you may imagine, juveniles typically are overwhelmed by police interrogation, and states differ on whether a parent is required to be present during the juvenile's interrogation. A study found that juveniles either admitted their guilt or made a damaging admission in nearly 90 percent of interrogations and that juveniles constituted at least one-third of individuals making false confessions (Feld 2013: 145–147, 239–240).

False confessions are inevitable given the combined impact of determined interrogators convinced of suspects' guilt, the impressionability and vulnerability of suspects, and the police practice of providing suspects with a complete account of the crime (Kassin and Gudjonsson 2004). Individuals who are easily intimidated or mentally challenged and juveniles as previously noted comprise a high percentage of individuals who have falsely confessed to crimes they did not commit. A summary of six studies documenting wrongful convictions finds between 14 percent and 16 percent of wrongful convictions result from false confessions. Leo reviews six studies of false convictions and finds roughly 250 of these convictions resulted from false confessions, the majority of which occurred during the past two decades. Juries find confessions a strong indication of a defendant's guilt. One study finds jurors will convict a defendant who has confessed even when they are aware of exonerating evidence between 78 percent and 85 percent of the time (Leo 2008: 243–245, 250).

Brandon L. Garrett studied forty defendants who confessed to crimes but later were exonerated by DNA evidence. In each instance, the confession was rich in detail and provided information that only the perpetrator of the crime could have known. Twenty-six of the men were "mentally disturbed" or under 18 years of age or both. Thirteen were taken to the crime scene by the police. Their interrogations were lengthy and pressurized, and the police provided the defendants with the details of the crime. In some instances, the jury was persuaded of the defendants' guilt despite the existence of exonerating evidence (Garrett 2011: 14–44).

Dan Simon notes that innocent individuals are willing to talk to the police because they believe that their innocence will be apparent to the police. This, however, may place them at risk for a false confession. He points out that studies indicate that the police at times rely on faulty physical cues in evaluating a suspect's likely guilt and that an interrogator who believes that a suspect is guilty will exert coercive pressure on the suspect and use a broader range of tactics to elicit a confession, including use of "false evidence" and promises of leniency (D. Simon 2012: 136–140).

The Central Park jogger case has become synonymous with the vulnerability of suspects who are subjected to custodial interrogation by the police. In 1990, five juveniles, four African American and one Hispanic, were variously prosecuted for assault, robbery, riot, rape, sexual abuse, and attempted murder of Trisha Meili, a young Wall Street investment banker. They were convicted in two separate trials and received sentences ranging from five to fifteen years. The convictions of four of the young men were affirmed on appeal (Weiser 2014).

In 2002, Matias Reyes, a convicted serial rapist and murderer who was serving a life sentence, confessed to raping the jogger, and DNA evidence subsequently confirmed that he was responsible for the rape. Yusef Salaam, one of the five defendants, stated that he had falsely confessed after having been mistreated by police and deprived of food, drink, and sleep for over twenty-four hours and after being falsely told by the police that his fingerprints were found on the victim's clothing. The defendants spent between six and thirteen years in prison before their exoneration and release. New York City subsequently settled a lawsuit brought by the Central Park Five for $41 million.

Leo concludes that *Miranda* has failed to achieve the goal of protecting defendants' right against self-incrimination. Once the police establish *Miranda* has been read, confessions generally are admitted into evidence by judges. This is a much easier burden for prosecutors than being required to establish in each case that the defendant voluntarily confessed. Prosecutors benefit from the fact that defendants who have confessed want to avoid trial and are eager to plead guilty in return for a lesser sentence. As a result, in many instances, courts are never asked to review the reliability of a defendant's confession (Leo 2008: 281).

Miranda has several lessons for the capacity of judicial decisions to usher in social change. What accounts for the fact that *Miranda* has not been proven more effective in protecting the rights of suspects?

Self-interest. The *Miranda* rule is counter to the self-interest of the police. The job of the police is to solve crimes, and they will find ways to get around a rule that interferes with the accomplishment of their main goal.

Scope. The courts cannot supervise every interrogation that is undertaken throughout the United States. There simply are too many arrests, too many defendants, and too many interrogations and confessions. Only a small number of jurisdictions tape interrogations, making it difficult to determine precisely what transpired.

Counter-strategy. The past forty years have demonstrated that the *Miranda* decision failed to anticipate the various strategies developed by the police to minimize the impact of the decision.

Psychology. The Supreme Court relied on suspects to invoke the *Miranda* rights. Most suspects are too intimidated and scared to invoke their *Miranda* rights or do not understand the *Miranda* rights.

Feedback. The Supreme Court has decided a number of cases that have weakened defendants' protections under *Miranda*. For example, a confession that is inadmissible in evidence may be used to cross-examine a suspect who takes the stand at trial in his or her own defense (*Harris v. New York*, 401 U.S. 222 [1971]). The Court also has provided the police with significant flexibility on the required reading of the *Miranda* rights (*Florida v. Powell*, 559 U.S. 50 [2010]).

Expertise. An understanding of the interrogation process by Supreme Court justices may have given them a better appreciation of the limitations of *Miranda* in protecting defendants' right against self-incrimination.

Since the *Miranda* decision, police have been able to elicit confessions at roughly the same rate that they had elicited confessions prior to the *Miranda* decision. Although initially subject to criticism by some members of the law enforcement community, *Miranda* has become an ally of law enforcement. Once the warnings have been given and waived by a defendant, the confession typically is admitted into evidence with little basis for objection by the defense (Zalman and Smith 2007).

The police have implemented the reform-minded judicial judgment in *Miranda* to limit the capacity of the decision to restrict their ability to obtain confessions. The Supreme Court in deciding *Miranda* seemingly failed to appreciate the creative capacity of a bureaucratic organization to impede and evade legal change.

Keep in mind that police and prosecutors respond to criticism by noting that defendants are free to exercise their right to silence and are not mere pawns in the hands of law enforcement. They also note that coerced confessions are the exception and the vast majority of confessions are carried out with scrupulous regard for the rights of suspects.

In the next section, we consider the difficulties of introducing legal changes into prisons.

Prison Reform

Courts historically adopted a "hands off" attitude toward prisoners. In the famous case of *Ruffin v. Commonwealth of Virginia*, the Virginia Supreme Court observed that the prisoner "has, as a consequence of his crime, not only forfeited his liberty, but all his personal rights except those which the law in its humanity accords him. He is for the time being the slave of the state." The hands-off doctrine also was based on the belief that courts lacked authority to tell prison officials how to run correctional institutions (*Ruffin v. Commonwealth of Virginia*, 62 Va. 790 [1871]).

The U.S. Supreme Court began to turn away from the hands-off doctrine in the late 1960s. Conservative and liberal justices realized that substandard prison conditions led to anger and frustration and had transformed correctional institutions into "colleges of crime" (Goldfarb and Singer 1973: 369). In *Cooper v. Pate*, the Supreme Court sent a strong message of a shift in thinking when it ruled without explanation that a black Muslim inmate had the same right to possession of religious materials as did Christian inmates (*Cooper v. Pate*, 378 U.S. 546 [1964]). In 1969, in *Johnson v. Avery*, the Supreme Court recognized that inmates possessed a Sixth Amendment right to an attorney when it ruled that prisons that failed to provide inmates with adequate access to lawyers could not deny inmates access to "jail-house lawyers." The Court reasoned that the failure to allow inmates to consult with such lawyers would effectively prevent the poor and the illiterate from appealing their convictions (*Johnson v. Avery*, 393 U.S. 483 [1969]). The rights of inmates were limited by the need to maintain institutional security and safety and were not as extensive as the rights of individuals in the "free world." Federal courts recognized the rights of inmates in a number of areas, some of which are listed below (Goldfarb and Singer 1973: 370).

Physical security. Prison inmates have the right to be free from violent attack and abuse.

Civil rights. Inmates retain freedom of religion, freedom of speech, and the prohibition on racial discrimination.

Access to justice. Inmates should have access to an adequate law library and the right to consult with lawyers or with "jail-house lawyers."

Procedural protections. Inmates have the right to modified due process hearings before certain punishments may be imposed for misconduct. An example is the loss of good-time credits.

Medical care. Inmates have the right to adequate medical care.

In a series of cases, the federal courts relied on the Eighth Amendment prohibition against cruel and unusual punishment to hold that the "totality of conditions" in various state prison systems violated inmates' constitutional rights. In *Holt v. Sarver*, an Arkansas federal district court found that the combined effect of the "dreary and disgusting" conditions at the Cummins Prison Farm constituted cruel and unusual punishment. The decision in *Holt* specified nine areas in which the prison was deficient and singled out the trustee system for particular criticism. To maintain order and security, the prison administration turned authority and power over to a group of prisoner trustees who ruled the inmate population with force and fear and extortion. This was not the only problem at Cummins. Inmates were forced to sell their blood in order to find the funds to afford food and medical care. Prisoners were crowded into open barracks, worked to exhaustion, and arbitrarily beaten and robbed (*Holt v. Sarver*, 309 F.Supp. 362 [E.D. Ark. 1970], *aff'd* 442 F.2d 304 [8th Cir. 1971]). Judge J. Smith Henley wrote:

> For the ordinary convict a sentence to the Arkansas Penitentiary today amounts to a banishment from civilized society to a dark and evil world completely alien to the free world, a world that is administered by criminals under unwritten rules and customs completely foreign to free world culture.

Seventeen years after the federal court asserted jurisdiction over the Arkansas prison system, Arkansas was given a clean bill of health (Feeley and Rubin 1998: 78–79).

The *Holt* decision inspired a number of challenges to prison conditions. By 1983, prison systems in eight states had been determined to be unconstitutional. Three years later, thirty-seven states had at least one individual prison or an entire prison system under the supervision of a federal court (G. Rosenberg 2008: 306).

As of 1966, only 218 inmates had filed lawsuits challenging their conditions of confinement in federal court. Six years later, over three thousand suits had been filed, and by 1984, eighteen thousand "condition of confinement" suits had been filed. The prisoners' rights movement was fueled by the writing of legendary African American inmate-writers like George Jackson, political-activist inmates such as L. Eldridge Cleaver and Huey P. Newton, and the prominent academic Angela Davis. These charismatic figures linked the prisoners' rights movement with the claims of the civil rights movement and the anti–Vietnam War student movement of the 1960s. Jackson was killed in 1971 in an alleged attempted escape from San Quentin State Prison in California. Tension was further fueled by a prison revolt at Attica Correctional Facility in New York State involving close to 1,300 inmates. Attica was regained by force resulting in the death of thirty-two inmates (Thompson 2016).

The most controversial and conflict-ridden "totality of conditions" decision involved the Texas Department of Corrections (TDC). The TDC was a legendary correctional system headed in the 1960s and early 1970s by George Beto, a larger-than-life figure who was famous for introducing the "control system." "Walking George" imposed a military regime on the twelve prisons in the Texas system. New inmates were assigned to toil in the fields. Prisoners who displayed "good behavior" were rewarded by an assignment to work in a factory and ultimately could look forward to being designated as "building tenders" (BTs) charged with supervision over other inmates. Rebellious inmates were subjected to a harsh regimen of solitary punishment. The mistreatment of African Americans in the Texas system was reminiscent of the slave system of the Old South (Perkinson 2010: 230–240, 246–250).

The legal challenges to prison conditions reflected a growing prisoners' rights movement. The plaintiff in the Texas case was David Ruiz, a rebellious inmate with a lengthy prison record who was serving a twenty-five-year sentence. Ruiz's sentence was extended when he unsuccessfully attempted to escape from the Texas penitentiary at Eastham. He found himself confined to the disciplinary wing of the prison where he encountered a new breed of politically aware prisoners who had been influenced by the civil rights movement and by the music and culture of the 1960s (*Ruiz v. Estelle*, 503 F.Supp. 1265 [S.D. Tex. 1980], *aff'd* 688 F.2d 266 [5th Cir. 1982]).

While confined in the disciplinary wing, Ruiz met Fred Cruz, an activist inmate who had already filed lawsuits against prison authorities. In 1974, Cruz and Ruiz joined with several dedicated lawyers to file a complaint on behalf of every Texas prisoner against the TDC, a suit that received support from the U.S. Department of Justice (Perkinson 2010: 260–271).

Beto had been replaced at the time of the legal action by his handpicked former assistant W. James Estelle, who denied virtually every allegation. Estelle vowed that he was not about to compromise with "pathologically maladapted inmates" dedicated to tearing down the system and spreading "institutional anarchy" and "terror" (Perkinson 2010: 271–272). The trial lasted 159 days and involved 349 witnesses. Fourteen months later, Judge William Wayne Justice issued a 118-page decision in which he held that the "totality of conditions" in the TDC violated the Constitution in a number of areas: the space provided for each inmate, disciplinary procedures, access to the court system, and medical care and sanitation. The following excerpt partially captures Judge Justice's findings (*Ruiz v. Estelle*, 508 F.Supp. 1265 [S.D. Tex. 1980]):

> It is impossible . . . to convey the pernicious conditions and the pain and degradation which ordinary inmates suffer within the TCD units—the gruesome experiences of youthful first offenders forcibly raped; . . . the sheer misery . . . for prisoners housed with one, two or three others in a forty-five foot cell . . . the physical suffering . . . which must be endured by those . . . who cannot obtain adequate medical care; the . . . helplessness felt by inmates arbitrarily sent to solitary confinement . . . without the proper opportunity to defend themselves . . . the bitter frustration of inmates prevented from petitioning the courts . . . for relief from perceived injustices.

Judge Justice ordered what has been described as the most sweeping prison reform in U.S. history. The two sides were persuaded to negotiate an agreement on measures to be taken to reform the prison, which was approved by Judge Justice in 1981. It was agreed that Professor Vincent Nathan would be named as a "special master" by the court to monitor implementation of the reforms and to make recommendations to the court on additional steps that might be required. Nathan was provided with a staff of thirteen and a budget of well over $1 million. He insisted that the TDC submit detailed plans on virtually every aspect of the corrections system, including health care, heating and ventilation, the hiring of officers, and promotion policies. The TDC's willingness to enter an agreement undoubtedly was encouraged by the fact that the state legislature had opened investigations into the TDC and its financial practices. The revelations about the TDC led Estelle to resign (Perkinson 2010: 284–285).

A new TDC director, Ray Procunier, was appointed who expressed a willingness to work with the special master. Procunier announced that his priorities were dismantling the BT system and hiring new guards. Prison discipline deteriorated, and Procunier resigned after one year in the job. He was replaced by Lane McCotter, a no-nonsense military man who had spent twenty years directing military prisons (Feeley and Rubin 1998: 85–91).

The long process of reform reached an end on September 11, 1992. Judge Justice proclaimed the TDC had "remade itself into a professionally operated agency whose goals are to achieve the highest standards of correctional excellence." Malcolm M. Feeley and Edward L. Rubin, in their book on prison reform, conclude that "massive changes had occurred" and that Judge Justice had achieved a "decisive" victory. The BT system disappeared, harsh living conditions improved, professional guards were introduced, medical care was upgraded, and educational programs were introduced.

As much as a billion dollars had been spent to improve prison facilities and programs (Feeley and Rubin 1998: 95).

Robert Perkinson, although recognizing the accomplishments of the Texas prison litigation, notes that Judge Justice in reviewing the progress of Texas prisons in 1999 condemned the continuing preying on weak inmates by prison gangs, the often sadistic and cruel behavior of guards, and the use of administrative segregation against mentally ill patients who were housed in unimaginably harsh conditions (Perkinson 2010: 236).

In a 1985 article, James Marquart and Ben M. Crouch analyzed the impact of *Ruiz v. Estelle* on the Eastham, a large maximum-security institution housing nearly three thousand inmates. They find that as a result of *Ruiz*, informal means of dispute resolution were replaced by a rigid legalistic bureaucratic approach. This new system treated all inmates alike, according to established rules and procedures.

In the past, the BTs and the guards controlled the institution. The BTs would settle small disagreements between inmates and inform the guards of developing problems and were authorized to severely beat defiant inmates. In general, the BTs were the most intimidating and most feared inmates. The guards ran the institution with an "iron hand" through verbal intimidation and coercive force. Inmates who posed a problem were "roughed up," and inmates who dared to attack an officer, destroy property, or attempt to organize a work strike were severely beaten. Estelle replaced the BTs with 141 new guards who were assigned to police the dormitories. The guards were instructed to avoid the unnecessary use of physical force, and a guard was fired and two guards were suspended for beating an inmate (Marquart and Crouch 1985).

Marquart and Crouch, based on reports and interviews, report that inmate threats toward guards and attacks on guards increased over 500 percent during the two years following the elimination of the BTs, the hiring of new guards, and the introduction of a new disciplinary regime. Inmates no longer feared physical retaliation when they confronted guards, and the guards no longer could look to the BTs for assistance. A guard who resorted to physical force against an inmate was required to submit a written report, and the entire episode was investigated. When a physical confrontation was anticipated between the guards and prisoners, the episode was required to be videotaped. Inmates no longer were "slaves of the state." They were entitled to a due process hearing before they could be punished, and the law now recognized the rights of prisoners to bring legal action in court against guards. Guards were hesitant to confront inmates and overlooked minor violations of the rules and made an effort to reach an understanding with inmates. Newly hired guards expressed a fear of inmates.

The increased attacks on guards resulted in a significant increase in the use of solitary confinement against inmates responsible for serious disciplinary violations.

The abolition of the BTs created a competition for dominance among the inmates. Violence between inmates increased following *Ruiz* at the same time that the prison population declined by three hundred inmates. Disputes that previously were settled by BTs now resulted in physical attacks, and inmates now found it necessary to carry weapons to protect themselves. Gangs attracted members by offering inmates protection. Violence erupted within gangs as inmates jockeyed for positions of leadership.

Many of the reforms introduced by prison litigation in recent years have been undercut by the explosion in prison populations. California prisons, which were built to house 100,000 inmates, by 2008 had a population of 170,000. A federal district court described the system as "criminogenic" in that the lack of rehabilitation services and frustration among inmates was a breeding ground for recidivism and crime. The federal court accordingly ordered California to reduce its prison population by roughly 47,000 inmates, a holding later endorsed by the U.S. Supreme Court.

Much of this increase in the prison population has resulted from the fixed-time punishment of first-time drug offenders. Between 1968 and 1973, the rate of imprisonment per 100,000 in Texas septupled, and the prison population grew by 1,300 percent (991 per 100,000 in 2008 compared to 788 per 100,000 nationally). During the six years of Governor George W. Bush's term in office, the Texas prison budget increased nearly a billion dollars, and roughly forty-six thousand prison beds were added. In 2000, Texas possessed 7 percent of the country's population and 12 percent of the country's prisoners.

The composition of the inmate population also changed. Texas witnessed the growth of racially based prison gangs that accelerated the spread of drugs and violence in the prisons. African Americans were incarcerated at five times the rate of Caucasians. As the number of prisoners continued to grow, the economic downturn experienced in the United States led to the slashing of the prison budget, leading to a further decline in discipline and control and to a cutback in prisoners' access to reading materials and to the law library and correspondence (Perkinson 2010: 313, 318–320, 341, 343–344, 345, 365).

In recent years, the nonprofit Sentencing Project reports that twenty-nine states have adopted reforms that have reduced their prison populations and thirty-nine states have experienced a decline in their prison populations. The Texas prison population has declined by 1 percent as a result of sentencing reforms, although the Texas prison system population of roughly 147,000 would qualify as the twentieth largest municipality in the state and the $3.4 billion budget would make it one of the largest local budgets in Texas. African American and Latino men presently constitute two-thirds of the inmates locked up in Texas's 109 facilities.

In 1996, the U.S. Congress passed the Prison Litigation Reform Act (PLRA), which was intended to curb the authority of federal courts to assume supervision over state prisons. The PLRA limits attorney fees for lawyers who bring "condition of confinement" suits, imposes filing fees on inmates, limits the ability of judges to appoint special masters, establishes expiration dates on consent decrees, and prohibits unsuccessful litigants from filing multiple legal actions. Perkinson notes the PLRA would have made it impossible for Judge Justice to have intervened to correct the abuses in the TDC (Perkinson 2010: 329).

The Violent Crime Control and Law Enforcement Act of 1994 requires a federal court to find that prison overcrowding constitutes cruel and unusual punishment before ordering a state prison system to take corrective action (Feeley and Rubin 1998: 382).

What is the final verdict on the impact of judicial intervention in the correctional system? Feeley and Rubin argue that prison reform litigation provided inmates with rights and privileges that were inconceivable before the initiation of the legal reform movement. They also point to the fact that the southern model of a racially divided institution in which the African American inmates functioned as modern-day slave labor has been abolished. Reform-oriented correctional officials ironically have been able to rely on federal court judges to implement changes in response to inmate legal suits that otherwise would have been impossible to achieve.

The cases brought by activist attorneys have helped to articulate a reform agenda for correctional institutions that has set a standard to be satisfied by correctional systems across the country. The American Correctional Association responded by developing standards for accreditation that today are accepted by prison officials as the standards to be met by correctional institutions. Feeley and Rubin caution that merely because legal challenges did not bring about a utopian change in prisons does not mean that a great deal has not been accomplished (Feeley and Rubin 1998: 366–380; Yackle 1989: 256–260). John DiIulio has been a critic of judicial intervention into prison and, in contrast to Feeley and Rubin, concludes judges lacked the expertise to reform correctional institutions and that their idealism inevitably led to the type of breakdown in order that characterized Texas prisons (DiIulio 1987: 227–231, 246–250).

Kitty Calavita and Valerie Jenness's comprehensive study of the California prison grievance system found that inmates have developed a "rights consciousness" and an awareness of their constitutional rights. Although inmate grievances were rarely, if ever, successful and were met with bureaucratic indifference, decision-makers were conscious of the threat of litigation in adjudicating complaints and made an informal effort to ensure that correctional officers complied with legal norms. Calavita and Jenness unsurprisingly conclude that despite the promise of the "rights revolution," inmates' claims inevitably are subordinated to the demands of organizational order and control (Calavita and Jenness 2015). Their findings generally are supported, with few exceptions, by a number of other studies (Steiner 2017).

Rosenberg observes that the central factor in the determination of the success of judicial intervention in correctional institutions is whether the court's reform agenda was supported by wardens and prison officials. Reform-minded administrators welcomed the court-ordered reforms in Texas and in other states as a vehicle for obtaining increased funding and for improving prison conditions. It also is crucial that prison staff support the reforms and do not resent courts forcing change "down their throats." Changes that undermine the authority of guards by loosening their capacity to discipline and control inmates or that make their job more difficult are met with resistance. Prison reform is not a politically popular area, and absent judicial intervention, state legislators are not likely to act on their own (G. Rosenberg 2008: 309–314).

10.3 YOU DECIDE

Solitary confinement is the isolation of an inmate in a prison cell for twenty-two to twenty-four hours a day with little human contact. The small cells typically measure no more than eight by ten feet and have solid metal doors. Food and communication arrive through slots in the door. Inmates are released into a walled yard for an hour a day for exercise. They may possess books and reading material and typically are authorized to see visitors through a Plexiglas barrier (Casella, Ridgeway, and Shourd 2016).

Prison systems typically call these segregation units by euphemisms such as Special Housing Units,

Security Housing Units, Special Management Units, and Behavioral Management Units. Inmates refer to these units as the SHU ("shoe"), the Box, the Hole, the Bing, or the Block.

The use of solitary confinement initially was conceived as a mechanism to control the most dangerous inmates. The federal system and as many as forty-four state correctional systems developed supermax institutions in which the most dangerous inmates are held in solitary confinement for their entire sentence. Solitary confinement evolved as a mechanism to segregate gang members from the general population (administrative segregation); to protect juveniles, individuals who are mentally challenged and vulnerable, and lesbian, gay, bisexual, and transgender inmates (involuntary protective segregation); and as a punishment for a long list of both violent and nonviolent violations of institutional rules and regulations (punitive or disciplinary segregation).

An inmate may find him- or herself in solitary confinement for weeks or months, and in some instances, he or she may be confined in solitary confinement for years on end.

Roughly twenty-five thousand inmates presently are held in federal and state supermax institutions, and over eighty thousand inmates at any given time are held in restricted confinement. This figure does not include solitary confinement in juvenile institutions, immigration detention centers, and local jails.

The annual financial cost of housing an individual in solitary confinement is roughly $75,000, which is two to three times the cost of housing an inmate in the general population.

A number of studies of solitary confinement have documented the destructive psychological impact of a lack of interaction with other individuals, limitations on visual stimulation, and a lack of physical activity on human beings. Associate Supreme Court Justice Anthony Kennedy, in a concurring opinion in *Davis v. Ayala*, called attention to the "terrible price" of "near-total isolation" (*Davis v. Ayala*, 576 U.S. ___ [2015]). The "[c]ommon side-effects . . . include anxiety, panic, withdrawal, hallucinations, self-mutilation, and suicide thoughts and behavior." Legal challenges to solitary confinement claiming that the practice violates the Eighth Amendment prohibition on cruel and unusual punishment have proven unsuccessful. Judges have reasoned that inmates are provided with the basic human needs of food, health, and safety and that restrictive confinement is necessary for institutional safety and security (*Mickle v. Moore*, 174 F.3d. 464 [4th Cir. 1999]).

Juan E. Mendez, the United Nations Special Rapporteur on Torture and Other Cruel, Inhuman and Degrading Treatment or Punishment, in 2015 issued a report on the global use of solitary confinement and concluded that restrictive confinement for more than fifteen days and under the best of conditions for thirty days constitutes torture.

In July 2015, President Obama called for a review of the use of solitary confinement in the federal system. He subsequently adopted a number of steps that have been followed by several states to limit the use of solitary confinement for juveniles and for low-level infractions. President Obama recounted the story of 16-year-old Kalief Browder, who was sent to Rikers Island in New York City in 2010 to await trial after being accused of stealing a backpack. Browder was released in 2013 after spending nearly two years in solitary confinement without ever standing trial, let alone being convicted. Browder subsequently committed suicide at age 22 as a result of the trauma he experienced during his confinement. President Obama noted that "social science shows that [solitary confinement] is likely to make inmates more alienated, more hostile, potentially more violent. Do we really think it makes sense to lock so many people alone in tiny cells for 23 hours a day for months, sometimes for years at a time? That is not going to make us safer."

Should inmates continue to be subjected to solitary confinement?

■ LAW AND SOCIAL MOVEMENTS

There is a persuasive argument that social change requires a legal reform that is promoted and pushed by a social movement. Social movements are both liberal and conservative and include Tea Party members; environmentalists; lesbian, gay, bisexual, and transgender activists; antinuclear and antiwar groups; and immigrant rights and affordable housing coalitions. Tactics range from demonstrations and letter writing to lobbying for legislation and voter mobilization (Stout, Dello Buono, and Chambliss 2004).

Litigation strategies often are criticized as expensive and time-consuming; even when a case is successful, a legal judgment may not result in social change for several years.

The decision in *Brown v. Board of Education* ordered the integration of schools with "all deliberate speed." The judgment in *Brown* and other discrimination cases, although highly important in guaranteeing equal rights in education, did not remedy the social conditions that contribute to inequality in education: poverty, unemployment, inadequate housing and transportation, and spending formulas that favor suburban schools. These underlying issues are political questions that can be addressed only in the political arena and not in the courts. Lawyers also can suffocate a social movement, cautioning activists that their demonstrations and loud demands may alienate judges, legislators, and the public (Gabel and Kennedy 1984).

Stuart Scheingold in his classic work, *The Politics of Rights*, calls attention to what he refers to as the "myth of rights." The myth of rights, according to Scheingold, is the misguided belief that when courts recognize that individuals possess rights, this automatically results in social transformation. Scheingold cautions that courts have a limited ability to bring about social change. He argues that judicial decisions nonetheless perform an important role in reinforcing the belief of activists that their cause is just and legitimate and in energizing people and inspiring them to continue their struggle (Scheingold 1974; see also Klarman 2006).

Michael W. McCann adopts a **legal mobilization approach** in illustrating how a social movement combined political action with the law to achieve pay equity (McCann 1994). McCann explains that a pay equity movement originated in the 1980s to provide equal pay for women in the workforce. At the time, a woman earned roughly 55 percent of the income of a man. This gap in pay was significant because women increasingly are the "breadwinners" in a family, and roughly 66 percent of working women were single, separated, divorced, or widowed and had to support themselves and their families. Female-headed households were five times more likely to be below the poverty line than other households (McCann 1994: 23–46).

Pay equity activists argued that only a portion of this differential in salary could be accounted for by skills, work experience, and education. They contended that the differential could be explained by discrimination against women. The problem in their view was that women were in jobs that were not highly valued but required the same sophisticated skills as the positions staffed by men. Pay equity activists argued for the use of job evaluation tools that factored in the skill, training, experience, and responsibility of a job in comparison to other positions. Individuals opposing pay equity argued wage determinations should be left to the functioning of the economic marketplace and to the law of demand and supply. Free market advocates also pointed out that the differential in pay between men and women could be explained by the fact that women with children often were unable to devote themselves fully to their jobs (McCann 1994: 24–32).

The Civil Rights Act of 1964 in Title VII prohibits employers from paying unequal wages to men and women. The law contains various exceptions for pay based on seniority or merit. Federal courts initially dismissed claims based on pay equity. In 1981, the U.S. Supreme Court changed the legal landscape in *County of Washington v. Gunther* and held that the Civil Rights Act could be relied on to claim that the government or a private firm was discriminating in pay against women based on the fact that men were paid more money for a different job (*County of Washington v. Gunther*, 452 U.S. 161 [1981]).

McCann notes that this decision "jump started" the pay equity movement and led to a finding that public workers in the states of Washington and Connecticut were the victims of gender discrimination. A formerly obscure and difficult-to-understand concept like pay equity suddenly attracted media attention and became a primary focus of the movement for gender equality. Virtually every state hurried to initiate "comparable worth" studies to evaluate pay equity among workers (McCann 1994: 53–64).

The primary strategy of pay equity activists involved unions making demands on employers on behalf of their members and feminist groups encouraging women to demand pay equity. The majority of activists agreed that legal actions were an important tool for raising the issue of comparable worth and for helping to organize women in the workplace to demand pay equity. Women were encouraged by the fact that although there were a number of legal setbacks, the Supreme Court decision in *Gunther* assured women that they had a legal right, not merely a moral claim, to an equitable wage and placed employers on the defensive.

Activists, however, did not place all their eggs in the legal basket. They viewed law as only one of several strategic tools that could be used to organize a broad-based movement for equal pay. Legal actions were viewed as too slow, too time-consuming, too expensive, and too unpredictable to rely on as the sole strategy. Litigation was viewed as a last resort and was considered decidedly less important than lobbying legislatures, holding rallies, appearing on the media, and bargaining with employers for pay equity (McCann 1994: 75–85).

In the second phase of the movement for comparable worth, the focus was on exacting concessions from employers. The threat of legal action was used as a "club" activists relied on to pressure employers to agree to negotiated settlements. Activists realized that employers would rather settle than spend the time and money to defend themselves in court. Employers also did not want to risk a setback in court, which would result in a judge's determining the appropriate salary for various jobs (McCann 1994: 138–179).

The third phase of the struggle for pay equity involved the implementation of agreements between employers and activists. Activists in this stage called on judges to ensure the agreements were fully implemented and that workers received compensation for lost wages and the agreed-on pay raises, promotions, and training required to move into new positions (McCann 1994: 180–226).

The last phase in the struggle for comparable worth was what McCann terms the "legacy" that the law left to the equitable pay movement. The workers involved in the movement for comparable worth developed a sense of "rights" within the workplace and worked to achieve additional rights for women, such as equity in hiring (McCann 1994: 518).

McCann concludes that activists should not overlook the contribution of a legal strategy to the success of a social movement. Judicial decisions can inspire and mobilize a social movement and provide leverage during negotiations. Characterizing pay equity as a right provided a powerful moral claim for women in negotiating with employers. Women received more than a half-billion dollars as a result of the movement for comparable worth, and a number of women went from low-wage jobs to moderate-income jobs. McCann's study also teaches that a movement is best advised to use a variety of tactics to achieve social reform and should not place all its hopes in the courts. The results of legal actions are unpredictable, and a legal strategy is time-consuming and can drain a small movement of money and resources (McCann 1994: 229, 295).

Sameer Ashar studied workers displaced from the Windows on the World restaurant in New York City following the September 11, 2001, attack. Windows of the World management opened a new non-union restaurant in Times Square and refused to hire the old union restaurant staff.

The workers relied on demonstrations and media publicity to embarrass the restaurant into hiring them. The workers successfully expanded their campaign to agitate on behalf of workers at chain restaurants throughout New York City. They relied on protests, media, and strategic legal actions and successfully pressured restaurants across New York City into improving wages, improving working conditions, and providing damages for workers terminated because of their union activities.

Like their counterparts in the pay equity movement, the restaurant workers captured the moral high ground by claiming they were defending their right to a living wage and to basic human dignity (Ashar 2007). Social activists also have successfully relied on a combination of non-legal and legal strategies to reform housing policies (B. Harris 2004).

Susan Coutin, in her study of Guatemalan and Salvadoran refugees who fled violence in Central America and unlawfully entered the United States, discusses how lawyers can define the agenda (frame the issues) to be pursued by activists. A significant number of these refugees faced repression, imprisonment, or death if sent back to their homes. American authorities nonetheless were deporting Guatemalans and Salvadorans back to Central America although Nicaraguans who were fleeing a left-wing, anti-American government typically were granted asylum.

Various church groups believed Central American refugees confronted a well-founded fear of persecution at home and deserved to be granted political asylum in the United States. They offered Guatemalan and Salvadoran refugees sanctuary, and a number of American activists were arrested for helping refugees cross the U.S. border. Various volunteer lawyers represented U.S. sanctuary activists charged with the criminal smuggling of refugees (Coutin 1993).

The lawyers in a series of cases framed the plight of the Central American refugees in legal terms and successfully argued that the U.S. government was prohibited by various international treaties from returning refugees to their country of origin. The lawyers ultimately succeeded in persuading the government to grant temporary, extended residence visas to several hundred thousand Central American refugees.

Coutin notes that even cases that proved unsuccessful had the benefit of defining the focus of the sanctuary movement and helping to educate the American public on the situation confronting Central Americans (Coutin 1993).

Charles R. Epp, in his study of the growth of rights and liberties throughout the world, stresses that the expansion of rights is dependent on social movements and organizations willing to fund litigation. He notes that cases do not appear by magic before the U.S. Supreme Court and supreme courts across the globe, and there must be groups dedicated to supporting legal litigation challenges to government policies (Epp 1998).

David Cole argues that significant legal change in most instances is the product of the efforts of an organized social moment. He argues that there are several tactical steps to achieving social change that are listed below. One of the organizations that Cole focuses on is the National Rifle Association (NRA). Originally founded in the nineteenth century to improve marksmanship among former Union soldiers, the NRA has evolved into a "gun rights" organization. The NRA succeeded in persuading the U.S. Supreme Court to recognize the individual right to bear arms in 2008 (*District of Columbia v. Heller*, 554 U.S. 570 [2008]) and two years later succeeded in persuading the Supreme Court that the Second Amendment applied to the states as well as to the federal government (*McDonald v. City of Chicago*, 561 U.S. 742 [2010]; see also D. Cole 2016: 95–148, 221–230).

Constitutional change often begins in other forms of state, federal, and international law. The NRA initially focused on change at the state level and succeeded in persuading all but six states to incorporate the right to bear arms in their constitutions and succeeded in nearly every state in passing a law recognizing a right to "concealed carry" in public. Federal courts subsequently required every state to recognize a right to concealed carry.

Most of the work of constitutional law reform takes place outside the federal courts. The NRA funded academics who argued that the Supreme Court decision in *United States v. Miller* in 1939, holding that the Second Amendment was intended to protect the rights of states to form militias and did not provide for an individual's right to bear arms, was historically inaccurate (*United States v. Miller*, 307 U.S. 174 [1939]). These studies provided support for the arguments before the U.S. Supreme Court that the Court should overturn existing precedent and recognize the Second Amendment right of individuals to bear arms.

The work of constitutional reform is intensely political. The NRA has provided money to support the election campaigns of candidates supportive of gun rights and to oppose the election of opponents of gun rights at both the state and federal levels. The organization focuses on votes that affect gun rights and ranks every candidate for state legislative office and every member of Congress on his or her support for gun rights. These rankings are used to determine which candidates will receive campaign donations, and the rankings are distributed to members of the organization to guide their votes. The NRA worked against twenty-four members of Congress who voted in 1994 to support a federal "assault weapons" ban and defeated nineteen of the legislators at the polls.

Framing and messaging are as essential to a constitutional campaign as formal legal argument. The NRA focuses on the right to own a weapon as an individual right that is essential to protection of the home, important to counter governmental repression, and essential to individual liberty.

Constitutional reform is slow, difficult, and incremental. The NRA succeeded in recognition of the Second Amendment as an individual right after nearly thirty years.

Constitutional reform is a continual process that involves protection of hard-won gains. The NRA has remained involved in persuading over thirty states to adopt stand your ground laws, which expand the right of self-defense in and outside of the home, and has defeated efforts to expand federal background checks and to hold gun manufacturers civilly liable for the consequences of gun violence. The NRA continues to challenge efforts to restrict the Second Amendment in state and federal courts.

Civil society organizations play a crucial part in constitutionalism. The NRA has five million members, an average of one hundred thousand per state. The organization claims the support of another thirty-nine million individuals who are supportive of the organization's goals. NRA members generally are "single-issue voters" who will vote on the basis of "gun rights." In contrast, supporters of gun control tend to list gun control as one of several issues on which they base their vote. The NRA has managed to defeat efforts like the expansion of background checks even when supported by an overwhelming majority of the American public.

In summary, we have seen throughout this chapter that there is a question whether law can immediately and independently impact social change. Our discussion of social movements reinforces the theme that runs through this chapter that law, when combined with other tactics, can effectively assist a social movement to achieve its goals. Legal actions can activate individuals, publicize grievances, translate grievances into the language of constitutional rights, and place pressure on elites to negotiate and to implement promised reforms. By funding legal cases to further their cause, social movements also help expand the rights of all members of society (Sarat and Scheingold 2006). Social movement analysis should be balanced by the reality that strong vested interests may be able to stand firm against even the most determined activists (Brisbin 2002).

In thinking about the material in this section, consider the impact of the Occupy Wall Street movement in New York City and in other cities across the country. This movement was criticized for failing to capitalize on its popular support and to get involved in running candidates for office and in mounting legal challenges to corporate policy. On the other hand, the movement succeeded in drawing attention to income inequality, the lack of economic mobility, the inadequacy of the minimum wage, and the greed and corruption of corporations. The most important legacy of Occupy's focus on what the movement viewed as excessive corporate profits may be the "Fight for Fifteen" movement, which through mass demonstrations has managed to achieve minimum wage increases for twenty-two million fast-food and other workers in California, New York, and Washington, D.C., and in fifteen cities. In November 2016, voters in Arizona, Colorado, Maine, and Washington voted in favor of raising the minimum wage.

We may be entering a new era of activism in which mass movements to protest government policies on immigration, the environment, health care, and other issues are combined with legal challenges in an effort to achieve social change. An example of this dual strategy was the protest by the Standing Rock Sioux and their supporters over the Dakota Access Pipeline, which the tribe states threatens their treaty rights and sacred land. In reaction to this renewed activism, at least sixteen states have passed legislation intended to curb demonstrations and increase the penalties for individuals arrested during protests (M. Smith and Wines 2017).

Civil disobedience historically has been relied on by activists to bring about legal change and to resist laws that are viewed as unjust and unfair.

■ CIVIL DISOBEDIENCE AND SOCIAL CHANGE

We have seen the limits of law in achieving social change. As noted in the last section, there are scholars who contend that significant social change occurs when there is a movement that is working toward social change that employs the courts and law as one of several tactics in its struggle. In some instances, individuals may resort to the intentional violation of the law to draw attention to their cause, energize their supporters, and influence public opinion.

Ran Hirschl focuses on the role of law and courts in frustrating rather than promoting social change. He argues that the rise of powerful judicial branches around the world reflects the desire of politicians and elites to avoid the "political thicket" and to delegate decisions to non-elected judges. He notes that in countries with powerful judges with constitutions that contain bills of rights, courts have refused to address issues of income equality and have protected the rich and powerful. The rhetoric of rights has been relied on by judges to extend freedom of speech to corporations and to facilitate the unlimited development of environmentally vulnerable wilderness areas (Hirschl 2004).

There is a long history of **civil disobedience** in the United States by groups seeking to change government policy. Direct civil disobedience involves the violation of laws by individuals seeking social change. An example is African Americans insisting on being served at a racially segregated lunch counter. Indirect disobedience involves a violation of unrelated laws. Civil rights protesters might conduct a sit-in at the mayor's office to protest segregated schools.

In 1850, Congress required federal marshals to assist in the apprehension of fugitive slaves and to take the fugitive slaves back to their "owners." Individuals assisting slaves were subject to a fine of one thousand dollars and imprisonment for up to six months. The federal government sent a strong signal that it was determined to return fugitive slaves to their "owners" when one thousand marshals and soldiers were sent to Boston to escort fugitive slave Anthony Burns back to Virginia.

The anti-slavery abolitionist movement helped tens of thousands of slaves escape involuntary servitude. In Philadelphia alone, over nine thousand fugitive slaves received assistance between 1830 and 1860 (Cover 1975).

A number of abolitionists who assisted fugitive slaves were prosecuted in federal courts. Judges presiding over the trials lectured jurors on the need to convict the defendants to demonstrate respect for the law and the property rights of slave owners and to prevent an influx of fugitive slaves into northern states. The judges warned jurors that there could be no compromise with the principle that objectionable laws should be changed only through the legislative process. The defendants who violated the Fugitive Slave Law were dismissed as fanatics and agitators. Northern juries on occasion defied judges and acquitted defendants, although most of the abolitionists were convicted (Cover 1975).

Abolitionists imprisoned in the South confronted harsh treatment. In 1844, Jonathan Walker was arrested off the Florida coast when his boat with fugitive slaves on board was stopped by naval authorities. Walker was convicted and pilloried for one hour while citizens pelted him with garbage. He was branded on his hand by a federal marshal (Florida was federal territory) with the letters "SS" (for slave stealer) and imprisoned for eleven months (Aptheker 1989: 111).

The non-violent protest and writings of the abolitionists profoundly influenced the thinking of Mohandas K. Gandhi, the Indian activist whose nonviolent campaigns against British colonialism and writings inspired non-violent activity throughout the world. Gandhi termed his philosophy of non-violence *satyagraha*, which literally means "holding onto the truth" or "truth force."

Gandhi's technique for vindication of the truth was *ahimsa*, or non-violence. This involves school boycotts, picketing, strikes, marches and rallies, and a refusal to cooperate with the government. Gandhi's central *ahimsa* tactic for the vindication of the truth was civil disobedience. This entails the open, non-violent violation of the specific law to which an individual objects. Gandhi believed violence obscures issues by inviting retaliation and diverts attention from the protesters' original grievance. Non-violence compels the individuals against whom the protest is directed to consider that protesters believe so deeply in a cause that they are willing to risk arrest. Protesters always are uncertain whether their cause is "just," and the resort to violence risks harming another in pursuit of what may be an unjust cause.

Another central feature of *satyagraha* is a demonstration of respect for the law by accepting punishment. The protester may object to a particular law while demonstrating respect for the rule of law. The acceptance of guilt and punishment is a concrete illustration of the individual's depth of commitment and willingness to suffer for a cause (Gandhi 1957).

Gandhi's philosophy had a profound influence on the Reverend Martin Luther King Jr., who was one of the foremost leaders of the American civil rights movement. During the 1960s, King led nonviolent protests against southern segregation. The primary tactic of civil rights demonstrators was to peacefully seek service in segregated restaurants. Scenes of non-violent demonstrators being arrested, sprayed by fire hoses, and attacked by dogs flashed across American television screens. American civil disobedients believed that they were acting to uphold their constitutional rights and, unlike Gandhi, did not always plead guilty and passively accept a jail sentence (Garrow 1979).

The Supreme Court vindicated the cause of civil rights protesters when it held that the Civil Rights Act of 1964 prohibited segregation in places of public accommodation such as hotels and restaurants (*Hamm v. Rock Hill*, 379 U.S. 306 [1964]). Southern authorities did not back down and instead resorted to criminal charges such as disturbing the peace to arrest demonstrators protesting segregation on buses, discrimination in education, and the exclusion of African Americans from voting. In Alabama, protests were met by violence. Between 1957 and 1963, there were seventeen unsolved bombings of African American churches and the homes of civil rights leaders (M. King 1963: 49).

Birmingham, Alabama, was perhaps the most segregated city in the United States. African Americans constituted two-fifths of the city but only one-eighth of the electorate. King organized protests, and the jails overflowed with arrested protesters. The city leaders limited protests by prohibiting protests by individuals who had not obtained a permit from the city commission (M. King 1963: 68–71). In April 1963, King refused to apply for a permit from the city commission and defied a court order prohibiting him from leading the march; as a result, he was arrested. The U.S. Supreme Court, in upholding King's conviction, advised that

> [i]n the fair administration of justice no man can be judge in his own case, however exalted his station, however righteous his motives, and irrespective of his race, color, politics, or religion. . . . One may sympathize with the petitioners' impatient commitment to their cause. But respect for judicial process is a small price to pay for the civilizing hand of law, which alone can give meaning to constitutional freedom. (*Walker v. City of Birmingham*, 388 U.S. 307 [1967])

In *Cox v. Louisiana*, the Supreme Court overturned the conviction of a defendant who had been arrested for picketing in front of a courthouse after being assured that he was picketing in a lawful location. Justice Tom Clark, though voting to acquit the defendant, criticized the resort to "mobocracy" (*Cox v. Louisiana*, 379 U.S. 559 [1965]). Justice Hugo Black, a former member of the Ku Klux Klan who later in life had become a strong guardian of civil liberties, later observed that

> [i]t is an unhappy circumstance in my judgment that the group [African Americans], which more than any other has needed a government of equal laws and equal justice, is now encouraged to believe that the best way for it to advance its cause, which is a worthy one, is by taking the law into its own hands from place to place and from time to time. . . . I say once more that the crowd moved by noble ideas today can become the mob rule by hate and passion and greed and violence tomorrow. (*Brown v. Louisiana*, 383 U.S. 131 [1966])

Opposition to the Vietnam War led to an upsurge in civil resistance against the foreign policy of the U.S. government. On November 2, 1965, Quaker Norman Morrison read an article describing the bombing of Vietnamese civilians. Morrison felt helpless to stop the war and doused his body with kerosene and immolated himself fifty yards from the office of Secretary of Defense

Robert McNamara. Seven days later, activist Roger LaPorte set himself on fire in front of the United Nations.

The Selective Service System was a major focus of protest and civil disobedience. During the Vietnam conflict, 10,055 individuals were prosecuted for draft resistance, 8,750 of whom were convicted. An analysis of four thousand resisters finds that they served an average of three years in prison (Baskir and Strauss 1979: 69).

In 1967, fifty prominent intellectuals endorsed the statement *A Call to Resist Illegitimate Authority* and expressed their intent to assist draft resisters by providing legal counseling and representation, bail, and financial assistance (Mitford 1970: 255–258). Students began to publicly burn their draft cards. In 1965, Congress responded by penalizing the burning of a Selective Service certificate with a prison term of up to five years and a fine of not more than ten thousand dollars. Congressman L. Mendel Rivers of South Carolina, the sponsor of the amendment, explained the law was aimed at individuals who "thumb their noses at their own government." Protesters were not deterred. In 1966, David Paul O'Brien and three companions burned their Selective Service certificates on the steps of the South Boston courthouse and were charged with knowingly destroying or mutilating a draft certificate.

The Supreme Court affirmed O'Brien's conviction, stating that the government had a legitimate and substantial interest in ensuring that individuals did not damage or burn their draft cards because the draft provides indisputable proof that an individual was registered with the Selective Service System. In dissent, Justice William Douglas proclaimed that the "underlying and basic problem" that the Court was avoiding was whether a draft is permissible in the "absence of a [formal] declaration of war" (*United States v. O'Brien*, 391 U.S. 367 [1968]).

The Second Circuit Court of Appeals, in an earlier case involving the burning of a draft card, asked what would be next, "turning on water faucets, dumping of garbage in front of City Hall, stalling cars, an event attracting heavy traffic, burning an American flag . . . or tearing up on television a court order or document required to be kept under internal revenue regulations" (*United States v. Miller*, 367 F.2d 72 [2d Cir. 1966])? The Eighth Circuit Court of Appeals stressed that there were great opportunities for peaceful change through the ballot box (*United States v. Kroncke*, 459 F.2d 697 [8th Cir. 1972]).

In *United States v. Berrigan*, Catholic priests Philip and Daniel Berrigan and Mary Moylan entered a Baltimore draft board and poured blood on Selective Service files. The defendants claimed they had acted out of the good motive of halting an unlawful and genocidal war. The Court reasoned that a civilized nation "cannot endure where a citizen can select what law he would obey because of his moral or religious belief" (*United States v. Berrigan*, 283 F.Supp. 336 [D. Md. 1968]). In a related case, the Fourth Circuit Court of Appeals asked, if these defendants were acquitted, would other individuals feel entitled to break the law to "demonstrate their sincere belief that the country is not prosecuting the war vigorously enough be entitled to acquittal?" (See *United States v. Moylan*, 417 F.2d 1002 [4th Cir. 1969].)

In the decades of the 1980s and 1990s, the American judicial system confronted a challenge from antinuclear protesters who claimed that nuclear weapons were unlawful and threatened the future of humankind. Civil disobedients termed their protests "plowshares disarmament actions" based on the biblical passage in Isaiah 4 to "beat swords into plowshares and spears into pruning hooks" (Laffin and Montgomery 1987).

Disobedients were inspired by Jonathan Schell's influential book *The Fate of the Earth*. Schell predicted that a nuclear exchange between the United States and Russia would result in hundreds of millions of deaths and injuries. The United States would be transformed into "A Republic of Insects and Grass," an urban desert without communication, transportation, utilities, electricity, food, or water and a complete breakdown of social organization. The resulting damaging of the environment would endanger the world's food supply and reduce human beings to an "endangered species" (Schell 1982: 3–96).

In *United States v. Quilty*, the Seventh Circuit Court of Appeals concluded that it was "impossible" to argue that the defendants had no alternative other than to unlawfully enter the Rock Island Arsenal. The court of appeals observed that there are "thousands of opportunities" for the lawful propagation of the nuclear message (*United States v. Quilty*, 741 F.2d 1031 [7th Cir. 1984]). In *United States v. Moylan*, the Fourth Circuit Court of Appeals observed that no legal system could long survive if every individual disregarded any law that by his or her "personal standard was judged morally untenable. Toleration of such conduct would not be democratic . . . but [would be] inevitably anarchic" (*United States v. Moylan*, 417 F.2d 1002 [4th Cir. 1969]).

Antinuclear protesters in many cases received relatively harsh sentences. In *United States v. Kabat*, the defendants damaged a nuclear weapon silo and were charged with a number of criminal offenses, including sabotage. The four defendants were sentenced to prison terms ranging from eight to eighteen years. Judge Myron Bright, in his dissent, pointed out that the defendants' protest activities "injured no one and did not, and could not, damage the missile's capacity." He noted that the sentences were "akin to penalties often imposed on violent criminals, such as robbers and rapists, or on those guilty of crimes considered heinous, such as drug dealers" (*United States v. Kabat*, 797 F.2d 580 [8th Cir. 1986]).

Civil disobedience has played a role in calling attention to, and creating debate over, issues ranging from abortion rights to the federal government's refusal to approve various drugs to treat HIV. In the view of disobedients, the claim that individuals can work effectively for change through legal channels is unrealistic. These individuals believe they will be heard only by taking direct action. Disobedients are motivated by the belief that the policies and laws they protest are immoral and are contrary to the U.S. Constitution and international law. They view themselves as vindicating the rule of law and believe that the government is employing its resources to uphold unlawful policies and frustrate social change.

10.4 YOU DECIDE

Aaron Swartz was a software developer and Internet activist who on January 11, 2013, committed suicide. He was one of the developers of the Web feed format RSS and a successful Internet entrepreneur. At the time of his death, Swartz, age 26 and a Stanford graduate, was a research fellow at Harvard University.

On January 16, 2003, Swartz was arrested by Massachusetts Institute of Technology (MIT) police and later held by federal authorities on charges that carried a potential sentence of thirty-five years in prison and $1 million in fines.

Swartz was considered an Internet genius who developed a commitment to open access and progressive political reform. In 2010 and early 2011, Swartz used his Harvard JSTOR account to download a large number of academic journal articles through the MIT computer system. JSTOR is a database of scholarly articles available to students and faculty at universities subscribing to the database. His purpose was to make the journal articles available to individuals who lacked an affiliation with a university. Swartz wrote in his *Guerilla Open Access Manifesto* that the world's scientific heritage increasingly was being digitalized and "locked up by a handful of private corporations." He urged scientists to ensure their work, much of which was supported by federal grant funds, was available on the Internet with open access.

Swartz was indicted by a federal grand jury of charges of obtaining information from and recklessly damaging a protected computer. Several months later, federal prosecutors added nine additional felony counts. The essence of the charge against Swartz was violating the terms of service of JSTOR by excessive downloading of articles although the articles were never distributed.

Following Swartz's death, his family and girlfriend issued a statement that "Aaron's death is not simply a personal tragedy, it is the product of a criminal justice system" based on "intimidation and prosecutorial overreach." The

decisions made by the U.S. attorney in Massachusetts "contributed to his death." The U.S. attorney responded that Swartz had been offered and refused a deal of six months in prison. His refusal to plead guilty, according to the U.S. attorney's office, was putting MIT through needless time and aggravation. In 2013, Swartz was posthumously honored with the American Library Association's James Madison Award for his "outspoken advocacy" of "unrestricted access to peer-reviewed scholarly articles."

An internal MIT report found that although MIT did not push for Swartz's prosecution, the university never articulated its opposition to his prosecution.

More than fifty thousand individuals signed an online petition to the White House urging the firing of U.S. Attorney Carmen Ortiz for "overreach in the case of Aaron Swartz."

On the other hand, JSTOR pays for the right to carry journals on its system, and libraries pay for the right to make the journals available to faculty and students.

What is your view?

 ## INTERNATIONAL PERSPECTIVE: FGM AND THE IMPLEMENTATION OF INTERNATIONAL HUMAN RIGHTS

The practice of female genital mutilation (**FGM**) or female circumcision provides insight into the process of implementing universal human rights documents.

Elizabeth Heger Boyle and Sharon E. Preves studied the adoption of anti-FGM laws across the globe. FGM is practiced widely in twenty-five countries and by a majority of the families in fourteen of these twenty-five countries. These countries are concentrated in Africa and Asia. FGM is primarily a cultural practice intended to preserve the purity of young women (Boyle and Preves 2000).

There are three types of FGM. *Sunna* is the least intrusive procedure and may be compared to male circumcision. Genital excision, or *clitoridectomy*, involves removal of some or all of the clitoris and the labia minora but does not entail cutting the labia majora. *Pharaonic* is the most extreme procedure and is performed on 15 percent to 20 percent of women and involves the excision of the clitoris, labia minora, and labia majora and the sewing together of the vulva. As a result, there only is a small hole for urination. The woman remains in this condition until marriage. Complications involve hemorrhaging, infections, shock, bleeding, and pain during intercourse. Most of the various explanations for FGM are based on the preservation of female purity prior to marriage (Boyle 2002: 26).

In the 1950s and 1960s, United Nations agencies like the World Health Organization refused to investigate FGM, claiming the practice involved issues of cultural practice that were within the sovereignty of states. In the late 1960s, there was a shift in the view of FGM: FGM came to be viewed as a health issue because the practice typically was conducted without sterilization and posed a significant health risk to women (Boyle 2002: 45–52).

A significant development in 1979 was the UN Convention on the Elimination of All Forms of Discrimination Against Women (CEDAW). Feminist activists argued that FGM violated the human rights and dignity of women protected under CEDAW and that states had an obligation to abolish the practice. The movement against FGM gathered momentum when European countries passed legislation in the early 1980s prohibiting FGM.

In 1994, the UN International Conference on Population and Development issued a strong statement calling FGM a violation of the human rights of women and advocating the total elimination of FGM. The U.S. Congress responded a year later by passing legislation that made FGM a crime and denying foreign assistance to countries that failed to take educational efforts to eradicate the practice. African anti-FGM groups criticized their governments for tolerating a practice that was harmful to women and violated "universal human rights."

African countries responded with a wave of reform laws outlawing FGM. However, in a number of countries in which FGM was widespread, traditionalists persuaded their national parliaments to stand firm against efforts to prohibit FGM. Government leaders in these countries went around the legislative process and relied on presidential decrees to prohibit FGM (Boyle 2002: 93–98; Boyle and Preves 2000).

What does this brief history of FGM tell us about the process of translating international human rights into national legislation?

International law. African governments were more concerned about their global reputation for human rights than with appeasing local pro-FGM groups and responded to international pressure to abolish FGM. Abolishing FGM also was a practical step because a reputation for respecting human rights assisted countries in attracting investment and foreign assistance and in obtaining access to markets in Europe and in North America.

Lawmaking. Anti-FGM laws resulted from a combination of international and domestic pressure.

Activists. African activists received support and encouragement from American and European groups and successfully characterized FGM as an issue of the repression of women and universal human rights.

Egypt illustrates the challenges countries encountered in abolishing FGM. In Egypt, 97 percent of women are circumcised, 82 percent of women favor continuation of the practice, and 6 percent have no opinion. After taking an early position against public hospitals performing radical forms of FGM in the 1950s, the government failed to enforce the law for forty years.

In 1994, a CNN report documented the cutting of a young girl in Cairo, Egypt. The government lashed out at the western media but quickly promised to enact a law prohibiting FGM. Parliament refused to pass an anti-FGM law, and the government responded by directing the health ministry to issue a decree prohibiting infibulation in public hospitals but allowing clitoridectomies at the request of parents.

Religious figures objected, arguing FGM was required by Islam. A government task force condemned a proposed plan to criminalize FGM. The government retreated and attempted to save face by reissuing the decree restricting FGM in state hospitals. The ban subsequently was repudiated as a result of pressure from religious leaders (Boyle 2002: 103–105).

In 1996, the United States adopted legislation linking foreign aid to anti-FGM laws. In response, the government of former president of Egypt Hosni Mubarak issued a health ordinance prohibiting FGM from being carried out in any government health facility. Egypt also launched an educational campaign in its schools to educate young women on the dangers of FGM and initiated symbolic prosecutions of individuals who carried out flawed FGM operations (Boyle 2002: 103–105).

This is an important story that indicates that although countries are sovereign and independent, international pressures in some cases can profoundly impact domestic policies. The international community provided support to domestic activists and was the primary influence behind the government's anti-FGM efforts. In the case of Egypt and other countries, international human rights "trumped" democracy. Anti-FGM activists in Africa, however, continue to be accused of imposing western values and undermining local culture.

Countries that at the time were less powerful than Egypt were in an even weaker position to resist pressure from the international community. In Tanzania, only 18 percent of the women are circumcised, and it is practiced in 20 of the 130 ethnic groups. In these groups, uncircumcised women are viewed as "unclean" and "impure" and are excluded from important social functions. Tanzania is heavily dependent on foreign assistance, and politicians all endorsed the view that FGM was a violation of fundamental human rights. In 1998, Tanzania passed a criminal law with little political opposition that declared FGM was "cruel to children" and punished parents who subjected their daughter to FGM with five years in prison and a fine. The law followed the terminology of western human rights groups in characterizing FGM as "mutilation" (Boyle 2002: 102–108).

Keep in mind that despite the passage of legislation, FGM is not easily eliminated. Ellen Gruenbaum notes that so long as men insist on a wife who has undergone FGM, the practice will be difficult to eradicate (Gruenbaum 2001: 192). Elizabeth Heger Boyle, Barbara J. McMorris, and Mayra Gómez analyzed the results of surveys of women in Egypt, Kenya, Mali, Niger, and Sudan conducted by the World Health Organization. Each of these countries has laws prohibiting circumcision, and Sudan had a policy of opposing circumcision. Despite anti-FGM laws and policies, the authors find nearly all the girls they surveyed in Egypt, Mali, and Sudan had been circumcised and roughly one-third of the women in Kenya and 14 percent in Niger were circumcised. Roughly 85 percent of the women in the study who had been circumcised intended to circumcise their daughters despite national opposition to the practice (Boyle, McMorris, and Gómez 2002).

Women in the study who had been circumcised were more likely than women who had not been circumcised to favor the practice and to circumcise their daughters. The small number of women who had been circumcised and opposed the practice based their opposition on the grounds of health and physical pain. The authors find that women who are educated are particularly receptive to anti-FGM messages. The more education a woman received, the less likely she was to support circumcision or to circumcise her daughter. College-educated women were especially receptive to arguments based on health and human rights.

The other influential factors in addition to education in whether a woman opposed FGM and would not circumcise her daughter were whether a woman owned a radio and worked for pay.

These women, according to the authors, were exposed to a new cultural universe through education or the media or through exposure to a world of independence outside the home. They were exposed to "scripts" or messages that they possessed the right to make their own decisions and that there was a human right to be free from FGM. These women also were trusting of modern medicine and opposed FGM on the grounds that it posed a medical risk. Christian women generally were more receptive to the anti-FGM message than were Muslim women (Boyle 2002: 120–138).

Rosemarie Skaine reports that a survey of women between the ages of 15 and 49 in Egypt finds that 63 percent of urban women approve of FGM as compared to more than 85 percent of rural women, and 47 percent of women with secondary education oppose the practice (Skaine 2005: 44–45).

FGM raises the profound question whether the global community should insist on a single standard of human rights. Are all human rights universal? Human rights purists insist that despite differences in social customs and practices, the Universal Declaration of Human Rights embodies the single standard of rights to which all people are entitled. The notion that women are entitled only to the rights recognized in their own culture may condemn women to a life without full control of their bodies, in which they may be compelled to enter into arranged marriages at an early age, are unable to gain custody over their children in the event of a divorce, do not enjoy the same rights of inheritance as their brothers, and are left destitute in the event of the death of their husbands. It is convenient for men to claim that the denial of equal rights to women is a part of a culture rather than a practice intended to maintain male dominance.

On the other hand, how can we talk of a single standard for human rights in a world of more than 195 countries and two billion people comprising a diversity of ethnic groups, religions, and races? Some people would find the American practice of the death penalty inhumane and barbaric.

CHAPTER SUMMARY

This chapter poses the question whether law reflects society or whether law changes society. There is a strong argument that social attitudes and practices shape the law and that a law that moves too rapidly to change societal customs and beliefs will be resisted. Other commentators point to examples of the law affecting social change. A third approach adopts a more complicated perspective and views social change as resulting from a combination of political activism and law. The social movement framework stresses the role of political activism and civil disobedience in achieving social change.

There are a range of factors that determine the impact of a law and whether a law will be effective in bringing about social change. These factors include the source of the law, the extent to which the law is consistent with fundamental values, the acceptance of the law by an individual's peer group, and whether the law is enforced through rewards and punishments. There may be compliance, resistance, or evasion of the law.

Courts in the United States have been receptive to issuing broad-based decisions intended to accomplish significant public policy reform. The dynamic view of the role of courts stresses that judges, as unelected individuals, are positioned to make decisions in areas that elected representatives may want to avoid for political reasons. Elected representatives, for example, have nothing to gain and much to lose by becoming involved in prison reform. The constrained view of the capacity of courts to bring about social change focuses on the fact that judges must wait for cases to appear on their docket before they are able to address an issue and do not possess the ability to force compliance with their judgments.

The judgment in *Brown v. Board of Education* became fully accepted when supported by threats by the U.S. Congress to restrict funding of segregated school districts. Abortion was accepted and on the increase before the issuance of the decision in *Roe v. Wade*, and Rosenberg argues *Roe* had a limited impact in promoting abortion. Support for *Roe* has somewhat eroded as a result of the failure of the pro-choice movement to mobilize political support for the judgment. Recognition of same-sex marriage initially depended on judicial decisions, although as public opinion shifted to support same-sex marriage, state legislators in an ever-increasing number of states have broadened the definition of marriage to include same-sex marriage.

These case studies suggest social change is brought about by the combined efforts of courts, legislatures, and political activism.

Courts have a particular challenge in setting standards to be followed by criminal justice organizations. Criminal justice personnel may perceive a conflict between court-ordered procedures and their ability to maintain order and detect and investigate crime. The police have been able to incorporate the requirements of *Miranda* into their interrogation procedures, and *Miranda* has had a limited impact in protecting suspects' Fifth Amendment rights.

Prison reform was successfully implemented because courts were able to employ special masters to monitor implementation. On the other hand, prison reform had unanticipated consequences and reportedly disrupted prison discipline and led to an upsurge in institutional violence. In both instances, courts lacked expertise in criminal justice and failed to appreciate the consequences of their decisions.

The case study of FGM illustrates how, in the international arena, the United States and Europe assisted local activists to pressure economically weak developing countries to adopt social reforms, even when such reforms were contrary to local practices.

There likely is no single theoretical perspective that fully captures the relationship between law, society, and social change. Law can indirectly or directly bring about social change, and in other instances, law reacts to society. Social change typically requires a combination of law, social activism, and political pressure.

CHAPTER REVIEW QUESTIONS

1. Discuss the role of society in bringing about a change in the law.

2. What is the capacity of the law to change society?

3. List the factors that determine whether there will be compliance with a law, evasion of a law, or resistance to a law.

4. What is the judicial path and extra-judicial path to bringing about social change?

5. Did *Brown v. Board of Education* result in the desegregation of public schools? What was the contribution of the 1964 Civil Rights Act?

6. Was *Roe v. Wade* responsible for women gaining access to abortions? Why has a woman's right to choose remained unsettled?

7. Did the recognition of same-sex marriage result from a political movement or from judicial decisions?

8. Has *Miranda v. Arizona* been effective in protecting a suspect's right to self-incrimination?

9. What has been the role of judicial decisions in prison reform?

10. Discuss the role of social movements in combination with legal challenges in bringing about social change.

11. Explain the reasons countries have abandoned the practice of female circumcision.

TERMINOLOGY

civil disobedience   431

compliance   389

evasion   389

FGM   435

impact of law   413

legal mobilization approach   426

ANSWERS TO TEST YOUR KNOWLEDGE

1. True

2. False

3. False

4. False

5. False

CHAPTER  11

LAW AND RACIAL AND ETHNIC INEQUALITY

TEST YOUR KNOWLEDGE: TRUE OR FALSE?

1. Critical race theory views the law as central to maintaining white privilege and the subordinate status of African Americans and people of color.

2. The law of stop and frisk as stated by the Supreme Court is based on the explicit argument that young males commit a disproportionate number of crimes.

3. Police use of force disproportionately is directed at young African American males.

4. There is no evidence that drug laws are enforced in a racially discriminatory manner.

5. Hate crimes are punished no more seriously than the same underlying crime that is not considered a hate crime.

6. American immigration policy in the nineteenth and twentieth centuries was fully welcoming of individuals of every country and background.

7. The criminal law generally recognizes as a defense that an individual did not follow the law because he or she is from a different culture.

Check your answers on page 502.

■ INTRODUCTION

We tend to view law as protective of individual rights and as ensuring equality. When we suffer what we view as an injustice, our response is "There ought to be a law against this type of behavior." The immediate reaction is to threaten to take the other person to court.

The law is not invariably a force for social equality and justice. In some instances, law may reflect and reinforce social prejudices and help maintain inequality and discrimination. Consider that for over one hundred years, the law in the southern United States regarded African Americans as slaves who had no rights whatsoever. In 1857, the U.S. Supreme Court in *Dred Scott v. Sandford* held that African Americans were "beings of an inferior order, and altogether unfit to associate with the white race, either in social or political relations, and [are] so far inferior that they had no rights which the white man was bound to respect" (*Dred Scott v. Sandford*, 60 U.S. 393 [1857]).

A law that appears fair on its face may be enforced in a discriminatory manner. The legislature or the courts also may require an individual alleging discrimination to meet a demanding legal standard that prevents acts of ethnic, race, or gender discrimination from being easily proven in a court of law. In 1942, President Franklin Delano Roosevelt in Executive Order 9065 ordered Japanese American citizens and residents to vacate the West Coast of the United States and to relocate to internment camps in the interior of the country. The U.S. Supreme Court dismissed claims that the relocation constituted, in the words of dissenting justice Frank Murphy, "legalized discrimination" (*Korematsu v. United States*, 323 U.S. 214 [1944]). The Court reasoned,

> Korematsu was not excluded from the Military Area because of hostility to him or his race. He was excluded because we were at war with the Japanese empire, because the properly constituted military authorities feared an invasion of our West Coast and felt constrained to take proper security measures, because they decided that the military urgency of the situation demanded that all citizens of Japanese ancestry be segregated from the West Coast temporarily, and, finally, because Congress, reposing its confidence in this time of war in our military leaders—as inevitably it must—determined that they should have the power to do just this.

In 1988, President Ronald Reagan signed congressional legislation apologizing for the internment after initially opposing the measure. The law was based on the findings of a commission appointed by President Reagan that concluded government actions in interning the Japanese had been based on "race prejudice, war hysteria, and a failure of political leadership." The U.S. government subsequently disbursed more than $1.6 billion in compensation to Japanese Americans who had been interned and their heirs.

This chapter looks at the influence of race in the enforcement of the criminal law and in U.S. immigration policy.

■ CRITICAL RACE THEORY

Critical race theory (CRT) is an intellectual movement that analyzes how the law maintains the dominance and privileges of white society and how the law perpetuates the subordinate status of African Americans. CRT scholars look at the interaction between law and society. They ask how the law shapes social attitudes toward race and how society shapes the law on race. CRT is an outgrowth of the critical legal studies (CLS) movement. The scholars who work in the critical race field agree with CLS that the law is not rational and objective and favors the powerful. Proponents of CRT, however, tend to focus their energies on critically examining the relationship between race and the law, a topic that they believe does not receive sufficient attention from CLS.

Professor Derrick Bell's articles in the 1970s challenging some of the "sacred cows" of the civil rights movement are credited with sparking the development of CRT. For example, Bell questioned whether litigation directed toward the integration of schools served the interests of African American parents and children who may have been better served by a movement directed toward securing greater resources and opportunities for existing schools rather than integrating the children into new schools. The long-term impact of integrated schools has been "white flight" from urban communities and a return to segregated schools, some of which lack adequate resources (D. Bell 1976). There are some general themes listed below that are emphasized by CRT (Delgado and Stefancic 2001).

Perspective. CRT scholars, unlike mainstream white scholars, take the perspective of racial minorities toward the law and use stories to educate readers on the challenges confronting African Americans and other minority groups (Delgado 1995: 37).

Racism. Racial discrimination is viewed as an essential feature of American society (Delgado and Stefancic 2001).

Construction of race. There is no firm biological or scientific basis to the racial categories of "white" and "African American" or "Hispanic." Historically in the American South, a "single drop" of black blood resulted in an individual being considered African American. Minority racial categories historically have been associated with negative characteristics although "whiteness" possesses positive associations (Gotanda 1995).

Property. White racial identity is a property right that confers a "white privilege" in areas ranging from education to housing and employment (C. Harris 1993).

Law and subordination. Law, although formally "color blind," is a mechanism for maintaining white dominance (L. Green 1995; S. L. Johnson 2000). For example, anti-discrimination laws, by requiring demonstration of an intent to discriminate rather than looking at, for example, the percentage of minorities who were hired and promoted or who leased an apartment, make it difficult to prove discrimination (Freeman 1978).

Law in context. The law focuses on the narrow issue whether an individual was discriminated against in a hiring decision or in a prosecutor's decision to bring a death penalty charge against a defendant. CRT scholars adopt a broader view and focus on the factors that keep African Americans and other minorities in a subordinate status. These factors include poor schools, poverty, unemployment, high incarceration rates, and discriminatory attitudes (Gotanda 1995: 265–266).

Legal equality. CRT argues that legal efforts to combat discrimination are taken by the white establishment to maintain their dominant position rather than out of a genuine commitment to equal rights. Viewed from a CRT perspective, the U.S. Supreme Court decision in *Brown v. Board of Education* was an effort to win the hearts and minds of the population of the developing world as part of America's cold war competition with the Soviet Union (D. Bell 1980).

Intersectionality. Minorities are disadvantaged by a combination of race, gender, and class. This is termed **intersectionality**, or being situated in the middle of various forces (D. Roberts 1995: 384).

Essentiality. Minorities, on account of race, suffer discrimination and disadvantages beyond that directed at women or the poor (Crenshaw 1995: 357).

Alternative legal analysis. Existing legal approaches often fail to offer full legal protection to minorities. Critical race scholars, for example, have challenged inclusion of racial insults as freedom of speech (Delgado 2000: 131).

Kimberlé Williams Crenshaw develops a series of arguments that are central to CRT in her essay on rape. Rape law in the past few decades has been reformed to eliminate those aspects of the common law that placed an unfair burden on women. For example, very few states continue to require that women place themselves at risk by demonstrating "resistance to the utmost" to establish a lack of consent. Crenshaw, while applauding these types of reform, notes that African American women continue to confront prejudice in the criminal justice system that is not experienced by white women (e.g., essentiality). Defendants charged with the rape of an African American woman, whether they are white or African American, are less likely to be charged and convicted and less likely to receive a lengthy prison sentence than defendants charged with the rape of a white woman. Crenshaw argues that the lenient treatment of individuals alleged to have raped African American women, in part, results from the historic view of African American women as "earthy" and "gratification oriented" and as conforming to the stereotype of a "bad woman." In other words, as compared with white women, African American women continue to be judged by "who they are rather than what has been done to them" (Crenshaw 1995).

Khalil Gibran Muhammad argues that crime is central to understanding discrimination against African Americans. He demonstrates how popular and academic publications beginning in the late nineteenth century identified African Americans as violent criminals. Commentators, for the most part, resisted explaining African American crime as a product of poverty, unemployment, and segregation. African Americans' alleged criminality instead was portrayed as a product of their biology and later was explained as a product of a culture in which crime was accepted, encouraged, and celebrated. African Americans migrating from the South to northern cities during World War I were singled out for police harassment and violence and high rates of arrest and imprisonment. The *Uniform Crime Reports* started in 1930 to record the national incidence of crime and soon thereafter began to highlight the racial divide in society by distinguishing between crimes committed by whites and crimes committed by African Americans and included no other racial or ethnic categories. Muhammad concludes that the identification of African Americans with crime and violence continues to this very day and has helped to justify racial discrimination and inequality (Muhammad 2010). This conclusion is reinforced in Ibram X. Kendi's study of the history of racist ideas in America, which he traces from the arrival of the first European settlers in America. Kendi notes that any "negative behavior" by an African American has been viewed as evidence of "what was wrong with Black people" although "negative behavior" by a white individual "only proved what was wrong with that person" (Kendi 2016).

Professor Osagie K. Obasogie showed how deeply racism is embedded in society and how racial characteristics are constructed by studying the attitude of individuals who are blind since birth. He finds that white individuals who are blind learn from an early age through the actions or statements of family and other individuals that African Americans are of a "different" race who engage in negative behavior. They then bring these biases and prejudices into their daily interactions and relationships with African Americans (Obasogie 2014).

Consider an example of how the social construction of race reinforces race privilege and legal subordination. Ian Haney López argues that race is "legally constructed." American law between 1879 and 1952 for the most part limited citizenship and for many years entry into the United States to "white" individuals and to individuals of "African nativity." There was no fixed definition of white, and courts held that whiteness should be determined in accordance of the views of the "common individual" rather than on the basis of scientific analysis. In the vast majority of cases, race would be "evident" by looking at an individual. Armenians initially were categorized as "Asiatics." Judges after some debate changed their minds and categorized Armenians as white and eligible for citizenship. López notes that the decision as to who is white and eligible for citizenship had significant consequences because whiteness carried privileges that were not available to non-whites. In California, for example, non-citizens were prohibited from owning or possessing long-term leases on agricultural land in the Fresno Valley, which meant that rural Japanese and other Asians were ineligible to purchase, cultivate, and sell property and to accumulate wealth. Another example of the social construction of race was the historic definition of white and African American in the South. The southern states in the United States practiced legal segregation until the 1960s. Race determined where you could live, go to school, and marry. The law in southern and border states variously followed a "one drop," "one-half drop," or "one-eighth drop" rule whereby the smallest amount of non-white blood resulted in an individual being assigned to a non-white and segregated status (I. López 2006).

The next section introduces the topic of the experience of African Americans in the criminal justice system.

■ AFRICAN AMERICANS AND THE CRIMINAL JUSTICE SYSTEM

Six of the original thirteen states provided for the legal enslavement of African Americans. A 1680 Virginia statute was the model for the "slave codes" adopted throughout the South, laws that remained in effect for the next 180 years. Slaves did not possess a legal personality. They were bought and sold as property. They could not bring a lawsuit, testify against a free white man or woman, make a contract, own property, sell goods without a permit, or offer their labor on the open market. Slaves could not fight or use profane language, beat drums or blow horns, or preach religious doctrine. Slaves who resisted a "Christian" lifestyle were punished by twenty lashes. They could not leave the plantation without a permit and were subject to curfews and arbitrary searches and seizures. Assemblies of several slaves were prohibited unless monitored by a white man. Escape was punishable by death (Higginbotham 1978).

The law prohibited teaching slaves to read or write, giving them books or pamphlets, teaching them to set type, and educating them about poisons. Whipping was the customary punishment for acts that did not carry the death penalty. Most states limited the number of lashes to thirty-nine, although Alabama authorized up to one hundred lashes.

In the 1829 North Carolina decision of *State v. Mann*, the court stated that the "power of the master must be absolute to render the submission of the slave perfect." The decision stated that a slave possessed no "remedy" against the power of "his master" whose authority is "conferred by the laws of man . . . if not by the law of God" (*State v. Mann*, 13 N.C. 263 [1829]).

At the time of the drafting of the U.S. Constitution, there were 675,000 slaves in thirteen states; almost one of every five Americans was a slave. The Constitution dealt with slaves as three-fifths of a person for purposes of the apportionment of Congress. The importation of slaves was not to be prohibited by Congress before 1808. The "Fugitive Slave" provision provided that a slave who fled to a "free state" could be reclaimed by his or her owner.

Any hopes of limiting the number of slave states in the Union was undermined by the 1857 U.S. Supreme Court decision in *Dred Scott v. Sandford*. Chief Justice Roger Taney held that the assertion in the Declaration of Independence that all men were created equal did not include African Americans. African Americans were "beings of an inferior order, and . . . unfit to associate with the white race . . . and so far inferior that they had no rights which the white man was bound to respect." African Americans, whether free or slaves, were not entitled to U.S. citizenship. Slaves were property, and slave owners could not be deprived of their property interest in slaves by federal law (*Dred Scott v. Sandford*, 60 U.S. 393 [1857]).

In 1865 as the Civil War drew to a close, Congress and twenty-seven states endorsed the Thirteenth Amendment abolishing slavery. Roughly eighteen months later, Congress voted to support the Fourteenth Amendment to the Constitution providing that "nor shall any State deprive any person of life, liberty or property, without due process of law; nor deny to any person within its jurisdiction the equal protection of the laws." A third step toward racial equality was the Fifteenth Amendment providing that the "right of citizens of the United States to vote shall not be denied or abridged . . . on account of race, color, or previous servitude." Congress was authorized to enforce each of these three amendments.

African Americans flocked to the polls in the South and elected hundreds of African Americans to local and state office, served on juries, created school systems, and abolished barbaric forms of punishment. White southerners did not accept the rising tide of African American emancipation. Throughout the South, African American voters were disenfranchised though poll taxes, literacy tests, and the prohibition on individuals convicted of a felony from voting. The U.S. Supreme Court in a series of cases affirmed these discriminatory practices, and by 1910, African Americans effectively had been eliminated as a force in southern politics. In Mississippi, 140,344 African Americans registered to vote in 1896; in March 1900, only 5,320 African Americans remained on the voting role.

African Americans were subjected to a reign of terror. In the twenty years between 1883 and 1903, there were three thousand documented lynchings of African Americans by white mobs, almost none of which resulted in criminal prosecution. In 1893 alone, there were 231 lynchings of African Americans.

Southern states began to reintroduce segregation in public facilities. In 1896, in *Plessy v. Ferguson*, the U.S. Supreme Court held that "separate" and "equal" railway facilities for the races were not in violation of the Fourteenth Amendment. The segregation of the races, according to the Court, does not stamp African Americans with a "badge of inferiority." Political equality in voting or in running for office did not require equality in public facilities, theaters, or schools. This type of separation does not "imply the inferiority of one of the two races." Each race, according to the Court, preferred to socialize with its own group (*Plessy v. Ferguson*, 163 U.S. 537 [1896]).

Discrimination was most apparent in the criminal justice system. In March 1932, nine African American, semi-illiterate teenagers were pulled off a railroad train at Paint Rock, Arkansas, and charged with the gang rape of two white women. The so-called Scottsboro Boys became global symbols of injustice. The defendants were sentenced to death although their appointed defense attorney only conferred with the defendants for thirty minutes, failed to cross-examine key witnesses or to challenge the all-white composition of the jury, did not offer a closing statement, and neglected to move for a change in the location of the trial despite the mob atmosphere surrounding the trial. The U.S. Supreme Court overturned their convictions based on ineffective assistance of counsel and subsequently overturned a second guilty verdict because of the exclusion of African American jurors. In the end, the four youngest defendants were released after serving six years in jail, and all but one of the five remaining Scottsboro defendants was paroled (J. Goodman 1995). In April 2013, the Alabama House of Representatives and Senate, in recognition of the defendants' unjust treatment, voted to pardon the Scottsboro defendants, all of whom were deceased.

The failure of the criminal justice system in the trial of the Scottsboro defendants was part of a larger pattern of mistreatment of African Americans. In the often-cited case of *Brown v. Mississippi*, the defendants were convicted of murder although witnesses freely admitted having obtained the confessions through the use of physical coercion.

One of the defendants was "hanged by a rope to the limb of a tree and, having let him down, they hung him again . . . and [when] he still protested his innocence, he was tied to a tree and whipped." The defendant was subsequently arrested and once again "severely whipped" and was told the whippings would continue until he confessed. The two other defendants "were laid over chairs and their backs were cut to pieces with a leather strap with buckles on it . . . and, as the whippings progressed and were repeated, they . . . confessed the crime" (*Brown v. Mississippi*, 297 U.S. 278 [1936]).

The Supreme Court in reversing the defendants' convictions held "it would be difficult to conceive of methods more revolting to the sense of justice than those taken to procure the confessions . . . and the use of the confessions thus obtained as the basis for conviction and sentence."

In 1955, Emmett Till, a 14-year-old African American from Chicago, was visiting his extended family in Money, Mississippi. He was accused of whistling at Carolyn Bryant, a 21-year-old store clerk. Her husband Roy Bryant and his half-brother J. W. Milam retaliated by kidnapping Till and beating him, gouging out one of his eyes, and shooting him in the head. They were acquitted by an all-white

PHOTO 11.1   The Scottsboro Boys were nine African American teenagers falsely accused and prosecuted in 1931 of the gang rape of two white females. Their struggle for justice in a series of trials before all-white juries and appeals before the U.S. Supreme Court lasted for several decades. The Scottsboro Boys case frequently is cited as a shameful miscarriage of justice. In November 2013, the Alabama parole board voted to grant a posthumous pardon to the Scottsboro Boys. From left to right, the accused are Clarence Norris, Olen Montgomery, Andy Wright, Willie Roberson, Ozie Powell, Eugene Williams, Charlie Weems, Roy Wright, and Haywood Patterson.

jury after sixty-seven minutes of deliberation. Roy Bryant and Milam later confessed to the killing in a national magazine in exchange for $4,000. In 2017, Carolyn Bryant admitted that she lied about Till. In 1963, the 16th Street Baptist Church in Birmingham, Alabama, was bombed, killing four young African American girls between the ages of 11 and 14. The trial of one of the perpetrators did not take place until 1977, and it was not until twenty-five years later that the two other perpetrators were brought to justice. In the last decades, federal authorities have reviewed over one hundred "cold case" killings that took place in the 1950s and 1960s during the civil rights movement in the South, and over twenty men have been sentenced to jail for the racially motivated murder of African Americans and African American and white civil rights workers (Leamer 2016; Romano 2014: 1–66).

Michelle Alexander, in her important book *The New Jim Crow*, notes that "Jim Crow" (a system of legal discrimination) collapsed following the historic 1954 Supreme Court decision in *Brown v. Board of Education* in which the Supreme Court ordered the desegregation of public schools with "all deliberate speed." Today, African Americans are repressed through the criminal law. Massive numbers of young people of color are incarcerated far from their home and, as a result of their imprisonment, are ineligible to vote, are excluded from various areas of employment, and are ineligible for public housing, welfare, and student loans. This "new Jim Crow" results in a significant number of African American males being prevented from participation in mainstream white society (Alexander 2010: 182–208).

Harvard law professor Charles Ogletree observes that there remains an "alarming prevalence of racial disparity in the Criminal Justice System" and there is a "presumption of guilt" rather than a "presumption of innocence" when it comes to African Americans (Ogletree 2010: 75). He cites a 2009 report from the Pew Research Center indicating that 1 in every 15 African American males aged 18 or older are in prison or in jail versus 1 in every 36 Hispanic males and 1 in every 106 white males. A 2003 Department of Justice report finds the lifetime risk of incarceration for a child born in 2001 is 1 in 3 for African American males, 1 in 6 for Hispanic males, and 1 in 17 for white males. Ogletree concludes by citing a report from the Sentencing Project stating that "one of every three black males born today will go to prison in his lifetime, as will one of every six Latino males" (quoted in Ogletree 2010: 15–16).

The next two sections discuss two examples of the legal bias against African Americans. The first section discusses stop and frisk of African Americans, and the second section discusses the differential prosecution and punishment of crack cocaine and powder cocaine. In reading this material, ask yourself whether, despite the racial progress achieved in America over the past several decades, the criminal justice system continues to unfairly treat African Americans.

■ RACIAL PROFILING

Racial profiling is defined as the reliance on race as the basis for detaining an individual for investigation or for arrest. In other words, an individual is detained based on "who he or she is" rather than "what he or she does." Consider two people of different races walking down the street. A decision by the police to stop one of these individuals based on his or her race would violate the Equal Protection Clause of the U.S. Constitution.

Discriminatory justice may occur in a variety of situations. A pretext arrest involves the police stopping an individual on a minor crime when their real motivation is to investigate a more serious offense. This may involve discriminatory justice or a decision by the police to detain an individual for investigation or arrest solely because he or she is African American or Hispanic. The police may overlook the same offense when committed by an individual of another race or nationality or gender. Judges have recognized there are instances in which race may be a factor to take into consideration. For example, an individual may give the police a description of an assailant that includes the offender's race.

The overwhelming perception of minority groups is that the police engage in racial profiling. A 2004 Gallup poll found that 67 percent of African Americans, 63 percent of Hispanics, and 50 percent of whites believe racial profiling is widespread (Walker, Spohn, and Delone 2007: 125, 127, 129). In a CBS/*New York Times* poll, 67 percent of African Americans responded they felt that they had been stopped by the police because of their race or ethnic background. This compares to 9 percent of whites (Ogletree 2010: 110). An October 2014 poll sponsored by *Reason* found that 70 percent of Americans oppose racial profiling and 25 percent support racial profiling; 81 percent of African Americans strongly disapprove of racial profiling as compared to 62 percent of Hispanics and 40 percent of white Americans (Ekins 2014). There was somewhat less opposition in a poll reported by the *International Business Times* (Morrison 2015).

The Fourth Amendment to the U.S. Constitution prohibits unreasonable searches and seizures. A reasonable seizure of an individual may be based on either probable cause (arrest) or reasonable suspicion (an investigative stop).

The Supreme Court in its 1996 ruling in *United States v. Whren* made it difficult for defendants to establish racial profiling. In *Whren*, two young African American defendants claimed that Washington, D.C., vice squad officers subjected them to a **pretext stop**. They argued that the true reason for the stop was their race and that they were suspected of drug possession rather than that they failed to signal a turn and had driven at an "unreasonable" speed.

The officers observed the defendants' SUV stopped at an intersection for an "unusually long time," and the officers executed a U-turn. The SUV accelerated, and the officers overtook the defendants' truck and spotted two large bags of cocaine in the front seat. The defendants contended that it was unreasonable under the Fourth Amendment for two plainclothes vice officers to have stopped them for a minor traffic violation in a congested area of the city. Police regulations specified that vice squad officers were to execute motor vehicle stops only for serious traffic violations. The defendants argued there are so many traffic regulations that the police always can find a reason to pull someone over for a violation. The U.S. Supreme Court held that so long as the police possess reasonable suspicion or probable cause to stop a vehicle, the Court would not explore the officers' motivation for a stop. The Court did indicate that the defendants' remedy lay in a violation of the Equal Protection Clause based on intentional racial discrimination, a difficult hurdle to overcome so long as the police had legal grounds to seize an individual (*United States v. Whren*, 517 U.S. 806 [1996]).

Racial profiling became a topic of intense public attention in 2013 when federal district court judge Shira A. Scheindlin held in *Floyd v. City of New York* that the New York City Police Department (NYPD) engaged in what she termed "indirect racial profiling" (*Floyd v. City of New York*, 959 F.Supp.2d 540 [S.D.N.Y. 2013]).

New York City mayor Michael Bloomberg, in an effort to reduce the crime rate, implemented an aggressive policy of "stop and frisk" in "impact zones" where crime was concentrated. In 2003, the second year of Mayor Bloomberg's first term in office, the police seized 604 weapons in 160,651 encounters or one gun for every 266 stops. In 2011, 780 guns were seized in 685,724 stops or one gun for every 879 stops. An estimated 8,000 guns and 80,000 other weapons were seized by the NYPD in the first ten years of New York's stop-and-frisk policy.

The NYPD credited its stop-and-frisk policy for reducing the number of murders in New York City to significantly below the number of murders reported a dozen years ago. The police explained that knowing there was a risk of being stopped, individuals would not carry firearms, realizing they faced a lengthy prison term under New York's strict gun control law. As a result, the NYPD claimed to have saved the lives of thousands of minority young people. Individuals who were stopped often were found to have outstanding warrants for their arrest and as a result were taken into custody.

Critics asserted that whatever the effectiveness of New York's stop-and-frisk policy was, the question was whether the stop-and-frisk policy was constitutionally permissible.

In 1968, in *Terry v. Ohio*, the U.S. Supreme Court held that it is reasonable under the Fourth Amendment for the police to detain individuals based on a reasonable suspicion the individual has committed a crime or is about to commit a crime. The facts are to be judged in accordance with a reasonable person standard and not based on what the officer (subjectively) believed. The police may not rely on a hunch, generalization, or stereotype in deciding to detain an individual based on reasonable suspicion of criminal activity (*Terry v. Ohio*, 392 U.S. 1 [1968]).

A police officer, when nothing in the initial stages of the encounter serves to "dispel" the officer's reasonable fear for his or her own or others' safety, is entitled to conduct a carefully limited search for weapons that might be used for an assault against the officer or the public. In 1993, in *Minnesota v. Dickerson*, the Supreme Court expanded police stop-and-frisk powers and held if a police officer lawfully pats down a suspect's outer clothing and feels an object and it is immediately apparent that the object is unlawful narcotics, the officer is justified in seizing the object (*Minnesota v. Dickerson*, 508 U.S. 366 [1993]).

Terry is intended to provide the police with the capacity to conduct a brief stop for purposes of crime investigation and detection. The Court anticipated these stops would be undertaken in situations requiring "swift action predicated upon the on-the-spot observations of the officer on the beat." In *Terry*, Martin McFadden, a thirty-nine-year veteran of the Cleveland police, spotted individuals "casing" a store, approached the men, and when the men proved unresponsive, conducted a carefully limited frisk for weapons. The Supreme Court reasoned that because unlawful *Terry* stops and unlawful *Terry* frisks would result in the exclusion of evidence, the police would be deterred from violating individuals' Fourth Amendment rights.

A *Terry* search policy that intentionally singled out members of one racial group for stop and frisk would violate the Equal Protection Clause of the Constitution, even if there were reasonable suspicion to stop members of the group. Harvard Law School professor Randall Kennedy notes courts have held that although race may not be the sole factor in a reasonable suspicion stop, it may be one of several factors relied on by the police. Individuals may be stopped for investigation who fit the victim's description of the perpetrators of a robbery where the individuals' size, gender, and race matches the victim's description and the individuals are detained within several blocks of the robbery. Kennedy argues that relying on race as the sole factor other than in "extraordinary circumstances" promotes distrust, interferes with minority–police relations, and leads to a perceived abuse of authority (R. Kennedy 1998: 137, 151, 153).

District Court Judge Scheindlin held that New York City's stop-and-frisk policy was unconstitutional, in violation of the Fourth Amendment and Equal Protection Clause of the U.S. Constitution. Judge Scheindlin appointed a federal monitor to supervise a reform of the New York City policy of stop and frisk, including the use of body-worn cameras for officers in some precincts, community consultation on the use of stop and frisk, and a modification in training. New York City subsequently implemented a series of reforms to the police department's use of stop and frisk.

Judge Scheindlin concluded that although NYPD policy formally prohibited racial profiling, the police practiced a policy of conducting stops in a "racially discriminatory manner." Between January 2004 and the middle of 2012, roughly 4.4 million stops were recorded by the police. Eighty-three percent of the stops involved African Americans (52 percent) or Hispanics (31 percent), although these two groups constitute close to 50 percent of New York City residents. In 2011, over 40 percent of stops targeted African American and Hispanic males between the ages of 14 and 24, a demographic group that comprises 4.7 percent of the New York City population.

Mayor Bloomberg and the police defended the stop-and-frisk policy based on the fact that young minority men commit a disproportionate percentage of crime. Judge Scheindlin noted that this argument might be valid if the "people stopped were criminals." However, she pointed out that the data indicate that 88 percent of individuals stopped are "overwhelmingly innocent" and their seizure results neither in an arrest (6 percent of detainees) nor in a summons (6 percent of detainees) to appear in court for a minor violation of the law. Judge Scheindlin wrote, "It is impermissible to subject all members of a racially defined group to heightened police enforcement because some members of that group are criminals." There also was little evidence that the *Terry* stops resulted in the seizure of weapons.

Judge Scheindlin went on to note that roughly half of all individuals detained are frisked, although only 1.5 percent of frisks led to the seizure of weapons. Weapons were seized in 1 percent of stops involving African Americans, 1.1 percent of stops involving Hispanics, and 1.4 percent of stops involving whites. Contraband other than a weapon was seized in 1.8 percent of stops involving African Americans, 1.7 percent of stops involving Hispanics, and 2.3 percent involving whites. Once stopped, African Americans and Hispanics were treated differently than whites. African Americans were 14 percent more likely and Hispanics 9 percent more likely than whites to be subjected to physical force during a stop.

Judge Scheindlin concluded that the focus on African American and Hispanic young people for investigative stops was based at least "in part" on the fact they were viewed as the "right people." She pointed to police supervisors lecturing officers to stop "the right people, the right time, the right location," which she concluded, based on the testimony of high-ranking police officials, was a code for targeting African American and Hispanic young people.

Judge Scheindlin noted that police reports indicated that minority youth were detained based on broad categories of behavior such as "furtive movement" or a "suspicious bulge" in their pocket. Furtive movements might encompass being "fidgety, changing directions, walking in a certain way, grabbing at a pocket or looking over one's shoulder." Eleven percent of African Americans and 9.6 percent of Hispanics were stopped based on a "suspicious bulge" as compared to 4.6 percent of whites. In most instances, the bulge turned out to be a wallet or cell phone. Judge Scheindlin stressed that a wallet or cell phone does not justify a stop, nor does the presence of a wallet or cell phone entitle the officer to continue to conduct a search. She observed that if the NYPD mistakenly believed this type of behavior constitutes reasonable suspicion, it should come as no surprise that so many stops yield so little evidence of criminal activity.

In other instances, individuals aged 14 to 21 were stopped because they allegedly fit the profile of the individuals responsible for committing crimes. Individuals falling into this category were stopped even if they were not acting in a suspicious fashion or did not fit the description of the perpetrator of a crime.

Judge Scheindlin stressed that the Equal Protection Clause does not authorize treating similarly situated members of different racial groups differently based on racial disparities in crime data.

The result was that minorities were being detained based on a lesser standard of reasonable suspicion than was being used to detain whites.

Judge Scheindlin cited the seizure of Cornelio McDonald, who was walking down the street in Queens late at night. He was stopped based on the fact that two African American males had committed robberies and a burglary in the vicinity. "In other words, because two black males committed crimes in Queens, all black males . . . were subject to heightened police attention." The larger impact of this stop-and-frisk policy was to make individuals fearful of walking down the street, distrustful of the police, and afraid to venture into white areas of the city.

Despite the awareness of government and police officials that the stop-and-frisk policy was being carried out in an unlawful and racially discriminatory fashion, Judge Scheindlin concluded these officials were indifferent to the discriminatory application of stop and frisk. Police officers were pressured to increase the number of stop and frisks regardless of whether the stops were justified, and as a result, the number of stops increased sevenfold between 2002 and 2011 (from 97,000 stops in 2002 to 686,000 in 2011).

Judge Scheindlin concluded that New York City's highest officials "have willfully ignored overwhelming proof that the policy of targeting 'the right people' is racially discriminatory and . . . violates the United States Constitution."

New York mayor Bill de Blasio implemented a number of agreed-upon reforms of NYPD's stop-and-frisk policy, which resulted in a dramatic decline of seizures (twenty-four thousand in 2015) that was accompanied by a decline in the crime rate. An audit of the department's practice of stop and frisk nonetheless found that the reforms were not being fully implemented by officers in the field (A. Baker 2016).

Michael D. White and Henry F. Fradella reviewed the social science literature on stop and frisk in New York and in other cities, and their analysis led them to several conclusions (M. White and Fradella 2016: 81–115):

Crime. The impact in New York and in other cities indicates that stop and frisk at best had a "minimal to modest" impact on crime.

Constitutional rights. Stop and frisk as practiced in New York violated the constitutional rights of thousands of individuals, particularly African American and Hispanic young people.

Consequences. The widespread misapplication of stop and frisk had negative emotional and psychological consequences for individuals who were detained and searched, and in some instances, detainees were physically or sexually abused.

Community relations. The use of stop and frisk in minority communities has contributed to a lack of trust of the police and has strained relations between the police and these communities.

Legal experts who are critical of stop and frisk note that although stop and frisk may be effective in regard to deterring and preventing crimes by individuals, it never was intended to be used as a dragnet tactic to control crime in an entire community (M. White and Fradella 2016: 113).

In 2016, New York City entered into a consent decree and paid $75 million in damages for nine hundred thousand summonses issued to individuals between 2007 and 2015 who had been falsely charged with minor offenses such as disorderly conduct, trespassing, and drinking in public. The plaintiffs bringing the legal action alleged that this was part of a pattern and practice of selectively and disproportionately stopping young minority males and that the police in order to meet a quota of arrests had been told to issue a summons regardless of whether they could establish a violation of the law (Weiser 2017).

A 2012 *New York Times* poll revealed that New Yorkers were fairly equally divided on whether stop and frisk was an acceptable method to make New York City safe. Among white voters, 55 percent believed stop and frisk made New York safer, and 39 percent did not believe the policy made New York safer; 35 percent of African American voters believed stop and frisk made New York safer while 56 percent believed stop and frisk had not made New York safer; and 48 percent of Hispanics agreed that stop and frisk had made New York City safer while 44 percent believed stop and frisk had not made New York safer. An October 2016 Rasmussen poll found that 47 percent of the public oppose stop and frisk, 41 percent favor stop and frisk, and 12 percent have no opinion. The public was divided on whether stop and frisk reduces crime although two-thirds were concerned that the policy violated civil liberties. The Rasmussen poll notes that support for stop and frisk has been rising slightly perhaps in reaction to widely publicized police–citizen interactions and the endorsement of stop and frisk by Donald Trump during the presidential campaign.

Professor Ogletree reviewed a study conducted by the American Civil Liberties Union of police stops in Los Angeles between 2003 and 2004. The report concludes that minorities are "over-stopped, over-frisked, over-searched, and over-arrested." Ogletree notes:

- Per ten thousand residents, the African American stop rate is 3,400 stops higher than the white stop rate, and the Hispanic stop rate is almost 360 stops higher.

- Relative to stopped whites, stopped African Americans are 12 percent more likely and stopped Hispanics are 43 percent more likely to be frisked.

- Relative to stopped whites, stopped African Americans are 76 percent more likely and stopped Hispanics are 16 percent more likely to be searched.

- Relative to stopped whites, stopped African Americans are 29 percent more likely and stopped Hispanics are 32 percent more likely to be arrested.

- Frisked African Americans are 42.3 percent less likely to be found with a weapon than frisked whites, and frisked Hispanics are 31.8 percent less likely to have a weapon than frisked non-Hispanic whites (Ogletree 2010: 110–111).

Several important studies of racial profiling involve traffic stops in New Jersey and in Maryland. The New Jersey study found that African Americans and whites violated traffic laws at the same rate. Minorities comprised 15 percent of drivers on the New Jersey Turnpike while constituting 42 percent of all individuals stopped and 73 percent of all individuals arrested. The New Jersey attorney general conducted a second study that found that 77 percent of all consent searches conducted by the police involved African Americans. Consent searches are significant because they involve the police asking a driver's permission to search an automobile in situations in which they may otherwise lack a legal basis to conduct a search (Alexander 2010: 131–132).

The Maryland study found that African Americans were 17 percent of drivers on I-95 outside of Baltimore and were 70 percent of drivers stopped and searched on the highway. Racial minorities (Hispanics, Asians, and African Americans) constituted 21 percent of all drivers and comprised almost 80 percent of drivers pulled over and searched (Alexander 2010: 141).

The Maryland data are based on police reports that were made available as a result of a lawsuit filed by an African American, Harvard-trained lawyer who had been stopped while traveling with his family on I-95. One explanation for the focus on stopping African American drivers is that a memo distributed to the state police advised the officers that drug traffickers are predominantly African American and are armed and dangerous and travel I-95 in the early morning. The reality was that whites driving on I-95 were four times more likely to be carrying narcotics than were African Americans (Ogletree 2010: 107–108). In New Jersey, whites were twice as likely to possess unlawful drugs as were African Americans and five times more likely than Hispanics to be in possession of unlawful narcotics (Walker et al. 2007: 131). Similar findings of racial profiling were found in studies in Florida, Illinois, and California (Alexander 2010: 132).

A 2002 study by the Bureau of Justice Statistics stressed that traffic stops are important because they account for 80 percent of police–citizen contacts and shape citizens' perceptions of the police. African Americans and Hispanics, according to the study, are more than twice as likely as whites to be arrested in a traffic stop. They are more than three times as likely to have force used against them during the stop (Walker et al. 2007: 128–129).

Charles Epp, Steven Maynard-Moody, and Donald Haider-Markel in a study of traffic stops in Kansas City, Kansas, distinguish between police safety stops and investigative stops. There is little difference in the racial identity of drivers who are stopped in safety stops because they are driving at a rapid rate of speed that threatens road safety. Drivers are treated the same regardless of their race. However, African Americans are 270 times more likely than whites to be subjected to an investigatory stop, and during these stops, the police are five times more likely to search African Americans than whites although they are less likely to find a gun or contraband in searches of African Americans (Epp, Maynard-Moody, and Haider-Markel 2015).

A study of 250,000 traffic stops in Durham, North Carolina, between 2002 and 2013 also found a pattern of racial discrimination along with a report released by Missouri Attorney General Chris Koster in 2014 (Koster 2015). In 2015, then attorney general Eric Holder updated the Department of Justice's 2003 Guidance Regarding the Use of Race by Federal Law Enforcement Agencies. The new guidelines provide that federal law enforcement officers may not use race, ethnicity, national origin, religion, sexual orientation, or gender identity to "any degree in making routine or spontaneous law enforcement decisions" such as ordinary traffic stops. Federal officers may rely on the listed characteristics in those instances in which this is part of a suspect's physical description or characteristic. More than half of the states have legislation addressing racial profiling by the police.

In July 2009, the issue of racial profiling was thrust into the national political stoplight when Sergeant James Crowley of the Cambridge, Massachusetts, police arrested esteemed Harvard professor Henry Louis Gates Jr., an African American, for a crime against "decency and good order." Crowley had been called to Gates's home when a neighbor reported seeing two men push open the front door, which, as it turns out, was jammed. A confrontation developed when Gates refused to exit his home in response to a request from Sergeant Crowley. Gates responded to being suspected of breaking and entering by loudly calling the officer a racist and shouting several times that this is "what happens to a black man in America." Professor Gates subsequently agreed to leave the house and showed Crowley his Harvard identification and driver's license indicating this was his home.

Ogletree, in analyzing the situation, concludes Crowley believed because of his "prejudice" that the 59-year-old Gates could not be the owner of the home and a crime was being committed. Crowley could have waited for the Harvard police to arrive to corroborate Gates's explanation before arresting him. The legally questionable charges later were dismissed (Ogletree 2010: 15–64).

President Barack Obama later commented that the "Cambridge police acted stupidly" and invited both men to a "beer summit" at the White House. The episode illustrates the continuing racial divide on race and criminal justice. According to a CNN poll, 61 percent of African Americans as compared to 29 percent of whites sympathized with Professor Gates. Forty-five percent of whites sympathized with Sergeant Crowley as compared to 19 percent of African Americans.

■ POLICE-INVOLVED VIOLENCE

The police under the common law possessed the right to employ deadly force against an individual who the officer reasonably believed had committed a felony. The authorization of deadly force was based on the notion that felons were a lawless element whose lives could be taken to safeguard the public. This presumption was strengthened by the fact that felons were subject to capital punishment and to the forfeiture of property. Felons were considered to have forfeited their right to life, and the police were merely imposing the punishment that awaited offenders in any event. Keep in mind that the fleeing felon rule developed prior to the equipping of law enforcement officers with firearms, and that as a result, an officer only would be in a position to employ deadly force when directly confronted by a threatening felon.

The U.S. Supreme Court restricted the fleeing felon rule in 1985 in *Tennessee v. Garner* and held that the fleeing felon rule constituted an unlawful seizure under the Fourth Amendment prohibition on unreasonable searches and seizures. The Court in *Garner* balanced the intrusion on a suspect's privacy interest against the need for the seizure and held that probable cause to arrest a suspect did not justify the employment of deadly force in *every instance*. On the other hand, "[w]here the officer has probable cause to believe that the suspect poses a threat of serious physical harm, either to the officer or to others, it is not constitutionally unreasonable to prevent escape by using deadly force" (*Tennessee v. Garner*, 471 U.S. 1 [1985]).

The FBI only recently began to comprehensively record nationwide police-involved shootings. The *Washington Post*, to provide insight into the incidence of police use of deadly force, in 2015 began to track police-involved fatal shootings. In 2015, the *Post* recorded 900 fatal police-involved shootings, and in 2016, the *Post* recorded a nearly identical 991 fatal police-involved shootings. In most instances, the individual killed was found to be armed, and the killing was found to be justified or the shooting was still under investigation. The shootings occurred in all varieties of departments and in various circumstances including routine patrols, undercover operations, and SWAT team operations (Lowery 2016a, 2016b).

In 2015, 40 percent of unarmed individuals killed by the police were African American although African American men constituted 6 percent of the population. Thirteen percent of African Americans fatally shot by the police were unarmed as compared to 7 percent of whites. An unarmed African American was determined to be five times as likely to be shot and killed by a police officer than an unarmed white American. In 2016, African Americans were three times more likely than whites to be killed by the police and constituted 34 percent of unarmed individuals killed by the police.

As of July 2016, the *Washington Post* recorded and analyzed 1,502 police killings by on-duty police officers. The *Post* found that 732 victims were white and 381 victims were African American (the other victims were of another race or of an unknown race). Based on each racial group's representation in the population, African Americans were determined to be 2.5 times more likely to be shot and killed by the police.

A study of 19,000 police use-of-force incidents between 2000 and 2015 in twelve jurisdictions concluded that the mean use-of-force rate against African Americans was 273 per 100,000 as compared to 76 per 100,000 for whites and 108 per 100,000 for all other individuals. Examining individuals arrested, the rate of use of force against African Americans was 46 for every 100,000 and against whites was 36 per 100,000.

An analysis of the data in this study indicates that African Americans who are killed by the police are no more likely to pose an imminent threat to the police at the time they are killed than whites who are fatally shot by the police. The only significant factor predicting whether an unarmed individual is shot was whether they are African American (T. Williams 2016b).

A blue-ribbon panel in San Francisco found that between January 2010 and July 2015, although African Americans comprise 5.8 percent of the city's residents, they constitute 40 percent of the victims of officer-involved shootings. The study also revealed racial disparities in the stop and search of African Americans (T. Williams 2016b, 2016c). A study of one thousand cases in police departments in California, Florida, and Texas found no racial bias in police shootings although the study found that African Americans were more likely to be handcuffed, pushed to the ground and against a wall, and pepper sprayed even when they were compliant with the officer's demands (Bui and Cox 2016).

Frank Zimring has closely analyzed the *Guardian* newspaper database on police use of deadly force. Zimring's overall conclusion is that police killing of civilians is a significant problem and that a substantial number of the civilian deaths are preventable by reasonable adjustments to the police policy regulating the use of deadly force. Examples of reforms worth considering are a limitation on the police use of deadly force when confronted by an individual with a weapon or object other than a firearm, a modification of the rule that authorizes the use of deadly force when an assailant is within twenty-one feet of the officer, and a limitation on multiple wound firings by the police. Zimring also identifies situations that should be studied that enhance the risk of police shootings, such as when a single police officer confronts a citizen, particularly an African American (Zimring 2017). The *Interim Report of the President's Task Force on 21st Century Policing* makes a number of recommendations regarding police use of force, including training officers to de-escalate rather than escalate confrontations (President's Task Force on 21st Century Policing 2015).

A *New York Times*/CBS News poll in 2016 found that 75 percent of African Americans believed that the police are more likely to use deadly force against an African American and only half as many whites agreed with this statement. Fifty-six percent of whites and 18 percent of African Americans agreed that the race of a suspect makes no difference in the decision of the police to resort to deadly force. Eighty percent of whites believed that the police department in their community was good or excellent. A majority of African Americans rated the job of their department as poor or fair. More than 40 percent of African Americans stated that the police make them feel apprehensive rather than safe. Whites and Hispanics overwhelmingly stated that the police make them feel safer (Russonello 2016).

There is a clear divide between the perceptions of African American and white officers regarding community relations. More than 60 percent of Caucasian and Hispanic police officers in one poll believed that police relations with African Americans are either excellent or good while only 32 percent of African American officers agreed with this statement. Ninety-two percent of white officers stated that the United States has achieved equal rights for African Americans while 29 percent of African American officers agreed with this statement (Bromwich 2017).

Black Lives Matter

The acquittal of George Zimmerman in 2012 for the killing of Trayvon Martin, an unarmed 17-year-old in Sanford, Florida, reignited the debate over whether the criminal justice system was fair and protective of African Americans. Zimmerman was acting as a volunteer neighborhood watchperson and suspected that Martin, who was walking home while talking on the phone and wearing a "hoodie," was a burglar. This was followed in August 2014 by the shooting of 18-year-old Michael Brown by Officer Darren Wilson in Ferguson, Missouri. The story circulated that Brown had been shot after raising his hands over his head to indicate his cooperation with the officer. The phrase "Hands up, don't shoot" became a national rallying cry. The St. Louis County elected prosecutor Bob McCulloch refused to appoint a special prosecutor and convened a grand jury that voted against indicting Officer Wilson. A Department of Justice investigation subsequently found that Wilson had shot Brown eight times as the physically imposing teenager allegedly moved toward him. The investigation concluded that it was not "objectively unreasonable" for Wilson to have used deadly force. The African American community nonetheless questioned whether it was necessary to kill Brown. The shooting became a symbol for the disrespect and disregard that the Ferguson community felt was exhibited by the police. Community members asked why Brown's body had been left for over four hours on the asphalt following the killing. Hundreds of individuals joined demonstrations and proclaimed that "I am Michael Brown" (Department of Justice 2015b).

A civil rights investigation by the Department of Justice found that Ferguson police engaged in "intentional discrimination on the basis of race" and that the police engaged in a "pattern and practice" of unconstitutional violations. "Officers violate the Fourth Amendment . . . [by] stopping people without reasonable suspicion, arrest[ing] them without probable cause, and using unreasonable force." Officers also "frequently" violated individuals' First Amendment rights, "making enforcement decisions based on the content of individuals' expression" (Department of Justice 2015a: 7, 25).

The failure to pursue charges against Officer Wilson was viewed by activists as emblematic of a national trend toward not pressing charges against police officers who killed citizens, particularly African Americans and other minorities. A national investigation by Professor Phil Stinson on behalf of the *Washington Post* found that between 2004 and 2014, fifty-four officers had been indicted for on-duty shootings, eleven had been convicted, twenty-one were acquitted, and nineteen prosecutions were pending. The officers convicted served an average of four years in prison. The analysis determined that several conditions were met in those instances in which a police officer was prosecuted: there was a combination of a victim shot in the back, an incriminating videotape, a police cover-up, and the incriminating testimony of fellow officers (Lowery 2016b: 46, 113). Zimring writes that assuming there are one thousand killings of civilians by the police, the expectation is that there will be one felony prosecution of a police officer (Zimring 2017).

The sense of outrage over police-involved killing of African Americans escalated over the killing of 12-year-old Tamir Rice on November 22, 2014, in Cleveland, Ohio. Officers Timothy Loehmann and Frank Garmback responded to the report of an armed individual outside a recreation center. The officers were not informed by the dispatcher that the 9-1-1 caller had cautioned that the individual possibly was a child playing with a toy gun (Lowery 2016b: 102–108).

The video of the Tamir Rice shooting showed the officers pulling directly in front of the gazebo where Rice had been playing with his pellet gun for the last hour. Loehmann leapt out of the passenger side of the cruiser and claimed that he yelled at Rice to raise his hand and that Rice instead lifted his shirt and reached for his waistband. Loehmann stated that he fired two shots when he saw Rice removing his weapon from his pants. The entire episode took a total of two seconds. Local prosecutor Timothy McGinty, following a thirteen-month investigation, announced that he had told the grand jury that he was opposed to filing charges and that they agreed with his decision. He called the killing a "perfect storm of human error, mistakes and miscommunication by all involved." McGinty explained that although Rice may have intended to give the gun to the officers or to show it to them, "there was no way for the officers to know that, because they saw the events rapidly unfolding in front of them from a very different perspective" (Lowery 2016b: 74–77).

In a number of other cases, police officers also were not prosecuted or were not convicted for the death of an African American citizen. In July 2014, a video recorded a number of New York City police officers subduing Eric Garner, a 43-year-old unarmed African American, who was arrested for selling loose cigarettes on the street. Garner died as a result of a chokehold by Officer Daniel Pantaleo combined with a number of officers piling on his stomach. A grand jury accepted Officer Pantaleo's account that he did not intend to apply a chokehold and, despite Garner's plea that "I cannot breathe," he did not believe that Garner was in danger (Lowery 2016b: 116). A mistrial was declared in the prosecution of Officer Michael Slager for the April 2015 murder of Walter Johnson in North Charleston, South Carolina. A video clearly showed Slager shooting Johnson in the back as Johnson fled a traffic stop for a missing tail light. The video showed Slager placing a stun gun next to Johnson's body. The speculation is that Johnson, a 50-year-old Marine Corps veteran, may have panicked because of a fear that he would be arrested because of an outstanding warrant for a failure to pay child support. Slager subsequently pled guilty to a federal civil rights violation in return for the dropping of other federal and state charges. A grand jury held police officers responsible for the July 2015 death of Sandra Bland, who allegedly hanged herself after being arrested for resisting arrest following a traffic stop in Waller County, Texas (Lowery 2016b: 111–115, 162–167, 171–172). In June 2017, police officers in Cincinnati, Milwaukee, and a Minneapolis suburb were acquitted of the killing of African Americans.

The U.S. attorney general, when he or she has "reasonable cause" to believe that a police department has engaged in a "pattern or practice of constitutional violations," may ask a court to direct a police department to correct the practice. This request for a pattern or practice decree is a mechanism to address a widespread practice of unlawful behavior rather than an isolated incident. Departments typically negotiate with the Department of Justice and voluntarily agree to the Department of Justice's request to avoid a court-imposed decree. The Trump administration has expressed skepticism about these "pattern and practice" investigations because they interfere with local law enforcement, which is best positioned to address community problems, and has indicated that it will not pursue federal "pattern and practice" investigations (Pérez-Peña and Stolberg 2017; Stolberg 2017).

The Obama administration conducted more than two dozen investigations into the "pattern and practice" of police departments. A number of these departments entered into agreements pledging to improve training, increase monitoring of police misconduct, investigate excessive and deadly force, and reform citizen complaint procedures and internal disciplinary mechanisms. Progress is evaluated by court-supervised monitors. The Baltimore police, for example, in a 2016 report, were determined to have engaged in "enforcement strategies that produce severe and unjustified disparities in the rates of stops, searches and arrests of African Americans" and to have engaged in a pattern and practice of unconstitutional stops, searches, and arrests and of excessive force against detainees (Department of Justice 2016).

A 2017 report on the Chicago Police Department concluded that the Chicago police routinely employed excessive force including shooting civilian suspects who did not pose a threat and unnecessarily employing stun guns on individuals who verbally challenged officers or resisted following commands. Eighty percent of Chicago police-involved shootings involved African Americans, and police officers were ten times more likely to use excessive force against African Americans. Complaints to the city's Independent Police Review Authority by whites were found justified by the review authority in 6 percent of the cases as compared to 2 percent of complaints by African Americans and 1 percent of complaints by Hispanics. Between 2009 and 2014, the Chicago police killed seventy people, most of whom were African American, the highest number of police-involved killings among the ten largest cities in the United States. The report also found that the police regularly engaged in a pattern of degrading speech directed at African Americans (Department of Justice 2017).

The Black Lives Matter movement developed in reaction to the killings of Trayvon Martin, Michael Brown, and nine individuals by white nationalist Dylann Roof at the Emanuel African Methodist Episcopal Church in Charleston, South Carolina. Black Lives Matter is a loosely organized network largely composed of young activists across the country (Cobb 2016).

The phrase "Black Lives Matter," according to Jelani Cobb, first appeared in July 2013 in a social media post by Alicia Garza, then 31 years of age, titled "a love letter to black people." Garza was a union activist involved with the National Domestic Workers Alliance, which represents and works on behalf of caregivers and housekeepers. She also was an active participant in the queer and transgender rights and anti-police-brutality movements.

Garza wrote, "I continue to be surprised at how little Black lives matter. And I will continue that, stop giving up on black life. . . . black people. I love you. I love us. Our lives matter." Garza, together with her friend and fellow activist Patrisse Cullors, posted the message under the hashtag #BlackLivesMatter and subsequently enlisted Opal Tometi to build a social media presence to promote Black Lives Matter (Cobb 2016).

Black Lives Matter started as a message and quickly emerged as the most important activist organization protesting police abuse. In the aftermath of the killing of Michael Brown in Ferguson, Missouri, Black Lives Matter activist Darnell L. Moore, a writer in Brooklyn, New York, coordinated "freedom rides" to Ferguson from New York, Chicago, Portland, Los Angeles, Philadelphia, and Boston. Hundreds of young people participated in protests and came to see Ferguson as a symbol and embodiment of institutional racism in the United States.

There are more than thirty Black Lives Matter chapters in the United States and Canada. The local groups are united by several guiding principles but are relatively free to pursue local concerns. Black Lives Matter is self-described as "an ideological and political intervention in a world where Black lives are systematically and intentionally targeted for demise. It is an affirmation of Black folks' contributions to this society, our humanity, and our resilience in the face of deadly oppression."

Black Lives Matter sets forth a broader agenda than police reform and also is committed to the rights of workers, to gender and sexual equality, and to including a diverse group of individuals and their concerns in the movement. The organization is dedicated to social activism and protest and has doubts about the effectiveness of electoral politics after what it views as the failure of the election of African American president Barack Obama to achieve the promise of a post-racial America. The focus is on a "flat organization" in which individuals and groups of individuals work to bring about social change rather than on centralized control and direction by a small set of leaders. During the 2016 presidential election, Black Lives Matter activists confronted Democratic presidential candidates in an effort to ensure that the candidates confronted issues of police and criminal justice reform.

As of March 2016, the hashtag #BlackLivesMatter had been used more than twelve million times, making it the third most tweeted hashtag related to a social cause. The first most frequently used hashtag is #Ferguson, which had been tweeted twenty-seven million times (Lowery 2016b: 87–89).

Black Lives Matter has been blamed for a number of controversial acts that the movement claims are the responsibility of individuals who are unaffiliated with the organization. Following the sniper attack and killing of five police officers in 2016 in Dallas, Texas, by an assailant who was not affiliated with Black Lives Matter, former New York City mayor and Trump surrogate Rudolph Giuliani blamed Black Lives Matter for "placing a target on the back of the police" and called the group "inherently racist." Giuliani claimed to have saved more lives through his aggressive stop-and-frisk policy than Black Lives Matter had saved through its protests. Other critics have confronted the movement with the claims that "all lives matter" and that "blue (police) lives matter."

A *New York Times*/CBS News poll found that 41 percent of Americans agree with Black Lives Matter, 25 percent disagree, and 29 percent have no opinion. Support is strongest among individuals under 30 and weakest among those over 50 years of age. Seventy percent of African Americans support Black Lives Matter as opposed to 37 percent of whites (Russonello 2016). A majority of African American police officers believed that Black Lives Matter protests were motivated at least in part by an apppropriate desire to hold the police accountable as compared to 27 percent of white officers (Bromwich 2017).

Stand your ground laws and the difference in punishment of crack versus powder cocaine are two other frequently cited examples of racial bias in the enforcement of the criminal law.

11.1 YOU DECIDE

Corey Menafee, a 38-year-old African American dining hall worker at Yale University, climbed on top of a table in the Calhoun College dining hall in June 2016 and smashed a stained glass window picturing slaves owned by nineteenth-century Yale alumnus John C. Calhoun. Calhoun during his political career served as a South Carolina senator, U.S. vice president under John Quincy Adams and Andrew Jackson, secretary of state, and secretary of war. His lasting legacy, however, is his uncompromising and outspoken support of slavery. The window that was broken portrayed African American slaves picking cotton on Calhoun's plantation. Menafee, a graduate of Virginia Union University, had worked at Yale for eight years and had worked at Calhoun since December and was described by his managers as a "very good employee." He was charged with a misdemeanor for reckless endangerment and felony criminal mischief. Menafee told the police that "no

employee should be subject to coming to work and seeing slave portraits on a daily basis."

Menafee later explained that "[l]ike they say, a picture's worth a thousand words. . . . That picture might have been worth a million words. I don't know, it just hit me. It just touched my heart to look up in 2016 and to see . . . a picture depicting real slaves in a field picking cotton. There's no real place for that in today's society. It's degrading, it's disrespectful and it shouldn't be there. Period."

Menafee subsequently apologized and resigned and was supported in his court hearing by forty Yale students, faculty members, and community members. Megan Fountain, a Yale alumna, stated that "Yale has to decide which is more valuable: a stained-glass window, or the dignity and humanity of the black people who live and work at Yale." Yale requested that the state's attorney not prosecute Menafee and later announced that the university would not pursue restitution.

Menafee, following the dismissal of charges, conceded that "looking back at the situation, it was a very juvenile thing to do" and that "there's [a] better way you can handle problems than just smashing something physically." He was rehired by Yale following a five-week suspension.

Yale removed several of the stained glass windows from Calhoun College, and President Peter Salovey, after announcing that the university would keep the college's name, announced in early 2017 that Yale would change the name of the college and name the college after renowned computer scientist Grace Murray Hopper. Yale took the additional step of stating that the faculty head of the residential colleges no longer would be referred to as "master" and that this designation would be replaced by the term "head of the college." The university explained that the designation "master" was suggestive of a slave master. President Salovey also announced that Yale would diversify the faculty and sponsor events addressing issues of diversity.

A number of universities have removed the name of white supremacists and segregationists from campus buildings. Duke and the University of North Carolina at Greensboro, for example, have removed the name of Charles B. Aycock, an early twentieth-century segregationist governor of North Carolina, from buildings. The State of South Carolina, following the killings in Charleston, South Carolina, by Dylann Roof, announced that the Confederate "stars and bars" flag would no longer fly on the grounds of the state capitol building. Note that some universities keep the name of controversial figures on buildings and provide a plaque detailing the individual's historical record as a means of provoking thought and debate.

The larger issue is that a number of elite American universities were entangled with the slave trade. For example, in 2016, it was revealed that Georgetown University had, in 1838, sold 272 slaves owned by the school in order to pay off debt.

As part of the Yale University administration, would you have advocated bringing criminal charges against Corey Menafee? Changing the name of the residential college?

■ RACE AND STAND YOUR GROUND LAWS

In 2013, George Zimmerman was acquitted based on self-defense in the homicide of 16-year-old Trayvon Martin. Although Zimmerman's defense was not based on Florida's controversial stand your ground law, the jurors appear to have been influenced by the law in evaluating Martin's claim of self-defense.

The **stand your ground** law authorizes an individual who is "lawfully situated" to rely on self-defense to "prevent death or great bodily harm to himself or herself or another or to prevent the commission of a forcible felony." The law eliminates the traditional requirement that an individual outside the home is required to exhaust all alternatives (e.g., retreat to the wall) before resorting to deadly force in self-defense. Claims of self-defense are adjudicated in a preliminary hearing in which the assailant is required to establish self-defense by a preponderance of the evidence (the Florida Supreme Court will determine whether the burden of proof may be placed on the prosecution). This modifies the standard procedure in which a defendant invokes self-defense at trial. The law absolves individuals acting in self-defense from criminal as well as civil liability (Light 2017).

The law originally was proposed by the National Rifle Association (NRA) and the American Legislative Exchange Council, a conservative coalition of state legislators and businesses. The NRA believed the law had tipped too far in favor of criminals, and stand your ground was an effort to provide protection for victims. Stand your ground law, after being adopted by Florida in 2005, spread to more than thirty-three other states.

An evaluation of the impact of stand your ground laws in Florida and other states is difficult because the police and prosecutors typically do not keep track of cases in which they decide against pressing charges.

There is little evidence that stand your ground laws have lowered the crime rate. Cheng Cheng and Mark Hoekstra of Texas A&M compared homicide rates in states before and after adopting stand your ground laws and compared homicide rates in states with stand your ground laws and states without stand your ground laws. Cheng and Hoekstra determined that homicides rose by 8 percent in states with stand your ground laws, which translates into roughly six hundred additional homicides per year in stand your ground states than otherwise would have been expected. Cheng and Hoekstra speculate that the increased killing results from ordinary interpersonal conflicts that escalate into violent confrontations (Cheng and Hoekstra 2012).

In Florida, there was an average of twelve justifiable homicides per year in the five years before the state adopted the stand your ground law. In the five years following adoption of the law, there was an average of thirty-five justifiable homicides per year. Cheng and Hoekstra explain that stand your ground laws "lower the cost of using force" and as a result you "get more of it." A study by Chandler McClellan and Erdal Tekin found that between 4.4 and 7.4 additional white males are killed each month as a result of stand your ground laws but that the law had no impact on the death rate among African Americans (McClellan and Tekin 2012).

The *Tampa Bay Times* notes that although stand your ground generally is applied in a responsible fashion by Florida prosecutors, a number of similar cases are treated differently by local prosecutors. The newspaper also finds cases that make a "mockery" of the law. "In nearly a third of the cases . . . defendants initiated the fight, shot an unarmed person or pursued their victim—and still went free" (Hundley, Martin, and Humberg 2012).

A central debate is whether stand your ground is applied in a racially discriminatory fashion.

In 2010 and again in 2013, the *Tampa Bay Times* analyzed over two hundred stand your ground cases in Florida and found that individuals relying on stand your ground avoided conviction in 70 percent of the cases. Defendants who killed a black person were found not guilty 73 percent of the time, while those who killed a white person were found not guilty 59 percent of the time (B. Montgomery and Jenkins 2010; "Florida's Stand Your Ground Law" 2013). An analysis of data from Florida between 2005 and 2013 by public health researchers at the University of St. Louis found that a defendant is twice as likely to be acquitted if his or her victim is non-white as opposed to white (Ackermann et al. 2015).

John Roman of the Urban Institute analyzed homicides between 2005 and 2010 in states he considered to have stand your ground laws. In states without stand your ground, 1.68 percent of white-on-white shootings were ruled justifiable as compared to 9.51 percent of defendants in white-on-black shootings. In those states with stand your ground laws, these statistics were even more skewed—3.51 percent of white-on-white shootings were considered to be self-defense. In contrast, 16.85 percent of white-on-black shootings ultimately were held to be justifiable (Roman 2013).

In 2015, the American Bar Association (ABA) published a comprehensive study of stand your ground laws. Among the task force's findings was that states with stand your ground laws experienced an increase in homicides and that stand your ground laws lead to "unpredictable, uneven" outcomes, result in "racial disparities," and undermine victims' rights. The ABA concludes that individuals' rights to self-defense were adequately protected prior to stand your ground laws and that the laws do not enhance individuals' personal security (ABA National Task Force on Stand Your Ground Laws 2015).

In brief, stand your ground laws are criticized as allowing fearful whites to rely on claims of self-defense to justify violence against young African Americans whom they stereotype as violent gang members. Jurors share this fear and invariably find that a white defendant acted reasonably in killing an African American male. Proponents of stand your ground laws argue that African American victims of crime benefit the most from these laws. The difference in the percentage of defendants found guilty who killed an African American assailant is explained in part by the fact that African American attackers were more likely to be armed and engaged in committing a crime when shot.

PHOTO 11.2 A demonstrator holds a "Justice for Trayvon and Byron Carter" poster at a rally protesting the acquittal of George Zimmerman on July 13, 2013, for the killing of Trayvon Martin. Byron Carter, a 20-year-old African American, was shot in the head and killed by a police officer in Austin, Texas, in May 2011 who was not charged with a criminal offense.

College students in Florida have organized to demand repeal of the state's stand your ground law although a state commission endorsed the law. What is your view?

There was a clear racial divide in reactions to the verdict in the Trayvon Martin case. In a Pew poll, 39 percent of white respondents were dissatisfied with the verdict, as compared to 86 percent of African Americans who said they had problems with the jury's decision. A majority of Americans support stand your ground laws, although unsurprisingly there are clear racial divisions. A Quinnipiac University poll in August 2013 found that 53 percent of Americans favor stand your ground laws and 40 percent oppose them. Fifty-seven percent of whites support stand your ground laws while 37 percent of whites oppose stand your ground laws. Thirty-seven percent of African Americans support stand your ground laws, and 57 percent oppose these laws. Hispanics are more evenly divided: 44 percent support stand your ground laws while 43 percent oppose stand your ground laws.

11.2 YOU DECIDE

The prohibition on discrimination traditionally has been limited to the categories of race, gender, ethnicity, nationality, age, and sexual preference. Deborah L.

Rhode of Stanford University argues that physical appearance is a distinct advantage in life and that there should be laws prohibiting discrimination

(Continued)

(Continued)

against individuals based on physical appearance, particularly against women. Discrimination against individuals who are overweight and against individuals viewed as unattractive is called the "last acceptable prejudice." You might be surprised to learn that the State of Michigan and the City of San Francisco prohibit discrimination based on height and weight. Urbana (Illinois), the District of Columbia, Madison (Wisconsin), and Howard County (Maryland) prohibit "appearance discrimination." Santa Cruz (California) bans discrimination based on height, weight, and any conditions stemming from birth, accident, disease, or natural physical development. The Australian state of Victoria also prohibits discrimination based on appearance. Discrimination laws in most American localities, states, and federal statutes are limited to the traditional categories of race, gender, ethnicity, nationality, age, and sexual preference.

Rhode points out that "appearance discrimination" can be hurtful to the individual.

People are judged on their appearance rather than on their ability, education, and performance.

Discrimination against individuals helps reinforce stereotypes. This, in turn, leads to other acts of discrimination.

Discrimination against individuals based on their appearance or dress is a limitation on individuals' self-expression and freedom of speech.

There are various types of appearance discrimination. This may range from inherent characteristics such as height or baldness to voluntary characteristics such as clothing and grooming. There are traits such as obesity that may be related to genetics as well as to personal lifestyle.

Rhode points out that under existing law, individuals may be denied a job because of their appearance or denied a job because they do not fit a company's image or because they refuse to adopt the style of dress required by the employer. Individuals are prohibited in some workplaces from braiding their hair and wearing headscarves or turbans. Of workers, 12 to 16 percent report having been discriminated against based on appearance, which roughly is the same percentage of individuals who report they have suffered discrimination based on gender, race, ethnicity, age, or religion.

Examples of discrimination based on appearance or based on a refusal to conform to a dress code include an individual dismissed from a job as a hotel clerk because of his or her weight or an individual fired as a cocktail waitress in a casino because she fails to maintain an "hourglass figure" or refuses to wear high heels and a revealing dress.

There is no question that there is a premium on beauty and there is discrimination against "unattractive" individuals. Teachers give less attention to children who are considered unattractive, and unattractive children are subject to teasing and are rejected by their peers. These early experiences can impact an individual's entire perspective on life. As adults, unattractive individuals are less likely than attractive individuals to be perceived as intelligent or interesting and are less likely to attract a financially successful spouse. The less attractive an individual is, the less likely he or she is to be interviewed, hired, or promoted. Overweight workers are the target of jokes and are perceived as lazy, sloppy, and lacking in discipline and psychological stability; they also are discriminated against in hiring and in promotions. College students report that they would marry an embezzler, drug user, or shoplifter before they would marry an obese individual. Attractive people receive special treatment in restaurants, hotels, and stores. When asked to grade papers with photos attached, professors are inclined to award a higher grade to attractive students. On the other hand, attractive women often are not taken seriously and are not viewed as competent.

There are good reasons why Americans spend billions of dollars on diets, cosmetic surgery, and health clubs. A fitness company denied a franchise to Jennifer Portnick, a 240-pound aerobics instructor. Sharon Russell was expelled from nursing school because she was overweight and would provide a bad "role model for good health habits." Russell went on to graduate from another school and has enjoyed success in a career in hospital administration. Television anchor Christine Craft was dismissed because she no longer met the standards of beauty, and her employers believed the audience would no longer find her attractive.

Should a company be free to hire employees who project a certain physical image and to insist that employees conform to certain standards of appearance and dress? Consider the following case. Cocktail waitresses at an Atlantic City hotel and casino entered into employment contracts in which the "Borgata Babes" agreed to maintain a "clean smile" and an "hourglass figure" that was "height and weight appropriate." The casino limited women to a 7 percent weight gain. One of the "Babes" was a dress size 4 when hired. She developed a thyroid condition that caused her weight to fluctuate. She asked for a size 6 dress and was told that the Borgata Babes are prohibited from going up in dress size. The only exception was for women who received breast implants (Rhode 2010).

Does a casino have the right to fire a waitress for gaining weight?

■ RACE AND THE WAR ON DRUGS

The Eighteenth Amendment to the U.S. Constitution provided for Prohibition, the banning of the manufacture, sale, or transportation of intoxicating liquors or the import or export of intoxicating liquors. In 1917, both the Senate and the House of Representatives approved the Eighteenth Amendment, and within five years of congressional passage, forty-four states had ratified the Amendment. Doris Marie Provine characterizes the temperance movement as the first anti-drug crusade in the United States. She attributes the success of the movement to the fact that anti-liquor crusaders from rural and small-town America skillfully identified alcohol with immigrants, ethnic Catholics, and Jews. The prohibition on alcohol took on symbolic importance and marked the dividing line between American values and foreign and alien values. Anti-liquor activists argued that immigrants' excessive use of alcohol threatened to undermine their capacity to work and to contribute to American society and threatened to encourage immoral behavior and social instability. They also warned that if African Americans were given access to alcohol, they would "run wild" and engage in crime, riots, and the rape of white women.

Federal law enforcement agents directed their anti-liquor efforts against the poor and minorities while the wealthy escaped enforcement. Provine observes that Prohibition established a pattern that was repeated in the "war on drugs": the identification of substance abuse with minorities and the blaming of minorities for social unrest and instability (Provine 2007: 37–62).

Opium in the eighteenth century and for most of the nineteenth century along with marijuana was viewed as a remedy for pain relief. Babies were given opium to calm them down, and the elderly used opium for rheumatic pain. Morphine was injected by artists and writers for inspiration and creativity. At the end of the nineteenth century, cocaine, heroin, and barbital were popular in the United States and in Europe as an alternative to alcohol, which had become increasingly expensive as a result of the growing movement for prohibition (Provine 2007: 64–67).

The Dutch in the 1600s introduced opium smoking into China. The smoking of opium became a concern in America with the influx of the Chinese into California and into the western United States in the 1850s.

Chinese immigrants largely built the Central Pacific Railroad, and an estimated eighteen thousand were employed by San Francisco factories in the 1870s. The influx of Chinese workers led to a backlash against low-wage Asian workers, who were viewed as a threat by white workers. San Francisco barred the Chinese from public employment, the purchase of real estate, and business licenses. Pigtails were considered a violation of the health ordinance. In Los Angeles, the "Anti-Chinese Union" engaged in a drumbeat of anti-Asian propaganda, provoking a mob attack in 1871 on the Chinese quarter of the city, resulting in the death of eighteen Chinese residents. The movement against the Chinese led to the adoption of a provision in the California Constitution prohibiting "aliens" from owning land or voting, restricting their employment, and encouraging their deportation.

Anti-Chinese riots broke out throughout the western United States, and the American labor movement denounced the Chinese as sources of disease and contamination. In 1892, Congress responded by prohibiting all immigration by Chinese laborers and restricting the ability of those Chinese who left the country from reentering (Provine 2007: 65–70). Kitty Calavita recounts that the congressional debate on Chinese exclusion characterized the Chinese as a "terrible scourge," "a great and growing evil," and "an inferior race" who were "incapable of assimilation." They were described as a threat to American workers because of their ability to work longer hours for less pay and in poorer conditions (Calavita 2010: 55–56).

Opium smoking and opium dens in Chinatowns were a central focus of anti-Chinese agitation. The media warned against the forced addiction and enslavement of white women and children by the Chinese. Anti-Chinese organizations warned that African Americans were using cocaine and heroin in increasing numbers and that the "cocaine-crazed Negro brain" and the "Negro cocaine fiends" posed a threat to the white women of the South.

The first federal criminal law punishing the non-medical use of drugs was the Harrison Narcotics Tax Act of 1914. The law regulated opium, morphine, cocaine, and their derivatives. The U.S. Congress drafted the law as a tax measure. Doctors, in return for paying a dollar, were authorized to prescribe these drugs. An individual who obtained narcotics outside of the health care system was subject to a criminal penalty of up to five years in prison and a $5,000 fine. In 1919, the U.S. Supreme Court held that the Harrison Act was a valid exercise of the federal government's authority to raise revenues. That same year, the Court determined that prescribing drugs for narcotics addicts "maintained" their drug habit rather than medically treated it. As a consequence, the Court held that doctors were not authorized under the act to prescribe drugs to narcotics addicts. The result of the decision was that narcotics addicts were "driven underground" and could only obtain drugs on the criminal black market. Within a short period of time, narcotic addicts comprised roughly 40 percent of inmates in federal prisons (Provine 2007: 63–90).

Marijuana or hemp was raised in the United States and initially was used as fiber for the manufacture of rope and as an ingredient of medicine. Marijuana (cannabis), in other parts of the world, was a source of recreation and relaxation, and by the twentieth century, marijuana had become an accepted part of the recreational drug culture in the United States. Following the repeal of the prohibition of alcohol in 1933, federal and state authorities turned their attention to curbing the use of marijuana. Prohibitionists identified marijuana use with Mexican workers and farm laborers, who in the 1930s were blamed for taking jobs from Americans.

By 1937, forty-six states prohibited the growing, possession, use, and sale of cannabis. The Marihuana Tax Act of 1937 placed a tax of $100 an ounce on anyone who dealt commercially with cannabis, hemp, or marijuana. A failure to pay the tax was punishable by five years in prison and a $2,000 fine. An individual who paid the tax confronted the catch-22 that he or she would be prosecuted for violation of state criminal laws prohibiting growing, possession, use, and/or sale of marijuana (Provine 2007: 81–86).

The next step was the criminalization of heroin. In the 1950s, Harry Anslinger, first head of the Federal Bureau of Narcotics, warned that Communist China was waging chemical warfare by addicting U.S. servicemen in Korea and in Japan. Government officials warned that drug peddlers threatened to spread heroin to African Americans and then to the white middle class. The 1951 Boggs Act and the 1956 Narcotic Control Act imposed imprisonment for the first offense of possession of heroin and the death penalty for selling heroin to minors (Provine 2007: 86–87).

The movement for criminalization of alcohol and narcotics identified the use of intoxicants with immigrants and minorities and warned that these substances inevitably would spread to the white middle class. This same pattern of the "racialization" of narcotics was followed in the movement for criminalization of cocaine (Provine 2007: 85).

In the past three decades, crack cocaine has become the center of anti-narcotics policy in the United States. Cocaine is an addictive stimulant drug. The powdered hydrochloride salt form of cocaine typically is snorted or dissolved in water and injected. **Crack cocaine** is produced by cooking cocaine powder with baking soda and water. This forms cocaine rocks. "Crack" refers to the crackling sound produced by the rock as it is heated by a user in preparation for smoking the rock. Powder cocaine is sniffed or injected, while crack, when mixed with baking soda, can be smoked, which allows the drug to be delivered in an efficient and powerful fashion. Moments after smoking crack, individuals desperately desire another "exhilarating rush of 2 minutes and a half." This is the perfect commodity for consumers, inexpensive and immediate. Crack typically is sold in small, less expensive quantities and in open-air drug markets. Powder more often is sold in larger quantities and is not typically sold on the street. The low cost of crack is deceptive because the user quickly becomes addicted and will do whatever is required to maintain his or her habit. Philippe Bourgois, in his study of selling crack in the barrio, writes that crack cocaine created thousands of "mom-and-pop entrepreneurs." These immigrants had few economic options in a declining economy and embraced this "high profit, high retail crack business" (Bourgois 2003: 75).

Elijah Anderson in his study of "code of the street" finds that the ease of entering the drug trade attracts young men with limited economic alternatives. There also is the incentive of the "fast life" and the status of a powerful drug dealer. Many of the young men drawn into the drug trade become addicted. It is a violent lifestyle. The intense nature of crack cocaine addiction drives users into violent behavior, a violence that is encouraged by the need to feed their habit. The competition for customers, turf wars, retribution against individuals who have failed to pay, and inevitable misunderstandings all contribute to a culture of violence (Anderson 1999: 114–121).

In 1980, the drug issue took on a higher profile with the election of President Ronald Reagan. First Lady Nancy Reagan urged young people to "just say no" to narcotics. Crack cocaine was the symbol of the Reagan administration's campaign to "get tough on drugs." The administration argued the war on drugs possessed an added urgency because the sale and distribution of crack supported the criminal activities of African American and Hispanic street gangs. In 1986, President Reagan signed the $1.7 billion Drug-Free America Act. The president's drug czar, William Bennett, endorsed doubling the capacity of federal prisons in order to house dealers and users (Provine 2007: 105).

The crack issue fully registered in the minds of Americans with the tragic deaths in the spring of 1986 of University of Maryland basketball star Len Bias and of Cleveland Browns football player Don Rogers. The media turned its spotlight on what was described as an avalanche of drug-induced violence.

In September 1989, President George H. W. Bush in his first national televised address called crack cocaine the "most pressing problem facing the nation." He held up a bag of cocaine that he stated had been purchased in Lafayette Park across from the White House. Undercover federal agents initially had not been able to find anyone selling cocaine in the park. They resorted to arranging to drive 18-year-old Keith Timothy Jackson to the park with the promise that he would be paid $2,400 for cocaine. Following President Bush's address, 64 percent of individuals in a poll identified drug abuse as the most important problem confronting the country. A year earlier, only 1 percent of respondents labeled illegal narcotics as the single most important issue in America (Provine 2007: 108).

Congress responded to the alleged narcotics crisis by passing the 1986 Anti-Drug Abuse Act. The act created a two-tier system of punishment for cocaine. The punishment was based on the amount of narcotics seized at the time of an individual's arrest. Possession of five grams of crack cocaine by a first offender was punishable by a mandatory minimum term of five years in federal prison; possessing fifty grams of crack cocaine was punishable by a ten-year term. The sentence for crack cocaine is one hundred times longer than the prison term for a comparable amount of powder cocaine. The penalty for the possession of crack cocaine was much greater than the possession of a comparable amount of any other unlawful narcotic. Individuals convicted of drug offenses were ineligible for public housing or for federal benefits such as student loans (Provine 2007: 106–119). A number of states adopted their drug laws along the lines of the federal pattern although the ratio between crack and powder cocaine generally was not as severe as the hundred-to-one federal ratio (Provine 2007: 120).

Provine notes that during the debate on the law punishing crack cocaine, the drug was linked to young African American males. The thinking behind the law was that crack is sold in small, relatively inexpensive amounts on the street, ravages communities, and leads to street violence between street gangs competing for control of the drug trade. The law was criticized for resulting in the disproportionate arrest and imprisonment of African Americans for lengthy prison terms while Caucasian sellers and users of powder cocaine received much less severe prison terms.

Supporters of the law predicted that if not combated, crack cocaine would spread into the suburbs and place white teenagers at risk. Provine describes the emotional campaign against crack cocaine as a "moral panic." She writes that crack was transformed into a "folk devil" that was blamed for crime, educational failure, and poverty. Between 1987 and 1998, the U.S. budget for combating drug abuse rose from $6 billion to $20 billion. Two-thirds of this total went to law enforcement and to prisons, and one-third was directed at treatment (Provine 2007: 110, 117–119).

The Fair Sentencing Act of 2010 constituted a major reform of U.S. narcotics laws. The sentencing reform law reduced the hundred-to-one ratio between crack and powder cocaine to an eighteen-to-one ratio. It is estimated the new law will reduce sentences for crack-cocaine-related offenses by an average of twenty-seven months in prison and save the federal government $42 million during the following five years. In June 2012, the Supreme Court held that the new more lenient penalty provisions apply to offenders who committed a crack cocaine offense before the law went into effect and are sentenced after the date that the law went into effect. The Court reasoned that sentencing these offenders under the old sentencing scheme would "seriously undermine . . . uniformity and proportionality in sentencing" (*Dorsey v. United States*, 567 U.S. ___ [2012]).

In August 2013, then attorney general Eric Holder announced an additional reduction in the federal sentencing of drug offenders. He stated that the United States has 5 percent of the world's population and 25 percent of the prison population. Federal prisons house roughly 219,000 inmates, one-half of whom are incarcerated for narcotics-related crimes. Federal institutions are 40 percent over capacity and cost $80 billion per year. Attorney General Holder observed that "too many Americans go to too many prisons for far too long and for no good law enforcement reason. . . . Although incarceration has a role . . . widespread incarceration . . . is ineffective and unsustainable" (Savage 2013: A1).

Attorney General Holder stated the Justice Department would look to state courts to handle more cases, implement drug treatment programs as an alternative to incarceration, and expand "compassionate release" for nonviolent elderly inmates who have completed a significant portion of their sentence.

In terms of drug prosecutions, Holder instructed local prosecutors that they should not write the specific quantity of drugs in the indictment of drug offenders who meet four criteria: their crime did not involve violence, the use of a weapon, or a sale to minors; they are not leaders of a criminal organization; they have no significant ties to large-scale gangs or cartels; and they have no significant criminal history. In other words, the indictment would state that the defendant conspired to distribute cocaine without specifying the quantity of the drugs. The quantity would remain a factor for the judge to consider at sentencing. Sentencing would be returned to judges and to some extent prosecutors rather than being based on the length specified in the statute or sentencing guidelines. Attorney General Holder noted states like Texas, New York, Colorado, Michigan, and Arkansas already had undertaken reform of drug prosecutions and realized that "we cannot simply prosecute or incarcerate our way to becoming a safer nation." In April 2014, Attorney General Holder announced that nonviolent felons who had served at least ten years and would have received a lesser sentence under current reformed federal laws would be considered for clemency.

Drug sentencing policies, according to then attorney general Holder, have created a "vicious cycle of poverty, criminality and incarceration" that traps "many Americans" and weakens communities. The federal system contains roughly 14 percent of the nation's prison population, and absent reform at the state level, there likely will be no significant change in the treatment of narcotics offenders.

In 2017, Attorney General Jeff Sessions reversed Holder's policy toward the prosecution of criminal defendants and instructed federal prosecutors to seek the harshest criminal charges and sentences that are supported by the evidence. Attorney General Sessions argued that drug trafficking is associated with violent crimes and other types of criminal activity and that the aggressive prosecution of narcotics offenses will reduce the crime rate. Sessions also expressed opposition to any move toward sentencing reform (Ruiz 2017).

Mass Incarceration and Crack Cocaine

Mandatory minimum sentences for drug offenders are identified as the cause of what has been termed *mass imprisonment* or **mass incarceration** (Gottschalk 2015). During the past thirty years, the U.S. prison population has exploded from three hundred thousand to more than one and a half million. Roughly a half-million people are in prison or jail for narcotics offenses as compared to forty-one thousand in 1980. Drug arrests have tripled since 1980; more than thirty-one million individuals have been arrested since the initiation of the war on drugs (Alexander 2010: 59).

The United States has the highest rate of incarceration in the world and "dwarfs" the rates in Russia, China, and Iran. In the United States, the rate is roughly eight times that in Germany (discussed in Chapter 9). The U.S. incarceration rate is significantly greater than the incarceration rate in countries with comparable crime rates and is six to ten times greater than that of other industrialized countries. Alexander writes that by the end of 2007, more than seven million Americans (one in every thirty-one adults) were in prison, on probation, or on parole (Alexander 2010: 6, 8, 59).

Jonathan Simon states that mass incarceration in the United States has the following characteristics (J. Simon 2007: 141–175):

Scale. The present trend will result in one in fifteen Americans born in 2001 serving time in prison (6.6 percent of the birth cohort).

Selective incarceration. Based on current trends, one in three African American men, one in seven Hispanic men, and one in seventeen white men will spend time in prison. The statistical odds of an African American man going to prison are greater than the odds that he will obtain a college degree, marry, or serve time in the military.

Drugs. Bruce Western writes that 45 percent of the increase in the state prison population is explained by the incarceration of narcotics offenders. He notes that African American young men are no more likely than white young men to use drugs and yet are more likely to be arrested and go to prison for drug offenses (Western 2006: 50).

Warehousing. Jonathan Simon characterizes prisons as based on a model of waste management. Financial resources do not allow for adequate recreational or treatment programs for inmates. The purpose of the supermax prison is to incapacitate offenders and deter crime rather than to rehabilitate offenders. The emphasis, up until recently, has been on building larger institutions to house the growing prison population (J. Simon 2007).

Zero tolerance. The discretion of judges to sentence defendants based on their individual characteristics has given way to a system of mandatory minimum sentencing. The system of parole and release of offenders who have been "rehabilitated" has been replaced by a system in which inmates serve at least 85 percent of their sentence.

The courts have stepped aside and imposed few if any restraints on the legislative power to fix sentences for drug offenses. In 1982, in *Hutto v. Davis*, the U.S. Supreme Court held that a prison sentence of forty years for possession of and attempt to sell nine ounces of marijuana was not disproportionate to the offense (*Hutto v. Davis*, 454 U.S. 370 [1982]). This was followed by *Harmelin v. Michigan* in which the Supreme Court affirmed a sentence of life imprisonment for a first-time offender who sold 672 grams of crack cocaine (*Harmelin v. Michigan*, 501 U.S. 957 [1991]). A third sentencing case is *Ewing v. California*. In *Ewing*, the Supreme Court upheld a sentence of twenty-five years to life for an offender with two previous burglary convictions who was convicted of the grand theft of three golf clubs, each of which was worth roughly $400. Under the California "three strikes and you're out" law, Ewing would be eligible for parole after twenty-five years. The Court majority found that California's response was not disproportionate to the threat posed to public safety by the recidivism of offenders (*Ewing v. California*, 538 U.S. 11 [2003]). Despite judicial acceptance of these mandatory minimum sentences, judges have expressed significant dissatisfaction over being compelled to hand down harsh sentences to low-level drug offenders (Alexander 2010: 91).

Race and Crack Cocaine

Alexander argues that following the successful struggle for racial integration and civil rights, conservative politicians turned to the issues of race and crime to attract support from white working-class voters. She contends our image of crime, especially drug crimes, is "racialized." In one study involving a video game, individuals were shown photos of white and African American individuals holding either a gun or another object (such as a wallet, can, or cell phone). Participants were more likely to mistake an African American as armed and to mistake a Caucasian as unarmed. African Americans demonstrated the same amount of "shooter bias" as whites (Alexander 2010: 42–44, 104).

A 2002 study in Seattle concluded the police pursued a "racialized" conception of drug use that targeted African Americans and Hispanics and largely ignored crack cocaine use by whites. The police focused their counter-narcotics efforts on crack cocaine, the one drug market in Seattle that was dominated by African American traffickers and did not expend the same resources on open-air drug markets in white areas. African American dealers were more likely to be arrested than white dealers even when dealers of both races were present at the same location. Despite police concentration on open-air drug markets, police records indicate citizen complaints regarding drug activity focused on drug houses rather than on street sales. The police conceded that there were drugs other than crack that were associated with higher levels of violence and deaths from overdose (Beckett and Bowen 2005; Beckett, Nyrop, and Pfingst 2006).

The same pattern of racialized enforcement is evident in the enforcement of laws prohibiting marijuana, a drug that is prevalent among all racial groups and is highest among whites. In California, there were 850,000 arrests for marijuana between 1990 and 2009 and a half-million between 2000 and 2009. Seven times more African Americans were arrested than whites. In Los Angeles, the average arrest rate per 100,000 African Americans between 2006 and 2008 was 523, and the arrest rate per 100,000 whites was 73. In San Diego, an average of 835 African Americans were arrested per 100,000 between 2006 and 2008, and the arrest rate per 100,000 whites was 145. The same pattern is found in cities throughout the country (Levine, Gettman, and Siegel 2010).

The American Civil Liberties Union and Human Rights Watch in 2016 published a report on narcotics enforcement. In 2015, the police made 13.6 percent more arrests for possession of small amounts of marijuana for personal possession than for all violent crimes combined. Four times as many people were arrested for possessing drugs as for selling them. Fifty percent of those charged with possession were charged with possessing marijuana for personal use.

According to the report, the rate of drug use by African American adults is similar to or even lower than the rate of drug use by white adults. African Americans, however, are more than two-and-a-half times more likely to be arrested for drug possession and nearly four times more likely to be arrested for simple marijuana possession. The racial disparities were six to one in Montana, Iowa, and Vermont. In Manhattan, African Americans are nearly eleven times as likely as whites to be arrested for drug possession (Stauffer 2016). Federal judges have sentenced fifty-four people to life without parole for marijuana crimes since 1996 (Schatz 2015).

Alexander writes that in major cities, as many as 80 percent of young African American men have criminal records and form an "undercaste" that is "locked out" of mainstream society (Alexander 2010: 7). African American men born in the late 1960s were more likely in 1999 to have spent time in a penitentiary than to have graduated from college or to have served in the military, and African American males with little schooling were more likely to be in prison or jail than in a labor union or enrolled in a government welfare or training program. Western studied a two-block area in the District of Columbia and documented that in a twelve-month period, 64 African American men were arrested for narcotics violations, and 120 received prison sentences (Western 2006: 31, 38).

The African American prison population grew at a rapid rate as a result of the war on drugs. The proportion of African Americans in state prisons grew from 7 percent in 1986 to 25 percent in 1991. Between 1980 and 1999, the overall incarceration rate in federal prison of African Americans tripled from 1,156 per 100,000 to 3,620 per 100,000. The racial difference in the length of federal sentences for African Americans and whites, "largely because of the new crack law," widened from 11 percent in 1986 to 49 percent in 1990. The difference in the length of sentence between African Americans and whites for other drug offenses grew from 6 percent in 1984 to 93 percent in 1990 (Provine 2007: 127).

The major burden of the differential treatment of crack cocaine and powder cocaine has been borne by African Americans. A survey found that 95 percent of respondents, when asked to close their eyes and describe a drug user, identified an African American. Yet African Americans comprise only 15 percent of drug users. Studies find that 65 percent of individuals who report using cocaine during their lifetime are white, 26 percent are African American, and 9 percent are Hispanic (Provine 2007: 127). Alexander notes that white students use cocaine at seven times the rate of African American students, use crack cocaine at eight times the rate of African American students, and use heroin at seven times the rate of African American students. The same percentage of white and African American students use marijuana. Studies also indicate that individuals tend to buy drugs from individuals of their own race (Alexander 2010: 96–97, 103).

A hidden impact of the war on drugs is that felony convictions carry significant disabilities. Individuals convicted of felony drug offenses are barred from public housing, ineligible for food stamps and student loans, discriminated against in employment, denied licenses for a wide range of professions, and in many states are ineligible to vote. Individuals who are released on parole or who receive probation rather than prison also must adhere to a range of rules (e.g., a prohibition on associating with other felons, passing drug tests), which, if violated, result in imprisonment. Roughly one-third of individuals admitted to prison are incarcerated as a result of parole violations rather than because of a new criminal conviction (Alexander 2010: 93; Pager 2007; Western 2006).

An important point that often is overlooked is that prosecutors have exercised their discretion to plea bargain the sentence of whites while pursuing the prosecution of African Americans. A study of defendants eligible for a mandatory minimum sentence found that African Americans were 21 percent more likely and Hispanic offenders were 28 percent more likely than white offenders to receive at least a minimum sentence (Provine 2007: 128).

The Supreme Court has decided two cases that have largely shut the door on defendants challenging what they argue is the discriminatory application of narcotics laws. In *United States v. Armstrong*, four African American defendants were arrested for conspiracy to distribute more than fifty grams of crack cocaine. The public defenders assigned to the case realized that of the fifty-three crack cocaine cases handled by their office over the past three years, forty-eight of the defendants were African American, and five were Hispanic. Yet the defenders were aware that most crack cocaine users were white and suspected the defendants were being diverted to the state system where the penalties were less severe.

The lawyers asked for a court order allowing them to inspect the files of prosecutors and submitted sworn affidavits (statements) from a halfway house intake coordinator stating that, in his experience, both whites and African Americans were fully represented among users of crack cocaine. A defense attorney testified that as a matter of policy, non-African American defendants were prosecuted in state rather than in federal court.

The Supreme Court held that Armstrong failed to identify similarly situated white defendants whom federal prosecutors had failed to charge with possession of crack cocaine. The Court stressed that prosecutors exercise almost complete discretion in bringing criminal charges. Armstrong, in order to obtain an order of "discovery" for the material in the prosecutors' files, was required to demonstrate some evidence that prosecutors' charging decisions were motivated by a discriminatory intent and that there was a pattern of "selective prosecution." The catch-22 is that Armstrong was required to produce the names of white defendants whom prosecutors had decided not to prosecute in federal court for possession of crack cocaine, the very information Armstrong sought to obtain from the government's files (*United States v. Armstrong*, 517 U.S. 456 [1996]). Alexander concludes that the decision in *Armstrong* makes it practically impossible to challenge prosecutorial decision-making on the grounds of racial bias (Alexander 2010: 114–115).

The Supreme Court also has created a high barrier for defendants to overcome to successfully challenge their prosecution and sentencing on the grounds of racial discrimination. The Court in *McCleskey v. Kemp* held that a defendant claiming that a prosecutor was motivated by racial discrimination in bringing criminal charges was required to demonstrate that the prosecutor acted with discriminatory intent. McCleskey had been convicted of killing a police officer and received a sentence of death. He claimed the sentence was influenced by racial bias and submitted a sophisticated statistical study of two thousand murder cases in Georgia conducted by David Baldus. The Baldus study, after taking thirty-five nonracial factors into account, found that defendants charged with the death of white victims were 4.3 times more likely to receive capital punishment than defendants charged with killing African American victims. Georgia prosecutors sought the death penalty in 70 percent of cases involving African American defendants and white victims and in 19 percent of cases involving white defendants and African American victims (*McCleskey v. Kemp*, 481 U.S. 279 [1987]).

The Supreme Court held that McCleskey was required to establish in his specific case that either the prosecutor or the jury acted on the basis of a racially biased intent. The statistical pattern that suggested the death penalty was being imposed in a racially discriminatory fashion was not sufficient to establish discrimination because the data reflected the decisions of prosecutors and juries throughout the state of Georgia who had made a decision on a number of cases, each of which involved a range of factors that needed to be weighed and balanced. Naomi Murakawa and Katherine Beckett argue that the requirement that defendants challenging their conviction based on racial discrimination demonstrate that their conviction was based on a racially discriminatory intent has made it virtually impossible for defendants to raise claims based on race (Murakawa and Beckett 2010). A close reading of *McCleskey* suggests that although the judgment addressed the death penalty, the Supreme Court was concerned that African American, Hispanic, and female defendants convicted of non-capital offenses would claim that their convictions and sentences were racially biased. The Court in *McCleskey* concluded that based on the evidence presented at trial, the risk of racial discrimination was "constitutionally acceptable."

Alexander points to the case of Edward Clary to illustrate the impact of *McCleskey* on African American defendants. Eighteen-year-old Clary was persuaded by friends in California to take some narcotics back home to St. Louis. He was stopped and searched at the airport and arrested for possession of more than fifty grams of cocaine, which triggered a five-year prison sentence. The same sentence for possession of powder cocaine required the possession of five thousand grams of powder cocaine. Clary's lawyer argued that 93 percent of defendants convicted at the time for possession of crack cocaine were African American and that African Americans were being treated unequally as compared to individuals convicted of possession of powder cocaine. This argument was embraced by federal district court judge Clyde Cahill, who declared that the hundred-to-one ratio was discriminatory. He held that the "presumption of innocence was a legal myth" and the sentencing scheme "reeks with inhumanity and injustice," and if white males were "being incarcerated at the same rate as young black males, the statute would have been amended long ago." Judge Cahill proclaimed that the law was based on a "lynch mob" mentality inspired by a fear of young African American males shaped by a media image of African American males as violent and dangerous. He sentenced Clary to the sentence that he would have received had Clary been convicted of possession of powder cocaine. The Eighth Circuit Court of Appeals reversed Judge Cahill and ordered Cahill to resentence Clary to ten years in prison (Alexander 2010: 109–112; *United States v. Clary*, 846 F.Supp.768 [E.D. Mo. 1994], reversed 97 F.3d 1457 [8th Cir. 1996]).

Alexander cites Chicago as an example of the impact of the war on drugs. Eighty percent of the African American adult male workforce in Chicago have a felony record. In the Chicago area, the number of individuals sent to prison annually for drug crimes increased from 469 in 1985 to 8,755 in 2005. Roughly 70 percent of African American men between ages 18 and 45 in the impoverished North Lawndale neighborhood are former offenders. The majority were convicted of drug offenses. There were 20,000 more African American males in the Illinois prison system in June 2001 than were enrolled in public universities in Illinois. In 1999, 992 African American males received a bachelor's degree from an Illinois state university as compared to the 7,000 African American males released from prison for drug offenses the following year (Alexander 2010: 184–185, 191).

In 2016, federal district court judge Frederic Block sentenced Chevelle Nesbeth, who was charged with drug smuggling, to probation rather than convict her of a felony, explaining that the collateral consequences of a felony conviction "served no useful purpose." Judge Block noted the "disastrous consequences, such as losing child custody or going homeless," which lead to individuals "becoming recidivists and restarting the criminal cycle" (Weiser 2016a).

In December 2013, President Obama commuted the sentences of eight federal prisoners convicted of crack cocaine offenses. All of these individuals were serving sentences of at least fifteen years in prison; two were sentenced to life imprisonment. President Obama noted that the inmates would have received significantly shorter sentences under current, reformed drug laws and already would have completed their sentences. Clarence Aaron, for example, was sentenced to three life terms for a drug crime committed when he was 22 years old. Stephanie George received a life sentence in 1997 at age 27 based on allowing her boyfriend to store a box of crack in her home. By the time he left office, President Obama had granted clemency to a total of 1,927 mostly non-violent drug offenders, a figure that includes 1,715 commutations and 212 pardons.

11.3 YOU DECIDE

Between 2013 and 2016, legislation was introduced in as many as twenty-four states that limited access to restrooms, locker rooms, and other sex-segregated facilities on the "basis of a definition of sex or gender consistent with sex assigned at birth" or "biological sex." The intent was to require transgender individuals to use the facilities that coincided with the assigned sex or gender on their birth certificate.

In February 2016, the Charlotte, North Carolina, City Council voted to prohibit businesses from discriminating against gay or transgender individuals. At the time, there was no explicit federal or state law prohibiting discrimination against lesbian, gay, bisexual, and transgender individuals. The ordinance agreed with transgender individuals using the public bathroom designated for the gender with which they identified rather than the gender on their birth certificate.

In March 2016, the North Carolina State Senate passed the Public Facilities Privacy and Security Act, also known as HB2, prohibiting Charlotte and other state municipalities from adopting their own anti-discrimination ordinances and taking the additional step of passing a so-called bathroom bill. The federal government informed North Carolina that HB2 was in conflict with the U.S. Department of Education and U.S. Department of Justice guidelines for schools' obligations under Title IX of the Education Amendments of 1972 prohibiting sex discrimination by schools and universities. The federal directives issued on May 13, 2016, do not carry the force of law and are an interpretation of Title IX. The directive advises that an educational institution receiving federal funds "must not treat a transgender student differently from the way it treats other students of the same gender identity" and is to provide "transgender students access to sex-segregated activities and facilities consistent with their gender identity." Schools are obliged to provide

transgender students "equal access to educational programs and activities even in circumstances in which other students, parents or community members raise objections or concerns." Gender identity in the federal guidelines is defined as "an individual's internal sense of gender," and notes that "a person's gender identity may be different from or the same as the person's sex assigned at birth."

North Carolina Republican governor Pat McCrory proclaimed that the state would not be "bullied" by the federal government. He argued that establishing separate bathrooms for men and for women based on their identity at birth does not constitute unlawful discrimination under Title IX. Governor McCrory noted that if Congress wanted to protect transgender individuals, it should explicitly include this language in Title IX rather than relying on the Department of Education's interpretation of the law. The federal directive, according to Governor McCrory, violated the right to privacy of individuals who would be required to reveal intimate portions of their anatomy to transgender individuals who in many instances possessed different "body parts." Governor McCrory also argued that the definition of a transgender individual was hopelessly unclear. He asked who decides who is a man and who is a woman? Is this purely a matter of self-definition? Does this require a certain number of years of hormone therapy? Sex reassignment surgery? The failure to define *transgender* opened the door to predators pretending to be transgender gaining access to bathrooms and placed children at risk.

Advocates for transgender individuals responded that compelling transgender individuals to use bathrooms based on their assigned sex or gender exposes them to harassment, intimidation, and violence. The claim that predators will take advantage of the law to commit

(Continued)

(Continued)

sexual assaults or that transgender individuals will commit sexual assaults against children has no basis in fact and is an effort to promote fear and apprehension.

Following passage of the "bathroom bill," Bruce Springsteen canceled a concert in protest, the National Basketball Association withdrew the all-star game from Charlotte, and the National Collegiate Athletic Association announced that NCAA-sponsored events would not be held in North Carolina. PayPal canceled plans to expand its offices in Charlotte, and the chief executives of Apple, Google, Hilton, and Starbucks wrote an open letter to Governor McCrory criticizing the bathroom bill. Various groups canceled conventions, and in aggregate, North Carolina lost over $400 million in spending and investment.

In April 2016, the federal government filed a legal action alleging that the North Carolina law violated the civil rights of transgender individuals. Attorney General Loretta E. Lynch, who was raised in North Carolina, compared the law to the Jim Crow laws intended to maintain a segregated society. The Obama White House termed the bathroom bill "mean spirited." North Carolina and nine

states in a separate legal action claimed that the federal government had unreasonably interpreted the prohibition on sex discrimination in Title IX and that the federal guidelines represented "unlawful federal expansionism."

The Trump administration in February 2017 reversed the Obama administration's position and issued a letter from the Departments of Justice and Education stating that Title IX did not protect access to bathrooms for transgender students. This was a matter to be decided by states and local school boards. The letter did clearly state that schools must ensure that students are able to learn in a safe and secure environment.

In the November 2016 gubernatorial contest, North Carolina attorney general Roy Cooper defeated Governor McCrory by ten thousand out of four million votes cast. McCrory became the first North Carolina governor ever to lose reelection. In March 2017, the Republican-dominated North Carolina legislature adopted a compromise measure repealing the bathroom bill.

What is your view of the North Carolina bathroom bill?

■ HATE CRIMES

The Civil Rights Act of 1968, 18 U.S.C. § 245, authorizes federal prosecution of any person who "willingly injures, intimidates or interferes with another person or attempts to do so, by force because of the other person's race, color, religion or national origin." Individuals violating the law confront a fine or imprisonment of up to one year, or both. A sentence of life imprisonment is provided for kidnapping, sexual assault, or murder. In 1994, the Violent Crime Control and Law Enforcement Act expanded the law to include disability.

On October 18, 2009, President Obama signed the Matthew Shepard and James Byrd Jr. Hate Crimes Prevention Act, expanding U.S. federal hate crime law to offenses targeting individuals because of their "actual or perceived" gender, sexual orientation, gender identity, and disability. The act eliminated the requirement in the 1968 law that victims are engaged in a federally protected activity such as voting.

The Hate Crime Statistics Act of 1990, 28 U.S.C. § 534, requires the attorney general to collect data on "hate crimes" committed because of a victim's race, religion, disability, sexual orientation, or ethnicity. In 1997, statistics began to be recorded based on disability.

Forty-five states and the District of Columbia have **hate crimes** statutes. State statutes cover crimes motivated by race, religion, and ethnicity; thirty-two cover disability, thirty-one extend protection to sexual orientation, twenty-eight include gender, sixteen encompass transgender/gender identity, thirteen include age, five include political affiliation, and three and the District of Columbia extend protection to homelessness. Roughly thirty states and the District of Columbia provide for a civil cause of action in addition to criminal liability. Twenty-seven states and the District of Columbia require the collection of hate crimes statistics.

In *Wisconsin v. Mitchell*, the U.S. Supreme Court affirmed Todd Mitchell's conviction for racially motivated aggravated battery. Aggravated battery ordinarily is punished by a maximum of two years in prison in Wisconsin, and the sentence was enhanced to seven years when committed as part of a hate crime. The Court held that Wisconsin possessed a compelling interest in enhancing the punishment for bias-motivated crimes because these offenses were associated with "negative secondary effects." These negative effects include the provocation of retaliation, the infliction of emotional harm on the victim, and the incitement of unrest. The Court dismissed as speculative the contention that the prosecution of hate crimes would suppress freedom of expression, explaining it was unlikely that a defendant would refrain from expressing discriminatory views because the statements might be introduced at a later trial to establish the requisite intent for a hate crime (*Wisconsin v. Mitchell*, 508 U.S. 476 [1993]).

In 1998, Matthew Shepard, a 21-year-old openly gay student at the University of Wyoming, met two men in a bar who offered him a ride home. They robbed Shepard, brutally beat and pistol-whipped him, tied him to a fence post, and left him to die in freezing temperatures. The defendants pled guilty in return for sentences of life in prison.

In the same year, James Byrd, a 49-year-old African American, was offered a ride from Shawn Berry (age 24), Lawrence Russell Brewer (age 31), and John King (age 23). Instead of taking Byrd home, the three men took Byrd to an isolated location, beat and urinated on him, chained Byrd to their pickup truck by the ankles, and dragged him while still alive for three miles. Byrd died after his right arm and head were severed from his body. They dumped Byrd's mutilated body in front of a church and went to a barbecue. Two of the men received the death penalty, and Berry was sentenced to life in prison.

Of the 5,818 hate crimes reported in 2015, roughly 59.2 percent were motivated by race/ethnicity/ancestry, 19.7 percent were based on religious bias, 17.7 percent were based on sexual orientation, 1.7 percent were motivated by gender identity bias, and 1.2 percent were motivated by disability bias. Of the 4,482 hate crime offenses categorized as crimes against persons, intimidation accounted for 41.3 percent of these offenses, 37.8 percent involved simple assault, and 19.7 percent involved aggravated assault. There were over 2,300 hate crimes offenses classified as crimes against property. Caucasians constituted 48.4 percent of offenders, and African Americans constituted 24.3 percent of offenders.

The federal sentencing guidelines punish hate crimes more severely than the same crime committed without a discriminatory intent. An aggravated assault ordinarily is punished by eighteen to twenty-four months in prison, but when committed as a hate crime, it is punished by twenty-seven to thirty-three months in prison. State statutes enhance the punishment of hate crimes by as much as twice the normal sentencing range.

In January 2017, Dylann Roof was sentenced to death in a federal court for the murder of nine African Americans engaged in prayer at the historic Emanuel African Methodist Episcopal Church in Charleston, South Carolina (Blinder and Sack 2017). Hate returned to the national agenda in the first few months of 2017 when Jewish community centers across the country received bomb threats and historic Jewish cemeteries in St. Louis, Missouri, and in Philadelphia, Pennsylvania, were vandalized. This was followed by the fatal shootings of two Indian men in Overland Park, Kansas.

In 2017, Joshua Vallum became the first defendant convicted under the federal Hate Crimes Act for killing a transgender person and was sentenced to forty-nine years in prison (Stack 2017).

Why not punish the crime of assault or kidnapping rather than punish the hate crime of assault or the hate crime of kidnapping? Should the law enhance the punishment for hate crimes beyond the punishment that ordinarily is provided for the crime? In the next section, we look at race and immigration law.

11.4 YOU DECIDE

The Washington Redskins football franchise is valued at $2.8 billion and is the third most valuable National Football League (NFL) franchise, the eighth most valuable sports franchise in the world. The team moved to Washington, D.C., from Boston in 1937 and has been embraced as a beloved part of the city. Controversy swirled around the team's racial policies in the early 1960s. The federal government warned the original owner, George Preston Marshall, that he should take steps to integrate the team, and in 1962, the Redskins became the last NFL franchise to have an African American player.

Over the last twenty-five years, Native American groups have protested against the team's use of the term *redskins* and have argued that the team should be denied federal trademark protection over the name, which these groups contend is a disparaging racial slur. A trademark is a property right that gives the holder of the trademark the exclusive right to use the trademark and to prevent others from using the mark and profiting from the history, tradition, use, and performance associated with the name. An organization that wanted to use "Washington Redskins" on a baseball hat or potato chips or as the name of its team would have to purchase a license from the Washington football club. The law allows the U.S. Patent and Trademark Office to deny protection to trademarks that "disparage . . . persons, living or dead, institutions, beliefs, or national symbols."

The claim is made by Native American activists that although the Washington football club is free to use the term *Washington Redskins*, the federal government should not in effect sponsor offensive speech by providing protection against other professional teams or businesses using the name on their merchandise or in their advertising.

The Washington football club responded that use of *redskins* is protected under the First Amendment to the U.S. Constitution. The notion of offensiveness is vague and subjective, and there are a number of registered trademarks that some individuals may view as offensive that refer to African Americans, Italians, Jews, Poles, and other groups. In a public letter, team owner Dan Snyder explained that the term *redskins* was adopted to honor Native Americans and that the team's current logo was designed in conjunction with the elders of the Navajo Nation.

In June 2014, the Trademark Trial and Appeal Board (TTAB) of the U.S. Patent and Trademark Office in response to a complaint filed by five Native American activists voted 2–1 to cancel six trademarks held by Washington Pro Football, Inc., on the grounds that the term *redskins* is disparaging to a "substantial" number of Native Americans and that this is evidenced "by the near complete drop-off in a usage of 'redskins' as a reference to Native Americans beginning in the 1960s." The TTAB noted as evidence of disparagement that the term *redskins* was used in books and movies when Native Americans were being portrayed as savages and barbaric.

Virginia federal district court judge Gerald B. Lee upheld the decision of the TTAB, finding that "the evidence before the Court supports the legal conclusion that . . . the Redskin [trademarks] consisted of matter that 'may disparage' a substantial [number] of Native Americans." Judge Lee also pointed to the fact that well-recognized dictionaries documented that the term *redskins* as far back as the eighteenth century was viewed as "often contemptuous." Lee stressed that while his decision denied Washington trademark protection, the team was free to use the name Washington Redskins and fans were free to purchase paraphernalia bearing the name.

Polls consistently have found strong support among Native Americans and among fans of the Washington football club for the team's continuing to use the name Redskins although the number of people supporting use of the name has significantly declined.

The challenge to the name Washington Redskins is part of a larger challenge to the use of Native American names and symbols by sports teams, which has led the National Collegiate Athletic Association to ban the use of Native American nicknames and logos by colleges absent agreement by Native American tribes.

The U.S. Supreme Court, while declining to review Judge Lee's decision regarding the Redskins, agreed to hear a case raising the issue of trademark protection for offensive speech brought by an Asian American ban seeking trademark protection for the name "The Slants." The Court held that it is a "bedrock principle" of the First Amendment that speech may not be "banned on the grounds that it expresses ideas that offend." This decision appears to provide federal trademark protection to the name *Washington Redskins*.

Should the Washington Redskins change the name of the team?

■ THE COLOR OF IMMIGRATION LAW

Critical race scholars from various ethnic and racial backgrounds have cautioned against "binary thinking," which views the racial divide as involving only whites and African Americans. They point to legal regulation of immigration as an example of laws that have singled out a number of minority groups for harsh treatment. Immigration policy is influenced by factors ranging from the economy to the need for workers to foreign policy. There also is the undeniable fact that, historically, immigration has been influenced by racial considerations (Delgado and Stefancic 2001).

Immigration law regulates the process through which individual residents abroad are authorized to enter and remain in the United States. Every country is a sovereign entity that possesses the legal authority to control its borders. In the United States, immigration and deportation are the responsibility of Immigration and Customs Enforcement (ICE) and Customs and Border Protection, which both are part of the Department of Homeland Security (DHS).

Individuals wishing to enter the United States apply for—and, if found to be eligible, receive—a visa from the American government that regulates the terms of their entry and residence. There are a number of visa categories. These include a visitor's visa for tourists, student visas, work visas, and resident visas. Individuals who receive a green card may work while in the United States. Asylum is a separate procedure that provides that individuals who confront persecution in their country of nationality may be granted residence in the United States based on humanitarian considerations. In some instances, the United States has recognized that individuals from countries that are experiencing internal violence and civil wars should be allowed to remain in America on a temporary basis.

In discussing immigration, we should not overlook that upwards of 645,000 Africans arrived in the United States and were forced into slavery. The African population in the United States by 1860 reached roughly 4 million.

Immigration has been subject to intense political disagreement and debate from the early years of the American Republic. On the one side were individuals who favored unlimited immigration into the country while the others questioned whether immigrants shared the country's democratic values and warned that too much diversity would introduce social tensions. Nearly three million individuals arrived in the United States between 1845 and 1854; this flood of immigrants from Scotland, France, Sweden, and Norway accounted for 15 percent of the American population. As the country's territory expanded as a result of the Louisiana Purchase and the Mexican American War, there was a need for new immigrants willing to settle in these territories and willing to work in the industries that powered the Industrial Revolution. By the late nineteenth century, a consensus emerged in favor of the continued immigration of northern and western Europeans into the United States (Tichenor 2002: 62, 70).

Strong opposition emerged to the immigration of southern and eastern Europeans. Opposition to these groups was based on a reservoir of anti-Catholic and anti-Semitic sentiment. European Jews in particular were viewed as genetically inferior and were thought to be at a lesser stage of intellectual and moral development (Higham 1974).

The conventional wisdom is that most immigrant groups, despite early opposition and prejudice, have been absorbed and assimilated into the American "melting pot." Lina Newton argues that the "straight line assimilation model" may not accurately capture the view of Americans toward Asians and Hispanics. Newton criticizes the failure to appreciate the contribution of these groups and argues that a combination of language, skin color, and broadly categorizing people from these regions as "all the same" has led to Asians and Hispanics being viewed as "permanently foreign" and as "unassimilable."

According to Newton, many Americans view Hispanics as temporary residents who are expected to return to Mexico after working in the United States for several years and do not view Hispanics as a permanent part of American society. Another narrative toward Hispanics identified by Newton is the "criminal alien," undocumented outsiders who are involved in crime and in the distribution of unlawful narcotics. Despite the diversity of Hispanics, they all are viewed as from "across the border," a region that, in the popular imagination, is identified with lawlessness and immorality.

Another false narrative is that Hispanic women cross the border to give birth so as to enable their babies to obtain American citizenship. The threat of "border babies" has motivated some politicians to advocate repeal of the Fourteenth Amendment to the Constitution, which establishes "citizenship by birth in the U.S." (Newton 2008: 22–41).

An extreme version of these various narratives is a controversial article in 2004 by the late Samuel Huntington of Harvard University. Huntington argued that Mexican Americans within the United States resist adopting the American work ethic, language, and culture; support returning portions of California and Texas to Mexico; and pose an internal threat to the country (Huntington 2004). Newton writes Hispanics, unlike European immigrant groups, are not given credit for having fought for the United States and are not recognized for their sacrifice and contribution to the building of America. The "word 'Mexican' in the United States is a negative; it automatically conjures a vision of something un-American, even menacing" (Newton 2008: 26).

The "negative narratives" about Hispanics and Asians are reflected in American immigration law. The immigration of Chinese workers in the nineteenth and early twentieth centuries elicited the same type of opposition that today is expressed toward Mexican immigration. Between 1850 and 1882, an estimated one-quarter of a million Chinese workers were recruited to build the American railroad system and to work in the mines and in agriculture. Labor unions in California blamed the

Chinese for depriving "white men" of jobs and for driving down wages. Politicians catered to this prejudice and denounced the Chinese as an inferior race associated with paganism, narcotics addiction, prostitution, polygamy, disease, and criminality. The Chinese were subject to special taxes, barred from California public schools, and prohibited from appearing as witnesses in court (Tichenor 2002: 87–196).

In 1882, the U.S. Congress passed the Chinese Exclusion Act. The act suspended Chinese immigration for ten years, prohibited the naturalization of Chinese immigrants, and provided that Chinese who left the United States required special reentry certificates. In 1884, Congress prohibited the entry of Chinese immigrants from the American territories of Hawaii and the Philippines and declared null and void the reentry certificates issued to Chinese immigrants (Tichenor 2002: 106–115).

PHOTO 11.3 The Chinese Exclusion Act of 1882 restricted Chinese immigration into the United States and denied basic freedoms to the Chinese in the United States. The drawing illustrates the type of ethnic stereotyping and discrimination practiced against the Chinese in the United States.

Calavita writes that a predominant theme in the congressional debate over the exclusion of the Chinese was the assertion that the Chinese were an inferior race incapable of assimilation into western society. American workers were at a disadvantage competing against these "insignificant, dwarfed, leathery little" men of the Orient "who could subsist on reduced rations and air." Congress was firm that the "purity and sweetness" of America's "national waters" were not to be "polluted by the mingling of its pure streams" with the "impure" of the Chinese. The Chinese Exclusion Act remained in effect until repealed in 1943 (Calavita 2010: 54–56).

During the 1880s, anti-Chinese riots took place in Denver, Wyoming, Seattle, Portland, and thirty-one California cities. In 1888, America entered into a treaty with China prohibiting Chinese entry into the United States for an additional twenty years. Congress followed this with legislation directed at Chinese aliens (non-citizens) living within the United States. Chinese who desired to remain in the country were required to obtain certificates of residence and were required to present a white male witness willing to swear that the Chinese applicant had lived in the United States before 1882. The Chinese also were required to carry a certificate of residence at all times (Tichenor 2002: 106–108).

The U.S. Supreme Court in a series of rulings recognized that Congress had complete authority over immigration and that the exercise of this power was not subject to judicial review by the courts. According to the Court, the presence of the Chinese in the United States was a privilege that could be revoked at the discretion of Congress. In 1889, Justice Stephen Field wrote, "[If Congress] considers the presence of foreigners of a different race in a country, who will not assimilate with us, to be dangerous to its peace and security . . . its determination is conclusive upon the judiciary" (*Chae Chan Ping v. United States,* 130 U.S. 581 [1889]).

Congress renewed the prohibition on Chinese immigration in 1902 and two years later declared a permanent ban on Chinese immigration. The Chinese population in the United States declined from 107,000 to 71,000 during the early years of the twentieth century although nine million Europeans were welcomed into the country. Six million of these new European immigrants were from the southern and eastern European countries of Italy, Russia, Hungary, and Greece. In 1910, President A. Lawrence Lowell of Harvard conceded that he had once thought the exclusion of the Chinese was "all wrong," although he now believed the exclusionary policy "preserved a beneficial homogeneity in American society" (Tichenor 2002: 114–120). In 1917, Congress adopted an "Asiatic barred zone" prohibiting immigration from Asia, India, and parts of Africa (Newton 2008: 12).

The Congress next turned its attention to the threat of continuing immigration of "inferior" Jewish, Italian, Greek, and Portuguese migrants. Highly questionable studies of newly arrived immigrants indicated that these "inferior" groups were of substandard intelligence and ability and did not share the outlook and civilization of the Swedish, Dutch, and German immigrants. In 1924, immigration was limited to 2 percent per year of each nationality already residing in the United States in 1890. This formula, along with the continuing prohibition on Asian immigration, resulted in 84 percent of new immigration coming from northern and western Europe (Tichenor 2002: 114–149).

The entry of Mexicans into the United States was unrestricted by quotas, although the Immigration Act of 1917 imposed a tax on entering Mexicans as well as a literacy test. The tax did not pose a barrier to entry because the U.S. Border Patrol lacked the resources to control the movement between the two countries.

The labor shortages caused by World War I led to the active recruitment of Mexican labor. In the early 1920s, Mexican workers comprised three-quarters of all California farmworkers, and in 1930, Mexican laborers picked 80 percent of the crops in the southwestern United States. It is estimated that as many as one million Mexicans migrated to the United States between 1910 and 1930. The workers lived in substandard conditions and the average wage was 38 cents an hour for men and 27 cents for women (the average wage in the United States in 1927 was 61 cents for men and 40 cents for women). There was no sick pay, workers compensation, or job security (Strum 2010: 4–9).

Despite the need for Mexican labor, the United States experienced periods of anti-Mexican agitation and policies. Large-scale unemployment during the depression fed resentment toward Mexican workers. Between 1929 and 1939, the U.S. government launched the Mexican Repatriation Program, and close to a million Mexicans were deported or forced to leave the United States. One-third of the entire Mexican population in the United States either were forced to leave or left voluntarily. It is estimated that 60 percent of these individuals were legal citizens (Strum 2010: 10).

In 1942, the agricultural labor shortage during World War II led to the United States and Mexico entering into a series of agreements for the importation of temporary contract labor into the United States. The program continued until 1964. A separate program assisted the railroads. In 1945, seventy-five thousand *braceros* ("arms") were building and maintaining railroad tracks, and fifty thousand *braceros* were working in agriculture. Despite assurances to the Mexican government that the *braceros* would receive the same wages and medical care as domestic workers, they generally were treated badly. In 1965, the Immigration and Nationality Act introduced a system of visas for Western Hemisphere immigrants and opened the door to Mexicans obtaining permanent residence status (Tichenor 2002: 167–174, 211–216).

The Bracero Program had limited impact in halting the flow of undocumented workers from Mexico, and western agricultural and ranching interests depended on undocumented workers and opposed a program of punishing employers. Although he supported the Bracero Program, President Dwight D. Eisenhower was convinced that undocumented workers lowered wages and placed a burden on American schools and public safety and medical care. In 1954, President Eisenhower launched Operation Wetback, a military-style operation in which thousands of Mexicans were deported and as many as five hundred thousand left voluntarily. Attorney General Herbert Brownell claimed the immigration sweeps were required to combat the "wetback invasion" (based on the notion that Mexican immigrants swim across the Rio Grande), which he asserted was responsible for disease, crime, and social instability. Federal agents combed Mexican neighborhoods in Los Angeles, detaining and asking Hispanics for identification, and raided factories in Chicago. The federal government reported they had broken the back of unlawful immigration (Tichenor 2002: 202).

The H-2A visa program currently provides for temporary agricultural workers to enter and work in the United States for a limited period of time. Employers are required to pay workers the minimum wage and provide adequate working conditions and housing. The H-2B visa program allows nonagricultural businesses to hire temporary workers. This program was used to bring workers from Mexico and Central America to the United States to work in New Orleans following Hurricane Katrina. American businesses complain that these programs do not provide a sufficient supply of workers and that they are forced to hire workers off the street, some of whom are in the United States unlawfully (Newton 2008: 50–51, 101).

President Ronald Reagan succeeded in persuading Congress to pass the Immigration Reform and Control Act of 1986. The act declared an amnesty for three million undocumented individuals who had entered the United States before January 1, 1982. In an effort to prevent additional unlawful immigration, the United States fortified the border. In 1993 and 1994, a combination of border patrol agents, stadium lighting, fencing, and tracking technology was introduced. A fence along vulnerable points on the border employs electronic sensors and other devices to detect individuals crossing into the United States from Mexico. The 1996 Illegal Immigration Reform and Immigrant Responsibility Act authorized $12 million to strengthen border defenses. In recent years, National Guard troops and drones and twenty-one thousand border patrol agents have been deployed at a cost of $18 billion to further strengthen border security. The United States has spent $132 billion since 2005 on border security. Roughly 58 percent of undocumented individuals attempting to cross the border are either apprehended or deterred from entering the United States. In contrast, in 2005, the apprehension rate was approximately 36 percent. The Department of Homeland Security calculates that the probability that a migrant will abandon efforts to cross the border due to stepped-up border enforcement increased from 11 percent in 2005 to 58 percent in 2015 (González 2016; Newton 2008: 56, 60; Tribune News Service 2016).

These steps, along with the declining U.S. economy and the modest strengthening of the Mexican economy, have significantly slowed but not halted the flow of undocumented workers into the

United States. Another factor is a policy of prosecuting repeat border crossers for illegal entry and reentry, which results in a minimum one-month imprisonment. In 1994, 1.5 million individuals were detained crossing the border. In 2012, the number of individuals detained dropped to 356,000 as a result of a decreased flow of undocumented individuals. In 2015, apprehensions fell to an all-time low of roughly 186,000 (González 2016).

The National Center for Border Security and Immigration of the University of Arizona finds that a majority of individuals detained at the border are low-skilled workers who lack economic opportunity in Mexico; most stated they will try again to cross the border. A government investigation of forty meatpacking plants in Nebraska found that 4,762 workers out of a workforce of 24,310 workers had Social Security numbers that did not match their names. A check of 1,700 workers in apple-packing sheds in the state of Washington resulted in finding 500 workers whose names did not match their Social Security number. The flow of immigration is the inevitable result of limited economic opportunity in Mexico. David Bacon points out that in the Mexican state of Oaxaca, only a third of the population have access to health care, the illiteracy rate is 21.8 percent, and the average educational level is 5.8 years. The monthly average income for non-governmental employees is less than $200 per family, which, according to Bacon, means that seventy-five thousand children are forced to work to help to support their families. The money that immigrants from Oaxaca send home from the United States is crucial to support their family and friends (Bacon 2008: 24–26, 146–147).

One consequence of the bolstering of border security is to force individuals to take risky routes into the United States. In 2011, 373 individuals died crossing the border; there were 477 deaths in 2012.

Arizona has been "ground zero" for debates on unlawful immigration in the United States for a number of years. There are an estimated eleven million "undocumented individuals" in the United States, and roughly 52 percent are immigrants from Mexico. It is estimated that the number of undocumented individuals in Arizona has increased five times over the past twenty years and that at present there are over 460,000 undocumented individuals in the state. Arizona shares a seven-hundred-mile border with Mexico, and it is the state with the most illegal crossings from Mexico into the United States and the highest number of arrests.

Arizona complained for a number of years that the state was bearing a heavy economic burden for schooling, health care, and public safety and that the federal government had not acted aggressively to limit the flow of immigration. Roughly 10 percent of adult workers in Arizona are undocumented and are concentrated in agriculture, construction, and low-wage service industries. An estimated 81 percent of undocumented individuals in Arizona are of Mexican origin. Undocumented adults and their children comprise a fifth of Arizonians living in poverty, a third of those without health insurance, and a sixth of school-age students (Francis 2010a).

On March 27, 2010, 58-year-old Robert Krentz was shot to death while working on his ranch, which was roughly nineteen miles from the Mexican border. The killing allegedly was committed by an individual entering from Mexico. In April 2010, Governor Jan K. Brewer of Arizona signed into law Senate Bill 1070, the Support Our Law Enforcement and Safe Neighborhood Act. The law was aimed at protecting Arizona from what was described as an influx of individuals "unlawfully in the U.S." from Mexico into Arizona. The law created a firestorm of protest, and the State of Arizona was criticized for enacting legislation authorizing racial profiling against Hispanics.

The Support Our Law Enforcement and Safe Neighborhood Act was a complicated and lengthy law that cannot be easily summarized. In 2012, in *Arizona v. United States*, the Supreme Court held that the Arizona law was unconstitutional because it interfered with federal jurisdiction over immigration (*Arizona v. United States*, 567 U.S. ___ [2012]). The main features of the Arizona law were as follows:

Reasonable suspicion. Police officers may determine an individual's immigration status during any lawful stop, detention, or arrest where reasonable suspicion exists that the person is unlawfully present in the United States. Reasonable suspicion is a fairly low standard of proof that may be roughly translated to mean in the neighborhood of 15 percent likelihood. This provision was not addressed by the Supreme Court and remains in effect.

Arrests. The police are to check the immigration status of individuals who are arrested to ensure that they are legally present in the United States before being released.

Documents. "Aliens" are required under federal law to register with the federal government and to carry their registration documents with them at all times. The Arizona law made it a misdemeanor punishable by a $100 fine and twenty days in jail to fail to possess a registration document. A second offense was punishable by thirty days. A police officer is to presume a person is lawfully present in the United States if he or she is able to present a valid Arizona driver's license, Native American tribal enrollment card, or other valid U.S. federal, state, or local form of identification that constitutes proof of citizenship.

Discrimination. Police officers are not permitted to consider, race, color, or national origin in enforcing the law.

Enforcement. Any citizen of Arizona may sue public officials to force them to fully enforce the law.

A public opinion poll by the Morrison Institute for Public Policy at Arizona State University indicated that 60 percent of Arizona voters support the law, and 23 percent oppose the law (Francis 2010b) although roughly the same percentage support a path to citizenship for undocumented individuals and another 15 percent favor providing individuals permanent residence without a path toward citizenship (Nevarez 2016). A national Gallup poll found 51 percent of the public favored the law and 39 percent were against the law (D. Wood 2010). The Pew Research Center for U.S. Politics and Policy indicated in a poll that 59 percent supported the law and 32 percent opposed the law (Pew Research Center 2010).

Critics alleged that the law encouraged the police to "racially profile" Hispanics. The police would be tempted to stop Hispanic drivers for minor traffic violations to determine whether they are lawfully in the United States. Hispanic citizens or lawfully present residents ran the risk of being stopped by the police and, in the event they did not possess the required identification, could find themselves in jail until they were able to establish their citizenship or lawful residence. Critics complained that "you could go out to pick up a pizza without any identification and find yourself arrested and jailed until you are able to demonstrate proof of citizenship or of lawful residence." There was particular objection to the requirement that American citizens and individuals lawfully in the United States were required to show their papers to the police, a requirement reminiscent of a "totalitarian police state."

President Felipe Calderón of Mexico, during a visit to the White House, condemned the law as a violation of human rights. Mexico issued a travel advisory warning its citizens that in traveling to Arizona they risked harassment and police interrogation. A poll conducted by the Pew Research Center for Hispanic Trends found that more than six in ten Hispanics in the United States reported that discrimination in schools is a "major problem," and nearly six in ten Hispanics believed that discrimination in the workplace is a "major problem." Thirty-six percent felt "immigration status" was the leading cause of discrimination, and 31 percent believed the debate over immigration had a negative impact. Seventy-five percent of Hispanics opposed the Arizona law, and 86 percent favored providing the roughly twelve million undocumented workers a path to citizenship (Lopez, Gonzalez-Barrera, and Motel 2011; Lopez, Morin, and Taylor 2010; Pew Research Center for Hispanic Trends 2012).

The State of Arizona explained that the law explicitly prohibited racial profiling and that the police would be trained to avoid discrimination against Hispanics. Arizona also pointed out that while the state had taken strong action against the "invasion of unlawful immigrants," only three states absorbed more refugees per capita: Arizona welcomed 4,700 refugees in 2009, almost twice as many refugees per capita as California and twice as many as New York (DeParle 2010).

On May 1, 2010, protests were held in seventy cities, and as many as sixty thousand people protested in Los Angeles. Protesters at the White House were arrested during a demonstration urging President Obama to work for immigration reform. Denver, Los Angeles, Oakland, San Francisco, and St. Paul (Minnesota) all announced they would ban business-related travel to Arizona and would halt all business with Arizona-based companies. Various professional groups decided that they would move their conventions to cities outside of Arizona. These protests sent a strong warning that a high economic price would be paid by states considering legislation similar to the Arizona law (Lacey 2010).

President Obama called the act misguided and warned that the law risked the arrest and harassment of Hispanics and might damage the relationship between the police and the public. Then attorney general Eric Holder announced that the Department of Justice would challenge the law in court.

In July 2010, federal district court judge Susan Bolton issued a preliminary injunction at the request of the Obama administration that prevented several sections of the law from being implemented pending a final legal judgment on the constitutionality of the law. An injunction is granted when the judge concludes that there is a strong likelihood that a law will be found to be unconstitutional. Judge Bolton explained immigration was a matter for the federal government rather than for state governments and that federal law is enforced by U.S. agencies. The Arizona law would impose a burden on the federal government by requiring the government to check into the immigration status of individuals arrested in Arizona. This inevitably would divert federal resources from other tasks (Archibold 2010).

In 2012, in *United States v. Arizona*, the U.S. Supreme Court struck down the Arizona law although it did not rule on the constitutionality of the "papers please provision." This is the portion of the law allowing police officers to request papers from individuals whom they have stopped and reasonably believe are unlawfully in the United States. However, in 2016, Arizona entered into an agreement with various civil rights groups establishing nonbinding guidelines for the police that prohibit racial profiling and extending the seizure of individuals solely to determine their immigration status.

Arizona is the most visible of the roughly thirty-five states and a number of localities that between 2005 and 2013 adopted three or more ordinances aimed at unlawful immigrants. None of these laws has survived a legal challenge (Provine et al. 2016: 44–45). Prince William County, Virginia, adopted a law requiring the police to check the immigration status of arrestees when there is probable cause to believe that the arrestee is unlawfully in the United States. A study by the University of Virginia and the Police Executive Research Forum found that the passage of the law resulted in the number of unlawful immigrants in the county declining by between three thousand and six thousand from 2006 to 2009 (Tavernise 2010). A 2006 city ordinance in Hazleton, Pennsylvania, struck down by the courts required landlords to evict illegal immigrants and directed businesses to fire undocumented workers. City workers were instructed to communicate in "English only," and individuals living in Hazelton were required to obtain a "residency card." The law reportedly reduced the Hispanic population of the city and forced small businesses that serviced these individuals to close (Newton 2008; Provine et al. 2016: 37, 132).

A combination of factors in recent years has led to a decline in the undocumented population in states that traditionally attracted immigrants. The number of undocumented individuals in Arizona stood at 500,000 and in recent years has stabilized at between 300,000 and 325,000. Border apprehensions in 2015 on the Arizona border decreased nearly 25 percent and continue to decline. Other states experiencing dramatic declines in their undocumented population include New York, Illinois, and California (Nevarez 2016).

In 2008, the Department of Homeland Security announced a Secure Communities program. The Obama administration subsequently extended the program to 1,210 jurisdictions and hoped to implement the program across the country. The policy, which was presented as voluntary, was intended to increase immigration enforcement by using state and local law enforcement officers. The fingerprints of individuals arrested and taken into custody were to be sent automatically to the FBI and to DHS were to be held held for seventy-two hours while ICE decided whether to deport them. Individuals who were unlawfully in the United States or who were lawful immigrants with a criminal record were all but certain to be deported. Studies found that the Secure Communities program led to racial profiling and pretextual stops by the police and too lengthy detentions while ICE processed the record of the individual arrested. Among those deported in 2013, only 12 percent had committed a serious crime, and for half of the detainees, the serious offense was a traffic violation or an immigration violation such as unlawful entry or over-staying a student or tourist visa. Several hundred U.S. citizens were falsely detained (Provine et al. 2016: 100–102).

A number of cities and counties declared themselves to be "sanctuary cities" and refused to participate in the Secure Communities program. These cities explicitly prohibited the police from asking arrestees, witnesses, and victims about their immigration status and prohibited the police from communicating the immigration status of citizens to federal immigration authorities. Officials in these "sanctuary" jurisdictions asserted that the Secure Communities program bred distrust of the police and, as a result, immigrant groups would not cooperate with the police in detecting and investigating crimes. Secure Communities also was criticized as burdening local law enforcement resources. Several studies have confirmed that Latinos are reluctant to report crimes in which they are victims or witnesses because of a fear that authorities will inquire into their immigration status. Local officials also claimed that the federal government has no constitutional right to require local law enforcement to enforce federal law (Provine et al. 2016; Semple 2010).

The Obama administration in 2014 abandoned the Secure Communities program after allegations that local authorities had engaged in racial profiling and that the program resulted in the mistaken detention of American citizens and lawful residents. At the same time, the DHS announced a new more limited federal–local program, the Priority Enforcement Program (PEP). The sanctuary cities movement subsequently spread to over thirty-nine cities and three hundred counties and to various college campuses and churches. New York attorney general Eric Schneiderman in January 2017 issued a set of guidelines to local governments setting forth basic principles for sanctuary cities, as outlined below. Keep in mind that entering the United States unlawfully is a crime although being present in the United States without proper documentation is not a crime (Yee 2017a).

Police. The police should not ask arrestees, victims, or witnesses about their immigration status and should not act on behalf of federal law enforcement agents in immigration matters. Individuals should not be stopped or arrested based solely on their suspected immigration status.

Registry. Local resources should not be used to create a registry of undocumented immigrants in the community.

Detention. Local officials at the request of federal authorities should not detain arrestees beyond the date on which they ordinarily would be released unless the individuals have been convicted of a serious felony, have illegally entered the United States after having been deported, or there is probable cause that the individual is involved in terrorist activity or a federal court has issued a criminal warrant requiring the individual's arrest and detention. New York City, for example, turns individuals accused of 170 serious felonies over to immigration authorities.

The Immigration Policy of President Donald Trump

In February 2017, the head of the DHS, General John Kelly, released two memos implementing President Donald Trump's campaign promise and executive orders calling for the deportation of undocumented individuals resident in the United States. The memos repealed President Barack Obama's deportation policy of focusing on hardened criminals and terrorists and, in effect, declared that all individuals unlawfully present within the United States were subject to deportation. Critics termed the Trump administration's announced policy of "taking the shackles off" of deportation and "carrying out a military operation" as a "blue print" for mass deportation (Santos 2017; Shear and Nixon 2017).

DHS announced plans to hire as many as ten thousand new agents and five thousand border patrol officers to enforce the memos. The memos also called for an increase in administrative judges to conduct hearings and expanding the thirty-four thousand available beds in detention facilities, most of which are in private prisons. ICE and border patrol will partner with local and state law enforcement under a more energetic federal program to enforce immigration law. DHS has characterized the use of local law enforcement as a "force multiplier" in the enforcement of immigration law. DHS also declared that it would seek funding for a wall between the United States and Mexico as previously announced in a January executive order issued by President Trump.

Immigration agents may expedite without a hearing the deportation of individuals who have been in the country for up to two years, a policy that under President Obama was limited to individuals within the country less than two weeks who were detained within one hundred miles of the border. This short-circuits the ordinary procedure of providing a hearing before an immigration judge with the possibility of appeal to the Board of Immigration Appeals and to a federal court. According to the new DHS policy, which has yet to be implemented, individuals awaiting a deportation or asylum hearing, rather than being housed within the United States, may be sent to Mexico. Parents and other individuals in the United States may be criminally prosecuted for smuggling or human trafficking and deported if they arrange to bring their children across the border. This is intended to curb the influx of children from Central America into the United States.

The Trump administration in justifying its immigration policy explained that individuals entering the United States unlawfully "present a significant threat to national security and public safety" and directed DHS to publish a weekly list of criminal actions committed by undocumented individuals. Studies, however, generally find that undocumented individuals commit crimes at a slightly higher rate than non-citizens in the United States legally and at a much lower rate than citizens (Pérez-Peña 2017).

A number of sanctuary cities announced that they would resist President Trump's announced policy of restricting funding to their jurisdictions. San Francisco, home to thirty thousand undocumented residents, filed a legal action to prevent the federal government from cutting off $1.2 billion in funding. The city had been targeted by President Trump after Kathryn Steinle, 32, was shot and killed by Juan Francisco Lopez Sanchez, who had a criminal record and had been deported five times. San Francisco admitted to mistakenly having failed to turn Sanchez over to federal authorities and noted that their policy requires cooperation with DHS in detaining felons (T. Fuller 2017).

Federal court judge William H. Orrick issued a temporary injunction holding that the Trump administration could not constitutionally withhold funding from San Francisco on the grounds that it was a sanctuary city. He reasoned that the Trump administration could not impose conditions on the receipt of federal grant funds that were not included by Congress as a condition for receiving the funds. Judge Orrick also reasoned that funds could not be withheld from programs that were unrelated to immigration enforcement (Medina and Bidgood 2017; D. Montgomery and Fernandez 2017; Yee 2017b). The withholding of funds from Sanctuary Cities will be decided by Congress and the courts in the coming years.

An additional executive order suspended the refugee program in Syria indefinitely and from other countries for 120 days and then cut admissions in half in 2017. The order also suspended issuance of visas for 90 days to individuals from seven Middle Eastern and African predominantly Muslim countries in which terrorist organizations have a "proven history" of terrorism against the United States or its allies. The seven countries listed in the order were Iran, Iraq, Libya, Somalia, Sudan, Syria, and Yemen. Admissions of refugees prioritized individuals fleeing religious rather than political persecution from countries in which the individuals are a religious minority (Liptak 2017a).

President Trump argued that the entry of individuals from these seven countries presented an immediate threat to the safety and security of the United States because the vetting process by the United States in these countries was flawed and a more intensive process needed to be developed. The president, according to federal law, may "suspend the entry of all aliens or any class of aliens as immigrants or nonimmigrants" if he determines that their entry "would be detrimental to the interests of the United States." This is somewhat at odds with another legal provision that states that "no person shall receive any preference or priority or be discriminated against in the issuance of an immigrant visa because of the person's race, sex, nationality, place of birth or place of residence."

Opponents of the measures argued that these measures although focusing on seven (predominantly Muslim) countries were intended as a "Muslim ban." A number of former American secretaries of state in a joint letter claimed that President Trump's order, rather than protecting the United States, assisted terrorist groups in painting the United States as an enemy of the Islamic world and assisted these groups in recruiting terrorists. Leading tech companies complained that the order interfered with their ability to recruit talent from across the globe. Others pointed out that there is no anti-Christian bias in refugee admissions: although less than 1 percent of Iranians identify as Christian, almost 50 percent of Iranian refugees since 2012 have been Christian (Qiu 2017).

Individuals from the seven designated countries, particularly Syria, already were subject to an intense, multilayered vetting process by the United Nations and by the United States involving biographic and biometric information that lasts between one and two years (Nixon 2017; Park and

Buchanan 2017). The immigration order resulted in hardship to a wide variety of individuals from the seven designated countries who without warning suddenly were prohibited from entering the United States, including permanent non-citizen residents of the United States (green card holders) who were abroad; Syrian refugee families, many of whom had been thoroughly vetted and had waited years to enter the United States; individuals whose entry had been approved on a special visa program for individuals who assisted the U.S. military in Iraq; student visa holders and foreign-trained doctors on special visas; individuals in need of medical treatment; and visiting artists. An estimated 746 individuals were detained after arriving in the United States, an unknown number of whom were sent back to the country in which their flight originated (Robbins 2017).

The States of Washington and Minnesota obtained a temporary restraining order from federal district court judge James L. Robart in Seattle prohibiting enforcement of the order and allowing the entry of two thousand refugees who had been vetted along with visa holders and permanent residents (green card holders) into the United States. Judge Robart found that the order was causing "immediate and irreparable injury" to individuals prohibited from entering the United States and that Minnesota and Washington had a "substantial likelihood" of winning once their challenge to the constitutionality of the order was fully litigated.

The Trump administration appealed to the Ninth Circuit Court of Appeals, which unanimously held that the government had failed to establish an immediate and imminent threat to national security from individuals in the seven countries listed in the executive order that required reinstatement of the travel ban. Out of nearly four hundred non-deadly Jihadist terrorist attacks in the United States since 9/11, three involved individuals connected to Iran or Somalia; all twelve deadly Jihadist attacks in the United States since 9/11 involved American citizens or residents. There were seventy-two instances of terrorist activity that were alleged to involve individuals from these countries, thirty-eight of which involved criminal activity that was not terrorist-related (Qiu 2017).

In *Washington v. Trump*, a three-judge panel of the Ninth Circuit Court of Appeals, one of whom was appointed by President George W. Bush, rejected the argument that the president has absolute authority over immigration and that his or her decisions may not be reviewed by the federal judiciary. The appellate panel also significantly held that the government was unlikely to win the case on the merits and noted that the order raised serious issues of religious discrimination that were unnecessary to address at this point in the process. The Ninth Circuit decision did not address the decrease in the number of refugees that may enter the United States in 2017, which is within the president's discretion.

The Trump administration announced a revised travel order on March 6, 2017. The order left much of the original order in place but exempted visa holders, individuals with dual passports, and refugees who already have been accepted; removed Iraq from the countries from which immigration was suspended; and omitted language expressing a preference for individuals fleeing religious prosecution. The order was justified on the grounds that three hundred people admitted as refugees had been subject to counterterrorism investigations (Thrush 2017).

The Ninth and Fourth Circuit Courts of Appeal blocked the revised travel ban on the grounds that it constituted religious discrimination (Liptak 2017c). Judge Robert L. Gregory, writing for the full Fourth Circuit Court of Appeals, held that President Trump's order prohibiting travel from six majority-Muslim countries "speaks with vague words of national security, but in context drips with religious intolerance, animus and discrimination" (*International Refugee Assistance Project v. Trump*, Case No. 17-1351 [4th Cir. 2017]).

In June 2017, the U.S. Supreme Court decided that it would determine the constitutionality of the travel ban when it reconvened later in the year. In the interim the Court held that the ban may be partially enforced. Individuals with a "bona fide" connection to the United States such as foreign students admitted to an American university, individuals with a job offer, and family members remain eligible to enter the country.

What is the future of immigration in the United States? Is it possible to find a solution to the problem? A philosophical question is the meaning of borders. In an interdependent world, perhaps national boundaries are less meaningful, and the United States, Canada, and Mexico should view themselves as a single integrated community. On the other hand, there are strong arguments that people within a country share common values and history and goals and are committed to the welfare of their communities. Individuals whose primary loyalty is to other countries are less willing to sacrifice and work for the common good (Macedo 2007).

11.5 YOU DECIDE

An undocumented student is a student who has remained in the United States following the expiration of his or her visa (legally authorized permission to enter) or who entered the United States without legal authorization. Many of these students have been in the United States for many years and share the same interests and dreams as students who are citizens and legal residents.

In *Plyler v. Doe*, the U.S. Supreme Court held that undocumented students have the right to an education up until high school. The Court explained that the denial of education severely impeded a young person's future (*Plyler v. Doe*, 457 U.S. 202 [1982]).

The judgment in *Plyler* guarantees the educational rights of roughly 1.8 million students under the age of 18. An estimated 65,000 undocumented students graduate from high school each year. The Supreme Court decision did not guarantee access to higher education (there are approximately 3.4 million undocumented young people between the ages of 18 and 29). It is estimated that 10 percent of undocumented males and 16 percent of undocumented females between the ages of 18 and 24 attend institutions of higher education.

A significant barrier to higher education is that only eighteen states grant full or partial in-state tuition to undocumented students. Most states do not have legislation that addresses the eligibility of undocumented students for in-state tuition. Three states explicitly declare these students ineligible for in-state tuition (Arizona, Georgia, and Indiana). Undocumented students in most instances are ineligible for federal Pell Grants or other federal assistance. South Carolina and Alabama explicitly prohibit undocumented students from enrolling in public colleges, and North Carolina bars them from community colleges.

The Obama administration deported 2.5 million individuals, a record number of undocumented individuals, from the United States. At the same time, the Obama administration supported the DREAM Act, which would grant permanent resident status to young people brought involuntarily into the United States as children. The bill failed to attract the necessary votes in Congress.

Individuals favoring the DREAM Act stressed that young people were brought involuntarily as children into the United States and have grown up and developed as Americans. America can benefit from the energy and enthusiasm and ability of these students. Opponents note that undocumented students are present unlawfully in the United States and will fill seats in colleges that should be reserved to students legally resident in the country.

(Continued)

In January 2011, President Obama, after failing to secure passage of the DREAM Act, issued an executive order without consulting Congress: the Deferred Action for Childhood Arrivals (DACA). The original DACA remained in effect and allowed an individual who arrived in the United States as a child to request deferred deportation if the individual

1. Was under the age of 31 as of June 15, 2012;

2. Came to the United States before reaching his or her 16th birthday;

3. Has continuously resided in the United States since June 15, 2007, up to the present time;

4. Was physically present in the United States on June 15, 2012, and at the time of making his or her request for consideration of deferred action;

5. Entered without inspection before June 15, 2012, or lawful immigration status expired as of June 15, 2012;

6. Is currently in school, has graduated or obtained a certificate of completion from high school, has obtained a GED, or is an honorably discharged veteran of the Coast Guard or Armed Forces of the United States; and

7. Has not been convicted of a felony, significant misdemeanor, or three or more other misdemeanors and does not otherwise pose a threat to national security or public safety.

An individual requesting consideration" for deferred action must be at least 15 years of age or older, unless he or she is currently in removal proceedings or has a final removal or voluntary departure order. DACA must be renewed after two years.

In 2016, the Supreme Court was divided 4–4 in *United States v. Texas*, which had the effect of upholding the Fifth Circuit Court of Appeals blocking implementation of President Obama's November 2014 executive order broadening the coverage of DACA and providing for Deferred Action for Parents of Americans and Lawful Permanent Residents (DAPA). DAPA extended protection from deportation to parents of children lawfully in the United States. An estimated 3.7 million individuals would have received lawful residency status under DAPA.

On September 5, 2017, President Trump rescinded DACA, although stating he would sign a DACA bill if passed by Congress in the following six months.

Do you favor DACA? DAPA?

■ LAW AND DIVERSITY: THE CULTURAL DEFENSE

Jill Norgren and Serena Nanda describe the **cultural defense** to a criminal charge as follows: "[Persons] socialized in a minority or foreign culture who regularly conduct themselves in accordance with their own cultural norms should not be held fully accountable for conduct that violates official United States law, if those individuals conduct prescriptions of their own culture" (Norgren and Nanda 1996: 265).

American and English law historically has not recognized the cultural defense.

In *Rex v. Esop* in 1836, a native of Baghdad (later established as the capital of Iraq) was convicted in England of a sexual offense that was not a crime in his homeland. The British court affirmed his conviction and held that "custom had to be subordinated to the law of the land" (*Rex v. Esop*, 173 Eng.Rep. 203 [Cent.Crim.Ct.1836]). In 1872, in *Carlisle v. United States*, the U.S. Supreme Court held that an undocumented immigrant who enters the United States is bound by American law (*Carlisle v. United States*, 83 U.S. 147 [1872]). The Court quoted U.S. Secretary of State Daniel Webster, who in 1851 wrote that every "foreign born residing in a country" owes to "that country allegiance and obedience to its law so long as he remains in it. . . . This is the universal understanding in all civilized States, and nowhere a more established doctrine than in this country" (Norgren and Nanda 1996: 266).

In 1986, a student note in the *Harvard Law Review* argued for recognition of a cultural defense. This defense would allow individuals who are charged with a criminal offense to plead that their act was justified based on their culture. The note argued a failure to recognize that a cultural defense "may send a message that an ethnic group must trade in its cultural values for that of the mainstream if it is to be accepted as an equal by the majority. It is . . . a system . . . likely to convince a person that the majority regards her culture as inferior" (Note 1986: 1293, 1302, 1311).

The notion of a cultural defense rests on the belief that individuals' attitudes and beliefs are shaped by the practices and values they learn at home, in school, in church, and in the media. The law, on the other hand, assumes that despite our differences, we should be held to a single standard of behavior. Consider how these two perspectives clash in the Kong Moua case (Norgren and Nanda 1996: 266–267).

Moua, a member of the Hmong tribe, had lived in the United States for six years after immigrating to America from Laos. The Hmong practice "marriage-by-capture," in which a man consummates marriage with a woman by abducting her and forcing her into sexual intercourse. The woman demonstrates her virtue by resisting the man, and the man demonstrates his masculinity by forcing her into sexual relations. Moua abducted a 19-year-old "Americanized" Laotian woman from a college campus and forced her to engage in sexual intercourse (Evans-Pritchard and Renteln 1994).

A defendant's reasonable belief that a woman consented to sexual intercourse may constitute a defense to rape. The judge determined Moua sincerely believed that the woman consented and that the woman's protests were nothing more than part of the ritual requirements of marriage-by-capture. However, the judge also was convinced the woman had vigorously resisted and had not consented. After consulting with Hmong clan elders, the judge approved a plea agreement in which Moua pled guilty to the reduced charge of false imprisonment and received ninety days in jail. He was fined $1,200, $900 of which went to the woman's parents (Cohan 2010: 234–235).

The "true cultural defense" would authorize a defendant to raise culture as a complete defense to a criminal charge. This potentially would result in Moua's acquittal. The culture defense would include a four-step process.

1. An individual is a member of an ethnic or religious or other distinct group.

2. The individual's behavior was required by the group's cultural tradition.

3. The individual was aware and a reasonable person would be aware that the individual's act violated U.S. domestic criminal law.

4. The social interest in preventing the criminal behavior is outweighed by the interest in respecting and recognizing the individual's cultural tradition. For example, the interest in punishing marijuana possession may be outweighed by a religious group's use of marijuana in a religious ritual. On the other hand, preventing murder outweighs the interest in recognizing an individual's cultural claim.

A number of arguments are made in support of recognition of the cultural defense.

Pluralism. An appreciation of diversity and equality of groups are important American values.

Individualized justice. The justice system should treat each defendant as a distinct individual and should not follow a "one size fits all" approach.

Knowledge. A recent immigrant may not realize that his or her act is criminal.

Deterrence. Individuals who are not members of the group will not mistakenly believe that if they commit a crime, they will benefit from the cultural defense.

Social stability. Immigrant groups whose values and traditions are appreciated will be strong and stable and loyal Americans.

There are several objections to the cultural defense outlined below.

Conformity. Individuals should abide by the law.

Equality. Immigrants and members of ethnic groups should be held to the same standard as other Americans.

Ignorance. Ignorance of the law traditionally is not recognized as a defense.

Uniformity. Individuals who commit the same crime should be treated in the same fashion. Society cannot function if there are different standards for different groups. The goal is to integrate groups into society rather than to encourage groups to follow their own standards of behavior.

Legitimacy. Different standards of criminal conduct will lead to disrespect for the law. People will resent the double standard for determining criminal conduct and will disregard legal rules.

Vulnerable groups. Recognition of the cultural defense threatens the rights of women and children who may be subject to sexual and physical abuse.

Fraudulent claims. Individuals may attempt to rely on the cultural defense who, in fact, may be aware their conduct violated U.S. law.

Judicial resources. The judge or the jury will spend time listening to expert witnesses debate the requirements of an individual's culture rather than focusing on the facts of the case.

One well-known case that has been at the center of the debate over the cultural defense is *People v. Kimura.* In 1984, Fumiko Kimura's husband revealed he had been having an extramarital affair and supporting a mistress for several years. Two months later, after having failed to achieve a reconciliation, Kimura, while holding her 6-month-old daughter and 4-year-old son, walked into the Pacific Ocean in an effort to commit parent–child suicide. Kimura and her two children were pulled from the water, but only Kimura survived (Chiu 2006: 1318).

Kimura was charged with two counts of premeditated and deliberate murder and confronted a possible penalty of death. A petition was submitted to the judge signed by twenty-five thousand individuals from the United States, Japan, and Europe. The petition asserted that in Japan,

Kimura likely would confront a maximum charge of voluntary manslaughter (manslaughter in the heat of passion) and likely would receive a suspended sentence with probation and supervised rehabilitation. The petition explained Kimura had followed a practice known as *oyako shinju,* parent–child suicide. Her actions were an expression of Japanese culture and were committed without an "intent to do harm to her children whom she deeply loved." Her lawyer did not raise a cultural defense and instead presented psychiatric evidence that Kimura was temporarily insane. The prosecutor agreed to reduce the charge of first-degree murder to voluntary manslaughter (murder in the heat of passion) (Chiu 2006: 1349).

Kimura lived in a closed Japanese community. She washed her husband's feet every night and never learned to drive. After being rescued from the ocean, her reaction was that the rescuers must have been Caucasians because the Japanese would have let her drown (Chiu 2006: 1354).

Oyako shinju was common in Japan in the 1950s and 1960s and occurred at a rate of two cases every three days. At the time of Kimura's act, *oyako shinju* no longer was a regular practice in Japan. Kimura's decision to take her life was a response to the humiliation of a failed marriage and is an appropriate response in Japan to an insurmountable and painful situation. She accepted blame as a bad wife and mother. The belief is that the child and parents form a closely connected unit and that it is more merciful to take the child's life than to leave the child alone without a mother.

The cultural defense would have permitted Kimura to explain her actions to the judge and to the jury and would have enabled her to be judged in accordance with the standards of her culture. Her attorney portrayed Kimura as temporarily insane rather than explain her motivation. On the other hand, the law generally limits the taking of the life of another to self-defense, and there is no legal justification for the taking of the life of two innocent children. Kimura nonetheless received a relatively light sentence for homicide that was similar to the sentence she would have received in Japan.

Several states have what are called *de minimis* statutes that courts on occasion have relied on to drop charges against immigrants who the judges believed were acting in a lawful fashion. Mohammad Kargar, an immigrant from Afghanistan, was arrested for kissing the penis of his 18-month-old son and explained that this was a traditional method of displaying affection in Afghanistan. Members of the Afghan community testified the penis is considered a "dirty" portion of the human anatomy and kissing this area of the child's anatomy is a selfless display of affection. The Maine court recognized that Kargar violated the sexual assault statute but dismissed the charge because Kargar did not act out of a sexual motive and the child was not subjected to pain or embarrassment (*State v. Kargar*, 679 A.2d 81 [Me. 1996]).

Commentators have cautioned that the cultural defense may be used to justify the abuse of women and children. Male defendants allege that the woman's conduct provoked the violence or that the punishment of children reflected cultural norms (Cohan 2010: 247).

In *People v. Chen*, Dong Lu Chen, an immigrant from Hong Kong, had been in America for roughly a year where he worked as a dishwasher. Chen lived in an insular Chinese community and had not learned English. He became embroiled in an argument with his wife of twenty-three years, Jai Wan. Dong became enraged when Jai Wan refused to sleep with him and announced that "this need was being taken care of elsewhere." Dong interpreted this comment as indicating that Jai Wan was having an affair and hit his wife over the head eight times with a claw hammer. He later admitted through an interpreter to his son and to the police that he had killed Jai Wan (*People v. Chen*, N.Y. Sup. Ct. Mar. 21, 1989).

An anthropologist testified that marriage is a sacred institution in China. Dong had experienced dishonor and humiliation and knew that other Chinese males would view his marriage as a failure. Dong's shame and embarrassment would prevent him from being accepted in the Chinese community or remarrying. Judge Edward Pincus accepted that Dong had been provoked and reduced the charge from murder to manslaughter and sentenced Dong to five years' probation discounted by the time that he had already served. Judge Pincus explained Dong had brought his culture with him to the United States and "was not entirely responsible for his actions. . . . [H]e was the product of his culture." The judge recognized that culture, although not a complete defense to the murder charge, explained why Dong had "cracked more easily" (Norgren and Nanda 1996: 272–273).

Brooklyn district attorney Elizabeth Holtzman was "enraged" at the verdict and insisted anyone who enters the United States should be prepared to abide by the laws of this country and there should be one standard of justice. Asian American groups complained that the judge's verdict placed women at risk and that the message was that Asian women would not be protected against domestic violence under American law. Experts on Chinese culture contended that domestic violence was condemned under modern Chinese law and the judge had relied on an outmoded stereotype in reasoning that domestic violence was tolerated in China (Norgren and Nanda 1996: 274).

In some instances, defendants have relied on cultural arguments to support their reliance on a traditional criminal defense. In *People v. Aphaylath*, Aphaylath killed his wife when he discovered her talking on the phone with her former boyfriend. Aphaylath's attorney successfully appealed the trial judge's refusal to hear the testimony of two anthropologists. The New York Court of Appeals held that the judge should have permitted the jury to hear evidence that the phone call had resulted in Aphaylath feeling shame and humiliation and losing control. The prosecutor reduced the charge to manslaughter, and Aphaylath pled guilty (*People v. Aphaylath*, 502 N.E.2d 998 [N.Y. 1986]; see also Chiu 2006: 1356).

In summary, individuals are products of their culture, and the question arises in a multicultural society whether the law should provide some recognition to different cultural practices in considering a criminal charge. On the other hand, there is the argument that individuals within the United States should conform to a single standard, particularly with regard to serious criminal offenses (Donovan 2008). In the international perspective, we look at how global inequality has helped fuel human trafficking. See the study site for You Decide 11.6 on culture and honor killings.

 INTERNATIONAL PERSPECTIVE:
GLOBAL TRAFFICKING

In 1833, the British Parliament adopted the Slavery Abolition Act and freed all slaves within the British Empire. Twenty-three years later, the Thirteenth Amendment to the U.S. Constitution declared, "Neither slavery nor involuntary servitude . . . shall exist within the United States, or any place subject to their jurisdiction."

It may come as a surprise to learn that there are an estimated twenty-seven million slaves in the world. There are more slaves today than all the individuals enslaved during the height of the transatlantic slave trade in the eighteenth and nineteenth centuries. The number of slaves is greater than the population of Canada and is six times the population of Israel. Slaves are defined as individuals who are held against their will for the purposes of exploiting their labor (Bales 2004: 9).

A majority of slaves work in agriculture. They also are found manufacturing bricks and in mining, working in rock quarries, carpet weaving, and in the jewelry industry. Although individuals are enslaved throughout the world, slavery is concentrated in Bangladesh, India, Pakistan, Nepal, Southeast Asia, northern and western Africa, and parts of South America (Bales 2004: 9). David Batstone notes that slaves in Pakistan may have constructed your shoes and the carpet in your house while slaves in the Caribbean may have manufactured the sugar in your coffee and the toys you played with as a child. Your shirt may have been sewn and the ring on your hand may have been polished by slaves in India (Batstone 2007: 9). One of the most scandalous abuses of slave labor has been in the Southeast Asian fishing industry. Investigative reporting by the Associated Press and *New York Times* has revealed whipping, deprivation of food and water, and deprivation of pay (Urbina 2015).

Roughly 100,000 enslaved individuals are in the United States, and 17,500 individuals are trafficked into America each year. An additional 30,000 individuals are transported through the United States on their way to other countries. America is not alone in its involvement in the slave trade. More than 150 countries serve as a source, destination, or transportation hub for the slave trade. The European Union countries are the destination for the trafficking of more than 200,000 persons per year (Batstone 2007: 3–6).

In 2004, the United Nations issued a report titled *Ten Million Children Exploited for Domestic Labor*. The report recorded that 700,000 children were compelled to serve as household labor in Indonesia and over a half million in agricultural work in Brazil. Other countries with child labor are Pakistan (264,000), Haiti (250,000), and Kenya (200,000) (Batstone 2007: 6–7).

In 2003, President George W. Bush addressed the United Nations General Assembly and denounced the fact that each year eight hundred thousand to nine hundred thousand individuals are "bought, sold, or forced across the world's borders." He proclaimed that the "trade in human beings . . . must not be allowed to thrive in our time." Trafficking in human beings is the third most lucrative global criminal activity behind the drug trade and the shipment in unlawful arms (Batstone 2007: 3).

What accounts for what Kevin Bales terms the new slavery? **Globalization** is the term for the closer connection of countries and peoples resulting from the increasing ease of transportation, communication, and economic activity between countries across the globe. This process often is celebrated as allowing people across the globe to share in the benefits of trade, culture, and movement across borders. A number of individuals have not shared in the benefits of globalization (Stiglitz 2012).

Several factors have combined to create a low-skill, impoverished, youthful population that is desperate for economic security (Bales 2004: 1–33).

Population. The world population since 1945 has more than tripled. Much of the growth has occurred in the least developed countries, 50 percent or more of whose populations are under the age of 15. These young people often lack opportunity or the education required to succeed in the new global economy.

War. War and internal unrest and genocide have displaced people across the globe. The world is overwhelmed with over fifty million refugees and displaced persons, who offer an inexhaustible supply of workers.

Economic development. Countries have adopted development strategies that rely on the export of goods to the world. Western corporations contract with factories across the globe that compete with one another for business based on their ability to manufacture goods inexpensively. Workers in factories manufacturing goods destined for Europe and the United States typically are required to work long hours for low wages in undesirable conditions. Agricultural land has been consolidated into large holdings that cultivate export crops like flowers. This has removed people from the land, limited the production of agricultural crops, and driven up the domestic price of the food in the developing world.

Education. Developing countries suffer from limited government finances as a result of a small tax-paying population and tax evasion among the wealthy. Relatively little money is available for public education, particularly in science and technology. As a result, there is a shortage of skilled labor able to compete at an advanced level in the global economy.

Bales distinguishes between the "new slavery" and the traditional forms of chattel slavery practiced in the American South during the nineteenth century. Bales argues that in the past, slaves were purchased at a high price and maintained, supported, and bred for the remainder of their lives. The slaves were essential to the owner's economic survival and security and typically were ethnically distinguished from the owner. Bales argues that much of modern slavery is based on a contract or consent. These contract employees work long hours and yield a high profit. Workers are disposed of when no longer productive because there are countless individuals available to take their place. Keep in mind that whatever the merits of Bales's general argument, there is a great deal of evidence that African slaves were subject to inhumane treatment and abuse in the American South (Bales 2004: 15).

The new slavery is based on five types of arrangements (Bales 2004: 19–22), as shown in Table 11.1.

E. Benjamin Skinner writes that the global commercial sex industry is a $100 billion enterprise and claims that two million women are working in forced prostitution at any given point in time (Skinner 2008: 132, 143, 177). In eastern Europe, the economy fell apart with the end of Communism. Unemployment for women in the former Soviet republics during the 1990s was

Table 11.1 ■ Forms of Slavery

Chattel slavery	This involves a small number of the slaves in the world. Chattel slavery is close to the traditional form of slavery and is found in northern and western Africa. The clearest example is Mauritania, in which slaves are owned, sold, and born into servitude.
Debt bondage	A person works to pay off a debt although the terms of service and the nature of the required work are left undefined. Children may be exchanged in return for a loan or seized in the event of a default. Debt bondage is common in India and Pakistan and accounts for over half of the slaves in the world.
Contract slavery	An individual signs a contract to work in heavy industry, a factory, or a restaurant or as a domestic. The contract is used to intimidate the worker into cooperation. This is common in Southeast Asia, Brazil, and the Middle East.
War slavery	Young people are seized and forced to fight as child soldiers. In countries like Burma, civilians are required to work under armed military guard on construction projects.
Religious slavery	In Africa and India, families may give a young woman to priests to atone for her sins. The young woman is required to clean and cook and often is released after bearing several children.

between 80 percent and 90 percent, and three of every four young women between the ages of 10 and 19 expressed the aspiration of working abroad. Roughly 25 percent of the population of Moldova emigrated in the 1990s. Another source of recruitment for the global sex trade is the overcrowded orphanages in Romania and Moldova, where orphanage directors are accused of selling children to the operators of brothels (Batstone 2007: 103–104, 166).

Young women are recruited with the promise of work in western Europe. The women, on arriving at their destination, find that they have been tricked and are told they owe thousands of dollars to cover the cost of transportation. The pimp typically sells the young girl to a brothel, and the brothel owners demand that the woman work to pay the cost of her purchase. This amount is compounded by rent, food, cigarettes, and interest. Women are threatened that a failure to pay off a debt will result in their death or in the death of their family members or children.

On arrival at their destination, the women are beaten, raped, and abused, and their passports are seized. They lack money to return home and lack knowledge of the local language and culture. A young woman might find herself sold four or five times and trafficked from Turkey to Italy and to Spain and to the Netherlands and to Japan and to Dubai. Skinner visited a brothel in Dubai and found women from China, Korea, Africa, eastern Europe, and Russia. The police often turn a blind eye to trafficking, and a woman who manages to contact the police often confronts a language barrier and may find herself jailed for prostitution and unlawful presence in the country and confronted with deportation back home where she faces certain retribution.

In the Netherlands, a woman who services fourteen or twenty men an evening reportedly earns her handlers $250,000 per year. The women ultimately are left with HIV, post-traumatic stress, and psychological disorders, and their lives are in constant risk from customers. As a woman's income-earning potential declines, she is discarded by her handlers (Skinner 2008: 117–191).

The same model is followed in countries in Asia. Bales reports that young women are tricked into signing contracts to work in urban areas, or they are sold by their parents to traffickers. A young woman between the ages of 12 and 15 can be purchased for $2,000, and the profit is as high as 800 percent per year. The young woman is exploited for three or four years before becoming ill or contracting HIV. Recruitment often is undertaken by women who visit rural villages and promise young girls the opportunity to travel, make money, and support their families.

The demand for virgins by Asian clients who are willing to pay a premium price makes it imperative for the pimps continually to recruit a new group of young women. Virgins are viewed as bringing good luck and do not present the risk of HIV (Bales 2004: 18–19). Batstone notes that on rare occasions a wealthy Asian businessman may support a young rural woman with the understanding he can have sex with her when she reaches puberty (Batstone 2007: 61).

Once recruited, the young women are beaten, abused, and threatened. Young women who resist are drugged, starved, locked in closets, stripped naked, and beaten with steel coat hangers. Women who are pregnant are forced to submit to abortions or to give birth, after which the child is sold (Bales 2004: 59–60).

The thirty-five thousand women held in debt bondage in Thailand generate an annual total revenue of roughly $1.7 billion. These figures do not include "sex tourism" from Asia and Europe, which draws more than seven million visitors to Thailand each year. Bales claims this accounts for thirteen times the income Thailand generates from its profitable computer industry (Bales 2004: 55–57, 65, 75–77).

Criminal gangs have entered into the **sex trafficking** industry. There is a global sex trade network that connects the sex industry throughout the world. A club in San Francisco can order young women from eastern Europe or Asia. Brothels are prepared to move to another location in the event that there is a crackdown or the economy begins to decline. Recruitment of women shifts from one country to another depending on the economy (Batstone 2007: 171–172). Misha Glenny, in his study of international organized crime, writes that the trafficking of women is attractive because it does not involve a significant financial investment, women can be moved easily across borders, and a single prostitute can generate a significant profit and continue to be sold and resold (Glenny 2008: 19). Thousands of women are trafficked along the so-called Balkan trail, which extends through the former Soviet Union and into Italy and from there to Asia and western Europe (Batstone 2004: 158).

In 2014, the Nigerian terrorist group Boko Haram kidnapped close to three hundred young girls from their school and threatened to sell them into slavery to raise money for arms and equipment (Nossiter 2014: A1).

The 2016 global report on human trafficking issued by the United Nations Office on Drugs and Crime (UNODC) finds that although most victims are women and children, men now constitute an increasing percentage of trafficked persons. Roughly four out of ten individuals trafficked between 2014 and 2016 were trafficked for forced labor, and 63 percent of these victims were men. Another development is that 42 percent of detected victims of trafficking between 2012 and 2014 were trafficked within the same country. An additional trend is the increased trafficking of individuals from sub-Saharan Africa as a result of regional armed conflicts. These migrants have been targeted for kidnapping for ransom and for the forcible removal of organs that are sold for significant profit (UNODC 2016).

Countries play different roles in the global trafficking network, and they may play more than one role, as shown in Table 11.2.

The most important international statement on trafficking is the 2000 United Nations Protocol to Prevent, Suppress and Punish Trafficking in Persons. This is a comprehensive document that requires states signing the protocol to take a number of steps to counter trafficking across international borders by "organized crime groups." The document has been ratified by 170 countries and is a supplement to the UN Convention against Transnational Organized Crime, which also includes a protocol against the smuggling of migrants. Signed by 117 countries, the Protocol to Prevent, Suppress and Punish Trafficking in Persons calls on states signing the treaty to achieve four goals:

1. *Prevention.* Prevent and combat trafficking in persons, paying particular attention to women and children. States are required to subject trafficking to criminal penalties.

2. *Protection.* Protect and assist the victims of such trafficking, with full respect for their human rights. States are to provide victims with housing, economic support, and medical and psychological care.

Table 11.2 ■ Countries' Roles in Global Trafficking

Supplier countries	These are the poor countries that offer limited opportunities for women.
Transit countries	These are countries in which women temporarily are housed and subsequently transported to their destination. These countries are situated on trafficking routes.
Consumer countries	Countries in northern and western Europe, the United States and Canada, and Japan provide a market for the sex trade.

3. *Contributing factors.* Protect and prevent trafficking by addressing the factors that lead to trafficking, such as poverty, lack of equal opportunity, and unemployment.

4. *Cooperation.* Promote cooperation among states in order to meet these objectives.

States are to cooperate in detecting, detaining, and prosecuting traffickers. The United Nations reports that in 2002 only 33 countries had criminal statutes that are aligned with the UN Protocol and that 158 countries had such statutes in 2016 (out of the 179 counted). Overall, the ratio between the number of traffickers convicted and the number of victims detected is roughly five victims per convicted offender. An investigation of 136 countries found that 40 percent reported ten or fewer convictions per year between 2012 and 2014 and 15 percent reported no convictions. Over one-third of convicted traffickers are women who typically are involved in the trafficking of women and children, and the overwhelming majority of traffickers are of the same nationality as the victims (UNODC 2016).

There are several characteristics of human trafficking in the United States (Batstone 2004: 228).

Country of origin. Individuals are trafficked from thirty-five countries. The largest number are trafficked from China, Mexico, and Vietnam.

Destination. The largest number of trafficked individuals are in Florida, New York, and Texas.

Gangs. Mexican, eastern European, Russian, and Asian criminal gangs are involved in trafficking in the United States.

Economic sectors. The largest number of trafficked individuals are forced into prostitution and other commercial sexual activities (45 percent). The next largest number of trafficked individuals are engaged in domestic service and agriculture (26 percent).

CHAPTER SUMMARY

We commonly view law as a mechanism to guarantee that individuals are treated equally and to protect individuals from discrimination. Critical race theory challenges this view of law and argues that the law helps to maintain and perpetuate racial inequality. Two examples of the racialization of the enforcement of criminal law are the discriminatory enforcement of stop and frisk and traffic laws and the differential sentencing of crack versus powder cocaine. Laws, seemingly neutral on their face, such as stand your ground statutes, can have a racially disparate impact. Hate crimes punish criminal offenses directed at individuals because of various personal characteristics.

Racial prejudice historically has been a factor in immigration law. Both the Chinese and Hispanics historically have been relied on as a source of temporary manual labor and have been deemed unsuited to be permanent members of the American community. The recent Arizona law aimed at curbing undocumented individuals is an example of the continuing tension over the immigration of Hispanics.

CHAPTER REVIEW QUESTIONS

1. Discuss the major themes of critical race theory. Do you agree or disagree with the arguments of critical race theory?

2. What is racial profiling? How does racial profiling play a role in stop and frisk and in the enforcement of traffic laws?

3. Explain the racially discriminatory impact of the enforcement of narcotics laws.

4. Describe the background, elements, and reason for hate crimes.

5. Discuss the relationship between race and immigration policy.

6. What are the global causes of human trafficking? Why is human trafficking such a widespread and profitable crime?

TERMINOLOGY

crack cocaine   467

critical race theory   442

cultural defense   492

discriminatory justice   448

globalization   497

hate crimes   476

intersectionality   444

mass incarceration   469

pretext stop   449

racial profiling   448

sex trafficking   499

stand your ground   461

ANSWERS TO TEST YOUR KNOWLEDGE

1. True

2. False

3. True

4. False

5. False

6. False

7. False

WANT A BETTER GRADE?

Get the tools you need to sharpen your study skills. Access practice quizzes, eFlashcards, author podcasts, SAGE journal articles, hyperlinks for Law and Society on the Web, and more at **study.sagepub.com/lippmanls2e**.

PRIVACY AND SURVEILLANCE

TEST YOUR KNOWLEDGE: TRUE OR FALSE?

1. The protection of privacy is a fundamental right explicitly provided by the U.S. Constitution.

2. The phrase *panopticon society* refers to a society in which there is no freedom from observation by the government or by other people.

3. The constitutional right to privacy has been relatively unimportant and has been relied on by the U.S. Supreme Court in deciding minor and uncontroversial cases.

4. The police need a warrant to listen to a phone call by an American citizen although a search warrant is not required to listen to the phone calls of non-American citizens within the United States.

5. Private data aggregator firms may collect credit card information and information from phone companies but are prohibited from collecting information from Internet searches and other online activities.

6. People are more worried about their credit card information being hacked from stores and from their computer or smartphone than any other crime.

7. High school students may not be subjected to drug testing without a search warrant.

8. The police require a warrant to collect DNA from an individual who is arrested for a crime.

Check your answers on page 542.

■ INTRODUCTION

In February 2010, 16-year-old Blake J. Robbins and his family filed suit against the Lower Merion School District in Philadelphia for the invasion of Blake's privacy. Blake had been called into the assistant principal's office and told that he was being charged with drug possession and with attempting to sell drugs.

The school district is one of the wealthiest in the Philadelphia area and had distributed laptops to all of the district's 2,300 high school students. The students and their parents had not been told the computers were equipped with webcams that, when remotely activated, could capture students' pictures and screen images of the students' e-mails. The cameras took a photo every fifteen minutes and in two years had captured fifty-six thousand images. Blake's parents alleged that he had candies rather than drugs in his possession at the time that the photo had been taken. The school explained that the cameras had been installed to locate missing laptops.

Blake argued that the school had invaded his privacy by taking his photo and by taking a photo of his computer screen without his consent in his own home. He also contended the school had a limited interest in observing students outside school hours. On the other hand, the school argued it had an interest in ensuring its laptops were safe and secure and had a responsibility to ensure students were not abusing drugs. A student who has nothing to hide has no reason to object to being observed, the school reasoned. Do you believe that Blake J. Robbins's right to privacy was violated? The school district ultimately settled two lawsuits for $610,000.

In October 2000, James Turner rented a car from a national rental car business. Turner was startled to learn that a computer in the vehicle enabled the company to chart Turner's progress on a website. The company also had the capacity to kill the ignition at any moment. Turner stopped to buy gas and was told that his debit card did not have enough value. He called his bank and was informed the company had deducted money from the card because he had been recorded as speeding in three instances. Turner's experience is a hint of the future. Some new cars are equipped with personal security alert systems that enable the security company to listen to conversations in the automobile. Systems currently in development will enable the police to remotely check whether a driver has unpaid traffic tickets, proper insurance coverage and vehicle registration, and a current driver's license (O'Harrow 2005: 292–293).

We may not think about the data collected on each of us on a daily basis. Robert O'Harrow Jr. notes that when we sign on to the Internet and browse the Web, all of our activities are recorded. As we move on to a newspaper site and sign in, more data are recorded. You may have the time before school or work to view a program you recorded on TiVo, which once again leaves data points. Driving to work, you use your E-ZPass to pay the tolls, and your movements are recorded. You have thirty minutes before class and use your debit card to pay for breakfast or get money from the ATM. Once again, your movements are recorded. During the day, cameras record you as you walk through campus and in the parking garage. You leave school and may use a magnetic strip ID card or other technology to enter the building. The computer at work records your e-mails and Web surfing. You stop at a pharmacy to fill a prescription as you leave work; once again, this information is recorded. You arrive home and call an 800 number and order some clothes. Your name, address, and other details are recorded. Virtually all of this information is sent to a "data aggregator" company that sells your name to various retailers seeking to market products to people who fit your profile. Much of this information also is being downloaded onto government computers (O'Harrow 2005: 284–285).

In this chapter, we explore the notions of **privacy** and **surveillance**. The cyber revolution has introduced technology that, as illustrated by the story of Blake J. Robbins, challenges us to define the limits of the right to privacy. Some may see Blake's situation as an ominous sign that we are moving toward a surveillance state in which we all are constantly observed. Others may see the notion of privacy as outmoded and as interfering with public safety and protections.

In contemporary society, we seemingly always are under the gaze of a camera or are being monitored by technology. Our information is being collected continually as we go about our daily lives. The protection of privacy against the intrusions of technological change poses one of the significant challenges in coming years.

As you read this chapter, consider whether our right to privacy remains strong or has been diminished. Ask yourself whether privacy is an outmoded and unnecessary concept and whether we spend far too much time discussing the topic. Another question to reflect on is whether technology has outstripped legal regulation.

■ DOES PRIVACY MATTER?

You may be thinking you have "nothing to hide" and see no reason to be concerned about privacy. Each of us may differ on his or her need for privacy. You may feel a need to live alone while your friends may enjoy living with a number of roommates. Consider why some people may argue that privacy does not matter (Solove 2011: 22):

> "I have nothing to hide from the government, and I doubt whether the government cares about what I have on my computer or what I tell my neighbor in any event."

> "I have nothing to hide, and neither do most people. The government knows everything anyway."

> "I have nothing to hide, and if we can uncover a terrorist plot, then it is worth all of us turning over personal information to the government."

There are several reasons why privacy is important and why Justice Louis Brandeis described privacy as "the right most valued by civilized men" (*Olmstead v. United States,* 277 U.S. 438, 478 [1928]). The justifications for privacy listed below are difficult to measure or to satisfactorily prove (Solove 2008: 80).

Anxiety and pressure. Privacy allows us to retreat from the commotion and confusion of the world and regain a sense of personal balance and perspective.

Creativity. Privacy allows us to think, to reflect on our experiences, and to exercise our imagination. We all know the reclusive genius who has retreated from the world to create art or music.

Individuality. Privacy allows us to express our personality and gives us freedom to determine what we eat, read, think, watch on television, or listen to on the radio. In other words, privacy allows us to shape the environment in which we live without being concerned about whether we are conforming to the crowd.

Democracy. Some commentators argue that privacy is vital for democracy. Privacy allows us to listen to and learn from one another and to experiment with various points of view without fear of retaliation.

Security. Control over our personal information provides security against someone stealing our identity and jeopardizing our financial security.

Privacy is not celebrated by everyone. Some commentators believe privacy is harmful to society and is the product of a bygone era and that we are moving to a more open or transparent society. The ancient Greeks viewed privacy as a retreat from involvement in society and from the responsibility to make a contribution. They believed an individual has no right to place his or her own selfish interests above what is good for the group. In other words, they believed the concern with privacy elevates the individual interest over responsibility to society and individuals should keep the larger collective interest in mind.

Some people believe privacy interferes with the smooth and efficient functioning of society. The more information we have about people, the better able we are to make judgments about whether to trust them. You clearly would want to know whether someone you are considering as a roommate or as an employee is a felon, drug addict, or alcoholic. Privacy allows individuals to hide their personality and to present a false image to the world (Solove 2008: 81–83).

A national identification card that contains all of your personal information on a computer chip would help to confirm whether you are a legal resident, could centralize your medical information (e.g., medications, allergies), and would allow a store to instantaneously establish that you have enough money in your account to cover a check that you wrote.

Privacy can inhibit our ability to solve crimes and to protect ourselves. Swipe cards that record the time we enter or leave a building have allowed people accused of crimes to establish that they were not at the crime scene at the time of the incident. The electronic tracking of sex offenders and domestic abusers can help to protect the community. A comprehensive national DNA database would assist the police in solving crimes.

Historically, the law has been concerned with the public sphere of life. The home has been protected by privacy from intrusion by the government. Various feminist scholars have argued that this separation gives men the space and opportunity to abuse women and children (Mackinnon 1987: 93–102).

In the next section, we look at the development of the law of privacy.

■ A BRIEF HISTORY OF THE LAW OF PRIVACY

The late nineteenth century witnessed the growth of "tabloid" journalism. The motto of Joseph Pulitzer's *New York World* was "Spicy, Pithy, Pictorial." The 1884 presidential contest pitted Grover Cleveland, the Democratic governor of New York, against James G. Blaine, the former Republican Speaker of the U.S. House of Representatives. A number of Blaine's letters were leaked to the media, lending credibility to the allegation that Blaine had been on the payroll of the railroads while in office. Blaine refused to offer an explanation, insisting the letters were within his "sacred right to privacy" (quoted in Lane 2009: 48–49).

Governor Cleveland also was the topic of press attention. It was disclosed that while practicing law in Buffalo (New York), Cleveland had fathered a child out of wedlock, leading the Republicans to coin the famous slogan: "Ma, Ma, where's my pa? Gone to the White House, ha, ha, ha." Cleveland emerged victorious in the election and was exposed to increased media examination of his personal life. The press reported Cleveland planned to marry the much younger daughter of his former law partner and revealed several embarrassing events in the life of the president's prospective new spouse, Frances Folsom. Media interest in the new Mrs. Cleveland intensified following marriage, and her image was used without her permission to endorse products ranging from candy to underwear to soap. One of Cleveland's strong supporters reported the president was horrified to see his wife's image being used to advertise products and unsuccessfully introduced legislation to criminalize the unauthorized use of individuals' image in advertisements (Lane 2009: 50–51).

One of Frances Cleveland's close friends was Mabel Bayard Warren, whose role as a Washington socialite had resulted in her own activities being the subject of tabloid journalism. Her marriage to attorney Samuel D. Warren Jr. in 1883 had been the subject of widespread press attention (Lane 2009: 53).

In the same year that the Warrens were married, George Eastman perfected a process to take photographs without having to cart chemicals around to coat the slide. In 1888, Eastman introduced a camera under the brand name Kodak that was able to take multiple photographs. Newspapers roughly ten years earlier had developed a process of efficiently reproducing photographs. The combination of these technologies meant that prominent individuals could be not only discussed but also easily pictured in the print media (Lane 2009: 52).

Another important development was the growth of "yellow journalism." This sensationalistic approach to the news was featured in inexpensive papers that focused on gossip and human-interest stories. In 1850, one hundred papers were read by eight hundred thousand readers; in 1890, nine hundred papers attracted a total of eight million readers (Solove 2008: 16).

These events undoubtedly influenced Warren and his law partner, Louis D. Brandeis, in 1890, to publish one of the most important law review articles in history in the *Harvard Law Review* titled "The Right to Privacy." Warren and Brandeis argued that the development of intrusive technology required courts to recognize that individuals have a right to privacy. The authors defined privacy as the "right to be left alone" and proposed that the law provide a remedy for individuals who suffer "pain and distress" when "what is whispered in the closet shall be proclaimed from the house-tops" (Warren and Brandeis 1890: 195).

Brandeis later would be appointed to the U.S. Supreme Court. He authored an important dissent in *Olmsted v. United States* in which the majority held that the Fourth Amendment's prohibition on unreasonable searches and seizures did not protect individuals against wiretapping and the seizure of their "words." Brandeis once again stressed that individuals had a "right to be left alone" and that "unjustifiable intrusion by the Government upon the privacy of the individual, whatever the means employed, must be deemed a violation of the Fourth Amendment." Brandeis predicted that "ways may someday be developed by which the Government, without removing papers from secret drawers, can reproduce them in court, and by which it will be enabled to expose to a jury the most intimate occurrences of the home" (*Olmstead v. United States*, 277 U.S. 438, 478 [1928]).

The notion of privacy being based on a right to be left alone has been criticized for lack of clarity. A definition that lumps together both an uninvited punch in the stomach and a "Peeping Tom" clearly lacks precision. Can we reasonably claim a right to be left alone when we leave our house and walk down the street no matter how much we may desire to be free from intrusions?

Despite this criticism, Warren and Brandeis should be credited with providing the foundation for the development of the law of privacy. In the next section, we look at what we mean by the notion of privacy and what aspects of our lives fall within the notion of privacy.

■ THE LAW OF PRIVACY

We could spend the entire chapter discussing definitions of privacy. The search for a universal definition of privacy may be futile. Most commentators agree that it is far too complicated a topic to be captured in a simple definition. The so-called reductionists argue privacy is merely an expression of other, more fundamental rights. The right to the privacy of religious beliefs, for example, merely is another way of articulating that we have freedom of association and belief. Freedom from intrusion into our private affairs is merely an extension of the right to be free from unreasonable searches and seizures (Solove 2008: 171–197).

The consensus is that the best way to think about privacy is to view privacy as involving a group of loosely related concerns. There are various dimensions of privacy to keep in mind. We already have talked about the right to be left alone, which includes freedom from unwanted phone solicitations, protection from panhandlers on the street, protection from unreasonable searches and seizures of your person and property, and the right to insist that your neighbor turn down his or her overly loud radio. Another conception of privacy stresses control over personal information that could result in prejudice or harm. An employer, for example, may gain access to an individual's medical records and refuse to hire the individual because his or her genes indicate a high probability of a serious disease (Westin 1970: 7). A third approach views privacy as "personhood" or the ability to make important choices in our lives. This may involve the use of contraceptives, the decision whether to give birth, and the decision regarding whom we want to love and marry. These different approaches suggest that privacy has various broad dimensions.

Information. Ability to limit access to certain types of information and to control how that information is distributed and used by other people.

Intimate activities. Freedom to make decisions about our health, including decisions about medications, procreation, medical treatment, and death.

Daily decisions. Ability to make day-to-day decisions that define our unique personality: what we eat, read, and watch; where we live and how we spend our time; how we dress and how we act; and with whom we associate and work.

Spiritual decisions. Freedom to make decisions regarding our religion, marriage, divorce, and whom we love and marry.

Communication. Freedom from the monitoring and surveillance of our conversations, mail, and e-mail.

Home and other physical locations. The right to the home as a haven in which family life can be pursued, and to certain areas of the workplace as under individuals' personal control and in which they are not subject to searches by employers.

Public portrayal. The right to prevent our photo or endorsement from being used in a commercial advertisement without our permission.

In a democracy, these types of decisions are made by individuals. A totalitarian state centralizes many of these decisions in the government. Privacy of course has limits. Merely because you are in your home does not mean that you can engage in unlawful behavior. The utilitarian approach balances an individual's claim to control his or her personal freedom against the social interest in limiting claims to privacy. An example is the fact that the police may search your home if they have a warrant based on probable cause that the home contains contraband or evidence relating to a crime. The government has the right to limit privacy in those instances in which courts have recognized that there is a compelling governmental interest; these areas include the following (Mills 2008: 120):

Public safety. Limits on possession of lethal chemicals and explosives and requirements that individuals use safety belts and motorcycle helmets.

Public health. Requirements that individuals obtain vaccinations and avoid use of unlawful narcotics.

Public morality. Laws prohibiting prostitution and incest.

Public welfare. The requirement of compulsory education.

In the next two sections, we outline the legal scope of the right to privacy.

■ THE CONSTITUTIONAL RIGHT TO PRIVACY

The U.S. Constitution does not mention the word *privacy*. This is understandable because the eighteenth-century framers of the Constitution could not have anticipated the developments of twenty-first-century technology and the threats to privacy stemming from government and private industry. The Supreme Court nonetheless in 1965 held that there is a constitutional right to privacy that protects individuals against state and federal governments. The growing concern with privacy is indicated by the fact that in the 166 years that elapsed between the establishment of the U.S. Supreme Court and Earl Warren's inaugural term as chief justice in 1953, the word *privacy* appears in 88 Court decisions, most of which did not discuss the term. The term *privacy* appears in 107 opinions in the fifteen and a half years that Warren was chief justice (Lane 2009: 153).

The constitutional right to privacy protects persons "from unwarranted governmental intrusions." The U.S. Supreme Court has recognized the right to privacy in four areas: (1) an individual's right to intimate relationships, (2) the reproductive rights of women, (3) the right to be free from widespread exposure of personal data, and (4) the right to be free from unreasonable searches and seizures (Soma and Rynerson 2008).

Intimate Relationships

In 1965, in the famous case of *Griswold v. Connecticut*, the U.S. Supreme Court held unconstitutional a Connecticut criminal law prohibiting the use and distribution of contraceptives and counseling individuals in the use of contraceptives.

The defendant Griswold was convicted in Connecticut of providing advice to married couples to prevent procreation through the use of contraceptives (*Griswold v. Connecticut*, 381 U.S. 479 [1965]).

Justice William O. Douglas noted that, although the right to privacy is not explicitly set forth in the Constitution, this right is "created by several fundamental constitutional guarantees." According to Justice Douglas, these fundamental rights create a "zone of privacy" for individuals. Justice Douglas noted that the various provisions of the Bill of Rights possess "penumbras, formed by emanations from those guarantees . . . [that] create zones of privacy." This right to privacy provided individuals with independence in making "certain kinds of important decisions."

Justice Douglas cited a number of constitutional provisions that together create the right to privacy. The right of association contained in the penumbra of the First Amendment, and the Third Amendment, in its prohibition against the quartering of soldiers "in any house" in time of peace without the consent of the owner, is another facet of that privacy. The Fourth Amendment explicitly affirms the "right of the people to be secure in their persons, houses, papers, and effects against unreasonable searches and seizures." The Fifth Amendment's Self-Incrimination Clause "enables the citizen to create a zone of privacy that Government may not force him to surrender to his detriment." The Ninth Amendment provides that "the enumeration in the Constitution of certain rights shall not be construed to deny or disparage others retained by the people."

Justice Douglas held that there is little doubt that married couples enjoy a right to privacy in controlling their intimate relationships that is "older than the Bill of Rights." "Marriage is a coming together for better or for worse, hopefully enduring, and intimate to the degree of being sacred."

In 2003, in *Lawrence v. Texas*, the U.S. Supreme Court overturned Daniel Lawrence's conviction under a Texas statute for "deviate sexual intercourse, namely anal sex, with a member of the same sex." Justice Anthony Kennedy held that Lawrence and his partner were "entitled to respect for their private lives. The State cannot demean their existence or control their destiny by making their private sexual conduct a crime" (*Lawrence v. Texas*, 539 U.S. 558 [2003]).

Reproductive Rights

In 1972, in *Eisenstadt v. Baird*, the Supreme Court extended *Griswold* and ruled that a Massachusetts statute that punishes individuals (other than doctors and pharmacists) who provide contraceptives to unmarried individuals violated the right to privacy. Justice William Brennan wrote, "If the right to privacy means anything, it is the right of the individual, married or single, to be free from unwarranted governmental intrusion into matters so fundamentally affecting a person as the decision whether or not to get or bear a child" that was at the "very heart" of the "right to privacy" (*Eisenstadt v. Baird*, 405 U.S. 438 [1972]).

The Supreme Court, in *Carey v. Population Services International*, next declared a New York statute unconstitutional that made it a crime to provide contraceptives to minors and for anyone other than a licensed pharmacist to distribute contraceptives to persons over the age of 15 (*Carey v. Population Services International*, 431 U.S. 678 [1977]).

The Court earlier held in *Roe v. Wade* that a woman possessed the privacy right to an abortion during the first two trimesters of a pregnancy. Justice Harry Blackmun wrote that the right to privacy "encompass[es] a woman's decision whether or not to terminate her pregnancy" (*Roe v. Wade*, 410 U.S. 113 [1973]). This line of cases establishing the right to privacy over intimate personal decisions culminated in *Lawrence v. Texas*, in which the Court held a Texas statute unconstitutional that punished sodomy between individuals of the same sex. The Court proclaimed that individuals are "entitled to respect for their private lives. . . . It is a promise of the Constitution that there is a realm of personal liberty which the government may not enter" (*Lawrence v. Texas*, 539 U.S. 558 [2003]).

Personal Information

In 1977, in *Whalen v. Roe*, the U.S. Supreme Court addressed the privacy interest in information. The case involved a New York law that required doctors and pharmacists to report to the State of New York the name and address and other information of all individuals who received a prescription for addictive drugs. The plaintiffs feared that reporting this information to the government created a risk of disclosure and that individuals would be deterred from getting the prescriptions they required. The Court held that the government had a significant interest in monitoring the use of drugs that threatened the health of individuals, and because that interest outweighed individuals' privacy interest, the State of New York had taken reasonable precautions to safeguard the data. The Supreme Court recognized that the reporting requirement may have deterred some people from obtaining drugs but noted that a large number of prescriptions had been filled despite the law (*Whalen v. Roe*, 429 U.S. 589 [1977]).

The Supreme Court significantly concluded its opinion by noting the threat to privacy posed by the "vast amounts of personal information in the computerized data banks or other massive government files" and recognized that the unreasonable intentional or unintentional disclosure of private information may threaten the right to privacy.

The Supreme Court also has recognized an individual's right to the privacy of his or her intellectual life. In 1969, in *Stanley v. Georgia*, a search of Stanley's home for bookmaking paraphernalia led to the seizure of three reels of film, portraying obscene scenes. Justice Thurgood Marshall concluded that "whatever the power of the state to control public dissemination of ideas inimical to the public morality, it cannot constitutionally premise legislation on the desirability of controlling a person's private thoughts" (*Stanley v. Georgia*, 394 U.S. 557 [1969]).

Searches and Seizures

Barry Friedman estimates that local and state police conduct more than eight million searches each year of pedestrians and automobiles. This does not include searches of homes or businesses or searches by the federal government (B. Friedman 2017).

In the famous *Katz* case, the FBI placed a monitoring device on a phone booth the agents suspected Katz used to transmit unlawful interstate gambling information. The Supreme Court held that Katz retained a privacy interest in the content of the phone conversations and that the government required a warrant founded on probable cause to seize the contents of the conversations. The Court rejected the government's contention that because the agents could see Katz inside the phone booth, he had no expectation of privacy. The U.S. Supreme Court established a two-prong legal test for privacy. First, the individual must have an expectation of privacy in the area that is searched. Second, society must consider the expectation of privacy to be reasonable (*Katz v. United States*, 389 U.S. 347 [1967]).

In the well-known case of *California v. Greenwood*, the Supreme Court held that Greenwood had no reasonable expectation of privacy in the garbage he placed on the street in front of his house to be picked up by the garbage company. The Court as a result held that the police did not require a search warrant issued by a judge to rummage through the trash that was contained in an opaque plastic bag. The Supreme Court reasoned that Greenwood intended to turn the garbage over to a third party (the trash collector) and garbage left on the curb easily could be examined by children and animals. As a result, the narcotics discovered in the bag were admissible against Greenwood (*California v. Greenwood*, 486 U.S. 35 [1988]).

In *Smith v. Maryland*, the Supreme Court held that we assume the risk that the phone numbers we voluntarily dial and turn over to the phone company will be revealed to the police (*Smith v. Maryland*, 442 U.S. 735 [1979]). In *United States v. Miller*, the Court held that individuals take the "risk, in revealing his affairs to another, that the information will be conveyed . . . to the government . . . even if the information is revealed on the assumption . . . it will be used only for a limited purpose and the confidence . . . in the third party will not be betrayed" (*United States v. Miller*, 425 U.S. 435 [1976]).

The Court in 2012 in *United States v. Jones* indicated that there are limits on the government's assertion that individuals by exposing themselves or their activities to public view lose their expectation of privacy. Law enforcement officers attached a GPS tracking device to Jones's car for the purpose of monitoring the movement of his vehicle on a public street. Jones claimed that his reasonable expectation of privacy had been violated by the warrantless twenty-day surveillance of his public movements. Justice Samuel Alito in a four-judge concurring opinion held that the use of "longer term GPS monitoring of most offenses impinges on expectations of privacy" (*United States v. Jones*, 565 U.S. ___ [2012]).

Technology may limit whether an individual possesses a reasonable expectation of privacy. The Supreme Court has held that drugs that were discovered by the police through the use of aerial surveillance are admissible because it is not uncommon for helicopters to fly over the enclosed yard and that the resident did not have a reasonable expectation of privacy in the backyard. Keep in mind that aerial surveillance enabled the police to spot narcotics that were not visible from the street (*Florida v. Riley*, 488 U.S. 445 [1989]).

An additional point to keep in mind is that the Supreme Court remains protective of the privacy rights in the home. In the *Kyllo* case, the police employed a thermal imaging device to measure the heat emanating from Kyllo's home. The intense heat, along with utility bills and information furnished by an informant, provided the police with probable cause to believe Kyllo was employing high-intensity lights to grow marijuana. A search of the home resulted in the seizure of more than one hundred plants. The Supreme Court condemned the warrantless use of technology to penetrate Kyllo's home and stressed that the Fourth Amendment "draws a firm line at the entrance to the home" (*Kyllo v. United States*, 533 U.S. 27 [2001]). In 2014, the Supreme Court held that a search incident to an arrest does not permit the police to search a suspect's cell phone absent a search warrant (*Riley v. California*, 573 U.S.___ [2014]).

The Supreme Court has carved out an exception to the probable cause and warrant requirement in regard to "special needs" searches or searches that are intended to protect the public safety rather than to investigate whether a particular individual is involved in criminal activity. This doctrine has been used to justify brief stops at automobile checkpoints (*Michigan Department of State Police v. Sitz*, 496 U.S. 444 [1990]), border searches (*United States v. Flores-Montano*, 541 U.S. 149 [2004]), and searches of individuals boarding planes and trains (*MacWade v. Kelly*, 460 F.3d 260 [2d Cir. 2006]).

Statutory Protection

The U.S. Congress and state legislatures have filled in the gaps in the Supreme Court's decisions and, in particular, have addressed the responsibilities of government agencies and the right to privacy against private companies that collect information about Americans.

The central statute is the Privacy Act of 1974, which requires federal agencies to inform people of the purpose for which information is being collected and prohibits the government from collecting information for one purpose and then using the information for another purpose. Government agencies also are required to establish procedures to protect data and must obtain your consent before releasing information. The major exceptions are law enforcement agencies that are authorized to release information regarding criminal activity. Critics point out that it is difficult to obtain damages for a breach of the law because you must prove that the information was intentionally released and that the release was not merely a result of negligence or sloppiness (Solove 2004: 134–139).

Federal laws addressing the privacy obligations of private businesses fall into several areas (Mills 2008: 135–136):

Medical records. The release of sensitive personal medical information and genetic information by doctors and hospitals is restricted.

Financial credit and consumer records. Statutes limit banks and financial institutions from releasing credit information. Individuals have access to their credit information and the right to correct the information.

Educational records. Information collected by educational institutions is protected.

Video records. Video rental records are confidential, and a number of states also protect records of bookstore sales and library records.

Federal law also protects privacy against state government in various areas. Two examples are listed below.

1. *Driver's licenses.* Motor vehicle records may not be released.

2. *Personal identity information and personally sensitive information.* Information is protected against disclosure that could result in identity theft, such as Social Security numbers. Sensitive information is protected against disclosure, such as autopsy photos and adoption records.

We should note that roughly ten state constitutions explicitly provide for the right to privacy. Various other state supreme courts have interpreted their constitutions to protect the right to privacy, and every state legislature has passed laws protecting privacy. These laws, for example, require businesses to maintain reasonable security for employee and customer information. An obligation is imposed on businesses to disclose security breaches, and businesses that raise money by selling stock to investors are required to disclose their security measures. Another set of laws requires the destruction of personal data that no longer is required by the business (Soma and Rynerson 2008: 170–185).

■ THE PANOPTICON SOCIETY

Jeremy Bentham, the influential eighteenth-century legal intellectual and godfather of the philosophy of utilitarianism, proposed a "panopticon" design for monitoring prisoners. A **panopticon** literally means a building with a comprehensive or panoramic view. The panopticon as envisioned by Bentham is a circular structure with open prisoner cells surrounding an observation tower. Guards monitor the prisoners from the observation tower in the middle of the structure.

The guards are able to observe the prisoners in each and every cell twenty-four hours a day. The inmates never are certain whether they are being observed and monitored by the guards and are motivated to follow the rules of the institution to avoid being disciplined. This is an open and transparent world in which the inmates are under constant observation and surveillance and possess no privacy and thus are constantly regulating their own behavior (Foucault 1977: 200–228).

John L. Mills terms this self-regulation the "panopticon effect" and notes that in contemporary society we are under constant observation and, in turn, constantly observe others. He quotes Christopher Slobogin, who calls the spread of closed-circuit television "panopticism," a form of "subtle coercion" whose constant "gaze" influences our behavior. In London, the average individual is on camera three hundred times a day, and the sense of being observed is intensified because the images from government cameras are downloaded onto home computers across the country (Mills 2008: 72–73). More than one million cameras are deployed in public places in England, and an average of five hundred cameras are added each week. These cameras are capable of recognizing the face of individuals whose image is on a database of known criminals and terrorists. In one test of the system, cameras on a major thoroughfare scanned sixty thousand license plates in an hour, leading to the detection of one thousand driving offenses and to sixty-five arrests of offenders (Rule 2009: 69).

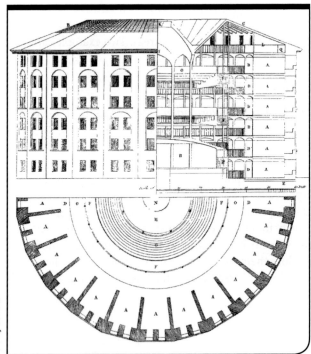

Jeremy Bentham

PHOTO 12.1   The panopticon is a prison design created by social theorist Jeremy Bentham (1748–1832), which allows a single guard to observe all the inmates. The term frequently is used to refer to the diminishing privacy of individuals in contemporary society.

The London borough of Newham has installed cameras equipped with automated face recognition software and boasts of having reduced crime by 60 percent (O'Harrow 2005: 165–166). The leading American study of the impact of cameras found that the cameras had little impact in limiting crime in a housing project. Residents frequently disabled the cameras, the community distrusted the police, and the community members who operated the cameras were reluctant to report the criminal behavior of their neighbors (Musheno, Levine, and Palumbo 1978).

There is no right to be free from observation by the government or by other people. The law assumes that while in public, we voluntarily expose ourselves to the cameras and have waived our expectation of privacy. The use of cameras is further justified as promoting the social interest in criminal prevention and detection that far outweighs the slight intrusion on the individual.

The American Civil Liberties Union found that roughly 250,000 resident

New Yorkers encountered either a public or a private camera each day. Many of these cameras are stationary, whereas others are capable of rotating and zooming in to follow a particular individual. Most people in New York City, of course, welcome the cameras and point to the cameras that led to the arrest of the Times Square bomber in May 2010. Other major cities have blanketed their downtown and subways with cameras, and suburban jurisdictions rely on cameras to capture images of drivers who run red lights or stop signs (Staples 2000: 59–60).

The use of cameras and electronic monitoring has spread to the workplace. William Staples describes workplaces in which the workers are under constant observation to determine whether they are meeting their work quotas and workers' keystrokes on their computers are constantly measured. Long-haul track companies install monitors that permit them to measure the average speed, fuel consumption, idle time, and location of their trucks. Roughly 67 percent of major employers utilize some form of electronic surveillance of workers (Staples 2000: 1, 75, 81).

Many of us are eager to be the "star of the show" and videotape our lives to reinforce our sense of importance and to attract the attention of other people. A high school student in Omaha, Nebraska, had his friend videotape his assault on a younger student, and two Ohio college students recorded the rape of an unconscious woman that they showed to their friends. There also are people like Jennifer Ringley of Washington, D.C., who hooked up a digital camera to her computer and posted a photo of herself on the Web every two minutes, twenty-four hours a day, seven days a week (Staples 2000: 63, 144). We also should note the unauthorized photos and videos posted on the Internet shot in high school locker rooms, clothing store dressing rooms, tanning booths, and "upskirt" views of women (Staples 2000: 141–146).

In a recent case, sportscaster Erin Andrews was awarded $55 million in a lawsuit against a hotel and against Michael David Barrett, who videotaped her naked in her hotel room without her knowledge. Barrett pled guilty and served two years in prison for traveling across state lines to videotape Erin Andrews. Barrett confessed to secretly taping other women and reported that he used a hacksaw to alter the peepholes of Andrews's room and then posted the videos online. The federal government and forty-eight states prohibit nonconsensual photographs or video recordings of individuals in a "state of undress" or "nudity" in a location in which the individual has a reasonable expectation of privacy (Mills 2008: 164–165).

One interesting issue involved the Girls Gone Wild videos. These videos record young women dancing and partying during Mardi Gras or spring break celebrations. Courts generally have found these young women voluntarily and publicly engaged in this conduct and that there was no violation of their privacy "even if the publicity has caused embarrassment, offense, or damage" (Mills 2008: 192).

Cameras increasingly are supplemented by microphones sufficiently powerful to pick up conversations. A leading donut chain restaurant reportedly monitors the conversations of customers and employees to detect planned criminal activity (Staples 2000: 64–65).

The future may lie in the use of radio-frequency identification (RFID) chips. These chips can be programmed with information, photos, and unique codes. They already are being used at schools to track students as they enter the building and to monitor their movements throughout the day. We may see the day when we are required to carry identification cards that contain an RFID chip. The police with this technology could ride down the street and instantly track the name and address of everyone on the street or check the name and insurance information of motorists stopped for traffic violations (O'Harrow 2005: 286).

A central pillar of the law of privacy is the notion that we waive our expectation of privacy by disclosing our image or activities to the public or by confiding in other people.

The European Court of Human Rights in *Peck v. United Kingdom* has taken a much different approach. Peck's suicide attempt was captured by a closed-circuit television camera. The image of Peck attempting to slit his wrists was released by the government to a newspaper and appeared on television. The European Court noted that Peck had not intended to participate in a public event and that the media had disseminated his image to a much larger number of people than possibly could have observed him in public. The British government, according to the European Court, should have asked Peck's consent to release his image and should have obscured his image. In other words, the European Court is questioning whether we really lose our complete expectation of privacy and control over our image when we enter the public domain (*Peck v. United Kingdom* [2003] 36 EHRR 41).

■ GOVERNMENTAL SURVEILLANCE

The events of September 11, 2001, ushered in an era of public fear and panic in the United States and in nation-states across the globe. Five weeks following the attacks of September 11, Congress passed the Uniting and Strengthening America by Providing Appropriate Tools Required to Intercept and Obstruct Terrorism Act (2001), popularly known as the **USA PATRIOT Act**. This is a complicated 324-page bill intended to make it easier to investigate terrorism by, among other provisions, expanding the ability of government to seize documents and records and to wiretap telephone, e-mail, and other modes of communication.

Another important counterterrorism statute, the 1996 Antiterrorism and Effective Death Penalty Act, provides for the federal death penalty for acts of terrorism, prohibits financial transactions with nation-states that sponsor terrorism, and authorizes the secretary of state to designate a private entity as a terrorist organization that is forbidden to raise funds in the United States.

In 1987, the U.S. Congress enacted the **Foreign Intelligence Surveillance Act** (FISA, rhymes with "Eliza") to provide procedures for electronic surveillance of threats to national security. In 1994, FISA was extended to cover physical searches of dwellings and other structures.

FISA established the **Foreign Intelligence Surveillance Court** (FISC) composed of eleven federal district court judges selected by the chief justice of the United States and by three other federal judges. Requests for a warrant to conduct surveillance of a threat to national security or for a warrant to conduct surveillance involving international terrorism are filed before a single judge. In the event that the order is turned down, the application is reviewed by the entire court. The proceedings and orders of FISC are secret, and the "target" of the warrant is not represented at the hearing. Critics assert FISC has failed to exercise an effective check on security agencies.

FISA is concerned with international threats to the United States. The individuals who may be a target of a FISA warrant for surveillance are individuals who work for a foreign organization or government (e.g., diplomats), foreign agents (e.g., persons involved in espionage), individuals affiliated with foreign terrorist groups, or individuals engaged in international terrorism.

FISA warrants are necessary for both electronic surveillance (e.g., wiretapping) and physical searches. An American or resident of the United States may not be singled out for surveillance based on the exercise of his or her First Amendment rights.

Following September 11, 2001, it was revealed that security agencies were not sharing information with one another. Section 218 of the USA PATRIOT Act addresses this issue by requiring that a significant purpose (rather than the sole purpose) of surveillance under FISA must be national security or international terrorism. This language has been interpreted as opening the door to the sharing of information and coordination between national security officials and criminal investigators. The FISC has issued a judgment that so long as a "significant purpose" of the surveillance is to gain foreign intelligence information or information regarding terrorism, the government also may have the simultaneous objective of investigating the individual for a criminal activity. As a result of the breakdown of the wall, an investigator who is conducting a national security investigation who overhears information regarding credit card fraud now is free to communicate this information to federal investigators (*In re Sealed Case No. 02-001, 02-002*, 310 F.3d 717 [2002]).

The 9/11 Commission Report recommended the integration of all foreign and domestic intelligence (National Commission on Terrorist Attacks 2004: 401–402). One of the important reforms is the Terrorist Threat Integration Center headed by the Director of National Intelligence (DNI) charged with bringing together intelligence gathered by the roughly nineteen American intelligence agencies. The government has depended on private companies with their vast databases to help create a network of digital surveillance. The reliance on data to track the activities of Americans has been termed **datavalence** (Webb 2007: 88–89).

The process of bringing information together is termed **data mining**. Traveling abroad does not raise suspicions that an individual is involved in terrorism. A foreign trip, however, may raise suspicions when combined with telephone calls to a terrorist leader, travel to a region where terrorist groups possess training camps, and membership in a group with terrorist sympathies (O'Harrow 2005: 147,152). The National Security Agency (NSA) is charged with monitoring electronic surveillance to detect threats both within the United States and across the globe. The agency also is tasked with combating threats to the U.S. communication systems. The NSA budget in 2013 was $10.8 billion, and the agency employs thirty-three thousand individuals in addition to hiring independent contractors. The total U.S. intelligence budget for all seventeen intelligence agencies in 2013 was an estimated $72 billion (Schneier 2015: 45).

In 2005, it was disclosed that the U.S. government was engaged in extensive warrantless surveillance of conversations between individuals in other countries and individuals in the United States. President George W. Bush in 2002 signed a secret order authoring the NSA to intercept communications within the United States without a warrant. President Bush explained that this "Terrorist Surveillance Program" was part of his responsibility as commander-in-chief to protect the United States. FISA procedures were too complicated and slow to permit the government to respond to terrorist threats. The disclosure of the warrantless surveillance program led Congress to revise FISA. The attorney

Laura Poitras/Praxis Films

PHOTO 12.2 Edward Snowden, a 31-year-old contractor for the National Security Agency, leaked thousands of classified documents to the press, which revealed the agency's mass surveillance of phone calls. Snowden obtained political asylum in Russia and has been charged with espionage by the United States. He is viewed as a traitor by many individuals, although others hail him as a hero.

general and the DNI (head of all U.S. intelligence agencies) may continue to engage in warrantless electronic surveillance of individuals abroad and in each instance must specify how they will avoid collecting personal information without a warrant on Americans who may be involved in the phone conversation or electronic communications. The law grants immunity (from being sued) to the phone companies that cooperated in President Bush's surveillance program.

The executive branch of the U.S. government subsequently established a large-scale electronic surveillance program to collect the phone numbers called by Americans ("metadata"). The full scope of NSA programs remains classified, although material released by former NSA analyst Edward Snowden indicates the government requires telecommunication companies to provide the phone numbers called by Americans. The numbers called from each phone were analyzed (*chaining*). In those instances in which a telephone call or e-mail was linked to an individual suspected of terrorism, a warrant could be sought to listen to the phone call or to open e-mails or phone calls connected to the number. The phone numbers collected were held by NSA for five years (President's Review Group on Intelligence and Communications Technology 2014; Privacy and Civil Liberties Oversight Board 2014).

The scope of the domestic surveillance program is illustrated by an order issued by FISC leaked to the British *Guardian* newspaper. The order is based on Section 215 of the USA PATRIOT Act, which allows the government to require organizations to provide information necessary to combat international terrorism or secret intelligence activities. Verizon was directed to provide the NSA with the call records of every Verizon customer between April 23, 2013, and July 19, 2013. These types of orders were issued every few months and required the records to include "on an ongoing daily basis" all records of calls "wholly within the United States, including local telephone calls" and any call "between United States and abroad."

The NSA is authorized to collect a wide range of data, including a defendant's home and work addresses, age, gender, income, ethnicity, marital status, sexual orientation, number of children, level of education, and location information.

A related surveillance program involves the infiltration of online games and Second Life (an online virtual world) to monitor the communication between players and to recruit informants. The NSA explained that the games are being used by terrorists to communicate with one another and to plot terrorist attacks. Another avenue of surveillance is the U.S. Postal Service tracking of the front and back of ten billion pieces of mail a year (Schneier 2015: 29).

Snowden, in addition to revealing the NSA's domestic surveillance program in June 2013, disclosed that the NSA conducted an extensive warrantless surveillance program abroad. This included monitoring the communication of thirty-five leaders of European countries aligned with the United States. The NSA collected 79.3 million recordings of telephone calls by French citizens alone between December 10, 2012, and January 8, 2013. The U.S. Constitution does not limit the ability of the NSA to examine the content of telephone calls and e-mails and other information collected abroad.

A vast $2 billion storage facility was created in Utah to store the collected data. The collection includes private e-mails, cell phone calls, Google searches, social media, bank records and transfers, medical prescriptions, parking tickets, travel records, and credit card purchases.

The metadata collection program of the phone records of all Americans is based on Section 215 of the USA PATRIOT Act. Section 215 authorizes the FBI to order any person or entity to turn over "any tangible things," so long as the FBI "specif[ies]" the order is "for an authorized investigation . . . to protect against international terrorism or clandestine intelligence activities."

The FBI under Section 215 is not required to demonstrate probable cause or reasonable suspicion to believe the person whose records are required is engaged in criminal activity or is an agent of a foreign power. Critics contend the government was abusing this provision by collecting the phone records of all Americans.

The foreign surveillance program of non-Americans is based on Section 702 of FISA, which allows the attorney general and DNI for up to a year to engage in "the targeting of persons reasonably believed to be located outside the United States to acquire foreign intelligence information." This provision does not allow individuals to be "intentionally" targeted who are inside the United States or American citizens currently in or outside of the country. There are questions whether the NSA's extensive foreign surveillance program is consistent with the language of the statute. Once again, this language may not be decisive. Non-citizens outside the United States have no right to be free from American surveillance. Barry Friedman alleges that because it is difficult to determine the location of a target, a significant amount of information on Americans is being collected under the 702 program (B. Friedman 2017: 295–296).

Bruce Schneier writes that, on a single day in 2013, the NSA had 117,675 individuals under active surveillance and that, including individuals with whom they were in contact, there may have been millions being monitored under the metadata program. Keep in mind that a search of telephone numbers and the timing, length, and frequency of conversations reveal a great deal about an individual. A Stanford University experiment analyzed the phone metadata of five hundred volunteers over several months and, by examining the numbers they dialed, was able to identify individuals who were pregnant, had an abortion, suffered from various serious illnesses, and owned a firearm (Schneier 2015: 22).

U.S. government officials argued that the surveillance program of Americans was essential for combating terrorism and counterterrorism. The largely unverified claim was that the program prevented or, at a minimum, "contributed" to the foiling of fifty-four terrorist plots, including twenty-five in Europe, thirteen in the United States, eleven in Asia, and five in Africa. The NSA claims that cyber attacks on the United States have increased by 17 percent in the past year. However, a special review committee appointed by President Barack Obama concluded that the metadata program had not been essential to detecting terrorist plots, and the information obtained through the metadata program would have been obtained by relying on the traditional warrant procedure (President's Review Group on Intelligence and Communications Technology 2014).

Despite the sophistication of these surveillance systems, their effectiveness ultimately depends on the competence of human beings. The United States narrowly avoided a terrible tragedy on Christmas Day 2009 when Umar Farouk Abdulmutallab attempted to ignite explosives hidden in his underwear as his plane was landing in Detroit. Abdulmutallab had boarded in Lagos, Nigeria, and changed planes in Amsterdam for Detroit without being singled out for investigation. Abdulmutallab, aged 23, was from Nigeria, and his British visa had not been renewed because of his involvement with radical Islamists in London. Abdulmutallab had come to Lagos from Yemen, and the United States had intercepted two conversations by **al Qaeda** members in Yemen referring to a Nigerian trained to carry out an attack on Christmas Day. Abdulmutallab paid for his ticket in cash and had no luggage—two key indicators of suspicious behavior. He had been in communication with a radical American Yemeni cleric, Anwar al-Awlaki, who also had been in contact with Major Nidal Malik Hasan, the Fort Hood killer. Abdulmutallab's father had been so worried about his son that he approached the American Embassy in Lagos in November, and his concern was relayed to the National Counterterrorism Center, which failed to place

Mr. Abdulmutallab's name onto a list of individuals who were to be closely examined or on the "no fly" list (Lipton, Schmidt, and Mazzetti 2010: A1).

In May 2015, the Second Circuit Court of Appeals fundamentally changed the debate over the bulk metadata program when it held that Congress had not intended for Section 215 to authorize the metadata program and that the language of the provision could not be read to justify such an extensive surveillance program (*ACLU v. Clapper*, 785 F.3d 787 [2d Cir. 2015]).

The disclosure of the metadata program led President Obama to propose reforms in the program. Congress after an extended debate adopted the USA Freedom Act, which provided that phone providers retain metadata rather than turning the data over to the government. NSA only may obtain access to these records by obtaining a warrant from FISC. The act also declassifies most FISA court opinions, provides for lawyers to represent civil liberties concerns in significant issues before the FISA court, and increases the penalty for material support for terrorism from fifteen to twenty years. The act limits the chain that the NSA may analyze to "two hops," meaning all numbers dialed by the target number (one hop) and all numbers dialed by the numbers dialed by the target (second hop). The goal of the metadata program is to determine whether various numbers are linked together in a terrorist network. It is a more efficient method of analysis than listening to the content of thousands of phone calls.

Torin Monahan raises the question whether we are too quick to embrace surveillance and sacrifice our civil liberties without evaluating whether the surveillance is effective. For example, Monahan notes that the creation of rigorous entry requirements for foreign travelers to the United States is intended to prevent the entrance of terrorists. The costs of this counterterrorism program include discouraging tourism, creating travel delays, encouraging other countries to create barriers to entry by Americans, and harming America's image abroad. Terrorists are able to avoid the restrictions on entry by entering illegally across the Mexican or Canadian border. There also is the challenge of managing and keeping current a trustworthy watch list and ensuring we have properly trained officers to administer the system. Focusing on foreign terrorists overlooks that we have witnessed a number of attempted attacks by home-grown terrorists lawfully residing in the United States (Monahan 2006).

The controversial Internet site WikiLeaks proclaims that it works to combat government secrecy and surveillance and in July 2010 released 251,287 documents, including secret reports on combat operations in Afghanistan that it had obtained from army intelligence officer Chelsea Manning, who was granted clemency by President Obama as he left office and subsequently was released from custody. The reports were "leaked" to three leading international newspapers, which helped to publicize the story. WikiLeaks earlier had released a secret video showing a U.S. Apache helicopter attack in Iraq that resulted in the death of civilians and of two journalists and has published reports on tax evasion by politicians, toxic dumping, and membership in racist organizations.

In February 2017, WikiLeaks released information on the ability of the CIA to access audio and written messages on encrypted devices and to use smart televisions as recording devices. The organization appears to have lost standing based on its efforts to influence the 2016 U.S. presidential election. Another hacker organization, Anonymous, which is a decentralized group of self-described freedom fighters and Robin Hoods, in 2012 was named as one of the most influential "people" in the world by *Time* magazine. There also is a growth industry in technological applications that enable individuals to protect themselves against surveillance (Schneier 2015: 167–238).

Much of the information about the surveillance of Americans is based on information Snowden handed over to newspapers in the United States and England. Snowden fled to Russia, where he was granted temporary asylum. He has been variously labeled as a "traitor" and a "hero." Should

Snowden be criminally prosecuted for leaking this information, or should he be recognized as a "whistle-blower" whose actions halted government illegality?

■ GOVERNMENT SURVEILLANCE AND DOMESTIC CRIME

Surveillance technology is not limited to the international "war on terrorism" and in recent years has been relied on by the police in an increasingly sophisticated "war on crime in the streets." Christopher Slobogin notes that American police are moving toward "panvasive surveillance" in which significant numbers of citizens are routinely monitored (Slobogin 2014).

Police departments in Chicago and in Kansas City and in dozens of other cities employ *predictive policing* to determine which individuals are likely responsible for the violence in the community and which individuals are likely to be targeted by violence. The police in Chicago developed a computer algorithm that identified 1,400 violence-prone individuals who were placed on a "strategic subjects list." The Chicago Police Department (CPD) in support of the program's effectiveness pointed to the fact that 85 percent of the more than 2,100 individuals shot in the first seven months of 2016 were on the list. Individuals on the strategic subjects list receive "custom notifications" in which they are visited by police officials, clergy, and community members and are warned that they are being monitored by the police and that their life is at risk. They are offered the opportunity and support to "turn their life around." The police responding to a 9-1-1 call in Chicago in some instances are able to check the "violence score" of the individuals involved to determine whether they should anticipate a dangerous confrontation (Gorner 2016).

Various variables are analyzed and assigned weights in computing individuals' "strategic" scores including their criminal history, weapons offenses, crimes of violence, age at first arrest, and whether they have been the victim of a shooting. An individual with a score of 500 or more is considered many times more likely to be involved in violence than the average Chicago resident. Critics assert that predictive policing is moving away from the requirement that the police arrest individuals based on their conduct in a specific instance rather than for their background or status. Another complaint is that the police target individuals on the list for arrest in order to take them off the street and that predictive policing overlooks the fact that crime is an inevitable product of a lack of economic opportunity, social services, and education.

Another technique of modern policing pioneered in New York and employed in Chicago is the use of data to locate crime "hot spots" to determine which areas are likely to see a spike in crime. The police then flood these areas with police. Critics claim that when the police presence is increased in an area, they start arresting individuals for minor crimes and inevitably push serious crime into other areas (Hardy 2016; O'Neil 2016: 84–104).

Roughly twenty states use "evidence-based sentencing" in which judges use data-based predictions of defendants' risk of future dangerousness in determining defendants' sentences. Critics object that risk scores rely too heavily on factors that are not based on defendants' criminal conduct such as employment, marital status, education, neighborhood, and the criminal history of family members (S. Starr 2014).

The police, as is apparent, no longer rely solely on the "eyes and ears" of police officers on the street to detect criminal conduct. According to the Bureau of Justice Statistics, the percentage of police departments employing some type of technological surveillance increased from 20 percent in 1997 to more than 90 percent in 2013. The most common forms of surveillance are cameras and automated license plate readers although there also is an increased reliance on the use of handheld biometric scanners (e.g., fingerprints or facial features), social media monitoring software, and tools to collect cell phone data and drones. The power of these technological tools is illustrated by the fact that in Montgomery County, Maryland, a single officer using a license plate reader for one hundred hours over a twenty-seven-day period collected nearly fifty thousand license plate scans. This resulted in over two hundred traffic citations, twenty-six suspended licenses, sixteen emissions violations, four stolen and one expired set of license plates, and three arrests. These investigative tools promise to be even more powerful in the future as individuals' name, license plate, criminal record, outstanding warrants, biometric data, photographs, and personal information all are linked into a unified national law enforcement database. A single item will give the police instantaneous access to a wealth of information (B. Friedman 2017: 230).

The police already scan and integrate content from social media networks in a specific geographic area. The technology was most prominently employed in Baltimore to determine when demonstrations were being planned to protest the death of Freddie Gray, who died in police custody. Aircraft equipped with cameras and digital technology have been employed to film protests and to identify protesters engaging in unlawful behavior. Another controversial investigative tool whose constitutionality has yet to be determined is stingrays, which simulate cell phone towers and allow the police to sweep up all cell phone data in an area without a search warrant (M. Goodman 2015: 7).

In most major metropolitan areas, a vast reservoir of information is centralized in sophisticated command centers that track police activity, monitor public and private surveillance cameras across the city, and employ technology to sweep up license plate numbers. All of this information, in turn, is linked to various databases and will become even more powerful in the future (Jouvenal 2016).

12.1 YOU DECIDE

On June 5–6, 2014, the British *Guardian* and the *Washington Post* disclosed that an anonymous source had leaked classified information that the U.S. government was requiring large telecommunications providers to turn the telephone numbers dialed by Americans over to the National Security Agency (NSA). On June 9, the *Guardian* released a video interview with Edward Snowden, the individual responsible for leaking the information. The 33-year-old Snowden was a former CIA and NSA contractor. After fleeing the United States and being denied asylum in Hong Kong and unsuccessfully seeking asylum in several other countries, Snowden received temporary asylum for three years in Russia.

Little is known about Snowden's background. He reportedly never received a high school diploma and briefly attended a community college. There is little doubt that he had a strong interest and aptitude for computers and maintained an active online presence. In 2004, Snowden, whose father was a veteran of the Coast Guard, joined the military in the aftermath of 9/11 and enlisted in a program that fast-tracked him into the Special Forces.

Snowden's slight build and various physical limitations made him an unlikely candidate for the Special Forces. In the summer of 2005, he was discharged from the Army after allegedly breaking both his legs. Snowden spent the next several months as an IT security specialist at the University of Maryland Center for Advanced Study of Language, a joint enterprise with the U.S. government.

In 2007–2008, Snowden worked in Geneva, Switzerland, as a contractor for the CIA maintaining network security. He later claimed that he grew disillusioned with the agency, and in 2009, Snowden terminated his relationship with the CIA, perhaps in response to an investigation into his attempt to access classified files.

Snowden next was hired by Dell as a contractor engaged in computer analysis for the NSA. He was sent to Japan, which fulfilled a longtime interest in Japanese culture and language. At some point, Snowden was certified as an "ethical hacker" employed by the NSA to counteract efforts to penetrate the agency's computer system. Snowden subsequently was transferred to Hawaii to work at an NSA regional cryptologic center.

A central event in shaping Snowden's attitudes toward U.S. security services was his inadvertent discovery of a report that provided a detailed account of the George W. Bush administration's warrantless wiretapping of both Americans and foreigners following 9/11. His sense of alienation was heightened in March 2013 when James Clapper, the director of national intelligence, denied before a congressional committee that the NSA had been collecting data on American citizens, a claim that Snowden knew to be false.

Snowden next took a job with the technology consulting firm Booz Allen Hamilton (BAH), which like Dell contracted to work with the NSA. Snowden worked as a professional hacker charged with detecting vulnerabilities in American technology that might be exploited by foreign countries. His responsibilities allowed him access to top-secret Internet programs and provided him with the opportunity to illicitly transfer data onto a thumb drive that he transmitted to journalists whom he trusted at the British *Guardian* newspaper and at the *Washington Post*.

Snowden believed that the government's bulk collection and storage for five years of all the numbers dialed by Americans without any basis to suspect that American citizens or residents were agents of a foreign power or were engaged in criminal activity violated the Fourth Amendment prohibition on unreasonable searches and seizures and violated the privacy of American citizens. He explained that his goal in revealing large amounts of information to selected journalists was to spark a worldwide discussion on privacy and on the secret state surveillance of individuals across the globe.

The American government has charged Snowden with espionage, and government officials labeled him a coward for fleeing rather than remaining in the United States and assuming responsibility for his actions. Critics asked how Snowden could portray himself as a defender of liberty and human rights and yet seek asylum in a repressive regime like Russia. Some high-ranking intelligence officials claim that Snowden's disclosures have made the United States less safe and have placed Americans at risk. Although Snowden's Russian visa has been extended for two years, Moscow has hinted that he may be sent back to the United States.

Polls indicated that the majority of Americans view Snowden as a whistle-blower rather than a traitor. Absent his unlawful leaking of information, the metadata program would not have been revealed. Snowden's revelations led to the disclosure of other surveillance programs, such as the U.S. Postal Service's extensive monitoring of the mail sent and received by Americans; the Barack Obama administration's approval of the warrantless search for suspicious addresses or computer codes that might be linked to malicious hackers regardless of whether they were affiliated with a foreign government; and the NSA's integration of online information to construct social network profiles of American citizens and residents.

The journalistic community recognized Snowden's contribution to public awareness of government surveillance by awarding him the Ridenhour Award for "truth telling," and the journalists who worked with him also were the recipient of prestigious awards for their reporting.

Should Edward Snowden be permitted to return to the United States and plead guilty to a minor criminal violation?

■ PRIVATE SECTOR ONLINE DATA COLLECTION

Information is big business. We would be shocked to learn there are databases compiled by private companies with records of our education, consumer purchases, travel, and attitudes. This information is marketed to businesses that sell products and to insurance companies that want to know whether we are a good risk for auto insurance and even to employers who want to know "whom they are hiring." O'Harrow writes that personal data "has become a commodity that is bought and traded . . . like sow bellies, or soybeans, or newsprint." We cast a shadow of information as we shop and go about our daily lives (O'Harrow 2005: 145).

In the good old days, a credit company would compile lists of consumers who did not pay their debts. An automobile dealer would pay a fee for the opportunity to consult the list to determine whether it should risk letting a consumer pay a portion of the price of the car and pay the rest of the cost of the car over the course of several years. Landlords wanted to ensure that individuals renting an apartment were a good risk. Today, our credit worthiness is reduced to a single, three-digit score. Three companies—Equifax, Experian, and TransUnion—maintain comprehensive dossiers of virtually every adult U.S. citizen. These scores change continuously in response to whether our payments are on time or are late, whether we have a solid employment history, and whether our home mortgage payments are on time. In 2004, the credit industry sold nearly one billion reports on American consumers (Rule 2009: 98–102).

Another program is the Comprehensive Loss Underwriting Exchange (CLUE). CLUE contains almost two hundred million files submitted by major insurance companies. The analysis of this information results in every individual being assigned a "score" that determines the amount of money he or she is required to pay for homeowner's or auto insurance. One difficulty is that unless you request a copy of your credit report, you may be unaware of inaccurate information in your file that is influencing your credit score or insurance rates (O'Harrow 2005: 140).

Daniel J. Solove writes that over 550 firms are involved in the information industry. The companies generate billions of dollars in profits (Solove 2004: 19). These companies realized that businesses would buy profiles of consumers who might be interested in their products. These information specialists gathered information on individuals from newspapers and knocked on the doors of neighbors and friends. The collection of data snowballed as businesses began to sell the names and addresses and purchases of their customers to these companies. Information companies offered free gifts and booklets on health and exercise to consumers who called a toll-free number, and while the consumer was on the phone, the operator asked questions about the caller's income, health, exercise habits, and other medical history. The company then turned around and sold these data to one of the major **data aggregator firms**.

As the use of credit cards spread, it became easier to trace all of a consumer's purchases, and the files on individuals continued to snowball. Courts have held that by using a credit card, you voluntarily turn the information over to the credit card company, which is free to sell your file to interested businesses (*Dwyer v. American Express Company*, 652 N.E.2d 1351 [Ill. App. Ct. 1995]). Another rich source of data is the questionnaires that individuals voluntarily complete. One major magazine publisher surveys readers each year on seven hundred items, including twenty-five health-related matters and the precise date of their marriage.

Data aggregator firms also began to tap into a vast amount of easily accessible government data. This includes voter lists, arrest records, legal actions, marriage licenses, home purchases and sales, property taxes and mortgage payments, credit card payments, and various other types of data. The federal government and state governments have protected certain types of data (e.g., health records; adoption records; records involving cable television, video rentals, credit, and driver's licenses) although a vast amount of data is easily obtained.

The greatest growth in the aggregation of information has resulted from the Internet. Websites sell data on users. The privacy policy of a site is based on the privacy terms posted on the site. These "terms of service" often establish "default rules" in which you give the site permission to contact you by e-mail with consumer solicitations or to sell your information for a profit to an aggregator. The user has the option of "opting out" of these terms of service. This market-based approach is premised on the view that in exchange for using the site, it is reasonable to allow the sponsor to sell your data. The user has the option of opting out of these terms of service. This of course assumes that a user is sufficiently motivated to learn about a site's privacy policy and possesses the capacity to understand the often difficult-to-comprehend privacy policies.

One English experimental study found that 7,500 Gamestation customers in one day unknowingly and willingly gave the company ownership of their "immortal soul." The Federal Trade Commission (FTC) is considering requiring Internet providers to enable individuals to select a "do not track" option. Providers warn that individuals who do not want their activity tracked may have to pay to access content because websites will not be able to make the individual's activity available to advertisers (Solove 2004: 76–92; M. Goodman 2015: 57).

Online retail sales continue to rise, with the average individual spending close to $1,750 in online purchases and Internet businesses generating well over $320 billion per year. Young people are the most wired part of the population and are one of the greatest sources of revenue. There are various ways that a site gathers information on visitors. First is registration information and the use of questionnaires. Second, visitors to a website leave a "clickstream" or an electronic record of their browsing. Sophisticated sites are able to display products that fit the customer's interests in order to extend the time ("stickiness") that they spend browsing the site and to increase the amount of money that they spend. E-mails are generated promoting products that will appeal to the customer in order to encourage him or her to revisit the site (Staples 2000: 133–137).

Another method of gathering information is spyware, software that traces an individual's exploration of the Web. The data gathered through use of spyware are used for pop-up ads and advertising. "Third-party tracking" involves assigning a number to a computer that visits a website. The tracker records other sites visited by the computer, and these sites are combined to form a profile that is auctioned to businesses (Mills 2008: 32).

New developments allow advertisers to access weeks or even months of user data, including the user's location, photographs, blogs, the content of shopping carts, e-mails, and a list of Web pages visited (Vega 2010). Roughly 1 percent of Americans have signed up for location-sharing software that tracks their location and shares this information with their friends. Location-sharing software allows for the collection of information on where an individual eats, shops, and vacations and how individuals spend their leisure time (C. Miller and Wortham 2010).

This information overload is the foundation of "cybernetic capitalism." There are millions of consumers, and the ability to single out individuals who are likely to be receptive to a product saves time and money. The general rule in the past was that only 2 percent of consumers contacted by a business would respond. Focusing in on consumers who are receptive to an appeal is a significant advantage. The process of profiling and "market segmentation" is the basis of the science of psychographics. Companies have compiled dossiers on almost 90 percent of families and offer twelve thousand separate mailing lists. A firm can locate a suburban male who owns a BMW who previously owned a Honda. Several additional clicks on the program will enable you to "target" male, white Republicans who earn more than six figures. Data brokers can sell companies lists of car owners, recently married couples, urban singles, and gun owners (O'Harrow 2005: 134).

Companies can subscribe to publications offering information on twenty-eight million households divided into one hundred different "lifestyles" based on their investments, hobbies, and vacations. *Information America* includes the basic information and average income of seventy million Americans (Staples 2000: 88). Most adults are "clustered" into a category such as "Blue Blood," "Bohemian," "Young Literati," "Shotguns and Pickups," or "Young Professional" (Solove 2004: 18–19). The search firm Spokeo provides subscribers with virtually every fact on an individual. It is estimated that more than a million people search the Spokeo database on a daily basis in deciding whether to hire an individual, extend someone credit, or enter into a relationship with someone (Andrews 2012: 9–10).

Marc Goodman writes that the Acxiom corporation of Little Rock, Arkansas, has a data bank in which 96 percent of American households and seven hundred million consumers across the globe are profiled. These profiles are sold to credit card companies, banks, and telecommunication and insurance companies. Each individual is assigned a thirteen-digit code and is categorized into one of seventy "clusters based on behaviour and demographics." "Cluster 38," for example, contains African American and Hispanic working parents who are lower middle class and shop at discount outlets (M. Goodman 2015).

You may believe that your lifestyle is invisible to the outside world. Information companies, however, are busy sweeping your magazine subscriptions, online purchases, restaurants you've visited, and airline destinations and hotels where you've stayed in order to build a profile on you. In Europe, this type of "secondary analysis" of your history would be unlawful without your consent. The one area of protection is the ability to be on a "no-call list" to avoid telephone solicitations. The law makes exceptions for charities, political campaigns, and organizations with an "established business relationship" (Rule 2009: 104–105).

Lori Andrews offers the example of an individual who writes a post on a medical site about his or her anxiety disorder and then searches for life insurance. A data aggregator may use these two entries to categorize the individual as a risk for suicide. He or she now may be viewed as a poor credit risk and may have difficulty obtaining a low interest rate on a home mortgage or a credit card with a high limit (Andrews 2012: 34). A researcher at the FTC created a dummy account on the dating site OkCupid and was able to track that his answers, including his purported drug usage, were forwarded in real time to dozens of data brokers (M. Goodman 2015: 74–75).

Marc Goodman relates the story of an angry father who marched into a Target department store demanding an explanation why his 15-year-old daughter received coupons for baby clothes and cribs. A few days later, after learning his daughter was pregnant, he called the store to apologize. Target had aggregated the young woman's purchase history and had concluded, based on a pregnancy prediction algorithm, that she was pregnant. This model allowed Target to identify thousands of pregnant women among the millions of women in its customer files (M. Goodman 2015: 73).

O'Harrow relates the story of an employee of a major drug company who, following the September 11, 2001, terrorist attacks, was removed from his position when the database mistakenly assigned him his nephew's Social Security number and falsely reported he had two criminal convictions. A 46-year-old single mother lost her job as a pipe insulator when a background check revealed that she had bounced a check for $60 two years earlier. Another worker lost his job after five years when his background check revealed a conviction for possession of one pound of marijuana ten years earlier (O'Harrow 2005: 132, 141–142).

Universities and companies, as a matter of course, hire firms to compile information on applicants, check employees' posts on social media sites, and monitor their Google searches (Andrews 2012). Associate professor Gloria Gadsden of East Stroudsburg University was suspended for the status updates posted on her Facebook page. The university explained that her sarcastic references to having a good day in which she did not want to "kill even one student" had to be taken seriously as a "security threat" (Andrews 2012: 76–77).

In a 2008 survey, one in ten college admissions officers stated they had viewed applicants' social networking sites, and almost 40 percent stated the posts had a negative impact on the admissions decision (Andrews 2012: 122).

Students have been suspended based on their online activities after posting criticism of teachers or coaches or making statements critical of school resources and creating fake school websites. A number of these suspensions have been overturned by federal courts on the grounds of freedom of speech (Andrews 2012: 76–78).

A relatively new development is analyzing an individual's social media friends in evaluating individuals' suitability for employment or loans. Your creditworthiness may drop if you are friended on Facebook by individuals who are behind on their loans. The thinking is that if your friends are poor credit risks, you also will prove to be a poor credit risk. Various public employers are requiring applicants as well as current employees to provide the passwords to their social media sites. High school students and college athletes increasingly also are being asked to reveal their passwords (M. Goodman 2015: 75–77).

A survey by the American Management Association found that 67 percent of firms are engaged in some form of electronic surveillance of their employees. In one-fifth of the cases, employees were not informed their computers or e-mail were being searched or that they were being subjected to video surveillance (Staples 2000: 77).

A Consumer Reports poll reported that over 60 percent of Americans incorrectly believe their online activities remain private and are not shared without their authorization. An overwhelming majority of Americans are opposed to being tracked on the Web and believe they should have control over their information (Andrews 2012: 22). In April 2016, President Trump signed a law to make it easier for cable and telecommunications companies to monitor and sell customers' online information to advertisers (Lohr 2017).

■ IDENTITY THEFT

The U.S. Government Accountability Office defines **identity theft** as "'stealing' another person's personal identifying information . . . and then using that information to fraudulently establish credit, run up debt, or take over existing financial accounts." In other words, the offender gains access to personal information that he or she uses fraudulently to "impersonate" the victim (Solove 2004: 110).

Identity theft is a growth industry. Solove explains that one reason for the increase in identity theft is that the private companies and government agencies that compile "dossiers" containing our personal information do not adequately safeguard these files. He observes that once having obtained our Social Security number, it is fairly easy for someone to exploit our identity. Gangs that formerly robbed banks now are hacking into computers and amassing the "data elements," including Social Security and credit card numbers, home addresses, telephone numbers, our mother's maiden name, and other data. John Soma and Stephen Rynerson report that between January 1, 2005, and November 1, 2007, five hundred security breaches occurred in the United States that resulted in the theft of millions of records (Soma and Rynerson 2008: 178).

Over six hundred thousand Facebook accounts are compromised each day. This may yield useful information ranging from date and place of birth to mother's maiden name and family photographs. Once having detected an individual's Facebook credentials, a hacker can access a range of online services. The overwhelming majority of people also use the same log-in information and password for multiple sites, and a hacker may gain access to bank, credit card, and e-mail sites (M. Goodman 2015: 88).

Identification thieves are able to sell a package of identifiers, and the identification information is used by a "middleman" to apply for credit cards, withdraw money from bank accounts, borrow money, and obtain mortgages. The FTC in 2013 estimated that thirteen million individuals had experienced identity theft. The FTC study concluded that identity theft had cost the economy roughly $18 billion. A victim spends an average of two years and roughly two hundred hours to remedy the damage from identity theft. This can cost thousands of dollars, and so long as the liabilities remain on the victim's credit report, the victim may find it almost impossible to obtain the credit required to lease an apartment, buy a home or car, establish phone or Internet service, or even obtain a job (O'Harrow 2005: 78; Solove 2004: 110).

The Department of Justice Bureau of Justice Statistics found that in 2014, 17.6 million individuals over the age of 16 had their personal information compromised at least once. Although half of the victims resolved their problems within a single day, 1.7 million found their experience "severely distressing." The financial loss from identity theft in 2014 totaled $15.4 million. Eighty-six percent of the Americans whose identity was stolen reported that the thieves attempted to open up a credit card or bank account in their name shortly after seizing the information. The threat of identity theft no longer is that a single computer will be hacked; the true threat of identity theft is the hacking of a large database. In 2013, millions of credit card numbers were stolen from Adobe Systems, and in 2014, over sixty million credit card numbers were stolen from Home Depot's network and eighty-three million were taken from JPMorgan Chase (Schneier 2015: 116).

April 2006 found that 69 percent of individuals were found to be very worried or somewhat worried about their identities being stolen. Identity theft was viewed as a greater concern than being a victim of crime, contracting cancer, or experiencing a terrorist attack (Mills 2008: 240–241). In 1998, Congress responded by passing a bill criminalizing identity theft; states also have adopted laws criminally punishing identity theft. Other laws prohibit cable television providers, driver's license bureaus, and other types of entities from releasing information. Solove has questioned the effectiveness of identity theft laws and explains that the state and federal governments have not devoted sufficient resources to the problem because it does not seem important when compared to solving crimes of violence. Investigations require trained officers working long hours. The estimate is that only one of every seven hundred identity thefts results in a conviction. One problem, according to the FTC, is that the average victim does not learn about the theft immediately. A theft may not come to light until the victim tries to apply for credit or examines his or her credit report (Solove 2004: 112).

A 2014 Gallup survey found that people are more worried about their credit card information being hacked from stores (69 percent) or about their credit card information being hacked from their computer or smartphone (62 percent) than any other crime. Eighty-five percent of individuals making over $75,000 worry about hacking as compared to 50 percent of individuals making less than $30,000. Roughly a quarter of individuals have had their credit card information stolen from their computer by a hacker.

O'Harrow tells the story of Michael Berry, who in 2002 inadvertently discovered that his credit report indicated that he had spent thousands of dollars on credit cards at a number of stores, charged hundreds of dollars of gasoline, and purchased an expensive new phone. Berry, who lived in Virginia, also was listed as having given expensive gifts to a woman in Los Angeles named Joan.

Some months later, Demorris Andy Hunter, posing as Berry, rented an apartment in Orlando, Florida. Hunter was a convicted killer who had spent thirteen years in prison. He had a California driver's license with Berry's name and a fake Social Security card with Berry's number. Hunter used these documents, along with the rented apartment, to obtain a job as a dishwasher at a local barbecue restaurant. Several weeks later, a resident of the complex, Theresa Green, was found murdered, and a national arrest warrant was issued for Berry's [Hunter's] arrest. *America's Most Wanted* featured Berry as someone who was being sought by the police for murder. As a precaution, Berry obtained a letter from the police in Oakland, California, explaining the warrant was for an individual who was impersonating Berry. In December 2003, Hunter was apprehended, and in the same month, the real Berry was singled out by President George W. Bush at the White House as an example of what can happen to an innocent individual who is the victim of identity theft (O'Harrow 2005: 74–97).

Because our information is being processed by groceries, pharmacies, restaurants, and banks, our identity easily can fall into the wrong hands. Credit card solicitations can be stolen from mailboxes or through "phishing" (an Internet fraud scheme intended to trick individuals into revealing information). A lost or stolen wallet or identifying information that is found in the trash may create a real risk of financial chaos for the victim. In July 2010, a government worker in Utah, in an apparent effort to call attention to the issue of immigration reform, released a list of names of undocumented individuals living in Utah, which included confidential medical information (O'Harrow 2005: 74–82).

Simon A. Cole and Henry N. Pontell note that consumers are told to take precautions, while the core of the problem may be the lack of protection of data by the information industry. An entire industry has developed that promises to protect us from identity theft (S. Cole and Pontell 2006: 125–146).

One company hired prison inmates to enter data. An inmate began sending sexually explicit letters to individuals on the database. A television reporter in Pasadena, California, using the name of a well-known child molester and murderer, paid $277 to the same company and obtained information on five thousand children. In another instance, a Navy sailor responded to an e-mail soliciting contributions to a toy drive sponsored by his ship on an e-mail account registered to "bosyrch." This came to the attention of the ship's legal advisor, who investigated the account and found that it was registered to "Tim," who identified himself as gay. A Navy paralegal tricked AOL into unlawfully revealing "Tim's" full name, and he was dismissed from the Navy under its former "don't ask, don't tell" policy (Solove 2004: 4).

Keep in mind that hacking also may be motivated by political motives. An example is Russia's apparent hacking of the Democratic Party during the 2016 campaign and North Korea's hacking of Sony in 2014 in retribution for the release of a movie spoofing leader Kim Jong-un.

Intelligence experts warn that cyber attacks by foreign governments are the number-one threat confronting the United States (Sanger 2017).

Computer hacking reached a new level of sophistication in November and December 2013, when the confidential credit and debit card data of as many as forty million Target customers were stolen along with the personal information of as many as seventy million additional individuals. Retail giant Neiman Marcus also suffered a breach of its security system. In both instances, the hackers installed malware and copied information directly off the magnetic strips of credit and debit cards. The stolen data were sent to a server inside Target, where it then was transferred to a Web server and eventually to a server in Russia.

In April 2017, Russian national Roman Valerevich Seleznev was convicted of identity theft and sentenced to twenty-seven years in prison. He was alleged to have stolen two million credit card numbers from 3,700 financial institutions and five hundred businesses, leading to incalculable financial losses (Perlroth 2017).

Identity theft, when it involves hacking into a computer, is a form of **cybercrime**.

■ CYBERCRIME

Cybercrime may be divided into two categories: crimes that involve an attack on a computer network and "net crime," or crime that is facilitated through use of the Internet.

Attacks on a network include the following:

- *Viruses.* Corrupting of computer programs.
- *Denial-of-service attacks.* Preventing access to computer programs.
- *Hacking.* Breaking into a website.
- *Malware.* Spying on a user's operation of a computer and recording information to break into confidential files.

Crimes that are carried out through the Internet include the following:

- *Identity theft.* Theft of personal information.
- *Fraud.* Tricking an individual out of money or something of value.
- *Phishing.* E-mails intended to trick a user out of his or her identifying information.
- *Pretexting.* Creating a false scenario to obtain information.
- *Child pornography.* Possession of unlawful portrayals of juveniles and unlawful solicitation of juveniles.
- *Copyright infringement.* Taking text, music, or a creative product without payment.

The FBI Internet Crime Complaint Center's annual report recorded 288,012 complaints filed by victims of cybercrime in 2015, an increase from 269,422 complaints in 2014; 12,145 involved a monetary loss. Over the past five years, the center has received an average of almost 300,000 complaints a year. Keep in mind that only 15 percent of all Internet crimes are reported to law enforcement authorities. The total dollar loss was $1,00,711,522, the average dollar amount lost by a victim was $8,421, and the median dollar loss was $560. The top categories of complaints were non-payment/non-delivery of goods, overpayment schemes in which individuals are asked to pay the expenses involved in collecting a substantial amount of money, identity theft, online auctions in which the quality of an item is misrepresented, personal data breaches, employment scams, extortion, credit card fraud, and e-mail scams and harassment. More than 50 percent of the complaints were received from California, Florida, Texas, New York, Illinois, Pennsylvania, Virginia, New Jersey, Washington, and Ohio (FBI 2015: 14–16).

In 2015, a "hot topic" was business e-mail compromise (BEC), defined as a scam focusing on businesses working with foreign suppliers and/or businesses that regularly send wire transfer payments. The victim-businesses are instructed to send funds owed to foreign suppliers to accounts controlled by the fraudsters. Other BEC scams involve romance, lottery, employment, and scams in which individuals are unknowingly used to launder money. In 2015, there were 7,838 BEC complaints with losses of over $263 million. A related offense is e-mail account compromise (EAC), which targets individuals rather than businesses. In 2015, there were 281 EAC complaints with losses of over $11 million. A third "hot topic" in 2015 was ransomware, in which business or hospital files are hacked and money is demanded for their return. There are instances in which hotel room access systems have been shut down until a ransom was paid. In 2015, there were 2,453 ransomware complaints resulting in losses of over $1.6 million (FBI 2015: 10–11).

In 2017, ransomware hackers seized data from computers in seventy-four countries, including British hospitals, the Russian Interior Ministry, and FedEx, and demanded payment in bitcoin. The malicious software was stolen from the U.S. government's catalogue of cyber spying tools Roughly a month later, a second attack was launched (Shane, Rosenberg, and Lehren 2017).

In past years, "FBI fraud" was widespread and involved an e-mail that falsely identified the sender as the FBI and requested personal information from the recipient. Other popular scams include "hitman scams" (an individual is threatened with physical retribution unless he or she sends money within seventy-two hours), astrological reading scams, economic scams (promises of government stimulus money), job-site scams, and fake pop-up ads for antivirus software. One new form of fraud involves advertisements posted on auction sites. The buyer poses as a wealthy individual presently out of the country. The buyer sends a fraudulent check for more than the asking price to a seller and later asks the seller to send the check for the excess funds back to the buyer.

Thirty-one states have passed legislation prohibiting "revenge porn" or the non-consensual posting of images, typically by an angry former or rejected lover. The Brookings Institution also recorded 1,397 victims of "sextortion" in 2015. In a typical case, an adult poses as a child on social media and persuades young women to send him sexually explicit photographs. He then threatens to post the photos online unless the young women send him additional photos or money (J. Smith 2016).

Some areas are not specifically addressed in the Internet crime report because they do not result in victim complaints. This includes the unlawful solicitation of juveniles and possession of child pornography and unlawful Internet gambling (FBI 2015: 12–13).

Three-quarters of offenders included in the 2009 Internet crime report were males, and half lived in California, Florida, New York, Texas, Washington State, and the District of Columbia. Offenders located abroad lived in Canada, Nigeria, Ghana, Malaysia, and the United Kingdom. The average complainant was a male, 40 to 49 years of age, who lived in California, Florida, Texas, or New York. The increased public awareness of Internet crime has led to a decline in complaints in recent years (Internet Crime Complaint Center 2009: 5–8).

Studies of cybercriminals indicate that these are individuals who spend a great deal of time online and are part of a social group in which these types of activities are encouraged and rewarded. Most cybercriminals are not deterred because they do not believe that they will be detected and believe the benefits of their activities outweigh the costs of apprehension. Some types of cybercrime, such as "piracy" of content and music, are viewed as normal and socially acceptable. A number of

12.2 YOU DECIDE

Encryption is one method of protecting the privacy of individual communication from governmental surveillance. American law enforcement agencies have resisted encryption and claim that it is vital that they are able to gain access to smartphones and other encrypted electronic devices.

In February 2016, the Department of Justice (DOJ) obtained a legal order from a federal magistrate requiring Apple to write code to bypass the security functions on the iPhone 5c of dead terrorist Syed Rizwan Farook so as to allow the FBI to detect the password and to search the data on the phone. Farook, along with his wife, killed fourteen people in a December 2015 terrorist attack in San Bernardino, California. The government later dropped the legal action when it successfully accessed the data stored on Farook's iPhone. The DOJ did not disclose how it managed to gain access to the phone or what it uncovered. The DOJ at the time it requested the court order stressed that it was asking Apple to allow the FBI to enter a single phone and did not intend to "break anyone's encryption or set a master key lose on the land."

Apple CEO Timothy D. Cook had earlier indicated that Apple would appeal the court order. He explained that even Apple did not have the present capacity to break into the iPhone and that the protection of user privacy was at the core of Apple's mission. He contended that this case was about the data security of "hundreds of millions of law-abiding people, and setting a dangerous precedent that threatens everyone's civil liberties," and making everyone vulnerable to "digital crime." Once created, "the [hacking] technique could be used over and over again on any number of devices." Apple also feared that governments in China and Russia and in other authoritarian countries would require that Apple provide them access to iPhones.

Various federal prosecutors asked in response whether Apple and Google were more important than combating terrorism. It was argued that preventing the government access to the iPhone was like preventing the police from searching a house for evidence of child pornography and impeding, if not making impossible, criminal prosecution.

A CBS/*New York Times* poll found that 50 percent of respondents believed that Apple should unlock the phone although 45 percent of respondents supported Apple. The major tech companies that control information belonging to millions of Americans indicated support for Apple protecting the privacy of consumers.

Did Apple have a moral responsibility to assist the government? A moral responsibility to protect users of the iPhone? A corporate responsibility to protect the profitability of the company for investors and for employees? Should corporations be required to give the government the capacity to access encrypted data?

commentators note that the anonymity of the Internet and the physical distance between the offender and victim make it easier for individuals to engage in computer crime (Higgins 2010: 89–109).

■ A DIGITAL CONSTITUTION

Lori Andrews has proposed a "Social Network" Constitution to safeguard individuals' digital rights; several of her provisions are listed below along with protections included in the Madrid Privacy Declaration signed by one hundred organizations in 2009. These principles are based on the proposition that everyone has the right to the protection of his or her personal data (Andrews 2012: 189–190; Schneier 2015).

The right to connect. Individuals should have access to the Internet and shall be free of monitoring of the sources and content of their exchanges.

Free speech and free expression. Freedom of digital expression is protected. Employers and schools are prohibited from accessing social network pages or taking action against people based on their expression or disclosures other than in the case of threatened imminent harm.

Privacy of place and information. Individuals should have privacy of networking profiles and should be protected against the tracking of their locations.

Control of image. An individual's image may not be used without his or her consent.

Due process. An individual is entitled to control, correct, and delete the individual's online information. Information shall not be collected or analyzed absent notice and consent of the individual.

Discrimination. Individuals shall not be discriminated against on their social network activities or profile.

Association. Individuals shall have the right to freedom of association on social networks and the right to keep their associations private.

Surveillance. Individuals also should be protected against the military or intelligence services' surveillance and collection of their personal information absent a judicial warrant issued based on probable cause.

Research. New technologies of mass surveillance should be subject to study and democratic debate.

James Rule reviewed privacy protections across the globe and, in addition to the protections proposed by Andrews, proposes that information collection for one purpose should not be used for another purpose. Rule also advocates strong civil and criminal penalties and argues that remedies should be provided for the unlawful collection of information and for the misuse of information (Rule 2009: 26).

Drug testing and the collection of DNA discussed below also pose a challenge to the right of individual privacy.

12.3 YOU DECIDE

In reaction to the intolerance to free speech that led to the terrorist killing of twelve French cartoonists and journalists and the wounding of eleven others working on the satirical magazine *Charlie Hebdo* in January 2015, a number of books appeared defending the value of free expression in an increasingly diverse world. One challenge is how to organize an open Internet that at the same time regulates, if not prohibits, hateful and harmful speech (Ash 2016; Neuborne 2015).

(Continued)

(Continued)

In 2016, Twitter permanently banned Milo Yiannopoulos, technology editor for Breitbart.com, who tweeted as @Nero and referred to himself as the "most fabulous supervillain on the internet." Yiannopoulos, an infamous young right-wing personality, at the time that he was banned had over thirty-three thousand followers. Yiannopoulos gained notoriety for his controversial views that the incidence of rapes on campus were exaggerated (a "fantasy" like Harry Potter) and as a leader in the Gamergate movement, which attacked the "sociopathic feminist programmers and campaigners" who advocated for a more diverse and politically progressive online gaming community. He notoriously posted a poll asking whether parents would prefer their child to have cancer or be a feminist. The events that precipitated the removal of Yiannopoulos's Twitter account involved his alleged incitement of crude attacks on African American actress and comedian Leslie Jones for her role in the remake of the movie *Ghostbusters*. Yiannopoulos, several months earlier, had his blue verification check mark removed by Twitter. He subsequently launched his "dangerous faggot" college tour, which led to vocal protests at universities including a violent confrontation at the University of California at Berkeley.

Yiannopoulos claimed that Twitter was discriminating against him because he was a Republican and outspoken supporter of Donald Trump. The statement by Twitter suspending his account explained that Yiannopoulos had violated the site's terms of service, which prohibited "behavior that harasses, intimidates, or uses fear to silence another user's voice." Twitter stated that "people should be able to express diverse opinions and beliefs on Twitter. But no one deserves to be subjected to targeted abuse online, and our rules prohibit inciting or engaging in the targeted abuse or harassment of others."

Yiannopoulos posted a response asserting that his suspension was "cowardly" and that Twitter was a "no-go zone for conservatives. . . . Like all acts of the totalitarian regressive left, this will blow up in their faces, netting me more adoring fans. We're winning the culture war, and Twitter just shot themselves in the foot."

Twitter, after banning Yiannopoulos, also removed 360,000 accounts of individuals who allegedly promoted terrorism and violent extremism.

In June 2016, the European Commission of the European Union and Facebook, Google, Twitter, and Microsoft entered into an agreement to "review the majority of valid notifications for removal of hate speech in less than 24 hours and remove or disable access to such content," as well as to "educate and raise awareness" with their users about these guidelines.

In the past, social media sites took an "anything goes approach." In part, this policy was motivated by the fact that monitoring and policing posts requires time and energy and may limit the user base of a site. On the other hand, mean-spirited posts may lead users to abandon a site, and there is a risk that a site may be held responsible for posts that are considered libelous or defamatory.

In 2017, YouTube confronted a massive loss of advertising because the automated advertising placement system often placed brands next to what companies considered to be objectionable material on the Internet.

Sites like Twitter and Facebook are private entities, and individuals have no First Amendment rights to express themselves on these social media sites. However, these sites are increasingly important avenues of communication that serve as public fora for debate and discussion. What is your view on whether there should be limits on expression on social media sites? Would a better alternative be the type of additional steps taken by Twitter to allow users to mute words, phrases, or entire topics? Should terrorist videos or advocacy on behalf of terrorist organizations be permitted?

■ DRUG TESTING

The growth in science, technology, and medicine has facilitated the monitoring of individuals to ensure they are living healthy lives and not engaging in deviant behavior. Drug testing is increasingly prevalent in the schools and workplace. The collection of DNA and fingerprinting have developed into a powerful tool in the investigation of criminal activity. In the future, we can anticipate technological innovations that will allow each of us to be identified as we walk down the street or enter a building with a minimum degree of intrusion.

More than fifteen million individuals were tested for drugs in 1998 at a cost of $600 million. Roughly 90 percent of businesses involved in manufacturing and transportation tested their employees. The U.S. Supreme Court in two cases upheld federal regulations calling for the random drug testing of certain federal employees engaged in occupations that could endanger the public (*Skinner v. Railway Labor Executives' Association*, 489 U.S. 602 [1989]; *National Treasury Employees Union v. Von Raab*, 489 U.S. 656 [1989]).

The most highly debated area of drug testing involves the random testing of high school students. In *Vernonia School District 472 v. Acton*, the Supreme Court upheld a testing program that focused exclusively on high school athletes. The school district alleged that drug problems among athletes had reached epidemic proportions and that athletes were role models for other students and that their drug use encouraged other students to experiment with narcotics. The district was able to point to several incidents in which student athletes suffered injuries or narrowly avoided injuries as a result of drug abuse. The Court reasoned that the urinalysis was non-intrusive and that athletes were subject to a range of regulations and had a diminished expectation of privacy (*Vernonia School District 472 v. Acton*, 515 U.S. 646 [1995]).

Seven years later, in *Board of Education of Independent School District No. 92 of Pottawatomie County v. Earls*, the Court upheld the testing of all students involved in extracurricular activities. Although Tecumseh (Oklahoma) High School had yet to experience a drug problem, the Court reasoned that the nationwide epidemic of drug abuse among young people justified the imposition of preventive measures (*Board of Education of Independent School District No. 92 of Pottawatomie County v. Earls*, 536 U.S. 822 [2002]). Several judges dissented from these two opinions and contended that drug testing constitutes a search and seizure and that the Constitution required a demonstration that there was at least a reasonable suspicion that a student is dealing or using drugs before subjecting him or her to a drug test. Drug testing, of course, is not limited to the school. Parents in increasing numbers are purchasing various home drug testing kits from their pharmacy (Staples 2000: 101).

Roughly 16.5 percent of all school districts (two thousand districts) randomly test students. Two districts per week reportedly are adopting drug testing. Joseph A. Califano, former presidential advisor on narcotics, has claimed that the "corridors and classrooms" of our nation's middle and high schools are so "infested" with drugs that for many students "school days" are closer to "school daze." Califano went on to observe that drug use is as much a part of the curriculum as arithmetic and English. An array of studies have indicated that students using marijuana in their senior year are eight times more likely to use marijuana at age 35. The figures are similar with regard to the use of cocaine and excessive drinking. The conventional wisdom is that students who regularly use drugs also perform significantly below students who report that they do not use drugs (Student Drug Testing Coalition 2008).

Drug testing is an $800 million industry. Companies charge between $15 and $40 per each test that is analyzed. The interest in deterring students from using narcotics to most people seems well worth the price. The value of drug testing in deterring teenage drug use is challenged by a 2003 study authored by Yamaguchi, Johnston, and O'Malley of the University of Michigan. The authors tracked ninety-four thousand middle school and high school students. The study concluded that there was no significant difference in drug use between students whose school had random drug testing and students whose school did not have random drug testing. Why? Students simply believed they would not be caught. Students who used drugs likely had been using drugs for some time and had not been caught in the past, and there was no reason to believe that the drug testing program would prove effective in detecting their use of narcotics. They also believed that even if caught, there would not be serious consequences (Grim 2006; Yamaguchi, Johnston, and O'Malley 2003).

■ DNA

DNA (deoxyribonucleic acid) is perhaps the most powerful tool of criminal investigation developed in the past several decades. The DNA molecule forms the basic architecture of the human body, and each person has unique DNA. Law enforcement has found that DNA is a valuable tool for identifying the perpetrator of a crime; however, DNA also has been used to exonerate individuals falsely accused or convicted of a crime. In 1998, the federal government established the National DNA Index System, which gradually has been expanded to include the DNA of individuals convicted of federal felony offenses. Each of the fifty states also has a DNA database that includes the DNA of state offenders. These databases all are linked together, and state and federal law enforcement officials can search the database for DNA that matches the DNA discovered at a crime scene.

The FBI database is the largest in the world and includes eight million files. Courts have upheld the constitutionality of taking DNA samples from individuals convicted of crimes and of inmates prior to their release from prison. The rationale is that these individuals are reasonably likely to engage in crime in the future and may have been involved in unsolved crimes in the past.

In 2013, in *Maryland v. King*, the U.S. Supreme Court upheld the constitutionality of a Maryland law authorizing the collection of DNA from individuals arrested for a crime of violence, or an attempt to commit a crime of violence, a burglary, or an attempt to commit burglary. The DNA sample is destroyed if the individual is not convicted. DNA samples may not be tested for any purpose other than identification of an individual. More than twenty-eight states have laws similar to the Maryland law (*Maryland v. King*, 569 U.S. ___ [2013]).

Critics assert that the DNA database originally was intended to focus on the most violent offenders. An individual who has been arrested may be acquitted or have his or her charges dismissed. Arrestees for this reason should not have their DNA on a government database, even if ultimately removed. Minorities already are overrepresented on DNA databases, and collecting DNA from individuals who are arrested will mean that the database is disproportionately used to single out African Americans and Hispanics for investigation. DNA is able to reveal every aspect of an individual's medical makeup, and if revealed, the information could be used to deny an individual insurance or employment. The European Court of Human Rights found that Great Britain had violated individuals' human rights by retaining the DNA sample of individuals who had been arrested but not convicted of a crime.

DNA has limits in solving crimes. There may be a perfectly innocent explanation for the presence of DNA at a crime scene. DNA also can deteriorate and may not yield a good match. There is some suggestion that DNA may not be as unique as represented. A study of the Arizona DNA database resulted in one hundred instances in which DNA samples were so close that they could be considered matches.

A controversial technique is familial testing, in which a complete match cannot be found on the database. Law enforcement then searches for partial matches. They search for the relatives of the individual whose profile yielded a partial match, thinking that this may yield a complete match. Eight states have used this technique although it is prohibited in various states because it has led in the past to innocent individuals being named as a suspect in a case. On the other hand, California has solved seven cases using familial searching including the Grim Sleeper serial killer of women who escaped apprehension for decades and only was detected when investigators matched crime scene data with the DNA of the killer's son, whose DNA was in an offender database (E. Rosenberg 2017).

Fortunately, we are protected against the misuse of our genetic information. In response to employers testing employees for susceptibility for disease such as sickle cell anemia and using genetic information in hiring decisions, President George W. Bush in 2008 signed the Genetic Information Nondiscrimination Act. The act prohibits insurance companies from denying coverage based on genetic testing and prohibits employers from refusing to hire or refusing to promote an individual based on his or her genetic tests (Soma and Rynerson 2008: 117–128). Thirty-four states also have passed laws protecting genetic information; these laws further strengthen the protections surrounding genetic information (Mills 2008: 43).

■ FINGERPRINTS AND BIOMETRIC IDENTIFICATION

The traditional mode of identification is fingerprint analysis. The FBI fingerprint database contains over forty million prints of convicted criminals as well as citizens who have applied for federal jobs. Police increasingly are equipped with mobile technology that allows police officers conducting traffic stops or investigative stops to take a motorist's fingerprints and compare the print to the fingerprints on the database to determine whether the prints match the prints of an individual against whom there is an outstanding arrest warrant (O'Harrow 2005: 185).

In 2014, the FBI introduced Next Generation Identification (NGI), which links eighteen thousand local, state, and federal police agencies that share information. The system can process fingerprint analysis in a number of seconds (B. Friedman 2017: 264).

In California, any person applying for a driver's license is required to be fingerprinted. Fingerprinting also is being used in California to identify welfare recipients to prevent individuals from registering under multiple names. In many states, before you can cash a check at a bank where you

PHOTO 12.3 The use of fingerprinting to combat crime was first introduced into the United States in the early twentieth century. It was the beginning of the use of scientific evidence to solve crimes, a trend that has culminated in the use of DNA evidence.

do not have an account, you are required to place a thumbprint on a scanner. Various grocery chains require fingerprints in order to cash checks. The customer places his or her finger on the scanner, and the system reports whether the individual has a reliable payment history (O'Harrow 2005: 174–175). Fingerprint identification software instantly can scan a print and confirm an individual's identity (Staples 2000: 110).

The United States and Europe require individuals entering the country to provide ten-finger fingerprints that can be read by a scanning device (O'Harrow 2005: 185).

Once you are in a database, there always is the remote risk of being falsely identified as being involved in criminal conduct. In May 2004, Brandon Mayfield, an Oregon defense lawyer, was arrested as a material witness by the FBI, and his office and home were searched. The arrest warrant charged that Mayfield was involved in the Madrid train bombings of March 2004 that killed 191 and injured 1,800. Mayfield was a military veteran who had converted to Islam. He represented a controversial local Muslim activist in a child custody dispute and advertised his legal practice in the Muslim Yellow Pages. Spanish authorities had lifted a fingerprint from a bag of unexploded detonators that the FBI concluded belonged to Mayfield. The media all featured headlines linking Mayfield to the Madrid bombings.

Mayfield insisted that this was not his fingerprint although the FBI claimed that it had never made an error in fingerprint identification. FBI examiners claimed that they were 100 percent certain the print sent by the Spanish matched that of Mayfield. Spanish officials were less certain but went along with the FBI analysis. Mayfield was detained and subsequently released when Spanish authorities announced that Mayfield's print did not match the print that they had lifted from the bag of detonators and that the print belonged to an Algerian al Qaeda operative. An international panel later found several errors in the FBI analysis, and Mayfield's civil suit against the U.S. government was settled for $2 million. The FBI later attributed the error to the "substandard quality" of the Spanish sample (Wax 2008).

Fingerprints are merely the tip of a large iceberg of biometric identifications that will be employed by the government in the coming years. Efforts are under way to refine the capacity for computer-based facial recognition, iris recognition, and skin and voice recognition. These biometric identifications will be linked to individuals' files. Portable devices will make it possible for these systems to be available to the police, at airports, and at large public events (O'Harrow 2005: 186–188). Various banks are experimenting with iris identification at automatic cash machines (Staples 2000: 110). One of the first applications of facial technology was the 2001 Super Bowl in Tampa, Florida. The system identified nineteen individuals whose photos had been loaded onto the system prior to the Super Bowl. Facial recognition technology software can identify sixteen thousand points on a person's face and compare them with thousands of similar points in police booking photos or in other photos in a matter of seconds, and are being linked to criminal files, DNA, and other information. Photo identification systems are effective roughly 80 percent of the time, which means a significant percentage of innocent individuals are identified as potential suspects (O'Harrow 2005: 178–181; T. Williams 2015).

A device that is being introduced into investigations of sexual molestation of children is the plethysmograph, or p-graph. William Staples writes this involves a narrow metal or rubber band that is placed around a male's genitals. Computer software enables an examiner to determine whether an individual is aroused by photos of children or sexually provocative audiotapes. Lawyers in custody disputes in some instances have attempted to use the test to support the argument that a father is likely to abuse the children. The relevance of this test is open to question. The manufacturer concedes that although the test may reveal that an individual possesses an attraction to children, it does not reveal whether the individual committed crimes in the past or likely would commit the crimes in the future. Employers have used the polygraph to evaluate the credibility of allegations that teachers or police officers have molested children. It is relied on in more than four hundred sexual offender treatment centers across the United States (Staples 2000: 105).

We do not want to leave the topic of surveillance of the body without mentioning the extensive use of polygraph testing. Italian criminologist Cesare Lombroso (1836–1909) attempted to demonstrate a correlation between the blood pressure of suspects under interrogation and their truthfulness. This basic insight inspired the first polygraph machine, or lie detector. In 1987, one government agency estimated that two million lie detector tests were being conducted each year by private industry and government. The polygraph is based on the theory that a "lie" will be associated with rising blood pressure, respiration rate, and perspiration rate (Staples 2000: 103–104).

The important point to keep in mind is that polygraphs are viewed as scientifically unreliable and are not admissible in a court of law. A suspect in a criminal case nonetheless may voluntarily take a test to persuade the police that he or she is not a suspect in a case. Examiners on occasion attempt to encourage the subject to believe that the test is "scientific" by dressing in white laboratory coats and wearing stethoscopes and spraying the air with ethyl alcohol. CIA agent Aldrich Ames, despite his spying for the CIA, passed the lie detector on a number of occasions and later explained that the polygraph simply did not work (Staples 2000: 104).

The Employee Polygraph Protection Act of 1988 prohibits the use of lie detectors in hiring and limited the ability of employers to administer polygraphs to employees. Lie detectors may be legally used to investigate misconduct and may be relied on to justify the firing of workers (Staples 2000: 104).

We take free and unlimited access to the Internet for granted in the United States. This is not the case in China and other countries. The next section illustrates a society that comes close to being a "panopticon society." (You can find You Decide 12.4 on a national identification card on the study site.)

INTERNATIONAL PERSPECTIVE: INTERNET SURVEILLANCE

The human rights watchdog organization Freedom House tracks Internet freedom in sixty-five countries with 88 percent of the world's Internet users. Freedom House, in its 2016 report, finds that Internet freedom has declined for the sixth consecutive year. Governments are attempting to limit online activity, which increasingly is the tool used throughout the world to organize popular demonstrations and mass movements to protest government policies and corruption, protect human rights, and advocate. Thirty-four of the sixty-five countries evaluated by Freedom House have been on a "negative trajectory" since June 2015. Fourteen countries recorded modest gains in Internet freedom although in the last six months of 2015, individuals in thirty-eight countries were arrested for their social media activities, and individuals in twenty-one countries were arrested for content published on news sites or blogs. In Russia, mechanical engineer Andrey Bubeyev was sentenced to two years in prison for reposting material that he shared with only twelve other individuals that identified Russian-occupied Crimea as part of Ukraine rather than as part of Russia. Individuals in twenty-six countries were punished for posting social satire. A 22-year-old Egyptian student was sentenced to three years in prison for posting a photo of President Abdel Fattah al-Sisi with Mickey Mouse ears on Facebook (Freedom House 2016).

Sixty-seven percent of Internet users in the countries analyzed by Freedom House live in countries where criticism of the government, military, or ruling party is censored, and 60 percent of Internet users live in countries where Internet users were arrested or imprisoned for posting political or religious content. Nearly 50 percent live in countries where in 2015 individuals were attacked or killed for their online activities. One-third of Internet users live in one of eighteen countries where discussion of lesbian, gay, bisexual, and transgender issues can result in punishment, and 38 percent of users live in the fifteen countries where social media or messaging apps were blocked in recent years. Countries have used more subtle measures to control the Internet such as raising the price of online access.

Internet access in addition to being a human rights question is an economic issue. Internet shutdowns in nineteen countries between July 1, 2015, and June 30, 2016, cost these countries an estimated $2.4 billion in lost productivity by impeding bank transfers and by complicating the ordering and shipment of goods (Searcey and Essomba 2017).

Freedom House ranked as the worst countries in terms of barriers to access to the Internet, limits on permissible content, and violation of users' rights China, Syria, Iran, Ethiopia, Uzbekistan, Cuba, Vietnam, Saudi Arabia, Bahrain, Pakistan, the United Arab Emirates, and Thailand.

Freedom House lists China as the "worst abuser" of Internet freedom. China has one of the most dynamic economies in the world and yet is committed to controlling the dissemination of information. This is a particularly difficult challenge in a country with over 420 million Internet users and 181 million blogs.

In 2001, President Jiang Zemin of China warned of the spread of "pernicious information" on the Internet. The sending of "secret" or "reactionary" materials was declared a crime punishable by death. A number of broad categories of communication are criminally punishable, including "injuring the reputation of state organs" and material that "undermines social stability." Persons convicted of Internet crimes in most instances have been prosecuted under the conventional criminal code and have received two to four years in prison for their criticism of the regime. However, a criminal law amendment in 2015 provided for a seven-year prison term for spreading rumors on social media. An estimated seventy individuals are imprisoned for Internet activities, including recently deceased Nobel Peace Prize laureate Liu Xiaobo. As many as thirty journalists are imprisoned for posting prohibited material online.

"The Great Firewall of China" intercepts information from outside China. Data must flow through one of three large computer centers where the government scans content for a list of prohibited keywords and websites. A "match" results in the blocking of the information. China also has blocked access to Facebook, YouTube, and Twitter.

The Chinese government in addition limits information on domestic websites. The major method involves surveillance by Chinese domestic Internet providers. These companies employ tens of thousands of Web administrators to monitor search engines, chat rooms, blogs, and websites for content that violates government regulations. Internet providers constantly are guessing at what is allowed and what is prohibited and tend to restrict questionable information to avoid criticism from the government. The owners and staff of Internet cafés are subject to criminal penalties for failing to monitor the Internet, and Internet providers and the staff of Internet cafés are obligated to report violators to the police.

Censorship is particularly tight over issues of food and medicine contamination, local corruption, environmental accidents, unrest in Tibet, and human rights violations. The flip side of this censorship is the practice of "guiding public opinion," which involves overwhelming any critical comments with posts supportive of the government.

China also is involved in cyber hacking and in 2010 is alleged to have launched a major attack on Google in order to gain access to the accounts of millions of American and European activists critical of China's human rights practices. China's cyber hacking of American military files and global commercial enterprises, according to Marc Goodman, is the "greatest transfer of wealth in human history." He alleges that China is responsible for 41 percent of all government cyber attacks in the world including two major hacks of the U.S. government that compromised over twenty-two million personnel files. The hacks gave China the potential capacity to identify American intelligence operatives working throughout the world (M. Goodman 2015: 32).

CHAPTER SUMMARY

Privacy is thought to be essential to promoting creativity, individuality, democracy, and a personal sense of security. Others dispute the significance of privacy and contend that privacy is harmful because it allows individuals to conceal information that may pose a threat to society and to other people. The larger point is that, in the contemporary transparent world, some individuals no longer view privacy as important. The discussion of privacy illustrates the challenge of modifying the law to address changes in technology and society.

Privacy encompasses a broad range of activities and areas that are protected under the law. There nonetheless is a vast area of activity that is loosely regulated by the law.

The panopticon is the central metaphor for understanding privacy in the contemporary wired world. Individuals in the panopticon are subjected to continual observation and modify their behavior to avoid calling attention to themselves. In this chapter, we reviewed government surveillance, the aggregation of information by private firms, and the monitoring of the human body. The wired world has subjected individuals to the threat of identity theft and various forms of cybercrime.

China is a society that closely approaches a "panopticon society" in regulating access to the Internet.

Mark Andrejevic notes the "asymmetric loss of privacy." The data collection efforts of corporations and governments have become less open and controllable as our lives have become more open and transparent (Andrejevic 2009).

The discussion in this chapter suggests that we now have a radically reduced realm of privacy. The larger question is, what difference does it make? Are our lives negatively affected? Is it too late to turn back the legal clock to a bygone era before the cyber revolution?

CHAPTER REVIEW QUESTIONS

1. Discuss the importance of privacy for individual freedom and democracy. Are there negative aspects of individual claims to privacy? Is the loss of privacy unavoidable in twenty-first-century America?

2. Trace the development of the notion of privacy.

3. What is the constitutional basis of the right to privacy?

4. Discuss the notion of the panopticon society. How is this relevant for contemporary issues?

5. Describe government surveillance. Is surveillance necessary to ensure national security?

6. Does private data collection pose a threat to privacy?

7. Has law enforcement responded adequately to the threat posed by identity theft and cybercrime?

8. Outline the role of technology, biometric data, DNA, and fingerprints in law enforcement.

9. How has the Supreme Court ruled in cases challenging drug testing?

10. Do Americans have a meaningful right to privacy?

TERMINOLOGY

al Qaeda   519

cybercrime   530

data aggregator firms   524

data mining   517

datavalence   517

Foreign Intelligence Surveillance Act   516

Foreign Intelligence Surveillance Court   516

identity theft   527

panopticon   513

privacy   505

surveillance   505

USA PATRIOT Act   516

ANSWERS TO TEST YOUR KNOWLEDGE

1. False

2. True

3. False

4. False

5. False

6. True

7. False

8. False

adjudication: a court's resolution of a dispute.

administrative law: a law regulating administrative agencies.

adversarial model: two opposing lawyers zealously represent a client in court.

agency capture: an agency that works on behalf of the individuals or industry regulated by the agency rather than on behalf of the public interest.

al Qaeda: an Islamic terrorist group responsible for the 2001 attack on the World Trade Center and Pentagon.

alternative dispute resolution: negotiation, mediation, arbitration, and other methods employed as an alternative to the formal judicial adjudication of disputes.

American Bar Association: a national organization of lawyers.

amicus curiae: a "friend of the court" brief.

Article III courts: courts created under the authority of Article 111 of the U.S. Constitution.

attitudinal approach: judges decide cases based on their political philosophy.

balancing of interests: judges decide cases by weighing the competing policy interests.

bar examination: a state examination that qualifies an individual to practice law. (online Appendix A)

"black letter" law: legal rules, established by different states or by the federal government, for regulating a dispute.

blaming: attributing the harm to an individual or individuals or organization.

brief: a written argument by lawyers submitted to the court.

capital punishment: the death penalty.

casebook: a compilation of cases used to teach a legal subject that was first used by Professor Christopher Columbus Langdell at Harvard Law School.

categorical imperative: identified with eighteenth-century theorist Immanuel Kant, stating that an individual should act as he or she would like all other individuals to act under similar circumstances.

cause lawyering: lawyering on behalf of a political cause.

child soldiers: individuals serving in military organizations who are below the approved age. (online Appendix A)

civil commitment: involuntary detention of individuals who threaten themselves and others.

civil disobedience: the intentional violation of the law and the acceptance of punishment as a means to bring about social change.

claiming: confronting the individual or individuals or organization thought to be responsible for a harm and asking for a remedy.

class action: a legal case on behalf of a group of similarly situated individuals.

classical sociological theory: the early social theorists, the most prominent of which are Émile Durkheim, Max Weber, and Karl Marx.

common law: the judge-made law originating in England.

community policing: neighborhood involvement in policing.

comparative justice: individuals in a similar situation should be treated in a similar fashion.

compliance: obedience to law.

concurring opinion: an opinion by a judge who agrees with the majority opinion.

conflict perspective: conflict is a central aspect of society.

conflict resolution: settling a dispute.

consensus model: defense attorneys and prosecutors cooperate in the disposition of criminal cases.

consensus perspective: society shares common values and is relatively stable.

contingent fee: a lawyer represents an individual in return for a percentage of any monetary recovery or monetary settlement.

continuing legal education: the requirement that practicing lawyers continue their education.

Convention Against Torture and Other Cruel, Inhuman or Degrading Treatment or Punishment: prohibits the use of torture by signatory states. (online Ch. 13)

Conviction Integrity Unit: prosecutors assigned to prevent, detect, and remedy false convictions.

courts of general jurisdiction: state courts in which trials of serious matters take place.

courts of limited jurisdiction: state courts that hear minor matters.

crack cocaine: produced by cooking cocaine powder with baking soda and water, sold on the street, and punished more severely than powder cocaine.

crime control model: an emphasis on the swift and certain disposition of criminal cases.

critical legal studies: a contemporary legal theory that views law as political.

critical race theory: an intellectual movement that analyzes how the law maintains the dominance of white society and how the law perpetuates the subordinate status of African Americans, Latinos, and other minority groups.

cultural defense: recognition of a racial, ethnic, or religious group's traditional practice.

cybercrime: criminal acts directed against a computer network or criminal acts that use the Internet to commit a crime.

data aggregator firms: companies that collect and sell information.

data mining: analysis of data to find patterns.

datavalence: the use of data to monitor individuals.

derogable rights: human rights that may be suspended during emergencies. (online Ch. 13)

deterrence: the threat of a penalty that causes individuals who would have committed the behavior to refrain from committing the act.

diploma privilege: graduates of state law schools automatically become members of the state bar. (online Appendix A)

discretion: a decision-maker exercises choice.

discriminatory justice: the selective enforcement of the law against an individual based on an individual characteristic such as race, class, ethnicity, or gender.

dispute: a disagreement between two or more individuals.

dissenting opinion: the opinion of a judge who disagrees with the majority opinion.

distributive justice: the government directs resources to individuals.

double jeopardy: prohibition on prosecuting an individual twice for the same offense.

drone: a remote-controlled, unmanned aircraft. (online Ch. 13)

dual court system: a system of state and federal courts.

dual sovereignty doctrine: the prosecution for the same offense by different jurisdictions.

due process model: a model that emphasizes the protection of due process rights in the criminal justice process.

Durkheim, Émile: A French classical sociologist who theorized that law reflects the type of solidarity in society.

dysfunctional role of the law: the law promotes inequality or serves the interests of a small number of individuals rather than promoting the welfare of society or impedes the enjoyment of human rights.

enemy combatants: detainees who do not qualify as prisoners of war under the Geneva Conventions. (online Ch. 13)

evasion: avoiding the strict requirements of a law.

exoneration: a legal determination that an individual convicted of a crime is innocent of the crime and has been falsely convicted.

families of law: the major legal traditions in the world: the common law, the civil law, socialist law, and Islamic law.

family of civil law: a legal tradition in which statutes passed by the legislature are the only recognized source of law.

federal question doctrine: federal courts have jurisdiction over cases presenting federal questions.

feminist jurisprudence: contemporary legal theory, which views law as maintaining female inequality.

FGM: female genital mutilation.

folkways: the customs that guide our daily interactions and behavior.

Foreign Intelligence Surveillance Act: an act that regulates electronic surveillance and physical searches of terrorist activity within the United States.

Foreign Intelligence Surveillance Court: a court that authorizes electronic and physical monitoring and searches relating to terrorist activity.

functionalism: a theory that views law as performing various functions in society.

functions of law: social control, dispute settlement, and social change.

gacaca: village dispute resolution established in Rwanda following the genocide.

general deterrence: the threat of criminal punishment to prevent crime.

genocide: an act and intent to exterminate an ethnic, racial, religious, or national group.

globalization: the close connection and interdependence between countries.

government lawyers: lawyers employed by the local, state, or federal government.

grand jury: a panel of citizens who determine whether there is enough evidence to bring a case to trial.

grievance: a perceived wrong committed by another individual, individuals, or organization.

group legal services plans: members of the plan pay a yearly fee and in return are given access to legal advice and representation for a reduced fee or for no fee.

hate crimes: criminally targeting individuals because of their "actual or perceived" race, ethnicity, religion, sexual orientation, gender identity, or disability.

historical-institutional approach: judicial decisions shaped by judges' concern with maintaining the legitimacy of the judicial branch.

historical school: law is the product of the historical evolution of society.

Human Rights Council: a United Nations council charged with investigating human rights violations. (online Ch. 13)

humanitarian law of war: the legal regulation of the law of war. (online Ch. 13)

identity theft: the taking and use of another person's identity.

impact of law: the effect on society of a statute or judicial decision.

in-house corporate counsel: a counsel lawyer who works directly for a corporation.

inquisitorial system: a form of legal system in which judges rather than lawyers play the primary role in calling and questioning witnesses.

International Bill of Human Rights: comprising the Universal Declaration of Human Rights, the International Covenant on Civil and

Political Rights, and the International Covenant on Economic, Social and Cultural Rights. (online Ch. 13)

International Covenant on Civil and Political Rights: a binding international treaty requiring signatory states to protect civil liberties and political rights. (online Ch. 13)

International Covenant on Economic, Social and Cultural Rights: a binding international treaty requiring signatory states to take steps to protect economic rights and security, family rights, and the right to cultural expression. (online Ch. 13)

international criminal law: the law that punishes international crimes. (online Ch. 13)

international law: regulates the relationships between countries in the world.

International Military Tribunal at Nuremberg: the trial of major Nazi war criminals following World War II. (online Ch. 13)

intersectionality: the relationship between race, class, and gender.

judicial activism: judges overturn laws on the grounds that the laws conflict with the constitution.

judicial restraint: judges are reluctant to find laws unconstitutional.

judicial review: the Supreme Court is authorized to interpret the meaning of the Constitution.

jurisdiction: the power of a court to hear a dispute.

jurisprudence: study of the philosophical questions that underlie the law.

jury: a six- or twelve-person panel that decides a defendant's guilt or innocence at a trial.

jury nullification: the jury determines that the applicable law is unfair and acquits the defendant.

justice: giving everyone that which they deserve.

justiciable: a dispute satisfying the conditions to be adjudicated by a court.

Kant, Immanuel: argued individuals should be treated as ends rather than as means.

legal behavioralism: an analysis of judicial decision-making and legal system through the use of quantitative studies.

legal consciousness: attitudes and views of individuals toward the law and how these attitudes and views influence individuals' willingness and ability to pursue legal remedies.

legal mobilization approach: a theoretical approach that analyzes how social movements use law to help bring about social change.

legal positivism: the definition of law as written law.

legal realism: law is the product of social, political, and economic factors.

Legal Services Corporation: a government corporation that funds legal aid.

legalism: judicial decisions based on the law.

libertarianism: individuals and society should be free from legal regulation.

litigious: overreliance on the courts to settle disputes.

LSAT: the Law School Admission Test, an important part of the decision to admit a student to law school. (online Appendix A)

majority opinion: the opinion of a majority of the judges on a court.

Marx, Karl: a German classical sociologist who theorized that law reflects the economic organization of society.

mass incarceration: a policy that relies on incarcerating offenders as the primary method of crime control.

mechanical solidarity: social cohesion based on common work, experiences, values, and traditions.

military commissions: military tribunals established by President George W. Bush to prosecute members of al Qaeda and aliens charged with terrorism. (online Ch. 13)

Missouri Plan: a system for selecting state court judges combining merit and direct election.

Model Rules of Professional Conduct: the American Bar Association ethical code, which is a model for state bar association ethics codes.

mores: deeply and intensely held norms about what is right and wrong.

multiplex relationships: individuals are tied together by a number of connections.

naming: identifying the harm caused by an individual or individuals or an institution.

natural law: law based on certain universal principles.

negative rights: rights based on the absence of governmental action. (online Ch. 13)

new judicial federalism: state supreme courts broadly interpret state constitutional provisions to provide more rights than is required under the U.S. Constitution.

non-derogable rights: rights that are to be protected in times of national emergency. (online Ch. 13)

norms: the "action aspect" of values that tell us how to act in a situation.

organic solidarity: social cohesion based on individuals' performance of interdependent economic roles.

originalism: judges look to the intent of the drafters of the law or the framers of the constitution.

panopticon: a building with a comprehensive or panoramic view.

Panama Papers: documents disclosing the use of tax havens by wealthy individuals.

paralegals: non-lawyers who perform various legal tasks.

plea bargaining: pleading guilty in return for a lesser sentence or for some other benefit.

plurality opinion: a majority of judges favor a particular result although they cannot agree on the reason for the decision.

positive rights: rights whose implementation requires government action. (online Ch. 13)

precedent: the common law principle that "like cases are treated alike."

pretext stop: a police-motivated seizure of a person based on an unarticulated reason.

privacy: the right to be left alone.

pro bono publico: legal activities undertaken in the public interest without charge.

pro se: an individual who represents himself or herself.

procedural justice: people will respect and support the justice system as long as they believe that fair and objective standards are being employed.

profession: an occupation that has prestige and status based on specialized expertise, training, restricted access, and self-regulation.

public defenders: lawyers paid by the government to represent indigent defendants.

racial profiling: relying on race or ethnicity to determine whether an individual is engaged in criminal activity.

resistance: legal or extra-legal resistance to a legal system.

restorative justice: individuals who are harmed are compensated for their injuries and for damage to their property.

retributive justice: the government punishes individuals who criminally harm other individuals and/or society.

Rome Statute: the statute establishing the International Criminal Court.

sanctions: punishments.

sex trafficking: the transportation of individuals for the purposes of sexual exploitation.

Shari'a: Islamic law; literally means "path to follow" for salvation.

simplex relationships: individuals are tied together by a specific type of connection.

socialist law: the purpose is to cleanse the influence of the past and to prepare individuals for the transition to a classless society in which the people collectively own property.

sociological jurisprudence: law exists in social and economic context and should be used to achieve social reform.

Socratic method: the question and answer approach to teaching law school.

solo practitioners: lawyers who practice on their own and are not members of a firm.

specific deterrence: the ability of law to prevent an offender from once again committing a crime.

stand your ground: no duty to retreat when attacked.

state appellate courts: individuals in state court systems have the right to appeal a case from courts of general jurisdiction to appellate courts.

strategic approach: judges decide cases so as to advance their political goals.

stratified private legal profession: an American legal profession characterized by a small percentage of lawyers who represent the most powerful clients, make the most money, and possess the most prestige.

substantive justice: the fundamental civil and political and property rights of individuals are protected against governmental interference such as freedom of speech and the right to be represented by a lawyer at trial.

surveillance: monitoring of an individual or individuals.

textualism: a judge looks at the words of a statute or constitutional provision.

transitional justice: the creation of a legal system viewed as fair and legitimate by a regime that succeeds a government that disregarded the rule of law.

truth and reconciliation commission: a commission charged with uncovering what transpired during a period of human rights violations. (online Ch. 13)

Universal Declaration of Human Rights: a non-binding, UN document recognizing the inherent rights of all individuals. (online Ch. 13)

universal jurisdiction: all countries have jurisdiction over certain serious international crimes. (online Ch. 13)

USA PATRIOT Act: the Uniting and Strengthening America by Providing Appropriate Tools Required to Intercept and Obstruct Terrorism Act of 2001, a congressional legislation intended to make it easier to investigate terrorism.

utilitarianism: law is based on the greatest good for the greatest number.

values: core beliefs about what is moral and immoral, good and bad, acceptable and unacceptable.

victimless crimes: individuals voluntarily engage in a crime with no identifiable victim.

Victorian Compromise: acceptance during the late nineteenth and early twentieth centuries that individuals will engage in immoral unlawful behavior in private.

Washington lawyers: lawyers and firms that specialize in representing business interests before federal agencies and in influencing congressional legislation affecting their clients.

waterboarding: a method of interrogation simulating drowning. (online Ch. 13)

Weber, Max: a German classical sociologist who theorized that there are different forms of legal authority—charismatic, traditional, and rational-legal authority.

white-collar crime: crime committed by individuals in business and the professions to advance professional goals.

working group: the prosecutor, defense attorney, and judge who work together on a regular basis in the courtroom.

■■REFERENCES

Abel, Richard L. 1989. *American Lawyers.* New York: Oxford University Press.

———. 2008. *Lawyers in the Dock: Learning From Attorney Disciplinary Proceedings.* New York: Oxford University Press.

Abrams, Rachael. 2016. "Falling Short of Commitments to Overseas Factor Workers." *New York Times,* May 31.

Abrams, Rachael, and Maher Sattar. 2017. "Turmoil in a Global Apparel Hub." *New York Times,* Jan. 23.

Abramson, Jeffrey. 2000. *We the Jury.* Cambridge, MA: Harvard University Press.

Ackermann, Nicole, Melody S. Goodman, Keon Gilbert, Cassandra Arroyo-Johnson, and Marcello Pagano. 2015. "Race, Law and Health: Examination of 'Stand Your Ground' and Defendant Convictions in Florida." *Social Science & Medicine* 42: 194–201.

Albonetti, Celesta. 1987. "Prosecutorial Discretion: The Effects of Uncertainty." *Law & Society Review* 21: 291–313.

Albright, Madeleine A., and William S. Cohen. 2008. *Preventing Genocide: A Blueprint for U.S. Policymakers.* Washington, DC: U.S. Holocaust Memorial Museum.

Alexander, Michelle. 2010. *The New Jim Crow: Mass Incarceration in the Age of Colorblindness.* New York: New Press.

Allen, Harry E., Edward J. Latessa, and Bruce S. Ponder. 2012. *Corrections in America: An Introduction,* 13th ed. Upper Saddle River, NJ: Prentice Hall.

Alliance for Justice. 2016. Broadening the Bench: Judicial Nominations and Professional Diversity. Washington, DC: Alliance for Justice.

Alschuler, Albert W. 1968. "The Prosecutor's Role in Plea Bargaining." *University of Chicago Law Review* 36: 50–112.

———. 1975. "The Defense Attorney's Role in Plea Bargaining." *Yale Law Journal* 84: 1179–1314.

———. 1979. "Plea Bargaining and Its History." *Law & Society Review* 13: 291–313.

———. 1986. "Mediation With a Mugger: The Shortage of Adjudicative Services and the Need for a Two-Tier System in Civil Cases." *Harvard Law Review* 99: 1808–1859.

American Anthropological Association. 1947. "Statement on Human Rights." *American Anthropologist* 49 (October–December): 539–543.

American Bar Association. 2001–2002. *Commission on Billable Hours.* Chicago: American Bar Association.

———. 2004. *Gideon's Broken Promise: America's Continuing Question for Equal Justice.* Chicago: American Bar Association.

———. 2014. *Survey of Lawyer Disciplinary Systems.* Chicago: American Bar Association.

American Bar Association. 2016. *Lawyer Demographics.* https://www.americanbar.org/content/dam/aba/administrative/market_research/lawyer-demographics-tables-2016.authcheckdam.pdf

American Bar Association Commission on the Future of Legal Services. 2016. *Report on the Future of Legal Services in the United States.* Chicago: American Bar Association.

American Bar Association Commission on Women in the Profession. 2009. *A Current Glance at Women in the Law.* Chicago: American Bar Association.

———. 2016. *A Current Glance at Women in the Law.* Chicago: American Bar Association.

American Bar Association Consortium on Legal Services and the Public. 1994. *Legal Needs and Civil Justice: A Survey of America.* Chicago: American Bar Association.

American Bar Association National Task Force on Stand Your Ground Laws. 2015. *Final Report and Recommendations.* Chicago: American Bar Association.

American Bar Association Section of Legal Education and Admission to the Bar. n.d. *ABA-Approved Law Schools.* Chicago: American Bar Association. http://www.americanbar.org/groups/legal_education/resources/aba_approved_law_schools.html

American Bar Association Standing Committee on Lawyer Disciplinary Systems. 2015. *2015 Survey on Lawyer Disciplinary Systems.* Chicago: American Bar Association.

American Bar Association Standing Committee on Lawyers' Professional Liability. 2008. *Profile of Malpractice Claims 2004–2007.* Chicago: American Bar Association

American Gaming Association. *2016 State of the States.* Washington, DC: American Gaming Association.

American Medical Association. 1859. *Report on Criminal Abortion.* Chicago: American Medical Association. http://www.abortion-essay.com/files/1859ama.html

Andenaes, Johannes. 1974. *Punishment and Deterrence.* Ann Arbor: University of Michigan Press.

Anderson, Elijah. 1999. *Code of the Street.* New York: Norton.

Andrejevic, Mark. 2009. *iSpy.* Lawrence: University Press of Kansas.

Andrews, Lori. 2012. I Know Who You Are and I Saw What You Did: Social Networks and the Death of Privacy. New York: Free Press.

Appelbaum, Binyamin. 2010. "Putting Money on Lawsuits, Investors Share in the Payouts." *New York Times,* Nov. 15.

Appleman, John Alan. 1954. *Military Tribunals and International Crimes.* Westport, CT: Greenwood Press.

Aptheker, Herbert. 1989. *Abolitionism: A Revolutionary Movement.* Woodbridge, CT: Twayne.

Archibold, Randal C. 2010. "Judge Blocks Arizona's Immigration Law." *Christian Science Monitor,* July 28.

Arendt, Hannah. 1963. *Eichmann in Jerusalem: A Report on the Banality of Evil.* New York: Viking Press.

Armstrong, Ken, and Steve Mills. 1999a. "The Failure of the Death Penalty in Illinois. Part 1: Death Row Justice Derailed." *Chicago Tribune,* Nov. 14.

———. 1999b. "The Failure of the Death Penalty in Illinois. Part 2: Inept Defense Cloud Verdict." *Chicago Tribune,* Nov. 15.

Arnold, Thurman. 1962. *The Symbols of Government.* New York: Harcourt Brace.

Ash, Timoth Garton. 2016. *Free Speech: Ten Principles for a Connected World.* New Haven, CT: Yale University Press.

Ashar, Sameer M. 2007. "Public Interest Lawyers and Resistance Movements." *California Law Review* 95: 1879–1926.

Asimow, Michael. 2000. "Bad Lawyers in the Movies." *Nova Law Review* 24: 533–591.

Auerbach, Jerold S. 1976. *Unequal Justice: Lawyers and Social Change in Modern America.* New York: Oxford University Press.

———. 1983. *Justice Without Law?* New York: Oxford University Press.

Austin, James. 1986. "Using Early Release to Relieve Prison Crowding: A Dilemma in Public Policy." *Crime and Delinquency* 32: 391–403.

Austin, James, and John Irwin. 2001. *It's About Time: America's Imprisonment Binge,* 3rd ed. Belmont, CA: Wadsworth.

Austin, John. 1995 [1832]. *The Province of Jurisprudence Determined.* Cambridge: Cambridge University Press.

Babcock, Barbara. 2013. "'Defending the Guilty' After 30 Years." Pp. 1–13 in Abe Smith and Monroe Freedman, eds. *How Can You Represent Those People?* New York: Palgrave/Macmillan.

Bach, Amy. 2009. *Ordinary Injustice.* New York: Metropolitan Books.

Bacon, David. 2008. *Illegal People: How Globalization Creates Migration and Criminalizes Immigrants.* Boston: Beacon Press.

Bailey, William C. 1990. "Murder, Capital Punishment, and Television Execution Publicity and Homicide Rates." *American Sociological Review* 55: 628–633.

———. 1998. "Deterrence, Brutalization, and the Death Penalty: Another Examination of Oklahoma's Return to Capital Punishment." *Criminology* 36: 711–734.

Baker, Al. 2016. "City Police Still Struggle to Follow Stop-and-Frisk Rules Report Says." *New York Times,* Feb. 12.

Baker, Joe G. 2003. "Glass Ceilings or Sticky Floors? A Model of High-Income Law Graduates." *Journal of Labor Research* 24: 695–711.

Baker, Nancy V. 1995. "The Attorney General as a Legal Policy-Maker: Conflicting Loyalties." Pp. 31–58 in Cornell W. Clayton, ed. *Government Lawyers: The Federal Legal Bureaucracy and Presidential Politics.* Lawrence: University Press of Kansas.

Baker, Tom. 2005. *The Medical Malpractice Myth.* Chicago: University of Chicago Press.

Baldus, David C., and James W. Cole. 1975. "Statistical Evidence on the Deterrent Effect of Capital Punishment: A Comparison of the Work of Thorsten Sellin and Isaac Ehrlich on the Deterrent Effect of Capital Punishment." *Yale Law Journal* 85: 170–186.

Bales, Kevin. 2004. *Disposable People: New Slavery in the Global Economy,* rev. ed. Berkeley: University of California Press.

Barkan, Steven E. 2009. *Law and Society: An Introduction.* Upper Saddle River, NJ: Prentice Hall.

Barrow, Delece Smith. 2016. "U.S. News Data: Law School Costs." *U.S. News & World Report,* March 17.

Barton, Benjamin H. 2015. *Glass Half Full: The Decline and Rebirth of the Legal Profession.* New York: Oxford University Press.

Baskir, Lawrence M., and William A. Strauss. 1979. *Change and Circumstance: The Draft, the War, and the Vietnam Generation.* New York: Random House.

Batlan, Felice. 2015. *Women and Justice for the Poor: A History of Legal Aid, 1863–1945.* Chicago: Cambridge University Press.

Batstone, David. 2007. *Not for Sale: The Return of the Global Slave Trade—and How We Can Fight It.* New York: HarperCollins.

Baum, Lawrence G. 2013. *American Courts Process and Policy,* 7th ed. Boston: Houghton Mifflin.

———. 2016. *The Supreme Court,* 12th ed. Washington, DC: CQ Press.

Baynes, Leonard M. 2012. "Falling Through the Cracks: Race and Corporate Law Firms." *St. John's Law Review* 77, no. 4: 785–838.

Beccaria, Cesare. 1988 [1764]. *On Crimes and Punishments* (Henry Paolucci, trans.). New York: Macmillan.

Becker, Gary. 1968. "Crime and Punishment: An Economic Approach." *Journal of Political Economy* 76, no. 2: 169–217.

Becker, Theodore L., ed. 1969. *The Impact of Supreme Court Decisions.* New York: Oxford University Press.

Beckett, Katherine, and Melissa Bowen. 2005. "Drug Use, Drug Possession Arrests, and the Question of Race: Lessons From Seattle." *Social Problems* 52: 419–441.

Beckett, Katherine, Kris Nyrop, and Lori Pfingst. 2006. "Race, Drugs and Policing: Understanding Disparities in Drug Delivery Arrests." *Criminology* 44: 105–138.

Bedau, Hugo A. 1973. "Genocide in Vietnam?" *Boston University Law Review* 53: 574–622.

———. 2004. "An Abolitionist's Survey of the Death Penalty in America Today." Pp. 15–50 in Hugo Bedau and Paul G. Cassell, eds. *Debating the Death Penalty.* New York: Oxford University Press.

Belknap, Joanne. 2007. *The Invisible Woman: Gender, Crime, and Justice,* 3rd ed. Belmont, CA: Thomson Wadsworth.

Bell, Derrick A. 1976. "Serving Two Masters: Integration Ideals and Client Interests in School Desegregation Litigation." *Yale Law Journal* 85: 470–490.

———. 1980. "*Brown v. Board of Education* and the Interest-Convergence Dilemma." *Harvard Law Review* 93: 518–533.

Bell, Monica C. 2016. "Situational Trust: How Disadvantaged Mothers Reconceive Legal Cynicism." *Law and Society Review* 50: 314–347.

Bell, Peter A., and Jeffrey O'Connell. 1997. *Accidental Justice: The Dilemmas of Tort Law.* New Haven, CT: Yale University Press.

Benforado, Adam. 2015. *Unfair: The New Science of Criminal Injustice.* New York: Crown.

Bennett, W. Lance, and Martha Feldman. 1981. *Reconstructing Reality in the Courtroom: Justice and Judgment in American Culture*. New Brunswick, NJ: Rutgers University Press.

Bentham, Jeremy. 1962 [1843]. *The Works of Jeremy Bentham*, vol. 1 (John Bowring, ed.). New York: Russell and Russell.

Berk, Richard. 2005. "New Claims About Executions and General Deterrence: Deja Vu All Over Again." *Journal of Empirical Legal Studies* 2: 303–330.

Berlin, Isaiah. 2002. *Four Essays on Liberty*. New York: Oxford University Press.

Berman, Arie. 2015. *Give Us the Ballot: The Modern Struggle for Voting Rights in America*. New York: Farrar, Straus and Giroux.

Berman, Harold J. 1963. *Justice in the U.S.S.R.: An Interpretation of Soviet Law*. Cambridge, MA: Harvard University Press.

Berns, Walter. 1987. *Capital Punishment*. New York: Basic Books.

Best, Geoffrey. 1980. *Humanity in Warfare*. New York: Columbia University Press.

———. 1994. *War & Law Since 1945*. New York: Oxford University Press.

Bickel, Alexander, M. 1962. *The Least Dangerous Branch: The Supreme Court at the Bar of Politics*. New Haven, CT: Yale University Press.

Birkby, Robert H. 1966. "The Supreme Court and the Bible Belt: Tennessee Reaction to the *Schempp* Decision." *Midwest Journal of Political Science* 10, no. 3: 304–319.

Black, Donald. 1972. "The Boundaries of Legal Sociology." *Yale Law Journal* 81: 1086–1100.

———. 1976. *The Behavior of Law*. New York: Academic Press.

Black, Ryan C., Ryan J. Owens, Justin Wedeking, and Patrick C. Wohlfarth. 2016. "The Influence of Public Sentiment on Supreme Court Clarity." *Law & Society Review* 50: 703–752.

Blinder, Alan, and Kevin Sack. 2017. "Charleston Church Killer Is Sentenced to Death." *New York Times*, Jan. 11.

Bloch, Sidney, and Peter Reddaway. 1977. *Russia's Political Hospitals: Abuse of Psychiatry in the Soviet Union*. London: Victor Gollancz.

Bloom, Mia. 2005. *Dying to Kill*. New York: Columbia University Press.

Blumberg, Abraham S. 1979. *Criminal Justices: Issues & Ironies*, 2nd ed. New York: New Viewpoints.

Blumstein, Alfred, Jacqueline Cohen, Susan E. Martin, and Michael H. Tonry, eds. 1983. *Research on Sentencing: The Search for Reform*, vol. 1. Washington, DC: National Academy Press.

Bodley, John H. 2002. "Victims of Progress." Pp. 137–163 in Alexander Laban Hinton, ed. *Genocide: An Anthropological Reader*. Malden, MA: Blackwell.

Boggs, Sarah L. 1971. "Formal and Informal Crime Control: An Exploratory Study of Urban, Suburban, and Rural Orientations." *Sociological Quarterly* 12: 319–327.

Bogira, Steve. 2005. *Courthouse 302: A Year Behind the Scenes in an American Criminal Courthouse*. New York: Knopf.

Boister, Neil, and Robert Cryer. 2008. *The Tokyo International Military Tribunal: A Reappraisal*. London: Oxford University Press.

Boland, Mary, L. 2005. *Sexual Harassment in the Workplace*. Naperville, IL: Sphinx.

Bonsignore, John. 1977. "Law as a Hard Science." *ALSA Forum* 2: 65–74.

Bourgois, Philippe. 2003. *In Search of Respect: Selling Crack in El Barrio*, 2nd ed. Cambridge: Cambridge University Press.

Boyd, Christine L., Lee Epstein, and Andrew D. Martin. 2010. "Untangling the Causal Effects of Sex on Judging." *American Journal of Political Science* 54: 389–411.

Boyle, Elizabeth Heger. 2002. *Female Genital Cutting*. Baltimore: Johns Hopkins University Press.

Boyle, Elizabeth Heger, Barbara J. McMorris, and Mayra Gómez. 2002. "Local Conformity to International Norms: The Case of Female Genital Cutting." *International Sociology* 17: 5–30.

Boyle, Elizabeth Heger, and Sharon E. Preves. 2000. "National Politics as International Process: The Case of Anti-Female-Genital Cutting Laws." *Law & Society Review* 34: 703–737.

Brandeis, Louis. 1995 [1914]. *Other People's Money and How the Bankers Use It*. New York: St. Martin's.

Brennan Center for Justice and National Institute on Money in State Politics. 2015. *Bankrolling the Bench: The New Politics of Judicial Elections 2013–14*. New York: Brennan Center.

Brest, Paul. 1980. "The Misconceived Quest for the Original Understanding." *Boston University Law Review* 1954: 204–288.

Brickman, Lester. 2003. "Effective Hourly Rates of Contingency-Fee Lawyers: Competing Data and Non-Competitive Fees." *Washington Law Quarterly* 81: 653–734.

Bright, Steven, and Patrick J. Keenan. 1995. "Judges and the Politics of Death: Deciding Between the Bill of Rights and the Next Execution in Capital Cases." *Boston University Law Review* 73: 759–835.

Brisbin, Richard A., Jr. 2002. *A Strike Like No Other Strike: Law and Resistance During the Pittston Coal Strike of 1989–1990*. Baltimore: Johns Hopkins University Press.

Bromwich, Jonah Engel. 2017. "White and Black Police Officers Are Sharply Divided About Race, Survey Finds." *New York Times*, Jan. 12. https://www.nytimes.com/2017/01/11/us/police-officers-pew-poll.html?_r=0

Brownell, Emery A. 1951. *Legal Aid in the United States: A Study of the Availability of Lawyers' Services for Persons Unable to Pay Fees*. Rochester, NY: Lawyers Co-operative.

———. 1961. *Supplement to Legal Aid in the United States*. Rochester, NY: Lawyers Co-operative.

Browning, Christopher. 1998. *Ordinary Men: Reserve Battalion 101 and the Final Solution in Poland*. New York: HarperCollins.

Bruff, Harold H. 2009. *Bad Advice: Bush's Lawyers in the War on Terror*. Lawrence: University Press of Kansas.

Bryce, James. 1995 [1888]. *The American Commonwealth*. Indianapolis, IN: Liberty Fund Press.

Buckley, Chris. 2016. "TV Trials Show China's New Phase in Attack on Rights." *New York Times*, Aug. 6.

———. 2017a. "Detained Lawyer Details Torture by Chinese Police." *New York Times*, Jan. 21.

———. 2017b. "In Reversal, Chinese Lawyer Confesses, and Rights Groups Denounce His Trial." *New York Times*, May 9.

Buell, Samuel W. 2016. *Capital Offenses Business Crime and Punishment in America's Corporate Age*. New York: Norton.

Bui, Quoctrung. 2016. "The Most Detailed Map of Gay Marriage in America." *New York Times*, Sept. 12.

Bui, Quoctrung, and Amanda Cox. 2016. "Analysis Finds No Racial Bias in Lethal Force." *New York Times*, July 12.

Bumiller, Kristin. 1987. "Victims in the Shadow of the Law: A Critique of the Model of Legal Protection." *Signs* 12: 421–439.

Bureau of Justice Statistics. 2015. *Local Police Departments, 2013: Personnel, Policies, and Practices*. Washington, DC: Bureau of Justice Statistics.

Burleigh, Michael. 2009. *Blood and Rage*. New York: HarperCollins.

Burnet, Jennifer, E. 2010. "(I)nJustice: Truth, Reconciliation, and Revenge in Rwanda's *Gacaca*." Pp. 95–118 in Alexander Laban Hinton, ed. *Transitional Justice: Global Mechanisms and Local Realities After Genocide and Mass Violence*. Piscataway, NJ: Rutgers University Press.

Burns, James MacGregor. 2009. *Packing the Court: The Rise of Judicial Power and the Coming Crisis of the Supreme Court*. New York: Penguin.

Burns, Robert P. 2011. *The Death of the Great American Trial*. Chicago: University of Chicago Press.

Butler, Paul. 2009. *Let's Get Free: A Hip-Hop Theory of Justice*. New York: New Press.

———. 2013. "How Can You Prosecute Those People?" Pp. 15–28 in Abbe Smith and Monroe H. Freedman, eds. *How Can You Represent Those People?* New York: Palgrave/Macmillan.

Cahn, Edgar S., and Jean C. Cahn. 1964. "The War on Poverty: A Civilian Perspective." *Yale Law Journal* 73: 1317–1352.

Calabresi, Guido. 1970. *The Costs of Accidents: A Legal and Economic Analysis*. New Haven, CT: Yale University Press.

Calavita, Kitty. 2010. *Invitation to Law & Society*. Chicago: University of Chicago Press.

Calavita, Kitty, and Valerie Jenness. 2015. *Appealing to Justice: Prisoner Grievances, Rights, and Carceral Logic*. Oakland: University of California Press.

Carlin, Jerome E. 1962. *Lawyers on Their Own: A Study of Individual Practitioners in Chicago*. New Brunswick, NJ: Rutgers University Press.

———. 1966. *Lawyers' Ethics: A Survey of the New York City Bar*. New York: Russell Sage Foundation.

Carlin, Jerome E., Jan Howard, and Sheldon L. Messinger. 1966. "Civil Justice and the Poor: Issues for Sociological Research." *Law & Society Review* 1: 9–89.

Carter, Lief H. 1979. *Reason in Law*. Boston: Little Brown.

Casella, Jean, and James Ridgeway, Sarah Shourd, eds. 2016. *Hell Is a Very Small Place: Voices From Solitary Confinement*. New York: New Press.

Casper, Jonathan. 1971. "Did You Have a Lawyer When You Went to Court? No, I Had a Public Defender." *Yale Review of Law and Society* 1: 4–9.

———. 1972. *American Criminal Justice: The Defendant's Perspective*, 2nd ed. Englewood Cliffs, NJ: Prentice Hall.

Center for Responsive Politics. n.d. *Lawyers/Law Firms*. Washington, DC: Center for Responsive Politics. http://www.opensecrets.org/industries/indus.php?ind=K01

Centers for Disease Control and Prevention. 2017. *Marriage and Divorce*. Washington, DC: Centers for Disease Control and Prevention. https://www.cdc.gov/nchs/fastats/marriage-divorce.htm

Chalk, Frank, and Kurt Jonassohn. 1990. *The History and Sociology of Genocide*. New Haven, CT: Yale University Press.

Chambers, David L. 1989. "Accommodation and Satisfaction: Women and Men Lawyers and the Balance of Work and Family." *Law and Social Inquiry* 14: 251–287.

Chambliss, William, J. 1964. "A Sociolegal Analysis of the Law of Vagrancy." *Social Problems* 12: 67–77.

———. 1967. "Types of Deviance and the Effectiveness of Legal Sanctions." *Wisconsin Law Review* 1967: 703–719.

Chamlin, Mitchell B. 1991. "A Longitudinal Analysis of the Arrest-Crime Relationship: A Further Examination of the Tipping Effect." *Justice Quarterly* 8: 187–199.

Chan, Sewell, and Marlise Simons. 2016. "South Africa to Withdraw From International Court." *New York Times*, Oct. 21.

Chase, Anthony. 1996. "Legal Guardians: Islamic Law, International Law, Human Rights Law, and the Salman Rushdie Affair." *American University Journal of International Law and Policy* 11: 375–435.

Chayes, Abram. 1976. "The Role of the Judge in Public Policy Implementation." *Harvard Law Review* 89: 1281–1316.

Chemerinsky, Erwin. 2014. *The Case Against the Supreme Court*. New York: Viking.

Chen, Michele. 2014. "The U.S. Government Uses Sweatshops, Too." *Huffington Post*, Mar. 7. http://www.huffingtonpost.com/michelle-chen/the-us-government-uses-sw_b_4545134.html

Cheng, Cheng, and Mark Hoekstra. 2012. *Does Strengthening Self-Defense Law Deter Crime or Escalate Violence? Evidence From the Castle Doctrine*. Working Paper No. 18134. Cambridge, MA: National Bureau of Economic Research.

Chiu, Elaine M. 2006. "Culture as Justification, Not Excuse." *American Criminal Law Review* 43: 1317–1372.

Chung, Renwei. 2016. "Corroding Pipelines Prevent Partnership for Many Minority Lawyers." *Above the Law*, June 3. http://abovethelaw.com/2016/06/corroding-pipelines-prevent-partnership-for-many-minority-lawyers/?rf=1

Clark, Gerald. 2008. "An Introduction to the Legal Profession in China in the Year 2008." *Suffolk University Law Review* 41: 833–850.

Clark, Phil. 2010. *The Gacaca Courts, Post-Genocide Justice and Reconciliation in Rwanda*. New York: Cambridge University Press.

Clinard, Marshall, and Peter Yeager. 1980. *Corporate Crime*. New York: Free Press.

Cobb, Jelani. 2016. "The Matter of Black Lives." *New Yorker*, March 14. http://www.newyorker.com/magazine/2016/03/14/where-is-black-lives-matter-headed

Cohan, John Alan. 2010. "Honor Killings and the Cultural Defense." *California Western Law Journal* 40: 177–252.

Cohen, Adam. 2016. *Imbeciles: The Supreme Court, American Eugenics, and the Sterilization of Carrie Buck.* New York: Penguin.

Cole, David. 2016. *Engines of Liberty: The Power of Citizen Activists to Make Constitutional Law.* New York: Basic Books.

Cole, Simon A., and Henry N. Pontell. 2006. "'Don't Be Low Hanging Fruit': Identity Theft as Moral Panic." Pp. 125–147 in Torin Monahan, ed. *Surveillance and Security.* New York: Routledge.

Coliver, Sandra. 2006. "Bringing Human Rights Abusers to Justice in U.S. Courts: Carrying Forward the Legacy of the Nuremberg Trials." *Cardozo Law Review* 27: 1689–1701.

Commission on the Responsibility of the Authors of the War and on Enforcement of Penalties. 1920. *American Journal of International Law* 14: 94–154.

Conley, John M. 2004. "How Bad Is It Out There? Teaching and Learning About the State of the Legal Profession in North Carolina." *North Carolina Law Review* 82: 1943–2016.

Conley, John M., and William M. O'Barr. 2005. *Just Words.* Chicago: University of Chicago Press.

Cook, Philip J. 1980. "Research in Criminal Deterrence: Laying the Groundwork for the Second Decade." *Crime and Justice* 2: 211–268.

Corsi, Jerome R. 1984. *Judicial Politics: An Introduction.* Englewood Cliffs, NJ: Prentice Hall.

Cotterrell, Roger. 1989. *The Politics of Jurisprudence: A Critical Introduction to Legal Philosophy.* Philadelphia: University of Pennsylvania Press.

Constitution Project and National Legal Aid and Defender Association. 2009. *Justice Denied: America's Continuing Neglect of Our Constitutional Right to Council.* Washington, DC: Constitution Project. http://www.constitutionproject.org/wp-content/uploads/2012/10/139.pdf

Coutin, Susan B. 1993. *The Culture of Protest: Religious Activism and the U.S. Sanctuary Movement.* Boulder, CO: Westview Press.

Cover, Robert, M. 1975. *Justice Accused: Antislavery and the Judicial Process.* New Haven, CT: Yale University Press.

Crenshaw, Kimberlé Williams. 1995. "Mapping the Margins: Intersectionality, Identity Politics, and Violence Against Women of Color." Pp. 357–383 in Kimberlé Crenshaw, Neil Gotanda, Gary Pellar, and Kendall Thomas, eds. *Critical Race Theory: The Key Writings That Formed the Movement.* New York: New Press.

Cressey, Donald R. 1953. *Other People's Money: The Social Psychology of Embezzlement.* New York: Free Press.

Crockett, Zachary. 2015. "How to Be a Lawyer Without Going to Law School." *Priceonomics*, Nov. 15.

Cross, Frank B. 2007. *Decision-Making in U.S. Courts of Appeals.* Stanford, CA: Stanford University Press. https://priceonomics.com/how-to-be-a-lawyer-without-going-to-law-school/

Cushman, John, Jr. 1998. "Nike to Step Forward on Plant Conditions." *San Diego Union-Tribune*, May 13.

D'Alessio, Stewart, and Lisa Stolzenberg. 1998. "Crime, Arrests, and Pretrial Incarceration: An Examination of the Deterrence Thesis." *Criminology* 36: 733–761.

Daniels, Stephen, and Joanne Martin. 2015. *Tort Reform, Plaintiffs' Lawyers, and Access to Justice.* Lawrence: University Press of Kansas.

Dau-Schmidt, Kenneth, Marc S. Galanter, Laushik Mukhopadhaya, and Kathleen Hull. 2009. "The Impact of Gender on Legal Careers." *Michigan Journal of Gender & Law* 16: 49–145.

Davenport, Coral. 2017a. "After All-Night Fight by Democrats, Senate Confirms E.P.A. Nominee." *New York Times*, Feb. 18.

_____. 2017b. "Nominee Appears Poised to Cut E.P.A. With a Scalpel, Not a Cleaver." *New York Times*, Feb. 6.

Davey, Monica, and Mitch Smith. 2016. "2 Former Flint Emergency Managers Are Charged Over Tainted Water." *New York Times*, Dec. 21.

Davis, Angela J. 2007. *Arbitrary Justice: The Power of the American Prosecutor.* New York: Oxford University Press.

Davis, Julie Hischfeld. 2017. "Court Pick Says Trump's Censure Is 'Demoralizing.'" *New York Times*, Feb. 9.

Davis, Ken. 2017. *The Brain Defense: Murder in Manhattan and the Dawn of Neuroscience in America's Courtrooms.* New York: Penguin.

Davis, Kevin. 2007. *Defending the Damned.* New York: Atria Books.

Davis, Lennard J. 2015. *Enabling Acts: The Hidden Story of How Americans With Disability Act Gave the Largest U.S. Minority Its Rights.* Boston: Beacon Press.

Death Penalty Information Center. *2016 Year End Report.* Washington, DC: Death Penalty Information Center.

Defense Research Institute. 2005. *A Career in the Courtroom: A Different Model for the Success of Women Who Try Cases.* Chicago: Defense Research Institute.

Deflem, Mathieu. 2008. *Sociology of Law Visions of a Scholarly Tradition.* New York: Cambridge University Press.

de la Merced, Michael J. 2016. "Faiza Saeed to Become First Woman to Lead Cravath, Swaine & Moore." *New York Times*, July 8.

Delgado, Richard. 1995. "The Imperial Scholar: Reflections on a Review of Civil Rights Literature." Pp. 46–57 in Kimberlé Crenshaw, Neil Gotanda, Gary Peller, and Kendall Thomas, eds. *Critical Race Theory: The Key Writings That Formed the Movement.* New York: New Press.

———. 2000. "Words That Wound: A Tort Action for Racial Insults." Pp. 131–140 in Richard Delgado and Jean Stefancic, eds. *Critical Race Theory*, 2nd ed. Philadelphia: Temple University Press.

Delgado, Richard, and Jean Stefancic. 2001. *Critical Race Theory.* New York: New York University.

DeParle, Jason. 2010. "Hard on Illegal Migrants, Haven for Refugees." *New York Times*, Oct. 9.

Department of Justice. 2015a. *Investigation of the Ferguson Police Department.* Washington, DC: Department of Justice.

———. 2015b. Report Regarding the Criminal Investigation Into the Shooting Death of Michael Brown by Ferguson, Missouri

Police Officer Darren Wilson Summary of the Evidence. Los Gatos, CA: Progressive Management.

———. 2016. *Investigation of the Baltimore City Police Department*. Washington, DC: Department of Justice.

———. 2017. *Investigation of the Chicago Police Department*. Washington, DC: Department of Justice.

Dershowitz, Alan. 1994. *The Abuse Excuse and Other Cop-outs, Sob Stories, and Evasions of Responsibility*. Boston: Back Bay Books.

Des Forges, Alison. 1999. *Leave None to Tell the Story*. New York: Human Rights Watch.

Destexhe, Alain. 1994. *Rwanda and Genocide in the Twentieth Century*. New York: New York University Press.

Devine, Dennis. 2012. *Jury Decision-Making: The State of the Science*. New York: New York University Press.

Devins, Neal. 1995. "Toward an Understanding of Legal Policy-Making at Independent Agencies." Pp. 181–208 in Cornell W. Clayton, ed. *Government Lawyers: The Federal Legal Bureaucracy and Presidential Politics*. Lawrence: University Press of Kansas.

Devlin, Mary. 1994. "The Development of Lawyer Disciplinary Procedures in the U.S." *Georgetown Journal of Legal Ethics* 7: 359–387.

Devlin, Patrick. 1965. *The Enforcement of Morals*. Oxford: Oxford University Press.

Diamond, Stanley. 1971. "The Rule of Law Versus the Order of Custom." Pp. 115–141 in Robert Paul Wolff, ed. *The Rule of Law*. New York: Touchstone Books.

Dicey, Albert Venn. 1905. *Lectures on the Relation Between the Law and Public Opinion in England During the Nineteenth Century*. London: Macmillan.

Dilulio, John J., Jr. 1987. *Governing Prisons*. New York: Free Press.

Dillard, Rebekah, and Emily Savner. 2009. *A Call to End Federal Restrictions on Legal Aid for the Poor*. New York City: Brennan Center.

Dinovitzer, Ronit, and Bryant G. Garth. 2007. "Lawyer Satisfaction in the Process of Structuring Legal Careers." *Law & Society Review* 41: 1–50.

Dobbins, Frank, and John R. Sutton. 1998. "The Strength of the Weak State: The Employment Rights and Revolution and the Rise of Human Resource Management Divisions." *American Journal of Sociology* 104: 441–476.

Dolbeare, Kenneth M., and Phillip E. Hammond. 1971. *The School Prayer Decisions: From Court Policy to Local Practice*. Chicago: University of Chicago Press.

Donohue, John J., and Justin Wolfers. 2006. "Uses and Abuses of Empirical Evidence in the Death Penalty Debate." *Stanford Law Review* 58: 691–711.

Donovan, James M. 2008. *Legal Anthropology*. Lanham, MD: AltaMira Press.

Doob, Anthony N., and Cheryl Marie Webster. 2003. "Sentence Severity and Crime: Accepting the Null Hypothesis." Pp. 251–286 in Michael Tonry, ed. *Crime and Justice: A Review of Research*. Chicago: University of Chicago Press.

Downie, Leonard. 1972. *Justice Denied*. New York: Penguin Books.

Drake, Bruce. 2016. *5 Facts About the Supreme Court*. Washington, DC: Pew Research Center.

Drape, Joe, and Marc Tracy. 2016. "A Majority Ruled It Was Rape. That Isn't Enough at Stanford." *New York Times*, Dec. 30.

Dror, Yehezkel. 1959. "Law and Social Change." *Tulane Law Review* 33: 749–801.

Drumbl, Mark A. 2007. *Atrocity, Punishment and International Law*. New York: Cambridge University Press.

Drutman, Lee. 2015. *The Business of America Is Lobbying: How Corporations Became Politicized and Politics Became More Corporate*. New York: Oxford University Press.

Duneier, Mitchell. 1999. *Sidewalk*. New York: Farrar, Straus and Giroux.

Durkheim, Émile. 1964 [1893]. *The Division of Labor in Society* (George Simpson, trans.). New York: Free Press.

Eckholm, Erik. 2014. "Inmate Dies After Execution Is Interrupted." *New York Times*, April 30.

Edelman, Laura B. 1990. "Legal Environments and Organizational Governance: The Expansion of Due Process in the American Workplace." *American Journal of Sociology* 95: 1401–1440.

———. 1992. "Legal Ambiguity and Symbolic Structures: Organizational Mediation of American Civil Rights Law." *American Journal of Sociology* 97: 1531–1576.

Edelman, Laura B., Christopher Uggen, and Howard S. Erlanger. 1999. "The Endogeneity of Legal Regulation: Grievance Procedures and National Myth." *American Journal of Sociology* 105: 406–455.

Editorial Board. 2016. "Louisiana's Color-Coded Death Penalty." *New York Times*, May 9. https://www.nytimes.com/2016/05/09/opinion/louisianas-color-coded-death-penalty.html?_r=0

Ehrlich, Isaac. 1975. "The Deterrent Effect of Capital Punishment: A Question of Life and Death." *American Economic Review* 65: 397–415.

Eisenstein, James, Roy B. Flemming, and Peter F. Nardulli. 1988. *The Contours of Justice: Communities and Their Courts*. Boston: Little, Brown.

Eisenstein, James, and Herbert Jacob. 1977. *Felony Justice*. Boston: Little, Brown.

Ekins, Emily. 2014. "Poll: 70% of Americans Oppose Racial Profiling by the Police." *Reason*, Oct. 14. http://reason.com/poll/2014/10/14/poll-70-of-americans-oppose-racial-profi

Ellsworth, Phoebe C. 1984. "Death Qualification and Jury Attitudes." *Human Behavior* 8: 31–51.

Ely, John Hart. 1980. *Democracy and Distrust*. Cambridge, MA: Harvard University Press.

Engel, David M. 1987. "The Oven Bird's Song: Insiders, Outsiders, and Personal Injuries in an American Community." *Law & Society Review* 18: 551–582.

———. 2016. *The Myth of the Litigious Society: Why We Don't Sue*. Chicago: University of Chicago Press.

Engel, David M., and Jaruwan S. Engel. 2010. *Tort, Custom, and Karma Globalization and Legal Consciousness in Thailand*. Stanford, CA: Stanford Law Books.

Engel, David M., and Frank W. Munger. 2003. *Rights of Inclusion Law and Identity in the Life Stories of Americans With Disabilities*. Chicago: University of Chicago Press.

Engen, Rodney L. 2008. "Have Sentencing Reforms Displaced Discretion Over Sentencing From Judges to Prosecutors?" Pp. 73–90 in John L. Worrall and M. Elaine Nugent-Borakove, eds. *The Changing Role of the American Prosecutor*. Albany: State University of New York Press.

Epp, Charles R. 1998. *The Rights Revolution*. Chicago: University of Chicago Press.

Epp, Charles R., Maynard-Moody, Steven, and Donald Haider-Markel. 2015. *Pulled Over: How Police Stops Define Race and Citizenship*. Chicago: University of Chicago Press.

Epstein, Lee, and Jack Knight. 1998. *The Choices Justices Make*. Washington, DC: CQ Press.

Epstein, Lee, and Joseph F. Kobylka. 1992. *The Supreme Court and Legal Change*. Chapel Hill: University of North Carolina Press.

Epstein, Lee, William M. Landes, and Richard A. Posner. 2013. *The Behavior of Federal Judges: A Theoretical Study of Rational Choice*. Cambridge, MA: Harvard University Press.

Erikson, Kai T. 1966. *Wayward Puritans: A Study in the Sociology of Deviance*. New York: Wiley.

Evan, William M. 1980. "Law as an Instrument of Social Change." Pp. 554–562 in William E. Evan, ed. *The Sociology of Law*. New York: Free Press.

Evans, Gareth. 2008. *The Responsibility to Protect*. Washington, DC: Brookings Institution.

Evans-Pritchard, Deirdre, and Alison Dundes Renteln. 1994. "The Interpretation and Distortion of Culture: A Hmong 'Marriage by Capture' Case in Fresno, California." *Southern California Interdisciplinary Law Journal* 4: 1–48.

Ewick, Patricia, and Susan S. Silbey. 1998. *The Common Place of Law: Stories From Everyday Life*. Chicago: University of Chicago Press.

Faust, Drew. 2013. "Fossil Fuel Divestment Statement." *Harvard University Office of the President*, October 3. http://www.harvard.edu/president/news/2013/fossil-fuel-divestment-statement

Federal Bureau of Investigation (FBI). 2011. *Financial Crimes Report 2010–2011*. Washington, DC: Federal Bureau of Investigation. https://www.fbi.gov/stats-services/publications/financial-crimes-report-2010-2011

———. 2015. *Internet Crime Report*. Washington, DC: Federal Bureau of Investigation. https://pdf.ic3.gov/2015_IC3Report.pdf

Feeley, Malcolm M. 1979. *The Process Is the Punishment: Handling Cases in a Lower Criminal Court*. New York: Russell Sage Foundation.

Feeley, Malcolm M., and Edward L. Rubin. 1998. *Judicial Policy Making and the Modern State: How the Courts Reformed America's Prisons*. Cambridge: Cambridge University Press.

Feld, Barry C. 2013. *Kids, Cops, and Confessions: Inside the Interrogation Room*. New York: New York University Press.

Feldman, Eric A. 2006. "The Tuna Court Law and Norms in the World's Premier Fish Market." *California Law Review* 94: 313–380.

Felstiner, William L. F., Richard L. Abel, and Austin Sarat. 1980–1981. "The Emergence and Transformation of Disputing: Naming, Blaming, Claiming." *Law & Society Review* 15, no. 3/4: 631–654.

Ferguson, Niall. 1999. *The Pity of War*. New York: Basic Books.

Ferguson, Robert A. 2007. *The Trial in American Life*. Chicago: University of Chicago Press.

Fidler, Ann. 2003. "'A Dry and Revolting Study': The Life and Labours of Antebellum Law Students." Pp. 65–100 in W. Wesley Pue and David Sugarman, eds. *Lawyers and Vampires Cultural Histories of Legal Professionals*. Oxford: Hart.

Fijalkowski, Agtata. *From Old Times to New Europe: The Polish Struggle for Democracy and Constitutionalism*. New York: Taylor & Francis.

Finkel, Norma. 1995. *Commonsense Justice: Jurors' Notions of the Law*. Cambridge, MA: Harvard University Press.

Finnis, John. 2011. *Natural Law and Natural Rights*, 2nd ed. New York: Oxford.

Flemming, Roy B., John Bohte, and Dan Wood. 1997. "One Voice Among Many: The Supreme Court's Influence on Attentiveness to Issues in the United States, 1947–1992." *American Journal of Political Science* 41: 1224–1250.

Flemming, Roy B., Peter F. Nardulli, and James Eisenstein. 1992. *The Craft of Justice Politics and Work in Criminal Court Communities*. Philadelphia: University of Pennsylvania Press.

"Florida's Stand Your Ground Law." 2013. *Tampa Bay Times*, Aug. 13. http://www.tampabay.com/stand-your-ground-law/

Foote, Caleb. 1956. "Vagrancy-Type Law and Its Administration." *University of Pennsylvania Law Review* 104: 613–650.

Forst, Brian. 2004. *Errors of Justice*. New York: Cambridge University Press.

Fortado, Lindsay. 2008. "Thacher Proffitt, 160-Year-Old Law Firm, to Close." *Bloomberg*, Jan. 30.

Foucault, Michael. 1977. *Discipline and Punish the Birth of the Prison* (Alan Sheridan, trans.). New York: Vintage Books.

Francis, David, R. 2010a. "Arizona Immigration Law and Illegal Immigrants: State of Extremes." *Christian Science Monitor*, May 17.

———. 2010b. "Why Arizona's New Immigration Law Makes Sense." *Christian Science Monitor*, May 17.

Frank, Jerome. 1930. *Law and the Modern Mind*. New York: Coward McCann.

———. 1949. *Courts on Trial*. Princeton, NJ: Princeton University Press.

Frankel, Marvin E. 1978. *Partisan Justice*. New York: Hill and Wang.

Frankel, Marvin E., and Gary P. Naftalis. 1977. *The Grand Jury: An Institution on Trial*. New York: Hill and Wang.

Freedman, Lori H. 2010. *Willing and Unable: Doctors and Abortion*. Nashville, TN: Vanderbilt University Press.

Freedom House. 2016. *Freedom on the Net*. Washington, DC: Freedom House. https://freedomhouse.org/sites/default/files/FOTN_2016_BOOKLET_FINAL.pdf

Freeman, Alan. 1978. "Legitimizing Racial Discrimination Through Antidiscrimination Law: A Critical Review of Supreme Court Doctrine." *Minnesota Law Review* 62: 1049–1119.

Frey, Maurice. 1963. "Review of Jerome E. Carlin, *Lawyers on Their Own*." *Buffalo Law Review* 13: 293–295.

Friedman, Barry. 2009. *The Will of the People: How Public Opinion Has Influenced the Supreme Court and Shaped the Meaning of the Constitution*. New York: Farrar, Straus and Giroux.

———. 2017. *Unwarranted Policing Without Permission*. New York: Farrar, Straus and Giroux.

Friedman, Lawrence M. 1977. *Law and Society: An Introduction*. Englewood Cliffs, NJ: Prentice Hall.

———. 1993. *Crime and Punishment in American History*. New York: Basic Books.

———. 1994. *Total Justice*. New York: Russell Sage Foundation.

———. 2005. *A History of American Law*, 3rd ed. New York: Norton.

———. 2015. *The Big Trial: Law as Public Spectacle*. Lawrence: University of Kansas Press.

Friedman, Lawrence M., and Jack Ladinsky. 1967. "Social Change and the Law of Industrial Accidents." *Columbia Law Review* 67: 50–80.

Friedman, Lawrence M., Rogelio Pérez-Perdomo, and Manuel A. Gómez, eds. 2011. *Law in Many Societies: A Reader*. Palo Alto, CA: Stanford University Press.

Frohmann, Lisa. 1991. "Discrediting Victim's Allegations of Sexual Assault: Prosecutorial Accounts of Case Rejections." *Social Problems* 38: 213–226.

———. 1997. "Convictability and Discordant Locales: Reproducing Race, Class, and Gender Ideologies in Prosecutorial Decision-Making." *Law & Society Review* 32: 531–555.

Fuller, Lon L. 1958. "Positivism and Fidelity to Law: A Reply to Professor Hart." *Harvard Law Review* 71: 630–672.

———. 1964. *The Morality of Law*, rev. ed. New Haven, CT: Yale University Press.

Fuller, Thomas. 2017. "San Francisco Sues Trump Over 'Sanctuary Cities' Order." *New York Times*, Feb. 1.

Gabel, Peter, and Duncan Kennedy. 1984. "Roll Over Beethoven." *Stanford Law Review* 36: 1–55.

Galanter, Marc. 1974. "Why the 'Haves' Come Out Ahead: Speculations on the Limits of Legal Change." *Law & Society Review* 9: 95–160.

Galanter, Marc, and William Henderson. 2008. "The Elastic Law Tournament: A Second Transformation of the Big Law Firm." *Stanford Law Review* 60: 1867–1928.

Galanter, Marc, and Thomas Palay. 1991. *Tournament of Lawyers*. Chicago: University of Chicago Press.

Gandhi, Mohandas K. 1957. *An Autobiography: The Story of My Experiments With the Truth* (Mahadev Desai, trans.). Boston: Beacon Press.

Gandossy, Robert F. 1985. *Bad Business: The OPM Scandal and the Seduction of the Establishment*. New York: Basic Books.

Garland, David. 2010. *Peculiar Institution: America's Death Penalty in an Age of Abolition*. Cambridge, MA: Belknap Press.

Garrett, Brandon L. 2011. *Convicting the Innocent: Where Criminal Prosecutions Go Wrong*. Cambridge, MA: Harvard University Press.

———. 2014. *Too Big to Jail: How Prosecutors Compromise With Corporations*. Cambridge, MA: Harvard University Press.

Garrow, David J. 1979. *Protest at Selma: Martin Luther King, Jr., and the Voting Rights Act of 1965*. New Haven, CT: Yale University Press.

———. 1998. *Liberty and Sexuality: The Right to Privacy and the Making of* Roe v. Wade. Berkeley: University of California Press.

Geis, Gilbert, and Leigh B. Bienen. 1998. *Crimes of the Century From Leopold and Loeb to O.J. Simpson*. Boston: Northeastern University Press.

Gelman, Andrew, Jeffrey Lax, and Justin Phillips. 2010. "Over Time, a Gay Marriage Groundswell." *New York Times*, Aug. 22.

Gelman, Andrew, James S. Liebman, Valerie West, and Alexander Kiss. 2004. "A Broken System: The Persistent Pattern of Reversals of Death Sentences in the United States." *Journal of Empirical Legal Studies* 1: 209–261.

George, Tracey E., and Albert H. Yoon. 2016. *The Gavel Gap: Who Sits in Judgment on State Courts?* Washington, DC: American Constitution Society.

Gibbs, Jack J., and Peggy L. Shelly. 1982. "Life in the Fast Lane: A Retrospective View by Commercial Thieves." *Journal of Research in Crime and Delinquency* 19: 299–330.

Gilligan, Carol. 1982. *In a Different Voice: Psychological Theory and Women's Development*. Cambridge, MA: Harvard University Press.

Gilson, Ronald, and Robert H. Mnookin. 1985. "Sharing Among the Human Capitalists: An Economic Inquiry Into the Corporate Law Firm and How Partners Split Profits." *Stanford Law Review* 37: 313–392.

Glendon, Mary Ann, Paolo G. Carozza, and Colin B. Picker. 2016. *Comparative Legal Traditions in a Nutshell,* 4th ed. St. Paul, MN: West.

Glendon, Mary Ann, Michael W. Gordon, and Christopher Osakwe. 1982. *Comparative Legal Traditions in a Nutshell*. St. Paul, MN: West.

Glenny, Misha. 2008. *McMafia*. New York: Knopf.

Gluckman, Max. 1955. *The Judicial Process Among the Bartose of Northern Rhodesia*. Manchester, UK: Manchester University Press.

Goldfarb, Ronald, and Linda R. Singer. 1973. *After Conviction*. New York: Simon and Schuster.

Goldhagen, Daniel Jonah. 1996. *Hitler's Willing Executioners: Ordinary Germans and the Holocaust*. New York: Knopf.

———. 2009. *Worse Than War*. New York: Perseus Books.

Golding, Martin. 1975. *Philosophy of Law*. Englewood Cliffs, NJ: Prentice Hall.

Goldman, Sheldon, and Thomas P. Jahnige, ed. 1968. *The Federal Judicial System: Readings in Process and Behavior*. New York: Holt, Rinehart and Winston.

Goldman, Sheldon, and Austin Sarat, eds. 1989. *American Court Systems: Reading in Judicial Process and Behavior*, 2nd ed. New York: Longman.

Goldschmidt, Jona. 2002. "The Pro Se Litigant's Struggle for Access to Justice: Meeting the Challenge of Bench and Bar Resistance." *Family Court Review* 40: 36–62.

Goldsmith, Jack. 2007. The Terror Presidency: Law and Judgment Inside the Bush Administration. New York: Norton.

Goldstein, Mathew. 2014. "4 Accused of Systematic Fraud That Sank Global Law Firm." *New York Times*, March 7.

———. 2016. "Wall Street Scion Caspersen Gets 4 Years in Prison for Fraud." *New York Times*, Nov. 4.

Goldstein, Matthew, and Liz Moyer. 2017. "One Former Dewey & LeBoeuf Executive Is Convicted; Another Is Acquitted." *New York Times*, May 9.

Goluboff, Risa. 2016. *Vagrant Nation: Police Power, Constitutional Change, and the Making of the 1960s.* Oxford: Oxford University Press.

González, Daniel. 2016. "How Many Mexicans Actually Cross the Border illegally?" *Arizona Republic*, October 9. http://www.azcentral.com/story/news/politics/border-issues/2016/10/09/how-many-mexicans-actually-cross-border-illegally/91280026/

Goodman, James, F. 1995. *Stories of Scottsboro.* New York: Vintage Books.

Goodman, Marc. 2015. *Future Crimes: Everything Is Connected, Everyone Is Vulnerable, and What We Can Do About It.* New York: Doubleday.

Gorner, Jeremy. 2016. "CPD's List: Likeliest to Kill, Be Killed." *Chicago Tribune*, July 24.

Gotanda, Neil. 1995. "A Critique of 'Our Constitution Is Color Blind.'" Pp. 257–275 in Kimberlé Crenshaw, Neil Gotanda, Gary Peller, and Kendall Thomas, eds. *Critical Race Theory: The Key Writings That Formed the Movement.* New York: New Press.

Gottschalk, Marie. 2015. *Caught: The Prison State and the Lockdown of American Politics.* Princeton: Princeton University Press.

Goulden, Joseph. 1971. *The Superlawyers: The Small and Powerful World of the Great Washington Law Firms.* New York: Dell Books.

Gourevitch, Philip. 1998. *We Wish to Inform You That Tomorrow We Will Be Killed With Our Families.* New York: Farrar, Straus and Giroux.

Graber, Mark A. 1999. *Rethinking Abortion.* Princeton, NJ: Princeton University Press.

Granfield, Robert. 2007. "The Meaning of Pro Bono: Institutional Variations in Professional Obligations Among Lawyers." *Law & Society Review* 41: 113–146.

Grann, David. 2009. "Trial By Fire: Did Texas Execute an Innocent Man?" *New Yorker*, Sept. 7. http://www.newyorker.com/magazine/2009/09/07/trial-by-fire

Grasmick, Harold G., and George J. Bryjack. 1980. "The Deterrent Effect of Perceived Severity of Punishment." *Social Forces* 59: 41–49.

Grasmick, Harold G., and Robert J. Bursik. 1990. "Conscience, Significant Others, and Rational Choice: Extending the Deterrence Model." *Law & Society Review* 24: 837–861.

Green, Gary S. 1985. "General Deterrence and Television Cable Crime: A Field Experiment in Social Control." *Criminology* 23: 629–645.

Green, Kristen. 2015. *Something Must Be Done About Prince Edward County: A Family, a Virginia Town, a Civil Rights Battle.* New York: HarperCollins.

Green, Linda. 1995. "Race in the Twenty-First Century: Equality Through Law." Pp. 292–301 in Kimberlé Crenshaw, Neil Gotanda, Gary Peller, and Kendall Thomas, eds. *Critical Race Theory: The Key Writings That Formed the Movement.* New York: New Press.

Green, Thomas Andre. 1985. *Verdict According to Conscience.* Chicago: University of Chicago Press.

Greenhouse, Carol J. and Barbara Yngvesson, Engel David, J. 1994. *Law and Community in Three American Towns.* Ithaca, NY: Cornell University Press.

Greenhouse, Linda, and Reva B. Siegel. 2011. "Before (and After) *Roe v. Wade*: New Questions About Backlash." *Yale Law Journal* 120: 2028–2086.

Greenhouse, Steven, and Elizabeth A. Harris. 2004. "Battling for a Safer Bangladesh." *New York Times*, April 22, p. B1.

Grim, Ryan. 2006. "Blowing Smoke." *Slate*, March 21. http://www.slate.com/id/2138399

Gross, Samuel R., Kristen Jacoby, Daniel J. Matheson, Nicholas Montgomery, and Sujata Patil. 2005. "Exonerations in the United States 1989 Through 2005." *Journal of Criminal Law and Criminology* 95: 523–560.

Gruenbaum, Ellen. 2001. *The Female Circumcision Controversy: An Anthropological Perspective.* Philadelphia: University of Pennsylvania Press.

Guinier, Lani, Michelle Fine, and Jane Balin. 1997. *Becoming Gentlemen: Women, Law School and Institutional Change.* Boston: Beacon Press.

Gulati, Mitu, Richard Sander, and Robert Sockloskie. 2001. "The Happy Charade: An Empirical Examination of the Third Year of Law School." *Journal of Legal Education* 1: 235–266.

Gusfield, Joseph R. 1963. *Symbolic Crusade: Status Politics and the American Temperance Movement.* Urbana: University of Illinois Press.

———. 1986. *Symbolic Crusade: Status Politics and the American Temperance Move*ment, 2nd ed. Urbana: University of Illinois Press.

Guttmacher Institute. n.d. *An Overview of Abortion in the United States.* http://www.guttmacher.org/media/presskits/2005/06/28/abortionoverview.html

Hadfield, Gillian, K. 2008. "Framing the Choice Between Cash and the Courthouse Experiences With the 9/11 Victim Compensation Fund." *Law & Society Review* 42: 645–682.

Hagan, John, and Fiona Kay. 2007. "Even Lawyers Get the Blues: Gender, Depression, and Job Satisfaction in Legal Practice." *Law & Society Review* 41: 51–78.

Hagan, John, and Illene Nagel. 1982. "White-Collar Crime, White-Collar Time." *American Criminal Law Review* 20: 259–289.

Hagedorn, John. 2015. *The Insane Chicago Way: The Daring Plan by Chicago Gangs to Create a Spanish Mafia.* Chicago: University of Chicago.

Hall, Jerome. 1952. *Theft, Law, and Society.* Indianapolis, IN: Bobbs-Merrill.

Hall, Kermit. 1989. *The Magic Mirror Law in American History*. New York: Oxford University Press.

Hall, Melinda Gann. 2008. "State Courts: Politics and the Judicial Process." Pp. 229–244 in Virginia Gray and Russell L. Hanson, eds. *Politics in the American States: A Comparative Analysis*, 9th ed. Washington, DC: CQ Press.

Haltom, William, and Michael McCann. 2004. *Distorting the Law: Politics, Media, and the Litigation Crisis*. Chicago: University of Chicago Press.

Handler, Joel F. 1967. *The Lawyer and His Community*. Madison: University of Wisconsin Press.

Haney, Craig. 2005. *Death by Design*. New York: Oxford University Press.

Hans, Valerie P., and Neil Vidmar. 1986. *Judging the Jury*. Cambridge, MA: Perseus.

Hansen, Mark. 2016. "What Do Falling Bar-Passage Rates Mean for Legal Education and the Future of the Profession." *ABA Journals*, Sept. 1. http://www.abajournal.com/magazine/article/legal_education_bar_exam_passage

Hanson, Roger A., and Brian J. Ostrom. 2012. "Indigent Defenders Get the Job Done and Done Well." Pp. 195–212 in Casia Spohn and Craig Hemmens, ed. *Courts A Text/Reader*, 2nd ed. Thousand Oaks, CA: Sage Publications.

Hanson, Roger A., Brian J. Ostrom, and Christopher Lomvardias. 1992. *Indigent Defenders Get the Job Done and Done Well*. Williamsburg, VA: National Center for State Courts.

Hardy, Quentin. 2016. "The Risks to Civil Liberties When Big Data Is Put to Work Fighting Crime." *New York Times*, Nov. 7.

Harlow, Caroline Wolf. 2000. *Defense Counsel in Criminal Cases*. Washington, DC: Bureau of Justice Statistics.

Harper, Steven. 2013. *The Lawyers' Bubble: A Profession in Crisis*. New York: Basic Books.

Harriger, Katy J. 1995. "Independent Justice: The Office of the Independent Counsel." Pp. 107–142 in Cornell W. Clayton, ed. *Government Lawyers: The Federal Legal Bureaucracy and Presidential Politics*. Lawrence: University Press of Kansas.

Harring, Sidney L. 1994. *Crow Dog's Case: American Indian Sovereignty, Tribal Law, and United States Law in the Nineteenth Century*. New York: Cambridge University Press.

Harris, Beth E. 2004. *Defending the Right to a Home: The Power of Anti-Poverty Lawyers*. Burlington, VT: Ashgate.

Harris, Cheryl. 1993. "Whiteness as Property." *Harvard Law Review* 106: 709–791.

Hart, H. L. A. 1958. "Positivism and the Separation of Law and Morals." *Harvard Law Review* 71: 593.

———. 1961. *The Concept of Law*. Oxford: Oxford University Press.

———. 1963. *Law, Liberty, and Morality*. Oxford: Oxford University Press.

———. 1968. *Punishment and Responsibility*. Oxford: Oxford University Press.

Harvard Law School Program on Criminal Justice Policy. 2016. *Moving Beyond Money: A Primer on Bail Reform*. Cambridge, MA: Harvard Law School.

Hassan, Nasra. 2001. "An Arsenal of Believers Talking to Human Bombs." *New Yorker*, Nov. 19, 36–41.

Hassan, Riaz. 2009. "What Motivates the Suicide Bombers?" *YaleGlobal Online*, Sept. 3. http://yaleglobal.yale.edu/content/what-motivates-suicide-bombers

Hastie, Reid, Steven D. Penrod, and Nancy Pennington. 1983. *Inside the Jury*. Cambridge, MA: Harvard University Press.

Hazell, Robert, ed. 1978. *The Bar on Trial*. London: Quartet Books.

Hazfeld, Jean. 2005. *Machete Season: The Killers in Rwanda Speak* (Linda Coverdale, trans.). New York: Farrar, Straus and Giroux.

———. 2007. *The Antelope's Strategy: Living in Rwanda After the Genocide* (Linda Coverdale, ed.). New York: Farrar, Straus and Giroux.

Heinz, John P., and Edward O. Laumann. 1994. *Chicago Lawyers: The Social Structure of the Bar*, rev. ed. Evanston, IL: Northwestern University Press.

Heinz, John P., Robert L. Nelson, Rebecca L. Sandefur, and Edward O. Laumann. 2005. *Urban Lawyers: The New Social Structure of the Bar*. Chicago: University of Chicago Press.

Helba, Cynthia, Matthew Bernstein, Mariel Leonard, Erin Bauer. 2015. *Report on Exploratory Study Into Honor Violence Measurement Methods—Appendixes*. Washington, DC: Department of Justice.

Helland, Eric, and Alexander Tabarrok. 2002. "The Effect of Electoral Institutions on Tort Awards." *American Law and Economic Review* 4: 341–370.

Henderson, William. 2004. "The LSAT, Law School Exams, and Meritocracy: The Surprising and Undertheorized Role of Test-Taking Speed." *Texas Law Review* 82: 975–1051.

Hensler, Deborah R., M. Susan Marquis, Allan F. Abrahamse, Sandra H. Berry, Patricia A. Ebener, Elizabeth G. Lewis, E. Allan Lind, Robert J. MacCoun, Willard G. Manning, Jeannette A. Rogowski, and Mary E. Vaiana. 1991. *Compensation for Accidental Injuries in the United States*. Santa Monica, CA: Rand Corporation.

Herz, Michael. 1995. "The Attorney Particular: Governmental Role of the Agency General Counsel." Pp. 143–180 in Cornell W. Clayton, ed. *Government Lawyers: The Federal Legal Bureaucracy and Presidential Politics*. Lawrence: University Press of Kansas.

Heumann, Milton. 1978. *Plea Bargaining: The Experiences of Prosecutors, Judges, and Defense Attorneys*. Chicago: University of Chicago.

Higginbotham, Leon A., Jr. 1978. *In the Matter of Color: Race and the American Legal Process: The Colonial Period*. New York: Oxford University Press.

Higgins, George E. 2010. *Cybercrime: An Introduction to an Emerging Phenomenon*. New York: McGraw-Hill.

Higham, John. 1974. *Strangers in the Land*. New York: Atheneum.

Hinduja, Sameer and Justin Patchin. 2010. "Cyberbullying Research Summary: Cyberbulylling and Suicide." *Cyberbullying Research Center*, July 1. http://cyberbullying.org/cyberbullying-research-summary-cyberbullying-and-suicide

Hinton, Alexander Laban. 2002. *Annihilating Difference*. Berkeley: University of California Press.

Hirschl, Ran. 2004. *Towards Juristocracy*. Cambridge, MA: Harvard University Press.

Hirschman, Albert. 1970. *Exit, Voice, and Loyalty.* Cambridge, MA: Harvard University Press.

Hoebel, E. Adamson. 1979. *The Law of Primitive Man: A Study in Comparative Legal Dynamics.* New York: Atheneum.

Hoffer, Peter Charles. 2010. *A Nation of Laws.* Lawrence: University Press of Kansas.

Hogue, Arthur R. 1966. *The Origins of the Common Law.* Indianapolis, IN: Liberty Press.

Hollis-Brusky, Amanda. 2015. Ideas With Consequence the Federalist Society and the Conservative Counterrevolution. New York: Oxford University Press.

Holmes, Oliver Wendell, Jr. 1897. "The Path of the Law." *Harvard Law Review* 10: 457–478.

———. 1938 [1881]. *The Common Law.* Boston: Little, Brown.

Hood, Roger, and Richard Sparks. 1972. *Key Issues in Criminology.* London: Weidenfeld and Nicolson.

Horowitz, Donald L. 1977. *The Courts and Social Policy.* Washington, DC: Brookings Institution.

Horowitz, Irving L. 2005. *Taking Lives: Genocide and State Power.* New Brunswick, NJ: Transaction Books.

Horowitz, Irwin A. 2008. "Jury Nullification: An Empirical Perspective." *Northern Illinois Law Review* 28: 425–452.

Horwitz, Jill R., and Joseph Mead. 2009. "Letting Good Deeds Go Unpunished: Volunteer Immunity Laws and Tort Deterrence." *Journal of Empirical Legal Studies* 6: 585–635.

Horwitz, Morton J. 1992. *The Transformation of American Law 1870–1960: The Crisis of Legal Orthodoxy.* New York: Oxford University Press.

Houppert, Karen. 2013. *Chasing Gideon: The Elusive Quest for Poor People's Justice.* New York: New Press.

Howard, Linda Gordon. 2007. *The Sexual Harassment Handbook.* Franklin Lakes, NJ: Career Press.

Howard, Philip K. 2009. *Life Without Lawyers: Liberating Americans From Too Much Law.* New York: Norton.

Human Rights Watch. 2015. "Whoever Raises Their Head Suffers the Most Workers' Rights in Bangladesh's Garment Factories." Apr. 26. https://www.hrw.org/report/2015/04/22/whoever-raises-their-head-suffers-most/workers-rights-bangladeshs-garment

———. 2016. "China: New Rules Gag Lawyers." Oct. 25. https://www.hrw.org/news/2016/10/25/china-new-rules-gag-lawyers

Hundley, Kris, Susan Taylor Martin, and Connie Humburg. 2012. "Florida 'Stand Your Ground' Law Yields Some Shocking Outcomes Depending on How Law Is Applied." *Tampa Bay Times,* June 1.

Hung, Melissa S. 2008. "Obstacles to Self-Actualization in Chinese Legal Practice." *Santa Clara Law Review* 48: 213–242.

Hunt, Alan, ed. 1989. *Critical Legal Studies.* Totowa, NJ: Rowman & Allanheld.

Hunt, Lynn. 2007. *Inventing Human Rights: A History.* New York: Norton.

Huntington, Samuel. 2004. "The Hispanic Challenge." *Foreign Policy* (March/April): 30–45.

———. 2007. *The Clash of Civilizations and the Remaking of World Order.* New York: Simon and Schuster.

Hurdle, Jon, and Richard Pérez-Peña. 2017. "Kathleen Kane, Former Pennsylvania Attorney General, Is Sent to Prison." *New York Times*, October 24.

Hurst, James Willard. 1950. *The Growth of American Law: The Law Makers.* Boston: Little, Brown.

Hutchinson, Allan, C. 2011. *Is Eating People Wrong? Great Legal Cases and How They Shaped the World.* Cambridge: Cambridge University Press.

Hutteman, Emmarie, and Yamiche Alcindor. 2017. "DeVos Confirmed for Education by Pence's Vote." *New York Times,* Feb. 8.

Hyman, David A. 2006. "Rescue Without Law: An Empirical Perspective Under the Duty to Rescue." *Texas Law Review* 84: 653–737.

Inbau, Fred, John Reid, Joseph Buckley, and Brian Jayne. 2001. *Criminal Interrogation and Confessions*, 4th ed. Gaithersburg, MD: Aspen.

International Military Tribunal at Nuremberg. 1945–1946. *Trial of the Major War Criminals Before the International Military Tribunal.* https://www.loc.gov/rr/frd/Military_Law/NT_major-war-criminals.html

Internet Crime Complaint Center. 2009. *Internet Crime Report.* Washington, DC: National White Collar Crime Center. http://www.ic3.gov/media/annualreports.aspx

Jacob, Herbert. 1988. *Silent Revolution: The Transformation of Divorce Law in the United States.* Chicago: University of Chicago Press.

———. 1996. "Introduction." Pp. 1–15 in Herbert Jacob, ed. *Courts, Law, and Politics in Comparative Perspective.* New Haven, CT: Yale University Press.

Jacoby, Joan E. 1980. *The American Prosecutor: A Search for Identity.* Lexington, MA: Lexington Books.

Jaffer, Jameel, ed. 2016. *The Drone Memos Targeted Killing, Secrecy and the Law.* New York: New Press.

Jensen, Christopher. 2014. "In General Motors Recalls, Inaction and Trail of Fatal Crashes." *New York Times,* March 2, B1.

Johnson, Cathy, and Craig Haney. 1994. "Felony *Voir Dire:* An Exploratory Study of Its Content and Effect." *Law & Human Behavior* 18: 487–506.

Johnson, Earl, Jr. 1974. *Justice and Reform: The Formative Years of the OEO Legal Service Program.* New York: Russell Sage Foundation.

Johnson, Shane D., and Kate J. Bowers. 2003. "Opportunity Is in the Eye of the Beholder: The Role of Publicity in Crime Prevention." *Criminology and Public Policy* 2: 497–524.

Johnson, Sheri Lynn. 2000. "Black Innocence and the White Jury." Pp. 163–177 in Richard Delgado and Jean Stefancic, eds. *Critical Race Theory*, 2nd ed. Philadelphia: Temple University Press.

Jones, Adam. 2006. *Genocide: A Comprehensive Introduction.* New York: Routledge.

Jones, Nicholas, A. 2010. *The Courts of Genocide.* New York: Routledge.

Joseph, Sarah, and Melissa Castan. 2013. *The International Covenant on Civil and Political Rights*, 3rd ed. Oxford: Oxford University Press.

Jouvenal, Justin. 2016. "The New Way Police Are Surveilling You: Calculating Your Threat 'Score.'" *Washington Post*, Jan. 10.

Kadish, Mortimer R., and Sanford H. Kadish. 1973. *Discretion to Disobey: A Study of Lawful Departures From Legal Rules*. Stanford, CA: Stanford University Press.

Kadish, Sanford H. 1967. "The Crisis of Overcriminalization." *Annals of the American Academy of Political and Social Science* 374: 158–176.

Kagan, Robert A. 2001. *Adversarial Legalism: The American Way of Law*. Cambridge, MA: Harvard University Press.

Kalven, Harry, Jr. 1988. *A Worthy Tradition: Freedom of Speech in America*. New York: Harper & Row.

Kalven, Harry, Jr., and Hans Zeisel. 1966. *The American Jury*. Chicago: University of Chicago Press.

Kang, Cecilia. 2017. "New F.C.C. Chairman Wastes No Time Rolling Back Obama-Era Internet Rules." *New York Times*, Feb. 6.

Kang, Jay Caspian. 2016. "How the Daily Sports Industry Turns Fans Into Suckers." *New York Times*, Jan. 6.

Kant, Immanuel. 1993 [1785]. *Grounding for the Metaphysics of Morals*, 3rd ed. (James Ellington, trans.). Indianapolis, IN: Hackett.

Kar, Robin Bradley, and Jason Mazzone. 2016. "The Garland Affair: What History and the Constitution Really Say About President Obama's Power to Appoint a Replacement for Justice Scalia." *New York University Law Review Online* 91: 53–114. http://www.nyulawreview.org/sites/default/files/%20 NYULawReviewOnline-91-Kar-Mazzone.pdf

Kassin, Saul, and Gisli Gudjonsson. 2004. "The Psychology of Confessions: A Review of the Literature and Issues." *Psychological Science in the Public Interest* 5: 35–67.

Kassin, Saul, and Lawrence S. Wrightsman. 1988. *The American Jury on Trial: Psychological Perspectives*. New York: Hemispheres.

Katz, Alyssa. 2015. *The Influence Machines: The U.S. Chamber of Commerce and the Corporate Capture of American Life*. New York: Spiegel & Grau.

Katz, Ellis. 1965. "Patterns of Compliance With the *Schempp* Decision." *Journal of Public Law* 14: 396–408.

Katz, Josh. 2017. "Trump's Big Opportunity to Shape Federal Courts." *New York Times*, Feb. 16.

Kawar, Leila A. 2015. *Contesting Immigration Policy in Court: Legal Activism and Its Radiating Effects in the United States and France*. New York: Cambridge University Press.

Kawashima, Takeyoshi. 1969. "Dispute Resolution in Japan." Pp. 182–193 in Vilhelm Aubert, ed. *Sociology of Law: Selected Readings*. Baltimore: Penguin Books.

Kay, Fiona M., and John Hagan. 1998. "Raising the Bar: The Gender Stratification of Law Firm Capital." *American Sociological Review* 63: 728–743.

———. 2003. "Building Trust: Social Capital, Distributive Justice, and Loyalty to the Firm." *Law and Social Inquiry* 28: 483–519.

Kay, Fiona M., Stacey L. Alarie, and Jones K. Adjei. 2016. "Undermining Gender Equality: Female Attrition From Private Law Practice." *Law & Society Review* 50: 766–801.

Keegan, John. 1998. *The First World War*. Toronto: Key Porter Books.

Kelly, J. M. 1992. *A Short History of Western Legal Theory*. New York: Oxford University Press.

Kelly, Michael J. 2007. *Lives of Lawyers Revisited: Transformation and Resilience in the Organizations of Practice*. Ann Arbor: University of Michigan Press.

Kelsen, Hans. 1967. *Pure Theory of Law*. Berkeley: University of California Press.

Kendi, Ibram X. 2016. *Stamped From the Beginning: The Definitive History of Racist Ideas in America*. New York: Nation Books.

Kennedy, David M. 2010. *Deterrence and Crime Prevention: Reconsidering the Prospect of Sanction*. New York: Routledge.

Kennedy, Duncan. 1998. "Legal Education as Training for Hierarchy." Pp. 53–78 in David Kairys, ed. *The Politics of Law: A Progressive Critique*, 3rd ed. New York: Basic Books.

Kennedy, Randall. 1998. *Race, Crime, and the Law*. New York: Vintage Books.

Kidder, Robert L. 1983. *Connecting Law and Society*. Englewood Cliffs, NJ: Prentice Hall.

Kiernan, Ben. 2007. *Blood and Soil*. New Haven, CT: Yale University Press.

King, Martin Luther, Jr. 1963. *Why We Can't Wait*. New York: New American Library.

King, Ryan D., Kecia R. Johnson, and Kelly McGeever. 2010. "Demography of the Legal Profession and Racial Disparities in Sentencing." *Law & Society Review* 44: 1–31.

Kirkland, Anna R. 2016. "Think of the Hippopotamus: Rights Consciousness in the Fat Acceptance Movement." *Law and Society Review* 42: 397–432.

Kirkland, Kimberly. 2005. "Ethics in Large Law Firms: The Principle of Pragmatism." *University of Memphis Law Review* 35: 631–729.

Kitroeff, Natalie. 2016. "The Best Law Schools Are Attracting Fewer Students." *Bloomberg*, Jan. 26. https://www.bloomberg.com/news/articles/2016-01-26/the-best-law-schools-are-attracting-fewer-students

Kittrie, Nicholas N. 1971. *The Right to Be Different*. Baltimore: Johns Hopkins University Press.

Klarman, Michael. 2006. *From Jim Crow to Civil Rights: The Supreme Court and the Struggle for Racial Equality*. New York: Oxford University Press.

Kleck, Gary, Brion Sever, Spencer Li, and Marc Gertz. 2005. "The Missing Link in General Deterrence Research." *Criminology* 43: 623–660.

Klein, Lawrence, Brian Forst, and Victor Filatov. 1978. "The Deterrent Effect of Capital Punishment: An Assessment of the Estimates." Pp. 336–360 in Alfred Blumstein, Jacqueline Cohen, and Daniel Nagin, eds. *Deterrence and Incapacitation: Estimating the Effects of Criminal Sanctions on Crime Rates*. Washington, DC: National Academy of Sciences.

Kluger, Richard. 1976. *Simple Justice*. New York: Knopf.

Koster, A. C. 2015. "Vehicle Stops Report." *Office of the Missouri Attorney General*. https://www.ago.mo.gov/home/vehicle-stops-report

Kramer, Larry. 2005. *The People Themselves: Popular Constitutionalism and Judicial Review*. New York: Oxford University Press.

Kramer, Martin. 1998. "The Moral Logic of Hezbollah." Pp. 131–157 in Walter Reich, ed. *Origins of Terrorism*. Washington, DC: Woodrow Wilson Center.

Kritzer, Herbert M. 2002a. "Lawyer Fees and Lawyer Behavior in Litigation: What Does the Empirical Literature Really Say?" *Texas Law Review* 80: 1943–1983.

———. 2002b. "Seven Dogged Myths Concerning Contingency Fees." *Washington University Law Quarterly* 80: 739–784.

Kronman, Anthony T. 1993. *The Lost Lawyer: Failing Ideals of the Legal Profession*. Cambridge, MA: Belknap Press.

Lacey, Marc. 2010. "Arizona Law Said to Harm Convention Businesses." *New York Times*, Nov. 18.

Ladinsky, Jack. 1963. "The Careers of Lawyers, Law Practice and Legal Institutions." *American Sociological Review* 28: 47–54.

Laffin, Arthur J., and Anne Montgomery, eds. 1987. *Swords Into Plowshares: Nonviolent Direct Action for Disarmament*. New York: Perennial Library.

LaFountain, Robert C., S. Strickland, R. Schauffler, K. Holt, & K. Lewis. 2015. *Examining the Work of State Courts: An Overview of 2013 State Court Caseloads*. Williamsburg, VA: National Center for State Courts.

LaFree, Gary D., Barbara F. Reskin, and Christy A. Vishner. 1985. "Jurors' Responses to Victims' Behavior and Legal Issues in Sexual Assault Trials." *Social Problems* 32: 389–404.

Lai, K. K. Rebecca, and Jasmine C. Lee. 2016. "10 Percent of Florida Adults Are Ineligible to Vote. Why?" *New York Times*, Oct. 7.

Landon, Donald D. 1990. *Country Lawyers: The Impact of Context on Professional Practice*. Westport, CT: Praeger.

Lane, Frederic, S. 2009. *American Privacy*. Boston: Beacon Press.

Langbein, John. 1978. "Torture and Plea Bargaining." *University of Chicago Law Review* 46: 3–22.

———. 1979. "Understanding the Short History of Plea Bargaining." *Law & Society Review* 13: 261–272.

Langbein, John, and Lloyd L. Weinreb. 1978. "Continental Criminal Procedure: 'Myth' and Reality." *Yale Law Journal* 87, no. 8: 1549–1569.

Lansing, Paul, Michael Fricke, and Suzanne Davis. 2009. "The Ethics of Contingent Fees in Legal Service Businesses." *Journal of the Legal Profession* 33: 301–316.

Lantigua-Williams, Juleya. 2016. "Are Prosecutors the Key to Justice Reform?" *The Atlantic*, May 18. http://www.theatlantic.com/politics/archive/2016/05/are-prosecutors-the-key-to-justice-reform/483252/

Larson, Magali Sarfatti. 1977. *The Rise of Professionalism: A Sociological Analysis*. Berkeley: University of California Press.

Latané, Bibb, and John M. Darley. 1968. "Group Inhibition of Bystander Intervention in Emergencies." *Personality & Social Psychology* 10: 215–221.

Layson, Stephen K. 1985. "Homicide and Deterrence: A Reexamination of U.S. Time-Series Evidence." *Southern Economic Journal* 52: 68–89.

Lazarus-Black, Mindie. 2007. *Everyday Harm: Domestic Violence, Court Rites, and Cultures of Reconciliation*. Champaign-Urbana: University of Illinois Press.

Lazarus-Black, Mindie, and Susan Hirsch, eds. 1994. *Contested States: Law, Hegemony and Resistance*. New York: Routledge.

Leamer, Laurence. 2016. *The Lynching: The Epic Courtroom Battle That Brought Down the Klan*. New York: William Morrow.

Lebacqz, Karen. 1987. *Six Theories of Justice*. Minneapolis, MN: Augsburg Fortress.

Lee, Sophia Z. 2014. *The Workplace Constitution From the New Deal to the New Right*. New York: Cambridge University Press.

Legal Services Corporation. 2007. *Documenting the Justice Gap in America: The Current Unmet Legal Needs of Low Income Americans*, 2nd ed. Washington, DC: Legal Services Corporation.

———. 2015. *Annual Report 2015*. Washington, D.C.: Legal Services Corporation.

Lemkin, Raphael. 1944. *Axis Rule in Occupied Europe: Law of Occupancy, Analysis of Government Proposals for Redress*. Washington, DC: Carnegie Endowment for World Peace.

Lemmings, David. 2003. "Ritual, Majesty and Mystery: Collective Life and Culture Among English Barristers, Serjeants and Judges." Pp. 25–64 in W. Wesley Pue and David Sugarman, eds. *Lawyers and Vampires: Cultural Histories of Legal Professions*. Oxford: Hart.

Lempert, Richard, and Joseph Sanders. 1986. *An Invitation to Law and Social Science: Desert, Disputes, and Distribution*. Philadelphia: University of Pennsylvania Press.

Leo, Richard, A. 2008. *Police Interrogation and American Justice*. Cambridge, MA: Harvard University Press.

Lesieur, Henry R. 1992. "Compulsive Gambling." *Society* 29, no. 4: 43–50.

Lessig, Lawrence. 2006. *Code 2.0*. New York: Basic Books.

Levin, Leslie C. 2004. "The Ethical World of Solo and Small Law Firm Practitioners." *Houston Law Review* 41: 309–392.

———. 2009. "Guardians at the Gate: The Backgrounds, Career Paths, and Professional Development of Private US Immigration Lawyers." *Law & Social Inquiry* 34: 399–436.

———. 2015. "The Folly of Expecting Evil: Reconsidering the Bar's Character and Fitness Requirement." *Brigham Young Law Review* 2014, no. 4: 775–818.

Levine, Harry, Jon B. Gettman, and Loren Siegel. 2010. *Arresting Blacks for Marijuana in California: Possession Arrests in 25 Cities, 2006–08*. New York: Drug Policy Arrest Alliance.

Levinson, Sanford. 1982. "Law as Literature." *Texas Law Review* 60: 373–402.

Levit, Nancy, and Robert R. M. Verchick. 2016. *Feminist Legal Theory: A Primer*. New York: New York University Press.

Lewis, Anthony. 1964. *Gideon's Trumpet*. New York: Vintage Books.

Lichtblau, Eric, David Johnston, and Ron Nixon. 2008. "F.B.I. Struggles to Handle Financial Fraud Cases." *New York Times*, Oct. 19.

Lieberman, Jethro K. 1981. *The Litigious Society*. New York: Basic Books.

Liebman, James S., Jeffrey Fagan, Valerie West, and J. Lloyd. 2000. "Capital Attrition: Error Rates in Capital Cases, 1973–1995." *Texas Law Review* 78: 1839–1865.

Light, Caroline E. 2017. *Stand Your Ground: A History of America's Love Affair With Lethal Self-Defense*. Boston: Beacon Press.

Linowitz, Sol M., with Martin Mayer. 1994. *The Betrayed Profession: Lawyering at the End of the Twentieth Century*. Baltimore: John Hopkins University Press.

Lippman, Matthew. 1989. "Islamic Criminal Law and Procedure: Religious Fundamentalism v. Modern Law." *Boston College International and Comparative Law Review* 12: 36–62.

———. 1997. "Law, Lawyers, and Legality in the Third Reich: The Perversion of Principle and Professionalism." *Temple International and Comparative Law Journal* 11: 199–308.

———. 2002. "Genocide: The Trial of Adolf Eichmann and the Quest For Global Justice." *Buffalo Human Rights Law Review* 8: 45–121.

Lippman, Matthew, Sean McConville, and Mordechai Yerushalmi. 1988. *Islamic Criminal Law and Procedure*. New York: Praeger.

Liptak, Adam. 2008a. "1 in 100 U.S. Adults Behind Bars Study Says." *New York Times*, Feb. 28.

———. 2008b. "U.S. Prison Population Dwarfs That of Other Nations." *New York Times*, April 23.

———. 2016. "Justices Friendliest to White Men When Choosing Friends of Court." *New York Times*, May 12.

———. 2017a. "Judges Refuse to Reinstate Travel Ban." *New York Times*, Feb. 10.

———. 2017b. "White House Ends Bar Association's Role in Vetting Judges." *New York Times*, March 20.

———. 2017c. "Appeals Court Will Not Reinstate Trump's Revised Travel Ban." *New York Times*, May 25.

Lipton, Eric, Eric Schmidt, and Mark Mazzetti. 2010. "Review of Jet Bomb Plot Shows More Missed Clues." *New York Times*, Jan. 18.

Lipton, Eric, and Julie Creswell. 2015. "Documents Show How Wealthy Hid Millions Abroad." *New York Times*, June 6.

Liu, Sida. 2006. "Client Influence and the Contingency of Professionalism: The Work of Elite Corporate Lawyers in China." *Law & Society Review* 40: 251–281.

Llewellyn, Karl N. 1962. *Jurisprudence: Realism in Theory and Practice*. Chicago: University of Chicago Press.

Llewellyn, Karl N., and E. Adamson Hoebel. 1941. *The Cheyenne Way: Conflict and Case Law in Primitive Jurisprudence*. Norman: University of Oklahoma Press.

Lloyd, Henry Demarest. 2000 [1894]. *Wealth Against Commonwealth*. Avon, MA: Adams Media.

Loftin, Colin, and David McDowell. 1981. "'One With a Gun Get You Two': Mandatory Sentencing and Firearms Violence in Detroit." *Annals of the American Academy of Political and Social Science* 455: 150–167.

Lohr, Steve. 2017. "Trump Completes Repeal of Internet Privacy Rules." *New York Times*, Apr. 4.

López, Ian Haney. 2006. *White by Law: The Legal Construction of Race*, rev. and updated ed. New York: New York University Press.

Lopez, Mark Hugo, Ana Gonzalez-Barrera, and Seth Motel. 2011. "As Deportations Rise to Record Levels Most Latinos Oppose Obama's Policy." *Pew Research Center*, Dec. 28.

Lopez, Mark Hugo, Rich Morin, and Paul Taylor. 2010. "Illegal Immigration Backlash Worries, Divides Latinos." *Pew Research Center*, Oct. 28.

Lortie, Dan C. 1959. "Laymen to Lawmen: Law Schools, Careers, and Professional Socialization." *Harvard Educational Review* 29: 352–369.

Lovell, George I. 2006. "Justice Excused: The Deployment of Law in Everyday Political Encounters." *Law & Society Review* 40: 283–324.

Lowery, Wesley. 2016a. "Aren't More White People Than Black People Killed by Police?" *Washington Post*, July 11.

———. 2016b. *They Can't Kill Us All: Ferguson, Baltimore, and a New Era in America's Racial Justice Movement*. New York: Little, Brown.

Lowrey, Annie. 2014. "In-Depth Report Details Economics of Sex Trade." *New York Times*, March 12.

Luban, David. 1988. *Lawyers and Justice: An Ethical Study*. Princeton, NJ: Princeton University Press.

Luginbuhl, James, and Julie Howe. 1995. "Discretion in Capital Sentencing Instructions: Guided or Misguided?" *Indiana Law Journal* 70: 1161–1189.

Lund, Michael. 1995. "Counsels to the President: The Rise of Organizational Competition." Pp. 257–280 in Cornell W. Clayton, ed. *Government Lawyers: The Federal Legal Bureaucracy and Presidential Politics*. Lawrence: University Press of Kansas.

Ma, Yue, 2002. "Prosecutorial Discretion and Plea Bargaining in the United States, France, Germany, and Italy." *International Criminal Justice Review* 12: 22–52.

Macaulay, Stewart. 1963. "Non-Contractual Relations in Business: A Preliminary Study." *American Sociological Review* 28: 55–66.

Macedo, Stephen. 2007. "The Moral Dilemma of U.S. Immigration Policy." Pp. 63–81 in Carol M. Swain, ed. *Debating Immigration*. New York: Cambridge University Press.

MacKinnon, Catharine. 1987. *Feminism Unmodified: Discourses on Life and Law*. Cambridge, MA: Harvard University Press.

Maine, Henry Sumner. 1970 [1861]. *Ancient Law*. Gloucester, MA: Peter Smith.

Malinowski, Bronislaw. 1982. *Crime and Custom in Savage Society*. London: Rowman and Allanheld.

Manly, Lorne. 2014. "Legal Debate on Using Boastful Rap Lyrics as a Smoking Gun." *New York Times*, March 27.

Mann, Michael. 2005. *The Dark Side of Democracy: Explaining Ethnic Cleansing*. New York: Cambridge University Press.

Marcos, Cristina. 2016. "116th Congress Will Be Most Racially Diverse in History." *The Hill*, Nov. 17.

Marquart, James, and Ben M. Crouch. 1985. "Judicial Reform and Prisoner Control: The Impact of *Ruiz v. Estelle* on a Texas Penitentiary." *Law & Society Review* 19: 557–586.

Marquart, James, Sheldon Ekland-Olson, and Jonathan R. Sorensen. 1989. "Gazing Into the Crystal Ball: Can Jurors Accurately Predict Dangerousness in Capital Cases?" *Law & Society Review* 23: 449–468.

Marquart, James, and Jonathan Sorenson. 1988. "Institutional and Post-Release Behavior of Furman-Commuted Inmates in Texas." *Criminology* 26: 677–694.

———. 1989. "A National Study of the Furman-Commuted Inmates: Assessing the Threat to Society From Capital Offenders." *Loyola of Los Angeles Law Review* 23: 5–28.

Marvell, Thomas, B., and Carlisle E. Moody, Jr. 1994. "Prison Population Growth and Crime Reduction." *Journal of Quantitative Criminology* 10: 109–140.

———. 1995. "The Impact of Enhanced Prison Terms for Felonies Committed With Guns." *Criminology* 33: 249–281.

Marx, Karl. 1900 [1847]. *The Poverty of Philosophy.* Moscow: Foreign Language Publishing House.

———. 1972 [1859]. *A Contribution to the Critique of Political Economy.* New York: International Publishers.

Marx, Karl, and Friedrich Engels. 1955 [1848]. *The Communist Manifesto.* New York: Appleton-Century-Crofts.

Masci, David. 2016. "5 Facts About the Death Penalty." *Pew Research Center.* http://www.pewresearch.org/fact-tank/2016/11/14/5-facts-about-the-death-penalty.

Mather, Lynn. 1979. *Plea Bargaining or Trial?* Lexington, MA: DC Heath.

Mather, Lynn, Craig A. McEwen, and Richard J. Maiman. 2001. *Divorce Lawyers at Work: Varieties of Professionalism in Practice.* New York: Oxford University Press.

Matoesian, Gregory M. 1993. *Reproducing Rape: Domination Through Talk in the Courtroom.* Chicago: University of Chicago Press.

———. 1995. "Language, Law, and Society: Applied Implications of the Kennedy Smith Rape Trial." *Law & Society Review* 29, no. 4: 669–702.

———. 2001. *Law and the Language of Identity.* New York. Oxford University Press.

Matsuda, Mari J. 1989. "When the First Quail Calls: Multiple Consciousness as Jurisprudential Method." *Women's Rights Law Reporter* 11: 7–10.

May, Larry. 2010. *Genocide.* New York: Cambridge University Press.

Mayhew, Leon H. 1971. "Stability and Change in Legal Systems." Pp. 187–210 in Bernard Barber and Alex Inkeles, eds. *Stability and Social Change.* Boston: Little, Brown.

McCann, Michael W. 1994. *Rights at Work.* Chicago: University of Chicago Press.

McClellan, Chandler, and Erdal Tekin. 2012. "Stand Your Ground Laws: Homicides and Injuries." *NBER Working Paper No. 18187.*

McClelland, Kent A., and Geoffrey P. Alpert. 1985. "Factor Analysis Applied to Magnitude Estimates of Punishment Seriousness: Patterns of Individual Differences." *Journal of Quantitative Criminology* 1: 307–318.

McConville, Michael, and Chester L. Mirsky. 2005. *Jury Trials and Plea Bargaining: A True History.* Oxford: Hart.

McGill, Christa. 2006. "Educational Debt and Law Student Failure to Enter Public Service Careers: Bringing Empirical Data to Bear." *Law & Social Inquiry* 31: 677–708.

McGirr, Lisa. 2016. *The War on Alcohol and the Rise of the American State.* New York: Norton.

McGuire, Kevin J. 2016. "Birth Order, Preferences and Norms on the U.S. Supreme Court." *Law & Society Review* 49: 945–972.

McIntyre, Lisa. 1987. *The Public Defender: The Practice of Law in the Shadow of Repute.* Chicago: University of Chicago.

McMillion, Barry J. 2015. *U.S. Circuit and District Court Nominations During President Obama's First Six Years (2009–2014): Comparative Analysis with Recent Presidents.* Washington, DC: Congressional Research Service,.

McQueen, M. P. 2016. "Minority Women Still Struggling to Win Top Law Jobs." *American Lawyer,* Aug. 1. http://www.americanlawyer.com/id=1202762960538/Minority-Women-Still-Struggling-to-Win-Top-Law-Jobs-?slreturn=20161131160707

Medina, Jennifer, and Jess Bidgood. 2017. "California Moves to Add Protections for Immigrants; Other States Follow." *New York Times,* Apr. 11.

Mencimer, Stephanie. 2016. "Claim of Privilege." *Mother Jones,* March–April.

Mendelsohn, Oliver. 2014. *Law and Social Transformation In India.* New York: Oxford University Press.

Menkel-Meadow, Carrie. 1986. "The Comparative Sociology of Women Lawyers: The Feminization of the Legal Profession." *Osgoode Hall Law Journal* 24: 897–918.

Merry, Sally Engle. 1979. "Going to Court: Strategies of Dispute Management in an American Urban Neighborhood." *Law & Society Review* 13: 891–925.

———. 1990. *Getting Justice and Getting Even: Legal Consciousness Among Working-Class Americans.* Chicago: University of Chicago Press.

Merryman, John Henry, and Rogelio Pérez-Perdomo. 2007. *The Civil Law Tradition: An Introduction to the Legal Systems of Europe and Latin America,* 3rd ed. Palo Alto, CA: Stanford University Press.

Merton, Robert. K. 1968. *Social Theory and Social Structure.* New York: Free Press.

Mertz, Beth. 2007. *The Language of Law School: Learning to Think Like a Lawyer.* New York: Oxford University Press.

Mettraux, Guenael, ed. 2008. *Perspectives on the Nuremberg Trial.* New York: Oxford University Press.

Meyerstein, Ariel. 2011. "Between Law and Culture: Rwanda's Gacaca and Postcolonial Legality." Pp. 143–151 in Lawrence M. Friedman, Rogelio Pérez-Perdomo, and Manuel A. Gómez, eds. *Law in Many Societies: A Reader.* Stanford, CA: Stanford University.

Michaels, Walter Benn. 2007. *The Trouble With Diversity: How We Learned to Love Identity and Ignore Inequality.* New York: Holt.

Michelson, Ethan. 2006. "The Practice of Law as an Obstacle to Justice: Chinese Lawyers at Work." *Law & Society Review* 40: 1–38.

Midlarsky, Manus I. 2005. *The Killing Trap: Genocide in the Twentieth Century.* New York: Cambridge University Press.

Mill, John Stuart. 1979 [1859]. *On Liberty.* Harmondsworth, UK: Penguin.

Miller, Arthur S. 1965. "On the Need for 'Impact Analysis' of Supreme Court Decisions." *Georgetown Law Journal* 53: 365–401.

Miller, Claire Cain, and Jenna Wortham. 2010. "Technology Aside, Most People Still Decline to Be Located." *New York Times,* Aug. 29.

Miller, Ed, and Daniel Singer. 2015. "For Daily Fantasy-Sports Operators, the Curse of Too Much Skill." New York: McKinsey & Company, Sept.

Miller, Perry. 1965. *The Life of the Mind in America: From the Revolution to the Civil War.* New York: Harcourt Brace & World.

Miller, Richard E., and Austin Sarat. 1980–1981. "Grievance, Claims, and Disputes: Assessing the Adversary Culture." *Law & Society Review* 15, no. 3/4: 525–566.

Mills, John L. 2008. *Privacy: The Lost Right.* New York: Oxford University Press.

Milner, Neil A. 1971. *The Court and Local Law Enforcement: The Impact of* Miranda. Beverly Hills, CA: Sage.

Mitford, Jessica. 1970. *The Trial of Dr. Spock, The Rev. William Sloane Coffin, Jr., Michael Ferber, Mitchell Goodman, and Marcus Raskin.* New York: Vintage Books.

Monahan, Torin. 2006. "Questioning Surveillance and Security." Pp. 1–26 in Torin Monahan, ed. *Surveillance and Security: Technological Politics and Power in Everyday Life.* New York: Routledge.

Montgomery, Ben, and Colleen Jenkins. 2010. "Five Years Since Florida Enacted 'Stand-Your-Ground' Law, Justifiable Homicides Are Up." *Tampa Bay Times,* Oct. 15.

Montgomery, Dave, and Manny Fernandez. 2017. "Texas Immigration Law Draws Protesters." *New York Times,* May 2.

Morgan, Phoebe A. 1999. "Risking Relationships: Understanding the Litigation Choices of Sexually Harassed Women." *Law & Society Review* 33: 67–92.

Morrill, Calvin, Lauren B. Edelman, Karolyn Tyson, and Richard Arum. 2010. "Legal Mobilization in Schools: The Paradox of Rights and Race Among Youth." *Law & Society Review* 44: 651–694.

Morris, Andrew, and William D. Henderson. 2008. "Measuring Outcomes: Post-Graduation Measures of Success in *U.S. News & World Report* Law School Rankings." *Indiana Law Journal* 83: 791–834.

Morris, Norval, and Gordon Hawkins. 1969. *The Honest Politician's Guide to Crime Control.* Chicago: University of Chicago Press.

Morrison, Aaron. 2015. "Racial Profiling Laws: Most U.S. Residents Want a Ban on Biased Policy; Will Federal Government Prohibit Practice?" *IBT,* Oct. 26.

Moyer, Liz. 2009. "It Could Have Been Worse for Madoff." *Forbes,* June 29. http://www.forbes.com/2009/06/24/bernie-madoff-prison-sentence-business-beltway-madoff.html (accessed November 20, 2012).

Muhammad, Khalil Gibran. 2010. *The Condemnation of Blackness: Race, Crime and the Making of Modern Urban America.* Cambridge, MA: Harvard University Press.

Murakawa, Naomi, and Katherine Beckett. 2010. "The Penology of Racial Innocence: The Erasure of Racism in the Study and Practice of Punishment." *Law & Society Review* 44: 695–730.

Murphy, Walter, F. 1964. *The Elements of Judicial Strategy.* Chicago: University of Chicago Press.

Musheno, Michael C., James P. Levine, and Dennis J. Palumbo. 1978. "Television Surveillance and Crime Prevention: Evaluating an Attempt to Create Defensible Space in Public Housing." *Social Science Quarterly* 58: 647–656.

Nader, Laura. 1969. "Styles of Court Procedure: To Make the Balance." Pp. 69–117 in Laura Nader, ed. *Law in Culture and Society.* Berkeley: University of California Press.

Nader, Laura, and Harry F. Todd, Jr. 1978. "Introduction." Pp. 1–41 in Laura Nader and Harry Todd, Jr., eds. *The Disputing Process—Law in Ten Societies.* New York: Columbia University Press.

Nagin, Daniel S., and Raymond Paternoster. 1993. "Enduring Individual Differences and Rational Choice Theories of Crime." *Law & Society Review* 27: 467–496.

Nagin, Daniel S., and John V. Pepper. 2012. *Deterrence and the Death Penalty.* New York: National Research Council of the National Academies.

Nardulli, Peter F. 1986. "'Insider' Justice: Defense Attorneys and the Handling of Felony Cases." *Journal of Criminal Law & Criminology* 77: 379–417.

National Association of Women Lawyers. 2016. *Report of the Ninth Annual Survey on Retention and Promotion of Women in Law Firms.* Chicago: National Association of Women Lawyers.

National Center for State Courts. 2006. *Examining the Work of State Courts, 2005.* Williamsburg VA: National Center for State Courts.

National Coalition for the Homeless. 2014. *Vulnerable to Hate: A Survey of Hate Crimes & Violence Committed Against Homeless People in 2013.* Washington, DC: National Coalition for the Homeless.

National Commission on Law Observance and Enforcement. 1931. *Report on Lawlessness in Law Enforcement.* Washington, DC: U.S. Government Printing Office.

National Commission on Terrorist Attacks. 2004. *The 9/11 Commission Report.* New York: Norton.

National Conference of Bar Examiners and ABA Section of Legal Education and Admission to the Bar. 2016. *Comprehensive Guide to Bar Admission Requirements 2016.* Madison, WI: National Conference of Bar Examiners.

National Law Center on Homelessness and Poverty. 2016a. *Homelessness in America: Overview of Data and Causes.* Washington, DC: National Law Center on Homelessness and Poverty.

———. 2016b. *Homes Not Handcuffs: Ending the Criminalization of Homelessness in U.S. Cities.* Washington, DC: National Law Center on Homelessness and Poverty.

National Research Council of the National Academies. 2014. *Identifying the Culprit: Assessing Eyewitness Identification.* Washington, DC: National Academies Press. https://www.nap.edu/catalog/18891/identifying-the-culprit-assessing-eyewitness-identification

Nelson, Robert L. 1988. *Partners With Power: The Social Transformation of the Large Law Firm.* Berkeley: University of California Press.

Nelson, Robert L., and Laura Beth Nielsen. 2000. "Cops, Counsel and Entrepreneurs: Constructing the Role of Inside Counsel in Large Corporations." *Law & Society Review* 34: 437–491.

Neubauer, David W., and Henry F. Fradella. 2011. *America's Courts and the Criminal Justice System,* 10th ed. Belmont CA: Wadsworth.

Neuborne, Burt. 2015. *Madison's Music: On Reading the First Amendment*. New York: New Press.

Nevarez, Griselda. 2016. "Arizona's Undocumented Immigrant Population Inches Up While Nation's Holds Strong." *Phoenix New Times*, Sept. 23. http://www.phoenixnewtimes.com/news/arizonas-undocumented-immigrant-population-inches-up-while-nations-holds-steady-8668831

Newman, Leonard S., and Ralph Erber, eds. 2002. *Understanding Genocide*. New York: Oxford University Press.

Newton, Lina. 2008. *Illegal, Alien, or Immigrant*. New York: New York University Press.

Nielsen, Laura Beth. 2004. *License to Harass: Law, Hierarchy, and Offensive Public Speech*. Princeton, NJ: Princeton University Press.

Nietzel, Michael T., and Ronald C. Dillehay. 1982. "The Effects of Variations in Voir Dire Procedures in Capital Murder Trials." *Law and Human Behavior* 6: 1–13.

Nisen, Max. 2013. "How Nike Solved Its Sweatshop Problem." Business Insider, May 10, http://www.businessinsider.com/how-nike-solved-its-sweatshop-problem-2013-5

Nixon, Ron. 2017. "How People Entering the Country Are Monitored and Checked." *New York Times*, Jan. 31.

Nolette, Paul. 2015. *Federalism on Trial: State Attorneys General and National Policymaking in Contemporary America*. Lawrence: University Press of Kansas.

Nonet, Philippe. 1976. "For Jurisprudential Sociology." *Law & Society Review* 10, no. 4: 525–545.

Nonet, Philippe, and Philip Selznick. 1978. *Law and Society in Transition: Toward Responsive Law*. New York: Harper & Row.

Norgren, Jill, and Serena Nanda. 1996. *American Cultural Pluralism and Law*, 2nd ed. Westport, CT: Praeger.

Nossiter, Adam. 2014. "New Kidnappings in Nigeria Lead U.S. to Offer Aid." *New York Times*, May 7.

Note. 1986. "The Cultural Defense in the Criminal Law." *Harvard Law Review* 99: 1293–1311.

Nownes, Anthony J., Clive S. Thomas, and Ronald J. Hrebenar. 2008. "Interest Groups in the States." Pp. 98–126 in Virginia Gray and Russell L. Hanson, eds. *Politics in the American States: A Comparative Analysis*, 9th ed. Washington, DC: CQ Press.

Nozick, Robert. 1977. *Anarchy, State and Utopia*. New York: Basic Books.

Nussbaumer, John. 2011. "The Door to Law School." *University of Massachusetts Law Review* 6: 1–35.

Obasogie, Osagie K. 2014. *Blinded by Sight: Seeing Race Through the Eyes of the Blind*. Stanford, CA: Stanford University Press.

O'Brien, Timothy L. 2006. "Why Do So Few Women Reach the Top of Big Law Firms?" *New York Times*, March 19.

Ogletree, Charles J., Jr. 2010. *The Presumption of Guilt*. New York: Palgrave/Macmillan.

O'Harrow, Robert, Jr. 2005. *No Place to Hide*. New York: Free Press.

O'Malley, Pat. 2009. *The Currency of Justice*. New York: Routledge-Cavendish.

Olson, Elizabeth. 2016a. "Gender-Bias Suits Target Law Firms' Pay Practices." *New York Times*, Sept.1.

———. 2016b. "Law Firms, Struggling Financially, Cull Partnership Ranks." *New York Times*, Nov. 22.

———. 2016c. "Law Graduate Loses Suit Against School on Enticing Enrollment Data." *New York Times*, March 25.

———. 2017. "Discrimination Suit Presses Issue of Lower Pay for Female Lawyers." *New York Times*, May 8.

Olson, Walter K. 1991. *The Litigation Explosion*. New York: Dutton.

O'Neil, Cathy. 2016. *Weapons of Math Destruction: How Big Data Increases Inequality and Threatens Democracy*. New York: Crown.

Onishi, Norimitsu, and Ken Belson. 2011. "Culture of Complicity Tied to Stricken Nuclear Plant." *New York Times*, April 22.

Organ, Jerome. 2013. "Understanding Trends in Demographics of Law Students—Part Two." *Legal Whiteboard*, October 17. http://lawprofessors.typepad.com/legalwhiteboard/2013/10/understanding-trends-in-demographics-of-law-students-part-two.html

———. 2014. "The Composition of Graduating Classes of Law Students—2013–2016—Part One." *Legal Whiteboard*, Dec. 29. http://lawprofessors.typepad.com/legalwhiteboard/2014/12/the-composition-of-graduating-classes-of-law-students-2013-2016-part-one-.html

Orucu, Esin. 2007. "A General View of 'Legal Families' and of 'Mixing Systems.'" Pp. 169–187 in Esin Orucu and David Nelkin, eds. *Comparative Law: A Handbook*. Portland, OR: Hart.

Packer, Herbert, L. 1968. *The Limits of the Criminal Sanction*. Stanford, CA: Stanford University Press.

Pager, Devah. 2007. *Marked: Race, Crime, and Finding Work in an Era of Mass Incarceration*. Chicago: University of Chicago Press.

Pape, Robert. 2005. *Dying to Win: The Strategic Logic of Suicide Terrorism*. New York: Random House.

Park, Haeyoun, and Larry Buchanan. 2017. "Refugees Entering the U.S. Already Face a Rigorous Vetting Process." *New York Times*, Jan. 29.

Parsons, Talcott. 1962. "The Law and Social Control." Pp. 56–72 in *Law and Society* (William M. Evan, ed.). New York: Macmillan.

Passell, Peter, and John Taylor. 1977. "The Deterrent Effect of Capital Punishment: Another View." *American Economic Review* 67: 445–451.

Paternoster, Raymond, Robert Brame, and Sarah Bacon. 2008. *The Death Penalty*. New York: Oxford University Press.

Patrice, Joe. 2013. "Unhappiest Job in America? Take a Guess." *Above the Law*. http://abovethelaw.com/2013/03/unhappiest-job-in-america-take-a-guess/

———. 2015. "Law School Deans Whine About *New York Times* Calling Out the Debt Crisis." *Above the Law*, Nov. 2. http://abovethelaw.com/2016/03/the-law-schools-with-the-highest-and-lowest-lsat-scores/

Payne, Brian. 2013. *White-Collar Crime: The Essentials*. Thousand Oaks, CA: Sage.

Payne-Pikus, Monique R., John Hagan, and Robert I. Nelson. 2010. "Experiencing Discrimination: Race and Retention in America's Largest Law Firms." *Law & Society Review* 44: 533–584.

Peresie, Jennifer I. 2005. "Female Judges Matter: Gender and Collegial Decisionmaking in the Federal Appellate Courts." *Yale Law Journal* 114: 1759–1790.

Pérez-Peña, Richard. 2017. "Contrary to Trump's Claims, Immigrants Are Less Likely to Commit Crimes." *New York Times*, Jan. 26.

Pérez-Pena, Richard, and Sheryl Gay Stolberg. 2017. "Police Unions Hail Less Oversight. Local Officials Fear Repercussions." *New York Times*, Apr. 5.

Perkinson, Robert. 2010. *Texas Tough*. New York: Metropolitan Books.

Perlez, Jane. 2015. "Conviction of Lawyer Affirms China's Resolve to Muzzle Rights Advocates." *New York Times*, Dec. 23.

Perlroth, Nicole. 2017. "Russian Hacker Sentenced to 27 Years in a Credit Card Case." *New York Times*, Apr. 22.

Peterson, Ruth D., and William C. Bailey. 1988. "Murder and Capital Punishment in the Evolving Context of the Post-Furman Era." *Social Forces* 66: 774–807.

Peterson, Todd David, and Elizabeth Waters Peterson. 2008. *Stemming the Tide of Depression: What Law Schools Should Learn From the Science of Positive Psychology*. George Washington Law School Public Law Research Paper No. 448.

Pew Research Center for Hispanic Trends. 2012. "U.S. Public, Hispanics Differ on Arizona Immigration Law." *Pew Research Center*, June 25.

Pew Research Center on the States. 2009. *One in 31: The Long Reach of American Corrections*. Washington, DC: Pew Memorial Trust.

Pew Research Center for U.S. Politics and Policy. 2010. "Broad Approval for New Arizona Immigration Law." *Pew Research Center*, May 12. http://pewresearch.org/pubs/1591/public-support-arizona-immigration-law-poll

Pfaff, John F. 2017. *Locked In: The True Causes of Mass Incarceration and How to Achieve Real Reform*. New York: Basic Books.

Pierce, Glenn L., and William Bowers, 1981. "The Bartley-Fox Gun Law's Short-Term Impact on Crime." *Annals of the American Academy of Political and Social Science* 455: 120–137.

Pierce, Jennifer. 1995. *Gender Trials: Emotional Lives in Contemporary Law Firms*. Berkeley: University of California Press.

Pinello, Daniel. 1995. *The Impact of Judicial Selection Method of State Supreme Court Policy: Innovation, Reaction, and Atrophy*. Westport, CT: Greenwood Press.

———. 1999. "Linking Party to Judicial Ideology in American Courts: A Meta-Analysis." *Justice System Journal* 20: 219–254.

Pizzi, William T. 1999. *Trials Without Truth*. New York: New York University Press.

Posner, Richard A. 1973. *Economic Analysis of Law*. Boston: Little Brown.

———. 2008. *How Judges Think*. Cambridge, MA: Harvard University Press.

Pound, Roscoe. 1908. "Mechanical Jurisprudence." *Columbia Law Review* 8, no. 8: 603–623.

———. 1930. *Criminal Justice in America*. New York: Da Capo Press.

———. 1942. *Social Control Through Law*. New Brunswick, NJ: Transaction.

———. 1943. "A Survey of Social Interests." *Harvard Law Review* 57: 1–39.

———. 1954. *An Introduction to the Philosophy of Law*. New Haven, CT: Yale University Press.

Power, Samantha. 2002. *"A Problem From Hell": America and the Age of Genocide*. New York: Basic Books.

President's Commission on Law Enforcement and Administration of Justice. 1967a. *The Challenge of Crime in a Free Society*. Washington, DC: U.S. Government Printing Office.

President's Commission on Law Enforcement and Administration of Justice. 1967b. *Task Force Report: The Police*. Washington, DC: U.S. Government Printing Office.

President's Review Group on Intelligence and Communications Technology. 2014. *The NSA Report: Liberty and Security in a Changing World*. Princeton, NJ: Princeton University Press.

President's Task Force on 21st Century Policing. 2015. *Interim Report of President's Task Force On 21st Century Policing*. Washington, DC: Office of Community Oriented Policing Services.

Pritchett, Herman. 1941. "Divisions of Opinion Among Justices of the U.S. Supreme Court, 1939–1941." *American Political Science Review* 35, no. 5: 890–898.

Privacy and Civil Liberties Oversight Board. 2014. *Report on the Surveillance Program Operated Pursuant to Section 702 of the Foreign Intelligence Surveillance Act*. Washington: U.S. Government Printing Office.

Provine, Doris Marie. 2007. *Unequal Under Law*. Chicago: University of Chicago Press.

Provine Doris Marie, Monica W. Varsanyi, Paul G. Lewis, and Scott Decker. 2016. *Policing Immigrants: Local Law Enforcement on the Front Lines*. Chicago: University of Chicago.

Quenqua, Douglas. 2015. "Lawyers With Lowest Pay Report More Happiness." *New York Times*, May 12.

Qiu, Linda. 2017. "Fact-Checking Claims About Trump's Travel Ban." *New York Times*, Feb. 24.

Quigley, John. 2006. *The Genocide Convention: An International Law Analysis*. Burlington, VT: Ashgate.

Quinney, Richard. 1974. *Critique of the Legal Order: Crime Control in Capitalist Society*. New Brunswick, NJ: Transaction.

Rabkin, Jeremy. 1995. "White House Lawyering: Law, Ethics, and Political Judgment." Pp. 107–142 in Cornell W. Clayton, ed. *Government Lawyers*. Lawrence: University Press of Kansas.

Radelet, Michael L., Hugo Bedau, and Constance E. Putnam. 1992. *In Spite of Innocence: Erroneous Convictions in Capital Cases*. Boston: Northeastern University Press.

Radelet, Michael L., and Traci L. Lacock. 2009. "Do Executions Lower Homicide Rates? The Views of Leading Criminologists." *Journal of Criminal Law and Criminology* 99: 489–508.

Rakoff, Jed S. 2016. "Why You Won't Get Your Day in Court." *New York Review of Books*, Nov. 24.

Ramirez, Mary Kreinder, and Steven A. Ramirez. 2017. *The Case for the Corporate Death Penalty*. New York: New York University.

Ramseyer, Mark, J. and Eric R. Rasmusen. 2010. *Comparative Litigation Rates*. Discussion Paper No. 681: Jon M. Olin Discussion Paper Series. Cambridge, MA: John M. Olin Center For Law, Economics, and Business.

Ran, Yanfei. 2009. "When Chinese Criminal Defense Lawyers Become the Criminals." *Fordham International Law Journal* 32: 988–1042.

Rappeport, Alan. 2017. "Consumer Watchdog Faces Attack by House Republicans, Memo Reveals." *New York Times*, Feb. 10.

Ratner, Seven R., and Jason S. Abrams. 2001. *Accountability for Human Rights Atrocities in International Law*, 2nd ed. New York: Oxford University Press.

Rawls, John. 1999. *A Theory of Justice*, 2nd ed. Cambridge, MA: Harvard University Press.

Reeves, Arin N. 2015. *Written in Black & White: Exploring Confirmation Bias in Racialized Perceptions of Writing Skills*. Chicago: Nextions.

Reichel, Philip L. 2008. *Comparative Criminal Justice Systems: A Topical Approach*, 5th ed. Upper Saddle River, NJ: Prentice Hall.

Reichstein, Kenneth J. 1965. "Ambulance Chasing: A Case Study of Deviation and Control Within the Legal Profession." *Social Problems* 13: 3–7.

Reiman, Jeffrey. 2007. *The Rich Get Richer and the Poor Get Prison*, 8th ed. Boston: Allyn and Bacon.

Reiman, Jeffrey, and Paul Leighton. 2017. *The Rich Get Richer and the Poor Get Prison: Ideology, Class and Criminal Justice*, 11th ed. New York: Routledge.

Rejali, Darius. 2009. *Torture and Democracy*. Princeton, NJ: Princeton University Press.

Resnick, Judith, and Dennis Curtis. 2013. *Representing Justice: Invention, Controversy and Rights in City-States and Democratic Courtrooms*. New Haven, CT: Yale.

Rhode, Deborah L. 1998. "The Professional Problem." *William & Mary Law Review* 39: 283–326.

———. 2000. *In the Interest of Justice: Reforming the Legal Profession*. New York: Oxford University Press.

———. 2004. *Access to Justice*. New York: Oxford University Press.

———. 2010. *The Beauty Bias: The Injustice of Appearance in Life and Law*. New York: Oxford University Press.

———. 2015. *The Trouble With Lawyers*. New York: Oxford University Press.

———. 2016. *Adultery: Infidelity and the Law*. Cambridge, MA: Harvard University Press.

Richards, Pamela, and Charles R. Tittle. 1981. "Gender and Perceived Chances of Arrest." *Social Forces* 59: 1182–1199.

Richardson, Richard, J., and Kenneth N. Vines. 1970. *The Politics of Federal Courts*. Boston: Little, Brown.

Richer, Alanna Durkin, and Curt Anderson. 2016. "Trial or Deal? Some Driven to Plead Guilty, Later Exonerated." *AP News*, Nov. 15. https://apnews.com/24cfa961d3444be49901496fdcaa3f da/trial-or-deal-some-driven-plead-guilty-later-exonerated

Robbennolt, Jennifer K., and Valerie P. Hans. 2016. *The Psychology of Tort Law*. New York: New York University Press.

Robbins, Liz. 2017. "U.S. Challenged on Tally of Travel-Ban Detainees." *New York Times*, Feb. 25.

Roberts, Dorothy E. 1995. "Punishing Drug Addicts Who Have Babies: Women of Color, Equality, and the Right of Privacy." Pp. 384–426 in Kimberlé Crenshaw, Neil Gotanda, Garry Pellar, and Kendall Thomas, eds. *Critical Race Theory: The Key Writings That Formed the Movement*. New York: New Press.

Roberts, Simon. 1979. *Order and Dispute*. New York: Penguin Books.

Robinson, Paul, H., and Sarah M. Robinson. 2015. *Pirates, Prisoners, and Lepers: Lessons From Life Outside the Law*. Lincoln, NE: Potomac Books.

Roman, John. 2013. *Race, Justifiable Homicide and Stand Your Ground Laws: An Analysis of FBI Supplementary Report Data*. Washington, DC: Urban Institute.

Romano, Renee C. 2014. *Racial Reckoning: Prosecuting America's Civil Rights Murders*. Cambridge, MA: Harvard University Press.

Rosen, Lawrence. 2006. *Law as Culture: An Invitation*. Princeton, NJ: Princeton University Press.

Rosenberg, Eli. 2017. "Family DNA Leads to Suspects, but Also Concerns." *New York Times*, Jan. 28.

Rosenberg, Gerald N. 2008. *The Hollow Hope: Can Courts Bring About Social Change?* 2nd ed. Chicago: University of Chicago Press.

Rosenthal, Alan. 2009. *Engines of Democracy Politics and Policymaking in State Legislatures*. Washington, DC: CQ Press.

Rosoff, Stephen, Henry Pontell, and Robert Tillman. 2010. *Profit Without Honor: White-Collar Crime and the Looting of America*, 5th ed. Upper Saddle River, NJ: Prentice Hall.

———. 2014. *Profit Without Honor: White-Collar Crime and the Looting of America*, 6th ed. Upper Saddle River, NJ: Prentice-Hall.

Ross, Edward Alsworth. 1965 [1907]. *Sin and Society: An Analysis of Latter-Day Inequity*. New York: Houghton Mifflin.

Ross, Laurence H. 1973. "Law, Science, and Accidents: The British Road Safety Act of 1967." *Journal of Legal Studies* 2: 1–78.

———. 1977. "Deterrence Regained: The Cheshire Constabulary's 'Breathalyzer Blitz.'" *Journal of Legal Studies* 6: 241–249.

Ross, Laurence H., Richard McCleary, and Thomas Epperlein. 1982. "Deterrence of Drinking and Driving in France: An Evaluation of the Law of July 12, 1978." *Law & Society Review* 16: 345–374.

Rossi, Jim. 2002. "What Lawyers Do When Nobody's Watching: Legal Advertising as a Case Study of the Impact of Underenforced Professional Rules." *Iowa Law Review* 87: 971–1022.

Rossi, Jim, and Mollie Weighner. 1991. "Contemporary Studies Project: An Empirical Examination of the Iowa Bar's Approach to Regulating Lawyer Advertising." *Iowa Law Review* 77: 179–268.

Rubenstein, Richard L. 1983. *The Age of Triage: Fear and Hope in an Overcrowded World*. Boston: Beacon Press.

Rubinstein, Jonathan. 1973. *City Police*. New York: Ballantine Books.

Rubinstein, Michael L., and Teresa J. White. 1979. "Alaska's Ban on Plea Bargaining." *Law & Society Review* 13: 267–383.

Ruiz, Rebecca, R. 2017. "Sessions Tells Prosecutors To Seek Harsher Penalties." *New York Times*, May 13.

Rule, James B. 2009. *Privacy in Peril: How We are Sacrificing a Fundamental Right in Exchange for Security and Convenience*. New York: Oxford University Press.

Russonello, Giovanni. 2016. "Race Relations Deemed Bleak by Most in U.S." *New York Times*, July 13. https://www.nytimes .com/2016/07/14/us/most-americans-hold-grim-view-of-race-relations-poll-finds.html?_r=0

Ruthven, Malise. 1984. *Islam in the World*. New York: Oxford University Press.

Saguy, Abigail C. 2003. *What Is Sexual Harassment? From Capitol Hill to the Sorbonne*. Berkeley: University of California Press.

Salokar, Rebecca Mae. 1995. "Politics, Law, and the Office of the Solicitor General." Pp. 59–84 in Cornell W. Clayton, ed. *Government Lawyers: The Federal Legal Bureaucracy and Presidential Politics*. Lawrence: University Press of Kansas.

Samuels, Suzanne. 2006. *Law, Politics, and Society*. New York: Houghton Mifflin.

Sandefur, Rebecca L. 2007. "Lawyers' Pro Bono Service and American-Style Civil Legal Assistance." *Law & Society Review* 41: 79–112.

———. 2014. *Assessing Justice in the Contemporary USA: Findings From the Community Needs and Services Study*. Chicago: American Bar Foundation.

Sandel, Michael J. 2009. *Justice: What's the Right Thing to Do?* New York: Farrar, Straus and Giroux.

Sander, Richard H. 2004. "A Systematic Analysis of Affirmative Action in American Law Schools." *Stanford Law Review* 57: 368–483.

———. 2006. "Empirical Studies of the Legal Profession: What Do We Know About Lawyers' Lives? The Racial Paradox of the Corporate Law Firm." *North Carolina Law Review* 84: 1755–1822.

Sander, Richard H., and E. Douglass Williams. 1989. "Why Are There So Many Lawyers? Perspectives on a Turbulent Market." *Law and Social Inquiry* 14: 431–479.

Sanger, David E. 2017. "Intelligence Officials Warn of Continued Cyberattacks." *New York Times*, May 12.

Sarat, Austin, Matthew Anderson, and Cathrine O. Frank, eds. 2014. *Law and the Humanities: An Introduction*. New York: Cambridge University Press.

Sarat, Austin, and William L. F. Felstiner. 1986. "Law and Strategy in the Divorce Lawyer's Office." *Law & Society Review* 20: 93–134.

Sarat, Austin, and Stuart A. Scheingold, eds. 2006. *Cause Lawyers and Social Movements*. Palo Alto, CA: Stanford University Press.

Santos, Fernanda. 2017. "The Road, or Flight, From Detention to Deportation." *New York Times*, Feb. 22.

Saul, Stephanie. 2017. "When Campus Rapists Are Repeat Offenders." *New York Times*, Jan. 24.

Saulny, Susan. 2003. "Lawyers' Ads Seeking Clients in Ferry Crash." *New York Times*, Nov. 4.

Savage, Charlie. 2013. "Justice Dept. Seeks to Curtail Stiff Drug Sentences." *New York Times*, Aug. 12. http://www.nytimes.com/2013/08/12/us/justice-dept-seeks-to-curtail-stiff-drug-sentences.html?pagewanted=all

———. 2016. "Before Scalia's Death, a Clash Between G.O.P. and Obama Over Appellate Judges." *New York Times*, Feb. 15.

———. 2017. "Lawyers Join Forces and Fan Out to Fight Trump Policies." *New York Times*, Jan. 31.

Savigny, Friedrich Carl von. 1975 [1831]. *Of the Vocation of Our Age for Legislation and Jurisprudence* (Abraham Hayward, trans.). New York: Arno Press.

Scalia, Antonin. 1997. *A Matter of Interpretation: Federal Courts and the Law*. Princeton, NJ: Princeton University Press.

Scalia, Antonin, and Bryan A. Garner. 2012. *Reading Law: The Interpretation of Legal Texts*. St. Paul, MN: West.

Schabas, William A. 2009. *Genocide in International Law*, 2nd ed. New York: Cambridge University Press.

Schatz, Bryan. 2015. "Waiting to Die in Prison—for Selling a Couple of Bags of Pot." *Mother Jones*, July/Aug. http://www.motherjones.com/politics/2015/05/life-sentence-marijuana-pot-prison-commuted

Schauer, Frederick. 2004. *Thinking Like a Lawyer: A New Introduction to Legal Reasoning*. Cambridge, MA: Harvard University Press.

Scheck, Barry, Peter Neufeld, and Jim Dwyer. 2000. *Actual Innocence: Five Days to Execution, and Other Dispatches From the Wrongfully Convicted*. New York: Doubleday.

Scheingold, Stuart A. 1974. *The Politics of Rights: Lawyers, Public Policy, and Political Change*. New Haven, CT: Yale University Press.

Scheingold, Stuart A., and Anne Bloom. 1998. "Transgressive Cause Lawyering." *International Journal of the Legal Professions* 5: 209–253.

Scheingold, Stuart A., and Austin Sarat, eds. 2004. *Something to Believe In: Politics, Professionalism, and Cause Lawyering*. Palo Alto, CA: Stanford University Press.

Schell, Jonathan. 1982. *The Fate of the Earth*. New York: Knopf.

Schiff, Benjamin. 2008. *Building the International Criminal Court*. New York: Cambridge University Press.

Schlitz, Patrick, J. 1999. "On Being a Happy, Healthy, and Ethical Member of an Unhappy, Unhealthy, and Unethical Profession." *Vanderbilt Law Review* 52: 871–960.

Schneier, Bruce. 2015. *Data Goliath: The Hidden Battles to Collect Your Data and Control Your World*. New York: Norton.

Schubert, Glendon A. 1965. *The Judicial Mind: The Attitudes and Ideologies of Supreme Court Justices, 1946–1963*. Evanston, IL: Northwestern University Press.

Schur, Edwin M. 1965. *Crimes Without Victims*. Englewood Cliffs, NJ: Prentice Hall.

———. 1968. *Law and Society: A Sociological View*. New York: Random House.

Schwartz, Richard D. 1954. "Social Factors in the Development of Legal Controls." *Yale Law Journal* 63: 471–491.

Schwartz, Richard D., and James C. Miller. 1975. "Legal Evolution and Societal Complexity." Pp. 52–62 in Ronald L. Akers and Richard Hawkins, eds. *Law and Control in Society*. Englewood Cliffs, NJ: Prentice Hall.

Scott, James C. 1985. *Weapons of the Weak: Everyday Forms of Peasant Resistance*. New Haven, CT: Yale University Press.

Searcey, Dionne, and Francois Essomba. 2017. "African Nations Are Increasingly Silencing the Internet to Head Off Protests." *New York Times*, Feb. 11.

Seelye, Katharine Q. 2017. "Harvard Law Review Has a First in 130 Years." *New York Times*, Feb. 2.

Segal, Jeffrey A., and Harold J. Spaeth. 2002. *The Supreme Court and the Attitudinal Model Revisited*. New York: Cambridge University Press.

Segal, Jeffrey A., Harold J. Spaeth, and Sara C. Benesh. 2005. *The Supreme Court in the American Legal System*. Cambridge: Cambridge University Press.

Sellin, Thorsten. 1959. *The Death Penalty*. Philadelphia: American Law Institute.

———. 1980. *The Penalty of Death*. Beverly Hills, CA: Sage.

Seltzer, Richard, Mark A. Venuti, and Grace M. Lopes. 1991. "Juror Honesty During the *Voir Dire.*" *Journal of Criminal Justice* 19: 451–462.

Selznick, Philip. 1961. "Sociology and Natural Law." *Natural Law Forum* 81: 84–110.

Semple, Kirk. 2010. "Program to Have Police Spot Illegal Immigrants Is Mired in Confusion." *New York Times*, Nov. 10.

Senate Intelligence Committee. 2014. *Report on Torture Committee Study of the Central Intelligence Agency's Detention and Interrogation Program.* Brooklyn, NY: Melville House.

Sentencing Project. 2016. *6 Million Lost Voters: State-Level Estimates of Felony Disenfranchisement.* Washington, DC: Sentencing Project.

Seron, Carroll. 1996. *The Business of Practicing Law: The Work Lives of Solo and Small-Firm Attorneys.* Philadelphia: Temple University Press.

Seron, Carroll, Gregg Van Ryzin, Martin Frankel, and Jean Kovath. 2001. "The Impact of Legal Counsel on Outcome for Poor Tenants in New York City's Housing Court." *Law & Society Review* 35: 419–434.

Shamir, Ronen. 1995. *Managing Legal Uncertainty: Elite Lawyers in the New Deal.* Durham, NC: Duke University Press.

Shane, Scott, Matthew Rosenberg, and Andrew W. Lehren. 2017. "Documents Said to Reveal Hacking Secrets of C.I.A." *New York Times*, March 8, A1.

Shapiro, Martin. 1981. "The Prototype of Courts." Pp. 1–64 in Martin Shapiro, ed. *Courts: A Comparative and Political Analysis.* Chicago: University of Chicago Press.

Shaw, Malcolm N. 1986. *International Law*, 2nd ed. Cambridge, UK: Grotius.

Shear, Michael D. 2017. "Discarding Obama's Legacy One Rule at a Time." *New York Times*, May 2.

Shear, Michael D., and Ron Nixon. 2017. "More Immigrants Face Deportation Under New Rules." *New York Times*, Feb. 22.

Shepard, Kris. 2007. *Rationing Justice: Poverty Lawyers and Poor People in the Deep South.* Baton Rouge: Louisiana State University Press.

Sherwin, Richard K. 2000. *When Law Goes Pop: The Vanishing Line Between Law and Popular Culture.* Chicago: University of Chicago Press.

Sherwood, Courtney. 2016. "Bundy Brothers Acquitted in Takeover of Oregon Wildlife Refuge." *New York Times*, Oct. 2.

Siegel, Larry J., Frank Schmalleger, and John L. Worrall. 2011. *Courts and Criminal Justice in America.* Upper Saddle River, NJ: Prentice Hall.

Siemsen, Cynthia. 2004. *Emotional Trials.* Boston: Northeastern University Press.

Silver, Carole. 2000. "Globalization and the U.S. Market in Legal Services—Shifting Identities." *Law and Policy in International Business* 31: 1093–1150.

Silverstein, Gordon. 2009. *Law's Allure: How Law Shapes, Constrains, Saves, and Kills Politics.* Cambridge: Cambridge University Press.

Silverstein, Lee. 1965. "The Continuing Impact of *Gideon v. Wainwright.*" *American Bar Association Journal* 51: 1023–1041.

Simon, Dan. 2012. *In Doubt: The Psychology of the Criminal Justice Process.* Cambridge MA: Harvard University Press.

Simon, Jonathan. 2007. *Governing Through Crime.* New York: Oxford University Press.

Simon, Rita J. 1967. *Juries and the Defense of Insanity.* Boston: Little, Brown.

Singer, Peter. 2007. *Corporate Warriors: The Rise of the Privatized Military Industry.* Ithaca, NY: Cornell University Press.

Singer, P. W. 2006. *Children at War.* Berkeley: University of California Press.

Skaine, Rosemarie. 2005. *Female Genital Mutilation.* Jefferson, NC: McFarland.

Skinner, E. Benjamin. 2008. *A Crime So Monstrous.* New York: Free Press.

Skogan, Wesley G. 2006. *Police and Community in Chicago.* New York: Oxford University Press.

Skolnick, Jerome H. 1967. "Social Control in the Adversary System." *Journal of Conflict Resolution* 11: 52–70.

Slobogin, Christopher. 2014. "Panvasive Surveillance, Political Process Theory, and the Non-delegation Doctrine." *Georgetown Law Journal* 102: 1723–1776.

Small, Jamie, L. 2015. "Classing Sex Offenders: How Prosecutors and Defense Attorneys Differentiate Men Accused of Sexual Assault." *Law & Society Review* 49: 109–142.

Smigel, Erwin O. 1969. *The Wall Street Lawyer: Professional Organization Man?* New York: Free Press.

Smith, Jada F. 2016. "As 'Sextortion' Proliferates, Victims Find Precarious Place in Legal System.*" New York Times*, May 11.

Smith, Mitch, and Michael Wines. 2017. "Across the Country, a Republican Push to Rein in Protesters." *New York Times*, March 2.

Smith, Reginald Heber. 1919. *Justice and the Poor.* New York: Carnegie Foundation.

Smith, Roger M. 2008. "Historical Institutionalism and the Study of Law." Pp. 46–59 in Keith Whittington, R. Daniel Kelemen, and Gregory A. Caldeira, eds. *The Oxford Handbook of Law and Politics.* New York: Oxford University Press.

Smith, Steven S., Jason M. Roberts, and Ryan J. Vander Wielen. 2009. *The American Congress*, 6th ed. New York: Cambridge University Press.

Snell, Kelsey, and Ed O'Keefe. 2017. "What's in the Spending Agreement? We Read It So You Don't Have To." *Washington Post*, May 1.

Soble, Jonathan. 2017. "Guilty Plea Moves Takata Toward Road to Recovery." *New York Times*, Jan. 17.

Solnit, Rebecca. 2009. *A Paradise Built in Hell: The Extraordinary Communities That Arise in Disasters.* New York: Penguin.

Solomon, Steven Davidoff. 2016. "Law School a Solid Investment Despite Pay Discrepancies." *New York Times*, June 22.

Soltes, Eugene. 2016. *Why They Do It: Inside the Mind of the White-Collar Criminal.* New York: Public Affairs.

Solove, Daniel J. 2004. *The Digital Person: Technology and Privacy in the Information Age.* New York: New York University Press.

———. 2008. *Understanding Privacy.* Cambridge, MA: Harvard University Press.

———. 2011. *Nothing to Hide: The False Tradeoff Between Privacy and Security.* New Haven, CT: Yale University Press.

Soma, John T., and Stephen D. Rynerson. 2008. *Privacy Law in a Nutshell.* St. Paul, MN: West.

Southworth, Ann. 2008. *Lawyers of the Right: Professionalizing the Conservative Coalition.* Chicago: University of Chicago Press.

Spangler, Eve. 1986. *Lawyers for Hire: Salaried Professionals at Work.* New Haven, CT: Yale University Press.

Spector, Malcolm. 1972. "The Rise and Fall of a Mobility Route." *Social Problems* 20: 175–185.

Spencer, Herbert. 1884. *Man Versus the State.* New York: Williams and Norgate.

Spiller, Pablo T., and Rafael Gely. 2008. "Strategic Judicial Decision-Making." Pp. 46–80 in Keith Whittington, R. Daniel Kelemen, and Gregory A. Caldeira, eds. *The Oxford Handbook of Law and Politics.* New York: Oxford University Press.

Spitzer, Steven. 1975. "Punishment and Social Organization: A Study of Durkheim's Theory of Penal Evolution." *Law & Society Review* 9: 613–635.

Spohn, Cassia. 2009. *How Do Judges Decide?* Thousand Oaks, CA: Sage.

Spohn, Cassia, Dawn Beichner, and Erika Davis Frenzel. 2001. "Prosecutorial Justifications for Sexual Assault Case Rejection." *Social Problems* 48: 206–235.

Spohn, Cassia, John Gruhl, and Susan Welch. 1987. "The Impact of the Ethnicity and Gender of Defendants on the Decision to Reject or Dismiss Felony Charges." *Criminology* 25: 175–292.

Spohn, Cassia, and Craig Hemmens. 2012. *Courts: A Text/Reader,* 2nd ed. Thousand Oaks, CA: Sage.

Squire, Peverill, and Gary Moncrief. 2010. *State Legislatures Today: Politics Under the Domes.* Boston: Longman.

Stack, Liam. 2017. "Killer of Transgender Woman Is Sentenced Under U.S. Hate Crimes Law." *New York Times,* May 17.

Stamp, Kenneth M. 1956. *The Peculiar Institution: Slavery in the Ante-Bellum South.* New York: Vintage Books.

Stanton, Gregory, H. 1998. "The Eight Stages of Genocide." *Genocide Watch.* http://www.genocidewatch.org/aboutgenocide/8stagesofgenocide.html

Staples, William G. 2000. *Everyday Surveillance.* Lanham, MD: Rowman & Littlefield.

Starr, June O., and Barbara Yngvesson. 1975. "Scarcity and Disputing: Zeroing-in on Compromise Decisions." *American Ethnologist* 2: 553–566.

Starr, Sonja B. 2014. "Evidence-Based Sentencing and the Scientific Rationalization of Discretion." *Stanford Law Review* 66: 803–873.

Staszak, Sarah. 2015. *No Day in Court: Access to Justice and the Politics of Judicial Retrenchment.* New York: Oxford University Press.

State Bar of California. 2014. *Attorney Disciplinary Report for the Year Ending December 31, 2014.* Sacramento: State Bar of California.

Staub, Ervin. 1989. *The Roots of Evil.* New York: Cambridge University Press.

Stauffer, Brian. 2016. *Every 25 Seconds: The Human Toll of Criminalizing Drug Use in the United States.* New York: Human Rights Watch/American Civil Liberties Union.

Steiker, Carol S., and Jordan M. Steiker. 2016. *Courting Death: The Supreme Court and Capital Punishment.* Cambridge, MA: Belknap Press.

Steiner, Benjamin. 2017. "Punishment Within Prison: An Examination of the Influences of Prison Officials' Decision to Remove Sentencing Credits." *Law and Society Review* 51: 70–98.

Steinzor, Rena. 2015. *Why Not Jail? Industrial Catastrophes, Corporate Malfeasance, and Government Action.* New York: Cambridge University Press.

Stephen, James Fitzjames. 1972 [1873]. *Liberty, Equality, Fraternity.* Chicago: University of Chicago Press.

Stern, Gerald M. 2008. *The Buffalo Creek Disaster.* New York: Vintage Books.

Stiglitz, Joseph F. 2012. *The Price of Inequality.* New York: Norton.

Stolberg, Sheryl Gay. 2017. "Justice Dept. to Re-examine Police Accords." *New York Times,* Apr. 4.

Stone, Christopher D. 1975. *Where the Law Ends.* New York: Harper & Row.

Stone, Geoffrey R. 2004. *Perilous Times: Free Speech in Wartime.* New York: Norton.

Story, Louise. 2016. "Report Describes Lawyers' Advice on Moving Suspect Funds Into U.S." *New York Times,* Jan. 31.

Stout, Kathryn A., Richard A. Dello Buono, and William J. Chambliss, eds. 2004. *Social Problems, Law, and Society.* Lanham, MD: Rowman & Littlefield.

Stover, Robert, and Howard S. Erlanger. 1989. *Making It and Breaking It: The Fate of Public Interest Commitment During Law School.* Urbana: University of Illinois Press.

Strom, Kevin, Marcus Berzofsky, Bonnie Shook-Sa, Kelle Barrick, Crystal Daye, Nicole Horstmann, and Susan Kinsey. 2010. *The Private Security Industry: A Review of the Definitions, Available Data Sources, and Paths Moving Forward.* Washington, DC: Bureau of Justice Statistics.

Strum, Philippa. 2010. Mendez v. Westminster: *School Desegregation and Mexican-American Rights.* Lawrence: University Press of Kansas.

Stuart, Forest. 2016. *Down, Out, and Under Arrest: Policing and Everyday Life in Skid Row.* Chicago: University of Chicago.

Student Drug Testing Coalition. 2008. http://www.studentdrugtesting.org

Sudby, Scott. 1997. "The Jury as Critic: An Empirical Look at How Capital Juries Perceive Expert and Lay Testimony." *Virginia Law Review* 83: 1109–1188.

Sudnow, David. 1965. "Normal Crimes: Sociological Features of the Penal Codes in a Public Defender Office." *Social Problems* 12: 255–276.

Sullivan, William M., Anne Colby, Judith Welch Wegner, Lloyd Bond, and Lee S. Shulman. 2007. *Educating Lawyers: Preparation for the Profession of Law.* San Francisco: Jossey-Bass.

Sumner, William Graham. 1906. *Folkways.* New York: New American Library.

———. 1911 [1883]. *What Social Classes Owe to Each Other.* New York: Harper & Brothers.

Sunstein, Cass. 2015. *Constitutional Personae.* New York: Oxford.

Sutherland, Arthur E. 1963. "Review of Jerome E. Carlin, *Lawyers on Their Own.*" *Harvard Law Review* 77: 395–398.

Sutherland, Edwin H. 1940. "White Collar Criminality." *American Sociological Review* 5: 1–12.

———. 1945. "Is 'White Collar Crime' Crime?" *American Sociological Review* 10: 132–139.

———. 1989 [1949]. *White Collar Crime: The Uncut Version*. New Haven, CT: Yale University Press.

Sutton, John R. 2001. *Law/Society Origins, Interactions, and Change*. Thousand Oaks, CA: Pine Forge Press.

Tamanaha, Brian Z. 2010. *Beyond the Formalist-Realist Divide: The Role of Politics in Judging*. Princeton, NJ: Princeton University Press.

———. 2012. *Failing Law Schools*. Chicago: University of Chicago Press.

Tanase, Takao. 1990. "The Management of Disputes: Automobile Accident Compensation in Japan." *Law & Society Review* 24: 651–692.

Taslitz, Andrew E. 1999. *Rape and the Culture of the Courtroom*. New York: New York University Press.

Tavernise, Sabrina. 2010. "Arizona-Style Law Reduced Immigrants, Study Shows." *New York Times*, Nov. 17.

Terrill, Richard J. 2016. *World Criminal Justice Systems*, 9th ed. Newark, NJ: LexisNexis.

Thomas, Katie. 2017. "Decades of Policies Could Fall at F.D.A." *New York Times*, Feb. 6.

Thompson, Heather Ann. 2016. *Blood in the Water: The Attica Prison Uprising of 1971 and Its Legacy*. New York: Pantheon.

Thrush, Glenn. 2017. "Trump's New Travel Ban Blocks Migrants From Six Nations, Sparing Iraq." *New York Times*, March 6.

Tichenor, Daniel J. 2002. *Dividing Lines: The Politics of Immigration Control in America*. Princeton, NJ: Princeton University Press.

Tigar, Michael, and Madeline R. Levy. 1977. *Law and the Rise of Capitalism*. New York: Monthly Review Press.

Tillman, Robert, and Henry Pontell. 1992. "Is Justice 'Collar- Blind'? Punishing Medicaid Provider Fraud." *Criminology* 30: 547–574.

Timmons, Heather. 2010. "Due Diligence From Afar." *New York Times,* Aug. 5.

Tittle, Charles R. 1977. "Sanction Fear and the Maintenance of Social Order." *Social Forces* 53: 579–596.

Tocqueville, Alexis de. 1973. *Democracy in America* (Henry Reeve, trans.). New York: Knopf.

Tonry, Michael. 2016. *Sentencing Fragments: Penal Reform in America, 1975–2025*. New York: Oxford University Press.

Travers, Max. 2010. *Understanding Law and Society*. London: Routledge.

Trevino, A. Javier. 2008. *The Sociology of Law: Classical and Contemporary Perspectives*. New Brunswick, NJ: Transaction.

Tribe, Meghan. 2017. "Study Shows Gender Diversity Varies Widely Across Practice Area." *American Lawyer*, Apr. 17. http://www.americanlawyer.com/id=1202783889472/Study-Shows-Gender-Diversity-Varies-Widely-Across-Practice-Areas

Tribune News Service. 2016. "Barely Half of Illegal Border Crossers Caught According to Homeland Security Report." *Chicago Tribune*, Oct. 7. http://www.chicagotribune.com/news/nationworld/ct-us-mexico-border-crossing-captures-20161006-story.html.

Tuchman, Barbara W. 1962. *The Guns of August*. New York: Ballantine Books.

Turow, Scott. 2003. *Ultimate Punishment*. New York: Picador.

———. 1977. *One L: The Turbulent True Story of a First Year at Harvard Law School*. New York: Grand Central.

Tushnet, Mark. 2000. *Taking the Constitution Away from the Courts*. Princeton, NJ: Princeton University Press, 2000.

Tyler, Tom R. 2006. *Why People Obey the Law*. Princeton, NJ: Princeton University Press.

Unger, Roberto Mangabeira. 1986. *The Critical Legal Studies Movement: Another Time, a Greater Task*. Cambridge, MA: Harvard University Press.

United Nations Office on Drugs and Crime (UNODC). 2016. *Global Report on Trafficking in Persons: 2016*. New York: United Nations.

Uphoff, Rodney J. 1992. "The Criminal Defense Lawyer: Zealous Advocate, Double Agent, or Beleaguered Dealer?" *Criminal Law Bulletin* 28: 419–456.

Urbina, Ian. 2015. "'Sex Slaves': The Human Misery That Feeds Pets and Livestock." *New York Times*, July 27.

Urofsky, Melvin I. 2015. *Dissent and the Supreme Court: Its Role in the Court's History and the Nation's Constitutional Dialogue*. New York: Pantheon.

U.S. Chamber, Institute for Legal Reform. 2015. *Trial Lawyer Marketing Broadcast, Search and Social Strategies*. http://www.instituteforlegalreform.com/research/trial-lawyer-ad

U.S. Government Accountability Office. 2016. *K–12 Education Better Use of Information Could Help Agencies Identify Disparities and Address Racial Discrimination*. Washington, DC: Government Accountability Office.

U.S. Sentencing Commission. 2012. *Federal Mandatory Minimum Sentencing: An Overview of the 2011 Report by the United States Sentencing Commission*. Sentencing Project, Aug. 1. http://www.sentencingproject.org/publications/federal-mandatory-minimum-sentencing-an-overview-of-the-2011-report-by-the-u-s-sentencing-commission/

Vago, Steven. 2012. *Law and Society*, 10th ed. Upper Saddle River, NJ: Prentice Hall.

Van Cleve, Nicole Gonzalez. 2016. *Crook County: Racism and Justice in America's Largest Criminal Court*. Palo Alto, CA: Stanford University Press.

Van den Haag, Ernest. 1975. *Punishing Criminals: Concerning a Very Old and Painful Question*. New York: Basic Books.

Van der Merwe, Hugo, Victoria Baxter, and Audrey R. Chapman, eds. 2009. *Assessing the Impact of Transitional Justice: Challenges for Empirical Justice*. Washington, DC: U.S. Institute for Peace.

Van Hoy, Jerry. 1997. *Franchise Law Firms and the Transformation of Personal Legal Services*. Westport, CT: Quorum Books.

Vega, Tanzina. 2010. "In Web Code, New Ways to See What Users Do." *New York Times*, Oct. 11.

Vidmar, Neil, and Valerie P. Hans. 2007. *American Juries*. New York: Prometheus Books.

Villamor, Felipe. 2017. "Ex-Officer in Philippines Says He Led Death Squad." *New York Times*, Feb. 21.

Vincent, Barbara S., and Paul J. Hofer. 1994. *The Consequences of Mandatory Minimum Prison Terms: A Summary of Recent Findings.* Washington, DC: Federal Judicial Center.

Vitiello, Michael. 2005. "Professor Kingsfield: The Most Misunderstood Character in Literature." *Hofstra Law Review* 33: 1–61.

Volokh, Eugene. 2015. "Judge Kozinski on Prosecutorial Misconduct." *New York Times*, July 17.

Wacks, Raymond. 2006. *Philosophy of Law: A Very Short Introduction.* New York: Oxford University Press.

Wagner, Peter, and Bernadette Rabuy. 2016. "Mass Incarceration: The Whole Pie 2016." *Prison Policy Initiative*, March 14. https://www.prisonpolicy.org/reports/pie2016.html

Waldron, Jeremy, ed. 1987. *"Nonsense on Stilts": Bentham, Burke and Marx on the Rights of Man.* London: Methuen.

Walker, Samuel. 2006. *Sense and Nonsense About Crime and Drugs: A Policy Guide,* 6th ed. New York: Oxford University Press.

Walker, Samuel, Cassia Spohn, and Miriam Delone. 2007. *The Color of Justice: Race, Ethnicity, and Crime in America,* 4th ed. Belmont, CA: Thomson/Wadsworth.

Walsh, Anthony, and Craig Hemmens. 2016. *Law, Justice, and Society: A Sociolegal Introduction,* 4th ed. New York: Oxford University Press.

Warden, Rob, and Steven Drizin, eds. 2009. *True Stories of False Confessions.* Evanston, IL: Northwestern University Press.

Warren, Samuel D., and Louis D. Brandeis. 1890. "The Right to Privacy." *Harvard Law Review* 4: 193–220.

Wasby, Stephen L. 1970. *The Impact of the United States Supreme Court.* Homewood, IL: Dorsey Press.

Wasserstrom, Richard, ed. 1971. *Morality and the Law.* Belmont, CA: Wadsworth.

Wax, Steven T. 2008. *Kafka Comes to America.* New York: Other Press.

Webb, Maureen. 2007. *Illusions of Security.* San Francisco: City Lights.

Weber, Max. 1954. *Law in Economy and Society* (Max Rheinstein, ed.; Edward Shils and Max Rheinstein, trans.). Cambridge, MA: Harvard University Press.

———. 1978 [1922]. *Economy and Society,* vols. 1–11 (Gunther Roth and Claus Wittich, eds.). Berkeley: University of California Press.

Weigend, Thomas. 1980. "Continental Cures for American Ailments: European Criminal Procedure as a Model for Law Reform." *Crime & Justice* 2: 381–428.

Weiser, Benjamin. 2014. "5 Exonerated in Jogger Case Agee to Settle Suit for $40 Million." *New York Times*, June 19.

———. 2016a. "Judge, in Striking Move, Keeps Felon out of Prison." *New York Times*, May 26.

———. 2016b. "Jury Trials Vanish and Justice Is Served Behind Closed Doors." *New York Times*, Aug. 8.

———. 2017. "Police Missteps Lead New York to Pay Millions." *New York Times*, Jan. 24, 2017.

Weiss, Debra Cassens. 2014. 2015b. "This Law Firm Will Spend More Than $25 M in Legal Advertising This Year, Report Says." *ABA Journal*, Oct. 2015. http://www.abajournal.com/news/article/ this_law_firm_will_spend_more_than_25m_in_legal_advertising_this_year_repor

Weitz, Eric D. 2003. *A Century of Genocide.* Princeton, NJ: Princeton University Press.

Westerland, Chad, Jeffrey A. Segal, Lee Epstein, Charles M. Cameron, and Scott Comparato. 2010. "Strategic Defiance and Compliance in the U.S. Courts of Appeals." *American Journal of Political Science* 54: 891–905.

Western, Bruce. 2006. *Punishment and Inequality in America.* New York: Russell Sage Foundation.

Westin, Alan. 1970. *Privacy and Freedom.* New York: Atheneum.

Whelan, Ed. 2016. "Law Professor Karl Mazzone on Senate Duty on Supreme Court Vacancies Part I." *National Review*, June 6. http://www.nationalreview.com/bench-memos/436237/kar-mazzone-senate-duty

White, G. Edward. 2016. *Law in American History, Volume II: From Reconstruction Through the 1920s.* New York: Oxford University Press.

White, Michael D., and Henry F. Fradella. 2016. *Stop and Frisk: The Use and Abuse of a Controversial Policing Tactic.* New York: New York University Press.

White House. 2017. *Executive Orders.* https://www.whitehouse.gov/briefing-room/presidential-actions/executive-orders

Wice, Paul B. 1978. *Criminal Lawyers.* Beverly Hills, CA: Sage.

———. 2005. *Public Defenders and the American Justice System.* Westport, CT: Praeger.

Wilkins, David B. 2008. "'If You Can't Join 'Em, Beat 'Em!' The Rise and Fall of the Black Corporate Law Firm." *Stanford Law Review* 60: 1733–1801.

Wilkins, David B., Elizabeth Chambliss, Lisa Jones, and Haile Adamson. 2002. *Harvard Law School Report on the State of Black Alumni 1869–2000.* Cambridge, MA: Harvard Law School.

Wilkins, David B., and Mitu Gulati. 1996. "Why Are There So Few Black Lawyers in Corporate Law Firms? An Institutional Analysis." *California Law Review* 84: 493–625.

Wilkinson, Charles F. 1987. *American Indians, Time, and the Law.* New Haven, CT: Yale University Press.

Williams, Franklin P., III. 1980. "Conflict Theory and Differential Processing: An Analysis of the Research Literature." Pp. 213–232 in James A. Inciardi, ed. *Radical Criminology: The Coming Crises.* Beverly Hills, CA: Sage.

Williams, Marian R., Stephen Demuth, and Jefferson E. Holcomb. 2007. "Understanding the Influence of Victim Gender in Death Penalty Cases: The Importance of Victim Race, Sex-Related Victimization, and Jury Decision Making." *Criminology* 45: 865–891.

Williams, Timothy. 2015. "Facial Recognition Software Moves From Overseas Wars to Local Police." *New York Times,* Aug. 12.

———. 2016a. "Correctional Population Hit 13-Year Low in 2015." *New York Times*, Dec. 30.

———. 2016b. "San Francisco Police Search Blacks at Unequal Rate Report Says." *New York Times*, July 12.

———. 2016c. "Study Supports Suspicion That Police Use of Force Is More Likely on Blacks." *New York Times*, July 8. https://www.nytimes.com/2016/07/08/us/study-supports-suspicion-that-police-use-of-force-is-more-likely-for-blacks.html?_r=0

Willis, James F. 1982. *Prologue to Nuremberg: The Politics and Diplomacy of Punishing War Criminals.* Westport, CT: Greenwood Press.

Wolfenden Report. 1957. *Report of the Committee on Homosexual Offences and Prostitution.* London: British Parliament.

Women Lawyers of Utah. 2010. *The Utah Report: The Initiative on the Advancement and Retention of Women in Law Firms.* Salt Lake City: Utah Bar Association.

Wood, Arthur Lewis. 1967. *Criminal Lawyer.* New Haven, CT: College & University Press.

Wood, Daniel B. 2010. "Opinion Polls Show Broad Support for Tough Arizona Immigration Law." *Christian Science Monitor,* Apr. 30.

Yackle, Larry W. 1989. *Reform and Regret.* New York: Oxford University Press.

Yamaguichi, Ryoko, Lloyd D. Johnston, and Patrick M. O'Malley. 2003. "Relationship Between Student Illicit Drug Use and School Drug-Testing Policies." *Journal of School Health* 73: 159–164.

Yee, Vivian. 2016. "Lashing Out in New Jersey Over Limits for Drivers." *New York Times*, Aug. 18.

———. 2017a. "Schneiderman to Advise 'Sanctuary Cities' How to Resist a Trump Deportation Push." *New York Times*, Jan. 19.

———. 2017b. "Trump Can't Withhold Funding to Sanctuary Cities, Judge Rules." *New York Times*, April 26.

Zalman, Marvin, and Brad W. Smith. 2007. "The Attitudes of Police Executives Toward *Miranda* and Interrogation Policies." *Journal of Criminal Law and Criminology* 97: 873–942.

Zalman, Marvin, Brad W. Smith, and Angie Kiger. 2008. "Officials' Estimate of 'Actual Innocence' Convictions.'" *Justice Quarterly* 35: 72–100.

Zaretsky, Staci. 2016a. "The Law Schools With the Highest (and Lowest) LSAT Scores." *Above the Law*, Mar. 22. http://abovethelaw.com/2016/03/the-law-schools-with-the-highest-and-lowest-lsat-scores/

———. 2016b. "The Global 100: The Richest Law Firms in the World." *Above the Law*, Sept. 26. http://abovethelaw.com/2016/09/the-global-100-the-richest-law-firms-in-the-world-2016/

Zemans, Frances, and Victor Rosenblum. 1981. *The Making of a Public Profession.* Chicago: University of Chicago Press.

Zimring, Franklin E. 2017. *When Police Kill.* Cambridge, MA: Harvard University Press.

Zimring, Franklin E., and Gordon Hawkins. 1973. *Deterrence: The Legal Threat in Crime Control.* Chicago: University of Chicago Press.

Zinn, Howard. 1971. "The Conspiracy of Law." Pp. 15–36 in Robert Paul Wolff, ed. *The Rule of Law.* New York: Simon and Schuster.

expenditures on prosecutor offices
by, 252
gambling determinations by,
352–353
grand jury, 260–261
hate crime statutes, 476–477
homicide rate in, 339
"no-fault" divorce in, 384–385
Statute of limitations, 214, 371
Staub, Ervin, 373–374
"Steel Seizure Case," 84, 108
Stefanic, Jean, 63
Steiker, Carol, 335
Steiker, Jordan, 335
Steinle, Kathryn, 489
Stephen, James Fitzjames, 342
Stephens, Edwin, 31
Sterilizations, 26–27
Stevens, John Paul, 36, 334
Stewart, Potter, 332
Stinson, Phil, 457
Stock fraud, 360
Stone, Christopher, 363
Stone, Geoffrey R., 32
"Stop and frisk" policy, 449–453
Story, Joseph, 139
"Straight line assimilation model," 480
Strategic approach, 100–101
Strategic lawsuits against public
participation (SLAPP), 27
Stratified private legal profession, 159
Strauder v. West Virginia, 290
Strickland v. Washington, 245, 337
Stuart, Forest, 357
Students, drug testing of, 535–536
Stuyvesant, Peter, 234
Style of law, 58
Substantive justice, 12
Substantive law, 52
Substantive rational thought, 53
Subsystems, 57
Sudan, 309–310, 371
Sudnow, David, 265
Suicide, 172–173, 516
Sullivan, Emmet G., 367
Summa Theologiae, 46
Sumner, William Graham, 50–51, 382
Sunna, 19–20
Sunstein, Cass, 100
Support Our Law Enforcement and
Safe Neighborhood drug
interactions, 484
Supreme court (state), 93, 201
Supreme Court (U.S.)
advertising-related decisions by, 181
amicus curiae briefs, 85

appeals heard by, 77–78
arbitration clause decisions, 237
Brown v. Board of Education
decision, 25, 28, 80, 97, 101,
386–387, 392, 394–397, 426
capital punishment decisions,
332–333
cases heard by, 77–78
civil commitment laws, 369
civil disobedience decisions, 432
Civil Rights Act decisions, 426–427
Congress and, 85–88
corporate liability decisions, 366
death penalty decisions by, 294,
332–333
decisions by, 78, 82–87, 96
discriminatory application of
narcotics laws, 472–473
dissenting opinion of, 78–79
drug offense sentencing
decisions, 470
drug testing decisions, 535
elitist character of, 79–81
execution methods decisions,
334–335
freedom of expression interpretation
by, 62
home of, 77
immigration decisions by, 482
interrogation decisions, 414
judge and jury decisions, 288, 298
judicial review by, 16, 82–85
jurisdiction of, 77, 82, 87
jury selection decisions, 290–291
jury sentencing decisions, 298
laws rejected or overturned by, 87
majority opinion of, 78
narcotics laws and, 472–473
plea bargaining decisions by, 264
police interrogation decisions, 414
presidents and, 84
prison overcrowding decisions, 318
privacy rights and, 509–513
prosecutorial discretion decisions
by, 256
public opinion of, 90–91
right to privacy decisions by,
509–513
same-sex marriage decisions,
408–410
size of, 88
slavery-related decisions by, 446–447
structure of, 79–80
Tennessee v. Lane decision, 36
vagrancy laws and, 355–356
women as lawyers, 164

Supreme Court (U.S.) judges. *See also*
specific judge
appointment of, 80–81, 88–90, 101
background of, 79–81
birth order influences on, 100
educational background of, 80
impeachment of, 90
net worth of, 80
nomination of, 88–90
retirement of, 81
Surrogacy, 387–388
Surveillance
governmental, 516–522
Internet, 539–541
protections against, 533
Suspension, 202
Sutherland, Edwin H., 358–359, 362
Sutton, John, 35, 396
Swann v. Charlotte-Mecklenburg Board
of Education, 399
Swartz, Aaron, 434–435
Sweatt v. Painter, 396
Symbolic Crusade: Status Politics and the
American Temperance Movement,
346
Symbolic speech, 7, 98
Syrian refugees, 489

"Tabloid" journalism, 506
Tabloid trial, 278
Takata, 368
Tanase, Takao, 217
Taney, Roger, 80, 446
Tanzania, 437
Target, 529–530
Taslitz, Andrew E., 276
Taxes
avoidance of, 361
corporate, 37
Taylor v. Louisiana, 289, 291
Ta'zir offenses, 19–21
Teale, Alan, 360–361
Tekin, Erdal, 462
Television advertising, 183
Tennessee v. Garner, 99, 455
Tennessee v. Lane, 36
Terrorism, 516–517, 519–520
Terrorist Threat Integration Center, 517
Terry v. Ohio, 450
Testimony, grand jury, 260
Texas
death penalty in, 337
prison gangs in, 423
Texas Department of Corrections,
420–421
Texas v. Johnson, 87, 98

Index ■ 597

Matthew Lippman is Professor Emeritus in the Department of Criminology, Law, and Justice at the University of Illinois at Chicago (UIC) and has taught criminal law and criminal procedure for more than thirty years. He has also taught courses on civil liberties, law and society, and terrorism and teaches international criminal law at John Marshall Law School in Chicago. He earned a doctorate in political science from Northwestern University and a master of laws from Harvard Law School, and he is a member of the Pennsylvania Bar. He has been voted by the graduating seniors at UIC to receive the Silver Circle Award for outstanding teaching on six separate occasions and also has received the UIC Flame Award from the University of Illinois Alumni Association, as well as the Excellence in Teaching Award, Teaching Recognition (Portfolio) Award, and Honors College Fellow of the Year Award. The university chapter of Alpha Phi Sigma, the criminal justice honors society, named him Criminal Justice Professor of the Year on three occasions. In 2008, he was recognized as a College of Liberal Arts and Sciences Master Teacher. He was honored by the College of Liberal Arts and Sciences, which named him Commencement Marshal at the May 2012 graduation. Professor Lippman is also recognized in *Who's Who Among America's Teachers*.

Professor Lippman is author of one hundred articles and author or co-author of six books. These publications focus on criminal law and criminal procedure, international human rights, and comparative law. He also is author of five other SAGE volumes, *Contemporary Criminal Law: Concepts, Cases, and Controversies* (4th ed., 2016), *Criminal Procedure* (3rd ed., 2017), *Essential Criminal Law* (2nd ed., 2017), *Criminal Evidence* (2016), and *Striking the Balance: Debating Criminal Justice and Law* (2017). His work is cited in hundreds of academic publications and by domestic and international courts and organizations. He has also served on legal teams appearing before the International Court of Justice in The Hague, has testified as an expert witness on international law before numerous state and federal courts, and has consulted with both private organizations and branches of the U.S. government. Professor Lippman regularly appears as a radio and television commentator and is frequently quoted in leading newspapers. He has served in every major administrative position in the Department of Criminology, Law, and Justice at UIC, including department head, director of undergraduate studies, and director of graduate studies.